CMT LEVEL I

CMT Level III

CMT Level III

The Integration of Technical Analysis

Readings Selected by

The Market Technicians Association

WILEY

CONTENTS

The Market Technicians Association (MTA) is a not-for-profit professional regulatory organization servicing over 4,500 market analysis professionals in over 85 countries around the globe. The MTA's main objectives involve the education of the public, the investment community, and its membership in the theory, practice, and application of technical analysis.

The MTA has the following stated mission:

- Attract and retain a membership of professionals devoting their efforts to using and expanding the field of technical analysis and sharing their body of knowledge with their fellow members.

- Establish, maintain, and encourage the highest standards of professional competence and ethics among technical analysts.

- Educate the public and the investment community of the value and universality of technical analysis.

The MTA's mission is to accomplish through the effective execution of a wide variety of professional services including, but not limited to, regional seminars, local chapter meetings, the maintenance of an extensive library of technical analysis material, and the regular publication of newsletters and journals.

MTA members and affiliates include technical analysts, portfolio managers, investment advisors, market letter writers, and others involved in the technical aspects of equities, futures, options, fixed income securities, currencies, international markets, derivatives, and so on.

Services provided to our members and affiliates are performed by a small NYC-based Headquarters staff, an active Board of Directors, Committee Chairs, and an extensive cadre of volunteers located in both U.S. and non-U.S. markets.

The Chartered Market Technician® (CMT) credential is the global standard for practitioners of technical analysis and technical risk management. It is a FINRA-recognized designation that sets apart CMT chartholders as specialists and value generators among active investment professionals.

The designation is awarded to those who demonstrate mastery of a core body of knowledge in risk management and portfolio management settings. The advanced technical expertise represented by the CMT charter immediately communicates to clients and employers the disciplined approach, academic rigor, and unique professional skill set that CMT chartholders possess.

The objectives of the CMT program are:

- To promote high ethical standards of education, integrity, and professional excellence.

- To guide candidates in mastering a professional body of knowledge.

- To professionalize the discipline of technical analysis.

Those candidates who successfully complete all three levels of the CMT examination and agree to abide by the MTA Code of Ethics are granted the right to use the CMT credential.

The curriculum for the Market Technician Association's CMT exam Level III is comprised of selected readings in the areas of technical analysis and other financial disciplines. The MTA curates each level of the three-volume curriculum, reviewing the available academic literature as well as practitioner scholarship. The process for selecting content for the curriculum and exams has three phases: (1) a job-analysis effort that reviews current practices among professionals who use technical analysis, (2) focus groups with subject matter experts, and (3) a review and deliberation by the CMT Test and Curriculum Committee to determine the best readings needed for exam quality.

From this effort the MTA is able to fashion these readings into a consolidated study curriculum for CMT candidates. The curriculum is designed to help candidates gain a broad understanding of the core body of knowledge and best practices for using technical analysis in forecasting and active money management. The MTA is indebted to the fine work of each author whose work is included in the curriculum as well as the volunteers who donate their time to the improvement of these publications.

■ About the Content Selections for Level III

Level III readings are designed to help candidates be prepared to integrate technical analysis into their practices, regardless of the work in which they are engaged. The chapters in this book are organized in such a way as to help candidates begin integrating what they learned in Level I and Level II into a cohesive activity of analysis, advisement, trading, or active investing. The book's readings are presented by category, in the order of the first six knowledge domains each Level III candidate should master: Risk Management, Asset Relationships, Portfolio Management, Behavioral Finance, Volatility Analysis, and Classical Methods. The final domain, Ethics, is not covered in this book, but rather by the *Standards of Practice Handbook* published by the CFA Institute.

Congratulations on qualifying for the CMT Level III Exam. This exam is designed to test the candidate's ability to **integrate** their understanding of concepts identified in Level I studies with the practical application learned in Level II studies. The Level III Exam requires candidates to **implement** critical analysis to arrive at well-supported recommendations in an investing/trading context. This exam provides an opportunity for you to show, in real time, that you know how to properly apply technical analysis concepts to produce excellent analysis as a financial professional. A successful Level III candidate demonstrates that he or she is ready to apply technical analysis in a variety of roles in an institutional setting.

The CMT Level III Exam uses a combination of multiple-choice questions and short-answer format questions. Price information, data, and charts will be displayed on-screen during the test, and a printed chart packet will also be provided.

The curriculum is organized into exam-specific knowledge domains that provide a framework for recognizing and implementing investment/trading decisions. The CMT Level III Exam tests the candidate's knowledge in seven domains. The first domain is ethics; the remaining domains are listed here:

Domain/Chapters	Topics Included
Risk Management/1–9	System Development and Management, Risk Control, Behavioral Techniques, Multiple Time Frames
Asset Relationships/10–17	Regression, Asset Indices and Measures, Intraday Correlations, Intermarket Indicators, Visualizing Asset Relationships
Portfolio Management/18–21	Analyzing Macro Environments, Business Cycles, Portfolio Risk, Performance Measures, Statistical Analysis, System Validation
Behavioral Finance/22–27	Causality and Statistics, Illusions, Biases, Protecting against Bubble Behavior
Volatility/28–29	Historical and Implied Volatility, the VIX Index, Hedging with VIX Options, Forecasting with the VIX Index and Futures
Classical Methods/30–57	Candlestick Patterns, Price Patterns, Statistics of Pattern Performance, Momentum Investing, Technical Indicator Performance

■ Exam Topics and Question Weightings

1. Risk Management	a.	risk management (e.g., basics of probability and statistics, basics of modeling risk factors, number of assets and impact on portfolio, managing risk through correlation, value-at-risk, performance and risk metrics, market volatility and fat-tailed distributions, correlation and diversification, managing individual trade risk, managing risk for an entire portfolio	21%
	b.	position sizing	
	c.	quantitative and statistical analysis	
	d.	system development and testing	
2. Asset Relationships	a.	intermarket analysis	18%
	b.	relative strength	
	c.	sector rotation	
3. Portfolio Management	a.	portfolio management (performance measurement, tactical asset allocation, asset correlation, alternative investments)	18%
4. Behavioral Finance	a.	behavioral finance	10%
5. Volatility Analysis	a.	volatility analysis	7%
6. Classical Methods	a.	candlestick analysis	21%
	b.	momentum investing	
	c.	oscillators or various technical studies	
7. Ethics	a.	ethics	5%

CHAPTER 1

System Design and Testing

From Charles D. Kirkpatrick II and Julie R. Dahlquist, *Technical Analysis: The Complete Resource for Financial Market Technicians*, 3rd Edition (Old Tappan, New Jersey: Pearson Education, Inc., 2016), Chapter 22.

Learning Objective Statements

- Explain the importance of using a system for trading or investing
- Compare and analyze differences between a discretionary and nondiscretionary system
- Describe the mind-set and discipline required to develop and trade with a system
- Explain the basic procedures for designing a system
- Describe the role that risk management plays in system design
- Identify and evaluate various ways to test a system
- Compare and analyze standard measures of system profitability and risk

We have covered most of the methods used by technical analysts to analyze the trading markets. We now enter into the field of how to utilize this knowledge to produce profits and reduce risk. Any constant and consistent management of assets requires money management, which we cover in the next chapter, and some type of system. Haphazardly investing or trading on intuition, rumor, or untested theories is a road to disaster. It is why most amateur traders and investors lose money.

A fundamental investor may use price-to-earnings, debt ratios, and so forth, whereas a technical investor will likely use relative strength, price trend, or volatility, and both investors will believe they are doing the correct analysis. They are not. In both cases, the methods may be correct, but making money requires a tested system. There are many myths in investing, and most investors succumb to them without further analysis. To trade or invest successfully, we need to know not only how profitable a method has been, but also what the risks of capital loss were. Not having an understanding of tested methods is flying blind in the financial markets. How do we test these methods? We create a system. The system must include not only the method for profit but also the means of controlling risk of loss. Both aspects of investing are extremely important. Some would argue that controlling loss is even more important than the profit method, that by buying and selling at the flip of a coin, one could make a decent return just by controlling risk of loss.

Let us begin this chapter by looking a little more closely at what a system is. Then we focus on what risk is and how to control losses. Once we have these foundations, we can focus on the mechanics of developing a system and testing investment strategies.

▪ Why Are Systems Necessary?

No stock market goes up forever. Indeed, most world stock markets have declined to zero at one time or another. The buy-and-hold strategy so popular in the United States today is based on a statistical anomaly. It is a strategy based on a survival bias in the U.S. and the U.K. markets, the only countries in history, so far, whose markets have not completely disappeared at some time (Burnham, 2005). This has caused a misleading assumption that U.S. stocks and stocks in general will necessarily continue to rise. "It would be naïve to expect the future of U.S. stocks to be as bright as the past" (Burnham, 2005, p. 175).

We certainly know that individual stocks can go to zero. How about buggy whips in 1910, or canals in 1830, or bowling in 1950, or junk bonds and REITs in 1980, or more recently the autos and the banks? Thus, a long-term plan that excludes a means of controlling risk is eventually doomed.

On the other hand, most technical and fundamental methods, by themselves, are not profitable over time either. Some of the exceptions have been covered earlier in this book, but these methods primarily depend upon the market circumstances at the time, on the method used, and on controlling risk. Traders' and investors' greatest misconception is that the market has order and that by finding and acting on that order, profits will be consistent and large. It presumes that a magic formula exists somewhere that can predict markets. This belief is not true. In looking at the previous studies in this book, there is no magic order to the markets beyond the fact that they sometimes trend and, more often, remain in trading ranges. The money made is based on the use of well-controlled entries and exits, especially those that limit the amount of loss that can occur and that will react to changing conditions in the market. A system will aid the investor or trader in timing these market entries and exits.

Discretionary Versus Nondiscretionary Systems

Systems are the next step in the development of an investment plan after understanding the methods of either technical or fundamental investing. Systems can be discretionary, nondiscretionary, or a combination of both. In discretionary systems, entries and exits are determined by intuition; in other words, the trader or investor exercises some discretion in making trades. Nondiscretionary systems are those in which entries and exits are determined mechanically by a computer.

Think for a minute of the stereotypical discretionary trader. Imagine the ultimate discretionary trader behaving like the man in the antacid advertisement with two or three phones yelling, "Buy" in one, "Sell" in another, with computer screens showing prices and charts of securities all over the world, with ringing phones, with news broadcasts from financial TV stations, and with a large contact list of people in different specialties. This type of trader is generally looking for the home run. It is a great image, one that has in it a bit of the swashbuckler, the gunslinger, and so on. In fact, many truly exceptional traders are like this. They have the gifted intuition to be able to do this consistently and profitably.

Most people, however, do not have the time, the knowledge, the contacts, the equipment, the quickness of thought, or the stomach to do this. In fact, most people who attempt to trade like this either burn out or go broke. They have no way of evaluating what they are doing except from the equity in their account at the end of the day. It is as if the excitement is more important than making profits.

The nondiscretionary trader, on the other hand, is usually calm, calculating, and likely bored. The majority of successful traders and investors use nondiscretionary systems (Etzkorn interview of Babcock, 1996). Some have been engineers; others have that type of mind, familiar with statistics and systems. They have studied the markets, the methods of profit-making—both fundamental and technical—and have tested the techniques using modern statistical methods. They understand that nothing is perfect and that markets change character over time. However, by testing their methods and strategies, they have derived a mechanical system that minimizes risk of loss and maximizes return.

Rules are the structure of a system. An example of a rule would be "buy when one moving average A crosses above another moving average B." Variables are the numerical inputs required in the rules (length of moving average A and length of moving average B). Parameters are the actual values used in the variables (two days and seven days). A system will include all these factors; their usefulness is determined by testing different rules, variables, and parameters over varied markets and market conditions.

A purely nondiscretionary system is one that runs by itself on market data that is continually fed into it. If our rule is to buy when the two-day moving average crosses above the seven-day moving average, for example, a buy order automatically is placed when this occurs. Once the trader has determined the rule to follow, the system is on autopilot and the trader does not make decisions.

A trader or investor can also choose to use a partial discretionary system. The partial discretionary system is one that generates signals that then are acted upon by the investor based on personal confidence in them and experience with them. By having some discretion, however, the system cannot be tested accurately because emotion can enter into the trading decisions and cause unquantifiable errors.

Is it always better to choose a nondiscretionary, mechanical system over a discretionary one? Let us look at some of the advantages and disadvantages of this approach.

Benefits of a Nondiscretionary, Mechanical System   A nondiscretionary, mechanical system provides a mathematical edge as determined by testing and adjusting. This is the principle behind the casino and an insurance business, both of which profit from many small profitable trades and occasional losses.

Using a nondiscretionary system avoids emotion. This is an advantage because traders often lose money due to emotional decisions. The nondiscretionary system also reduces other trading pitfalls—overtrading, premature action, no action, and constant decision making. Trading with a properly designed mechanical system also prevents large losses and risk of ruin, which most traders have never quantified or understood. In fact, risk control can be one of the most important advantages of a mechanical system.

Trading with a nondiscretionary system also provides certainty, develops confidence, and produces less stress. Anxiety comes from uncertainty and ambiguity. Although a nondiscretionary system cannot predict the future, it can structure how to react to possible outcomes. It gives a list of responses to events beyond one's control.

Pitfalls to a Nondiscretionary, Mechanical System   Although there are many benefits to a nondiscretionary, mechanical system, pitfalls also exist. For one, extrapolating will not have the same results as tests; history does not repeat itself precisely. The more a system is optimized or curve-fitted, the less reliable it will be in the future. In fact, in their book *The Ultimate Trading Guide*, Hill, Pruitt, and Hill (2000) suggest that you should generally expect half the profits and twice the drawdowns as shown in tests of past data. Having been tested, the system designer expects results that are often unrealistic. The designer must be careful not to lose confidence when unrealistic expectations are not achieved.

Nondiscretionary systems often will make profits in clumps, especially if it is a trend-following system. The trader then loses small amounts waiting for the next clump and protecting from large losses. In other words, great creativity may have gone into inventing the system, but its operation is boring. In addition, some system designs allow large drawdowns but still eventually produce profits. The emotional problem for the user is the wait for the drawdown to be recovered and meanwhile the possible loss of confidence in the system. A loss of confidence results in fiddling with the rules or giving up just as the system is about to kick in.

Although a good system adjusts to a changing market, it does require periodic updates. This can often be a source of confusion for the designer. Is it time to update an underperforming system because of a changing marketplace? Alternatively, is the lackluster performance period a time for the trader to sit by patiently waiting for the system to kick in? The answers to these questions are not always obvious.

Remember that the system falls apart if it is not followed precisely. This is what the testing was for, and violations of the rules established from the testing negate the value of the system. This requires considerable discipline.

Using a nondiscretionary, mechanical system is not easy—otherwise, everyone would do it. There is a lot of work in coming up with a system, testing it, adjusting it, and trying it correctly and convincingly. The tendency for many people is to "wing it" and see if it works. That method leaves the trader nowhere.

A Complete Trading System

The following is from The Original Turtle Trading Rules by Turtle member Curtis Faith (bigpicture.typepad.com/comments/files/turtlerules.pdf):
Decisions required for successful trading:

- Markets—What to buy or sell

- Position Sizing—How much to buy or sell

- Entries—When to buy or sell

- Stops—When to get out of a losing position

- Exits—When to get out of a winning position

- Tactics—How to buy or sell

How Do I Design a System?

Now you are convinced that you need to design a system for trading. However, how do you do that? Let us look at some of the requirements and steps involved in creating an effective system.

Requirements for Designing a System

What is needed to design a successful system? Before even considering the components of a system, we must begin with something even more basic—designing a workable, profitable system begins with some basic personal attitudes. Some of the characteristics of the necessary mind-set include the following:

- Understand what a discretionary or nondiscretionary system will do—be realistically knowledgeable, and lean toward a nondiscretionary, mechanical system that can be quantified precisely and for which rules are explicit and constant.

- Do not have an opinion of the market. Profits are made from reacting to the market, not by anticipating it. Without a known structure, the markets cannot be predicted. A mechanical system will react, not predict.

- Realize that losses will occur—keep them small and infrequent.

- Realize that profits will not necessarily occur constantly or consistently.

- Realize that your emotions will tug at your mind and encourage changing or fiddling with the system. Such emotions must be controlled.

- Be organized—winging it will not work.

- Develop a plan consistent with one's time available and investment horizon—daily, weekly, monthly, and yearly.

- Test, test, and test again, without curve-fitting. Most systems fail because they have not been tested or have been overfitted.

- Follow the final tested plan without exception—discipline, discipline, discipline. No one is smarter than the computer, regardless of how painful losses may be and how wide spreads between price and stops may affect one's staying power.

Initial Decisions

Once you are committed to the mind-set and discipline of creating a system, you must make certain decisions about the characteristics of your system. The actual fundamental or technical method used as the basis for the system is relatively unimportant. What is important is that whatever is used can be defined precisely. Most fundamental and technical methods, by themselves, have a sketchy record of performance. Performance in the system will depend more on filters, adjustments, and the entry and exit strategies than the method itself. This does not mean that any old method will work. Pick a model (entry and exit method that has some statistical probability of success) that is familiar, sensible, comfortable, and has a decent record. Be sure it is based on facts, not opinion, and then concentrate on the process of developing a system.

Most systems designers argue that the simpler the system, the better. A system can become bogged down with large numbers of conditions and statistically will lose degrees of freedom, requiring more data and more signals to establish its significance. The market has **entropy**, an inherent disorder that changes periodically in unexpected ways. A system with few variables will reflect the patterns in the market with a certain accuracy. As more variables are added to the system, entropy causes the nonpattern variables to increasingly influence the results, causing the system to eventually decrease profitability because it can account only for the patterns but not the internal market changes. Indeed, when testing a system, the added variables should be tested for their effect on the system results, and if the performance declines, those variables should be eliminated even if they appear logical. Some designers such as Richard Dennis argue against simplicity (Collins, 2005), but they have enormous computer power and knowledge behind them. Hill and others argue that even with modern technology and mathematics, the success of systems now is no greater than the classic systems designed with a hand or crank calculator.

First, you must decide what kind of input and tested model is to be used to generate signals. Some investors depend on fundamental information; most traders depend on technical methods. Others use a combination. The important aspect is to have a clear understanding of the system's premises and to know that the rules will be easily quantifiable and precise. Specificity is much easier to use and to test than generality. You must also understand the logic of the system and be sure that it suits your style of trading or investing.

Second, you must decide on which markets to focus. Is the market suitable for the intended system? Are there opportunities for diversification between markets or instruments? How much volatility and liquidity is required, and what specific instruments will be traded?

Third, you must establish the time horizon for the system. For example, most trend-following systems work better over longer periods, but most pattern systems work in hours and days. Does the system intend to scalp trades, swing trade, or long-term invest? In addition, what is the psychologically best-suited time not only for system logic but also for ease of use? Do you have time to spend all day with the system, or can you monitor the system only daily, weekly, or monthly?

Fourth, you must have a risk control plan; otherwise, you will not know what to do when markets change. Understand that losses are inevitable, but be sure to keep them under control. Admitting losses separates the professional from the amateur. Rationalizing or excusing losses never helps. The market is never wrong—get out, the quicker the better. To do this, devise a stop-loss strategy—"no clinging to the mast of the sinking ship." This strategy should include protective and trailing stops, price targets, and adjustments for volatility, type of market, and any other state that the market might be in. Another option is to have a filter that shuts down the system when the market enters a trading range or has other characteristics that detract from the model's performance. Otherwise, the account may suffer a larger loss. Emotions and judgment become adversely affected, causing missed opportunities, selling profitable positions to get even, and other mistakes. Stop-losses free up nonproductive capital and cause less stress once accepted. In addition to risk control, you must decide whether you should use leverage or pyramiding.

Fifth, establish a time routine, which should include when to update the system and necessary charts, plan new trades, and update exit points for existing trades. As part of your system administration, maintain a trader's notebook, a trader's diary, and a daily equity chart. Maintain a daily trading sheet (similar to an accounting ledger) and a position sheet.

Types of Technical Systems

Technical analysts use a number of types of technical trading systems. Although there are numerous systems, they can be divided into four main categories: trend following, pattern recognition, range trading, and exogenous signals systems.

Trend Following From our knowledge of technical systems, we understand that markets trend at times and trade in a range at other times. The most profitable background is a trending background because the moves are larger and generate fewer transaction costs. While periodically trend trading becomes difficult and many traders begin to believe it is dead, it is not. As Bill Eckhardt, partner of Richard Dennis and originator of the Turtles, has been quoted, "I have lived through the death of trend-following a half dozen times, and, like Mark Twain's death, it was highly exaggerated." (Collins, 2005). Most large-scale mechanical system hedge funds and commodity trading advisors use trend-following systems. Rather than attempting to catch the peaks and valleys, the trend-following system acts in the direction of the trend as soon after it has begun as can be reliably detected. Contrary to the buy low and sell high philosophy, the trend-following system will buy high and sell higher. Schwager believes that slower, longer trend systems work better because the gains are larger, although less frequent, and the whipsaws are minimal. Most trend-following systems add a trend indicator such as the ADX to their set of rules to be sure that a trend is in existence. As we know from earlier studies on trends, the performance of a trend-following system can suffer during a trading range market.

Moving Average Systems   The classic trend-following system is composed of two moving averages that generate signals when they cross over each other. In his book *The Definitive Guide to Futures Trading*, Larry Williams discusses how, as early as the 1940s, Donchian demonstrated the validity of this method and showed that it was more successful than the older system of using price versus a single moving average.

If two moving averages are better than one, would three be even better? No, studies have shown that adding more moving averages weakens performance because of the increased number of rules required. Although practitioners frequently report success using moving averages, we must mention that academic studies have shown that moving average crossover systems, even with simple filters, are generally unprofitable. However, academics have not used any kind of risk control in their experiments. Without the use of these important risk-control strategies, the academic studies are not a true measure of the profitability of using a moving average crossover system.

Breakout Systems   A variation of the trend-following system is the breakout system. These systems generate buy and sell signals when price moves out of a channel or band. The most popular of these systems is based on a variation of the Donchian channel breakout system or some kind of volatility breakout system using Bollinger Bands or other measures of range volatility. The breakout system can be long term and use weekly figures, or short term, such as the open range breakout systems used intraday.

Problems with Trend-Following Systems   Given their profitability, the moving average and breakout strategies are popular. Because many of these trend-following systems are being traded, many others will receive the same signal at roughly the same time and price you will. Liquidity can become strained, and slippage costs from wider spreads and incomplete fills will increase the transaction costs over what may have been anticipated. The solution to this problem is to devise an original system or to spread out or scale entry orders.

Another problem with trend-following systems is that whipsaws are common, especially during a trading range market, as the system attempts to identify the trend. In fact, trend-following systems often produce less than 50% wins because of the many whipsaws during ranging markets. This problem can be reduced with the use of confirmations, such as special price requirements (penetration requirement, time delay, and so on), once a signal has been given, or through filters and diversification into uncorrelated markets.

Inevitably, to avoid whipsaws, a trend-following system will be late in the trend and will thus miss profit potential at both ends of the trend. Unfortunately, this is the cost of a trend-following system. If an attempt is made to clip more profit at each end of the trend, the number of losses will increase from the ranging nature of the trend at its terminal points. On the exit side of a trend, specific trailing stops or such can be used to receive better prices, but again there is the risk of missing another leg in the trend by exiting prematurely.

Losses occur primarily in the trading range preceding the establishment of a trend, as the system tries to identify the next trend as closely as possible. One strategy to combat this is to use a countertrend system at the same time, even if it is not as profitable as the trend-following system. The gains from the countertrend system will offset some of the losses of the trend-following system, and the overall performance results will improve over the trend-following system alone.

Moving-average and breakout systems are usually limited to a one-directional signal only. Part of the advantage in following a trend is to pyramid in the direction of the trend as evidence of its viability becomes stronger. To accomplish this in a trend-following system, other indicators must be used, thus increasing the complexity and decreasing the adaptability of the system.

The greatest fault with trend-following systems is the large percentage of consecutive small losses that produce significant drawdowns. For example, let us say that the system suffers ten small losses in a row while in a trading range. The drawdown to the equity of the account accumulates during this period from the peak of the equity to the subsequent cumulative loss. A series of losses that cause a large drawdown affect not only the pocketbook but also the confidence in the system and often lead to further complications. One strategy to lessen a sequence of losses is the strategy mentioned previously of using a countertrend system. Another is to initiate only small positions on a signal until the trend is well established. Yet another is to run another trend-following system parallel that has a longer or shorter period.

Because a trend-following system often is characterized by clumps of large profits from the trend and many small losses from the trading range, extreme volatility occurs in equity. We will look at this later when we study equity curve smoothness, but the most-often-used countermeasure is to diversify into other markets or systems.

As with most mechanical systems, a trend-following system can work well during testing and then bomb in practice. In most cases, this is due to improper testing and adjusting. Some-times the improper testing is due to unrealistic assumption about transactions costs. Unrealistic assumptions including spreads during fast markets, limit days in the futures market, and other possible anomalies may have given false results during the testing stage of the system under consideration. Remember that the popularity of trend-following systems can affect slippage; this fact often is erroneously ignored in the testing phase.

Occasionally, substantial parameter shifts will occur that the adaptive system will not be able to recognize and accommodate. Again, by diversifying by using more than one system or using market character adjustments to volatility, such problems can be reduced.

Pattern Recognition Systems

"Every ship at the bottom of the sea had plenty of charts" is attributed to noted systems trader Jon Najarian (Patel, 1997). Using patterns requires considerable testing and overcoming the problem of defining patterns. Larger patterns do not succumb to easy computer recognition because of their variable nature. System traders such as Larry Williams, Larry Connor, and Linda Raschke use short-term patterns, some of which we discussed in Level I, Chapter 8 and Level II, Chapter 9, "Short-Term Patterns," and limit their exposure with specific position stops and price or time targets. Generally, such systems are partially discretionary because they require some interpretation during the trade entry.

Reversion to the Mean

Reversion to the mean systems are based on the buy-low-sell-high philosophy within a trading range and are also called **trading range** systems. This type of system requires a certain amount of volatility between the peaks and valleys of ranges; otherwise, transaction costs, missing limits, and being stopped out on false moves chew up any potential profits. Generally, these systems are discretionary. They profit from **fading** small counter-trend moves or moves within a flat trend and using oscillators such as the stochastic, relative strength index (RSI), the Moving-Average Convergence/Divergence (MACD), or cycles. The largest potential problem in trading with one of these systems is the possibility of a trend developing that creates the risk of unlimited losses. Protective stops are a necessity.

Generally, this type of system does not perform well. A number of publicly available tests—for example, of buying and selling within Bollinger Bands—have been conducted, and invariably the best performance comes from buying and selling on breakouts from the bands rather than trading within them. The major use of countertrend systems is to run coincident with trend-following systems to dampen the series of losses in the trend-following system during a trading range.

Exogenous Signal Systems

Some systems generate signals from outside the market being traded. Intermarket systems, such as gold prices for the bond market, would be an example of an exogenous signal system. Other examples are sentiment such as the VIX for S&P futures, volume, or open interest warnings of activity that trigger price systems or act as confirmation of price systems, or fundamental signals such as monetary policy or consumer prices.

Which System Is Best?

Which type of system is the best? John R. Hill and George Pruitt, whose business is to test all manner of trading systems (www.futurestruth.com), maintain that the best and most reliable systems are trend-following systems. Within trend-following systems, the breakout systems have the best characteristics—specifically the Bollinger Band breakout systems, and the Don–chian, or channel, breakout systems. Closely behind are the moving-average crossover systems.

How Do I Test a System?

Testing a hypothetical system is absolutely necessary, and the testing process can be tedious because so many ideas of how to trade turn out to be unsuccessful. This is the most difficult aspect of designing a system, and unfortunately, because it is so time-consuming and discouraging, many analysts take short-cuts, such as not performing out-of-sample tests, and end up with a system that eventually blows up on them. The process begins with being sure the data being used in the testing is clean and the same as the data that will be used later when the system goes live. The next is to establish the rules for the model being chosen as the basis for the system and **optimize** the variables chosen. These rules include entry and exit signals at first and will have other filters added later depending on the results of the first series of tests. If a **walk-forward** program is not available, a large portion of the data, called **out-of-sample data**, must be kept aside to use later when testing the system for **robustness**. Once a viable system has been adequately optimized, the resulting parameters are then tested against the out-of-sample data to see if the system works with unknown data and was not the result of **curve-fitting** or **data mining**. This is the disheartening part of system design because invariably the out-of-sample test will fail, and the development must return to the beginning. It is at this point that most amateurs give up.

Clean Data

Not surprisingly, for an accurate evaluation of any system, the data must be impeccable. Without the correct data, the system tests are useless. Data should always be the same as what will be used when the system is running in real time. Not only the data but also the data vendor should be the same source as what will be used in practice. Different vendors receive different data feeds. This is especially a problem in short-term systems, where the sequence of trades is important for execution and for pattern analysis.

The amount of data required depends on the period of the system. A general rule of thumb is that the data must be sufficient to provide at least 30 to 50 trades (entry and exit) and cover periods where the market traveled up, down, and sideways. This will ensure that the test has enough history behind it and enough exposure to different market circumstances.

The real-time trader has enough difficulty with "dirty" data on a live feed, and this becomes just as crucial when testing back data. Cleanliness of data is a necessary requirement. Any anomalies or mispriced quotes will have an effect on the system test and will skew the results in an unrealistic manner. Cleaning of data is not an easy task and often must be relegated to the professional data providers.

Special Data Problems for Futures Systems

Although stock data has a few historical adjustments such as dividend payments, splits, offerings, and so on, the futures market has another more serious problem: which contract to test. Most futures contracts have a limited life span that is short enough not to be useful in testing most systems. The difficulty comes from the difference in price between the price at expiration and the price of the nearest contract on that date into which the position would be rolled. Those prices are rarely the same and are difficult to splice into something realistic that can be used for longer-term price analysis. To test a daily system, for example, two years or more of daily data is required at the very least, but no contract exists that runs back for two years. Of course, testing can be done on nearest contract series, but it is limited to the contract length. This is satisfactory if the system trades minute by minute but not for daily signals in a longer-term system.

To rectify this problem, two principal methods of splicing contract prices of different expirations together in a continuous stream have been used. These methods are known as perpetual contracts and continuous contracts. Neither is perfect, but these methods are the ones most commonly used in longer-term price studies.

Perpetual contracts, also called **constant forward contracts**, are interpolations of the prices of the nearest two contracts. Each is weighted based on the proximity to expiration of the nearest contract to the forward date—say, a constant 90 days. As an example, assume that today is early December, only a few days from expiration of the December contract of a commodity future and a little over three months from the expiration of the March contract, the next nearest. The 90-day perpetual would be calculated by proportioning each contract's current price by the distance each is in time from the date 90 days from now. This weighting in early December favors the March contract price, and each day as we approach the December expiration, the December contract receives less weight until expiration when the perpetual is just the March contract price. The following day, however, the March contract price begins to lose weighting as the June contract price begins to increase its weighting. This process gives a smooth but somewhat unrealistic contract price; it eliminates the problem of huge price gaps at rollover points, but you cannot literally trade a constant forward series. As Schwager points out, "the price pattern of a constant-forward series can easily deviate substantially from the pattern exhibited by the actual traded contracts—a highly undesirable feature" (1996, p. 664).

The continuous, or spread-adjusted, contract is more realistic, but it suffers from the fact that at no time is the price of the continuous contract identical to the actual price because it has been adjusted at each expiration or each rollover date. The continuous contract begins at some time in the past with prices of a nearby contract. A rollover date is determined based on the trader's usual rollover date—say, ten days before expiration. Finally, a cumulative adjustment factor is determined. As time goes on and different contracts roll over to the next contract, this spread between contracts is accumulated and the continuous contract price adjusted accordingly. With this method, the continuous prices are exactly what would have been the cost to the trader had the system signals been followed when they occurred. There is no distortion of prices. Price trends and formations occur just as they would have at the time. The only difference is that the actual prices are not those in the continuous contract. Percentage changes, for example, are not accurate. Nevertheless, the method demonstrates exactly what would have happened to a system during the period of the continuous contract, which is precisely what the systems designer wants to know.

As Schwager points out, "a linked futures price series can only accurately reflect either price *levels*, as does the nearest futures, or price *moves* as does continuous futures, but not both…" (1996, p. 669). Students interested in trading futures can refer to the book *Schwager on Futures: Technical Analysis*, to learn more about these techniques.

Testing Methods and Tools

Fortunately, the wheel need not be reinvented when it comes to testing software. Many trading software products include a testing section. Some are reliable; however, some are not. Before purchasing any such software, you should understand the testing methods and resulting reports of the software. Almost all such programs leave out crucial analysis data and may often define terms and formulas differently from others. For example, the term *drawdown* has different meanings, depending on intraday data, closing data, trade close data, and so forth. You must understand the meaning of all terms in any software program to correctly interpret tests performed by it. With this in mind, the systems analyst must establish exactly what information is desired, what evaluation criteria would be useful, and how the results should be presented.

Test Parameter Ranges

The initial test of a system is run to see if the system has any value and, if so, where the problem areas might lie. When the testing program is run, the parameters selected initially should be tested to see if they fall in a range or are independent spikes that might or might not occur in the future. A parameter range, called the **parameter set**, which gives roughly the same results, bolsters confidence in the appropriateness of the parameter value. If, when the parameter value is changed slightly, the performance results deteriorate rapidly, the parameter will not likely work in the future. It is just an aberration. When the results remain the same or similar, the parameter set is said to be stable—obviously a desirable characteristic.

BOX 1.1   DESIGNING A SYSTEM: "HAL" (NAME OF THE COMPUTER IN
2001: A SPACE ODYSSEY)

Let us look at a simple case study of how to develop a trading system. Suppose we decide that we will trade International Business Machines (IBM), traditionally a less volatile blue chip. We also decide that we will start with an oscillator called the **Commodity Channel Index (CCI)**. The CCI is an oscillator similar to the Stochastic only it includes a volatility component and thus makes it a more realistic indicator of overbought or oversold. The signals will come from the CCI crossing levels determined by the optimization.

Looking at the monthly chart of IBM (see Figure 1.1) from 2005 through mid-2015, we see several periods of upward and downward trends and trading ranges. This is an ideal history to analyze and test because it includes the three possible trends in any market: up, down, and sideways. It also covers a period of more than nine years, roughly 2250 days, enough to give us plenty of signals.

Normally the CCI is contained with +300 and –300 but is not explicitly bounded. The only variables are the length of the moving averages used in its construction and the level of the two signal lines.

The account will assume a capitalization of $30,000, and commissions and slip-page will be 10 cents per share for each entry and exit or 20 cents per share total. The entries will be limited to 100 shares per trade and only one 100-share position allowed. The reason for this model in our exercise is that we know it has worked well over the past two years, and we want to see if changing the parameters can improve its performance.

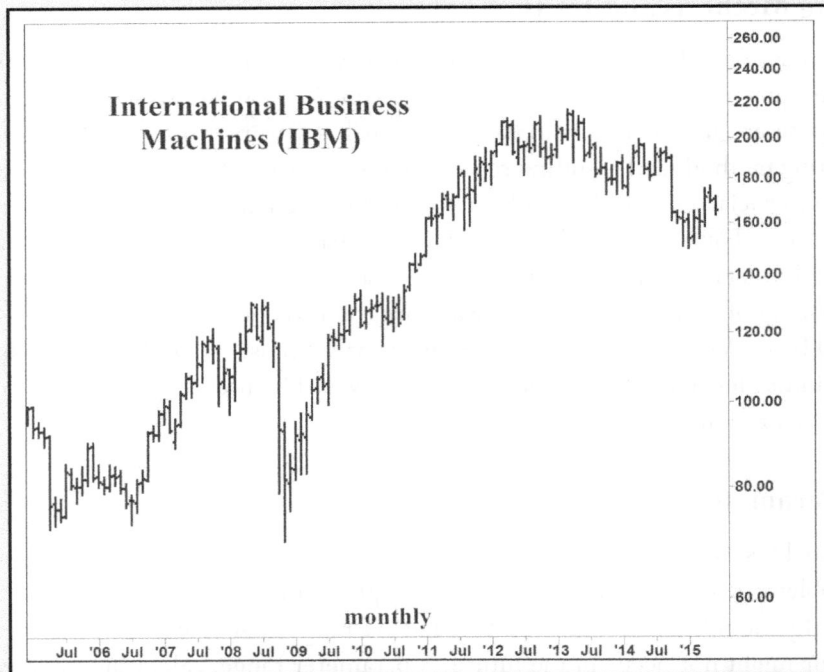

Created using TradeStation

FIGURE 1.1   International Business Machines Corporation common stock price (monthly: January 2005–June 2015)

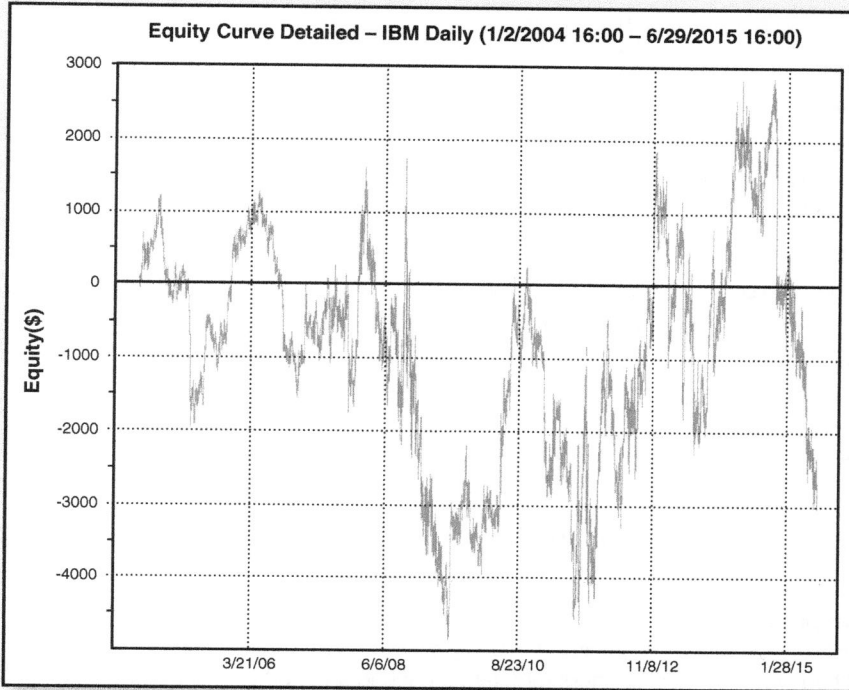

FIGURE 1.2 **Equity curve for trading IBM using a Bollinger Band reversion to the mean model (IBM weekly: January 2, 2004–June 29, 2015)**

The equity curve for this system with the default length parameter of 14 and signal levels as +100 and –100 is shown in Figure 1.2. An equity curve is a chart of the equity in the account (vertical axis) versus time measured either by trade number or by time (horizontal axis). In Figure 1.2, time is along the horizontal axis. Looking at the chart, we can see that the system had a mixed performance and could easily be discarded as just another oscillator. However, if we change the parameters through optimization and walk-forward testing, perhaps we can find a more reliable formula that worked in the past for the entire period and will have a good chance of working in the future.

The tabulated data in Table 1.1 is from this one run using the standard Bollinger Band parameters.

TABLE 1.1 **HAL Initial Test Statistics**

Trades	All	Long	Short
Net profit	($2,153)	$2,991	$(5,144)
Gross profit	$32,773	$17,229	$15,544
Gross loss	($34,926)	($14,238)	($20,688)
Profit factor	0.94	1.21	0.75
Number of trades	139	69	70
Percent profitable	57.55	65.22	50.00
Average trade net profit	($15.49)	43.35	($73.49)
Largest winner as a % of gross profit	5.92%	6.32%	12.47%
Largest loser as a % of gross loss	7.76%	19.04%	9.60%

(continued)

TABLE 1.1 *(Continued)*			
Trades	All	Long	Short
Maximum consecutive losing trades	4	3	5
Average days in winning position	14.41	15.2	13.5
Average days in losing position	29.51	26.13	31.83
Buy-and-hold return	80.7%		
Return on account	(40.41 %)		
Monthly average return	($31.63)		
Standard deviation of monthly return	$887.80		
Sharpe ratio	(0.01)		
System MAR (intraday)	(negative)	0.666	(negative)
Trade MAR	(negative)	0.883	(negative)

Source: TradeStation

Let's look at some of these statistics and learn what they tell us about the HAL system so far:

- **Net profit** is the difference between gross profit and gross loss. It is negative for this system as a whole but positive for long positions. This problem can be attacked in one of two ways: using different parameters for selling short or just using it for long signals. If we use long signals only, we already have a viable system that has worked in the past but not very well. We decide we will adjust both long and short signals with an optimization and walk-forward test.

- **Gross profit and gross loss** are the totals under each category for each trade. Gross profit is the total profit from profitable trades; gross loss is the total from all losing trades.

- The **profit factor** is the absolute value of the ratio of gross profit to gross loss. It shows the profitability of the system. In this case, for every dollar of loss, 0.94 dollars of profit are generated; in other words, it is a losing system. The long side only was favorable at 1.29. The better systems are above 2.00.

- Looking at the **number of trades,** this system generated 139 trades: 69 long trades and 70 short trades. This is a large enough number of trades for reliable statistics. Generally, at least 30–50 trades are required to test a system.

- **Percent profitable** is the percent of all trades that were profitable. In our example, 57.55% of the trades were profitable, yet the system lost money. This suggests that there is something wrong with the losing trades; although fewer in number, they are losing more than the winners.

- **Average trade net profit** is the average profit received per trade. This is negative and suggests that the system is vulnerable to transaction costs.

- The **largest winner or loser versus gross profit or gross loss** figure gives a hint as to whether the gain or loss was accounted for by only one trade. In this case, the largest winning trade accounted for 5.92% of the total gross profit. This is a reasonable size when considering that the total number of trades was greater than 139.

- The **maximum consecutive losing trades** is important because a long string of consecutive losses invariably causes a large drawdown and, thus, a high potential risk for the system. In this case, the number of successive losses is four trades in a row.

It suggests that two whipsaws took place during the test period. Whipsaws can be controlled with stops.

- Considering the **average weeks in winning and losing positions,** there is not much question that the HAL has a problem with losing trades. There should be considerably less time in losing trades. The rule of thumb is that one-quarter of the time can be spent on losing trades versus winning trades, but with a long holding period, the system isn't kicking the losers out soon enough.

- **Buy-and-hold return (80.7%)** is the return gained if the investor bought the IBM on the first day and held it for the entire time period through all its gyrations. This is the number to beat.

- **Return on account (–40.41%)** is the total return on the minimum account size as determined by the maximum drawdown. It should be compared to the buy-and-hold return to see if the system outperforms a do-nothing approach. In this case, the system failed to exceed the do-nothing approach. Of course, such comparisons are not as easy as they look because the concept of risk has not been introduced to either method. The buy-and-hold method has infinite risk because the drawdown can be 100%. The risk of the system has been limited to a much smaller percentage, but we are still observing losses.

- **Average monthly return and standard deviation** of the monthly return are used to determine the volatility of returns. The average monthly return for this system is –$31.63, but it is highly volatile with a standard deviation of $887.80. Ideally, a system should have a standard deviation less than five times the monthly return. In this case, it is 31.5 times, far above the limit, and likely due to the large number of losses.

- The **Sharpe ratio** is a common measure of the return versus risk of a portfolio or system. As we saw in Level II, Chapter 21, "Selection of Markets and Issues: Trading and Investing," it is a ratio of return—in this case, adjusted for the risk-free return of T-bills, to the standard deviation of return, a proxy for risk. As we stated earlier, however, risk is not just volatility, but is also the risk of capital loss. The Sharpe ratio fails to account for drawdown and fails to account for skewed deviations of return. An investment that deviates more to the upside, for example, will not be fairly represented by the Sharpe ratio, which assumes a normal distribution. These problems are why system designers shy away from the Sharpe ratio and have designed other ratios of return to risk that are more realistic. In this system, the Sharpe ratio is close to zero, suggesting that the return does not exceed the risk-free return of T-bills.

- **System MAR** is the ratio of annual percentage net gain for the system to the maximum percentage drawdown (MDD). The maximum percentage draw-down is the maximum percent that the equity curve corrected from a peak. The ratio measures the greatest decline that occurred during the system run and thus the potential loss in the future for the system. A ratio of greater than 1.0 is preferred.

  Naturally, one wants a system that has no drawdown, but barring that, one wants a system that has profits considerably higher than any drawdown potential. A large drawdown lowers trust in the system and may cause a premature close of the system before it has a chance to perform. The HAL has a negative gain versus a maximum drawdown. The favored standard is anything above 1.00. The ratio is, thus, a gauge for comparing systems.

- **Trade MAR** is the ratio of the net annual gain percentage to the largest trade drawdown in a trade, sometimes called the **Maximum Adverse Excursion.** Where maximum system drawdown may include many trades, the individual trade risk is also needed to gauge the systems performance and isolate where losses are occurring.

HAL may have promise if we can fix the problem with lengthy losing trades and the short selling losses. The long only section is satisfactory and will improve with improvement in the losses, but the entire system is bogged down by poor performance in the short side. This is not surprising in a market that has a generally upward trend, but it still is disappointing. We look next at ways to improve this system with optimized parameters and changes in the model logic.

▨ Optimization

Once you determine that the parameters in your system are valid, you may optimize the system. **Optimizing** is simply changing the parameters of a system to achieve the best results. The most important benefit of optimization is that the designer may find parameters that do not work under any circumstances. If parameters do not work with the past data, it is highly likely they will not work in the future. Thus, optimizing can eliminate useless rules and parameters.

Optimizing is also useful in determining whether certain types of stops are useful. Often the designer finds that there is a limit—for example, to a protective stop—beyond which the stop does not add to the system performance. Often, the distance of trailing stops is too close to the last price, causing premature exits. These determinations can be analyzed more closely with optimization.

Although it can be beneficial, optimization does come with major hazards. With modern computers and sophisticated software, we can take any series of prices and find the best parameters for any predefined system. The problem is that by doing such an optimization, we are just fitting the data to a curve of results and have no idea whether the parameters we have derived will perform in the future. Because the future is what we are attempting to control, most optimization is useless and even dangerous because it gives us a false sense of confidence.

The principal concern with optimization is the tendency to **curve-fit**. Curve-fitting occurs when the optimization program finds the absolute best set of parameters. What the program is really doing is fitting the parameters to the data that is being tested. Thus, it is forming a mathematical model of that data and fitting parameters to that particular time in history. The only way that the parameters will work in the future is if the future exactly duplicates the history that was optimized. Of course, we know this will never happen and, thus, the parameters determined by optimization likely will be useless in the future. Any system could be made to look profitable if optimized; this is a problem that buyers of systems must face when considering purchasing an existing system for investing or trading. The trick is to optimize over a certain period and then test the parameters derived through optimization on a period in which no optimization has been conducted. This is called **out-of-sample (OOS) testing**. Invariably we will find that the results in the optimization will overstate the results in the out-of-sample period and, thus, the optimized parameters should never be used to evaluate the system's usefulness. Optimization should be kept simple. Fine-tuning the system just increases the level of false confidence that eventually will be dashed in real time when the system fails.

There is, thus, some controversy about the use of optimization in arriving at workable mechanical systems. The basic principles of realistic optimization are to keep it simple, test out-of-sample data against in-sample optimization results, preferably use baskets of securities, determine parameter sets instead of single parameters, understand that the best results are high profits with minimal risk, and avoid expecting to find the Holy Grail. Next, we discuss some optimization methods and some tests for statistical significance to perform after the most realistic parameter sets have been determined.

Before optimizing, the analyst must decide what the optimization is looking for in the data. Is it looking for net profit, maximum drawdown, Sharpe ratio, percentage of winning trades, or any other **objective function**? This objective function is an important aspect of the investigation for the best system. What is best? Many analysts use as their objective function a ratio of net profit to maximum drawdown, called the **MAR ratio**, to account not only for profits but also for risk of loss. Others use a **regression line** fit to the resulting profits. A tight fit suggests less volatility and thus less drawdown. A variation is called the **perfect profit correlation**. It assumes that the perfect system would buy every trough and sell every peak and thus generate a certain "perfect" profit. The tested system results are then compared to the perfect system to see how well it correlated.

Methods of Optimizing

As a general rule, an optimization should be done over a considerable period of price data and include those periods when the prices are in trends and in trading ranges. We do not know ahead of time whether the future will be similar, but we do know that there will be trends and trading ranges. Any system must be able to deal with both of these situations and have developed adjustable parameter sets or rules that will account for them. Parameters determined in this manner should be suitable for future conditions.

Whole Sample One method of optimizing is to take the entire price sample and run an optimization of the parameters. This is usually frowned upon because it is the closest to curve-fitting. To avoid curve-fitting, optimization should optimize only a portion of the data, called **in-sample (IS)** data, and test the resulting parameters on another portion of the data, called **out-of-sample (OOS)** data, to see if positive results continue in data not seen before by the optimization process. The selection of data can be a basket of stocks or futures rather than a single market average or issue and should have sufficient data to produce over 30 trades. The diversification of securities reduces the likelihood that any results are solely the result of peculiarities in a particular security, and the large number of signals increases the statistical significance of the results. After determining the optimal parameter sets—those that are consistent and give decent results (but not necessarily the best results)—the next step is to divide the optimization period into segments and run a test on each using the derived parameter sets. The results from these different periods then can be analyzed for consistency to see if the system generated similar results under all conditions. Things to look for are the amount of drawdowns, the number of signals, the number of consecutive losses, the net profit as a percentage of maximum drawdown, and so on. The actual amount of net profit is less important for each stage than are the determinants of risk and the consistency of results (Ruggiero, 2005). If the results are not consistent, the system has a major problem and should be optimized using other means or discarded.

Out-of-Sample Optimization (OOS) This is a method most often used in **neural network** and **regression** studies. We do not cover these particular methods because they are more useful with other data series. They can be used in market analysis, and some people, such as Lou Mendleson (www.profittaker.com), claim to have successfully been able to correlate different markets using neural network patterns. However, for purposes of this study of optimization, we ignore neural networks, multiple regressions, and others such as expert systems and artificial intelligence. Instead, we focus on the most common and productive methods—those used by the majority of systems designers.

One variation of OOS that is commonly used is to take the entire price data series to be optimized and divide it into sections, one of 70%–80% being the IS data and the remaining 20% to 30% being the OOS data. The out-of-sample data can include the first small portion of the total period and the last, or just the last, most recent data. As with all other test methods, the sample must include bull, bear, and consolidation periods. The total amount of data necessary is large in all optimization processes to account for periods of upward, downward, and sideways trends. All must be included so that the system can learn to adjust to any future change in direction or habit.

This method optimizes the in-sample data and then tests it on the out-of-sample data. The out-of-sample results are theoretically what the system should expect in real time. Invariably, the out-of-sample performance will be considerably less than the performance generated in the optimization. If the out-of-sample results are unsatisfactory, the method can be repeated with different parameters, but the more that the out-of-sample results are used as the determinant of parameter sets, the more that the objectivity of the optimization is compromised and the closer to curve-fitting the process becomes. Eventually, if continued in this manner, the out-of-sample data becomes the same as the sample data, and the optimization is just curve-fitting. One other method of reducing the effect of curve-fitting is to use more than one market as the out-of-sample test. It is difficult to have the same parameter set in different markets and at the same time curve-fit. This appears counterintuitive because most analysts would think that each market is different, has its own personality, and requires different parameters. Indeed, when looking at publicly available systems for sale, one method of eliminating a system from consideration is if it has different parameters for different markets. This usually indicates that the results are from curve-fitting, not real-time performance. A reliable system should work in most markets.

Walk Forward Optimization Walk forward optimization is also an OOS method that uses roughly the same price data series as the one described previously. Although there are many variations of this method, the most common procedure is to optimize a small portion of the data and then test it on a small period of subsequent data—for example, daily data over a year is optimized and then tested on the following six months' data. The resulting parameters of this test are recorded, and another year's data is optimized—this time, the in-sample data used includes the earlier OOS data plus six months of the earlier IS data. Again, the results are recorded, and the window is moved forward another six months until the test reaches the most recent data. Each optimization, thus, has an out-of-sample test. The results from all the recordings are then analyzed for consistency, profit, and risk. If some parameter set during the walk forward process suddenly changes, the system is unlikely to work in the future. The final decision about parameter sets is determined from the list of test results.

Optimization and Screening for Parameters We look next at all the different summaries and ratios that a system designer considers in measuring **robustness** (the ability of the system to adjust to changing circumstances), but first we must mention those that are used to screen out the better systems during optimization.

When optimization is conducted on a price series, the results will show a number of different parameter sets and a number of results from each parameter set. We can look at the net profit, the maximum drawdown, and any of the other statistics shown in Box 1.1. Many analysts screen for net profit, return on account, or profit factor as a beginning. They look at the average net profit per trade to see if the system generates trades that will not be adversely affected by transaction costs. Most important, they look at the net profit as a percentage of the maximum drawdown. The means of profiting from a system—any system of investing—are determined by the amount of risk involved. Remember the law of percentages. Risk of capital loss is the most important determinant in profiting. The net profit percentage of maximum drawdown describes quickly the bottom-line performance of the system. Unfortunately, the optimizing software of some commercial systems fails to include this factor, and it must be calculated from other reported statistics.

Measuring System Results for Robustness

When analyzing a system, we look at the system components, the profit, the risk, and the smoothness of the equity curve. We want to know how robust our results are. Robustness simply means how strong and healthy our results are; it refers to how well our results will hold up to changing market conditions. It is important that our system continues to perform well when the market changes because, although markets trend and patterns tend to repeat, the future market conditions will not exactly match the past market conditions that were the basis for our system design.

Components   The most important aspect of the optimization and testing process is to be sure that all calculations are correct. This sounds simple, but it is surprising how often this is overlooked and computer program errors have led to improper calculations. The next aspect is to be sure that the number of trades is large enough to make the results significant. The rule of thumb is between 30 and 50 trades in the OOS data, with 50 or more being the ideal. We have mentioned previously that the comparisons between in-sample and out-of-sample results should differ in performance but should not materially differ in average duration of trades, maximum consecutive winners and losers, the worst losing trade, and the average losing trade. We should also be aware of the average trade result in dollars and the parameter stability. We could apply a student t test to the parameters and their results to see if their differences are statistically significant, and we should test for brittleness, the phenomenon when one or more of the rules are never triggered. Once we are satisfied that the preceding inspection shows no material problems, we can look at the performance statistics more closely.

Profit Measures   Remember that the point of practicing technical analysis is to make money—or profit. On the surface, it seems as if this is a simple concept: if I end up with more money than I began with, then the system is profitable. Actually, measuring and comparing the profitability of various potential systems is not quite so straightforward. There are several ways in which analysts will measure the profitability of systems. The major ways are as follows:

- Total profit to total loss, called the **profit factor**, is the most commonly used statistic to initially screen for systems from optimization. It must be above 1.0, or the system is losing, and preferably above 2.0. Although a high number suggests greater profits, we must be wary of overly high numbers; generally, a profit factor greater than ten is a warning that the system has been curve-fitted. As a measure of general performance, the profit factor only includes profits and losses, not drawdowns. It, therefore, does not represent statistics on risk.

- **Outlier-adjusted profit** to loss is a profit factor that has been adjusted for the largest profit. Sometimes a system will generate a large profit or loss that is an anomaly. If the profit factor is reduced by this anomaly and ends up below 1.0, the system is a bust because it depended solely on the one large profit. The largest winning trade should not exceed 40% to 50% of total profit.

- **Percentage winning trades** is a number we use in the next chapter on the makeup of risk of ruin. Obviously, the more winning trades there are, the less chance of a run of losses against a position. In trend-following systems, this percentage is often only 30% to 50%. Most systems should look for a winning trade percentage greater than 60%. Any percentage greater than 70% is suspect.

- **Annualized rate of return** is used for relating the results of a system against a market benchmark.

- The **payoff ratio** is a calculation that is also used in the risk of ruin estimate. It is a ratio of the average winning trade to average losing trade. For trend-following systems, it should be greater than 2.0.

- The **length of the average winning trade** to average losing trade should be greater than 1. Otherwise, the system is holding losers too long and not maximizing the use of capital. Greater than 5 is preferable for trend-following systems.

- The **efficiency factor** is the net profit divided by the gross profit (Sepiashvili, 2005). It is a combination of win/loss ratio and wins probability. Successful systems usually are in the range of 38% to 69%—the higher the better. This factor is mostly influenced by the win percentage. It suggests that reducing the number of losing trades is more effective for overall performance than reducing the size of the losses, as through stop-loss orders.

For a system to be robust, we should not see a sudden dip in profit measures when parameters are changed slightly. Stability of results is more important than total profits.

Risk Measures What happens if you find a system that has extraordinarily high profit measures? Chances are you have a system with a lot of risk. Remember, high profits are good, but we must balance them against any increased risk. Some of the major ways that analysts will measure the risk within their system are as follows:

- The **maximum cumulative drawdown** of losing trades can also be thought of as the largest single trade paper loss in a system. The maximum loss from an equity peak is the **maximum drawdown (MDD)**. The rule of thumb is that a maximum drawdown of two times that found in optimizing should be expected and used in anticipated risk calculations.

- The **MAR ratio** is the net profit percent as a ratio to maximum drawdown percent. It is also called the **Recovery Ratio**, and it is one of the best methods of initially screening results from optimization. In any system, the ratio should be above 1.0.

- **Maximum consecutive losses** often affect the maximum drawdown. When this number is large, it suggests multiple losses in the future. It is imperative to find out what occurred in the price history to produce this number if it is large.

- **Large losses** due to price shocks show how the system reacts to price shocks.

- The **longest flat time** demonstrates when money is not in use. It is favorable in that it frees capital for other purposes.

- The **time to recovery** from large drawdowns is a measure of how long it takes to recuperate losses. Ideally, this time should be short and losses recuperated quickly.

- **Maximum favorable and adverse excursions** from list of trades informs the system's designer of how much dispersion exists in trades. It can be used to measure the smoothness of the equity curve but also give hints as to where and how often losing trades occur. Its primary use is to give hints as to where trailing stops should be placed to take advantage of favorable excursions and reduce adverse excursions.

- The popular **Sharpe ratio,** the ratio of excess return (portfolio return minus the T-bill rate of return) divided by the standard deviation of the excess return. The excess rate of return has severe problems when applied to trading systems. First, it does not include the actual annual return but only the average monthly return. Thus, irregularities in the return are not recognized. Second, it does not distinguish between upside and downside fluctuations. As a result, it penalizes upside fluctuations as much as downside fluctuations. Finally, it does not distinguish between intermittent and consecutive losses. A system with a dangerous tendency toward high drawdowns from consecutive losses would not be awarded as high a risk profile as others with intermittent losses of little consequence.

Individual analysts will choose, and even create, the measure of risk that is most important to their trading objectives. Some of the other measures of risk mentioned in the literature are as follows:

- **Return Retracement ratio**—This is the average annualized compounded return divided by MR (maximum of either decline from prior equity peak [that is, worst loss from buying at peak] or worst loss at low point from any time prior).

- **Sterling ratio** (over three years)—This is the arithmetic average of annual net profit divided by average annual maximum drawdown; it is similar to the gain-to-pain ratio.

- **Maximum loss**—This is the worst possible loss from the highest point; using this measure by itself is not recommended because it represents a singular event.

- **Sortino ratio**—This is similar to the Sharpe ratio, but it considers only downside volatility. It is calculated as the ratio of the monthly expected return minus the risk-free rate to the standard deviation of negative returns. It is more realistic than the Sharpe ratio.

Smoothness and the Equity Curve Some analysts prefer to analyze risk in a graphic, visual manner. Two graphs commonly are used as a visual analysis of a system's performance: the **equity curve** and the **underwater curve**.

An equity curve chart is shown in Figure 1.2. It shows the level of equity profit in an account over time. Ideally, the line of the equity profits should be straight and run from a low level at the lower-left corner to a high level at the upper-right corner. Dips in the line are losses either taken or created by drawdowns.

The common measure of smoothness is the standard error of equity values about the linear regression trend drawn through those equity values. Smoothness of a system is affected by changes in the entry parameters or adjustments, such as filters. Because the majority of price action has occurred by the exit, the exit parameters and stops have little effect on smoothness.

The second type of graph used to look at system performance is the underwater curve chart. An example of this type of chart is shown in Figure 1.3. This displays the drawdown from each successively higher peak in equity. It is calculated in percentages and gives a representation not only of how much drawdown occurred, but also of how much time passed until equity recovered from that drawdown. As Figure 1.3 shows, the maximum percentage drawdown in the initial HAL system was a little over 90% of the original capital of $30,000. This chart helps us see that a major problem with the system is not only the size of the drawdowns but also the time it takes for the system to recover. In Box 1.2, we outline a method for improving the system.

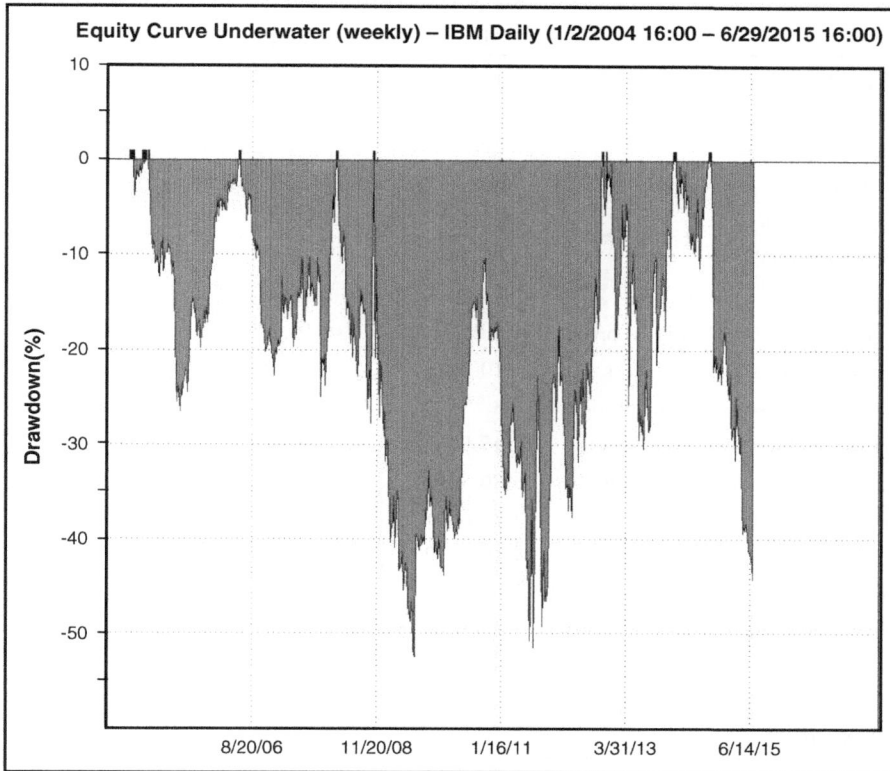

FIGURE 1.3 Weekly underwater curve for HAL in Box 1.1

BOX 1.2 UPGRADE IN THE HAL

Now it is time to upgrade our system based on the results of our initial testing. We first optimize the parameters of the given variables to see if there is a possibility of an improved system just by changing the parameters. This is the first step, and it showed that with curve-fitting, the net profit of over $35,000 was possible versus the loss incurred without adjustments. The second step is that we run a walk-forward test of the results and arrive at a system that we can expect to work in the near future. This is the one we report on here.

The changes made to HAL are threefold. First, we include a filter that will prevent the system from trading when the market is dull. We do this using a requirement that the ADX be higher than its predecessor some unknown number of days prior.

We use the ADX because it is a measure of trend and we don't want to play if there is no trend. There are other configurations of the ADX as a filter, but this is the one that worked best with HAL. Second, we add a percentage protective stop to lower the number of losses that accumulated time and loss while waiting for a buy signal. Third, we run optimizations on the parameters of ADX length, ADX lookback, CCI length, and upper and lower signal levels. The optimal results, using the perfect profit correlation as the objective function, were then run through a walk-forward optimizer to see which combination of parameters has the most likely chance of profiting in the next year.

TABLE 1.2 **Tabulated Data for the Final Optimized System for HAL**

Trades	All	Long	Short
Net profit	$31,437	$20,294	$11,143
Gross profit	$40,879	$23,179	$17,700
Gross loss	($9,442)	($2,885)	($6,557)
Profit factor	4.33	8.03	2.70
Number of trades	68	32	36
Percent profitable	64.71%	78.13%	52.78
Average trade net profit	$462.31	$634.19	$609.53
Largest winner as a % of gross profit	8.03%	14.17%	16.77%
Largest loser as a % of gross loss	10.19%	31.85%	14.67%
Maximum consecutive losing trades	3	2	5
Average weeks in winning position	45.59	50.44	39.21
Average weeks in losing position	26.54	53.86	15.29
Buy-and-hold return	85.66%		
Return on account	1057.42%		
Monthly average return	$475.07		
Standard deviation of monthly return	$906.07		
Sharpe ratio	0.23		
System MAR (intraday)	5.09	3.68	2.75
Trade MAR (intraday)	10.57	22.08	2.94

Source: TradeStation

Look at how the system improves with the additions. Figure 1.4 shows the new equity curve for the system. Notice how smooth the curve is now. Net profit has increased from $2,000 to $31,000. The number of trades has decreased because of the ADX filter; the

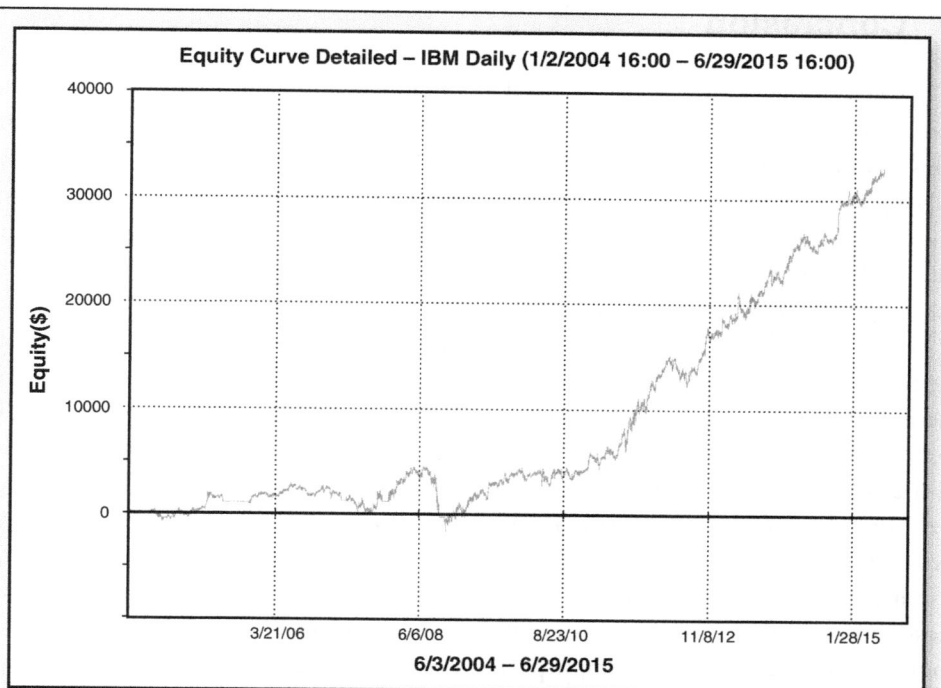

FIGURE 1.4 Equity curve of final optimized HAL

eliminated trades were obviously losers because the percentage of winners increased. The profit per trade is now high enough to withstand any extra trading costs, and the profit factor is now above the 2.00 standard threshold for a favorable system. The higher monthly return versus the standard deviation is well below the 5.00 normal ratio and explains why the equity curve is so smooth.

Do not use this system as it stands in any stock. It is presented only as an example of the process of looking for parameters, variables, and rules in a system development.

However, we hope that you can see the process of developing a reliable and profitable system and some of the types of adjustments that can be applied to systems—especially the use of stops—to improve performance and reduce risk. System development is a difficult and time-consuming task.

BOX 1.3   WHAT IS A GOOD TRADING SYSTEM?

In his book *Beyond Technical Analysis*, Tushar Chande discusses the characteristics of a good trading system. Chande's Cardinal Rules for a good trading system are the following:

- **Positive expectation**—Greater than 13% annually.
- **Small number of robust trading rules**—Less than ten each is best for entry and exit rules.
- **Able to trade multiple markets**—Can use baskets for determining parameters, but rules should work across similar markets, different stocks, different commodities futures, and so on.
- **Incorporates good risk control**—Minimum risk as defined by drawdown should not be more than 20% and should not last more than nine months.
- **Fully mechanical**—No second-guessing during operation of the system.

■ Conclusion

Throughout this book, we have looked at a number of technical indicators to guide our buying and selling of securities in reaction to particular market conditions. In this chapter, we turned our attention to mechanizing these reactions. A model is simply a plan or set of rules of when to buy and sell securities. A system uses the model as its base and lets us determine *a priori* how we will react to particular market situations. Having a system in place helps us follow a well-thought-out plan and prevents us from haphazardly trading based on emotion.

Of course, our basic objective in creating a system is to make a profit. Although this sounds like a straightforward goal, the goal of making a profit is not as simplistic as it sounds. Of course, we test our system to see how well it performs. But—and this is an important but—just because a system performs well using past, historical data in a trial situation does not guarantee that we will have the same stellar results in future, real-time trading. The most basic reason for this performance differential is that the market never repeats itself exactly; the system is operating in a different market environment than the one in which it was tested. There are also some system design and testing issues of concern. The system designer must be careful about data choice and not to overfit the data in the sample period. As we have seen in this chapter, even a system that has a high net profit in a test period is not necessarily a system that will perform well in the future. The system designer must consider a host of statistics about the system performance to determine whether the system is suitable for future trading. By following the guidelines laid out in this chapter, you should be ready to design systems and test them to determine their appropriateness for your trading situation.

■ References

Burnham, Terry. *Mean Markets and Lizard Brains*. New York, NY: John Wiley & Sons, Inc, 2005.

Chande, Tushar. *Beyond Technical Analysis*. New York, NY: John Wiley & Sons, Inc, 2001.

Collins, Art. "The Legend and the Lore of Richard Dennis." *Technical Analysis of Stocks & Commodities* 23, no. 4 (April 2005): 46-53.

Etzkorn, Mark. "Bruce Babcock: Market Realities." *Futures Magazine* (December 1996): 36-42.

Faith, Curtis. Way of the Turtle: The Secret Methods that Turned Ordinary People into Legendary Traders. New York, NY: McGraw-Hill, 2007.

Hill, John R., George Pruitt and Lundy Hill. *The Ultimate Trading Guide*. New York, NY: John Wiley & Sons, Inc, 2000.

Patel, Alpesh. *The Mind of the Trader*. London, UK: Financial Times/Pitman, 1997.

Ruggiero, Murray A., Jr. "Walking Before You Run with System Optimization." *Futures Magazine*. February 2005.

Ruggiero, Murray A., Jr. "Out of Sample, Out of Mind." *Futures Magazine*. April 2005.

Schwager, Jack D. *Schwager on Futures: Technical Analysis*. New York, NY: John Wiley & Sons, Inc, 1996.

Schwager, Jack D. *Technical Analysis*. New York, NY: John Wiley & Sons, Inc, 1996.

Sepiashvili, David, PhD. "How to Best Evaluate System Performance." *Futures Magazine*. March 2005.

Williams, Larry. *The Definitive Guide to Futures Trading*. Brightwaters, NY: Windsor Books, 1988.

CHAPTER 2

Money and Portfolio Risk Management

From Charles D. Kirkpatrick II and Julie R. Dahlquist, *Technical Analysis: The Complete Resource for Financial Market Technicians,* 3rd Edition (Old Tappan, New Jersey: Pearson Education, Inc., 2016), Chapter 23.

Learning Objective Statements

- Calculate and measure risk as it relates to money management
- Describe the significance of a martingale betting strategy to trading applications
- Differentiate between diversifiable versus correlated risk
- Compare and analyze the various types of stops used to manage risk
- Describe how to calculate the minimum capital needed for trading a system
- Determine an appropriate percentage of capital to allocate toward one system

> They [great traders] have all been humbled by the market early on in their careers. This creates a definite respect for Mr. Market. Until one has this respect indelibly engraved in their (sic) makeup, the concept of money management and discipline will never be treated seriously. (Cooper, 2004)

Money management is the next and final step in portfolio design after having established a reliable system or systems. We have concentrated on the reward side of investment because that is the more interesting and the part that most investors or traders find enjoyable. Unfortunately, the reward side is only half of the portfolio equation. The other half is portfolio risk and money management, a much-neglected aspect of portfolio management that should receive as much attention as the reward side. We can refer to money management as the risk side of investment, the means of preventing financial ruin. It is principally concerned with how to measure and manage risk of loss and, therefore, how to utilize one's capital most efficiently. In most aspects of investing, there is a trade-off between reward and risk. Neither can be measured precisely, and the amount of risk to reward is a personal decision based on one's tolerance for risk. Everyone is happy with reward, but different investors have different thoughts on what they can accept as risk. Unfortunately, reward is not guaranteed, but risk is. A system might not return profits, but a system will always have losses. Just how much risk is acceptable, how to measure it, and how to control it is the subject of this chapter.

When we set out to create a system, we are usually concentrating on profits. Remember our underlying objective is to make profits. However, we must be careful not to focus so much on earning profits that we forget about the critical concept of risk.

The amateur investor or trader usually uses a discretionary system. Testing and analyzing and evolving a workable nondiscretionary system takes too much time, knowledge, experience, and thought. Most people would rather just take the word of others and act spontaneously. Profitable professionals, however, always have a system. Although they may use a discretionary system, professionals know the results of investment action from experience and know the risks. Successful professionals always apply some form of risk control, even if it is just a series of mental stop-loss levels. Considering risk marks the difference between amateurs and professionals. Those who consider profit potential and not risk are mostly amateurs, even if they think they are professionals, and generally have or manage portfolios that considerably underperform the markets over the long term.

Risk is a vital concept, but what exactly is it? Academics have long characterized risk as equivalent to volatility. The Capital Asset Pricing Model (CAPM) and options theory consider volatility not only an important variable in markets, but also a measure of risk. These ideas are partially correct, but as anyone who has operated in the markets knows, the real definition of risk is: "How much money am I going to lose?" This is how the technical analyst focuses on risk.

The amount of money lost, or potentially lost, is called **drawdown**. It is defined as that amount by which the equity in an account declines from a peak. In other words, a drawdown is how much investors would suffer if they became invested in an account at its peak value. In a specific trade, the drawdown also can be defined as the amount that the trade value declines between the entry and the exit, even if the exit is above the entry and produces a final profit. Drawdown is sometimes referred to as the "pain" of holding a position. Although volatility can contribute to drawdown, as we will see later in looking at the smoothness of equity curves, the major concern for any investor or trader is the amount that can be lost.

We saw in Level II, Chapter 21, "Selection of Markets and Issues: Trading and Investing," that a 50% decline requires a 100% advance to return to even and that a 100% gain can be wiped out with only a 50% loss. This law of percentages is against the investor. Thus, a profit and a loss are not equivalent. A minor loss always requires a larger gain to offset it. The purpose in quantifiable systems is to minimize that potential loss.

Risk to the investor or trader in the markets also includes many intangibles. Loss comes not only from asset loss but also from emotional loss. Nothing is more disturbing to the psyche than losing money and at the same time being proven wrong. Both these risks can be reduced by systems. Losing money can be prevented through proper exit strategies, and the emotional loss can be alleviated through the confidence that although one may make small mistakes, one's equity curve continues upward. A well-devised and well-understood system can produce that confidence, making small losses just an inconvenience rather than a traumatic event.

■ Risk and Money Management

"Risk is the amount and probability of an adverse or series of adverse events occurring" (Rotella, 1992). Substituting "losses" for "adverse events" results in the following: *Risk is the amount and probability of a loss or series of losses occurring.* Note that the probability of occurrence is as important as the total amount.

There has never been a system that was 100% profitable, that never took a loss on any trade or investment. Although such a system is the ideal, it has never been achieved despite the brilliant minds, sophisticated mathematics and theories, and superfast computer abilities that have addressed methods of investment. It likely never will be achieved. The search for such a perfect strategy can become an obsession but is genuinely futile, and losses are, therefore, inevitable in investing and trading.

Ruin is also likely. Every day some traders and investors are wiped out, largely because they did not utilize a portfolio method that included an assessment and control of risk. The area between perfection and ruin is a compromise between the gains and losses, known more commonly as **rewards** and **risks**, of a system or portfolio strategy. As can be imagined, the possibilities between perfection and ruin are limitless and have much to do with personal preference for risk. The reward side of a strategy we can fairly well quantify, as was shown in the previous chapter on systems, but the risk side is not so easily understood. The trade-off between the two will affect the ultimate success or failure of a portfolio strategy. That is the essence of money management—to maximize return at minimum risk. No home runs, no Holy Grails, no perpetual money machines—just plain and simple, consistent profits with minimum chance of losing all of one's capital. The extremes, of course, range between highly leveraged options or futures contracts in a seat-of-the-pants, untested, untried system, and on the opposite side, strictly cash. The cash investment theoretically has no risk, whereas hotshot investments and systems are likely doomed. (A cash position does not have the risk of losing capital. Economists, however, will consider the inflation risk—the risk of the cash position losing purchasing power during inflationary periods.)

Ironically, a good system can lose money if it is not applied with concern for risk. Money management can turn it into a profitable, reliable system, but money management cannot help a system that does not work. Thus, as we covered in the previous chapter, the first step in creating a portfolio strategy is to find a workable system, preferably more than one. It need not be a supersystem—just one that consistently shows higher profits than losses. It can be based on fundamentals, technicals, or both. If you read interviews with successful traders and investors, you will find every one of them has a different method or system of entering the markets, but they all have in common a money-management system to protect against loss. Indeed, most will admit that money management is more important than any system. The second step is to decide on what markets and in which issues the system will trade or invest. The third step is to combine these systems and issues into a portfolio strategy. At this point, the subject of money management arises.

Because the theories of money management largely concern price and position size, the evaluation and control of risk are technical. Fundamental investors cannot assess risk in the marketplace with fundamentals alone. What should be the initial capital? What should be the trade size in contracts, shares, or dollars? What should be the risk strategies applied to these positions? What should be the execution style? Should the strategies be combined into one portfolio system, or should each system be treated separately? All these questions must be answered to manage the portfolio successfully, and all of them rely on technical studies and use of price action and signals. Generally, the systems will take care of themselves if properly tested and will give adequate entry signals, leaving the investor with the problem of how to best position from those signals and what exit strategies to use. The object of money management is to maximize the best situations and avoid or minimize those situations that can cause capital loss.

Because money management has much to do with determining the size of positions, it has also been called **position sizing**. However, there is more to it than just sizing. The parameters for risk avoidance, such as stops and exit strategies, are also important, as are diversification and execution methods. We cover some of the principal money-management strategies you should know and demonstrate methods of testing for and reducing the risk of ruin.

■ Testing Money-Management Strategies

We covered the standard method of testing a system in Level II, Chapter 22, "System Design and Testing," but now we are looking at complete portfolio systems that include, hopefully, many subsystems and many issues traded using each subsystem with different objectives that satisfy the requirement for diversification. Of course, we should already have tested each subsystem by itself with a diversified number of issues and have confidence in its results alone. By merging it into a portfolio system, however, we now need a method to test the entire model. We will see that the model often will produce better results than any of the separate subsystems do individually. To test the model, we can use the same methodology as used in Level II, Chapter 22, or we can use what is called a **Monte Carlo simulation**.

Because the testing system in Level II, Chapter 22 is plagued with the risk of curve-fitting and the inability to determine the success or failure of the system under varying circumstances, we need a testing method that looks at a multiple set of possibilities and tells us how well the rules, variables, and parameters in the combined subsystems handle change. The Monte Carlo simulation is one of the better and more often used testing methods of portfolio risk.

Without discussing the mathematics behind a simulation (because it can become complicated), we instead just outline what it does. A simple simulation can be performed on a spreadsheet, with considerable work, and a more sophisticated software program called Equity Monaco is available from www.tickquest.com for free. More sophisticated software is available elsewhere for a fee. More information on the mathematics of Monte Carlo simulations can be seen at www.montecarlosimulations.org.

As we will see later in this chapter, with the martingale betting system, a system may be profitable, but the bettor must be able to withstand a long series of losses (a large drawdown). This means that the trading system results, even if spectacular from the optimization tests, could be just the result of chance or luck.

In the martingale betting system, the system is profitable only as long as the bettor is able to withstand a long series of losses, a large drawdown. To measure whether the system is valuable in all circumstances and what the odds of failure from a series of losses might be, especially because the trader usually has limited capital, the trader (or investor) needs to test for as many different circumstances as possible. The Monte Carlo simulation does not use the rules, variables, or parameters in the original trading system. It uses only the actual trades, entry and exit, and the profit or loss from each. It looks at the sequence of these trades from various angles to see the probability of a series of losses leading to ruin in the system. It, thus, is a money-management test rather than a system test, although obviously the system determines the trades. If the money-management test fails by showing a high probability of ruin, the original system must be discarded, adjusted to improve these results, or other safeguards installed to prevent such a possible disaster.

The simulation takes the original trade data, profits, and losses and scrambles them in a random manner. This is done many times, usually at least 100 times and better if 1,000 or 2,000 times. An equity curve is then created for each scrambled sequence of trades. The results from each equity curve are then assembled to give the results and related to a normal distribution curve. The simulation is testing to see if the system is random and by how much. The less the system is random, the more likely it will be profitable with minimum risk of failure.

■ Money-Management Risks

We have defined risk in many ways in earlier chapters. Variability of returns, amount of loss per trade, beta, and maximum amount of loss per trade, drawdown, maximum drawdown, and volatility of prices have all been used. One of the principal difficulties in the use of standard linear statistics in evaluating markets is that it assumes that each price, each trade, and each profit or loss is independent. In other words, it stands by itself and is not related to any other price, trade, or trade return. When using such statistics, one must, therefore, be careful not to believe absolutely in what the statistical tests might show.

Concepts

For our purposes, the important risk consideration is loss of capital. This comes from losses on trades, realized or unrealized, and, thus, we will use drawdowns as the best definition of risk. Because drawdowns, if not controlled, can lead to ruin, our intention in this chapter is to develop means that will keep us from losing all our capital.

Drawdown and Maximum Drawdown   When we discussed drawdowns in the previous chapter, we found that more than one drawdown can occur, and it may result from one trade or many trades. If we look at all the drawdowns over a period, the one that has the highest equity percentage loss is called the **maximum drawdown (MDD)**. The MDD is the worst case that occurred in the system and often is used as an estimate of the worst case that can occur in the future. Of course, it could have been a fluke and exaggerate potential drawdowns in real trading, or it could underestimate and make drawdowns appear less damaging than they would be in real trading. We will find that we can reduce risk of loss on single trades with stops, but we cannot reduce the risk from a series of losses. All we can do is find a realistic estimate of the odds of a long run of losses against us and then take our chances or change the system. Even assuming a large MDD, we must design the money-management strategy such that enough capital is always available to withstand a loss in the magnitude of the known MDD. Otherwise, the system goes broke.

Drawdowns, for statistical purposes, are not independent, especially if the loss occurs in multiple systems at one time based on some adverse news. Uncontrollable loss, called **an act of God** in the insurance industry, or a **Black Swan** after the subject of the book by that name by Nassim Taleb (2010), cannot be anticipated and thus is never included in any estimate of risk. These events, however, usually only affect a single trade rather than a series of trades.

Theory of Runs   A drawdown is usually the result of a series of losses. We can estimate the chances of a series of losses using the theory of runs. This theory states that the probability of a series of independent events is the product of the probability of each event occurring. Thus, if a system has a losing percentage of 40%, the odds of a run of five losses in a row are $(0.40 \times 0.40 \times 0.40 \times 0.40 \times 0.40) = .01$ or 1%. If a system has a losing percentage of 60%, the odds of a run of five losses in a row are 8%. Although this calculation does not account for money lost in each transaction, it does suggest that to avoid a series of losses, the lower the losing percentage of the system, the better. Even so, a large number of losses together may not be harmful to a system specifically—many trend-following systems have long runs of losses—but create an additional risk of loss of confidence in the system and the potential premature abandonment just before it becomes profitable. Psychology is a major component in trading, and confidence is usually fragile when trades are going against the trader.

Martingale Betting System   A martingale betting system often is used in a situation where the bet size can be changed but the odds are relatively even, such as gambling at a roulette wheel. The basis for the method is the theory of runs and the odds against a long series of losses when probability is about even. The method is to double up on the next bet after a loss and return to the standard bet after a win. Eventually, a winning bet will cover all the previous losses and return a profit on the original bet. Unfortunately, the system requires substantial capital to withstand an unexpectedly long series of losses in a row.

For example, assume you make a $100 standard bet that takes the $100 bet and either returns the bet plus $100 on a win or pays nothing on a loss with even odds of winning or losing (50% win percentage). After a run of five successive losses occurs, using a martingale system, the next bet will require $3,200 above the $3,100 that has already been lost ($100 + $200 + $400 + $800 + $1,600 = $3,100). Thus, betting the sixth time after five successive losses would require $6,300, hoping for a win that would net $100 above our previous commitment. It is a tough way to make $100. Nevertheless, as long as the bettor can ante up the funds for the next bet in a losing series of bets, he will profit eventually by the amount of the original bet ($100) when the final winning bet occurs.

If the payoff ratio is greater than one-for-one and the win percentage is greater than 50%, the martingale approach may be profitable in the trading markets, but that long series of losses is always hanging out in space somewhere waiting to occur. Furthermore, in the trading markets, the profit from each bet is not constant. It could, for example, be larger for losses than for gains. Of course, a maximum loss or stop can be used to get out of the game, but by then so much capital has been lost that the chances of recovery are slim. Needless to say, the martingale approach rarely is used in trading markets.

Reward to Risk

The objective in all investment is to have a high reward to risk. Return on investment, or ROI, is the standard calculation of reward. ROI is calculated as net profit divided by initial capital at the beginning of the measured period.

The standard method for analyzing portfolios and systems for reward and risk is to calculate the ratio of CAGR (compound annual growth rate) to the %MDD. This is called the **MAR ratio** and is how we initially evaluated the system design parameters in Level II, Chapter 22. Some analysts use other ratios. The profit/loss ratio, also called the **profit factor**, is commonly used, and the **payoff ratio**, which is the average gain per profitable trade to the average loss per unprofitable trade, is often used.

A recent myth about MDD, derived from the risk-reward relationship in Modern Portfolio Theory, is that a higher MDD percent suggests a higher return. This is not true. Capital risk and reward are not proportional. MDD percent cannot be greater than 100%, but return can theoretically be infinite.

Normal Risks

The most important aspect of money management, beyond establishing where and what kind of stops to use to protect capital, is the determination of position size for each trade. Too much in a position can incur unwarranted risks in case of failure, including complete ruin, and too little can reduce profit potential beyond the risk-free rate. Position size is directly related to capital risk, the amount of money that can be lost, and it is the aspect of money management that most traders and investors overlook.

Position Size By **position size**, we mean the amount of capital committed to a system or investment that incurs a specific risk. This is usually based on the difference between the entry price and exit price multiplied by the number of shares or contracts. As an example, let us assume we can only risk $500 in a trade. We have a breakout system that will buy a stock at $50. We place a protective sell stop at $45. This $5 difference in price is the capital risk we are taking per share. The entire position is not at risk because it will be liquidated on the stop. Without a stop, of course, we have no idea what risk we are taking. This is one reason fundamental analysis has trouble controlling capital risk. It has no means of determining when to exit a position. Knowing we have a $5 dollar per share risk, however, we know we can buy 100 shares for a total capital risk of our limit of $500.

In systems, position size has two levels of importance. The first is the determination of the minimum size of account required to trade a system with a minimum level of potential risk of ruin. The second is the determination of the optimal size of each position taken in a system that meets the predetermined risk level of the system owner. Generally, the position size in either determination is based on the maximum drawdown of the system and the margin required for a futures contract or price of a stock.

One problem does arise, and it has to do with short-term trading when the difference between prospective entry and exit price is small. This is best explained with an example. Say we have a $100,000 account and want to limit our losses to 2% of capital (that is, $2,000 per position). We find a $50 stock that we believe we can scalp for $2 with a risk of only $0.50. Using the risk formula and a 2% limit, we can buy 4,000 shares ($2,000 / $0.50 = 4,000). However, 4,000 shares of a $50 stock is $200,000, twice the amount of our capital. What do we do? We can borrow the extra $100,000 for the trade, but that leaves us with absolutely no room for another trade and exposes us to the risk of the debt. We can also cut back on the

4,000 shares to 2,000 shares, but by doing so we still haven't freed enough capital for another trade and have cut our potential profit in half. To combat this problem, most traders use a smaller percent risk than 2% as their risk limit on a position. This makes sense not only for this situation, but because a scalper makes many trades a day, any one of which can go wrong, resulting in an increased risk of a long series of losses and a large drawdown. This method reduces that risk by limiting the potential trade loss to a smaller amount and allows more bad trades to occur without the risk of ruin.

Number of Shares or Contracts In the stock market, the question of how many shares to use in a system is relatively easy because margin requirements are comparatively small and the number of shares flexible. In the futures markets, however, the number of contracts to use can become a problem. Margin requirements frequently change. The two standard methods of determining the number of contracts are either to use the system on a fixed number of contracts or to determine the risk as a percentage of the trading account and divide that by the margin required for each contract. After a successful series of trades, if the account capital has increased, a decision must be made as to whether to continue with a set number of contracts or continue with the percentage risk proportion on a continuous capital adjustment. Some traders use a capital step process whereby the number of contracts is only adjusted when the account capital reaches certain thresholds.

Evstigneev and Schenk-Hoppe (2001) argue that constant proportion strategies produce wealth more rapidly than other proportional methods. This is an outgrowth of the Kelly formula discussed next and implies that keeping a portfolio equally proportionally invested is the best method of accumulating profits. This concept goes against the grain of some analysts. They maintain that, although the system is working, the accumulation of profits is favorable. However, at some time, a significant series of losses will occur, when the capital is larger than its initial size. In that case, the losses will be proportionately larger because they depend on the proportion of the capital in the account. For now, we will go with the statistical evidence from Evstigneev and Schenk-Hoppe. They are not alone in their conclusions. As such, we will look for the optimal proportion of capital to invest in a system that will avoid the risk of total loss of capital. This sometimes is referred to as the fixed fractional method.

Determining Optimal Position Size There are three methods of determining the position size: (1) risk of ruin formula, (2) theory of runs formula, and (3) optimal f or Kelly formula. To calculate the best position size, all three formulas should be used, and that formula with the smallest percentage of capital to be risked should be the one used in the system or model.

Risk of Ruin Formula   The risk of ruin (ROR) formula uses three pieces of data from the historical or testing data: (1) the probability of success or the percentage of wins; (2) the payoff ratio, or average win trade amount divided by the average loss trade amount; and (3) the fraction exposed to trading.

The risk of ruin formula (Kaufman, 1998) is

$$ROR = ((1 - ta) \div (1 + ta))^{cu}$$

Where: ROR is the risk of ruin

ta is the trading advantage (percent wins minus percent losses)

cu is the number of trading units, shares, or contracts

Because the ratio is always less than one, the greater "cu" is, the less chance of ruin using a fixed dollar amount. In addition, the greater the "ta," the less chance of ruin. The risk of ruin, therefore, is proportional to the percentage wins. The formula demonstrates that trend-following systems with a high percentage of losses often should end in ruin. This formula, however, fails to account for the amount of each win and loss.

To determine the optimal percentage of capital to use in any system with win and loss amounts, use this formula:

$$PCT = ([(A + 1) \times p] - 1) / A$$

Where: PCT is the percentage of capital to use

A is the average payoff ratio

p is the percentage of wins

Theory of Runs   The chance of going broke from a series of losses is the amount of trading times the percentage of losses to the power of the largest string of losses.

BOX 2.1   OPTIMAL PERCENTAGE OF CAPITAL TO AVOID RISK OF RUIN

Using the figures from the example in Level II, Chapter 22, let us calculate the percentage of capital to use from the risk of ruin formula.

Data

(p) Percent profitable trades (profitable trades) = 64.71%
Average win trade amount   = $929.07
Average loss trade amount = $393.42
(A) Average payoff ratio (average win/average loss) = 2.36

Formula

Optimal percentage of capital = $\{[(A + 1) \times p] - 1\} \div A$

Substituting

Optimal percentage of capital   = $\{[(2.36 + 1) \times 0.6471] - 1\} \div 2.36 = 49.8\%$
That is, any amount over 49.8% of capital in this system has a high chance of ending in ruin. The high percentage suggests that the risk of ruin is low for normal commitments of 2%.

Most analysts will assume a minimum run of ten consecutive losses as the baseline. In any case, most calculations end with a maximum suggested percentage investment of around 2% to avoid the risk of going broke.

Optimal f and the Kelly Formula   The Kelly formula was invented by John L. Kelly, Jr. of Bell Labs in the early 1940s to measure long-distance telephone noise and was later adopted by gamblers to determine optimal betting sizes. Its application to the trading markets is somewhat tenuous because it does not account for MDD and, thus, risk of ruin. However, it is used in conjunction with other position-size calculations to determine the optimal size of a position relative to capital. In any profitable system, capital growth increases in proportion to the percentage of capital risked. After a certain threshold in the percentage, however, the rate of growth decreases and eventually reaches zero. The Kelly ratio or optimal f is the threshold of maximum growth. Optimal f is, therefore, a method of determining the optimal percentage of capital that should be invested in a particular system.

The optimal f percentage $=$ (percentage of wins $\times$ (profit factor $+$ 1) $-$ 1) / profit factor

Where: Percentage of wins is the percentage of winning trades

Profit factor is the ratio of total gains over total losses

Once f is determined, it is multiplied times capital for the amount to be used in each position. This amount can be divided by the contract margin requirement for each contract to determine the number of contracts. In the stock market, the amount for each position can be divided by the price of the shares to determine the number of shares. Because this method often suffers from extraordinary drawdowns, the percentage of capital is usually limited to 0.8 of optimal f, or a maximum optimal f of 25%.

To account for MDD that is otherwise not in the f formula, another method called **secure f** (Zamansky and Stedhahl, 1998) is to divide the MDD by optimal f to determine the amount that can be risked on one contract or convert this amount to a percentage of capital for stock shares. The Larry Williams formula for the number of contracts to trade is to take the amount of money at risk (account balance times risk percent from whatever formula) divided by the largest single loss. A loss in the future can be controlled by stops.

Final Position Size   The smallest percentage of capital suggested by the three formulas is used as the final percentage for trading the specified system. Generally, because the theory of runs limits the percentage to around 2%, most professional traders use this figure, or less, as a maximum commitment to any system. In the HAL system, however, the percentage of losses is so small that the odds of a run of five losses is almost negligible. Thus, the other methods should take precedence, and each shows that a substantial portion of assets could have been invested in the system.

Initial Capital   The reason for concern about initial capital requirements is the risk of a series of losses right in the beginning of the system use. The problem at start-up is not the problem of individual loss in a trade. That can be controlled with stops. The problem is the risk of complete loss of capital. This problem is related to the possibility of a run of losses that wipes out capital and eliminates the trader from being able to reenter the system. Later, when profits have accrued, the accumulated profit cushion lessens the risk of losing all, but at the start, the risk of being wiped out is the highest.

A general rule of thumb for initial capital is to have at least three times the margin required for a single contract for each contract traded, or at least two times the amount of the MDD plus the initial margin for stocks and contracts. A more precise number can be determined from the Monte Carlo simulation described previously, estimating the odds of complete failure of the system using history. As in any simulation, the levels determined from the test should be doubled or tripled as a precaution against extraordinary initial surprises.

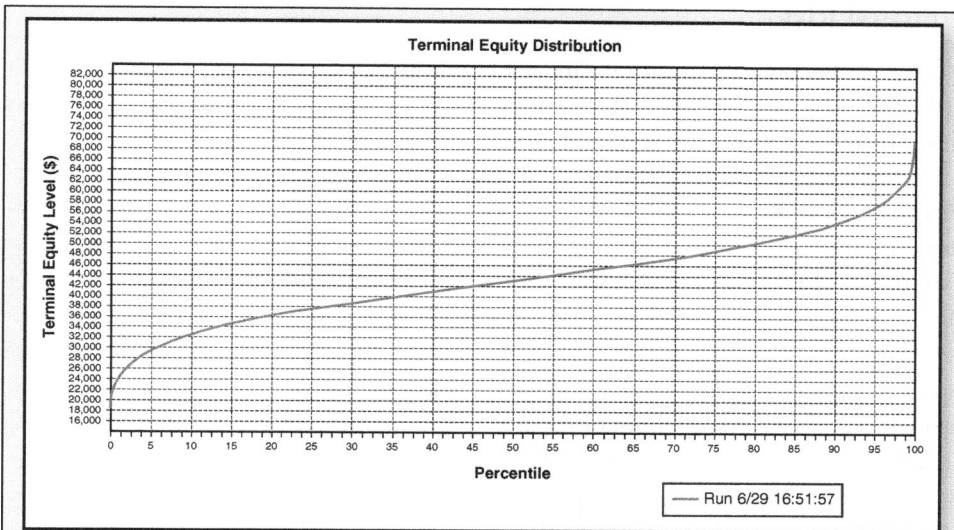

FIGURE 2.1 Monte Carlo simulation projected terminal equity of HAL system
Source: www.tickquest.com—equity montecarlo

Leverage   Leverage, or the borrowing of capital to increase the potential for gain, of course, also increases the risk. Leverage generally increases the volatility of the portfolio or system and, thus, magnifies all those dangerous possibilities from increased volatility, including larger drawdowns and more potential for complete failure.

Risk is proportional to leverage. If we find that our system or combination of systems produces an MDD that is unacceptably high, we can adjust the portfolio mix to include a risk-free investment, such as Treasury bills, in the proportion necessary to bring down the potential MDD. For example, if the model estimates a 40% MDD, and we will accept only a 20% MDD, we can adjust the model to invest 50% of the capital in risk-free investments and the remainder in the systems. On the other hand, if the systems suggest a 10% MDD, and we are willing to accept a 20% MDD, we can borrow 100% of the model's capital and double our return as well as our risk.

Pyramiding   Pyramiding is a more complicated method of adding leverage to a position. It consists of adding to a profitable position to gain leverage. Of course, the risks are not as clear because gaining size in the position after it is profitable may result in a larger position just as the inevitable drawdown begins. The best manner of pyramiding is to test it within the system as a set of rules. Specific rules of thumb for pyramiding include the following:

1. Never adding to a position until its profit becomes positive
2. Placing stops at the break-even level as size increases
3. Entering the largest positions first and diminishing the size of subsequent entries
4. Being sure that the position risk is still within the limits established by the system and by the maximum acceptable position size

Unusual Risks

Before we become involved in standard portfolio risks, we must be aware of other risks that we have some control over but that will not usually show up in standard tests of performance. These are outlined next.

Psychological Risk As we have mentioned many times earlier, trading and investing are largely psychological. The motion of investment vehicles is due largely to rational and to irrational decisions on the part of buyers and sellers. Taking advantage of this price motion through technical analysis is an emotional exercise for the trader or investor as well. The participant in the markets must be careful not to be swept up in the emotion of the crowd; indeed, in many instances, she must act against the crowd and, thus, against human nature. Many inputs can affect the psychological stability of the trader. Lack of sleep, family fight, sickness, or any other nonstandard outside intervention can upset one's attitude and ability to act successfully. Unfortunately, once lack of success begins, lack of confidence also begins, and lack of confidence can cause even more errors in judgment. The purpose in designing a nondiscretionary system is to reduce those outside emotional effects and let the system operate by itself. However, a losing system or series of losses can cause even the slightest override of the system; simply a change in orders, a wait after a breakout, or any other minor action unknowingly can upset the expected results even more. Many system overrides are not even recognized by the trader—just a little change here and there. Thus, there is a constant battle between the psyche and the markets. A supersystem will not avoid one's own nature. Only one can control one's nature. It is a risk that cannot be eliminated by a computer—only reduced—and the system must be followed religiously. Some writers argue that the psychology of trading accounts for better than 70% of success. This is likely true, but unfortunately, it is perverse and unquantifiable.

Knowledge of the Market "I didn't realize that option expired today" or "I didn't realize that contract traded at night in Singapore" can be costly mistakes. The trader or investor must be fully aware of the markets being traded, their history, their method of execution, their various peculiarities, their people, their structure, and their operation. There is no excuse for losing money from simple ignorance. Most investors learn from experience about the oddities of particular markets, but that experience can be costly.

Diversifiable Risk Diversification is a complex subject. As we saw in Level II, Chapter 22, the complexity has to do with the weighting amount of different vehicles or systems in a portfolio, as well as whether the behaviors of the components are similar or different from each other. Various mathematical models have been developed; but as we said before, diversification is the commonsense approach of "not putting all your eggs in one basket" that is needed. Obviously, if different vehicles or systems are used, they should not act in concert. Otherwise, they are essentially the same system, and risk has not been diversified away.

Risk is both correlated and uncorrelated. Correlated risk cannot be eliminated through diversification. We must use other means. This nondiversifiable, or market, risk is the risk generated by the overall market itself and accounts for a large portion of portfolio risk. Uncorrelated risk, however, can be reduced through diversification. Uncorrelated risk comes from the effects of all sorts of exogenous variables on individual issues and has more to do with the risk of the individual issue than the overall market. Uncorrelated risk can be reduced by diversification into dissimilar or uncorrelated issues or systems.

An example of correlated, nondiversifiable risk would be the risk that the Federal Reserve tightening the money supply will have a widespread impact on security values and affect almost any stock in a portfolio. On the other hand, the risk that a Vioxx lawsuit will decrease the value of Merck stock is uncorrelated, diversifiable risk. The lawsuit would not impact the stocks of other companies.

Reduction in uncorrelated risk can reduce MDD and enhance ROI. Indeed, the results of a diversified portfolio are often superior to the results from the best individual system by itself. The Capital Asset Pricing Model suggests that a properly structured 9-stock portfolio reduces the uncorrelated risk to that of one-third the risk of a single stock. A 16-stock portfolio can reduce uncorrelated risk to one-fourth that of a single stock. The relationship is based on the inverse square root of the number of stocks in the portfolio. As such, the portfolio can never eliminate uncorrelated risk, but with just a few different issues or systems, it can reduce it enough to make it irrelevant. The real problem then becomes the effect of correlated risk as in the debt crisis in 2008–2009 when many investments that had earlier been uncorrelated suddenly became correlated and declined together. What constitutes correlation in investments or systems, then, is a subject equally difficult to assess. Some investors believe that diversification detracts from performance because it dilutes reward along with risk. Using specific selection methods to concentrate on the investments with the most potential, they use exit strategies in individual issues to reduce uncorrelated risk and market timing for the entire portfolio to reduce correlated risk.

One further complication in the subject of correlations is that often a lead-lag relationship occurs that is invisible to the system tester, and most correlations themselves change over time. Efficient diversification is, thus, a useful and important subject but not a simple one.

Trade Frequency   Ten losing trades in different markets is the same as ten consecutive losses in one market. The drawdown is the same. Thus, diversification can bring problems as well as reduce risk. The frequency of trading in different markets will increase the risk of a series of losses across markets.

Temporal   Risk increases with time. The longer a position is held, the more risky it becomes. This is why long-term interest rates are usually higher than short-term rates. On the other hand, in the markets, reward does not increase with time. Thus, to reduce risk, a position should not be held beyond the time that reward ends. Then, only risk remains.

Security Quality   If given the choice of trading a high-quality issue (as determined by some financial rating service) that has the same market characteristics as a low-quality issue, including volatility, liquidity, and volume, which would you choose? The high-quality issue, of course. Erroneously, quality is a concept that normally is not addressed and certainly is not a factor in most systems models.

■ Money-Management Risk Strategies

In addition to determining the optimal position size, optimal initial capital, and leverage, risk strategies include the timing and placement of exits.

Entry strategies carry no risk until executed. An entry can be made at any time, when the situation or setup is right, or not at all. Perhaps you would rather go to the beach. Because you must now watch your investment, you cannot go to the beach. Once entered into a position, however, an exit strategy is necessary because the position is now at risk. It is the most important action decision in any system.

Exit strategies are usually twofold: prevention of loss of capital or closing at a target profit or price. Prevention of capital loss can come after a loss, as in a protective stop, or after a profit, as in a trailing stop. There is always a trade-off between potential reward and potential risk. An exit stop placed too tightly to the trading price prevents a single large loss, but many small losses that are equally devastating can occur instead. An exit stop can also be too loose, resulting in a larger-than-necessary loss. It must be wide enough to avoid being triggered by random noise and intrinsic volatility of the issue but not sacrifice too many profitable trades. At other times, a profit may have accrued, and rather than a risk of loss, the question of stop placement or target exit is necessary. All these decisions, naturally, should be tested before the situation arises. There are advantages and disadvantages to all of them.

Slippage is a problem with stops. Any stop that suggests an exit in the direction of the short-term trend rarely will be executed at the same price as the system test suggests. A volatility stop, for example, often will occur when price volatility exceeds the estimated volatility, and a technical stop at a specific price, depending on where it is located within a price pattern, may occur along with many others and receive a poor execution. A target exit often receives a better execution and less slippage because the trend is directed into the target limit. However, it might not be executed at all if the price fails to reach the target, or the price might roar through the target and lose profit opportunity. There is no easy answer about slippage except that these potential problems should be addressed in the testing of a system.

Protective Stop

All entries must have a protective stop under all circumstances, and that stop must be inviolate. The protective stop is placed at the level of maximum limit of loss from entry, accounting for the maximum loss that the trader can allow on any one position on any one trade. It is often called a **money-management stop** because it prevents the complete loss of capital. It is determined by the level of risk that the trader is willing to take with his capital in any one position on any one trade. There are numerous methods of determining where the protective stop should be placed.

Hard Money or Dollar Stop When we decide how much money we are willing to risk in a trade, we can place a protective **hard money stop** at a price level that reflects that potential loss and no more. In the earlier example of position size risk, we considered a stock trading at $50, with the maximum amount we wanted to risk at $500. We can buy 100 shares at $50 and place a sell stop at $45, or we can buy 200 shares at $50 and place a sell stop at $47.50. The same dollar risk appears to be present in each transaction. This is not accurate, however, because the odds of being triggered at $47.50 are higher than at $45. The consideration of where to place the stop, therefore, should be one based on the best price rather than on how many shares can be bought. Once the price is determined, the amount of shares to purchase can be adjusted accordingly. Let us say there is a large support level at $46. It would be wiser to use the $45 stop than the $47.50 stop, even though fewer shares are originally purchased, because the support level has a better chance of holding the stock from falling through $45 and triggering the stop. Furthermore, as technical traders, we know that if the support level at $46 is broken, we do not want to own the stock. At $47.50, we do not know anything about the stock prospects, and the market does not care.

Maximum Winning Adverse Excursion The protective stop is placed to prevent loss if something goes wrong with the system. A method of determining when the system is going wrong is called the **maximum adverse excursion** method. Taking each winning trade in the system test or from the past real-time use of the system, one plots the frequency of adverse excursions. These are the amounts by which the value of the entered position in each trade goes against the initial value before it is closed at a profit. It is similar to a drawdown except limited to winning trades. If an entry is made and the trade eventually is a profitable one, the adverse excursion is the amount of money that the trade was in the hole before it turned profitable. Some profitable trades immediately profit. These are not a problem. Looking at those winning trades that do have initial problems, you will find that, over time, the excursion from entry value reaches a limit. If the system is trouble free, that price is the level beyond which a profitable trade should not go in the future. A price just beyond that level is where the protective stop should be placed. Losing trade adverse excursions are not considered because they will become a problem and will be stopped out at the protective stop. Once the maximum adverse excursion from winning trades is established, it also determines how many contracts or shares can be entered on the system entry signal. If the maximum adverse excursion for one contract is greater than the maximum limit of loss allowed by the trader, the position should not be taken. Otherwise, the number of shares or contracts can be determined by dividing the maximum adverse excursion by the margin required for the contract or the price of the shares. The maximum winning adverse excursion should be recalculated periodically to maintain consistent with any changes in the market or the system.

Trailing Stop

With the protective stop in place and inviolate, the market issue will either trigger that stop or will begin to profit. Once a certain amount of profit in the trade has occurred, the next problem for the system is to maximize the profit without giving up too much of what has been gained. A trailing stop is used most frequently to lock in the gain.

Breakeven Level and Breakeven Stop A trailing stop often is not placed until a certain gain level is accumulated. This is called the **breakeven level**, the profit level at which a stop can be placed at the entry price to lock in a breakeven on the trade but not be triggered by noise. In the preceding example, we bought the stock at $50, and after a little erratic motion, the stock rose to $55. The ATR (Average True Range) is $1.50. If we had earlier set three times the ATR, or $4.50, as the break-even level, then when the stock reached $54.50 ($50 + $4.50), we would automatically raise the protective stop to a break-even stop at the entry price of $50. This eliminates the risk of any loss on the transaction from then on. At the same time as the break-even stop is placed, a trailing stop strategy is initiated.

Another method of handling the break-even level is to exit half the position when the profit has reached the break-even level. The break-even stop is then raised to the entry price. This method locks in a profit, keeps a portion of the position open, and cannot lose capital once it is entered. The potential for profit is reduced, but a smaller profit has already been stashed, and the risk of loss is zero on the remaining portion. A trailing stop strategy then is applied to the remaining position.

Technical Point Versus Money Point The decision about a trailing stop usually centers on whether to use a technical point or a money point. A **money point stop** is similar to a hard money stop described previously, only in this case it defines the amount that the trade should not lose from its maximum profit level. If $500 is the money point stop, the stop-price level changes with the value change in the market issue, such that if a correction of more than $500 occurs from the maximum unrealized profit, the system will exit the trade. A technical stop is one placed at a price that represents a technical level beyond which it is obvious that the trade is reversing direction. It is sometimes called a **critical threshold stop** (Katz and McCormick, 1998) because breaking the specified stop level is critical to the trade. Technical points often are used more in investment and swing trading trailing stops. Money point stops are used more in short-term trading, where price action is often more erratic. The market itself does not accommodate a money point stop because that level is unrelated to the market price and is a matter of the personal risk decision of the trader, but the market does respect the technical stop if properly placed.

Volatility Stop   We discussed volatility stops in Level I, Chapter 5, "Breakouts, Stops, and Retracements." A trailing stop is placed at a certain level based on the historical volatility of the issue. As such, the stop price will adjust to changes in volatility; it will loosen when volatility increases and tighten when volatility decreases. It is commonly used for this reason.

Maximum Winning Favorable   A maximum winning favorable excursion, as opposed to the adverse used in establishing stops, also can be used to establish a trailing stop. The maximum favorable excursion is the highest amount that a profitable trade reaches before it is exited. It is similar to a target. A fraction of this calculation is added to the entry price, and the fraction is increased over time.

Trend Line   A trend line stop can be used because a trend line follows the price action. As a technical point stop, it has advantages in that a bunching of orders at a critical level, such as a support or resistance zone, usually is not seen along a trend line, such that when triggered, the execution of the exit will be less influenced by competing orders.

Adaptive   Special formulas, such as Wilder's parabolic, can be used. These formulas follow the price trend and adjust to market conditions along the way. They and volatility stops also are called **adaptive stops**, and their details can be complicated.

Other Kinds of Stops

We have just considered a number of protective and trailing stop strategies, which are generally based on price action. Other exit strategies may be employed, such as those based on a particular technical signal or those based on time.

Signal   One obvious stop is the signal stop. This occurs when the system gives a signal to enter a position in the opposite direction from the existing position. It is part of a stop-and-reverse system.

Time   Because of the multidimensional aspect of time and reward versus risk, a **time stop** often is used in short-term trading when time, cost of money, and opportunity cost are important. This stop is placed to exit the position a certain time after the entry. If a profit has not been gained within the time specified, the odds of it not occurring in the future increase, and the position is best closed to avoid further risk. A variation of the time stop is to reduce the position size as certain time passes. This reduces the risk but leaves room for some further gain. Time stops are also used in swing trading where the trade horizon is only a few days.

Targets

In our look at point-and-figure charts and, in some instances, at bar chart patterns, a price target often is established. Exiting at a target can be an exit strategy. In short-term trading, money targets are often used: "If I make $500 on this trade, I'm out." Targets can be tested as long as the target calculation method is easily quantified. At a target, especially a longer-term target, position size may be reduced or trailing stops tightened using technical barriers, a money stop, or volatility adjustment. In addition, once a target is reached, the system might have a reentry signal that enters the position again if the target is exceeded by a certain amount or the trend continues. Finally, a combination of target and time stop can adjust the target prices as time moves along. This reduces the possibility of the added risk with time affecting profits. All target limits should be accompanied by a trailing stop to avoid losing any profits already gained in case a target is not reached.

Execution

Execution risk strategies are useful in short-term trading where profit margin often is related to executed prices and slippage. Entry execution in most instances is related to when the system gives a signal. A breakout system often has competition at the breakout level, for example. Exit execution, on the other hand, can be controlled through experiment. A short-term system must establish, when the system is not a stop-and-reverse, the time at which a better exit can be obtained. Should the trade exit on the close for the day, the opening of the next day, or at some time between when volatility usually declines? The opening is usually emotional and can be either an advantage or a disadvantage. The closing is used in most systems because it is the most rational and eliminates overnight risk.

Another means of executing an entry or exit is scaling. This is done more by institutions, which have large positions they need to accumulate or distribute, but it can equally be useful for the smaller-sized trader or investor, who can accommodate more than one standard position size. Scaling is the entering or exiting a position over time in small pieces. The initial execution accomplishes part of the goal of the system, and over time, entries may be added at more advantageous prices. If they do not, at least a small position has been entered.

Monitoring Systems and Portfolios

All systems and portfolios must be monitored for changes in behavior. The obvious change is when the system is running a series of losses larger than usual. There are methods of monitoring the system that will warn of changes, however, before any substantial loss is incurred.

Bryant (2001) suggests the following methods. Calculate the average profit factor over a moving number of trades—say the last 20 trades—just as in an oscillator such as the stochastic. Plot this calculation and then run a moving average through the plot and watch the behavior of the profit factor window to its moving average. The profit factor should always be above 1.0, and minor oscillations should be ignored. Any drift lower, however, is a warning of something potentially wrong. The recent calculation of a profit factor window should be compared with the entire history of profit factors with a t-test to see if the deviation from the moving average is significant.

Perform a test run to see if the strings of wins and losses are within a normal distribution—that is, if they are random or not. If no dependency is present, smaller size positions should be traded after a win and larger after a loss. If the test shows a positive dependency, the run streak is significant and positions should be reduced until the last trade is a win, at which point position size can be increased.

The equity curve of the system should be checked periodically. One method is to sum the profits and losses over a specified number of trades—say 30—and plot this figure in time. The sum should remain positive, or equity momentum is declining. Another common method of watching the equity curve is to calculate a moving average of equity. Breaking of the moving average is not necessarily a signal for action but a warning. If a forward line is calculated or a trend line plotted and broken, action likely should be taken, as the system performance is deteriorating for some reason. Often when these signals of danger arise, the position size in the system is reduced until evidence of recovery is seen or the problem is resolved.

The sum or average of the percent of winning trades over a specified number of trades will tell if there is a change in runs. A z-test can test whether the differences in proportions or percentages are significant and worth investigating further.

If Everything Goes Wrong

Occasionally a portfolio model breaks down completely. Murphy's Law takes hold, and everything that can go wrong does. At that point, the remedy is to close down the system and exit all positions. A standard for closing the entire portfolio model is a dollar or percentage stop, usually around 20%. No system should sustain that amount of loss without adjustment.

Conclusion

It pays to understand that trading and investing are not just a matter of entry into positions. Technical signals are useful for entry, but technical understanding of risk is even more important. Remember the law of percentages and how difficult it is to recover from losses. Investing and trading are a matter of determining and controlling loss of capital. Entry is easy; best exit is difficult. Money management consists of a number of ways to measure and to protect from the risk of loss either in individual trades or in complete systems. Exit strategies and the principles of position size are likely the most important aspects of any portfolio model. Amateur investors and traders do not often utilize these risk control measures, but if they did, considerably fewer disasters to pride and portfolios would result.

References

Bauer, Richard J., Jr. "Basic Statistics." Charles D. Kirkpatrick II and Julie Dahlquist, eds. *Technical Analysis*. 3rd ed. Old Tappan, NJ: Pearson, 2016.

Bryant, Michael R. "Money Management Indicators." *Technical Analysis of Stocks & Commodities* 19, no. 10 (2001): 42-50.

Cooper, Jeff. *Hit and Run Trading II: Capturing Explosive Short-Term Moves in Stocks*. Columbia, MD: Marketplace Books, 2004.

Evstigneev, Igor V. and Klaus Reiner Schenk-Hoppe. "From Rags to Riches: On Constant Proportions Investment Strategies." Working paper no. 89, Institute for Empirical Research in Economics, University of Zurich, 2001.

Katz, Jeffrey and Donna McCormick. "Barrier Stops and Trendlines." *Technical Analysis of Stocks and Commodities* (July 1998): 44-49.

Kaufman, Perry J. *Trading Systems and Methods*. 3rd ed. New York, NY: John Wiley & Sons, Inc, 1998.

Rotella, Robert P. *The Elements of Successful Trading*. New York, NY: NY Institute of Finance, 1992.

Taleb, Nassim N. *The Black Swan: Second Edition: The Impact of the Highly Improbable: With a New Section: On Robustmness and Fragility*. New York, NY: Random House, 2010.

Zamansky, Leo and David Stedhahl. "Secure Fractional Money Management." *Stocks and Commodities Magazine* 15, no. 7 (July 1998): 318-323.

CHAPTER 3

Behavioral Techniques

From Perry J. Kaufman, *Trading Systems and Methods, +Website*, 5th Edition (Hoboken, New Jersey: John Wiley & Sons, 2013), Chapter 14.

Learning Objective Statements

- Identify the three major time frames in which the American media could be viewed as providing trading signals

- Using the Volatility Ratio, compare the volatility of an event day in a stock to most other days in the same stock
- Summarize the results of event studies referenced in this chapter
- Apply the guidelines for reading the Commitment of Traders reports into a rule for a trading system or investing methodology

Some approaches to trading are directly dependent on human behavior and cannot be represented by pure mathematical techniques. Short-term systems are more likely to target investor behavior than economic factors because, over a few hours of one day, the influence of macroeconomic policy and long-term trends is very small. The concepts presented in this chapter deal specifically with the interpretation of human reactions, although the interpretations are all systematic. The section "Measuring the News" covers an area that has always been important to a floor trader, yet has been greatly overlooked by technicians; it offers great opportunity for research. "Event Trading," the study of the market's reaction to price shocks, has become increasingly important for both proactive and reactive traders. "Opinion and Contrary Opinion" takes the form of a poll or consensus of opinions of traders and market publications. It may help answer the question, "What is everyone else doing?"—or at least—"What are they thinking of doing?"

The principal works of Elliott and Gann are included in this chapter with a complete discussion of the Fibonacci series and its ratios. Fibonacci forms a singular part of their techniques, and has been applied to most other forms of charting. The way in which traders respond to market moves and the remarkable similarity that can be found in Nature give serious underlying substance to these methods. Because not all of the assumptions upon which these systems are based can be quantified, they can only be substantiated by the performance of the systems themselves. All of these behavioral methods are fascinating and open areas of creativity essential to broadening system development. They are grouped together with discussions of natural phenomena and the rapidly growing area of financial astrology, all of which should stimulate your grey matter.

■ Measuring the News

> If you can keep your head when all about you are losing theirs, maybe you haven't heard the news.
>
> —*Rudyard Kipling, adapted by H.L. Menken*[1]

The news is likely to be the greatest single element affecting pricing of free markets. It broadcasts both official statistics and interpretation, and can express information directly and by innuendo. It is indispensable to traders. If the news services are not objective, they could materially alter any opinion by including unverified claims or omitting relevant information. Occasionally, one news service releases an economic report too soon, throwing the market into a turmoil. On the whole, financial reporting is good, but cannot be without bias. The very act of interviewing the CEO of some company may give viewers the impression that the company has credibility, which is not always the case.

The impact of news is so great that a speculator holding a market position according to a purely technical system would do best not reading, listening to, watching, or in any sense being exposed to news, because whether pro or con, it is impossible to ignore. In a study commissioned by the *Wall Street Journal,* it was shown that 99% of the financial analysts polled read the paper regularly, and 92% considered it the *most valuable* publication they read.[2]

As an element of a trading program or as an indicator of its own, the news has exceptional value, but its interpretation can be very complex. We believe that, if we could measure the impact of unexpected news, the importance of the *Wall Street Journal* or other wire service articles, earnings releases, economic reports, the USDA crop reports, and the CFTC Commitment of Traders report,[3] we would be able to anticipate the direction of prices, or at least react profitably. But first we must be aware of the complications of analyzing the news. There is the problem of objectively selecting which items are relevant and which are most important. And then there is the difficulty of quantifying the news—how do you rank each item

---

[1] Adam Smith, *The Money Game* (New York: Random House, 1967). Based on the poem "If" by Rudyard Kipling.

[2] Frederick C. Klein and John A. Prestbo, *News and the Market* (Chicago: Henry Regnery, 1974), 3.

[3] A thorough analysis of the CFTC *Commitment of Traders* report can be found later in this chapter. It should be noted that other government reports released on the same day may complicate the interpretation.

that is measured, and on what scale do you determine cumulative importance? Some news items clearly have a greater impact on the market—weather disasters, terrorist activity, economic reports, a change of interest rates, major trade agreements, changes in government policy, key crop reports—but these must be ranked as bullish (+) or bearish (−) in a way that produces a numerical system of analysis. On a single day, an address by the president about foreign trade may be ranked −3, a meeting of the Federal Reserve +7, unemployment −4, a bombing in the Middle East −3, a continued lack of rain in the West +2, larger-than-expected retail inventories −4, and a key article in the *Wall Street Journal* on the improved Libyan crude oil production +5, giving a net score of −5 to the overall economic picture. This would be interpreted as moderately bearish.

Klein and Prestbo attempted such a study by assigning values of 3, 2, and 1 to articles in the *Wall Street Journal* of decreasing importance. Their interest was the stock market, and their work was straightforward and some of the conclusions general in nature. They showed a direct correlation between the relevant positive and negative news articles and the direction of the stock market. As it was scored over 6-week intervals before and after major turning points in the Dow Jones Industrial Averages, the news would stay about 70 percent favoring the current market direction. Having eliminated the possibility of the market influencing the news, they could conclude that, in retrospect, the market reflected the nature of the news. A victory for common sense.

With the continued globalization of world futures markets, there is a noticeable reaction in all financial markets to significant economic reports released by any major economy. The correlations are especially high during a crisis when markets are under stress. Rising consumer confidence in Germany is interpreted as bullish in the United States because it is positive for American exporters. Surprisingly lower earnings or disappointing growth of a major microchip manufacturer reflects badly on the entire tech sector everywhere in the world. News of the need to restructure Greek or Italian debt will cause a movement away from the euro, while the resolution will strengthen the euro.

There are exceptions when news is of limited scope and relevant to a specific commodity, such as a lack of rain in the Corn Belt during prime growing season, or a winter freeze in Florida's orange orchards or Brazil's coffee region. The news is watched carefully during the last phase of a bull or bear move. Commodity traders will wait for a crop report to show the final numbers on yield, in the same way the financial market traders will wait for initial claims to fall or the Fed or European Central Bank to raise rates, signaling a final change in the economic trend. Chicago weather traders are notorious for watching news that affects U.S. crops. It is the anticipation of weather, rather than the actual weather, that drives most price moves, as it is the anticipation of interest rate changes, or employment numbers, that moves the markets. The news items that affect prices the most are:

- Release of economic statistics (PPI and CPI for inflation, retail sales, balance of trade, employment and initial claims, consumer confidence, housing and refinancing).

- Action by the Federal Reserve or other central banks to change rates or change their *bias* (the way they express future policy).

- Changes in the money supply that indicate easing or tightening.

- Government reports on commodities production and inventories.

- Unexpected news or price shocks, such as an assassination or terrorist attack.

- Trade negotiations, agreements, legislation, and occasionally rulings by the U.S. Supreme Court that affect business.

- Weather and natural disasters, such as the Japanese earthquake, or a hurricane that affects the sugar crop or causes large payouts by insurance companies.

- In-depth studies by the *Wall Street Journal*.

- Front-page news articles and dominant television coverage of high prices, strikes, etc., and their potential effects on business.

- Market letters, research reports, and comments from accepted authorities, major brokerage houses, and influential organizations.

Ranking and Measuring

The problem of ranking and assigning numeric value to news items is that it requires knowledge of how others see the news. Klein and Prestbo studied this problem for the stock market and concluded that about 90% of the *Wall Street Journal* readers perceived news in the same way, when classified as bullish, bearish, or neutral. A reason for the consistent interpretation of the news articles is the published analysis. Within minutes of the release of an economic report or Central Bank action, the financial news services broadcast expert opinions. When this study was done, interpretations were supplied by the brokerage houses and transmitted to the media to be relayed to traders. The *professional analysis,* then and now, is assumed to be correct and is an overwhelming influence shaping public opinion. The report of an upgrade of Ford from *hold* to *buy* by Bank of America will bias investors towards being long Ford.

News can also be measured empirically, by studying the immediate impact of an expected or surprise news item. For statistical reports, such as Initial Claims, Consumer Confidence, or the Producer Price Index, care must be taken to use the correct figures. Market reaction is a combination of expectations compared with actual figures and corrections to the previously released data. In some cases, it is difficult to know whether a jump in prices was due to an upwards revision of the previous data or current values that are higher than expectations. You can find this week's list of economic reports on the Internet, along with the previous report data, expectations of the economists for the new data, and expectations of the market. Logical Information Machines (LIM), a data service, provides all of the historic reports, including revisions, and provides tools for analyzing the impacts. Combined with a record of trader expectations, there is enough information to evaluate trader reactions. Following the release of an economic report, we can then expect the price change to be expressed as:

Price change $= a \times$ (*Current value* $-$ *Expectations*) $+ b \times$ (*Revision* $-$ *Previous value*) where a and b are weighting factors, $a > b$ implying that the current value is more important than the previous one. The values of a and b can be found using a regression analysis. It is necessary to make the assumption for this type of measurement that the effects of a news release are most important in the short term, and that their influence on the market is diluted each day (and often each hour) following the release. A starting point for representing the way in which the news decreases in importance is to use the relationship in physics:

$$I = \frac{1}{T^2}$$

where I = the net impact

T = the elapsed time since the release of the news

In science this relationship, which represents the physical impact declining with the square of the distance or time, applies directly to sound and light.

The impacts of economic reports are significant, frequent, and worth studying. For futures markets, the CFTC releases its *Commitments of Traders* (COT) report each week. It tells the distribution of holdings among large and small speculators and hedgers as a percentage of total open interest. This report is watched with the idea that the small speculators are usually holding the wrong positions and the positions of large hedgers are normally right. The COT report is covered in a later section of this chapter.

Trading on the News

Even without a sophisticated method of measurement, there are many professional speculators who trade on the news. When a bullish news item appears and the market fails to respond upwards, the experienced trader looks for a place to sell. It shows that expectations exceeded reality and prices had already anticipated the bullish interpretation of the news. Sometimes there are a large number of sell orders placed above the market in anticipation of one last rally after the report is released. An increasing number of traders watch the early morning price movement on 24-hour electronic exchanges, before the primary market opens. The *primary market* is the local stock market or the beginning of the normal business day. One strategy is to sell a higher overnight move when there is little news to support the rise. If prices have been rising steadily in the premarket session in anticipation of a bullish economic report, selling early may be the only opportunity. Prices frequently gap lower after a bullish report that did not meet market expectations. Most U.S. economic reports are released at 8:30 A.M., New York time, one hour before the U.S. stock markets open. The response to the report can be seen on Globex, where most major index markets are traded. If you are trading individual stocks or ETFs then you may be able to trade through an ECN (Electronic Communication Network), the first of which was Instinet in 1969. Since then, the most successful, Island and Archipelago (Arca), have been absorbed by NASDAQ and the New York Stock Exchange, respectively. These off-exchange providers allow you to trade at any time and match your order with others within their own network. Good executions depend on finding other orders at your price. You may also find access to off-market trading through the major electronic order entry platforms, Think or Swim (TD AmeriTrade), Schwab, E*Trade, and Interactive Brokers.

Agricultural *weather markets* function purely on news. When there is a potential for a drought, traders with long positions wait for the 5-day forecast hoping for no rain; they anticipate a loss of a specific number of bushels per acre for every dry day once rainfall is below a specific level. Weather markets are nervous, with prices often gapping higher and lower at the open, and are characterized by evening-up on weekends; they rely heavily on anticipation. It is said that a farmer loses his crop three times each year, once for drought, once for disease, and once for frost. In 1976, the news carried numerous articles on the desperate wheat crop in the western states, showing films of virtually barren fields, and yet the United States harvested one of its largest wheat crops on record. Weather markets have a history of volatile price movement but rarely materialize as the disaster that is anticipated, thanks to new drought-resistant strains of hybrid corn.

The *discounting of news* is as important as the news itself. An old saying in the market, *buy the rumor, sell the fact*, implies that anticipation drives the price past the point where it would realistically account for the news. When the actual figures are released, there is invariably an adjustment back to their proper level. The pattern of anticipation for each economic report or news event should be watched closely. A later section in this chapter, "Trading the Reaction of Treasuries to Economic Reports," shows that price reversals are more common than continued movement following a report.

Market Selectivity

The market seems to focus on one news item at a time and one remedy at a time. Although the same factors are always there to affect prices, they must reach a point of newsworthiness before they become the primary driving force. For heating oil, the combination of unexpected, sustained cold weather compared to inventories will activate a weather market. Although professionals may monitor thermals, published by the U.S. Weather Service, the market will react quickly to a weather report that anticipates a cold front over the next five days.

Since 2003, when the economic recovery became the leading driver of stock prices, U.S. traders have focused their attention on weekly Initial Claims and the monthly employment report. The news broadcasts repeatedly stated that 400,000 claims was the balancing point between job growth and job loss. A sustained economic recovery needed job growth which would translate into consumer spending. The weekly Initial Claims data, released each Thursday at 8:30 A.M. in New York, is still followed by a sharp reaction in Treasuries and Index futures in U.S. and foreign markets. After years of terrorist attacks, wars in Iraq and Palestine, political upheaval in the mid-East and northern Africa, and the subprime crisis, the market still responds to Initial Claims and ignores most other news. It is a classic case of crowd behavior.

Media Indicators

In a delightful article,[4] Grant Noble argues that the news recognizes events when they are cresting, and most often provides a countertrend trading opportunity. First, the American media should be viewed as providing trading signals in three major time frames:

1. *Long term,* as given by the large circulation news magazines such as *Time, Newsweek,* and the *Economist.* With the timeliness of a brontosaurus, they profile moves that last many years.
2. *Medium term,* represented by *Barron's, Forbes,* and *BusinessWeek,* covering a period of about 3 months.
3. *Short term,* held captive by the *Wall Street Journal* and the *New York Times,* which provide intermediate predictions as well as medium-term outlook.

By reading these periodicals you find that the *Wall Street Journal* has run headlines on a "killing drought," "dust bowl," and the *New York Times* on "Drought...imperils crucial wheat crop" just as the wheat price makes its highs for the current move. In another case, *Barron's* cover article asked, "Is the bull leaving you behind?" in August 1987 just ahead of the precipitous drop in October of that year. It is not surprising that the media would highlight events only after they have become a popular concern. We might say that the proportion of news coverage corresponds to a high public consensus, a topic addressed in the section "Contrary Opinion." It may be perfectly valid to construct a consensus indicator based on the number of square inches of news coverage given to an event in a combination of publications, each weighted by its circulation. This may be easier now by scanning the most popular electronic news websites. Even with the increased access of electronic news, broad coverage and recognition of consensus remains a lagging indicator.

■ Event Trading

There are two situations that trigger *event trading.* The most common are scheduled economic reports, earnings announcements, and recommendations by financial institutions and independent analysts. The price moves tend to be modest, and traders usually take a position opposite to the market reaction, looking for a correction. In this section we will look at larger reactions to reports and unexpected events, and address specific situations.

The largest price moves with the greatest volatility, called *price shocks,* are the result of reactions to perceived important, unexpected news. These market events pose the greatest risks to all traders because they are unpredictable and of such great magnitude that they are out of proportion with normal trading risk. It may be possible to trade for a number of years without experiencing a large, adverse price shock;

---

[4] Grant Noble, "The Best Trading Indicator—The Media," *Technical Analysis of Stocks & Commodities* (October 1989).

therefore, many traders do not plan properly for these situations. Yet surviving a price shock is often the difference between the end of a trading career and a long, successful one. This section presents a strategy for trading immediately after a price shock.

Not all price shocks are of such magnitude that they present an unmanageable problem. It may be that most price moves, big and small, are either the reaction to news or the anticipation of news. Larger price moves are the result of an act that affects the global economy, such as a terrorist attack, declaration of war, assassination, or natural disaster associated with weather or earthquakes. Smaller shocks come from the periodic release of economic reports by a government agency or monetary authority; financial commentary on television, radio or newspaper; earnings releases; unexpected bankruptcy; rulings by the Supreme Court; statements by the Department of Agriculture with respect to a new drug; and countless other sources. The U.S. government releases economic data on a preannounced schedule, many of them at 8:30 A.M. New York time. These create regular disruptions.

The frequency and size of these price moves, triggered by unexpected news, make these events a natural candidate for a trading system.[5] The profit opportunity, however, does not lie in taking a position ahead of the report and anticipating the market reaction, but in studying the systematic patterns that come after the initial price reaction to the news. Because the news is unexpected, you cannot predict the results or the extent of the reaction; therefore, taking a market position in advance of a government report would have a 50% chance of success and often very high risk. Studies might show that there is a bias in the direction of the price shock due to the way the monetary authority plans economic growth and controls inflation; however, the risks would remain high. This section only looks at positions entered on the close of the *event day*, the day on which a sharp market move occurred.

Market Reactions to Reports

To determine whether there is ample opportunity to profit from the price move that follows an *event,* it is necessary to study the direction of the price changes that occur over the following few days. These lagged reactions are the results of market inefficiencies. When a surprise occurs, no one can know what the correct price should be; it takes time for the market to reach equilibrium. The premise proposed by the Efficient Market Hypothesis, that the market will immediately find the correct price, is ridiculous. It may the correct price at the moment, given the time to react and the size of the orders flowing into the market. With large price shocks there is often an over- or underreaction that is corrected during the next few days. Sometimes prices jump one direction and immediately begin to go the other way until they have completely discounted the price shock by the end of the trading day. The initial reaction to a price shock may not be the profitable direction for a trader.

[5] Ben Warwick, *Event Trading* (Chicago: Irwin, 1996). Also see Andrew Busch, *World Event Trading* (Hoboken, NJ: John Wiley & Sons, 2007) and Peter McKenna, *The Event-Trading Phenomena* (Wilkes-Barre, PA: TradeWins, 2003).

Figure 3.1 illustrates the types of price movements that are expected following an upwards price shock. When there is an underreaction, or a structural change, prices move higher over the next few days; when there is an overreaction, or a short-lived event, prices reverse. Patterns are not as orderly as shown in Figure 3.1 because volatility is high and many traders react impulsively (or by financial necessity) to the move, covering their losses. A move that is a candidate for event trading:

- Must have enough volatility to generate a follow-up move large enough to generate a profit.

- Must have a favorable likelihood of success.

- Must hedge another position, thereby reducing overall risk.

When studying these events, there should be a direct relationship between the size of the reaction and the type of pattern that follows. For example, a small reaction to news may be followed by a steady continuation of the direction of the price shock. Therefore, if Initial Claims or total unemployment jumps by 0.2% in a month, the market expects a reaction by the government to stimulate job growth by lowering interest rates. The same initial reaction would occur if unemployment jumped by 1 full percent, but the number would be so unexpectedly large that it may be considered an error, in which case it is not clear to what extent the government would respond. The market may overreact to a large shock but underreact to a small one. The best way to discover this is to study the reaction to events.

We could reason that, if trend-following is profitable for a market, and all moves are the results of price shocks of different sizes, then the normal price shock will occur in the direction of the trend.

Fundamental to understanding price shocks that occur as a reaction to economic reports or corporate earnings is that the size of the shock is based on the difference between the *expectations* and the *actual* reported data. The best assessment

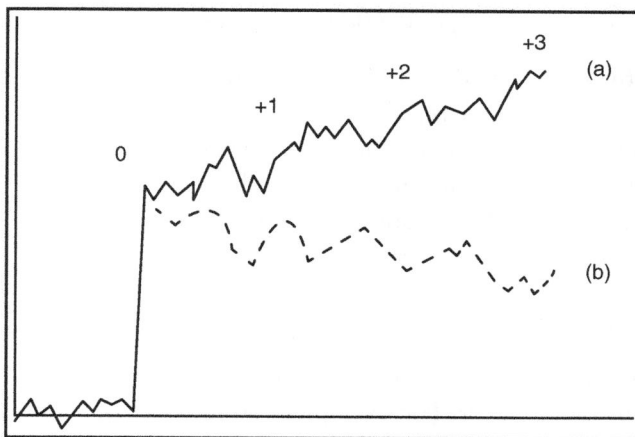

FIGURE 3.1   Price Reaction to Unexpected News, Including Delayed Response. The Upwards Price Jump on the Event Day (0) May be Followed by (a) a Continuation Move Up or (b) a Reverse Move Down Over the Next 3 Days.

of expectations is the market price just ahead of an economic report. The market always discounts what it believes is its best guess at what the report will say; therefore, if bond prices rise in advance of an important unemployment report, we can say that the market expects unemployment to increase. If the futures price of short-term rates have moved up by the equivalent of ½% drop in yield in anticipation of a very bad report, and the report comes out neutral, then prices will drop sharply to offset the incorrect expectation. When studying market reactions from historic records of economic data, you must use price to represent expectations. A study of how much prices have moved between releases of the same economic report can tell you whether the current price fully discounts the anticipated announcement.

Measuring an Event

The most practical way of measuring the surprise effect of an event is to compare the volatility on the day of the shock to the average volatility. This can be done by comparing the volatility of the current day with the average volatility of the recent past, using the *true range* calculation:

$$Volatility\ ratio_t = \frac{True\ range_t}{Average\ true\ range_{\text{previous }n\text{-days, lagged }m\text{-days}}}$$

where the average true range is calculated over n days but the value used is the average lagged m days. Typically, $n = 60$ and $m = 30$. The use of 60 days for an average will reduce the effect of any other price shocks that occur within that period, and the lagging avoids missing two shocks that follow one another. When the ratio is greater than 3.0 we are likely to have identified a day in which a news event caused a significant price shock. The larger the ratio, the greater the surprise to the market. Note that the true range is used because the shock can occur overnight, causing an opening gap, in which case the best measurement of volatility includes the price move relative to the previous close. To get the best results, use only *pit session* data.

Volatility Pattern   During the declining stock market beginning in 2000 and subsequent rally, the key economic reports watched by traders were weekly Initial Claims and the monthly Unemployment. One study of volatility shows that price movement in the Treasury futures is greatest on the day of the report and lowest on the day after the report. There are cyclic variations in volatility that seem to occur in a weekly pattern between the monthly releases of these reports.

Trading the Event Lag

Once you have studied the way prices move following an event day or a price shock, you can create trading rules. For example, you find that a monthly change in the Consumer Price Index of between 0 and 0.2% has no particular reaction, provided market expectations were similar to the data released. A change between +0.2 and +0.4 or −0.1 and −0.4 should provide enough surprise for a noticeable market reaction, when accompanied by lower or higher expectations. Data greater than a change of ±0.4 should cause a price shock regardless of the anticipation. In addition, we might find that changes over +0.4 tended to react in the opposite direction to the normal government action because of overanticipation or disbelief.

Based on the results of studying these patterns, Warwick established the following trading rules:

1. Buy on the close if the market closes in the upper 20% of the trading range on an event day, and if prices have shown an historic continuation pattern.
2. Hold for a predetermined number of days, based on the lag pattern of the market.
3. Use a stop-loss to limit risk.

In an older study applied to the corn market, Arnold Larson[6] found that 81% of the price changes occurred on the event day. There was a typical price reversal of 8% over the next 4 days, and a net change in price of 27% in the original direction over 45 days. An update of this study, shown at the end of this section, confirms that human behavior is not easily changed.

Results of Event Studies

In his book *Event Trading,* Warwick showed the test results of some of the major markets, allowing us to compare the effects of the systematic reaction of U.S. 30-year bonds with that of the S&P 500 and other financial markets. Unexpected news that causes bond prices to rally sharply (causing yields to decline) would result in a rise in the stock market, unless the news was particularly bad for the long-term economy of the country. Therefore, a drop in the consumption of durable goods should be followed by lower interest rates and a slightly lagged upwards response in the stock market. This pattern is shown in Table 3.1 where the bond and S&P results are side by side.

In general, we expect a price shock to impact interest rates first, then currencies, and finally equities markets. Typically, the interest rates react in a way to offset the economic effects and stabilize the equity market; this preempts the action that would be expected from the Central Bank. The foreign exchange (FX) markets react positively to raises in rates, and negatively to decreases, tempered by the reason for the rate change. The exception is when the news is much more extreme than usual and targets the stock market first. Investors, because of a lack of confidence, will shift their funds from equities to interest rates in what is called a *flight to safety*. This will cause a decline in the stock market and a corresponding drop in yields, although Warwick normally expects the two markets to move in the same direction. Lower yields (higher bond prices) should lower debit and facilitate business, thereby raising stock prices. However, investors are cautioned that the time lag in the reaction of Treasuries and equity index markets may vary considerably due to the state of the economy and current interpretation of economic policy.

---

[6] Arnold Larson, "Measurement of a Random Process in Futures Pricing," *Food Research Institute Studies* 1, no. 3 (November 1960), referenced in Warwick, *Event Trading* (1996).

| TABLE 3.1 | Results of Upwards Breakout of U.S. Bonds (left) and S&P 500 (right) for the Period 1989–1994 |

	U.S. Bonds			S&P 500		
	Holding Period	Buy or Sell	Confidence Level	Holding Period	Buy or Sell	Confidence Level
Durable goods	0–1	B	97	0–4	B	> 99
Retail sales	0–1	B	90	0–2	B	96
Retail sales	1–5	S	95	2–4	S	96
CPI	Low confidence			0–3	B	92
PPI	0–5	S	95	0–1	B	97
NAPM	0–2	B	91	0–4	S	97
Industrial production	0–1	S	94	Low confidence		
GDP	0–3	B	90	0–4	B	96
Employment	0–2	B	91	0–1	B	93

Table 3.1 shows the way the markets move after both the interest rates and stock market initially react with an upwards price shock. When both markets continue in the same direction, such as following retail sales, GDP, and employment data, then the full impact of the data takes longer to be assessed by the market, or there is expectation of some continued response by the government. The PPI and National Association of Purchasing Managers (NAPM) reports do not show this consistency, indicating that the market takes this information differently. When the pattern of confidence is low, the market may do a good job of reaching the best price level in immediate response to the news; therefore, there is no consistency in the price move that follows.

Table 3.2 shows the side-by-side test results of reactions that cause a drop in bond prices and a corresponding drop in the S&P 500. The frequency of low-confidence results may represent the conflict between the normal upwards bias of the stock

| TABLE 3.2 | Results of Downwards Breakout of U.S. Bonds (left) and S&P 500 (right) for the Period 1989–1994 |

	U.S. Bonds			S&P 500		
	Holding Period	Buy or Sell	Confidence Level	Holding Period	Buy or Sell	Confidence Level
Durable goods	Low confidence			0–2	B	92
Retail sales	Low confidence			0–4	B	94
Retail sales	Low confidence			Low confidence		
CPI	0–4	S	97	Low confidence		
PPI	Low confidence			Low confidence		
NAPM	Low confidence			Low confidence		
Industrial Production	0–4	S	93	Low confidence		
GDP	0–3	S	91	0–3	B	>99
GDP	3–4	B	>99	0–3	B	>99
Employment	0–1	S	93	Low confidence		
Trade balance	0–3	S	93	0-3	S	>99

market or the unusually bullish trend during the test period. The GDP results that show the most confidence indicate that the stock market moves higher even when the interest rates rise in reaction to positive GDP data. Balance of Trade data, which is not always the primary focus of the market, has a very consistent pattern, but is not clearly related to the interest rate move as are most of the other statistics.

Although this work concentrates on the short-term reaction to unexpected news, the long-term trend should not be overlooked. Economic data can exhibit trends over long time periods, and the response by the Fed is usually moderate but consistent. If the CPI or PPI show early signs of inflation, then the monetary authority will push rates up slightly; if this doesn't work, as seen in the next series of economic reports, they will move rates slightly higher again. This pattern creates an underlying trend that can be used to filter the direction of trades and add confidence to the results.

Readers are cautioned that the Treasury-stock index relationship can change for long periods due to the state of the economy. While the underlying economic principles will eventually surface, it is always important to study the market yourself and verify the patterns that you will use for trading. The process will build understanding and confidence in the method.

Reaction to Unemployment Reports   During the recent economic downturn, unemployment has been the focus of the recovery, and tracking those people filing unemployment claims has been the key measure in the past. Using Logical Information Machines (LIM), it was found that when the market underestimated its expectations of the monthly unemployment figure (issued on the first Friday of the month) by at least 0.2%, there was an average return of 4.5% in the S&P 500 during the following 27 days from the close of the report day. Similarly, U.S. 30-year Treasury bonds showed an average return on a long position of 3.2% during the period from 3 to 28 days following the report.[7] The interpretation is that the economy is worse than expected and will continue that way.

Trading the Reaction of Treasuries to Economic Reports   Treasury prices are often the market most affected by economic reports. A good report implies that interest rates will rise, and a poor report will cause them to fall; the reaction presumes that the government will use interest rates to counterbalance economic growth, above or below its target level. As discussed in the previous sections, futures markets reflect the expectation of these reports. In a study by Ruggiero[8] that covered 175 report days, Treasuries were seen to overreact to the numbers released in the Producer Price Index (PPI), Unemployment, and Retail Sales on the day of the report, plus the days of Treasury auctions.

To profit from the reaction of Treasuries, Ruggiero used a 1-day raw stochastic, *(close-low)/(high-low)*. He then bought Treasuries when the value was below 0.50 and sold when it was above 0.50 on the next open following the report day. Positions were held for 3 days. Based on the results of bonds, the reaction to the PPI was best, retail

---

[7] Gibbons Burke, "Event-Based Analysis," *Futures* (April 1995).

[8] Murray A. Ruggiero, Jr., "Exploiting Report Day Tendencies in Treasuries," *Futures* (February 2001).

sales next, and unemployment last, although still profitable. We can conclude that traders overreact to all three reports, but higher volatility will yield better returns.

Raschke Trades the News

In her popular book with Laurence Connors, Linda Raschke[9] trades only the reaction to the morning economic reports. Using 30-year U.S. bonds as an example, if a report such as the Producer Price Index or Gross Domestic Product causes bond prices to jump more than 4/32 above the high of the previous day, then

- Place a sell stop 3/32 below the high of the previous day to enter a short sale on a reversal.

- Once the new trade is entered, place a stop-loss 1/32 above the high of the current day.

- Move that stop down as soon as possible to a break-even point.

Raschke takes a businesslike approach to trading, keeping risk as low as possible and the chances of success as high as possible, even during the unusually high volatility that follows the release of morning reports. The same method is suggested for currencies, but there is no reason why it could not be used for any market that is directly affected by the economic numbers, such as stock indexes. European interest rate and index markets might be particularly interesting because they also react to U.S. reports but then must adjust to their own economic situation.

Finding Recent Patterns

We can write a program to find the patterns that follow any price shock. As discussed earlier, the average true range will allow us to find relatively large shocks. Start with the 60-day average true range, then calculate the ratio of today's true range divided by the average true range lagged 30 days (lag = 30). The subscript *ndays* is needed because we inspect the ratio *ndays* ago and look to see how price moved from *ndays* + 1 to today.

```
ATR = AvgTrueRange(60);
if ATR[lag] = 0 then ratio = 0
else ratio = truerange[ndays] / ATR[lag];
```

Whenever the *ratio* > *T*, where *T* is a threshold value of, for example, 2.0, we print the ratio, the price change on the day of the price shock, then the cumulative price change starting on the close of the day of the price shock (shown as *Start* on the *x*-axis). The cumulative price changes show what would have happened if a long or short position had been taken on the day of the price shock and held for 10 days.

Results are shown for three different markets over the past 10 years, ending April 2011. The threshold level for the ratio was 2.0, indicating a price shock in which today's volatility was at least twice the average volatility, all based on the closing prices. Figure 3.2a shows that the largest positive and negative price shocks during the last

[9] Laurence A. Connors and Linda Bradford Raschke, *Street Smarts* (Malibu, CA: M. Gordon Publishing, 1995).

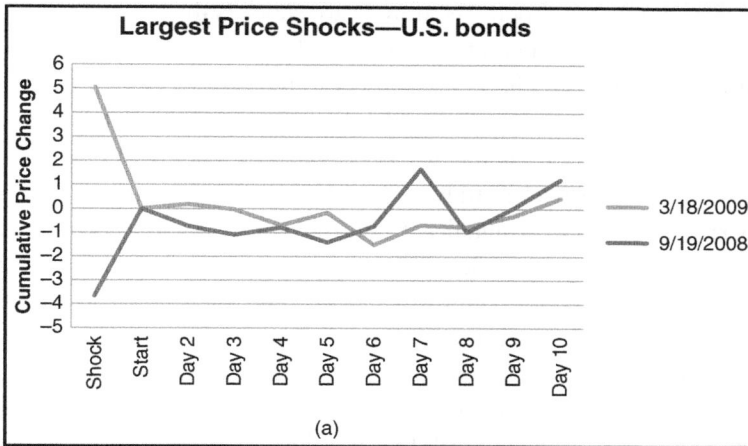

FIGURE 3.2a U.S. 30-Year Bond Price Shocks and Cumulative Reaction for 10 Years Ending April 2011. (a) The Two Largest Upward and Downward Shocks, (b) The Average of All Shocks with a Closing Price Move of More Than 1.5 Points (48/32nds).

10 years occurred in 2008 and 2009. The starting point on the chart shows the closing gap on the day of the shock, $5\frac{2}{32}$ higher and $3\frac{15}{32}$ lower. Positions are taken at the close of the day of the shock, and the accumulated net price change shown on days 2 through 10. After 10 days the downward price shock ends more than 1 point higher while the upwards price shock shows only a small gain. At its best point, we could have gained $1\frac{16}{32}$ in 4 days by selling the upwards price shock on the close. We could have also gained the same amount in 5 days by buying the downward shock on the close. It was mentioned earlier that volatility drops off quickly, and this chart shows that the accumulated reaction to the largest price shocks is moderate. Both shocks end higher after 10 days, showing that the long-term trend surfaces once the impact of the shock fades.

Looking at the largest shocks is not representative of the returns from trading. Figure 3.2b shows the average of all price shocks greater than $1\frac{16}{32}$. It shows a steady move

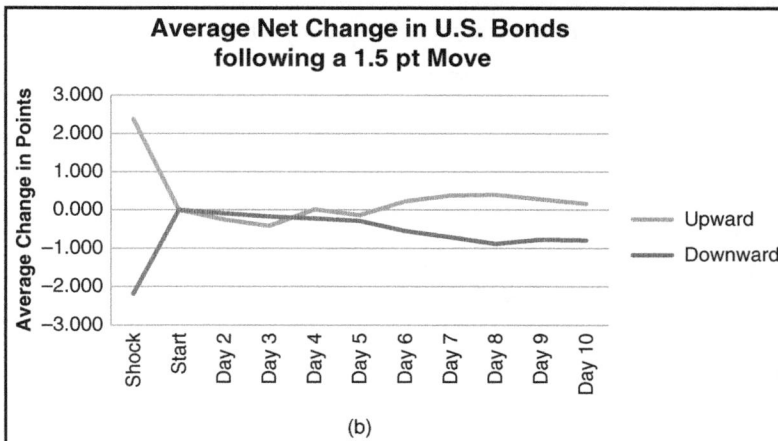

FIGURE 3.2b Average Shock > 48/32nds and Subsequent Cumulative Price Changes.

back in the direction of the shock. The downward shock is the most profitable, with an average return of nearly 1 full point by selling on the close of the day of the shock. The average volatility is very low. This is very similar to the case shown in Figure 3.1 where price continues slowly in the direction of the shock for a few days afterward.

The underlying direction of the market should be considered when evaluating results. In the case of Warwick's study, from 1989 to 1994, there is a shorter, volatile sideways period followed by a significant bull move. You would expect greater confidence buying downward price shocks. In the pattern found in Figure 3.2b we would also expect either upwards or downwards shocks to be followed by an upwards move, but that doesn't happen. Instead, they are quite symmetric, a sign that the underlying direction did not bias the results. A chart of 30-year bond futures is shown in Figure 3.3.

The results of crude oil tests are shown in Figure 3.4. The price shocks in the crude market are different from bonds because they most often come from geopolitical events rather than weekly API or economic reports. For large shocks, where the market closed higher or lower by at least $4/barrel, averaging nearly $6/barrel, the biggest opportunities were selling. Both upward and downward shocks ended nearly $2 lower after 3 and 4 days, and although the downward shocks ended much lower after 10 days, we should assume that it was reverting to the trend. The memory of a price shock should be less than 10 days.

To see if the large price shocks are different from the more frequent, smaller shocks, Figure 3.4b shows the average of all shocks greater than $1. The results are muted compared to the shocks greater than $4, and the upside price shocks have a modest downside reaction while the downside price shocks offer little opportunity.

The S&P is of interest to nearly everyone, and Figure 3.5 shows that upward price shocks greater than 30 points are followed by steady substantial declines, netting about 40 big points, or $2000 per contract. Downward price shocks fail to produce either a profit or a loss, indicating that once a large drop occurs, prices sit at that level for a number of days. It should be noted that a shock of 30 points is more likely to occur at higher price levels, which represent a smaller percentage. During the past 10 years, the price of the S&P index has fluctuated higher and lower, essentially ending where it began. The period of highest frequency of price shocks, both up and

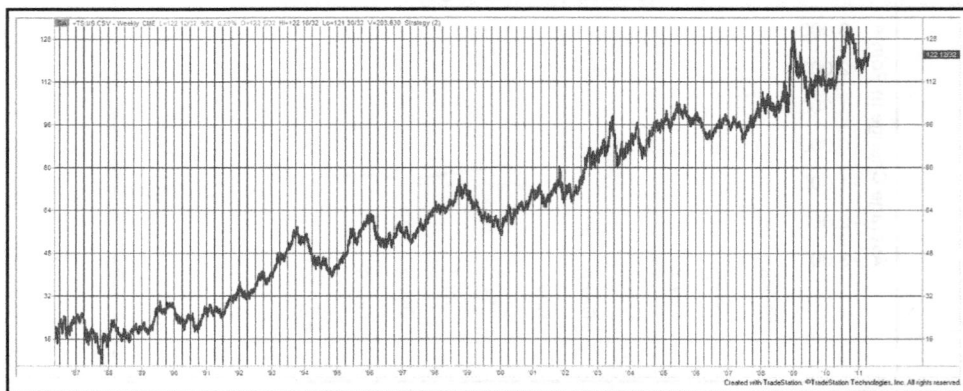

FIGURE 3.3   U.S. 30-Year Bond Futures, 1986 to April 2011.

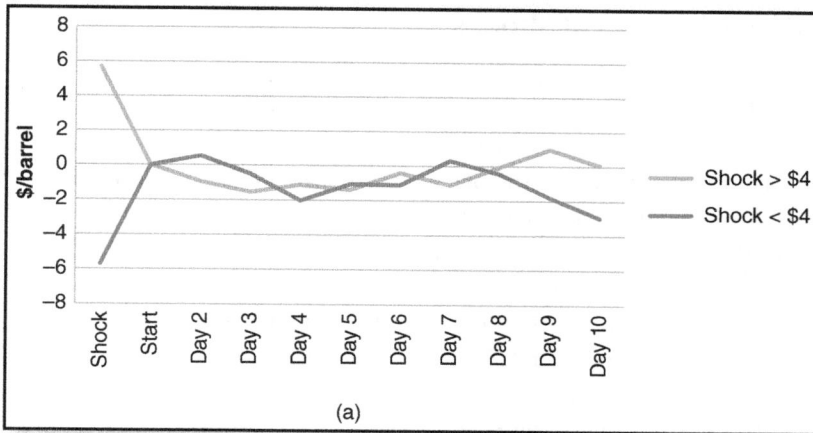

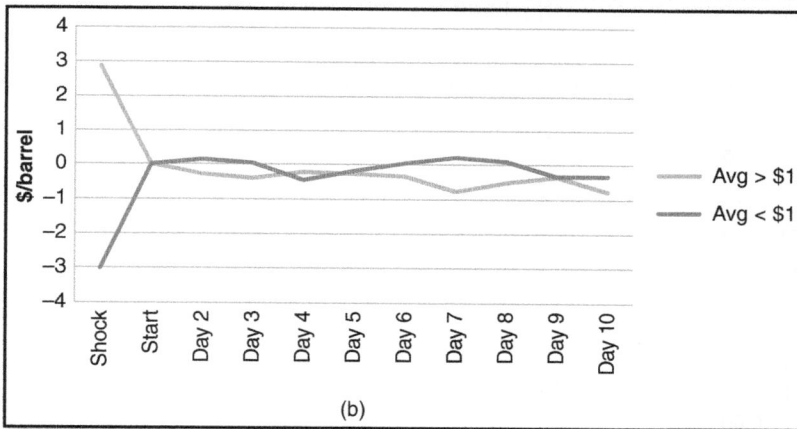

FIGURE 3.4 Results of Price Shocks in Crude Oil Futures for 10 Years. (a) Shocks Greater Than $4/barrel, and (b) Shocks Greater Than $1/barrel.

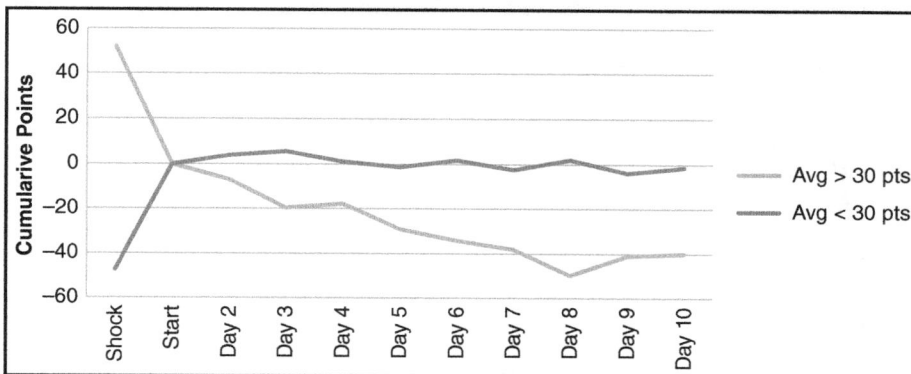

FIGURE 3.5 S&P Price Shocks Greater Than 30 Points.

down, occurred in the fall of 2008, during the subprime mortgage crisis. Although the pattern was more prevalent years ago, there should still be a bias for price shocks to the downside. Most traders/investors prefer to be long in the equity markets, causing a vacuum underneath when a large number of them want to exit at the same time.

Conditional Analysis of Shocks

So far, the analysis of shocks has only considered the direction of the closing price, above or below the previous close by some large threshold value. Even with daily data, there are patterns that can refine this study and make it more practical. What if on the day of the large move, the price closed near the high or near the low? If the shock was upwards, and prices closed near their highs, then we might expect a continuation of that move into the next day. If an upwards shock closed near the lows of the day we might expect a reversal.

Using U.S. 30-year bonds as an example because it has frequent shocks of varying size, a test was run using a 1.5 threshold for the price shock (prices close 1.5 times higher or lower than the average true range), and the close was in the highest or lowest 20% of the daily trading range. Figure 3.6 shows that the results for the 6 days following the shock are much different from the study that ignores the relative position of the close. For upwards shocks, part a, a lower close has the distinct tendency to continue lower, although an average of only 17 basis points, while a higher

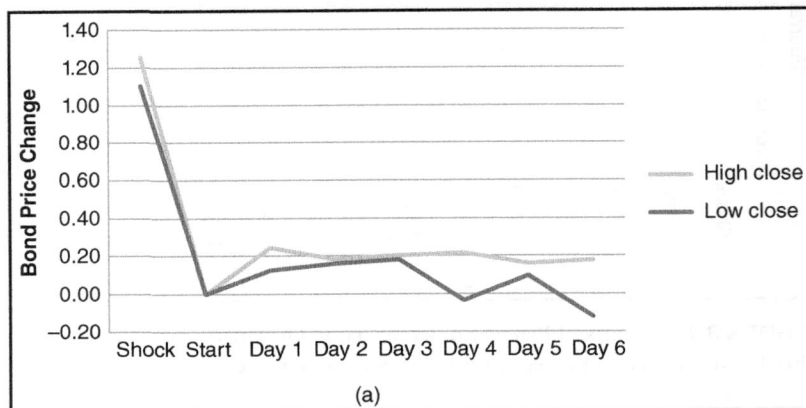

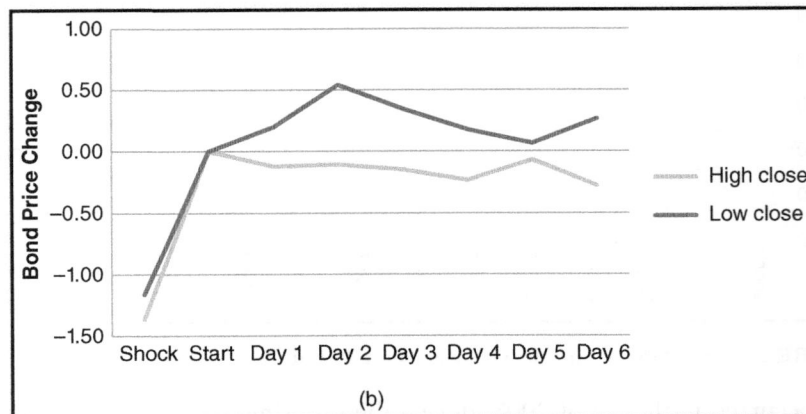

FIGURE 3.6   Results of Price Shocks of 1.5 with Prices Closing in the
Highest or Lowest 20% of the Daily Trading Range. (a) Upwards Price
Shocks. (b) Downwards Price Shocks.

close fails to follow through. For downward shocks, part b, the upward reaction is much stronger when prices close near the highs of the day. During the two days after the shock, prices gain 50 basis points before settling back to the original level of the price shock. Keeping these reactions in context, bonds have been in an uptrend for 25 years, so that an upwards move following a downwards price shock could simply be a reversion to the trend.

■ Commitment of Traders Report

Drawing from more than 20 years of experience in analyzing the CFTC's *Commitment of Traders Report* (COT), William L. Jiler described an approach to identifying a major trend in his *1985 CRB Commodity Yearbook*.[10] With his usual thoroughness and clarity, Jiler presents material that had previously been unsuccessfully interpreted.

Originally released on the 11th day of each month, the publication of the COT report changed to twice each month in 1990, biweekly in 1992, and has been released every Friday since January 2000. The content of the report has remained essentially the same; however, in 2010 the CFTC made a new attempt to classify the traders more accurately. The *short form COT Report* summarizes the open interest (open positions) of *reporting* and *nonreporting* traders as of the close of trading on the Tuesday of the reporting week. *Reported positions* are those exceeding a minimum level determined for each futures market (e.g., 750,000 bushels for corn, 500,000 for soybeans, 500 contracts for 30-year Treasury bonds, and 300 contracts for the S&P 500). These levels are based on the total activity of the market and may change over time. As of January 2000, those traders with reportable positions must aggregate all smaller positions held in the same market into one number. Previously, only the individual orders in excess of the reporting limit needed to be identified. Additional information is available that subdivides the open interest into positions held by hedgers, who are commercial users of the commodity, and speculators. By subtracting the reported positions from the total open interest, the total positions of small hedgers and speculators can be found.

The short form, shown in Figure 3.7, gives a brief breakdown of speculative and commercial positions. In the long form, Figure 3.8, grain positions are further divided into *old crop* and *other* positions, including new crop and intercrop spreads. At the bottom are the concentration of positions held by the largest four and eight traders.

In order to analyze the shifts in position, Jiler compiled tables of *normal patterns,* similar to a seasonal study (see Figure 3.9). When the open interest of one group is significantly greater than their normal holdings, they express a definite opinion on the direction of the market. By tracking these changes for many years and observing the corresponding price changes, Jiler concludes that the large traders have the best forecasting record, with the large hedger better than the large speculator. The small

---

[10] William L. Jiler, "Analysis of the CFTC Commitments of Traders Reports Can Help You Forecast Futures Prices," *1985 CRB Commodity Year Book* (Jersey City, NJ: Commodity Research Bureau, 1985).

WHEAT – CHICAGO BOARD OF TRADE								
FUTURES-ONLY POSITIONS AS OF 12/12/06								
							NONREPORTABLE POSITIONS	
NONCOMMERCIAL			COMMERCIAL		TOTAL			
LONG	SHORT	SPREADS	LONG	SHORT	LONG	SHORT	LONG	SHORT
(CONTRACTS OF 5,000 BUSHELS) OPEN INTEREST: 417,081								
COMMITMENTS								
73,598	56,045	69,448	237,539	232,901	380,585	358,394	36,496	58,687
CHANGES FROM 05/25/2004 CHANGE IN OPEN INTEREST: –7,043								
–10,463	–1,186	126	3,462	–6,610	–6,875	–7,670	–168	627
PERCENT OF OPEN INTEREST FOR EACH CATEGORY OF TRADERS								
17.6	13.4	16.7	57.0	55.8	91.2	85.9	8.8	14.1
NUMBER OF TRADERS IN EACH CATEGORY (TOTAL TRADERS: 317)								
102	89	92	67	96	233	256		

FIGURE 3.7 Commitment of Traders Report (Short Form) From the CFtC.gov Website.

WHEAT – CHICAGO BOARD OF TRADE										
Commitments of Traders – Futures Only, May 10, 2011										
	Total Open Interest	Reportable Positions							Nonreportable Positions	
		Non-Commercial			Commercial		Total			
		Long	Short	Spreading	Long	Short	Long	Short	Long	Short
(CONTRACTS OF 5,000 BUSHELS)										
All	455,903	100,101	89,939	65,413	253,366	243,455	418,880	398,807	37,023	57,096
Old	415,581	100,159	95,463	46,454	237,460	227,124	384,073	369,041	31,508	46,540
Other	40,322	11,869	6,403	7,032	15,906	16,331	34,807	29,766	5,515	10,556
Changes in Commitments from May 3, 2011										
	–4,544	–4,092	–1,627	2,347	–3,085	–8,434	–4,830	–7,714	286	3,170
Percent of Open Interest Represented by Each Category of Trader										
All	100.0	22.0	19.7	3.3	55.6	53.4	91.9	87.5	8.1	12.5
Old	100.0	24.1	23.0	11.2	57.1	54.7	92.4	88.8	7.6	11.2
Other	100.0	29.4	15.9	17.4	39.4	40.5	86.3	73.8	13.7	26.2
Number of Traders in Each Category										
All	421	123	132	153	84	132	311	337		
Old	418	121	141	138	79	127	294	326		
Other	171	37	31	19	33	86	84	129		

Percent of Open Interest Held by the Indicated Number of the Largest Traders

	By Gross Position				By Net Position			
	4 or Less Traders		8 or Less Traders		4 or Less Traders		8 or Less Traders	
	Long	Short	Long	Short	Long	Short	Long	Short
All	22.3	18.6	37.4	25.5	20.0	13.5	34.1	19.0
Old	23.5	20.2	39.5	27.7	22.1	15.8	36.7	22.3
Other	32.5	23.5	48.5	31.8	25.1	3.8	38.5	20.5

FIGURE 3.8 Commitment of Traders Report (Long Form), May 10, 2011.

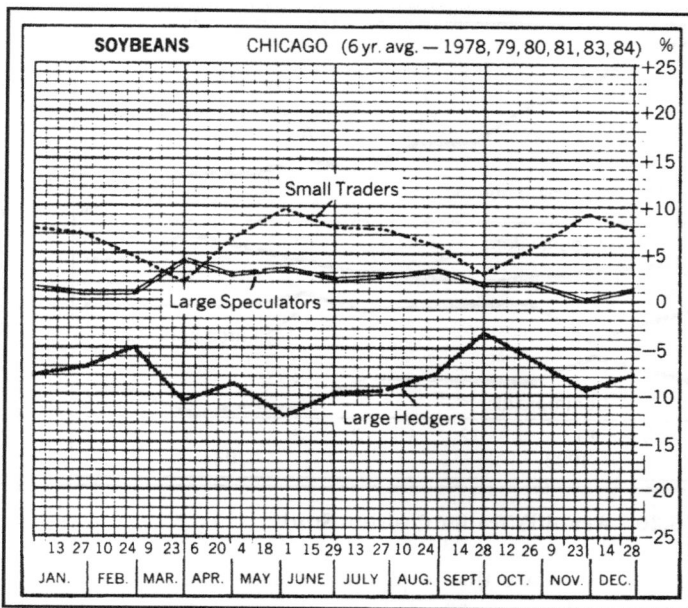

FIGURE 3.9 Jiler's Normal Trader Positions.

traders were notably worse. Guidelines, referring to agricultural products, were stated as:

> The most bullish configuration would show large hedgers heavily net long more than normal, large speculators clearly net long, small traders heavily net short more than seasonal. The shades of bullishness are varied all the way to the most bearish configuration which would have these groups in opposite positions—large hedgers heavily net short, etc. There are two caution flags when analyzing deviations from normal. Be wary of positions that are more than 40% from their long-term average and disregard deviations of less than 5%.

This result was confirmed by Curtis Arnold,[11] who compared positions of large and small speculators with commercials for 1-year periods spanning 1983–1984. Arnold shows in Figure 3.10 that the positions of commercials and small speculators tend to be opposite, with the commercials positioned to profit from the subsequent price move.

Over a wider group of 36 markets from 1983 to 1989, a study conducted by *Bullish Review*[12] showed that a large weighting of long or short positions held by commercial hedgers correctly forecast significant market moves 67% of the time. In retrospect, it seems likely that a large commercial trader, bank, investment house, or other institution would take a longer-term view of the market, setting positions to take advantage (or avoid the risk) of a potential price move. Because of their size, institutions are not likely to change their positions on minor price variations.

[11] Curtis Arnold, "Tracking 'Big Money' May Tip Off Trend Changes," *Futures* (February 1985).

[12] Steve Briese, "Tracking the Big Foot," *Futures* (March 1994).

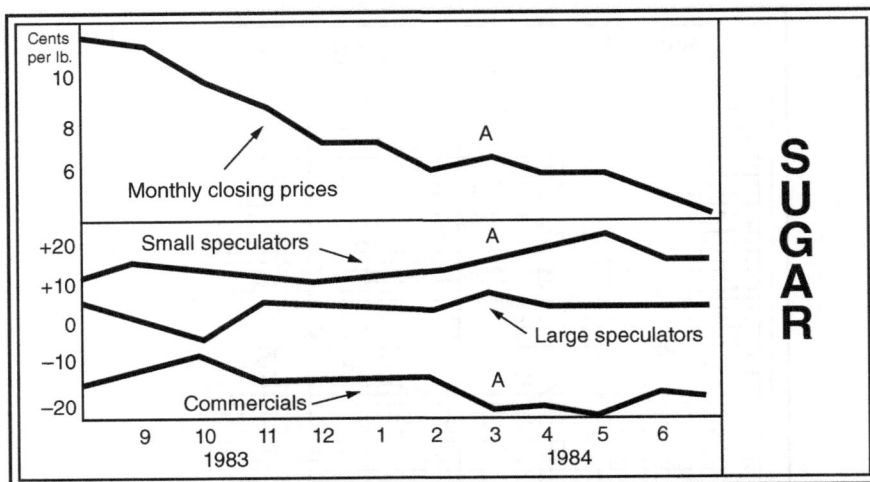

FIGURE 3.10 Arnold's Trader Position Study.

Analysts should be aware that a qualified *hedger*, one that is registered with the CFTC in order to set large positions due to their ongoing risk of holding physicals, may also take large speculative positions under the same umbrella. Given this ambiguity, the new COT classifications will make it clearer where the "smart money" is positioned. The old report combined commercials and swap dealers; however, swap dealers can side with the speculator or commercial given market conditions. By separating them, the report now shows "true commercials."

Creating an Oscillator for the COT Numbers

Briese uses a *COT Index*[13] as an oscillator to plot the results of the COT report.

$$COT\ Index_t = 100 \times \frac{NL_t - Lowest(NL, n)}{Highest(NL, n) - Lowest(NL, n)}$$

where NL = the net long positions of a given group of reporting traders
n = the look back period, ranging from 1.5 to 4 years

This should be recognized as the formula for a stochastic, giving the bullish percentage.

In order to see the cycle of the three reporting groups, Ruggiero[14] plotted the stochastic of each group using a calculation period of 1 year. The positions of commercial and those of small-lot traders are completely out of phase. The stochastic indicator shows that the commercial traders reach an extreme level of bullishness (high stochastic values) just ahead of an upwards price move, and a low stochastic value just before prices drop. This implies that they are usually holding the right position. Ruggiero interprets the other values to mean that funds trading these markets become bullish or bearish when the commercials are beginning to exit their

[13] In Murray A. Ruggiero, Jr., *Cybernetic Trading Strategies* (New York: John Wiley & Sons, 1997). Also see Stephen Briese, *Commitment of Traders Bible* (Hoboken, NJ: John Wiley & Sons, 2008).

[14] Murray A. Ruggiero, Jr., "Seeking a Commitment," *Futures* (April 2002).

positions, about halfway through the move. Small-lot traders tend to become bullish, with a high stochastic reading, as prices peak.[15]

While this study is consistent with previous works, the use of a stochastic makes a strong visual impact, showing how the bullishness and bearishness of these different groups are remarkably out of phase. The best short sale signals occur at just these times, when the positions of the commercials are strongest, well above 80, and the two other groups are weakest, under 20. Buying opportunities are just the opposite. Extreme differences precede change in the positions of each group and the market price. The holding time for this trade corresponds to the time it takes for the stochastic to switch from high to low, and low to high, for the different groups. This may take 3 to 6 months, depending on the market.

Trading Signals An additional trading refinement was applied to the reported positions for the S&P 500. When the stochastic for the commercials crosses above 80 and the S&P closes lower than it did 4 weeks ago, we get a buy signal. The position is closed out when the stochastic touches 40, which is just before the neutral level of 50. It is not safe to assume that stochastic values will move from overbought to oversold; it is much better to only expect them to return to neutral.

Ruggiero also used the COT Index for both commercials and small traders to create a basic timing model:

If COT Index Commercials[lag] > *Ctrigger* and COT Index Small < *Strigger* then *buy*
If COT Index Commercials[lag] < *Ctrigger* and COT Index Small > *Strigger* then *sell*[16]

The results are bullish when the COT Index for commercials is high and the COT Index for small traders is low. The results are bearish when the COT Index for commercials is low and the COT Index for small traders is high. The COT Index for commercials is lagged by one or more weeks because the actions of commercials are interpreted as leading the market. *Ctrigger* and *Strigger* are levels that are determined to be significant turning points. In Ruggiero's tests, this method was highly successful for Treasury bonds using *Ctrigger* = 30, *Strigger* = 50, and *lag* = 1 (one week).

Capturing the Cycle in the COT In another more extensive strategy, Ruggiero created a method that anticipated price direction based on extreme bullishness and bearishness in the COT report; however, he chose to only take long positions.[17] The pattern being exploited is called the *markup phase*, which occurs after the commercials have stopped buying and start selling the rallies. At the same time, funds enter the market as it accelerates. The public enters when prices are very bullish and commercials are turning bearish.

---

[15] The same conclusion is reached by Jon D. Andersen in "Analyze Net Positions," *Technical Analysis of Stocks & Commodities* (July 2002), although Andersen plotted the actual COT values—rather than convert to an indicator—and observed the diverging patterns.

[16] In Ruggiero, *Cybernetic Trading Strategies*, this was written as a *buy* signal; however, it seems that it should have been a *sell* signal.

[17] Murray Ruggiero, "Trading off the Big Boys," *Futures* (January 1998).

The purpose of this strategy is to enter the market at the time of upwards acceleration and exit after at least *n* days and after the acceleration has stopped. To implement this, Ruggiero finds the correlation of price and volume and converts that to an oscillator rescaled to the range +1 to –1. He finds the Herrick Payoff Index (HPI) using a conversion factor of 100 and a smoothing constant of 0.10, which combines price, volume, and open interest. A *markup* occurs when the correlation oscillator > 0.3 and HPI > 0 but not the highest value of the recent period and the payoff has not retraced by some threshold percentage.

Once the markup has been determined, another oscillator is formed from the net commercial position, longs minus shorts, ranging from 100 to 0. If the oscillator > 85 and a markup occurred within the past 3 days, a long position is entered. Trades are held for at least *n* days and until there is no markup.

The numbers in the COT report can be turned into a *Sentiment Index,* as shown in the next section of this chapter.

■ Opinion and Contrary Opinion

Market sentiment, the collective opinion of investors, is a driving force in the market, yet it is very difficult to measure and even harder to deliver those results in a timely fashion. For that reason, analysts often substitute a combination of volume, open interest, and price for true sentiment, hoping that the recorded actions of traders closely relate to what they are thinking. Opinion, however, weighs on the marketplace and governs future actions in the same way that high volume may not move prices today, but provides a platform for a potentially large price move. The *Consumer Confidence Index*, released monthly by the Conference Board and conducted by Nielson, is the most common example of opinion that moves the market.

Public opinion is also fast to change. A prolonged bull market in stocks may show a gradual increase in bullish sentiment; however, the collapse of a bank, an increase in rates by the central bank, a sharp downturn in the economy of another region, or a single sharp drop in the stock index could quickly change the public's opinion. In reality, sentiment indicators are most popular for trading in the direction opposite to the unified public opinion.

Contrary Opinion

The *contrarian* lies somewhere between the fundamentalist and the technician, basing actions on the behavior of crowds, in this case the market participants.[18] The contrarian sees the end of a bull market occurring when everyone is bullish. Once all long positions have been set, there is diminishing influence by the bulls; moreover, the contrarian believes that opportunities always lie in the reverse direction from crowd thinking.

---

[18] For the most definitive works, see Humphrey Neill, *The Art of Contrary Thinking* (Caldwell, OH: Caxton Printers, 1960), who is credited with having first formulated the concept, and Earl R. Hadady, *Contrary Opinion* (Pasadena, CA: Hadady, 1983).

Contrary opinion alone is not meant to signal a new entry into a position; it only identifies situations that qualify. It lacks the timing. It is more of a filter than a trading system, a means of avoiding risk and finding an opportunity. Consider the patterns that appear in every prolonged bull or bear move. First, there is a place where the direction is generally accepted as the major trend. After that, traders wait for a pullback to enter in the direction of the trend at a more favorable price. These price *corrections* within a trend become smaller or even disappear when everyone wants to *buy a lower open* or in the case of a bear market, *sell a higher open,* until finally there is a *blow-off* and a major reversal. The dramatic end to a prolonged move is generally credited to the entrance of the public; when the masses are unanimously convinced that prices are going higher, who else is left to buy?

The other important ingredient for a contrarian is that all the facts cannot be known. The widely accepted belief that prices will go higher must be based on presumptions; if the final figures were out and the reality known, the market would adjust to the proper level. This idea is older than *The Art of Contrary Thinking.* In 1930, Schabacker[19] advised,

> It is best to follow the crowd when fundamental considerations for the industry, for the stock and for the group are improving and indicate that there is really something to the move. But it is best to reverse the action of the crowd and desert them, or play the opposite side of the market, when their action is based more on rumors, on prospects, on paper talk, on public gossip, on results of pool publicity, etc., than upon a genuine raison d'être. Another clue is that when the resulting movement is sharper than usual and enthusiasm is higher than seems logical, it is also best not to follow the crowd.

The practical application of the theory of contrary opinion is the *Bullish Consensus*[20] and the *Market Sentiment Index*, created from a poll of market letters prepared by the research departments of brokerage firms and professional advisors. In the *Bullish Consensus* (see Figure 3.11), these opinions are weighted according to the estimated circulation of these letters.

$$Bullish\ Consensus = \frac{Sum\ of\ (Each\ source \times Relative\ circulation \times Bullish\ opinion)}{Sum\ of\ (Each\ source \times Relative\ circulation \times 100)}$$

The value of the bullish consensus ranges from 0 to 100%, indicating an increasingly bullish attitude. Because of the bullish tendency of the novice trader, and the long-term upwards bias of the stock market, the neutral consensus level is 55%. The normal range is considered from 30 to 80%, although each market must be individually evaluated.

Hadady also devised a simple mathematical way of displaying the bullishness of the market.[21] Using the formula below, he shows that when 80% of traders are bullish,

[19] R.W. Schabacker, *Stock Market Theory and Practice* (New York: B. C. Forbes, 1930), 517. This book was the definitive study of the market. In it he quotes Theodore Price as saying that speculation is "hazard plus intelligence" while gambling is "hazard without intelligence."

[20] The Bullish Consensus is a product of Sibbett-Hadady, Pasadena, CA; a Market Sentiment Index is published in Consensus, Kansas City, MO.

[21] R. Earl Hadady, "Contrary Opinion," *Technical Analysis of Stocks & Commodities* (August 1988).

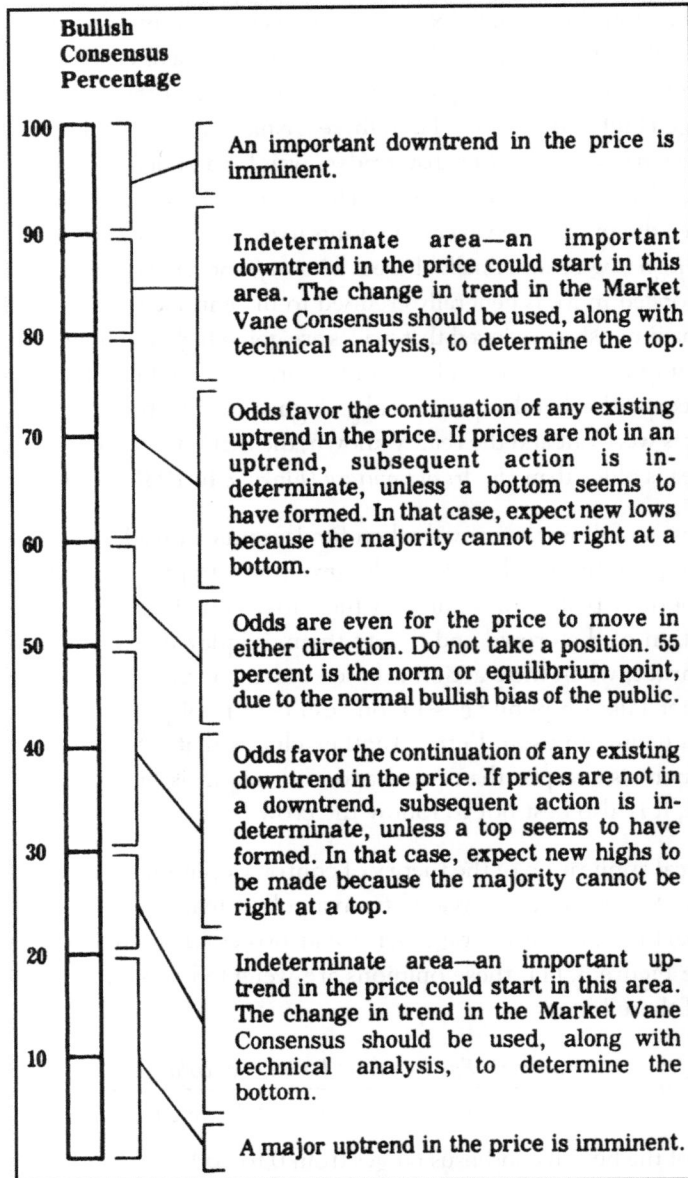

FIGURE 3.11   Interpretation of the Bullish Consensus.

Source: R. Earl Hadady, *Contrary Opinion* (Pasadena, CA: Hadady, 1983).

then the average buyer will hold only ¼ the number of contracts as the average seller. This leads to a precipitous drop in prices once a decline begins.

$$N_t = \frac{20\%T \times N_s}{80\%T} = \frac{1}{4} \times N_s$$

where T = the number of traders in the market

N_t = average number of contracts held by a single bullish trader

N_s = average number of contracts held by a single bearish trader

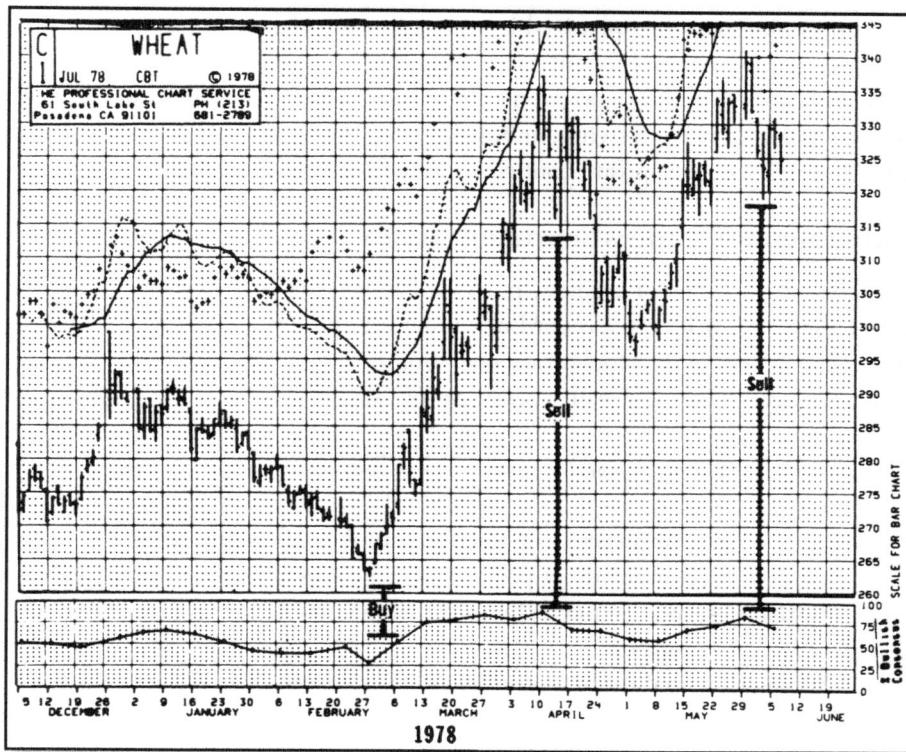

FIGURE 3.12 Typical Contrarian Situation—Wheat, 1978.

The principles of contrary opinion do not require that trades only be entered in the direction opposite to the current price movement. Within the normal range, the contrarian will take a position in the direction of the trend. Frequently, the Bullish Consensus will begin increasing prior to the price turning higher, indicating that the attitude of the trader is becoming bullish. It is considered significant when the index changes 10% in a 2-week period. Once the Bullish Consensus reaches 90% during an upward move, or 20% during a bear move, the market is considered overbought or oversold, and the contrarian looks for a convenient point to exit from the current trade. Positions are not reversed until prices show that they are changing direction. This could be identified using a moving average. Remembering Schabacker's advice, the occasion of a general news release that moves the market further than would seem reasonable in the direction of the general opinion is an opportune moment to enter a contrary trade; specific news that fails to move prices would be a good indication of an exhausted trend when the consensus is overbought or oversold. A typical contrarian situation identified by Hadady is given in Figure 3.12.

R. Earl Hadady said, "The principle of contrary opinion, by definition, works 100% of the time. The problem is getting an accurate consensus."[22] Timeliness is the difficulty with this index; if 60 to 70 market letters are reviewed, read, and weighted to form an index, the results may be outdated before they can be used. The theory

[22] George Angell, "Thinking Contrarily," *Commodities* (November 1976).

of contrary opinion also emphasized its use as a timing device for entering trades at an opportune moment and for filtering out the ambiguous trades; the theory is not readily applicable to exiting a position unless the reverse consensus occurs. Because a consensus does not have to switch uniformly from bullish to bearish, it is not always prudent to wait for an opposite confirmation before exiting a trade.

Commitment of Traders Sentiment Index

The reported positions of traders, published in the CFTC's *Commitment of Traders Report*,[23] may be considered a recording of market opinion into categories. By combining the idea behind the stochastic calculation with a method originally developed by Curtis Arnold, you can create a *Sentiment Index*:

$$COT\ Sentiment\ Index = \frac{Current\ net - Minimum\ net}{Maximum\ net - Minimum\ net}$$

Where   *Net* = commercial net position (number of contracts) minus the total combined net position of large speculators and small traders

     Maximum = greatest net difference that occurred during the comparison period

     Minimum = smallest net difference that occurred during the comparison period

The intent of the Sentiment Index is to rank the current spread between the commercial and speculative positions within the context of the historic range, in a manner similar to a stochastic. There seems to be uniform agreement that the commercials are the group that determines the correct direction of prices. A shift in the position of the commercials should be closely watched.

A Lesson from Put-Call Ratios

The ratio of put option volume to call option volume, called the *put-call ratio*, is the major sentiment index for listed options. It too is used for its contrary value. Unlike the sentiment indexes derived from analyst opinions, this ratio is available daily. The interpretation of extreme levels of the put-call ratios, in particular for the major equity index options, points out a problem that may reflect on the proper use of all contrary indicators.[24]

Prior to 1986, the market was considered ready for an upturn when the total put volume exceeded 65% of the total call volume. Similarly, when the put volume fell to 35% of the call volume, it was a bearish indication. In the volatile markets of 1986 and 1987, these levels proved to be far too close, and as McMillan said, "Not surprisingly, the put-call ratios fell into some disfavor at that point." This could easily happen with a contrary indicator, or any indicator that rarely reaches its extreme

THE INTEGRATION OF TECHNICAL ANALYSIS

[23] Stephen E. Briese, "Commitment of Traders as a Sentiment Index," *Technical Analysis of Stocks & Commodities* (May 1990).

[24] Lawrence G. McMillan, "Put-Call Ratios," *Technical Analysis of Stocks & Commodities* (October 1995).

values (even a relative strength index that has no maximum and minimum bounds). Because contrary opinion is a valuable addition to analysis, the use of these indicators now focuses on relative highs and lows. This can be accomplished by smoothing the ratio using a standard moving average or momentum indicator, a simple difference over *n* days. When the ratio moves over 65% *and turns down* it is time to sell. This approach gives up a timing edge but greatly reduces risk and increases reliability. After selling, if the momentum indicator reversed and made new highs, short positions should be exited or reversed.

Dogs of the Dow and the Small Dogs

Another recognizable contrarian method is the *Dogs of the Dow*, popularized by Michael O'Higgins in *Beating the Dow*.[25] The method shows that if, on January 1 of each year, you bought the 10 members of the Dow with the lowest stock dividend yields from 1973 through 1989, you would have beaten the average return of the Dow by 6.8% per annum. It assumes that good companies pull themselves up after a bad period. While not always profitable during the turn of the market between 2000 and 2002, it is reported to have done much better than the Dow Index.

For the small investor, O'Higgins proposed the *Small Dogs of the Dow*, also fondly called the *puppies*. Out of the 10 stocks selected as the Dogs of the Dow, buy the ones with the lowest stock value. In Robert Sheard's book, *The Unemotional Investor*, he presents the *Foolish Four*, a way of selecting 4 of the 10 Dogs.[26] As described on *winninginvestments.com*, Sheard sorts the 5 stocks of the Small Dogs, lowest price at the top, and places them alongside the 10 Dogs, lowest yields at the top. If the same stock appears at the top, it is eliminated because it is trading at a low price for a good reason. If there is no match, he takes the top 4 stocks from the Small Dogs.

Watching the Big Block Transactions

Big block transactions are those that are equal to or greater than 100,000 shares or have a transaction value of $1 million or more. *Corporate insiders* are the corporation's officers, directors, and beneficial owners of more than 10% as specifically named in the 1934 Securities and Exchange Act, Section 16. Corporate insiders must register their holdings with the SEC and must disclose any share transactions by filing a report within 30 days after the purchase or sale. Due to slowness in these filings, the Sarbanes-Oxley Act became effective in August 2003 to accelerate reporting (among other things), which now must be done within 2 days of the transaction. Insiders can also file a plan with the SEC, in advance, to buy or sell shares on specific dates or at specific prices. Not all of the shares traded by insiders are "timed."

Insider trading is not the same as *trading on inside information*, which is illegally making a trade based on nonpublic or privileged information. Insider selling is a

---

[25] See Harry Domash, "Winning Investing.com," winninginvesting.com.
[26] See the website for the Motley Fool, fool.com.

common occurrence, as executives who have accumulated stock options, and venture capitalists who see the appreciation in share value, convert their holdings into cash. Some of these transactions are done at regular intervals and have no relationship to market direction, while others are at opportune moments and may offer insight into the future direction of prices.

The combination of big block trades by corporate insiders is a special case that was studied by Bjorgen and Leuthold,[27] who concluded in 1998 that

- Since 1983, when net selling, measured in dollars, reached historically high levels, the stock market performed poorly over the next 12 months. At the time this article was written, 1998, corporate insiders were selling at levels approaching historic highs.

- When net selling reaches historic lows, the market has performed significantly above average over the next 12 months.

The authors also noted that the number of net buy or sell transactions, regardless of total dollars, may also follow the same relationship. The combination of these two items, large transaction size and privileged information, seems analogous to the positions of commercial traders in the *Commitment of Traders* report published weekly by the CFTC. Earlier in this chapter it was shown that commercials tend to be on the right side of the market while the small speculator is not.

THE INTEGRATION OF TECHNICAL ANALYSIS

---

[27] Eric Bjorgen and Steve Leuthold, "Corporate Insiders' Big Block Trades," *Journal of Technical Analysis* (Winter-Spring 2002). This study was written in May 1998 and won the 1999 Charles Dow Award.

CHAPTER 4

Pattern Recognition

From Perry J. Kaufman, *Trading Systems and Methods, +Website*, 5th Edition (Hoboken, New Jersey: John Wiley & Sons, 2013), Chapter 15.

Learning Objective Statements

- Analyze potential patterns in price data and describe why they may be valid as a trading signal
- Analyze potential trading opportunities based on gaps in price data
- Distinguish those signals based on gaps that are likely to be worthwhile trading signals from those which are not likely to be worthwhile

Pattern recognition forms the basis for most trading systems. Patterns are most obvious in traditional charting, which is primarily the identification of common formations; even moving averages attempt to isolate, using mathematical methods, what has been visually determined to be a trend. Traders have always looked for patterns in price movement. Because the earliest technicians were not equipped with computers, their conclusions are considered market lore rather than fact, and are handed down from generation to generation as proverbs, such as "Up on Monday, down on Tuesday," "Locals even-up on Fridays," and "Watch for key reversals." Because these three sayings have endured, they are candidates for analysis later in this chapter. Readers should also note the early work of Arthur Merrill, whose well-known pattern studies are still quoted; these studies are referenced throughout this chapter.[1]

The earliest technical systems based on patterns were of the form: "If after a sharp rise the market fails to advance for 3 days, then sell." As computers became more powerful, more complex approaches could be taken. For example, by observing the closing prices starting on an arbitrary day, *all* patterns of higher and lower closes can be recorded to find their tendency to repeat. A computer is well-equipped to perform this task. First, the 2-day combinations of price changes—*up-up, up-down, down-up,* and *down-down*—are tallied to see if there is a greater chance of, for example, an up day following an up day and a down day following a down day. Next,

---

[1] Arthur A. Merrill, *Behavior of Prices on Wall Street* (Chappaqua, NY: Analysis Press, 1966).

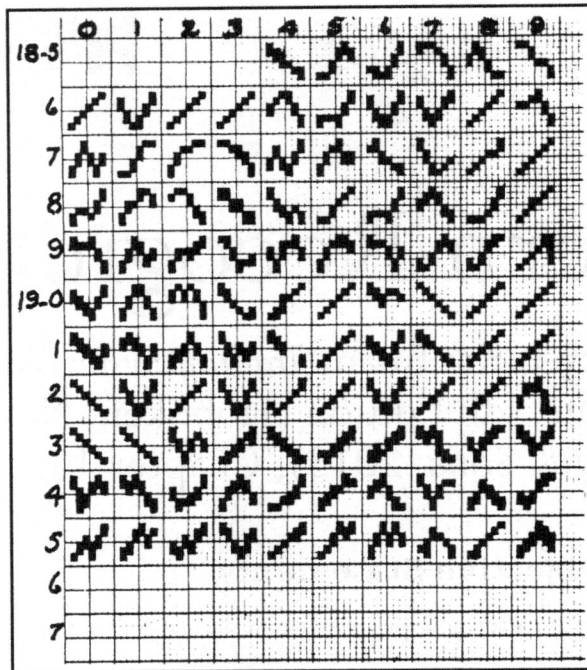

FIGURE 4.1 Graph of the New York Stock Market.

the eight 3-day patterns are tested for the same possibility of a high-probability price move, then sixteen 4-day patterns, and so on. When you get to larger sequences, such as *up-up-down-up-down-up,* every six consecutive prices must be tested for that pattern. From the price moves that follow this pattern, we can conclude whether it has any predictive ability. This approach as well as the combination of events used to forecast profitable situations are discussed later in this chapter.

Pattern recognition may appear to be more of a game than a business, but it is a source of many valuable ideas as well as false paths. Figure 4.1, a graph of the New York Stock Exchange (1854–1959), shows a very simple way to visualize the price pattern throughout the year. Each box represents the net movement of consecutive 2-month intervals, and is either up or down. When viewing all the patterns for 104 years in one glance, it is difficult not to count the recurrences of the more obvious patterns and then look for the formations that precede them in order to see whether they could be predictive. For example, in 1922, 1924, and 1927, there were sharp advances in the market; the years preceding those showed identical *V* patterns. When we look for all other *V* patterns, we see that 3 of 5 were followed by the same bull moves. Another pattern that stands out is that of two consecutive years of sharp rise, 1862–1863, 1908–1909, 1918–1919, and 1927–1928; in no case was there a third consecutive year but neither the preceding nor following years seem consistent.

Patterns frequently provide the foundation for a trading method or the motivation to begin the development of a method. They have been applied in many ways to price analysis, from the time of day to place an order to the complex relationship of price, volume, and open interest. Daily trading opportunities may be a function of patterns based on the strength or weakness of the daily opening price. These are discussed in the next section. Weekly and weekend price patterns are studied, as well as types of reversals and their effects. These techniques can be used sequentially by following a weekday pattern with a weekend pattern, or they can confirm the results of each other when used together. The end of this chapter discusses more general issues in pattern recognition. Because patterns are implicit in many trading systems throughout this book, readers are encouraged to use the index if they are looking for a discussion of a specific pattern.

◼ Projecting Daily Highs and Lows

Statisticians claim that the best forecast of tomorrow's price is today's price; for longer-term projections, the best forecast is the mean. They state that no one has been able to reliably account for the numerous combinations of price moves that would be needed to accurately project the changes that result in the high and low prices for tomorrow. Nevertheless, many traders project these values and seem to use them with success.

Pivot Points

The simplest approach to projecting tomorrow's highs and lows is to base those figures on the average price of today plus or minus a value that somehow relates to the current trading range, or volatility. One technique, based on a *pivot point*,[2] projects two levels of support and resistance:

Pivot point	$P = (H + L + C)/3$
Resistance 1	$R1 = 2 \times P - L$
Support 1	$S1 = 2 \times P - H$
Resistance 2	$R2 = (P - S1) + R1$
Support 2	$S2 = P - (R1 - S1)$

As an example, take the high, low, and close of the day to be 12.50, 11.50, and 11.75. Then

$$P = (12.50 + 11.50 + 11.75)/3 = 11.916$$
$$R1 = 2 \times 11.916 - 11.50 = 12.332$$
$$S1 = 2 \times 11.916 - 12.50 = 11.332$$
$$R2 = (11.916 - 11.332) + 12.332 = 12.914$$
$$S2 = 11.916 - (12.332 - 11.332) = 10.918$$

The projected support and resistance levels show a downward bias consistent with the close that was in the lower part of the trading range.

---

[2] Mark Etzkorn, "All in a Day's Work," *Futures* (January 1995). This technique is attributed to William Greenspan.

Another method takes the average range (*high* − *low*) over the past 14 days, then adds and subtracts ½ of that range to yesterday's close, so that the projection is symmetric around the prior close and equal to the average range.

DeMark's Projected Ranges

Another author and trader, Tom DeMark,[3] has based his projections on the positioning of today's opening price relative to yesterday's closing price, which gives him added timely information. If today's open is higher than the previous close, the projections are biased upwards; if lower than the close, they are biased downwards. If today's close is below today's open, then

Tomorrow's projected high $= (H + C + 2 \times L)/2 - L$
Tomorrow's projected low $= (H + C + 2 \times L)/2 - H$

If today's close is above today's open, then

Tomorrow's projected high $= (2 \times H + L + C)/2 - L$
Tomorrow's projected low $= (2 \times H + L + C)/2 - H$

If today's close is the same as today's open then

Tomorrow's projected high $= (H + L + 2 \times C)/2 - L$
Tomorrow's projected low $= (H + L + 2 \times C)/2 - H$

Once the basic formula is determined, which biases tomorrow's projection in the direction of today's close relative to today's open, the *projected high* is found by removing two units of the low price, and the *projected low* is found by removing two units of the high price from the formula. This effectively shifts the projection in the direction of the new high by one-half the difference of today's close and today's low, $(C - L)/2$, and the new low by one-half the difference of today's close and today's high, $(H - C)/2$.

Comparing the Two Ranges

Because the two methods of calculating the projected ranges use the same basic prices, combining them with slightly different arithmetic, it is not clear whether they give values that are the same or different. For example, if the Swiss franc had a high, low, and close of 6600, 6450, and 6500, respectively, the first pivot method would give a projected first resistance level (high) of $2 \times (6600 + 6450 + 6500)/3 - 6450 = 6583$. DeMark's projected high is different, based on the way today's opening price relates to the previous close. If the open is lower than the previous close, we get $(6600 + 6500 + 2 \times 6450)/2 - 6450 = 6550$; if the open is higher, we have $(2 \times 6600 + 6450 + 6500)/2 - 6450 = 6625$; and, if the open is about the same as the previous close, then the projected high is $(6600 + 6450 + 2 \times 6500)/2 - 6450 = 6575$. It seems reasonable that the pivot point method returns a value close to DeMark's neutral case when the market opens unchanged from the previous close.

[3]Tom DeMark, *The New Science of Technical Analysis* (New York: John Wiley & Sons, 1994).

THE INTEGRATION OF TECHNICAL ANALYSIS

▥ Time of Day

Market participants, especially floor traders and day traders, are the cause of periodic movement during the day. Angas called these the "tides of the daily prices." Over the years, the great increase in participants has added liquidity to nearly all markets but has not altered the intraday time patterns. Even high frequency trading seems to have added huge trading volume without altering the basic patterns. The classic pattern in both stocks and futures shows the greatest volume near the open, the next highest volume near the close, and the lowest volume at midday.

Trading Habits Form Lasting Patterns

There are a number of reasons for this normal pattern of trading. Many investors evaluate their positions and study market reports in the evenings and then place their orders in the morning. In Europe, where business begins six hours earlier, economic reports are released before the main trading sessions in the United States, and can affect the early market direction. However, U.S. business reacts to U.S. reports, so U.S. markets readily change direction once U.S. business begins. Although futures in all the major index markets are trading throughout the night, price movements during these off hours are not considered important to the direction of prices the next day. Even now, European markets are open until the U.S. stock markets close; however, that's 10 p.m. in Frankfurt, and most traders have gone home. Only a few brokerage houses have desks that will accept orders late in the evening. The only practical way of trading is using an electronic order entry program. With all the globalization, overnight trading has not materially changed the patterns that occur during the day sessions.

The close of the day is a common time for trading because many investors believe that the closing price best represents the correct value. In the futures markets, a large part of the daily volume is the result of day trades by floor traders, or *locals*. Positions entered in the morning will be closed out by the end of the day to avoid depositing the margin required of positions held overnight. Accounts are settled using the closing price.

Once the opening orders have been executed—the order flow that has accumulated from decisions made since the last close—volume declines. Scalpers and floor traders are active during the opening minutes but frequently have a mid-morning coffee break, and more take a lunch break; this natural phenomenon causes liquidity to decline and may result in a temporary price reversal. All traders and investors develop habits of trading at particular times. Some prefer the opening, others 10 minutes after the open. Large funds and managed accounts have a specific procedure for entering the market, such as using close-only orders. Institutions with large orders must trade during times when the volume is heavy in order to keep slippage under control, or they may take advantage of VWAP orders (volume-weighted average price) where partial orders are automatically fed into the market based on an algorithm that balances time intervals and volume.[4] Without these orders, most institutions will favor trading at the more active times.

A day trader must watch certain key times. The opening moments of the trading session are normally used to assess the situation. The stock market will gap up or down to align itself with the futures market, which has been trading continuously. Most other markets have electronic sessions in which the prices reflect current news. The day session opens with the bid-asked at the level already trading in the electronic session; therefore, there is little opportunity for profit in the first few seconds of trading. After a short delay, as the first burst of activity slows, floor traders will sell a strong open and buy a weak one; this means the trade must be *evened up* later, reinforcing the opening direction. On a strong open without a downward reaction, all local selling is absorbed by the market, and later attempts of the locals to liquidate will hold prices up, preventing a reversal. Floor traders can normally be expected to take the opposite position to the opening direction, usually causing a reversal early in the session.

Tubbs' Intraday Patterns

In Chapter 13 of Tubbs' *Stock Market Correspondence Lessons* ("Tape Reading") he explains the six dominant patterns in the stock market (based on a 10:00 a.m. to 3:00 p.m. session).

1. If a rally after the open has returned to the opening price by 1:00 p.m., the day is expected to close weaker.
2. If the market is strong from 11:00 a.m. to 12:00 p.m., it will continue from 12:00 p.m. to 1:00 p.m.
3. If a reversal from 1:00 p.m. to 1:30 p.m. finds support at 1:30 p.m., it will close strong.
4. If the market has been bullish until 2:00 p.m., it will probably continue until the close and into the next day.
5. A rally that continues for 2 or 3 days (as in Pattern 4) will most likely end on an 11:00 a.m. reversal.
6. In general, a late afternoon reaction down after a strong day shows a pending reversal.

Putting these together, the following two patterns (among others) can be expected:

1. A strong open with a reversal at 11:00 a.m. not reaching the opening price, then strength from 11:00 a.m. to 1:00 p.m., a short reversal until 1:30 p.m., and then a strong close; according to Pattern 5, there will be a strong open the following day.
2. A strong open that reverses by 11:00 a.m., continuing lower until 1:00 p.m., then reverses again until 1:30 p.m., will close weak.

---

[4]At the time of this writing, source code for automatically generating VWAP orders can be found on www.codeproject.com/KB/recipes/VWAP.aspx.

TABLE 4.1	Merrill's Hourly Stock Market Patterns					
	Time during Trading Session					
	10:00	11:00	12:00	1:00	2:00	3:00
1962	−	+	−	−	+	−
1963	+	+	+	+	+	−
1964	+	+	−	−	+	−
1965	+	+	−	−	−	−

Merrill's Intraday Patterns

Merrill's work shows the hourly pattern of the stock market in Table 4.1, where a plus or minus sign indicates rising or falling prices during the preceding period. During the four years shown, the grid clearly indicates a strong opening and follow-through to 11:00 a.m. During 1963, the bullishness lasted all day, trailing off at the close. Except for 1963, we cannot say from this table that there was a bullish or bearish price move because there is no volatility, or average price move, associated with these hourly intervals.

The pattern in Table 4.1 supports what we would expect as a normal intraday pattern. Prices begin strong and continue the first hour. Having exhausted the early orders, volume decreases, and price reverses due to lack of buyers. By 2 p.m. the short sellers who faded the first hour move to cover their positions, causing a move back in the direction of the opening hour. The only inconsistency in the pattern is the weak close, which contradicts the strong open. Had there been both a strong open and a strong close, we could declare these as bull years. Nevertheless, the pattern of a weaker close persisted for at least four years, offering an opportunity for day traders.

Updating Intraday Time Patterns, 2000–2011

Every decade is unique, and 2000 was no exception. Prices began at extreme highs, fell for three years, languished for a year, then rallied only to collapse in 2008 and rally again. We can expect a bias to the upside during a sustained bullish period, such as the 1990s, but the last decade is much more interesting. It gives us an opportunity to understand the intraday patterns under very different market scenarios. The 11 years in Figure 4.2 can be separated into four distinct periods:

1. 2001–2002, strong bear market
2. 2003–2007, normal bull market
3. 2008, extreme collapse
4. 2009–May 2011, strong bull market

First using the entire 11 years, the patterns are evaluated in three ways:

1. The cumulative change in returns for each 30-minute period throughout the day.
2. The change relative to the direction of the open from the previous close (as in Merrill's Table 4.1).
3. The change relative to the opening 30 minutes of trading.

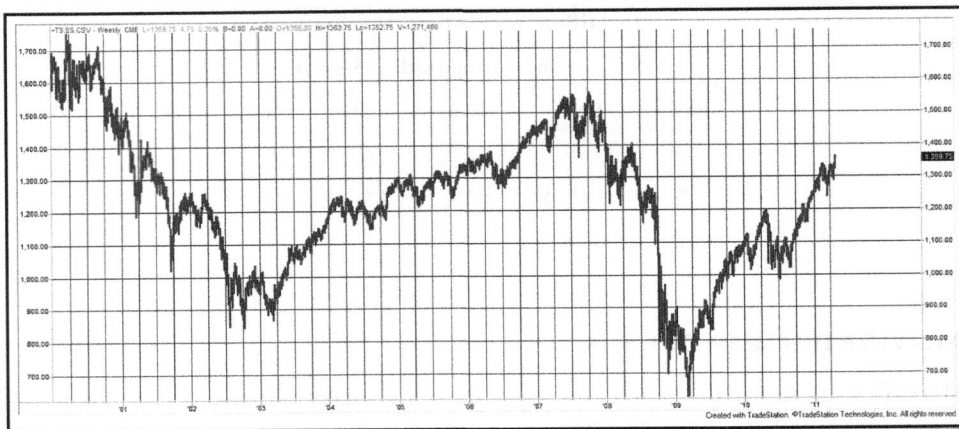

FIGURE 4.2 S&P Back-Adjusted Futures from 2000 Through May 2011.

These are shown in Figure 4.3 as *Average move, Same as previous close,* and *Same as first bar.* The bottom line, *Average move,* shows that the net returns over the full period were near zero. The top line, *Same as previous close,* indicates that there was a modest continuation of the prior close to end of first bar direction throughout the day. That is, if the end of the first bar was higher than the previous close, then it was likely to close even higher, and if it opened lower, then it would continue lower throughout the day. The middle line, *Same as first bar,* shows that there is essentially no change after the opening bar, so that most of the daily move occurs overnight and on the opening bar.

If the 11 years are separated into the four periods that represent clear regimes, the results are more interesting. Figures 4.4a–d show the results, which can be summarized as

a. 2001–2002, a strong bear market shows that the average move ends the day lower and the direction at the close of the first bar persists slightly throughout the day.
b. 2003–2007, a normal bull market shows the average move steadily increasing throughout the day as did the direction from the previous close. However, prices tended to reverse slightly relative to the direction of the opening bar.

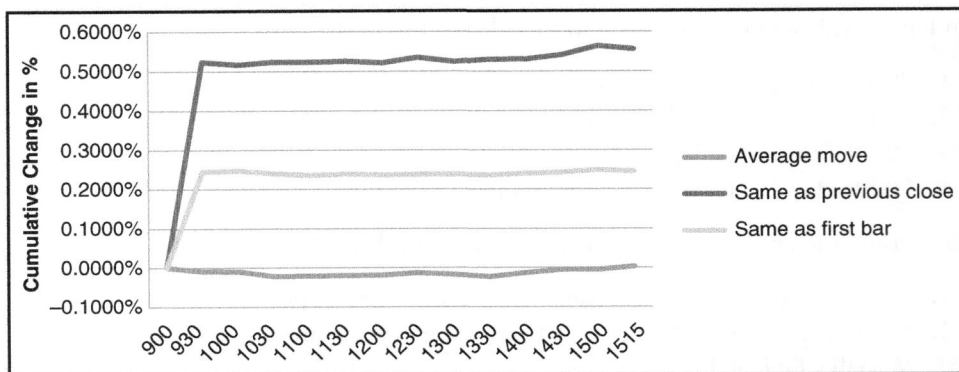

FIGURE 4.3 S&P Futures Intraday Time Patterns for 2000 Through May 2011.

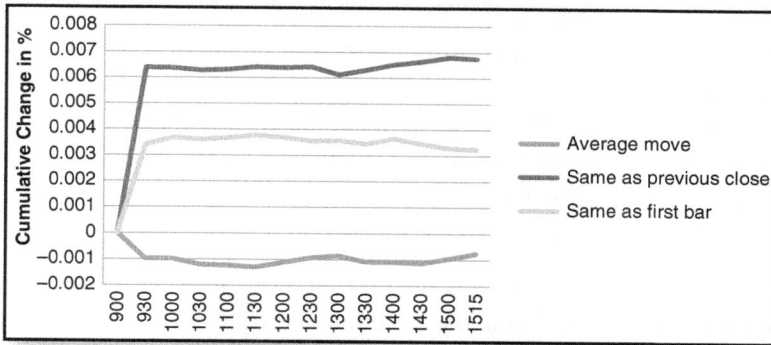

FIGURE 4.4a   S&P 2001–2002, Strong Bear Market.

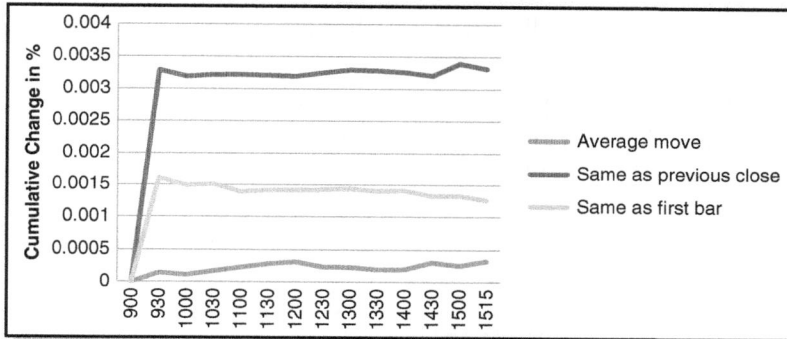

FIGURE 4.4b   S&P 2003–2007, Normal Bull Market.

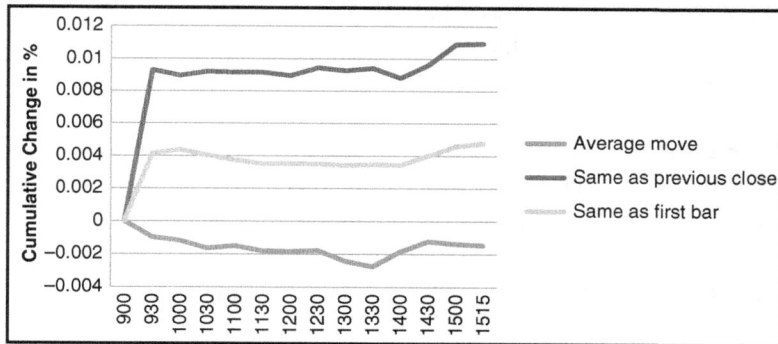

FIGURE 4.4c   S&P 2008, Extreme Collapse.

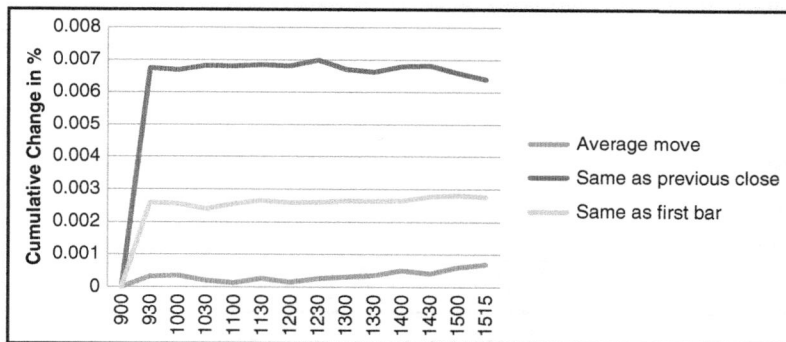

FIGURE 4.4d   S&P 2009–May 2011, Strong Bull Market.

c. 2008, the extreme collapse due to the subprime crisis, is the most consistent. All three measures continued in the direction of the opening moves and the overall market direction.

d. 2009–2011, a strong bull market, shows in the average move, but is different in the other measurements. Rather than continuing in the direction given by the prior close to end of first bar, or from the open to the end of the first bar, prices reverse, giving back earlier gains or losses.

Overall, we can say that there is a small profit that can be extracted by taking a position at the end of the first bar in the direction of the previous close, and holding to end of first bar. Unfortunately, the four cases were classified after the fact; therefore, it will take more time to recognize when a bull or bear market is in effect. The only case that fails is the strong bull market, which still leaves reasonable opportunity in the other three scenarios.

The overall intraday time pattern of the S&P can be summarized in the same way as Merrill in the following table, where a "+" represents a net gain from the close of the previous bar and "−" a net loss:

Time	1000	1100	1200	100	200	300	400
2000	−	+	+	+	+	+	+
2008	−	−	−	−	+	+	+

For the full 11-year period, the opening bar was generally lower, but each subsequent bar was higher. From 2008 through May 2011 the first half of the day was lower and the last half higher. This does not show whether the day was a net gain or loss, only the relative direction of prices.

EURUSD Time Patterns   Is the pattern of the S&P typical of other markets? We would expect it to be similar to other index markets, but other sectors, such as commodities and currencies, could have unique patterns of their own. As an example, the same analysis was run on the EURUSD currency futures for the same 11-year period from 2000 through May 2011. Results are shown in Figure 4.5.

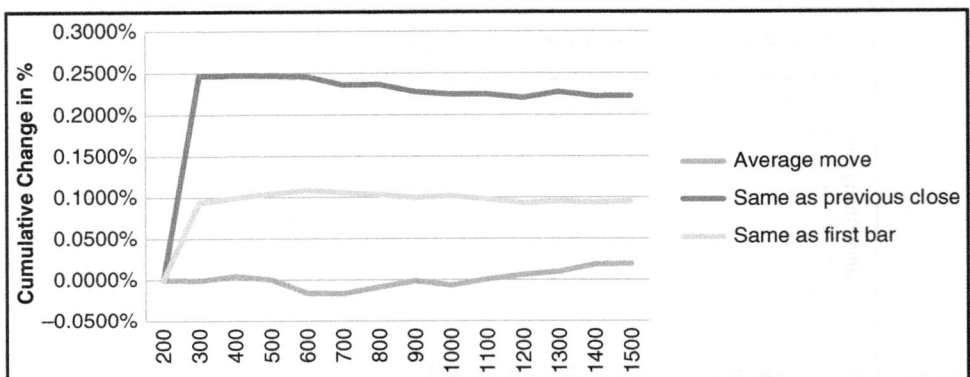

FIGURE 4.5   Time Patterns for EURUSD Futures from 2000 Through May 2011.

The overall pattern is only slightly different from the S&P. There was a net gain in the EURUSD, shown by the *Average move*; however, that gain was all in the overnight move. From the end of the first bar, which occurs at 3 a.m. in New York (9 a.m. in Frankfurt), prices tend to reverse. The move relative to the direction of the open-close of the first bar is essentially flat. Another way of viewing these patterns is by indicating which markets are open during each time interval. In the following table, trading begins at 2 a.m. in Europe and ends at 3 p.m. in New York. The first 5 hours are actively traded in Europe but not the United States. There are 3 hours of over-lapping trading after which Europe closes (at 4 p.m. local time). The U.S. trades for another 5 hours, with only small volume coming from Europe.

Time	Europe is open at 200					U.S. is open			Europe is closed				
	300	400	500	600	700	800	900	1000	1100	1200	1300	1400	1500
2000	−	+	−	−	−	+	+	−	+	+	+	+	+
2008	+	+	−	−	−	+	−	−	+	+	+	+	+

The table shows that, from 2000 through May 2011, despite the net gain in the EURUSD, that gain came mostly when the U.S. session was open. During the past 2½ years, the larger gain in the EURUSD is reflected in both the European open and in the U.S. session. It appears as though the U.S. trading is driving the U.S. dollar lower.

Refining the Patterns for Trading To increase the chance of a profitable trade, it might be best to observe only stronger or weaker openings. For example, if the end of the first 30 minutes of S&P trading shows a gain greater than 1% from the previous close, we can expect the entire day to be more volatile than a day that posted a gain of only 5 or 10 basis points. Restricting trading to days of higher volatility will reduce the trading opportunities but should improve results. By allowing very small opening price changes, we include days that might drift sideways because of the lack of news.

Repeating the same test of the S&P for 2009 through May 2011, but with the addition of a 50 basis point filter, Figure 4.6 shows that the average gap from the

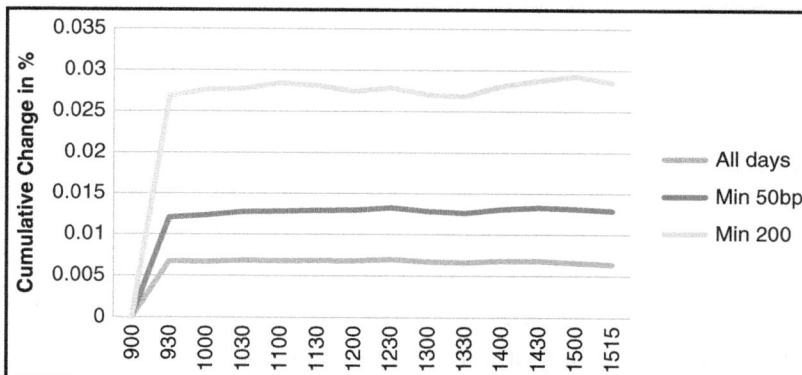

FIGURE 4.6 S&P Futures Time Patterns, 2009–2011, with 50 bp and 200 bp Minimum Gap Filters.

previous close to the end of the first 30-minute bar nearly doubles to 1.2% with a 50 bp threshold, and the balance of the day continues modestly in the same direction as the gap, while the unfiltered test reverses slightly. If the minimum gap filter is increased to 200 bp, the balance of the days seems to continue at perhaps a slightly increased rate, but certainly the same pattern. As the gap filter increases, it is possible that prices will show a reversal pattern.

One possibility for trading is to first decide that price will continue to move in the direction of the opening gap, then wait for a pullback. Even in Figure 4.6, which shows the average of a large number of days, there is a pullback low at 13:30 and a rally shortly afterwards. Individual days will have a much wider price range and higher volatility that could produce profits.

Intraday Highs and Lows

In selecting a place to enter the market for a single day trade, it would be a great advantage to know the time of day at which the highest or lowest price is likely to occur. It would also be useful to know if that pattern changes when the market opens higher or lower, and when there is a large price gap on the open. The same markets, the S&P and the EURUSD, will be used in case there is an opportunity to combine the previous time patterns with the likelihood of a high or low occurring.

S&P 500 Highs and Lows   The pattern shown for the S&P futures in Figure 4.7 is typical of most markets. The open is the time of day with the greatest chance of being the day's high or low price, twice as likely as the closing time and eight times more likely than near the middle of the trading session. This pattern should not be a surprise because it has not changed in 50 years. What could be a surprise is that the close of the day is less likely to be a high or low than the open. We often remember strong or weak closes, rather than strong or weak opens.

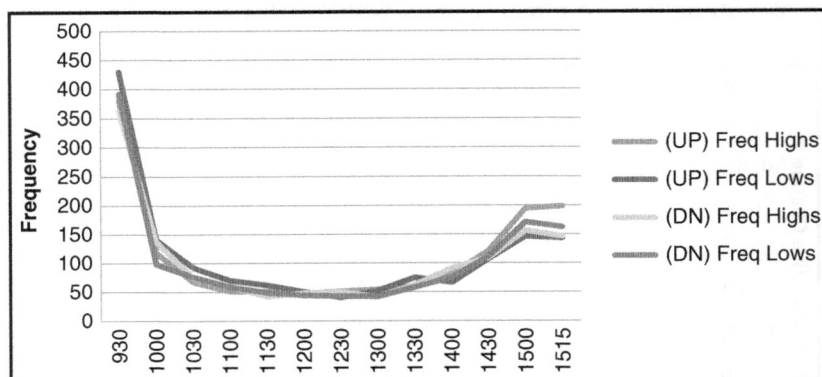

FIGURE 4.7   **Frequency of Intraday Highs and Lows for SP Futures, 2000 Through May 2011.**

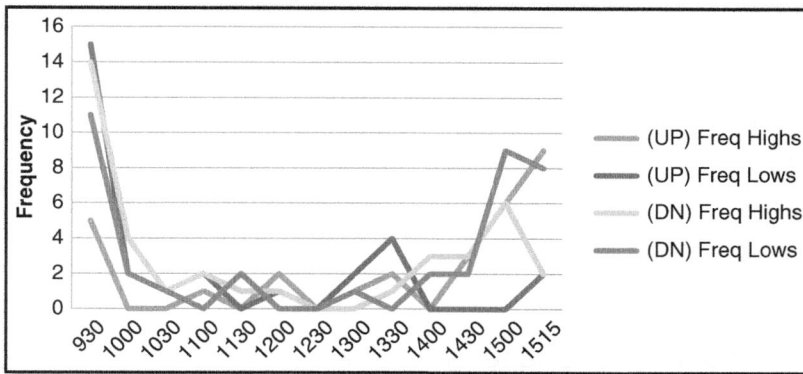

FIGURE 4.8 S&P Intraday Highs and Lows When There Is a Gap Open, Higher or Lower, Exceeding 2.0%.

Can this be turned into a trading opportunity? Once the market has been open for an hour and trades away from the opening price, that early high or low becomes a strong candidate for a daily high or low. Then, if that level is broken, the close becomes the next likely time for a high or low. The concept of a new high or low after midday could be the basis for an intraday breakout signal.

This pattern could change if there is a strong or weak gap open. Figure 4.8 shows the frequency of highs and lows following a gap of ±2.0%. There are two significant differences. First, the difference in the frequency of the open and close is much smaller. Instead of 2.5:1, as in the first chart, it is now about 1.6:1. More important, the other times of day are much less likely to post a high or low. For the case of the strong upwards gap, the low of the day is overwhelmingly going to be at the open. Consistent with that is the high of the day, which is more likely to be at the close than the open.

EURUSD Highs and Lows Because currencies are actively traded around the world, the pattern for EURUSD is different from the S&P. In the previous section, the analysis of time-of-day patterns showed that activity could be separated into three parts: from the open of Europe to the open of the U.S., from the open of the U.S. to the close of Europe, and from the close of Europe to the close of the U.S. The same is true for the frequency of highs and lows. From 2 a.m. to 8 a.m. the frequency of EURUSD highs and lows is very similar to the S&P chart. This is when Europe is the dominant player. The difference between this and the S&P chart is that the early open is far more likely to be the high or low of the day. From 8 a.m. to 10 a.m. both Europe and the United States are open and the frequency of both highs and lows are essentially sideways. Once Europe closes, the normal pattern repeats, but in a more subdued manner (see Figure 4.9).

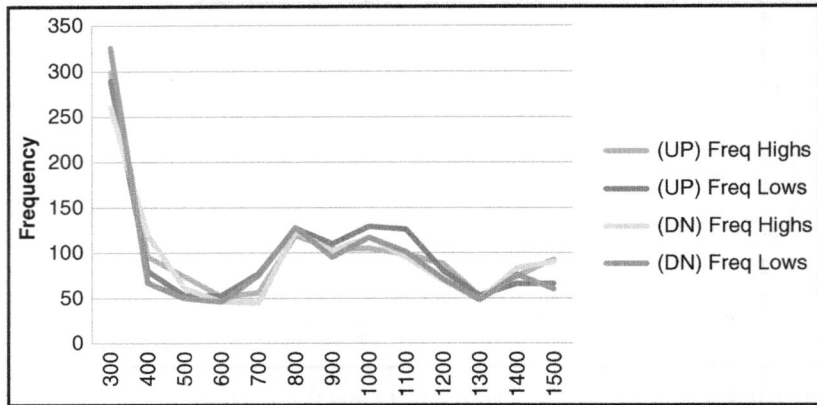

FIGURE 4.9 Frequency of Intraday Highs and Lows for EURUSD Futures, 2000 Through May 2011.

Using the Intraday High and Low Patterns for Trading There are few simple rules that come out of the intraday high-low patterns that could help trading. Because there is a high frequency of the high or low occurring during the first bar of the day, you become more confident as the day progresses that an early extreme is a high or low. For example, the S&P gaps up 12.00 points after a bullish employment report. It then runs up to a high of up 4.00 points at the end of the first 30 minutes, then falls back to trade up 11.00 points by the end of the second bar. Have we seen a high or a low? It may still be too early to tell. If prices continue lower and make new lows, then we are much more confident that the high was made during the first bar. If prices make a new high, then we are equally confident that we have seen the low of the day. As each bar passes, we are more confident that we have seen the high or low. We can then trade in the direction of the high or low not yet seen, expecting that it will occur on the close. The sooner we make this decision, the more profit potential we can capture. A breakout of a high or low later in the day increases the chance of a close in that direction. Always place a stop-loss at the point where a new low would occur if you are long, or a new high if you have sold short.

Midday offers another trading opportunity because of the small chance of seeing a new high or low. If you have decided that the low occurred near the open, then buying on a test of the lows during the quiet midday session could provide good entry timing.

An exception to every rule During the 1990s, the stock market experienced one of the greatest bull markets in history. From 1995 through 1996 nearly everyone was talking about the 20% annual returns that were easily achieved in the stock market. This affected the intraday patterns. Investors would most often buy on the open of trading, but they would also buy on any pullback during the day. The result was that the *U*-shaped pattern that we clearly see in Figures 4.7 through 4.9

were replaced by a jump at the open and a straight line throughout the rest of the day.

Opening Gaps

To any trader, an opening gap looks like an opportunity for a profit. Certainly, a large *gap opening* implies greater volatility for the day, and we expect a greater reaction. Based on the way the market closes, it may also forecast the direction of the next opening price. At least we would expect a volatile open to offer more information than a quiet open. Using only daily data, a gap analysis was performed to study the combination of patterns that followed a gap opening of various strength or weakness. A strong open followed by a stronger close would allow a trader to buy on a pullback after the open. A consistently weak close after a strong open would be an opportunity to sell short near the open. Specific entry timing can be improved by using the patterns discussed in the previous sections.

The output for these tests are shown in Table 4.2 (a) and (b). Part (a) shows the frequency of occurrence of ABX (Barrick Gold) gaps from January 2000 through May 2011 based on increments of 25 basis points, shown on the left. In the center row are then the number of days that prices opened unchanged from the previous close. Below that are the days when prices gapped lower on the open, and above are the days prices gapped higher. The top and bottom rows have all those days when prices gapped greater than and less than 2.5% from the previous close. Part (b) uses the same values but expresses them as a percentage of the number of cases on each line. The percentages are most useful, but we also need to know the frequency to assess the significance. If there are only three cases on a line, the results are not very helpful.

Both parts (a) and (b) of Table 4.2 show the following columns:

1. The opening gap expressed in basis points (e.g., 150 is 1.50%).
2. The number of cases for that opening gap. The 150 line would include 150 up to 175 but not including 175.
3. Three columns explaining the closing price of the day:
   a. *Cont Dir.* The close continued (extended the move) in the direction of the gap.
   b. *Below Open.* The close was between the gap opening and the prior close.
   c. *Rev Dir.* The close reversed the direction of the opening gap, that is, if the open was higher, the close was lower.
4. The next three columns show the trading range pattern.
   a. *Cross Prev Close.* Prices crossed the prior closing price at least once during the trading session.
   b. *Adj from Open.* Prices reversed from the open but did not cross the prior close.
   c. *Cont Only.* Prices continued in the direction of the open and never reversed.
5. The last column shows the frequency of prices continuing on the next open in the direction of today's gap.

TABLE 4.2(a) ABX Gaps in Increments of 25 bps

		Closing Prices			Trading Range			
Gap	Cases	Cont Dir	Below Open	Rev Dir	Cross Prev Close	Adj from Open	Cont Only	Cont Next Day
250	131	62	44	25	40	85	5	68
225	48	27	18	3	6	39	2	27
200	60	31	15	13	24	34	1	31
175	85	39	25	19	36	47	2	41
150	131	66	33	29	59	59	9	75
125	151	77	32	40	71	66	9	95
100	167	85	26	52	93	62	7	92
75	222	103	34	75	146	57	16	107
50	240	102	17	112	184	25	25	145
25	246	114	7	115	218	10	14	146
0	196	0	0	0	0	0	0	0
−25	191	102	6	78	166	10	13	79
−50	228	117	13	83	176	29	11	97
−75	159	79	24	54	100	36	16	71
−100	157	74	38	42	93	50	6	70
−125	97	61	16	20	45	42	6	35
−150	89	48	18	19	40	43	4	42
−175	49	26	9	14	22	23	3	23
−200	47	29	11	7	13	31	3	18
−225	34	15	13	6	17	16	1	18
−250	94	57	23	11	20	68	5	37

TABLE 4.2(b) ABX Results in Percentages

		Closing Prices			Trading Range			
Gap	Cases	Cont Dir	Below Open	Rev Dir	Cross Prev Close	Adj from Open	Cont Only	Cont Next Day
250	131	47.33	33.59	19.08	30.53	64.89	3.82	51.91
225	48	56.25	37.50	6.25	12.50	81.25	4.17	56.25
200	60	51.67	25.00	21.67	40.00	56.67	1.67	51.67
175	85	45.88	29.41	22.35	42.35	55.29	2.35	48.24
150	131	50.38	25.19	22.14	45.04	45.04	6.87	57.25
125	151	50.99	21.19	26.49	47.02	43.71	5.96	62.91
100	167	50.90	15.57	31.14	55.69	37.13	4.19	55.09
75	222	46.40	15.32	33.78	65.77	25.68	7.21	48.20

TABLE 4.2(b) (*Continued*)

Gap	Cases	Closing Prices			Trading Range			
		Cont Dir	Below Open	Rev Dir	Cross Prev Close	Adj from Open	Cont Only	Cont Next Day
50	240	42.50	7.08	46.67	76.67	10.42	10.42	60.42
25	246	46.34	2.85	46.75	88.62	4.07	5.69	59.35
0	196	0	0	0	0	0	0	0
−25	191	53.4	3.1	40.8	86.9	5.2	6.8	41.4
−50	228	51.3	5.7	36.4	77.2	12.7	4.8	42.5
−75	159	49.7	15.1	34.0	62.9	22.6	10.1	44.7
−100	157	47.1	24.2	26.8	59.2	31.9	3.8	44.6
−125	97	62.9	16.5	20.6	46.4	43.3	6.2	36.1
−150	89	53.9	20.2	21.4	44.9	48.3	4.5	47.2
−175	49	53.1	18.4	28.6	44.9	46.9	6.1	46.9
−200	47	61.7	23.4	14.9	27.7	66.0	6.4	38.3
−225	34	44.1	38.2	17.7	50.0	47.1	2.9	52.9
−250	94	60.6	24.5	11.7	21.3	72.3	5.3	39.4

Gaps in Futures Markets

Although the example above used ABX, we will start with gaps in futures markets, the most popular being the *e*mini S&P contract. Instead of showing the detail in a comparable table, Figure 4.10 compares the frequency of gaps in ABX with those in the *e*mini S&P. While ABX has most of its gaps greater and less than 1%, as shown by the peaks at both ends, the S&P is exactly the opposite, with essentially no gaps greater or less than 1%. How can that happen? We know that the stock market has gapped higher and lower fairly often.

The answer is that the *e*mini S&P trades on Globex from 6 p.m. to the following 4:15 p.m. (New York time). Because the new session opens only 1 hour, 45 minutes

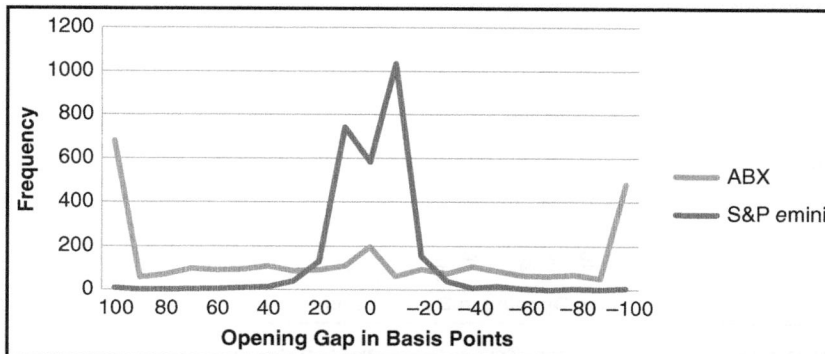

FIGURE 4.10 Comparison of Gap Frequency for ABX and the *e*mini S&P.

after the previous session closes, and there is rarely any news to surprise the market; most gaps will occur on Sunday evening when the new week begins. Otherwise, the new opening price is very close to the previous closing price. To get a pattern similar to ABX we would need to look at the floor session for the big S&P contract, which has been declining in volume. Alternatively, we could set the time for the emini session to only look at prices from 9:30 a.m. when the stock market opens. In the next section, we will look at gaps for individual stocks, which will have great similarity to the index.

Five futures markets, U.S. 30-year bonds, the German DAX, the EURUSD currency, gold, and wheat were studied, and a comparison of the frequency of gaps is shown in Figure 4.11. The data was from January 2000 through May 2011, continuous futures, which makes some of the percentage results slightly off due to back-adjusting. In general, they all follow a normal distribution, with the tails curving up at the end when gaps exceeded +1% and −1%. Of the five markets, the DAX is much more volatile than the others, with fewer cases in the middle and more in the tail. The EURUSD is at the other extreme, with more in the middle and fewer in the tail. U.S. bonds (US) is the only market that shows the unchanged cases greater than the small gaps on either side of the center and very little in the tail. This can be explained because the futures markets open at 8:20 a.m. (New York), 10 minutes ahead of the economic reports. On reporting days the market often opens very quiet in anticipation of the report. Had we moved the opening time to 8:40 a.m. using intraday data then there would be a large number of gaps in the tails.

Tables 4.3 (a) through (e) show the statistics for the five futures markets, each expressed as a percentage of the number of cases in the row and all from January 2000 through May 2011.

Looking at the same statistics across the five markets is a helpful way of understanding the patterns and deciding if there is an opportunity for a trading profit.

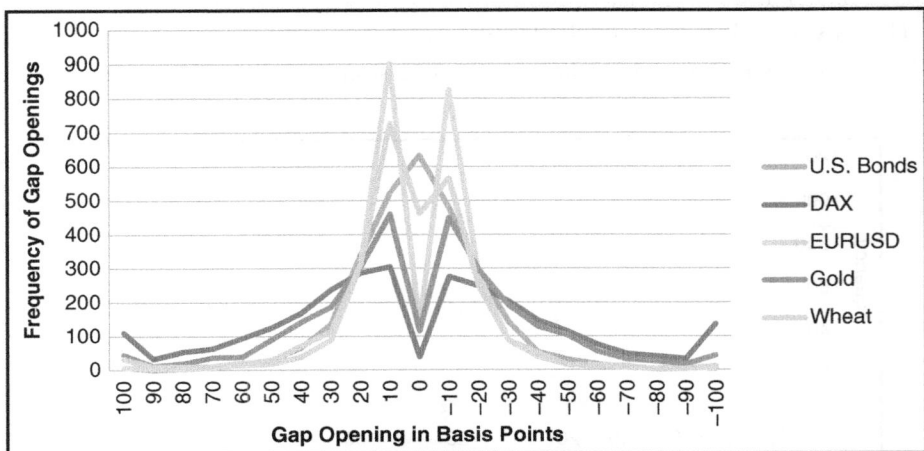

FIGURE 4.11 Frequency of Gap Opening in Basis Points for Five Futures Markets, from January 2000 Through May 2011.

TABLE 4.3(a)	U.S. 30-Year Bonds							
		Closing Prices vs. Open			Trading Range			
Gap	Cases	Cont Gap Dir	Below Open	Rev Gap Dir	Crossed Prev Close	Pullback from Open	No Pullback	Cont Next Day
100	7	71	29	0	43	57	0	57
90	0	0	0	0	0	0	0	0
80	3	100	0	0	0	100	0	33
70	8	25	38	0	50	50	0	88
60	19	47	5	42	63	37	0	63
50	29	45	24	24	55	28	10	62
40	66	56	9	26	61	30	2	62
30	136	45	13	34	74	19	1	51
20	340	49	5	36	82	9	3	53
10	522	53	0	39	87	2	5	50
0	633	0	0	0	0	0	0	0
−10	479	48	0	46	87	1	4	48
−20	289	42	6	46	86	8	2	51
−30	142	50	9	39	74	20	1	45
−40	53	51	21	21	58	30	6	47
−50	30	50	20	20	53	37	0	40
−60	17	24	18	59	82	12	6	53
−70	6	83	0	17	33	67	0	50
−80	3	33	67	0	33	33	0	0
−90	5	40	20	40	80	20	0	20
−100	4	75	25	0	0	100	0	25

TABLE 4.3(b)	German DAX							
		Closing Prices vs. Open			Trading Range			
Gap	Cases	Cont Gap Dir	Below Open	Rev Gap Dir	Crossed Prev Close	Pullback from Open	No Pullback	Cont Next Day
100	111	64	21	14	35	60	5	49
90	32	38	28	34	56	44	0	59
80	54	54	20	26	52	46	2	39
70	63	41	21	37	57	40	2	49
60	94	49	19	30	60	37	3	45
50	125	47	18	34	60	37	2	50
40	168	54	16	30	65	32	2	46
30	237	48	14	38	78	22	0	49
20	286	54	7	39	83	14	3	58
10	305	55	3	40	91	5	3	54
0	38	0	0	0	0	0	0	0
−10	276	50	3	46	94	3	3	46
−20	248	42	9	48	86	12	1	42
−30	203	48	12	38	81	16	1	45
−40	147	49	11	39	75	24	1	48
−50	114	53	18	28	65	33	2	42
−60	75	55	20	25	60	35	4	51
−70	47	55	15	30	60	40	0	43
−80	40	58	8	35	45	48	8	43
−90	32	50	34	16	34	59	6	38
−100	136	44	33	22	43	57	1	48

TABLE 4.3(c) **EURUSD Currency**

Gap	Cases	Closing Prices vs. Open			Trading Range			Cont Next Day
		Cont Gap Dir	Below Open	Rev Gap Dir	Crossed Prev Close	Pullback from Open	No Pullback	
100	7	29	71	0	14	71	14	57
90	4	25	50	25	100	0	0	50
80	3	67	0	33	67	33	0	0
70	8	38	25	25	63	38	0	63
60	15	53	20	27	47	53	0	53
50	17	41	18	41	82	18	0	53
40	39	51	23	26	67	31	0	33
30	88	48	16	36	69	22	5	65
20	310	48	9	43	84	14	1	50
10	902	53	4	42	94	3	1	54
0	130	0	0	0	0	0	0	0
−10	824	51	2	45	92	4	2	50
−20	277	45	8	45	85	14	1	44
−30	87	33	21	45	83	16	1	48
−40	38	50	13	37	82	18	0	55
−50	15	53	20	27	73	27	0	67
−60	10	70	20	10	40	60	0	10
−70	6	83	0	17	67	33	0	33
−80	2	50	0	50	50	50	0	0
−90	4	25	75	0	50	50	0	25
−100	5	20	60	20	60	40	0	40

TABLE 4.3(d) **Gold**

Gap	Cases	Closing Prices vs. Open			Trading Range			Cont Next Day
		Cont Gap Dir	Below Open	Rev Gap Dir	Crossed Prev Close	Pullback from Open	No Pullback	
100	45	49	24	24	38	60	2	42
90	11	45	27	27	36	55	9	64
80	19	42	16	37	47	47	5	63
70	37	65	22	14	43	49	8	57
60	38	58	21	18	53	42	5	55
50	90	58	21	19	43	50	7	52
40	142	58	24	18	50	40	8	47
30	186	49	15	34	70	26	4	48
20	304	56	8	32	72	20	6	54
10	460	52	3	41	87	5	5	50
0	116	0	0	0	0	0	0	0
−10	449	42	2	52	94	3	2	51
−20	295	41	11	46	80	15	2	52
−30	191	48	18	32	63	33	1	51
−40	129	50	25	24	51	47	0	49
−50	103	41	31	26	42	54	0	53
−60	55	49	35	15	42	55	0	49
−70	31	48	29	23	39	58	0	58
−80	25	40	40	16	28	72	0	48
−90	16	50	31	13	31	63	0	63
−100	43	42	44	12	28	72	0	51

TABLE 4.3(e)   Wheat

Gap	Cases	Closing Prices vs. Open			Trading Range			Cont Next Day
		Cont Gap Dir	Below Open	Rev Gap Dir	Crossed Prev Close	Pullback from Open	No Pullback	
100	32	47	22	28	63	34	3	75
90	9	33	33	33	67	33	0	44
80	9	67	22	11	44	56	0	56
70	12	42	25	33	83	17	0	67
60	20	65	5	30	45	45	5	65
50	28	64	4	32	64	32	4	61
40	71	46	17	35	70	23	3	65
30	114	53	7	39	79	16	3	71
20	312	50	5	42	78	12	5	58
10	727	46	2	48	87	3	6	58
0	462	0	0	0	0	0	0	0
−10	566	56	2	38	89	3	4	44
−20	246	52	5	39	83	10	4	56
−30	87	51	3	41	72	21	5	40
−40	50	54	12	32	72	20	4	44
−50	14	57	7	36	57	29	0	64
−60	14	64	14	21	71	29	0	50
−70	11	45	0	55	73	18	9	36
−80	1	100	0	0	100	0	0	0
−90	3	67	33	0	0	100	0	33
−100	11	55	36	9	64	36	0	36

Figure 4.12 shows the results of prices continuing the next day, on the open, in the same direction as today's gap. Only two markets stand out as different from the others, U.S. bonds and the EURUSD. Bonds have a high probability of continuing when the gap is +70 bp but nearly the opposite when the gap is +80 bp. However, the

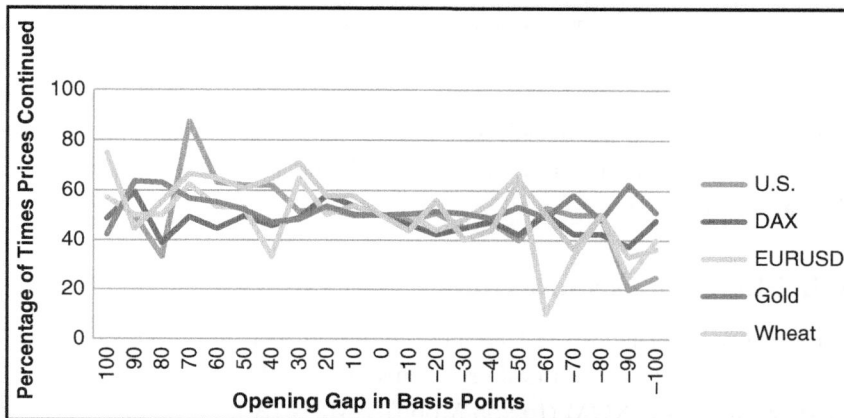

FIGURE 4.12 Likelihood of Continuing in the Same Direction on the Next Open.

conclusion is based on too little data, which makes it unreliable to trade. However, when there is a large downward gap in either bonds or euros, there is a low probability of continuing the next day, as seen in the lower right part of the chart. In addition, wheat and the DAX have the same pattern, although not as significant. Then any gap opening that shows a drop of at least 90 bp is likely to reverse on the next open. Unfortunately, there were only about 10 cases for each in 11 years; therefore, these results also lack confidence. If we look closely at wheat, we can see that all upwards gaps from 30 bps and higher had a 63% chance of continuing the next day, a more interesting outcome.

While the results of continuing the next day are not as clear as we would like, there are other values that have more potential for trading. For example, in looking at U.S. bonds, consider the two columns, *Closing below the open* and *Crossing the previous close*, and the rows that include gaps from +40 to −30 bps. That area of the table has been extracted below:

		Closing Prices vs. Open	Trading Range
Gap	Cases	Below Open	Crossed Prev Close
40	66	−9	−61
30	136	−13	−74
20	340	−5	−82
10	522	0	−87
0	633	0	0
−10	479	0	−87
−20	289	−6	−86
−30	142	−9	−74

For bonds, the chance of a small upwards gap closing below the open, or a downwards gap closing above the open, is very low. In addition, the chance of either an upward or downward gap crossing the previous close is high. We can then expect that an upwards gap that retraces below the previous close should be bought with expectations of a close that will be above the open. The opposite would be true of a lower gap opening. This is really a confirmation that interest rate markets trend. Any unexpected move to the upside will close in that direction and the same for the downside. The results for the DAX are not at all the same, but the results for the EURUSD are very similar.

Do Individual Stocks Show Unique Gap Patterns?

Earlier there was a chart of the frequency of emini S&P gaps compared to ABX, showing that ABX had a large number of gaps greater than 1%. Now we will look at more detail for ABX, XOM (Exxon Mobil), AMZN (Amazon), and LUV (Southwest Airlines), shown in Tables 4.4(a) through (d). The data is all from January 2000 through May 2011 and the gaps are in increments of 25 basis points.

TABLE 4.4(a) **ABX (Barrick Gold)**

Gap	Cases	Closing Prices			Trading Range			Cont Next Day
		Cont Dir	Below Open	Rev Dir	Cross Prev Close	Adj from Open	Cont Only	
250	131	47	34	19	31	65	4	52
225	48	56	38	6	13	81	4	56
200	60	52	25	22	40	57	2	52
175	85	46	29	22	42	55	2	48
150	131	50	25	22	45	45	7	57
125	151	51	21	26	47	44	6	63
100	167	51	16	31	56	37	4	55
75	222	46	15	34	66	26	7	48
50	240	43	7	47	77	10	10	60
25	246	46	3	47	89	4	6	59
0	196	0	0	0	0	0	0	0
−25	191	53	3	41	87	5	7	41
−50	228	51	6	36	77	13	5	43
−75	159	50	15	34	63	23	10	45
−100	157	47	24	27	59	32	4	45
−125	97	63	16	21	46	43	6	36
−150	89	54	20	21	45	48	4	47
−175	49	53	18	29	45	47	6	47
−200	47	62	23	15	28	66	6	38
−225	34	44	38	18	50	47	3	53
−250	94	61	24	12	21	72	5	39

TABLE 4.4(b) **XOM (Exxon Mobil)**

Gap	Cases	Closing Prices			Trading Range			Cont Next Day
		Cont Dir	Below Open	Rev Dir	Cross Prev Close	Adj from Open	Cont Only	
250	19	47	47	5	16	84	0	58
225	9	67	33	0	22	78	0	44
200	9	67	22	11	11	89	0	44
175	27	63	15	22	33	63	0	37
150	35	60	23	17	51	40	9	49
125	72	44	25	28	42	57	1	42
100	151	54	24	17	42	52	3	54
75	263	47	22	31	59	37	2	55
50	408	52	11	35	68	25	5	50
25	386	54	4	40	84	11	4	58
0	202	0	0	0	0	0	0	0
−25	375	47	5	46	89	6	3	46
−50	312	46	11	40	77	19	3	47
−75	234	47	21	29	63	36	0	52
−100	107	43	27	29	53	45	2	41
−125	75	41	36	17	45	52	1	48
−150	45	53	22	24	36	62	2	42
−175	25	52	24	24	40	60	0	60
−200	20	30	35	30	65	30	0	50
−225	10	50	50	0	50	50	0	60
−250	37	62	32	5	27	70	3	41

TABLE 4.4(c) AMZN (Amazon)

Gap	Cases	Closing Prices			Trading Range			
		Cont Dir	Below Open	Rev Dir	Cross Prev Close	Adj from Open	Cont Only	Cont Next Day
250	153	55	24	21	37	61	1	45
225	30	30	20	50	67	30	3	43
200	33	58	21	18	42	55	3	33
175	66	53	15	29	55	42	3	39
150	70	47	20	33	74	24	0	66
125	87	49	15	36	59	39	0	44
100	144	53	13	33	69	27	2	48
75	187	47	9	43	79	19	1	42
50	259	46	7	46	86	12	2	47
25	297	49	4	44	91	4	2	46
0	50	0	0	0	0	0	0	0
−25	286	48	1	48	92	5	2	48
−50	302	43	11	46	86	10	1	55
−75	217	46	14	39	73	24	2	45
−100	147	46	16	37	67	31	0	51
−125	93	51	22	28	63	33	1	53
−150	83	51	20	28	61	35	2	51
−175	71	52	20	28	62	34	1	52
−200	38	42	24	29	61	39	0	50
−225	37	43	27	30	54	41	0	62
−250	173	49	25	24	40	55	2	49

TABLE 4.4(d) LUV (Southwest Airlines)

Gap	Cases	Closing Prices			Trading Range			
		Cont Dir	Below Open	Rev Dir	Cross Prev Close	Adj from Open	Cont Only	Cont Next Day
250	74	42	32	19	45	54	0	59
225	20	50	25	10	50	40	0	50
200	38	47	32	18	45	53	3	42
175	48	54	21	23	48	40	4	40
150	56	43	25	30	59	34	4	54
125	95	44	24	24	54	35	4	53
100	111	50	19	26	63	26	4	53
75	196	49	12	36	68	22	5	51
50	304	47	4	44	75	13	7	45
25	301	49	1	46	83	2	10	45
0	283	0	0	0	0	0	0	0
−25	301	48	1	46	88	3	5	47
−50	299	49	12	36	76	14	6	56
−75	262	48	15	32	71	18	5	47
−100	143	52	20	24	55	34	6	51
−125	92	50	23	24	51	37	3	54
−150	58	55	16	26	41	50	7	47
−175	34	47	29	24	44	53	3	50
−200	34	38	38	15	53	41	3	50
−225	23	35	35	26	57	43	0	61
−250	51	43	35	20	29	67	4	47

As with futures, it seems that the most interesting combinations are smaller gap openings that persist in closing in the direction of the gap after crossing through the previous closing price. There seems to be a low chance of a reversal during the trading day, but there are no numbers that indicate that the direction will continue the next day.

A Simple Gap Trading Method for Stocks

A basic approach to trading gaps was taken by Reverre.[5] Beginning with a 1-year study of the distribution of opening gaps for General Electric, Reverre noted that the distribution was very narrow, with 85% of the days opening with less than a 1% gap, and only 5% of the days showing gaps greater than 2%. Apply the following rules:

- Place limit orders to buy if prices open more than 1% lower, and sell if they open more than 1% higher, than the previous close.

- Exit the trade at the close of the day.

Although there may be additional profits from holding the trade for more than one day, this simple method produced small but consistent profits when applied to the Dow stocks. Reverre makes two important observations:

1. Trading the medium-sized gap of 1% showed consistency because gaps often represented noise and were likely to correct.
2. Trading gaps greater than 2% gave much larger profits and losses. Larger gaps were more likely to be structural and may not correct.

Test results showed that a 1% gap yielded an average long profit of $0.057 and average short profit of $0.034, which makes the brokerage commissions an important factor. When optimizing the gap size in 2004, 1.25% showed the best results; however, this is likely to change with the overall volatility of the market.

Updating this method, using GE data from January 2000 through May 2011 and a 2% gap filter, gave the cumulative profits, in $/share, shown in Figure 4.13. For a 1% filter, the program returned only 2.13¢ per share (without costs), and with a 2% filter it increased to 3.39¢ per share, with longs doing somewhat better than shorts. The period for mid-2003 until the subprime crisis in 2008 had very low volatility and few trades; however, if we remove that from the statistics, the profits per trade should increase significantly and make this simple approach a viable possibility.

Close-to-Close Gaps Reverre also applied a similar approach to large 1-day moves, looking for a correction over the next one to three days. Using the largest 20% moves in General Electric, or about 1.28 standard deviations, during the period December 1995 to February 1999, a *buy* signal occurred when prices fell by more than 1.96% and a *sell* signal when prices rose by more than 2.24%. Although

---

[5] Stéphane Reverre, "Trading the Opening Gap," *Technical Analysis of Stocks & Commodities* (November 1999); and Stéphane Reverre, "Trading against the Gap," *Technical Analysis of Stocks & Commodities* (Bonus Issue 2003).

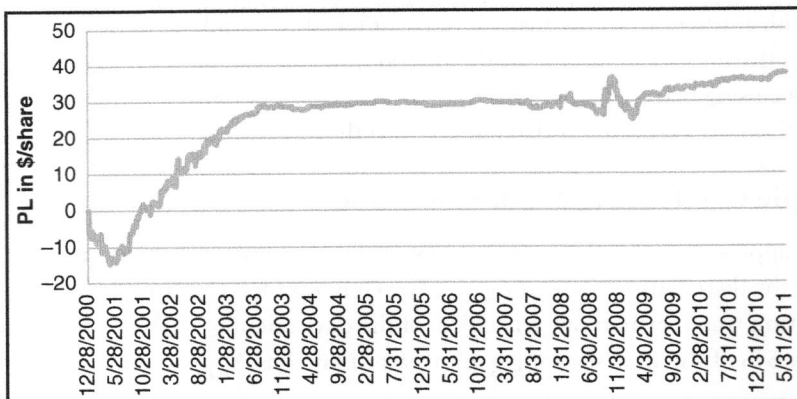

FIGURE 4.13 General Electric Cumulative PL Using a Simple Gap Filter Day Trading Method.

70% of the corrections occurred by the close of the following day, best results came by holding the trade for two days. Entries could be placed as limit orders in advance of the close.

Tested over the 30 Dow stocks, maximum returns came from 1-day moves with gaps of 4% to 5%, holding for 1 day. A wider range of gaps, from 2.5% to 5%, gave good results holding for 2 days. While less than half of the Dow stocks showed net profits, the overall profitability was good. Both long and short positions performed well, even though the test period was near the end of a strong bull market.

From 2000 to May 2011, the same tests were still profitable, but returned only 2 to 3¢ per share using the smaller gaps of about 2%. Larger gaps of 4% showed losses, which means that limiting the gaps to between 2% and 4% could be highly profitable if you can decide whether a range of gaps is sensible or a case of overfitting.

CHAPTER 5

Multiple Time Frames

From Perry J. Kaufman, *Trading Systems and Methods*, *+Website*, 5th Edition (Hoboken, New Jersey: John Wiley & Sons, 2013), Chapter 19.

Learning Objective Statements

- Demonstrate that you can evaluate price and chart data using one of the three multiple time frame methods described in this chapter
- Explain two benefits for using Multiple Time Frames in trading

In Level II, combinations of two trends and two momentum periods were used to create well-known systems and indicators such as Donchian's 5- and 20-day Moving Average, the two-trend crossover systems, double smoothing, the MACD, and the Turtle method, among many others. Each of those methods used daily data for all calculations. This chapter looks at systems where the components use a combination of intraday, daily, and/or weekly data in order to improve both timing and results.

Although the use of multiple time periods by floor traders has been popular for decades, few professionals have talked about it. It is only since better quote equipment has allowed this technique to be accessed by a wider audience that this approach has seeped into the public domain. The combination of multiple time periods allows the trader to time entries into the market using very short-term data, such as 10-minute bars, while watching the longer-term picture for the daily or weekly trend. Because it is agreed that most trends are best identified over a longer time period, and choosing the specific entry point requires a much faster response, the combination of two or even three time intervals is very sensible when each one targets a specific purpose. If the trend can be identified profitably, then the trader can filter or select short-term trades that have a better-than-average chance of becoming winners.

For most traders, the use of any one time frame presents special problems. The very short term contains a high percentage of noise that obscures the market direction. The numerous individual patterns that can be found in a 5-minute bar chart can divert your efforts away from the big picture. The use of only weekly charts, although they clearly show the direction of prices, presents higher risk and little opportunity for a good entry point. The obvious solution is to combine both time frames into a program that uses each to its best advantage.

■ Tuning Two Time Frames to Work Together

Throughout most of this book the individual systems and methods have been discussed on their own merits. When using a momentum indicator, an analyst would look for the specific RSI or stochastic that generated the most profits by showing a timely trend change or overbought/oversold condition. However, very few indicators work on their own as successful trading systems. They are combined with other indicators, and their trading signals are subject to selection using trend lines or divergence.

Once you have decided to combine two techniques, such as a moving average to identify the longer-term trend and an RSI or stochastic to provide improved entry timing, the two techniques must be tuned to work together. The best RSI signals, taken on their own, may no longer be the best entry timing points. You will want the time period for the indicator to be much shorter than the time period used to calculate the trend. For example, if your trend system has a typical holding period of one month (about 23 business days), you will want your timing oscillator to have a good chance of giving you a better entry point within the first 3 to 5 days (10%–20%) of that trade.

To get an indicator to reach overbought and oversold levels an average of every 5 days, you will need to use less than 5 days to calculate the indicator value. It does not matter if the indicator returns a loss when all of its buys and sells are totaled because the profitable part of the program comes from the longer-term trend component. It is most likely that the oscillator will generate five overbought or oversold conditions during the typical holding period for the trend trade, but only one of them will be used—the first one after the new entry signal. It is only important to see how this selective timing helps to improve overall profits and risk of the combined strategy. Readers might remember that Linda Raschke used this technique in *First Cross*.

Figure 5.1 gives an example of the timing needed to coordinate a short-term stochastic indicator with a longer-term trend. The top of the chart shows euro futures (EURUSD) with a 60-day moving average. Trading signals would normally be generated when the trendline turns up or down. In the first case, the trend turns up on July 30 at a closing price of 1.2986. It turns down on December 16 at 1.3152 for a gain of $2075. Instead, if we used the 3-day raw stochastic in the center panel and waited for the first oversold condition in the stochastic following the upturn, we would have entered on August 11 at 1.2810 and exited on December 31 at 1.3306 for a gain of $6200. At the same time, trades would be entered against the direction of the current price move, generally resulting in less slippage.

Again using the center panel for timing, the long position entered on December 31 would have changed direction on February 22 at 1.3600 using the trend, but on March 10 at 1.3736 waiting for an oversold condition. That causes an entry at a worse price, a

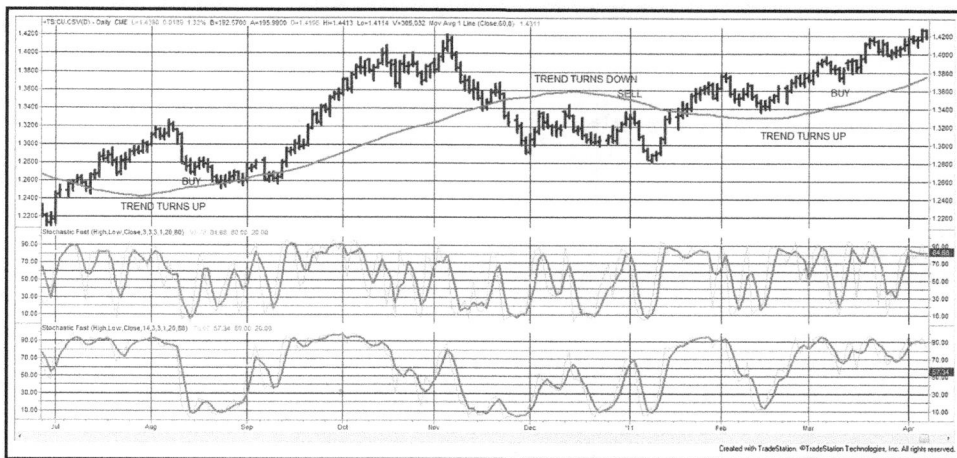

FIGURE 5.1 Timing the Entry into a 60-Day Moving Average with a Stochastic, Applied to Euro Futures, July 2010 to March 2011. A 3-Day Raw Stochastic is in the Center Panel and a 14-Day Raw Stochastic at the Bottom.

situation that happens when prices move steadily in one direction. Overall, entering on a price reversal using a short-term momentum indicator can greatly improve both performance and the percentage of profitable trades; however, not every entry is better.

Now consider the standard 14-day stochastic in the bottom panel. Had it been used for timing, some trades might have been missed because this longer calculation period has fewer swings from overbought to oversold, and those signals that did occur would have resulted in a significantly delayed entry into the trend trade.

▨ Elder's Triple-Screen Trading System

The *Triple Screen*[1] popularized a method often used by floor traders who had access to more sophisticated quote and graphics equipment beginning in the early 1980s. It combines trend-following and oscillators using three time frames, each serving a specific purpose. The oscillators are normally associated with timing, while the trend determines the direction of the trade, similar to the process discussed in the previous section. Dr. Elder has observed that each time frame relates to the next by a factor of 5. That is, if you are using daily data as the middle time period, then the shorter interval will be divided into five parts, bars of 1 to 2 hours in length, and the longer period will be five days, or one week.

To be practical, it is not necessary to divide a 6-hour trading day into five intervals of 1 hour and 12 minutes. Rounding to 1 hour is close enough. If, for example, you want to focus on trading a 10-minute chart, then the middle interval is 10 minutes, the short-term is 2 minutes, and the long-term is 1 hour (not 50 minutes).

In the following description, Screen 1 holds the longest time frame while Screen 3 shows the shortest one. Figure 5.2 is an example of the Triple Screen, with 60-minute gold futures in the top panel, daily prices in the second panel, and weekly prices

---

[1] Dr. Alexander Elder, *Trading for a Living* (New York: John Wiley & Sons, 1993).

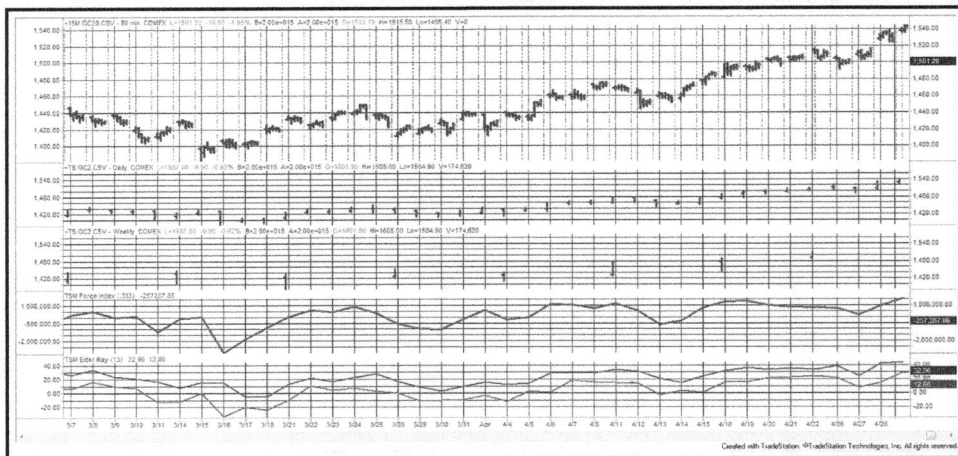

FIGURE 5.2 The Triple Screen for Gold Futures, March and April 2011. From the Top, the Panels are 60-Minute Bars, Daily, Weekly, the Force Index, and the Elder-Ray.

in the third (middle) panel. The bottom two panels show indicators for the intermediate (daily) move, discussed below. In the original Triple Screen, each of the price charts was actually on separate screens, not combined into one.

Screen 1: The Major Move (Lowest Frequency Data)

The long-term view is used to see the *market tide,* a clear perspective of the major market trend, or sometimes the lack of trend. Weekly data is used for this example (the third panel from the top in Figure 5.2), which is consistent with the experience that less frequent data (i.e., weekly or monthly) smoothes the price movement by eliminating interim noise. Although there are many other choices for a long-term trend, the Triple-Screen approach uses the slope of the weekly MACD, where the histogram that represents the MACD value is very smooth, equivalent to, for example, a 13-week exponential smoothing (1 rolling calendar quarter). The trend is up when the MACD bar, or 13-week exponential value, is higher than that of the previous week; the trend is down when this week's value is lower.

Screen 2: The Intermediate Move (Middle Frequency Data)

The oscillator applied in Screen 2 (the second panel) identifies the time period in which we would trade. Again, the specific oscillator is not as important as the time frame and the ability to identify *market waves* in the major moves of Screen 1. Two oscillators are suggested, the *Force Index* and *Elder-Ray,* both described below. A stochastic can also be used.

1. *Force Index*

$$Force\ Index_t = Volume_t \times (Close_t - Close_{t-1})$$

The Force Index is then smoothed using a 2-day exponential smoothing, equivalent to a 0.333 smoothing constant, and the resulting value is used to determine overbought and oversold levels. The Force Index is shown in panel 4.

Entering a long position using the Force Index is not as clear as when using the Elder-Ray. The steps are:

1. Identify the trend in Screen 1, which shows that the major move is up.
2. Confirm the long position if the 2-day exponential of the Force Index falls below its center line and does not fall below the multiweek low. When using a stochastic instead of the Force Index, buy when the stochastic falls below 30.

2. *Elder-Ray*

Elder-Ray is a technique for separating bullish and bearish movement.

$$Bull\ Power_t = High_t - 13\text{-}day\ exponential\ smoothing$$

$$Bear\ Power_t = Low_t - 13\text{-}day\ exponential\ smoothing$$

To determine when to buy using the Elder-Ray and Screen 1, the following two steps are necessary:

1. The trend in Screen 1, the major move, must be up.
2. Bear power is negative but rising; bear power must not be positive.

Two additional steps may be used to filter trades and improve performance, but are not required:

3. The last peak in bull power is higher than the previous peak (the most recent bull power should not be significantly lower than the previous peak).
4. Bear power is rising from a bullish divergence.

The opposite rules apply for sell signals. The Elder-Ray is shown in panel 5 of Figure 5.2.

Screen 3: Timing (High Frequency Data)

The final screen is for fastest response, primarily for identifying *intraday breakouts*. It is shown as 60-minute bars in the top panel of Figure 5.2. To improve the point of entry, the intraday bars can be used to set long positions when the current price moves above the previous day's high. There is no calculation involved, simply a *Buy Stop* order using the shortest time period. In this example, a new buy signal occurs when the high of the hourly bar moves above the highest high of the hourly bars of the previous day.

Stop-Loss

Every system needs risk control, and that most often comes as a stop-loss order. The Triple Screen approach positions the stop as a three-step process. For a long position,

1. First place the stop below the low of the day of entry, or the previous day's low, whichever is lower.
2. Move the stop to the break-even level as soon as possible. Naturally, there must be some room between the stop-loss level and the current price; otherwise the stop will always be hit.

3. Continue to change the stop to protect 50 percent of the highest profits. In addition, you may consider taking profits when the stochastic or Force Index moves above the 70 percent level.

■ Robert Krausz's Multiple Time Frames

The most robust and fully automated approach to multiple time frames was taken by Robert Krausz, a well-known trader who provided an extensive course on his method. To understand the importance of first arriving at a sound theory before implementing and testing a trading program, we need to briefly review the characteristics of performance that indicate a robust method.

When testing a trend-following system, we should expect that a trend of 100 days, compared to a trend of 50 days, will produce larger profits per trade, greater reliability, and proportionally fewer trades. As you increase the calculation period, this pattern continues; when you reduce the calculation period this pattern reverses. You are prevented from using very short calculation intervals because relative market noise increases, and slippage and commissions become proportionally larger; on the other hand, the longest periods are undesirable because of large equity swings. When viewing test results as a flowing picture, there must be a clear, profitable pattern and continuity when plotting returns per trade versus the average holding period.

The sophistication in Krausz's work lies in his understanding of this pattern, and its incorporation into the structure of his program, *The Fibonacci Trader*.[2] Krausz also worked in three time frames. Each time frame has a logical purpose, and they are said to be modeled after Gann's concept that the markets are essentially geometric. The shortest time frame is the one in which you will trade; in addition, there are two longer time frames to put each one into proper perspective. The patterns common to time frames are easily compared to fractals; within each time frame is another time frame with very similar patterns, reacting in much the same way. You cannot have an hourly chart without a 15-minute chart, because the longer time period is composed of shorter periods; if the geometry holds, then characteristics that work in one time frame, such as support and resistance, should work in shorter and longer time frames. Within each time frame, there are unique levels of support and resistance; when they converge across time frames, then the chance of success is increased. In Krausz's work, the relationships between price levels and profit targets are interwoven with Fibonacci ratios and the principles of Gann.

One primary advantage of using multiple time frames is that you can see a pattern develop sooner. A trend that appears on a weekly chart could have been seen first on the daily chart. The same logic follows for other chart formations. Similarly, the application of patterns such as support and resistance is the same within each time frame. When a support line appears at about the same price level in hourly, daily, and weekly charts, it gains importance.

[2] Robert Krausz, *W. D. Gann Treasure Discovered* (Geometric Traders Institute, Fibonacci Trader Corp., 450-106 State Road 13 North, #206, Jacksonville, FL 32259-3863, FibonacciTrader.com).

Laws of Multiple Time Frames[3]

As a well-known, successful trader,[4] Krausz brought more than just three time frames and some unique strategies to one display screen. He endowed the program with six rules:

1. Every time frame has its own structure.
2. The higher time frames overrule the lower time frames.
3. Prices in the lower time frame structure tend to respect the energy points of the higher time frame structure.
4. The energy points of support/resistance created by the higher time frame's vibration (prices) can be validated by the action of the lower time periods.
5. The trend created by the next time period enables us to define the tradable trend.
6. What appears to be chaos in one time period can be order in another time period.

Using three time frames of about the same ratio to one another (10-minute, 50-minute, and daily) with daily being the longest, Figure 5.3 shows the June 1998 contract of U.S. bonds with a number of techniques applied over multiple time frames. Figure 5.3a uses only daily bars, while Figure 5.3b uses 10-minute bars; both charts are drawn on the same price scale to facilitate comparison.

To understand the application of these techniques, it is necessary to identify the following features:[5]

- The *Daily HiLo Activator* (in this case, it is the moving average of the daily highs) is presented as a stepped line. The 4 days of interest are marked by the letters *A, B, C,* and *D* and appear on both (a) and (b) of Figure 5.3.

- The *50-minute HiLo Activator* (seen in Figure 5.3b) is the moving average of the 50-minute highs, used as a *Buy Stop*, or the moving average of the 50-minute lows used as a *Sell Stop*.

- The *10-minute Gann swings* are based on 10-minute bars (in Figure 5.3b). The solid line shows when the Gann swing represents an upwards trend, and the broken line when it shows a downtrend.

The interpretation of these techniques relies on the faster response provided by the 10-minute bars, combined with the direction given by the longer time frames.

- Based on the 10-minute Gann swings, the trend turned from up to down at about 121-00, while the daily Gann swings placed the trend change much later, near 120-00.

---

[3] Copyright, Robert Krausz.

[4] See Jack Schwager, *The New Market Wizards* (New York: John Wiley & Sons, 1992).

[5] The following chart analysis was provided by Robert Krausz. Further analysis of bond moves relevant to this discussion can be found in two articles, "A Strategy for Trading Multiple Time Frames," *Futures* (November 2001), and "Intraday Strategies for Multiple Time Frames," *Futures* (January 2002).

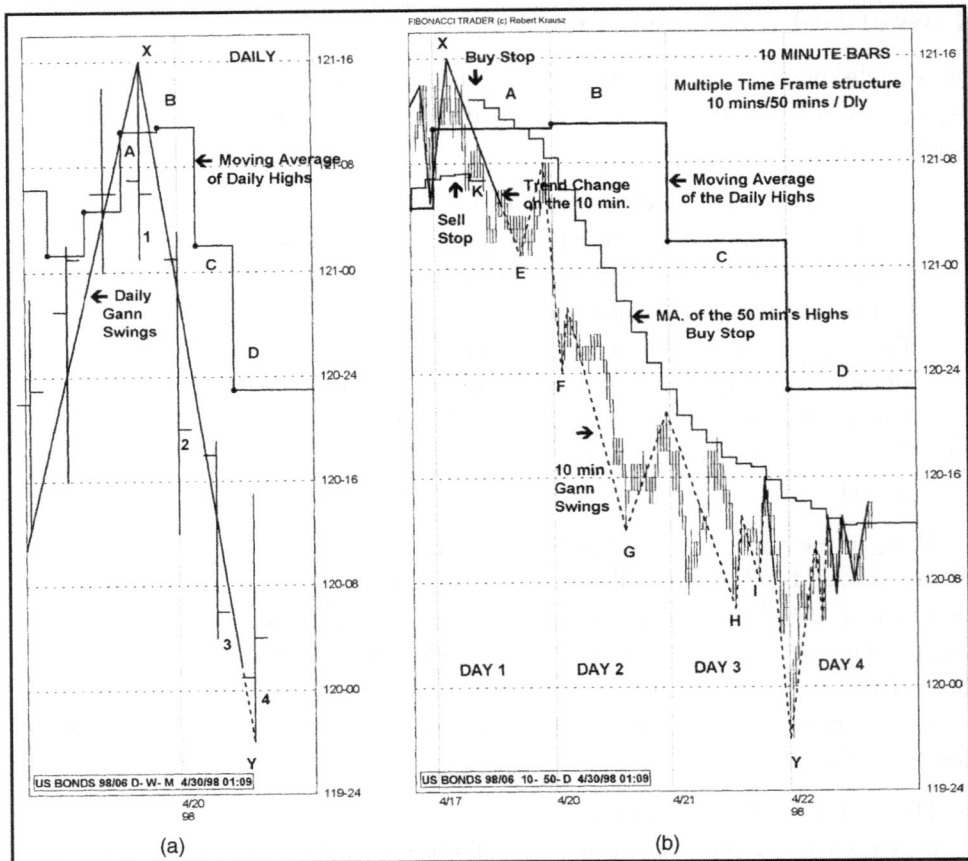

FIGURE 5.3 Krausz's Multiple Time Frames, June 1998 U.S. Bonds. (a) Daily Chart with Gann Swings and a Stepped Moving Average. (b) Multiple Time Frame Structure for the Corresponding Four Days.

Source: Chart created using *The Fibonacci Trader.* Used with permission from Fibonacci Trader Corporation, 450-106 State Road 13 North, #206, Jacksonville, FL 32259-3863, www.fibonaccitrader.com.

- The slope of the daily Gann swing, measured from point *X* to point *Y* on both charts, was down, defining the dominant trend. Short trades can be entered using the downward trend of the 10-minute time frame. The process of coordinating the trend of the higher time period with that of the lower time period, and acting in only that direction, seems to be the most advantageous approach. The low of each 10-minute swing, marked *E, F, G, H,* and *I* on the 10-minute bar chart, provides opportunities to add to the original position.

- At the top left of the 10-minute chart, the 10-minute close falls below the *Sell Stop* of the 50-minute HiLo Activator at point *K* (about 120-06). The *Buy Stop* then applies and follows declining prices for 3 days. These changes occur in the same area where the Gann swing indicates a trend change from up to down.

THE INTEGRATION OF TECHNICAL ANALYSIS

■ The 50-minute moving average of the highs, shown in a step formation on the 10-minute chart, tracks the highs of the market rallies on Days 1, 3, and 4. The daily moving average of the highs (the Daily HiLo Activator) remained level on Day 2 and turned down on Day 3. The trend can only change to up when the Daily HiLo Activator turns up again.

More on Selecting the Three Time Frames

In thinking out the use of multiple time frames, it is necessary to understand that you cannot substitute a 10-period moving average of 1-hour bars with a 40-period moving average of 15-minute bars. Similarly, you cannot replace a 10-week average with a 50-day average. It seems natural to think that any two trends covering the same time span will give the same result, but that is not the case. Although we can average many data points, we cannot get rid of all the noise; fewer data points over the same time span will always yield a smoother result. Therefore, the use of hourly, daily, and weekly time periods—multiple time frames—gives a much different picture of the market than simply using three different moving averages of the equivalent calculation periods. It is much easier to see the major trend using weekly data, find the short-term direction based on daily data, and time your entry using hourly bars.

■ Martin Pring's *KST System*

Martin Pring approaches multiple time frames using *rate-of-change* (ROC) indicators in his *KST System*.[6] Note that rate-of-change is the same as returns multiplied by 100 (i.e., whole percent). Because each ROC applied to a specific calculation period has a unique cycle, the combination of three calculation periods will provide a valuable confirmation of a trading signal. Although Pring prefers to begin with a long-term view of the market, using 6-, 12-, and 24-*month* ROC calculation periods, Figure 5.4 shows the 6-, 12-, and 24-*week* ROC applied to the S&P 500 futures. Vertical lines show where the cycles of the three time frames align at major and intermediate tops and bottoms. These points will form the basis of the trading rules.

The cycles formed by the ROC are used in conjunction with a trend. The cycles not only confirm the trend change, but the size and frequency of the cycles will help to set objectives. The best trend moves occur when all three ROC indicators are moving in the same direction following a coordinated turning point.

The second stage in the process is to smooth the ROC indicators, making them more reliable. Using the 6-, 12-, and 24-month ROC preferred by Pring, the 6- and 12-month indicators are smoothed by a 6-period moving average, and the 24-month smoothed by a 9-period moving average. Because the ROC calculation actually

---

[6] Martin J. Pring, *Martin Pring on Market Momentum* (Gloucester, VA: International Institute for Economic Research, 1993). Also see www.pring.com.

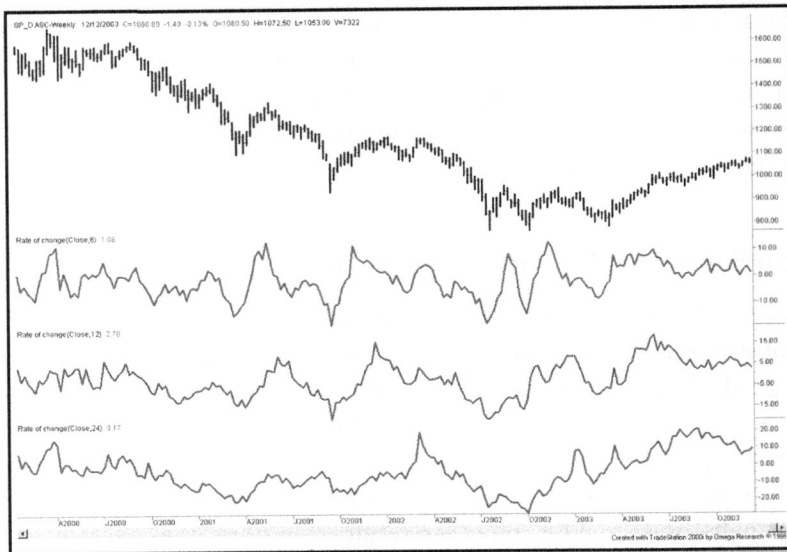

FIGURE 5.4 6-, 12-, and 24-Week ROC (Top to Bottom) Applied to the S&P 500 Continuous Futures, January 2000 to December 2003.

speeds up the price movement, instead of introducing a lag, this small amount of smoothing shows very little lag in the smoothed values. Using the three smoothed ROC indicators, Pring selects trades using the following guidelines:

1. A trendline based on about half of the longest ROC period determines the direction of the trade.
2. The longer 24-period ROC identifies the major move.
3. The strongest price moves occur when all three ROC values are moving in the same direction.
4. If the 24-period ROC peaks while the other two indicators are rising, the sell-off is minor. Similarly, when the 12- and 6-period indicators peak but the 24-period is rising, the sell-off is also mild.

We can conclude that all three indicators need to peak at the same time, followed by all three values declining, to see a significant sell-off.

Creating a Composite Indicator

Pring observed that trading signals generated by combining the ROC indicators with a trend reversal were out of phase with the major moves in the S&P. To correct that problem, he created the *KST indicator*, a composite of four smoothed ROC calculation periods, each step-weighted in proportion to its period.

1. A 24-period ROC weighted 4.
2. An 18-period ROC weighted 3.
3. A 12-period ROC weighted 2.

4. A 9-period ROC weighted 1.

$$KST = (4 \times Average(ROC(price, 24), 9)) + (3 \times Average(ROC(price, 18), 9))$$
$$+ (2 \times Average(ROC(price, 12), 6)) + (1 \times Average(ROC(price, 6), 6))$$

where $ROC(price, 24)$ is a function that returns the 24-period ROC of the *price* series
$100 \times \left(\dfrac{P_t}{P_{t-24}} - 1 \right)$, and *Average (series, 9)* is a function that returns the 9-period average
of *series.* In this formula, *series* is the result of the ROC calculation. In his description
of KST, Pring does not give the weighting of 18-period ROC; the value 9 is used here.

To generate trading signals, Pring plots the 9-month ROC along with the KST
indicator, plus the 12-period moving average trendline. In Figure 5.5 the bottom
panel has an 18-period ROC smoothed using a 9-period average, one of the KST
components. Using weekly data, the 18-period ROC seemed to track better. Trading
signals are taken in the direction of the moving average trendline in the upper panel,
but timed when the KST indicator crosses the ROC line after the first turn in the
trendline. With the proper choice of ROC periods, the trade could be exited when
the KST crosses the ROC in the other direction. If the ROC is too fast, then it will be
difficult to take bigger profits from the trend moves; therefore, it seems preferable to
use one of the slower ROC calculations.

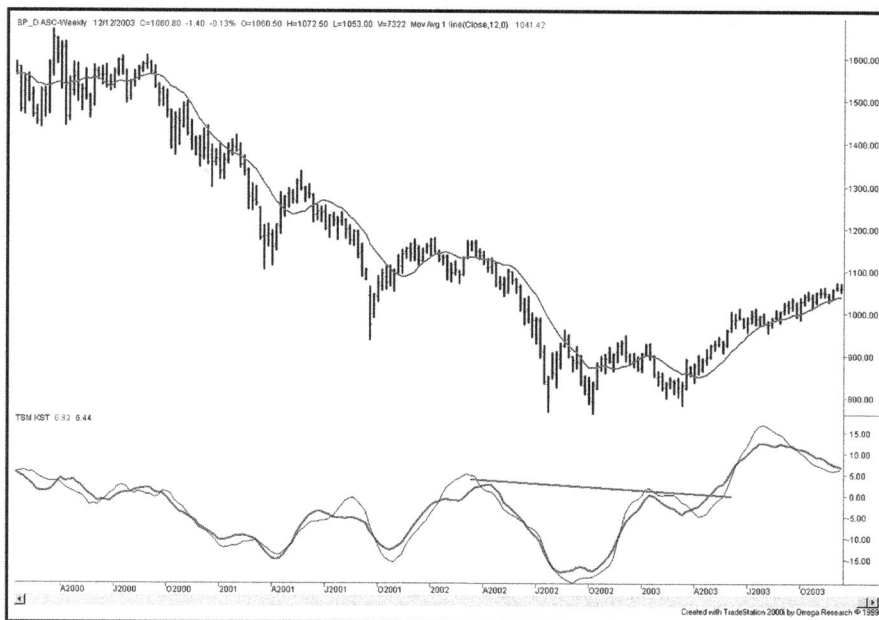

FIGURE 5.5 **KST Combined with an 18-Period ROC and a 12-Period Trendline can Improve Timing and Selection of Major Price Moves. Prices are S&P
500 Continuous Futures, Weekly Data, January 2000 to December 2003.**

The major trends are clearer, and the signals more reliable, when applied to monthly data, although the method is generalized to work using any size data bar. A faster version of KST can be constructed from daily data and used to filter trades or improve their timing. It is a requirement, however, that the KST signals be used in combination with a trendline.

The KST is an exceptionally smooth indicator with very little lag, making its signals more timely than most other indicators. It can also be used in the same way as an RSI or stochastic, applying divergence and trendlines to generate additional, reliable trading signals. In Figure 5.5, a trendline has been drawn across the tops of the KST indicator beginning in April 2002, showing the breakout of a descending pattern in April 2003, a very timely entry into the stock market.

CHAPTER 6

Advanced Techniques

From Perry J. Kaufman, *Trading Systems and Methods, +Website*, 5th Edition (Hoboken, New Jersey: John Wiley & Sons, 2013), Chapter 20.

Learning Objective Statements

- Analyze the relationship between a system's entry signals and changes in market volatility
- Distinguish whether a system's entry signal should be filtered based on liquidity
- Calculate the expected move of an index or security based on volatility measures
- Explain the basics of using Fractal Efficiency, Chaos Theory or genetic algorithms in trading
- Explain the basics of using Neural Network (Machine Learning) programming to trade with market data

After price, volatility has the greatest impact on trading, so it is worth spending time understanding how to measure it and how to use it when trading. Those methods cover a wide range. Volatility has already been discussed as part of many indicators and as a way to make stop-losses, profit-taking, and even the charting scale variable so that the trading methods adjust automatically to changing market conditions.

Volatility can be used as a trading filter, avoiding high risk or standing aside when the volatility is too low. It is the key measure of risk and will be the dominant ingredient in structuring a portfolio. As systematic programs mature, there seems to be a greater, justifiable concentration on how to include and manage volatility. Here, we will look at it in more detail.

▍ Measuring Volatility

In general, the volatility of most price series, whether stocks, financial markets, commodities, or the spread between two series, is directly proportional to the increase and decrease in the price level. Higher prices translate into higher volatility. This *price-volatility relationship* has been described as *lognormal* in the stock market, and is similar to a percentage-growth relationship.

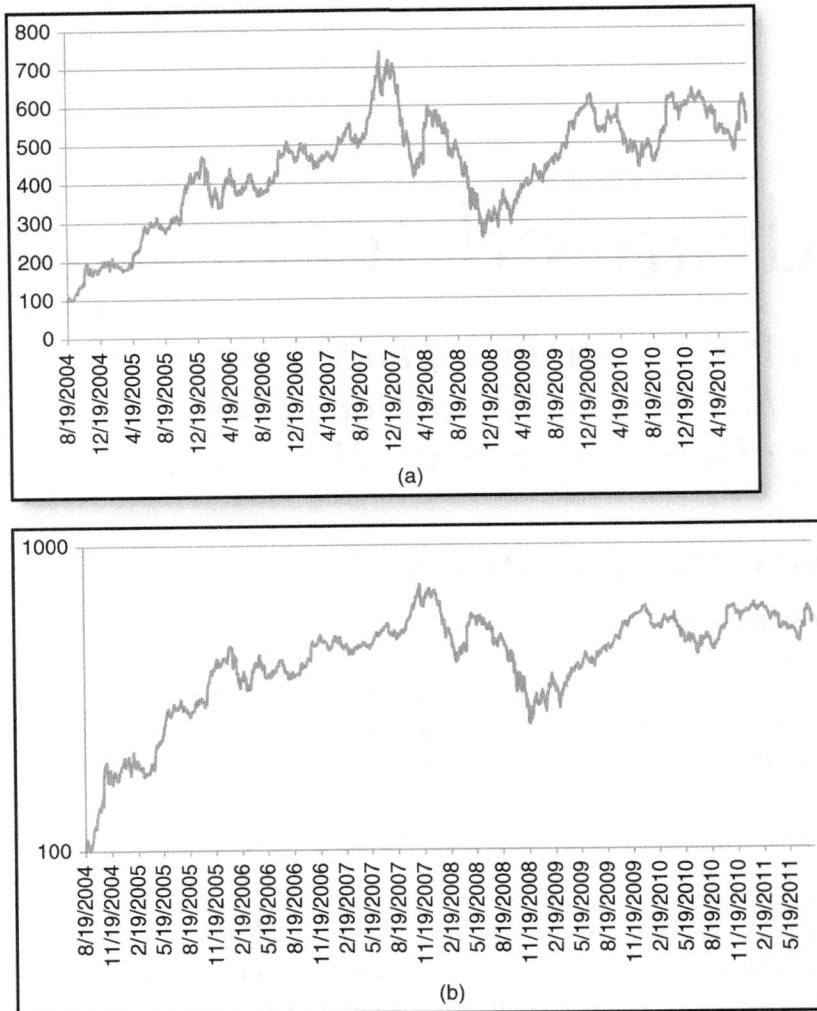

FIGURE 6.1 A Comparison of (a) Google Prices and (b) a Semi-Log
Plot of the Same Prices.

Consider Google in Figure 6.1a, a plot of the price since inception, and 1b, a semi-log plot, available on Excel under *format axis/axis scale/logarithmic*. In a semi-log plot, the *y*-axis is plotted on a log scale, where each equal space up is 10 times the previous level. By showing them side by side, the log scale is clearly less volatile. The faster moves up and down near the highest levels are much smaller on the log chart. Then using a log relationship is one way of explaining the relationship between price and volatility.

The Price-Volatility Relationship

Before getting immersed in various measurements of volatility, be aware that two stocks trading at the same price can have very different volatility. It may not only be the nature of their business, but those stocks in the news tend to have more volatility. This becomes important in many ways:

- When sizing positions in order to equalize risk.

- When balancing position sizes for pairs trading or market neutral baskets.

- For assessing risk in portfolios.

While each of these issues is covered in other places in this book, it is volatility that is the key driver of risk, and measuring volatility correctly is necessary to control that risk.

Adjusting for a Base Price

While a stock price can go to zero, commodities always have an intrinsic value. Wheat, for example, has a production cost below which farmers are reluctant to sell. During times of surplus, or when an individual farmer is in need of cash, wheat could be sold below cost, but not at zero, and not usually far below cost. When prices get very low because of exceptionally high inventories, they tend to settle near the cost of production and volatility drops significantly. Farmers are not interested in selling so there is little activity. Speculators do not see prices changing until there is more information about the next year's crop; therefore, they also stand aside. From this we can say that, somewhere below the cost of production, volatility goes to zero. Call that level the *base price* for the purpose of calculating volatility.

Then prices can be adjusted by dividing the current price by the base price (p_0) or subtracting the base price from the current price, then taking the natural log (ln) of the adjusted value.

$$Adj\, p_t' = \ln \frac{P_t}{P_0} \quad \text{or} \quad Adj\, p_t' = \ln(p_t - p_0)$$

The charts of either of these adjusted prices will look similar to the unadjusted semi-log plot; however, when the base price is high, the adjusted price will be more useful.

Exceptions

There are three noteworthy exceptions to the price-volatility relationship, and these exceptions will lead to a more general way of measuring volatility.

1. Interest rates trade as prices on the futures markets, which is inverse to the yield. When evaluating long-term volatility for rates, and in most cases when using percentages, yield should be used.
2. Foreign exchange has no base price, only equilibrium, the price that all traders, and the governments, accept as fair value for the moment. This situation is always short-lived. Prices get more volatile when they move away from equilibrium in either direction.
3. Energy is controlled by a cartel. They attempt to set the supply and target a price range. This was very effective when prices were in the range $18 to $32/bbl, but does not seem to have much effect at higher levels. Changing the supply can cause shocks to the market in either direction.

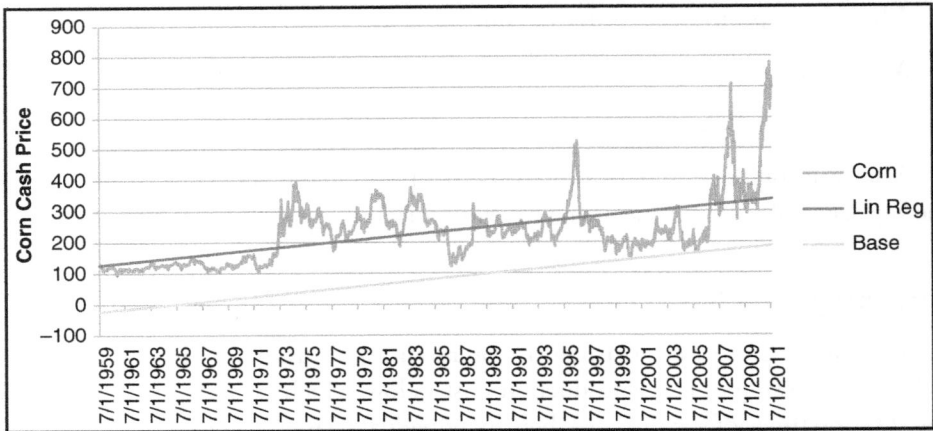

FIGURE 6.2 Using the Linear Regression to Define the Base Price Level.

Determining the Base Price

Finding the real base price of a commodity can have uses beyond volatility, in fundamental analysis. There are two straightforward ways this can be done.

1. *Use a linear regression of prices.* Apply a standard least squares regression, available on Excel in Data/Data Analysis, with sequential integers as x and the closing prices as y. Then create the regression line as $p'_t = a + bx$, where a is the y-intercept and b the slope. To find the base price, calculate the residuals, $res_t = p_t - p'_t$, then find the minimum residual value. Subtract that minimum value from the regression line to get the base price line, shown in Figure 6.2. The base price continues to increase with time.

2. *Use a linear regression of volatility.* Instead of price, using a measure of volatility related to the price level will give a more direct view of the price-volatility relationship.

Consider monthly copper prices and two measurements of volatility, the returns and the price range for that month. These numbers will not be annualized because that is only multiplying them by a constant, the square root of 12. From a spreadsheet of copper cash prices, calculate the returns of the past 21 days whenever the month changes. At the same time, find the difference between the highest high and the lowest low price for the past 21 days. Put them into a table along with the monthly ending price. Using Excel, choose a scatter diagram with a linear regression line for the combinations of price with returns, and price with range. Both of these are shown in Figures 6.3a and b. Using the monthly price ranges gives a clear picture of the price-volatility relationship, increasing in direct proportion to price and going to zero somewhere near $0.50/lb. Using returns is not as clear, with a large indistinguishable cluster in the bottom left corner and low volatility occurring at high prices. Using the price range whenever possible turns out to be a more robust solution because it has the advantage of using more data, namely the high and lows rather than only the close.

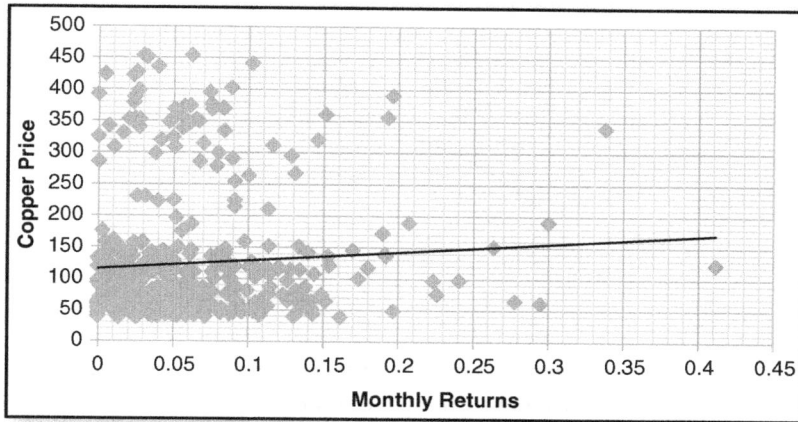

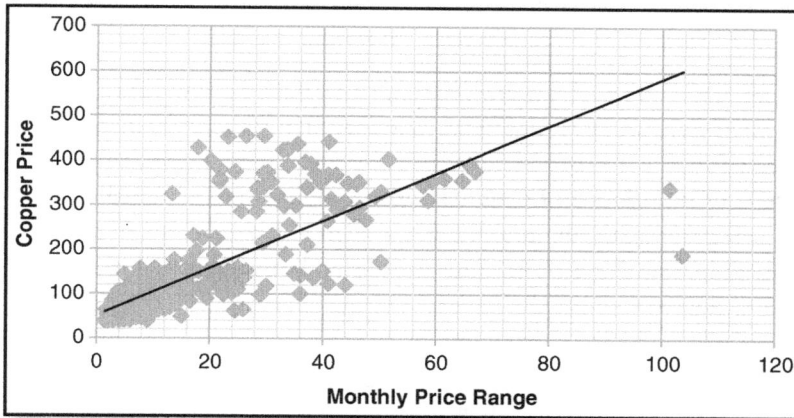

FIGURE 6.3 Scatter Diagrams of Volatility Against Price for Monthly Copper, 1974 to July 2011. (a) Price and Monthly Returns. (b) Price and Monthly Price Range.

There are many other ways to find the base price and the price-volatility relationship; however, simple is often best. In this case, a linear regression shows the relationship clearly, even if a nonlinear fit may have been more accurate. For the purpose of using volatility in trading systems, the comparison of returns to price range shows that the price range is a more effective measurement when high and low data are available.

The Time Interval

The time period over which volatility is measured is also a significant factor in the price-volatility relationship. A longer period means that the net changes over *n* days may turn into months or years. Longer measurement periods give higher volatility values; however, the rate at which volatility increases will decline over time. The maximum time period over which volatility increases will be equal to the period of the largest price move, taken as a percentage. Options traders are familiar with this relationship because option pricing is all about volatility, how much could a stock or

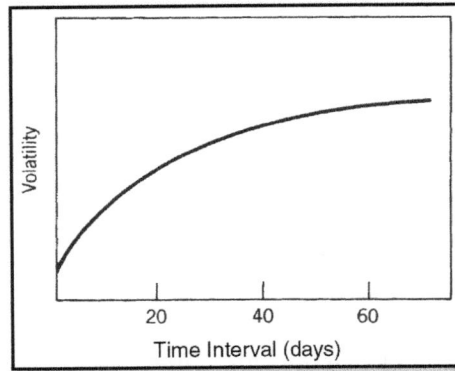

FIGURE 6.4 Change in Volatility Relative to the Interval Over Which It Is Measured.

futures price move before expiration. Figure 6.4 shows a general representation of how volatility increases over time. This may vary slightly for specific markets.

An Example of a Lognormal Calculation A lognormal relationship in prices can be shown using the math function *natural log, Ln,* in Excel. Over the long term and under average market conditions, the relationship between actual price changes and volatility is expected to be:

$$\frac{|P_t - P_{t-1}|}{\ln p_t} \approx \frac{|P_s - P_{s-1}|}{\ln p_s}$$

This formula says that the absolute value of the change in price on day t divided by the natural log of the price on day t is approximately equal to ($\approx$) the change in price on any other day, s, divided by the natural log of the price on day s.

For example, if the price on day t is 20 and the price on day s is 40, then the natural log of prices on those days are ln (20) = 2.99 and ln (40) = 3.99. If the volatility is $1.00 when $p_t = 20$, then the volatility is expected to be $1.23 when $p_s = 40$.

$$\frac{volatility\ at\ p_t = 20}{\ln(20)} \approx \frac{volatility\ at\ p_s = 40}{\ln(40)}$$

If the volatility at 20 is 1.00, then the volatility at 40 is 1.23. When using a spreadsheet for your calculations, note that the function *ln* is not the same as the function *log*.

Volatility Measures

There are five practical measures of volatility that can be easily used to satisfy the need to show expanding and contracting volatility, but are not tied to an underlying price level. They simply measure volatility over the most recent n days, or n bars using price differences or ranges. Referring to Figure 6.5 in conjunction with the

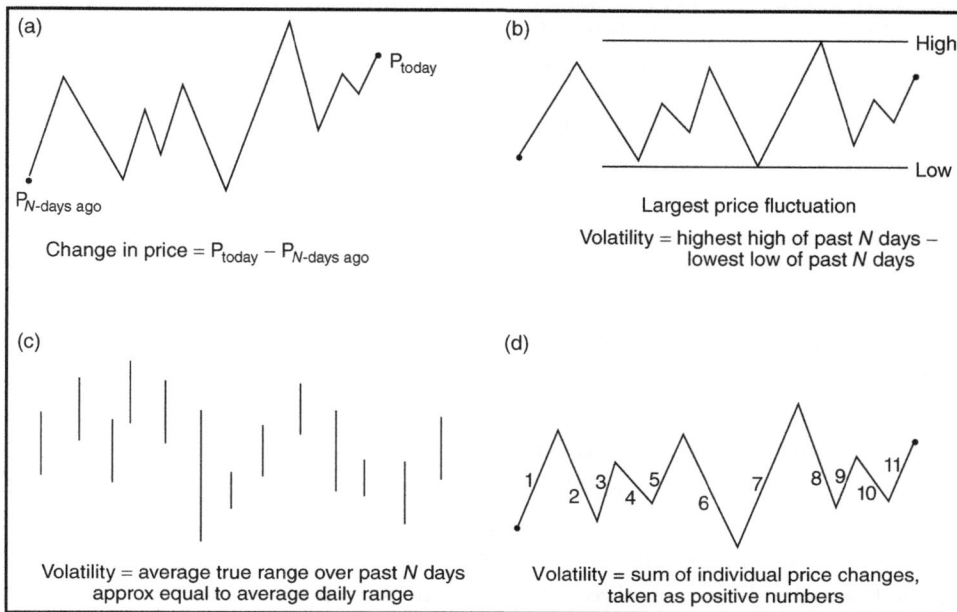

FIGURE 6.5 Four Volatility Measures.

Source: Perry J. Kaufman, *A Short Course in Technical Trading* (Hoboken, NJ: John Wiley & Sons, 2003). Reprinted with permission.

formulas below, the five volatility measures for today, V_t, calculated using the past n days, are:

1. The *change in price* over n days (Figure 6.5a):

$$V_t = Close_t - Close_{t-n}$$

2. The *maximum price fluctuation* during the n days (Figure 6.3b):

$$V_t = Max(High_t, \ldots, High_{t-n}) - Min(Low_t, \ldots, Low_{t-n})$$

   where *Max* and *Min* are the same as the *TradeStation* functions *Highest* and *Lowest*.
3. The *average true range* over the past n days:

$$V_t = Average(Truerange, n)$$

   where *Truerange* is a function that returns the maximum range from the combination of today's high, low, and previous close.
4. The *sum of the absolute price changes* over n days:

$$V_t = \sum_{i=t-n+1}^{t} |Close_t - Close_{t-1}|$$

   For stocks, the sum of the returns should be used.
5. Classic *annualized volatility* for daily data

$$V_t = Stdev(r_i) \times \sqrt{252}, \text{ where } i = t - n + 1, t$$

In (1), the volatility is entirely dependent on the value of the two points, p_t and p_{t-n}, regardless of the price activity that occurred during the days between them. If prices are very volatile but close to where they began n days ago, this method would show zero volatility. Over many calculations, this method returns a reasonable measure of volatility, but will always be lower than those using the highs and lows.

The maximum range (2) corrects for the dependence on only two points and will produce a more meaningful measure of volatility, which may also be used as an estimate of risk. This method may be effective as the basis for a stop-loss or profit target if you know the average holding period of the trade, because it estimates the maximum move for that period.

The average true range (3) is the most popular measurement of volatility and gives a reasonable guideline for future volatility. Many strategies use a factor times the average true range to place a stop-loss, take profits, or decide the current level of risk.

The sum of the absolute price changes (4) is similar to the average true range but misses the connection to the previous day. Then a large gap that does not retrace to the previous close will appear to have lower volatility. This may be better for intraday trading.

The last method (5), *annualized volatility*, is the most popular and accepted among financial analysts. It is the standard deviation of the returns over the past n periods, times the square root of the number of periods, P, in a year. The generalized formula is

$$V_t = \sigma(r_i) \times \sqrt{P}$$

For daily data based on a 60-day rolling calculation, $i = t - 59$ to t and $P = 252$. For monthly data, $P = 12$. In the case of back-adjusted futures prices, the returns, $r_t = p_t / p_{t-1} - 1$ or $\ln (pt/p_{t-1})$ will be incorrect because older data gets distorted due to the continuous adjustment.

Of the five measurements, the two of most interest are the average true range and annualized volatility.

Comparing Annualize Volatility and Average True Range   Results from annualized volatility and average true range can be very different and can significantly affect trading decisions, position size, and risk assessment. Figure 6.6 shows a daily chart of Merck (MRK) from April 2010 to May 2011. The average true range (ATR) is shown in the center panel and the annualized volatility in the lower panel, both calculated over 20 days. The ATR is considerably smoother on a daily basis and shows smaller jumps when prices gap. In some cases, such as the far right, the true range is increasing while the annualized volatility is flat. Both can be converted to dollar values by multiplying by the current price.

Ratio Measurements

Bookstaber[1] presents a volatility measurement V, in the traditional notation of a return series, that is, the ratio of successive closing prices. He adds alternate measures using the high and low, or a combination of the three as follows,

---

[1] Richard Bookstaber, *The Complete Investment Book* (Glenview, IL: Scott, Foresman, 1985), 349.

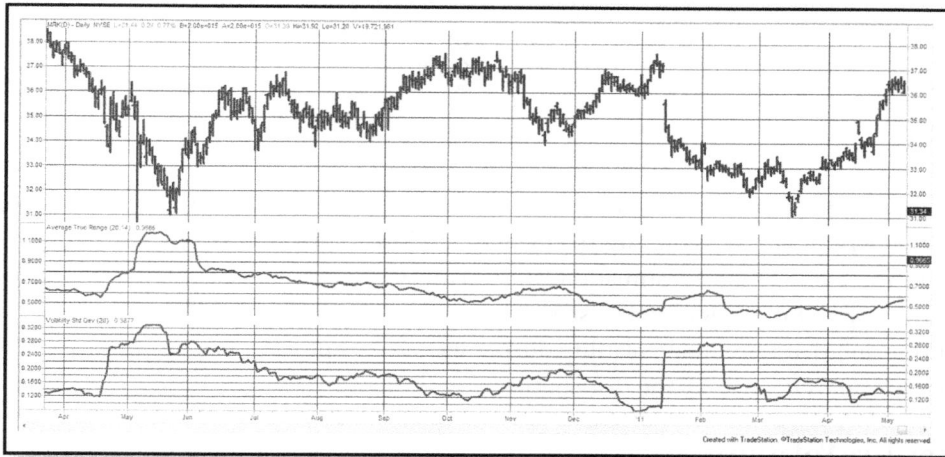

FIGURE 6.6 Merck (MRK) with a 20-Day Average True Range (Center Panel) and a 20-Day Annualized Volatility (Bottom Panel).

where C_t = the closing price on day t
H_t = the high price on day t
L_t = the low on day t
V_t = the volatility on day t

(a) Close-to-close volatility (for stock prices or cash data)

$$R_t = \frac{C_t}{C_{t-1}}$$

and

$$A = \frac{1}{n}\sum_{i=1}^{n} \ln R_{t-i}$$

then

$$V_t^2 = \frac{1}{n-1}\sum_{i=1}^{n} (\ln R_{t-1} - A)^2$$

and

$$V_t = \sqrt{V_t^2}$$

(b) High-low volatility

$$V_t = \frac{0.601}{n}\sum_{i=1}^{n} \ln\left(\frac{C_t}{C_{t-1}}\right)^2$$

(c) High-low-close volatility

$$S_t^2 = 0.5\ln\left(\frac{H_t}{L_t}\right)^2 - 0.39\ln\left(\frac{C_t}{C_{t-1}}\right)^2$$

$$V_t^2 = \frac{1}{n} \sum_n^n S_{t-i}^2$$

$$V_t = \sqrt{V_t^2}$$

Note that t may be a time interval rather than a single day. Then C_t is the last price of the period, and H_t and L_t are the highest and lowest prices of the interval.

In the close-to-close estimation, the volatility V_t is the standard deviation of the closing price ratios. Bookstaber states that this measurement will follow a χ^2 distribution and that the actual volatility during the current period t can be set within the error bounds defined by the distribution.

Relative Volatility

It is often convenient to filter trades by either high or low volatility. Sometimes, the absolute lows and highs are important, but relative highs and lows may work in many cases. *Relative volatility* (*RV*) can be defined as the volatility over a short period divided by the volatility over a longer period, where the longer period is typical of the normal volatility,

$$RV_t = \frac{V_t(n)}{V_t(m)}$$

where V_t is any of the volatility measures, and n and m are calculation periods, where $f \times n = m$, where $f >= 5$, but $f >= 10$ would be better.

Lagging the Longer Period One problem with the relative volatility, and many other comparative measures, is that the shorter calculation period is contained in the longer one. A better measure would be to lag the longer calculation so that it ends before the shorter one starts,

$$RV_t = \frac{V_t(n),\ i = t - n + 1, t}{V_t(m),\ j = t - m - n + 1, t - n}$$

Then the shorter calculation, n, goes from $t - n + 1$ to t, and the longer one, m, goes from $t - m - n + 1$ to $t - n$, non-overlapping periods. This method will also help on the back side of a volatile period, when the typical calculation includes the recent volatility, making the declining volatility seem normal, rather than still volatile.

Implied Volatility, *VIX*

Even easier than calculating the volatility yourself is to have a good measurement accessible at all times. The CBOE's volatility index, *VIX*, reflecting the *implied volatility* of the S&P options, is available on a real-time basis. The VIX was introduced in 1993 and only recently started trading as futures, valued at 1000 times the price. VIX was originally the volatility of an options index, OEX, a weighted value of the implied volatilities of 8 puts and calls in the S&P 100, expressed as a percentage of the index price. However, the futures contract is constructed from the forward 3-day volatilities of the S&P 500.

Although the OEX is no longer quoted, it is important to understand how the value of the VIX is calculated. If the VIX is 25%, and the SPX is 1600, then VIX is forecasting 25% volatility for at-the-money options, relative to the price of the SPX for 30-day rolling expiration period.[2] Because the 30-day calendar period is equivalent to about 21 trading days, and there are 252 trading days in the year, 1 standard deviation of the volatility (equal to a 25% move in the SPX at 1600) becomes

$$Implied\ range = 1600 \times 25\% \times \sqrt{\frac{21}{252}} = 115.47$$

Then, an implied volatility of 25% when the SPX is at 1600 is equal to a 68% (1 standard deviation) chance of a price change of ±115.47 within the next 30 calendar days (21 trading days).

The VIX is based on a very specific set of criteria that make it generic, rather than specific to any index or stock; however, its relative changes and extreme highs and low can make it very useful for trading. Figure 6.7 shows the VIX plotted below the cash S&P 500 index, SPX, for the now-famous period, March 2008 through March 2009. When the S&P hits its lowest price on October 24, 2008, VIX peaks at 89.53. Previously the VIX was trading near its lows of about 20. The VIX pattern, which is generally inverse to the S&P, leads to the belief that the S&P rises on low volatility and falls on high volatility. Another way of seeing this is that investors are exiting on high volatility and entering on low volatility. For that reason traders talk about buying the S&P when VIX is high and selling when it is low.

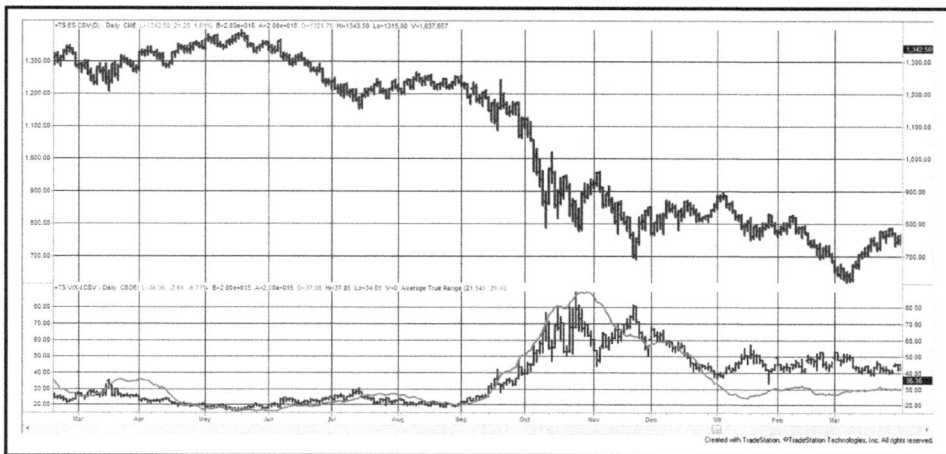

FIGURE 6.7 *e*Mini S&P (top) and the CBOE VIX Index with the Average True Range in the Bottom Panel.

[2] Andrew Fisher, "Teaching the Old VIX New Tricks," *Futures* (August 2001). Fisher explains the VIX calculations in addition to proposed improvements in iVIX.

For comparison, Figure 6.7 also shows the historic volatility in the lower panel. This is actually the 21-day average true range of the emini S&P, but it tracks the implied volatility closely except when prices are under stress. Remember that the implied volatility is what options traders believe will be the volatility *over the next 30 days*, while historic volatility is the actual market volatility *over the past 30 days* (actually 21 trading days). Note the key difference is that, right after the October decline the implied volatility dropped faster than the actual market volatility, then the implied volatility spiked again in late November when the actual volatility continued to fall.

■ Using Volatility for Trading

For many traders, volatility is essential to success. It has been embedded in many of the systems and methods discussed throughout this book, but this section will look at specific applications that use volatility.

Intraday Volatility and Volume

Intraday volume forms a smooth *U*-shaped pattern for domestic markets, and a similar but more complex pattern for markets that open in Europe but span U.S. trading hours.

Intraday volatility has a pattern that is identical to volume, highest at the open, then declining to its lowest point at mid-session, and rising again as the trading day ends. The closing volatility and volume are typically lower than the opening activity.[3] For this purpose, volatility (*VT*) was calculated

$$VT_t = \sqrt{\frac{1}{n-1} \sum_{i=t-n+1}^{t} \left(\ln\left(\frac{P_i}{P_{i-1}}\right) - \overline{P} \right)^2}$$

where n = calculation period
$\ln$ = natural log
P_i = price at time i
$\overline{P}$ = arithmetic mean of the natural log of price differences:

$$\overline{P} = \frac{1}{n} \sum_{i=t-n+1}^{t} \ln\left(\frac{P_i}{P_{i-1}}\right)$$

To find the correlation between the intraday pattern of volatility and that of volume, a simple linear regression can be solved

$$Volatility_t = a_t + b_t \times Volume_t + e_t$$

[3] Gunter Meissner and Sarp Cercioglu, "Trading Trends and Correlations," *Futures* (January 2003).

TABLE 6.1   Predicting the Trading Range of the S&P 500

Rule	Conditions Tested	Conclusion
1	`0 < L[1] - x`	Very good predictor, but few cases (161 at $x = -0.10$)
2	`0 > H[1] + x`	Modest predictor, but few cases (101 at $x = 0.60$)
3	`C[1] + x > 0 > C[1]`	Range got smaller when $x = 0.35$
4	`C[1] - x < 0 < C[1]`	Range got smaller when $x = 0.30$
5	`0 < C[1] - x`	Range tended to increase as x increased
6	`H[2] <= H[1] and L[2] >= L[1]`	No significance
7	`H[2] > H[1] and L[2] < L[1]`	Modest predictor of lower volatility
8	`Day of week`	Mon had lowest volatility, Tues and Fri the highest
9	`Average(TrueRange,3)[1] > x`	Higher average true range for 3 days was a very good predictor of higher volatility
10	`RSI(close,3)[1] < x`	When RSI < 40 good predictor of higher volatility

Source: William Brower, *The Inside Edge.*

where all values are calculated at time t. The resulting correlation, $R = 0.595$, is statistically significant for NASDAQ 100 volatility and volume. The correlation between volatility and volume are highest at the beginning and end of the day. Meissner and Cercioglu suggest that this volatility pattern, with the corresponding volume that provides liquidity, can be traded by being long options at the beginning and end of the day, profiting from the *gamma* (the rate of change of *delta*, which is the rate of change of the futures price with respect to the rate of change of the underlying asset). During the quiet mid-session period, a short options position may be used to profit from *theta,* the time decay.

Predicting Volatility with Trading Ranges

William Brower, in his publication *The Inside Edge,*[4] performed a thorough study of trading ranges, looking for when there would be a higher volatility tomorrow. This is an advantage for day traders and systems with short holding periods, and breakout systems in general. A summary of his results is shown in Table 6.1 for the S&P from 12/23/87 through 12/15/95. *O, H, L,* and *C* are the opening, high, low, and closing prices, and the notation [1] and [2] represent the prices 1 and 2 bars back.

Thomas Bierovic—On-Balance True Range

To visualize the change in volatility, Thomas Bierovic has created an *On-Balance True Range* by following the same rules as On-Balance Volume (*OBV*), but substituting the true range calculation for volume. He then calculates a 9-day exponential smoothing of the

---

[4] William Brower, *Inside Edge* (Inside Edge Systems, 24 Old Stagecoach Road, Redding, CT 06896, March/April 1996).

On-Balance True Range and uses the crossovers of the oscillator and smoothed oscillator to confirm signals. Although the highs and lows may come at nearly the same time as other oscillators, the relative peaks and valleys may offer the trader new insights. For many traders, this simple interpretation can help separate high and low volatility conditions.

VIX Trading Systems

The *VIX*, the index of implied volatility (see details in the previous section), can also be interpreted as the level of risk in the market. VIX is considered a mean-reverting indicator as the following strategies show.

Connors   Larry Connors has based a number of trading systems on the VIX. This strategy, called *Connors VIX Reversal 9, CVR 9*, is based on VIX range expansion, looking for higher prices in the S&P Index following a VIX expansion and lower prices following a VIX contraction.[5] Connors treats volatility as mean-reverting. Entries are based on a minor reversal in the VIX. The rules for buying (selling are the reverse) are:

1. Today's VIX high must be higher than the VIX high of the past 10 days.
2. Today's VIX must close below its open.
3. Yesterday's VIX must have closed above its open.
4. Today's VIX range must be greater than the ranges of the past 3 days.
5. If conditions 1–4 are met then *buy* S&P futures on the close and *exit* in 3 days.

Connors is actually looking for turning points in the VIX. The specific pattern that precedes a buy signal in the S&P ends with a range expansion. This expansion is likely to mark the end of a short-term upwards move in the VIX. A decline in the VIX that follows eases the way for a short-term rally in the S&P. Traders are more comfortable buying when volatility is dropping, or at least not at noticeably high levels. As with many other systems, this requires additional protective stops and position size management.

Another Connors mean-reverting VIX strategy[6] uses the RSI for timing. If

1. The S&P > 200-day moving average
2. The 2-day RSI of the VIX > 90
3. Today's VIX open > yesterday's VIX close

then *buy* on the close and *exit* when the 2-day RSI closes > 65.

MarketSci Blog   One of the more interesting websites is *MarketSci Blog*, which offers numerous creative strategies for equities trading. This one, published on March 1, 2011, takes a 10-day exponential smoothing (*EMA*) and a 10-day simple moving average (*SMA*), both applied to the VIX index, and *buys* the VIX when the EMA falls below the SMA, then *sells short* when the EMA moves above the SMA. It does this based on the concurrent closing prices. The rationale is that the EMA is faster than the SMA, given the same calculation period; therefore, it acts as a timing

---

[5] Larry Connors, "Timing Your S&P Trades with the VIX," *Futures* (June 2002).
[6] Connors, Larry, *Short-Term Strategies That Work* (Jersey City, NJ: Connors, 2008).

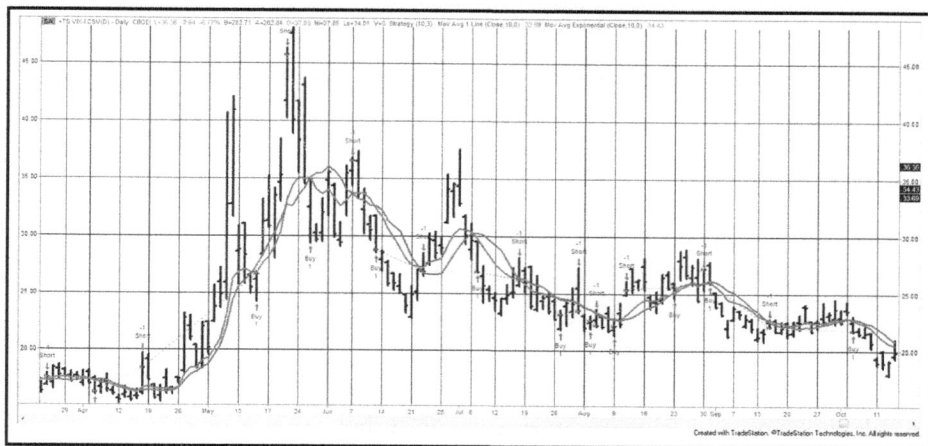

FIGURE 6.8 VIX Mean-Reverting Strategy from MarketSci Blog, Triggered by the EMA Crossing the SMA.

trigger. A fast execution is essential for mean-reverting trades. Figure 6.8 shows the VIX prices and the two trends for April to October 2010.

Figure 6.9 breaks down the profits from the VIX mean-reverting strategy into long only, short only, and both long and short. Unlike most other strategies, this is remarkably symmetric, with longs and shorts performing equally. It is important to note that this study was done using the VIX cash index, which is not tradable. There is a futures contract for VIX, but not enough data for a valid study.

Gerald Appel on VIX Gerald Appel[7] gives his own thoughts on trading VIX as

- *Buy* when there are high levels of VIX, implying broad pessimism.

- There are no reliable sell signals using VIX.

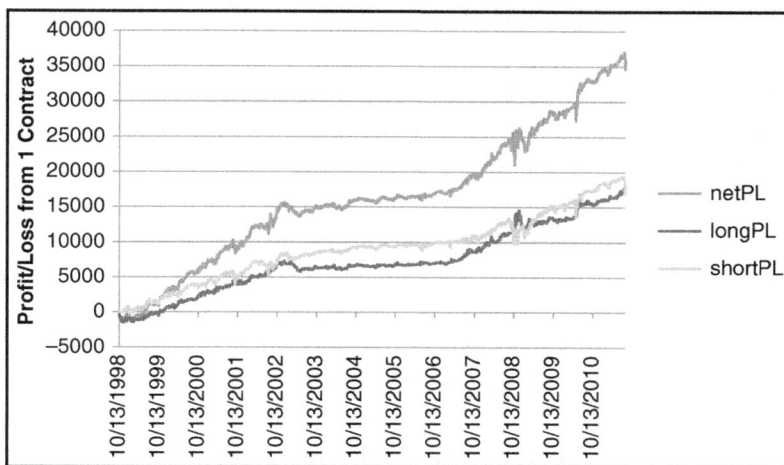

FIGURE 6.9 Profits from VIX Mean-Reverting Strategy, 1998–2011.

---

[7] Gerald Appel, *Power Tools for Active Traders* (Upper Saddle River, NJ: Financial Times, Prentice-Hall, 1999), 155.

- Volatility tends to increase during weaker market climates.

- The stock market is likely to advance for as long as volatility remains stable or decreasing.

Volatility System

Bookstaber[8] uses the average true range (*ATR*) over the past *n* days as the basis for a simple volatility strategy:

- *Buy* if the next close, C_t+_1, rises by more than $k \times ATR_t(n)$ from the current close C_t

- *Sell* if the next close, C_t+_1, falls by more than $k \times ATR_t(n)$ from the current close C_t

The volatility factor *k* is given as approximately 3, but can be varied higher or lower to make the trading signals less or more frequent, respectively. This method falls into the category of *volatility breakout*.

Profit Targets and Stop-Loss Orders

One of the most common uses of volatility is to make both profit-targets and stop-loss orders adapt to current market conditions. For that purpose, a method identical to Bookstaber, in the previous section, is most often used to define both; however, they are often applied differently.

Profit targets are best used for short-term trading and determined at the time of entry

$$PT_t = p_E \pm k \times ATR_{t-1}$$

where *PT* is the profit target, p_E is the trade entry price, and *k* is a constant, usually about 3. If the last entry was long, the target is added, and when it is short, the target value is subtracted from the entry price. The profit target is triggered by the intraday high or low price, rather than the close. The reason that profit targets are used most often in short-term trading, rather than in long-term trend following, is that shorter time intervals have a higher degree of market noise. Once profits are taken, you want prices to reverse and allow you to reenter at a better price, or reverse direction entirely. For long-term trend following, it is necessary to capture the *fat tail*; therefore, taking profits works counter to that notion. Once you exit a long-term trend by taking profits, and the trade continues to be profitable, it is necessary to reenter the trade to avoid losing that rare chance at an exceptionally large profit.

For *stop-losses*, the same $k \times ATR_{t-1}$ is used, but it is subtracted from the long entry and added to the short entry. In this case, when applying stops in a noisy market it is best to use the high and low to trigger the stop, but actually exit the position on the close. That way you take advantage of the market noise to improve the exit price. Stop-losses have the same problem as profit-targets when applied to long-term trend systems. If you are stopped out, but the trend is still intact, it is necessary to reenter the trade in order to avoid missing the rare but large profit.

---

[8] Richard Bookstaber, *The Complete Investment Book* (Glenview, IL: Scott, Foresman, 1985), 224–236.

▦ Trade Selection Using Volatility

High volatility is clearly related to greater risk, but low volatility may also mean that there is a smaller chance for profits. The following are reasonable expectations for selecting trades based on volatility:

- ▪ *Entering on very high volatility* is exposure to very high risk. Returns from high volatility trades may range from large profits to large losses. The net results may be a profit, but the return-to-risk ratio is likely to decline. Long-term performance may be best if these trades are avoided.

- ▪ *Entering on extreme low volatility* seems safe, but prices often have no direction and produce small, frequent losses. Waiting for an increase in activity before entering might improve returns. Contrary to this, some traders advocate entries when prices have had a short-term drop in volatility.

- ▪ *Exiting a position when prices become very volatile* should reduce both profits and risk, but may come too late. This is an issue best resolved by evaluating the specific system.

Eliminate or Delay?

Whenever a high or low volatility situation occurs at the time of an entry signal, there are two choices. The trade can be completely eliminated by *filtering,* or it can be delayed until the high volatility drops or the low volatility increases to an acceptable level. When a trade is filtered, it is necessary to track the trade that was not entered, to know when it was completed. Each new trade is subject to the volatility threshold at the time of its entry. A trade that is delayed pending a change in volatility can be entered any time volatility moves back into the acceptable range. The following sections look at these cases in more detail. Before starting, we can theorize that short-term trading would most likely eliminate, not delay, trades that fall outside the acceptable volatility range because there are many trades and each is held for a short time. At the other end of the spectrum are the long-term trend trades, held for weeks, that would suffer if the exceptionally large profit was missed. Then delaying the entry would be the best solution.

Constructing a Volatility Filter   Calculating the volatility is simple to program using any spreadsheet or strategy testing software. The following steps were used here:

1. Calculate a moving average trend. Use one fast trend and one slow trend.
2. Calculate the volatility, using any one of the methods described early in this chapter, but not including the volatility of the current day.
3. Enter a new trade (on the close) if today's volatility is (a) above the low filter threshold or (b) below the high filter threshold.
4. Exit a current position if the volatility is above the high filter threshold *and,* based on testing, (a) the current price change has moved in a profitable direction or (b) the current price change has moved in a losing direction.

These six different conditions will be applied to five very different markets: Eurodollars, Japanese yen, crude oil, IBM, and the S&P 500 over the period 1990 through mid-2011 to allow enough trades for the long-term trend to show valid results. We know that this interval contained exceptional and varied price moves.

The two trends used will be 10 and 60 days. A charge of $15 per trade per side will be used so that there will be some impact of trading more often. It is likely that some of these markets will not be profitable using these trends, but the results are more concerned with improvement rather than absolute profits.

Standard Deviation Measurement A standard deviation was used to determine the volatility threshold level because these levels are associated with probabilities. A high-volatility filter with a *1-standard deviation threshold* means that no trades were taken if the volatility was above the average volatility plus 1 standard deviation, the top 16% occurrences. A *2-standard deviation threshold* filters out volatility in the top 2.5%, and 3 *standard deviations* restricts only the top 0.13%. In all cases, a 20-day standard deviation will be used, comparable to VIX. Because the period is short, volatility can jump well beyond the normal 3-standard deviation maximum, and it may be necessary to test filter values above 3.

The program *TSM Moving Average* will used as the underlying strategy. This enters and exits trades based entirely on the direction of the moving average trendline, not on the price penetration of the trendline.

Entry Filter Results Table 6.2 shows the results of a 40-day moving average system (a moderately slow trend), buying when the trendline turns up and selling when it turns down, using a volatility entry filter that delays the entry until the threshold conditions are met. The data used was back-adjusted futures from 1990 through July 2011, except for Amazon, which began in May 1997. Costs were $15. Results are expressed as total profits or losses, profit factor (gross profits divided by gross losses), number of trades, percentage of profitable trades, and profits per contract or per share (for Amazon). Each market has three lines, the first showing the results of the moving average system with no entry filters, the second reflecting only trades below the low filter, and the third only trades above the high filter.

The low filters shown on each of the second lines in column 2 were found by optimizing the filter times the standard deviation of returns over the past 20 days over the range from 0.05 to 1.0 in steps of 0.05. Eurodollar interest rates show that the optimal threshold was 0.25, which reduced trades by 30% and increased profits per trade by 47%. All of the markets show significant increases in performance when only low volatility trades were taken. In the case of the S&P, a losing moving average performance will normally be improved by removing trades. All markets show improvements when the threshold level is below 0.35.

With the high volatility filter, which allows trades only above its threshold level, we expected to show profits but at higher risk; however, it did better than expectations. Test inputs were 0.25 to 3.0 in steps of 0.05. The S&P was the only market that chose the maximum filter value, trying to remove as many trades as possible. Other

TABLE 6.2 Tests of Low and High Threshold Filters, from 1990 through July 2011, Except for Amazon, Which Began in May 1997

Market	Test	$PL	Profit Factor	Number of Trades	% Prof Trades	Profits/ Trade
Eurodollars	No filters	41,087	2.11	247	31.5	166
	< 0.25	42,537	2.5	175	34.5	244
	> 1.60	42,425	2.56	158	37.4	268
Euro FX	No filters	100,062	1.33	302	35.4	331
	< 0.30	91,225	1.36	233	37.7	391
	> 0.55	102,975	1.36	282	36.5	365
Crude oil	No filters	121,450	1.49	323	36.8	376
	< 0.35	135,170	1.67	246	41.9	549
	> 2.55	126,560	2.11	105	41.9	1205
S&P	No filters	−37,187	0.83	378	28.3	−98
	< 0.05	6,650	1.07	153	29.4	43
	> 3.0*	3,825	1.06	88	30.7	43
AMZN	No filters	58.41	1.16	190	32.6	0.31
	< 0.15	124.10	1.51	115	36.5	1.08
	> 1.30	96.09	1.33	133	37.6	0.72

markets all showed good improvement, but the threshold levels were not consistent, depending on the nature of price movement. Crude oil, which has had the most volatility and the largest price moves, shows best profits with a threshold at 2.55, a level that would eliminate most trades in other markets.

Figure 6.10 shows the net equity from the Eurodollar interest rate futures using the high and low filters separately. Results are similar because the 20-day standard deviation is

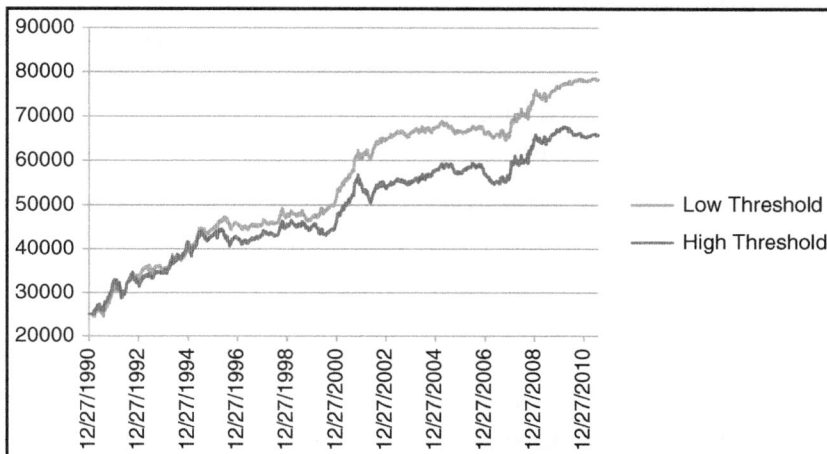

FIGURE 6.10 Net Equity Resulting from Eurodollar Rates Using a 40-Day Moving Average and a Low Filter of 0.25 Compared to a High Filter of 1.60.

highly variable and both filters will eventually allow an entry to the same trade, but at different places. As we can see from the chart, the low volatility entries outperform the high volatility and produced a smoother return stream. If we calculate the information ratios for the two tests, rather than use the profit factor, we see that the low-volatility filter has a return of 6.08% with a volatility of 5.32% while the high filter has a return of 4.85% with volatility of 5.59%. That gives the low filter a ratio of 1.143 compared to 0.867 for the high filter, considerably better.

This test confirms the popular notion that entering on low volatility is preferable. Even without any high-volatility trades, this seems to be a safe approach. The program *TSM Moving Average Filtered*, available on the Companion Website, was used for testing.

High Volatility Exits: Reducing the Risk   It seems natural to think that you may be able to reduce risk by exiting a trade when volatility becomes very high. It also may be too late because you may have already been exposed to the worst of the volatility. If prices jumped because of a price shock, then the highest volatility would have occurred at the moment of the shock. On the other hand, if prices have been moving higher for weeks, and are becoming very volatile at the top of a move, then exiting could save a lot of aggravation. If a market is noisy, then volatile price jumps are frequent and short-lived. In those situations, you should close out positions when a volatile move is profitable because profits will soon disappear. Or, if the volatile move is an immediate loss, then waiting before you exit should recover at least part of the loss. The opposite is true for a trending market. A good price move should be followed by more profits, and a bad move by further losses.

A high-volatility exit is not the same as profit-taking because it is not targeting a specific profit for the trade, but looking only at the risk of a 1-day move. One of the more difficult tests should be U.S. 30-year bonds with a long calculation period because profits are normally the result of holding onto the trade until the end, capturing the fat tail. Nevertheless, we will test high-volatility exits with the following rules:

1. Use a 40-day moving average and generate buy and sell signals when the trend-line turns up and down.
2. Calculate the 20-day volatility as the standard deviation of the 20-day price returns.
3. Exit the current trade, whether long or short, when today's returns are greater than the previous 20-day volatility times a factor.
4. If a high-volatility exit occurs, do not reenter until the trend changes.

Based on bond futures prices from 2000 through July 2011, Table 6.3 shows the results. Line 1 is the benchmark performance of the 40-day moving average without

TABLE 6.3	Test Results for High-Volatility Exits, 30-Year Bonds, 2000 through July 2011				
Test	Net PL	Profit Factor	Number of Trades	% Prof Trades	Profit / Trade
No HV exits	4,500	1.02	350	36.0	12
Exit factor 10	12,968	1.07	350	40.0	37
Exit and reenter	34,781	1.16	387	40.8	89

high-volatility exits. Line 2 has the same entries but exits when the returns are 10 times the 20-day volatility. Results are somewhat better, but then only the most extreme moves were used to exit.

Remembering that trend systems need to capture as much of the very good moves as possible, we will add a *reset rule*. We will be able to reenter the market in the same direction as the trade just exited, but only when the volatility drops to one-quarter the volatility (the daily return) on the day of the exit. The concept is that, at one-quarter the volatility, the market is more-or-less back to normal. Results of that test are shown on line 3 and are considerably better.

Ranking Based on Volatility   Gerald Appel[9] offers an additional approach to trade selection by creating a ranking method for mutual funds.

- Select only funds with average to below average volatility.

- Add the 3-month and 12-month performance together to get a single value.

- Rank the funds.

- Only invest in the top 10%.

Trade Selection Summary

Once you have a basic system, the next step is to decide whether you can eliminate some of the losing trades without eliminating the profitable ones. In the extreme, we want to eliminate *all* of the losing trades, even if we reduce some of the profits; of course, that is impossible. Every system has a risk, even so-called riskless trades. Arbitrage, when done properly, has virtually no risk; however, it may be so competitive that the opportunities are rare and the margin of profit small. In the final analysis, you can't remove the risk, only delay it or move it around. If your system shows that it has essentially no risk, then it's important to rethink your development process to find the flaw.

Nothing is free. Good trading is not a matter of hitting it rich on a single short position, it is grinding out a profit day by day and week by week. Occasionally, if you follow new markets, you might find an opportunity that others have not yet seen. If you act fast, you can capitalize on this for a short time, until others see the same situation. Then bigger players come in and push you out. In turn, they are followed by other investors who combine to remove all the profit opportunity, even for themselves. At the same time, other opportunities surface.

When selecting trades to eliminate, the easiest place to begin is by associating performance with volatility or price level. While some systems perform better in an environment of higher volatility, your strategy may show the best return relative to risk when there is less volatility. When you filter trades you will always get rid of good ones while, hopefully, removing more of the bad ones.

---

[9] Gerald Appel, *Power Tools for Active Traders* (New Jersey: Financial Times, Prentice-Hall, 1999)

▪ Liquidity

Many systems that have excellent historic backtests fail when they are actually traded. These include models based on both intraday and daily data. One reason for this disappointing performance is the lack of understanding of market liquidity at the time of execution. Consider two systems:

1. A *trend-following method,* which will trigger buy or sell orders as prices rise or fall during the day.
2. A *countertrend system,* which sells and buys at relative intraday highs or lows.

Although each system intends to profit with their opposing philosophies, both act when prices make a relatively unusual move. Figure 6.11 shows the normal distribution of intraday volume and the profitability associated with this distribution.[10]

The solid line *bb'* is the actual volume on an ideally normal day. Volume is greatest at the median *M* and declines sharply to the high and low endpoints *H* and *L,* where only one trade may have occurred. As we know from previous sections, the time of highest volume will be near the open and close of trading; therefore, *M* will actually occur at the beginning or end of the day, while the end points of *bb'* will occur near midday.

The dotted line *cc'* represents the apparent profit for a countertrend system that makes the assumption of a straight-line volume distribution. The endpoints are shown to contribute the largest part of the profits when, in reality, no executions may have been possible near those levels. Assuming the ability to execute at all points on the actual distribution *bb'*, the approximate profit contribution is shown as *dd'*.

For trend-following systems, no profits should be expected when buy or sell orders are placed at the extremes of the day. The actual price distribution *bb'* is the maximum that could be expected from such a system; in reality, the first day is usually a loss.

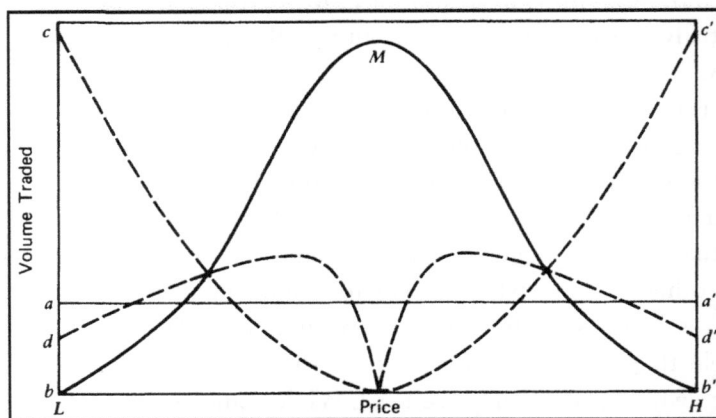

FIGURE 6.11 **Daily Price/Volume Distribution Shows Liquidity.**

[10] Gary Ginter and Joseph J. Ritchie, "Data Errors and Profit Distortions," in Perry J. Kaufman, ed., *Technical Analysis in Commodities* (New York: John Wiley & Sons, 1980).

◼ Trends and Price Noise

Throughout this book there are techniques that try to find the underlying trend when the price direction is not clear. The trader who enters a new trend sooner will be more profitable, but the erratic behavior of prices makes a faster response less reliable. What makes a trend so difficult to identify is *noise*. Noise is the erratic movement of price and, by definition, it is unpredictable. In engineering, this type of behavior that shows no patterns is called *white noise,* yet the noise that we see in price movement has very definite statistical attributes. When measuring noise using the efficiency ratio, or fractal efficiency, different markets had different levels of noise, but that the equity index markets had the most noise and short-term rates the least. Also, developing markets had low noise while markets in the major industrialized countries had more noise. As the financial systems mature, more investors participate, and noise increases. In this section we will look at another aspect of noise, how it directly affects trading. It is still treated as a big picture item, more important conceptually.

Noise is the product of a large number of market participants buying and selling at different times for different purposes. Each has its own objectives and time frame. Noise can be the result of price shocks—unexpected events, in particular news or economic reports, that causes change that persists for varying periods into the future. Noise has most of the qualities of a sequence of random numbers. Nearly half of all price moves change direction on the next day; about 25% of all price moves continue in the same direction for two days, 12.5% for three days, and so on. These patterns should already be familiar to analysts. The size of a price move, or price shock, also appears to be random; that is, 50% are quite small, 25% are twice as large, 12.5% are four times as large, and a few are extremely large.

Then how can you tell if a price move up is an indication of a new direction or simply more noise? The answer is that you cannot know for sure until prices continue in the same direction. If you are a fundamental analyst, a structural change in the market is as close as you get to a definite change. For example, the Fed continued to lower interest rates following the stock market peak in 2000 in order to stimulate economic growth and prevent a deep recession. By the end of 2003, equity prices had been rising for six months and interest rates were at a 50-year low. A move by the Fed that raises rates would be a structural change, a clear sign that it was more concerned with the prospects of inflation and convinced that that economic growth would continue without further stimulation. A trader would expect that a short position in long-term maturity, fixed income futures, would be sound.

A systematic trader, studying only the numbers, could identify this specific structural change by following the government's lending rate, the prime rate, or a combination of short-term rates, in combination with the price of market being traded. But at this point we are only concerned with how to recognize a trend change looking at a single price series.

Figures 6.12 a–c show how noise varies for different markets and how it affects trend trading. The first is Eurodollar interest rates, typical of a very low-noise market.

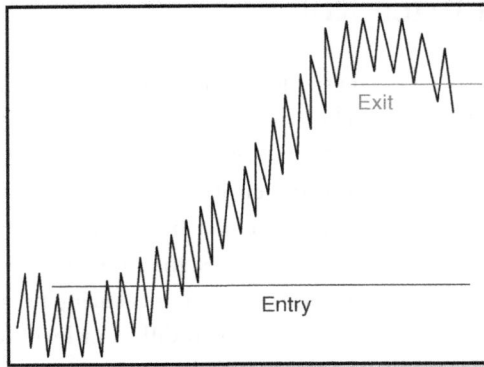

FIGURE 6.12a **A Low Noise Market Allows Sooner Entries and Exits Resulting in Larger per Trade Profits.**

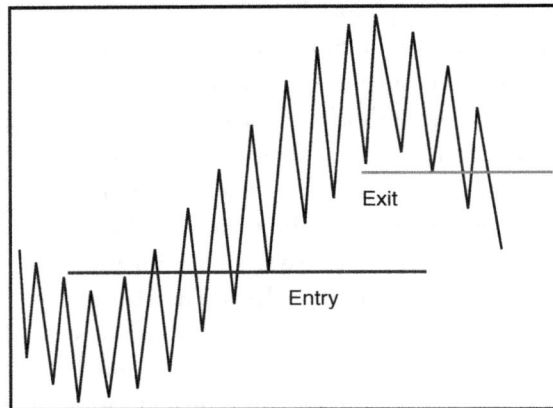

FIGURE 6.12b **Increased Noise Causes Entries and Exits to be Delayed, Resulting in Less Profit for the Same-Size Move.**

Because of less noise, a simple breakout strategy would be able to identify a change of direction in time to capture a large percentage of the price move. The second part represents a market with more noise, but still identifiable trends, such as the EURUSD. A higher level of noise means that the trend is identified later and the exit later, resulting in smaller profits for about the same size move as Eurodollars. The third figure represents the equity index markets, which have exceptionally large noise. By the time the new trend can be identified, entered, and finally exited, there is no profit.

We can improve our chances of entering a new trend, and not being fooled by noise, by waiting until the price changes direction by a larger amount. A small price change could easily be noise, but as the price change gets larger, the chance of being a true trend increases quickly. This is the reason why a long-term trend is more reliable than a short-term one.

Figure 6.13 tries to visualize the way noise and the trend calculation period work together. Along the bottom are the absolute returns, showing frequent "normal" returns and occasional price shocks, some smaller, some larger. When a fast trend period is used,

THE INTEGRATION OF TECHNICAL ANALYSIS

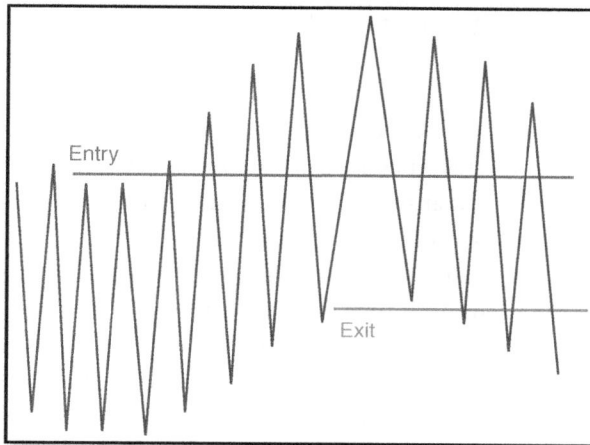

FIGURE 6.12c High-Noise Markets, Typical of an Equity Index in a Major Industrialized Country, Cause Entries and Exits That Are Too Late to Net a Profit.

it experiences a large number of price shocks that might cause the trend to change. As the trend period gets longer, the trend lags behind, and fewer shocks will trigger a trend change. This results in the longer trends being more reliable, although they will suffer from markets swings while holding onto the same trade. There is always the exceptional price shock that affects any trend, as shown toward the right part of the illustration.

As markets evolve, noise increases. To capture the same returns, it may be necessary to use a longer calculation period for trends. If you are already doing that, then expect smaller returns. One alternative is to take advantage of the noise and use mean reversion methods, emphasizing the shorter holding periods. Noise is dominant in the short term and trends in the long term.

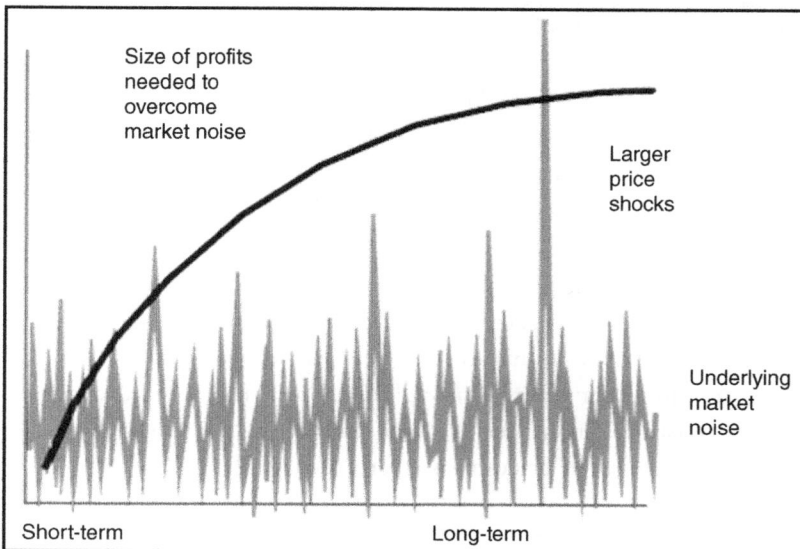

FIGURE 6.13 How the Trend Calculation Period (the Curved Line) Relates to Market Noise.

Trends and Interest Rate Carry

In the environment of exceptionally low interest rates during 2010–2012, an interesting new situation has developed expressed by the question "Can you profit from using a trend system for interest rates when rates are near zero?" Certainly, there seems to be a good reason for believing that there is little upside profit trading 10-year notes and much greater downside risk if yields suddenly increase. Yet, this is not really the case.

Trading interest rate futures involves rolling into the new contract every three months ahead of expiration. Each time the data rolls into the next delivery month, it shifts from about 15 days to expiration to at least 105 days to expiration. The net interest on 105 days is much greater than 15 days, so the price of the contract will be lower because it is either discounted (as in the case of short-term rates) or simply reflecting a higher yield-to-maturity. If this situation persists for many months, or even years, then staying long the interest rates continues to extract the carry. While that may not be a large profit in any one contract, the accumulated returns can be significant.

Fractals, Chaos, and Entropy

Another area that has captured the interest of market analysts is chaos. *Chaos theory* is a way to describe the complex behavior of nonlinear systems, those that cannot be described by a straight line. It is also called *nonlinear dynamics*. Chaotic systems appear, at first, to be random but turn out to be "not without any form or method." One explanation is that small occurrences significantly affect the outcomes of seemingly unrelated events. If we think of the effects of the continuous flow of news on prices, the most recent may be most significant, but that fades at the same time other news arrives.

One method of measuring chaotic systems is with various geometric shapes. This effort has resulted in an area of mathematics now called *fractal geometry;* its approach strikes a true note about how the real world of numbers actually works.[11] All of us have been taught Euclidean geometry in school; it is the world of straight lines and clean edges in which we can measure the length of a line or the area of a rectangle very easily. In the real world, however, there are no straight lines; if you look closely enough—using a microscope if necessary—all "straight lines" have ragged edges and all may be described as chaotic.

Fractal Dimension

In fractal geometry we find that there is a way of representing the irregularity of numbers and the formations seen in nature. We first must accept the notion that there are no *whole* numbers in nature, that real-world objects are more likely to be described as fractional, or having a *fractal dimension*. The classic example of this is the algebra of coastline dimension. We will see that the questions "How long is the coastline?" and "How far did prices move?" are very similar.

---

[11] An excellent discussion of this topic can be found in Edgar Peters, *Chaos and Order in the Capital Markets* (New York: John Wiley & Sons, 1991). The coastline example is originally credited to Benoit Mandelbrot. Other books can be found by searching the Internet for "Chaos Theory in Financial Markets."

The answer to both of these questions is "That depends on how it is measured." Expanding on an example earlier in this book, consider the problem of measuring the coastline of Australia using a large wall map. If we take a 12-inch ruler, and placed each end on a part of the coastline, we might find that the coastline is about 10 feet (perhaps 10,000 miles according to the scale). Using a 12-inch ruler requires that we cross over parts of the coast that jut out into the water; in other cases we might span a large harbor in order to get both ends of the ruler to touch the coastline. Had we taken a slightly smaller ruler we would have been more accurate and perhaps have found the coastline to be 15,000 miles; an even smaller ruler would have followed the contours better and found 20,000 miles of coast. As the ruler gets smaller the coastline appears to get longer. If we had an infinitely small ruler, the coast would be infinitely long. There is really no correct answer to the question, "How long is the coastline?" It all depends on your ruler.

Fractal dimension is the degree of roughness or irregularity of a structure or system. In many chaotic systems there is a constant fractal dimension; that is, the interval used for measuring will have a predictable impact on the resulting values in a manner similar to a normal distribution. Therefore, if we used a 12-inch ruler to get 10,000 miles of coastline, we might expect a predictable relationship of coastline to ruler:

24-inch ruler	5,000-mile coastline
12-inch ruler	10,000-mile coastline
6-inch ruler	20,000-mile coastline

Note that the large 24-inch ruler returns a value that is actually smaller than what we believe is a reasonable answer. This is because, when you place a long ruler from one coastal point to another on the map, it cuts across part of the land mass.

Using Fractal Efficiency

The Kaufman's *Efficiency Ratio* is formed by dividing the absolute value of the net change in price movement over n periods by the sum of all component moves, taken as positive numbers, over the same n periods. If the ratio approaches the value 1.0 then the movement is smooth (not chaotic); if the ratio approaches 0, then there is great inefficiency, chaos, or noise. This same measurement has been renamed *fractal efficiency*. Kaufman related this to trending and nontrending patterns, when the ratio approached 1.0 and 0, respectively. While each market has its unique underlying level of noise, the measurement of fractal efficiency should be consistent over all markets. Markets may vary in volatility although their chaotic behavior is technically the same; therefore, theoretically, the characteristics of one market may be compared to others by matching both the fractal efficiency and volatility. In reality, there are small differences in fractal efficiency due to the various participation and liquidity of markets; however, once these differences have been considered, the treatment of price behavior can be the same.

The interpretation of fractal efficiency as noise allows trading rules to be developed. For example, a market with less noise should be entered quickly using a trending system, while it would be best to wait for a better price if the market has been rated as high noise. A noisy market is one that continues to change direction, while an efficient market is smooth. When viewed in the long term, the level of market noise should determine the type of strategy that should be applied to each market. These characteristics are important in choosing trading rules and in turning a theoretical model into a profitable trading system.

Chaotic Patterns and Market Behavior

Chaotic patterns in prices are easy to visualize but very difficult to measure. There would be no problem in predicting price direction if every participant reacted in the same way to the same event, much the way a single planet would smoothly orbit a single sun. In the real world nothing is quite as simple. Consider the pattern of prices represented as nearby moons, *a* and *b*, that are each circling nearby planets of equal mass, *P1* and *P2*. Because the planets are larger than the moons, they are called *attractors*. We will get a wobbly pattern whenever the moon passes across the midpoint where one attractor is stronger than the other, shown as a straight line in Figure 6.14a. A moon at point *a* is most affected by the nearest attractor, *P1*, but as it circles it becomes closer to *P2* and tries to form an orbit around that planet. It might form a figure-8 pattern as it switches between *P1* and *P2*, ending up in location *b* on the far side of *P2*. The possible patterns are too complex, and they vary based on the distance between *P1* and *P2* and the size of *P2* compared to *P1*. If attractor *P2* is much larger than *P1*, as in Figure 6.14b, there will simply be a distortion

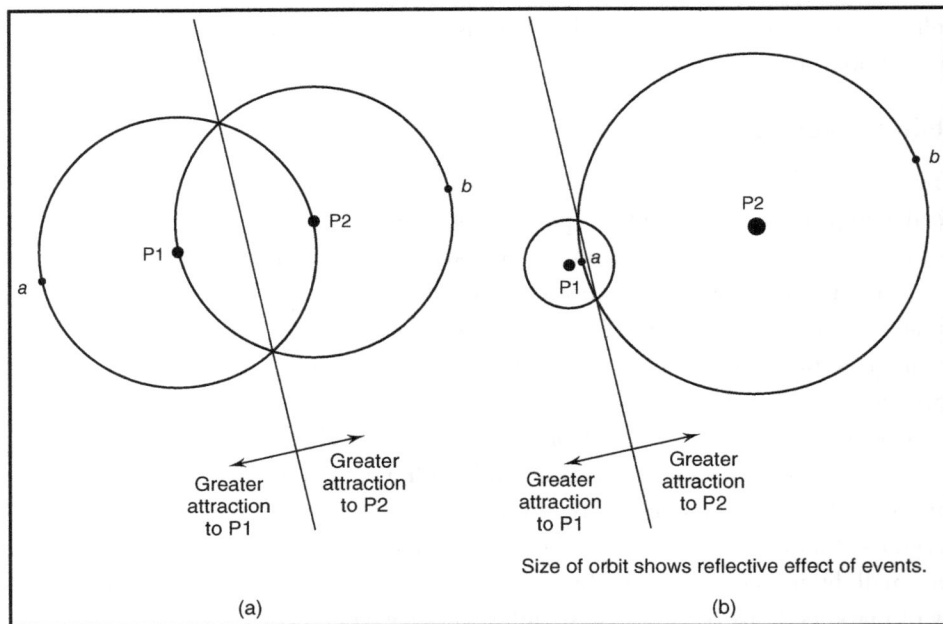

FIGURE 6.14 (a) Equal Attractors Cause a Symmetric Pattern, Often a Figure 8, that Switches between P1 and P2. (b) Very Unequal Attractors Show Only a Small Disturbance in a Regular Orbit.

in the orbit around *P2* at the location of the straight line, rather than a switching of orbits from one planet to another.

As complex as these patterns might get, they are simple when compared to reality. Each day brings events of varying importance into the market, acting as attractors. Each attractor has an initial importance that loses value over time. To make matters worse, we cannot always predict when a new attractor, or news event, will appear. When we can predict the time, such as an economic report, we cannot predict the impact. This makes the chaotic pattern very similar to raindrops falling on a pond. Each new drop, equivalent to a new event, hits at an unpredictable time and place, with variable size, and forms circular ripples. These ripples dissipate as they get further away from the point of contact in the same way that the importance of an event fades away over time. The interesting aspect of the raindrop analogy is that, while we cannot predict where the next raindrop will fall, once it has landed we can completely determine its effects—until the next drop hits. This analogy is remarkably similar to the market. The frequency and size of price shocks are like rain drops; occasionally there is a large one that overwhelms the smaller events, the market noise, for a short time.

Entropy—Predicting by Similar Situations

Forecasting the future by finding a similar combination of factors, *similar conditions,* that occurred in the past has always been a technique used by fundamental analysts. It is necessary to match the state of major economic indicators with the less quantifiable government policy, then look at how the prices reacted to these similar setups.[12] The entire area of charting, traditionally called *technical analysis,* is based on a predictable outcome following a specific chart pattern. These patterns can be simple or very complex, exist in a single time frame or be the composite of multiple time frames.

There is one mathematical method that comes closest to being able to identify similarities in price patterns. *Conditional entropy* can measure the probability that two patterns are similar. The higher the value of conditional entropy, the more likely the results of a past pattern will predict the results of a current pattern.[13] This has an analogy in *autocorrelation,* which measures the ability of past data to predict future data.

Entropy *Entropy,* the basis for this more advanced form, is a measurement of expectations. If the output of a system is known, and there is no uncertainty, the value of the entropy formula is zero. When entropy is low, the state of the system is easy to predict. As the output becomes less certain, the value approaches 1, and there is more disorder. Entropy, *H,* is defined as a function of price, *x,*

$$H(x) = -\sum_{x=i}^{n} p_i(x) \log_2 p_i(x)$$

[12] A data service, LIM (Logical Information Machines), provides both extensive fundamental and price data along with tools for comparing past events and their outcomes.

[13] The mathematics for conditional entropy, with excellent examples, is located on the website http://tecfa.unige.ch and was written by Phillippe Lemay. This section is adapted from his work.

where x can have n different values, and $p_i(x)$ is the probability that the outcome will be the ith value of x. When the system has only one possible outcome, $n = 1$, then $H(x) = 0$. If all n possible outcomes have an equal probability, then uncertainty is maximized, and $H(x) = \log(n)$. Therefore, if there are 16 possible outcomes, the maximum entropy is 4. It is convenient to normalize the value of the entry by dividing by the maximum value $\log(n)$.

As an example, consider the price moves that follow a particular chart pattern, where prices close in the upper 10% of the daily trading range and the stock is above its 200-day moving average. The hypothetical frequency of the next day's move is shown in Table 6.4. The calculations in the columns follow the formula $H(x)$ and show the result $H(pattern) = 2.20$. The maximum entropy for a 6-scale variable is $\log_2(6) = 2.58$; therefore, there is considerable uncertainty in the ability of this pattern to forecast 1 day ahead.

Conditional Entropy   *Conditional entropy* will give us the probability of the outcome based on the current price pattern being similar to a previous price pattern. But first we need to create a frequency distribution to use as a basis for the calculations. Table 6.5 gives the number of times that an upwards price change occurred given the

TABLE 6.4   **Frequency of Price Moves Following a Known Pattern, plus Entropy Calculations**

Price Move in %	Frequency	Probability	$\log_2(\text{prob})$	$\text{prob} \times \log_2(\text{prob})$
+3	33	0.13	−2.98	−0.38
+2	87	0.33	−1.58	−0.53
+1	84	0.32	−1.64	−0.53
−1	35	0.13	−2.90	−0.39
−2	14	0.05	−4.22	−0.23
−3	8	0.03	−5.03	−0.15
Sum	261	1.00	−18.35	−2.20

TABLE 6.5   **Frequency of Price Moves Following the Completeness of the Chart Pattern When Prices Are above the 200-Day Moving Average. The value 1 represents the completed pattern and 5 is the beginning of the pattern.**

Completeness of Chart Pattern	Price Change Next Day in %					
	+3	+2	+1	−1	−2	−3
1	19	4				
2	11	63	64	3	1	
3	2	16	18	20	2	2
4	1	4	1	9	6	2
5			1	2	4	3
6				1	1	1

TABLE 6.6 **Conditional Probabilities of a Price Change Given the Completeness of a Pattern. Values Correspond to Table 6.5.**

Completeness of Chart Pattern	Price Change Next Day in %					
	+3	+2	+1	−1	−2	−3
1	0.83	0.17				
2	0.08	0.44	0.45	0.02	0.01	
3	0.03	0.27	0.3	0.33	0.03	0.03
4	0.04	0.17	0.04	0.39	0.26	0.09
5			0.1	0.2	0.4	0.3
6				0.33	0.33	0.33

completeness of a chart pattern while the current price was above the 200-day moving average. The value 1 on the left scale indicates that the pattern was complete; the value 6 is a minimum recognition of the pattern. The top scale shows the percentage change in price on the next day. The frequencies show that price changes of 1% and 2% were most common when the chart pattern was near completion but not yet fully completed.

Conditional probabilities can be calculated from the frequency distribution in Table 6.5. These are shown in Table 6.6. To compute the conditional probability of state j of variable Y (the dependent variable) given state i of variable X (the independent variable, the past pattern), we write $p(Y = j \mid X = i)$. Then the conditional probability is computed by dividing the frequency of occurrence of the two states, n_{ij}, by the total frequency of state i, given as n_i. Then the probability of Y conditioned on X is

$$P_{j|i} = \frac{n_{ij}}{n_i}$$

In this hypothetical example, the probability is highest, and the price moves the most, when the chart pattern is complete. In a test with real data, we might expect the two values in row 2, columns +2 and +1 to show the greatest probabilities. The values in the lower right corner are high, but are based on a sample of only 1 value; therefore, they are not reliable.

The conditional probabilities can then be entered into the final formula for conditional entropy. The conditional entropy is the average sum of the entropies based on the conditional probability, H, of Y (the second event or price change) conditioned on X (the first event or completeness of pattern)

$$H(y \mid x) = -\sum_{x=i}^{t_1} P_i(x) \sum_{y=j}^{t_2} P_{ij}(y \mid x) \log_2 P_{ij}(y \mid x)$$

The higher the value of H, the greater the predictive value.

■ Neural Networks

Neural networks are recognized as a powerful tool for uncovering market relationships.[14] The technique offers exceptional ability for discovering nonlinear relationships between any combination of fundamental information, technical indicators, and price data. Its disadvantage is that it is so powerful that, without proper control, it will find relationships that exist only by chance.[15]

Although the idea and words for the computerized neural network are based on the biological functions of the human brain, an *artificial neural network* (ANN) is not a model of a brain, nor does it learn in the human sense. It is simply very good at finding patterns, whether they are continuous or discrete, appearing at different times.

The operation of an artificial neural network can be thought of as *a feedback process,* similar to the Pavlovian approach to training a dog:

1. A bell rings.
2. The dog runs to 1 of 3 bowls.
3. If right, the dog gets a treat; if wrong, the dog gets a shock.
4. If trained, stop; if not trained, go back to Step 1.

Terminology of Neural Networks

The terminology used in the computerized neural network is drawn from the human biological counterpart, shown in Figure 6.15. The following are the principal elements.

■ *Neurons* are the cells that compose the brain; they process and store information.

■ *Networks* are groups of neurons.

■ *Dendrites* are receivers of information, passing it directly to the neurons.

■ *Axons* are pathways that come out of the neuron and allow information to pass from one neuron to another.

■ *Synapses* exist on the path between neurons and may inhibit or enhance the flow of information between neurons. They can be considered *selectors.*

THE INTEGRATION OF TECHNICAL ANALYSIS

---

[14] Parts of this section are based on Perry Kaufman, *Smarter Trading* (New York: McGraw-Hill, 1995), 164–171.

[15] Readers are referred to E. Michael Azoff, *Neural Network Time Series Forecasting of Financial Markets* (New York: John Wiley & Sons, 1994); Robert Trippi, *Neural Networks in Finance and Investing*, 2nd ed. (New York: McGraw-Hill, 1996); Apostolos-Paul Refenes, *Neural Networks in Capital Markets* (New York: John Wiley & Sons, 1995); and Edward Gately, *Neural Networks for Financial Forecasting* (New York: John Wiley & Sons, 1996), for a more introductory approach. It seems that very little has been published during the past 10 years although there is more software available.

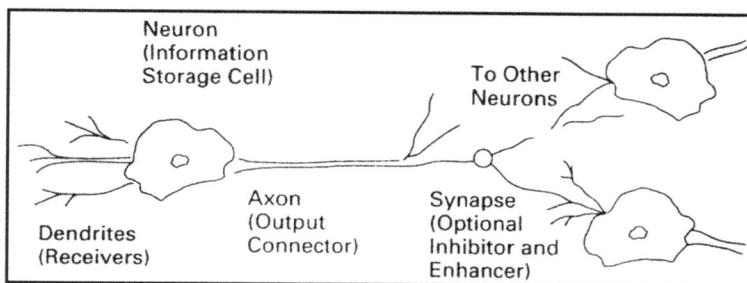

FIGURE 6.15 A Biological Neural Network. Information is received through dendrites and passed to a neuron for storage. Data are shared by other cells by moving through the output connector, called an axon. A synapse may be located on the path between some individual neurons or neural networks; they select the relevant data by inhibiting or enhancing the flow.

Source: Perry Kaufman, *Smarter Trading* (New York: McGraw-Hill, 1995), 165.

Artificial Neural Networks

Using essentially the same structure as a biological neural network, the computerized or artificial neural network (ANN) can generate a decision on the direction of the stock market.[16] It relies heavily on the synapses, which are interpreted as weighting factors in this process. To achieve its result it will also combine inputs that interact with one another into a single, more complex piece of data using layers of neurons, as shown in Figure 6.16, a classic 3-layer neural network. The ANN will modify these weighting factors in order to minimize the output error when compared to known results (the learning phase). It differs from a least squares regression because it includes linear, nonlinear, and pattern recognition relationships.

To be most efficient and avoid overfitting, the inputs to the ANN should be those factors considered most relevant to the direction of stock prices. The five items chosen here were the Gross Domestic Product (GDP), unemployment, manufacturing or inventories, interest rates, and the value of the U.S. dollar—all readily available data. Each of these items is input and stored in separate Layer-1 neurons. Changing the values in these neurons may have a positive or negative effect on the final output, which is the expected direction of stock prices. An improved GDP, lower unemployment, lower inventories, and a lower U.S. dollar are all good signs for economic growth and result in the possibility of higher interest rates. Higher rates are a defensive action by the Federal Reserve to prevent inflation with the eventual consequence of a decline in stock prices. Interest rates themselves have a direct effect on stock prices, improving corporate profits as the cost of borrowing declines.

---

[16] The website www.cs.stir.ac.uk, featuring a description by Professor Leslie Smith, Centre for Cognitive and Computational Neuroscience, University of Stirling, U.K., was found to have very useful information.

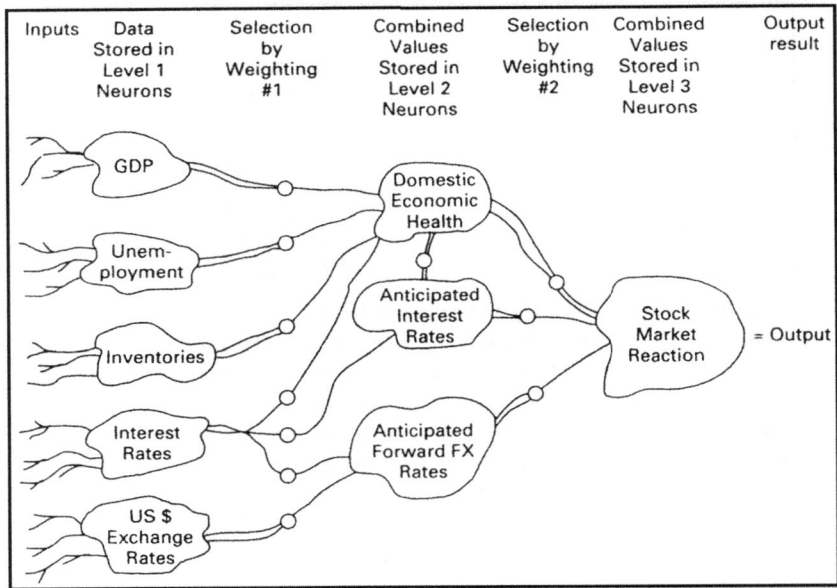

FIGURE 6.16 A 3-Layer Artificial Neural Network to Determine the Direction of Stock Prices.

Source: Perry Kaufman, *Smarter Trading* (New York: McGraw-Hill, 1995), 166.

Each neuron in Layer 1, which receives the data from the dendrites, is connected to a second layer of neurons through a synapse. Each synapse can be used to restrict or enhance information by assigning a weighting factor. For example, if changes in unemployment have a greater ultimate impact on stock prices than changes in the GDP, then it may receive a weight of 1.5 compared to 0.9 for the GDP. If very small changes in any of the data are deemed unimportant to the result, then the synapse can act as a threshold and only allow data to pass if it exceeds a minimum value. If the data is irrelevant, it gets a weighting factor of zero; if it reacts contrary to the result, the weighting factor will be negative.

The second layer of neurons is used to combine initial data into significant subgroups by trial and error. To allow this to happen, every neuron in Layer 1 must be connected to every neuron in Layer 2 by its own axon containing a synapse. Figure 6.16 shows the significant groupings that might result, ignoring the other connecting axons which would clutter the illustration. GDP, unemployment, and inventories are combined into a single item called Domestic Economic Health (DEH). The synapses allow each element to be assigned a specific level of importance relative to DEH using weighting factors. Also note that the neuron DEH is altered by anticipated interest rates, which is the result of data flowing to another neuron in Layer 2. Finally, the three neurons in Layer 2 are combined according to importance, giving the net stock market reaction to the input data.

Layer 2 may be called a *hidden layer,* because you normally only see the input and output layers. Layer 2 has the complex interconnections that allow feedback to occur. It is possible to have more complex connections by adding another hidden

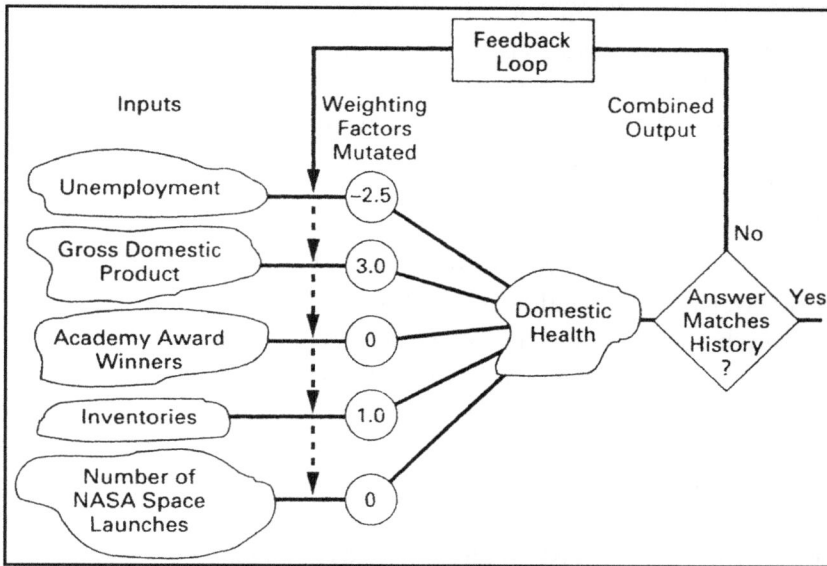

FIGURE 6.17   Learning by Feedback.

Source: Perry Kaufman, *Smarter Trading* (New York: McGraw-Hill, 1995), 166.

layer. In general, the more hidden layers, the longer the solution time and the more finely tuned the answer.

The human brain works in a way very similar to the artificial neural network shown in Figure 6.16. It groups and weighs the data, combines them into subgroups, and finally produces a decision. The human process of weighing the data is complex and not necessarily transparent; that is, we may never know the precise flow of data, how many layers exist, and how weights are assigned and reassigned before the final decision.

Because a computerized neural network cannot *know* whether its answer is correct, you must tell it. This is done by giving the computer the historic data and the corresponding answers. By giving the artificial neural network a long history of information, it can determine, using *feedback,* the weighting factors that would have given the correct results most often. The more history that is given to the computer, the more likely it will find a robust answer. Figure 6.17 shows the results of using five different inputs to predict the direction of the stock market. Two of the inputs, the Academy Award Winners and the Number of NASA Launches, are not likely to be useful in the long term, but *may appear* to provide valuable information about economic activity for short intervals. By using enough comparisons, the weighting factors are found to show that unemployment has a strong negative effect on prices, the GDP a strong positive effect, and inventories have a weak positive effect. The other items had no consistent predictive ability and received a weight of zero. This feedback process is called *training.*

Selecting and Preprocessing the Inputs

There is considerable debate over the inputs needed to find a successful solution using a neural network; however, everyone agrees that the selection of inputs is critical. These inputs must be presented in the most direct form because the neural network will not be able to change them. This step is called *preprocessing*. We must decide which factors are most likely affecting the direction of stocks and the ability to anticipate that direction, then prepare data that contains information with those qualities. For example, we may want to know the short-term and long-term trends, the direction of interest rates, the Dow Jones Utility Index, the ratio of interest rates to gold, economic data such as the GDP and the Balance of Trade, technical indicators such as the RSI, stochastic, and ADX, and a 20-day moving correlation between the U.S. stock market and other major equity markets. There are countless factors that might influence the direction of stocks; the more you choose, the slower the solution and the greater the chance of a less robust model. If you choose too few, they may not contain enough information; therefore, the preprocessing problem requires practice. You may also construct a number of simple trading systems that show profits and include their basic components as inputs to the neural network. You might create a performance series for a specific system that has only values −1, 0, and 1, representing short, neutral, and long market positions. In that way, the neural net may be used to enhance an existing trading strategy.

Selecting the Success Criteria

In a manner similar to evaluating any backtesting result, the training process requires that you select the success criteria. One possibility for the success criteria is a combination of frequency of trading, the size of the profits per trade, a reward/risk ratio, and a frequency of profitability.

According to Ruggiero,[17] neural networks can be used to predict price direction, such as the percentage change five days into the future; however, they are much better at predicting *forward-shifted technical indicators* because these tend to have smoother results. Most technical indicators, such as trend and momentum calculations, smooth the input data, which is most often the price. The longer the time period used in the calculation, the greater the smoothing. Ruggiero suggests an output function such as

```
Average((close[-5] - Lowest(Close[-5],5))/(Highest(close[-5],5) -
                    Lowest(close[-5],5)),5)
```

which is the 5-day average of a 5-period stochastic shifted forward by 5 periods. In this notation, the bracketed value [−5] represents 5 periods into the future.

The Training Process

At the heart of the neural network approach is the feedback process used for training shown in Figure 6.17. This is the part of neural networks that many people refer to as the *learning process*. To observe sound statistical practice, it is advised that only about 70% of the data be used for training. As the neural net refines the weighting factors for each of

---

[17] Murray A. Ruggiero, Jr., "Build a Real Neural Net," *Futures* (June 1996), the first of a series of excellent articles on this subject.

the inputs and combinations of inputs (in the layers between the input and output), it will need more data to test these results. Of the remaining 30% of the data, 20% should be designated for testing. The success or failure of the method to find a solution is based on the performance of the test data. The remaining 10% is saved for out-of-sample validation.

Weighting factors are found using a method called a *genetic algorithm*. For now, we need to know that the training process begins with an arbitrary or random value assigned to the weighting factors of each input. As the training proceeds, these weighting factors are randomly *mutated,* or changed, until the best combination is found. The genetic algorithm changes and combines weighting factors in a manner referred to as *survival of the fittest,* giving preference to the best and discarding the worst.

Testing is completed when the results, as measured by the success criteria, cannot be improved. That is, after a number of feedback loops on the historic data (the oldest 70% of the data), the test data (the next 20%) is used with the new weighting factors. If the results are improving (also called *converging*) the process continues. If the results are improving at a very slow rate, or have stopped because a better combination cannot be found, the neural network process is completed. Sometimes the results get worse rather than better. This can be fixed by beginning again using new random weighting factors. If this fails to solve the problem, then it is most likely that there are too many inputs that are irrelevant. Starting with a smaller number of basic inputs should get the process back on track.

Because the genetic algorithm is a trial-and-error process, rather than an analytic approach, the best results could be found by chance, rather than by cause and effect. With enough data, it is always possible that two series of events will appear related even when they are not. It is necessary to review the results to avoid obvious mistakes.

A Training Example

We would like to train an ANN to tell us whether we should buy or sell stocks. As inputs, we select what we believe to be the five most relevant fundamental factors: GNP, unemployment, inventories, the U.S. dollar index, and short-term interest rates. This test does not use any preprocessed data, such as trends or indicators. To simplify the process, the following approach is taken:

1. Each input is normalized so that it has values between +100 and −100, indicating strength to weakness, with 0 as neutral.
2. When the combined values of the five indicators exceeds +125, we will enter a long position; when the combined value is below −125, we will enter a short.
3. Values between +125 and −125 are considered neutral to the trading strategy.

To show how the training process works, two combinations of starting values are shown in Table 6.7 and Table 6.8 as Case 1 and Case 2. Table 6.7 is the initial state of the neural network, where we begin by arbitrarily setting all of the weighting factors to 1.0. In actual training, the network might require that the sum of all weights total 1.0. The actual values of the normalized inputs are shown in the columns marked *Relative Value*, and the correct historic answers are at the bottom, marked as *Strong* and *Weak* stock market reactions to these values. For the neural network to return

TABLE 6.7 Two Training Cases (Initial State)

Input	Case 1 Relative Value	Weight	Net	Case 2 Relative Value	Weight	Net
GNP	Strong	50	1.0	50	Weak	−60	1.0	−60
Unemployment	Low	−25	1.0	−25	High	40	1.0	40
Inventories	Low	−50	1.0	−50	Neutral	15	1.0	15
U.S. dollar	Very Strong	75	1.0	75	Neutral	0	1.0	0
Interest rates	Falling	−25	1.0	−25	Rising	45	1.0	45
Total value		75				40		
Threshold		±125				±125		
Current response		None				None		
Actual market reaction		Strong				Weak		

Source: Perry Kaufman, *Smarter Trading* (New York: McGraw-Hill, 1995).

the correct answers, it must produce a result greater than +125 for Case 1 and below −125 for Case 2. By assigning initial weights of 1.0 to all inputs, the value of Case 1 is +75, and the value of Case 2 is +40; both fail to produce the known historic answer and testing continues searching for better weighting factors.

In Table 6.8 the weighting factors have undergone mutation using a genetic algorithm. This example attempts to use only weighting factors of +1.0, 0, and −1.0. By reversing the effect of unemployment and interest rates on the direction of the stock market, and by random selection of weighting factors, the results now match the historic pattern of stock movement. Using fractional values for weighting factors, and many more training cases, the ANN method should find the current underlying relationship between these inputs and stock market movement.

TABLE 6.8 Two Training Cases (After Mutated Weighting Factors)

Input	Case 1 Relative Value	Weight	Net	Case 2 Relative Value	Weight	Net
GNP	Strong	50	1.0	50	Weak	−60	1.0	−60
Unemployment	Low	−25	−1.0	25	High	40	−1.0	−40
Inventories	Low	−50	1.0	−50	Neutral	15	1.0	15
U.S. dollar	Very Strong	75	1.0	75	Neutral	0	1.0	0
Interest rates	Falling	−25	−1.0	25	Rising	45	−1.0	−45
Total value		125				−130		
Threshold		±125				±125		
Current response		None				None		
Actual market reaction		Strong				Weak		

Source: Perry Kaufman, *Smarter Trading* (New York: McGraw-Hill, 1995).

Success Criteria

Determining success during the learning process is a matter of measuring the ANN output against the training data, looking for convergence. The common measurements are the average correlation (adjusted for the number of parameters), the t-statistic, the t^2-statistic, and the F-statistic. The t^2-statistic is unique to neural networks and measures the nonlinear relationships between two variables[18]

$$t^2 = \sqrt{AS} \times \frac{\sigma_I}{\sigma_O} \times \sqrt{n-k}$$

where σ_I is the standard deviation of the input data
σ_O is the standard deviation of the output data
n is the number of observations
k is the number of model inputs
AS is the average squared slope of the cross-section

As with most comparisons, it is also necessary to include a measurement of accuracy based on the size of the sample. The *root mean square (E)* and the *mean absolute percentage error (MAPE)* can be used,

$$E = \sqrt{\frac{\sum_{i=1}^{n} e_i^2}{n}}$$

$$MAPE = \frac{\sum_{i=1}^{n} \frac{|e_i|}{|A_i|}}{n}$$

where n is the number of observations,
e_i is residual error of observation i
A_i is the actual value of observation i

Reducing the Number of Decision Levels and Neurons

The robustness of a neural network solution is directly related to the number of decision levels, the number of neurons in each level, and the total number of inputs. Fewer elements produce more generalized and therefore more robust solutions. When there are many decision layers and many neurons, the inputs can be combined and recombined in many different ways, allowing very specific patterns to be found. The more specific, the greater the chance that the final solution will be overfitted, that is, it will be fine-tuned to such specific patterns in the past that those patterns will not occur in the future.

Failure to converge to a solution can also occur if there are too many inputs and the genetic algorithm allows too much mutating (discussed in the next section). Neural networks can be highly complex and require experience before they can be used efficiently.

---

[18] Stephan Kudyba, "Are Neural Networks a Better Forecaster?" *Futures* (October 1998).

The trade-offs using a neural network are the same as with most other optimization methods. Too many inputs and combinations increase the time of testing and increase the chance of a solution that is overfit. Too few values can produce a result that is too general, has large risk, and is not practical. It is best to begin with the most general and proceed in clear steps toward a more specific solution. In this way you will understand the process better, ultimately save time, and be able to stop when you have reached the practical limitations of this method.

Modeling Human Behavior

Neural networks are considered a learning process similar to the parallel architecture of the human brain. It can be trained on a classification of data, then used to find new data of the same class, or it can be trained on a number of points in a function (for example, a logarithmic curve or more complicated cycle), then used to find other points on that function.

One application that is relevant to price forecasting is to make each of the Layer-1 neurons contain the results of the major economic indicators. The synapse between level 1 and level 2 would discard any indicator when its value was not significantly different from zero. This reflects the way the public views economic reports. During the scenario of economic recovery, such as early in 2003 as well as after the subprime crisis of 2008, corporate earnings and income growth were most important. Other reports were, for the most part, ignored. After earnings improved and the stock market had rallied, traders looked for employment statistics to improve as a means for sustaining economic growth and the stock market rally. At that point, earnings were no longer as important as more jobs. A neural network can be constructed to reflect this selection process that makes one or two economic reports more important than others given the state of the economy. Using previous GDP, stock market trends, and the direction of Fed funds, we can limit the entire neural net solution to the relationship between one or two economic indicators and the future direction of stock prices, setting the synapse weighting factors to zero for the other reports in Layer-1 neurons. A similar method might have the synapses assume a weighting factor of 1 when the economic report has a change that is large enough to attract the attention of the public (at least a 1.5 standard deviation change) and a value of 0 at any other time. In that way a minor change in all indicators does not have a cumulative impact on the neural network while the public shrugs off the data.

A Final Comment about Neural Networks

When using neural networks and other powerful searching tools, every analyst must keep in mind that neural nets will nearly always find the correct solution in a *closed system*, one where the output is fully defined by all the inputs. An ANN is often used when it is too difficult to find a solution by other means. For example, in a chemical or manufacturing process, the formula may have too many variables. A neural network will not only solve the problem, but solve it quickly. The stock market, however, is different. No one is sure that there is a solution to the problem *as we are specifying it*. Because of this uncertainty, there is no guarantee that the answer will work. You will then need to test the results on out-of-sample data to verify the success.

▓ Genetic Algorithms

The concept of a genetic algorithm is based on Darwin's theory of survival of the fittest. In the real world, a mutation with traits that improve any creature's ability to survive will continue to procreate. This has been applied to system development using a technique called a *genetic algorithm*. Although a genetic algorithm[19] is actually a sophisticated search method that replaces the standard optimization, it uses a technique that parallels the survival of the fittest. It is particularly valuable when the number of tests or combinations is so large that a test of all combinations is impractical. Instead of the typical sequential search, it is a process of random seeding, selection, and combination to find the best set of trading rules or parameter values. Standard statistical criteria are used in the selection process to qualify the results. Searching for a large, optimal set of parameters or finding the best portfolio allocation takes minutes using a genetic algorithm; a standard sequential search may take weeks at the same computing speed.

Representation of a Genetic Algorithm

Using the words common to this methodology, the most basic component of a genetic algorithm is a *gene;* a number of genes will comprise an *individual,* and a combination of individuals (and therefore genes) is a *chromosome.* Each chromosome represents a potential solution, a set of trading rules or parameters where the genes are the specific values and calculations. These in turn form individuals that represent rules that ultimately form a trading strategy. For example, Chromosome 1 might be a rule to buy on strength:

> If a 10-day moving average is less than yesterday's close and a 5-day stochastic is greater than 50, then *buy.*

Chromosome 2 could be a rule that buys on weakness:

> If a 20-day exponential is less than yesterday's low and a 10-day RSI is less than 50, then *buy.*

If we rewrite these two chromosomes in a notational form, the genes and individuals in its structure become more apparent:

> Chromosome 1: MA, 10, <, C, [0], &, Stoch, 5, >, 50, 1
> Chromosome 2: Exp, 20, <, L, [1], &, RSI, 10, <, 50, 1

Each of these chromosomes has 11 genes, any one of which can be changed. In addition, each chromosome has two individuals, separated by an "&" operator. In Table 6.9, the description of the genes indicates other values that can replace the current ones.

---

[19] This technique is attributed to John H. Holland, *Adaptations in Natural Language and Artificial Systems* (Ann Arbor: University of Michigan Press, 1975).

TABLE 6.9 Functional Description of the Genes in Chromosomes 1 and 2

Gene	Chr 1	Chr 2	Function
1	MA	Exp	Trend type (moving average, exponential smoothing, breakout)
2	10	20	Calculation period for gene 1
3	<	<	Relational operator (<, <=, >)
4	C	L	Price used in gene 1 calculation ((H + L + C)/3, indexed value)
5	0	1	Reference to past data ([0] = current day, [1] = previous day)
6	&	&	Method of combining individuals (and, or)
7	Stoch	RSI	Indicator type (RSI, stochastic, MACD)
8	5	10	Calculation period for gene 7
9	>	<	Relational operator (<, <=, >)
10	50	50	Comparison value for relational operator
11	1	1	Market action (1 = Buy, −1 = Sell)

Table 6.9 is a way to represent the chromosomes and individuals in a general form. It is easy to see that each gene can be changed, and each change will represent a new trading rule. For example, the 10- and 20-day averages in gene 2 of chromosomes 1 and 2 could be changed to 5 and 15 days; or, the indicators *Stoch* and *RSI* could be changed to *MACD* and *Momentum*. A combination of trading rules, or chromosomes, will create a trading strategy. Before continuing, the following steps will be needed to use the genetic algorithm to find the best results:

1. A clear way of representing the chromosomes and their component individuals and genes.
2. A *fitness* criterion to decide that one chromosome is better than another.
3. A *propagation* procedure that determines which chromosomes will survive and in what manner.
4. A process for *mutation* (introducing new characteristics) and *mating* (combining genes) to give chromosomes with greater potential a better chance for survival.

Representation of the genes and chromosomes has been shown in Table 6.9. However, there is one additional step needed to get started: creating an initial chromosome pool.

Initial Chromosome Pool

To begin, an initial pool of chromosomes must be created. These will look just like those in Table 6.9; however, each gene will be chosen at random from a list of candidates that has been previously defined. Eleven lists are needed, one for each unique gene.

1. *Trend type,* 1 of 5 choices: a moving average, exponential smoothing, linear regression, breakout, or step-weighted average.
2. *Trend calculation period,* a number between 1 and 200.

3. *Trend relational operator,* 1 of 3 choices: $<, <=, >$.
4. *Price used in the trend calculation,* 1 of 4 choices: C, (H + L + C)/3, (H + L)/2, indexed value.
5. *Reference data or lag:* a number between 1 and 10.
6. *Method of combining individuals,* 1 of 2 choices: *and* or *or.*
7. *Indicator type,* 1 of 5 choices: RSI, stochastic, MACD, momentum, Fisher transform (all indicators must be transformed to return values between -100 and $+100$).
8. *Indicator calculation period,* a number between 1 and 50.
9. *Relational operator,* 1 of 2 choices: $>$ or $<$.
10. *Comparison value for indicator and relational operator,* a number between -100 and $+100$.
11. *Market action,* 1 of 2 choices: *buy* or *sell.*

These 11 lists offer the possibility of 4.8×10^{10} combinations, or 48,000,000,000 possibilities. Regardless of the computer speed, trying each combination would be a daunting task. However, the genetic algorithm is likely to find the best solution, or a solution very nearly the best, in less than 1,000 passes through its process.

To assure a fast solution, it is necessary to start with a large chromosome pool. Each chromosome in the pool is created by selecting one item from each list randomly. This pool represents the *genetic population.*

Fitness

Having created a pool of chromosomes that look similar to those in Table 6.9, it is necessary to decide which are best. This is done by defining a *fitness* criterion, or *objective function,* which can be used to rank the chromosomes. Because fitness will lead to survival, it is very important to decide which chromosomes should be discarded and which should survive, or even flourish. A fitness criterion must combine the most important features associated with a successful trading strategy:

■ Net profits or profits per trade.

■ The number of trades or a sample error criterion.

■ The smoothness of the results or a reward-to-risk ratio

Ideally, preference is given to systems that have large profits, lots of trades, and very consistent performance. To measure that result, the following might be used:

$$Rank = PPT \times \left(1 - \frac{1}{\sqrt{NT}}\right) \times \frac{GP}{GL}$$

where PPT = the profits per trade
  NT = the number of trades
  GP = the gross profits
  GL = the gross losses

Alternatively, the term GP/GL can be replaced by the information ratio, AROR/ASD, the annualized rate of return divided by the annualized standard deviation, or volatility.

The fitness criterion *rank* favors large profits per trade, a large number of trades, and a high ratio of gross profits to gross losses, which is a measure of smoothness of returns. These factors are not weighted, but they serve as a simple measurement for ranking the chromosomes. For example, a trading method that returned $500 per trade for 10 trades, with a gross profit/loss ratio of 0.5 would have a rank of 170.75. Another system that returned only $250 per trade over 100 trades with a profit/loss ratio of 1.4 would rank 315.00. Therefore the system with the smaller returns has a much more agreeable trading profile according to the fitness criteria based primarily on the gross profit to gross loss ratio. Each analyst must create a criterion that allows those strategies that are most desirable to survive.

Propagation

The process of *natural selection* allows only the best individuals to survive. A strong *propagation* criterion is used to encourage the survival of chromosomes with the highest ranking, as determined by the fitness test. A weak criterion allows lower rankings to survive. The implementation of this selection process is also drawn from evolution. When an individual has a high fitness score, it is allowed to create more offspring; therefore, it becomes a larger part of the population. When it has a low score, it creates fewer offspring, or no offspring, and eventually disappears from the population.

The propagation step in a genetic algorithm determines how many offspring will be created from each existing chromosome based on its fitness score. For example, if there are only 10 chromosomes in the initial pool, with fitness scores from 1 to 5 (5 being the best), they are sorted in descending order of fitness as follows

Chromosome rank	1	2	3	4	5	6	7	8	9	10
Fitness score	5	4	3	3	2	2	2	1	1	1

The propagation criterion states that the fitness score of each chromosome is multiplied by 3 and divided by 5 in order to get the number of new offspring when the chromosome is propagated. Then the numbers of offspring, in the same order, are

Chromosome rank	1	2	3	4	5	6	7	8	9	10
New offspring	3	2.4	1.8	1.8	1.2	1.2	1.2	.6	.6	.6

The fractional number of offspring can be rounded or truncated (the fractional part dropped off) to get whole numbers. If rounded, there will be 3 offspring for the highest ranking chromosome, 2 for the next, 2 for the next 2, and 1 for the next 6, for a total population of 15. But it is necessary to keep the population fixed at 10 because the pool size should represent the maximum space available in the computer; therefore, the bottom 5 chromosomes do not survive. The new population, using the original chromosome ranking is 1, 1, 1, 2, 2, 3, 3, 4, 4, and 5. There are more offspring from the fittest chromosome 1; therefore, it has a better chance of surviving. The next few in line have a reasonably good chance of survival, and the ones at the bottom have disappeared.

One popular way to calculate the number of offspring is to divide the fitness of one chromosome, f, by the average fitness of all chromosomes, F. Therefore,

$$\text{Number of offspring} = \text{Current fitness} / \text{Average fitness} = f/F$$

This method works best when there are a large number of choices rather than only 10 possibilities. However, if the fitness of the linear regression chromosome was 4, and the average of all chromosomes was 2, the linear regression would propagate 2 or 3 offspring. The more offspring, the better chance of survival during both the real evolutionary process as well as the genetic algorithm process.

Mating

The new pool of offspring now moves to the next Darwinian test, *mating*. Remembering that a genetic algorithm is a sophisticated search method, it needs a way to combine the genes of individuals that have passed the fitness criteria in different ways so that we might create a better chromosome. This is very similar to cross-pollination, where you continue to pollinate two species with certain desirable but different features, hoping to get a new species that has the best of both. This is done through *mating* (also called *crossover*).

When mating, we must be careful to combine, or switch, the entire individual, and not just one gene (remember that individuals are separated by an "&" symbol). All of the genes that form an individual make sense only as a set. If we separate the individual, then the result could be an inferior offspring. Using chromosomes 1 and 2, we can switch the first individuals to get

Offspring 1: Exp, 20, <, L, [1], &, Stoch, 5, >, 50, 1
Offspring 2: MA, 10, <, C, [0], &, RSI, 10, <, 50, 1

In the actual genetic algorithm process, only a small percentage of offspring are mated, perhaps 10–15%. If all the offspring were mated, then we would lose the combination that had the highest fitness; there is no guarantee that any of the offspring will be better. The offspring that are chosen to be mated are randomly selected. Because there are more offspring for the fittest chromosomes, there is a greater chance that these will be used in the mating process.

Mutation

Mutation is the process of introducing new genes, or combinations of genes, into the gene pool. Up to this point, the genetic algorithm has propagated the fittest chromosomes, then created new chromosomes by combining entire individuals of an existing one through mating. The last step is to randomly introduce new genes on the chance that an even better chromosome, or a better individual, will be formed.

A new gene can replace any one of the genes in the chromosome; however, it must be chosen from the corresponding list for that gene, as shown in the initial creation of the *gene pool*. For example, the first gene of the chromosome, which represents a trend-following calculation, can only be selected from the five choices designated. In mutating the gene, one of these five techniques is chosen randomly, excluding the existing gene. Similarly, the calculation period and the way in which rules are combined are selected randomly from their corresponding lists. Typically, only one gene in one of the individuals in a chromosome is mutated; however, you could mutate all of the genes in an individual. Using the approach of changing all the genes in one of the individuals in Chromosome 1,

Chromosome 1: MA, 10, <, C, [0], &, Stoch, 5, >, 50, 1

the genes in the second individual (Stoch, 5, >, 50, 1) might be mutated to (RSI, 10, >, 40, 1). Of all the chromosomes, only 10% are chosen at random for mutation. If too many are mutated, then there is a strong chance of losing the best chromosomes. If too few are mutated, then there is little chance of introducing a new and better chromosome. This same balance was discussed during mating.

The two methods of mating and mutation provide the only tools needed to introduce new features into the optimization and to combine features in all ways. If you could continue this process indefinitely, you would see every possible mutation and combination.

Converging on a Solution

Each pass through the genetic algorithm process creates a new generation of chromosomes. Normally, the population remains the same but the average fitness (the measurement of success) of the pool keeps increasing through propagation, mating, and mutation. The solution is found when either

1. The average fitness of the entire pool does not increase after a few new generations are created, or
2. There is no improvement over the chromosome with the best fitness.

Finding the best solution requires a fine balance of how many chromosomes are mated and how many of the new offspring are mutated. If only a small percentage (less than 5%) are changed, there is little chance of creating better offspring. In that case the results converge quickly because they are limited to choices and combinations within the initial pool. If a large percentage of the offspring (more than 25%) are changed, there is a significant possibility that the best of the pool will be lost and the process will fail to converge.

Putting It into Practice: Simulated Performance

The technique for a successful search using a genetic algorithm requires that good test procedures be followed. Data is separated into the testing and out-of-sample parts, where 70% to 80% of the data is tested. Once a solution is found, it is applied to the remaining 20% to 30% of the data not yet seen. If there is a large amount of data, the two sets could be 60%–40% or 50%–50%. The performance of the out-of-sample data will normally deteriorate, but must still meet minimum success criteria. These expectations are discussed in the next chapter. Step-forward testing can also be applied.

Multiple Seeding

Both the genetic algorithm and neural network are capable of finding a solution in much shorter time than a sequential search. In many cases, the solution can be found in seconds instead of hours; however, it may not be the best solution, just a very good one. Because there are so many combinations, you will never know whether the solution is the best—that would require testing every combination. It is most likely that the solution is a local peak rather than a global one. The analogy can easily be seen on a contour map. If you are dropped at random on one point of the map, and you proceed to walk uphill looking for a peak, you will find the local high point, but you may have missed a much higher mountain across the valley.

Because the propagation, mating, and mutation processes all seek higher fitness values, they essentially move uphill from the best combinations in the initial pool. It is possible that a combination of trends and indicators that would produce the best system was never introduced during the random initialization of the pool, nor did it appear in the subsequent mutation process.

The most efficient solution is to run the genetic algorithm or neural network a number of times to see if it arrives at the same solution starting with different random values in the pool. While it is not a guarantee that you will cover all major combinations, especially when there is a massive number of variations, it is the simplest way of avoiding serious oversights. The search tools are so fast that running them 10 times is still a minute amount of time compared to a sequential search. If you think about the contour map, starting at 10 different points has a much higher chance of finding the highest peak than beginning at one point.

▓ Replication of Hedge Funds

Technology allows us to approach problems as never before. With the proliferation of hedge funds, some analysts have decided that they can replicate the performance of those funds using mathematical methods, and any inaccuracy would be offset by the lower cost of replication compared to hedge fund fees. Replication can also be applied to a set of hedge funds, such as a fund of funds, or a hedge fund index. The systematic process of replication is marketed as a conservative and algorithmic approach to investing.

In a simple example, say that a hedge fund allocates resources only to stocks in the mining sector, and within that sector there are 10 stocks. The program is always long. If we have the historic returns of the hedge fund, we can use Excel's *Solver* and find what percentage of the investment would need to be allocated to each of the 10 stocks in order to duplicate the returns. This assumes that allocations did not change over the period of analysis. It may be that positions are rebalanced once during the month, so that this regression may need to be done more often with some constraints on the size of the change allowed in each stock.

Alternatively, we try to replicate the returns each day by asking "What allocations would have given us yesterday's returns?" We then buy or sell shares to align with that solution. On the next day we ask the same question. If the hedge fund does not change positions often, we will adjust our positions until we align correctly with the hedge fund positions, similar to the way a Monte Carlo approach to sampling finds the right distribution. During the time it takes to find the same positions, there will be some tracking error, but this may be better or worse than the actual hedge fund.

The mathematics of replication has become a specialized area of application. Rebalancing of the replication model was initially done monthly; however, that would allow for large tracking errors. A better method would be to rebalance whenever the tracking error exceeded a threshold level. There is a trade-off between the tracking error and the cost of rebalancing. The Hedge Fund Replication Index (see *hedgefundreplication.com*) is said to be able to replicate 85% of hedge fund returns, leaving a tracking error of 15%, less than the fees associated with a fund of hedge funds.

CHAPTER 7

System Testing

From Perry J. Kaufman, *Trading Systems and Methods*, *+Website*, 5th Edition (Hoboken, New Jersey: John Wiley & Sons, 2013), Chapter 21.

Numbers are like people; torture them enough and they will tell you anything.

—Anonymous (quoted by John Ehlers in *Rocket Science for Traders*)

Learning Objective Statements

- Critique the use of performance and risk metrics based on a given objective
- Interpret data from a system test to determine lack of randomness in the results
- Explain the differences of various performance metrics and why one is more suitable than another for a given objective
- Interpret the Sharpe ratio for trading systems, portfolios, and individual securities

System testing remains a fight between computer power and common sense. Before 1980, testing a trading system was a simple concept. Conscientious traders and analysts applied their ideas to charts, marking the buy and sell signals manually and keeping a hand-written record of the trades. The process took a long time; therefore, they were careful not to begin unless they were reasonably sure that the method had a good chance of success. Ideas came from an understanding of the fundamentals or the awareness of market patterns, plus valuable experience. The tabulation of profitable results was verification that the idea was sound.

By the early 1990s, you were at the high end of technology if you had daily data that could be read by a computer and a program such as TradeStation or MetaStock to give you charts and indicators that could be combined into a trading system. Best of all, these programs showed the historic profitability of the trading strategies and, in particular, the best strategy. Moving averages and the RSI were still sophisticated tools, but the ability to test for the best calculation period and combine indicators began a step down a path that has now become very complex and taken the industry further from the simple solution.

That process has continued to advance, but not always for the better. Those who have applied diligence, selectivity, and most of all common sense to the automating systems are likely to have gotten better results, faster response, and more useful information than ever before. Those who have carelessly used the power of new computers and the convenience of trading strategy development software are not likely to be as successful. Bigger and faster computers and high-tech software do not mean better results.

The tools alone do not ensure a profitable trading program. It is the thought process, creativity, and knowledge that are needed to be competitive. Computers allow us to solve problems of magnitude and complexity that we could never have considered before, and they do it in a way that is easy to understand. We can manipulate massive amounts of data to find out not only whether our ideas are sound, but the risks associated with various events. But computers are still only highly sophisticated calculators, even when you call your technique "artificial intelligence." Giving it a catchy name does not make it true. Computers do not think, they compute.

One of the most misused techniques that has evolved from computerization is *optimization*. This is not the mathematical process of finding a *local maximum* on a map of continuous contours; instead it is the iterative process of repeatedly testing data to find the single best moving average speed, point-and-figure box size, stop-loss size, or a combination of multiple values that produce the highest trading profits, the lowest risk, or some other target result. That is not to say that optimization could not be effective. Traders seem to have an irresistible urge to know the system parameter values that would have generated the highest profits. Experience shows that the best test results never live up to their expectations and are often a financial tragedy when traded. They are the result of *fine tuning* or *overfitting*. Everyone using a computer for testing a strategy is guilty of overfitting the result at some time.

Computers present a serious, often futile, dilemma for the analyst. If the objective is to use a trend-following strategy—a moving average, exponential smoothing, or linear regression slope—how do you decide the right calculation period? More than 20 years ago, the 5-, 10-, and 20-day moving averages were most popular because they represented a 1-week, 2-week, and 1-month time interval. They were also easy to calculate. In fact, the 10-day moving average was the most common because no division was necessary to arrive at the average, you only needed to move the decimal point. Unfortunately, competition is now keener, markets more complex, and that simple approach is no longer viable.

Consider the process of creating a trading strategy. For a trend system, once the calculation period has been logically selected (e.g., 10 days) and the trading rules determined (buy and sell when the trend changes direction and use a 3% stop-loss), you will want to know the performance of that choice over past data for a selection of futures markets or stocks. If testing proves successful, you will trade using that method; however, if it does not meet expectations using the test data, what do you do? With a computer, the answer is easy: try another trend speed or a different stop-loss and see if the results are better. This follows a perfectly natural progression; after all, who would use a system that has failed to be profitable in the past?

Ultimately, we decide that testing all combinations of calculation periods and rules gives us a better understanding of how successful a trading system can be. Why guess at each parameter when you can try them all using specialized development software? We should know by now that this approach fails, but not everyone knows the approaches that are correct. The following sections discuss various aspects of testing and optimization, how to take advantage of it, and how to control it. There is a comprehensive summary at the end of the chapter.

■ Expectations

Expectations are an essential part of system development. They force you to define a plan in advance. The importance of this comes when you see the test results.

Testing should be the process of validating your ideas. That first requires that you define those ideas in a clear plan, deciding whether it should work for hourly, daily, or weekly intervals. You should have an idea of the relative risk of the method, and the percentage of profitable trades. If the test results confirm your ideas, then you can have confidence in the strategy. If they differ, you know that something is wrong. Without expectations, there can be no validation or confirmation; therefore, if you indiscriminately test all combinations of indicators, you will not know whether you have found a good idea or have simply overfit the data. Testing should be used for deciding between various trade-offs of risk and reward, but *not for discovery*.

Setting Your Objective and Measuring Success

There are a number of steps that must be carefully performed before testing can begin. These steps are more important than the actual testing and will require you to decide what you are looking for and how you will use the results. Correctly defined, the final system will have realistic goals and predictive qualities. Incorrectly done, it will look successful but fail in actual trading.

First, define the *test objective*. What measurement or statistic will show success? Is it the highest possible profit, the frequency of profitable trades, or the average profit to average loss ratio? Testing software gives you a choice, but does not allow a combination of these items; most likely, it will be a combination that you want. For example, if maximum profits are used as the performance criterion, the resulting system may have one or two large profits and an overwhelming number of small losses. This can be seen in energy strategies that captured the move to $150/bbl in June 2008, or in gold where the 20 years from 1985 to 2005 were losses, but those were all forgotten when prices neared $2000/oz. When seen as total performance, exceptional profits during the peak of the stock market in the late 1990s can overwhelm the results of the whole test, making it look acceptable; however, the profits were made in the past and not the current market. That strategy may not be profitable now. Later, this chapter will look at successful but decaying performance.

While there is no *right* way to define success, the industry has favored the *Sharpe ratio*, or the simple *information ratio* (without the risk-free returns)

$$Sharpe\ ratio = \frac{Annualized\ returns - Risk\text{-}free\ returns}{Annualized\ risk}$$

Later in this chapter, the section "Performance Criteria" explains many of the components that can be used to decide the relative success of a trading method. All traders want to know the maximum drawdown, not just the probabilities, and day traders will want to know the average profit per share or profit per contract to understand the impact of costs and slippage on the results.

■ Identifying the Parameters

Once the test strategy is known, the *parameters* to be tested must be identified. A *parameter* is a value within the strategy that can be changed in order to vary the speed or timing of the system. For example, parameters include:

- Moving average calculation period (number of days or bars).

- Exponential smoothing constant (a percentage).

- Band width around a moving average (percentage or number of standard deviations).

- RSI calculation period (number of days or bars).

- Stop-loss value (fixed number of points, a percentage, or a volatility factor).

- Maximum holding period for a trade (days or bars).

Suppose the strategy uses a moving average to identify the trend, an RSI to decide the entry timing, and a percentage stop-loss. The most basic test would be to choose the stock or futures contract, fix the calculation period of the RSI at 14 days, fix the stop-loss at 3%, and vary the calculation period for the moving average. The test would then simulate the results of the trading strategy, stepping through the possible range of moving average days: for example, 1 through 250 days. This is called a *1-parameter* optimization.

Most systems have more than one important parameter. In this example, the moving average period, the RSI period, and the stop-loss value are all important. If the stop-loss is held constant at 3%, the moving average and RSI can be tested together. The optimization process does a sequential test, selecting the first moving average value, then testing all of the RSI values; the next moving average value is then used, and all of the RSI values are retested. The process is repeated until all combinations of the moving average calculation periods and RSI calculation periods have been tested. This is a *2-parameter* optimization.

Range of Parameter Settings

It doesn't take much effort to create an optimization with a very large number of tests; it follows that the test time for the optimization will increase dramatically. For example, a test of 250 moving average values (1 to 250), 30 RSI calculation periods

(5 to 34), and 30 stop-loss values (0 to 3.0 in steps of 0.1) gives $250 \times 30 \times 30 = 225,000$ tests. If each test takes 0.01 second (much longer for intraday data, perhaps less for daily data), the total test time will be about 36 minutes. Tests with more parameters will quickly get out of control. It will be necessary to select fewer values to test for each parameter and choose them more carefully. Limiting the test is actually an advantage because it forces a decision, in advance, about the range of parameters that are reasonable for the strategy. Without these restrictions, the test process moves further away from validation and closer to indiscriminant exploration.

Distribution of Values to Be Tested

It is not necessary to test all of the calculation periods for a moving average or any trend method; however, the values should not be spaced evenly apart. For a moving average trend, it is best to use all of the smaller values for the number of days and then fewer values as the numbers become larger. For example, the sequence

$$1, 2, 3, 4, 5, 6, 8, 10, 12, 15, 20, 25, 30, 40, 50$$

would be a better choice than using all numbers between 1 and 50. Consider that the difference between a 49- and 50-day period is only 2%, while the difference between the 2- and 3-period test is 50%. The tests at the two ends of the test series therefore represent very different sensitivity. The difference in performance between a 1- and 2-day moving average will be significant, but the difference between a 49- and 50-day trend will be negligible.

Using equal increments will weight this set of tests heavily toward the long end; that is, average results or a plot of test returns versus calculation period will always reflect the results of the longer calculation periods. Using test values that increase in percentage increments would solve this problem. If the starting test value is multiplied by 1.5 to get the second value, and that is multiplied by 1.5 to get the third value, the final test series is improved. Beginning at 1, the series becomes

$$1, 1.5, 2.2, 3.3, 5.0, 7.6, 11.4, 17.1, 25.6, 38.4, 57.7$$

By specifying the tests using percentage increments you not only reduce the test time but you improve the distribution of results.

Ordering the Test Parameters   Testing one parameter at a time can give you a better understanding of the dynamics of a system. It is much more difficult, sometimes impossible, to see the way that test results vary when there are five parameters being tested simultaneously. For sequential testing, the most important feature must be tested first—the one that combines the big picture with the greatest impact on the results. In the example of a system with a moving average, RSI, and stop-loss, the moving average is the primary component. The success of the strategy will depend on selecting a profitable trend period. While the other indicator and risk control should improve the results, it is unrealistic to think that a strategy should be driven by the size of the stop-loss. In the same way, the second test should be the RSI to improve entry and/or exit timing. Risk control, using the stop-loss, should improve the final picture.

Types of Test Variables

Test variables can be of three forms: *continuous, discrete,* or *coded* (alphabetic). In order to interpret and display test results properly, these forms need to be identified in advance.

> *Continuous parameters* refer to values, such as percentages, which can take on any fractional number within a well-defined range. If a stop-loss level is defined as a percentage, it may be tested beginning with the fractional value .02% and increasing in steps of .005% until 2.0% is reached.
>
> *Discrete parameters* are whole numbers, or integer values, such as the number of days in a moving average.
>
> *Coded parameters* represent a category of operations, also called a *regime.* For example, when the parameter value is *A,* a single moving average is used; when the value is *B,* a double moving average system is tested; and when the value is *C,* a linear regression is used.

The first two parameter types, continuous and discrete, should be distinguished from the last one, coded. The analyst can expect a pattern in the results when testing parameters that take on progressively larger or smaller values. For example, a moving average of 1 day may post the largest losses, and show progressively smaller losses until 30 days is reached, where it becomes profitable; performance peaks at 80 days and then starts to decay. The coded parameter, however, shifts rules for each value. There is no reason why a change of rules, which switches regimes, would result in any performance pattern that continues across these regimes. The first rule may be profitable, the second losing, and the third profitable. The display of results, discussed later, is only valid for continuous and discrete parameters tested in an incrementally ascending or descending manner.

■ Selecting the Test Data

It is assumed that strategy testing will be done using a computer. It will be necessary to have a database of prices and if more ambitious, a history of economic statistics as well. Data is readily available from numerous vendors and includes daily high, low, and closing prices, plus volume and open interest (futures) for nearly all exchange-traded markets in the world. Individual stock data is also available and may be found on the Internet at no cost (although some inconvenience). Intraday (tick) data on futures can be purchased from a limited number of vendors, the most well-known being CQG Data Factory and Tick Data, Inc. Stock data can usually be exported from whatever quote service you use. A complete database is an important asset. It can be kept current by automatic updating at the end of each day.

Some data vendors, aware that analysts will want to use the data for testing, have created special *continuous test series* specifically for that purpose. Prices of individual stocks will be corrected for stock splits by dividing the data prior to the split by the split ratio; therefore, a 3:1 split will be adjusted by dividing the data before the split by 3. If there was a previous split of 2:1 the data prior to that is divided by 6.

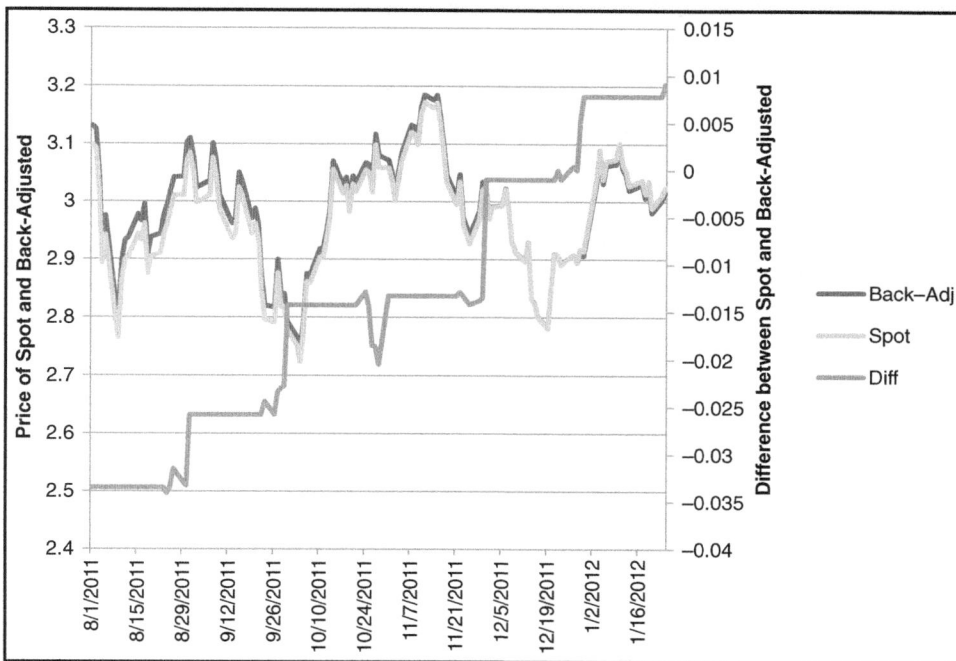

FIGURE 7.1 Comparing Back-Adjusted Data with the Nearest Contract.

Futures data, which expires every 1 to 3 months, is rolled by adjusting the gap between contracts on the date of the roll. Vendors allow you to specify exactly how and when the rolls should occur, or you can simply select the default method. Figure 7.1 gives an example of a recent period of heating oil futures, which rolls every 30 days. Over a short time period, the unadjusted and adjusted series look very similar, but the differences (Diff) show that the gaps cause sharp price changes each month, and the accumulated gaps over 10 or 20 years of data can be enormous. Without the gap adjustments, these differences become windfall profits and losses. Analysts may choose to use different data formats for testing.

1. *Individual full contracts.* The entire futures contract or a series of contracts is tested. Using full contracts is a tedious process and can result in overlapping test periods and duplication of results. Figure 7.2 shows the test bias resulting from carelessly using all of the data for futures contracts from July 1993 through December 1996. The horizontal bars represent the life of the contract for a futures market with delivery in May, July, September, December, and January. Because of the 18-month duration, there was only 1 contract tested in the last half of 1991, compared to 6 contracts tested during the middle period, and falling off to 2 contracts at the end of 1996. Figure 7.2b shows the frequency of testing for each time period.

2. *Backward- (or forward-) adjusted data.* Individual contract data segments are combined on a specific *roll date* by adjusting all the prices in the older contract by the difference between the prices of the new and old contract on the roll date. For example, if on the same date the new contract was trading at 80.00 and the old contract at 75.00,

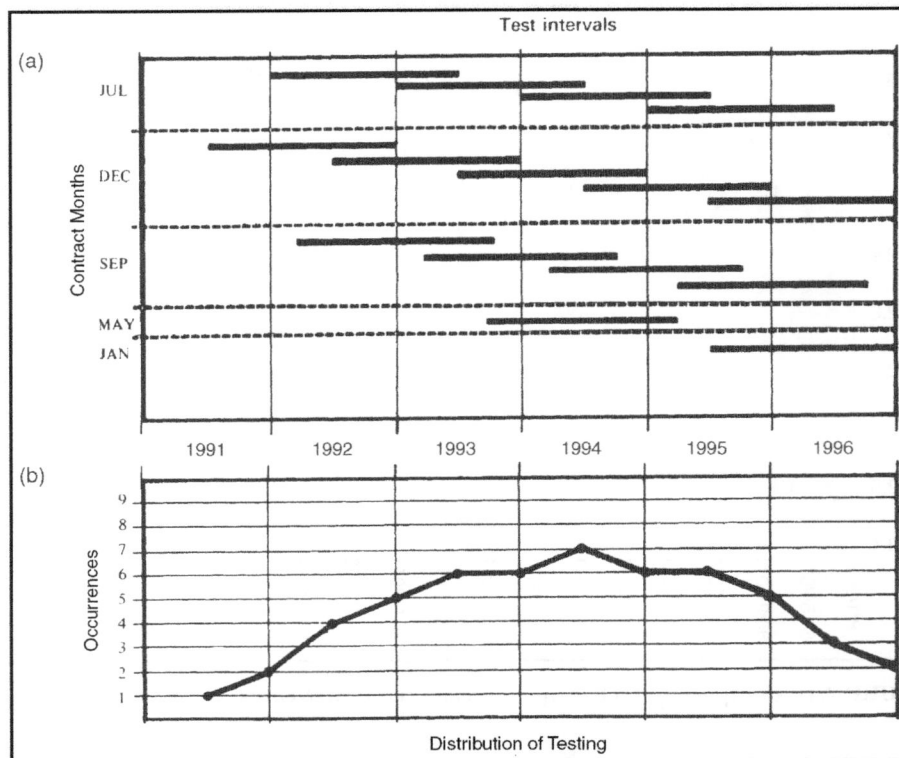

FIGURE 7.2 Testing Using All of the Data for Futures Contracts July 1993 Through December 1996. (a) Test Intervals. (b) Distribution of Testing.

then all the data in the old contract would be increased by 5.00. Moving backwards to the previous contract, if that showed a price of 78.00 when the third oldest contract showed 74.00, the prices in the third oldest contract would be increased by 9.00, the sum of the two roll values. Had the third oldest contract been higher than the second on the roll date, 81.00 versus 78.00, then its prices would be increased by only 2.00, the sum of 5.00 minus 3.00. The adjustment in every older contract is the cumulative adjustment of all previous roll values. A *forward-adjusted* series begins with the oldest data and adjusts newer data as it moves forward in time. At the end, the old data matches the actual prices, but the newest data is different.

This technique has become popular and works well for most systems. The adjustments will cause large differences in the oldest data, especially if that data goes back more than 10 years. In the extreme case, the adjusted price can even become negative! Calculations that use a percentage of price do not work with back-adjusted data.

The *roll date* can be one of the following choices:

a. *A fixed date*, such as the last day of the month before the delivery month. This is standard for interest rates, agricultural products, and some other commodities because margin requirements change significantly for those who trade into the delivery month. Therefore, for Treasury notes and Eurodollars, the

June contract is rolled on the last day of May, the September contract on the last day of August, and so on. For index markets, the expiration date may be the third Friday of the month, and the contract is actively traded until a few days before delivery. Software provided by data vendors allow you to choose *n* days before the contract expiration.

    b. The day on which *volume and/or open interest switches* from the nearest delivery to the next deferred. Using this method, the roll-adjusted series represents the contracts with the greatest liquidity.

3. *Indexed data series.* A continuous series is constructed to represent the daily percentage returns each day. This is essentially the way a stock index is constructed. If the price of copper moves 1.0% from $0.9000 to $0.9090 per pound, then the indexed value will be increased by 1.0%, from 100 to 101. When the contract rolls, the price change of the new contract is compared to its prior price. The conversion into an indexed series is useful for comparing two markets and for constructing portfolios.

4. *Constant n-day forward series.* In the same manner as the London metals and cash forward markets are quoted (for example, delivery 30 days forward), an artificial 30-day forward series can be created for any futures market. The 30-day price is calculated by interpolating between the delivery months on both sides of the date 30 days ahead. This type of data series is called a *perpetual contract* and presents its own set of problems. Deferred contracts are not as volatile as the nearby contract, and formulated values create a series that tends to be smoother than the one you are likely to trade. Your test results may appear to have less risk, probably less profit, and greater reliability in identifying trends. Most important, testing would be done on a price series where none of the prices actually occurred.

Cash Data

Cash data is available for most futures markets, but FX presents a particular problem. There are many more FX crossrates than there are futures markets, and some of these can be interesting to trade. Even the Euroyen, the second or third most active trading FX market, has very low futures volume on the CME; therefore, the data may not be as good as cash data. However, testing cash data and trading futures data is not a reliable approach. Futures prices can trade at a premium or discount to cash and will fluctuate with the difference in interest rates between the two countries as well as speculative anticipation. In the extreme, the cash market may be going up and the futures market going down. Approximate futures data can be created from cash data by calculating the interest rate parity, the forward difference in the interest rates of the two component countries in the crossrate.

Problems with Adjusted Data Series

Back-adjusted data, split-adjusted data, and indexed data are ideal for testing most methods, in particular trends and momentum indicators. They cannot be used if any of the calculations require percentages. Futures markets, especially energy, have large price differentials on the roll dates. This causes older prices to be shifted down so that the prices at the beginning of the adjusted series can be negative. This makes no difference to a moving average calculation, but a percentage of a negative number is likely to play havoc with the strategy's trading decisions. This problem is more subtle for back-adjusted stock splits because the prices all appear to be scaled correctly and never go negative. For example, if IBM had split twice (each 2:1) during the past 10 years, then the price 10 years ago would have been adjusted lower by dividing by 4. If the real price in 1990 was $50 per share, the adjusted series would show it as $12.50. If the trading range was $2 at $50 per share it will be $0.50 when back-adjusted to $12.50. But the volatility at a truly lower price might be proportionally higher than at $50. The $12.50 stock will have all the characteristics of a $50 stock.

Comparing historic highs and lows cannot be done with a back-adjusted series. Analysts may normally recognize an important resistance level when prices test the highs of the previous year; however, the older price has been adjusted and may be higher or lower than its original price. To make this comparison, it is necessary to have a second series that is rolled on the same dates but not back-adjusted. The second series can be accessed when the true historic price is needed.

An indexed series can be awkward when you trade because all the prices must be converted to indexed values in order to be evaluated by the strategy. You cannot simply test using an index series, then trade using a price series.

Which Data Series Is Best?

If all adjusted series have problems, which is best? It is the series constructed from the pieces of the contract that you actually trade. In most cases, it is a back-adjusted series rolled on the volume or open interest. It is also the most liquid. If the true prices are needed, then a second series should be used.

Indexed series are also very good, although more difficult to trade. The process of indexing comes very close to volatility-adjusting and may make the data easier to use and the parameter selection more consistent.

Synthetic Data

The ultimate answer to getting test data is to create it yourself. The more data the better. It would be ideal if *synthetic data* could be created that had the same characteristics as the data that will be traded, yet is different. Over the years analysts and mathematicians have attempted to create synthetic data.

> *Monte Carlo Method.* One of the first methods used a Monte Carlo process that first scanned actual data looking for a way to divide the data into equal-length segments by finding the period that resulted in the lowest autocorrelation (the dependence of one data segment on the previous). The real data could then be rearranged randomly into a new series. Unfortunately, mixing segments would separate a prolonged bull market from the inevitable decline that occurs at the peak. In actual trading, a system can suffer a large loss when

prices peak only after it has accumulated larger profits during the previous upwards trend. Separating the data so that these two events do not follow one another is unrealistic. The Monte Carlo approach was abandoned.

Random Numbers and Distributions. A synthetic series created mathematically begins with random numbers. It has been shown that a simple series of random numbers will look very similar to most price movement, especially during a sideways period. But price movement is not normally distributed and has much longer runs, both up and down, than would be found in a random series. Real data may have seasonality, a long, underlying directional bias due to government policy, changing volatility, and a certain level of underlying noise. But mathematics is powerful, and an artificial series can be created that has 10% trend and 90% noise, reflects a seasonal bias, and has a lognormal distribution.

A more recent and sophisticated attempt at creating synthetic data can be found in Wolberg's *Expert Trading Systems*.[1] The technique uses a Gaussian distribution to represent the skewed price distribution, and a noise component that is a function of the price trend, yet variable around the trend. The trend component is itself nonlinear, created using kernel regression. One process used for verifying that the synthetic data has the same characteristics as real data is the *Fraction Same Sign*, which is the percentage of synthetic records in which the predicted and actual data have the same sign. Other statistics of variance, noise, and distribution should match.

Synthetic data is an ideal solution to a difficult problem. It also brings to mind two computers playing chess with one another. In this case, one computer creates a data series to fool the other computer into thinking that it is real. The second computer is creating a strategy that can take advantage of the fact that it knows the data series is not real, and is constructed from components that are built systematically. If the series was real, then it would have a level of complexity that resists exploitation. If it is not random, then another computer should be able to identify the process used to create the series, then capitalize on it. The second computer should always win.

■ Testing Integrity

Traditionally, analysts use as much data as possible to determine whether their proposed strategy is sound. The use of long test periods assures a good sample of markets, including long periods of sideways movement, bull and bear markets, and a good number of price shocks of various sizes. As more data is used, it is most likely that the results will show larger profits and larger losses. More data allows the possibility of larger price runs, larger price shocks, and more complex patterns.

At the risk of offending someone, the testing process most often involves some level of cheating. Acknowledging that developing a system can be difficult, there is a right way and a wrong way to test in order to arrive at credible results. This section will outline the most acceptable methods.

---

[1] John R. Wolberg, *Expert Trading Systems: Modeling Financial Markets Using Kernel Regression* (New York: John Wiley & Sons, 2000).

In-Sample and Out-of-Sample Data

The basic scientific method begins with *in-sample* data for testing the idea. In-sample data is a part of the total data available that has been set aside for testing. Normally, it is about 50% of the data. The remaining part of the data will be used for *out-of-sample* testing, or validation. If, for example, there are 20 years of data, the in-sample data could be

1. The first 10 years.
2. The last 10 years.
3. Alternating, equal periods, such as the first 5 years, then years 11–15.
4. Alternating random time periods.

Setting aside the first 50% of the data is very common, but it suffers if the markets change, becoming more or less volatile or changing characteristics due to market dynamics. The same is true of using the last 50% of the data. Choosing parameter values that worked in older or newer markets is not a robust approach.

Alternating periods gives a better sample of changing markets, and good results will require some type of adapting rules. When using alternating periods, the system actually calculates performance on all data but only displays the in-sample periods. Results should always be shown as daily changes, not total profits. If you choose total profits, then the difference between the end of one in-sample period and the start of the next will show whether the trading method netted a profit or loss during that interval. That would be cheating. Instead, the daily returns can be combined into one continuous stream and analyzed.

Alternating random periods are the most robust testing method, but those periods must be fixed at the beginning of the development process and not changed. If you were working on two different systems, each one would have its unique set of test data. In that way, you are not always testing the same data for every method you create. To create random test periods requires a small program, but that could be implemented on a spreadsheet.

- Decide how many in-sample periods and multiply by 2. Let's say there are only 2 in-sample and 2 out-of-sample periods

- Does the in-sample come first? Let's assume *yes*.

- Then, for 20 years of data, each segment will have about 5 years. Let's say that the shortest will be 2 years and the longest 8 years.

- Start the first in-sample period on day 1.

- Find a uniform random number (between 0 and 1) and multiply that value by 6, the range of years in the in-sample period. If the random number is 0.72 then the adjusted value 4.32 is added to the 2-year minimum giving the length of the first period as 6.32 years.

- The same calculation is repeated for the next two segments. The last segment is whatever is left over.

Once calculated, these intervals can be assigned to specific data and all in-sample testing will use that data. This data can be used as much as needed. Rules and parameters can be changed, and a detailed inspection of performance should be done. The data can be tortured without mercy. Evaluating these results will be discussed in the next section.

Out-of-Sample Testing

When testing is completed, it is time to validate the results using the out-of-sample data. This is the critical part. You must have done all you can to create a good system before using the out-of-sample data, because there is no second chance.

It is best to use only the out-of-sample data in your final test, and not include the in-sample data. Rarely, it will have the same successful profile as the in-sample test. More often, it will show about 50% of the returns from the in-sample data. Because there is 50% new data containing price moves never seen in the original testing, the performance is often worse. A drop in the information ratio from 2.0 to 1.0 for the out-of-sample data is actually a reasonably good result. But what happens when the ratio drops from 2.0 to 0.4? When the detail is inspected, you realize that you overlooked a case where the volatility was extreme, and adding a simple volatility filter would fix it, increasing the ratio to 1.0. This is where *integrity* enters. You cannot fix anything once you have used the out-of-sample data. That is called *feedback*. The result is always overfitting, and the chance of the system working plummets. You can spend endless time using the in-sample data, but once the out-of-sample is used, you're done.

Step-Forward Testing

The repeated process of choosing parameter values from tests of in-sample data, then applying the results to out-of-sample data, has been developed into a process called *step-forward testing*[2] (also called *walk-forward testing* and *blind simulation*). In many ways this parallels what happens in reality. We choose the parameters on back data, then use them going forward. This process goes as follows:

1. Select the total test period—for example, 20 years of daily data from 1988 through 2007.
2. Select the size of the individual test intervals—for example, 2 years.
3. Begin testing with the first 2-year period, 1988 through 1989.
4. Select the best parameter values from those results.
5. Use the selected parameter values from Step 4 to find the performance of the next 6 months of data (the first half of 1990). Accumulate this out-of-sample performance throughout the test process.
6. If there is more data to test, move the test period forward by 6 months (the second test will be from the second half of 1988 through the first half of 1990), then test the data; otherwise, go to Step 8.
7. Repeat Step 4.
8. The result of the step-forward test is the accumulated results of the individual out-of-sample tests in Step 5.

---

[2] A thorough presentation of both step-forward testing and optimum search techniques can be found in Robert Pardo, *Design, Testing and Optimization of Trading Systems* (New York: John Wiley & Sons, 1992).

This process clearly simulates the traditional approach to test design, using in-sample and out-of-sample data in its proper order. It seems intuitively satisfying.

Short-Term Bias   Step-forward testing can introduce a bias that favors faster trading models. Because the in-sample test used only 2 years of data in our example, a long-term trading model may only post a few trades during this period. If there was a bull market during the entire 2 years, then any long-term trend would have captured the same results. Without enough data, testing cannot find which calculation period is best. Consequently, it would be difficult to evaluate the risk of these positions.

The problem of short-term bias can be identified by the optimum parameter values switching from short-term to long-term in successive test periods. For example, if you test moving averages from 5 to 50 days, you will find that one period shows 10 days as the best, followed by a period in which 50 days is best, followed again by a period in which 15 days is best. This erratic behavior is a sign that the data intervals are too short. It can be corrected by increasing the test intervals from 2 years to 5 years. Longer test intervals go a long way toward eliminating the short-term bias, but they must be considered in context with the type of trend envisioned by the developer. It also requires extra data at the beginning that cannot be used in the final results.

Feedback   The most serious concern about step-forward testing is feedback, discussed in the previous section on out-of-sample testing. Each application of the step-forward process uses all of the data, where the final performance is determined from the out-of-sample part. Then, if the test is performed more than once, there is no out-of-sample data, which violates our concept of scientific testing. To avoid this, additional data can be set aside for a final test, but that reduces the amount of data available for testing and validation.

■ Searching for the Best Result

The best result, or *optimal result,* of testing a strategy is the *most robust* set of parameters. That is different from the parameter set that yields the *maximum value* of the test objective, whether it is highest profits, most consistency, or highest information ratio. It unlikely that the maximum value will be the selection that represents the most robust strategy; however, many methods require that maximum be located in order to decide the most robust. This section will discuss some of the techniques used to find the maximum result.

Search methods have evolved with technology over the past 20 years. At the high end are genetic algorithms and Monte Carlo sampling that are used when test combinations are too large to scan all possibilities. They will be discussed toward the end of this chapter. The most basic approach, *sequential testing,* calculates the results of every combination of parameters in a preset order. For example, a single moving average system with a stop-loss might have the following parameter test ranges:

1. Moving average calculation periods from 1 to 50.
2. Stop-loss values from 0 to $1,000 per share, or the equivalent, in steps of $10.

The total number of tests would then be $50 \times 100 = 5{,}000$. When three parameters are tested, the number of tests increases rapidly. Taking care to use the best parameter distribution, as discussed earlier, is a simple way to reduce the test time and improve the usefulness of the results. When there are too many tests, even with carefully chosen values, a wider spacing of values can be used to locate the general pattern of performance. Once the approximate range of parameter values is known, more detailed retesting can be done.

Calculate the number of tests you will run before beginning an optimization. Although the time may not be a problem as computers have gotten faster, you may be limited by available storage space. All computers have limits. If you generate 10,000 combinations, remember that you will need to evaluate them using a spreadsheet. Large numbers of rows and columns, combined with numerous markets, can create an unmanageably large spreadsheet.

Mathematical Optimization

If you have created a system on a grand scale and the number of parameters combined with the number of tests for each parameter generates a test that is far too long, then *mathematical optimization* offers a testing solution. One caveat is that this method only applies to continuous results. Test values must be increased incrementally, as in a moving average calculation period, with results that are also continuous; that is, performance increases and decreases somewhat smoothly as parameter values are increased. You cannot use this method to test coded variables that cause an abrupt shift in the methodology. In the simplest example, the procedure is:

1. Test one parameter, such as the moving average calculation period. Initialize the other parameters to a reasonable value.
2. Find the best result and fix that value for the remaining tests.
3. Select the next parameter to test.
4. Continue at Step 2.

This technique is called *sequential optimization*. It has the advantage of reducing a 3-parameter test case from $n_1 \times n_2 \times n_3$ total tests to $n_1 + n_2 + n_3$. It has the disadvantage, however, of not always finding the best combination of parameter values when the test is very large. Figure 7.3 shows a 2-dimensional map of test results, a good way of visualizing the relationships between parameter sets. If Figure 7.3 shows all the tests, then the best choice is the 20-day moving average with a 0.30% stop-loss (shown as 30 basis points), netting a score of 400. Using sequential testing, beginning with the moving average days, and setting the stop-loss to its lowest value, the best result (in row 1, at the top) is 200, the 15-day calculation period. Fixing the first parameter value at 15 and testing the stop-loss values, the results appear in the same column. The best result is a score of 300 when the stop-loss value was 0.30%. While this result is good, it is not the peak result or even next best, 350. For this set of tests, the best results cannot be found regardless of whether the test begins with rows or columns—when the lowest value for the other parameter was chosen.

	Moving average days				
	5	10	15	20	25
10	100	150	200	150	150
20	200	150	250	300	300
Stop-loss (points) 30	250	200	300	400	350
40	200	150	200	300	300
50	100	100	150	250	250

FIGURE 7.3   **Visualizing the Results of a 2-Dimensional Optimization.**

There are two ways that avoid this problem. One method is to list the parameters in order of importance, that is, those that would have the greatest impact on profitability, or by its fundamental importance to the strategy. This was discussed in the section "Ordering the Test Parameters." In this example, the moving average is the primary parameter; however, that choice does not work. Fortunately, mathematicians are prepared for this problem.

The other alternative is to choose a series of random starting values for each of the parameters, including the primary one, and search horizontally and vertically from that point. For example, two random values, 1 and 4, are chosen for parameter 2, the stop-loss. The test begins by scanning row 1 for all values of the moving average, which was done in the first example. The maximum score was 300. The test is repeated, scanning row 4 for all values of the moving average. This time the value 300 is found in column 4. The next scan of column 4 finds the maximum, 400. Instead of testing all combinations, $n_1 \times n_2$, the answer was found searching $2 \times (n_1 + n_2)$. This is much faster when n_1 and n_2 are large. This process is called *seeding*.

The object of any search is to find the best results with as few tests as possible. Although each 3-parameter test is only $n_1 + n_2 + n_3$ tests, the total number of tests will accumulate quickly. When you have performed a number of searches beginning with a random seed and found the same results, you can conclude with some certainty that you have located the peak. For example, if you begin searching in Figure 7.3 in any row other than row 1, or in any column at all, you will find the maximum value. For a test of this size, after 3 seeded values show the same result, you can conclude that the peak has been found. For larger tests, more seed values would be needed, yet the total number of searches will be relatively small.

More on Test Continuity

Any system can be tested using a computer, but automatic selection of the best results only makes sense when they are continuous. A moving average system with stops is continuous in all directions. Adding a third dimension, an entry or exit delay (0, 1, or 2 days) will produce continuous results in three dimensions. But not all tests satisfy this principle. It has been briefly mentioned that rule changes are the most likely cause of discontinuity. Consider a test where one variable is the trend calculation period and the other is a set of rules, coded as *L, S,* and *B*, where *L* only takes long positions, *S* only takes short positions, and *B* takes both long and short positions. Although there may be interesting patterns and relationships, averaging these results does not make sense.

If each parameter tested has values that result in a continuous return curve, there are mathematical techniques available to locate the point of maximum profit with the minimum steps. One method, *optimization by steepest descent,*[3] uses both the returns and the rate of change of returns to determine the size of the steps taken during the optimization process. This method can be suboptimal if there is more than one return peak, but can be solved using seeding.

▣ Visualizing and Interpreting Test Results

Visualization is vital for avoiding gross errors in development. Looking at a price chart of what is being tested avoids data errors, and presenting test results in some logical form shows outliers, erratic results, or various levels of continuity. Some will argue that this can all be done by scanning the results and using various measurements, yet there is no real substitution for what the eye can see.

Test platforms, such as TradeStation, MetaStock, and Ninja Trading[4] are excellent alternatives for analysts who do not want to develop their own test platforms. Trade Station performs an optimization by sequentially processing every combination of parameters from a range specified by the user. The results are shown as a table, which can be exported to Excel, with one combination of parameters following another and the results of the test displayed on one line. As an example, if we are testing a moving average with a percentage band, an optimization was specified with

1. The moving average calculation period varying from 10 to 50 days in increments of 10 days.
2. The percentage band (based on the moving average value) varying from 1% to 4% in increments of 1%.

The system buys when the closing price penetrates the upper band and sells when it penetrates the lower band. The results of the optimization using NASDAQ 100 continuous futures from 1996 through 2003 are shown in Table 7.1. The user can choose the statistics that appear in the table. In this test, the columns (from left to right) are the moving average period (*MA Per*), the percent band (*% Band*), net profit (*Net Profit*), net profit for long positions (*Long NetPrf*), net profit for short positions

---

[3] F. R. Ruckdeschel, *BASIC Scientific Subroutines*, vol. 2 (Peterborough, NH: Byte/McGraw-Hill, 1983).
[4] There are an increasing number of test platforms available for a wide range of costs. Many of these will advertise in, or have been reviewed by, *Futures* magazine, *Technical Analysis of Stocks & Commodities, Active Trader*, and *The Technical Analyst*.

TABLE 7.1 Optimization Report from TradeStation for a Moving Average—% Band System Applied to NASDAQ Continuous Futures

MA Per	% Band	Net Profit	Long NetPrf	Short NetPrf	#Trds	#PftTrds	Avg W/L	Avg Trade	Avg Wbars	Avg Lbars	MaxDD	Pfact	ROA
10	3	−89895	−32540	−57355	89	30	2.03	−1010	42	12	−189510	0.884	−47.4
10	4	−243235	−127165	−116070	61	36	1.23	−3987	46	16	−421200	0.693	−57.7
10	2	−194545	−89410	−105135	136	32	1.66	−1430	25	8	−227740	0.792	−85.4
10	1	−108775	−48005	−60770	192	35	1.56	−567	18	5	−157850	0.876	−68.9
20	2	−158015	−72245	−85770	94	32	1.61	−1681	39	10	−338560	0.792	−46.7
20	4	93265	52115	41150	48	41	1.69	1943	62	21	−120550	1.209	77.4
20	3	118545	67580	50965	60	41	1.73	1976	53	15	−221180	1.238	53.6
20	1	−39195	−13215	−25980	134	31	2.07	−293	29	7	−153890	0.945	−25.5
30	3	89365	51445	37920	52	32	2.48	1719	69	19	−128395	1.202	69.6
30	4	−12345	−13990	1645	43	32	2.02	−287	73	23	−210745	0.974	−5.9
30	1	178315	95540	82775	96	33	2.7	1857	43	8	−164980	1.352	108.1
30	2	65770	39605	26165	68	32	2.37	967	55	15	−141660	1.131	46.4
40	3	198085	103005	95080	43	34	2.9	4607	79	21	−150670	1.555	131.5
40	2	285980	152810	133170	51	35	3.46	5607	74	16	−154510	1.885	185.1
40	1	200735	106750	93985	78	28	3.79	2574	58	11	−147845	1.489	135.8
40	4	176195	80480	95715	31	38	2.37	5684	91	31	−161050	1.496	109.4
50	2	197125	107520	89605	49	34	2.89	4023	78	17	−116830	1.537	168.7
50	1	267520	140480	127040	56	33	3.51	4777	75	12	−90680	1.805	295
50	4	225465	106965	118500	27	40	2.57	8351	111	29	−152850	1.764	147.5
50	3	247025	116200	130825	31	38	2.95	7969	98	27	−127050	1.865	194.4

(*Short NetPrf*), number of trades (*#Trds*), number of profitable trades (*#PrfTrds*), average win/loss ratio (*AvgW/L*), average profit per trade (*Avg Trade*), average number of bars in a winning trade (*Avg WBars*), average number of bars in a losing trade (*Avg LBars*), maximum drawdown (*MaxDD*), profit factor (*PFact*), and return on account (*ROA*). *Profit factor* is the ratio of gross profits to gross losses, and *return on account* is the ratio of net profits to the absolute value of the maximum drawdown.

The optimization report is shown in the order that it appears after testing is completed. The moving average period increases from 10 to 50; however, the % band is not always in ascending order. Nevertheless, there is a clear pattern that shows profits begin with a 30-day moving average using a 2% and 3% band, then become profitable for longer calculation periods with all band values. When the optimization is completed, a final report is available showing the returns for the best combination of parameters, the 40-day moving average with a 2% band.

Seeing Continuity in Test Results

Visualizing the test results properly can make interpretation far easier. Table 7.1 is easy to read for the short test example, but combinations of 2 or more parameters can produce hundreds of lines of statistics that are not easy to organize. Figure 7.3 has already given a preview of how results might be presented in 2 dimensions to show continuity, rather than as a list of one test result after another, one line under the other. Consider the most basic test, a 1-parameter optimization of the moving average calculation period. Figure 7.4 shows three possible patterns that might result.

In all three patterns, the total profit/loss is shown on the left, and the moving average calculation period is shown along the bottom. Figure 7.4a indicates that both fast and slow parameters generate losses, although the midrange is profitable. It is easy to select the number of moving average days that produced the highest profit because of good continuity around that point.

Figure 7.4b shows two possible areas of success. Because both are about equal in size, the choice between the two would be based on frequency of trading and size of the profits per trade. The short calculation period has more trades, a shorter holding period, and smaller profits per trade. Another possibility is to trade the moving averages represented by the peaks. If you must choose one, then it is most likely that the longer calculation period will be considered a more conservative selection. A fast trading system can result in errors, poor execution prices, and large transaction costs. Unless these factors have been incorporated into the trading strategy, a highly profitable simulation may result in disappointing real performance.

The pattern in (b) appears exaggerated in (c), but is actually more realistic. The fast system has much higher profits in a very narrow range while the long-term trend has a wide range of success. The spike in the area of the 3-day moving average is surrounded by losses, indicating that the high profits may have been caused by a short-lived price shock or an actual window of opportunity for a fast trader. This pattern also occurs when there are no transaction costs. There are fast trading strategies that can be highly profitable without slippage or commission! The pattern in (c) is also exaggerated by

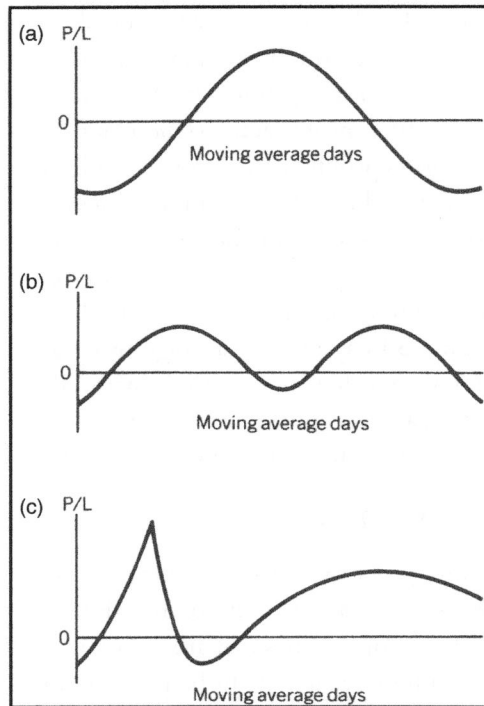

FIGURE 7.4 Possible Resulting Patterns from a Test That Varies Only the Moving Average Days.

testing calculation periods with equal increments. As discussed earlier, calculation periods of 90 and 100 days will have similar results compared to periods of 10 and 20 days.

The three patterns in Figure 7.4 are all good results, showing a wide range of calculation periods that produce profits. An erratic pattern, one that does not have these smooth return relationships, shows that the underlying strategy is unreliable, or that the test program has errors.

Two-Parameter Tests

The most common tests are those that have two or more parameters, a combination of one or two trends, an indicator for timing, a stop-loss for risk control, and sometimes profit targets. Table 7.1 showed the results of a moving average with a percent band. The results of a 2-parameter test, for example, a moving average and a stop-loss, can be shown as a *grid* (a 2-dimensional table) in the same form as Figure 7.3, with the moving average calculation period along the left (rows) and the stop-loss values at the top (columns). Figure 7.5 shows that the fewest number of days and the smallest stop-loss value will give the score in the top left corner box. The bottom right box will show the result of the longest trend and largest stop-loss. With this presentation, there is continuity of performance in all directions. The patterns in the upper right may be similar to those of the lower left if the system displays some symmetry.

Although the combination of markets, trading rules, and parameter values can produce a very large combination of results, three patterns are most likely to appear

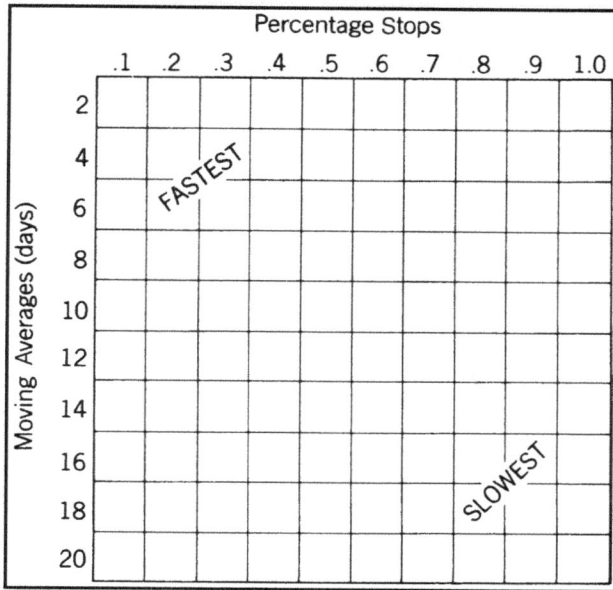

FIGURE 7.5 Standard Configuration for a 2-Dimensional Optimization.

in this 2-dimensional presentation. Figure 7.6a shows the simplest case, where a single area of successful performance is broad and gradually tapers off. This is analogous to the single parameter test shown in Figure 7.4a. Selecting the parameters associated with the center of the best performance area seems the most logical based on the reasoning that moderate shifts in price patterns are still likely to be profitable.

Two areas of profitability are usually the results of a highly volatile market (Figure 7.6b). Prices that are moving quickly and sustain a major trend can be traded using a fast or slow model. The fast model is often more profitable because it captures more of the trend; it then reacts faster to change of direction. It also has more losing trades and higher cost. The slower trend-following approach captures less of the price move by entering later and exiting later, but has a higher percentage of profitable trades. It may also have a lower information ratio because it holds those trades through larger price swings. Choosing the parameters to use in actual trading follows the same reasoning applied to Figures 7.4b and 7.4c.

The third case, shown in Figure 7.6c, has erratic returns. The absence of a consistent pattern in the performance indicates that the trading strategy does not work with this data.

Alternate Ways of Visualizing Results

A wide range of statistical software provides user-friendly ways to show results as a *contour* or *topological relief map*. The patterns shown in Figure 7.6 can be seen in multiple colors, graded from one shade to another as returns increase and decrease, making it much easier to see the peaks and valleys of performance and get a sense of smoothness. Any spreadsheet program will allow a *surface plot* which will give you a rough look at the continuity of a 2-parameter test, as shown in Figure 7.7. This 3-dimensional graph

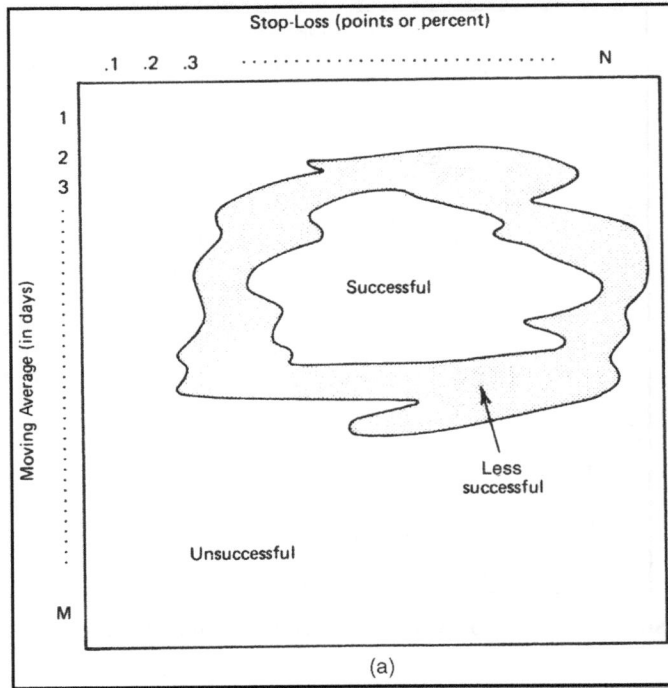

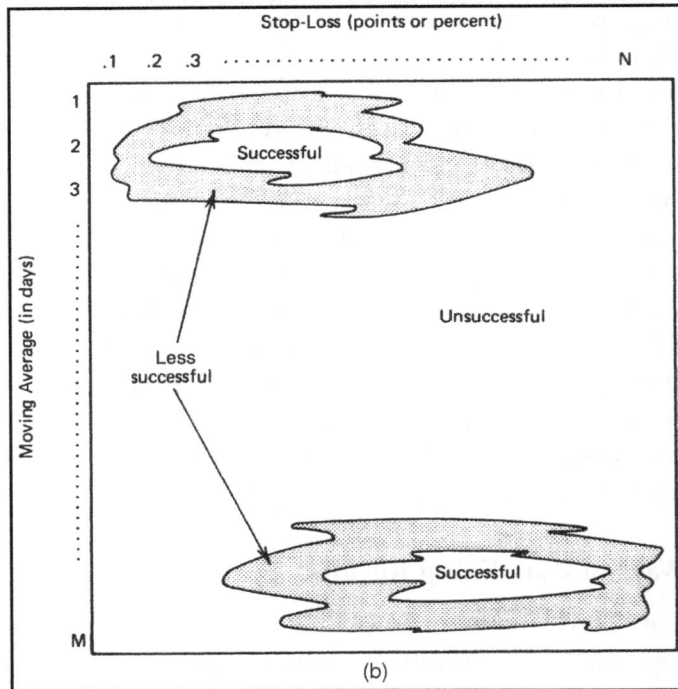

FIGURE 7.6 **Patterns Resulting from a 2-Dimensional Optimization. (a) Single Profitable Area. (b) Two Distinct Profitable Areas. (c) No Obvious Pattern.**

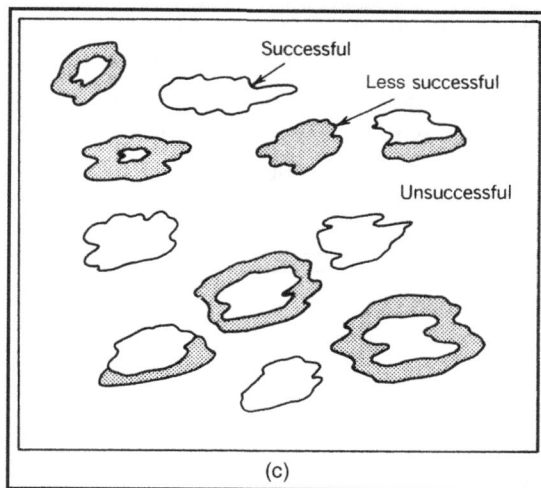

FIGURE 7.6 *(Continued)*

gives the profit factors for the moving average–stop-loss strategy shown in Table 7.1. The moving average calculation periods are shown along the bottom right scale (*Y*), the stop-loss percentages along the bottom left (*X*), and the profit factor on the upright axis (*Z*). The returns shown on the surface have the best returns as the moving average calculation periods get larger, and the best stop-loss is in the center, about 2.5%. The fastest trends and the largest stop-losses have the worst performance. Overall, the stop-loss choices do not contribute as much as the trend. If smaller increments were used for testing the variables, the surface diagram would be smoother.

Visualizing with Scatter Diagrams Unfortunately, technology does not yet allow us to chart more than 3 dimensions. If the system has three parameters, a moving average, RSI, and stop-loss, it will be necessary to have more than one chart in order

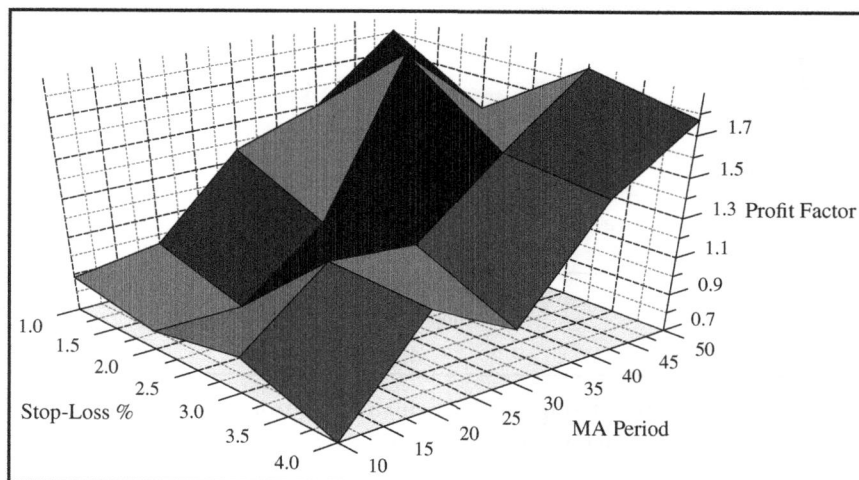

FIGURE 7.7 **3-Dimensional Surface Plot of Moving Average–Stop-Loss Strategy.**

to visualize the results. In Figures 7.8a and b, there are only two parameters, a moving average and a stop-loss. Each chart will show the results of only one. To accomplish this, the results of an optimization were exported to PSI-Plot software,[5] although a similar result could be achieved with Excel using an *XY plot*. Each circle represents the results of an individual test where the moving average or the stop-loss had the value shown along the bottom.

THE INTEGRATION OF TECHNICAL ANALYSIS

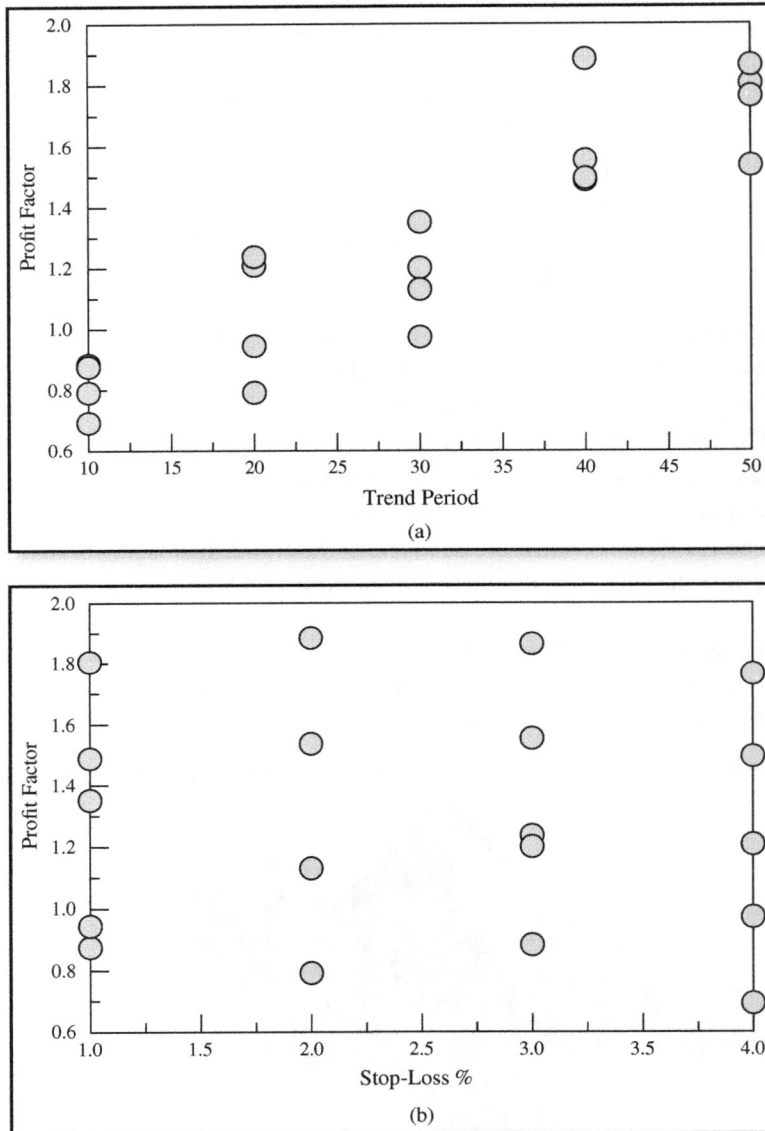

FIGURE 7.8   Visualizing the Performance of Multiple Parameters. (a) Moving Average Calculation Periods. (b) Stop-Loss % Values.

[5] *PSI-Plot* and *ProStat* are products of Poly Software International. They provide excellent statistical analysis and graphics at a reasonable cost.

The moving average results in Figure 7.8a show a clear progression of success as the calculation period increases, except for the last two cases, the 40- and 50-day periods. While the range of results is the same, the 50-day clusters near the top, and the 40-day near the bottom, favoring the 50-day. Overall, we see that long-term moving averages perform better than shorter-term. Of course, this is only one market, one time period, and a very small test, so much more testing would need to be done to be confident of this conclusion.

Figure 7.8b shows that the stop-loss results are far less convincing. The 4% stop can be eliminated as the worst performer because it has lower highs and lower lows; however, the other three are not as clear. The one good note is that about 80% of the tests are above the profit factor value of 1.0, which indicates a net profit (gross profits greater than gross losses). While the 1% stop has the smallest range of results, the 2% the largest, and the 3% in between, it is not clear which is best. We can suggest that, if the averages are the same, the stop-loss value with the smallest standard deviation of profit-factors would show the greatest stability.

Standardizing Test Results

When testing a single system, the results of one set of parameters can easily be compared to other sets because the test period, commissions, and other basic values are all the same. However, over time you will test many different systems and variations of those systems, and you will want to compare them to decide which strategy is best. This requires some advanced planning. Standardizing test results is the best way to increase the usefulness of extensive testing. This should include:

1. *Annualizing all values.* Tests not performed using the exact same test intervals (for example, 10-year and 12-year periods), or tests on different futures markets, are likely to use data that starts and ends on different dates. Annualizing the results will not give a perfect comparison, but will make comparisons more relevant.
2. *Risk adjusting.* A profit of $10,000 with a drawdown of $5,000 is effectively the same as a profit of $20,000 and a drawdown of $10,000, given adequate reserves. Expressing the results as profits divided by risk, called the *information ratio*, is a better way to view returns.
3. *Adjusting for standard error.* The important difference between two tests that yield the same results, one test with two trades and the other with 50 trades, is that the one with only two trades is a less reliable result. If both posted 50% profitable trades, another losing trade would make the reliability of the second test drop to 49%, while the first case would drop to 33%. Instead, results should be presented at the same confidence level, which means subtracting the standard error from the current result.

Averaging the Results   Because the testing process is computer-dependent, it is desirable to make the selection of the best parameters automatically. This

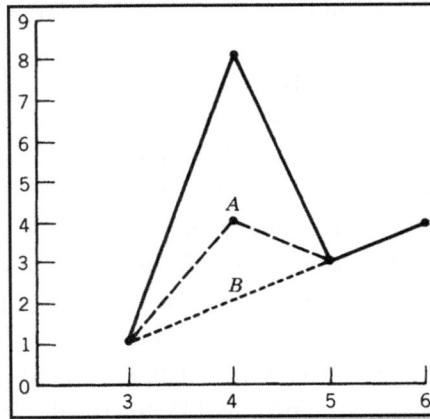

FIGURE 7.9 Replacing a Spike with the Average A or an Interpolation B.

can usually be done effectively by averaging either the annualized returns or the return ratio displayed in the test map. In the case of a moving average system, you may choose to eliminate distortions in performance caused by spikes. For example, the results of a 3-, 4-, 5-, and 6-day test show profits of 1,000, 8,000, 3,000, and 4,000, respectively. The 4-day case appears to be a profit spike and could be minimized by replacing its value with the average of the three values or, preferably, by the interpolated value of the two adjacent points (Figure 7.9). In general, the substitution process in which every value is replaced by the average of its neighbors

$$\overline{PL}_i = \frac{PL_{i-1} + PL_i + PL_{i+1}}{3}$$

will smooth out the returns. The best parameter set is the highest value of $\overline{PL}_i$ once all averages have been substituted for the raw test results. This may help find the overall performance pattern rather than an outlier.

2-Parameter Averaging The results of a 2-parameter test may also be averaged to create a smoother set of values. Using a 2-dimensional grid shown in Figure 7.10, the original net profit or loss of each test will be denoted as PL_{ij}, associated with row i and column j of the display. The object is to replace each PL_{ij} with $\overline{PL}_i$, the average value of its neighbors. This is done, as seen in Figure 7.10a, by taking an average of the 8 test results adjacent to the ijth value as well as the center value. There are special cases when the ijth result is not fully surrounded but on the perimeter of the test grid. Figures 7.10b, c, and d show the averaging technique used when the ijth box is a top, side, or corner value. The 9-box average shown here is comparable to the 3-point average in the 1-parameter test. If the test has relatively small increments between tests and more test cases, an average of a larger area would be better. A generalization of this method can be found later in this chapter under "Sensitivity Testing."

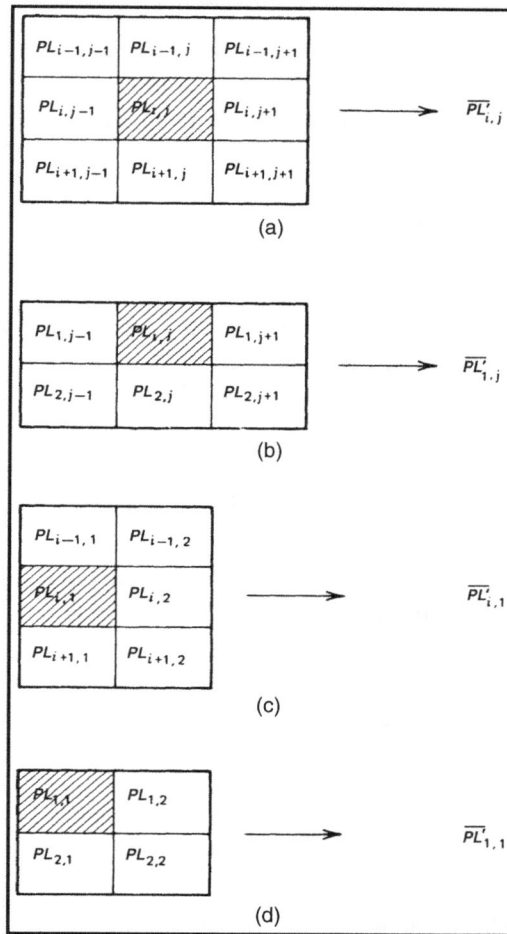

FIGURE 7.10 Averaging of Map Output Results. (a) Center Average (9 Box). (b) Top Edge Average (6 Box). (c) Left Edge Average (6 Box). (d) Upper Left Corner Average (4 Box).

◼ Large-Scale Testing

A strategy with many parameters, each with a wide range of values, will result in a large-scale test—an optimization of hundreds of thousands (or even millions) of tests. It would be impossible to use any form of sequential testing to reduce the test time to something reasonable. Yet there are search methods that can arrive at a likely solution quickly. Two of these are *genetic algorithms* and *Monte Carlo* sampling.

Genetic Algorithms

A genetic algorithm is a very practical and very powerful searching tool.[6]

---

[6] Readers are encouraged to read Murray A. Ruggiero, Jr., "Using Genetic Algorithms for Trading Applications," Chapter 20 in *Cybernetic Trading Strategies* (New York: John Wiley & Sons, 1997).

In the previous discussion, a trend and an oscillator were combined into a trading strategy and the rules for applying each component could be randomly changed. In this example, the rules will be fixed, but the parameter values are unknown; only the range of parameter values can be specified. Define the strategy and the range of calculation values as:

1. A long-term moving average trend, 30 to 250 days, increments of 5.
2. A percentage band around the long-term moving average, 0.5% to 4.0%, increments of 0.25%.
3. A short-term moving average trend, 3 to 30 days, increments of 3.
4. A percentage band around the short-term moving average, 0.1% to 1.5%, increments of 0.1%.
5. An RSI for entry timing, 5 to 20 days, increments of 1.
6. RSI overbought and oversold thresholds, 40 to 95 for overbought, −40 to −95 for oversold (only one set is needed if these values are symmetric), increments of 5.
7. A percentage stop-loss, 0.25% to 3.0%, increments of 0.25%.
8. A moving average trend for equity, 5 to 50 days, increments of 5.

These 8 parameters seem innocent enough, but total 2,332,800,000 tests. At 10 tests per second, the processing time would be 64,800 hours, more than 7 years!

Initialization
1. A *string* of 8 cells is created to represent each of the parameters. A string is the general term given to a single set of parameter values, called a *chromosome*.
2. Each cell in the string is assigned a random number that determines which parameter value will be used.
3. A pool of 1,000 to 5,000 strings is created, the larger, the better.

Propagation
4. The *objective function* (ranking score such as the information ratio) is calculated for each string.
5. The pool is sorted in descending order by objective function.
6. Multiple copies are made of the highest-ranking strings and added to a new pool.
7. The new pool is sorted by highest objective function, and culled to the best 5,000 strings. The new pool replaces the old pool so there is only one pool.

Mating
8. Two strings, not previously selected, are chosen at random from the pool.
9. A random number between 1 and 8 divides the cells of the strings into left and right parts.

10. The left part of the first string is switched with the left part of the second string, creating two new strings.

11. The mating process continues until 10% to 15% of the strings have been combined.

Mutating

12. One string is chosen at random from the pool.

13. One of the 8 cells is chosen at random.

14. Based on the range of values for the parameter assigned to this cell, a new value is chosen at random and replaces the old value.

15. Mutation continues until one cell in 10% of the strings has been changed.

Converging

16. The best objective function, or score, is saved at the end of each pass, and the parameter values associated with this string are saved.

17. The genetic algorithm process continues at Step 4 until the objective function converges. That occurs when, after a number of passes, the objective function does not increase significantly.

18. The genetic algorithm process is repeated up to 5 times, beginning with the initialization, in order to produce different seeded strings.

19. After 5 passes, the string previously saved with the highest objective function is the solution.

Saving a set of best results will improve your understanding of its success. If, for example, the best 20 strings all cluster at a similar solution, it is likely to be more robust. If the cells of the top 20 vary considerably, then the integrity of the results are in question.

For a trading strategy with 8 parameters and over 2 billion combinations, the genetic algorithm should converge within 100 passes. Repeating the process five times in order to seed the cells differently increases the number of passes to 500. It is likely that the elapsed computer time will be 30 minutes. It does not guarantee that the maximum combination will be found. The chances of finding a maximum can be increased with a larger pool and by reseeding more times. However, the parameter values chosen from this short search will be astoundingly good. We will never know how close the results come to finding the maximum because no one is going to run a full test.

Monte Carlo Sampling

The problem with the genetic algorithm solution is that it returns only the maximum results. There is no information on the depth of success that is needed to determine robustness. It is helpful to know the parameter values that are most successful, but it is not always enough. *Monte Carlo* sampling is used to create a statistically valid subset of tests when the total number of tests is too large. The results of this smaller set of tests can be analyzed as though it were the complete set.

Monte Carlo simulation (MCS) was created by the famous mathematicians Johann von Neumann and Stanislaw M. Ulam; they devised the method shortly after

World War II to help them simulate the behavior of an atomic weapon. There is an interesting example of how the Monte Carlo process has been used to find the area of a lake with an extremely irregular shoreline. A picture of the lake is taken from above and the scale is determined (e.g. $1'' = 100$ feet). Think about the picture as $10'' \times 10''$, displayed in color on a computer screen, with the lake clearly blue and the surroundings green. The picture is then superimposed with a fine grid, so that there are 100 (or even 1,000 if more accuracy is needed) pixels per inch, for a dimension of $1,000 \times 1,000$ representing the entire screen, an unknown part of which is the lake. Now pick two *uniform random numbers* between 1 and 1,000 to represent the x and y coordinates, and say the first values are 135 and 441. Remember that a uniform random number has an *equal chance* of being any of the values between 1 and 1,000. The position (135,441) is marked on the display and the computer determines whether it falls in the lake or on the shore. This process is repeated for 1,000 pairs of random numbers. When completed, the computer has counted 520 pairs that were in the lake; therefore, 52% of the display area is lake, or 520,000 square feet. If more accuracy was needed, the grid would be divided into more pixels, and more random pairs would be generated. The process works because the probability of a pair of random numbers falling in the lake is equal to the ratio of the lake's area to the entire picture.[7]

Random numbers can also be used to generate parameter values in a test of a trading strategy. Using the same 8 parameters applied to the genetic algorithm solution, a value is picked at random for each parameter from the list of ranges specific to that parameter. This is the same step as the initialization of the pool of strings used in the genetic algorithm. Every time a value is picked a counter is incremented. Every parameter has a counter for every possible value used in the test. After the first string is created and saved in a table along with its performance statistics, the counter for each random value that was used is increased by 1. After 1,000 random strings, the total count for the list of values in any parameter will total 1,000.

The first opportunity to end the test is when the distribution of all values within a parameter list is normal. For a truly random selection, each value should have approximately the same count. Because there were 10 values for parameter 8, after 1,000 strings each value should have a count of very close to 100. If there were 20 values, each would have a count of 50. Once the minimum distribution criterion is satisfied, the more strings that are generated, the better the sample. These strings can now be analyzed as though they were the entire test set, although academics will argue that the statistical quality of the sample data (e.g., variance) may vary significantly from the whole set.

As with the genetic algorithm solution, the Monte Carlo sampling can be performed a number of times. If the best results are similar, then you can be confident that the smaller sample is a good representation of the entire set. The use of random values has the additional advantage of avoiding unfair targeting of values that may be known in advance to perform well.

---

[7] Adapted from an example in Wolf von Ronik, "System Testing via Monte Carlo," *Futures* (April 2001).

▓ Refining the Strategy Rules

As testing progresses, still using the in-sample data, it is inevitable that the analyst will want to modify a rule or add a new feature to the trading strategy. This usually follows from inspecting the results of tests and noting that a specific pattern was not treated properly (or profitably). After some work, the analyst introduces a carefully constructed rule, which turns a previous loss into a profit. Figure 7.11 shows two possible changes in the performance pattern for 1-parameter test based on this change.

If the rule change improves the specific situation that was intended, but loses money in other market situations, the complete test pattern will appear as shown in Figure 7.11a. Higher peak profits occur where the new rule works best, but other parameter values have been turned from profits to losses or to larger losses. The average returns may remain the same, but the results are more extreme. Because the new rule caused the fitting of a specific pattern at the cost of added losses in other patterns, it is not an improvement. Statistically, this performance change can be measured by kurtosis. A very high value of kurtosis is a sign of overfitting.

In Figure 7.11b, the new rule improves performance in all cases. This pattern is an ideal solution. It is possible, of course, that an improvement is defined in such a way that it corrects only that specific problem without affecting any other trades. That type of rule fitting, which affects only one or two cases, is unlikely to work in the future. If it falsely raises expectations of success, it puts the investor at risk.

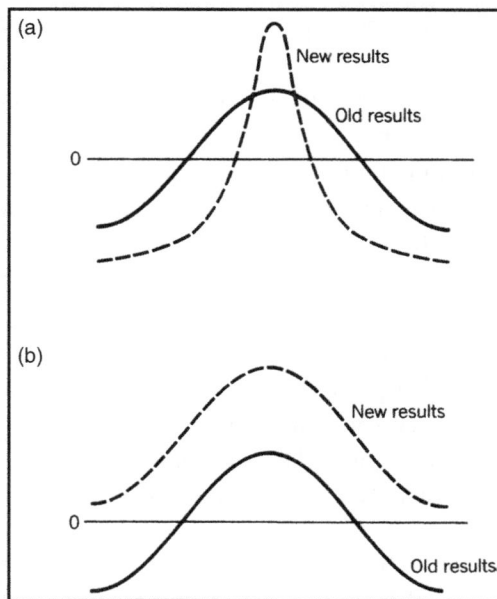

FIGURE 7.11 Patterns Resulting from Changing Rules. (a) A Rule Change that Improves One Situation at the Cost of Others. (b) A Rule Change Resulting in General Improvement.

■ Arriving at Valid Test Results

It is not unusual for the results of an optimization, especially one with many parameters, to appear perfect. All the trades could be profitable, the equity drops might be small, and the strategy might perform in changing markets, and yet, the final system will consistently lose money when traded. Creating a system with predictive qualities (rather than one that is historically fitted) requires preparation in advance of testing.

There is no "best" place to say this, and it should be said in more than one place. *We have a tendency to accept good test results, but look closely for errors when there are bad results.* It is important that all results be verified carefully.

Common Sense versus Statistics

You can always find a particular moving average or indicator that gave a signal to sell the S&P just before the 1987 crash, or ahead of the 2008 mortgage crisis. It is not difficult when a computer can combine millions of combinations of trend speeds, filters, momentum indicators, divergence rules, and so on, using powerful search engines. It is also easy when you are willing to sacrifice performance at other times to capture the biggest profits in recent history. However, what works in a specific case, and often an unusual one, is not likely to work in general. Manipulating the rules is a wasted effort. Showing that a combination of technical indicators would have profited from the last market crash has no bearing on how it will respond to the next crisis.

The adage that "there are lies, half lies, and statistics" is true. Statistics can prove a point or prove just the opposite, depending on how the numbers are presented. A frequent contradiction in the news is when an anticrime group states that burglaries doubled in the past year while the police department states that burglaries rose by the slowest rate in 5 years. A market can be in an uptrend and a downtrend at the same time, based on the time interval over which you view it.

The most profitable test results may not be the ones you want. If you tested the S&P from 1990 through 2003, the results would be overwhelmed by the 10-year bull market. The parameter values may be biased toward longer-term trends that captured most of the market's upwards move; however, it would have lost money during the sideways prices moves of 2002–2003. The statistical profile will still look good because the bull market profits were far greater than the more recent losses; however, using a strategy that capitalized on an unusual bull market is not a good choice. As Jack Schwager has stated, "The mistake is extrapolating probable future performance on the basis of an isolated and well-chosen example from the past."[8]

Omissions and Scenarios The more difficult problems to overcome are the ones you cannot see, the price moves that are not part of your test data, and the *omissions*. Every few years the market experiences a price shock, most recently the subprime collapse

---

[8] Jack D. Schwager, *Schwager on Futures: Technical Analysis* (New York: John Wiley & Sons, 1996), 673.

of 2008, before that the terrorist attack of September 11, 2001. Price history is full of small price shocks caused by economic reports, but the very large ones are years apart. If your test does not include data with a significant price shock, then you cannot know if you will survive the next one. If you have tested a strategy using data that is highly skewed in one direction, as the equity markets were in the 1990s, then the resulting strategy will be biased. You must be constantly looking for potential problems. As of early 2012, the best strategy would have been long bonds from the early 1990s, ignoring all information to the contrary. But eventually inflation and an improved economy will change that, and a long-only strategy will give back its gains. You must question the ability of your strategy to perform under different scenarios. The following guidelines were developed over many years and are intended to avoid the most basic and costly errors that occur in testing. You may be able to add your own experiences to this list.

Searching for Robustness

A *robust* system is one that performs consistently in a wide variety of situations, including patterns that are still unforeseen. From a practical view, this translates into a method that succeeds with the fewest parameters tested over the most data. In tests by Futures Truth,[9] the best performing systems commonly have four or fewer variables.[10] The characteristics of a system with the best forecasting ability are:

1. *It must be based on a sound premise.* Each rule and formula must capitalize on a real fundamental or price phenomenon. *Discovering* a price pattern or cycle through optimization may seem to be a revelation, but it is more likely to be an illusion. By testing enough patterns, it is statistically probable that one of them will seem to fit. Without a fundamental reason for the existence of that pattern, it is not safe to use it. For example, the use of a very long-term trend to trade interest rates is intended to mimic the direction of U.S. economic policy; a shorter 1-month trend may be best for capturing the seasonal moves in agricultural commodities. A short-term trader may hypothesize that a strong close on increasing intraday volatility will have follow-through on the next open. Observations based on experience and confirmed by testing are usually sound.

2. *It must adapt to changing market conditions.* A system that assumes that markets do not change or that everything has been seen in past data will suffer large equity swings. Self-adjusting features do not use absolute price levels or fixed dollar amounts. They might include an inflator or deflator, stop-loss values that adjust to volatility, rule shifts based on whether the current year shows a seasonal or nonseasonal pattern, and a variation in position size based on changing risk.

3. *It must be tested properly.* The principles of statistics say that the best tests use the most data. More data includes bull, bear, and sideways markets, large and small price shocks, and periods of instability and doldrums. There is no substitute for

[9] John Hill and George Pruitt, Futures Truth, Hendersonville, N.C., is an organization that validates and monitors trading systems. It publishes *Futures Truth Magazine,* www.futurestruth.com.
[10] John Hill, "Simple vs. Complex," *Futures* (March 1996), 57.

more data, even when some analysts say that old data is no longer valid. Proper test procedures include using in-sample and out-of-sample data periods, discussed earlier. Alternately, you can paper trade until there are enough trades to compare the out-of-sample profile with the expectations defined by your tests.

From time to time, each of the three points above will seem to be the most important. In the long run, they must all be included to create a robust program.

Performance Criteria

Assuming that the proper principles have been followed, are the test results good enough? Although the strategy shows steady profits with a low equity drop, could a simpler system have done better? It can be a rude awakening to be pleased with your system's 20% returns only to realize that the average stock return was 25%. The industry has become highly competitive.

Benchmarks   It is necessary to have a *benchmark* that provides a way of measuring success. It is best if this is a well-documented indicator, such as the S&P Index, the Lehman Brothers Treasury Index, a class of funds, such as Fidelity, or a Commodity Trading Advisor (CTA) Index as published by BarclayHedge. Benchmarks add a note of reality to expectations. The reason for developing a trading strategy is to have more consistent profits, or less risk during volatile periods, or a different return profile, than an investment program already offered by, say, the Royal Bank of Scotland. Depending on the period you measure, the S&P 500 has a return-to-risk ratio ranging from about 1.0 to zero, meaning that, at the better end, there is a 16% chance that the risk during any one year will exceed the annualized returns.

The spectacular profits or losses of one manager that get spotlighted in the news is not a good measure of anything, but simply a rare event. The focus should be on consistency, having very good gains each year. The largest gain can only come with high risk. You should not be surprised that those investment advisors posting the highest monthly returns have had very erratic performance in the past. It is all too common to see a fund with the largest monthly gains, up 20% in June, but still down 5% for the year.

Inaccuracies can hide in the benchmarks. Two important idiosyncrasies of published benchmarks are *survivorship bias* and *asymmetric measurement of returns.* Considering the last, some hedge funds that lost 50% in 2008 then gained 50% in 2009. Did they recover their investors' losses? Of course not. A gain of 50% after a loss of 50% still leaves the investor with a loss of 25%. Survivorship bias is a different type of problem. If a hedge fund has been reporting its performance each month, but has a fatal loss and closes down its fund, it most often will not report the returns of the last month. It has no motivation to do that. Therefore, the performance benchmarks often omit the largest of the negative monthly returns.

Measuring Test Results   As a preamble to measuring results, specify the test range for each parameter in advance. An optimization should represent a broad sampling of tests over a wide but reasonable range of parameter values. This range should be established before testing begins and not changed. For example, if a short-term moving average is being tested from 3 to 15 days, then an RSI used for timing would have a range of 3 to 10 days. You would not test the RSI from 3 to 50 days because the longer periods do not make sense in the context of the original plan. Even worse, if the 45-day RSI proved the best, the initial concept may be discarded in order to pursue a solution that is most likely to be an overfitted dead end. If the common-sense ranges are used and are not profitable, the concept should be reviewed.

There are a number of popular performance criteria used to evaluate any trading strategy.

1. *Information ratio.* This single, most important measure is the annualized returns divided by the annualized standard deviation of returns. It gives you a clear way to value the return relative to risk and the smoothness of returns. Other measures, such as TradeStation's *profit factor*, the gross profits divided by the gross losses, can also be used.

2. *Net profits or losses.* Although not the best criterion for picking a parameter value, profits are the reason for trading. While no one would select a system that produces a net loss, it is the other statistics that will tell which are the best choices for parameter values.

3. *Number of trades.* This simple value indicates whether your test was long enough to generate dependable results. A few trades can appear very profitable, but small numbers are statistically unreliable. A system that has more trades with the same returns has a better chance of performing up to expectations.

4. *Percentage of profitable trades.* Also called *reliability,* a value above 60% can be interpreted as a method that captures profits regularly. A trend system will be working correctly if its reliability is between 30% and 40%.

5. *Average net return per trade.* The average return per trade gives you an indication of how difficult it will be to realize the system returns. An average return of $50 per trade for a currency is likely to be overwhelmed by the slippage, which typically exceeds 4 bps for each side, a total of $100 for a round-turn futures contract. Many very fast trading systems look good until you apply realistic costs. Slippage per side on the S&P should be 50 basis points, fixed income $\frac{1}{32}$ to $\frac{2}{32}$ (about $45), and energy products up to 20–30 basis points (about $100). The slippage executing stocks varies with the liquidity and market volatility. Slippage should be as accurate as possible, determined from actual trading. While it is good to be conservative by using a larger slippage, it eliminates faster trading systems that may be highly profitable.

6. *Maximum drawdown.* The largest equity swing from peak to valley is the maximum drawdown. This measurement can be very erratic and is not likely to be the largest risk seen in the future; however, it gives a rough idea of the minimum capital needed to trade this market. A surprisingly small maximum drawdown is a sign of overfitting or a very small test period. It is safer to take the average maximum drawdown from a range of tests than the one from the best result. An investor will typically capitalize a trading account with three times the maximum drawdown.

7. *Annualized rate of return.* The rate of return requires that the size of the initial investment be known. The investment can be calculated after the fact from the risk-to-equity ratio based on the maximum drawdown or standard deviation of historic returns, linked to a *target volatility level.* Annualized returns allow you to compare one test against others or against a benchmark.

8. *Average time-to-recovery.* A large drawdown may be inevitable in a realistic system, but a shorter time-to-recovery is most desirable. *Time-to-recovery* is the time between two successive equity highs. A larger drawdown with a much faster recovery seems to be a better trade-off for most investors.

9. *Time in the market.* All else being equal—profitability and risk—a trading system that is in the market less than another system is preferable. If two systems have approximately the same performance profiles, then the one that is in the market less is exposed to fewer price shocks. It may be a good trade-off to sacrifice some potential profit in order to be out of the market more often. As discussed, being out of the market is the only defense against event risk.

10. *Slope of periodic returns.* If the quarterly or annualized returns are saved and a linear regression line drawn through those returns, the slope of that line would indicate whether the performance of the strategy is constant over time. A declining slope should be interpreted as better performance in the past, perhaps a trend system that did exceptionally well in the equity market of the 1990s but is not doing well now. A rising slope means that the strategy does better under current price patterns than older ones. A horizontal slope is best, indicating consistent performance across all time periods.

Having decided the measurements needed to understand the results of an individual test, there are other rules that must be established, including how to assess the end results. This will help to avoid bending the rules to fit the results.

Average Results   *Use the average of all test results.* Specifying reasonable parameter ranges is important when evaluating the test results. Nearly all sets of tests will show losses, but hopefully, there will be some areas of attractive profits. If you tested 1,000 cases and 30% of the tests showed returns of about 25% per year, 30% showed breakeven results, and the last 40% showed various profits and losses, you might say that the 30% profitable tests are a broad area from which parameter values can be chosen. That assumes that the market will continue to perform in a way that allows those parameters to generate profits during the next year. It is better to assume that the price patterns change; you cannot tell which combination of parameters will be the best. Regardless of the past returns for the parameters you choose, your expectations should be the average performance of all tests.

It would be optimistic to expect the average return of all tests to be highly profitable; however, that is the correct goal. When comparing systems, the best one has the highest average of all tests as well as the most profitable number of tests. If you accept the premise that actual trading performance is represented by the average of all tests, then your expectations are realistic. A statistical indication of the likely success of a strategy would be

Adjusted returns = Average of all tests − 1 Standard deviation of all test returns

A system satisfying this requirement should have an 84% chance of achieving the adjusted returns.

Review Outliers   Realistically, a system should not base its profitability on a single major market move over the test interval. In particular, if the move that generated the profit was actually a price shock, the system had only a 50% chance of posting that profit and has an equal chance of a loss in the future. It may be practical to re-move the profits generated on the first day or two of a move that began with a price shock, allowing for the possibility of holding the wrong position in the future. By posting a windfall profit, the risk of the system is erroneously reduced.

Concentrate on large profits and large losses   The largest profits and losses are critical to the net performance of any system; therefore, you should make a special effort to study those trades. In doing that, you may find that the largest profits were the results of price shocks, as discussed in the previous point, or that there is an erroneous piece of data that was not seen before. If there are a number of large profits and no large losses, you can be sure that you have over fit the data.

Sensitivity Testing

Once the parameter values have been selected, a sensitivity test should be performed. *Sensitivity testing* is simply a way of finding out how much performance changes when the individual and combinations of parameter values are shifted up and down by small amounts. A robust solution should be modestly sensitive to changing values; in some cases, the performance will improve, but generally, as larger changes in values are used, some decay is expected. Overall, small changes in parameter values should not jeopardize the profitability of the strategy. If the performance declines for all other parameter values, then the current model is a peak solution, which usually means it was overfit and will not meet expectations.

Sensitivity in n-Space   When using multiple parameters, sensitivity needs to be viewed as an *n*-dimensional problem, commonly called *n-space*. Let's try to visualize what this means and find a way to show sensitivity given changes in each of *n* parameters.

Using four parameters in our example, assign w_0, x_0, y_0, and z_0 as the chosen, or *core*, parameter values with the resulting performance at location (0,0,0,0). As the parameter values change, the new results will be away from the core in any of 4 directions. With *n* parameters they would move in *n* directions. We can measure where they are by finding *the radius of an n-dimensional "sphere,"*

$$r_i^2 = (w_i - w_0)^2 + (x_i - x_0)^2 + (y_i - y_0)^2 + (z_i - z_0)^2$$

Because the position of the test is defined by the radius, the distinction between these tests will be how far they are from the core. All *i* sets of parameters can be sorted, smallest to largest. If they are partitioned into, for example, 10 equal sets, they represent concentric layers of the same sphere going outward. By averaging the performance statistics of each of the tests within the same layer, we can see how much that average decays as it moves away from the core in any direction. We then have an *n*-dimensional sensitivity test. An enterprising analyst might take this a step farther and use random numbers for the parameters (within a predefined range), calculate the radius from the midpoint parameter values, along with the performance statistics, and find the most robust layer.

Reading Between the Lines

It is easy to show specific examples of rules, indicators, and systems that produce large profits, while the overall performance is bad. Many books and systems for sale base the "proof" of a trading method on specific examples. These examples look reasonable in isolation. There is an inclination to accept these examples if the concept is sound, when there is fundamental or economic substantiation, such as expecting a seasonal low in the U.S. crops at harvest. Nevertheless, proving that a system is likely to be successful can only be done with a long-term test and disclosure of the statistical performance profile, not with a few well-chosen examples.

The Significance of "Significant"

It is often the case that *statistically significant* results are not actually significant. This goes back to the problem of testing, retesting, and knowing how many combinations have been included in the sample. Using a less-than-statistical method, we previously suggested that a trading method was robust if 70% of all tests were profitable. Naturally, that would be initial tests using a reasonable range of test values. If we subsequently narrowed that range to eliminate calculation periods that always lost money, that rule would no longer apply.

If 1,000 different parameter values, spread over a wide range, were tested on a 10-year period of historic data, how many of them need to be profitable to consider the system statistically successful? That's not clear. But, given the number of tests, one highly successful parameter is certainly not significant. In addition, if you continue to try new trading ideas and one is finally successful, is that really significant? Isn't it the cumulative number of tests across all strategies that should be considered? Finding 1 strategy in 100 does not seem as comforting as finding the first one successful based on a sound premise. Cranking out combinations of indicators and trends is sure to find an occasional but insignificant success.

Systems That Work in Only One Market

If a system is developed for the emini S&P futures, should it work on the NASDAQ 100, or on the Dow? Seen on a quote machine, and statistically, the price moves of those markets are very similar. When an Initial Claims report is surprisingly high, they all drop together; and when Retail Sales are lower than expected, they all fall together. Each of the three markets represents a different set of stocks, and each has a different volatility profile, and while a disappointing earnings report by Intel will impact NASDAQ more than the S&P or Dow, there are implications in the Intel earnings that inevitably affect stocks in all markets.

Then the answer should be *yes,* a strategy that is profitable for one index market should be profitable for similar index markets, unless it is using certain characteristics unique to one class of market. While profitability may vary, if it generates good profits for the S&P and losses for NASDAQ, then the parameter values are most likely overfit. The two other index markets serve nicely as out-of-sample data.

Advertised Systems for One Market   From time to time, all traders receive mail that offers a highly specialized system called "The Cattle Trader," "The Gold Day-Trading System," or "Easy Profits through Stock Index Trading." It is best to assume that each of these systems has been finely tuned with rules unique to one market. Optimization is a well-known process and can be used responsibly or easily abused. Because these offers tend to have big profits with little risk, it seems reasonable that the proclaimed results are unrealistic. It is a clear case of "too good to be true." And, because the rules of the program are not revealed, it is impossible to test them yourself.

▦ Comparing the Results of Two Systems

The easiest way to understand the use of testing is by example. Using daily NASDAQ 100 data from January 1997 through December 2003, we compare the results of two trend systems, one based on a moving average and the other on the slope of a linear regression, in order to decide which of the two is best. In both cases, the system generates a buy signal or a sell signal when the trendline or slope turns up or down, respectively. There are no other trading rules. Table 7.2 shows the results of varying the calculation interval from 10 to 250 days in steps of 10 days. Transaction costs of $125 per trade were used to cover commissions and slippage.

Which System Is Better?

The first point to notice is that most test results are profitable. This is seen in both the net profits (column 2) and the profit factor (column 3). The high percentage of good tests justifies the underlying premise—that the market has trends. We should always expect all basic trend systems—moving averages, regression, and swing—to be profitable if one is profitable because they all benefit from the same price moves, some more, some less. Figure 7.12 is a good example of the similarity. At the short end, both methods suffer from trading too quickly and paying a large commission. On the far right they track closely.

The next interesting statistic is the number of trades. This is a 6-year test, so if the number of trades is less than one per year, some investors may not consider it "active." In the *# Trds* columns for both systems, the number of trades declines in an orderly manner until it reaches 8, then it seems to stall. In addition, the profit factor (*PFact*) jumps up at the moving average period of 190 and the regression period of 140. This is exaggerated because TradeStation only counts closed-out profits, rather than the daily change in profits. Using an information ratio based on daily prices would be much more uniform.

TABLE 7.2 Comparison of NASDAQ Trend Tests

	(a) Moving Average						(b) Linear Regression Slope				
Period	NetPrft	PFact	#Trds	%Prft	AvgTrd	Period	NetPrft	PFact	#Trds	%Prft	AvgTrd
10	−338005	0.71	229	28	−1476	10	−44455	0.95	173	34	−257
20	−70065	0.91	181	30	−387	20	49995	1.09	81	29	617
30	104715	1.17	157	34	667	30	267190	1.77	50	38	5344
40	226065	1.61	89	37	2540	40	109005	1.32	37	37	2946
50	198930	1.5	74	29	2688	50	130605	1.39	27	40	4837
60	284610	1.91	80	37	3558	60	157965	1.61	23	34	6868
70	261670	1.97	72	36	3634	70	300015	2.94	19	36	15790
80	−21600	0.95	86	26	−251	80	313145	3.39	15	40	20876
90	93940	1.25	78	34	1204	90	165265	1.85	15	33	11018
100	−9640	0.98	74	24	−130	100	190660	1.97	16	37	11916
110	62100	1.15	74	24	839	110	134610	1.55	12	33	11218
120	273470	2.17	50	38	5469	120	270560	3.17	12	41	22547
130	312970	2.73	36	33	8694	130	416630	6.96	8	62	52079
140	325790	2.57	48	27	6787	140	531740	16.53	6	66	88623
150	469530	5.52	32	40	14673	150	468600	14.72	6	66	78100
160	445130	5.23	38	34	11714	160	499400	10.11	6	66	83233
170	455190	8.58	20	35	22760	170	418800	9.63	6	66	69800
180	434260	6.17	18	27	24126	180	493850	27.05	4	75	123463
190	515210	36.35	10	50	51521	190	594060	100	2	100	297030
200	480260	76.04	8	50	60033	200	524160	100	2	100	262080
210	401590	10.01	10	40	40159	210	540260	100	2	100	270130
220	409960	13.19	8	62	51245	220	463710	100	2	100	231855
230	338160	5.29	18	55	18787	230	401260	100	2	100	200630
240	359210	9.18	10	50	35921	240	404310	100	2	100	202155
250	346560	16.99	8	37	43320	250	417560	100	2	100	208780
Average	254400	8.57	60	37	16324	Average	328756	32.32	21	61	91267
Avg 10–180	194948	2.62	80	32	5951	Avg 10–130	189322	2.30	38	38	12754

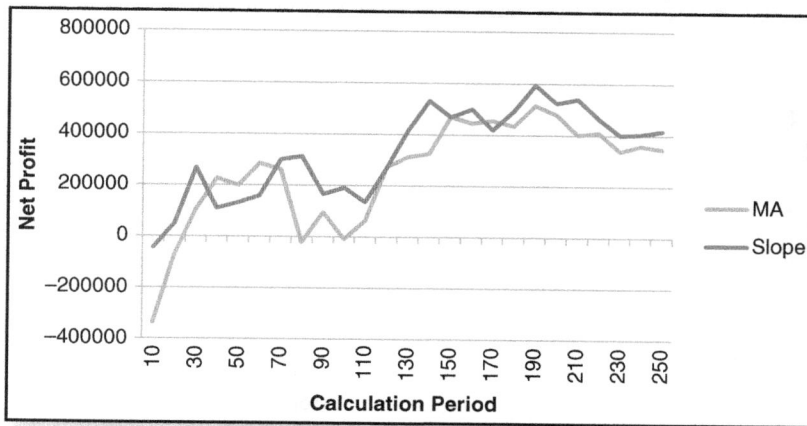

FIGURE 7.12 Net Profit for Moving Average and Slope Methods, NASDAQ, 1997–2003.

We try to get a better picture of comparative performance by looking only at the moving average system through 180 and the regression slope through 130. The feature that ties them together will be the number of trades. It gives us an idea of the sensitivity of each trend indicator. You should notice that the number of trades declines faster with the regression method. Figures 7.13a and b compare the number of trades and the corresponding profit factor for each method. In part a, the moving average trades start higher (the left scale) and decline slower than the slope results in part b. While both methods now span the same ranges, the moving average results are more orderly.

Then which is the better trading system? The moving average method has the highest net profit at calculation period of 150 with 32 trades. The slope method peaks at 200 with only 2 trades. In our limited test range, it peaked at the longest calculation period of 130 with lower profits and few trades. Perhaps more important, the *average* ratio for the moving average is 2.62 and for the slope 2.30 when we consider the smaller, more realistic ranges. *Because we cannot know which trend speed will be best in the future, the more robust system would be the one with the highest average ratio over given reasonable test ranges.* Check for performance decay as discussed earlier.

Using Correct Transaction Costs Transaction costs have a significant impact on short-term trading. Faster trading has the advantages of smaller actual losses and more transactions. A system that performs well with more transactions will give more confidence of future performance. A system that only had two trades during the past 10 years may show high historic profits but also high risk and a poor sample.

On the negative side, short-term trading is a fight against slippage and overall transaction costs. There may be times when prices are moving so fast that you miss the trade completely. Most profits from short-term trading occur at the beginning of the trade and require good entry timing. Using a simple moving average method, this time for NASDAQ futures from 1991 through 2011, tests were run using no costs, then $50, $100, and $150 round-turn total costs. The results are shown in Figure 7.14. With no costs most of the tests that use more than a 15-day calculation period are profitable. As higher costs are added, the profitable part of the performance gets narrower, limited

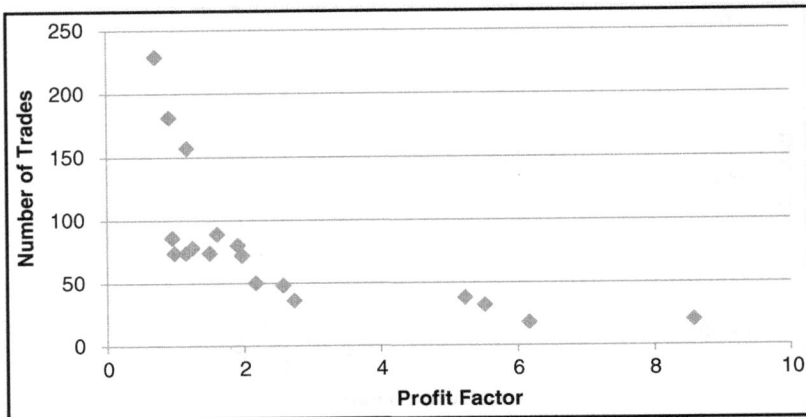

FIGURE 7.13(a) Comparison of Number of Trades Versus Profit Factor, Moving Average.

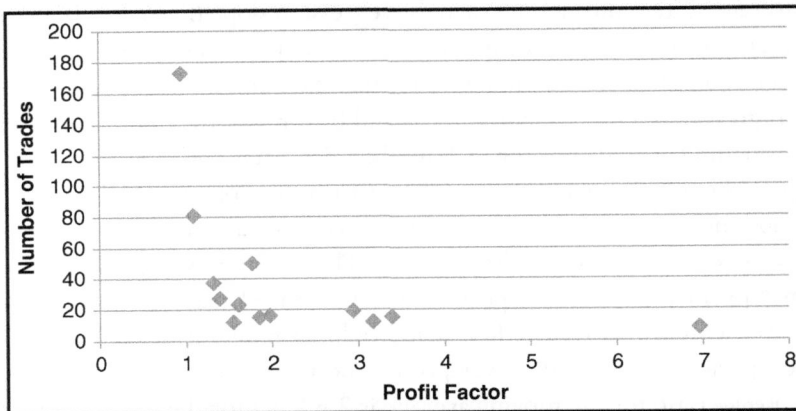

FIGURE 7.13(b) Number of Trades Versus Profit Factor, Regression Slope.

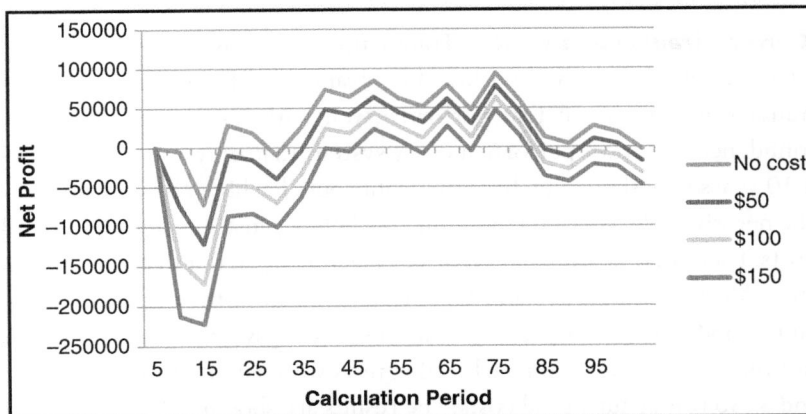

FIGURE 7.14 Comparison of Net Profits with Varying Transaction Costs, Applied to a Moving Average System on NASDAQ, 1991–2011.

to calculation periods between 45 days and about 75 days. For many markets all tests above 45 days might be profitable; NASDAQ is not the best trending market.

The lesson in this simple exercise is that transaction costs must be included to be realistic, but costs that are too high will make everything seem to be a loss. Realistic costs are necessary.

◼ Profiting from the Worst Results

The worst results of an optimization or test sequence may hold valuable information. If the loss was the result of a single drawdown, then it is important to know how that drawdown was reflected in each of the tests. If a 30-day trend lost on a price shock but the 40-day trend profited, then the next time there is a price shock the opposite might occur. Price shocks are an extremely important concept. Here it is only important to know that price shocks cannot be avoided, and generally cause losses. Choosing a parameter that side-stepped a price shock has no bearing on the future.

A persistent area of losing performance is different. Consider moving average results for NASDAQ from 1991 to 2011 all using faster calculation periods, shown in Figure 7.15. Any calculation period from 1 to 11 produced significant losses. From the previous discussions of trends and price noise, we know that nearly all equity index markets are noisy, and that noise generates losses in short-term trends. We can take advantage of this characteristic by using the short-term trend as entry timing for a longer-term trend that is profitable on its own.

If we consider this conceptually, we expect noise to cause losses for most trend systems using faster calculation periods. The results of a typical optimization of one variable can be seen in Figure 7.16a, very similar to Figure 7.15. When two moving averages are tested, there tend to be two clusters of returns, one showing losses where both averages

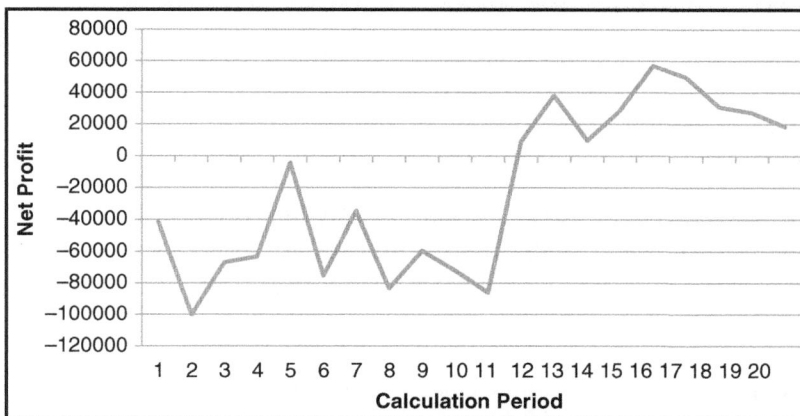

FIGURE 7.15   Net PL for a NASDAQ Moving Average System, 1991–2011, Where the Calculation Periods Are Short.

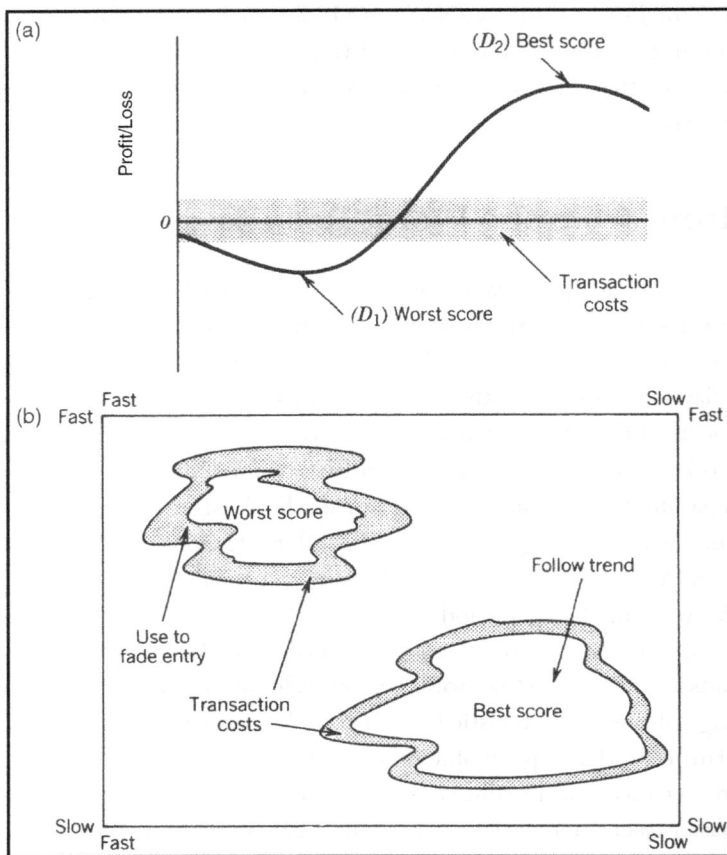

**FIGURE 7.16 Dual Use of Test Map. (a) Single-Variable Test.
(b) Two-Variable Test.**

have shorter calculation periods, and another with profits in the area of longer averages, seen in Figure 7.16b. An alternate strategy that *fades* the faster trend is,

> *Buy* when the slow average is up and the fast average turns down.
> *Sell short* when the slow average is down and the fast average turns up.
> *Exit the long position* when the slow average turns down.
> *Cover the short position* when the slow average turns up.

Following this strategy, performance is greatly improved over the simple trend. Although the *Net PL* is lower, all the other statistics are far better, as seen in the table below. In addition, trades are not reversed from long to short, so that liquidity is improved and some unexpected risk may be avoided.

Strategy	Net PL	Profit Factor	Trades	%ProfTrades	Profit/Trade
MA	64385	1.51	212	35	277
MA w/Fade	53380	2.26	72	47	741

■ Retesting for Changing Parameters

One optimization is never the end of the testing process. If the system development is completed, the parameter values selected, and the most recent data used for out-of-sample verification, then you have *proved the concept*. One final test must be done on all of the data before beginning to trade the program. Using more data always gives a more robust solution. The final parameter choices may be slightly different from the previous values but should not change significantly. A large change is a warning of problems, either a test period that was too short, or a poor selection of parameter values.

As in step-forward testing, some analysts prefer to retest a system periodically using a fixed amount of data, dropping off the oldest. Longer test intervals are always better, unless there is a reason to believe that the oldest data is no longer relevant. In some cases, there are structural changes, such as the formation period preceding the emergence of the European Currency Unit, which put controls on the variance in exchange rates between the participating countries. A new market with low liquidity during its earlier years may be considered different from more active, current market conditions. Retesting remains an important way to adjust the system to characteristics of new data.

Retesting should be considered after 5% to 10% of new data is available, relative to the original test interval. Using the 2-variable test as an example, a shift may be expected in the area of best performance as shown in Figure 7.17.

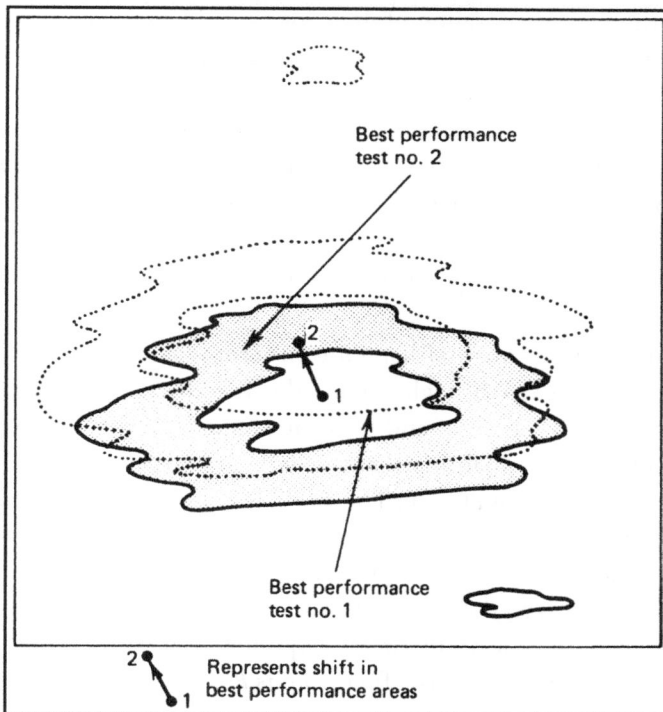

FIGURE 7.17 Consecutive Tests.

Because only a small amount of data was added, the size of the shift in Figure 7.17 should be small. If a large shift actually occurs, then two possibilities should be considered:

1. The data was unusually volatile and introduced patterns not previously seen in the data. In this case the shift in parameters is justified.
2. The data period for the original tests was short and did not include enough patterns to make the parameter choice robust. With a small amount of test data, there is a greater likelihood that a faster trading model will be selected. As the data shifts and that faster model is no longer good, the parameters may jump to a very slow model.

Retesting after a Major Move   When your system fails to perform as expected, often after a price shock, it is natural to question whether the system has the right parameters. Is the trend fast enough? Is the stop-loss too close? If you have used enough data for your original tests, then it is very likely that retesting won't change anything. If you make up new rules to fix this one problem, you are overfitting and therefore accomplish nothing. While using more data for testing is always safest, markets will continue to offer new patterns, bigger swings, and more risk than anything contained in the history.

Is the Model Broken?   Some trading systems, when based on an economic scenario, will have a limited life. A fully technical program, such as a moving average, should adapt to trends of varying lengths that occur over time, taking larger and smaller profits, and cutting losses short. The way to judge if a model is performing as expected is by measuring the size and duration of drawdowns and comparing that to the tested profile, understanding that, as the amount of data increases, so will the likelihood of larger profits and larger losses. If a new system begins trading and posts steady losses until it reaches the previous maximum drawdown, chances are that something is wrong. Systems should not systematically decay from the first day of trading.

The probability of a drawdown greater than P can be calculated as[11]

$$Probability\ of\ a\ drawdown \geq P = \left(1 - \frac{P}{100}\right)^{2\mu/\sigma^2}$$

This formula assumes a normal distribution of returns (although trading returns should have a longer tail to the right). The value μ is the average fractional change in equity (percentage returns), and σ is the standard deviation of the returns. The equation gives the probability that the daily drawdown from the peak equity will be greater than or equal to P. The same formula works for monthly data. For example, during the test, the annualized return was 30% with a daily return ratio of $\sigma/\mu = 9$. Based on 250 trading days per year, the daily value of μ is calculated using $(R_y/R_0)^{1/y} - 1$, or $\mu = (1.3/1.0)^{1/250} - 1$, and $\mu = 0.00105$. Then $\sigma = 0.00945$ and the value of the exponent $2\mu/\sigma^2 = 23.51$. If we want the 95% confidence level, then the final step is $P = (1 - 95/100)^{1/23.51} = 0.880$.

---

[11] John R. Wolberg, *Expert Trading Systems* (New York: John Wiley & Sons, 2000), 181–183.

Then the probability of a drawdown of at least 12% can be expected in 5% of the months.

Testing across a Wide Range of Markets

A comprehensive test that applies one trading strategy to a broad selection of markets is basic to the concept of *robustness*. When a system performs well in many markets over the same test period and calculation ranges, it is fair to assume that the method is sound. If a technique works in the Swiss franc but not the euro, in 10-year Treasury notes but not 5-year Notes, in Intel but not Microsoft, then the method is most likely not robust but fine-tuned to each market. Markets have individual characteristics that might justify differences in performance; however, a strategy that can generate profits in a broad range of markets with the same rules and calculations is robust. At the same time, we should expect the results to be *suboptimal*; that is, performance will vary considerably across markets because fewer parameters and rules will be used. As Ken Tropin, founder of Graham Capital says, "Loose pants fit everyone."

Robert Colby, in *The Encyclopedia of Technical Market Indicators,*[12] has given an excellent comparison of market indicators by presenting each of their test results in a common form. Thomas Bulkowski has done the same in his *Encyclopedia of Chart Patterns.*[13] Viewing the results of a set of indicators gives a much better idea of the success of that approach than testing any one of them. For example, if one volume indicator was successful during the past 10 years, but three others were inconsistent, then the use of any volume indicator becomes questionable. While there are always exceptions, robustness is found when a number of strategies, all applied to volume, show similar, profitable returns.

Classic Tests by Davis and Thiel, Maxwell, and Hochheimer

There are three previous (if somewhat dated), well-known comprehensive studies of moving average systems by Davis and Thiel, Maxwell, and Hochheimer. In addition, Lukac, Brorsen, and Irwin studied 12 different trading methods across 12 futures markets. These studies are interesting because of the techniques and the conclusions. Strategy development software now allows us to test, in seconds, what once took hours or days, so the actual results of these older studies will be omitted in favor of our own tests.

Davis and Thiel

Davis and Thiel, the authors of the oldest of the studies,[14] completed before 1970, analyze the greatest variety of markets, covering virtually all of the U.S. crops as well as cattle, eggs, and the soybean complex. They include about 5 years of data and

---

[12] Robert W. Colby, *The Encyclopedia of Technical Market Indicators* (New York: McGraw-Hill, 2003).

[13] Thomas Bulkowski, *Encyclopedia of Chart Patterns* (New York: John Wiley & Sons, 2000).

[14] R. E. Davis and C. C. Thiel, Jr., *A Computer Analysis of the Moving Average Applied to Commodity Futures Trading* (West Lafayette, IN: Quiatenon Management, 1970).

use relatively fast moving averages (up to 10 days); they introduce variations in lead-oriented plotting and in testing nonconsecutive days; the data used is close-only. The results are clearly presented in both detail and summary, and yield generally good returns.

The study used combinations of simple moving average buy and sell signals, leading plots (moving the calculation forward), and skips (using every second or third price rather than every price). They test a total of 100 combinations of the three factors:

A *skip* from 1 day (none) to 5 days (1 week).
A *moving average* of 5, 6, 7, 8, or 10 days.
A *leap* of 0 or 2 days.

Before 1970, markets had fewer participants, less noise, and showed more short-term trending, and the moving average was state-of-the-art technology. Using a computer to study the markets in 1970 was very unusual; Digital Equipment was still selling their most popular PDP-5, and IBM had just introduced its first mini-computer, the System 3. Traders were using point-and-figure charts on the exchange floors, and the 10-day moving average was the most popular technical tool. Lower volume and a larger percentage of commercial participation made trends more consistent than today's markets. It was possible to trade using a 3- to 5-day moving average and post consistent profits.

In retrospect, the technique that skipped 1 or 2 days of data is another way of smoothing, similar to a 3-day momentum that compares today's price with the price 3 days ago. The success of the variations in rules is proof that markets trended in the 1960s and that a trending method, such as a moving average, was a viable strategy. Over time it has been necessary to increase the calculation period in order to avoid steadily increasing noise.

Maxwell

Maxwell's study is extremely comprehensive but applied only to the pork bellies futures market.[15] His idea was to perform a thorough test of combinations of trending methods and trading rules. As with Davis and Thiel, the computer was still not available to the general public, and the ability to perform a broad study was a groundbreaking event.

Trend combinations included a simple moving average of 3, 5, or 10 days, an average-modified or a weighted average. The second feature was the delay factor, used to improve the timing of both entries and exits. Some of the options were:

1. Act without delay.
2. Act if the signal condition persists for one additional day (a confirmation).
3. Enter if the signal condition persists for two additional days, but liquidate without a delay.

---

[15] Joseph R. Maxwell, *Commodity Futures Trading with Moving Averages* (Cupertino, CA: Speer, 1974).

Combinations of two types of moving averages and a delay factor were tested, with and without fixed or moving stops. With 10 types of averages, 6 delay factors, and different stops, Maxwell had a lot of combinations to examine.

The study is then expanded to 3-factor systems with a list of 18 combinations of rules to generate 324 systems of which the results of 285 are recorded, with 49% profitable systems. The largest *loss* was generated by a system with the rules:

1. Enter a new position when the price crosses both the weighted 3-day and weighted 10-day averages, as long as the signal condition persists for two additional days (*buy* if prices are higher, *sell short* if lower).
2. Liquidate positions when the 3-day average reverses its direction through the longer average as long as it continues for one additional day.
3. No fixed stops are used.

The best *profits* in the 3-factor system used the rules:

1. Enter a new position when both the 5-day average-modified and a 10-day weighted average move above the average price, provided the 5-day average lagged behind the 10-day (that is, the longer-term trend turned up first in order to get a buy signal).
2. Liquidate the position when the shorter-term average crossed the longer-term average in the direction opposite to the current position.
3. No fixed stops were used.

Maxwell's study represents a great amount of work and some simple and sound philosophy. The conclusion—that two trends, one twice the length of the other, will be profitable if the slow trend turns first—makes sense even with longer calculation periods in current markets. The slower trend finds the major move and the faster trend provides the timing. Identifying the major move comes first. In the rules that produced the worst results, the 2-day lag to confirm the signal is long with respect to the 3- and 10-day trends. When trading using fast signals, a delay will often reduce the net profits.

Unfortunately, Maxwell's studies only used a 50-day test interval for May 1972 pork bellies, which is not an adequate data sample to statistically justify his conclusions. Maxwell does test four other selected 50-day periods, but the reader cannot know how these periods were chosen. Considering the effort in outlining a testing program and establishing rules, in addition to the analysis of results, the test period is a very weak point. Because the final test rules and values are reasonable, the market may have been successfully traded with a broad range of trending strategies.

Comparing Methods of Calculation across Selected Markets

Hochheimer[16] performs two interesting studies: a comparison of three types of *moving average calculations* and a test of *channels* and *crossovers*. In the first analysis, Hochheimer

---

[16] Frank Hochheimer, "Moving Averages," and "Channels and Crossovers" in Perry J. Kaufman (Ed.), *Technical Analysis in Commodities* (New York: John Wiley & Sons, 1980).

compares *simple, exponentially smoothed,* and *linearly weighted* moving averages, tested on a good sampling of markets (without financials and currencies, which did not exist during the 1970–1976 test period). The *linearly weighted average* is actually *step-weighting,* where integer values are used as weighting factors, each successive day is incremented by one, and the most recent day has the highest weighting factor.

The same trading rules applied to all trends, regardless of the calculation method:

1. The trend calculation used the closing price only.
2. A *buy* signal occurred on an upwards penetration of the moving average by the closing price; a *sell* signal occurred on a downward penetration of the moving average.
3. The model is always in the market.
4. A trade cannot be executed when the day's high and low price are the same. This assumes that there was no trading, caused by a *locked-limit day,* the consequence of a price shock.

The test covered 7 years of data from 1970 to 1976 and calculation periods which ranged from 2- to 70-day periods (or the equivalent smoothing constant). In Hocheimer's results, the slower trends were consistently better than faster ones, regardless of which technique was used. With a few exceptions, the best selection of days ranged from 40 to 70. This may be the first sign of a shift to longer calculation periods, in contrast to the approach taken by Davis and Thiel as well as Maxwell.

Current Results   To bring this up to date, a sample of 17 liquid futures markets were tested for five different trend-following strategies using calculation periods from 2 to 80 days, in steps of 2 days, and data from 1990 through mid-2011. The methods are

1. Moving average
2. Exponential smoothing
3. Linearly weighted average
4. Slope of a least-squares regression
5. *N*-Day breakout

All trades were charged a round-turn cost of $40 to cover commissions and slippage. Where markets were not yet trading at the beginning of the test period, data was used from the inception of that market. Table 7.3 gives a summary of the moving average results. The columns that are not obvious are:

Best Period, the calculation period with the highest Net Profit of all tests.
Best Range, the range calculation periods showing the best test performance, based on observation.
Profit Factor, the gross profits divided by the gross losses. This measure is the only risk measure available on TradeStation and does not always show the relative return and risk correctly. It is based on closed-out trade results; therefore, any large losses held during the trade are ignored if that trade closes out at a better level.

TABLE 7.3 Results of a Simple Moving Average Model

Market	Best Period	Best Range	Net PL	Profit Factor	Trades	% Prof Tests
U.S. bonds	72	62–80	36291	1.25	228	30%
Eurobund	80	48–80	55540	1.87	156	73%
Eurodollars	28	22–80	33867	1.64	289	78%
S&P	72	64–72	3197	1.02	288	5%
DAX	42	58–72	213135	1.51	318	80%
NASDAQ	70	44–78	80785	1.87	162	73%
EURUSD	74	24–36	169332	1.80	216	85%
USDJPY	66	62–80	98295	1.50	256	75%
CADUSD	64	38–68	9670	1.08	290	3%
Crude oil	20	64–80	161070	1.50	152	85%
Heating oil	74	16–80	174687	1.85	247	75%
Natural gas	24	58–80	692640	1.65	132	90%
Gold	50	14–24	11830	1.07	322	3%
Copper	74	40–50	153137	2.03	250	80%
Wheat	14	60–80	23420	1.12	556	10%
Cotton	80	10–70	106855	1.97	223	83%
Soybeans	24	58–80	33970	1.15	466	10%
Average	55	22–26	121042	1.52	268	55%

% Prof Tests, the percentage of profitable tests out of the total of 40 calculation periods. This gives us a notion of the robustness of the method. If 30 of the 40 tests were profitable, regardless of the amount, the result is 75%.

Caveats   The test range selected was 2 to 80 days, which can be criticized as an unrealistic choice. First, we do not expect profits using a 2-day trend because it is too fast, and generates too many trades with small profits and losses that will not be greater than the cost of $40. Nevertheless, all of the systems that will be compared suffer the same burden. Second, the number of days in the test should not be evenly distributed because the difference in performance between a 2- and 4-day trend is far greater than the difference between a 78- and 80-day trend. However, it is more complex to create tests this way, and the intention here is to present something that can easily be replicated by any analyst with modest system development software.

Moving Average Conclusions   We can draw some useful conclusions from this first test.

1. The best choice is often near the high (longer calculation periods) end of the test range.
2. The best range of results often includes the maximum test period, 80 days.
3. Those markets that showed unusual results can, for the most part, be explained.
4. The percentage of profitable tests, a measure of robustness, is high for most markets.

This confirms that a moving average is a viable strategy and the slower calculation periods tend to be uniformly better.

Of all test results, robustness *(% ProfTests)* is the first one to be reviewed. A market that does not trend has few tests that are profitable. The worst of those markets are the S&P, the Canadian dollar, and gold. Of these, gold may be the most surprising because it has increased dramatically during the past few years; however, it languished at low prices for 15 of the 20 years tested. If a closer look at the results of gold showed that it was highly profitable for the past 5 years, you might want to include it based on the assumption that volatility will continue and that it adds important diversification to a portfolio.

The Canadian dollar does not have the impact of gold. It reflects a decline in the value of the U.S. dollar, but is often subdued in price movement and, in many cases, has a difficult time overcoming costs. It also has made bigger moves recently, but may not offer enough positive arguments to offset its poor historic performance.

The S&P presents the most difficult problem. It is a very important, liquid market, but has been shown to have a large component of noise that fights with the trend. Robustness of 5% means that only 2 of 40 tests were profitable, and those do not necessarily show profits recently. While the DAX and NASDAQ were both very successful under this strategy, it is difficult to argue why the S&P should be included. Each analyst will need to resolve this dilemma himself.

One way to get to see the big picture of the results is to chart the average net profit and average profit factor for all 17 markets by their calculation periods. Figure 7.18 shows that the faster trends are uniformly losses, while progressively longer trends are profitable. This argues for the success of the *macrotrend*, which tends to track the bigger price moves caused by economic policy. It also shows that the profit factor does not offer much additional information on risk than the net profits.

Exponential Smoothing Smoothing is different from a moving average because it is front-loaded; that is, it puts more weight on the nearest data while decreasing the

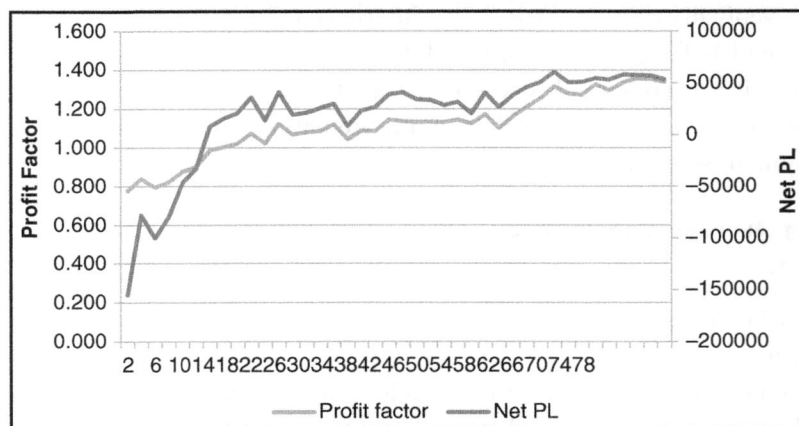

FIGURE 7.18 Average Results of Moving Average Tests for 17 Markets Based on Calculation Period, Showing the Similarity Between the Profit Factor and the Net PL.

TABLE 7.4 Results of Exponential Smoothing Tests

Market	Best Period	Best Range	Net PL	Profit Factor	Trades	% Prof Tests
U.S. bonds	78	70–80	43068	1.32	230	35%
Eurobund	78	64–80	73140	2.64	134	70%
Eurodollars	80	24–80	28310	1.72	178	78%
S&P	60	58–74	555	1.00	319	3%
DAX	12	12–22	228282	1.31	651	90%
NASDAQ	70	58–68	67260	1.71	160	75%
EURUSD	68	38–80	206447	2.08	223	83%
USDJPY	54	60–76	125892	1.63	294	83%
CADUSD	66	38–64	12810	1.11	314	10%
Crude oil	42	62–66	140650	1.56	329	88%
Heating oil	72	38–80	201814	2.07	251	78%
Natural gas	28	48–80	266180	1.62	369	93%
Gold	70	26–46	15210	1.09	306	13%
Copper	74	68–76	154582	2.13	216	85%
Wheat	58	56–80	1840	1.01	297	3%
Cotton	80	56–62	135495	2.51	223	75%
Soybeans	20	56–80	15175	1.05	580	8%
Average	**59**	**18–22**	**100983**	**1.62**	**298**	**57%**

importance of older data each day. One important characteristic is that the trend always turns up when prices move above the trendline and turns down when they move below the trendline. This increases the number of trades and offers no advantage to using the direction of the trendline as the buy and sell signal rather than the price penetration of the trendline. Table 7.4 summarizes the results in the same form as the moving average tests. Other than having more trades, these results are very similar to the moving average.

Linearly Weighted Average   The linearly weighted average is also frontloaded, giving the largest weight to the most recent data. Unlike exponential smoothing, the oldest data does not retain any residual value, but drops off at the end of the calculation period. Table 7.5 shows the test.

Linear Regression Slope   The linear regression slope is popular among economists, but the method is very different from the previous three averages. The regression line slope shows the trend of prices that continue in the same direction and will trigger a signal sooner than a moving average. This can be seen in the results of the Canadian dollar and the S&P, although wheat and soybeans do not perform well. (See Table 7.6.)

N-Day Breakout   This last trending method is very different from the others because it does not have a "trendline" but identifies the trend based on new highs and lows. The N-day breakout is deceiving in that it is both very reliable in finding the correct trend but at exceptionally high risk. The risk cannot be seen in these numbers;

TABLE 7.5   **Results of Linearly Weighted Average Tests**

Market	Best Period	Best Range	Net PL	Profit Factor	Trades	% Prof Tests
U.S. bonds	18	10–20	55215	1.16	627	30%
Eurobund	80	56–80	42140	1.46	248	63%
Eurodollars	40	30–52	22957	1.38	311	73%
S&P	62	62–74	50662	1.24	405	20%
DAX	62	60–72	267080	1.63	319	78%
NASDAQ	68	50–80	72605	1.56	232	63%
EURUSD	30	26–32	142825	1.31	475	83%
USDJPY	44	64–80	98847	1.31	418	73%
CADUSD	64	40–66	35690	1.29	385	30%
Crude oil	80	62–68	157190	1.75	281	80%
Heating oil	74	64–80	132282	1.52	319	80%
Natural gas	18	44–78	244480	1.34	634	68%
Gold	78	10–20	41300	1.27	318	13%
Copper	70	78–80	178655	1.93	329	88%
Wheat	10	42–80	−15525	0.94	850	0%
Cotton	80	68–80	118475	1.84	301	83%
Soybeans	34	60–80	9205	1.03	469	5%
Average	**54**	**34–56**	**97299**	**1.41**	**407**	**54%**

TABLE 7.6   **Results of Linear Regression Slope Tests**

Market	Best Period	Best Range	Net PL	Profit Factor	Trades	% Prof Tests
U.S. bonds	80	16–32	68377	1.99	57	65%
Eurobund	80	60–80	54420	2.52	46	83%
Eurodollars	50	28–60	45632	2.73	76	85%
S&P	74	74–08	20550	1.19	75	28%
DAX	74	66–76	239747	2.19	63	88%
NASDAQ	80	64–80	87655	2.94	38	80%
EURUSD	38	28–44	173272	1.99	54	93%
USDJPY	76	64–80	119555	2.17	59	88%
CADUSD	72	64–80	44050	1.74	75	33%
Crude oil	26	20–34	146150	1.67	173	83%
Heating oil	70	66–80	176939	2.36	74	70%
Natural gas	24	16–36	250020	1.64	201	88%
Gold	26	22–40	−1550	0.99	177	0%
Copper	80	56–80	151302	2.68	57	83%
Wheat	24	22–34	18557	1.14	206	18%
Cotton	80	60–80	77110	1.79	65	88%
Soybeans	26	22–44	44022	1.27	208	38%
Average	**58**		**100930**	**1.94**	**100**	**65%**

however, every trade has an initial risk equal to the highest high minus the lowest low over the calculation period. For the longest period of 80 days, that risk can be very large and is the reason why many traders prefer the basic moving average over the breakout. Table 7.7 shows the results.

TABLE 7.7 Results of *N*-Day Breakout Tests

Market	Best Period	Best Range	Net PL	Profit Factor	Trades	% Prof Tests
U.S. bonds	62	60–80	121698	1.85	41	70%
Eurobund	62	58–74	83290	6.86	29	90%
Eurodollars	80	56–80	52175	5.10	25	46%
S&P	58	46–60	16007	1.17	51	38%
DAX	64	62–80	260477	2.69	37	75%
NASDAQ	40	16–50	149510	2.66	46	85%
EURUSD	32	22–40	157917	1.96	79	90%
USDJPY	60	56–70	100355	2.08	44	88%
CADUSD	68	62–80	48630	2.75	32	53%
Crude oil	60	56–80	134920	2.09	46	88%
Heating oil	60	50–80	174513	2.48	44	85%
Natural gas	80	14–24, 68–80	247060	3.08	33	39%
Gold	18	14–18, 74–80	11720	1.08	161	13%
Copper	44	26–56	127400	2.22	60	78%
Wheat	80	66–80	37530	2.06	34	38%
Cotton	78	64–80	91645	2.65	31	93%
Soybeans	24	22–28	26645	1.20	126	35%
Average	**57**		**108323**	**2.59**	**54**	**65%**

Comparing the Five Strategies

We can draw some important conclusions from looking at the average results of the five trend-following tests, shown in Table 7.8. The first and most significant point is that the averages are all profitable. That means trend-following works. If prices trend, then any strategy that profits from the trend should work to some degree. It is not the method, but the market that is most important. Each strategy extracts slightly different parts of the same trends.

Of the five methods, the weakest is the linearly weighted average. It has the most trades and the lowest robustness, although only 1 point below the moving average. The two that show the best performance are the linear regression slope and the breakout, but they also have far fewer trades and much higher risk. An average of 54 trades over 20 years means that the breakout system had only 2.7 trades per year. In some years it may have had 5, and in others it held the same trade all year. That

TABLE 7.8 Average of Statistics of Five Trend-Following Strategies

Strategy	Best Period	Net PL	Profit Factor	Trades	% ProfTests
MA	55	121042	1.52	268	55%
EXP	59	100983	1.62	298	57%
LWA	54	97299	1.41	407	54%
LRS	58	100930	1.94	100	65%
BO	57	108323	2.59	54	65%

TABLE 7.9   Average Robustness of Trend Tests by Market

Market	MA	EXP	LWA	LRS	BO	Average
U.S. bonds	30%	35%	30%	65%	70%	46%
Eurobund	73%	70%	63%	83%	90%	76%
Eurodollars	78%	78%	73%	85%	46%	72%
S&P	5%	3%	20%	28%	38%	19%
DAX	80%	90%	78%	88%	75%	82%
NASDAQ	73%	75%	63%	80%	85%	75%
EURUSD	85%	83%	83%	93%	90%	87%
USDJPY	75%	83%	73%	88%	88%	81%
CADUSD	3%	10%	30%	33%	53%	26%
Crude oil	85%	88%	80%	83%	88%	85%
Heating oil	75%	78%	80%	70%	85%	78%
Natural gas	90%	93%	68%	88%	39%	75%
Gold	3%	13%	13%	0%	13%	8%
Copper	80%	85%	88%	83%	78%	83%
Wheat	10%	3%	0%	18%	38%	14%
Cotton	83%	75%	83%	88%	93%	84%
Soybeans	10%	8%	5%	38%	35%	19%
Average	**55%**	**57%**	**54%**	**65%**	**65%**	**59%**

translates into high risk. Then the breakout system should reward you for taking that risk, yet the basic moving average system had the highest average net profit without that exposure.

The next big picture item is robustness. If a market trends, then we can expect any of the trend systems to be profitable for that market. Certain characteristics of a strategy will cause the results to vary. For example, the two extremes are the simple moving average, which cuts losses short, and the breakout, which holds the trade as long as possible. For the S&P, the moving average posted only 2 tests of 40 with profits, while the breakout had 15 profitable tests. By looking at the average of all systems, the far right column in Table 7.9, we can see which markets are trending and are likely to perform best with a trend-following strategy.

Sorting the results in the right column of Table 7.9 and charting them in Figure 7.19, we can see that there is a sharp delineation between trending and non-trending markets. Of the 17 markets, 11 show robustness above 70%, which would be a good threshold for acceptance. However, a decision cannot always be made on a single criterion. For example, interest rates, represented by U.S. 30-year bonds, reflect interest rate policy, and have been the biggest component of profits for macrotrend portfolios for the past 20 years. They consistently produce profits using long-term trends but fail for faster calculation periods. As mentioned earlier, gold has been very profitable during the past few years and has increased in volatility. If gold continues to be an alternate currency choice for investors, then performance during the 1990s may not be important.

Of the remaining markets, wheat and soybeans have not been discussed. In the same way that interest rates perform only for longer-term trends, grains are dominated by

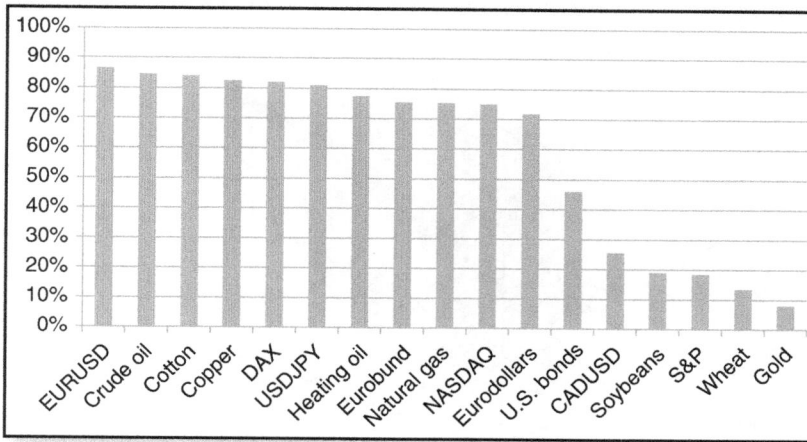

FIGURE 7.19 Robustness of Trend-Following Tests, by Market.

seasonality. The very long-term trend will identify structural changes as well as shifts in the U.S. dollar, but profits from that are minimal compared to seasonal price swings.

Crossover Strategy

In Hochheimer's *crossover of two simple moving averages,* the short-term average (the faster trend) ranged from 3 to 25 days and the longer one from 5 to 50 days. The objective was to eliminate the whipsaws that were evident in the first study. The rules for this system were:

1. Each moving average used closing prices only; the calculation period for the long-term trend was always greater than the period for the short-term trend.
2. *A buy* signal occurred when the short-term average moved above the long-term average; a *sell short* signal occurred when the short-term average moved below the long term.
3. The model was always in the market.
4. If the high and low prices of the day were equal, a *locked-limit* day was assumed, and no trading signals were generated.

In the current test of two trends, the short period will vary from 3 to 21 in steps of 2, and the long period from 10 to 80 in steps of 5. That gives 150 combinations of which 11 are eliminated because the short period will be greater than the long period (for example, the combination of a 15-day fast trend with a 10-day slow trend is not allowed).

Results are more difficult to display because each test is a 3-dimensional surface, as shown in Figure 7.20 for the DAX index. In general, the best results favor the longest calculation periods of both parameters, seen as the rounded area running up the front right of the chart. The conclusion here is that this method does best with the slowest signals, the same conclusion as the single trend approach.

The results of testing the same set of markets are shown in Table 7.10. Notice that the average profit factor is lower than any of the single-trend strategies and the

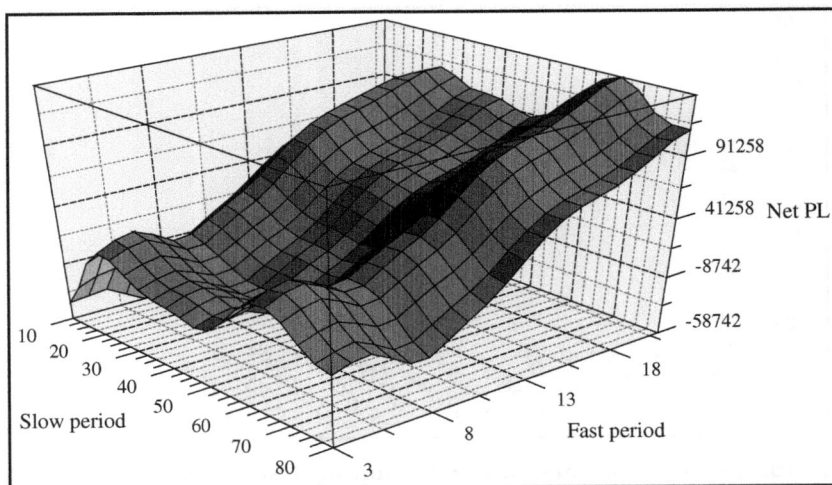

FIGURE 7.20 Surface Plot of the DAX Index Optimization Results.
(Plot Created with PSI-Plot by Poly Software International)

average number of trades is higher than all but the linearly weighted average. A high number of trades is likely to mean smaller profits per trade. Traders have a minimum unit return below which the return is unrealistic. In Table 7.11, the per contract returns show that the average for the 2-trend system is only 62% of the simple moving average and 17% of the linear regression slope. And, while $222 is large enough overall, the Eurodollar interest rates show only $81, which is at the low end of what most analysts would regard as a safe margin of error.

TABLE 7.10 Results of a Moving Average Crossover Strategy

Market	Best Slow	Best Fast	Net PL	Profit Factor	Trades	% Prof Tests
U.S. bonds	80	17	35265	1.19	342	27%
Eurobund	75	17	53270	1.60	277	55%
Eurodollars	30	21	23685	1.48	299	56%
S&P	75	13	2290	1.01	452	1%
DAX	60	21	185795	1.48	326	73%
NASDAQ	70	17	53415	1.41	238	41%
EURUSD	25	19	131607	1.36	426	89%
USDJPY	65	15	59682	1.24	401	54%
CADUSD	75	15	−32020	0.77	394	0%
Crude oil	65	19	156120	1.75	328	63%
Heating oil	70	19	158159	1.58	356	53%
Natural gas	20	17	27396	1.58	423	91%
Gold	50	19	22600	1.13	381	6%
Copper	75	19	114415	1.56	352	72%
Wheat	15	13	11452	1.06	527	9%
Cotton	80	15	74180	1.48	381	84%
Soybeans	25	21	26432	1.12	476	8%
Average	56	18	64926	1.34	375	46%

Market	2 MA	MA	LRS
U.S. bonds	103	159	1199
Eurobund	192	356	1183
Eurodollars	81	117	600
S&P	5	11	274
DAX	569	670	3805
NASDAQ	224	498	2306
EURUSD	308	783	1533
USDJPY	148	383	2026
CADUSD	−81	33	587
Crude oil	475	354	844
Heating oil	444	707	2391
Natural gas	647	753	1243
Gold	59	36	−8
Copper	325	612	2654
Wheat	21	42	90
Cotton	194	479	1186
Soybeans	55	72	211
Average	222	357	1301

TABLE 7.11 Per Contract Returns for the 2-Moving Average, the Simple Moving Average, and the Linear Regression Slope Strategies

The measure of robustness is also lower than any other system, indicating that nearly half of all moving average pairs that were tested generated losses. For the S&P and Canadian dollar, there were essentially no combinations that were profitable, but then the ranking of successful markets is similar to the previous tests. In reviewing the single-trend systems, we could conclude that, in general, they favored the longer calculation periods. In the 2-trend system, there is also a tendency to pick the longest of the fast trend, which had a maximum calculation period of 21 days. Had we allowed both trends to assume the same range up to 80 days, it is very likely that some of the combinations would have chosen both trends at 80, or very close to it. This method has forced us to choose a suboptimal combination because, from the robustness measurement, the 2-trend method is not as good as any of the single-trend strategies. To verify that observation, we would need to measure the information ratio for all of the systems, keeping in mind that the average results should be the criterion for comparison, and not the best results.

More on Comparing Strategies and Markets

The key to robustness is to test more data, more markets, more of everything, and then to study the results looking for a common areas of success and broad patterns of consistency. There is no better way to tell if a market has trends than to test it for a variety of trending methods. A market that performs well using a daily breakout, but fails with a regression slope, is not a good candidate for trend system.

A comprehensive look at 12 trading methods applied to 12 futures markets provides an opportunity to evaluate generalized performance.[17] The annualized percentage returns for a variety of U.S. markets are shown for 12 well-defined technical methods in Table 7.12. These trading systems are:

CHL *Channel breakout,* the closing price penetration of the *N*-day high and low.

PAR Wilder's *Parabolic system,* in which the stop and reverse point (SAR) gets closer each day.

DRM *Directional Movement,* a Wilder method that averages the up days and down days separately.

RNQ *Range Quotient,* basing a breakout of a ratio of current change to past change.

DRP *Directional Parabolic,* combining the DRM and PAR systems.

MII *MII Price Channel,* a breakout system using only the oldest and most recent prices.

LSO *L-S-O Price Channel,* using two parameters, including an interval of oldest prices, to decide a channel breakout.

REF *Reference Deviation,* determines a volatility breakout based on a standard deviation of past closing price changes.

DMC *Dual Moving Average Crossover,* holding a trend position when both moving averages are moving in the same direction.

DRI *Directional Indicator,* a ratio of the current price change to the total past price change.

MAB *Moving Average with % Price Band,* gives a signal when prices penetrate the band.

ALX *Alexander's Filter Rule,* generates signals when prices reverse from a previous swing high or low by a percentage amount.

To create the results in Table 7.12, each market was tested for 3 years and the best parameters used to generate the returns for the next years, in a step-forward approach. It is easy to see that some markets are not profitable for any strategy and that some strategies are generally poor. Unless you were creating a strategy for a specific group of markets, you would not want to trade a system that was not profitable in at least 50% of the markets, nor would you want to trade a market that failed in most of the trend strategies. For example, cattle lost in every system, and the RNQ, REF, and MAB systems were consistently unprofitable; therefore, none of those would be good candidates for trading. The most consistent systems were CHL, PAR, MII, and DMC, each posting 8 of 12 winning markets; however, each has a noticeably different technique. T-bills present an interesting choice because the highest profit, 239.8%, occurred in one of the least reliable systems, REF; DRP, MII, or CHL are likely to be better choices because of their overall consistency.

[17] Louis P. Lukac, B. Wade Brorsen, and Scott H. Irwin, "How to Test Profitability of Technical Trading Systems," *Futures* (October 1987).

TABLE 7.12 Percentage Returns by System and Market, 1978–1984*

	CHL	PAR	DRM	RNQ	DRP	MII	LSO	REF	DMC	DRI	MAB	ALX	Average
Corn	22.4	3.8	29.8	-6.2	30.1	43.3	10.7	4.6	37.9	-2.9	-4.7	22.9	16.0
Cocoa	10.0	-101.7	-121.9	-345.0	-112.1	-73.6	-256.9	-120.5	-72.9	-281.8	-219.2	-35.2	-144.2
Copper	-15.4	2.9	-46.1	-78.4	-4.2	-31.4	-83.0	-66.2	-39.8	-94.3	-118.4	-16.8	-49.3
Cattle	-12.2	-28.4	-12.4	-72.5	-16.5	-34.8	-44.9	-56.3	-11.4	-70.0	-58.9	-5.5	-35.3
Pork bellies	-30.8	22.0	-6.8	-134.4	4.8	20.6	-117.4	-145.3	-6.5	-127.6	-112.0	-12.1	-53.8
Lumber	38.7	-43.6	-0.4	-19.2	-40.6	31.3	-46.3	-18.4	36.6	-19.1	-47.1	24.6	-8.6
Soybeans	7.7	-19.1	25.8	-57.9	-10.0	13.3	-21.5	-45.6	2.6	-10.7	-22.5	13.1	-10.4
Silver	60.5	54.4	0.2	-15.9	82.3	-19.1	12.5	-72.4	34.2	-76.2	-18.0	55.9	8.2
Sugar	103.4	46.2	61.2	-42.1	63.4	72.6	-0.8	-47.3	82.3	17.6	15.2	71.6	36.9
British pound	-3.5	8.1	20.7	-36.1	30.3	1.9	-7.8	3.5	25.9	-10.2	-65.8	-39.8	-6.1
German mark	66.5	35.4	68.2	18.8	78.0	63.3	19.2	-17.8	46.3	24.6	6.6	-50.0	29.9
T-bills	108.7	48.5	132.7	-40.1	225.5	189.9	221.8	239.8	127.8	39.2	-12.0	32.9	109.6
Average	29.7	2.4	12.6	-69.1	27.6	23.1	-26.2	-28.5	21.9	-51.0	-54.7	5.1	-8.9

*Calculation of annual percent returns assumes that 30% of the initial investment is used for initial margin, in which margin is estimated as 10% of contract value.

TABLE 7.13	Percentage Returns by System and Year*						
System	1978	1979	1980	1981	1982	1983	1984
CHL	6.1	47.9	81.6	21.8	28.3	19.9	28.0
PAR	18.5	16.4	54.5	29.9	−31.7	−43.2	−19.4
DRM	29.3	21.7	92.2	−31.6	−22.7	7.8	−7.3
RNQ	−57.2	−69.0	−9.6	−152.1	−31.2	−135.5	−100.1
DRP	34.8	63.8	88.7	31.0	−13.4	−20.0	38.5
MII	12.9	41.6	87.8	54.6	−30.7	3.1	7.1
LSO	−47.1	−4.0	39.1	−55.1	−55.1	−37.6	−59.5
REF	−13.5	23.3	53.2	−85.2	2.0	−109.6	−69.2
DMC	17.6	26.8	85.4	5.9	22.9	1.9	−1.6
DRI	−60.7	−15.4	46.3	−108.1	−114.4	−105.3	−34.0
MAB	−38.0	−44.3	−7.7	−114.4	−91.1	−81.8	−45.7
ALX	28.3	38.6	82.6	−34.4	−8.2	−2.0	−14.4
Average	−5.8	12.3	57.8	−36.5	−28.8	−41.9	−23.1

*Equal percentage amounts of margin are assumed to be invested in each market.

Although this study is now dated, the trending nature of these markets remains the same. The German mark (now the euro) and T-bills are the best performers, and we would expect the same outperformance in 2011. Displaying the system results by year for all markets is another way to look at robustness. In Table 7.13, RNQ and MAB had net losses over all markets in all years, while CHL, MII, and DMC stand out as very consistent. The combined presentation of results across all markets and systems is one way of avoiding overfitting by looking at the big picture.

▪ Price Shocks

Ignoring or underestimating the significance of a price shocks will result in a catastrophic loss—if not now, then sometime in the future. Price shocks are large changes in price caused by unpredictable and significant events. The impact of price shocks on historic tests can change the results from profits to losses; it varies the risk from small to extremely large. Unfortunately, not enough thought is given to how these moves affect test results and future performance. A discussion of price shocks could easily fill an entire book, but the concepts that are most important can be explained briefly. When it comes to actual trading, the difference between the expected results and actual performance (not attributed to slippage) is greatly dependent on the number of price shocks.

By its very nature, a price shock must be unexpected. However, not all similar events cause shocks. An assassination, abduction, or political coup is likely to be a surprise, while a crop freeze can be anticipated as weather turns unusually cold. Some economic reports, such as a 0.5% increase in the Producer Price Index or a jump in the balance of trade, will come as a shock, but a low carryover supply of soybeans or a tightening of the money supply after steady economic growth can be anticipated. During times when good economic news is important to support a continued bull market in equities, any disappointing surprise will cause a shock. Every word used by the Fed when stating its current policy on interest rates, following an FOMC meeting, is dissected by the traders, often resulting in large, sudden price changes. The market always tries to anticipate the results of a scheduled economic report. When it is right, prices remain calm; when it is wrong, prices react in proportion to how poorly it was anticipated.

Misinterpreting the Past

In this chapter, our interest in price shocks is how it affects test results and, consequently, the selection of parameters used for trading. At the time of a price shock, such as 9/11, we know that the event could not have been anticipated; at best we might have been lucky and held a short position in equities or a long in bonds. We would never attribute that profit to trading skill. The problem comes when testing a strategy with historic data, which always contains price shocks. The computer cannot know the difference between a profit from a consistent move in the right direction or a windfall profit from a price shock; results only show the set of parameters that had the best performance. For example, if there were 10 major price shocks in 20 years of data, and your historic tests profited from 8 of those shocks, then you have overestimated your profits by profiting from at least 3 shocks that in all probability should have been losses. Even worse, you have *underestimated your risk* by posting profitable results that should have been losses. It is the erroneously low risk that is fatal to trading because it allows overleveraging.

Consider that a price shock only occurs because traders and investors are liquidating their positions or entering new positions in the direction of the price shock. If the shock favored lower interest rates or a stronger U.S. dollar and most traders already held those positions, then there would be little trading activity due to the news and

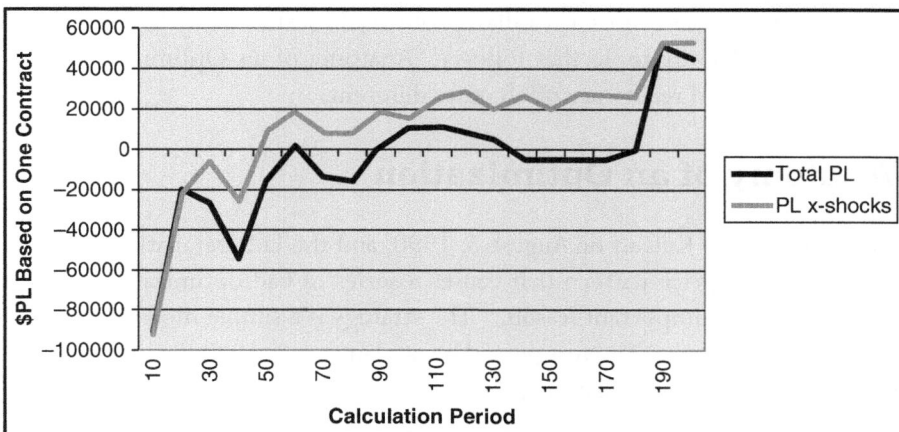

FIGURE 7.21 Price Shocks Consistently Reduce the Returns of a Moving Average System Applied to the S&P, 1991–2009.

correspondingly little price movement. The news was correctly anticipated, hence no price shock. The only time a price shock is important is when its interpretation is contrary to the direction held by traders. Unless you are a contrarian, a price shock is more likely to cause a loss than a profit.

To better understand the effects of price shocks on performance, a test was run that removed the profits and losses from 1-day moves where the current trading range was more than 5 times the average true range of the previous 10 days. Figure 7.21 shows that price shocks consistently had a negative effect on trend performance. Then choosing parameters that netted a profit on all price shocks would be unrealistically optimistic.

How can this problem be avoided? First, look at the pattern of profits and losses from a series of tests. If a 20-day and 30-day moving average each showed a maximum drawdown of $10,000, but the 25-day average only lost $5,000, assume that the 25-day results could have had the same drawdown as the nearby tests. By some quirk of timing one test was able to avoid a loss while a nearby test was not. It would be risky to assume such good fortune in trading. It is safer to average the returns of a series of tests, but use the largest drawdown.

Create a list of major price shocks. This can be done in a spreadsheet by finding 1-day price ranges that are at least 3.5 times the size of recent average ranges. Then look at them on a chart for confirmation. Verify how many of these events produced profits or losses. If the results profited from more than 50% of the shocks, then both profits and risk are wrong. Reverse the average of the 1-day profits with the equivalent loss. Be sure only one day is changed because the system should adjust after the day of the price shock. Also check to see that there is an even distribution with regard to the size of the price shocks. Not only should there be an even number of profits and losses from price shocks, but they should be of comparable size. The system may show good results by taking losses on the minor price shocks and large profits on major ones.

Price shocks must be treated as a serious risk; otherwise, any trading account can be overleveraged and undercapitalized. This is the most common cause of catastrophic loss. A price shock that causes a windfall profit could just as easily have produced a devastating loss. The example that follows, "Anatomy of an Optimization," shows how expectations and reality are often quite different.

■ Anatomy of an Optimization

The Iraqi invasion of Kuwait on August 6, 1990, and the U.S. retaliation on January 17, 1991, create a price pattern that causes a series of bad optimization tests; this pattern can teach an important lesson.[18] The strategy is a simple moving average applied to crude oil futures. The test period began January 2, 1990, but 100 days were needed to initialize the calculations; therefore, the first trade was entered May 24,

---

[18] Perry Kaufman, "Price Shocks: Reevaluating Risk/Return Expectations," *Futures Industry* (June/July 1995).

	TABLE 7.14	Test 1. Optimizing Crude Oil, January 2, 1990, through August 3, 1990*

Period	Net Prft	ROA	MaxDD	Trds
5	2615	82.9	−3155	11
10	6765	959.6	−705	5
15	6975	989.4	−705	3
20	4975	705.7	−705	3
25	6975	989.4	−705	3
30	4635	657.5	−705	3
35	3635	313.4	−1160	3
40	3215	276.0	−1165	3
45	3255	187.6	−1735	3
50	255	10.6	−2415	3
55	−715	−21.1	−3385	5
60	2625	156.7	−1675	5
65	2785	239.1	−1165	5
70	−385	−12.6	−3055	7
75	1955	112.7	−1735	3
80	−5040	−100.0	−5040	2
85	−5040	−100.0	−5040	2
90	−5040	−100.0	−5040	2
95	−5040	−100.0	−5040	2
100	−5040	−100.0	−5040	2

Trade Detail from Testing

Trade Date	B/S	Price	Profit/ Loss	Cum P/L
May 24, 1990	Buy	23.58		
May 25, 1990	Sell	23.55	−55	−55
Jul 11, 1990	Buy	22.49	1035	980
Aug 3, 1990	Sell	28.51	5995	6975

*Testing stopped the day before the invasion of Kuwait.
Test selects 15-day moving average.
Holding short on August 6, 1990, when Iraq invades Kuwait.

1990 (see Tables 7.14 through 7.16). The first test could have used more data; however, the results would have been similar.

In both Test 1 and Test 2 the moving average calculation periods selected were those that produced the highest profits. By accepting these choices the trader would have held a short position before the invasion of Kuwait, and a long position before the U.S. retaliation. In reality, there would have been large losses—the best past parameter values could not predict the price action on the next day. When a price shock is an important part of the data being tested, the best optimized result is the one that took the most profits out of that move, even at the cost of losing on most other trades. The system is not robust; it is finely tuned to one price move.

TABLE 7.15	Test 2. Optimizing Crude Oil, January 2, 1990, through January 16, 1991*			
Period	Net Prft	ROA	MaxDD	Trds
5	−6010	−32.3	−18610	32
10	3660	22.3	−16430	20
15	12350	103.8	−11895	14
20	19810	345.4	−5735	10
25	8410	105.5	−7970	10
30	8420	86.8	−9705	8
35	18075	1348.9	−1340	5
40	11150	308.9	−3610	6
45	9335	304.1	−3070	5
50	8265	246.7	−3350	3
55	2485	55.0	−4515	7
60	9075	184.8	−4910	5
65	7155	100.4	−7130	7
70	3815	53.3	−7160	7
75	7195	83.9	−8580	9
80	−8540	−82.6	−10340	12
85	−3860	−54.2	−7125	8
90	1960	35.7	−5485	4
95	440	9.5	−4615	4
100	−3950	−85.6	−4615	2

Trade Detail from Testing				
Trade Date	B/S	Price	Profit/ Loss	Cum P/L
May 24, 1990	Buy	23.58		
May 25, 1990	Sell	23.55	−55	−55
Jul 12, 1990	Buy	23.49	35	−20
Oct 19, 1990	Sell	40.10	16585	16565
Oct 30, 1990	Buy	41.23	−1155	15410
Oct 31, 1990	Sell	41.92	665	16075
Nov 19, 1990	Buy	38.39	3505	19580
Nov 21, 1990	Sell	37.30	−1115	18465
Nov 26, 1990	Buy	40.62	−3345	15120
Nov 27, 1990	Sell	40.53	−115	15005
Jan 7, 1991	Buy	35.70	4805	19810

*Testing stopped the day before the U.S. retaliation.

Test selects 20-day moving average.

Total profits are $3,225 without price shock.

Holding long when U.S. attacks Iraq.

In Test 2, although there were large profits from the first price shock, the trader would have still held the wrong position when the second shock occurred. This method of testing hides the real trading risk, focuses on profits that cannot be predicted, and does it all at the expense of everyday trading profits.

TABLE 7.16	Test 3. Optimizing Crude Oil, January 2, 1990, through March 28, 1991*			
Period	Net Prft	ROA	MaxDD	Trds
5	−17255	64.0	−26975	45
10	−13195	−45.0	−29295	31
15	4480	26.6	−16840	20
20	8430	67.6	−12475	16
25	−4690	−22.6	−20725	20
30	−1395	−6.4	−21775	17
35	28335	2114.6	−1340	9
40	−360	−2.5	−14420	12
45	18245	594.3	−3070	7
50	8265	246.7	−3350	3
55	2485	55.0	−4515	7
60	9075	184.8	−4910	5
65	7155	100.4	−7130	7
70	3815	53.3	−7160	7
75	7195	83.9	−8580	9
80	−18225	−81.3	−22410	13
85	−12945	−70.4	−18390	9
90	−4065	−40.3	−10080	5
95	−8645	−56.0	−15430	5
100	−3485	−75.5	−4615	5

Trade Detail from Testing

Trade Date	B/S	Price	Profit/ Loss	Cum P/L
May 24, 1990	Buy	23.58		
May 25, 1990	Sell	23.55	−55	−55
Jul 16, 1990	Buy	24.16	−635	−690
Nov 9, 1990	Sell	40.58	16395	15705
Jan 14, 1991	Buy	38.76	1795	17500
Jan 16, 1991	Sell	39.36	575	18075
Mar 8, 1991	Buy	29.89	9445	27520
Mar 13, 1991	Sell	30.89	975	28495
Mar 19, 1991	Buy	30.75	115	28610
Mar 28, 1991	Sell	30.50	−275	28335

*Test period includes both price shocks.
Test selects 35-day moving average.
Total profits are $2,495 without price shocks.
Optimization profits include both Iraqi invasion of Kuwait and the U.S. attack on Iraq.

Test 3 looks back at the best results when the data includes both price shocks, August 6, 1990, and January 17, 1991. Instead of calculation periods of 15 and 20 days, selected in the first two tests, this optimization shows best returns for a 35-day calculation period. A look at the sequence of results in the optimization places the peak returns in an uncertain position between two losses, indicating instability. The trading detail shows that the system would have shorted oil on the day before the invasion of Iraq, a likely case of overfitting. The most reasonable selection would be in the area of the 60-day period, although profits are far lower, and there is still no assurance that this choice would be profitable the next time.

■ Summarizing Robustness

We return to the concept of robustness. Earlier we listed the criteria that are important in "Searching for Robustness," the first being a sound premise. In showing test results we concluded that a large number of profitable tests was a good measurement of robustness. For the testing process, it was necessary to set performance expectations and make realistic assumptions about the parameter values that were likely to work; realistic costs also must be used. The process of testing needed to be done scientifically, using in-sample and out-of-sample data.

If we pass the hurdle of in-sample success, followed by good out-of-sample results, we have *proved the concept*. We can retest with all the data then trade, using a small commitment to begin.

Practically speaking, a *robust* trading strategy is one that produces consistently good results across a broad set of parameter values applied to many different markets tested for many years. *Robustness* is a term used to describe a system or method that works under many market conditions, one in which we have confidence. In the best scenario, a robust system is not sensitive to moderate changes in parameter values.

A strategy can also be robust if the underlying premise has a single set of rules with no parameter values and is successful across a specific set of markets during a specific time period, provided there is a large sample of trades. Ideally, if a long-term moving average system is robust, then someone unfamiliar with the system should be able to choose a calculation period between 100 and 300 days, specify a market and a time interval, and expect the system to show net profits from trading. This would be most likely if a large percentage of all the parameter values were profitable.

The highest profit or the best risk ratio is not important when looking for robustness, and focusing on these values can be distracting. Instead, it is the average values of all tests that are important, that is, the average net profit, average number of trades, average drawdown, and average profit per trade. In addition, the standard deviation of profits for all tests will give a very good idea of the consistency of returns over the range of tests.

The following is a checklist and brief explanation that outlines the steps for testing, evaluating the test results, selecting parameter values, and monitoring actual trading, consistent with the purpose of finding a robust trading strategy:[19]

THE INTEGRATION OF TECHNICAL ANALYSIS

---

[19] A more detailed explanation of testing "robustness" can be found in Perry Kaufman, *Smarter Trading* (New York: McGraw-Hill, 1995).

1. *Deciding what to test.* Testing should be used for validation of an existing idea, not for discovery.
   a. *Is the underlying premise sound?* It should be based on careful observation of the market, or an awareness of relationships between different factors that drive the market, or between different markets themselves. It may be implemented using trends, oscillators, and other techniques, but it is trying to capture a pattern in human behavior, or an economic or fundamental process.
   b. *Can you program all the rules?* Programming a system guarantees that all of the contingencies have been thought out. Rules can even account for exceptional situations, such as crisis intervention following a dramatic price shock, where a different set of rules is applied.
   c. *Does the strategy make sense only under certain conditions?* A strategy can apply to a smaller set of specific situations, provided there are enough cases and those patterns can be extracted from a varied set of test data. When there are fewer cases it is more important that the justification be explained in advance, based on a clear market phenomenon, and not discovered by testing.
   d. *Take a guess as to the expected results.* Based on the rules of the strategy, a rough estimate of the number of trades, percentage of profitable trades, and even the net profits should be written down before testing begins. Testing then becomes a way of confirming these estimates.
   e. *Be critical of good results.* Getting good test results in a pattern that is different from expectations may mean that the rules are specified incorrectly, or that you misunderstood the risk of the method. It is the best time to rethink the problem before moving forward. While we always try to understand and fix bad results, there is an inclination to accept good results without questioning whether they could be wrong. Getting good results for the wrong reason is still an error.
2. *Deciding how to test.* There are a number of steps necessary before the test process begins:
   a. *Choose the testing tools and methods.* Select a test platform, such as TradeStation, MetaStock, or Ninja Trading, that can speed up the test process and keep it objective. Programming in these platforms prevents the strategy from looking ahead at the data before making a decision about today, an error that can easily happen when programming in BASIC, C, or even using a spreadsheet. Many perfect strategies have been created by accidentally looking at tomorrow's prices.
   b. *Use as much of the right data as possible.* More data is best, but if there is less data available it should have a wide variety of price patterns, such as bull and bear markets, price shocks, and sustained sideways periods.
   c. *Separate the data into in-sample and out-of-sample sets.* The only way to assure that no overfitting has occurred is by reserving a substantial part of the data for validation. Once the out-of-sample data has been used, you cannot change the program.

d. *Choose the range of parameter values that applies to the strategy.* The nature of the trading strategy, for example, a long-term or short-term breakout, will determine the parameter values that should be tested. Test only the range that makes sense for the strategy. This serves to validate the concept and avoids discovering an isolated profitable situation that can be distracting and misleading.

e. *Decide the order in which to test the parameters.* Not all parameters should be tested at the same time. A few of the most important parameters should be tested first to see if the basic structure is profitable. These parameters, such as the calculation period for the trend, will have a wide range of results. These results may show that faster trading cannot be profitable after transaction costs. Other parameters, such as a stop-loss, are used to refine the risk profile, and should not turn a losing method into a profitable one. They can be tested later.

f. *Be sure the parameter test values are distributed properly.* Testing equal increments of trend periods can be misleading. The difference between a 3- and 4-day moving average is 33%, while the difference between a 99- and 100-day average is only 1%. When testing periods from 1 to 100 days, in steps of 1, the average results are heavily weighted toward the long end, which has similar performance. Commercial testing platforms may not allow unequal test increments; therefore, it is necessary to weight the results in a way that compensates for the distribution.

g. *Define the success criteria.* Highest net profits are not the best measurement of success for individual tests. Risk-adjusted returns, high reliability, frequency of trading, and time in the market can be combined to give very good objective criteria.

h. *Presentation and visualization of the results.* A table of test results, in the order they are processed by the testing program, is a very difficult format for evaluation. The availability of charts via a spreadsheet allows a visual presentation of how the values of each parameter interact with all other parameter values. It becomes clear which parameters are stable and which are not performing properly. Two- and 3-dimensional contour maps and scatter diagrams can give a better view of the interaction between parameters; they also show the sensitivity of each parameter value at the same time—in easy-to-read colors.

3. *Evaluating the results.* Careful review of the test results can avoid many hours of unnecessary work later on. Looking at a good sample of individual test results (one result for each combination of parameter values), and even the individual trades of a few selected parameter values, will give insight into the good and bad aspects of a trading strategy. The statistics are not enough information to be sure that the program is performing correctly. An exceptionally large trading loss, and too many trades that ended with a stop-loss and not enough with profit-taking, will indicate a problem that cannot be seen without studying the detail.

a. *Verify a reasonable sample of calculations.* Just because calculations were done by a computer doesn't mean they are correct. Someone had to tell the computer what to do, and people make mistakes. This is the time to remember the Carpenter's Rule: *measure twice, cut once.*

b. *Were there enough trades to have reliable results?* Results that show excellent performance with only a few trades are a problem. When there is not enough data, there is no way to be sure that the results are robust.

c. *Does the trading system produce profits for most combinations of parameters?* The best assurance of robustness is when most parameters produce profitable results, even though the returns and risk vary.

d. *Did rule changes improve overall test performance?* When a special rule is added to improve performance or to correct a specific problem, the average statistics of all tests must improve, while the standard deviation remains unchanged. Or, the standard deviation of all tests must decline while the average returns remain unchanged. Both profiles indicate a change that is a global improvement; otherwise, the changes have targeted a single problem, which is a sign of overfitting.

4. *Choosing the specific parameter values to trade.* Choosing the final values to be used in trading is a unique and difficult problem. There is no sure way of knowing if the final selection of values will perform in the future. The testing process tries to separate robust performance from success by luck or chance.

a. *The final parameter selection can include all data.* Good test procedures call for using in-sample and out-of-sample data, but once that has been completed successfully, a final test can be run on all data. Staying as current as possible improves the chances for success.

b. *Choose values from a broad area of success not biased by the one test that had peak profits.* Peak performance of any sort is an exception not likely to be repeated. Select the final parameter values that represent average returns in an area of consistency that is not sensitive to moderate changes in parameter values.

c. *Profits must be distributed evenly throughout the test period.* The best parameter value choices are those that show consistency over time. The stock index futures have a tendency to be highly profitable for trending methods during the bull market of the 1990s, but have a decaying profit profile during the more recent years. A set of values that show a moderate increase in performance in recent years is more desirable that one that shows a decay in returns; however, uniformity across the entire period is best.

d. *Verify whether a disproportionate amount of profits came from price shocks.* It is not possible to avoid large price shocks in real trading because you never know when they will come. Historic results that do not show large (negative) equity jumps due to price shocks are not realistic, and result from overfitting. The final values chosen may have produced conservative results by avoiding all of the price shocks. Even worse, those results that profited from more than 50% of the price shocks, or from the largest price shocks, have erroneously low risk. In real trading, far fewer than 50% of the price shocks will become a windfall profit.

e. *Scale the risk to a personally acceptable risk level.* Every return is associated with a comparable level of risk. For example, the final system performance shows a risk-adjusted annualized return of 50% with an associated annualized risk of 20%, measured as 1 standard deviation of the monthly returns. Then there is a 2.5% chance that the system can lose 40% in one year. A trader that will only accept a 2.5% chance of a 20% loss will need to reduce the leverage by one-half, reducing the expected returns to 25% per annum.

f. *When there is a choice between two sets of parameter values, choose the one that causes less time in the market.* Parameter values that generate comparable returns and have less time in the market are best. Being out of the market is the only defense against price shocks. If a strategy holds a position only 60% of the time, then there is a 40% chance that a price shock can be avoided. Strategies that are out of the market most often do not reverse positions. Separating exits and entries improves slippage and liquidity.

g. *Out-of-sample performance must validate the results.* Before beginning trading, an out-of-sample test should confirm that the system can perform on data never seen before. If there is no recent out-of-sample data available, a test of a similar market or older data can be used. While this is not as good as more recent data in the tested markets, a further decay in performance when applied to a similar index would still be a strong sign that the model was overfitted.

5. *Trading and performance monitoring.* The development of a system is never complete. There is a continuous evolution in the markets, seen in the changing participation, volatility, interrelationships between markets, and the introduction of new markets. The only way to see how these changes affect a trading program is to carefully monitor the system signals and the corresponding execution prices. From this evaluation, funds can be reallocated, the method of placing orders can be changed, and better rules can be introduced. Without monitoring the trading, and comparing the results to the test expectations, there is no basis for saying that a system is performing correctly.

a. *Trade using exactly the same rules that were tested.* It is often convenient to program a simple version of an idea, but trade a more complex set of rules. Or, a new rule may be added at the end without testing, because the test process takes too long. What appears to be an inconsequential change can cause substantially different results. If the tested method and traded method are not identical, there is no basis for assessing success.

b. *Trade the same data that was used in testing.* The use of a continuous back-adjusted series for testing futures will not give you the same results as testing each contract, beginning at the time it becomes the most active delivery month. Some artificial continuous price series are smoother than real prices and appear to perform better, but are not real data; at the least, it does not include the cost of rolling contracts. Forex data is a unique problem because test data may represent the quotes of one set of banks, while the data on any quote machine will be from an entirely different set of banks. These can vary dramatically. Testing using cash FX data is not the same as futures. The best trading results come when the test data and trading data are from the same source.

c. *Monitoring the difference between the system and the actual entries and exits.* Slippage, the difference between the system price and the actual market execution, can change performance from theoretically profitable to a real trading loss. Monitoring this difference will tell you the realistic execution costs, the maximum volume that can be traded, and the best time of day to trade.

A Final Comment on Testing

Testing is the only way you can know if a strategy can be successful, but it provides no guarantee of profits. Testing can be done on many levels. It can be as simple as validating a single set of rules with no choice of parameter values, applied to past data. It can be as complex as a multidimensional analysis of results based on parameters that are so interdependent that they must all be tested simultaneously.

Testing that follows a sound procedure and a test evaluation that looks for robust solutions will improve the chances for success. Bad testing can be tragic—it is a waste of time and resources, and leads to a system that has little chance of success.

The extent of testing is a matter of judgment. Simple tests can outline the performance profile and provide an understanding of the risks and rewards. Complex tests may introduce subtle errors in the process, just as complex strategies may be flawed due to their intricacy. Begin simply, increase the complexity slowly, and stop as soon as possible.

Remember that, as hard as we try, real-time results will not be as good as historic results. Historic price patterns never repeat themselves in the same way. The best system rules and the best parameter values are the simplest and the most general. They may show lower returns and greater risk than the ideal optimized results, but they are much more likely to represent the future returns.

Other areas of interest to readers actively testing and evaluating test performance are *genetic algorithms*.

CHAPTER 8

Practical Considerations

From Perry J. Kaufman, *Trading Systems and Methods, +Website*, 5th Edition (Hoboken, New Jersey: John Wiley & Sons, 2013), Chapter 22.

Learning Objective Statements

- Explain what checks can be made to verify the validity of daily data
- Differentiate between general problems encountered when testing a system with deeper issues such as the assumptions of the developer
- Construct a rule to take advantage of combining the Theory of Runs with the direction of a trend

This chapter discusses areas of technical and mathematical analysis that are not systems by themselves yet are essential to the successful development of a system and to trading. The first part concerns the use—and the misuse—of the computer. Technical analysis and computers have become inseparable and, with the simple steps provided by development software such as *TradeStation, MetaStock*, and spreadsheets, it would be rare to trade a new technical system without first running it through a computer to simulate its past performance.

The second section, "Extreme Events," is the most underestimated deterrent for finding the best system, for generating realistic expectations, and the most common reason for catastrophic loss. Unpredictable events, once they become part of price history, are often treated as though they could have been anticipated. This can inflate performance returns and minimize risk during strategy testing with serious consequences to actual trading. This section tries to explain how to close the gap between testing and reality.

"Gambling Techniques—The Theory of Runs," the third section, is actually an application of gambling techniques, primarily Martingales, to trading. What would seem more reasonable than assuming that the odds are against you in the stock or futures markets and treating it as a gambling scenario?

The final sections start by combining systems that focus on different market characteristics, and then explore the trade-offs inherent in the basic types of strategies. There is also a short analysis of trading limits in futures markets to show some of the problems and flaws of moving from a test to an operating environment. The last section reviews the similarity of systems and the impact of technical systems on the markets.

■ Use and Abuse of the Computer

Make sure your present report system is reasonably clean and effective before you automate. Otherwise your new computer will just speed up the mess.
—Robert Townsend[1]

Computers are not a substitute for thinking. They excel in performing the same tedious task, over and over again, quickly and accurately—provided, of course, that correct information was entered. But even though technology has not yet reached the stage depicted in *Star Wars, Star Trek*, or even in H. G. Wells' *The War of the Worlds*, the computer has become an essential part of trading, from viewing charts to order entry to system development. This section will consider both good and bad ways to approach a computer problem.

Speed and capacity are no longer a concern when choosing a computer. Even the basic models have sufficient power to solve all but specialized problems. Storing tick data on all stocks from their inception would still present a problem, but there are servers that can easily handle that. Even laptops have storage measured in terabytes and perform multitasking. Still, buying the high-end hardware ensures some added longevity to your purchase.

During the 1980s the average life of a computer *generation* was about 10 years; however, advances in technology have reduced that to about 3 years, if you don't mind 1 year when you feel obsolete. Each year, computers become faster and more sophisticated. It is said that the capacity and speed of the computer doubles every year and a half.

Because not everyone knows how to program a computer, software companies have developed *turn-key* packages, programs that are *user-friendly,* operated by a click of the mouse and driven by menu selection. The combination of these two factors, cheap and powerful hardware and sophisticated, user-friendly software, has made individual and institutional investors dependent upon this technology. Generally, development software falls into two groups:

1. *Daily market analysis,* with price updates and orders placed at the end of the day.
2. *Intraday trading platform,* providing users with online data feeds and real-time executions.

---

[1] Robert Townsend, *Up the Organization* (New York: Knopf, 1970), 36.

Both types of software provide the ability to enter your trading strategies and test them on historic data. The software that operates on daily data, also called *end-of-day data,* is considered "off-line" and is used by traders who prefer to evaluate the market after it closes and prepare orders that can be executed the next day without having to constantly watch the market. The intraday trading platform, however, is much more complex and more expensive. It requires active data feeds, provides real-time graphics, and generates trading signals that change as price patterns develop during the day. It can make decisions based on each price print or based on a bar size defined by the user, for example, every 30 minutes.

Acquiring Data

Daily historic data is readily available from a wide range of providers and may even come with the purchase of the software development program. A convenient list can be found on *DataVendors.com*, however, it is missing CQG and perhaps other important sources. It is common to see 25 years of historic data on all U.S. equity and futures markets, but not as common to have European and Asian data provided as well. More data and markets are always available at an added cost. Specialized data vendors, such as Dial Data and Commodity Systems Inc., provide an easy way to update data each day in a format readily used by most testing and trading platforms.

If futures data is needed, check to see if the vendor provides a continuous, back-adjusted data series, which will be necessary for testing. The types of back-adjusting were discussed in Chapter 7. You will need to understand the exact way in which data is back-adjusted so that it corresponds to the way in which you trade.

Intraday data is available from a few major vendors, such as the CQG Data Factory, Tick Data Inc., and of course, Bloomberg; however, Bloomberg does not provide an automatic download and update. Intraday trading platforms, such as TradeStation and Thomson-Reuters MetaStock, provide data feeds that are integrated with the trading strategies and can also generate orders when trading signals occur. One-stop shopping has come to trading. The Chicago Mercantile Exchange has made most of its tick data available, but it is not necessarily in a format that can be read by your trading strategy software. You may still find it easier to buy the data in the right format.

If you are using a live charting service, or a trading platform with live data, that data can be downloaded to a text file and used for historic testing. Most services will provide an "export" feature in a drop-down menu or by right-clicking on the prices that appear on the screen.

Data Accuracy It may seem surprising, but even daily data—open, high, low, and close—can vary from one provider to another. Most often the settlement prices are the same, but the highs and lows can be off by small amounts. For most developers this is not important, but for posting the settlement value of an ETF or listed fund the differences need to be resolved each day by using multiple data sources. Occasionally, there will be a large error in the closing price that passes through, so it falls to the user to have some validity checks for unusually large moves.

PRACTICAL CONSIDERATIONS

Even though historic data has been available for many years, you may find short periods where the decimal point shifts within a data series. A simple visual check, displaying the historic data as a chart, will show any problems that need fixing. Smaller errors may never be found.

Combining data from different vendors may also introduce problems. One source may record a price as 135.50 and the other as 13550 or 1355.

Cleaning the Data Tick data is notorious for including bad data with the good, simply because of the magnitude of the numbers. Errors were pervasive when futures markets were open outcry and prices were recorded by a clerk with a data entry machine, standing above the pit. Now that nearly everything is electronic, the prices are far more accurate, but not always perfect. When using high frequency data (for example, every tick), it may turn out that not all ticks are flowing through to your computer due to the speed of access. In other cases, when there is a *fast market*— extremely high volume—you will either receive the data late or miss pieces of data.

There is still good reason to check the integrity of the data. Some markets are still open outcry, and even computers make mistakes. Simple checks of daily data should include:

1. *Outliers*, those data points that are more than 4% away from the previous data (or some preset percentage).
2. *Missing dates*, more than 4 days in sequence without data should be flagged as a potential problem.
3. *Open and closing prices outside the high-low range* are not possible, and the data should be corrected or removed.

For intraday data, some additional checks are:

4. *Frequency of data*, a comparison of the average ticks per 5-minute interval with the current frequency, looking for those times when there was no data.
5. Unusually large intraday price jumps that reverse within a few seconds indicate a data error or a large order that couldn't be absorbed easily.

One dilemma presented by cleaning data was most pronounced in the energy markets when it was only open outcry. If you developed a system based on clean data, then applied that strategy to intraday live data, you would find that there were a large number of additional signals due to bad prices. Your theoretical, profitable results would instead be filled with bad trades, netting a loss instead of the expected profit. The solution was to use the original, dirty data in the development to force the system to be less sensitive to price movement.

Combining Standard Techniques into a System

Strategy development programs provide a wide assortment of standard techniques in the form of indicators and preprogrammed systems. Choose a stochastic oscillator or an RSI, a moving average or an *N*-day breakout, and combine them in various ways with different calculation periods, such as a 10-day and 40-day smoothing, or even vary the frequency of data using 30-minute, 1-hour, and daily bars. These existing techniques can satisfy most needs. It has already been shown that trend profits are the result of prices trending rather than the formula used to create a trendline. The trend speed is more important than the method. Adding an oscillator or momentum indicator for entry timing is also a broad concept that can be satisfied by a number of indicators. Somewhere in the combination of these techniques should be a trading strategy that matches the time frame and risk profile that you want. Before taking the path of specialized programming, there is a lot to be learned by using these standard tools.

Programming a New Idea

Computer programming talent is no longer rare, but in high demand and sometimes expensive. However, many of us have become proficient at spreadsheets and some simple programming tasks, so we have a better idea of what is good and bad. Fortunately, the data management, the complex bookkeeping, and order entry are already built in to the programmable section of trading development software. Functions such as *buy on the close* or *sell at 125 stop* allow orders to be entered as they would in actual trading. It is only necessary to code the actual strategy and the list of trades, and a performance summary will be produced automatically. Large-scale testing is also a well-used feature. Most important, the software prevents you from looking ahead at tomorrow's price in order to decide whether to buy or sell today. Throughout this book, there are many examples of strategies in both Excel and TradeStation. Anyone able to program can take the simple TradeStation instructions and change them to Basic, C, or any other language.

The prevailing philosophy about software development is to try to use as much third-party software as possible. For example, after an optimization has been run (resulting in hundreds of lines of test results, one line for each combination of parameter values), save the results to a spreadsheet. This test detail can then be sorted, organized, analyzed, and charted with all the facilities in the spreadsheet program. If a series of tests are saved, they can be compared in the spreadsheet. Results can be averaged, and the variance can be found in order to find the most robust strategy. For the more popular platforms, such as TradeStation and MetaStock, a number of users' groups, support groups, and newsletters can be of great help. Some companies provide alternate statistical measurements for your tests, while others have an add-in portfolio program. It is a good idea to check to see if these services satisfy your needs before attacking the programming yourself.

Too Much Power

It is tempting to let the computer solve the problem of finding the ideal trading system, but it can't do that. In Chapter 7, we discussed the process of finding a successful trading system beginning with a sound premise. Instead, you can throw all indicators, trend calculations, fundamental data, and rules into a big pot and let the computer find the best combination using brute force optimization, neural networks, or genetic algorithms, but by now you should know that an overfit solution does not work. More computer power does make processing faster, but is not essential to finding a successful system. There is a good argument for saying that less power means that the solution should be reasoned out in advance to be most effective. But then, it should be reasoned out anyway.

Looking into the Past

The advantages of using as much data as possible have been discussed thoroughly—it reflects a broader variety of market conditions; therefore, results based on more data will be more robust. There is often a concern that older data does not represent current conditions. While there may be some truth in that, there is usually more to be gained with a system that can survive those years and still perform well in current markets. Unless there has been a structural change that makes the old data invalid, longer tests and more data are better. If the older years represent a period of low volatility that is not likely to be seen again, a strategy should, at the very least, not post losses for that period. Price patterns never seem to repeat themselves; however, there are characteristics of the past that continually reappear.

Paper Trading

With all good intentions, when a new strategy is developed, the plan is to hold the most recent data aside for out-of-sample testing. However, before testing is completed, that data has been used at least once, most often many times. No matter how careful you are, it is possible that the system has been overfitted to the data by fine-tuning the rules and parameters. Even if there was no conscious overfitting, the returns from real trading will be different from the tested results.

The safest alternative is a period of *paper trading*. Only by monitoring the program daily can its performance be seen under real market conditions. Even before doing that, the performance expectations must be documented. You should know the frequency of trading, holding period, percentage of profitable trades, size of profits, and size of losses in order to measure comparative results.

It is always a relief when the system posts its first profit, but it is the overall profile that is most important. When paper trading, assume that the execution is the worst price of the 5 minutes immediately following an intraday signal, or the highest price of the futures market closing range if trades are executed *on the close*. A touch of reality can point out problems before they happen and save a lot of money. Don't start trading a new system without monitoring its performance first. After that, start with a small amount.

It Should Work, but It Doesn't

It was hard work, and all of the steps were followed as conscientiously as possible. The rules were logical, and well-defined, and the strategy was tested on enough data. Your effort has resulted in proving one of four things:

1. The strategy is profitable.
2. The strategy is not profitable.
3. The strategy cannot be implemented effectively.
4. The whole process takes too long or is too expensive.

Of course, a successful outcome is the best result, but it is not the most likely result from the first attempt. If you are convinced that the method should work but the results were not good enough, each step in the process will need to be reviewed. Trading strategies should be built slowly; each piece must be proved to be sound before going on to the next step. You should never have gotten to the end without knowing that the final product was going to be profitable. If the performance deteriorated as new rules and features were added, you should have stopped until the problems were resolved.

Vertical or Integrated Solutions

There are two philosophies for system development, *vertical,* using individual building blocks, one upon the other, and *fully-integrated,* similar to a puzzle box where all pieces fit together in just one special way. The fully-integrated method takes advantage of the interrelationship between features, such as the calculation speed of a trend and a filter that blocks entering a new trade and forces the liquidation of the current trade when volatility is too high. It is possible that, as the filter blocks more trades, the trend speed will change to be profitable in markets with less volatility. Therefore, the two parameters, trend speed and filter threshold, are interdependent and must be tested together.

Using the vertical method, the primary rule is tested first and must be profitable without any other features. In this case, the trend is tested and found to be successful when the calculation period is above 40 days. Next, the volatility threshold is tested with the selected trend period. The volatility threshold is therefore dependent upon a specific trend. It becomes clear that the volatility feature works or does not work.

What happens when the vertical solution shows that volatility does not help, but there is a very successful integrated solution? This will happen when the trend period is not profitable on its own, but is profitable when selected trades are made based on the volatility filter. To some analysts, this is a more sophisticated solution; to others, it is overfit. The answer can be found by tabulating the percentage of profitable test combinations, a measure used in Chapter 7 that was called *robustness*. If the percentage of profitable tests of the combined parameters is greater than the percentage of successful tests using only the trend, then the volatility feature is an improvement.

Transparent or Complex Solutions   A *transparent strategy* is one that is easy to understand. If it was capitalizing on a chart pattern, it could be explained by showing that pattern, or combination of patterns, on a chart. If a trading signal was generated, another trader who knew the rules could look at the prices on a screen and confirm that a signal should have occurred at that point.

A complex system is not transparent. A chart pattern that is filtered by price volatility and volume, then confirmed by the pattern of other stocks in the same sector as well as the S&P 500 index, would be difficult to calculate manually. If the underlying premise is a trend based on a portion of a trigonometric curve, it is not clear that anyone could intuitively know that a trade should have occurred on any specific price bar.

Complex solutions may be wrong without anyone knowing. They are more difficult to create, especially difficult to debug, and cannot be visually confirmed by studying the signals on a chart. Acceptance is based on historic testing and profitability. A complex solution can be successful, but it is a very difficult road to follow, and difficult to fix when it goes wrong.

Isolating the Problems   A few of the more common problems that cause disappointing test results are:

1. The rules were interpreted incorrectly. When the rules were programmed, choices were made in order to satisfy a rule that was not definitive. For example, the rule could have been buy only if confirmed by volume. When that rule was programmed, it was interpreted as buy only if today's volume is greater than yesterday's volume. Because volume is erratic, the statement should have been buy only if today's volume is greater than the average volume of the past 10 days.

2. The techniques did not work for the parameter value range that was tested. The original concept was to find a medium-length trend to avoid very long holding periods that have high risk, or very short-term trading that is too intense. However, none of the parameter values in the range from 15 to 70 days worked and the stop-loss of 1% to 3% did not seem to be effective.

   Systems do not always work as expected. It turns out that medium-speed trends have highly variable holding periods; that is, sometimes the price move is sustained for 1 to 2 weeks, other times 2 months. The same trend period cannot capture both. Negative results are important feedback. They help create a better strategy before it is too late. After all, if the answers were known in advance, this would all be unnecessary.

   Instead of finding a single, medium-speed trend, combine a longer trend with the medium one. The longer one will find the fundamental direction, dictated by economic policy; the medium calculation period will capture shorter moves within that trend, at the same time avoiding the losing scenario of trading against the fundamental direction. Take the time to understand why two trends worked when one did not. This is an opportunity to increase your understanding of how the market works and find a successful strategy at the same time.

3. *It worked in some markets but not in others.* Some markets have clearer trends, while others have more noise. Not all markets will work with the same strategy; however, all markets within the same sector should work. Don't expect Raytheon and IBM to trade the same way, or Intel and General Electric, but two wireless telephone companies or two auto manufacturers should produce similar results. In futures, the fixed-income markets show the longest trends, while the equity index markets have the most noise. You should be concerned when similar markets perform differently, but expect different markets to have unique characteristics.

Just Because It Doesn't Work in Practice Doesn't Mean It Won't Work in Theory   If the more general issues are not the problem, then you need to look deeper.

Did you make assumptions? When the initial idea was verified, was it probably done with selected data, representing markets that were most likely to be successful.

It may work during a particular type of market, but fail during other times. Try to isolate the same type of price patterns in other markets by filtering periods of high or low volatility or isolating intervals of high correlation.

Ignoring a few large losses. Long-Term Capital made the mistake of rationalizing a few large losses, convincing themselves that the combination of events that caused the largest equity drawdowns during historic testing would not occur again. If those losses were removed, then the expected risk was much lower, trading could be leveraged, and profits would be increased proportionally. They were right and wrong. The same events did not happen again, but different circumstances resulted in losses just as large. Because of their high leverage and massive positions, they shook the entire financial system when they fell. If anything, history does not show enough risk. The increased correlation between markets, and greater participation, will result in faster, larger, and more volatile price swings with less protection from diversification. Large historic losses should not be ignored, but accepted as a likely but infrequent event. There is more about this important problem in the next section, "Extreme Events."

Misjudging market volatility. If the year was 1996 and the equity markets were moving steadily higher, a newly developed system trading the S&P or NASDAQ 100 could be very profitable. As time advances towards 2000, the system continues to perform in the same bull market, but volatility increases significantly. If the system trades the same number of NASDAQ contracts in 2000 as it did in 1996, then it is exposed to 6 times the volatility as prices moved from 600 to 4,000. Individual trade risk must account for changing volatility by varying the stop-loss and the position size. In a diversified portfolio that included soybeans and NASDAQ futures, soybeans remained within a narrow range of volatility, while NASDAQ volatility kept growing. Did the historic tests account for this dramatic imbalance over time?

Failing to recognize an evolving marketplace. Not only will volatility increase with price, but price patterns will change with growing market participation. Increased volume from a broad set of participants introduces more noise into short-term price movement. Economic policy still creates the major trends; however, theoretical market efficiency does not stop the increase in erratic price movement caused by large and small traders acting with similar or opposite strategies. The net effect is that a trend system will take longer to recognize a trend change. It will enter later and exit later, resulting in a reduction in net profits. Over a long test interval, this will show a noticeable decay in performance.

Taking Control

It is not necessary to create or acquire a system that is exceptionally complex in order to be successful. Simple systems, such as long-term trends or a dual moving average crossover, can be profitable as well. A simple trend approach, applied to the S&P or NASDAQ, would have gotten you out of the long positions after the 2000 tech bubble peak, and well before the largest losses from the subprime crisis in 2008. While most financial managers and brokers were encouraging clients to hold their positions, that it was just a temporary setback, the trend had turned down. The problem with advice based on market "know-how" is that there is no specific point that would cause a change. It is only clear that positions should have been exited well after the fact, when it is too late. At the very least, even a passive investor needs to recognize that the money is more important to him or her than it is to the broker. Being proactive can cause a small opportunity to be missed but can also avoid a big loss.

■ Extreme Events

Price shocks are the most likely reason for catastrophic loss. Although very large price shocks are infrequent events, experiencing only one is enough. Price shocks cause the largest gap between expectations (formed by historic testing) and real trading results. The implications of price shocks in testing were discussed in Chapter 7.

A *price shock* is an unexpected, unpredictable event. Price shocks are a normal part of price movement and happen often. Most are the result of economic reports that differ from expectations, such as the Fed raising rates by ½% when only ¼% was anticipated, unemployment rising when it was expected to fall, or a drug company's latest miracle cure being denied by the FDA. But the largest price shocks are unexpected events with global impact, such as the terrorist attack of 9/11/2001. A significant unexpected political event, such as the abduction of Gorbachev in 1991, caused havoc in the foreign exchange markets for 3 days. The collapse of Lehman Brothers may have been a shock, but the subprime crises evolved over days and weeks. The key word to remember is *unexpected*.

Money Moves the Markets

As technology has made communication instantaneous, everyone seems to know of a price shock at the same time. The world watched while the second airplane flew into the World Trade Center. Markets plummeted until trading was halted in the United States. Drops in the S&P 500 were mirrored in the equity markets of every country.

During a price shock, diversification is ineffective. Markets all move together, or all reverse together. While the equity markets dropped, fixed income prices skyrocketed in a *flight to safety*. Both of those price moves are easily explained. However, other markets, such as soybeans and cocoa, uniformly reversed direction because of large-scale liquidation. The fundamentals are no longer important—investors are simply cashing out of all positions. It is the money that moves the market during a price shock. It was exactly the same scenario in the subprime crisis of 2008. Correlations went to 1, not because those markets had anything fundamentally similar, but because investors were moving money out as quickly as possible. Markets that are entirely unrelated to the events will become volatile in what appears to be a sympathetic move. This usually compounds the trading risk while it presents great opportunities for profits after the price shock has been fully absorbed.

Fooling Yourself with Hindsight

If an event was expected, then it would not cause a price change, let alone a price shock. No one can profit from a price shock by clever planning, but only by luck. We can never assume that an open trade would be on the right side of a price shock in more than 50% of those events, and it may be far fewer. Unfortunately, backtesting a trading system using historic data does not attempt to identify price shocks, but treats them as normal, everyday events. The final selection is often the parameter values that produced the best returns or return ratio, without concern about specific profits that may have been the result of shocks. Regardless of the way the best performance was judged—higher profits, lower risk, least sensitive, or a combination of statistical values—you can be sure that selection has been the greatest beneficiary of these unpredictable price shocks. It goes a long way toward explaining why out-of-sample and real trading is never as profitable as the simulated test results.

While there are no other alternatives for validating a proposed trading strategy, back-testing is weakest because of its handling of price shocks. In an attempt to understand the enemy, four important prices shocks since 1990 were:

1. *The abduction of Gorbachev.* A particularly difficult price shock on August 16, 1991, was followed by an opposite shock two days later. Russian Premier Gorbachev was abducted and then surprisingly released (see Figure 8.1). European currencies dropped sharply against the dollar because of anticipated disruption of Russian trade. Most financial markets were affected at the same time, as were the energy markets. Many currency traders profited from this shock because

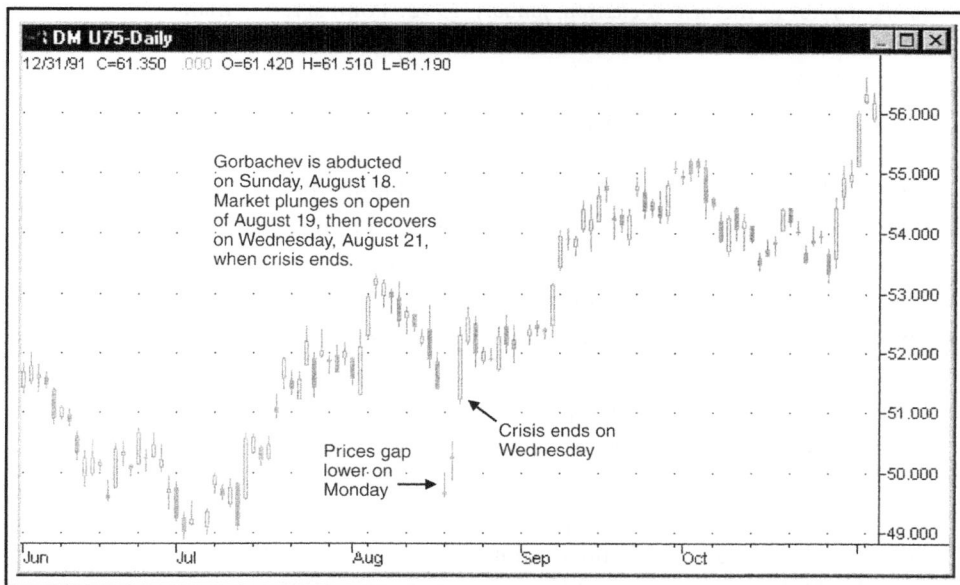

FIGURE 8.1   The Gorbachev Abduction Caused a Double Price Shock, with Most Impact on the European Currencies, Such as the US$/German Mark.

Source: Chart created with TradeStation® by Omega Research, Inc.

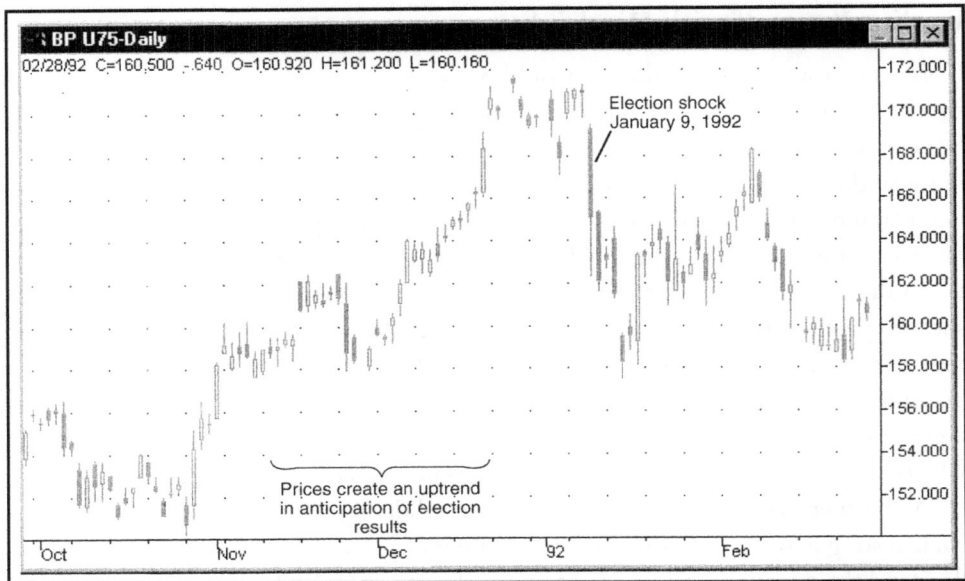

FIGURE 8.2 Labour's Victory in the British Election of 1992 Represents a More Common Shock.

Source: Chart created with TradeStation® by Omega Research, Inc.

they were holding short positions over the weekend when Gorbachev was abducted on a Sunday. They continued to hold shorts looking for a further decline, but gave back their profits when prices abruptly reversed on Wednesday.

2. *Labour's loss in the British election, January 1992.* Politics holds many surprises, but the victory of John Major's Conservative party in 1992 was unexpected (see Figure 8.2). After a 2-month uptrend, prices gapped lower and posted a daily range of nearly £10, close to 6%. The low was made on the fifth day after the election results and was followed by a 3-week recovery that retraced 90% of the fall. Unlike the Gorbachev abduction, this price shock had limited effect on other markets.

3. *The Gulf War, August 1991 through January 1992.* Oil prices are notorious for volatility, but the Gulf War marked a period of unprecedented price shocks driven by news (Figure 8.3). Because Iraq had been moving troops near the Kuwait border, Iraqi intentions were not a surprise. In Figure 8.3 prices were rising from the second week of July as news of Iraq's plans circulated in the marketplace. The threat of an oil supply disruption and a failing diplomatic solution resulted in a rise of $4, or 28%. Therefore, many systematic traders and commercials would have been long on August 7, 1990, when Iraq invaded Kuwait. During the next months, oil prices show a number of gaps and wide-ranging days, fueled by news and uncertainty. The most dramatic price shock was on the day of the U.S. invasion of Kuwait, January 17, 1991. Futures prices opened near their high of $30.80/bbl and by the close of trading had fallen to $20.50. The first cash trade in oil, after the invasion was known, exchanged hands at about $40/bbl. Preceding the U.S. invasion, oil prices were exceptionally

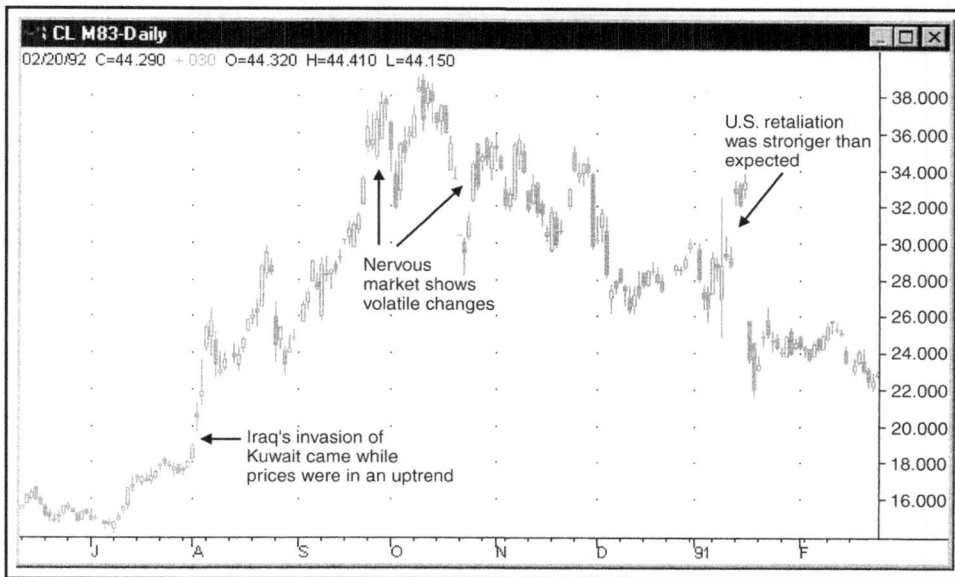

FIGURE 8.3 Crude Oil Prices from Iraq's Invasion of Kuwait through the Beginning of the Gulf War, August 1990 to February 1991.

Source: Chart created with TradeStation® by Omega Research, Inc.

volatile but showed an upwards trend. There would have been no trend system holding a short position ahead of the $10 drop in futures prices.

4. *The terrorist attack on September 11, 2001.* This generation will remember where they were on 9/11, just as the last generation remembers where they were when John F. Kennedy was assassinated. In an unprecedented move by the exchanges, all trades executed in the morning before the attack were canceled (Figure 8.4). After the S&P close on September 10 at 1101.4, prices of futures opened 6 days later on September 17 at 1041.4, 5.4% lower, posting the low for the move of 939.0 on September 21, after 5 days of steady declines.

The price shock of 9/11 favored the trend followers. The two months prior to 9/11 show an increasing bearish move, with the last two weeks steadily declining. The shock itself, the difference between the close of 9/11 and the open of 9/17 was not as severe as the other examples. The surprising 42-point rally on September 28 may have produced more losses for systematic traders than the actual price shock. The steady rise that followed during the next few months is similar to the recovery after the October 1987 plunge. Traders see the extreme lows as the farthest prices can be pushed, and most sentiment turns to the other direction.

The interesting elements in the four examples are:

- *Price shocks do not always generate losses for trend traders.* The British election and the U.S. invasion of Kuwait caused prices to change direction. The Iraq invasion of Kuwait and 9/11 favored current trend positions. The Gorbachev abduction was good on one day and bad two days later, or just the opposite, depending on your position.

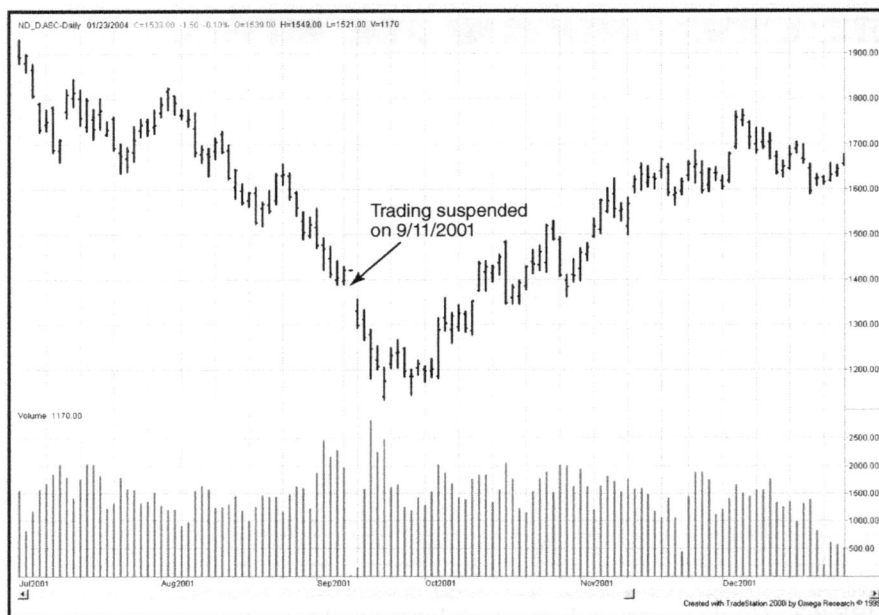

FIGURE 8.4 The Price Shock of 9/11/2001.

■ *Prices change direction after the shock has been absorbed into the market.* A price shock pushes prices to an extreme, and after the market has absorbed the news, it is most likely to move in the other direction for a longer period. If a trading account was capitalized adequately to absorb these shocks, a crisis management strategy may be able to recover much of the loss or even net profits from the second phase of the reaction.

■ *Volatility always increases.* If the initial shock resulted in a windfall profit, reducing the size of the position, or even exiting the entire position, is a reasonable way to deal with exceptional risk.

Not all news is a complete surprise. In the agricultural markets, a crop freeze in orange juice or coffee is often anticipated by a change in weather. Before a freeze can occur, the temperature must drop, and below-freezing temperatures must be sustained in order to cause damage. This weather change causes processors to protect themselves by buying forward contracts or futures. In turn, prices move up in anticipation of problems. However, on January 9, 2012, the USDA announced that it was looking into the possible contamination of Brazilian orange juice from a chemical fungicide. Brazil provides $1/3$ of all the orange juice in the U.S. market. Prices jumped 16% in 2 days, then reversed 15% on the following 2 days when the report turned out to be questionable.

Identifying Price Shocks

If we cannot predict price shocks, and they seriously impact our historic tests, then we must understand their effects. In Chapter 7, it was shown that price shocks always added profits to historic performance, but in actual trading, this is not likely to be true. This was done by identifying a price shock as a 1-day trading range five times the size of the previous trading ranges, as measured using the average true range. By accumulating the net change relative to your trading position, on those days identified as a price shock, you can see the impact on performance.

Crisis Management

One aspect of crisis management is having sufficient financial reserves to survive an extreme, correlated price reversal, if not a worst-case scenario. For most trading programs, holding enough reserves aside to weather a worst-case scenario will lower the annualized rate of return to a level below the return on government bonds. Nevertheless, the potential for a large loss is real and must be taken into account. That means some tactical method must be used.

In the previous examples of well-known price shocks, prices reversed direction within a few days and continued in that direction for some time. If the original position was held after its initial loss, then part of that loss would have been recovered. The strategy that evolves is

1. If there is a windfall profit from the price shock, exit the position.
2. If there is a large loss from the position, hold the position expecting a reversal. This may take a few days and may increase the risk.
3. If there are adequate reserves, the position can be increased on peak volume or when volatility declines at a later point.

Holding a position during a price shock seems very risky; however, the trade has already seen most of the risk by the time the first order to exit could be placed. In the book *Trading Systems and Methods*, Chapter 14, it was shown price patterns that included a price shock and following reaction. In most cases, the reactions were orderly and the increased risk from holding the trade for a few days is small in proportion. During Gorbachev's abduction, a short position should have been liquidated, getting the low price, while a long position would have begun its recovery immediately, reaching new high profits 13 days later. The British election had two legs down and only recovered to unchanged after 3 weeks. During the U.S. invasion of Kuwait, a long position, liquidated immediately, would have been highly profitable; a short position held for only a few hours more would have been even more profitable. Shorts held on 9/11 should have been liquidated immediately, even though they would not have captured the full profits, but longs would have suffered additional losses for the next 5 days. In 2012, the orange juice price shock reversed the entire move within 4 days. All of these situations require careful monitoring, but all have the same characteristic that the shock of the news carries prices to extreme levels, followed by a substantial reversal.

System Disconnect during a Crisis A large price shock can create a disconnect between a trading system and the market. This is particularly true for trending methods. During 1987, the stock market began an accelerated decline in mid-October,

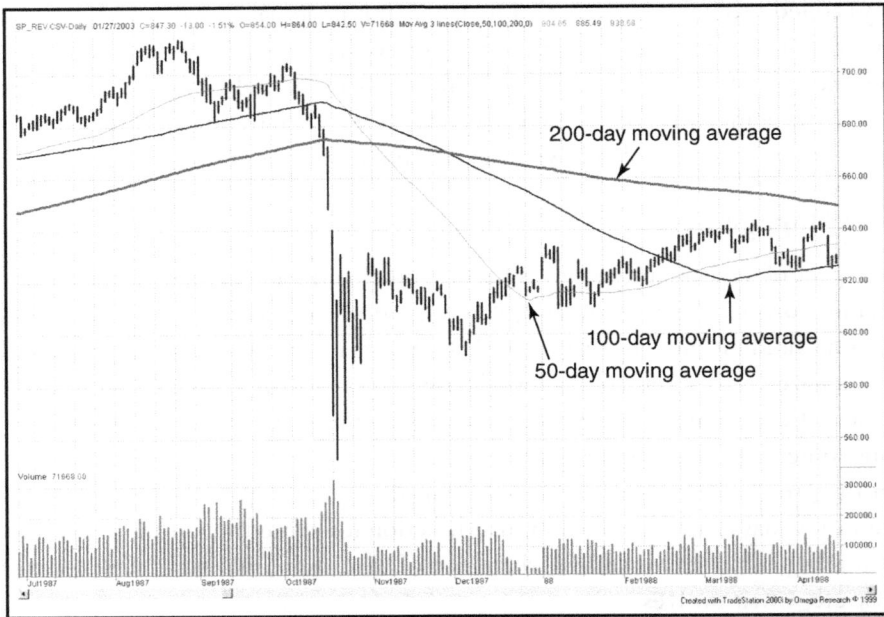

FIGURE 8.5 S&P 500 Futures. Moving average trendlines become out-of-phase during a crisis.

leading to a 2-day drop of large proportion on very high volatility and confirmed by a peak in volume. Figure 8.5 shows how 50-, 100-, and 200-day moving averages reacted to that move. All three moving averages turned down on the day of the largest drop, and following a trend signal to sell would have captured the lowest price of the move. Switching to crisis management rules, where shorts are liquidated and longs are held, would have been a far better strategy.

Equally important is the direction of the price movement compared to the direction of the three trendlines after the low price. The fastest, 50-day moving average turned down, crossing the prices that were moving higher in mid-December, and finally turning up in late December. The 100-day moving average turned up in the following March, and the benchmark 200-day moving average turned up in August of 1998. It seems clear that these moving averages are out of phase with the price movement after the shock. The moving averages are not reflecting the market trend; they are catching up to an event long past. Dogmatically holding a short position from mid-October onward because the trendline is down puts the trader out-of-phase with reality.

The collapse of the world stock markets in the fall of 2008 was not technically a price shock, and there was no one day that could be attributed to the decline. The news came out slowly, steadily, and clearly in favor of an economic disaster. Figure 8.6 shows that any long-term trend follower would have been short ahead of the decline, which, on this portion of the price movement, was a drop of 55% in the S&P futures. Here again there is a disconnect in the moving averages, but the sustained concerns over the future of the economy allowed the moving averages to catch up to the lower prices and trigger an upturn at a reasonable point. Had prices turned up sooner, the trends would still be

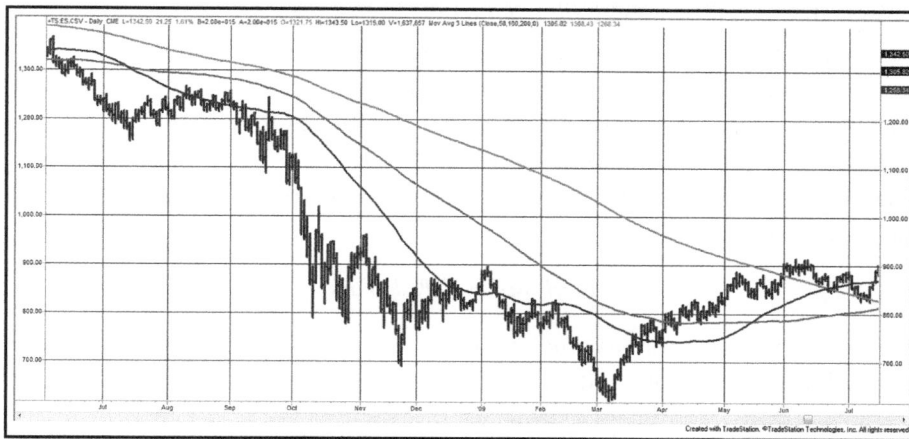

FIGURE 8.6 The S&P Decline Due to the Subprime Crisis Generated Large Profits for Trend Followers Who Were Already Short. They were fortunate that the depressed prices allowed the trends to catch up to lower prices.

declining. Because of this fortunate pattern, and their ability to hold shorts, trend followers trading futures posted their best year in the history of that industry.

Crisis management must be invoked to correct unusual situations that are not handled by the main strategy. These events can be identified using a technical measure of a price shock. The new rules can be well-defined in advance or they can be handled by a team of competent managers. They must recognize that, as in the Crash of 1987, the trendlines are no longer useful. Once the extreme period has passed, which can be determined by a drop in volatility, the trends can be reinitialized at the new price levels and follow the new price direction.

Gambling Techniques—The Theory of Runs

The application of gambling theory to highly leveraged or short-term trading satisfies two important conditions. First, it presumes no statistical advantage in the occurrence of profits and losses but concerns itself instead with the probable patterns. Viewed simply as an up or down price move, or a trading profit or loss, each daily change could be treated as an occurrence of red or black in roulette. Second, gambling theory stresses money management under adverse conditions. A successful professional gambler and an active trader must be highly disciplined and conserve capital. This section will look at a gambler's approach to money management and risk, using the *Theory of Runs*.

If the assumption is made that the profit or loss of each trade is unrelated to the previous trade, or that each successive price has an equal chance of going up or down, the situation closely resembles roulette. In Monte Carlo, the roulette wheel has 37 compartments: 18 black, 18 red, and 1 white, assuring a loss of 2.7% in the same way that transaction costs are a handicap to trading. Continuously betting on only red or black will break even, less 2.7%, over long betting periods. The only way to change the odds is by money management—varying the size of the bets. Although the variables in trading are more complex, we will look at this first.

The most well-known method for winning in a gambling situation is based on the probability of sequences occurring, the Theory of Runs. On each spin of the wheel, the likelihood of the same color (red or black) reoccurring is 50%, or 1:2 (1 out of 2, ignoring the white slot). In order to define a run of 3 reds, it is necessary to show a black on each side, that is,

Black-Red-Red-Red-Black

otherwise the run may not be complete. If each color has a 50% chance of occurring, the probability of a run of 3 reds is

$$\frac{1}{2} \times \frac{1}{2} \times \frac{1}{2} \times \frac{1}{2} \times \frac{1}{2} = \left(\frac{1}{2}\right)^5 = 0.03125$$

or about 3%. One run of 3 can be expected for every 32 spins of the wheel (called *coups*). Extending that to runs of n consecutive reds gives $(1/2)^{n+2}$. For 256 coups, which is both a power of two and the approximate number of trading days in a year, there are the following possibilities for runs of red:

Run of Length	Probability of Occurrence	Expected Number of Occurrences	Total Appearances of Red
1	$\frac{1}{8}$	32	32
2	$\frac{1}{18}$	16	32
3	$\frac{1}{32}$	8	24
4	$\frac{1}{64}$	4	16
5	$\frac{1}{128}$	2	10
6	$\frac{1}{256}$	1	6

Total appearances: 120

There is less than a 1% chance that a run greater than 6 will occur, and that only 4 will occur out of 10,000 spins. Notice, however, that the total appearances of red is only 120, short by 8. These 8 appearances could increase any of the runs from 1 through 6, or become a run of 7 or 8. The likelihood of a run greater than 6 is calculated using a geometric progression to get the sum of all probabilities greater than 6, or $(1/2)^{n+2}$, where $256 \geq n \geq 7$:

$$P = (1/2)^9 + (1/2)^{10} + \cdots + (1/2)^{256}$$

$$= \frac{(1/2)^9}{1-(1/2)} = \frac{1}{256}$$

There is a single chance that there will be a run greater than 6 in 256 tries. The average length of a run greater than 6 turns out to be 8, based on the decreasing probability of occurrences of longer runs. The average length of all runs greater than *n* will be *n* + 2. That makes the table of runs complete, with the number of occurrences of red equal to 128.

Each time you double the number of spins, you increase the length of the longest run by 1, so that for 512 spins there should be a run of 7 and for 1024 spins, a run of 8.

Martingales and Anti-Martingales

The classic gambling application of the Theory of Runs is called *Martingales*. In the simple version of this approach, an initial bet is doubled each time a loss occurs; whenever there is a win, the gambler nets one unit of gain and the betting begins again at the initial size. To demonstrate how this works, it is necessary to use a table of uniform random numbers (which can be found in Appendix 1). These numbers vary from 0 through 99999, but should be interpreted from 0.0 to 1.0. If you are using Excel, then select the *uniform random numbers* which return values equally across the range from 0.0 to 1.0. Let all the random numbers from 0 to less than 0.5, be assigned to red and larger values to black. Figure 8.7, read left to right, where open squares are red and solid squares are black, shows the first 257 assignments according to the Appendix 1. Assuming that we bet on black, losses will depend on the longest run of red. We must decide the size of the initial bet in advance, which should be as large as possible and still withstand the longest run of red that is likely to occur. By using the results from the analysis of the length of runs, we find that for every 256 coups it is likely that only 1 run greater than 6 will occur, and that run would most

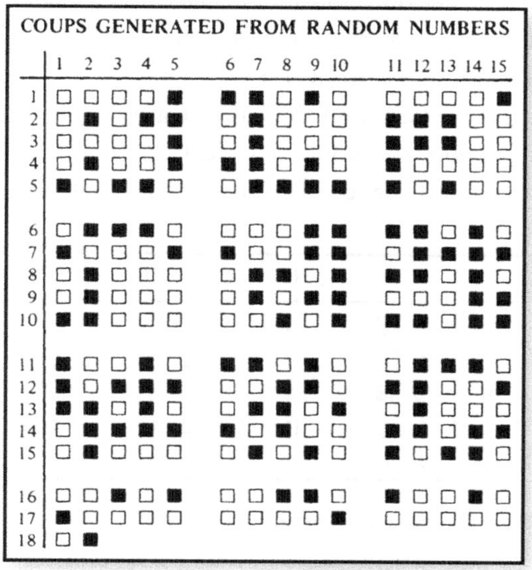

FIGURE 8.7 Sequence of Random Numbers Representing Occurrences of Red and Black.

TABLE 8.1	Simulated Runs	
Red	**Black**	
35 runs of 1	35 runs of 1	
12 runs of 2	14 runs of 2	
7 runs of 3	11 runs of 3	
7 runs of 4	3 runs of 4	
2 runs of 5	2 runs of 5	
2 runs of 6		
1 run of 8		
138 total occurrences	118 total occurrences	

probably be 8 in length. The probability of a run of 9 is $(1/2)$,[11] or one in 1024. In 256 coups, the odds are about 3 to 1 against a run of 9 occurring.

Having decided that capitalization must withstand a run of 8, we calculate that a bet of $1 doubled 8 times is $128. Divide the maximum amount of money to be risked by 128 and the result is the size of the initial bet. If the available stake is $1,000, then when divided by 128 gives $7.8125, which must be rounded down to $7; therefore, on the eighth consecutive occurrence of red, the bet will be $897. Counting the occurrences of runs on the simulated roulette table (Table 8.1), it is interesting to see that a run of 8 (but not 7) appears.

The results are within expectations, and no runs greater than 8 occurred in either red or black. For the purposes of this example, the betting would then proceed as shown in Figure 8.8, using an initial bet of $7. Every occurrence of black is a winner. Although as much as $897 may be won on a single black coup after a run of 8, each sequence of runs nets only the initial bet of $1 because of the accumulated losses during that sequence. For the 256 coups shown in Table 8.2, there were a total of 65 distinct runs resulting in a profit of $455, a return of 45.5% on capital. Instead of using Martingales, if we had used the basic strategy of betting equal amounts on black to win on every coup, we would have lost $140 on a $7 bet. The Martingales method therefore has a good chance of winning a moderate amount.[2] In a casino, the

	1	2	3	4	5		6	7	8	9	10		11	12	13	14	15
1	1	2	4	8	[16]		[1]	[1]	1	[2]	1		2	4	8	16	[32]
2	1	[2]	1	[2]	[1]		1	[2]	1	2	4		[8]	[1]	[1]	1	2
3	4	8	16	32	[64]		1	[2]	1	2	4		[8]	[1]	[1]	1	2
4	4	[8]	1	2	[4]		[1]	[1]	1	[2]	1		[2]	1	2	4	8
5	[16]	1	[2]	[1]	1		2	[4]	[1]	[1]	[1]		[1]	1	[2]	1	2

FIGURE 8.8 Betting Pattern.

[2] The Martingales approach is likely to work if the player could withstand adverse runs of 11, but casinos tend to limit bets to amounts significantly less than 210 times the minimum bet.

drawback is the occasional run of 9. The house sets the maximum bet for the table, which always prevents doubling down after a run of 8.

Anti-Martingales

The *anti-Martingales* approach offers a smaller chance of winning a large amount; it is exactly the opposite of applying Martingales. Instead of doubling each losing bet, the winners are doubled until a goal is reached. Because there is an excellent chance of 1 run of 6 in 256 coups and a similar chance of a longer run, this method wins if the long run occurs in the first half of the number of coups to be played (256 in this case). Once a run of 6, occurs you must immediately stop playing.

We already know that a run of 6 returns $32 on a bet of $1, and a run of 8 nets $128. This method would have lost if it had been applied to black in the test sequence; because there were 138 red coups with no black runs greater than 5, there would have been a loss of $138. If the bet had been on red, looking for a run of 6, there would have been three wins, each for $94, and a loss of $118 for that many appearances of black. Waiting for a run of 8 would have won $128 and lost $117 on black by stopping right after the win. The success of anti-Martingales depends on how soon the long run appears. In 4,096 coups, a run of 11 will occur once, returning $1,024 on a bet of $1. In the same 4,096 spins, there will be 2,048 losses, showing that if the long run happens in the middle of play, the method breaks even; if it occurs sooner, you win.

The Theory of Runs Applied to Trading

Before applying either Martingales or anti-Martingales to the markets, it must be determined whether the movement of prices up or down is as uniform as in roulette. A simple test was performed on 15 diverse futures markets from 2000 through mid-2011 and the combined results of all up and down runs are shown in Table 8.2. The top section of the table shows the total days in each market, followed by the total number of up and down days and the average upwards and average downward price change. This allows us to understand the bias in the data. The lower part shows the differences between the normal occurrence of sequences and those that actually occurred in each market.

The two most extreme differences are the DAX and Eurodollar interest rates. The DAX shows an unusually high number of 1-day reversals, with most of the other combinations less. The Eurodollars are the opposite, showing far fewer reversals for sequences 1 through 5 (with an exception at 3), adding those differences to the longer sequences to create a fat tail. The differences between these two markets and the normal sequences, as well as the average of all markets, are shown in Figure 8.9. For both the DAX and the Eurodollar, and for all markets on average, there are fewer runs of 4 and 5 days.

Earlier tests of these runs had shown that there were fewer short-term sequences and most markets had shifted those differences to the fat tail. That no longer seems to be the case. The DAX, with many more 1-day reversals, exhibits an increasing amount

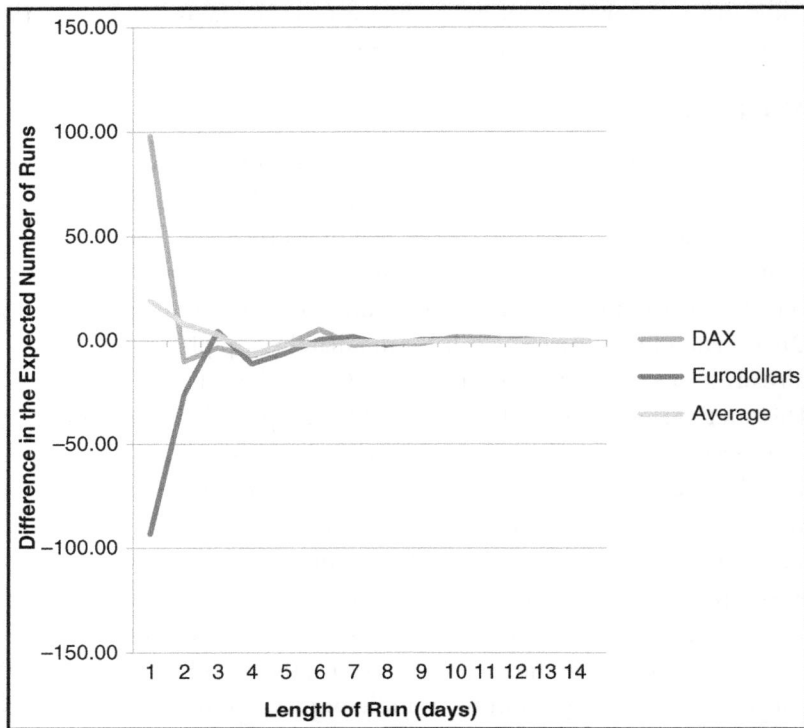

FIGURE 8.9 The Two Most Extreme Markets That Differ from the Normal Sequence of Runs, as Well as the Average of 15 Diverse Markets.

of noise compared to expectations, while the trend characteristics of the Eurodollars have fewer short-term changes but do not increase the tail by an obvious amount.

One way of incorporating these results into a trading program is to treat the higher or lower frequency of short-term reversals as a way to improve entry prices:

- After a new trend signal, wait for the DAX to reverse before entering the new trade.

- When there is a new trend signal in the Eurodollars, enter immediately.

The most interesting applications are in the betting strategies of the Martingales and anti-Martingales methods, applied to futures markets. The following sections show two possibilities.

Martingales within a Trend By combining the Theory of Runs with the direction of the trend, the chances of being on the correct side of the longest run are increased, and the size of the price move in the direction of the trend may also tend to be larger. Long-term trends will offer the best chance of identifying the direction of prices. We can create rules to take advantage of this:

1. If the trend has just turned up, based on a moving average, enter a long position with 1 contract.
2. If the trend is still up and the price closes lower, double the size of the long position.

TABLE 8.2 Expected Occurrences of Ups and Downs for a Diverse Set of Markets

	Normal	S&P	NASDAQ	DAX	30-Year Bond	Euro-bund	Euro-dollars	EURUSD	USDJPY	Crude	Heating Oil	Natural Gas	Gold	Copper	Wheat	Cotton
Total days	2632.6	2617	2634	2678	2577	2657	2443	2622	2616	2632	2634	2568	2612	2614	2604	2623
Days up		1425	1397	1422	1371	1392	1301	1373	1324	1363	1320	1226	1417	1349	1242	1309
Days down		1192	1237	1256	1206	1265	1142	1249	1292	1269	1314	1342	1195	1265	1362	1314
Avg up		9.175	18.404	53.833	0.579	0.307	0.0467	0.0061	0.0047	0.9899	0.0286	0.1552	5.881	3.312	8.6457	0.9803
Avg down		−11.062	−21.136	−61.362	−0.613	−0.306	−0.0434	−0.0063	−0.0047	−1.0419	−0.0279	−0.1563	−6.017	−3.252	−8.1863	−0.9799

Length of Run	Normal	S&P	NASDAQ	DAX	30-Yr Bonds	Euro-bund	Euro-dollars	EURUSD	USDJPY	Crude	Heating Oil	Natural Gas	Gold	Copper	Wheat	Cotton	Average
1	658.15	22.85	−16.15	97.85	−39.15	16.85	−93.15	27.85	−5.15	28.85	45.85	26.85	36.85	69.85	56.85	9.85	19.12
2	329.08	−6.07	−16.08	−10.08	28.93	32.93	−26.08	12.93	32.93	−3.07	13.93	−9.07	23.93	46.93	−10.08	6.93	7.93
3	164.54	1.46	1.46	−3.54	1.46	−6.54	4.46	5.46	−0.54	16.46	19.46	−7.54	−0.54	−23.54	15.46	20.46	2.93
4	82.27	5.73	2.73	−7.27	−3.27	−13.27	−11.27	−19.27	2.73	−12.27	−22.27	−1.27	−13.27	−2.27	2.73	−11.27	−6.87
5	41.13	−6.13	5.87	−2.13	−5.13	7.87	−6.13	−3.13	−3.13	3.87	−2.13	−2.13	−5.13	−2.13	−10.13	1.87	−1.87
6	20.57	−0.57	−5.57	5.43	−3.57	−2.57	0.43	4.43	−5.57	−1.57	−4.57	4.43	−4.57	−3.57	−7.57	−4.57	−1.97
7	10.28	1.72	4.72	−2.28	1.72	−3.28	1.72	−2.28	−5.28	−3.28	−2.28	−1.28	−2.28	−2.28	4.72	0.72	−0.62
8	5.14	0.86	−0.14	−1.14	−1.14	0.86	−2.14	−2.14	−2.14	−2.14	0.86	−3.14	4.86	−3.14	−1.14	−2.14	−0.88
9	2.57	−2.57	−2.57	−1.57	−0.57	2.43	0.43	3.43	0.43	2.43	1.43	−1.57	−0.57	−1.57	−2.57	−0.57	−0.24
10	1.29	−1.29	1.71	1.71	−0.29	−0.29	0.71	−1.29	−0.29	−0.29	0.71	−1.29	−0.29	−1.29	−1.29	−1.29	−0.29
11	0.64	0.36	−0.64	1.36	−0.64	−0.64	0.36	−0.64	0.36	−0.64	−0.64	−0.64	−0.64	0.36	−0.64	−0.64	−0.24
12	0.32	−0.32	−0.32	−0.32	−0.32	−0.32	0.68	−0.32	−0.32	−0.32	−0.32	0.68	−0.32	−0.32	−0.32	0.68	−0.12
13	0.16	−0.16	0.84	−0.16	−0.16	−0.16	−0.16	0.84	−0.16	−0.16	−0.16	−0.16	−0.16	−0.16	−0.16	−0.16	−0.03
14	0.08	−0.08	0.92	−0.08	−0.08	−0.08	−0.08	−0.08	−0.08	−0.08	−0.08	−0.08	−0.08	−0.08	−0.08	−0.08	−0.01

TABLE 8.3	Comparison of Moving Average Results with Martingales with and without Cap, Applied to Eurodollar Rates, 2000 through Mid-2011		
	Net PL	ASD PL	Ratio
MA 60	16375	2456	6.67
MA 60 x 8	131000	19648	6.67
Martingales	549518	67262	8.17
Martingales cap 8	529243	63898	8.28

3. If the trend is up and the price closes higher, remove all positions in excess of the original 1 contract.
4. If the trend turns down, exit all longs and sell short 1 contract.
5. If the trend is down and prices close higher, double the size of the short position.
6. If the trend is down and prices close lower, cover all short positions in excess of the original 1 contract.

Because no one has unlimited money and it is possible for price to go the wrong way for up to 8 days, possibly 9 over a long test period, we need to cap the number of times we can double down. For this test, we will start with 1 contract and allow up to 8 contracts. At that point we will hold the current position until prices move in our favor, then reduce the size back to 1, the initial amount. To find the results, the program *TSM Martingales with Trend* was used, available on the Companion Website.

Two markets were tested, Eurodollar interest rates and the S&P, because they represent the extremes of a very trending and very noisy market. Only a 60-day trend was used. Because there will be a lot of entering and exiting positions, a $25 round-turn cost was charged to avoid unrealistic results. Table 8.3 gives a comparison of three results for Eurodollars. The first row are the results of a straight 60-day moving average, using 1 contract only, where the trading signal is based on the direction of the trendline. In the second row the same method used 8 contracts for each trade. The third row gives the results of the Martingales strategy with rules 1–5 above, and the last row is the Martingales strategy with a cap of 8 contracts.

The second row, using 8 contracts, is needed to compare the last row, where the contract size varies from 1 to 8. In that case, there must always be enough money in the account to trade 8 contracts, even when 1 is the current position size. In Table 8.3, the first column of numbers, *Net PL*, is the total accumulated profits for the strategy, the next column is the annualized standard deviation of the daily profit/loss changes, and the last column is the ratio of the two previous columns, essentially an information ratio. For our purposes, the information ratio is the best measure of results and shows that the capped version exceeds all others. The *Net PL* of rows 2, 3, and 4 are shown in Figure 8.10. The Martingales results might be good in this one case, where the Eurodollars are extremely trending, but what about the highly noisy S&P futures?

One would think that a noisy market would benefit from doubling the position size on a negative move because there would be a high likelihood of a reversal and a

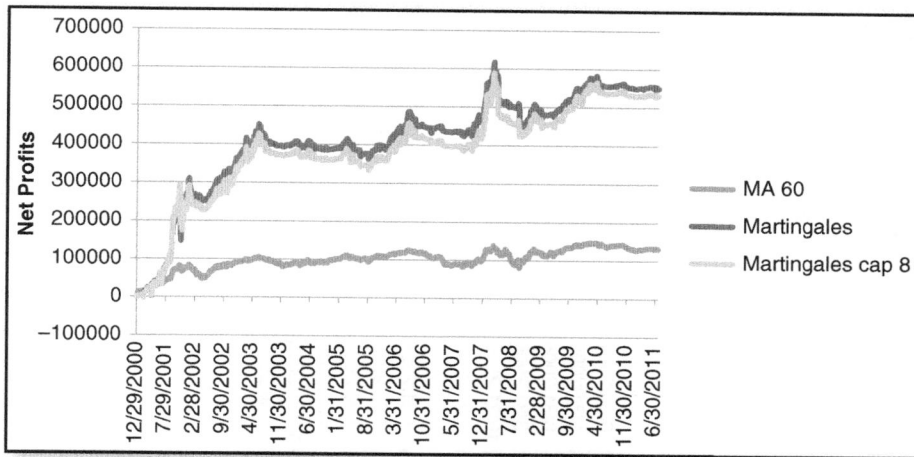

FIGURE 8.10 Comparison of Net PL for a 60-Day Moving Average System Trading 8 Contracts, a Martingales Approach, and a Martingale Capped at 8 Contracts, Eurodollars 2000 to Mid-2011.

fast recovery of the losses. But the S&P noise hurts the ability to identify the trend with any consistency, so that even a 60-day trend filter does not improve the chances of being right by much. Table 8.4 shows that the S&P performance ratios are much lower than those of Eurodollars and the capped Martingales, the only one we could really trade, underperforms all the other combinations. But then, none of the combinations are particularly good. A chart of the net profits is given in Figure 8.11.

Anti-Martingales Applying anti-Martingales to a trading situation presents more of a problem. The approach calls for adding to the position size when we are profitable and resetting the size to some nominal amount when we have a loss. Unless you trade a very large account, the size of the profits from a normal gain may not be enough to add one more contract. Then, if you have a small losing day, you would need to reduce the position size fractionally, but there is no benchmark size if you have been increasing the position size as the equity grows.

The only practical applications seems to be doubling the number of contracts each time prices move in a profitable direction, then reverting to 1 contract after 3 or more profitable days, much like the gambling approach. Success depends on having a large number of runs in the profitable direction. The original anti-Martingales

TABLE 8.4 Martingales Comparison Applied to the *emini* S&P, 2000 through Mid-2011

	Net PL	ASD PL	Ratio
MA 60	13363	11371	1.18
MA 60 x 8	106900	90966	1.18
Martingales no cap	1365112	355856	3.84
Martingales cap 8	252687	243369	1.04

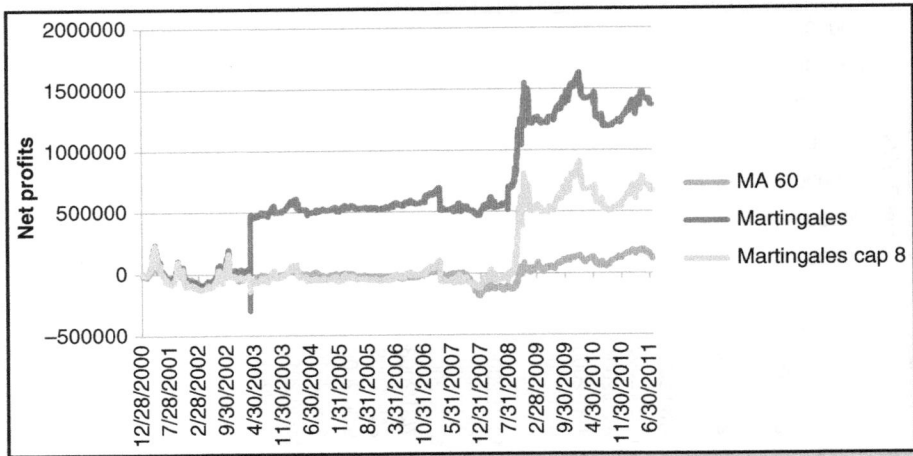

FIGURE 8.11 Comparison of Martingales Net Profit for the emini S&P Futures, 2000 through Mid-2011.

method calls for leveraging up in anticipation of 6 moves in the profitable direction then moving to another table, hoping that the run of 6 came in the first 50% of the 100 flips. There is no counterpart for stopping if the market goes the right direction, so we need to play for the continuous sequences of runs. Table 8.5 shows the results of Eurodollar tests using a 60-day moving average to decide the direction of leveraging. The rules were identical to the Martingales approach except that, when a profitable day occurred, the position size was doubled, and when a losing day occurred the position was reduced to the initial size. The cap limits the size of the position, so that a cap of 4 allowed the position to be doubled twice.

In Table 8.5, row 2 is simply the *Net PL* and volatility of row 1 multiplied by 8 to allow better comparison with the cap 8 row. The ratio does not change by scaling all positions. The *no cap* result is most interesting because it posts a net loss. That can be seen clearly in Figure 8.12.

Except for the *no cap* case, allowing the position to double for up to three times beats the simple moving average method. The *no cap* method continues to double the position until there is a loss, which then occurs while holding the largest position. There are three cases where this happens, once where the net return is still profitable

TABLE 8.5	Anti-Martingales for Eurodollar Futures, 2000 through Mid-2011, Filtered with a 60-Day Moving Average		
	Net PL	ASD PL	Ratio
MA 60	16375	2456	6.67
MA 60 x 8	131000	19648	6.67
Anti-Martingales no cap	−16443	535752	−0.03
Anti-Martingales cap 2	916037	83639	10.95
Anti-Martingales cap 4	815743	78707	10.36
Anti-Martingales cap 8	742093	75667	9.81

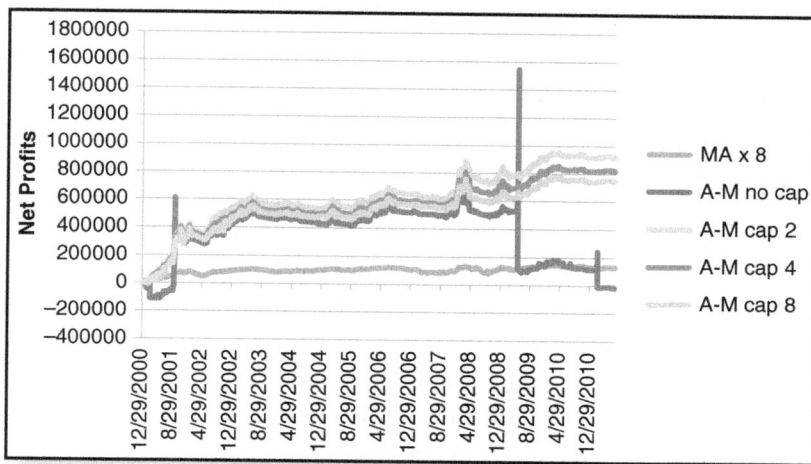

FIGURE 8.12 Comparison of Anti-Martingales Method with Different Caps, Applied to Eurodollar Futures, 2000 through Mid-2011.

and two times where the system takes a huge loss. On the other hand, the frequency of two positive days in a row is high, so that adding extra risk paid off.

A similar case was run for the emini S&P, but the results were poor. Because of its high level of noise, there were more losses when positions were doubled, resulting in worse results than the simple moving average. This method can be tested using *TSM Anti-Martingales with Trend*, available on the Companion Website.

Fractional Martingales

The simple Martingales and anti-Martingales just discussed offer one possibility for applying gambling theory to position management but always double the position size. If a large account is being traded, it may be better to use the actual profits to decide the number of contracts for anti-Martingales. Another approach would be to scale down the risk by trading 1.5 times the previous position size rather than twice. This was the approach taken by Furguson,[3] and should give the same relative improvement over the basic trend method.

Delayed Countertrend Entry into a Run For Martingales, rather than doubling the size on the first down day in an uptrend, waiting until prices posted two or three lower closes should increase the chances of a move back in the trend direction. Although there are fewer opportunities, the chances of a continued move in the same direction quickly become smaller.

There has always been conflicting interpretation about the chances of a continued price move following a series of moves in that direction. In a purely random event, there is always a 50% chance of prices moving in either direction; however,

[3] James William Furguson, "Martingales," *Technical Analysis of Stocks & Commodities* (February 1990), and "Reverse Martingales," *Technical Analysis of Stocks & Commodities* (March 1990).

the market is not a random event, and behavioral finance advocates will argue that there is enough predictability to be profitable. This premise can be substantiated by measuring the distribution and size of the average up and down moves within a long-term trend.

Gustafson[4] studied the S&P from 1988 to 1995 and created a trading strategy that entered a long position after prices closed lower 4 days in a row, exited after an upwards run of 5 days, and always exited after 8 days. Admittedly, this method is only long and takes advantage of the upwards bias in the stock market, which was particularly strong in the mid- and late-1990s. The results for the in-sample period had 78% of the trades profitable, a $35,030 net profit and a $5,847 maximum drawdown. Applying this to data from 1982 through mid-2001, the results showed 76% reliability, profits of $348,460, and a drawdown of $56,370, showing that this pattern was successful out-of-sample, but still in the same bull market. The rules are:

1. If $C_t > C_{t-1}$ then $up = up + 1$ else $up = 0$
2. If $C_t < C_{t-1}$ then $down = down + 1$ else $down = 0$
3. If $down = 4$ then buy on next open
4. If $up = 5$ then $exit\ longs$ on next open
5. If $days\text{-}in\text{-}trade = 8$ then $exit\ longs$ on next open

■ Selective Trading

It may be unrealistic to think that you can always follow a technical, fully automatic system without manual intervention. Overriding system signals may occur for reasons of sound risk management during a crisis when you decide that the system is not programmed to deal with the current volatility, that a more conservative action is the best business policy, or that the market has temporarily disconnected from the strategy.

The beginning system trader often has concerns that the impersonal buy and sell orders will not react properly to the underlying forces that are driving prices. This can cause the trader to override the system signals. For example, if the program is geared to take profits after a move of 2%, the trader might judge that the current price move is going to continue and opt for holding the trade rather than taking profits. The application of this special *intuitive* filter generally favors holding a position through ups and downs until it shows a profit (if ever), rather than applying consistently good risk management. Judgment tends to interpret all news in favor of holding the position in anticipation of a profit someday. An experienced trader has learned to control these urges to override the system, not to take a loss personally, to keep losses small, to establish and stay with a trading plan, and to filter out unsupported opinions. Trading is a business, and business principles must take precedence over emotions.

[4] Gordon Gustafson, "Price Persistency," *Technical Analysis of Stocks & Commodities* (January 2002).

Filtering Out the Losing Trades

An investor once told a trading advisor that, "I would be happy to take smaller profits if you can eliminate the losing trades." If that were only possible, there would be many more rich investors. Nevertheless, a lot of effort goes into an attempt to automatically select the profitable trades, or reduce the number of losing trades.

Two approaches to this are most common. The use of multiple indicators, such as two moving averages, or more than one oscillator, such as a stochastic or RSI. Or, signals can be confirmed by another market, or by seasonality, or weekly patterns. Given the power of computers, some combination will produce the appearance of a very, very good system. However, we should know by now that this is just an exercise in overfitting. The simple solution, even with risk that is larger than we want, is most often the best solution. There is no way to filter out all the losing trades and leave only the profitable ones.

There are many trading systems that can be bought that promise profits. Those that do not disclose their rules are called a *black box*. Trying to incorporate a black-box approach to improve the performance of your own program is not a good idea. Without knowing everything about the other system, there may be duplicate techniques—a fast trend, a 3-day cycle, or an increase in position size and risk. Although a correlation analysis of the black-box approach and your system may show that the methods work well together, there are still too many uncertainties. The unknown system may have been overfitted and will not show its real risk, or it may have a particular weakness to a market pattern that has not occurred during your testing period. You must understand every method that you trade, know how the parameter values were selected, and verify its results. It's your money and your risk.

■ System Trade-Offs

Although traders are continually searching for a system that has no losses, they are realistic enough to know that most profit, loss, and other characteristics of a trading system are dependent on one another. Just as in gambling theory, a system can be structured to have frequent small losses and occasional large profits—or frequent small profits with some large losses. It is simply not possible to create a system with such small losses that these losses are essentially zero without increasing the frequency of the losses to the point where profits rarely occur. In short-term or high-leveraged trading, the *cost of doing business*, transaction costs, prevents such an approach from working. Even "risk-free" arbitrage turns out not to be risk free.

The basic principles of systematic trading require that the trader choose between the frequency of profits to losses, the relative size of those profits and losses, and the number of opportunities that will be available to trade. These interrelationships will be different for various types of systems.

Trend-Following Systems

The relative risks and rewards of trend-following systems change based on the selection of the calculation period. Using a simple moving average system applied to

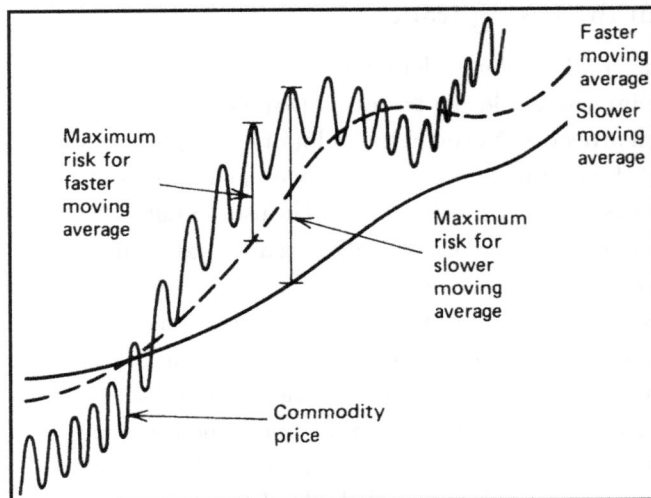

FIGURE 8.13 Relative Risk of a Moving Average System.

closing prices, the example in Figure 8.13 shows that a faster moving average will stay closer to the current price than a slower moving average. The maximum risk is measured from the current price to the corresponding moving average value.

The other changing pattern is that longer trends capture more of the fat tail. In fact, a fast trend cannot capture the fat tail at all, although the average profit should still be larger than the average loss. Basic trend following will always have many more small losses compared to fewer larger profits. At the same time, the risk, due to the lag, increases with the trend period.

The risk of a single trade being small or large is an incomplete measure of trading risk. Because there are more losses than profits in normal trend-following systems, it is important to consider the sequence of losses as part of the ultimate risk of trading. It is the aggregation of these losses that provides a reasonable comparison in determining whether a slow or fast moving average system has the best profit-to-loss ratio.

The attraction of a trend system is that it cuts losses short. This is called *conservation of capital.* On the other hand, it is unrealistic to expect a smoothing technique to produce more than 40–45% profitable trades; 30–35% is normal.

Mean-Reverting Systems

Mean-reverting systems are those that take advantage of nondirectional price movement or a fundamental divergence between two markets, selling when prices move higher and buying when they move lower. The belief is that prices will return to the mean. The risk-and-reward profile of a mean-reverting method is different from that of a trend-following approach. Although the size of the profits and losses relates to the holding period of the trade in a manner similar to trend following, positions must be set in advance of an expected price reversal, or while two markets are diverging. This introduces more risk and makes the success of the method dependent upon good timing. When mean-reverting methods are discussed here, those techniques that require a confirmation—that is, they wait until prices reverse direction—are not included. Waiting until prices turn introduces a trend element.

Due to the greater risk of a mean-reverting system, its objectives are generally well-defined. In a trend system, you let the profits run until prices reverse and the trend changes direction; however, most mean-reverting methods rely on an overbought/oversold indicator, contrary opinion, or divergence, and set goals for exiting when that condition disappears or becomes neutral. This results in a performance profile that limits profits; therefore, those profits must be more frequent. To accomplish results with limited but more frequent profits, you cannot also limit the size of the losses.

Trade-Offs

The performance profile goes together with particular trading styles. Ideally, you would want very large profits, high reliability, and small losses. Unfortunately, these combinations are not possible. The realistic trade-offs that are associated with the two primary systematic strategies are:

Trend Following	Mean Reversion
Many small losses and a few large profits	Many small profits and a few large losses
Lower average risk per trade	Higher average risk per trade
Improve reliability with larger risk	Reduce number of trades to lower risk

The last trade-off for trend following refers to longer calculation periods being generally more successful, but at the cost of larger lags. For mean reversion, making the entry threshold further away means lower risk once the trade is entered, but far fewer opportunities.

An example of mean-reverting trade-offs are shown in Figure 8.14, where prices are moving sideways, with no apparent trend bias. This can also be viewed as a price series with the trend removed. Assuming that there is a normal distribution of prices, there is a clustering near the center and less frequent peaks and valleys as prices move further away from the middle. If high values are treated as overbought and low

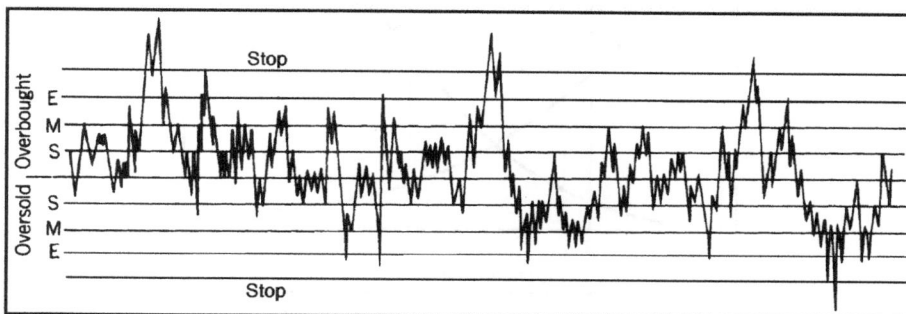

FIGURE 8.14   Entry Point Alternatives for a Mean-Reverting Strategy.

values as oversold, the area above and below the center line can be divided into three zones, *slightly* (S), *moderately* (M), or *extremely* (E) overbought or oversold.

In Figure 8.14 there are more opportunities to buy a *slightly oversold* market and sell a *slightly overbought* market, the points where prices cross the innermost set of horizontal lines. Profits are taken when prices return to the mean, the center horizontal line. All prices must pass through the area closest to the center before reaching a more overbought or oversold condition; therefore, the *opportunities* must decrease as profit goals increase.

But what about the risk? If trades were entered at the *S* lines, and the *M* lines were used as a stop-loss, then almost one-half the trades would be stopped out, and the size of the losses would equal the size of the profits. Because price changes are not normally distributed, there are actually fewer losses than profits using this method; however, the net returns would not be impressive. If the entry were at the *S* lines and the exit at the outermost *Stop* lines, then most trades would be profitable, but the losing trades would be large. The net of profits and losses would be better because relatively few trades reach the stop. If trades are entered at the *E* lines and exited at the *Stop* lines, then profits would be larger than losses and risk greatly reduced. However, there would be very few opportunities and a larger percentage of them would be stopped out. Theoretically, the minimum risk occurs if a trade can be entered at the absolute extreme points, an unlikely possibility, and there would be only one trade. Figure 8.15 shows the relationships that exist for a standard mean reversion system.

All systems have trade-offs. In order to reduce the risk, there must be more small losses or fewer opportunities—whether a trending or mean-reverting strategy. A trend-follower looking for the big move must also take a big risk and many small losses. In the development of a system or trading philosophy, each person must settle on the combination of risk, reward, and opportunity that best suits him or her. There is no *best* combination.

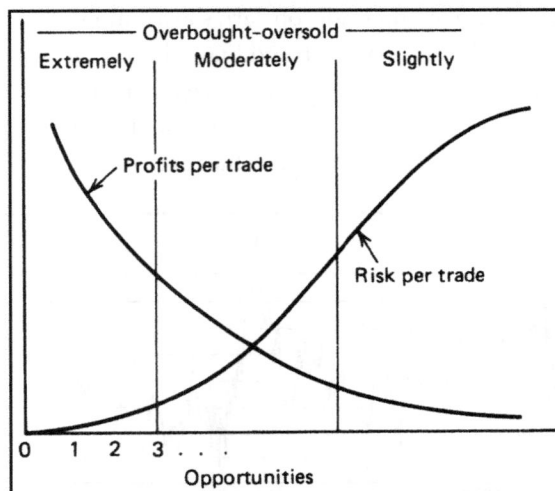

FIGURE 8.15 Relationship of Profits to Risk per Trade Based on Opportunities.

The Commodex Method of Combining Elements

The *Commodex* system was first presented in 1959 and is still actively run by second-generation Philip Gotthelf.[5] Commodex combines the components most acceptable to the experienced trader in a unique weighting method. It includes moving averages, price momentum, and open interest to calculate a trend index.

The most interesting aspect of the Commodex system is its ranking process, intended to produce a relative strength value for each trend. Using 10- and 20-day moving averages, the system scores the current market performance to establish the value of the trending component. Bullish and bearish values are calculated by looking at three situations independently: the simple moving average signals derived from both the long- and short-term trends, and the double moving average signal generated by combining the two trends. The two techniques of single and double moving averages are treated exactly as covered in Level II, Chapter 4. The most important of the three factors is the long-term trend, second is the short-term trend, and last the relative position of the fast to the slow moving average. The highest-ranking upward-moving trend occurs when current prices are above both the faster and slower moving averages, and the faster average is below the slower. The opposite positions would result in the strongest downward-trending component. Trends are considered neutral if the most important element, the long-term moving average, conflicts with the other two factors.

The rate of change in open interest (for futures) is considered a reinforcement of the trend. Using a concept different from the usual charting techniques, Commodex considers it a bullish sign if there is increasing *growth momentum* in open interest combined with rising prices. The growth momentum is the difference between the rate of increase of the open interest and the 20-day moving average of the open interest. Confirming a bull move with rising prices and rising open interest is a classic concept of charting. The bear move is confirmed with rising open interest and falling prices. Commodex also considers a drop in open interest along with falling prices to be a bullish factor. The movement of volume is treated in the same manner as open interest and can confirm a bull or bear trend. An increasing volume momentum with rising prices is support of an upward move; other combinations indicate bear trends.

Added together, the signals are ranked from a *strong buy* to a *strong sell* with lesser degrees in between. The system must be given credit for the quantification and balancing of these elements, which are generally treated as highly interpretive charting techniques. The rules for applying the daily signals to trading combine both the individual strength of the signal with the movement of the Commodex trend index. The trend index itself acts as an overbought/oversold indicator, encouraging profits at specified levels and considering a position reversal in more extreme situations; stops are placed using the 20-day moving average with predetermined band penetrations. Additional objectives are based on the profits

---

[5] More on Commodex can be found at their website, Commodex.com.

accrued from a trade, with a 50% return justifying a protective stop on part of the positions, and a 100% profit requiring the liquidation of half the position. These money-management concepts are an important aspect of any system and tend to round out Commodex.

Combining Trends and Trading Ranges

Price movement is classified as being in either a trend or a trading range, and most traders decide that one or the other of those regimes will be their sole focus. Trading ranges and trends take turns dominating price movement, with the trading range most common, but those conclusions depend on your time horizon. In 2011, the interest rates continued to post historically low yields, while the EURUSD moved between 1.23 and 1.45. Whenever the S&P breaks above a recent high or below a previous low, analysts are quick to point to the next level of resistance or support as the price target. They imply that prices will move to those levels then hesitate or reverse direction. Because this is a well-known concept, we can put rules on combining the trend direction with clear support and resistance levels. These are shown in Figure 8.16.

The exact rules for combining the two techniques depend on the size of the trading range, the speed of the trend, and whether the support and resistance levels have been established over time. Recent range formations offer less of an obstacle than those that have survived for some time. If the range is narrow, a moving average buy or sell signal invariably occurs at the resistance or support level and is met with an initial reversal. For a larger range, a medium-speed moving average signal may occur closer to the center of the range and allow some opportunity for trend profit before resistance is encountered. For very wide ranges, there may be ample latitude for a moving average to signal entry and close out without the interference of support and resistance levels. One method of combining the two techniques is to use whichever

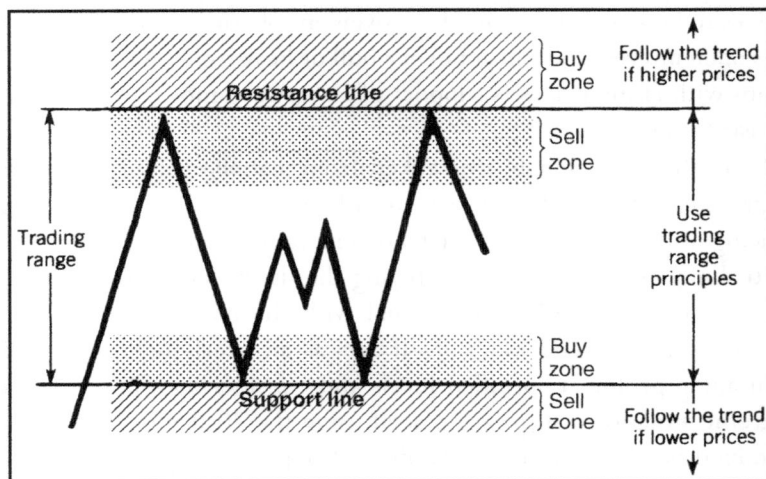

FIGURE 8.16 Combining Trends and Trading Ranges.

THE INTEGRATION OF TECHNICAL ANALYSIS

signal is generated, regardless of the system. The following combinations of short position entry and exit would be used for medium to wide ranges:

1. Enter a new short position when the moving average turns down.
2. Enter a new short position when prices enter the sell zone below the resistance level.
3. Enter a new short position when prices fall below the support area, then close out the short position when the moving average turns up.
4. Close out a short position when prices enter the buy zone above the support level.
5. Close out a short position when prices break through a resistance level moving up.

The same rules apply in reverse for long positions. The advantage of this filtering method is that new short trades are not entered at support levels, which causes immediate losses or prolonged trades with little return.

▪ Trading Limits and Disconnected Markets

Trading limits, which were unique to futures markets, have infiltrated the stock market. On February 18, 2011, the SEC adopted a *limit up/limit down rule* that halts trading for 5 minutes in any single stock or ETF if that market moves more than 10% in 5 minutes. The intention is to control excess volatility; however, it would not stop an event such as the *flash crash* that occurred on May 6, 2010. There is some doubt that this rule will accomplish its objective.

Curbs on excess price movement in futures, which can be highly leveraged, were intended to allow those traders on the losing side to meet margin calls in an orderly manner. Rules require that accounts must have a minimum deposit equal to 75% of the initial margin; otherwise, positions are liquidated by the brokerage firm. Clients have up to 24 hours to meet margin calls. Limits also prevent overreaction to false news, so that a price shock based on a rumored assassination would be corrected by the next day's opening if not true, and an extreme move that could ruin many investors would be avoided.

While futures contracts are halted at the limit, the cash market is not. This can create a severe disconnect between those two markets. Soft commodities, such as coffee, sugar, and cocoa, are trading in New York as well as in London. Traditionally, New York has had trading limits and London has not, presenting interesting dynamics in extreme cases.

Rules for limits have changed over the years. At first there was a simple limit of 20¢ per bushel for soybeans; then, it was changed to expanding limits, 20¢ the first day, 30¢, then 40¢, then no limits. As of 2008, after a very volatile period, soybean limits were raised to 70¢ and corn to 30¢; there are no longer expanding limits. Trading simply stops at the limit and continues again the next day. All agricultural futures markets have trading limits.

Effects of Limits on Trading Systems

When developing a trading system, especially one that trades on the close, it is necessary to test prices for limit moves. This is particularly difficult because those limits have changed many times during the years. Using today's soybean limit of 70¢ would not allow the program to recognize any limit moves before 2011.

The easiest way to recognize a *locked-limit day* is that the open, high, low, and close are all the same. No trading occurred on that day. However, most days trade up to the limit then stop, so that the high and close are the same, or the low and close, on a limit-down day. On those days you can test the change from the previous day. If that change is some even amount, say 20¢ or 40¢, there is a good chance is was a limit move. Allowing a trend system to change from a long to a short position on a limit day may produce a large gain when there may have been a large loss.

Most recently, cotton has been the center of extreme moves. Floods in Pakistan two years in a row, political disruption in Egypt, and drought in the southern United States have put pressure on prices, as shown in Figure 8.17. During February 2011 there are a number of days with gap openings representing limit moves. Figure 8.18 shows the closing price changes for the same period. Without knowing the daily limits, which can vary under certain circumstances, we can see that there are a large number of moves at even number, $4, $5, $6, and especially $7 (the maximum limit), with one exception above $8 (a data error?). Given the frequency of these limit moves, ignoring them in an historic test of a system would give highly incorrect results.

Note that rules about limit moves can be different for each market and each exchange, and they have changed from time to time. In some cases, limits do not apply to the front month or the second month, so it is important to check the rules before trading.

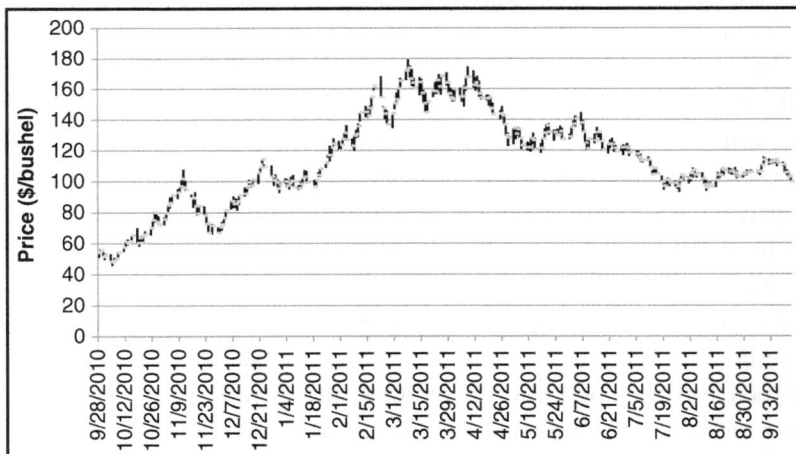

FIGURE 8.17 Cotton Futures Prices during the Recent Period of Stress.

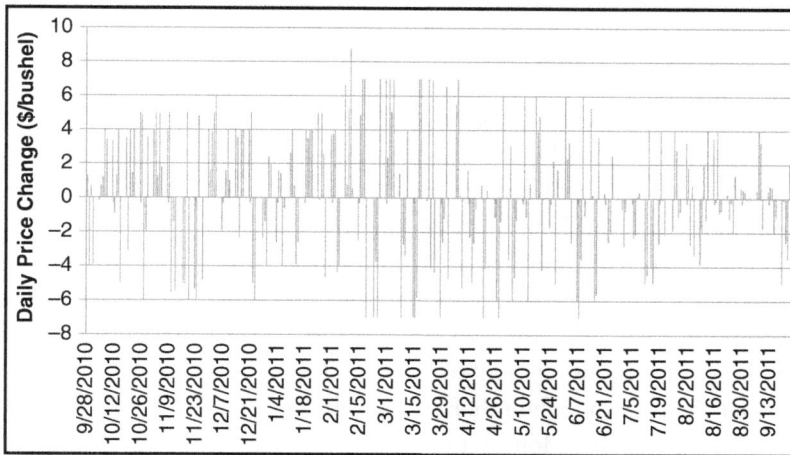

FIGURE 8.18 Cotton Futures Daily Price Changes.

Similar to Price Shocks

Limit moves are always the result of price shocks. If there is a comparable cash market open, then it will reflect the correct market price. In most cases, cash prices move quickly to the extreme, then start the slow, prolonged reversal. If you cannot liquidate a futures position because of a limit move, using the cash market to hedge the risk is not effective. The cash market would have already jumped to the price considered fully discounted by the traders. Buying in the cash market is more likely to add to your loss. Being long both futures and cash will simply double your risk. If there were no limits, then the full loss would have been seen on the day of the price shock. With limits, there is a chance that the some easing of the problem will occur and losses will be smaller by the time you exit the trade.

▣ Silver and NASDAQ—Too Good to Be True

This story of silver trading could have applied to the NASDAQ or S&P index during the late 1990s, or perhaps gold in 2011. The word "silver" could be replaced by "Intel" or by "Apple." There is no doubt that the same circumstances will reappear from time to time.

In 1974, public awareness of inflation caused an overwhelming interest in all forms of hedging, with large numbers of naive investors purchasing silver and gold as currency protection. Many sophisticated investors turned to the futures markets, which offered leverage on their purchases.

One investment system that was sold at that time was more of a leveraged substitute for the purchase of bullion than a trading strategy. At the time it was published, it had *always* worked—the sponsor of the system stood behind it with his reputation. The rules of the system were:

1. Trade silver futures because of their intrinsic value, historic performance, potential, and fundamental demand with short supply.
2. Use the futures contract between three and seven months from delivery to combine the advantages of liquidity and duration.
3. Always buy, never sell, because it is always successful.
4. Buy whenever you like. Although any sophisticated method can be used, it won't matter in the long run—any guess will do just as well. Follow the same method for adding to positions or reentering after closing out a trade.
5. Close out the position when there is a profit, not before.
6. Meet all margin calls—don't let the market beat you.
7. Invest $5,000 per contract (5,000 troy ounces). This will allow a $1 per ounce adverse move (silver was at $4.50 per ounce).
8. Whenever you need reinforcement, reread the reasoning behind this system.
9. Do not let anyone or anything interfere with following this system.

How did the investors do? It depended on when they started. Entering in the first half of 1975, shortly after the system was released, showed individual contract returns ranging from profits of 51¢ to losses of 18¢ per ounce. A drop in silver prices then produced losses of up to $1.02 per ounce for the next 9 months (slightly over 100%), followed by a 2-month rally, and losses again. This system would have worked from 1979 to February 1980 and then lost for the next 6 years. An investor following these rules, entering at a chance place, would have had more than a 10:1 likelihood of losing. Any profit made would have been given back if the investor persisted in following the method. Of course, had you held silver into 2011, you would have been profitable even after entering at the worse price—unless you consider inflation. Then prices again dropped by 25%.

The same results would have followed trading the NASDAQ. Buying anytime during the 1990s would have produced profits. No matter what trend method, indicators, filters, or dart board you use—if you buy and prices go higher, you always make money. If a trader continued to buy from 2000 through 2003, he would have faced the same total loss as the silver trader. The only true test of a strategy is the ability to make money in different types of markets.

In trying to understand how a system such as this can have a chance of reaching the public, remember the time in which it was introduced. With prices increasing drastically, food shortages, and publicity over the devaluing U.S. dollar, the rationale of the system seemed justifiable. The same arguments seem to apply to gold in 2011. There was serious talk about *leveraged inflation funds* using futures. We saw the same euphoria on the part of inexperienced traders who bought NASDAQ in the late 1990s. They had no expectation of losses. These systems fill an immediate need, without regard to long-term consequences. There is no doubt that, if high inflation or another major bull market returns, systems just like this one will reappear right near the top.

■ Similarity of Systematic Trading Signals

A primary concern of both the government regulatory agency (CFTC) and individual traders is the similarity of trading signals generated by computer-based systems that are used to manage large positions. Throughout this book, we have noted that the market is the driver of trends, and that the specific trend-following method is less important. These systems may appear different in their rules and parameters, but they could be essentially quite similar—for any of them to be profitable, they need to extract those profits from the same price moves, even though they may enter and exit as somewhat different points.

The S&P index affects the price patterns of those stocks within the index. Traders enter orders to buy and sell the S&P based on S&P price support and resistance, or on trends applied to the S&P index. That, in turn, causes an arbitrage between the index and the individual stocks comprising the index; therefore, those stocks stop rising at the S&P resistance levels, even though that price may not align with the stock's own resistance point.

If systematic trend-following systems with different calculation periods are not highly correlated, then it is possible to reduce portfolio risk by trading a variety of different techniques and time periods; however, the reality may be different from the theory. Lukac, Brorsen, and Irvin[6] performed a study that compared 12 popular trading techniques (mostly trend-following) over 12 varied futures markets for the years 1978–1984. Each system was optimized, using 3 years of data, and the best parameter values were used to trade the next year. The systems selected were:

- ▪ Channel systems
  - — Closing price channel (CHL)
  - — MII price channel (MII)
  - — L-S-O price channel (LSO)

- ▪ Momentum/oscillators
  - — Directional Indicator (DRI)
  - — Directional Movement (DRM)
  - — Range quotient (RNQ)
  - — Reference deviation (REF)

- ▪ Moving averages
  - — Moving average with percent band (MAB)
  - — Dual moving average (DMC)

---

[6] Louis P. Lukac, B. Wade Brorsen, and Scott H. Irwin, *Similarity of Computer Guided Technical Trading Systems* (CSFM-124, Working Paper Series, Columbia Futures Center, Columbia University Business School, New York, March 1986). Also by the same authors, "Do Similar Signals from Trading Systems Move Prices?" *Futures* (November 1987).

- Systems with trailing stops
    — Parabolic Time/Price System (PAR)
    — Alexander's Filter Rule (ALX)
    —Combined Directional Movement and Parabolic Time/Price System (DRP)

The study used three measures to test system similarity:

1. The percentage of the time that systems are on the same side of the market (long or short).
2. The percentage of buy or sell signals that occurred on the same day or within a few days of one another.
3. The correlation of aggregate monthly portfolio returns.

The results show a significant positive correlation in the system profitability (Table 8.6). However, there is no pattern that shows that one particular type of system is notably more correlated than others. The Parabolic and Directional Parabolic systems are most similar because one is based on the other. In Table 8.7, the percentage of trades that occur on the same day is very low. A more informative comparison is seen in Table 8.8, which tallies the percentage of days that each system held the same position.

The study concludes that computer-based systems trade on the same day significantly more often than would randomly be expected, but the actual percentage of trades that occur on the same day is small. These systems have

TABLE 8.6   **Correlations of Aggregate Monthly Returns from 12 Systems**

System	CHL	PAR	DRM	RNQ	DRP	MII	LSO	REF	DMC	DRI	MAB
PAR	0.57										
DRM	0.72	0.61									
RNQ	0.70	0.41	0.70								
DRP	0.65	0.81	0.79	0.57							
MII	0.75	0.54	0.67	0.73	0.67						
LSO	0.59	0.43	0.53	0.68	0.54	0.70					
REF	0.55	0.37	0.57	0.66	0.52	0.54	0.60				
DMC	0.72	0.41	0.68	0.78	0.55	0.74	0.58	0.57			
DRI	0.71	0.42	0.69	0.77	0.55	0.70	0.59	0.66	0.64		
MAB	0.72	0.55	0.75	0.74	0.69	0.69	0.63	0.60	0.78	0.72	
ALX	0.58	0.55	0.62	0.55	0.57	0.57	0.58	0.51	0.52	0.56	0.57

All coefficients significant at the 0.01% level with the exception of REF and PAR coefficient, which is significant at the 0.05% level.

Source: Reprinted with permission of *Futures* magazine (250 S. Wacker Drive, #1150, Chicago, IL 60606, November 1987).

TABLE 8.7 **Percentage of Trades That Occur on the Same Day**

System	CHL	PAR	DRM	RNQ	DRP	MII	LSO	REF	DMC	DRI	MAB
				Trading System							
PAR	19*										
DRM	25**	21**									
RNQ	22**	9	15								
DRP	30**	93**	48**	10							
MII	20*	15	10	28**	17						
LSO	22**	13	17	27**	18	23**					
REF	12	7	7	11	9	12	14				
DMC	16	6	8	28**	6	12	18	19*			
DRI	18	9	14	38**	10	32**	22**	15	25**		
MAB	28**	18	23**	23**	27**	18	25**	11	19*	23**	
ALX	12	20*	12	19*	20*	9	17	10	10	16	17

Percentage of trades that occur on the same day by each pair of systems. Significance assuming a binomial distribution with *denoting 95% confidence limits and ** denoting 99% confidence limits.

Source: Reprinted with permission of *Futures* magazine (250 S. Wacker Drive, #1150, Chicago, IL 60606, November 1987).

TABLE 8.8 **Percentage of Trading Days Systems Hold the Same Positions**

System	CHL	PAR	DRM	RNQ	DRP	MII	LSO	REF	DMC	DRI	MAB
				Trading System							
PAR	70										
DRM	82	76									
RNQ	75	61	73								
DRP	68	83	75	59							
MII	82	69	80	75	65						
LSO	73	58	71	73	57	73					
REF	72	57	69	69	55	72	69				
DMC	81	62	77	79	61	79	76	78			
DRI	70	56	68	72	54	71	69	67	73		
MAB	65	54	66	62	53	63	61	57	65	59	
ALX	72	64	71	68	59	73	65	67	73	63	58

Percentage of the trading days each pair of systems is on the same side of the market (long or short) at the same time. All coefficients are significant, assuming a binomial distribution with 99% confidence limits.

Source: Reprinted with permission of *Futures* magazine (250 S. Wacker Drive, #1150, Chicago, IL 60606, November 1987).

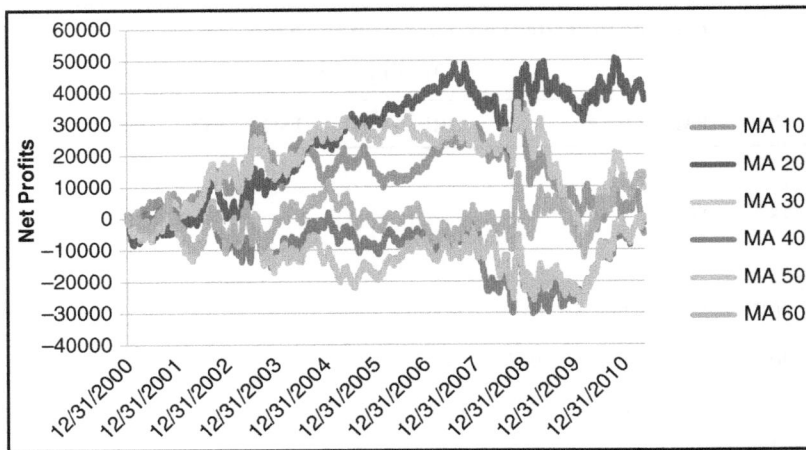

FIGURE 8.19 Net PL for Six Moving Average Systems, U.S. 30-Year Bond Continuous Futures, from 2000 through Mid-2011.

the potential to move market prices. One must be concerned, as the assets under management of macrotrend trading programs get larger, that they compete with each other for both entries and exits, which now may span up to three trading days.

Comparison of Moving Average Systems

Using U.S. 30-year Treasury bonds as an example of a trending market, apply a simple moving average system to continuous futures prices from 2000 through mid-2011. The net profits of 6 calculation periods, from 10 to 60 days, are shown in Figure 8.19. Results seem to vary considerably.

If we take the daily changes in PL for each of the six systems and find the correlations (see Table 8.9), we can see a clear pattern. Looking down in column 1, the 10-day calculation period, the correlations decline as the difference in the calculation periods increases. They also drop faster when the percentage difference in the calculation days is larger. Then the correlation difference between the 10- and 20-day trend is larger than the difference between the 50- and 60-day trends. This supports the statement that the calculation periods used for testing should not be in equal increments because they favor the slower periods. Also notice that the correlation between any two calculation periods will always be positive because they are extracting profits from the same trends. This was even more pronounced in the Lukac study over a period when the market had stronger trends.

Similarity of Long-Term Performance

The similarity of signals also implies the similarity of performance. It was shown that trend-following systems of about the same calculation periods had similar

TABLE 8.9 Correlations of PL Changes for Moving Average Systems of Different Calculation Periods, U.S. Bond Futures, 2000 through Mid–2011

	MA 10	MA 20	MA 30	MA 40	MA 50	MA 60
MA 10	1					
MA 20	0.511	1				
MA 30	0.428	0.678	1			
MA 40	0.365	0.555	0.712	1		
MA 50	0.315	0.478	0.593	0.711	1	
MA 60	0.265	0.382	0.458	0.579	0.747	1

performance over time. The conclusion was that all of the methods identified the same trend, some sooner and some later, but the effect was that they all made money or lost money, to different degrees, during those trends. It was the market, not the strategy, that was most important.

A recent paper by ISAM[7] attempts to show that all trend systems converge on the same performance over time. By defining three systems, but focusing on the N-day breakout, they show that various combinations of calculation periods and asset allocations cause variation in the year-to-year returns but total returns converge to similar results over time. Does this mean that it does not matter which parameters we choose, or how we allocate funds within a portfolio, because it will all come out the same in the end? Or, does it mean that, if we traded all combinations of parameters and allocations, that we would get an average result? Or, are the systems in the study not really representative of the set of trend-following systems that we have been discussing?

High Correlation at the Best and Worst Times

Different systems and the same system with different calculation periods will hold the same trade for varying periods of time. Typically, when they are in the same trade, prices are moving in a profitable direction. That is easy to understand. If a 10-day average was long and the 20-day average turned from short to long, then the 10-day would have continued to be profitable. In order to get the 60-day average to turn up, all of the trends of shorter periods are likely be profitable.

Once they are all in the same position, they also pose the greatest risk. The portfolio returns will increase and decrease by larger percentages each day, and, in the event of a price shock, all systems drop together. The process of controlling correlated risk, and overall risk, is discussed in Chapter 9.

---

[7] "Trend Following: The Myth of Return Dispersion," *International Standard Asset Management* (ISAM) (August 2011). See www.isam.com.

Risk Control

From Perry J. Kaufman, *Trading Systems and Methods, + Website*, 5th Edition (Hoboken, New Jersey: John Wiley & Sons, 2013), Chapter 23.

Learning Objective Statements

- Explain how to measure probability of price change and returns over a given time frame
- Explain how to measure risk factors such as news, volatility, etc.
- Interpret calculations of VaR
- Compare VaR calculation to confirm selection of stop placement
- Calculate the amount of money at risk in a portfolio based on a specified scenario
- Differentiate between risk and performance metrics derived from one of the following: Sharpe ratio, Information Ratio, Treynor Ratio, calmar Ratio, Sortino Ratio

Every trading style has losing streaks that will ruin an investor who begins trading at the wrong time or is undercapitalized; therefore, the size of the position, the markets to trade, and when to increase or decrease leverage become important for financial survival. Some risks, called *systematic risk,* can be controlled or reduced while *market risk,* which can take the form of a price shock, can never be eliminated.

This chapter covers a broad range of topics related to risk, including individual trade risk, collective risk, leverage, and a continuation of the effects of price shocks and catastrophic risk. It is not possible to say that one is more important than another. In a specific situation, any one of the areas discussed may be the answer to preventing a substantial loss. The first part of this chapter discusses capitalization and shows why many traders are successful for months and then lose everything in only a few days. It explains the choices in dynamic leveraging and offers alternatives of less risk. Profit-taking and stops, the two most common ways to control risk, are shown to apply to specific types of trading, rather than used as a generalized solution. The last section tries to distinguish between a system that is temporarily performing properly and when it has failed to live up to expectations of it.

■ Mistaking Luck for Skill

Embracing risk is more important than measuring risk. Understanding and accepting each day's losses and series of losses is essential for survival. Risk cannot be eliminated, as much as traders try to make each trade a profit or engineer systems to minimize losses. You can move the profits and losses around, but you cannot eliminate them or make them so small that they are meaningless. And measuring risk as a 10% chance of losing 20% of your equity is not as sobering as actually losing 20%. It is even devastating when you thought you could only lose 5%.

Daily market volatility gives a good approximation of short-term risk, and volatility of the actual profits and losses of a trading method provides a way to estimate how much risk must be absorbed to achieve the expected profits. Price shocks are the fly in the ointment. They add an unpredictable aspect to risk, coming at unexpected times and cause losses that are larger than anything seen in the past. Chapter 8 continued a discussion of some practical aspects of price shocks, with examples of how to manage both profits and losses caused by these large moves. This review only serves as a reminder of a very important problem.

A price shock represents the greatest risk for traders. In most cases, a price shock causes a loss, but when it is a windfall profit it can be disarming.[1] A price shock, such as 9/11, cannot be anticipated, and any profit that might have been gained is the result of luck, not skill. Traders must realize that the profit could have been a loss; they should assess how their account would have survived a drop of the same magnitude. Mistaking luck for skill ignores the risk and exposes the trader to future risk for which he or she is now unprepared. Long-Term Capital Management, a home for some of the smartest financial minds, believed they could engineer the risk out of each trade by explaining away all of the previous price shocks, then failed to survive the next price shock. Without including these larger, infrequent losses in the performance profile, trading accounts are likely to be undercapitalized.

The only way to reduce the possibility of loss from a price shock is to be out of the market as much as possible. This translates into two practical trading rules:

1. *Do not hold a position longer than necessary.* Choose a strategy that has good entry timing and has many opportunities for exiting the trade. It is best to be in the market when prices are moving and out when volatility drops and prices are no longer active. A trading method that is in the market only 40% of the time has a 60% chance of avoiding a price shock. A strategy that is always in the market will be exposed to all price shocks.

2. *Try to earn as much as possible while investing as little as possible.* The less you have invested, the less you have at risk. Futures and options offer an opportunity to leverage price moves by as much as 20:1; however, that works against you when a price shock causes a large loss. A fully leveraged trading program that has a theoretical return of 200% per annum will also be a total loss after an adverse

---

[1] A book entirely devoted to price shocks and the "black swan" is Nassim Nicholas Taleb, *Fooled by Randomness* (Texere, 2001). Taleb has popularized the phrase "mistaking luck for skill."

price shock. A deleveraged program may return only 20% but is 10 times more likely to survive a price shock, a much better long-term alternative. A small reduction in returns for a larger reduction in exposure is a good trade-off.

■ Risk Aversion

Traders react differently to risk, and most are risk-averse. A primary reason for the popularity of trend systems is that they provide some degree of *conservation of capital*. They take small losses when prices move the wrong way, and hold a trade for much longer when it shows a profit. By taking small losses, the investor can wait until a sustained trend comes along. This gives the trending system its familiar profile of a large number of small losses offset by a few large profits. But each trader has her personal tolerance level for risk and not all of them find conservation of capital appealing. Some are risk seeking.

Daniel Bernoulli, a famous mathematician, proposed a theory of utility in 1738 that distinguished between price and value, where price is the same for everyone but value (utility) depends on the personal circumstances of the individual making the estimate.[2] Bernoulli's approach defined a concept of *diminishing marginal utility*, shown in Figure 9.1, which indicates that as wealth becomes greater, the preference for more wealth diminishes (unlike the concept of power). In the lower left part of the chart, where the investor has a small net worth, the likelihood of accepting risk is much higher, although the magnitude of the risk is still small. When risk becomes greater, even proportional to reward, all investors become cautious. Bernoulli's graph shows the curve beginning at zero and moving up and to the right in a perfect

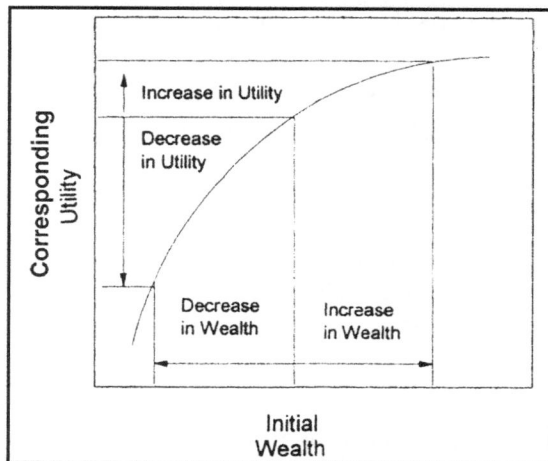

FIGURE 9.1 **Changes in Utility versus Changes in Wealth.**

Source: Peter Bernstein, *The Portable MBA in Investment* (New York: John Wiley & Sons, 1995), 38. © 1995 Peter Bernstein. Reprinted by permission of John Wiley & Sons, Inc.

[2] Peter L. Bernstein, ed., *The Portable MBA in Investment* (New York: John Wiley & Sons, 1995), 37.

quarter-circle, ending horizontally where risk is no longer attractive. This implies that people are risk-averse. Most people are not interested in an even chance of gaining or losing an equal amount. Other theories that have been proposed are that the market maximizes the amount of money lost and the market maximizes the number of losing participants. All of these concepts appear to be true and are significant in developing an understanding of how the market functions.

Naturally, there are exceptions to most rules. People will spend small amounts to have a very small chance of winning a very large amount, as with various state lotteries. Young people with a small amount of money are willing to take greater risks, rationalizing that a small amount of savings is not significant for their future.

Risk Preference

The Bernoulli theory of utility recognizes that each investor has his or her unique objectives and attitudes toward risk. Some investors would like to keep risks low and returns steady; more speculative investors would risk a sizable amount of their capital for a chance at the big move. This trait is called the investor's *risk preference*. The *risk preference, P,* or *utility* of an investor for a specific venture (in this case a trade) can be found by adding the expected value of the investor's utilities or preferences, p_i, for the various outcomes of that event,

$$P = w_1 p_1 + w_2 p_2 + \cdots + w_n p_n$$

where $\sum w_i = 1$

n = possible outcomes

The weighting factors may be the results of personal bias or may be the calculated probabilities of each outcome. For example, consider a gold trade that has a likely profit of $4,000 and a risk of $1,500. For convenience, adjust the reward values by dividing by 1,000. If the probability of success is 60%, the total utility of the trade is:

$$P(\text{trade}) = 0.60 \times 4 + 0.40 \times (-1.5) = 1.8$$

If the probability of success were increased, the utility P would increase linearly. But investors do not feel the same about different rewards. Given a scale of 0 to 100 (negative to positive reaction), an investor may rank a 60% chance of a $4,000 profit and a 40% chance of a $1,500 loss both as a 65. If the reward is increased to $8,000 while the risk remains at $1,500, the investor might only raise the preference of the trade to 80, although the utility would be 4.2, more than twice as large.

The various curves drawn through the computed utilities represent the risk preference of the individual. Figure 9.2 shows these curves progressing from extreme risk aversion to extreme risk seeking. As the risk increases in (1), the trader is risk-averse and less likely to participate in the trade; in (3), there is equal chance of taking the trade at all risk levels; and in (5), the trader is risk seeking and is more likely to enter a trade that has higher risk.

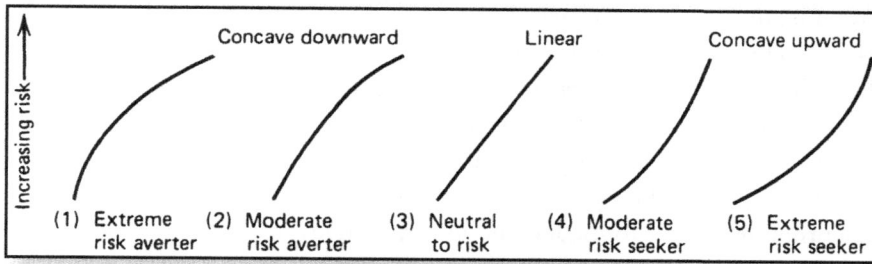

FIGURE 9.2 Investor Utility Curves.

Source: R. J. Teweles, C. V. Harlow, and H. L. Stone, *The Commodity Futures Game: Who Wins, Who Loses, Why?* (New York: McGraw-Hill, 1974), 133. © 1974. Reprinted with permission of The McGraw-Hill Companies.

The Efficient Frontier

There are a large number of performance profiles that result from combining trading strategies, a diverse selection of stocks, futures, ETF, and funds, and the amount of leverage used. Each of these investments can be described in terms of its annualized rate of return and its annualized risk. Risk is most often the standard deviation of the annual returns; however, other measurements will be discussed in the next sections.

The *efficient frontier* is a way of visualizing which choices would be made by any rational investor. Suppose there were 8 different investment programs, and all of them reported their annualized rate of return and the annualized risk. These could then be plotted in Figure 9.3. Let us also assume that these investments represented a good sample of all risk and return combinations.

A *rational investor* is one who wants the highest return for the lowest risk. Therefore, given a choice between investment D and investment C, we would choose C because it had the same risk but a substantially higher return. Similarly, if we were given a choice between investment D and investment A, we would choose investment A because it has the same return with a much lower risk. Given a choice of any two

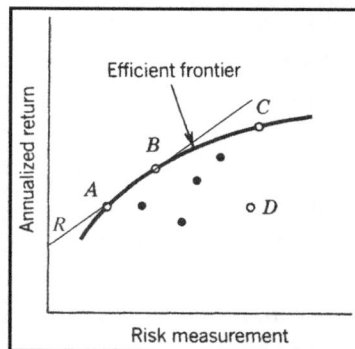

FIGURE 9.3 The Efficient Frontier. The line drawn from R, the risk-free return, touches the efficient frontier at the point of best return to risk ratio, B.

investments, displayed on a chart of risk and return, a rational investor will always choose the one that is higher and to the left.

The efficient frontier is a curve plotted through those investment alternatives that have the highest returns for a given risk, or the lowest risk for a given return. An investor seeking greater returns with a higher tolerance for risk will choose an investment further to the right on the curve; one with a lower risk tolerance must select a program farther to the left and lower, with less return.

The optimal point on the efficient frontier is where the return-to-risk ratio is a maximum. This is also the point where a line, drawn from the risk-free return on the left scale upwards to the right, is tangent to the curve. Nevertheless, not all investors choose this point because the absolute level of risk may be too high, or the absolute returns too low. Investors' risk preferences are personal and unique.

Common Sense Management of Risk

Risk control is as much an issue of common sense as it is complex rules and mathematics. Most of this chapter shows how various rules, measurements, and leveraging techniques can reduce risk for both discretionary and algorithmic trading; however, successful traders have applied common sense, without complex formulas, for a long time. Some of these successful principles are:

1. *Only risk a small amount of total capital on any one trade.* The total amount risked should allow you to comfortably survive a number of losses in a row. No trade should ever risk more than 5% of the invested capital.
2. *Know your exit conditions in advance.* There should be a clear exit criterion for every trade, even if the exact loss cannot be known in advance.
3. *Large profits mean large risk.* If the average profits or average losses are too large relative to the investment, then smaller positions should be taken.
4. *Exit a trade quickly.* Exit a trade as soon as you recognize that it has gone wrong. Don't try to manage the loss. Many floor traders believe that the smartest trader is the first one out.
5. *Don't meet margin calls.* Experienced traders believe that a margin call is an objective statement of a trade that's gone wrong, or a system that is not meeting expectations. It is a time to review trading performance rather than invest more.
6. *Liquidate your worst position first when lightening up.* The profitable trades have proved that they are trending or performing properly; the losing ones have proved they are not. Stay with the good positions and liquidate the worst.
7. *Be consistent with your trading philosophy.* If you are a trend follower, then keep losses small and let profits run. You cannot be a trend follower by taking profits whenever they occur.
8. *Be sure the trading profile is compatible with your risk preference.* You cannot follow a strategy that takes risks that are uncomfortably large. Be sure that profile is agreeable to you.

9. *Plan for contingencies.* Nothing ever goes as planned, and you must be prepared for infrequent but important exceptions, such as a price shock. Do not be undercapitalized.

◼ Liquidity

The ability to implement any trading program is directly related to the liquidity of the market. Even though liquidity can have more than one meaning, lack of liquidity has only one trading result—poor execution. A *liquid* market does not necessarily mean good fills, but an *illiquid* market assures bad ones. Two types of illiquidity most often encountered in the markets are:

1. *Fast markets,* in which there are mostly buyers or sellers, and few traders willing to take the other side of the position.
2. *Inactive markets*, usually the smaller cap stocks, deferred futures contracts, and many ETFs, where there is less commercial or institutional interest.

The fast market is the result of developing news or an economic report where everyone has the same interpretation of the direction that prices should move. In futures this may be combined with a supply/demand imbalance or a perceived imbalance. Once a large number of buy orders flood the market, specialists, market makers, and locals all stand aside (or widen the bid-asked spread and offer very small quantity) rather than be run over. The few arbitrageurs, hedgers, and risk-seeking traders willing to take the opposite position do little to offset the vast number of orders that continue to push prices in one direction. In the inactive market, a large premium must be paid to attract another trader to take the opposite side. This only succeeds when the bid or offered price clearly appears to give the other trader a guaranteed short-term profit.

An illiquid market causes poor executions, which is the largest part of transaction costs and is sometimes too large to overcome. Ginter and Richie[3] have described this as a function of the order size, volume, and the speed of the market, in a single formula that applies to the futures markets, but could be adapted to individual equities:

$$C = K \times \frac{Q \times V}{L_c \times L_o}$$

where C = cost of execution due to liquidity
Q = size of the order entered
V = volatility of the market
L_c = volume of the market (all contract months for futures or possibly the combined volume of highly correlated equities)
L_o = volume of the specific delivery month or individual equity
K = constant factor

---

[3] G. Ginter and J. Richie, "Data Errors and Price Distortions," in Perry J. Kaufman, ed., *Technical Analysis in Commodities* (New York: John Wiley & Sons, 1980).

The volatility V might be the daily price range, annualized volatility, or implied volatility. This provides a way to measure how much volume would move the market a specified number of points. The total volume (liquidity) L_c is important because it implies liquidity due to interdelivery spreading in futures. If applied to stocks, added liquidity may come from activity in a closely correlated industrial group. Volume also serves as a measurement of the general interest in the product or in the related stock group. Increased trading in other futures market delivery months, or in similar stocks, is a sign of growing interest.

The constant factor K varies according to the type of the execution order being placed and the current direction of the price with regard to that order. If prices are moving higher and a buy order is placed, K will be large; if prices are moving higher and a sell order is placed, K will be smaller. The investor can see that transaction costs, including commissions and execution slippage, will have considerably greater impact on systems that trade more often, have smaller average profits, and trade in the direction of the trend. Given a choice between systems of equal gross profits, the investor should favor the method of fewest trades in the most liquid markets.

■ Measuring Return and Risk

Risk and return are the two most important criteria for measuring performance and for determining that one trading method is better than another. Looking at only returns is not enough. However, the ways in which these and other measures can be combined to express the quality of performance varies considerably. For example, returns are often the annualized rate of return but they can also be expressed as the slope of a straight line drawn through the daily or monthly returns. Risk has many more variations from the annualized standard deviation of returns to measurements of drawdown and time to recovery. The following section gives an overview of these techniques.

Risk Characteristics of a Trading Model

Before either risk or returns can be measured, it is necessary to have a strategy that has produced historic results, whether real or theoretical. The use of actual trading results is always better because it will show larger equity swings than hypothetical performance, regardless of how conscientiously you have performed the development and testing. Hypothetical results are always optimistic. In some cases, techniques such as analyzing trends in returns do not work with theoretical results but can be a great benefit in real trading.

Suppose there is a choice of systems to trade, and the daily equity of each is available. If only one can be selected, which should it be? There are some characteristics of performance that are normally considered better:

1. Larger profits rather than smaller profits because it leaves more room for execution error.

2. Upwards equity surges (profits) over downward surges (losses).
3. A shorter time-to-recovery rather than prolonged drawdowns.
4. Less time in the market because it avoids price shocks.

Results are always relative. If your choice is between a buy-and-hold portfolio in stocks with a return of 8% and risk of 11%, compared to a simple moving average system of S&P futures with 12% returns and 13% risk, then the moving average system is clearly better, although far from being a money machine. To find the best choice always include a benchmark. Most often this is the result of a theoretical portfolio of 60% stocks (using the S&P) and 40% Treasury bonds (using the Lehman Brothers Treasury Index).

The Sharpe Ratio and Information Ratio

The classic measurement of performance is the *Sharpe ratio* (SR), expressed as

$$SR = \frac{E - I}{\sigma}$$

where E = the expected return (the annualized rate of return)
   I = the risk-free interest rate (usually the 3-month rate)
   σ = the standard deviation, or fluctuation, of the periodic returns (the annualized volatility)

In calculations for the annualized rate of return and annualized volatility, for practical purposes, I is often omitted, with the simplified form called the *information ratio*, the most common performance statistic. The risk-free return, I, cannot be omitted when there is interest income on unused capital, or on some part of the account balance, that has been imbedded in the performance. For futures trading, interest can be earned daily on a large part of the market-to-market value of the account. For a comparison of different investments, it is necessary to specifically identify which returns include interest income. In the world of Commodity Trading Advisors (CTAs), there may be a performance hurdle, such as the yield on the 3-month Treasury bill, before any incentive is paid.

The Sharpe and information ratios satisfy the first universal criterion of system selection, that all else being equal (primarily risk), higher profits are better. It does not satisfy either of the other criteria illustrated in Figure 9.4 because it cannot distinguish between:

1. Consecutive small losses (System B) and alternating small losses (System A), shown in Figure 9.4a.
2. Large surges of profits and large losses, shown in Figure 9.4b.

Clearly, System *A* is best in both cases. Also note that performance of monthly returns is always better than results based on daily returns because it is inherently smoothed. It is unlikely that the end-of-month net asset value (NAV) will be either the lowest or highest of the month, although highest is more likely than lowest.

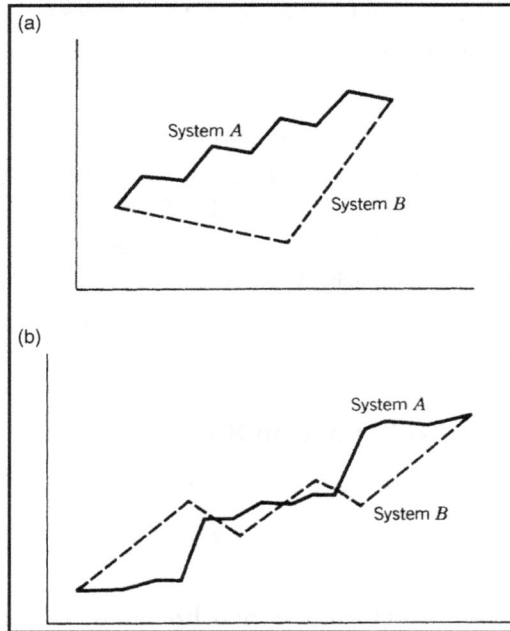

FIGURE 9.4 Two Cases in Which the Sharpe Ratio Falls
Short. (a) The order in which profits and losses occur.
(b) Surges in profits versus evenly distributed losses.

Treynor Ratio An additional measure of return to risk is the *Treynor ratio* (TR), the annualized return less the risk-free return, all divided by beta, the relative volatility of the current portfolio compared to a benchmark, usually the S&P

$$TR_t = \frac{AROR_t - I}{\beta_t}$$

Average Maximum Retracement

Schwager[4] has presented a comprehensive study of risk and return evaluation techniques. Although each method may emphasize a particular equity trait, he seems to favor the *Average Maximum Retracement* (AMR). This method finds the average equity drawdown, the difference between the current value in the account and the highest past value, by ignoring all days when equity was on new highs.

$$AMR_t = \frac{1}{n} \sum_{i=t-n+1}^{t} POS\left(MCE_i - TE_i\right)$$

where $POS(X) = \begin{cases} x & \text{if } x > 0 \\ 0 & \text{if } x < 0 \end{cases}$

---

[4] Jack D. Schwager, *A Complete Guide to the Futures Markets* (New York: John Wiley & Sons, 1984).

and MCE = closed-out equity (realized profits) on any trade entry date prior to i
$\quad\quad TE_i$ = total equity on day i
$\quad\quad\quad n$ = total number of days of equity data or the calculation period

When $TE_i > MCE_i$, then equity is on a new high and all traders will have a profit on day i, regardless of when they began. Schwager suggests that a much simpler computation would use only the low equity day of each month; it would give a rough but good approximation.

Measuring only the drawdowns is a concept similar to *semivariance* and is valuable because the distribution of profitable returns compared to losing returns is not symmetric; therefore, the standard deviation does not express it correctly and may bias the results in favor of profitable days, giving you an understated picture of risk.

Largest Loss and the Calmar Ratio

Measurements such as Schwager's AMR, and even the basic standard deviation, are good for comparing the long-term performance of one system against another; however, they lack a certain reality of simply looking at the largest loss seen over the test period. John Sweeney calls this the *maximum adverse excursion*,[5] advocating that traders should minimize the size of their largest loss.

Consider the standard deviation of equity changes, showing that in any month there is a 68% chance that your returns will be between 15% and −5% (a mean of 5% and a standard deviation of 10%). There is only a 2.5% chance that you will lose more than 15% in one month (2 standard deviations, one sided); therefore, there is a 50% chance you will lose that 15% in one of the first 20 months (20 ÷ 2.5). Yet probability shows that you should lose more if you keep trading or less if you stop sooner.

The largest historic loss, called the *maximum drawdown,* is a practical alternative. It simply states that the trading program *did* lose 15% during one month of a 3-year test. While it is possible, and even likely, that the program will have a larger loss in the future, you must be prepared for a 15% loss in a single month. The relationship of the drawdown to the returns are expressed as the *Calmar ratio*

$$Calmar\ ratio_t = \frac{AROR_t}{Max\ drawdown_t}$$

where *max drawdown* as of day t is the largest historic drawdown, peak to valley, from the beginning of the data to today.

Using the historic drawdown is practical but not without problems. In Chapter 8 on testing, there were many cases where final system profile benefitted from unintentional overfitting. Even when parameters were chosen from a robust section of the test surface, they might all have looked good because the timing avoided a particularly bad price shock. Then the theoretical maximum drawdown might be

---

[5] John Sweeney, "Maximum Adverse Excursions for Stops," *Technical Analysis of Stocks & Commodities* (April 1987).

understated. Even if not overfitted, then the future always brings larger profits and especially larger drawdowns.

Sortino Ratio

A variation on both the Sharpe ratio and semivariance, the *Sortino ratio* includes only the downside risk in the denominator and replaces the risk-free threshold with a minimum acceptable return (MAR) in the numerator. Then the Sortino ratio is calculated as

$$SR_t = \frac{AROR_t - MAR}{\sigma(PE_t - E_t)}$$

MAR may be the risk-free rate of return or any other threshold set by the investor. The denominator is the standard deviation of all the negative equity excursions, the difference between the peak equity (*PE*) and the current equity (*E*), not equal to zero, on each day during the calculation period.

Ulcer Index

Investors have increased anxiety as current returns drop farther below the highest returns previously achieved. This can be measured by the *Ulcer Index (UI)*[6] a form of semivariance, similar to Schwager's *Average Maximum Retracement*, that produces a statistical measure of relative declines on all days that were not new high returns.

$$UI_t = \sqrt{\frac{\sum_{i=t-n+1}^{t} D_i^2}{n}}$$

where D = the difference between the highest equity as of day i and the actual
           equity on day i
         n = the number of days in the equity stream

If the equity on day i is a new high equity, then $D_i = 0$. As *UI* increases, investors are more anxious about performance.

Potential Risk

Risk is never a single value; it is a probability, and the standard deviation is the tool most often used for finding that relationship. Even if a drawdown has occurred that is larger than the previous maximum drawdown, there is still a small chance that another, even larger drawdown will occur. It is unreasonable to think that all future losses will be smaller than the maximum already experienced. This *potential for loss* can be expressed as a probability with two different measurements over *n* days:

---

[6] Created by Peter Martin in 1987, it appeared in a book by Peter Martin and Byron McCann, *The Investor's Guide to Fidelity Funds* (New York: John Wiley & Sons, 1989).

1. *Probability of a drawdown* (DP). This is essentially the method used by Schwager and the Ulcer Index. Calculate the standard deviation of all daily drawdowns, D_i, measured from the most recent equity high to today's equity value. When today's equity is also a new high equity, the value used is zero.

$$DP = stdev(D_i)$$

   where $i = 1, n$, and n is only those days where a drawdown existed, that is $D_i \neq 0$.
2. *Semivariance (SV)*. Calculate the linear regression of the equity stream or *NAV*, then find the standard deviation of all drawdowns, D_i, below the corresponding value of the straight line fit, $p'i$. Semivariance will produce a smaller value than DP because the values on the straight line will be lower than the peak equity.

DP is a more conservative version of both Schwager and the Ulcer Index because it omits those days on which the equity made a new high. The standard deviation will be increased in proportion to the number of days omitted. With either measure, DP and SV represent the value of 1 standard deviation. Therefore, there is a 16% chance that there will be a drawdown greater than DP or SV over the next n days. There is only a 2.5% chance of a drawdown of twice that amount over the next n days.

Either of these measurements can be used to form a ratio of return to risk, called a *drawdown ratio* (DR):

$$DR_t = AROR_t / DP_t$$

or

$$DR_t = AROR_t / SV_t$$

where $AROR_t$ = the annualized return on investment on day t.

These ratios satisfy all three of the original criteria: higher profits are favored because the rate of return is in the numerator, the order of profits and losses will result in larger and smaller net equity drops, and large gains are not penalized because only the drawdowns are used to measure risk.

Conservative investors may want to include some additional simple considerations of potential risk. All else being equal, systems will have greater risk if:

1. They are tested with smaller samples.
2. They have few historic equity drops (also likely to be a poor sample).
3. They concentrate on fewer product groups (not well diversified).
4. They compound positions.

Annualized Volatility The *annualized volatility* is mentioned separately because is it the most common way to express risk. It is simply the annualized standard deviation.

$$V_t = \sigma(r_i) \times \sqrt{252}, \ i = t - n + 1, \ t$$

where r represents the returns for the past n days and 252 is the number of trading days in the year. Analysts simply call this *volatility*. Even though we know that returns are not symmetric, this remains the most common measurement of risk. In portfolio analysis, this will be used to determine the *target volatility*.

Value at Risk   *Value at Risk* (VaR) is used in most companies to assess whether the current market positions are likely to produce a loss that is unacceptably large over the next few days. It is different from volatility given in the previous section because it attempts to *anticipate risk*, even though it is done using historic risk. This is done by finding the probability of loss of the current market positions based on past market movement. For example, Bank Two holds large short positions in fixed income futures to protect loan commitments at current levels. They also hold a wide variety of foreign currencies, of which 50% are hedged with forward contracts. If interest rates drop or the U.S. dollar strengthens, they could show large losses in their futures positions. According to bank policy, the loss allowed in a single day must be kept to under 0.5% of cash value of these commitments. If there is a potential risk exceeding that amount, the futures position must be immediately reduced.

VaR is a combination of cross-correlations between markets for which there is exposure, the position sizes, the volatility of those markets, the projected time period over which the risk will be forecast, and a confidence interval to determine the risk tolerance. Using the return series for the interest rate and FX exposure held by Bank Two, the *variance-covariance* solution for VaR can be calculated as[7]

$$VaR = \sqrt{\sigma_{IR}^2 + \sigma_{FX}^2 + (2 \times \rho_{IR,FX} \times \sigma_{IR} \times \sigma_{FX})}$$

where σ = the standard deviation of the return series for the individual markets
p = the cross-correlation between the two return series

In this example, the return series reflects the position size and volatility of the exposure. This formula implies a VaR projected period of 1 day.

For example, Bank Two holds 1 million in EURUSD, which have a daily standard deviation of 0.565%. If the current EURUSD rate is 1.25, then the market value of the position is USD 1.25 million. It also holds a EUR 1 million position in 10-year Eurobunds, which show a standard deviation of 0.605% and a market value of USD 1.25 million. Using 1.65 standard deviations to represent the 95% confidence level, and making the assumption that r_i/σ_i is normally distributed, and the EURUSD exchange rate should not drop more than $0.565 \times 1.65 = 0.932\%$ (less than 1%) on a single day, 95% of the time. The Eurobunds should drop less than $0.605 \times 1.65 = 0.998\%$ on a single day. We could then expect the approximate risk of the FX position to be USD 1.25 million $\times 0.932\% =$ USD 11,650 and the risk of the Eurobund position to be \$1.25 million $\times 0.998\% =$ USD 12,475 over the next 24 hours.

---

[7] Jacques Longerstaey, *RiskMetrics*™ *Technical Document*, 4th ed. (Morgan Guaranty Trust Company, riskmetrics@jpmorgan.com).

The total risk of the FX and Eurobund positions is not the sum of the two risks, because correlations between the two markets may show that price movement of one market is partially offset by opposite movement in the other market. In this example, the correlation of the returns of two markets is −0.27, showing that there is a noticeable offsetting effect. Applying these values to the previous formula gives

$$VaR_t = \sqrt{12475^2 + 11650^2 + \left(2 \times -0.27 \times 12475 \times 11650\right)}$$

$$VaR_t = \text{USD } 17,068$$

The value at risk for the next 24 hours is far less than the sum of the two individual market risks because their price movements tend to offset each other.

A more general calculation of VaR uses separate values for the underlying prices, the position size, the time period, and the confidence interval. For three assets, this is

$$VaR_i = CI \times \sqrt{P}$$

$$\times \sqrt{w_1^2 x_1^2 \sigma_1^2 + w_2^2 x_2^2 \sigma_2^2 + w_3^2 x_3^2 \sigma_3^2 + 2w_1 w_2 x_1 x_2 \sigma_1 \sigma_2 r_{12} + 2w_1 w_3 x_1 x_3 \sigma_1 \sigma_3 r_{13} + 2w_2 w_3 x_2 x_3 \sigma_2 \sigma_3 r_{23}}$$

where CI = the confidence interval (expressed as 1.65 standard deviations for a 5% probability

P = the VaR calculation period (5 is a projected period of 5 days)

w_i = the weighting factor, or relative position size

x_t = the current value or price of the asset on the current day t

σ_i = the annualized volatility, shown below

r_{ij} = the cross-correlation between market i and market j

Cross-correlations can be found using the spreadsheet function *correl* or can be calculated directly from the formula in Level II, Chapter 14. The volatility, σ_i, is calculated using the prices, x_i, over n days, as the standard deviation of the price changes, annualized:

$$\sigma_i = \sqrt{252} \times stdev(d_i)$$

$$d_i = \frac{x_t - x_{t-1}}{x_{t-1}} \text{ over the past } n \text{ days}$$

The square root of 252 is used to annualize the daily values.

In the practical implementation of risk control, VaR would be calculated before the close of trading and, if its value exceeds the threshold amount, action can be taken to reduce the exposure on the same day.

Generalized VaR Calculation   The probability of loss at the end of a forecast period, P_E, is calculated as the difference between the cumulative percentage loss over that period and the cumulative expected return, dividing this value by the cumulative standard deviation, and applying the standard deviation of a normal distribution to give a probability estimate.[8]

---

[8] Mark Kritzman and Don Rich, "The Mismeasurement of Risk," *Financial Analysts Journal* (May/June 2002). This entire section uses material from the Kritzman and Rich article.

$$P_E = N\left[\frac{\ln(1+L) - \mu T}{\sigma\sqrt{T}}\right]$$

where $N[\ ]$ = the cumulative normal distribution function
           L = the cumulative percentage loss in periodic units
           μ = the annualized expected return in continuous units
           T = the number of years in the horizon, where 1 day is $\frac{1}{252}$
           σ = the standard deviation of continuous units

In this process, the compounding of periodic returns results in a lognormal distribution, while the continuous returns and standard deviation are normally distributed. To calculate VaR, this calculation is changed to specify the probability, Z, and solve for the size of the threshold loss.

$$VaR = -(e^{\mu T - Z\sigma\sqrt{T}} - 1)W$$

where e = the base of the natural logarithm (2.7128)
           Z = the chosen probability deviate (for example, 5% is 1.65)
           W = the initial value of the asset

The result of this calculation gives the probability of loss at the end of the period, T, and does not reflect any losses that might have occurred during the period (if T is greater than 1 day). Losses during the period will always be at least as large as the loss at the end of the period.

A Simpler Value at Risk   There are three calculation methods associated with Value at Risk: variance-covariance, historical, and Monte Carlo. The section above discussed the classic variance-covariance approach, but most analysts will find the historical method easier to implement and intuitively simpler. In essence, to calculate the VaR for today, take today's market positions and apply them to the data from the past, say, 1 year (252 days). Specifically,[9]

1. Given n markets or assets, each with positions (contracts or shares) $w_1, w_2, \ldots, w_n$.
2. Calculate the returns for the past k days ($k = 252$) as $r_i = p_i/p_{i-1} - 1, i = t - k + 1, t$.
3. Calculate the total returns for day i as $R_i = w_1 r_{1i} + w_2 r_{2i} + \ldots + w_n r_{2i}$. Include the forex and conversion factors (for futures) if applicable so that the total returns are all in USD, euros, or any single currency.
4. Find the average, $\overline{R}$, and standard deviation, s, of R over the k days.
5. Given a confidence level specified in standard deviations (e.g., 99% = 2.33), the VaR for the current day, t, is $\overline{R} - 2.33s$. VaR is always expressed as a negative number.

Price Shocks and Realistic Distributions   Value at risk is a good indication of risk under most market conditions, but is known to be a poor measurement during

THE INTEGRATION OF TECHNICAL ANALYSIS

---

[9] Thanks to Robert Ehbar, Mizuho Alternative Investments, for his help in this section.

extreme, highly correlated price moves across market sectors. It has been said that VaR works *except* when you need it the most—when the risk is greatest. A *stress test* is used to find out how VaR performs under extreme cases. This isolates specific market periods, such as price shocks (discussed in Chapter 8), or can use simulated data in which all prices reverse direction and make a 2-to-3 standard deviation move with very high correlation, as in the subprime collapse in late 2008.

The assumption of a normal distribution in either returns or price movement is not realistic, an opinion held by Benoit Mandelbrot, among others, who maintained that using the standard deviation of equity changes underestimates the real risk of the financial markets.[10] Most return distributions are skewed and have a fat tail due to the application of conservation of capital and the unusually long, nonrandom distribution of runs. A log distribution could be substituted for a normal distribution, but this tends to be more extreme than necessary. The degree of fat tail present in the distribution can be measured using *kurtosis*,

$$ k = \frac{\sum_i^n r_i^4}{n\sigma^4} $$

where r_i = the return on day i
σ^2 = the variance
n = the number of days

A normal distribution has a kurtosis of 3, but the actual returns series might have a kurtosis as large as 25, indicating a significant fat tail. Although the non-normal distribution can be identified, there does not seem to be a simple solution for the form of the distribution that can be applied to VaR. When extreme distributions exist, the practical solution is to perform stress tests to recognize the potential risk during extreme cases and treat these as exceptions in the same way that crisis management might be used during a price shock. Advanced work with VaR focuses primarily on alternative distributions and unexpected, extreme risk.

Hindenburg Omen   The *Hindenburg Omen*[11] is a price pattern that attempts to forecast a stock market crash. It is named after the famous Hindenburg disaster of May 6, 1937, during which the German Zeppelin *Hindenburg* exploded and burned. The basis for the calculation is Norman Fosback's *High Low Logic Index* (HLLI), which is the lesser of the NYSE new highs or new lows divided by the number of NYSE issues traded, then smoothed using an exponential moving average. The premise is that, under normal conditions, a large number of stocks either make new highs or new lows, but not both at the same time. The existence of both indicates a specific case of potential volatility. Specifically, on a given day,

---

[10] B. B. Mandelbrot, "A Multifractional Walk Down Wall Street," *Scientific American* (February 1999).
[11] According to Wikipedia, the Hindenburg Omen originated with Jim Miekka, and the name was suggested by the late Kennedy Gammage.

- The number of NYSE new 52-week highs and the number of new 52-week lows are greater than or equal to 2.8% of the total issue that advance or decline that day. Note that the percentage 2.8, was raised from a previous level of 2.5 as overall market volatility has increased.

- The NYSE index is greater than it was 50 trading days ago.

- The McClellan Oscillator is negative (see Level II, Chapter 6).

- The new 52-week highs cannot be more than twice the 52-week lows, although the new lows may exceed the new highs by any amount.

- The combination of events must occur on 3 consecutive days.

Once the signal has occurred, a stock market crash is expected within 30 trading days, but only when the McClellan Oscillator is negative.

Depending on your definition of a "crash," a drop between 5% and 50%, you could expect the Hindenburg Omen to be successful about 25% of the time. Most recently, these included August 12, 20, 24, 25, and 31, 2010.

Risk Characteristics of Systems

Every trading method has its unique risk and return pattern. The difference between trend and mean-reverting systems was discussed in the section "System Trade-Offs" in Chapter 8. In general, a trend system has many smaller losses and fewer larger profits. A mean-reverting system has the opposite; many smaller profits and fewer larger losses. This is similar to the choices available with gambling strategies.

Even among trending systems there are enormous differences in trading risk. A typical moving average system, which qualifies under *conservation of capital,* keeps individual trade losses small compared to individual profits, but may have a series of losses that when combined, add up to one very large loss. In addition, trend systems fail when they encounter a sideways period, and frequently reverse from long to short and back again until prices finally pick a direction. Tests show that the number of trend trades cannot be reduced below a threshold level, even if the trend calculation period is very long. All trends seem to get caught in a sideways price pattern that generates a series of small losses.

A breakout system, the other very popular trending technique, exchanges a much larger risk for much greater reliability than moving average or exponential smoothing. When a new long position is entered at a new high price for a specific time period, the risk is defined as the price needed to make a new low for the same period. Therefore, the trade risk at the time of entry is the difference between the highest and lowest closing prices, or the highest high and lowest low for the period, n,

$$Trade\ risk = Max(High, n) - Min(Low, n)$$

Risk-Adjusted Returns In order to choose one trading method over another, it is necessary to test them over the same time period and risk-adjust the returns. For example, if system *A* had an annualized return of 15% and an annualized risk of 10%, while system *B* had returns of 25% and a risk of 16%, we would multiply the returns of system *A* by 16/10 or 1.6 to get an adjusted return of 24%. Then system *B* would be slightly better. If you are not interested in the size of the returns then finding the information ratio, dividing the returns by the corresponding risk, 1.5 for system *A*, and 1.56 for system *B*, would give you the normalized relationships.

Time to Recovery   A trading program that recovers quickly from losses is more desirable than a program that lingers at its lowest level of loss. The fact that a program recovers quickly does not change its level of absolute risk (maximum drawdown), but it will change the annualized volatility, measured using a standard deviation, or any statistic that averages the daily negative excursions.

Stability of Returns   The most common calculation of returns is the average of the individual annualized returns; therefore, if a trading program returned 24%, 18%, 20%, 15%, and 19% in 5 consecutive years, most investors would see this as an average return of 19.2%. Another equally valid method is to find the slope of a straight line through the cumulative returns, 24%, 42%, 62%, 77%, and 96%. This gives the annualized returns as 17.9% because it reflects the slight tendency for returns to decline.

A systematic way of determining if your system worked better in the past but has been struggling in more recent markets is to find the slope through the annualized returns (monthly returns if much less data). If the slope is rising or sideways, then the system is performing well. If the slope is noticeably declining, then performance is decaying; it is not adjusting to current or changing markets.

How Much Bigger Could the Risk Really Be?   Many of the risk measurements described in this section attempt to express the probability of a future loss. Within reason, many of them succeed, with VaR being the most likely. An investor must distinguish between the calculated probability and the effects of a real loss. If there was only a 1% chance of a 50% loss in a single month, then by the 50th month there would have been a 50% chance of a 50% loss. There is also a large error factor in most of these calculations because the amount of data used to find the statistics was too small. If 100 cases were used, there is a 10% chance of error in the results. The value of the measurement is also dependent upon the period in the market that was used to create these values; the risk in crude oil was exceptionally high during the Gulf War and then again in 2007. If those periods are not included, based on the assumption that they were outliers, the results will not reflect the future risk of trading crude oil.

It's Not the Markets, It's the Money

At the risk of repeating this too many times, market trends and market shocks are caused by institutions and investors moving money. When all markets move together it is not the fundamentals, it is simply panic. Under stress, investors withdraw money from every type of investment, causing them all to reverse and the correlations to go to 1.

Money seeks a safer place during times of extreme uncertainty, and this is seen as stock prices drop on widespread selling and bond prices rise on widespread buying. In 2011 and 2012, short-term rates went negative—investors were willing to pay the government to hold their money just to gain safety. No amount of correlation analysis or diversification will protect an investment from a price shock in which all markets move the same way based on a flight to safety. No amount of insightful analysis would have allowed for interest rates to go negative.

Leverage

Leverage is controlling an asset using less money than the face value of that asset (also called the *exposure*). If you bought a gold futures contract on 10% margin, then you are depositing only $16,000 to control the value of an asset worth $160,000, 100 ounces of gold at $1600/ounce. Then every price changing in gold, up or down, is magnified 10 times. If gold drops $10/ounce, then you make or lose $10 × 100 ounces = $1000. In the current volatile environment, gold can easily move $25 each day, or $2500, over 15% of your deposit. That is great when it's a profit, and horrible when it's a loss.

The consequences of leverage are readily seen by measuring the volatility of returns, and the consequences of high and low leverage will be discussed; however, leverage also plays a crucial role in both the trading strategy and the portfolio structure. Futures and options markets offer exceptionally high leverage opportunities, and some traders and analysts act as though they are obligated to take advantage of the maximum allowable. Without leverage, many futures prices show less risk than stocks. In stocks, leverage is only achieved by borrowing up to 50% of the face value of the stock, and that works best when interest rates are low. For the most part, the discussion in this chapter applies to futures. Leverage also allows you the flexibility to balance the risk of a portfolio.

Rules for Trading on Margin   A few rules should be understood at the beginning. Trading in futures is highly risky because of the leverage. Each exchange sets the *minimum margin* based on price volatility, but the investment house, or broker, often sets that number higher for their smaller customers. In addition, they may require a minimum deposit. They need to protect themselves in the event that a price shock wipes out the entire value of their customer's account and they are left making up the loss.

Commercials, those businesses dealing in commodities, can often put up only 5% rather than 10%. In some cases they substitute a letter of credit rather than any cash. In addition, they *sweep the account* each evening, removing any excess profits and replenishing any losses. There is no audit of how the positions taken by commercials offset business risk, so it is very common for these businesses to speculate under the guise of hedging. When the CFTC publishes its Commitment of Traders report, separating the open interest into speculators and commercials, those who believe that the hedge positions are offsetting physical exposure might be surprised.

Margin Rules and Volatility   The rules of brokerage houses require that an investor replenish the amount in his or her account back to the full amount if the loss on any futures position exceeds 25% of the initial margin. If you were required to put up $16,000 for one gold contract, and gold fell $40, you would get a margin call that required another $4,000 deposited by the next day. If you capitalized the account at more than the initial margin, which is the usual process, then that $4,000 can be taken from the excess in the account. Because $40 is a move of only 2.5%, it is very impractical to have only $25,000 in an account that trades 1 contract of gold. If you started with $50,000, then your leverage is not really 10:1, based on margin, but only about 3:1, based on the entire investment. The minimum funds required by your broker is negotiable, based on your financial solvency and the size of the positions you trade, but can never be less than the minimum exchange margin.

Volatility will vary across markets, and the margin does not always reflect the difference in risk. Exchanges do not change the margin requirements often, and volatility must increase or decrease substantially, and remain at that level, before the exchange governors meet for their review.

Reserves and Targeted Risk Levels

How much do you really need in your trading account to be "safe" and still leverage your returns? During the past 10 years, the hedge fund managers and CTAs have gotten much more conscientious about identifying risk and figuring out the leverage needed to target a particular level of risk. Using the daily profits and losses from a simulated trading history, the process goes as follows:

1. Record the daily profits and losses.
2. Calculate the standard deviation of those profits and losses.
3. Decide your *target volatility*. That is the amount of risk you are willing to take, expressed as annualized volatility. Typically, this is about 15%.
4. Divide the standard deviation of returns (2) by the target volatility to get the investment size needed to achieve that volatility. If the investment is too big by say 25%, then your positions sizes are too big for the investment. Reduce the size of all your positions by 25%.

As an example, Table 9.1 shows a segment of daily returns. Column 2 (*P/L*) shows the daily profits and losses trading 1 contract of EURUSD futures using a trend system. At the bottom on column 2 is the annualized standard deviation (the standard deviation $\times \sqrt{252}$). Using a target volatility of 15%, we divide the annualized standard deviation by 0.15 to get the initial investment needed for that volatility, $266,592, which starts column 3. Each P/L change is then added to the initial equity to get the running equity totals. The returns, in column 4, are the P/Ls in column

TABLE 9.1	Calculating the Investment Size Based on Target Volatility			
Date	P/L	Equity	Returns	NAV
7/19/2011	0	266592		100.00
7/20/2011	−486	266107	−0.0018	99.82
7/21/2011	−1155	264952	−0.0043	99.38
7/22/2011	1692	266643	0.0064	100.02
7/25/2011	1248	267892	0.0047	100.49
7/26/2011	537	268428	0.0020	100.69
7/27/2011	−198	268230	−0.0007	100.61
7/28/2011	−198	268032	−0.0007	100.54
7/29/2011	1750	269782	0.0065	101.20
8/1/2011	−1108	268673	−0.0041	100.78
8/2/2011	2648	271322	0.0099	101.77
8/3/2011	2544	273865	0.0094	102.73
8/4/2011	−863	273002	−0.0032	102.40
8/5/2011	−852	272150	−0.0031	102.08
8/8/2011	7164	279314	0.0263	104.77
8/9/2011	3477	282791	0.0124	106.08
8/10/2011	4819	287609	0.0170	107.88
8/11/2011	−3827	283782	−0.0133	106.45
8/12/2011	−1038	282744	−0.0037	106.06
8/15/2011	1797	284541	0.0064	106.73
Ann StDev	39989		14.5%	
Target Vol	15%			
Investment	266592			

2 divided by the previous equity value, so that a P/L on 7/26/2011 uses the equity from 7/25/2011. Finally, the NAVs are calculated using $NAV_t = NAV_{t-1} \times (1 + r_t)$. When the annualized standard deviation of the returns is calculated at the bottom of column 4, it comes very close to the target of 15%.

It may seem surprising that an average daily P/L of $1968 requires an investment as large as $266,592, 135 times the average, but one standard deviation of this sample is nearly $40,000, and we can expect to lose at least 2 or 2.5 standard deviations over time, or $100,000. That would be 37% of the initial investment. Then 15% volatility is an aggressive target.

Reserves are the excess funds in the account not used for margin or committed for other purposes. Reserves are needed to cover losses and continue to trade at the targeted level of volatility. Reserves will vary as the position sizes are adjusted in order to keep volatility stable. Most investors, as well as professional managed accounts, set a maximum risk, at which point the positions are liquidated. The maximum level of risk is usually 50%, but it can be as low as 10%. In the previous paragraph, 2.5 standard deviations of the volatility gave a 2.5% chance of a loss greater than 37%, which would be reasonable with a maximum drawdown of 50%. However, a 10% maximum would be equivalent to a target volatility of $\frac{1}{5}$ of 15%, or 3%, which would also reduce the expected returns by 80%. In the real world, the lowest practical volatility target is 6%, more often 8%.

▤ Leverage Based on Exposure

The traditional way to measure leverage uses *exposure*, the actual value of goods purchased. For example, the margin for 1 gold futures contract was raised to $9,450 on August 24, 2011, when gold was trading at about $1,800. That is 5.25% of the contract value, or leverage of 19:1. As mentioned before, a brokerage firm would never allow a customer to open a futures account with $10,000 to buy or sell 1 gold contract. A move of $25, only 1.4%, which happens often, would create a gain or loss of $2,500. If a loss, then the account value would fall to $7,500, generating a margin call and requiring replenishing the account by the next day. Each brokerage firm decides on the minimum account value based on what will be traded, as well as some assessment of the experience and credit history of the trader. For 1 contract of gold, it is likely that the broker will require $50,000, reducing the leverage to 3.6:1, a more likely scenario.

In Europe, some registered funds have leverage limits set by the government. Typically, this can be 2.5 times the current account value. Compared to U.S. regulation, this is very severe. For the gold contract valued at $180,000, the account must set aside $72,000. The biggest problem is with interest rate futures, which are also assessed at face value, although the risk is actually a function of the yield, which goes in the opposite direction. Then when Eurodollar rates are trading at 99.50, yielding only $\frac{1}{2}$% interest, the regulatory authorities require 0.9950 × $1,000,000 (face value), or $995,000 to trade one contract. That essentially eliminates trading Eurodollars in a small investment account because, as we will see in the next section on the calculation of position size, the current low volatility of Eurodollars requires a large position compared to other markets in a diversified portfolio. This risk calculation also causes most funds to choose a different method for calculating risk, such as VaR, which is permitted by European regulators.

▤ Individual Trade Risk

Risk control begins at the moment a position is entered. There are two distinct issues at that time, the strategic element of the trade, for example, the risk and reward of a single share or contract, and the total exposure of that trade relative to the investment amount. We will look at the second one first.

Position Sizing

The traditional way of deciding how many shares to trade in a stock is to divide the total investment by the number of stocks in the portfolio, then divide that portion of the investment by the share price. Then each stock has the same invested amount, but not the same risk. For example, if we were trading four stocks, Apple, Amazon, Microsoft, and Bank of America where each stock had a nominal risk amount of $10,000 on October 7, 2011, the position sizes (line 2 in Table 9.2) could be found as $10,000 divided by the share prices (line 1). Then Bank of America has a very large position, 1695 shares, compared to the other stocks. But it turns out that BAC, trading at a low price, is relatively more volatile than the other stocks and this position size focuses all the risk on BAC.

There are three basic ways to calculate the position size of any trade in stocks, given $10,000 to invest:

1. $10,000 divided by the share price
2. $10,000 divided by the dollar value of $100 \times$ annualized volatility
3. $10,000 divided by the average true range $\times \sqrt{252}$

Table 9.2 shows the considerable variation in the position size using these three methods. The upper part of the table gives the number of shares, and the lower part normalizes the shares by dividing each value on that row by the lowest value on the row. Then method 1 ("10000") shows that the low price of Bank of America results in a position size 62 times the size of the Apple position. In method 2, the annualized volatility, the results of Bank of America are reversed because the percentage returns of a volatile stock trading at a low price are unusually high. Instead of having the largest position, as in method 1, it has the smallest. Method 3 uses the highs and lows to find the average daily risk, then annualizes the value. This time Amazon has the highest risk and Microsoft the lowest. The three methods produce astonishingly different results.

The problem with calculating size for equities using a method other than (1) is that dividing the funds equally among the stocks does not work. Using method 1, the maximum number of shares for AAPL would be 27, so that there would not be enough money to buy 424 shares required by method 2, or 71 shares for method 3. It will be necessary to pool all of the money and redistribute it in proportion to the number of shares needed. For example, part 1 of Table 9.3 shows the dollar value

TABLE 9.2	Comparison of Position Sizes Based on Three Methods			
7-Oct-11	AAPL	AMZN	BAC	MSFT
Close	369.80	224.74	5.90	26.25
10000	27	44	1695	381
Ann Vol	424	246	134	345
AvgTR	71	66	1400	2033
	AAPL	AMZN	BAC	MSFT
10000	62.7	38.1	1.0	4.4
Ann Vol	1.0	1.6	62.7	14.1
AvgTR	1.1	1.0	21.1	30.6

needed to trade each of the stocks in each method given by Table 9.2. On the far right is the multiplication factor needed to reduce the totals of methods 2 and 3 to the $40,000 available. Part 2 multiplies the values in part 1 by the factor on the respective line, so that the investment required for each method comes to the same $40,000. Part 3 then divides the respective investment amounts from part 2 by the share price to get the actual shares traded.

Methods 2 and 3 in part 3 are fully risk-adjusted, but show a significant difference in the allocations. In method 2, there would be very low exposure to BAC, more to AAPL, and less to MSFT, while method 3 is very different. Which is better? The true range method is considered a better measure of risk; however, it would be best to test each method over a wide range of stocks and futures and use the average information ratio to draw your own conclusions.

As an example, we will compare the traditional method 1 with method 3 using BAC because it had the greatest variability, and apply a 200-day moving average strategy over the past 20 years. Before discussing the results, it is important to understand that a single test cannot be conclusive because the best method should work regardless of the calculation period or the strategy. First, the total P/L, shown in Figure 9.5, indicates that BAC is not a successful candidate for trend trading, but the average true range method shows far less volatility, 27% lower, than trading the same shares for each trade (this test used 2201, which was the average shares traded using the true range method). Figure 9.6 shows a history of the number of shares traded, with exposure dropping sharply from 1994 to 1996 while prices were moving steadily higher (see Figure 9.7). Position sizes dropped from about 6000 shares

TABLE 9.3 Adjusting the Shares Traded for Each Method of Position Sizing

1	Investment amount needed to trade each method						
Method	AAPL	AMZN	BAC	MSFT	Total	Factor	
10000	10000	10000	10000	10000	40000	1.000	
Ann Vol	156784	55331	793	9048	221956	0.180	
AvgTR	26241	14922	8262	53357	102782	0.389	

2	Total investment redistributed among stocks according to method					
Method	AAPL	AMZN	BAC	MSFT	Total	
10000	10000	10000	10000	10000	40000	
Ann Vol	28255	9972	143	1631	40000	
AvgTR	10212	5807	3215	20765	40000	

3	Shares actually traded after redistribution of investment			
Method	AAPL	AMZN	BAC	MSFT
10000	27	44	1695	381
Ann Vol	76	44	24	62
AvgTR	28	26	545	791

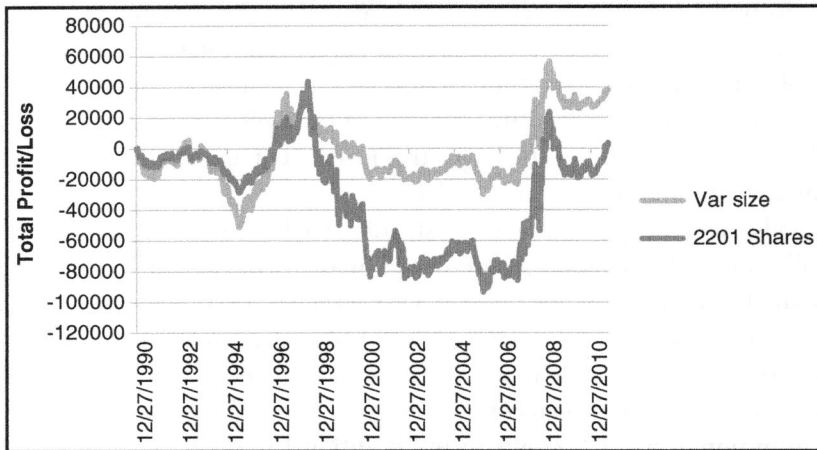

FIGURE 9.5   Total PL for BAC Using Methods 1 and 3, for 20 Years.

to 1000 shares. The exceptional volatility in 2008 did not cause as much of a reduction in position size, falling from about 1500 shares to 500 shares. Be reminded that varying the number of shares based on volatility constantly changes the amount needed as an investment, so that a rigorous test would need to define the investment size as the largest amount needed over time.

Even with all the qualifications and calculations, adjusting the position size to target the same risk on each trade gives each trade an equal chance to participate in the results. Unless you can select which trades are most likely to be better than another, equal risk is the most conservative approach. Reducing the position size when the market gets more volatility also prevents the volatility of returns from varying wildly. The price swings of the past 3 years would easily have resulted in portfolio volatility ranging from very low at 6% to as high as 25% if no attention was paid to position size.

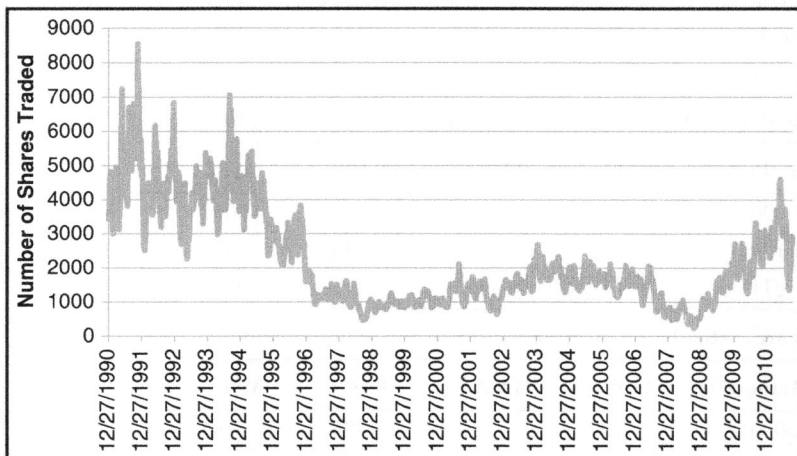

FIGURE 9.6   Number of Shares Traded in BAC Using the True Range Method.

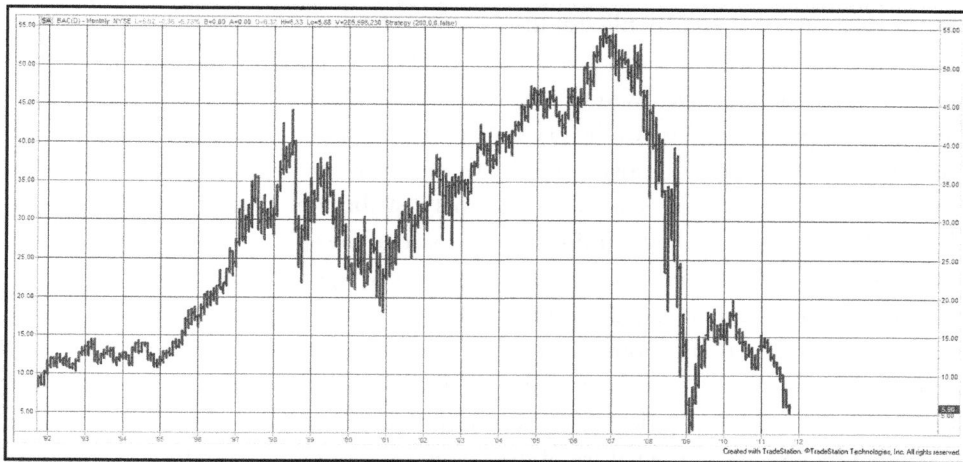

FIGURE 9.7 Bank of America, Monthly from 1992 through September 2011.

Initial Position Risk

The entry point of a trade is the time of greatest uncertainty. Systematic strategies identify the critical point where the trend should change, but when the calculation uses a large number of days, the lag may cause a delayed reaction. In the case of a moving average system, the trend will converge on current prices during a sideways pattern, at which point the trend direction may flop back and forth until prices move out of the range. The period of greatest trend uncertainty is the point at which it changes direction.

For mean reversion traders, the greatest profits are in anticipating the change in direction of prices. They must buy when prices are falling, clearly an uncertain time. They count on the likelihood that certain moves cannot be sustained for more than a few days or that large moves are overblown. There is considerable uncertainty at the point of entry.

Each trading style has its own intrinsic risk associated with initial entries. The trend philosophy is known for its tenacity, entering a long position whenever prices turn up, taking a small loss if prices then turn down, and reentering the next time they turn up. The breakout technique will limit losses to the size of the current trading range and any attempt to reduce this loss, which can be large in a volatile market, conflicts with the essence of the method. Mean reversion systems must take large losses in exchange for a high percentage of smaller, profitable trades. If losses are limited using stops, then the percentage of profitable trades is reduced, and the profit/loss balance is upset.

Stop-Losses

Stops provide the ability to control risk on individual trades. A *sell stop* is placed below the current price and becomes a *Market Order* to sell once that price is touched. Stops do not guarantee that you are filled at the stop price because opening gaps, fast markets (after an economic report), and low volume can result in large slippage. If the market gaps lower on the open, below your stop order to sell, the order gets filled at the market price. Stops placed close to the price currently being traded are hit frequently. Because of the nature of price movement, the farther away you place a stop, the less often it is hit. The pattern is very similar to a normal distribution. Using random numbers, the number of times reached multiplied by the size of the stop will always be constant. Then a stop must be better than a random event to be a good trading rule.

The beginning trader may decide that no trade should lose more than $500, and place a stop at that point. Some more experienced traders believe that you should never lose more than 3% of your total investment on a single trade. On some level, it makes sense to scale your losses to the amount of money at risk, but stops are more sensible if they relate to the nature of the system, the timing of the trade, the market volatility, or a chart pattern. Some worthwhile possibilities that change with market conditions are:[12]

1. Advance the stop by a percentage of the price change, as in Wilder's parabolic system.
2. Use a swing high or low point, based on a percentage minimum swing.
3. Use the highest high or lowest low of the recent *n* periods.
4. Apply a method such as Kaufman's *Adaptive Moving Average* (KAMA) as a stop.
5. Adjust the stop by the volatility, such as 3 times the current 10-day average true range.

Initial Stop   Because the greatest period of uncertainty is at the point of the trade entry, a stop can be placed at that time and never moved. But trend systems already cut losses quickly, and mean reversion systems need a high percentage of profitable trades, the result of holding trades that initially go the wrong way, so it is not clear that any stop-loss would improve those profiles. Under highly volatile situations, they may be a benefit, but that would need to be tested for specific strategies, and the frequency of occurrence would be small.

Trailing Stops   A *trailing stop* is one that captures an increasing part of the profits as prices move in a favorable direction. Some trailing stops advance, but never retreat, as in Wilder's *Parabolic*; others, based on volatility and price changes, may retreat. Trailing stops are usually constructed in one of the following ways:

1. *Fixed percentage.* A long position was entered in IBM at $75 using a moving average. A trailing stop of 3% is calculated based on the highest prior close. The trade is liquidated if either the trend changes or prices fall by 3% from the high point of the trade, whichever comes first. Alternatively, a stop may be a percentage of the trend value and placed at the trendline minus 3% of the trendline, forming a smooth band.

---

[12] Tushar Chande and Stanley Kroll, *The New Technical Trader* (New York: John Wiley & Sons, 1994).

2. *Volatility.* Because price volatility changes, a trailing stop may be calculated using any of the volatility measures discussed earlier, preferably annualized volatility or average true range, and placed below the highest high of the current price move. This method is more adaptable than the fixed percentage; however, when volatility increases, today's stop may move farther away than on the previous day. ISAM has suggested that a generic stop is 12 × *average true range* calculated over the past 252 days; however, this conflicts with the idea that the multiplier should vary based on the calculation period of the trend.

3. *Percentage of profits.* Placing a stop at a point that captures 50% of the profits is a sensible technique except at the beginning of the trade. When there are only small profits, the stop would be too close; therefore, this method can only be used after some profits have already been accumulated in the trade, a *trigger* value. Prior to that, an initial stop would be based on price volatility. Once the profit stop is triggered, the closer of the two stops would be used.

Standard Deviation Stop   The standard deviation is the basis for traditional risk assessment, and it can be used to determine stop-loss levels.[13] In her *Dev-stop,* Cynthia Kase uses the following steps to create stop-loss levels for both long and short positions:

1. Calculate the *true range* (TR) of the past two trading days using the highest high and lowest low of the 2-day period.
2. Calculate the rolling *average true range* (ATR) of TR (in Step 1), using 30 periods for intraday charts and 20 periods for daily charts. Note that each period combines 2 days.
3. Calculate the standard deviations (STDEV) of the true ranges in Step 1 using the same 20- and 30-day period as in Step 2.
4. The stop-loss values are $DDEV = ATR + (f \times STDEV)$, where $f = 1$, 2.06 to 2.25, and 3.20 to 3.50, where the larger values of the pairs correct for skew and allow for greater risk.
5. The *dev-stop* for long positions is *trade high − DDEV*; the dev-stop for short positions is *trade low + DDEV. Trade high* and *trade low* are the prices corresponding to the greatest profit in the long and short trades.

This method adjusts for volatility using a standard statistical measurement and is applied to the extreme profit of a trade, in the manner of a trailing stop. In Figure 9.8, an 80-day moving average, the smooth, heavier line, is shown with 30-year bonds. The two other lines above and below prices are the standard deviation stops based on the 80-day price differences and a multiplication factor of 8. That value is then subtracted from the highest price of a long position or added to the lowest price of a short sale. The chart shows that the trend change from long to short, which occurred about December 1, 2010, would have been stopped out at least 15 days earlier. In the following short position, the daily high penetrates the stop, but the stop is only activated if prices

[13] Cynthia Kase, "Redefining Volatility and Position Risk," *Technical Analysis of Stocks & Commodities* (October 1993).

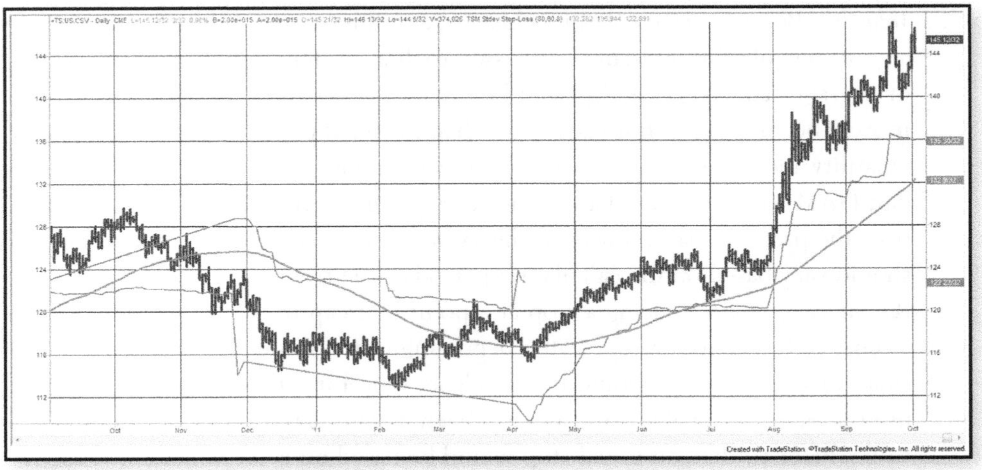

FIGURE 9.8 30-Year Bonds with an 80-Day Moving Average and an 80-Period Standard Deviation with a Factor of 8 Measured from the High or Low of the Trade.

close above that level. In the most recent long position, the stop is closer to prices than the moving average but manages to stay clear of being hit because it adapts to the price volatility. Two programs that use these stops and display them in an indicator are *TSM Moving Average Stop-Loss* and *TSM Stdev Stop-Loss*, both on the Companion Website.

Profit Targets Profit targets are points at which the system captures a profit expected to be larger than the return at the end of the trade, or a short-term windfall, such as a favorable price shock. "Profit taking" may actually net a loss on the trade if a sudden partial recovery from a larger loss looks attractive. Profit targets are essential in short-term trading, where the price noise makes it likely that any favorable move will reverse soon. They are more difficult to incorporate into a longer-term trend-following system because they risk missing the bigger profit (from the fat tail) in exchange for smaller but more frequent profits. As a trend-follower, once you take profits but the trend direction is still intact, you need to find a way to reenter that trade to avoid missing the rare, but very large price move.

Profit-taking is best when it is based on price volatility (V), and is most often calculated as

1. For longs, a multiple of the average true range or annualized volatility added to the system entry point (not the actual fill), $E + f \times V$.
2. A favorable move of $f \times V$ on any single day, or combination of successive days, where f is a multiplication factor.

While any profit target assumes that prices will not continue in the same direction, method 2 may not net a profit on the trade. A large, favorable move may occur after an initial trade loss, and the net return may still be a loss. However, if the extreme move cannot be sustained, then taking a small loss is preferable over a larger loss.

The factors used for the net size of the profit-taking level are usually arrived at by data mining. Not to be outdone, we will look at the various levels of profit-taking applied to a short-term and longer-term moving average system for 60-minute euro currency futures.

In Table 9.4 the 60-minute euro futures are shown with an 80-bar and a 5-bar moving average system where profit-taking has been applied using a factor (shown on the left) multiplied by the average true range over a 20-bar period. Once the profit target has been hit, the system waits for the next trend trade. It cannot reenter the same trend. The top line shows the results with no profit-taking. The longer 80-bar average has the smallest profits but the highest percentage of profitable trades when the profit target is smallest. As the target gets larger, profits get larger. The no-profit case at the top shows that returns were best if there was no profit-taking.

The faster trend on the right shows that profit-taking turned a losing strategy into a profitable one for factors from 5.50 to 9.0. They were not large profits, but because of the higher level of noise in 5-minute bars, profit-taking can take advantage of short-lived price moves. Because longer calculation periods emphasize the

TABLE 9.4	Profit-Taking Tests Using the Euro Currency Futures, 2002–2010							
	80-Bar Moving Average				**5-Bar Moving Average**			
PT Factor	Net Profit	% Profitable Trades	Avg Trade	Profit Factor	Net Profit	% Profitable Trades	Avg Trade	Profit Factor
None	121655	45	1580	2.738	−3278	32	−7	0.991
10.00	94405	45	1226	2.348	−3278	32	−7	0.991
9.50	85693	45	1113	2.224	−3278	32	−7	0.991
9.00	90880	45	1180	2.298	4723	32	11	1.013
8.50	86030	45	1117	2.229	4160	32	9	1.012
8.00	81630	45	1060	2.166	6498	32	14	1.018
7.50	75543	45	981	2.079	19098	32	43	1.053
7.00	68168	45	885	1.974	11485	32	26	1.032
6.50	71483	46	916	2.021	6635	32	15	1.019
6.00	63583	46	815	1.908	4448	32	10	1.012
5.50	53945	46	692	1.771	523	32	1	1.001
4.50	35533	46	456	1.508	−11915	32	−27	0.967
4.25	30608	46	392	1.437	2785	32	6	1.008
4.00	26345	46	338	1.376	−8728	32	−19	0.976
3.50	17583	46	225	1.251	−14153	32	−32	0.960
3.00	25383	49	325	1.385	−27478	32	−61	0.923
2.50	21033	51	270	1.324	−29538	32	−66	0.917
2.00	22208	54	285	1.363	−31050	34	−69	0.911
1.50	13658	56	175	1.233	−24525	38	−55	0.927
1.00	18220	62	234	1.448	−40113	43	−89	0.873
0.50	11308	69	145	1.306	−37775	54	−84	0.862

trending nature of prices, taking profits prevents the system from realizing all of the trend.

A program to test variable-size profit targets, *TSM Moving Avg Profit Targets*, can be found on the Companion Website.

Multiple Target Levels, Scaling Out of a Trade   Floor traders instinctively know how to reduce risk and give themselves the best opportunity for profit.[14] One technique that stands out is the way they take profits. Because they are dealing with trades that may last from minutes to hours, they are sensitive to market noise and realize that the size of the price move is very unpredictable. Instead of targeting a single price level as an exit point, they will often exit in three parts. For example, if you bought the emini S&P at 1125 and with an average daily volatility of 15 points, you might expect to target an exit of 1133. But what if the price reached 1132? Floor traders cannot count on being rigid about a target, so they are more likely to set three targets 1130, 1133, and 1135 to cover a wider range. If the first target is hit, they have reduced their risk considerably. If the second target is hit, they will never turn a profit into a loss. Then multiple targets, especially where the average is the same as your original target level, reduce your risk as the market goes yours way, and still give you a reasonable chance to capture the same total profit.

■ Kaufman on Stops and Profit-Taking

Both profit-taking and stop-losses are a duel with price noise. If volatility causes a sharp drop followed by a recovery, then hitting a stop captures the worst exit. On the other hand, if volatility gives you a windfall profit, then exiting that position will be a good move. Because there is so much market noise, stop-loss orders are usually based on the closing price, or, if they are triggered by intraday price moves, the actual exit is still on the close to take advantage of a pullback. The opposite would be true of profit-taking. You would want to exit at the time of the intraday spike rather than waiting for the end of day.

There is a lot of debate about whether a stop-loss improves results or simply seems to be a good idea but does not actually result in better performance. Every trader can tell a story of how a stop order was executed at the worst price of the day, or how it saved him from a devastating loss. In fast markets, you are lucky if your stop is executed near your price. Often it gets filled at the extreme of the move, where all the buyers and sellers cluster. But that does not mean that stops do not work. Some work, and some do not work. The ones that are most likely to work must adapt to volatility, such as the standard deviation stop, rather than a fixed dollar amount or a percentage of price. And trailing stops are more practical than initial stops.

---

[14] Courtesy of Barbara Diamond, the first woman trader on the floor of the Chicago Mercantile Exchange.

As an example, a test was run on U.S. 30-year bonds from 2000 to 2011, using a moving average trend strategy with calculation periods from 10 to 100 in increments of 10 days, and a standard deviation stop based on a fixed calculation period of 40 days but varying the factor from 2 to 10 in increments of 2. This produced 50 tests. Of course, we could have varied the calculation period for the stop and made the increments smaller, but then you would expand the number of tests considerably. This is only to give us the big picture.

Table 9.5 is a *heat map* arranged to see the continuous patterns. Although the tones may not be clear here, you can create the same chart using the *conditional formatting* option in Excel. The left scale is the moving average period, and the top is the stop-loss factor. The upper left has the slowing moving average and the largest stop, and the bottom right is the most sensitive. The right-most column gives the profits of the same moving average strategy with no stop. There are also averages of the columns and rows. In comparing the two columns on the right, every stop-loss average except one was better than the corresponding strategy with no stop-loss. On the bottom, every stop-loss factor was better than the average of all trends with no stop loss. By any standard, we would consider this a robust improvement. Keep in mind that this is a test of only one market and over one selected time period. Interest rate markets are well known to have trends, so that results might be very different applied to equity index markets that are typically noisy.

Risk Protection or False Hope? Stops are normally *resting orders,* that is, they are held by the floor broker or in the electronic queue, to be executed as a *market order* when the price is touched. When a price shock occurs and the market jumps through

TABLE 9.5 **Stop-Loss Test of 30-Year Bonds, 2000–2011, Applied to a Moving Average Strategy and Displayed as a Heat Map**

MA Period	Stop-Loss Factor					Average	No Stop
	10	8	6	4	2		
100	−11594	−6969	8625	11594	−6313	−931	−27875
90	10063	12250	35781	47594	35438	28225	688
80	11625	13063	33594	44688	21688	24931	4813
70	26063	32219	42406	41406	34063	35231	8531
60	1688	7844	13813	14250	16906	10900	6281
50	−10281	−1156	12750	22313	−344	4656	−8000
40	5906	13375	21375	30906	20156	18344	−3781
30	−19000	−13531	−3344	6781	7125	−4394	6938
20	33938	36156	34125	52500	44688	40281	36375
10	−1594	−813	1094	−188	17438	3188	−813
Average	4681	9244	20022	27184	19084	16043	2316

your stop order, it is very likely that you will get filled at the worst price of the fast move. So stops work as you planned most of the time, except when you need them most. It is very similar to other financial phenomena, such as correlation, where a portfolio normally benefits from diversification except during times of extreme stress.

Market Noise, Trends, and the Frequency of Stops   Because of market noise, stops that are close to the market price will get hit more often. As discussed briefly before, if we were dealing with random price data, the number of times that a stop is hit, times the distance of the stop from the market, will always be constant. Then a stop that is 100 points away may get hit 10 times for a total loss of 1000 points, and a stop that is 200 points away will get hit 5 times, also for a total of 1000 points. However, price data is not random, and the distribution implies that larger moves are more likely to change the direction of the trend. As you filter out more of the noise, those remaining events have a greater likelihood of being significant.

Proximity Risk   When many stop orders cluster around the same point, there is *proximity risk*. One way this can be seen is in a gap as price breaks through a key resistance level. Given the large number of trend-following systems, it would not be surprising to find that many of them are generating the same orders on the close, especially following a very volatile price move.

Large macro trend systems, those with substantial assets under management, may take up to 3 days to enter a trade. The likelihood of proximity risk is greatly increased, and the cost of execution could be significant.

Managing Risk without Stops

A stop-loss is not the only way to reduce risk. An alternative is to reduce the size of your positions as volatility increases. This can be done at different places within the trading process. At the beginning of this chapter, we showed how to calculate the position size based on price volatility. The greater the volatility, the smaller the position. You can also rebalance those positions' sizes as the volatility changes, although you must consider the added switching costs. That could be done using a testing platform as long as you correctly estimate and include the commissions and slippage each time you change position size.

Risk Control Overlay   Some traders include stop-loss orders based on factors other than the price or volatility of the specific market traded. They generally take one of the following three approaches:

1. *A percentage of initial margin,* for example, 50% to 70% of initial margin. This is loosely related to long-term volatility but lags considerably.[15] An estimate of long-term volatility may be a more satisfactory alternative.

---

[15] Tushar Chande and Stanley Kroll, *The New Technical Trader* (New York: John Wiley & Sons, 1994).

2. *A percentage of the portfolio value or total account value,* for example, 1.0% to 2.5%. This concept of equalized risk (and perhaps reward) across all markets is very popular; however, it is not sensitive to individual markets, and as with many stops, it imposes artificial overrides. If the volatility of one market increases or decreases faster than others, then this risk level would need to be adjusted to individual markets; otherwise, it could be reached on every trade or not reached at all.

3. *The maximum adverse excursion* determined by historic evaluation.[16] A stop is placed just beyond the maximum adverse excursion for each trade, or 2.5% of the price, whichever is smaller.

■ Ranking of Markets for Selection

Knowing which market to trade at the right time would clearly improve performance. To accomplish this, there are a number of ways to measure the *trendiness* of a market, from standard statistical techniques to more complex rules. Each method will measure some special characteristic of price movement. To take advantage of this, it is necessary to trade using a system that targets this type of price pattern. For example, if you use a correlation coefficient, r^2, to rank the trend over 20 days, then the highest-ranking markets may do best using a linear regression for the trend-following system, with a period no greater than 20 days. If the correlation is low then mean reversion would be favored.

To prove that ranking methods result in better performance, we would need to record their values in a table over various time periods.[17] For example, the five measurements below can be calculated for periods of 5, 10, 20, and 40 days.

1. Correlation coefficient, but only for values greater than 0.25.
2. Sum of the net moves, in dollars, over n, $2 \times n$, and $4 \times n$ days.
3. Slope of an n-day regression converted to a 1-day dollar-value change.
4. Wilder's Average Directional Movement Index (ADX), but only for values greater than 0.20.
5. Average of the absolute value of price changes.

Each measurement will need to have threshold values that determine when they represent significant trends. For the correlation coefficient, anything below 0.25 is most likely to be a sideways market; similarly, Wilder's ADX would need to be above 0.20 to indicate a trend. If the results are erratic, it may be necessary to smooth the last 3 days of each value. In the case of item 5, higher volatility is often associated with greater profits and greater risk for a trend-following system; therefore, it is necessary to take a careful look at how this ranking affects performance.

---

[16] John Sweeney, *Campaign Trading* (New York: John Wiley & Sons, 1997).

[17] Based on an idea suggested in Chande and Kroll, *The New Technical Trader* (New York: John Wiley & Sons, 1994).

Commodity Selection Index

Among Wilder's trading tools is the *Commodity Selection Index* (CSI),[18] a calculation for determining which products are most likely to make the greatest move for each dollar invested. In this case, the movement measured is *directional* and, therefore, should apply directly to trending models. The CSI combines directional movement, volatility, margin requirements, and commission costs into an index that allows for comparison and selection. It is the result of the following calculations.

Directional Movement

The trending quality of the market, as defined by Wilder, begins with *directional movement,* the greater of either:

1. Plus DM (PDM), today's high minus yesterday's high, $H_t - H_{t-1}$.
2. Minus DM (MDM), today's low minus yesterday's low, $L_t - L_{t-1}$.

Note that *plus DM* and *minus DM* are often written as $+DM$ and $-DM$; however, to avoid confusion in the following calculations, they will be shown as *PDM* and *MDM*.

The directional movement is either up or down, whichever is larger of PDM and MDM. It is the largest part of today's range that is *outside* yesterday's range. The value that is not used is set to zero. When an inside day occurs, both PDM and MDM are zero, and the directional movement is zero (Figure 9.9).

In the calculation of PDM and MDM, DM is expressed relative to today's *true range* (TR1), $\max(H_t - L_t, H_t - C_{t-1}, C_t - L_{t-1})$. The true range is always positive.

The relationship of the price direction to the true range is called the *Directional Movement* (DM). Today's directional movement is calculated using either the PDM or the MDM, whichever is greater. The notation "14" refers to the period over which the values are smoothed.

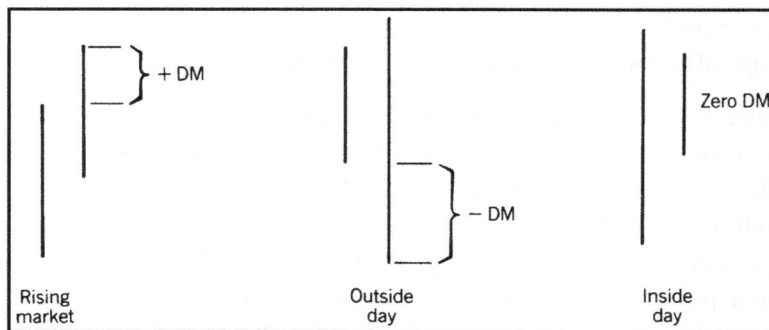

FIGURE 9.9 Defining the DM.

[18] J. Welles Wilder, "Selection and Direction" in Perry J. Kaufman, ed., *Technical Analysis in Commodities* (New York: John Wiley & Sons, 1980).

$$PDM14 = +\frac{DM14}{TR14} \quad or \quad MDM14 = -\frac{DM14}{TR14}$$

Once the first DM14 is calculated, using 14 days of price movement, an *average-off* technique is used to find each successive DM14 as follows:

$$PDM14_t = PDM14_{t-1} - \frac{PDM14_{t-1}}{14} + PDM14_t$$

$$MDM14_t = MDM14_{t-1} - \frac{MDM14_{t-1}}{14} + MDM14_t$$

The same procedure is followed for the true range:

$$TR14_t = TR14_{t-1} - \frac{TR14_{t-1}}{14} + TR14_t$$

These results can also be produced using a smoothing constant of 0.071, which is an approximation of the fraction $\frac{1}{14}$, where t is today's value:

$$PDM14_t = 0.071 \times PDM14_{t-1} + PDM14_t$$

$$MDM14_t = 0.071 \times MDM14_{t-1} + MDM14_t$$

$$TR14_t = 0.071 \times TR14_{t-1} + TR14_t$$

At this point, the Directional Movement components can be used as trading indicators; however, Wilder's interest was to use this in a more complete concept, shown in the following sections.

Directional Indicator and True Directional Movement Once the PDM14, MDM14, and the TR14 are calculated, the *directional indicators,* PDI14 and MDI14 follow,

$$PDI_t = \frac{PDM14_t}{TR14_t}$$

$$MDI_t = \frac{MDM14_t}{TR14_t}$$

and the *True Directional Movement* (DX) is the difference between PDI14 and MDI14. When an upward trend is sustained, the MDI current value is zero; therefore, the PDI14 becomes larger, the MDI14 becomes smaller, and DX becomes greater. This is then *normalized* in order to express the final value between 0 and 100.

$$DX_t = 100 \times \frac{\left| PDI14_t - MDI14_t \right|}{PDI14_t + MDI14_t}$$

where multiplying by 100 converts the percentage to a whole number, and the absolute value prevents DX from becoming negative. At the same time, the absolute value causes DX to lose the information about which direction prices are moving.

Average Directional Movement Index (ADX) The DX is then smoothed using the equivalent of a 14-day average (a 0.133 smoothing constant), and is called the *Average Directional Movement Index* (ADX).

$$ADX_t = ADX_{t-1} + 0.133 \times (DX_t - ADX_{t-1})$$

The ADX, the PDM, and the MDM are shown for NASDAQ 100 continuous futures in Figure 9.10. The heavier ADX line moves higher as the price trend becomes clear. The individual components, the PDM (shown as the thinnest line) and the MDM (the medium-weight line), indicate the relative strength of the upwards and downwards moves within the trend. As NASDAQ prices decline, the MDM remains above the PDM, which is shown along the bottom of the lower panel.

One last adjustment is made to the extreme variance of the ADX by taking the average of the current value and the value of the ADX 14 days ago. This final value is called the *Average Directional Movement Index Rating* (ADXR),

$$ADXR_t = \frac{ADX_t + ADX_{t-14}}{2}$$

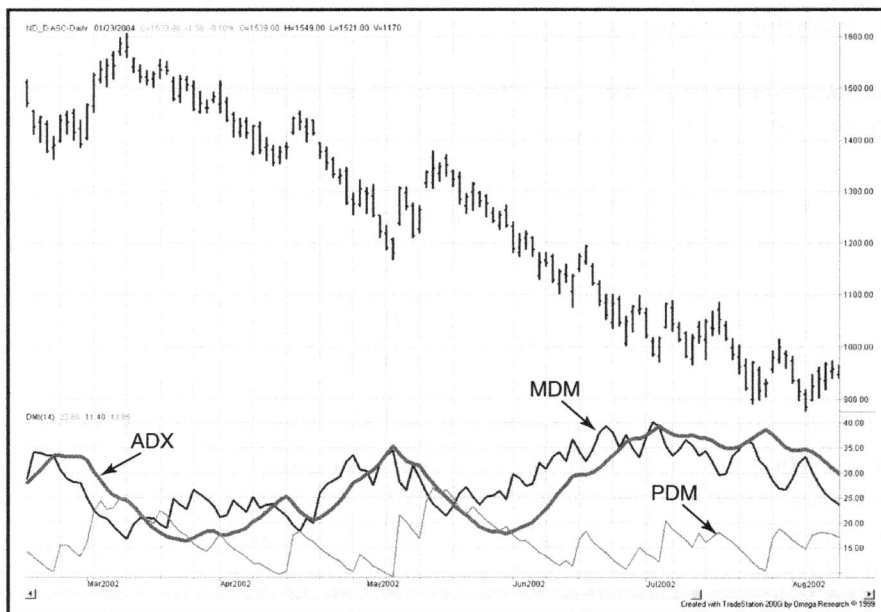

FIGURE 9.10 The 14-Day ADX, PDM, and MDM, Applied to NASDAQ 100 Continuous Futures Prices, February to August 2002.

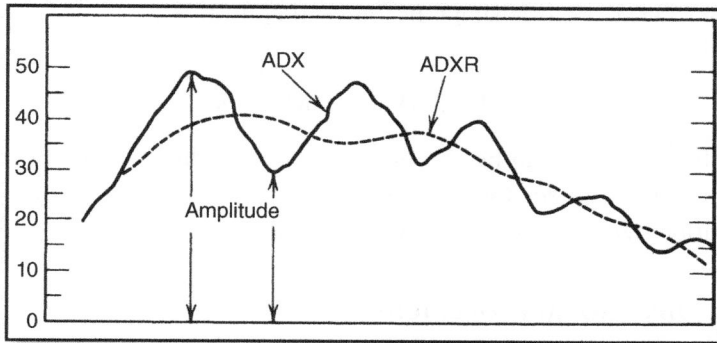

FIGURE 9.11   The ADX and ADXR.

The ADX and ADXR are shown plotted together in Figure 9.11. The ADX is seen to oscillate about the ADXR. Measuring the distance of the ADX from the zero line, a higher amplitude means higher directional movement and a stronger trend, whether up or down. The peaks are always the extremes. The distance between the ADX and ADXR is used to measure the overbought and oversold condition of the trend. The larger the value, the greater the reactions to the trend.

Using the ADX as a Trending Indicator. The ADX has become a popular tool. Ruggiero[19] uses it to determine the trend with the following rules:

1. If ADX crosses above 25, the market is trending.
2. If ADX crosses below 20, the market is consolidating.
3. If ADX crosses below 45 after being higher, the market is consolidating.
4. If ADX rises above 10 on 3 of 4 days after being lower, the market will start to trend.
5. A trend based on rule 4 remains in effect until the 5-day difference in the ADX is less than 0.

Commodity Selection Index   The creation of the Directional Movement Indicator, the different components, and finally the ADX leads to the *Commodity Selection Index* (CSI), which is calculated as:

$$CSI_t = ADXR_t \times ATR14_t \times \left[100 \times \frac{V}{M} \times \frac{1}{150 + C} \right]$$

where $ADXR$ = average directional movement index rating
$ATR14$ = 14-day average true range
V = conversion factor; value of a 1¢ move for a futures market (in dollars)
M = margin (in dollars)
C = commissions (in dollars)

The CSI can be applied to equities by setting $V = 1$ and M to the total share value of the investment. Note that for a particular futures market, or for equities, the value

---

[19] Murray A. Ruggiero, Jr., *Cybernetic Trading Strategies* (New York: John Wiley & Sons, 1997).

inside the bracket does not change. By calculating it once and calling that value K, the CSI can be expressed as:

$$CSI_t = ADXR_t \times ATR14_t \times K$$

A portfolio allocation can be chosen by calculating the CSI daily or weekly for each market. Simply select those products to trade that have the highest CSI or allocate position size in proportion to their CSI value.

Retesting Directional Movement

When these indicators were published in 1978, they were all based on a 14-day calculation period, which is why all of the notations include the number 14.[20] With the ability to test these indicators over different calculation periods, the "14" was dropped from the notation. The first study to use PDI and MDI, the directional indicators, in a trading strategy was by Hochheimer, known for his other studies of moving averages, crossovers, and channels. He defined the rules of a *Directional Movement System* in two ways.[21] The first set of rules is:

1. a. *Enter a new long position and close out any short sales* if the PDI crosses above the MDI. Enter a *buy stop* on the next day using today's high price. This order remains as long as it is not executed and PDI remains higher than MDI.
   b. *Enter a new short sale and close out any long positions* if the PDI crosses below the MDI. Enter a *sell stop* on the next day using today's low price. Maintain this order until it is executed and while PDI remains below MDI.

Hochheimer calls the first case "directional movement with delay." The second case is an immediate market entry following the crossing of the directional indicators:

2. a. *Enter a new long position and close out any short sales on the open of the next day* if the PDI crosses above the MDI.
   b. *Enter a new short sale and close out any long positions on the open of the next day* if the MDI crosses below the PDI.

In both cases the system is always in the market. Before seeing the actual results, it is possible to generalize the expected performance.

1. Rule 2 must have more trades than Rule 1 because it always takes a position when a crossing occurs, while the first set of rules requires a confirmation.
2. Because there is no commitment to stay in the trade once entered (for example, no price channel), there could be frequent whipsaws using Rule 2.
3. Because Rule 1 uses the high and low of the prior day, its entry prices will always be equal to or worse than those of Rule 2.

---

[20] For a general discussion of this topic, see Chapter 7.

[21] Frank L. Hochheimer, *Computerized Trading Techniques 1982* (New York: Merrill Lynch Commodities, 1982).

4. If the Directional Indicator gives a highly reliable signal, it would be better to enter immediately, as in Rule 2.

In Hochheimer's tests, the following parameter ranges were used:

1. The PDM varied from 7 to 20 days.
2. The MDM varied from 5 above to 5 below the PDM value.
3. Two *true ranges* (TR) were calculated, the first using the parameter value of the PDM, the other using the parameter value of the MDM.

The test data covered a wide range of those futures markets available from 1970 to 1981.

Rather than show the detail of those tests, which would be considered out of date with current markets and conditions, we ran a simpler test on directional movement using the first set of rules, varying only the basic calculation period. Tests include five most popular markets, one from each sector, and covered from 2000 through 2011. Results are shown in Table 9.6. The calculation periods were from 4 days to 80 days in increments of 4 days. While each market has areas of good profit, there was little consistency. The best period for bonds was 4, the DAX 54, EURUSD 28, crude 20, and copper 60. This alone does not satisfy our conditions for a robust system.

TABLE 9.6 Profits or Losses from the Directional Movement Test, 2000–2011

Period	U.S. Bonds	DAX	EURUSD	Crude	Copper
4	21969	−106738	30688	28350	25800
8	−13500	−22063	21250	9990	29100
12	15250	−23500	58475	−11010	17275
16	10156	−36188	15775	−3880	72188
20	13813	−75563	50625	66400	23938
24	−37281	−5038	68425	54780	37288
28	−14688	−33000	90925	−5870	85525
32	−48250	19075	86150	−10310	107213
36	−55281	−8863	61000	48230	56525
40	−54531	−45413	56350	−12370	963
44	−43844	97775	59350	−20800	38863
48	−37438	79625	37925	−28960	103575
52	−42281	−2300	37175	−81440	99600
56	−23094	129625	14125	−102380	93425
60	−32719	130600	29738	−97750	116225
64	−33031	98588	19425	−104220	68075
68	−48313	88563	−12513	−132010	98300
72	−56938	71863	−56538	−118340	95488
76	−47281	66638	6938	−63060	44650
80	−46156	35688	11450	−34950	52325

Trading Rules Combining PDM, MDM, and ADX   Most often, the three indicators, PDM, MDM, and ADX, are used to complement a trending strategy by improving the entry or exit timing. However, Colby[22] has found that using a 2-day calculation period and the following rules, the Dow Jones Industrial Averages were profitable for 72 years from 1928 to 2000:

> *Enter a new long position* when the 2-day PDI > the 2-day MDI *or* the 2-day ADX > the 2-day smoothing of the ADX.
>
> *Close out a long position* when the 2-day PDI < the 2-day MDI *or* the 2-day ADX < the 2-day smoothing of the ADX.

Entering a new short sale and exiting a short sale (buying to cover) are the opposite rules. All orders are executed on the close. The results show that a $100 investment would have returned $9,988 after profits were reinvested, which was better than a buy-and-hold strategy by 118%. Because of the strong bull market of the 1990s, this strategy would have lost money on its short sales during that period.

Ranking Trends Using Prices

Chande also created his own trend ranking based on a rolling period of 50 or 100 days.[23] His *trend strength* is calculated as

$$S_t = \frac{\ln \dfrac{P_t}{P_{t-n}}}{\sigma\left(\ln \dfrac{P_t}{P_{t-1}}, n \right) \times \sqrt{n}}$$

Where $\sigma(\ )$ is the standard deviation of the 1-period returns over n periods. The numerator is the net return over n days, divided by a volatility function. In this case, S_t can be either positive or negative to show the trend direction.

Kaufman's Strategy Selection Indicator

A market's *characteristic* is reflected in its price patterns. Some markets, such as the S&P 500 index, are very volatile with gradual upward moves and fast, sharp drops. In contrast, Eurodollar interest rates are very steady, often trading high volume at the same price. Qualifying markets by their underlying level of *noise* allows you to decide which trading strategy is most likely to be successful. Less noise favors trending systems and high noise makes mean-reverting techniques more appropriate.

[22] Robert W. Colby, *The Encyclopedia of Technical Market Indicators,* 2nd ed. (New York: McGraw-Hill, 2003).

[23] Tushar Chande, "Which Trends (and Markets) Are Best?" *Futures* (May 1997).

The concept of *noise* is of great value when choosing which system to apply to a market and identifying when a market is best treated as trending. In essence, noise is market movement that has no direction or price movement in which the amount of direction is overwhelmed by erratic up and down movement. As a simple reminder, noise is defined using the *efficiency ratio, ER,* the absolute value of the net price change divided by the sum of the individual price changes taken as positive values, over the same time interval. Closing prices are used.

$$ER_t = \frac{|C_t - C_{t-n}|}{\sum_{i=t-n+1}^{t} |C_i - C_{i-1}|}$$

ER is not the same as volatility and indicates that noise increases as *ER* gets closer to zero because the divisor increases with the amount of noise. Emerging markets have less noise and more trend because there are fewer participants and those that are active seem to have the same view of the direction of the market, or the lack of liquidity drives prices further in one direction than would be seen in a highly liquid market. But equity index markets could be a special case. To see if this process can be generalized, we compare the returns from a 65-day simple moving average system with the 65-day (quarterly) average noise. A program that calculates the average efficiency ratio is *TSM Efficiency Ratio Average*, available on the Companion Website.

Results of Efficiency Ratio Selection The results of calculating the average value of the efficiency ratio and the corresponding profit factor for a wide range of markets is shown in Figure 9.12 and Table 9.7. Data included 1990 through mid-2011, or whenever the data started. The left scale of Figure 9.12 shows the profit factor, the gross profits divided by the gross losses (a measure of return to risk) and along the bottom the efficiency ratio. Note that the range in the efficiency ratio is small because the calculation period of 65 days is long. It is not necessary to use more days

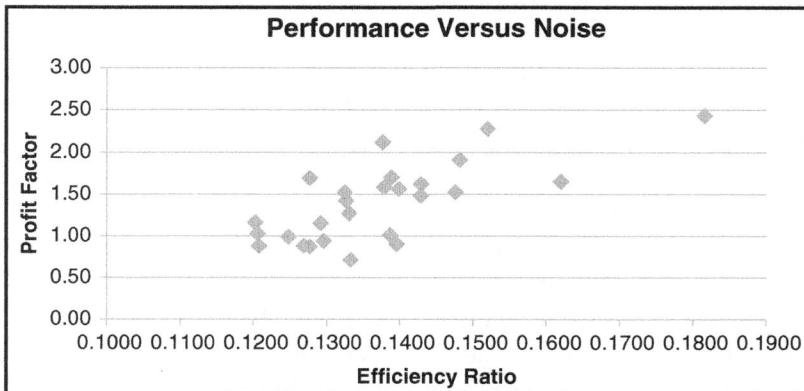

FIGURE 9.12 Scatter Diagram of the Profit Factor versus the Efficiency Ratio for a Wide Range of Futures and Equities, 1990 through Mid-2011.

TABLE 9.7	Values of the Efficiency Ratio (Noise) and Corresponding Profit Factor Sorted Highest to Lowest Average Noise	
Market	Average Noise	Profit Factor
Eurodollar	0.1816	2.43
Sht Sterling	0.1620	1.65
AAPL	0.1520	2.28
Eurobund	0.1482	1.91
Nat gas	0.1476	1.52
Euro	0.1429	1.62
U.S. 10-year	0.1429	1.48
Japan	0.1399	1.56
IBM	0.1396	0.90
Copper	0.1389	1.70
AMZN	0.1387	1.01
DAX	0.1379	1.58
Crude	0.1377	2.12
MRK	0.1333	0.71
US bonds	0.1331	1.27
NASDAQ	0.1327	1.42
Cotton	0.1325	1.52
Gold	0.1296	0.94
Canada	0.1292	1.15
HO	0.1277	1.69
Soybeans	0.1277	0.87
MSFT	0.1269	0.88
Wheat	0.1248	0.99
GE	0.1208	0.88
CAC	0.1206	1.03
S&P	0.1203	1.16

than the longest daily run of upward or downward price moves. Including more days only compresses the values, but 65 days was used for consistency. Results show that there is a pattern going from the bottom left to the upper right, consistent with lower returns when the efficiency ratio is small (indicating more noise) and higher returns when the ratio moves toward 1.

Table 9.7 gives the numbers used in Figure 9.12. The highest efficiency ratio and largest profit factors are for the short-term interest rates and Apple stock, which has had a spectacular move during the past 10 years. The interest rates tend to have strong trends based on the way monetary policy is implemented, and the short maturities track the government rates more closely than the long maturities, which include a greater degree of speculation about future policy.

At the bottom of the table are most of the other stocks as well as the most active equity index markets and grains. Index markets have greater noise than other sectors, and the grains have less long-term direction because of seasonality and their response to changes in the U.S. dollar.

Figure 9.12 shows that those markets with profit factors below 1.0 have net losses and are not good candidates for trend systems but may be best with mean-reversion strategies. Those farthest up and to the right are highly trending markets. When choosing markets to include in a diversified trading program, it is not necessary to include those that conflict with the nature of the strategy.

■ Probability of Success and Ruin

The relative size of trading profits and losses, the frequency of the losses, and the sequence in which they occur, combine to form an equity profile. This can apply equally to the returns of individual discretionary traders or fully automated trading systems. The profile can be used to determine the capitalization necessary to maintain trading during the losing periods and allow the system to continue uninterrupted trading. In investment terminology and probability theory, the level at which there is no longer enough money to continue trading is called the *point of ruin,* and the likelihood of getting there is the *risk of ruin.* The probability of the *risk of ruin* is expressed as

$$R = \left[\frac{1-A}{1+A} \right]^{c}$$

where $0 \leq R \leq 1$, and where 0 indicates no risk, and 1 is certain ruin
$A = P - (1 - P)$; P is the proportion of winning trades, also called the *trader's advantage*
$c =$ the beginning units of trading capital (subsequent units can be expressed in fractional increments)

A trading system that has 60% profitable trades and trading capital in $10,000 units will have a risk of ruin calculated as follows:

$$A = 0.60 - (1 - .060) = 0.20$$

$$R = \left(\frac{1-0.20}{1+0.20} \right)^{c} = \left(\frac{0.80}{1.20} \right)^{c} = \left(\frac{1}{3} \right)^{c}$$

When $c = 1$ unit, and the initial investment is $10,000, the risk of ruin $R = 0.33$, or 33%. When $c = 2$ units and the initial investment is $20,000, $R = 0.11$, or 11%. Therefore, the greater the trader's advantage or the greater the capital, the smaller the risk of ruin (Figure 9.13).

When using profit goals, the point at which trading would stop if the goal was achieved, the chance of ruin should decrease as the goal becomes closer. The relationship would be expressed as:

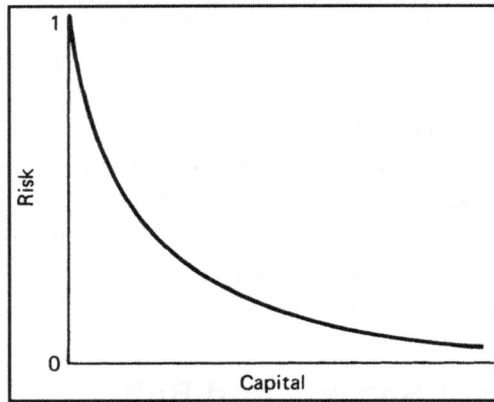

FIGURE 9.13 Risk of Ruin Based on Invested Capital.

$$R = \frac{[(1+A)/(1-A)]^G - 1}{[(1+A)/(1-A)]^{c+G} - 1}, \quad 0 \le R \le 1$$

where all terms are the same as above, and G is the goal in units of trading capital.

Wins Not Equal to Losses

The basic equations in the previous section are generally applied to gambling situations, where the size of profits and losses are the same. This requires that the percentage of winning events exceed the losing events in order to avoid ruin. Trading, however, often results in more losing trades than profitable ones and must therefore return much *larger* average profits than losses. This pattern is common to all conservation-of-capital systems, such as trend following. The risk of ruin of unequal profits and losses, including an unequal chance of a profit or loss, can be found as:[24]

C_T = the total capital available for trading (in units)
C_R = the cutoff point, where level of ruin is reached $(C_R < C_T)$
$C_A = C_T - C_R$, capital available to be risked
E = the expected mean return per trade, the probability-weighted sum of values that a trade might take

$$E = \sum_{i=1}^{N} (PL_i \times p_i)$$

where PL_i = the possible profit or loss value
            p_i = the probability of PL_i occurring $(0 < p_i < 1)$
            N = the number of trades

E_2 is the expected squared mean return per trade, the probability-weighted sum of all the squared values of a trade,

---

[24] Fred Gehm, *Quantitative Trading & Money Management*, rev. ed. (Chicago: Irwin, 1995).

$$E_2 = \sum_{i=1}^{N} (PL_i^2 \times p_i)$$

where PL_i and p_i are defined above.

$$D = C_A / \sqrt{E_2}$$

$$P = 0.5 + E / \left(2\sqrt{E_2}\right)$$

The risk of ruin is then

$$R = \left(\frac{1-P}{P}\right)^D$$

Introducing an objective and a desired level of capital L, the risk of ruin R becomes

$$R = 1 - \frac{[(1-P)/P]^D - 1}{[(1-P)/P]^G - 1}$$

where

$$G = 1 / \sqrt{E_2}$$

As in the first situation, using equal profits and losses, the risk increases as the objective L increases.

Ralph Vince[25] derived similar results from Griffin's work,[26] which claims to provide a "fair approximation" of risk. Vince's approach has been modified here for convenience and given in a way that allows a spreadsheet solution:

```
Risk of Ruin = ((1 - P)/P)^(MaxRisk/A)
```

where the following terms are defined in the order needed for calculation:

AvgWin is the average winning trade (e.g., $400)
AvgLoss is the average losing trade (e.g., $200)
Investment is the amount invested (e.g., $10,000)
ProbWin is the probability (percentage) of a winning trade (e.g., 0.40)
ProbLoss is the probability (percentage) of a losing trade (e.g., 0.60)
MaxRisk is the maximum part of the investment that can be lost, in percent (e.g., 0.25)
AvgWin% is ABS(*AvgWin/Investment*)
AvgLoss% is ABS(*AvgLoss/Investment*)
Z is the difference of possible events, (*ProbWin* $\times$ *AvgWin%*) $-$ (*ProbLoss* $\times$ *AvgLoss%*)
A is the square root of the sum of the squares of possible events, ((*ProbWin* $\times$ *AvgWin%*)^2 + (*ProbLoss* $\times$ *AvgLoss%*)^2)$^{(1/2)}$
P is $0.5 \times (1 + (Z/A))$

[25] Ralph Vince, *Portfolio Management Formulas* (New York: John Wiley & Sons, 1990).
[26] Peter A. Griffin, *The Theory of Blackjack: The Compleat Card Counter's Guide to the Casino Game of 21*, 6th ed. (Las Vegas: Gamblers Press, 1999).

TABLE 9.8 **Examples of Risk of Ruin with Unequal Wins and Losses**

	Case 1	Case 2	Case 3	Case 4	Case 5	Case 6
AvgWin	400	400	400	350	325	325
AvgLoss	200	200	200	200	200	200
Investment	10000	5000	2500	10000	10000	10000
ProbWin	0.4	0.4	0.4	0.4	0.4	0.4
ProbLoss	0.6	0.6	0.6	0.6	0.6	0.6
MaxRisk	0.25	0.25	0.25	0.25	0.25	0.15
AvgWin%	0.04	0.08	0.16	0.035	0.0325	0.0325
AvgLoss%	0.02	0.04	0.08	0.02	0.02	0.02
Z	0.004	0.008	0.016	0.002	0.001	0.001
A	0.0200	0.0400	0.0800	0.0184	0.0177	0.0177
Z/A	0.2	0.2	0.2	0.1085	0.0565	0.0565
P	0.6	0.6	0.6	0.5542	0.5283	0.5283
Risk of Ruin	0.63%	7.93%	28.17%	5.22%	20.21%	38.31%

A spreadsheet, *TSM Risk of Ruin*, and a function of the same name can be found on the Companion Website. Using the spreadsheet, Table 9.8 gives the risk of ruin for a few cases. Case 1 is the basic configuration using a $10,000 investment, a $400 average win, and a $200 average loss. The probability of a win or loss is 40% and 60% respectively, and the maximum loss in the account is set at 25%. That gives a risk of ruin less than 1%, shown at the bottom of the Case 1 column. In Cases 2 and 3, the size of the investment is halved, and the risk of ruin increases to 7.9% and 28.1%. The risk of ruin goes up faster than the decrease in the investment size. In Cases 4 and 5 the *AvgWin* is reduced from $400 to $350 and $325 and the risk of ruin also increases rapidly. In the last Case 5, the *AvgWin* is held at $325 but the *MaxRisk* drops from 25% to 15% causing the risk of ruin to jump to 38.3%.[27]

■ Entering a Position

In the equities market, most people with retirement programs choose to add to their stock portfolio as money is available, and to reinvest profits. Over the long run, if the stock market continues to rise, that method is good. On the other hand, if a systematic trader gets an entry signal, they have only a few choices,

■ Buy the entire amount at the time of the signal.

■ Average into the position (or some weighted average).

■ Wait for a better price.

We will compare these three choices, although the third, waiting for a better price, can be done at *any* better price or by applying some timing tool.

---

[27] A full discussion of risk of ruin can be found in Ralph Vince, *The Handbook of Portfolio Mathematics* (Hoboken, NJ: John Wiley & Sons, 2007), Chapter 9.

Averaging into a Position

It is not possible to cover all the different trading methods, but we can look at trend following as a popular example. We will take a small sample of markets, U.S. 30-year bonds, the emini S&P, and gold, to represent a trending, noisy, and popular market. We apply an 80-day moving average from 1990 through mid-2011 as the benchmark case.

First, consider the results if entry points are randomly distributed. That is, if there is no significance in the point at which a trend changes direction, then over time the technique of averaging into a trade should give the same results as simply entering the entire position at the point of the initial trend change.

The test will look at always entering 5 contracts (or in equities, 5 shares), spaced from 1 to 5 days apart. That is, the first case will enter 1 contract each day for 5 days, the next case 1 contract every 2 days for 10 days, and so on. The slowest will average every 5 days over 21 days (days 1, 6, 11, 16, and 21). The maximum range of 21 days would be too long for a fast trend system, so it is likely that the number of days used to average into a trade will depend on the average holding period of the trend system. This study simply looks at one trend period, 80 days.

When averaging into a trade, if the trend changes direction before the full position is set, then the loss on the trade will be less than if you had entered all contracts on day 1. On the other hand, if prices were to move steadily higher after a new long signal, then the average entry price will be worse than day 1, the point where the trend first changed.

Table 9.9 shows the results. The first column of values, *MA80*, is the benchmark 80-day moving average where the entire position of 5 contracts is set at the time of initial entry. The next column gives the results of setting 1 contract on each of the

TABLE 9.9	Results of Averaging into a New Position Based on an 80-Day Moving Average System. The Notation "5x2" Heading the Column Means 5 Total Contracts Entered 2 Days Apart.

		Total PL					
		MA80	**5 × 1**	**5 × 2**	**5 × 3**	**5 × 4**	**5 × 5**
U.S. Bonds	Volatility	53047	51559	50482	49487	48626	47765
	@15%	353646	343728	336548	329913	324173	318435
	Total PL	454375	440688	461719	429000	399844	358625
	Ratio	**1.28**	**1.28**	**1.37**	**1.30**	**1.23**	**1.13**
emini S&P	Volatility	241349	10128	46535	45284	44193	43290
	@15%	1608997	67522	310231	301892	294618	288597
	Total PL	−212375	−35175	−2950	30775	40825	51362.5
	Ratio	**−0.13**	**−0.52**	**−0.01**	**0.10**	**0.14**	**0.18**
Gold	Volatility	60732	58617	57227	56184	55289	54546
	@15%	404879	390780	381516	374558	368593	363638
	Total PL	117000	161260	179890	173950	172240	166750
	Ratio	**0.29**	**0.41**	**0.47**	**0.46**	**0.47**	**0.46**

first 5 days beginning on the day of the initial entry, The next column, 5×2, sets 1 contract on the initial day, the next four on days 3, 5, 7, and 9 (spaced every 2 days). The remaining columns space the entries every 3, 4, and 5 days, respectively. Then the final column takes 21 days to enter a trade, days 1, 6, 11, 16, and 21. The first row for each market is the annualized volatility of the daily profits and losses. The second row is the first row divided by 15%, which gives an estimate of the investment size needed if the target volatility of the portfolio is 15%. This allows a comparison across markets. The third row is the total profit from the 20-year test, and the fourth row is the ratio of the total profit divided by the investment (row 3, Table 9.8). The ratio gives a simple way to compare all results.

Bonds are a trending market, so it would not be clear if waiting to enter is better than entering immediately; however, results improve to their best point by waiting 2 days between entries. With the emini S&P, which represents a highly noisy market, results continue to improve as entries are spaced out. The waiting process turns results from negative to position. For gold, waiting is also an improvement but results seem to stabilize after 2 days. If we chose to wait 2 days between each of the entry orders, all three of the markets would show improvements.

It will be very difficult to generalize these results to all systems, even all trend systems, because the delayed entry must depend on the speed of the trend. If we had used a 10-day moving average instead of 80 days, then entering over 21 days does not make any sense. The total time to enter should be proportional to the speed of the trend or the average holding period of the trade. It is also not clear how a mean-reverting strategy would fare by averaging in, but it might also improve. Averaging into a trade removes the uncertainty of a single entry and replaces it with a more stable value. In doing that, there seems to be an overall improvement in trend-following results.

A program, *TSM Averaging In*, available on the Companion Website, was used to produce the results.

Waiting for a Better Price

A simple way to improve an entry is to wait for a price that is better than the system signal. The obvious problem is when prices give a new signal and keep going and there is never a chance to enter at a better price. Statistically, it is possible that many small improvements will offset the occasional time when a trade is missed completely. To avoid the worst-case scenario of missing the biggest profit, we can enter at the close if no opportunity has occurred within 5 days, with the results shown in Table 9.10. If no opportunity occurred, the trade was entered on close of the fifth day. There is one explanation needed. The test platform used does not post the open position profit or loss on the last trade. For fast systems, where the trades have a short holding period, that makes little difference. For the 80-day moving average, which was the basis of this test, the last trade may have lasted for many months, as it did with gold. Had the last trade been included, as it was in the previous study, gold

TABLE 9.10 Results Based on Waiting for a Better Price after the Initial Entry Signal

U.S. 30-Year Bonds					emini S&P					Gold				
Threshold	Total PL	Trades	% Prof TR	Prof /TR	Threshold	Total PL	Trades	% Prof TR	Prof /TR	Threshold	Total PL	Trades	% Prof TR	Prof/TR
None	61468	188	36.1	327	None	-44162	263	30.4	-168	None	-1580	246	32.9	-6
Min	72781	113	41.5	644	Min	-22337	155	26.4	-144	Min	12170	147	37.4	83
0.03125	71469	112	42.0	638	0.5	-22575	155	27.7	-146	1	10990	130	33.8	85
0.06250	69656	110	42.7	633	1.0	-21850	153	28.1	-143	2	14630	121	33.1	121
0.09375	69469	108	44.4	643	1.5	-22475	151	27.2	-149	3	14990	116	32.8	129
0.12500	69594	108	44.4	644	2.0	-20588	149	28.9	-138	4	14260	112	31.3	127
0.15625	68219	108	42.6	632	2.5	-22063	148	29.1	-149	5	15010	112	31.3	134
0.18750	69188	102	43.1	678	3.0	-20438	146	29.5	-140	6	15070	112	31.3	135
0.21875	70156	101	43.6	695	3.5	-18163	143	30.1	-127	7	14910	111	31.5	134
0.25000	73281	100	46.0	733	4.0	-14575	140	30.0	-104	8	15930	110	31.8	145
0.28125	71313	100	46.0	713	4.5	-14238	140	30.7	-102	9	16600	109	32.1	152
0.31250	71406	99	45.5	721	5.0	-13888	139	30.9	-100	10	12560	109	33.0	115
0.34375	72594	98	45.9	741	5.5	-11588	137	31.4	-85	11	13700	108	33.3	127
0.37500	70750	97	46.4	729	6.0	-11713	136	31.6	-86	12	13700	108	33.3	127
0.40625	67938	97	45.4	700	6.5	-11713	136	31.6	-86	13	13700	108	33.3	127
0.43750	69938	94	46.8	744	7.0	-11550	135	31.9	-86	14	14800	107	33.6	138
0.46875	69313	93	47.3	745	7.5	-10125	134	32.1	-76	15	15810	107	33.6	148
0.50000	70594	93	48.4	759	8.0	-9275	134	32.1	-69	16	19000	105	34.3	181
					8.5	-9175	134	32.1	-68	17	20890	103	34.0	203
					9.0	-9588	133	32.3	-72	18	20890	103	34.0	203
					9.5	-10250	131	32.1	-78	19	22420	103	34.0	218
					10.0	-9700	131	32.1	-74	20	22420	103	34.0	218

would show a large net profit. That does not change the effect of this rule, but should explain any inconsistencies between the results of the benchmark case here and in the previous example. The program, *TSM Wait for a Better Entry*, is available on the Companion Website. It allows you to change both the threshold and the maximum window in which the threshold will be applied.

We see that waiting, even for a minimum move pullback after the initial signal, results in a significant improvement in performance for the three markets during the period from 1990 through mid-2011. However, a different range of thresholds was used for each market because the threshold is defined as a point value. It may be worth trying this with a percentage, but back-adjusted futures prices can be distorted when the data goes back many years, so you need to be careful about using percentages.

The minimum threshold, shown in the second row of values, cut the number of trades by about 40% in all three markets. This shows that there are many trend trades that lasted only a few days, and, because of waiting for a better price, the trend turned back in the previous direction, and the false signal was not taken. The minimum threshold also turned the gold results from a loss to a profit, while it cut the S&P losses in half. It had the least improvement in bonds, which has the strongest trend. We would expect markets with a large noise component to work well with this rule, so that the S&P had the biggest improvement even though it never showed a profit. A secondary benefit is that the profits per trade improved significantly.

The need for a maximum number of days in which this rules is applied is a critical element for its success. While these results show improvements, it is possible that without the 5-day window, one exceptionally profitable trade would be missed. Even though it does not show in the tests, the possibility of that problem makes using a window necessary.

Using Timing for a Better Price

The last study applies a momentum indicator to find one better entry point after the initial trend signal. Linda Raschke's *First Cross* system used this as a primary rule for short-term trading. In this case, we will continue to use the 80-day moving average as a benchmark, and the popular RSI as a timing indicator. Long positions will be entered after the initial signal, or at the time of the initial signal, if the RSI is below a threshold level set at 30. The threshold for selling was 70. Again, a maximum window will be used to avoid missing a trade. The RSI will be 8 days rather than the default 14 days in order to find more opportunities within the window.

Table 9.11 shows results similar to the previous tests but with fewer trades. Even an 8-day RSI does not generate as many timing signals as the other studies, so that the trends reverse more often within the 5-day window without an entry occurring. The program, *TSM Timing the Entry*, available on the Companion Website, was used to produce these results.

TABLE 9.11 **Results of Timing the Entry Using an 8-Day RSI and an 80-Day Moving Average, and Threshold Entry Levels of 30 and 70 for Buy and Sell Signals over 20 Years**

Market	Total PL	Trades	% Prof Trades	Profit/Trade
Bonds	65750	90	47.7	731
S&P	−10550	124	34.6	−85
Gold	22180	105	34.2	211

From the three studies, we can conclude that these three markets, and hopefully markets in general, benefit from entry timing. These techniques were very specific, using a long-term trend as a benchmark, but the same concept should apply across a reasonably broad set of trend calculation periods until we get to short-term trading. When trades are held for only a few days, the application may require using hourly data to time the entry instead of daily data. Still, prices do not go only one way, and market noise should allow us a better place to enter a trade.

Compounding a Position

At some point, most traders find themselves adding to, or compounding, their position (or seriously considering it). Some view this as a means of concentrating their resources on those markets that have more potential. There are two lines of thinking. When a trade becomes more profitable, it is confirming its move and is thought to deserve more of a commitment than a trade that has not become profitable. The alternative, when prices move against you, is *scaled-down buying,* or *averaging down,* popular in the securities industry. In pension programs, where new money is added at regular intervals, regardless of market movement, the timing is arbitrary, and profits are entirely dependent on whether the stock market as a whole, or the fund in which you are invested, is higher in the long run. But that is not trading. If positions are not added specifically based on profits, losses, or some timing method, then it is the same as averaging into a position.

The types of compounding are illustrated in Figure 9.14. Part a shows smaller positions added, with the added size on the left and the total position on the right. Part b shows equal positions added, and part c shows adding then removing positions. Systematic traders may use a number of conditions for entering addition size, ideally,

- A sustained basing formation

- Expectation of substantial additional profits

- A clear risk level

They expect profits to accumulate soon after adding positions

No matter how well each entry is chosen, compounding will result in the largest holdings at the highest (or lowest) price; when the market reverses, losses occur on a larger base, and profits can disappear quickly. A compounded position can

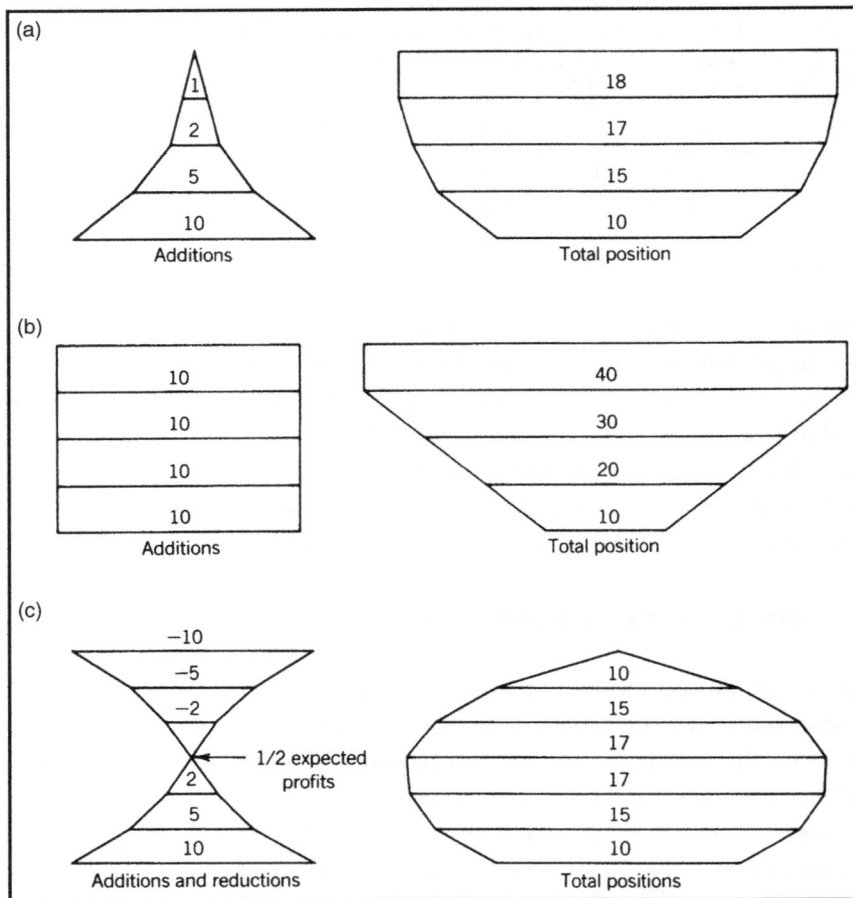

FIGURE 9.14 Compounding Structures. (a) Scaled-down size (up-right pyramid) offers a small amount of compounding. (b) Adding equal amounts (inverted pyramid) gives maximum leverage. (c) Reflecting pyramid combines leverage and profit-taking.

be very fragile and top-heavy; prices must be watched carefully for a change of direction. If you continue to leverage up with all available funds, then risk will become unmanageable.

Now consider building a position, similar to averaging in, rather than leveraging. If you plan to buy 1000 shares of Apple or 10 contracts of S&P, then you can start with 200 shares or 2 contracts and add the same amount at regular intervals, but only if you have new high profits. If prices go the wrong way, then you wait. If the trend reverses, the loss will be smaller if the maximum position was not set. Results could be similar to the previous study on averaging into a trade.

Adding on profits is not the same as waiting for enough profit and using those profits to add size. With both stocks and futures, the amount of profit would need to be very large to have enough to add, so the opportunities are small. For this method, there must be adequate funds set aside to carry the full position.

In the rest of this section, we will look at a few limited cases of entering a position in parts based on market conditions:

- Adding equal amounts on new high profits with a minimum number of days separating the entries

- Adding half the previous size with the same conditions as above

- Adding equal amounts on new losses with a minimum number of days between entries.

Intuitively, the last method should give a better entry price but might miss the move. In addition, if trend-following works, then we want the entire position set during those trades that capture the fat tail.

Adding on Profits

As with the previous studies, it is necessary to choose a trading system, and again we will use a simple moving average, but with a calculation period of 60 days. We will look at four markets, Apple (AAPL), Amazon (AMZN), 10-year Treasury notes (TY), and the *emini* S&P (ES). Both Apple and Amazon are popular stocks and have made big moves, 10-year notes are very trending, and the S&P is noisy, which gives us a somewhat varied sample. The data covers the past 20 years. The rules will be

1. Enter 1 unit on the new trend signal.
2. Enter another unit after *n* days only if the trade is on new high profits.
3. Stop entering after five units have been added.

Looking first at Apple, the first entry in Table 9.12, the largest total profits occur with the simple 60-day moving average without additional entries; however, the *Profit Factor* (gross profits divided by gross losses) improves steadily as the gap between entries increases. At the same time, the average return per share (*Profits/ Trade*) will decline because the average entry price will increase for longs and decrease for short sales. On the far right, the *Units Entered* give us an idea of how many units were traded on average. For example, for the 1-day wait, 2.62 units indicates that the average trade had 2.62 shares while the 60-day moving average would always have 5 shares. Amazon, the second set, is the exception, showing a decline in the profit factor.

The two futures markets both show improved total profits as well as higher profit factors as trades are entered over time; 10-year notes peak with a 3-day wait while the *emini* S&P peaks at 5 days for profits and 10 days for the profit factor. Overall, entering as profits accumulate rather than entering all at one time gives much better results for the two futures markets and reasonably good results for the two stocks. The program, *TSM Adding on Profits*, used to create Table 9.12, can be found on the Companion Website.

TABLE 9.12 **Building a Position on New High Profits**

	Method	Total PL	Prof Factor	Trades	Profits/Trade	Units Entered
Apple	MA 60	430.35	2.79	238	1.810	5.00
	1 Day	389.34	3.42	624	0.624	2.62
	3 Days	374.54	4.18	501	0.748	2.11
	5 Days	350.82	4.34	473	0.742	1.99
	10 Days	305.34	4.33	425	0.718	1.79
Amazon	MA 60	153.08	1.45	172	0.890	5.00
	1 Day	96.98	1.43	425	0.228	2.47
	3 Days	76.90	1.36	389	0.198	2.26
	5 Days	71.74	1.36	348	0.206	2.02
	10 Days	56.72	1.35	307	0.185	1.78
Notes	MA 60	13734	1.11	292	47.04	5.00
	1 Day	29825	1.42	647	46.08	2.22
	3 Days	30791	1.49	569	54.10	1.95
	5 Days	27700	1.48	519	53.36	1.78
	10 Days	17828	1.34	464	38.42	1.59
S&P	MA 60	22162	1.14	301	73.00	5.00
	1 Day	28875	1.28	719	40.16	2.39
	3 Days	28225	1.3	626	45.08	2.08
	5 Days	34463	1.43	564	61.10	1.87
	10 Days	30728	1.46	484	63.48	1.61

There are many combinations that could have been tested, a wide range of trend speeds, a mean reversion system, and different ways of adding to the trade. Analysts will always need to study these techniques in a conceptual framework as well as how it applies specifically to their set of trading systems.

Averaging Down

Because the practice of averaging down is pervasive in the equities markets, we would be remiss if we did not run the same test as *Adding on Profits* but reverse the logic so that we are *adding on losses*. Equal positions were added after at least *n* days provided that the open position was making new losses greater than remaining at the previous loss. There was an additional weaker test that allowed new positions to be entered as long as the trader showed a loss every *n* days, but those results were actually worse than this study.

Table 9.13 shows that Apple was the only market in which averaging down improved long-term performance, both in total profits and profit factor. The other three test markets produced noticeably worse results for all combinations of delay, given the same trend period of 60 days. Of course, other trend periods might have given

TABLE 9.13 Averaging Down by Adding Equal Amounts Whenever There Was a New Low Separated by a Minimum Number of Days

	Method	Total PL	Prof Factor	Trades	Profits/Trade	Units Entered
Apple	MA 60	430.35	2.79	238	1.810	
	1 Day	877.4	3.36	377	2.330	1.58
	3 Days	672.07	3.32	308	2.180	1.29
	5 Days	505.64	2.81	284	1.780	1.19
	10 Days	502.1	2.91	263	1.910	1.11
Amazon	MA 60	153.08	1.45	172	0.890	
	1 Day	−19.55	0.97	278	−0.070	1.62
	3 Days	65.83	1.13	226	0.290	1.31
	5 Days	70.13	1.16	207	0.340	1.20
	10 Days	102.42	1.26	191	0.540	1.11
Notes	MA 60	13734	1.11	292	47.04	
	1 Day	−7234	0.97	455	−15.90	1.56
	3 Days	7171	1.04	377	19.02	1.29
	5 Days	7000	1.04	357	19.61	1.22
	10 Days	8015	1.05	323	24.82	1.11
S&P	MA 60	22162	1.14	301	73.00	
	1 Day	−2475	0.99	456	−5.43	1.51
	3 Days	5437	1.03	378	14.38	1.26
	5 Days	10737	1.06	351	30.59	1.17
	10 Days	23712	1.14	324	73.19	1.08

different results, but a 60-day moving average is representative of the faster end of the macrotrend space and generally a conservative choice. Although a brief test, we would expect that any of the other methods, averaging in or adding on profits, are likely to yield better results. Readers interested in testing this will find the program *TSM Averaging Down* on the Companion Website.

◼ Equity Trends

Every system has profit and loss patterns that can be seen clearly by plotting its daily or weekly returns. Long-term trending techniques show that once or twice each year, there are major increases in profits corresponding to a trending market; at other times, returns show a steady decline or a stabilizing pattern.

Increasing position size as equity increases during a trending period always results in being fully invested at the top of the cycle, when losses begin. Losses will be on a larger base than profits, and equity will drop much faster than it increased. Decreasing size as profits increase will reduce risk but lose the advantage of capturing the fat tail. Similar changes can occur at the bottom of an equity cycle after a nontrending market period. A sustained losing streak may cause a speculator to reduce the investment in proportion to dwindling capital. If this happens, the result will be entering into a profitable period with a smaller investment than the prior losing period. The system must have disproportionately larger profits to recover the losses and achieve a net gain.

A classic example of a pattern in returns is one where there is a 100% gain for each profitable period, followed by an interval where there is a 50% loss. If this cycle is repeated twice each year then each year will have the following equity pattern:

	Change in Equity	Total Equity	
Original Investment		$10,000	
Gain of 100%	+10,000	20,000	First 6 months
Loss of 50%	−10,000	10,000	
Gain of 100%	+10,000	20,000	Second 6 months
Loss of 50%	−10,000	10,000	

Trading would be a great deal of effort for no return.

Some investors choose not to compound their returns, but let profits accumulate as *reserves*, also called *account excess*. Given the same profit/loss cycle as above, but holding the investment constant results in a very different equity pattern. The management of the reserves is the key to successful management. Starting with margin and reserves equal, reserves increase during profitable periods and decrease during losing ones. Proportionately more of the total equity is traded during losing phases. The results are:

	Change in Equity	Margin	Reserves	Total Equity	Reserves/ Equity
Original investment		10,000	10,000	20,000	50%
Gain of 100%	+10,000	10,000	20,000	30,000	67%
Loss of 50%	−5,000	10,000	15,000	25,000	60%
Gain of 100%	+10,000	10,000	25,000	35,000	71%
Loss of 50%	−5,000	10,000	20,000	30,000	67%

Using the natural pattern of trading returns, hold the number of positions the same and allow the reserve to increase during profitable periods; maintain the same position size through the beginning of the next losing period. When the drawdown has slowed or stabilized, the total account value can be redistributed into margin and excess according to the original 50% formula. In the next example, the total account value of $25,000 is distributed 40% to margin and 60% to reserve at the end of the first cycle. It is redistributed so that the next profit phase will be entered with a larger base than the previous losing cycle. The result is a gradual increase in profits:

	Change in Equity	Margin	Reserves	Total Equity	Reserves/ Equity
Original investment		10,000	10,000	20,000	50%
Gain of 100%	+ 10,000	10,000	20,000	30,000	67%
Loss of 50%	−5,000	10,000	15,000	25,000	60%
Redistribute		12,500	12,500	25,000	50%
Gain of 100%	+10,000	12,500	25,000	37,500	67%
Loss of 50%	−5,000	12,500	18,750	31,250	60%
Redistribute		15,625	15,625	31,250	50%

Trading on Equity Trends

It seems reasonable to think that the equity stream generated from a trend-following system, especially a long-term macrotrend system, would also trend. We would expect prices to move in a favorable direction the majority of the time, producing a chart with reasonably smooth swings. By applying a simple moving average to the accumulated profits and losses, we could exit positions when the trend of equity is down.

Using the results from an 80-day moving average applied to the same futures markets used earlier, 30-year bonds, the emini S&P, and gold, we applied both a 10-day and 60-day moving average to the cumulative profits over 20 years. When the trend of the equity was up on day t compared to $t - 1$, we used the returns on day $t + 1$; otherwise, we used a return of zero. While this is only one calculation period, 80 days represents the heart of the macrotrend system. For simplicity, only 1 contract was traded on each signal rather than a risk-adjusted position size. The results are shown in Figures 9.15a–c, and the calculations in the spreadsheet *TSM Equity Trends* are available on the Companion Website.

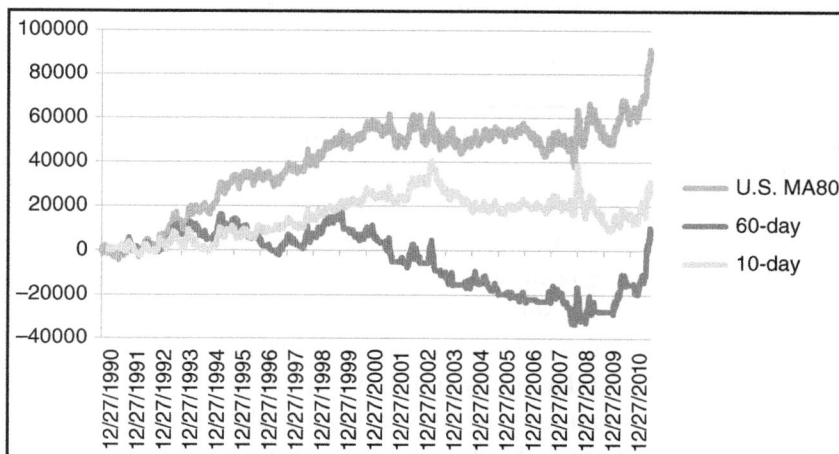

FIGURE 9.15a 30-Year Bonds Cumulative Profits Shown with a 10-Day and 60-Day Equity Trend Calculation.

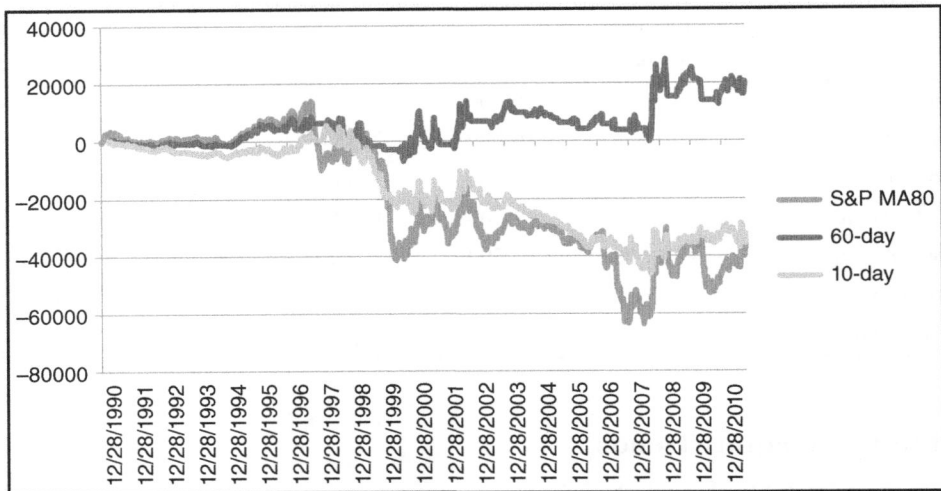

FIGURE 9.15b The *e*mini S&P Cumulative Profits Shown with a 10-Day and 60-Day Equity Trend Calculation.

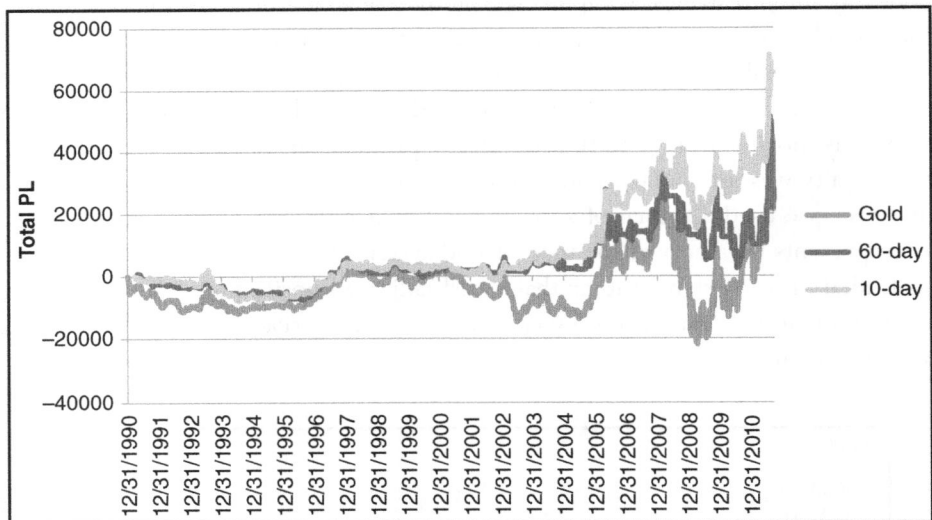

FIGURE 9.15c Gold Cumulative Profits Shown with a 10-Day and 60-Day Equity Trend Calculation.

None of the three cases show consistency, even though there were improvements for the S&P and gold using both the 10-day and 60-day equity trends. Bonds, the market with the most trend, show a significant deterioration using this method. The equity trend method also did not include any switching costs, which would be more significant for the 10-day equity trend. We can infer that this method would perform poorly on a diversified portfolio, which should have shorter periods of negative movement. Of course, this does not mean that a solution cannot be found, only that a simple approach to finding trends in systematic equity patterns is not going to be easy.

In pursuing this, you should first find out if the returns are positively autocorrelated, meaning that there is persistence in either positive or negative returns. You must also consider that applying this to hypothetical equity patterns is not likely to work because hypothetical results are always better than actual trading results.

■ Investing and Reinvesting: Optimal *f*

Optimal f is the optimal fixed fraction of an account that should be invested at any one time, or the size of the bet to place on any one trade. The amount to be risked is measured as a percentage of the portfolio size. The objective is to maximize the amount invested (put at risk) yet avoid the possibility of a loss greater than some target amount. Trading a very small part of assets can be a poor use of capital, while trading too much guarantees bankruptcy or ruin. Optimal *f* is the ideal portion of an investment that should be placed at risk at any one time.

Investing generally has a 2-level optimal *f*: (1) the part of the total portfolio put at risk compared to that part held in cash equivalents, and (2) the individual size of the commitment to each stock or futures contract within that portfolio. This is particularly important for futures, where the high leverage of individual markets makes it very easy to risk too much on each trade.

Risk Assessment

Then, how much should be invested? The optimal amount is difficult to pinpoint because you would have to know what risks lie ahead, and, of course, that's not possible.

The most extreme situation can be found by using the calculation for *risk of ruin* in a previous section of this chapter, most often applied to gambling situations in which the bet sizes, payout, and odds are well defined. When there are enough test data and trades, this technique has been applied to trading systems (see the section "Wins Not Equal to Losses"). All this depends on using historic data, which is often not a reliable indication of future price movement, which seems to get more correlated and more volatile.

Some analysts have tried to deal with the uncertainties of price movements by using a *Monte Carlo* technique in testing, which moves blocks of data, or sequences of returns, using a random process. This results in a distribution of possible risk combinations from which you can assign the probability of loss. Monte Carlo risk analysis is considered unusually severe because many of the worst combinations happen because the return series is identified without regard to possible cause-and-effect relationships. For example, a long-term trend-following technique expects to capture moves that are based on economic or government policy; therefore, sustained profits are most often followed by a reversal before the trade is ended. In fact, the size of the change of direction at the end of a trend is directly related to magnitude of the prior trend because of the lag. To move this data around so that the loss at the end of the trend comes at a different time may create a large loss without the preceding profit, a situation that is unfair to the trading strategy. Yet even an analysis of real performance is likely to understate the size of the future risk.

For an initial investment, optimal f is simply the maximum part of that portfolio that can safely be traded without any significant risk of ruin. For those investors who withdraw profits as they occur and continue to trade based on the same assumed initial investment, nothing need be changed unless exceptionally high risk requires a decrease in the amount of leverage. However, it is more common—and more complicated—for the investor to vary the amount committed to the market by either increasing or decreasing leverage. This involves (1) determining the right time to change the leverage, (2) calculating the amount to increase the investment when there are profits, and (3) figuring the size of the reduction when there are losses exceeding some designated amount. These are issues that are addressed by optimal f.

Finding Optimal f

Ralph Vince, in his popular book *Portfolio Management Formulas*,[28] focuses on optimal f, risk of ruin, and other practical items. The significance of this approach is the need to maximize the amount invested yet avoid the risk of ruin. Optimal f is the ideal amount of an investment that should be put at risk at any one time. First, we need to know what percentage gain is required to recover a percentage loss.

$$Required\ gain = \frac{1}{1 - Percent\ loss} - 1$$

That is, a 50% loss requires a 100% gain to restore the original value. Because the amount risked on each trade depends on our expectations of loss, the results obtained from the optimal f calculation will be the size of the bet, the invested amount, or the number of futures contracts to be traded, as a percentage of the maximum loss. The value used as a maximum loss will be an estimate, because losses can always be greater than those already experienced in the market, or those found by historic testing. In addition, the optimal f will be different for each system, depending upon its performance profile.

The mathematics needed to determine optimal f is based on the Kelly Betting System.[29] Kelly states that the optimum bet is the one that maximizes the growth function $G(f)$:

$$G(f) = P \times \ln(1 + B \times f) + (1 - P) \times \ln(1 - f)$$

---

[28] Ralph Vince, *Portfolio Management Formulas* (New York: John Wiley & Sons, 1990), 79–86. Also see Ralph Vince, *The Handbook of Portfolio Mathematics* (Hoboken, NJ: John Wiley & Sons, 2007), Chapters 4 and 5.

[29] John L. Kelly, Jr., "Kelly Betting System," *Bell System Technical Journal* (July 1956). Kelly's own method began with the optimal bet size based on unequal payouts as $p - (1 - p)/r$, where p is the probability of winning and r is the win/loss payout ratio.

where f = the optimum fixed fraction
  P = the probability of a winning bet or trade
  B = the ratio of the average winning return to the average losing return
  ln = the natural log function

The solution for finding the optimal fixed fraction to invest uses the geometric product and geometric mean, which represent the way in which profits and losses accrue.

$$Optimal\ f = \max\left(\prod_{i=1}^{n}\left(1+\frac{f\times(-R_i)}{Largest\ loss}\right)\right)^{1/n}, \quad for\ f = 0.01\,to\,1.0$$

where max = the function that returns the maximum value
  $\prod$ = the product function
  R_i = the series of individual trade returns
  n = the number of trades

By testing values of f between 0.01 and 1.0, and finding the geometric mean of all trades (each percentage profit or loss applied to the account value before the current trade), the value of f is found that gives the best return. That f-value is the optimal f, the percentage of the total account that should be invested for each trade. Another way of expressing optimal f, is given as[30]

$$f = [p \times (PLR + 1) - 1] / PLR$$

where PLR = the ratio of average profit to average loss
  p = the probability of a winning trade

Therefore, if $p = 0.50$, there is an equal chance of a profit or a loss, and the average profit is $400 while the average loss is $200 (giving $PLR = 2.0$), then $f = (0.50(2 + 1) - 1)/2 = 0.5/2 = 0.25$ or 25% of the available capital. Given an equal chance of a profit or a loss, it is not likely that there would be 4 losses in a row, each of 25%; however, the theory of runs shows that, out of every 100 trades, there should be one run of 6. Eventually, there will be a run of 4 or 5 losses in a row. Optimal f, however, invests a fraction of the current equity; therefore, after a loss of 25%, the next investment is 25% of the balance, or 18.75% of the initial equity. If there are further losses, that amount drops to 14.06%. After three losses in a row, instead of having lost 75% of the initial equity, the investment has only dropped by 57.81%. Over time, with profits twice as large as losses, and winning trades alternating normally with losing trades, the losses will be recovered.

---

[30] Robert P. Rotella, *The Elements of Successful Trading* (New York: The New York Institute of Finance, 1992), 549–550.

Observations of Optimal *f*

According to Alex Elder,[31] there are some difficulties in using optimal *f*. Because the value is based on every historic trade, the ideal amount to invest on the next trade will keep changing. In addition, if you trade a position larger than determined by optimal *f*, and get average results, you can expect to go broke eventually because you are overinvesting. On the other hand, if you invest less than the optimal amount, then your risk decreases arithmetically, but your profits decrease geometrically, which is another bad scenario. Because this is too complicated for most investors, the simple solution is to keep trading the same amount, with a reserve sufficiently large to absorb most extreme, adverse price moves.

On the positive side, Dr. Elder concludes that the most useful result of optimal *f* is that it shows the trader to:

- Never average down.

- Never meet margin calls.

- Liquidate the worst position first.

The application of optimal *f* uses the end value of individual trades, somewhat similar to the payout of a bet, while trades are comprised of many days of individual returns. The drawdown during a trade could be much larger than the final outcome of that trade. Then there is more risk than can be seen using only the final trader result.

Markowitz also took a look at this problem in 1959, with the following approximation:

$$Expected\ log\ return = Expected\ return - \tfrac{1}{2}\ Variance\ of\ returns$$

Using an amount of leverage *M*, the log returns becomes:

$$Expected\ leveraged\ log\ returns = M \times Expected\ return - \tfrac{1}{2}\ M^2\ Variance\ of\ returns$$

then

$$Optimal\ leverage = Returns / Variance = \mu / \sigma^2$$

As with other methods, this depends on the future being the same as the past. Because of the uncertainty, it may be best to consider using these methods only to reduce leverage, not increase it. Traders should measure success in terms of a return-to-risk ratio.

■ Comparing Expected and Actual Results

In the development of an economic model or trading system, the final selection, as well as the choices made along the way, are based on comparing the results of one method with another. Often the results are given in terms of information ratios,

---
[31] Dr. Alexander Elder, *Trading for a Living* (New York: John Wiley & Sons, 1995).

profit/loss ratios, annualized percentage profits, expected reliability, and drawdown ratios. Although these statistics are common, their predictive qualities and sometimes their accuracy are not known. On occasion, these results are generated by a sample that is too small; usually they are not the results of actual performance but an historic test. This does not mean that the model will be unsuccessful, but that the pattern of success might vary far from expectations. In actual trading, everyone experiences a series of losses far exceeding the maximum level that was expected; at that point, it is best to know whether this situation could occur within the realm of the system's profile or whether the system has failed. For example, a moving-average system is expected to have about 33% profitable trades with an average profit to average loss ratio of 4:1. But the first 10 trades of the system are losers. Should trading be stopped?[32]

Binomial Probability

Consider the application of a random-number sequence to the trading model. What is the probability of *l* losses in *n* trades when the probability of a loss is *p?* Most of the work in this area of probability is credited to Bernoulli, whose study of a random walk is called a *Bernoulli process.* A clear representation of a random walk is shown by Pascal's triangle (Figure 9.16), where each box represents the probability of being in a particular position at a specific time in a forward random walk. The result of this process is called a *binomial distribution.*

The forward random walk has an analogy to price movement, with the far edges of Pascal's triangle showing the probability of a continuous sequence of wins or losses using random numbers. The sequence $\frac{1}{2}, \frac{1}{4}, \frac{1}{8}, \ldots, (\frac{1}{2})^n$ is exactly the same as in the discussion of the Theory of Runs. The probability of successive losses can be calculated as the likelihood of a run of the same length, $(\frac{1}{2})^{n+2}$.

A binomial distribution is useful in considering the total number of losses that can occur in any order within a sequence of trades; it is the probability of getting to a

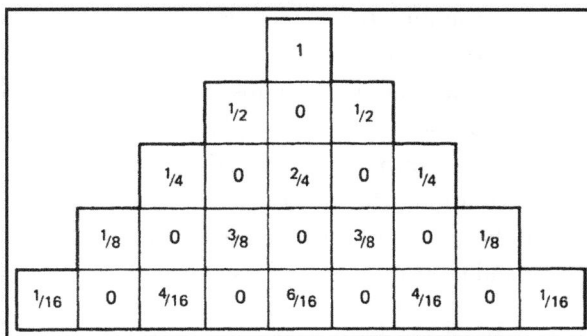

FIGURE 9.16 Pascal's Triangle.

---

[32] Another technique, the probability of a drawdown was discussed in Chapter 7, in the section "Is the Model Broken?"

specific point at the base of Pascal's triangle when there is a high probability of moving to the left (losses) rather than the right (profits). The formula for the binomial probability is:

$$B(l:p,n) = \frac{n!}{l!(n-l)!} p^l (1-p)^{n-l}$$

where $l =$ the number of losses
$n =$ the total number of tries
$p =$ the probability of a loss

and the symbol "!" is the *factorial* (e.g., $5! = 5 \times 4 \times 3 \times 2 \times 1$).

Consider the first 5 trades of a system with a probability of success of $1/3$. How many losses should be expected? To answer the question, it must be phrased differently. In this case, what is the probability of having 4 losses out of the first 5 trades? Let $l = 4$ and find the binomial probability B for all possibilities based on a normal distribution function. Then,

$$B(4:0.667,5)\frac{5!}{4!1!} \times (0.667)^4 \times (0.333)^1$$

$$= \frac{120}{24} \times (0.19792) \times (0.333)$$

$$= 5 \times 0.659 = 0.32954$$

The binomial probability of having 4 losses out of the first 5 trades is about 33%. Table 9.14 shows the probability of loss for the first 5, 10, and 15 trades of a system with a $\frac{1}{3}$ predicted reliability. Results show the highest probability of loss is at the $\frac{1}{3}$ point (mean) for each sequence, but the standard deviation gives the range of variance about the mean, so that from 2.3 to 4.4 losses are expected in every 5 trades, 5.2 to 8.2 in 10 trades, and 8.2 to 11.8 losses in 15 trades.

Note that in the 5-trade example, the chance of no loss is only 1% and there is a 13% chance of all losses. For the purpose of evaluation, it is easier to look at the maximum rather than the minimum number of losses. For 15 trades, there is an 8% chance of 13 or more losses; if the system has produced more than 12 losses in that period, there may be something wrong with the trading method.

Instead of the Pascal distribution, which is normal, the Poisson and various skewed distribution functions will be more appropriate for trading performance. It is well known that price changes and their returns have a skewed distribution with a fat tail.

χ^2—Chi-Square Test

Once a system has been traded and there is enough data to give a performance profile, a simple correlation between these actual results and the expected results can be found using the *chi-square test*. The sample error, $1/\sqrt{N}$, will tell you if there is enough data.

TABLE 9.14 The Probability of a Specific Number of Losses

5 Trades		10 Trades		15 Trades	
Losses	Probability (%)	Losses	Probability (%)	Losses	Probability (%)
0	1	0	0	0	0
1	4	1	0	1	0
2	16	2	0	2	0
3	33	3	2	3	0
4	33	4	5	4	0
5	13	5	14	5	1
		6	23	6	2
		7	26	7	6
		8	19	8	11
		9	9	9	18
		10	2	10	21
				11	20
				12	13
				13	6
				14	2
				15	0

$m = \frac{1}{3}$ $m = 6\frac{2}{3}$ $m = 10$

$sd = 1.05$ $sd = 1.5$ $sd = 1.825$

m = Mean.
sd = Standard deviation.

Assume that the real trading results show a reliability of 20% (1 out of 5 profitable trades) as compared to the expected reliability of 35%. What are the chances of getting the expected results? The chi-square test is

$$\chi^2 = \frac{(O-E)^2}{E}$$

where O = the observed or actual result
         E = the expected or theoretical result.

then,

$$\chi^2 = \frac{(20-35)^2}{35} + \frac{(80-65)^2}{65}$$
$$= \frac{(-15)^2}{35} + \frac{(-15)^2}{65}$$
$$= \frac{225}{35} + \frac{225}{65} = 6.428 + 3.46$$
$$= 9.89$$

The percentage of actual winning trades is compared with the anticipated winning trades and the losing trades with the expected losing trades. The answer must be found in the first row of Table 9.15, which gives the distribution of χ^2.

The probability is distributed unequally in the table because the results are only significant if the probability is small, showing less likelihood of the results occurring by chance. For this simple 2-element test, the result P is classified as

Highly significant   if $P \geq 10.83$ (0.1% or $1/1000$)
Significant   if $P \geq 6.64$ (1% or $1/100$)
Probably significant   if $P \geq 3.84$ (5% or $1/20$)

The answer $\chi^2 = 9.89$ is between 0.1% and 1.0%, which shows *significance*. For a large sample, the actual reliability should not have been 20% when 35% was expected.

The chi-square test can be used to compare actual price movement with random patterns to see whether there is appreciable variation. Based on the expected number of runs, discussed earlier in the section "Gambling Techniques—The Theory of Runs" in Chapter 8, Table 9.16 shows the difference between the expected runs of a random series compared to the actual runs of a price series.

Applying the actual data for runs of 1 through 8 against a random distribution, based on Table 9.16,

$$\chi^2 = \sum_{i=1}^{8} \frac{(O_i - E_i)^2}{E_i}$$

$$= \frac{(1214-1225)^2}{1225} + \frac{(620-612)^2}{612} + \frac{(311-306)^2}{306} + \frac{(167-153)^2}{152}$$

$$+ \frac{(67-77)^2}{77} + \frac{(41-38)^2}{38} + \frac{(16-19)^2}{19} + \frac{(13-19)^2}{19}$$

$$\overset{(1)}{= 0.09877} + \overset{(2)}{0.10457} + \overset{(3)}{0.08169} + \overset{(4)}{1.2810} + \overset{(5)}{1.2987}$$

$$\overset{(6)}{+ 0.23684} + \overset{(7)}{0.47368} + \overset{(8)}{1.8947}$$

$$= 5.470$$

From Table 9.15, the probability can be found in row 7 to be between 50% and 70% for 8 cases. These results are not significant; the Theory of Runs shows that all cases taken together give the same patterns as chance movement. Individual runs or sets of 2 or 3 adjacent runs can be inspected for distortion. In both cases, the results are further from normal but not mathematically significant. The two runs that differed the most were 4 to 5 days, which showed an 11% probability of occurring by chance.

Highly significant price runs can be found in the occurrence of extended runs, for example, 20 days, which is found occasionally in trending markets. By looking at the *asymmetry* of price movement, where a reverse run of 1 day is of negligible value, the

TABLE 9.15   Distribution of χ2

Cases Less	Probability of Occurring by Chance								
1	.70	.50	.30	.20	.10	.05	.02	.01	.001
1	.15	.46	1.07	1.64	2.71	3.84	5.41	6.64	10.83
2	.71	1.39	2.41	3.22	4.61	5.99	7.82	9.21	13.82
3	1.42	2.37	3.67	4.64	6.25	7.82	9.84	11.34	16.27
4	2.20	3.36	4.88	5.99	7.78	9.49	11.67	13.28	18.47
5	3.00	4.35	6.06	7.29	9.24	11.07	13.39	15.09	20.52
6	3.83	5.35	7.23	8.56	10.65	12.59	15.03	16.81	22.46
7	4.67	6.35	8.38	9.80	12.02	14.07	16.62	18.48	24.32
8	5.53	7.34	9.52	11.03	13.36	15.51	18.17	20.09	26.13
9	6.39	8.34	10.66	12.24	14.68	16.92	19.68	21.67	27.88
10	7.27	9.34	11.78	13.44	15.99	18.31	21.16	23.21	29.59

TABLE 9.16   Results from Analysis of Runs

Expected Length of Run	Actual Results (E)	Results (O)
1	1225	1214
2	612	620
3	306	311
4	153	167
5	77	67
6	38	41
7	19	16
8	10	5
9	5	3
≥ 10	4	5
≥ 8*	19	13

*The last groups were combined in order not to distort the results based on a small sample.

significance of these runs will dramatically increase. Price movement is not a simple matter of random runs and equal payout.

Yates Correction   Frank Yates, an English statistician, determined that the chi-square test often overestimates the significance for small amounts of data (under 5 data points). This can be corrected by subtracting 0.5 from the difference between each observed value and the expected value,

$$\chi^2_{Yates} = \sum_{i=1}^{N} \frac{\left(\left|O_i - E_i\right| - 0.5\right)^2}{E_i}$$

It should be noted that using a small number of data points is unreliable at best.

CHAPTER 10

Regression

From Markos Katsanos, *Intermarket Trading Strategies* (Hoboken, New Jersey: John Wiley & Sons, 2008), Chapter 3.

Man loves company, even if only that of a small burning candle.

–Georg Christoph Lichtenberg

Learning Objective Statements

- Identify the assumptions of regression
- Differentiate between data from a linear regression and data from a multiple regression

Regression involves the use of the concept of correlation in predicting future values of one security (dependent variable), in terms of another (independent or predictor variable). For example, if there is high correlation between the S&P 500 and the Euro Stoxx 50 index we can use the linear regression equation to predict future values of the S&P by extending the least squares or linear regression line into the future.

The mere fact that we use our knowledge of the relationship between the two indices to predict values of the S&P 500 from the Euro Stoxx doesn't imply that changes in the Euro Stoxx cause changes in the S&P. These could be caused by a number of economic or geopolitical reasons which affect both indices.

▨ 10.1 The Regression Equation

The general form of a simple linear regression is:

$$y = bx + a \tag{10.1}$$

where a (regression constant) is the intercept and b (regression coefficient) is the slope of the line, y is the dependent variable and x is the independent variable. Estimates for the values of a and b can be derived by the method of ordinary least squares. The method is called "least squares" because estimates of a and b minimize the sum of squared error estimates for the given data set. The regression constant a and the coefficient b are calculated using the following formulae:

$$b = \frac{\sum (x_i - \overline{x})(y_i - \overline{y})}{\sum (x_i - \overline{x})^2} = \frac{n \sum xy - \sum x \sum y}{n \sum x^2 - \left(\sum x\right)^2} \tag{10.2}$$

$$a = \frac{\sum y - b \sum x}{n} = \overline{y} - b\overline{x} \tag{10.3}$$

where $\overline{x}$ is the mean of the x values, and $\overline{y}$ is the mean of the y values.

The formula for the regression coefficient b can be alternatively expressed in terms of Pearson's correlation coefficient r:

$$b = r\frac{s_y}{s_x} \tag{10.4}$$

where s_x is the standard deviation of the predictor variable x and s_y is the standard deviation of the dependent variable y.

Table 10.1 shows an Excel sheet of one day changes between gold and the dollar index, illustrating the calculation of the regression coefficient and the constant.

Thus the regression equation to predict the dollar index in terms of gold is Y (dollar) $= -0.314 * X$ (gold) $+ 0.083$

In the following example only 15 data sets were used but in practice more than two years' data need to be taken into account for a reliable prediction.

■ 10.2 Multiple Regression

The concept of linear regression with a single predictor variable can be extended for more than one variable combined into the following equation:

$$y = b_1 x_1 + b_1 x_1 + \ldots + b_k x_k + a \tag{10.5}$$

In single regression we fitted a straight line to the scatterplot of points in a two dimensional graph. Extending this concept, the geometry of multiple regression (where two or more predictor variables are involved), would involve fitting a plane in multi-dimensional space (Figure 10.1).

However, since we live in a three-dimensional world, we cannot visualize the geometry when more than two independent variables are involved. We can extend, however, the same method only mathematically.

The practical problem in multiple linear regression is to select an effective set of predictor variables which will maximize the coefficient of determination, r squared, which is the proportion of variance in the dependent variable that can be explained by the variance of the predictor variables. Therefore, we want to include predictor variables that are highly correlated with the dependent variable but have low correlations among themselves.

As a rule of thumb, intercorrelation among the independents above 0.80 signals a possible problem and may cause the system to become unstable. The statistically

TABLE 10.1 Example of Calculating the Regression Coefficient b and the Intercept a Using Excel. The formula for calculating the other statistical metrics can be found in Table 13.2 (Level II, Chapter 13). The Greek letter μ depicts the mean for both the X and Y variables. The variables X and Y are the one day percentage change of gold (spot) and the dollar index respectively from 8 December 2006 to 29 December 2006.

A	B	C	D	E	F	G	H	1
Date	X	Y	X − μ	(X − μ)²	X − μ	(Y − μ)²	(X − μ)(Y − μ)	2
12/8/06	−1.344	0.640	−1.386	1.921	0.570	0.325	−0.790	3
12/11/06	0.929	−0.132	0.887	0.787	−0.202	0.041	−0.179	4
12/12/06	−0.008	−0.289	−0.050	0.003	−0.359	0.129	0.018	5
12/13/06	−0.325	0.470	−0.367	0.135	0.400	0.160	−0.147	6
12/14/06	−0.430	0.444	−0.472	0.223	0.374	0.140	−0.176	7
12/15/06	−1.664	0.406	−1.706	2.910	0.336	0.113	−0.573	8
12/18/06	0.163	−0.036	0.121	0.015	−0.106	0.011	−0.013	9
12/19/06	1.088	−0.667	1.046	1.094	−0.737	0.543	−0.771	10
12/20/06	−0.402	0.096	−0.444	0.197	0.026	0.001	−0.011	11
12/21/06	−0.250	0.072	−0.292	0.085	0.002	0.000	−0.001	12
12/22/06	0.332	0.263	0.290	0.084	0.193	0.037	0.056	13
12/26/06	0.613	0.298	0.571	0.326	0.228	0.052	0.130	14
12/27/06	0.401	−0.107	0.359	0.129	−0.177	0.031	−0.064	15
12/28/06	1.133	−0.179	1.091	1.190	−0.249	0.062	−0.272	16
12/29/06	0.394	−0.227	0.352	0.124	−0.297	0.088	−0.105	17

(Continued)

TABLE 10.1 *(Continued)*

A	B	C	D	E	F	G	H	1	2
Date	X	Y	X − μ	(X − μ)²	X − μ	(Y − μ)²	(X − μ)(Y − μ)		
Σ	0.630	1.052		9.223		1.733	−2.897	18	
n	15	15		Covariance σ_{xy} =			−0.207	19	
mean μ	0.042	0.070		Pearson's Correlation **r**			−0.725	20	
σ	0.812	0.352		Regression Coef. b (formula 3.2)			−0.314	21	
				Regression Coef. b (formula 3.4)			−0.314	22	
				Regression Constant a =			0.083	23	
				Regression Constant a =			0.083	21	

Formula for Column H

Row	
21	H18/E18
22	H20*C21/B21
23	(C18-H21*B18)/B19
24	C20-H22*B20

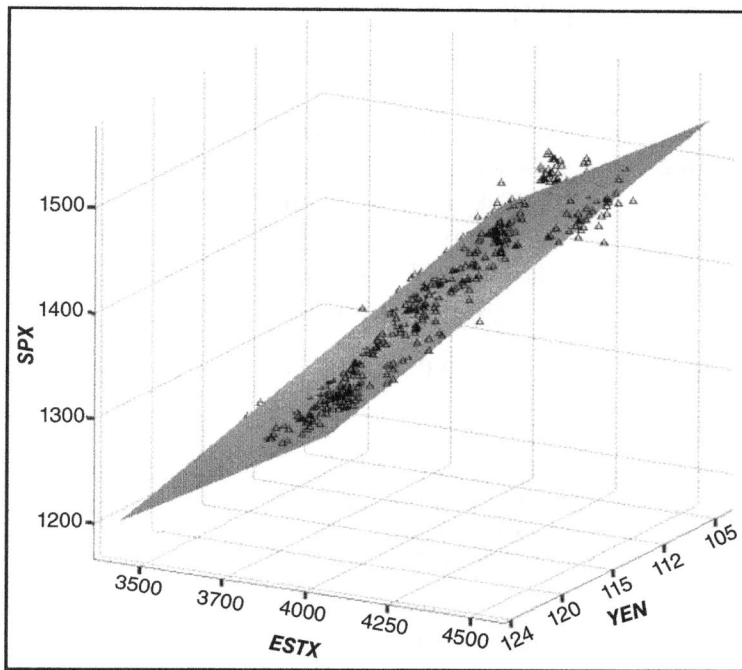

FIGURE 10.1 Three-Dimensional Scatterplot Visualizing the Relationship between the S&P 500 (on the Y-axis) vs. the Euro Stoxx 50 (on the X-axis) and the Yen (on the Z-axis) for the 2-Year Period from 1 January 2006 to 31 December 2007. The More Points Fall inside the Regression Plane the Better the Predictive Power of the Regression Model.

preferred method of assessing multicollinearity is to calculate the tolerance coefficient for each independent variable.

Tolerance is $1 - r^2$ (one minus the coefficient of determination) for the regression of each independent variable on all the other independents, ignoring the dependent. There will be as many tolerance coefficients as there are independents. The higher the intercorrelation of the independents, the more the tolerance will approach zero. As a rule of thumb, if tolerance is less than 0.20, a problem with multicollinearity is indicated.

High multicollinearity can be ignored when two or more independents are components of an index, and high intercorrelation among them is intentional and desirable. These are usually combined in an index prior to running regression, but when this is not practically possible they can be entered individually. For example, if data for an obscure index are not readily available some of the component stocks can be used instead of the index itself.

Perhaps this is better understood with an example. Let's say that we want to design an intermarket system to trade the S&P 500. The first step is to calculate the correlation between the S&P 500 with major international equity, commodity and financial indices.

Because of normality and linearity problems associated with raw index prices, these are converted to weekly percentage yields and the correlation matrix is calculated (depicted in Table 10.2). The next step is to add to the regression equation the predictor variables one at a time and calculate the coefficient of determination (r squared) and the tolerance for each variable. As you can see in Table 10.3, including more than three variables will only improve r squared marginally or not at all and the tolerance drops below 0.2 for a number of cross correlated variables. Thus the first step is to exclude the DAX, FTSE and CAC 40 since they are highly correlated with the ESTX (Euro Stoxx). The Nikkei is then dropped from the analysis as it doesn't improve the r squared coefficient at all. The remaining variables are the ESTX, VIX and UTY (model 3) and the regression equation becomes:

$$SP = 0.366*ESTX - 0.067*VIX + 0.206*UTY + 0.045 \qquad (10.6)$$

TABLE 10.2 Correlation Matrix of Weekly Percent Yields of Major International Indices, the CBOE Volatility Index (VIX,) the Utility Index (UTY) and the 10-Year Treasury Yield (TNX) with the S&P 500 for the 5-Year Period from 1 January 2001 to 31 December 2006

	S&P 500	ESTX	DAX	CAC 40	FTSE	Nikkei	VIX	UTY	TNX
S&P 500	1	0.81	0.80	0.80	0.74	0.42	−0.72	0.60	0.39
ESTX	0.81	1	0.94	0.97	0.88	0.49	−0.57	0.43	0.45
DAX	0.80	0.94	1	0.92	0.82	0.51	−0.56	0.39	0.49
CAC 40	0.80	0.97	0.92	1	0.89	0.49	−0.56	0.43	0.46
FTSE	0.74	0.88	0.82	0.89	1	0.45	−0.54	0.40	0.42
Nikkei	0.42	0.49	0.51	0.49	0.45	1	−0.36	0.21	0.29
VIX	−0.72	−0.57	−0.56	−0.56	−0.54	−0.36	1	−0.43	−0.25
UTY	0.60	0.43	0.39	0.43	0.40	0.21	−0.43	1	0.04
TNX	0.39	0.45	0.49	0.46	0.42	0.29	−0.25	0.04	1

TABLE 10.3 The Coefficient of Determination (r^2), the r^2 Change and the Tolerance Are Depicted for Each Model. The first model includes only the Euro Stoxx, the second includes the Euro Stoxx and the VIX and one more index is added for each subsequent model.

			Tolerance							
Model	r^2	r^2 change	ESTX	VIX	UTY	TNX	DAX	FTSE	CAC 40	Nikkei
1	0.65	0.65	1.00							
2	0.75	0.10	0.67	0.67						
3	**0.79**	**0.05**	**0.63**	**0.63**	**0.77**					
4	0.80	0.01	0.52	0.63	0.74	0.77				
5	0.81	0.01	0.12	0.62	0.74	0.74	0.12			
6	0.81	0.00	0.08	0.62	0.74	0.73	0.12	0.21		
7	0.81	0.00	0.05	0.62	0.73	0.73	0.11	0.19	0.05	
8	0.81	0.00	0.05	0.60	0.73	0.73	0.11	0.19	0.05	0.72

where SP, ESTX, VIX, TNX and UTY are weekly percentage changes of the corresponding indices.

Substituting the values for ESTX, VIX and UTY for 11/7/06 in (10.6):

$$SP = 0.366*1.7 - 0.067*(-0.09) + 0.206*(-1.6) + 0.045 = 0.343\% \text{ vs } 0.36\%$$

the actual S&P 500 weekly change for the specific week.

10.3 Assumptions

The correlation assumptions discussed in Level II, Chapter 13, are also valid for regression, since according to (10.4) regression is directly proportional to correlation.

The most important assumption is that of linearity. Checking that the linearity assumption is met is an essential task before using a regression model, as substantial violation of linearity means regression results may be more or less unusable.

Simple inspection of scatterplots is a common, if non-statistical, method of determining if nonlinearity exists in a relationship. An alternative is to fit a preliminary linear regression and to use the appropriate diagnostic plots to detect departures from linearity. Transforming one of the variables (for example by taking differences or logs) can sometimes help linearize a nonlinear relationship between two financial series.

Normality is also a problem when considering raw stock or index prices but it is less of a problem when taking log differences or percentage yields. The problem of the longer tails (discussed in Level II, Chapter 13) can be partially overcome by removing some of the most extreme outliers.

Normality can be visually assessed by looking at a histogram of frequencies. Alternatively you can use a formal normality test such as the Shapiro-Wilks W test or the Kolmogorov-Smirnov D test.

10.4 Nonparametric Regression

Nonparametric regression relaxes the usual assumption of linearity and makes no assumptions about the population distribution.

A more accurate estimate of the prediction is usually obtained by using nonparametric regression in cases of severe violations of linearity at the expense of much greater computation and a more difficult-to-understand result.

Two common methods of nonparametric regression are kernel regression and smoothing splines. The smoothing splines method minimizes the sum of squared residuals, adding a term which penalizes the roughness of the fit. The kernel regression algorithm falls into a class of algorithms called "SVMs" or "Support Vector Machines." SVM-based techniques typically use a kernel function to find an optimal separating hyperplane so as to separate two classes of patterns with maximal margin. SVM models are closely related to neural network models.

In recent years, SVMs have received considerable attention because of their superior performance in forecasting high noise and non-stationary financial time series. A major advantage of SVMs over other nonparametric methods is that they can have good performance even in problems with a large number of inputs. However, unlike other nonparametric methods the major difficulty of the SVM approach lies in the selection of its kernel, as choosing different kernel functions will produce different SVMs.

CHAPTER 11

International Indices and Commodities

From Markos Katsanos, *Intermarket Trading Strategies* (Hoboken, New Jersey: John Wiley & Sons, 2008), Chapter 4.

To conquer fear is the beginning of wisdom.

—**Bertrand Russell**

Learning Objective Statement

- Describe the different international indexes and commodities

Before proceeding with intermarket correlation, and for the benefit of US readers, I thought it might be useful to say a few words about the international indices used in the next chapters. I presume that readers who have bought this book are familiar with the Standard & Poor 500 and the Nasdaq so I will start with European stock indices.

11.1 The DAX

The leading index of the Deutsche Börse; the DAX (symbol: GDAXI) comprises of the 30 largest and most actively traded German equities (blue chips). The criteria for weighting the stocks in the index are trading volume and market capitalization. The DAX is a performance index, which means that all income from dividends and bonus distributions is reinvested into the index.

In addition to the DAX, the Deutsche Börse calculates a number of other indices, the most important being:

- The MDAX, which consists of the 50 largest companies from the classic sector of the Frankfurt Stock Exchange, that rank below the DAX components in terms of market capitalization and trading volume.

- The TecDAX, which consists of the 30 largest companies from the technology sector of the Frankfurt Stock Exchange, that rank below the DAX components in terms of market capitalization and trading volume. The TecDAX is equivalent to the US Nasdaq 100 index.

- The SDAX (small cap) which consists of 50 shares from the classic sector that rank directly below the MDAX in terms of market capitalization and trading volume. The SDAX is equivalent to the US Russell 2000 index.

- TheHDAX, which is a large cap index and includes the 110 largest German equities from all sectors of the economy. This is equivalent to the US Russell 1000 index.

- The L-DAX (symbol: GDAXIL) is a late index, indicating the price development of DAX 30 index's performance after the Xetra electronic-trading system closes and is based on the floor trading at the Frankfurt Stock Exchange. The L-DAX index is computed daily between 17:30 and 20:00 CET and takes over after the DAX closes at 17:30 hours CET.

- The Dax Volatility Indices: VDAX (symbol: VDAX) and VDAX-NEW (symbol: V1X). These are the German equivalents to the CBOE volatility index (VIX) and track the implied volatility of the DAX index. In simpler terms the volatility indices measure in percentage terms whether the DAX options are selling above or below their fair values (as generally estimated by the Black-Scholes formula).

The calculation of the new V1X index is based on DAX option contracts, which are quoted both "at the money" and "out of the money." Thus, VDAX-NEW has a broader volatility surface than the VDAX, which only takes into account options that are "at the money." The VDAX-NEW will replace VDAX in the medium-term.

Each September the Deutsche Börse decides whether changes are to be made to the composition of the index. More information about German indices can be found at the Deutsche Börse's website at http://boerse-frankfurt.com.

TheDAXis a highly cyclical index that now(May 2008) faces a potential downturn as fully one-fifth of the index is made up of financial stocks, which are sinking to multi-year lows.

Futures and options on the DAX trade in the Eurex Exchange (symbol: FDAX) from 8:00–22:10 CET; they have a contract value of 25 euro per index point of the DAX index and are highly liquid with an average volume of more than 200,000 contracts per day.

■ 11.2 The CAC 40

The CAC40 index (symbol: FCHI), which takes its name from the ParisBourse's early automation system "Cotation Assistée en Continu" (Continuous Assisted Quotation), is the main benchmark of the Euronext Paris. Tracking a sample of blue chip stocks, its performance is closely correlated to that of the market as a whole. The index contains 40 stocks selected from among the top 100 by market capitalization and the most active stocks listed on Euronext Paris, and it is the underlying asset for options and futures contracts. The base value was 1000 on 31 December 1987 and historical data are not available prior to that date.

The CAC 40 is a market value-weighted index. Since 1 December 2003, this index is no longer weighted by the total market capitalization of the component stocks but by their free float adjusted market capitalization. This method of calculation, already used for other major indices around the world, ensures greater coherence between the real allocation of companies on the market and how it is expressed in the indices. It also limits the manifestation of volatility caused by too much of an imbalance between the weight of a stock in the index and the corresponding free float or available shares in the market. The index composition is reviewed quarterly by an independent Index Steering Committee and a capping factor is used to limit an individual stock weight to 15%.

CAC 40 futures trade under the symbol FCE at the Euronext (MONEP) and they have a contract value of 10 euro per index point.

MONEP handles equity options, long- and short-term options, and index futures. Futures are liquid for trading purposes. An average of 120 000 contracts per day changed hands for the earliest expiring contract.

Listed below are the top 10 companies currently (as of 31 December 2007) contained within the index and below that a breakdown by industry group:

CAC 40 top 10 Constituents

1	Total – Oil & Gas	12.6%
2	Sanofi-Aventis – Pharmaceuticals	6.7%
3	BNP Paribas – Banking	6.2%
4	Suez – Utilities	5.6%
5	France Telecom – Telecommunications	4.7%
6	Axa – Insurance	4.5%
7	ArcelorMittal – Steel	4.5%
8	Société Générale – Banking	4.3%
9	Vivendi – Entertainment	3.6%
10	Carrefour – Retail	3.6%

CAC 40 breakdown by industry

1	Financials	19.2%
2	Industrials	12.6%
3	Consumer Goods	12.6%
4	Oil & Gas	12.5%
5	Utilities	11.9%
6	Consumer Services	9.6%
7	Health Care	7.6%
8	Basic Materials	6.7%
9	Telecommunications	5.2%
10	Technology	2.1%

Financials at 19.2% are the most heavily weighted group followed by Industrials and Consumer Goods (which includes famous French luxury goods manufacturer Louis Vuitton, Moet Hennessy (LVMH) and beauty products producer L'Oréal).

11.3 The FTSE

The FTSE 100 index (pronounced "footsie") is a share index of the 100 largest companies listed on the London Stock Exchange, weighted by market capitalization.

The index calculation began on 3 January 1984 and historical data are not available prior to that date. Component companies must meet a number of requirements set out by the FTSE Group, including having a full listing on the London Stock Exchange and meeting certain tests on free float and liquidity. The constituents of the FTSE 100 are reviewed and changed four times a year.

Trading lasts from 08:00–16:29 (when the closing auction starts), and closing values are taken at 16:35. The highest value of the index to date was 6950.6, set on 30 December 1999 at the height of the internet bubble.

Though it only contains the top 100 companies, the FTSE correlates closely with the All Share Index and, indeed, some broad US stock market indices.

Listed beloware the top 10 companies currently (31 August 2007) contained within in the index and below that a breakdown by industry group:

FTSE 100 top 10 constituents

1	BP Plc – Oil	7.1%
2	HSBC Holdings – Banking	7.0%
3	Vodafone Group – Telecommunications	5.6%
4	Glaxosmithkline – Pharmaceuticals	4.9%
5	Royal Dutch Shell Plc – A Shares – Oil	4.7%
6	Royal Bank Of Scotland – Banking	3.6%
7	Royal Dutch Shell Plc – B Shares – Oil	3.6%
8	Barclays – Banking	2.7%
9	Anglo American – Mining	2.6%
10	Astrazeneca – Pharmaceuticals	2.5%

FTSE 100 breakdown by industry

1	Financials	27.7%
2	Oil & Gas	17.2%
3	Consumer Services	10.5%
4	Consumer Goods	10.3%
5	Basic Materials	10.1%
6	Heath Care	8.2%
7	Telecommunications	7.6%
8	Utilities	4.7%
9	Industrials	3.5%
10	Technology	0.2%

With oil and gas stocks making up almost 17% of the index at the moment, the FTSE is very sensitive to oil prices. However, financials at 27.6% are the most heavily weighted group and the reason for the precipitous decline during the sub-prime crisis in 2007–2008, despite rising oil prices.

The FTSE 100 index reached a 5-year high on 13 July 2007; this was partly caused by the increase in the price of oil and the resultant increase in the share prices of BP and Shell.

The index is seen as a barometer of success of the British economy and is a leading share index in Europe. It is maintained by the FTSE Group, a now independent company which originated as a joint venture between the *Financial Times* and the London Stock Exchange (hence the abbreviation Financial Times Stock Exchange). According to the FTSE Group's website, the FTSE 100 companies represent about 81% of the UK share market.

FTSE futures trade at the London International Futures & Options Exchange (LIFFE) from 8:00–21:00 GMT (9:00–22:00 CET) under the symbol Z.

11.4 The Dow Jones Stoxx 50 and Euro Stoxx 50

The Stoxx 50 (STXX50) tracks the performance of the 50 most important and most actively traded shares in the pan-European area, while the Euro Stoxx 50 (STOXX50E or ESTX50) tracks the 50 most important stocks in the Eurozone. The Euro Stoxx covers 50 stocks from 12 Eurozone countries: Austria, Belgium, Finland, France, Germany, Greece, Ireland, Italy, Luxembourg, the Netherlands, Portugal and Spain.

The criteria for including a company in the index are market capitalization and trading volume of the European companies. Both indices are market capitalization-weighted.

Futures for both are highly liquid and trade at the Eurex (DTB) from 8:00–22:10 CET under the symbols FSTX and FESX respectively.

The Dow Jones Euro Stoxx 50 (Price) was developed with a base value of 1000 as of 31 December 1991 and uses float shares.

11.5 The Nikkei

The Nikkei 225 (N225) is Japan'smost widely watched index of stock market activity in the Tokyo Stock Exchange (TSE) and has been calculated continuously since 7 September 1950 by the *Nihon Keizai Shimbun* (Nikkei) newspaper. It is a price-weighted average (the unit is yen), and the components are reviewed once a year.

The Nikkei Stock Average is the average price of 225 stocks traded on the first section of the Tokyo Stock Exchange, but it is different from a simple average in that the divisor is adjusted to maintain continuity and reduce the effect of external factors not directly related to the market.

The Nikkei average hit its all-time high on 29 December 1989 when it reached an intra-day high of 38 957 before closing at 38 916. Thirteen years later, the Nikkei had plunged more than 80% from its 1989 highs.

The Nikkei's devastating decline was triggered by a real estate crisis similar to the one experienced in the United States in 2007–08. At the height of the Japanese market in 1989, Japanese banks were lending money secured by real estate. Investors took the borrowed money and ploughed it into the stock market. A snowball effect began when the real estate market crashed, pressuring further property and stock prices.

The Nikkei finally made a bottom on 28 April 2003 at 7608.

On 12 August 2005 it broke out from a 20-month rectangle formation and on 26 February 2007 rose to a six-year high of 18 215.

Nikkei futures trade in Osaka (symbol:N225), in the Chicago Mercantile Exchange (CME) in US dollars (symbol: NKD), in yen (symbol:NIY) and in Singapore (symbol: SGXNK). The Osaka exchange has recently introduced the Nikkei 225 mini contract (symbol: N225M).

■ 11.6 The Hang Seng

The Hang Seng (HSI) is a barometer of the Hong Kong stock market and includes companies from Finance, Utilities, Properties and Commerce, and Industry sub-indexes. The index calculation began on 24 November 1969 and Hang Seng Index futures (symbol: HSI) were introduced by the Hong Kong Futures Exchange in 1986.

Only companies with a primary listing on the Main Board of the Stock Exchange of Hong Kong (SEHK) are eligible as constituents. Mainland enterprises that have an H-share listing in Hong Kong will be eligible for inclusion in the Hang Seng Index (HSI) only when the H-share company has 100% of its ordinary share capital listed on the Hong Kong Stock Exchange.

Hang Seng futures trade in Hong Kong (symbol: HSI) from 9:45–12:30 (first trading session) and 14:30–16:30 Hong Kong time (second trading session). The multiplier is HK$50 per index point. Mini contracts are also available with a multiplier of HK$10 per index point.

■ 11.7 Trading Hours, Symbols and Volatility

In Table 11.1 you can find European and US trading hours of the major exchanges.

You can see that trading in some Asian markets is not very convenient for European traders as they open too late at night and close too early in the morning.

You can find current quotes and historical prices for most of the international indices in Yahoo Finance http://finance.yahoo.com which is free for 20-minute delayed

TABLE 11.1 Trading Hours in Local, US Eastern Time (EST) and Central European Time (CET) for Major World Exchanges. All the times shown are standard winter times. Please note that Japan and China do not currently observe the daylight saving time (DST) or summer time and consequently the CET and EST opening and closing time indicated should be moved forward by one hour. The transition to summer time starts on 25 March and ends on 28 October in Europe. In the United States the transition starts two weeks earlier, on 11 March and ends on 4 November.

		Time					
Country	Exchange	Local Open	Local Close	ET Open	ET Close	CET Open	CET Close
USA	NYSE, Nasdaq	9:30	16:00	9:30	16:00	15:30	22:00
Canada	Toronto	9:30	16:00	9:30	16:00	15:30	22:00
Germany	XETRA	9:00	17:30	3:00	11:30	9:00	17:30
Germany	Frankfurt	9:00	20:00	3:00	14:00	9:00	20:00
France	Paris	9:00	17:30	3:00	11:30	9:00	17:30
Britain	LSE	7:00	15:30	2:00	10:30	8:00	16:30
Japan	Tokyo	9:00	15:00	19:00	1:00	1:00	7:00
Hong Kong	Hong Kong	10:00	16:00	21:00	3:00	3:00	9:00
Australia	ASX	10:00	16:00	18:00	0:00	0:00	6:00

quotes. I thought it would be useful to include a list of symbols used by the most popular data providers or brokers for some international indices in Table 11.2 as each one uses a different symbol for the same index. You will notice that US brokers are still of the old fashioned mentality that foreign markets are irrelevant to US investors and do not provide any data for non-US indices. Of course US markets do not exist in a vacuum and it would be very helpful for US investors to check how the international markets are doing before the US market opens for trading. International indices would be also useful for traders of international ETFs or ADRs that are trading in the US exchanges.

I thought it would be useful for international traders to include the most likely daily percentage changes for some of the major international indices and commodities in order to assess risk adjusted positions in each market accordingly (see Table 11.3). Each value in Table 11.3 indicates the daily change that was exceeded by the percentile in the top row. For example the S&P 500 was up by more than 1.57% only 5% of the time. Frequency distribution values are included instead of standard deviations because, as discussed in Level II, Chapter 15, none of the indices conform to the normality assumption.

An interesting comparison between actual observations and theoretical probabilities as predicted by the normal distribution is depicted in Table 11.4. It can be seen that there is an exponential shift from the middle to the tails of the distribution making predictions beyond the 0.02 level of significance totally unreliable.

Since 6 July 2007 the Securities and Exchange Commission (SEC) have abolished the "uptick rule," a regulation that prohibited short selling following downticks. This

TABLE 11.2	Symbols for the Major World Indices Used by Different Data Providers and Brokers. They usually differ from provider to provider by a Prefix or a suffix. Blank cells indicate that the index was not available at that broker or data provider.

Index name	Reuters	Yahoo Finance	TC200	CSI Data	E*Trade/ Schwab	Interactive Brokers
S&P 500	.SPX	^SPX	SP-500	SPX-I	$SPX	SPX
S&P 100	.OEX	^OEX	OEX	OEX-I	$OEX	OEX
Dow Jones Industrials	.DJI	^DJI	DJ-30	DJIA-I	$DJI	INDU
Dow Jones Transports	.DJT	^DJT	DJ-20	DJAT-T	$DJT	TRAN
Nasdaq 100	.NDX	^NDX	NDX–X	NDX-I	$NDX	NDX
Nasdaq Composite	.IXIC	^IXIC	COMPQX	COMP-I	$COMPX	COMP
Russell 2000	.RUT	^RUT	RUT-X	RUT-I	$RUT	RUT
NYSE Composite	.NYA	^NYA	NYSE	NYA-I	$NYA	NYA
Canada TSX	.GSPTSE	^GSPTSE	TSX–X	TCMP-I	–	TSX
DAX	.GDAXI	^GDAXI	FDAC-X	GDAX-F	–	DAX
CAC 40	.FCHI	^FCHI	PCAC-X	FCHI-I	–	CAC40
DJ Euro Stoxx 50	.STOXX50E	^STOXX50E	–		–	ESTX50
DJ Stoxx 50	.STOXX50	^STOXX50	–	–	STX	
FTSE 100	.FTSE	^FTSE	FTSE-X	FTSE-F		Z
Greece General	.ATG	–	–	ATG-F		–
Nikkei 225	.N225	^N225	NIKI-X	N225-F	–	N225
Hang Seng	.HSI	^HSI	HKHS-X	HSI-F	–	HSI
Korea KOSPI	.KS11	^KS11	–	KS11-F	–	
Australia All Ordinaries	.AORD	^AORD	–	AORD-F	–	–
Brazil BOVESPA	.BVSP	^BVSP	–	BVSP-F	–	–
Mexico IPC	.MXX	^MXX	–	MXX-F	–	–
10 Yr Treasury Yield	.TNX	^TNX	TNX–X	TNX-I	$TNX	TNX
Amex Oil Index	.XOI	^XOI	XOI	XOI-I	$XOI	XOI
CRB Index	.CRB	–	CRY0	@CR	–	–
Euro	RD-EUR=	EURUSD=X	–	–	–	EUR.USD
Dollar Index	.DXY	NA	DXY0	–	–	–
Gold	XAU=	XAUUSD=X	XGLD	MAU0	–	–
Volatility Index	.VIX	^VIX	VIX–X	VIX-I	$VIX	VIX
Crude Oil	–	NA	XOIL	–	–	CL
Silver	XAG=	XAGUSD=X	XSLV	–	–	–
PHLX Gold/ Silver	.XAU	^XAU	XAU	XAU-I	$XAU	XAU

| TABLE 11.3 | Frequency Distribution of Daily Yields of Major Stock Market Indices and Commodities from 1992 to 2006. The daily changes are divided by percentiles according to values below which certain percentages of cases fall. So, for example, the 5% percentile of the S&P 500 Daily change is −1.59% which means that the S&P 500 declined by −1.59% or less only 5% of the time. |

| Daily Change % | Percentiles | | | | | | |
	5	10	25	50	25	10	5
S&P	−1.59	−1.08	−0.46	0.04	0.55	1.13	1.57
DJ-30	−1.52	−1.06	−0.47	0.05	0.57	1.13	1.56
Russell 2000	−1.84	−1.33	−0.50	0.11	0.60	1.25	1.78
NDX	−3.10	−2.18	−0.90	0.12	1.03	2.17	3.06
TSX	−1.34	−0.92	−0.39	0.06	0.52	0.99	1.32
Euro Stoxx	−2.40	−1.68	−0.76	0.05	0.82	1.69	2.36
DAX	−2.26	−1.58	−0.65	0.08	0.78	1.58	2.22
CAC	−2.12	−1.47	−0.68	0.02	0.77	1.52	2.10
FTSE	−1.60	−1.15	−0.51	0.02	0.57	1.15	1.62
ATG	−2.35	−1.59	−0.72	0.02	0.80	1.80	2.55
Nikkei	−2.34	−1.72	−0.80	0.00	0.79	1.69	2.27
Hang Seng	−2.43	−1.66	−0.70	0.04	0.83	1.79	2.47
10 Yr Tr Note Yield	−1.75	−1.34	−0.68	0.00	0.60	1.35	1.93
XOI	−1.99	−1.35	−0.63	0.05	0.76	1.50	2.01
OIL	−3.48	−2.50	−1.15	0.06	1.28	2.56	3.45
Canada Venture	−1.50	−1.02	−0.39	0.14	0.68	1.18	1.58
XAU	−3.47	−2.66	−1.41	−0.07	1.40	2.90	3.94
Silver	−2.46	−1.66	−0.71	0.00	0.82	1.81	2.48
Gold	−1.34	−0.89	−0.38	0.00	0.43	0.99	1.38
CRB	−1.06	−0.75	−0.37	0.02	0.39	0.76	1.09
Dollar Index	−0.86	−0.65	−0.31	0.01	0.31	0.64	0.86
Euro	−1.02	−0.74	−0.37	0.00	0.37	0.79	1.07
Yen	−1.07	−0.77	−0.37	0.00	0.39	0.80	1.06
Corn	−2.23	−1.76	−0.90	0.00	0.84	1.84	2.58
Wheat	−2.49	−1.95	−1.13	−0.07	1.09	2.22	2.85

rule was created after the 1929 stock market crash in order to prevent short-sellers from adding to the downward momentum of a sharp decline by requiring every short sale to be executed on a higher price than a previous trade. This rule has been in effect for 78 years. But can the recent volatility in the markets be blamed entirely on the rescinding of the uptick rule?

At the time of writing, not enough data were available for such a study as the recent volatility has been exaggerated by the combination of the housing and related financial upheavals. It would be interesting to see the effect that this rule had on the probabilities of daily changes of the S&P 500 (in Table 11.4).

S&P 500 daily % change	Actual probability	Normal probability
−5.10%	0.1%	0.000%
−3.08%	0.5%	0.091%
−2.60%	1.0%	0.418%
−2.22%	2.0%	1.200%
−1.90%	3.0%	2.636%
−1.75%	4.0%	3.695%
−1.59%	5.0%	5.219%
−1.08%	10.0%	13.253%
−0.46%	25.0%	30.983%
0.04%	50.0%	50.225%

■ 11.8 The Dollar Index

Just as the S&P 500 provides a general indication of the value of the US stock market, the US dollar index (symbol: DXY) provides a general indication of the international value of the US dollar and it is a measure of the value of the dollar relative to its most significant trading partners. Similar in many respects to the Federal Reserve Board's trade-weighted index, the dollar index does this by averaging the exchange rates between the US dollar and six major world currencies.

The dollar index is calculated by taking the geometric weighted average of the dollar's value against a basket of six major world currencies and is calculated by taking the product of each currency spot rate raised to the corresponding weight according to the following formula:

$$\text{USDXY} = 50.14348112 \times \text{EURO}^{-0.576} \times \text{YEN}^{-0.136} \times \text{GBP}^{-0.119}$$
$$\times \text{CAD}^{-0.091} \times \text{SEK}^{-0.042} \times \text{CHF}^{-0.036} \tag{11.1}$$

In the formula above all currencies are expressed in USD per unit of the foreign currency.

To express the yen, Canadian dollar, Swedish krona and Swiss franc in their more familiar format in yen per US dollar, CAD per US dollar, SEK per US dollar and CHF per US dollar you only need to change the sign of the weight exponent. The above formula (4.1) then becomes:

$$\text{USDXY} = 50.14348112 \times \text{EURO}^{-0.576} \times \text{USDJPY}^{0.136} \times \text{GBP}^{-0.119}$$
$$\times \text{USDCAD}^{0.091} \times \text{USDSEK}^{0.042} \times \text{USDCHF}^{0.036} \tag{11.2}$$

The constant, currently equal to 50.14348112, was set back at the initiation of the index in order to make the index equal to 100.00 at that time.

TABLE 11.5 Contracts to Trade Based on Either Equal Profit/Loss or Historical Volatility. The fourth and fifth columns are daily % changes exceeded only 10% of the time during a 5-year observation period. The sixth column is the wilder's average daily true range, the seventh and eighth columns are the suggested number of contracts to trade for equal profit/loss based on the expected historical 10th percentile of daily changes or based on the historical volatility, respectively. The last column is the 50-day average volume as of April 2007.

Name	Symbol	Multiplier	Max% Daily Change 10th Percentile		ATR	Contracts to Trade		Average Volume
						For Equal Profit/Loss	Volatility Adjusted	
S&P 500	SPX	250	1.1	−1.1	12.2	1	1	49000
S&P 500 mini	ES	50	1.1	−1.2	12.4	5	5	929000
DJ-30	DD	25	1.1	−1.1	104	1	1	7323
DJ-30 mini	YM	5	1.1	−1.1	106	6	6	91890
Nasdaq 100	NDX	100	1.8	−1.9	25.2	1	1	7600
Nasdaq 100 mini	NQ	20	1.8	−1.9	25.3	6	6	314000
Russell 2000 mini	ER2	100	1.6	−1.6	11.1	3	2	16000
Nikkei	NKD	5	1.7	−1.6	204	3	2	7500
Nikkei	JNI	1000	1.7	−1.6	214	2	2	83000
DAX	FDAX	25	1.7	−1.7	71.5	1	1	152635
CAC 40	FCE	10	1.4	−1.5	59.3	4	3	146530
Euro Stoxx 50	FESX	10	1.5	−1.6	46.0	5	4	863522
Euro	6E	125000	0.8	−0.7	0.01	3	3	171000
Gold	ZG	100	1.3	−1.2	7.2	5	2	44000
Gold mini	YG	33.2	1.3	−1.2	7.2	14	6	5200
10Year Note	ZN	1000	0.5	−0.5	0.5	8	8	919000
10Year Bund	GBL	1000	0.4	−0.4	0.5	7	6	1115000
Crude Oil	CL	1000	2.8	−2.6	1.7	2	2	430000
Crude Oil mini	QM	500	2.8	−2.6	1.8	4	4	30000
Wheat	ZW	5000	2.3	−2.1	0.1	7	4	57000
Corn	ZC	5000	1.9	−1.8	0.1	10	5	204000

Symbol	Underlying Index/ Commodity	Shares to Trade For Equal Profit/Loss	Volatility Adjusted	Average Volume
SPY	S&P 500	500	500	200000000
DIA	DJ-30	600	600	17000000
QQQQ	Nasdaq-100	1000	1000	170000000
IWM	Russell 2000	600	500	100000000
EWJ	Nikkei 225	3000	2500	24000000
EWG	DAX	1500	1500	2200000
EWQ	CAC 40	1500	1300	500000
EZU	EURO STOXX 50	500	400	640000
FXE	Euro	800	700	200000
GLD	GOLD	900	400	10000000
IEF	7–10-Year Treasury Bond	2000	2000	360000
USO	CRUDE OIL	600	600	13000000
DBA	Agricultural Commodities	1500	800	1500000

An example of calculating the dollar index on 8 February 2008 using formula (11.1) is depicted in Table 11.7. The FX rates (from Bloomberg) are raised to the negative of their weight, and the product, when multiplied by the index constant of 50.14348112, yields the dollar index level of 76.67 on that date.

The index was calibrated to par or 100 in March 1973 when the world's major trading nations abandoned the 25-year-old Bretton Woods agreement to fix their currency rates. Thus a quote of 84 means the dollar's value has declined 16% since the base period.

The dollar index component currencies and their weightings are: Euro (57.6%); yen (13.6%); British pound (11.9%); Canadian dollar (9.1%), Swedish krona (4.2%); and Swiss franc (3.6 %). These are depicted in the pie chart in Figure 11.1 and in Table 11.7.

Intraday values for the dollar index are generally not available from data providers. However, a rough indication of the dollar index intraday change can be estimated by the EUR/USD FX rate because, as you can see from Table 11.8, three of the dollar index components – the British pound, the Swedish krona and the Swiss franc – are highly correlated with the euro.

There's no doubt that the dollar index plays a dominant role in the financial markets and the dollar's daily changes have major effects on many other asset classes like commodities, precious metals, the bond and stock markets.

From the end of World War II until the early 1970s, the dollar was tied to other major currencies by the Bretton Woods fixed exchange rate agreement. After it

TABLE 11.7	Shows the FX Rates of the Dollar Index Constituent Currencies on 8 February 2008 (from Bloomberg). The weights applied to the FX rates are shown in the third column, and the FX rate raised to (the negative of) that weight in the last column. This product, when multiplied by the constant of 50.14348112, yields the dollar index of 76.67 on 8 February 2008. All FX rates are expressed in USD per unit of the foreign currency.

Currency	FX Rate	Weight	$(\text{FX rate})^{-\text{Weight}}$
Euro	1.4507	0.576	0.8071073384
Yen	0.0093	0.136	1.8892364628
Sterling	1.9460	0.119	0.9238298752
Canadian dollar	1.0008	0.091	0.9999272318
Swedish kroner	0.1540	0.042	1.0817430901
Swiss franc	0.9065	0.036	1.0035401646
Constant			50.14348112
Product (index level)			76.67

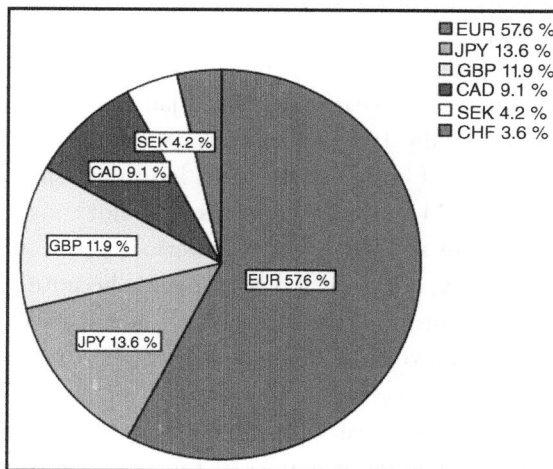

FIGURE 11.1   The Dollar Index.

TABLE 11.8	2- and 5-Year Nonparametric Correlation between the Euro and the Rest of the Dollar Index Component Currencies. Notice the high correlation between the Euro and the British pound, Swedish Krona, and Swiss franc. All rates are expressed in USD per currency.

	Correlations with the Euro				
Years	JPY	GBP	CAD	SEK	CHF
2	0.039	0.974	0.659	0.985	0.915
5	−0.077	0.957	0.638	0.983	0.953

became free floating, the dollar went through a roller-coaster ride. It rose to an all-time high of 160 in 1985 but then retreated to almost where it started. At the beginning of 2002 it rose again to 120, making a 16-year high and more recently, in 2008, mainly because of the huge US trade deficit, it plummeted to an all-time low of 70.

The main fundamental factors affecting the dollar index are:

- the US trade deficit;

- US, Japanese, Canadian and European interest rates and bond yields;

- CPI inflation;

- quarterly gross national product (GDP);

- non farm payroll figures.

A quantitative statistical analysis of the relationship between the dollar index and the factors mentioned above would reveal the magnitude of their correlation with the dollar index and to what extent they might have an influence on the dollar's future value.

While data on tradeable instruments such as bond yields, the dollar, international bonds etc. are readily available, it is sometimes difficult to find appropriate fundamental data because they are often subject to revision and not always reported in a data-compatible format.

Table 11.9 lists some markets with readily-available data that correlate well with the dollar index and covers the 5-year period from January 2003 to December 2007 (in the second column) and the 10 years from January 1998 to December 2007 (in the third column). I included both a short and a long time span because, as it becomes apparent from Table 11.9, the correlations were not constant over time, usually strengthening during the most recent 5-year period. This was more pronounced in the case of the CRB index, crude oil and gold, mainly because investors turned to commodities as a hedge against the recent disorderly dollar decline.

The British pound, the euro and the yen had the highest negative correlation in both time spans, but this was expected as they are all components of the dollar index. The commodity that correlated best with the dollar index was gold ($r = -0.51$). Of course this is nothing new and it is normal for gold, which is denominated in dollars, to have a negative correlation with the dollar. Surprisingly, the dollar index correlated better with the Australian dollar, which is not a dollar index component, than with Gold.

Lastly, the dollar index did not correlate well with equity indices. The correlation with the S&P 500 reversed sign from weak positive to weak negative during the latest 5-year period. The equity index that correlated best with the dollar index was Canada's Venture Index. This was no surprise as the Venture Exchange is heavily weighted with gold mining stocks.

Dollar index futures trade in the NYBOT (which has been recently acquired by the Intercontinental Exchange or ICE) under the symbol DX. The contract value is 1000 times the index and is currently trading at 73. Thus, if you sell one contract, you are basically shorting $73,000 against a basket of six foreign currencies.

| TABLE 11.9 | Correlation of Monthly (21 day) Percentage Yields between the Dollar Index and Related Commodities. In the second column is the correlation using more recent Data from 1 January 2003 to 31 December 2007 and the correlation using 10 years of data (from 1 January 1998 to 31 December 2007) in the third column. |

| | Correlation Data–Years | |
Index/Commodity	5	10
OIX	−0.23	−0.13
Crude oil (NYMEX)	−0.26	−0.13
Natural gas	−0.14	−0.16
S&P 500	−0.17	0.01
Nikkei	0.12	0.13
Venture (Canada)	−0.36	−0.31
XAU	−0.36	−0.35
Silver	−0.33	−0.29
Gold (cash)	**−0.51**	**−0.49**
CRB index	−0.39	−0.32
Utility Index	−0.29	−0.11
Japanese Bonds	−0.10	−0.10
Bund	−0.15	−0.20
Bonds	−0.16	−0.23
10-yr Australian bond	−0.10	−0.25
10-yr Treasury yield	0.16	0.26
Interest rates (short)	0.14	0.18
Euro	**−0.98**	**−0.98**
AUD	**−0.66**	**−0.56**
GBP	**−0.84**	**−0.80**
YEN	**−0.65**	**−0.56**

▓ 11.9 The Xoi and the Oix

The continued surge in the price of oil confirms that oil supply is scarcely meeting demand. The excess demand is coming from China and India and will only get stronger. The question is not whether, but when, world crude productivity will start to decline, ushering in the permanent oil shock era. While global information for predicting this "event" is not so straightforward as the data M. King Hubbert used in creating his famous curve that predicted the US oil production peak, there are indications that most of the large exploration targets have been found, at the same time that the world's population is exploding.

On 26 February 2008 crude oil prices crossed the $100 barrier. High crude prices imply higher profitability for the oil industry which, in turn, will propel their stock prices even higher.

The AMEX oil index (XOI) and the CBOE oil index (OIX) are the most popular indices designed to measure the performance of the oil industry through changes in the prices of a cross section of widely-held corporations involved in the exploration, production, and development of petroleum.

The XOI was established with a benchmark value of 125 on 27 August 1984 and currently has 12 component companies, all involved in exploring, developing, producing, and refining petroleum. These range in size from the tiny $29 billion (market capitalization) Hess to the mighty $440 billion Exxon Mobil, the world's largest publicly-traded oil company.

Both indices are price weighted. Perhaps surprisingly, considering its use with the DJIA, price-weighted indices have major problems. In the XOI's case, the smaller and less-important companies now have far higher share prices than the big ones. This allows these smaller companies to unduly influence and distort index performance.

For example Apache, because of its rich $100 share price, comprises 11.7% of the OIX by weight even though it is only a $33 billion company. Meanwhile, giant Exxon Mobil is weighted at 10% of the XOI even though it is a massive $440 billion behemoth. The problem is that share prices are meaningless, and a company of any size can have whatever share price range it wants by splitting or reverse-splitting its stock.

An alternative and better way to weight an index, which is more common in newer indexes, is by market capitalization. This weighting solves the problem of a $1 move in a $10 stock having the same impact as an identical move in a $100 stock, despite the fact that the former situation represents a 10% change, and the latter only a 1% change. Not surprisingly, market cap weighted indexes are by far the most common. The classic example always provided for the market-weighted index style is the Standard & Poor's 500 index.

With the XOI's current price weighting, the bottom four components – which represent a hefty 23% of the XOI's weight today – are a mere 9% of its market capitalization!

Despite these problems, the XOI remains the most popular measure of the oil-stock sector today with the OIX a close second.

For comparison purposes, both the XOI and OIX components are listed in the same Table 11.10. As you can see their composition and weight are very similar. The main difference between them is that the Amex used Apache Corporation instead of CBOE's Repsol and Valero.

Table 11.11 lists some markets that correlate well with the Amex oil index. The data are composed of equity indices, commodities, currencies and interest raterelated markets. I statistically correlated these against the XOI on a same month basis, meaning there was no monthly offset between the XOI data series and the related markets. The highest correlation in both time spans was between the XOI and Canada's TSX index, but this was to be expected as the TSX is heavily weighted with oil exploration stocks. Surprisingly, Japanese bonds correlated considerably better with the XOI ($r = -0.31$) than US Treasury bonds ($r = -0.1$). Interest rates had virtually no correlation with the XOI.

THE INTEGRATION OF TECHNICAL ANALYSIS

TABLE 11.10 Composition of the CBOE Oil Index (OIX) and Amex Oil Index (XOI) as of 2 February 2008. A blank cell indicates that the stock in that row is not included in the index.

Symbol	Name	Price 8/2/08	Market cap–billion	OIX weight	XOI weight
APA	Apache Corp	100.63	33.5	11.74%	—
HES	Hess Corp	56.46	28.6	10.41%	10.36%
XOM	Exxon Mobil Corp	64.30	439.8	10.38%	9.86%
CVX	Chevron Corp	75.38	165.5	10.24%	9.64%
TOT	Total	79.26	158.3	9.64%	8.30%
RDS.A	Royal Dutch Shell	88.96	124.0	9.28%	8.15%
COP	Conocophillips	49.38	119.9	9.09%	9.16%
OXY	Occidental Petroleum	66.68	55.1	8.49%	7.74%
BP	British Petroleum	67.53	202.8	8.02%	7.27%
APC	Anadarko Petroleum	70.29	26.4	6.84%	6.68%
MRO	Marathon Oil Corp	81.71	35.0	5.87%	5.34%
REP	Repsol Ypf S.A	31.88	37.1	—	3.64%
VLO	Valero Energy	59.06	32.1	—	6.75%

TABLE 11.11 Correlation of Monthly (21 day) Percentage Yields between the Amex Oil Index (XOI) and Related Indices. The correlation using more recent data from 1/1/2003 to 31/12/2007 is shown in the second column and the correlation using 10-year data (from 1/1/1998 to 31/12/2007) in the third column.

Index/commodity	Correlation Data–Years	
	5	10
OIX	0.99	0.99
Crude oil	**0.52**	0.42
Brent	0.49	0.43
Natural gas	0.3	0.31
S&P 500	0.48	**0.46**
TSX (Canada)	**0.74**	**0.47**
Venture (Canada)	0.49	**0.47**
Australia All Ordinaries	**0.54**	0.43
XAU	**0.54**	0.40
Gold	0.37	0.16
CRB index	**0.57**	0.44
Japanese bonds	−0.31	−0.31
Utility index	0.45	0.44
10 yr Treasury bond	−0.12	−0.1
10 yr Treasury yield	0.04	0.1
Dollar index	−0.21	−0.12
AUD	0.38	0.33
GBP	0.05	0.08
Yen	−0.06	0.05

As can be seen in Table 11.11 the correlations were not constant over time, some-times strengthening from weak to medium or strong during the most recent 5-year period. This was more pronounced in the case of the dollar and dollar denominated commodities such as gold, crude oil, and the CRB index.

The XOI correlated better with the Australian dollar than the US dollar index and there was also strong positive correlation with the Australian All Ordinaries index. This was certainly a surprise since Australia is not a major oil-producing country.

Options on the OIX trade on the CBOE under the symbol OIX expiring every three months from the March quarterly cycle (March, June, September and December). Options on the XOI are also available from the AMEX.

■ 11.10 The CRB Index

The history of the CRB index dates back to 1957, when the Commodity Research Bureau constructed an index comprised of 28 commodities to track the perfor-mance of commodities as an asset class.

Since then, as commodity markets have evolved, the index has undergone peri-odic updates. Its name was changed to the Reuters CRB Index in 2001 and it was again renamed as the Reuters/Jefferies CRB Index (RJ/CRB) in July 2005 when it underwent its tenth and most recent revision, the collaborative effort of Reuters Plc. and Jefferies Financial Products, LLC.

The original CRB index included 28 commodities until the list was reduced to 21 in 1987, where it remained until a major revision in 1995 when it was further sliced down to 17 commodities. Of the 28 commodities included in the original CRB of 1957, foodstuffs such as rye, potatoes, onions and lard – that aren't really relevant to an evolving industrial economy – were gradually removed.

During the latest revision in 2005 three new commodities were added (unleaded gas, aluminum and nickel) and an existing one (platinum) was eliminated for a net gain of two components. In addition, the CRB's traditional geometric averaging was also eliminated, in favor of a weighting arithmetic averaging which better tracks the true direction of commodities prices during today's volatile markets. By its very mathemati-cal nature geometric averaging effectively continually rebalanced the index, decreasing exposure to rising commodities and increasing exposure to declining commodities.

To refresh the readers' mathematics, the formula for the geometric mean of a data set [a1, a2, . . . , an] is the nth root of their product and it is useful for averaging quantities with the same or similar values in magnitude.

In the new CRB, crude oil has a weight of 23 times the weight of orange juice or hogs and 4.6 times the weight of sugar. You can see the composition of subsector weightings of the new RJ/CRB in Figure 11.2 and the individual commodities in Table 11.12.

By diversifying into commodities, investors are better able to obtain desirable long-term results, while at the same time lowering the overall volatility of their portfolio.

TABLE 11.12	Commodities Included in the Old and New CRB Index and the Goldman Sachs Commodity Index (as of April 2007)		
	Old CRB	New R/J CRB	GSCI
Crude oil	5.9%	23.0%	37.9%
Brent	0.0%	0.0%	15.5%
Heating oil	6.0%	5.0%	6.2%
Unleaded gas	0.0%	5.0%	1.3%
Natural gas	5.9%	6.0%	6.2%
Gas/Oil	0.0%	0.0%	5.4%
Corn	5.9%	6.0%	3.0%
Wheat	5.9%	1.0%	5.9%
Soybeans	5.9%	6.0%	2.1%
Sugar	5.9%	5.0%	0.9%
Cotton	5.9%	5.0%	0.8%
Coffee	5.9%	5.0%	0.6%
Cocoa	5.9%	5.0%	0.2%
Orange juice	5.9%	1.0%	0.0%
Cattle	5.9%	6.0%	2.8%
Lean hogs	5.9%	1.0%	1.1%
Gold	5.9%	6.0%	2.0%
Silver	5.9%	1.0%	0.3%
Aluminum	0.0%	6.0%	2.4%
Copper	5.9%	6.0%	3.0%
Nickel	0.0%	1.0%	0.9%
Platinum	5.9%	0.0%	0.0%
Lead	0.0%	0.0%	0.5%
Zinc	0.0%	0.0%	0.7%

The counter-cyclic nature of commodities to other financial assets such as equities makes commodities an ideal asset class to incorporate into a portfolio in order to achieve a more desirable return scenario. Attempting to find the right combination of contracts in obscure markets such as soybeans, pork bellies, cattle, and coffee would be difficult for a futures market professional and potentially disastrous for anyone else. Many mutual type commodity funds and money managers have surfaced, but most with unpredictable results and very few offering the true commodity portfolio necessary for proper asset diversification.

The Reuters/Jefferies CRB index has been recognized as the main barometer of commodity prices for many years and has been accepted globally as a standard for measuring the commodity futures price level.

To alleviate the need to choose individual commodities while facilitating the investment in a representative group, the New York Board of Trade (NYBOT) began offering futures contracts on the Reuters/Jefferies CRB index. The trading symbol is CR and the contract size is 200 times the index.

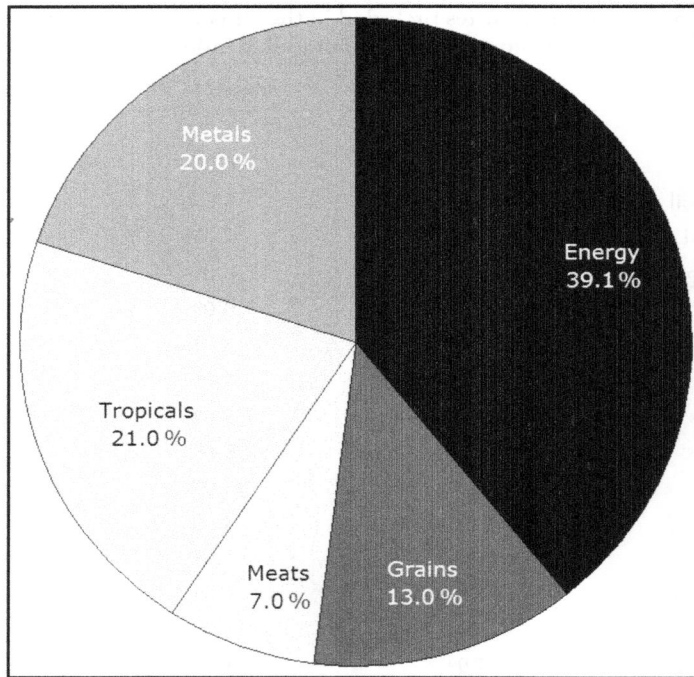

FIGURE 11.2 Sub-Sector Composition of the New RJ/CRB Index. The energy group includes crude oil, heating oil, unleaded gas and natural gas; the grain group includes corn, wheat and soybeans; the meat group includes live cattle and lean hogs; the tropicals include sugar, cotton, coffee, cocoa and orange juice and lastly, the metals group includes gold, silver, aluminium, copper and nickel.

Buyers of the Reuters/JefferiesCRBindex futures contract have direct participation in valuation changes of the component commodities (see Table 11.12 and also Figure 11.2). A "long" position provides opportunities for obtaining a hedge against inflation and dollar depreciation while at the same time reaping potentially extraordinary returns from commodity price appreciation.

■ 11.11 The Goldman Sachs Commodity Index (GSCI)

The GSCI, created in 1991, currently includes 24 commodities and is designed to provide investors with a reliable and publicly available benchmark for investment performance in the commodity markets. Individual components qualify for inclusion in the GSCI on the basis of liquidity and are weighted by their respective world production quantities in the last five years of available data. A list of the components and their dollar weights, as of April 2007, is presented in Table 11.12.

The GSCI is heavily weighted in energy futures contracts, which constitute 72.5% of the index compared with only 39%for the Reuters/Jefferies CRB index, which was the main factor for the GSCI becoming the top-performing commodity benchmark in

FIGURE 11.3 Weekly Chart of the S&P Goldman Sachs Commodity Index (thick bold line with the scale on the right), the RJ/CRB Index (thin black line) and Crude Oil Futures (thin grey line) from 2001 to February 2008. Notice how the Goldman Sachs commodity index closely follows crude oil prices.

2007. This, however, is not necessarily an advantage, as it limits the diversification into other commodities which is especially beneficial in periods of declining oil prices.

In Figure 11.3 you can see a comparison between the Goldman Sachs commodity index (thick line), the RJ/CRB index (normal line) and crude oil futures (thin line). Notice how the Goldman Sachs commodity index closely follows crude oil prices. Possible means of investing in the Goldman Sachs commodity index include the purchase of GSCI-related instruments, such as the GSCI futures contract traded on the Chicago Mercantile Exchange (CME).

In February 2007 the GSCI was acquired by Standard & Poor's and renamed the S&P GSCI.

11.12 The XAU and the HUI

The Philadelphia Exchange (PHLX) Gold and Silver Sector (XAU) Index is a capitalization-weighted index composed of 16 companies involved in the gold and silver mining industry. The XAU was set to an initial value of 100 in January 1979. Options on the XAU trade under the same symbol in the Philadelphia Exchange.

The component companies and their weighing can be seen in Table 11.13.

Another popular gold mining index is the AMEX's Gold BUGS index (HUI). BUGS is an acronym for Basket of Unhedged Gold Stocks. The index was introduced on 15 March 1996 with a starting value of 200.

TABLE 11.13	Composition of XAU Index as of 8 February 2008	
Company name	Symbol	Weight
Barrick Gold Corp.	ABX	22.04%
Agnico Eagle Mines Ltd.	AEM	4.39%
AngloGold Ashanti Ltd.	AU	5.64%
Yamana Gold, Inc.	AUY	5.15%
Coeur d'Alene Mines Corp.	CDE	0.62%
Freeport McMoran Copper	FCX	17.54%
Gold Fields Ltd.	GFI	4.63%
Goldcorp, Inc.	GG	13.00%
Randgold Resources Ltd.	GOLD	1.74%
Harmony Gold Mining Co.	HMY	2.10%
Kinross Gold	KGC	6.64%
Newmont Mining Corporation	NEM	11.97%
Pan American Silver Corp.	PAAS	1.34%
Royal Gold, Inc.	RGLD	0.44%
Silver Wheaton, Inc.	SLW	1.70%
Silver Standard Resources	SSRI	1.05%

The AMEX Gold BUGS index is comprised of 15 of the nation's largest "unhedged" gold mining stocks. It is a "modified equal-dollar weighted" index. As a result, most of the index's component stocks are equally weighted, yet the largest stocks still carry a greater weight than the smallest. The component companies and their weighing on the 31 January 2008 are depicted in Table 11.14.

TABLE 11.14	Composition of HUI Index as of 1/31/08	
Company name	Symbol	Weight
Barrick Gold	ABX	17.16%
Newmont Mining	NEM	14.53%
Goldcorp Inc.	GG	10.04%
Yamana Gold	AUY	5.83%
Randgold Resources Ads	GOLD	5.81%
Agnico Eagle Mines	AEM	5.42%
Kinross Gold	KGC	5.40%
Golden Star Resources	GSS	4.95%
Eldorado Gold Corp	EGO	4.89%
Gold Fields Ltd. Adr	GFI	4.61%
Harmony Gold Mining	HMY	4.38%
Coeur d'Alene Mines	CDE	4.38%
Hecla Mining	HL	4.32%
Iamgoldcorp	IAG	4.22%
Northgate Minerals	NXG	4.06%

The major difference between the two indices is that BUGS is made up exclusively of mining stocks that do not hedge their gold positions more than 18 months into the future. This makes the BUGS index much more profitable than the XAU when gold prices are rising, but can also compound its losses when gold declines.

◼ 11.13 The VIX

The CBOE Volatility Index (VIX) is designed to reflect investors' consensus view of future (30-day) expected market volatility by averaging the weighted prices of out-of-the money options on the S&P 500 (SPX) index.

The name might be misleading as the VIX is not really a measure of market volatility but only of the price level of the SPX options, which is somewhat subjective and varies by opinions about the options that have nothing to do with volatility. The VIX also tells us something very important about the price of the options from which it is derived: It indicates whether the options are expensive or cheap relative to their historical prices. When the VIX is high, options are expensive, and when it is low, options are cheap. The option premium usually goes up when the market declines and it is usually a sign of fear.

I consider the VIX as a sentiment indicator because, unlike surveys and collections of information about bullishness or bearishness, it is an indicator based on traders using their capital during the course of the trading day willing to pay more for SPX put options if they perceive that a market correction is imminent. In that sense the VIX is the collective wisdom of the market at that instant.

There are three variations of volatility indexes: the VIX which tracks the S&P 500, the VXN which tracks the Nasdaq 100 and the VXD which tracks the Dow Jones Industrial Average.

The original VIX, introduced by the CBOE in 1993, measured the implied volatility or the amount that the OEX (S&P 100) options were selling above or below their fair value (as calculated by the Black-Scholes formula). The use of the Black-Scholes formula (which embodied a number of other factors like interest rates, time to expiration and historical volatility) tended to sometimes distort the expected volatility and so, in September 2003 the CBOE decided to change the calculation method. The new VIX used a newly-developed formula to derive expected volatility by averaging the weighted prices of the 30-day to expiration, out-of-the money puts and calls and was independent of the Black-Scholes option pricing model. The second noteworthy change was that the new VIX calculation used options on the S&P 500 index (SPX) rather than the S&P 100 (OEX).

For the sake of consistency the CBOE has created a historical record for the new VIX dating back to 1986 and continued the calculation of the original OEX VIX, but under the new ticker symbol "VXO."

Generally VIX values greater than 30 are associated with a large amount of volatility as a result of investor fear or uncertainty, while values below 20 generally correspond to less stressful, even complacent, times in the markets. Traders who want to trade the VIX directly can do so by purchasing futures or options on the VIX which trade actively on the CBOE. The contract size is $1000 the VIX and the symbol is VX.

Futures traders are most familiar with the fair value of stock index futures derived from the cost-of carry relationship between the futures and the underlying stock index. Since there is no carry between VIX and a position in VIX futures, the fair value of VIX futures cannot be derived by a similar relationship. Instead the fair value is derived by pricing the forward 30-day variance which underlies the settlement price of VIX futures. The fair value of VIX futures is the square root of this expected variance less an adjustment factor.

The VIX has ranged from a high of 48 in 1998 to a low of about 9 in 1993 (Figure 11.4). The VIX generally declines during periods of orderly market advances and rises during periods of market declines. The steeper the decline, the greater the VIX. Certain levels of the VIX may predict turning points in the market. It is useful to examine selected periods and the relationship of the VIX and the market. For example, Figure 11.4 details some extremes in the VIX for the most recent 10-year period from 1998 to 2008.

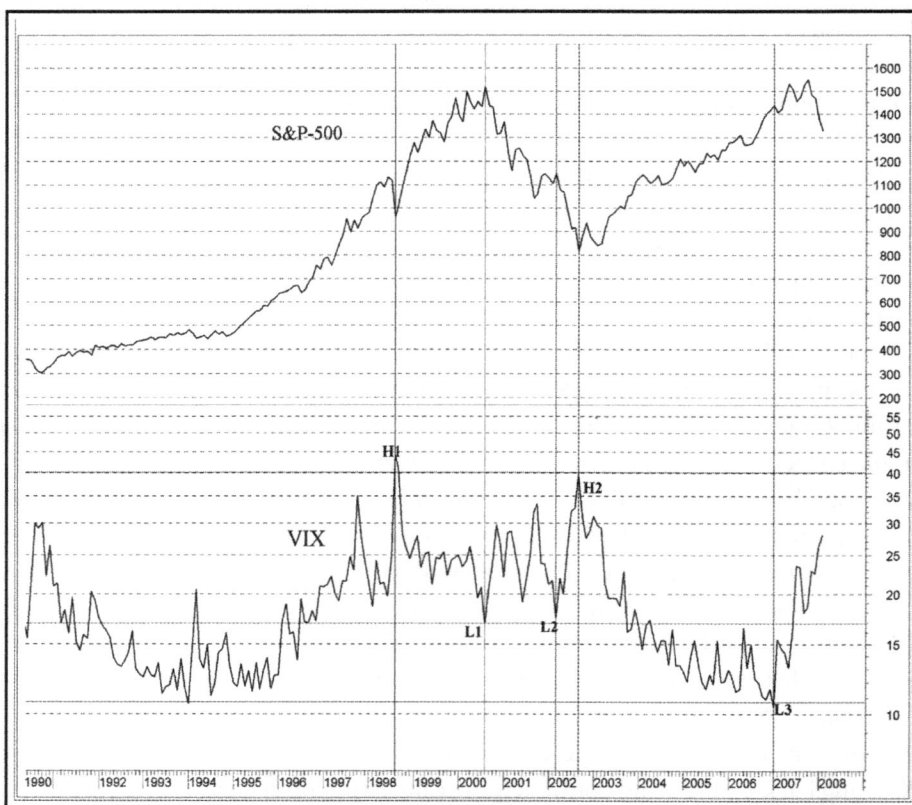

FIGURE 11.4 Weekly Chart of the S&P Goldman Sachs Commodity Index (thick bold line with the scale on the right), the RJ/CRB Index (thin black line) and Crude Oil Futures (thin grey line) from 2001 to February 2008. Notice how the Goldman Sachs commodity index closely follows crude oil prices.

Notice that the 2000 and 2002 bottoms in the VIX (marked L1 and L2 respectively in Figure 11.4) coincide with tops in the S&P 500. The VIX usually forms extreme tops or bottoms at the same time as the S&P forms bottoms or tops but sometimes it may lead the S&P 500. Notice that in January 2007 the VIX declined as low as 10 (marked L3 in Figure 11.4) which preceded a major market decline by more than six months.

The absolute level of the extremes in the VIX is not very important and varies over time. The first two bottoms (L1 and L2) occurred with the VIX around 17, but during the third extreme bottom in 2007 the VIX declined as far as 10.

Tops in the VIX indicate market bottoms. The VIX rose above 40 in August 1998 (marked H1 in Figure 11.5) and in October 2002 (marked H2) which coincided with the end of the correction in 1998 and the end of the bear market in 2002 respectively.

To determine whether the VIX is useful in predicting short-term market tops or bottoms in real-time trading, let's examine the 2-day chart in Figure 11.5. To help correctly identify the tops and bottoms in the VIX, I used the 150 day (75 bar in a 2-day chart) intermarket momentum oscillator, described fully in Chapter 16. The interpretation of this indicator is similar to the Williams' %R Oscillator. Buy signals

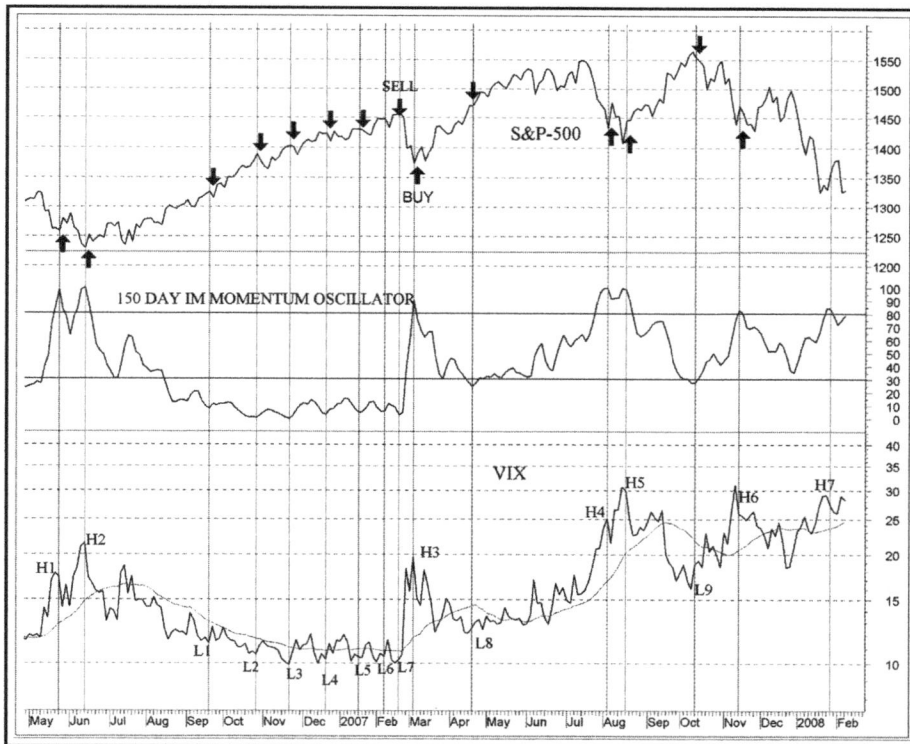

FIGURE 11.5 2-Day Chart of the S&P 500 (top) and the VIX (bottom) from May 2006 to February 2008. The 75 bar (150-day) intermarket oscillator is plotted in the middle chart. Extreme tops of the IM momentum oscillator (over 80) are marked H1–H7 and extreme bottoms (below 30) by L1–L9.

were considered when the oscillator rose above a specific level (e.g. 80), formed a peak and subsequently reversed direction and fell below that level. The oscillator indicated a sell signal when it fell below a specific level (e.g. 30) and then rose above that level.

According to the interpretation above, the oscillator issued seven buy signals and nine sell signals during the period from May 2006 to February 2008. These are overlaid in the chart in Figure 11.5. The signals marked H2, H3 and H5 correctly identified market bottoms while the other four buy signals were early by approximately two weeks on average. Only two signals (marked L7 and L9) correctly predicted market tops while the rest of the sell signals were premature. In these cases the time period that the VIX was early in predicting a market top ranged from two weeks to five months.

In view of the above we can conclude that the VIX, in spite of correctly predicting some market turning points, was early in predicting more than half of the market tops or bottoms. It is not, therefore, the "Holy Grail" that some people believe it is and should only be used together with other indicators for more accurate market timing.

CHAPTER 12

The S&P 500

From Markos Katsanos, *Intermarket Trading Strategies* (Hoboken, New Jersey: John Wiley & Sons, 2008), Chapter 5.

Interpretation is the revenge of the intellect upon art.

—Susan Sontag

Learning Objective Statement

▪ Describe general correlations noticed between the S&P 500 and International Indices

The calculation of the correlation coefficient between the index to be predicted and other related markets is the first step of a complete and thorough intermarket analysis. Of course, the final challenge comes from interpretation. Intermarket analysis relies on the premise that relationships in the past will be the same in the future so before making any conclusions it is always prudent to assess the stability of the correlation coefficient over time.

I chose to start this correlation analysis with a broad market index like the S&P 500 which is widely regarded as the best single gauge of the US equities market.

▪ 12.1 Correlation with International Indices

The first step in a correlation or regression analysis is to decide whether you want to analyze the price on a daily, weekly, monthly or quarterly basis. Using long time scales has the added apparent theoretical benefit that averaging over long periods suppresses windowing errors and daily noise, revealing the underlying long term correlations. The choice of time periods is therefore very important and should depend on a trader's time horizon. This is illustrated in Tables 12.3 and 12.4 where the correlation rises dramatically when weekly returns replace daily data. As the time

| TABLE 12.1 | Yearly Correlation Between Daily Prices of the S&P and Major World Indices. Symbols: DJ-30 is the Dow Jones Industrials, RUT is the small cap Russell 2000 index, NDX is the Nasdaq 100, TSX is Canada's S&P TSX Composite Index and Euro Stoxx is the Dow Jones Euro Stoxx 50 Index which tracks the 50 most important stocks in the Euro zone. The 10th percentile row shows the yearly correlations below which certain percentages of cases fall. So, for example, if the 10th percentile of the correlation between the S&P 500 and the DJ-30 is 0.61, it means that the correlation was below 0.61 only 10% of the time. The reverse is true for the 90th percentile row. Notice the significant improvement in correlation consistency during the latest 10-year period from 1998–2007 (bottom four rows). |

Year	DJ-30	RUT	NDX	TSX	Euro Stoxx	DAX	CAC	FTSE	Nikkei	Hang Seng
2007	0.93	0.69	0.70	0.92	0.90	0.84	0.76	0.86	0.21	0.46
2006	0.97	0.85	0.75	0.81	0.94	0.83	0.80	0.84	0.52	0.90
2005	0.77	0.952	0.92	0.82	0.84	0.83	0.80	084	0.73	0.76
2004	0.84	0.96	0.94	0.86	0.87	0.91	0.83	0.76	0.02	0.75
2003	0.99	0.98	0.98	0.95	0.93	0.97	0.95	0.97	0.84	0.87
2002	0.98	0.96	0.85	0.98	0.98	0.96	0.98	0.98	0.76	0.85
2001	0.92	0.86	0.94	0.96	0.95	0.95	0.95	0.95	0.84	0.93
2000	0.59	0.46	0.67	0.57	0.59	0.50	0.61	0.64	0.35	0.59
1999	0.87	0.83	0.81	0.89	0.87	0.84	0.83	0.86	0.81	0.89
1998	0.92	0.28	0.80	0.38	0.66	0.61	0.76	0.69	−0.02	0.20
1997	0.97	0.93	0.91	0.94	NA	0.93	0.90	0.96	−0.22	−0.04
1996	0.99	0.73	0.97	0.97	NA	0.95	0.89	0.85	−0.09	0.93
1995	0.99	0.96	0.95	0.90	NA	0.78	0.02	0.98	0.23	0.92
1994	0.95	0.75	0.77	0.72	NA	0.04	0.34	0.68	−0.18	0.70
1993	0.93	0.92	0.73	0.84	NA	0.89	0.87	0.88	0.15	0.83
1992	0.24	0.49	0.52	−0.24	NA	−0.52	−0.34	0.45	−0.18	0.14
1992–2007										
Average	**0.87**	0.79	**0.83**	0.77	NA	0.71	0.69	**0.82**	0.30	0.67
Median	**0.93**	0.86	0.83	**0.87**	NA	**0.87**	0.83	**0.86**	0.22	0.80
Std Dev	0.20	0.21	**0.13**	0.31	NA	0.41	0.37	**0.15**	0.40	0.31
Range	0.75	0.70	**0.46**	1.21	NA	1.49	1.32	**0.53**	1.06	0.97
10th Per	**0.49**	0.40	**0.52**	−0.24	NA	−0.52	−0.34	**0.45**	−0.22	−0.04
90th Per	**0.99**	**0.97**	**0.97**	**0.97**	NA	0.96	0.96	**0.98**	0.84	0.93
1998–2007										
Average	**0.88**	0.78	**0.84**	0.81	**0.85**	0.84	**0.84**	0.84	0.50	0.72
Median	**0.92**	0.85	0.83	**0.87**	**0.89**	**0.87**	0.83	0.86	0.62	0.80
Std Dev	**0.12**	0.24	**0.11**	0.19	**0.13**	0.16	**0.12**	**0.12**	0.34	0.24
Range	0.40	0.70	**0.31**	0.60	**0.39**	0.47	**0.37**	**0.33**	0.86	0.73
10th Per	**0.61**	0.30	**0.67**	0.40	0.60	0.51	**0.62**	**0.65**	0.00	0.23
90th Per	**0.99**	**0.98**	**0.98**	**0.98**	**0.98**	0.97	**0.98**	**0.98**	0.84	0.93

TABLE 12.2 Long- and Short-term Spearman's ρ Nonparametric Correlation between the S&P and Major World Indices. High correlations are in bold. Abbreviations: H = heteroscedasticity present (non homogeneous data), CL = curvilinear relationship, NL = non linear, NA = correlation coefficient not available because of insufficient data.

Year	DJ-30	RUT	NDX	TSX	Euro Stoxx	DAX	CAC	FTSE	Nikkei	Hang Seng
2	**0.98**	0.91	0.93	**0.96**	**0.98**	**0.97**	0.96	0.96	0.58	0.92
3	**0.98**	**0.97**	0.93	**0.98**	**0.99**	**0.98**	**0.98**	**0.98**	0.85	0.96
4	**0.97**	**0.99**	0.95	**0.99**	**0.99**	**0.99**	**0.98**	**0.98**	0.90	**0.98**
5	**0.98**	**0.99**	**0.97**	**0.99**	**0.99**	**0.99**	**0.99**	**0.99**	0.94 H	0.98 CL
10	0.88	0.57 H	0.93 CL	0.71 CL	0.89	0.89	0.91	0.90	0.81 NL	0.87 CL
15	0.96	0.87 H	0.98 CL	0.91 CL	NA	0.96	0.96	0.96	−0.3 NL	0.82 CL
20	**0.99**	NA	0.99 CL	0.94 CL	NA	NA	NA	**0.98**	NA	0.92 CL
25	**0.99**	NA	NA	0.94 CL	NA	NA	NA	NA	NA	NA

segment is reduced, noise becomes a bigger factor in the calculation and the correlation drops due to an abundance of change which is unfolding in the short term.

To better understand the evolution of correlations over time in Table 12.1, I have calculated price correlations between the S&P 500 and major world indices yearly from 1992 to 2007, in Table 12.2 up to 25 years long- and short-term nonparametric price correlations and in Table 12.3 nonparametric correlations between daily percentage returns of the S&P 500 and major world indices. The data used to derive the correlation coefficients are up to the end of 2007. You can find up-to-date values of nonparametric price correlations at http://www.csidata.com.

Care should be taken before using any of the numbers, especially the long-term price correlations in Table 12.2, as some of the relationships were not linear. I have marked these to indicate deviations from linearity, but in any case you should check a scatterplot or a chart of the related index before making a significant investment

TABLE 12.3 Long- and Short-Term Spearman's ρ Nonparametric Correlation between the S&P Daily Percent Returns and Major World Indices. The 15-year correlation of the DJ Euro Stoxx 50 was not calculated as only nine years of data were available for this index.

Year	DJ-30	RUT	NDX	TSX	Euro Stoxx	DAX	CAC	FTSE	Nikkei	Hang Seng
2	**0.95**	**0.89**	**0.88**	0.65	0.48	0.49	0.51	0.50	0.12	0.13
4	**0.95**	0.84	**0.88**	0.62	0.44	0.43	0.43	0.42	0.11	0.10
5	**0.96**	0.84	**0.88**	0.62	0.46	0.48	0.45	0.42	0.11	0.10
10	0.93	0.81	0.84	0.65	0.44	0.49	0.44	0.42	0.13	0.13
15	0.92	0.77	0.80	0.60	NA	0.40	0.39	0.39	0.11	0.13
avg.	**0.94**	0.83	**0.86**	0.63	0.46	0.46	0.44	0.43	0.12	0.12

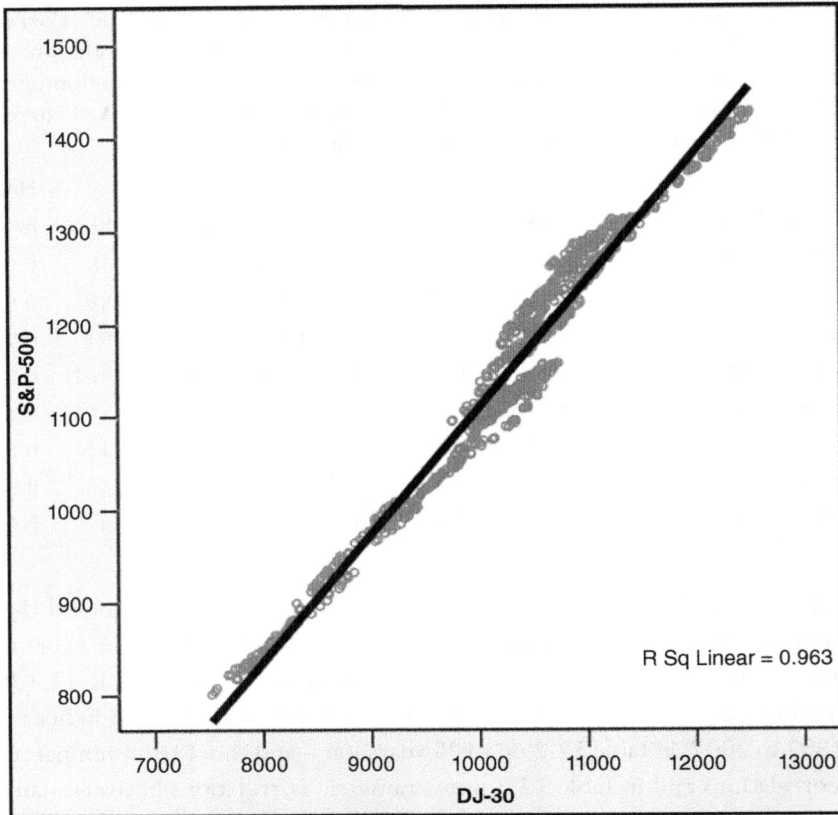

FIGURE 12.1 Scatterplot of 2-Year Closing Prices of the S&P 500 vs. the Dow Jones Industrials. Although the homogeneity of variance around the regression line is not perfect, it is still better than the plot in Figure 12.2.

decision based on these numbers. For example, in Tables 12.1 and 12.2 the correlation coefficient between the S&P 500 and Russell 2000 in 2004 and 2005 is indicated higher than the corresponding correlation with the DJ-30. However, looking at the relevant scatterplots in Figures 12.1 and 12.2, we can see that higher values of the Russell 2000 (Figure 12.2, top right) are not distributed evenly around the linear regression line and, as discussed in Level II, Chapter 15, this could distort the correlation coefficient between the two indices.

This is not usually a problem when transforming price data to differences or percentage yields. For example consider the scatterplots in Figures 12.3 and 12.4 which are both between the S&P and the VIX. In Figure 12.4 price data was converted to weekly yields.

As can be seen from Table 12.1, the correlations are not constant over time, sometimes (although rarely) alternating from weak negative to strong positive.

In order to examine more closely the volatility of these correlations I have calculated at the bottom of Table 12.1 the average, median, standard deviation and the

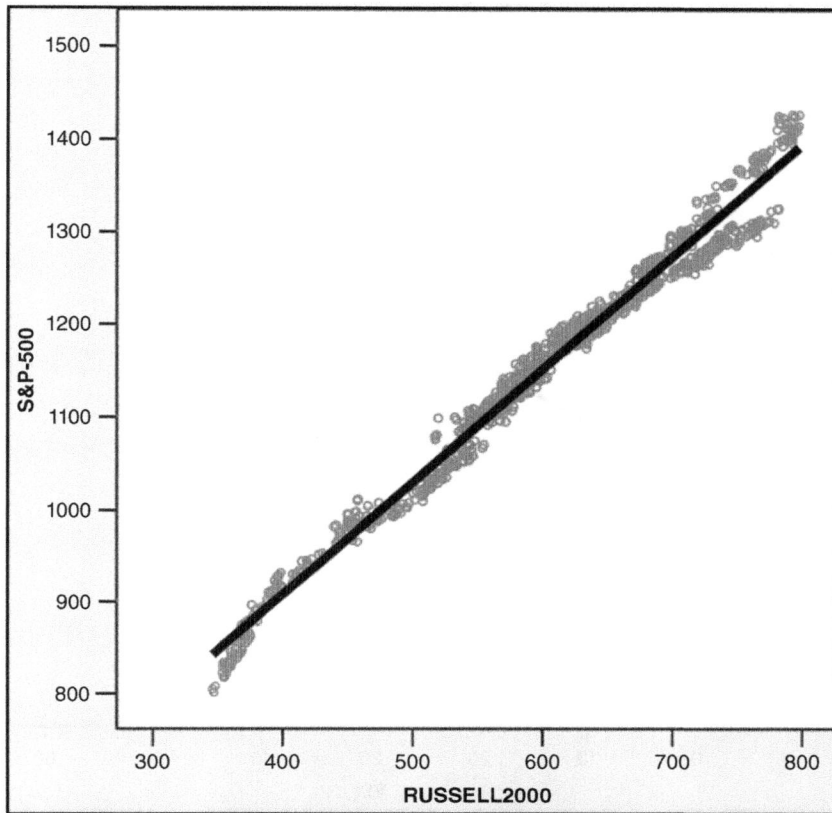

FIGURE 12.2 Scatterplot of 2-Year Closing Prices of the S&P 500 vs. the Russell 2000 Small Cap Index. Notice the increase in variance at the top right of the plot.

maximum range (highest minus lowest correlation value over each time span). The standard deviation, however, may not be the best measure of variance as most values were concentrated at the far right of the histogram (negative skew) and the correlation distribution deviated significantly from the normal Gaussian curve.

To deal with this problem I divided the yearly correlations in percentiles according to their level. So for example, if the 10% percentile of the correlation between the S&P 500 and the DJ-30 is 0.61, it means that only 10% of the yearly correlations were below 0.61. The correlation was more stable over time with high capitalization indices like the DJ-30 and the FTSE. Small capitalization stocks, represented by the Russell 2000, had the most unstable relationship. In fact, correlation with European stocks was less volatile than with its US compatriot. Their correlation with the Euro Stoxx broke down during the most recent 10-year period only twice, in 2000 and 1998.

The correlation between the S&P 500 and other international and emerging market equities was highly erratic when considering yearly time segments, and over the 16-year study (Table 12.1), the relationship also varied substantially. This is because international relationships can change as the forces that drive earnings in Europe, Asia and

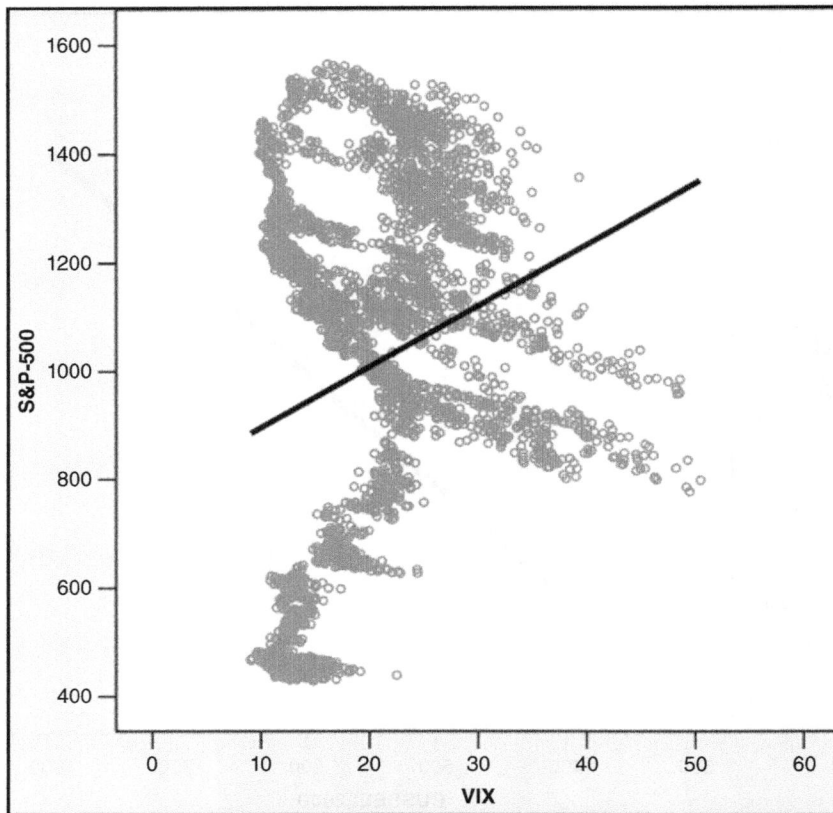

FIGURE 12.3 Scatterplot of the CBOE Volatility Index (VIX) vs. the S&P 500 over a 15-year Period from 1993 to the End of 2007.

elsewhere aren't identical to what is unfolding in Chicago and Silicon Valley. The correlation with British stocks was an exception because, although the correlation was not as strong as with the DJ-30, it was less volatile over time. The index with the weakest and most unstable correlation was the Nikkei 225 and this was evident in all time frames.

Rather than rely on historical correlations, a more comprehensive and dynamic approach is needed when making trading decisions. The number and frequency of these changes can complicate the design of intermarket trading systems as they rely on the principle that relationships in the past would be the same in the future. Markets may decouple and a strategy based on that assumption might produce considerable drawdown.

Taking into account the predicted future correlation rather than historical values could be advantageous in intermarket system design or long-term forecasting. One way of making a prediction of what the correlation is going to be in the future is to adjust the correlation coefficient, in order to take into account the most recent trend, by the trend or rate of change of the correlation during the most recent 5-year period.

The impact of globalization and free money flow across national borders can be seen in the rising correlations between the S&P 500 and international indices. The S&P 500 and Euro Stoxx 50 have been posting correlations in the range of 0.9 to

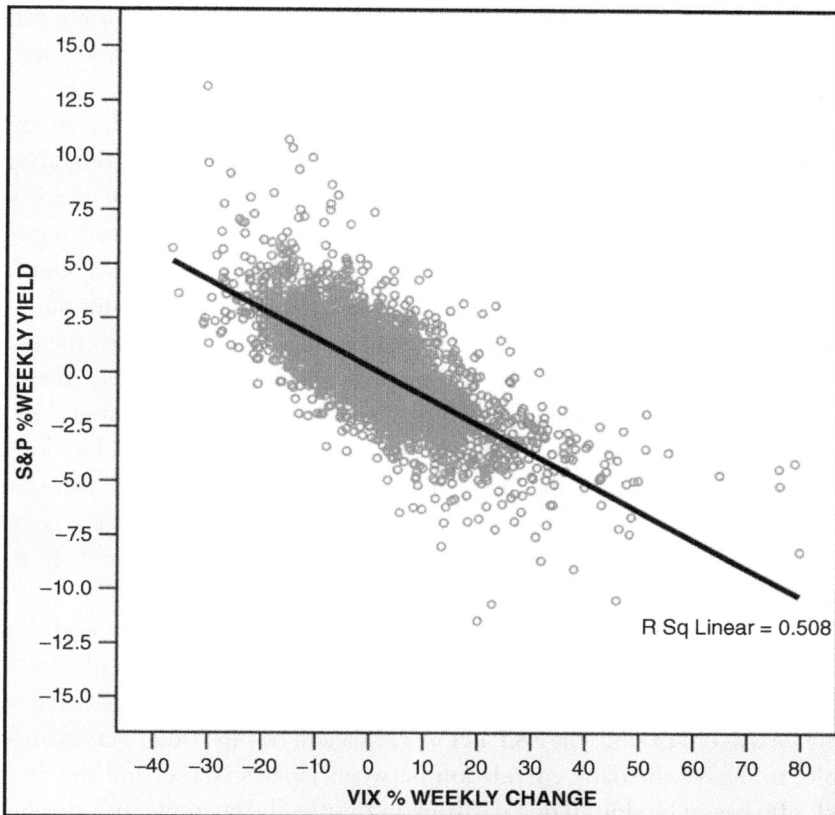

FIGURE 12.4 Scatterplot of Weekly % Changes of the CBOE Volatility Index (VIX) vs. Weekly % Returns of the S&P 500 over the 15-year Period from 1993 to the End of 2007. The relationship has become approximately linear when taking percent yields.

0.94 for the last two years (Table 12.1), up sharply from the 0.59 to 0.86 during the period from 1998 to 2000. Also the correlation of weekly yields with the FTSE has improved from 0.39 to 0.74 and with the DAX from 0.66 to 0.76 during the latest 2-year period (Table 12.4).

TABLE 12.4   Long- and Short-term Nonparametric Correlation between S&P Weekly % Returns and Major World Indices

Year	DJ-30	RUT	NDX	TSX	Euro Stoxx	DAX	CAC	FTSE	Nikkei	Hang Seng
2	**0.95**	**0.86**	0.84	0.69	0.77	0.76	0.78	0.74	0.46	0.49
4	**0.95**	**0.86**	0.85	0.67	0.75	0.73	0.73	0.67	0.44	0.46
5	**0.96**	**0.87**	**0.87**	0.69	0.75	0.72	0.74	0.68	0.46	0.47
10	0.92	0.82	0.84	0.74	0.74	0.73	0.73	0.70	0.43	0.50
15	0.92	0.79	0.79	0.70	NA	0.66	0.65	0.39	0.38	0.45
avg.	**0.94**	0.84	0.84	0.70	0.75	0.72	0.73	0.64	0.43	0.47

This trend is widely acknowledged for European indexes, but what is less accepted is that correlations between US and many other non-European indexes have also increased.

A comparison between Tables 12.2 and 12.3 reveals a significant deterioration of the correlation between the S&P and all non-US exchanges when comparing correlations between daily percentage yields instead of prices. This can be partly attributed (except for the TSX) to different time zones. Most European exchanges close at 11:30 US ET time, so only two hours of US trading is taken into account. This is a real problem in calculating the actual real-time correlation. One solution is to use Intraday 30-minute data and correlate the S&P change between 11:30 the previous day and 11:30 the next day but this will involve splitting a trading day in two. Obtaining 15 years of intraday data is also a problem. Another possible alternative is to compare the S&P with European index futures data as most of them close long after regular hours. Conveniently, the DAX and Euro Stoxx futures closing time happens to coincide with the US market closing time at 16:00 ET. Of course there is no overlap between the US and Asian markets so in order to predict Nikkei daily changes based on S&P changes the S&P has to be shifted one day in the past.

You should therefore take into consideration the trading hours of each index as non-US indices (except Canada's TSX and other American indices) trade during different time zones. The S&P is the last to close and therefore international indices can only be used to predict the S&P (short term) and not the other way around. For example, to derive the daily correlation between Japan's Nikkei and the S&P 500, the S&P 500 has to be shifted one day back in time as the current day's closing price is not known during Japanese trading hours. You can find trading hours for all the Exchanges in Chapter 11 (Table 11.1).

■ 12.2 Interest Rates, Commodities, Forex and the VIX

The importance of changes in interest rates and their impact on equity markets has long been recognized by astute Wall Street analysts and technicians. Martin Zweig in his classic *Winning On Wall* Street provided a stock market timing model which is based on changes in the prime rate.

The old "Don't fight the Fed" maxim for years suggested that when the Fed starts lowering rates, it is time to start buying stocks. Conversely, when the Fed begins to raise rates, it is usually time to head for the exit. Unfortunately, investors who responded to this old canard and began buying stocks when the Federal Reserve Board started lowering rates were burned badly twice: once in 2001, and again in August 2007.

Over the past seven years we have been confronted with a reversal of the normal negative correlation between interest rates and share prices. This proves that a system relying on the historical correlation alone is not the best approach and a broader assessment of factors affecting the future relationship between stocks and interest rates is also required.

In the search for factors influencing price correlation, market corrections, uncertainties or perceived risks play a fundamental part, as Figure 12.5 illustrates. The 1987 crash, the 1997 Asian financial crisis and the Long Term Capital Management crisis in conjunction with Russia's bond default triggered a sharp slide in stock prices and a subsequent rally in bonds, as investors fled to safety. This resulted in negative correlation between stocks and bonds (positive between stocks and bond yields).

An analysis of correlation at specific periods in the business cycle reveals a fundamental reason for the correlation reversal between stock prices and bond yields: The correlation with interest rates switches to positive during economic recessions. During the 1981–1982 recession bonds rallied, pushing yields lower, while stock prices

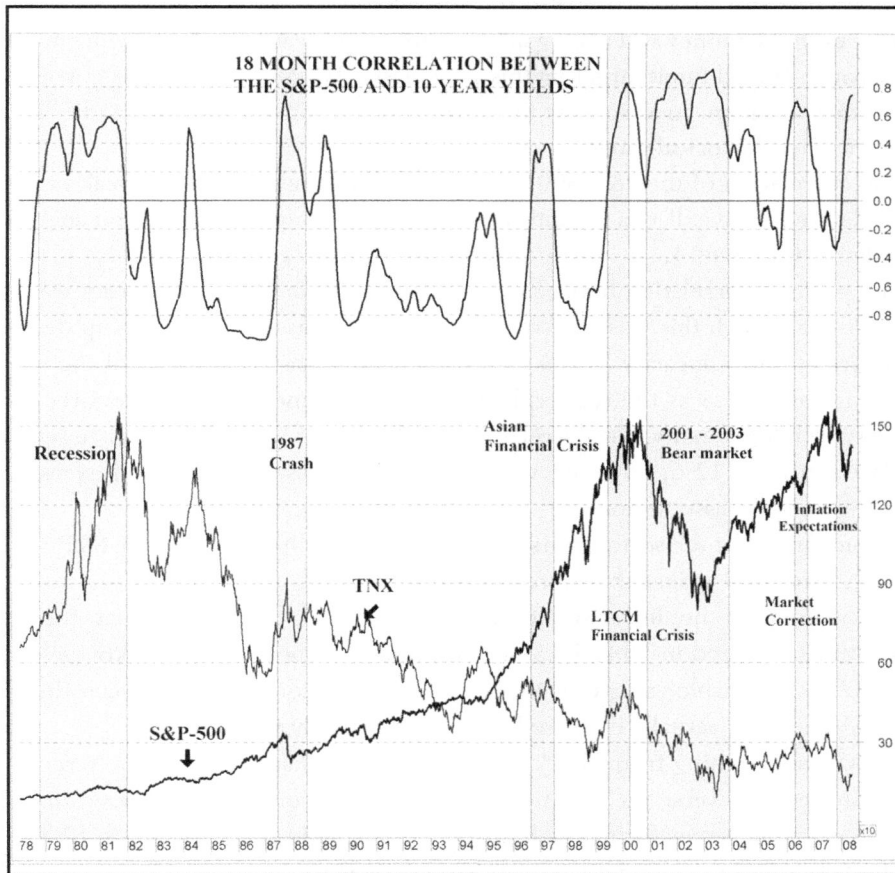

FIGURE 12.5 Weekly Chart of the S&P 500 and 10-Year Treasury Yields (TNX) from 1978 until May 2008. The top chart is the 18-month correlation between the S&P 500 and the TNX. Notice how the traditional long-term negative correlation turns positive in times of financial turmoil like the 1987 market crash, the 1997 Asian crisis and the Russian bond and subsequent Long Term Capital Management crisis (shaded in grey). Notice also how, at the beginning of 2000, the long-term correlation bias turned from negative to positive.

declined. This pattern was repeated during the more recent recession in 2001–2003 (see Figure 12.5).

Apart from the factors already discussed, inflation expectations or rising commodity prices can also induce a correlation reversal because rising inflation is negative for bonds and therefore positive for yields. Rising oil and agricultural commodity prices induced a correlation reversal again at the beginning of 2008 as illustrated in Figure 12.5.

The fluctuation of correlations, however, is hardly limited to stocks and bonds. The correlation of weekly yields between the S&P 500 and the CRB index strengthened from near zero or a non-existent historical correlation to 0.15 as commodities became everyone's new favorite asset class.

The increase may not seem a lot but the question is whether the trend will continue. Factors that may have caused the correlation upturn may be the dollar's demise or even the money still rolling into commodities by way of the growing number of exchange-traded funds targeting this asset class. My opinion is that the correlation will revert to the mean as soon as the dollar index stabilizes and commodity prices return to their historical range.

The correlation of the S&P 500 with gold has also reversed from weak negative to moderate positive. If you are interested in gold a complete correlation analysis is included in Chapter 14.

The positive correlation between the S&P and oil for the last 20 years was also a surprise, although this was not consistent over time as their relationship deviated considerably from linearity. This was also the case with the majority of the correlations in Table 12.5 as the scatterplots revealed that most of them deviated from linearity or homogeneity. The correlation coefficients of weekly percentage returns, displayed in Table 12.6, however, were more reliable as none deviated excessively from the linearity assumption.

A comparison of the scatterplots of the CBOE Volatility Index vs. the S&P in Figures 12.3 and 12.4 makes this more obvious.

Inconsistent or nonlinear relationships were also the reason that the high correlations depicted in Table 12.5 have faded away when taking weekly yields (in Table 12.6). A notable exception to the rule was the correlation between the S&P and the VIX which actually increased when using weekly yields.

Activities stemming from the "carry trade," which have emerged only recently, also managed to reverse the traditional weak positive correlation between the S&P and the yen to negative during the last three years (Table 12.5 and Figure 12.6).

The first step in running a correlation analysis is to decide on the best time interval for calculating price changes. To understand the basic financial factors behind a market's course over longer periods of time, more than 10 days of percentage returns should be used generally. On the other hand, weekly percentage yields are more suitable for shorter-term trading. The best time period for taking percentage differences can also vary from market to market. The objective is to take a variable that you're interested in (in this case the S&P 500) and see to what degree its changes

TABLE 12.5 Long- and Short-Term Nonparametric Correlation between the S&P, Commodities, Forex and the VIX as of 31.12.2007. TNX is the CBOE 10-year Treasury Yield Index, XOI is the AMEX Oil Index, XAU is the Philadelphia Gold/Silver Stock Index, GOLD is the World Gold Index (XGLD), CRB is the Commodity Research Bureau Index and YEN is the JPY/USD exchange rate. Abbreviations: H = heteroscedasticity present (non homogeneous data), CL = curvilinear relationship, NL = non linear, NA = correlation coefficient not available because of insufficient data.

Years	VIX	TNX	XOI	Crude oil	XAU	GOLD	CRB	Dollar index	YEN
2	0.3NL	−0.25H	0.83	0.2NL	0.4H	0.73H	−0.2NL	−0.83	−0.3H
5	−0.5H	0.65H	0.98CL	0.88NL	0.88	0.96 CL	0.81H	−0.77NL	0.3H
10	−0.3NL	0.5NL	0.54 NL	0.37NL	0.15NL	0.12NL	0.22 NL	−0.2NL	0.3NL
15	0.23H	−0.4NL	0.85 NL	0.61NL	−0.2NL	0.00	0.17 NL	0.09H	−0.3NL
20	NA	−0.8NL	0.93 NL	0.53NL	−0.3NL	−0.3NL	0.06	NA	NA
25	NA	−0.9NL	NA	NA	NA	−0.3NL	−0.06	NA	NA
30	NA	−0.8NL	NA	NA	NA	−0.070	−0.09	NA	NA

TABLE 12.6	Nonparametric Correlation between S&P and Major Commodity and Financial Weekly Percentage Returns								
Years	VIX	TNX	XOI	Crude oil	XAU	GOLD	CRB	Dollar index	YEN
2	−0.81	0.18	0.56	0.02	0.47	0.20	0.15	−0.17	−0.15
5	−0.75	0.20	0.51	−0.10	0.34	0.10	0.08	−0.08	−0.02
10	−0.77	0.19	0.44	0.03	0.15	0.02	0.07	0.06	−0.02
15	−0.70	0.02	0.46	0.01	0.12	−0.01	0.03	0.08	−0.04
avg.	−0.76	0.15	0.49	−0.01	0.27	0.08	0.08	−0.03	−0.06

FIGURE 12.6 Weekly Chart of the S&P 500 (in bold) and the Yen (Yen USD thin line) from 1992 until February 2008. Notice the alternating periods of positive (gray background) and negative (white background) correlation with the S&P 500 and how, in the beginning of 2005, the unwinding of the "carry trade" reversed the correlation from positive to negative.

can be explained by changes in some other potentially relevant variables for a range of different time spans.

Table 12.7 lists the correlation between the S&P and related markets using daily to quarterly percentage returns. As you can see, the correlation peaked at the three week interval for some markets (e.g. XOI), while a longer-term time span was more appropriate for calculating the correlation with other markets like interest rates (TNX). The VIX was an exception to the rule, as it actually correlated better with the S&P 500 on a short-term basis (daily yields). This is probably because the

THE S&P 500

TABLE 12.7 10-Year Correlation between the S&P and Major Commodity and Financial Indices Using Daily, Weekly, 10 Trading Day (2-week), 15 Trading Day (3-week), Monthly and Quarterly Returns for the 10-Year Period from the Beginning of 1998 to the End of 2007

Time segment	VIX	TNX	XOI	Oil	XAU	GOLD	CRB	Dollar index	YEN
Daily	−0.78	0.23	0.48	−0.02	0.08	−0.04	0.04	0.14	−0.09
Weekly	−0.75	0.24	0.46	−0.01	0.14	0.00	0.06	0.08	−0.06
10 day	−0.74	0.26	0.46	−0.02	0.13	−0.02	0.03	0.08	−0.03
15 day	−0.74	0.24	0.48	−0.03	0.13	−0.02	0.02	0.06	−0.01
Monthly	−0.75	0.24	0.46	−0.03	0.13	−0.03	0.03	0.05	0.03
Quarterly	−0.70	0.32	0.37	−0.13	0.12	−0.01	−0.11	0.13	−0.02

VIX is a sentiment indicator and not a fundamental factor affecting changes in the S&P 500.

12.3 Correlation Between the S&P 500 and Stocks

The 25 stocks with the best (positive) and the worst (negative) correlation with the S&P 500 are depicted in Tables 12.8 and 12.9 respectively, over a 5-year period until February 2007. Surprisingly, the five best correlated stocks are not S&P components

TABLE 12.8 Nonparametric Correlation between the S&P 500 and the 25 Best Correlated International Stocks during the 5-Year Period from February 2002 to February 2007. Column 3 shows the 5-year Spearman's correlation coefficient and Column 4 shows the stock's underlying index.

Company Name	Symbol	Correlation	Index
Axa	AXA	0.986	CAC40
Netherlands Index ETF	EWN	0.98	AEX
Sage GRP	SGE.L	0.978	FTSE
Sweden Index ETF	EWD	0.977	OMXSPI
European Equity Fund	EEA	0.976	ESTX
Emerson Electric	EMR	0.975	S&P
Tri-Continental Corp.	TY	0.973	NA
Lincoln National Corp.	LNC	0.972	S&P
Exxon Mobil	XOM	0.967	S&P
United Technologies	UTX	0.961	S&P
Boeing Co.	BA	0.96	S&P
Altria Group	MO	0.959	S&P
Chevron Corp.	CVX	0.958	S&P
American Express	AXP	0.956	S&P
Pearson Plc	PSO	0.956	FTSE
Pepsico	PEP	0.955	S&P
BP Plc	BP	0.95	FTSE
Caterpillar Inc.	CAT	0.949	S&P
Public Service Enterprise	PEG	0.947	S&P
Alltel Corp.	AT	0.946	S&P
COGECO	CGO.TO	0.941	NA
Merril Lynch & Co.	MER	0.934	S&P
Dover Corp.	DOV	0.93	S&P
Citigroup	C	0.908	S&P
Procter & Gamble	PG	0.905	S&P

TABLE 12.9 Nonparametric Correlation between the S&P 500 and the 25 Worst Correlated Stocks. The 5-year Spearman's correlation coefficient is shown in Column 3 and the stock's underlying index in Column 4.

CompanyName	Symbol	Correlation	Index
PRG-Schultz Int.	PRGX	−0.907	
Tenet Healthcare Corp.	THC	−0.864	S&P 500
European Diamonds Plc	EPD.L	−0.841	
Superior Industries Int.	SUP	−0.833	Russell 2000
Entercom Communications	ETM	−0.804	Russell 2000
Ramco Oil Services Plc	ROS.L	−0.8	
Farmer Bros Co.	FARM	−0.791	Russell 2000
Trimeris Inc.	TRMS	−0.791	Russell 2000
Fibernet Telecom Group	FTGX	−0.78	
Molins Plc	MLIN.L	−0.779	
Fifth Third Bancorp	FTB	−0.758	S&P 500
Libbey Inc.	LBY	−0.757	S&P 600
Blockbuster	BBI	−0.756	Russell 2000
Ninety Nine Only Stores	NDN	−0.751	Russell 2000
NTT Docomo ADS	DCM	−0.697	Nikkei
Enzon Pharmaceutical	ENZN	−0.696	Russell 2000
Fred's Inc.	FRED	−0.688	Russell 2000
Cray Inc.	CRAY	−0.686	Russell 2000
La-Z-Boy Inc.	LZB	−0.679	Russell 2000
Ballard Power Systems	BLDP	−0.678	TSX
Utstarcom Inc.	UTSI	−0.661	Russell 2000
Jardine Lloyd Thompson	JLT.L	−0.658	
GoAmerica Inc.	GOAM	−0.657	
Ariba Inc.	ARBA	−0.643	Russell 2000
Cabot Microelectronics Cp	CCMP	−0.639	Russell 2000

but European stocks or ETFs. The 25 worst correlated stocks were mostly companies that did not follow the bullish trend during the period under study because of various company specific problems.

I wouldn't advise investing in these stocks as a means of diversification. On the other hand, some of them might recover and catch up with the S&P 500 provided that their problems are resolved.

CHAPTER 13

European Indices

From Markos Katsanos, *Intermarket Trading Strategies* (Hoboken, New Jersey: John Wiley & Sons, 2008), Chapter 6.

A little uncertainty is good for everything.

—**Henry Kissinger**

Learning Objective Statement

■ Describe general correlations noticed between the European Indices and other indices or commodities

▒ 13.1 The DAX

Trading in DAX futures has recently become very popular among US traders as it provides an additional liquid market to trade. The main advantages are currency diversification and a wider range of trading times. The German futures exchange (Eurex) is open 14 hours a day from 8:00 to 22:00 CET (02:00–16:00 US EST) and the longer trading times are convenient for bothAustralian and US-based traders. In order to make modifications or design your own system for intermarket DAX futures trading, you will need a thorough understanding of its correlation with other international stock indices, currencies and commodities.

Correlations between the DAX and major international indices, forex and commodities are depicted in Table 13.1 and correlations with other European indices in Table 13.2. The DAX correlated best, with the Euro Stoxx 50. This was not surprising as both indices had a number of common component stocks. The second best correlationwas with the French CAC 40 index, as both nations—whether they like it or not—are joined in the economic community. American indices had to be shifted back one day in time in order for the correlation values to have some predictive usefulness for the DAX, as all American exchanges closed 4½ hours later. An alternative approach would be to correlate the DAX opening price with the previous day's

| TABLE 13.1 | Nonparametric Correlation between the DAX and Major World Indices for the 5-Year Period until 31 December 2006. The 5-year Spearman's price correlation coefficient is shown in column 3 and the correlation of daily and weekly yields (% changes) in column 4. All US indices were shifted one day back since the current day's closing price is not known at the time of the DAX close. |

		Yield %	
Index/Commodity	Daily Prices	Daily	Weekly
SP 500 (lag 1 day)	0.913	0.134	0.661
DJ-30 (lag 1 day)	0.884	0.125	0.652
NDX (lag 1 day)	0.847	0.167	0.614
TSX (lag 1 day)	0.881	0.097	0.505
Euro Stoxx 50	**0.992**	**0.878**	**0.928**
Stoxx 50	**0.971**	0.864	0.887
Tecdax	0.833	0.714	0.764
CAC 40	**0.995**	0.862	**0.904**
FTSE	**0.989**	0.724	0.767
Athens General	**0.980**	0.385	0.551
Utility index (lag 1 day)	0.912	0.085	0.242
Nikkei	0.900	0.231	0.535
Hang Seng	0.852	0.245	0.508
10 Yr tr. yld (lag 1 day)	0.715	0.062	0.375
Bund	0.372	−0.338	−0.377
Gold	0.660	−0.15	−0.113
Oil (Brent)	0.040	−0.039	−0.055
Euro	0.404	−0.21	−0.213
Dollar index (lag 1 day)	−0.25	0.080	0.170
Yen	0.030	0.082	0.074

closing price of the corresponding American index. This improves the correlation coefficient from 0.134 to 0.422 when comparing the last day's S&P 500 daily change with the DAX change between the current day's open and last day's close. Similar correlation analysis can be used to predict opening prices of lagging (in the time zone) international indices. For example the Nikkei opening price can be predicted based on the last day's closing price of the S&P 500, or a European index opening can be predicted based on both the last day's closing price of the S&P and the current day's closing of Asian exchanges using a multiple regression model.

Notice that correlations between DAX and all other non equity index assets (below the Hang Seng in Table 13.1) broke down and even reversed sign when taking daily or weekly yields. This is because their relationship with the DAX was non linear thus invalidating the correlation analysis.

■ 13.2 Correlation with Stocks

In Table 13.3 you can see 15 US stocks (including foreign ADR) with the strongest correlation with the DAX over a 5-year period. An analysis by industry reveals that

TABLE 13.2 Nonparametric Correlation between the DAX and Major European Indices for the Preceding 5 and 10 year Period as of 31 May 2007

Index	5 Year	10 Year
Euro Stoxx 50	**0.992**	**0.966**
Stoxx 50	0.971	0.944
CAC 40	**0.995**	0.94
Euronext 100	**0.996**	N/A
FTSE	0.99	0.925
SSMI (Swiss)	0.99	0.936
MIB-30 (Italian)	0.987	N/A
BEL-20 (Belgian)	0.986	0.734
Athens General	0.98	0.823
Irish Stock Index	0.987	N/A

TABLE 13.3 Nonparametric Correlation between the DAX and the 15 Best Correlated US Stocks (including ADRs) during the 5-Year Period from 1 June 2003 to 1 June 2007. The 5-year Spearman's correlation coefficient is shown in column 3 and the stock's industry group in column 4. As was expected, the DAX has the strongest correlation with European ADRs like Holland's Akzo and the Greek Telco OTE.

Company name	Symbol	Correlation	Industry
Akzo Nobel NV	AKZOY	0.985	Chemicals
Hellenic Telecomm	OTE	0.979	Telecomm
ING Group NV	ING	0.976	Financial
Orient Express	OEH	0.976	Lodging
Mexico Fund	MXF	0.976	Country fund
Chubb Corp.	CB	0.975	Financial
General Dynamics	GD	0.975	Defense
Cleco Corp.	CNL	0.975	Utilities
DPL	DPL	0.975	Utilities
Manitowoc	MTW	0.973	Farm Machinery
Be Aerospace	BEAV	0.973	Defense
Iconix Brand	ICON	0.972	Apparel
Laboratory Corp.	LH	0.972	Drugs
Nucor	NUE	0.972	Steel
Cemex	CX	0.971	Building materials

the DAX correlated best with interest rate sensitive groups like Utilities, Financials and Building Material stocks.

■ 13.3 European Futures

European futures trade long after the closing of equity trading in the corresponding exchanges so a more realistic analysis (for trading purposes) would be to correlate European index futures with the corresponding US futures. A comparison of the daily yields in Tables 13.1 and 13.5 reveals a significant improvement of the correlations of daily changes which can only be attributed to the time lag factor between indices. This was most pronounced in the case of the DAX, whose correlation with the S&P improved dramatically from 0.13 (cash index) to 0.55 (futures). There was no significant difference, however, when comparing the direct price correlation between future and cash prices in Tables 13.1 and 13.4 as US cash indices were shifted back one day in time.

TABLE 13.4 Nonparametric Correlation Matrix between International Futures for the 5-Year Period from 1 January 2002 to 31 December 2006. The FDAX is the DAX contract trading in the Eurex; the ES, YM, NQ and NKD are the S&P 500 e-mini, Dow, Nasdaq 100 and Nikkei contracts trading in the CME Globex; the ESTX is the Euro Stoxx 50 contract trading in the Eurex; the 6E is the Euro contract trading also in the Globex; the GC is the gold contract trading in the Comex; and the ZN is the 10-year Treasury note futures contract trading in the Globex.

Symbol index	FDAX DAX	ES SP 500	YM DJ-30	NQ Nasdaq	NKD Nikkei	FCE CAC 40	FESX Eurostx	6E Euro	GC Gold	ZN 10y TN
FDAX	1	**0.91**	0.89	0.85	0.90	**0.99**	**0.99**	0.41	0.66	−0.81
ES	**0.91**	1	**0.98**	**0.96**	0.92	0.93	0.88	0.68	0.86	−0.61
ER2	0.85	0.98	0.96	0.93	0.92	0.86	0.80	0.75	0.93	−0.53
YM	0.89	0.98	1	0.92	0.92	0.90	0.86	0.71	0.85	−0.60
NQ	0.85	0.96	0.92	1	0.85	0.86	0.82	0.63	0.81	−0.54
NKD	0.90	0.92	0.92	0.85	1	0.912	0.86	0.55	0.80	−0.69
FCE	0.99	0.93	0.90	0.86	0.91	1	0.99	0.44	0.69	−0.80
FESX	0.99	0.88	0.86	0.82	0.86	0.99	1	0.36	0.59	−0.82
EURO	0.41	0.68	0.71	0.63	0.55	0.44	0.36	1	0.82	−0.09
GC	0.66	0.86	0.85	0.81	0.80	0.69	0.59	0.82	1	−0.33
ZN	−0.81	−0.61	−0.60	−0.54	−0.69	−0.80	−0.82	−0.09	−0.33	1

TABLE 13.5 Nonparametric Correlation Matrix of Daily % Changes between International Index, Currency and Bond Futures for the 5-Year Period from 1 January 2002 to 31 December 2006. Significant correlations are depicted in bold. The ZN is the 10-year Treasury note futures trading in the Globex.

Symbol index	FDAX DAX	ES SP 500	YM DJ-30	NQ Nasdaq	FCE CAC 40	FESX Eurostx	6E Euro	ZN TN
FDAX	1	0.55	0.52	0.49	**0.81**	**0.89**	−0.2	−0.29
ES	0.55	1	**0.82**	0.86	0.43	0.52	−0.1	−0.19
YM	0.52	**0.82**	1	0.67	0.41	0.50	−0.1	−0.16
NQ	0.49	**0.86**	0.67	1	0.37	0.45	−0.1	−0.21
FCE	**0.81**	0.43	0.41	0.37	1	**0.84**	−0.2	−0.23
FESX	**0.89**	0.52	0.50	0.45	**0.84**	1	−0.2	−0.26
EURO	−0.22	−0.12	−0.09	−0.14	−0.19	−0.22	1	0.33
ZN	−0.29	−0.19	−0.16	−0.21	−0.23	−0.26	0.33	1

13.4 Time Factor

It is obvious from Table 13.1 that the correlation of weekly percentage yields is stronger than the corresponding daily one. But why stop there? What about higher time increments? I have calculated in Table 13.6 Pearson's correlation of percentage yields for time intervals ranging from 1 to 100 days between DAX and S&P

TABLE 13.6	Correlation Variation between DAX and S&P Futures (e-mini) for Different Time Segment Percentage Yields for the 5-Year Period from 1 July 2002 to 30 June 2007. In the 3rd column is the correlation % change (improvement) from the previous time increment.	
Days	Pearson's Correlation	% Change
1	0.617	
2	0.719	16.4
3	0.763	6.2
4	0.787	3.1
5	0.803	2.1
6	0.810	0.8
7	0.810	0.0
8	0.817	0.8
9	0.816	−0.1
10	0.824	1.1
11	0.825	0.1
12	0.822	−0.4
13	0.825	0.3
14	0.821	−0.4
15	0.822	0.1
16	0.824	0.2
17	0.823	0.0
18	0.824	0.1
19	0.823	0.0
20	0.825	0.2
25	0.831	0.8
30	0.847	1.9
35	0.853	0.7
40	0.863	1.3
45	0.872	0.9
50	0.876	0.5
75	0.890	1.6
100	0.893	0.3

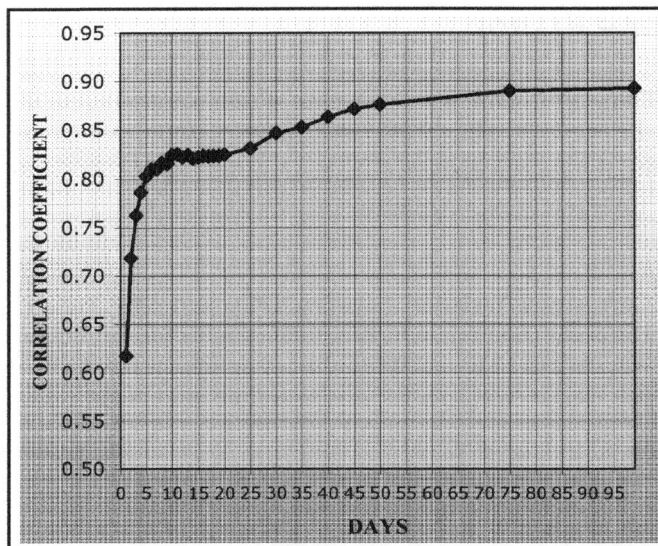

FIGURE 13.1 Graph of Correlation Variation for Time Intervals Ranging from 1 to 100 Days of Percent Yields between DAX and S&P Futures (e-mini) for the 5-Year Period from 1 July 2002 to 30 June 2007.

e-mini futures (ES). They are also plotted graphically in Figure 13.1. A visual inspection of the graph reveals that the correlation improved exponentially for the first 5-day period, made a short-term peak at the 10-day increment and actually decreased slightly up to the 15-day time increment. It then started sloping up slightly to level off at 75 days. It is worthwhile noting that for longer than 10-day percentage differences, the correlation coefficient improved by only 8 %. Therefore a time increment of five to ten days, when taking percentage differences, might be the optimum to use when designing short to medium term intermarket trading systems.

▆ 13.5 Intraday

The correlation of intraday percentage changes follows a similar pattern to the daily yields above.

In Table 13.7 I list Pearson's correlation for up to 1500 minutes (25 hours) of percentage yields between the DAX, Euro Stoxx 50 and S&P e-mini futures (ES). This was also plotted graphically in Figure 13.2. The correlation between the DAX and Euro Stoxx improved exponentially for the first 10-minute period, made a short-term peak at the 75-minute increment, making only marginal improvements for the next 200 minutes.

| TABLE 13.7 | Intraday Correlation of 1 to 1500 Minute (25 hour) Percent Changes between the DAX, Euro Stoxx and S&P 500 Futures for the 3-Month Period from 1 January 2007 to 31 March 2007 |

Minutes	Hours	ESTX	ES
5	0.08	0.877	0.724
10	0.17	**0.888**	0.741
15	0.25	0.891	0.754
20	0.33	0.893	0.763
25	0.42	0.895	0.768
30	0.50	0.897	0.774
35	0.58	0.899	0.780
40	0.67	0.900	0.782
45	0.75	0.901	0.787
50	0.83	0.902	0.789
55	0.92	0.904	0.793
60	1	0.905	0.797
65	1.08	0.906	0.802
70	1.17	0.907	0.807
75	1.25	**0.908**	0.810
80	1.33	0.908	0.812
85	1.42	0.908	0.813
90	1.50	0.909	0.814
95	1.58	0.909	0.815
100	1.67	0.908	0.816
125	2.08	0.910	0.823
150	2.50	0.910	0.830
200	3.33	0.913	0.836
250	4.17	0.915	0.842
375	6.25	0.916	0.850
500	8.33	0.918	0.862
750	12.50	0.925	0.884
1000	16.67	0.928	0.897
1250	20.83	0.928	0.900
1500	25	0.933	0.910

The correlation between the DAX and S&P e-mini futures (ES), on the other hand, made a short-term peak at the 75-minute (1¼ hour) increment but continued rising at a more moderate rate.

It is worthwhile noting that for longer than 10-minute percentage differences, the correlation coefficient between the DAX and Euro Stoxx futures improved by

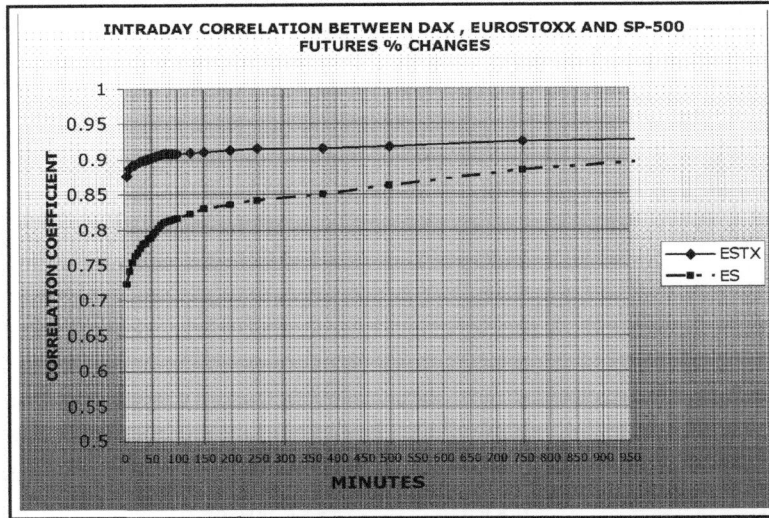

FIGURE 13.2 Graph of Correlation between Percent Changes of DAX, Euro Stoxx (solid line) and e-Mini S&P 500 Futures (dashed line) for Intraday Time Segments Ranging from 5 to 1500 Minutes (25 trading hours) for the 3-Month Period from 1 January 2007 to 31 March 2007. The correlation with Euro Stoxx futures flattens out after the first 75 minutes.

only 5% but its correlation with the S&P e-mini improved substantially (23%). It is therefore better to use longer time spans when designing short- to medium-term intermarket trading systems to trade the DAX based on its correlation with the S&P e-mini.

CHAPTER 14

Gold

From Markos Katsanos, *Intermarket Trading Strategies* (Hoboken, New Jersey: John Wiley & Sons, 2008), Chapter 7.

Good judgment is usually the result of experience and experience frequently is the result of bad judgment.

—**Robert Lovell**

Learning Objective Statements

▪ Describe general correlations noticed between the Gold and other indices

In 1925, in a speech at the University of Cambridge, the English economist John Maynard Keynes called the Gold Standard "a barbaric relic" but even though the Gold Standard has since been abolished the "barbaric relic" has not lost its value. Federal Reserve Board chairman Alan Greenspan once wrote about gold: "This is the shabby secret of the welfare statistics' tirades against gold. Deficit spending is simply a scheme for the confiscation of wealth. Gold stands in the way of this insidious process. It stands as a protector of property rights. . . ."

Gold topped $1000 an ounce in March 2008 as investors bid gold prices up amid worries about the falling dollar and the sub prime financial crisis. In fact, investors who bought gold in 2003 have more than tripled their initial investment, enjoying an annualized return of over 20%.

One of the reasons gold has surged so much is that it's much easier to buy. For many years it was difficult for ordinary investors to trade gold. The minimum amount needed in order to buy gold bullion was $1 million. Buying gold coins or jewellery was also a problem because of the hassle of storing and reselling them. An alternative way to buy gold was to trade gold futures on the New York Commodities Exchange (COMEX). Most investors, however, do not have a futures account or prefer to trade only stocks because of the volatility and also the rollover costs. Investors can now buy shares of SPDR Gold Trust, an exchange-traded fund that can be bought and sold like any stock under the ticker symbol GLD. Each share represents one-tenth of an ounce of gold, and the shares are highly liquid.

In times of a financial crisis, rising inflation, or a weak dollar, gold does well but is it a good long-term investment? Gold peaked at about $840 an ounce in 1980 and was in a continuous decline until 2002. Anyone who invested in gold in 1988 would have made only 72% on his initial investment and with inflation factored in would have made next to nothing over the 20 years from 1 January 1988 until the end of 2007. Meanwhile, a $1000 investment in the S&P 500 would have grown at a compound annual return of 10.6% a year to $7500 in that time. Taking inflation into account the stock investor would still have made a 360% profit and his initial $1000 investment would have grown to $4600 at an annualized rate of 7.4% a year during the past 20 years. Investing in stocks generally does better against inflation over the long term because companies raise prices when inflation goes up. Growing productivity also helps stock prices keep ahead of inflation, which is not the case with gold.

Another reason for gold's mediocre long-term performance is the most fundamental concept of economics: supply and demand. Unlike other commodities which are used in industry and need to be continuously replenished, gold stays in the market.

■ 14.1 Correlations with Equity and Commodity Assets

Gold was traditionally uncorrelated with equities until a character change occurred in 2003. Gold started moving in the same direction with the S&P 500 and other international equity indices (see Figure 14.1).

FIGURE 14.1 Weekly Composite Chart of the World Gold Index (thick black line with the scale on the right Y-axis) and the S&P 500 (thin gray line with the scale on the left Y-axis). Negative correlation is shaded in a gray background and positive with no background. Notice the correlation reversal in April 2003.

Before making any hasty conclusions, however, we should examine what the other asset classes were doing at the time. During that period the dollar was falling precipitously, inflation was rising and the rest of the commodities were also rising. I believe that the contemporaneous gold–equity appreciation only happened by chance and gold's gain had nothing to do with rising equity prices and more to do with the dollar's demise and the commodity-induced inflation.

Gold has been moving in lock step fashion with major averages until the summer of 2007 when fears of melt down in US financial markets triggered flight-to-safety demand for the yellow metal which decoupled from the S&P and moved to new highs in the following months.

In Tables 14.1 and 14.2 I list the correlation of weekly and two-week (10 working days) percent changes between gold and related equity indices, currencies and commodities. You can see that the correlation of weekly yields between gold and the S&P 500 changed from near zero to over 0.20 during the most recent 2-year period ending on 31 December 2007. For the reasons discussed above, I believe that this is only temporary and the correlation with equities will revert to the mean.

But this is not the only change in gold's intermarket relations, and whether they will also revert to the mean is doubtful. A close inspection of Table 14.1 reveals that, during the last 5-year period since 2003, gold started moving closer to the entire commodity complex as represented by the CRB Index.

TABLE 14.1 Long- and Short-Term Nonparametric Correlation of Weekly Percentage Changes between the World Gold Index and Related Commodity and Financial Indices up to 31 December 2007. TNX is the CBOE 10 Year Treasury Yield Index, XAU is the Philadelphia Gold/Silver Stock Index, CRB is the Commodity Research Bureau Index, Yen is the USD per yen exchange rate (JPY.USD) and TSX is the S&P Canada Composite Index.

Years	S&P 500	XAU	Silver	TSX	CRB	Dollar Index	Euro	Yen	TNX	Crude Oil
2	0.20	0.78	0.82	0.46	0.63	−0.55	0.54	0.24	0.03	0.41
5	0.10	0.74	0.74	0.31	0.55	−0.57	0.54	0.32	−0.08	0.23
10	0.02	0.71	0.66	0.18	0.45	−0.47	0.43	0.26	−0.10	0.17
15	0.00	0.71	0.66	0.18	0.43	−0.38	NA	0.23	−0.07	0.14

TABLE 14.2 Long- and Short-Term Nonparametric Correlation of 10-Day Percentage Changes between the World Gold Index (gold spot) and Related Commodity and Financial Indices up to 31 December 2007. TNX is the CBOE 10 Year Treasury Yield Index, XAU is the Philadelphia Gold/Silver Stock Index, CRB is the Commodity Research Bureau Index, Yen is the USD per yen exchange rate (JPY.USD) and TSX is the S&P Canada Composite Index.

Years	S&P 500	XAU	Silver	TSX	CRB	Dollar Index	Euro	Yen	TNX	Crude Oil
2	0.16	0.80	0.80	0.47	0.71	−0.63	0.61	0.32	0.00	0.51
5	0.09	0.74	0.71	0.34	0.59	−0.57	0.53	0.37	−0.10	0.25
10	0.02	0.72	0.64	0.20	0.47	−0.49	0.47	0.25	−0.11	0.19
15	0.01	0.73	0.63	0.21	0.45	−0.39	NA	0.23	−0.09	0.15

The traditional positive correlation between gold and silver has also recently increased significantly from 0.66 (strong) to 0.82 (very strong).

Gold and silver have always been positively correlated markets and their prices tend to move in the same direction. Their relationship, however, is not fundamental. The price of one does not move in a particular direction because the other market is moving the same way, as both markets are driven by the same fundamentals. This doesn't mean, however, that their relationship cannot be used in exploiting short-term market inefficiencies as the fundamental reasons (like the price of the US dollar) might not be reflected fully in the price of both at the same time.

Also, since gold is denominated in US dollars, it is reasonable to assume that it will be affected by the Federal Reserve monetary policy. In 2004 the Fed created excess liquidity. In the following 3-year period gold broke out from historical prices to new 10-year highs. After all, unlike paper money, gold cannot be printed. Longterm bullish factors for gold include explosive money supply growth, the US dollar, negative interest rates in the US, inflation and high commodity prices. Negative factors include Central Bank selling which can affect the yellow metal negatively in the short term.

Commodity prices may get seriously distorted by the underlying currency fluctuations and it pays to examine them with international eyes. Gold offers the best example in recent history.

To illustrate my point I have prepared two charts (Figure 14.2). They are both of gold, the only difference being the currency gold is priced in. The first one (bold line) is in US dollars, and the other in euro. For the 3½-year period from the beginning of 2002 and until about the middle of 2005 the first gold chart (in dollars) showed a

FIGURE 14.2 Weekly Chart of Gold Spot Prices in US Dollars (thick bold line with the scale on the right Y-axis) and Gold in Euro (thin line with the scale again on the same axis). As you can see, European gold investors didn't profit from the 2002–2005 rally in gold.

strong up trend but this was not the case with the second chart (in euro) which moved in a sideways range, finishing in April 2005 lower than it started in January 2002.

The gold's (in dollars) uptrend was caused by a bear market in the dollar, not a bull market in gold. During this period, the correct position for an international investor was a short dollar position, not a long gold position.

Gold is also tracking the crude oil market, for signals about futures inflation trends, and speculative sentiment towards the US dollar. Although its long-term correlation with crude oil futures is not as strong ($\rho = 0.41$ in Table 14.1) as it is with the CRB Index ($\rho = 0.63$), silver ($\rho = 0.82$) or the dollar index ($\rho = -0.55$), it can increase dramatically, in periods of rising volatility and sharp dollar declines (Figure 14.3). During the preceding 3-year period there were four such incidents of market sentiment shift resulting in extremely close correlation between gold and crude oil (marked A, B, C and D in the chart in Figure 14.3) which happened to coincide with the start of a sharp dollar decline. This is because, during periods of undisciplined dollar decline, their correlation with the dollar became the dominant price moving factor for both. Notice also that gold decoupled from

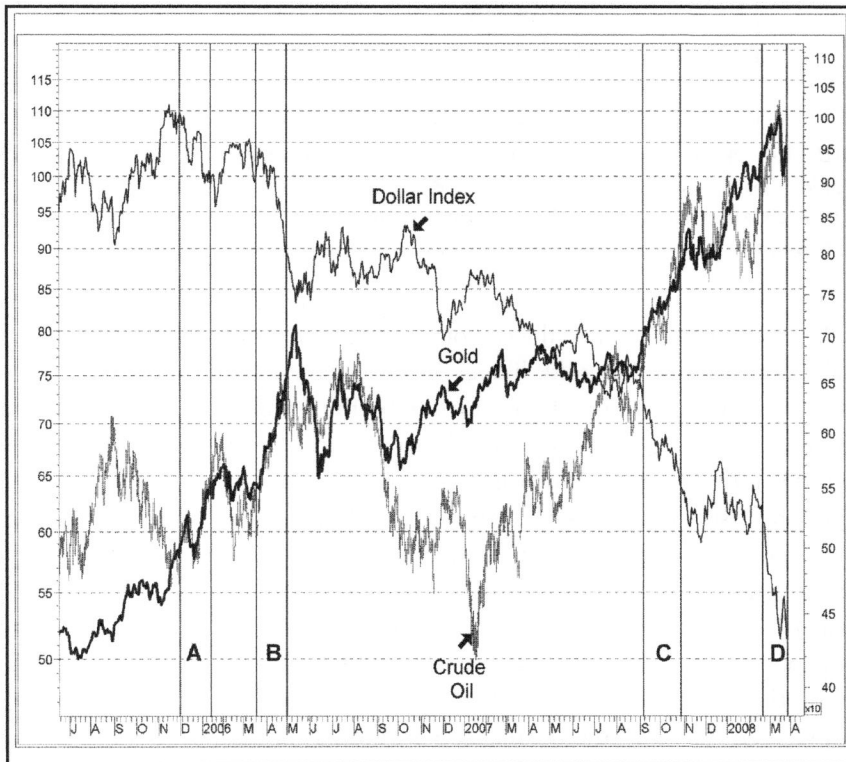

FIGURE 14.3 Daily Composite Chart of Gold Bullion Spot Prices (thick bold line with scale (divided by 10) on the right Y-axis), the Dollar Index (thin line) and Nymex Crude Oil Futures (gray price bars with the scale on the left Y-axis) from June 2005 to April 2008. Notice that in periods of sharp and uncontrollable dollar decline (bounded by vertical lines and marked A, B, C and D in the chart) the gold and oil charts coincide, indicating a market sentiment shift and resulting in a stronger correlation between the two commodities.

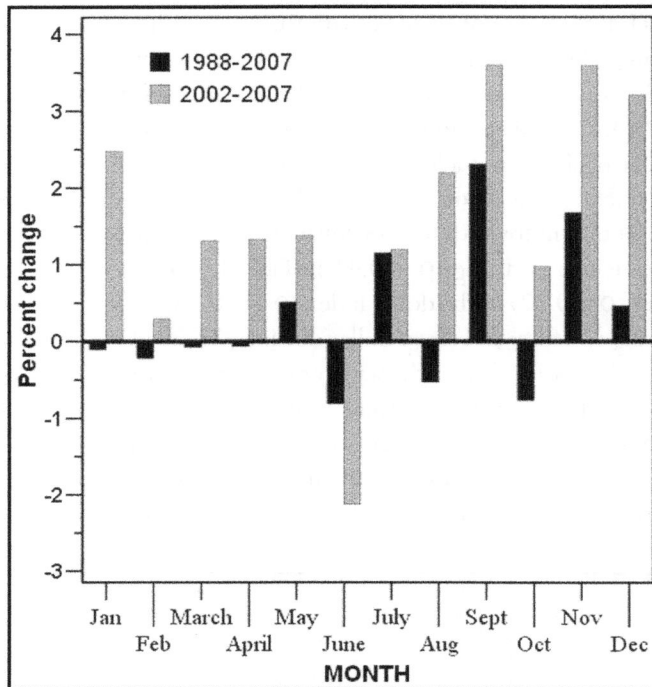

FIGURE 14.4 Average COMEX Gold Near-Term Contract Percent Changes for the 20-Year Period from 1988–2007 Are Shown in Black, and for the Most Recent 6-Year Period from 2002–2007 in Gray. Notice the seasonal strength in the September to December period when the jewellery industry is busy acquiring inventory for the holidays.

oil two to three weeks before the dollar actually bottomed out as the market is always forward looking and discounted the end of the dollar's decline in advance.

Finally don't forget that gold, like every other commodity, is subject to seasonal changes. Demand for gold is driven mainly by the jewellery industry. Gold prices usually spike up during the September through December period as jewellers stock up in gold prior to the year-end holiday shopping season.

Although seasonal patterns tend to recur each and every year in a more or less similar fashion, something that is more macro fundamental might override them. In the case of gold this factor was the dollar's weakness. In the bar chart in Figure 14.4 you can see how gold's long-term (20 year) seasonality has been distorted by the recent (since 2002) bullish secular trend. Although the normal seasonal pattern is still there, the recent bullish trend that has been in place since 2002 pushed toward higher prices. As a result, the normal seasonal low is not as pronounced as it might be otherwise. A secular bullish trend in energy and agricultural commodities has also caused anomalies in normal seasonal patterns, at least temporarily.

14.2 Leading or Lagging?

It is very difficult to establish whether gold bullion prices are leading or lagging other related commodities by inspecting a composite chart visually (Figures 14.5 and 14.6).

THE INTEGRATION OF TECHNICAL ANALYSIS

FIGURE 14.5 Weekly Chart of the World Gold Index (in bold with the scale on the Y-axis), the World Silver Index (thin line in gray), and the CRB Index (normal line). Vertical lines were drawn at major peaks. No lead or lag is apparent from the charts as all three indices seem to peak at the same time.

FIGURE 14.6 Weekly Chart of the World Gold Index (thick line in bold with the scale on the right Y-axis), the XAU Index (in gray), and the Dollar Index (normal line with the scale on the left Y-axis). Vertical solid lines were drawn at major peaks and dashed lines at major bottoms. No lead or lag is apparent from the charts as gold peaks at the same time that the dollar bottoms out and the XAU makes a top.

Sometimes it leads, other times it lags, sometimes it moves coincidentally and at other times it does not respond at all to other correlated commodities. A rigorous mathematical analysis, however, reveals some repetitive persistency in gold's elusive maneuvers. This was contrived by calculating, in Table 14.3, lagging and leading correlations of weekly yields between gold and related commodities by shifting gold yields from one to 10 days forward (positive values) and up to 10 days back in time (negative values). The leading/lagging correlations between gold and every other related commodity were then plotted individually in Figures 14.7 to 14.11. For

| TABLE 14.3 | Pearson's Correlation Coefficient of Weekly Percentage Changes between the World Gold Index and the XAU, the Dollar Index, Canada's Venture Index and the Reuters/Jefferies Commodity Research Bureau Index (CRB). The correlations (except for the Venture Index) were calculated for the 15-year period from 1992–2006. Column 1 depicts the number of days that the gold data was shifted in time. A +1 day lag indicates that yesterday's gold weekly change was correlated with today's XAU, and dollar, CRB or Venture data and a lag of −1 indicates that tomorrow's gold weekly change was correlated with today's of the corresponding commodity. Therefore higher correlations with positive lags indicate a gold lead and higher correlations for negative lags indicate that gold lagged. Lag avg. (at the top of Column 1) is the weighted average of the lagging correlations and lead avg. is the time weighted average of the leading correlations. | | | | |

Lagdays	XAU	Dollar Index	Silver	Venture	CRB
lag avg.	0.291	−0.098	0.209	0.256	0.142
−10	−0.012	0.024	−0.033	−0.011	−0.018
−9	−0.002	0.026	−0.035	−0.003	−0.031
−8	0.018	0.028	−0.029	0.033	−0.028
-7	0.039	0.023	−0.017	0.077	−0.017
−6	0.055	0.015	−0.007	0.093	−0.010
−5	0.096	−0.003	0.021	0.134	0.014
−4	0.250	−0.067	0.158	0.235	0.103
−3	0.375	−0.126	0.275	0.320	0.189
−2	0.478	−0.191	0.381	0.384	0.261
−1	0.589	−0.249	0.495	0.474	0.344
0	0.679	−0.315	0.612	0.574	0.428
1	0.476	−0.233	0.454	0.417	0.330
2	0.328	−0.187	0.334	0.310	0.244
3	0.196	−0.129	0.218	0.222	0.161
4	0.058	−0.082	0.091	0.118	0.074
5	−0.070	−0.028	−0.026	0.027	−0.015
6	−0.066	−0.033	−0.036	0.013	−0.036
7	−0.068	−0.030	−0.040	0.015	−0.045
8	−0.068	−0.032	−0.042	0.009	−0.043
9	−0.070	−0.021	−0.040	−0.003	−0.047
10	−0.063	−0.013	−0.044	−0.013	−0.042
lead avg.	0.150	−0.113	0.167	0.179	0.120

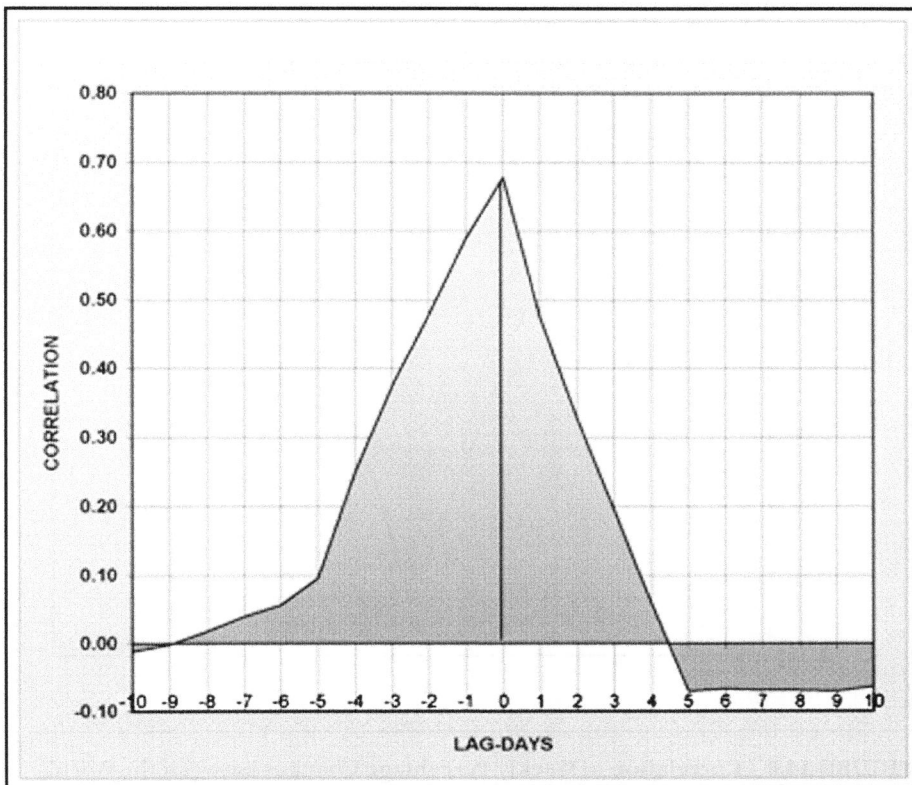

FIGURE 14.7 Correlation of Weekly Percentage Changes between the World Gold Index and the XAU, for 1 to 10 Day Lag or Lead. Higher correlations for negative values on the X-axis indicate that gold lags the XAU, and higher correlations for positive values on the X-axis that indicate that gold leads the XAU. In this case the gold correlations were higher for negative lag, indicating that it is lagging the XAU. The correlations were calculated for the 15-year period from 1992–2006.

predictive purposes, we wish to detect which commodities have stronger leading correlations with gold. These relationships can then be used to predict the future course of events in trading systems or forecasting models.

The moment of truth has arrived for gold since the leading/lagging correlation analyses shed some light on the existence and nature of the predictive capability of related markets in forecasting the yellow metal's next move. Keep in mind that these indicate only the average short-term tendency and are not appropriate to use for longer-term trends. Important conclusions are summarized below.

■ **The XAU** There was a strong positive contemporaneous (zero lag) correlation between the XAU and gold ($r = 0.68$ and $r = 0.62$ for weekly and daily yields respectively). Based on the lag analysis, the XAU is leading gold for both weekly (Figure 14.7) and daily yields (Table 14.4). The weekly yield weighted average of 10-day leading correlations was 0.29 compared with 0.15 for lagging correlations (Table 14.3). A longer-term lead of gold stocks over gold bullion was also noticed by John Murphy and mentioned in his book on intermarket analysis (see Bibliography).

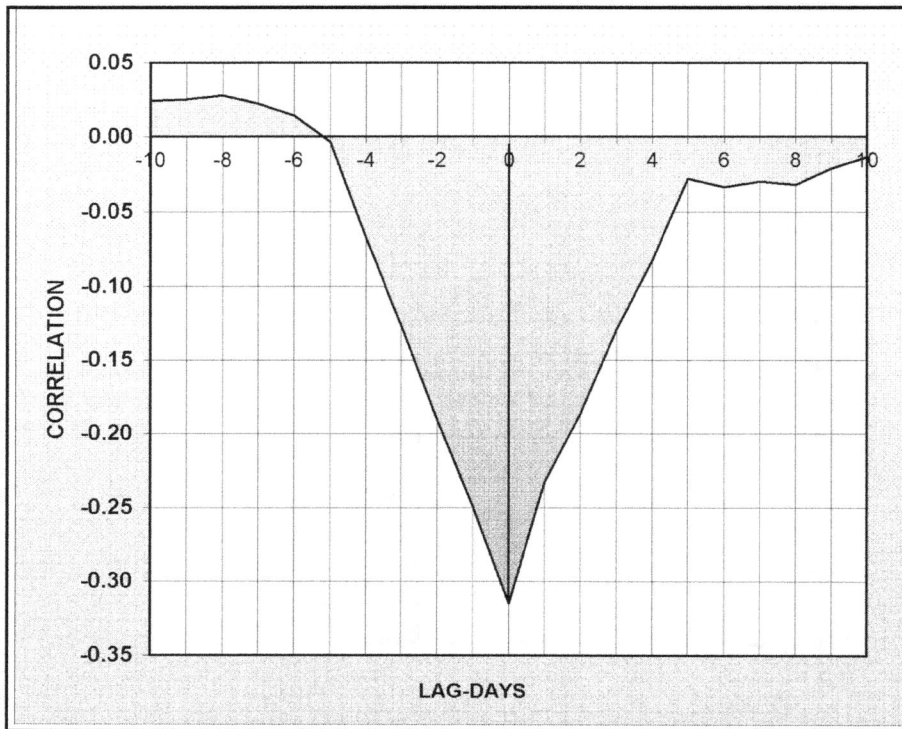

FIGURE 14.8 Correlation of Weekly Percentage Changes between the World Gold Index and the Dollar Index, for 1 to 10 Day Lag or Lead. Gold's initial lag reversed to a lead after the first couple of days. The correlations were calculated for the 15-year period from 1992–2006.

- **The dollar index** had relatively weak coincident negative correlation when taking daily percent differences but this improved on raw price correlations (Table 14.5). It is reasonable to assume that, as gold is denominated in US dollars, it should lag the dollar. This was confirmed, however, for only the first two days of lag before gold took the lead. Notice the correlation actually turned positive for more than five days of lead (see Table 14.3 and Figure 14.8).

- **Silver** had the second best (after the XAU) correlation of weekly and daily yields. Silver moves more or less coincidentally with gold. A slight lead is barely evident in the graph in Figure 14.9.

- **Canada's Venture Index** had the best coincident correlation based on raw prices (r = 0.965 in Table 14.5). The Venture Index is also leading gold prices (Figure 14.10).

- **The CRB Index** had the worst positive coincident correlation for both weekly and daily yields. No significant lead or lag was apparent in Table 14.3 or Figure 14.11.

We can therefore conclude, based on the correlation analysis above, that gold either lags or moves concurrently with other related commodities or indices. It is therefore better to use relatedmarkets in order to forecast gold rather than the other way

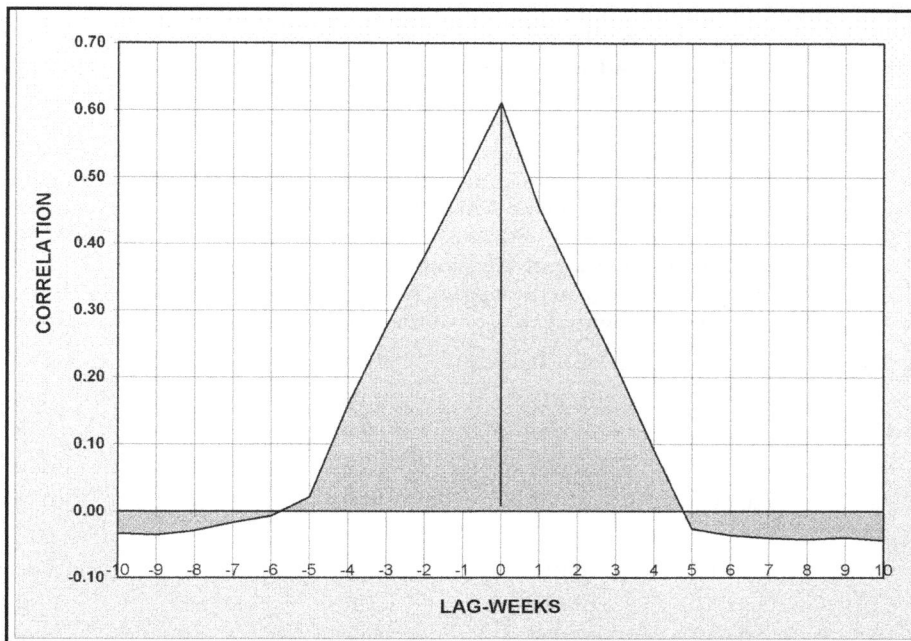

FIGURE 14.9 Correlation of Weekly Percentage Changes between the World Gold Index and the World Silver Index (XSLV), for 1 to 10 Day Lag or Lead. Silver correlated slightly better with leading (negative shift) gold values, suggesting that it is leading gold. The correlations were calculated for the 15-year period from 1992–2006.

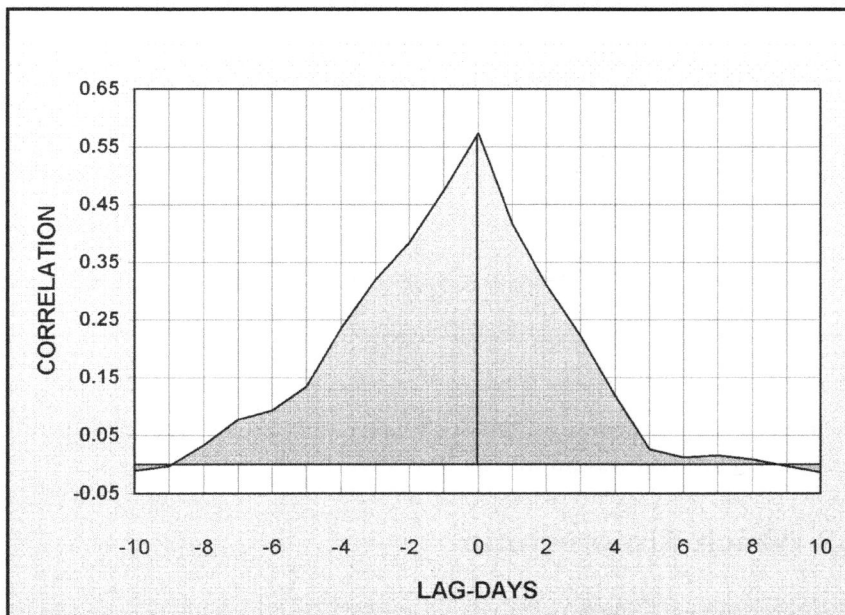

FIGURE 14.10 Pearson's Correlation of Weekly Percentage Changes between the World Gold Index and Canada's Venture Composite Index, for 1 to 10 Day Lag or Lead. The Venture Index correlated slightly better with leading (negative values on the X-axis) gold prices suggesting that it is leading gold. Data for the Venture Index were available only for the 5-year period from 2002–2006.

| TABLE 14.4 | Pearson's Correlation Coefficient of Daily Percent Changes between the World Gold Index and the Xau, the Dollar Index, Canada's Venture Index and the Reuters/Jefferies Commodity Research Bureau Index (Crb). The correlations were calculated for the 15-year period from 1992–2006. Column 1 shows the number of days that the gold data was shifted in time. A lag of 1 day indicates that yesterday's gold daily change was correlated with today's XAU, Dollar, CRB or Venture prices. Therefore higher correlations with positive lags indicate a gold lead and higher correlations for negative lag indicate that gold lagged. Lag avg. is the time weighted average of the lagging (negative shift) correlations and lead avg. is the time weighted average of the leading (positive shift) correlations. |

Lag days	XAU	Dollar Index	Silver	Venture	CRB
lag avg.	0.029	−0.005	0.007	0.033	0.008
−10	0.028	−0.009	0.025	0.031	0.000
−9	0.004	0.003	−0.008	−0.005	−0.013
−8	−0.006	0.001	−0.035	−0.004	−0.026
-7	0.015	0.019	0.013	0.030	0.015
−6	−0.013	0.014	−0.034	−0.007	−0.003
−5	0.033	−0.023	0.043	0.061	−0.002
−4	0.030	0.009	0.003	0.048	0.008
−3	0.028	0.002	0.010	0.059	0.021
−2	0.005	−0.010	0.012	0.014	−0.007
−1	0.092	−0.025	0.014	0.044	0.033
0	0.623	−0.313	0.619	0.572	0.409
1	−0.072	0.038	−0.064	0.009	−0.009
2	−0.029	−0.022	0.010	−0.017	0.013
3	0.001	0.006	0.003	0.030	0.001
4	0.005	−0.012	−0.002	0.010	0.002
5	0.004	−0.015	0.019	0.024	0.018
6	−0.034	−0.007	−0.032	−0.039	−0.034
7	−0.020	−0.001	−0.004	−0.003	−0.021
8	−0.017	−0.020	−0.028	−0.008	−0.004
9	−0.007	0.002	0.020	0.020	−0.006
10	0.006	−0.007	−0.002	0.014	0.012
lead avg.	−0.022	−0.001	−0.012	0.004	−0.002

around. The inferences drawn from this analysis are only useful for short-term predictions as the lag interval was limited to 10 days or less.

▥ 14.3 Which Time Frame?

There are two problems when using raw price data to calculate statistical metrics such as correlation:

- ▪ Prices are not normally distributed.

- ▪ Relationships between markets are not linear.

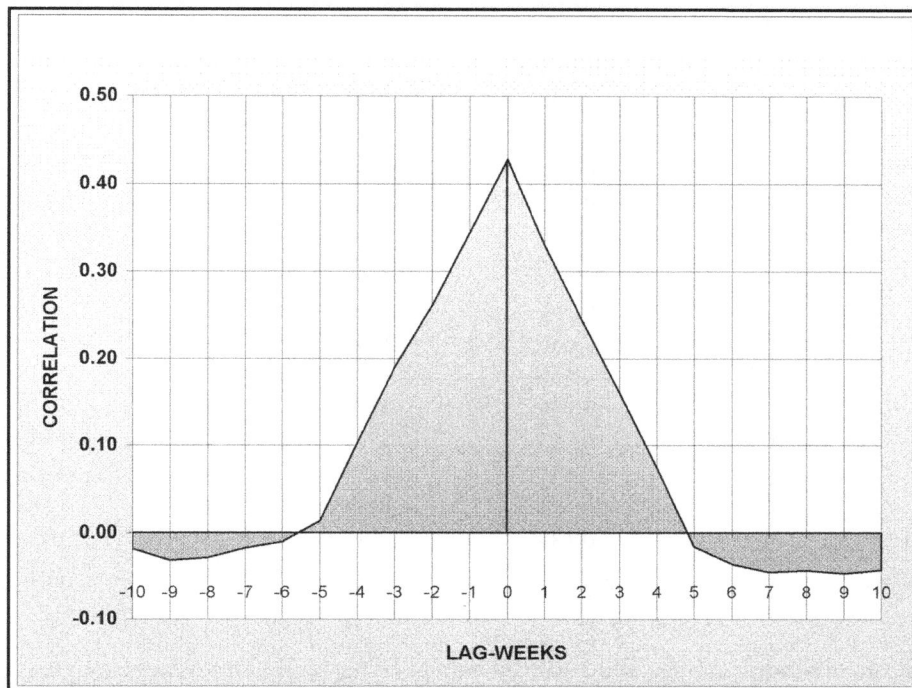

FIGURE 14.11 Pearson's Correlation of Weekly Percentage Changes between the World Gold Index and the Reuters/Jefferies Crb Index, for 1 to 10 Day Lag or Lead. The CRB correlated slightly better with leading gold values, suggesting that it is leading gold. The correlations were calculated for the 15-year period from 1992–2006.

| TABLE 14.5 | Pearson's Correlation Coefficient between the World Gold Index and the XAU, the Dollar Index, Canada's Venture Index and the Reuters/Jefferies Commodity Research Bureau Index (CRB). The correlations (except for Venture Index) were calculated for the 15-year period from 1992–2006. Column 1 shows the number of days that the gold data were shifted in time. A lag of 1 day indicates that yesterday's gold price was correlated with today's XAU, dollar index, CRB or Venture prices. Lag average is the time weighted average of the lagging correlations and lead average is the time weighted average of the leading correlations. |

Lag days	XAU	Dollar Index	Silver	Venture	CRB
lag avg.	0.766	−0.633	0.822	0.908	0.846
−10	0.757	−0.626	0.807	0.892	0.843
−9	0.758	−0.627	0.809	0.894	0.842
−8	0.760	−0.628	0.811	0.897	0.843
−7	0.762	−0.629	0.814	0.899	0.844
−6	0.763	−0.631	0.817	0.902	0.845
−5	0.766	−0.631	0.820	0.911	0.846
−4	0.767	−0.632	0.822	0.910	0.846

Continued

TABLE 14.5 (*Continued*)

Lag days	XAU	Dollar Index	Silver	Venture	CRB
−3	0.768	−0.634	0.824	0.910	0.847
−2	0.769	−0.635	0.826	0.911	0.847
−1	0.771	−0.637	0.829	0.916	0.848
0	0.790	−0.654	0.856	0.965	0.871
1	0.769	−0.638	0.829	0.916	0.846
2	0.767	−0.637	0.826	0.910	0.844
3	0.765	−0.636	0.825	0.909	0.842
4	0.763	−0.636	0.823	0.908	0.840
5	0.762	−0.636	0.822	0.910	0.839
6	0.760	−0.636	0.819	0.901	0.837
7	0.758	−0.635	0.816	0.897	0.835
8	0.756	−0.635	0.815	0.894	0.833
9	0.754	−0.634	0.813	0.892	0.831
10	0.753	−0.634	0.811	0.890	0.830
lead avg.	0.763	−0.636	0.823	0.907	0.840

Both problems are usually resolved when taking price differences or percent changes but what is the optimum time segment for calculating the difference?

In Table 14.6 I have calculated Pearson's correlation from 1 to 400 days percent changes between gold bullion, the XAU and the dollar index. This is also plotted graphically in Figure 14.12.

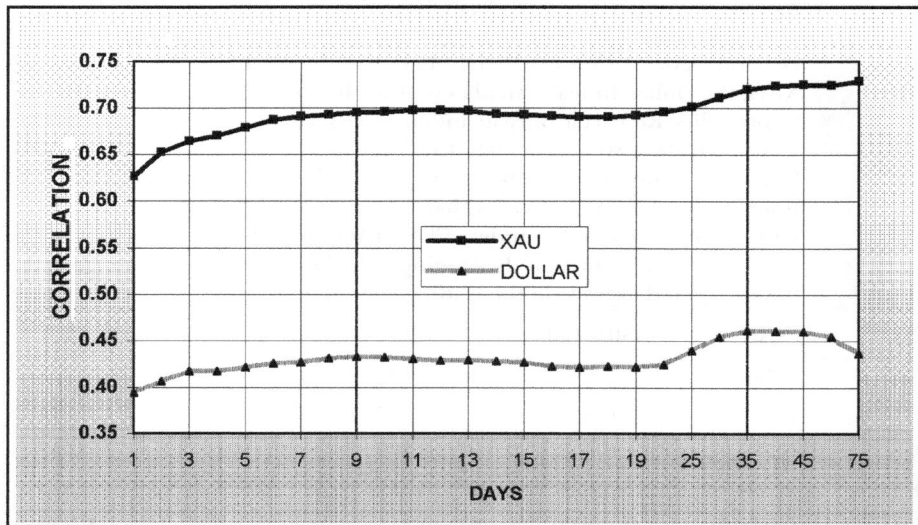

FIGURE 14.12 Graph of the Correlation between Gold Bullion, the XAU (bold black line) and the Dollar Index (gray line) for Variable Time Segment Percent Changes for the 10-Year Period from 1 January 1997 to 1 January 2007. The number of trading days used to calculate the percent changes is plotted in the X-axis and Pearson's correlation in the Y-axis.

TABLE 14.6	Pearson's Correlation for Different Interval Percent Changes between Gold Bullion, the XAU and the US Dollar Index Based on 10-year Data from 1 January 1997 to 21 December 2006. Columns 3 and 5 show the correlation % change from the previous time increment.			
Yield days	XAU	% Change	Dollar Index	% Change
1	0.626		−0.394	
2	0.652	4.2	−0.406	3.1
3	0.664	1.9	−0.418	2.8
4	0.670	0.9	−0.418	0.0
5	0.679	1.3	−0.422	1.0
6	0.688	1.3	−0.426	1.0
7	**0.691**	0.5	−0.427	0.3
8	0.693	0.2	−0.432	1.0
9	0.695	0.4	**−0.433**	0.4
10	0.696	0.1	−0.432	−0.2
11	**0.698**	0.2	−0.431	−0.4
12	0.698	0.0	−0.429	−0.4
13	0.697	−0.1	−0.429	0.1
14	0.693	−0.6	−0.428	−0.2
15	0.693	0.0	−0.427	−0.4
16	0.692	−0.2	−0.423	−0.9
17	0.691	−0.2	−0.422	−0.3
18	0.691	0.0	−0.423	0.2
19	0.692	0.2	−0.422	−0.1
20	0.696	0.6	−0.425	0.6
25	0.702	0.8	−0.440	3.6
30	0.711	1.4	−0.454	3.2
35	**0.720**	1.2	**−0.462**	1.7
40	0.724	0.6	−0.461	−0.2
45	0.725	0.1	−0.460	−0.1
50	0.725	−0.1	−0.455	−1.2
75	0.729	0.6	−0.437	−3.9
100	0.744	2.1	−0.432	−1.1
200	0.823	10.6	−0.450	4.1
300	0.873	6.0	−0.444	−1.4
400	0.886	1.5	−0.544	22.6

The correlation variation in time is very similar for both the gold–XAU and the gold–dollar relationships. The gold–dollar correlation peaked for nine day changes, two days sooner than the gold–XAU. Both correlations then declined until the 20th day. The similarity, however, ended there. The gold–XAU correlation kept rising when taking longer time differences whereas the gold–dollar correlation peaked at 35 days.

In choosing the best time frame to use in a trading system or indicator, one's time horizon should also be taken into consideration. A time increment of nine days, when taking percentage differences, might be the best to use when designing short to medium term intermarket trading systems.

■ Bibliography

Murphy, John J. (1991). *Intermarket Technical Analysis: Trading Strategies for the Global Stock, Bond, Commodity, and Currency Markets*. John Wiley & Sons Inc.

Murphy, John J. (2004). *Intermarket Analysis: Profiting from Global Market Relationships*. New York: John Wiley & Sons, Inc.

Intraday Correlations

From Markos Katsanos, *Intermarket Trading Strategies* (Hoboken, New Jersey: John Wiley & Sons, 2008), Chapter 8.

Probable impossibilities are to be preferred to improbable possibilities.

—Aristotle

Learning Objective Statement

- Identify the strongest correlations in various timeframes between the listed index futures in this chapter

15.1 Relationships between Different Time Frames

The analysis of correlations of weekly yields is not really very useful to day traders or short-term traders of stock index futures.

But what about intraday relationships?

In Table 15.1 you can see the correlation of percentage changes between the DAX, the Euro Stoxx 50 and the S&P 500 and the DOW e-mini futures for different time intervals ranging from five to 1500 minutes (25 hours). One trading day for the DAX and Euro Stoxx futures is 14 hours so the correlation study, although calculated over a three-month time span, involves only up to two days of percentage changes.

An empirical relationship between time (in minutes) and correlation, which is not so obvious from Table 15.1, unravels when the correlation is plotted vs. time in the graph in Figure 15.1. You can see that the correlation increases exponentially up to a certain time increment (about 75 minutes) when it suddenly loses steam and starts to level out.

To assist traders I have derived the following empirical equations to convert correlations between different time frames.

For the DAX–Euro Stoxx relationship:

$$r_i = 0.87*(T_i)^{.01} \tag{15.1}$$

and

$$r_i = r_j^* \, (Ti/Tj)^{.01} \tag{15.2}$$

TABLE 15.1	A Total of 10870 5-Minute Bars Were Used to Calculate Intraday Correlation of Percentage Yields (Changes) between the S&P 500 e-Mini Futures, the Euro Stoxx, the DAX and DOW e-Mini Futures for the 3-Month Period from 1 January 2007 to 31 March 2007. Significant correlations are depicted in bold.

Minutes	ESTX	DAX	YM
5	0.725	0.724	0.614
10	0.750	0.741	0.655
15	0.767	0.754	0.667
20	0.779	0.763	0.679
25	0.783	0.768	0.683
30	**0.788**	0.774	0.690
35	0.782	**0.780**	**0.694**
40	0.776	0.782	0.696
45	0.780	0.787	0.700
50	0.783	0.789	0.703
55	0.787	0.793	0.706
60	0.785	0.797	**0.707**
65	0.786	0.802	0.724
70	0.788	0.807	0.737
75	0.788	0.810	0.750
80	0.788	0.812	0.761
85	0.788	0.813	0.771
90	0.787	0.814	0.779
95	0.786	0.815	0.787
100	0.785	0.816	0.794
125	0.785	**0.823**	0.818
150	0.786	0.830	0.830
200	0.783	0.836	0.851
250	0.780	0.842	0.868
375	0.778	0.850	0.889
500	**0.786**	0.862	0.902
750	0.812	0.884	0.913
1000	0.830	0.897	**0.921**
1250	0.831	0.900	0.925
1500	**0.842**	**0.910**	0.928

and for the ES − DAX relationship:

$$r_i = 0.677 * T^{.04} \qquad (15.3)$$

and

$$r_i = r_j^* \, (T\,i\,/\,T\,j)^{.04} \qquad (15.4)$$

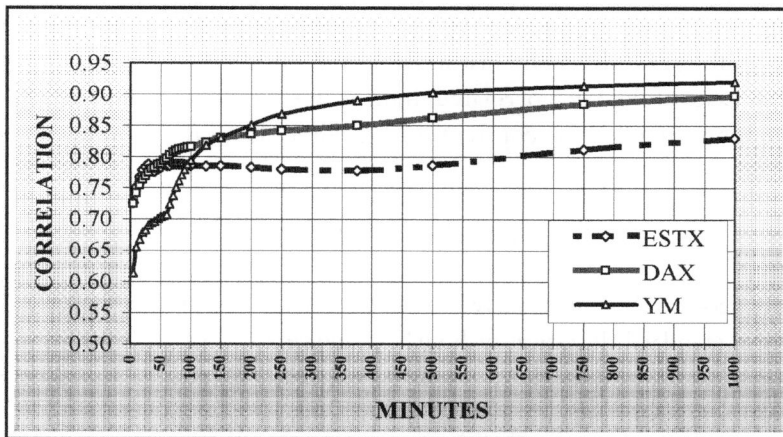

FIGURE 15.1 Intraday Correlation of Intraday Percentage Yields
(changes) between the S&P 500 e-Mini Futures, the Euro Stoxx, the
DAX and the DOW e-Mini Futures for the 3-Month Period from
1 January 2007 to 31 March 2007.

where r_i = Pearson's intraday correlation for time interval i; rj = Pearson's intraday
correlation for time interval j; T = time in minutes.

Equations 15.1–15.4 above are useful in calculating correlations and regression
coefficients for all intraday time frames. For examplewe can use formula (15.3) to
calculate an estimate of the 60-minute correlation between DAX and S&P e-mini
futures:

$$r = 0.677*60^{.04} = 0.797$$

Formula (15.4) can be used to convert correlations between intraday time frames.
For example we know that the 15-minute correlation between the S&P e-mini and
DAX futures is $r = 0.754$ and we want to know the corresponding 60-minute correlation coefficient. By substituting the 15-minute correlation in formula (15.4) we get:

$$r = 0.754*(60/15)^{.04} = 0.797$$

15.2 Intermarket Regression

The correlation coefficient calculated above can be used to forecast the expected
change of one equity index future in terms of the other using the regression equation
derived in Chapter 10. So for example:

- On 23 March 2007 and at 10:00 CET (02:00 US ET) the price of DAX futures
  was 6894.5 and the ES (S&P e-mini) was 1444.8.

- At 11:00 CET the DAX went up by 0.2% to 6908 but the ES did not move at all.

- Using the regression equation we can calculate the expected change of the ES in terms of the DAX, based on historical data of 60-minute intervals as follows: In the case of highly correlated indices the regression line usually crosses throughthe origin so the constant can be ignored and the regression equation is reduced to:

$$ES = r*sd(ES)/sd(DAX)*DAX$$

where: ES = S&P e-mini hourly % change; DAX = DAX futures hourly % change; sd = the standard deviation of hourly changes; r = Pearson's hourly correlation between the ES and the DAX. And the expected ES change based on historical correlations was:

$$ES = .797*.185/.239*.2 = .12\%$$

There was therefore a divergence between e-mini and DAX futures, most probably due to the lateness of the hour (for US traders) and the e-mini needed to catch up. During the next two hours the ES outperformed the DAX by more than 0.16%, thus nullifying the divergence.

THE INTEGRATION OF TECHNICAL ANALYSIS

■ 15.3 Which Time Frame?

In order to choose the best time span for calculating percentage yields in a trading system or indicator, I have listed in Table 15.1 Pearson's correlation for up to 1500 minutes (25 hours) of percentage yields between the S&P e-mini, the Euro Stoxx 50 (ESTX), DAX and Dow e-mini futures. These were also plotted graphically in Figure 15.1.

After carefully examining both the table and the graph the following conclusions can be drawn:

- Surprisingly, the S&P e-mini correlated better with the European futures than with its compatriot, the DOW e-mini, but only for shorter time segments up to 35 minutes of yields.

- Correlations with European futures peaked between 30 and 35-minute yields and this is probably the best value to use for short-term predictions based on Euro Stoxx futures.

- The S&P e-mini correlated better with the Euro Stoxx for very short yields (up to 35 minutes), with the DAX for medium (40 to 150 minute) yields and with DOW futures for longer term (over 150 minute or 2½ hour) yields.

- The correlation between the S&P e-mini futures (ES) and the Euro Stoxx, aftermaking a short-term top at the first 30-minute yield segment, went sideways forthe next 470 minutes (8 hours) but started rising again sharply.

- On the other hand, after rising sharply for the first 35 minutes, the correlation between the S&P and the DAX continued rising at a more moderate rate.

- Similarly, the correlation between the S&P and DOW e-mini futures (YM), after making a short term plateau between the 35-minute and 60-minute increment, kept rising rather steeply until the end.

- The correlation coefficient between the S&P and Euro Stoxx futures improved by only 7% for longer than 30-minute yields, whereas the correlation with the DOWimproved by more than 30%. It is therefore advantageous to use longer time frames when designing short-to-medium term intermarket trading systems to trade the S&P based on its correlation with the DOW.

Finally you should keep in mind that the values of the correlations in Table 15.1, although calculated from a big enough sample of 10 870 cases, are not written in stone but can vary considerably over time. For example, take a look at the chart of the S&P e-mini and Euro Stoxx 15-minute December 07 contracts. The correlation of 30-minute changes (in the top window) varies from a maximum of $r = 0.86$ on 19 September to a minimum of $r = 0.72$ on 9 October 2007. The corresponding average correlation calculated in Table 15.1 from a different sample from 1 January 2007 to 31 March 2007 was $r = 0.788$ (in bold) which is pretty close to the average in the chart in Figure 15.2. In addition to the short-term variations mentioned

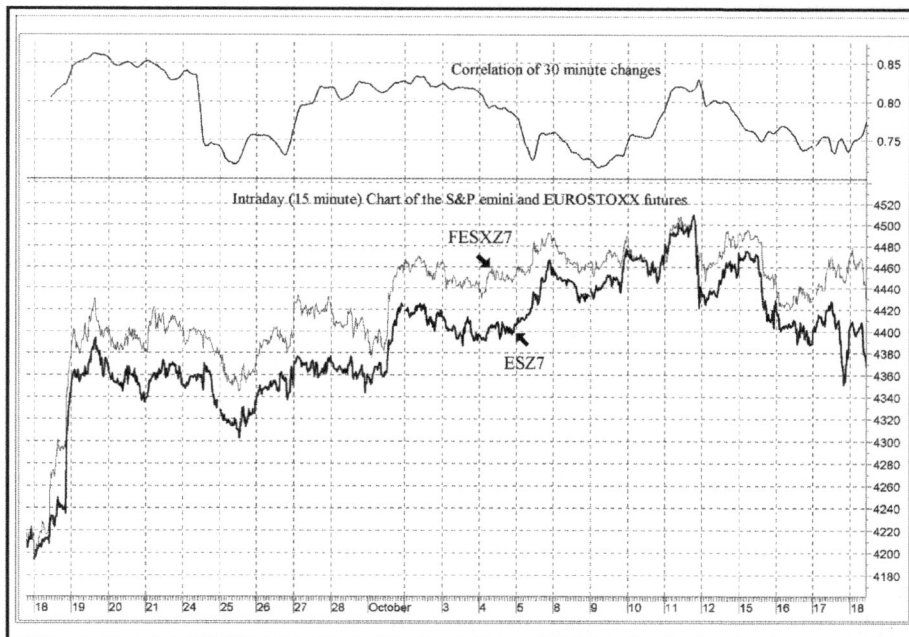

FIGURE 15.2 Intraday (15 minute) Composite Chart of the S&P e-Mini (ESZ7), Plotted with a Thick Bold Line and the Euro Stoxx 50 (FESXZ7) December 2007 Contracts from 18 September 2007 to 18 October 2007. The 10-day moving average of the correlation of the 30-minute changes is plotted in the top window.

above, the correlation can also digress from the mean during long time periods, caused by temporary decoupling of the underlying equity indices which is usually caused by a component stock specific problem not present in the other index.

■ 15.4 Lagging or Leading?

In practice, the main purpose of a predictive model is not to get the maximum explanatory value from a contemporaneous correlation analysis but to find a predictive market that shows changes and disparities between forecasted and observed values, warning of dangers and opportunities well ahead of time. In this context, we want the observed values to diverge from the statistically predicted values at times. This can only be accomplished by a leading/lagging correlation analysis which is simply a list of the correlations between values of a time series and other values of a related time series displaced at specified time intervals (lags).

Some problems arise in running a correlation analysis between US and European index futures, mainly because of the different time zones and trading hours. To deal with the time zone problem I had to convert all time zones to Central European time (CET) and in order to avoid division by zero errors in the correlation calculation (when one of the contracts was not trading), I deleted all US futures data when the European futures were closed (from 22:00 to 7:50 CET).

Although European index futures trade long after the underlying equity markets have closed, after 17:30 CET (when the European equity exchanges close) they move only on news from the other side of the Atlantic.

To deal with this problem and examine the effect of the US equity markets on European futures after the underlying main equity exchanges have closed or vice versa, I have divided the data into five separate groups according to the time of day. In the first group I have included only data until 14:30 CET (8:30 US EST). This is the time when European stock action and news are prevailing before the release of any important US economic news.

The second time segment was until US market open (15:30 CET or 9:30 US EST). The third group included only data until 17:30 CET (10:30 US EST) which is the closing time of most European stock exchanges. In the fourth group I have included all available data from 8:00 to 22:00 CET and, lastly, in the fifth group I have included only data after 15:30 CET (9:30 US EST). This is the time segment when the prevailing news that drives the markets originates mostly from the United States.

In addition, in order to determine which one was leading or lagging, the S&P e-mini was shifted both forward and backward in time.

Table 15.2 presents the leading, lagging and synchronous (coincident) correlations of 30-minute yields during the different time segments of the trading day between the S&P e-mini and Euro Stoxx futures, the DOW e-mini and the DAX, and in Table 15.3 you can see the intraday variability of the correlation between DAX and Euro Stoxx futures.

| TABLE 15.2 | Intraday Correlation of 30-Minute Intraday Yields (percentage changes) between S&P 500 e-Mini Futures, the Euro Stoxx, the DAX and DOW e-Mini Futures for Specific Time of Day Segments. Column 3 shows only data until 14:30 CET (Central European time) or 8:30 US EST, Column 4 shows only data until US market open (9:30 US EST), Column 5 shows only data until European close (17:30 CET) and Column 6 shows only data after US market open (9:30 US EST). The S&P data were shifted forward and back in time in order to calculate lagging and leading correlations. |

			TIME (CET)			
30 Min Yields	Lead/Lag	<14:30	<15:30 US Open	<17:30 EUR Close	08:00–22:00 All Day	>15:30
ESTX	synchronous	0.811	0.795	**0.781**	**0.788**	**0.815**
ESTX	lagging	0.663	0.65	0.632	0.652	**0.676**
ESTX	leading	0.668	0.655	0.634	0.649	0.665
YM	synchronous	0.606	0.596	0.680	0.690	**0.735**
YM	lagging	**0.512**	**0.503**	**0.569**	**0.583**	**0.615**
YM	leading	0.485	0.483	0.558	0.571	0.609
DAX	synchronous	**0.818**	**0.797**	0.776	0.774	0.798
DAX	lagging	**0.676**	**0.658**	0.635	0.644	0.663
DAX	leading	0.668	0.654	0.63	0.64	0.655

The following conclusions were drawn from the leading, lagging and synchronous time segmented correlations in Tables 15.2 and 15.3:

- The best synchronous correlation was between S&P e-mini and Euro Stoxx futures ($r = 0.788$ in bold in the Column-5 of Table 15.2 and $r = 0.815$ after 15:30 CET). The Euro stoxx was slightly leading the e-mini up to 15:30 CET but the lead reversed dramatically to a considerable lag (r lagging $= 0.676$ vs. r leading $= 0.665$) after the US market open. It is therefore better to avoid intermarket trading signals before 15:30 CET when designing an intermarket system to trade the Euro Stoxx based on its correlation with the S&P e-mini.

| TABLE 15.3 | Intraday Correlation of 30-Minute Intraday Yields (percentage changes) between the Euro Stoxx and DAX Futures for Specific Time of Day Segments. In the first row only data until US market open (15:30 CET) were used, in the second row only data until European market close (17:30 CET) were used, and in the fourth row only data after US market open (9:30 US EST) were used. In order to calculate lagging and leading correlation the Euro Stoxx data were shifted forward and back in time. |

		DAX		
	Time of Day CET	Synchronous	Lagging	Leading
<15:30	Before US open	0.857	**0.696**	0.687
<17:30	Before EUR close	0.883	**0.716**	0.707
10:00–22:00	All day	0.897	**0.740**	0.731
>15:30	After US open	0.948	0.789	0.781

■ The DAX futures lagged both the Euro Stoxx futures (Table 15.3) and the S&P e-mini (Table 15.2) for all time frames; a slight lag up to European close deteriorated significantly after 17:30 CET (European close). As the DAX correlated significantly better with Euro Stoxx futures than with the e-mini, it is better to use this relationship in designing an intermarket system to trade DAX futures, at least until US market open. After 15:30 both European futures lagged the US futures; therefore replacing the Euro Stoxx with the e-mini might have a lead time advantage, despite the lower correlation.

■ Surprisingly, the DOW e-mini, despite the underlying index sharing all of its component stocks with the S&P 500, did not correlate with the S&P e-mini as well as Euro Stoxx futures. In addition, the DOW lagged the S&P e-mini during all time segments. It is therefore preferable to trade the DOW e-mini based on its correlation with the S&P e-mini and not the other way around.

The variability of the correlation during the trading day, presented in Table 15.2 in tabular form, can also be seen graphically in the chart in Figure 15.3 where the

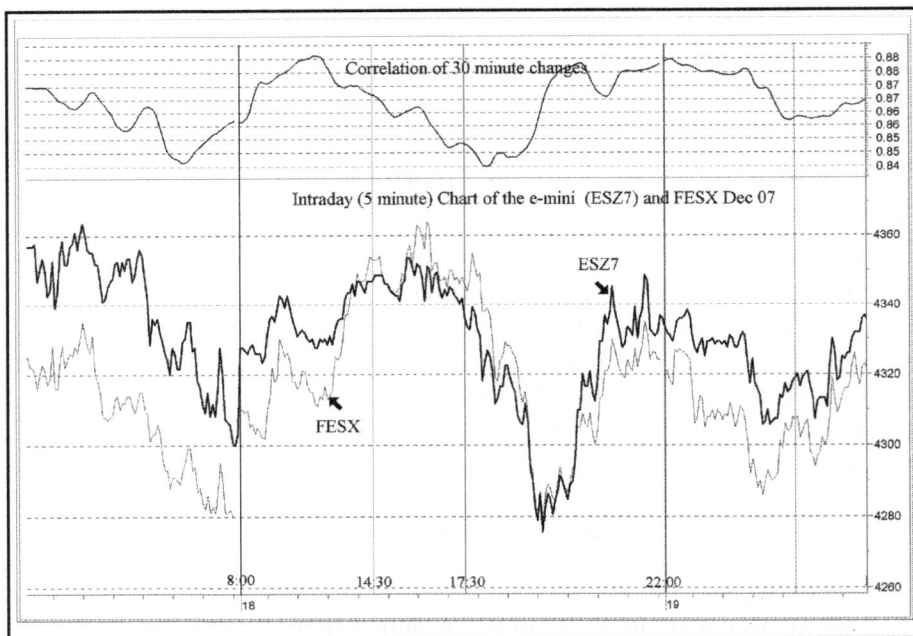

FIGURE 15.3 Intraday (5 minute) Composite Chart of the S&P e-Mini (thick bold line) and Euro Stoxx 50 (thin line with the scale on the right Y-axis) Contracts from 18–20 December 2007. The 5 bar moving average of the correlation of the 30-minute changes between the S&P e-mini and Euro Stoxx futures is also plotted in the top window. To illustrate the correlation variability during the trading day, vertical lines are drawn at the EUREX open (8:00 CET), at 14:30 CET (US pre-open), 17:30 CET (European equity close) and 22:00 CET (EUREX futures close). Euro Stoxx futures trade in the EUREX from 8:00 a.m. CET to 22:00 CET. To avoid division by zero errors in the correlation calculation when the Euro Stoxx doesn't trade, non overlapping e-mini data (from 22:00 to 8:00 CET) were deleted.

correlation of 30-minute changes between the S&P e-mini and Euro Stoxx futures is plotted in the top window. For example, you can see that on 18 December 2007, the correlation rose to a maximum during the first time segment (before 14:30 CET) and then fell to an intraday low during the second and third time segments. It then rose again exactly to the level of the morning high during the end of the last time segment (after about 22:00 CET).

In designing intermarket systems to trade stock index futures, it is therefore better to use intermarket generated signals only when the underlying equity markets are closed and the leadership switches to related markets that are still open.

CHAPTER 16

Intermarket Indicators

From Markos Katsanos, *Intermarket Trading Strategies* (Hoboken, New Jersey: John Wiley & Sons, 2008), Chapter 9.

I'm a great believer in luck, and I find the harder I work, the more I have of it.

—**Thomas Jefferson**

Learning Objective Statements

- Analyze and interpret relative strength of different assets
- Analyze and interpret Bollinger Band Divergence signals
- Interpret data from multiple regression divergence signals to predict a target market
- Prepare a recommendation or other response based on asset correlation data

Classic technical analysis indicators, such as moving averages, only indicate the possible likelihood of the continuation of the current trend and they are certainly no guarantee of future direction, which can reverse on a dime.

The indicators presented in this chapter, unlike moving averages, will help you judge the direction of tomorrow's price, and possible trend reversals using intermarket correlations.

16.1 Relative Strength

Relative strength (RS) is a popular indicator which compares one security with another or with a benchmark index, for example a specific US stock with the S&P 500.

Relative strength in the stock market was popularized in the 1980s by William O'Niel in his classic *How to Make Money in Stocks*. O'Niel is also the founder of *Investor's Business Daily*, where he publishes the IBD® 100 stock list featuring companies that show superior earnings and strong price performance relative to the market average.

The relative strength is calculated by dividing the price of one security by the benchmark. The ratio is further smoothed by a moving average in order to eliminate the effect of erratic price movements or "noise" from daily price fluctuations.

When this ratio is rising, the numerator is outperforming the denominator and vice versa.

In Figure 16.1 I use the ratio between the Gold ETF (GLD) and the dollar index (DXY). To remove daily noise the ratio is smoothed by its 3-day exponential moving average (EMA). This is plotted in the middle window and, to avoid confusing it with Wilder's Relative Strength Index, I called it Intermarket Relative Strength. Classic technical analysis trendlines can be drawn by joining tops or bottoms. On 27 March 2006 the gold/dollar ratio broke the trendline drawn over the three previous peaks (the first, shorter trendline on the left of the chart in Figure 16.1) and the price of the gold ETF surged 27% from 55.7 to 71.1. Similarly, on 27 October 2006 the ratio broke its 5-month down trendline (second trendline in the middle) which indicated a trend reversal for gold.

The relative strength, however, cannot keep rising indefinitely, flagrantly violating long-term relationships. To determine overbought and oversold levels, I normalize it on a scale from 1 to 100 using the intermarket momentum oscillator (the formula is included in Section 16.6 below).

THE INTEGRATION OF TECHNICAL ANALYSIS

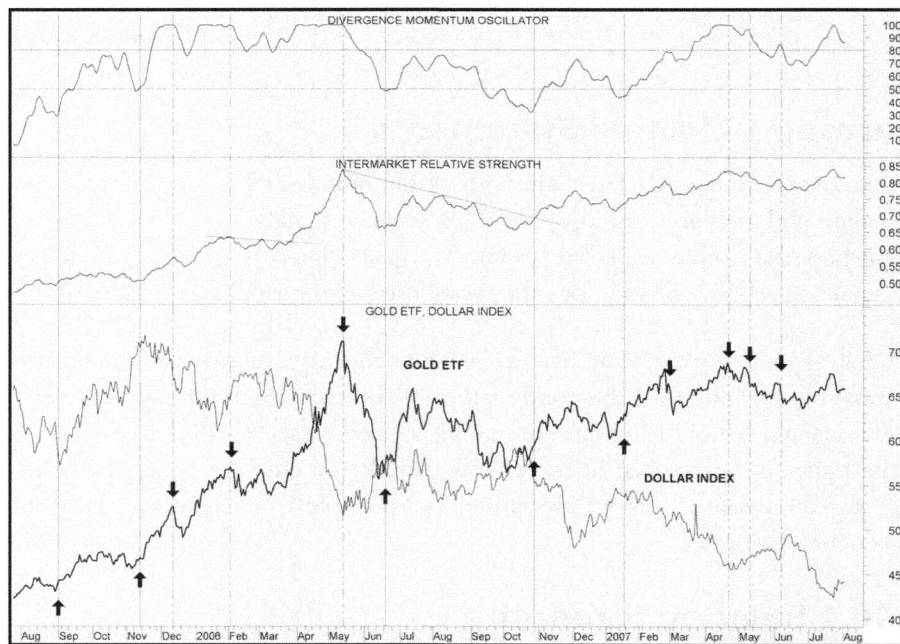

FIGURE 16.1 **Composite Chart of the Gold ETF (GLD) and the Dollar Index (DXY) for the 2-Year Period from July 2005 to July 2007.** The 3-day moving average of the gold/dollar relative strength is depicted in the middle window and the 2000-day intermarket momentum oscillator (see Section 16.6) in the top window. Up and down arrows indicate sell and buy signals triggered by the oscillator crossing its 4-day moving average at overbought (over 80) and oversold (less than 50) levels respectively.

Values over a specific value (e.g. 80) indicate overbought levels and below another lower value (e.g. 50) oversold levels. In Figure 16.1, I marked some possible buy and sell signals triggered by the oscillator crossing its 4-day moving average from below on oversold (less than 50) levels and crossing its moving average from above on overbought (over 80) levels respectively.

The relative strength between a stock and the appropriate index can also be used to evaluate one's stock portfolio. If the relative strength drops below its moving average while the price of the security is still rising, then it is time to consider heading for the exit while the stock is still strong.

This tactic can be combined with a moving average strategy to help you get out at a better price than if you were using a moving average of the price alone.

■ 16.2 Bollinger Band Divergence

This indicator was first introduced in my article "Detecting Breakouts" in *Technical Analysis of STOCKS & COMMODITIES* (see Bibliography) in order to calculate the divergence between price and money flow. It can also be used to calculate the divergence between a security and a related market. First the relative position of both securities in the Bollinger Bands is calculated and the divergence is derived by subtracting the relative position of the intermarket security from the base security. Indicator values vary from -100 to $+100$, values less than zero indicate negative divergence and over zero positive divergence. Buy signals are generated when the indicator reaches a peak above a certain level (usually 10 to 30) and subsequently declines. Similarly, sell signals are triggered when the indicator reaches a bottom below a certain level (usually -10 to -30) and rises.

The formula for the relative position of a security in the Bollinger Bands is derived as follows:

$$SEC1BOL=(C-BollingerBBottom)/(BollingerBTop-BollingerBBottom) \qquad (16.1)$$

$$\text{but } BollingerBandBottom=MA-2SD \qquad (16.2)$$

$$\text{and } BollingerBandTop=MA-2SD. \qquad (16.3)$$

Substituting from (16.2) and (16.3) in (16.1) we get

$$SEC1BOL=(C-MA+2SD)/4SD. \qquad (16.4)$$

The formula above will produce the relative position of a security in the Bollinger Bands. Values of 1 indicate that it has reached the top band and values of zero indicate that it has reached the bottom band. To eliminate negative values (when price falls below the bottom band) the final value is increased by one and the formula becomes:

$$SEC1BOL=1+(C-MA+2SD)/4SD \qquad (16.5)$$

The divergence is then calculated by taking the 3-day exponential moving average percentage difference between the relative position of the related intermarket security and the security to be traded as follows:

$$DIVERGENCE = EMA(3)[(SEC2BOL - SEC1BOL)/SEC1BOL^*100] \quad (16.6)$$

where SEC1BOL=Relative position of the base security in the Bollinger Bands; SEC2BOL=Relative position of the intermarket security in the Bollinger Bands; MA=Moving average; SD=Standard deviation; EMA=Exponential Moving Average.

There are some limitations with the underlying Bollinger Band theory that should be understood before applying it to trading:

- The formula involves the calculation of the standard deviation which makes the assumption of normality and it is therefore subject to errorwhen the price distribution deviates significantly from normality.

- Because of scaling factors the formula doesn't work so well with negatively correlated markets.

You can find the MetaStock code for all intermarket indicators in Appendix A. There are two ways of entering data for the intermarket security (SEC2). The first method (used in the relative strength indicator) is by referencing the symbol and folder in the first line of the code. For example in the line

SEC2:=Security("C:\MetastockData\INTERMARKET\DXY0",C);

C:\Metastock Data\INTERMARKET is the folder in my hard drive where historical data for the dollar index is located; DXY0 is the symbol for the Dollar Index; and C indicates that I want to reference only the closing price.

An alternativemethod (used in the case of the Bollinger Band divergence indicator) is to drag and drop the indicator on the dollar index chart until it changes color to pink (the dollar index and not the indicator). This method cannot be used, however, when back-testing an indicator. An advantage of using the first method is that there is no need to have a chart of the intermarket security plotted in order to use the indicator. Tradestation users can only use the second method and a chart of the intermarket security should be always plotted together with the base security.

■ 16.3 Intermarket Disparity

The disparity index was first introduced by Steve Nison in his book *Beyond Candlesticks: New Japanese Charting Techniques Revealed* (see Bibliography) and it has since been incorporated in the majority of popular technical analysis software.

It is defined as the percentage difference or "disparity" of the latest close to a chosen moving average, and the formula is:

$$((Close - MA(Close, 30))/MA(Close, 30))^*100.$$

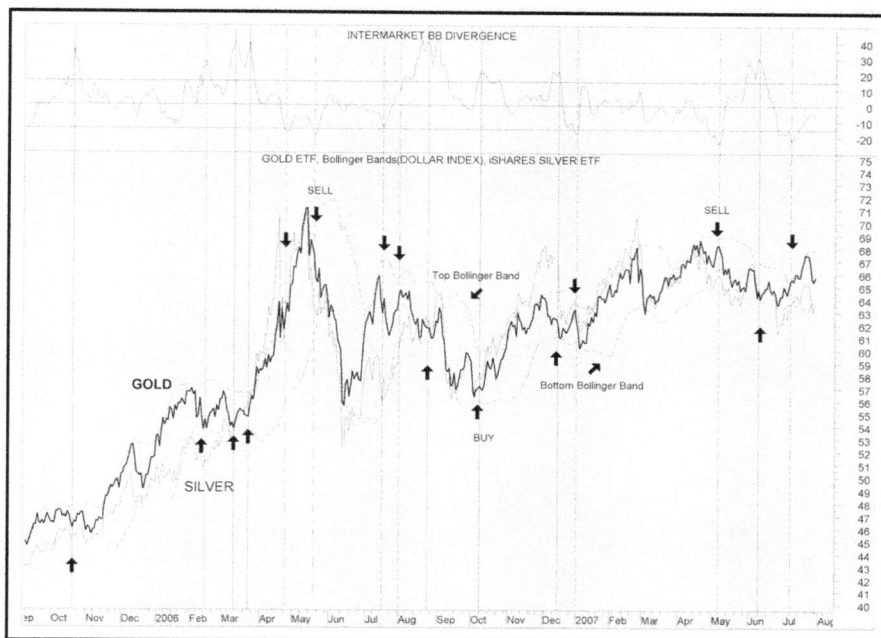

FIGURE 16.2 Composite Chart of the Gold (GLD) and Silver (SLV) ETF. The 20-day intermarket Bollinger Band divergence indicator is depicted in the top window. Horizontal lines are drawn at the 15, 0 and−15% divergence levels. Up arrows indicate buy signals triggered by Bollinger Band divergence peaks above the 15% divergence level. Similarly, down arrows indicate sell signals triggered by Bollinger Band divergence troughs but only below the −15% negative divergence level.

To calculate the intermarket disparity I subtract the disparity index of the base security from the disparity index of the intermarket security according to the following formula:

$$DS1=(SEC1-MA(SEC1))/MA(SEC1)^*100 \qquad (16.7)$$

$$DS2=(SEC2-MA(SEC2))/MA(SEC2)^*100 \qquad (16.8)$$

$$\text{Intermarket Disparity (ID)}=c^*DS2-DS1$$

where SEC1 = the base security (the security that you want to predict); SEC2 = the intermarket security. c has been introduced to take into account the sign of the correlation coefficient and can be either +1 in cases of positive correlation between SEC1 and SEC2 or −1 in case of negatively correlated markets (like gold and the dollar index).

The interpretation is similar to the Bollinger Band indicator. Positive and negative values indicate positive and negative divergence respectively. A sell signal is generated when the divergence reaches a bottom and reverses below a certain negative level and a buy signal is generated when the indicator reaches a top and falls above a certain positive level. Unlike the Intermarket momentum oscillator (see Section 16.6 below), there are no upper or lower limits as these vary according to the securities being compared and their correlation.

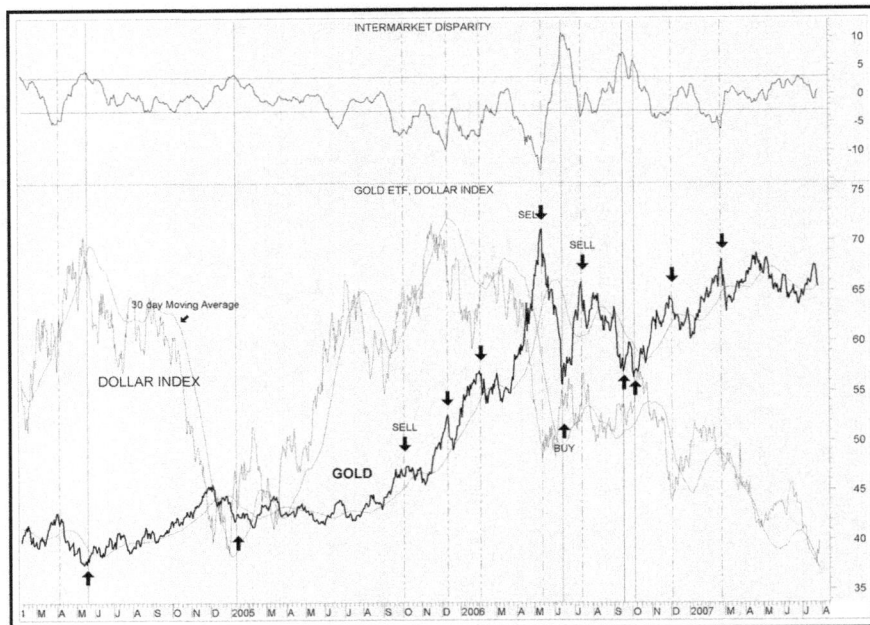

FIGURE 16.3 Composite Chart of the Gold ETF (GLD) and the Dollar Index (DXY). The 30-day intermarket disparity indicator is depicted in the top window. Buy signals are triggered by the intermarket disparity reaching a top and turning down on 3% or greater positive divergence. Similarly sell signals are generated by the intermarket disparity reaching a bottom and turning up but only for divergence values below −3% (negative divergence).

A similar method was used by Murray Ruggiero in his book *Cybernetic Trading Strategies* (see Bibliography) to develop the mechanical trading signals based on intermarket divergence.

The difference between the two methods is that Ruggiero considers buy signals between positively correlated markets only when *DS1<0 and DS2>0* and sell signals only when *DS1>0 and DS2<0* whereas the intermarket disparity indicator (ID) described above calculates the divergence precisely. It can issue buy signals when DS2-DS1 rises above a certain level even when both securities are above their moving average (both DS1 and DS2 are positive), which usually occurs when the disparity of the intermarket security (DS2) is considerably higher than DS1. Similarly Ruggiero's method issues buy signals between negatively correlated markets only when *DS1<0 and DS2<0* and sell signals when *DS1>0 and DS2>0* whereas the ID indicator can issue buy signals even when both DS1 and DS2 are negative, which occurs only when the disparity of the intermarket security (DS2) is considerably lower than DS1.

■ 16.4 Intermarket LRS Divergence

This indicator was first introduced in my article "Volume Flow Performance" in *Technical Analysis of STOCKS & COMMODITIES* (see Bibliography) in order to calculate the divergence money flow divergence between price and the volume flow indicator.

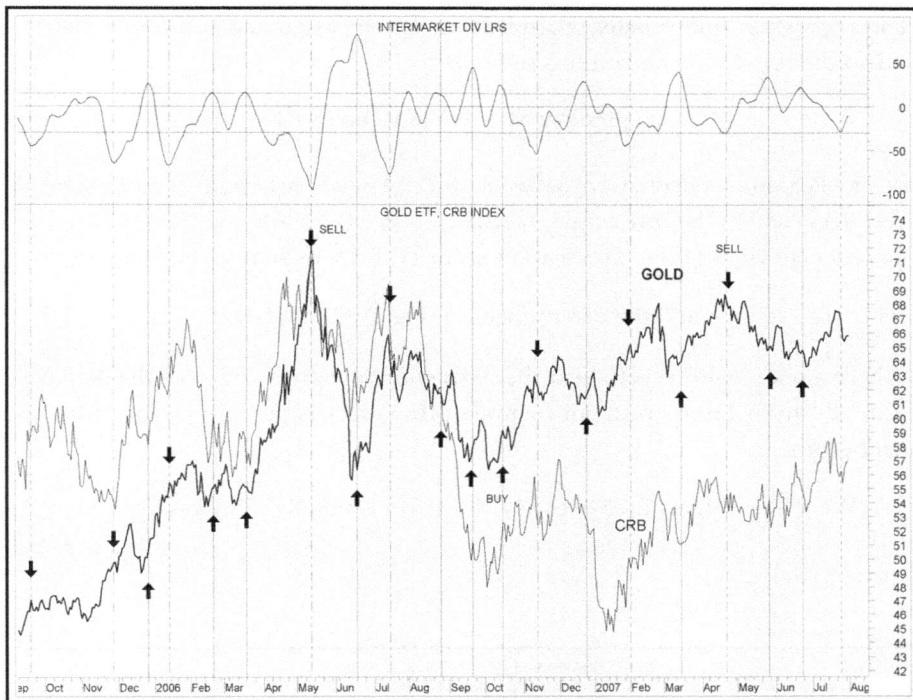

FIGURE 16.4 Composite Chart of the Gold ETF (GLD) and the CRB Index (CRB).
The 15-day intermarket divergence LRS indicator is depicted in the top window.
Buy signals are triggered by the intermarket LRS divergence reaching a top and
turning down on positive divergence levels of 15 or greater. Similarly, sell signals
are generated by the intermarket LRS divergence reaching a bottom and turning
up, but only for divergence values below the −30 level (negative divergence).

It can also be used (with some modifications) to calculate the divergence of a security from its related intermarket. First the linear regression slope of both securities
is calculated and the intermarket slope is then adjusted to take into account the difference in volatilities between the two securities. The divergence is then derived by
subtracting the base security slope from the intermarket. Values below zero indicate
negative divergence and values over the zero line positive divergence. Buy signals are
generated when the indicator reaches a peak above a certain level (usually between 10
and 40) and subsequently declines. Similarly, sell signals are triggered when the indicator reaches a bottom below a certain level (usually from −10 to −40) and rises. Divergence levels vary according to the intermarket securities chosen for comparison.

■ 16.5 Intermarket Regression Divergence

The linear regression equation, derived in Chapter 10, is used to make a prediction
of likely values of the dependent variable or the security to be predicted (gold in our
examples), based on values of a correlated market. This method can only be used
with price differences or yields as raw prices violate the two basic assumptions of
regression: linearity and normality.

The regression line usually crosses through the origin and can be therefore ignored so the regression equation is reduced to:

$$Y(Pred) = r^*StDev(Y)/StDev(X)^*X \qquad (16.9)$$

where r=Pearson's correlation between the related markets; Y=percentage yield of the security to be predicted (actual); Y(Pred)=predicted percentage yield; X=percentage yield of the intermarket security; StDev=standard deviation;

$$\text{and the divergence is } Y(Pred) - Y(actual). \qquad (16.10)$$

Where a scatterplot reveals that the regression line does not cross the origin then we can add the Y-Intercept from formula (10.3) in Chapter 10 to formula (16.9) which becomes:

$$Y(Pred) = r^*StDev(Y)/StDev(X)^*X + MA(Y) - MA(X)^*r^*StDev(Y)/StDev(X). \qquad (16.11)$$

FIGURE 16.5 Composite Chart of the Gold ETF (GLD) and the XAU. The 300-day intermarket regression divergence indicator of the 15-day Gold-XAU yields is depicted in the top window. Buy signals are triggered by the intermarket regression divergence reaching a top and turning down on positive divergence levels of 3 or greater. Similarly, sell signals are generated by the intermarket regression divergence reaching a bottom and turning up but only for divergence values below the −4 level (negative divergence).

■ 16.6 Intermarket Momentum Oscillator

A serious disadvantage in using all the above indicators is that extreme divergence levels vary according to the markets being analyzed. This is mainly because of price scaling differences between the base and intermarket security.

To automate the tedious work of identifying indicator extreme values, I use a simple momentum oscillator which I call the intermarket momentum oscillator. I use the following formula to calculate the new oscillator:

$$\text{Momentum} = MA,3(\text{Indicator} - \text{Lowest}(\text{Indicator}, 200))^* 100 /$$
$$(MA,3(\text{Highest}(\text{Indicator}, 200) - \text{Lowest}(\text{Indicator}, 200))$$

where $MA,3 = 3$-day moving average; Highest and Lowest are the highest and lowest values of the indicator over the previous 200-day period.

The formula above will normalize the divergence on a scale from 1 to 100. Trading signal interpretation is similar to that of the stochastic oscillator:

- Buy when the oscillator falls below a specific level (e.g. 30) and then rises above that level, and sell when the oscillator rises above a specific level (e.g. 80) and then falls below that level.

- Buy when the oscillator falls below a specific level (e.g. 30) and then rises above a higher level (e.g. 40), and sell when the oscillator rises above a specific level (e.g. 90) and then falls below a lower level (e.g. 80).

- Buy when the oscillator rises above its signal line (moving average) and sell when it falls below the signal line.

- A combination of either one of the first two methods with the third.

An example of this oscillator applied on the intermarket relative strength is shown in Figure 16.1. When the indicator is used to normalize divergence the buy and sell signals indicated above should be reversed as we want to buy at maximum positive divergence and sell at maximum negative divergence. Care should also be taken in interpreting indicator signals in trending markets. In this case the second method of interpretation would be more appropriate as the indicator can remain in the overbought area for a long period of time.

■ 16.7 Z-Score Divergence

A comparison of two securities on the same chart is sometimes difficult and misleading because of price scaling differences. A convenient method of normalizing both prices on an equal scale is by converting the prices to their Z-scores. These are computed by subtracting the mean and dividing by the standard deviation according to the formula:

$$Z = (C - MA)/SD$$

Z-scores use the standard deviation as a unit of measure and indicate how many standard deviations the price falls above or below the mean. In order to eliminate decimal places and negative values it is sometimes convenient to transform them into a different scale with a mean of 50 (instead of 0) by adding 50 and multiplying by 10.

The Z-score divergence is computed by subtracting the Z-score of the base security from the intermarket and multiplying the result by their correlation coefficient. A visual inspection of the Z-scores and their differences can help you determine if you are positioned in the market in the correct direction and which one is leading or lagging.

An interesting chart is that of gold and the euro in Figure 16.6. Although these markets have a fairly high degree of correlation, their relationship swings, with the euro switching position as follower and leader. Their spread is more accurate (because of scaling differences) when comparing the Z-scores (in the middle chart) rather than the prices themselves. Care should be taken when using this method for trading, because by using the standard deviation to convert prices to Z-scores we make the implicit assumption that the distribution of security prices is normal.

FIGURE 16.6 Composite Chart of the Gold ETF (GLD) (thick line with the scale on the right Y-axis) and the Euro (thin line on the left Y-axis). The 250-day (1 year) Z-scores of gold (thick line) and the Euro (thin line) are depicted in the upper window on the same scale. The Z-score illustrates more clearly the relation between gold and the Euro, especially in periods where both charts are very close in the bottom window.

Financial series, however, are rarely normally distributed. The Z-score will normalize prices regardless of statistical merit which is only absolutely correct in the case of perfectly normally distributed data. In the case of serious deviations from normality, unlikely events – such as the markets uncoupling even more – are more likely to occur than is the case in a normal distribution.

Nevertheless, the above limitations do not mitigate the usefulness of the Z-score indicator in comparing multiple related securities visually.

16.8 Multiple Intermarket Divergence

All the indicators discussed above involve the comparison between two correlated markets. This concept can be extended to multiple markets where a prediction of the future direction of a security is extended to include multiple predictor markets.

This can be achieved by adding the divergences for each market after taking into account the redundant cross correlation between the predictor (independent) variables.

This can be achieved by weighing each predictor variable according to its part (or semi-partial) correlation coefficient with the dependent variable (the security to be predicted).

The part correlation coefficient represents the proportion of the variance of a predictor market (independent variable) that is not associated with any other predictors and is calculated by removing all variance which may be accounted for by the other independent variables. The remaining unique component of the independent variables is then correlated with the dependent variable. The computational formula for the part correlation coefficient is:

$$r_{y1(2)} = \frac{r_{y1} - r_{y2}r_{12}}{\sqrt{1-r^2_{12}}} \qquad (16.12)$$

$$r_{y2(1)} = \frac{r_{y2} - r_{y1}r_{12}}{\sqrt{1-r^2_{12}}} \qquad (16.13)$$

where: $r_{y1(2)}$ is the correlation between y (the dependent variable) and 1 (the first independent variable) with the influence of the second independent variable removed from variable 1.

$r_{y2(1)}$ is the correlation between y (the dependent variable) and 2 (the second independent variable) with the influence of the first independent variable removed from variable 2.

r_{y1} and r_{y2} are the correlations between the dependent variable y and the independent variables 1 and 2 respectively.

r_{12} is the correlation between the independent variables.

In the example in Figure 16.7 the formula for the intermarket divergence LRS (top window) has been extended to include two predictor markets: silver and the

FIGURE 16.7 The 20-day double divergence between gold, the dollar index and the silver ETF is depicted in the top window. Extreme values of the divergence are indicated by the horizontal lines at +15 and −20.

dollar index by weighing each predictor variable according to its part correlation with the security to be predicted (gold). The complete double LRS divergence formula is included in Appendix A.

The linear regression slopes were compared over a 20-day interval. The time interval was used as a switch for increasing or decreasing the amount of trading signals. Decreasing the time segment produced more signals while increasing it reduced them.

Please note that because of gold's recent strength all examples presented in this chapter have a tendency to exaggerate negative divergence. To compensate for this divergence bias, asymmetrical divergence levels of +15 and −20 were chosen for the extreme positive and negative divergence levels respectively.

■ 16.9 Multiple Regression Divergence

In multiple regression, the goal is to predict the value of the dependent variable (the market to be predicted) from a set of k independent variables (related markets).

Multiple regression finds a set of partial regression coefficients b_k such that the dependent variable could be approximated as well as possible by a linear combination of the independent variables (with b_i etc. being the weight of the combination). Therefore, a predicted value, denoted Y, of the dependent variable is obtained from:

$$Y = a + b_1X_1 + b_2X_2 + \ldots b_kX_k \qquad (16.14)$$

The coefficients of the multiple regression equation represent the amount by which the dependent variable (to be predicted) increases when one independent (predictor) variable is increased by one unit and all the other independent variables are held constant. They will therefore vary depending upon the other independent variables included in the regression equation.

Part correlation, discussed above, is also the basis of multiple regression.

The values of the regression coefficients are found using ordinary least squares. In this case it is more convenient to express the regression coefficients in matrix form. When more than two variables are involved, the formula becomes too long and cannot be programmed into MetaStock because of formula space limitations. They can, however, be calculated using any other programming language.

However, for a trader who is only interested in a few markets, there is an easier method. The linear regression coefficients can be calculated using any off-the-shelf statistical package and substituted in the MetaStock code. This method has the advantage of being able to select an effective set of predictor intermarket securities that will maximize the coefficient of determination, R squared.

The practical problem in multiple regression is one of identifying predictor variables that are highly correlated with the dependent variable but have low correlations among themselves.

There might be a tendency to continue including variables as long as there seems to be an increase in R squared. In practice, however, it is simply not feasible to find more than three predictor markets that are uncorrelated.

In choosing the best independent variables to include in the regression equation it is important to ensure that these are not too highly correlated with each other (i.e. Pearson's correlation should not exceed 0.80), because the regression may become unstable.

A counterintuitive point worth noting is that sometimes an independent variable that has zero or very low correlation with the dependent can lead to improvement in prediction if it is included in the regression equation. This is because it removes the irrelevant variance or "noise" that it shares with the other predictors but is not present in the dependent variable.

The gold example can be used again to illustrate some of these points.

The first step is to choose independent variables that are known to be related to gold and choose the best time increment to use when calculating percent changes.

The correlation analysis in Chapter 14 (Table 14.6) indicates that gold has the stronger correlation with the XAU and the dollar index when taking 9-day yields. This time segment was therefore used to construct the correlation matrix with related markets in Tables 16.1 and 16.2 using 15 and 10 years of data respectively. The correlation coefficients were similar in both tables, except for the correlation between the dollar index and gold which improved considerably (from -0.33 to -0.43) when using 10 years of data.

Considering that the dollar is a major fundamental factor affecting gold, I decided to use the shorter time period when calculating the regression equation coefficients.

We can now proceed with the regression analysis to predict gold in terms of the XAU, silver, the dollar, the CRB and the yen. These were chosen because they correlatedwellwith gold but were not too highly related with each other. The eurowas not included because of its high cross correlation with the dollar index ($r = -0.97$).

TABLE 16.1 Correlation Matrix of 9-Day Yields. The TNX is the CBOE 10-year Treasury yield index. Data for the most recent 15-year period were used to calculate the correlations. Only 10 years of data were available for the euro and therefore it was not included in the matrix.

15 Year Correlation Matrix of 9-Day Yields

	Gold	XAU	Silver	Dollar	CRB	Yen	TNX
Gold	1	0.70	0.60	−0.33	0.43	−0.19	−0.09
XAU	0.70	1	0.54	−0.22	0.42	−0.17	−0.05
Silver	0.60	0.54	1	−0.17	0.44	−0.11	0.02
Venture	0.58	0.67	0.59	−0.27	0.47	−0.24	0.08
Dollar	−0.33	−0.22	−0.17	1	−0.18	0.55	0.18
CRB	0.43	0.42	0.44	−0.18	1	−0.18	0.08
Yen	−0.19	−0.17	−0.11	0.55	−0.18	1	0.08
TNX	−0.09	−0.05	0.02	0.18	0.08	0.08	1

The first aspect to consider is how well the independent variables predicted the dependent variable, in this case gold. This is determined by the coefficient of determination, R squared. Model 3 (see Table 16.3) has an R^2 of 0.587 implying that 58.7% of the variance in gold is explained by the predictor variables, the XAU, silver and the dollar.

Clearly the XAU is the largest contributor to the coefficient of determination, R^2 (Table 16.3). The first model (first line in Table 16.3) which consists of the XAU only has a coefficient of determination R^2 of 0.484, hence we can say that the contribution of the XAU to R^2 was 0.484. When silver is added (in model 2) R^2 increases 13% to 0.549 and the addition of the dollar index (model 3) adds a further 0.038 or 7% to R^2. The CRB and the yen, in the fourth and fifth model respectively, contribute very little to R^2 and consequently add very little value to the predictive ability of the regression equation. This is also verified by their near zero part correlation coefficients (their correlation coefficient with gold after removing the effects of all other variables) depicted in the last two columns of Table 16.3.

TABLE 16.2 Pearson's 10-Year Correlation Matrix of 9-Day Percentage Yields. Data for the most recent 10-year period were used to calculate the correlations.

10 Year Correlation Matrix of 9-Day Yields

	Gold	XAU	Silver	Dollar	Euro	CRB	Yen	TNX
Gold	1	0.70	0.58	−0.43	0.40	0.44	−0.22	−0.09
XAU	0.70	1	0.52	−0.31	0.28	0.43	−0.19	−0.03
Silver	0.58	0.52	1	−0.26	0.23	0.43	−0.13	0.01
Venture	0.58	0.67	0.59	−0.27	0.23	0.47	−0.24	0.08
Dollar	−0.43	−0.31	−0.26	1	−0.97	−0.27	0.54	0.24
Euro	0.40	0.28	0.23	−0.97	1	0.21	−0.35	−0.24
CRB	0.44	0.43	0.43	−0.27	0.21	1	−0.25	0.10
Yen	−0.22	−0.19	−0.13	0.54	−0.35	−0.25	1	0.10
TNX	−0.09	−0.03	0.01	0.24	−0.24	0.10	0.10	1

TABLE 16.3	Model Summary. The first model includes only the XAU. Silver, the dollar, the CRB and the yen are added one at a time in models 2, 3, 4 and 5 respectively. Adding the CRB and the yen make very little difference to the coefficient of determination R^2.

| | | | | Part correlations | | | | |
Model	R2	R^2 change	R^2 % change	XAU	Silver	Dollar	CRB	Yen
1	0.484	0.484	100	0.70				
2	0.549	0.065	13.4	0.46	0.26			
3	0.587	0.038	6.9	0.41	0.23	−0.20		
4	0.592	0.005	0.9	0.38	0.20	−0.19	0.07	
5	0.593	0.001	0.2	0.38	0.20	−0.18	0.07	0.03

The relative impact of each variable on gold is also of interest.

Each of the regression coefficients in Table 16.4 estimates the amount of change that occurs in the dependent variable (gold) for one unit change of the corresponding independent variable. We cannot say, however, that because the dollar index coefficient is larger than the corresponding coefficient for the XAU that the dollar is more important for predicting gold, as they use different scales of measurement. In order to make effective comparisons, all coefficients should be normalized. This is done by multiplying each variable by the ratio of its standard deviation to the standard deviation of the dependent variable (gold). The resultant normalized coefficients are then called standardized.

Examining the standardized coefficients in Table 16.5 and their percentage weight in Table 16.6 we can see that when including all potential predictor markets (last line in Table 16.6) the XAU has the greatest impact on gold (45 %). The CRB, in spite of a moderate correlation with gold (r = 0.44), has a very low standardized coefficient (0.085) because of its high cross correlation with the XAU and silver.

In view of the above the CRB and the yen can be removed from the regression equation with very little loss to its predictive ability. Thus the equation reduces to:

$$G9 = 0.07 + 0.216^*X9 + 0.166^*S9 - 0.43^*D9 \qquad (16.15)$$

where the variables G9, X9, S9 and D9 are the 9-day percentage yields of gold, the XAU, silver and the dollar index respectively.

TABLE 16.4	Unstandardized Regression Coefficients

| | Regression coefficients | | | | | |
Model	Constant	XAU	Silver	Dollar	CRB	Yen
1	0.121	0.31				
2	0.06	0.24	0.18			
3	0.071	0.216	0.166	−0.43		
4	0.068	0.207	0.153	−0.413	0.117	
5	0.066	0.207	0.151	−0.449	0.123	0.049

| | Standardized Regression Coefficients | | | | |
Model	XAU	Silver	Dollar	CRB	Yen
1	0.696				
2	0.540	0.299			
3	0.490	0.270	−0.208		
4	0.469	0.249	−0.199	0.080	
5	0.469	0.247	−0.216	0.085	0.034

TABLE 16.6 | Percentage Weight of Each Variable in the Model

| | % Weight | | | | |
Model	XAU	Silver	Dollar	CRB	Yen
2	64%	36%			
3	51%	28%	21%		
4	47%	25%	20%	8%	
5	45%	24%	21%	8%	3%

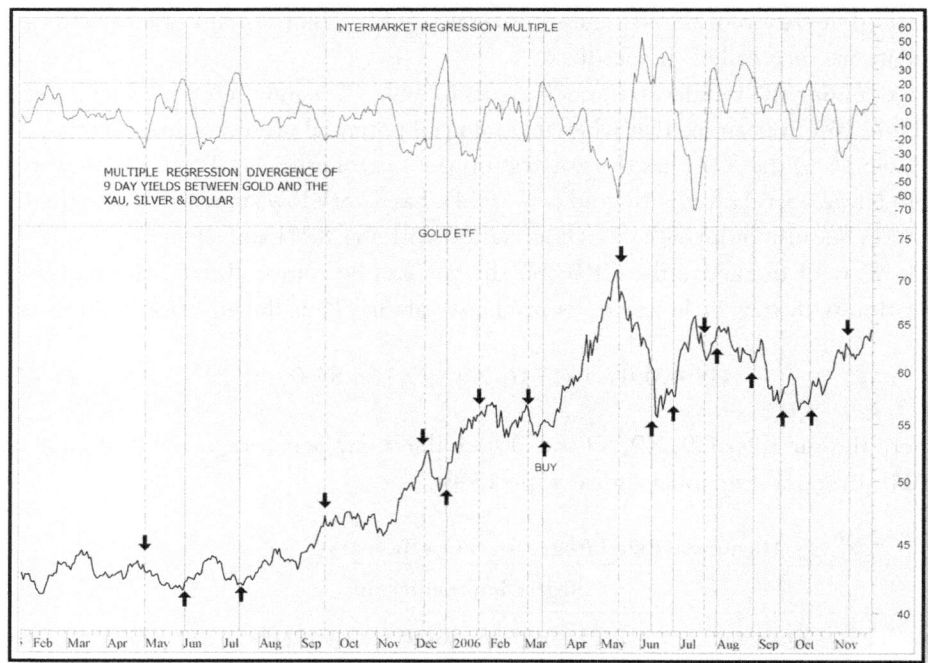

FIGURE 16.8 The multiple regression divergence between gold, the XAU, silver and the dollar index using 9-day percentage yields is depicted in the top window. Extreme divergences are indicated by the horizontal lines at +/−20 levels. Buy signals are triggered by the indicator forming a top above the extreme level and declining below 20, and sell signals are triggered by the indicator declining below −20, forming a bottom and rising above −20.

Thus we can calculate the divergence between the predicted (based on the related markets) and actual values of gold's 9-day yields using the above formula (16.15) by subtracting the second from the first.

The divergence was plotted in the top window of the chart in Figure 16.8. Unlike conventional technical analysis indicators, all divergence indicators are leading price and it is therefore prudent to wait until the indicator forms a top or bottom and reverses direction before making any buy or sell decisions.

It would be interesting to see which of the indicators described above performs better in predicting gold.

16.10 Intermarket Moving Average

I have seen the intermarket moving average mentioned in a book on intermarket analysis but unfortunately the author did not provide the formula. To calculate the predicted moving average I use the multiple regression formula (equation 16.16) to predict gold prices based on their correlation with the XAU, the dollar and silver. The indicator is plotted in Figure 16.9. Crossovers over the conventional (actual) moving average indicate that gold is undervalued and crossovers under the conventional moving average indicate that gold is overvalued relative to its related markets. Crossovers, however, cannot be used to generate buy and sell signals as gold can remain undervalued or overvalued for some time before following its peers.

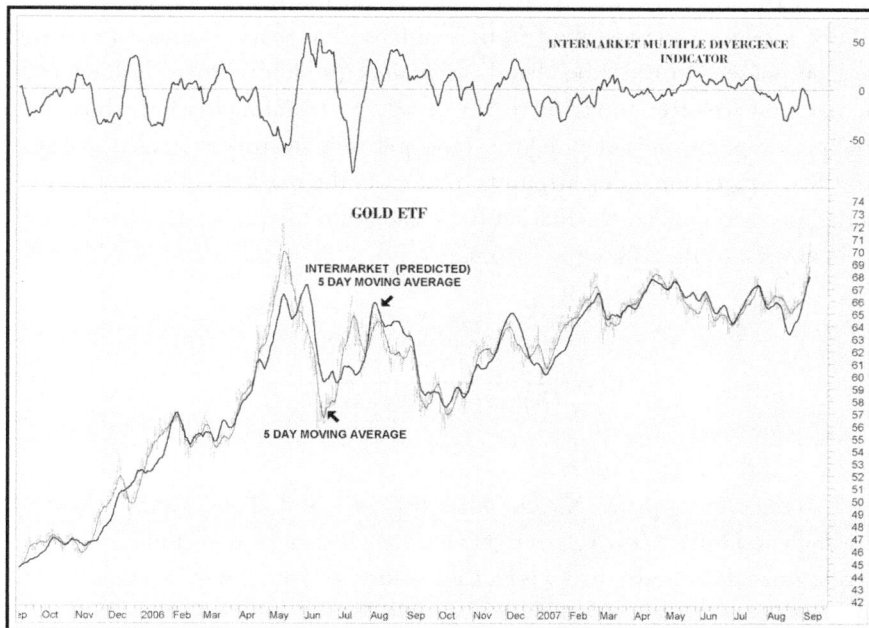

FIGURE 16.9 The intermarket (predicted) 5-day moving average (thick line) is plotted together with the classic 5-day moving average in the bottom window and the multiple divergence indicator in the top window. Notice that when the intermarket moving average crosses above the classic moving average the divergence (top window) turns positive.

This indicator, therefore, can only be used as a rough estimate of the price level relative to other correlated markets but can't be used in mechanical trading systems as these require precise and timely signals.

■ 16.11 Congestion Index

This indicator has nothing to do with intermarket trading but I thought that it would be a good idea to mention it in this chapter as it is used extensively with the trading systems in the second part of this book.

Market movements can be characterized by two distinct types or phases. In the first, the market shows trending movements which have a directional bias over a period of time. The second type of market behavior is periodic or cyclic motion, where the market shows no consistent directional bias and trades between two levels. This type of market results in the failure of trend-following indicators and the success of overbought/oversold oscillators.

Both phases of the market require the use of different types of indicator. Trending markets need trend-following indicators such as moving averages, moving average convergence/divergence (MACD), and so on. Trading range markets need oscillators such as the relative strength index (RSI) and stochastics, which use overbought and oversold levels.

The age-old problem for many trading systems is their inability to determine if a trending or trading range market is at hand. Trend-following indicators, such as the MACD or moving averages, tend to be whipsawed as markets enter a nontrending congestion phase. On the other hand, oscillators (which work well during trading range markets) are often too early to buy or sell in a trending market. Thus, identifying the market phase and selecting the appropriate indicators is critical to a system's success. The congestion index attempts to identify the market's character by dividing the actual percentage that the market has changed in the past x days by the extreme range according to the following formula:

$$CI = \frac{\dfrac{(C - C[X-1])}{C[X-1]}100}{\dfrac{Highest(H, X) - Lowest(L, X)}{Lowest(L, X)}} \qquad (16.16)$$

where C is the closing price; X is the time segment; and Highest and Lowest are the highest high and lowest low respectively for the chosen time period X.

To minimize daily noise the CI is further smoothed by a 3-day exponential moving average.

The congestion index fluctuates between 100 and −100. The larger the absolute value, the less congested the current market. Readings between +20 and −20 indicate congestion or oscillating mode. Crossing over the 20 line from below indicates the start of a rising trend. Conversely, the start of a down turn is indicated by crossing under −20 from above.

The CI can also be used as an overbought/oversold oscillator. The indicator signals an exhaustion of the prevailing price trend and warns of an impending price reversal when it reaches an extreme reading either above 85 or below −85 and then reverses direction.

Unlike similar indicators, like the vertical horizontal filter (VHF) or Wilder's ADX, the congestion index is directional for the following reasons:

- It is self-contained in the sense that it eliminates the need for a second indicator to identify the trend direction.

- It is better in identifying trend reversals.

- It provides more accurate readings in cases of temporary pullbacks.

- The chart space is less congested.

In the example of the S&P 500 in Figure 16.10, the CI was the first to identify a rising trend which started at the beginning of April 2007 and lasted until the end of

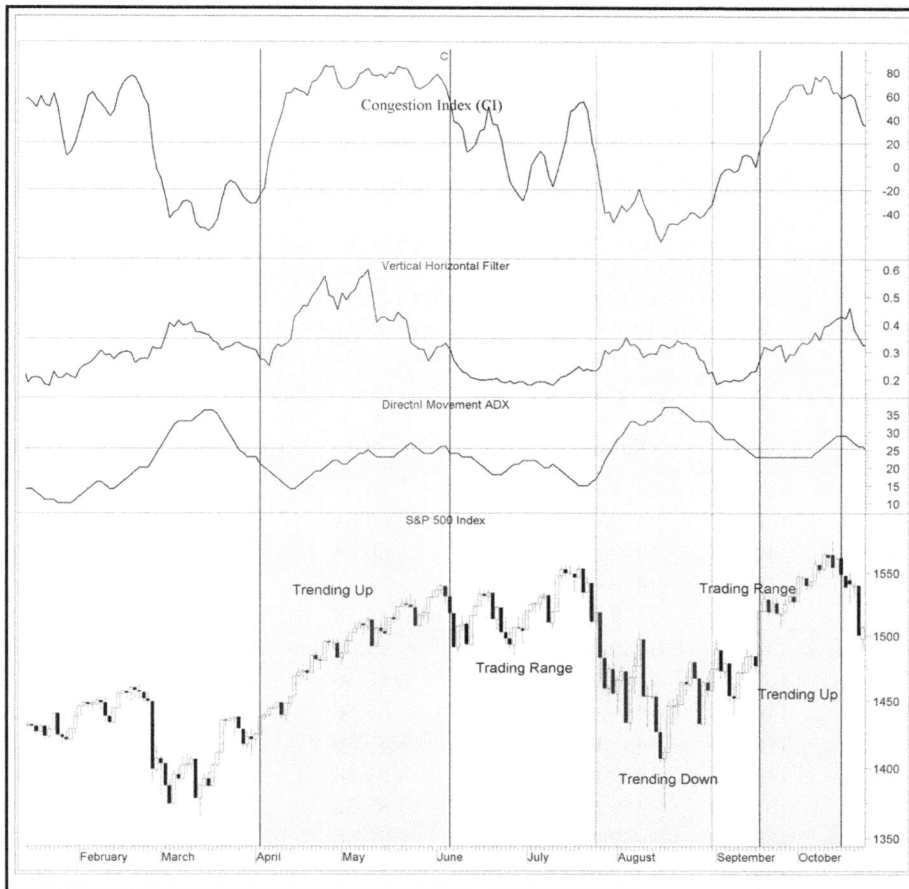

FIGURE 16.10 Chart of the S&P 500 from 1 February 2007 to 12 October 2007. The 3-day moving average of the 28-day CI is plotted in the top window, the 28-day vertical horizontal filter below and the 14-day ADX in the second from bottom window. CI detected both up trends (in gray) with virtually no lag.

May. On 5 April, the CI crossed over 20, decisively followed eight days later by the VHF crossing over 0.35 (the indicator's default value for a trend) on 16 April.

The ADX, on the other hand, missed the trend altogether. It was actually down at the beginning of the trend and started rising on 17 April, but by the time it crossed over 25 (indicating a trend) the trend was over.

But why the disparity between the indicators? The answer is in the calculation method. The VHF is calculated using the formula:

$$VHF = \frac{Highest(C,28) - Lowest(C,28)}{\sum ABS(C_i - C_{i-1})} \tag{16.17}$$

where Highest(C,28) is the highest close in the last 28 days; Lowest(C,28) is the lowest close in the last 28 days; and the denominator is the sum of the absolute value of the difference between consecutive daily closes for the last 28 days.

To help solve the mystery I calculated the 28 day readings, up to 5 April, for the VHF and CI indicators in the Excel sheets in Tables 16.7 and 16.8, respectively. Let's take a closer look what happened on 3 April (the first day of the breakout).

On that day the S&P was up 1%, and as a result the denominator of formula (16.17) increased while the numerator decreased because the new 28-day high was

TABLE 16.7	Calculation of the VHF. Column B is the S&P 500 closing price, Column C shows the highest close of the last 28 days, Column D shows the lowest close of the last 28 days, Column E is their difference, Column F is the absolute value of the difference between consecutive daily closes, Column G is their sum for the last 28 days and Column H is the VHF.

A	B	C	D	E	F	G	H
Date	Close	Highest	Lowest	H-L	$|(C-C[1])|$	$\sum$	VHF
2/27/07	1399.04	1459.68	1399.04	60.64	50.3	190.96	0.318
2/28/07	1406.82	1459.68	1399.04	60.64	7.8	194.49	0.312
3/1/07	1403.17	1459.68	1399.04	60.64	3.6	194.01	0.313
3/2/07	1387.17	1459.68	1387.17	72.51	16.0	202.46	0.358
3/5/07	1374.12	1459.68	1374.12	85.56	13.1	210.47	0.407
3/6/07	1395.41	1459.68	1374.12	85.56	21.3	219.62	0.390
3/7/07	1391.97	1459.68	1374.12	85.56	3.4	206.83	0.414
3/8/07	1401.89	1459.68	1374.12	85.56	9.9	215.03	0.398
3/9/07	1402.85	1459.68	1374.12	85.56	1.0	214.43	0.399
3/12/07	1406.6	1459.68	1374.12	85.56	3.8	209.98	0.407
3/13/07	1377.95	1459.68	1374.12	85.56	28.6	229.21	0.373
3/14/07	1387.17	1459.68	1374.12	85.56	9.2	230.73	0.371
3/15/07	1392.28	1459.68	1374.12	85.56	5.1	233.39	0.367
3/16/07	1386.95	1459.68	1374.12	85.56	5.3	237.32	0.361
3/19/07	1402.06	1459.68	1374.12	85.56	15.1	251.42	0.340
3/20/07	1410.94	1459.68	1374.12	85.56	8.9	258.28	0.331
3/21/07	1435.04	1459.68	1374.12	85.56	24.1	280.67	0.305
3/22/07	1434.54	1459.68	1374.12	85.56	0.5	270.92	0.316

TABLE 16.7 (Continued)

A	B	C	D	E	F	G	H
Date	Close	Highest	Lowest	H-L	|(C-C[1])|	Σ	VHF
3/23/07	1436.11	1459.68	1374.12	85.56	1.6	267.8	0.319
3/26/07	1437.5	1459.68	1374.12	85.56	1.4	259.55	0.330
3/27/07	1428.61	1459.68	1374.12	85.56	8.9	256.15	0.334
3/28/07	1417.23	1459.68	1374.12	85.56	11.4	266.02	0.322
3/29/07	1422.53	1459.68	1374.12	85.56	5.3	270.05	0.317
3/30/07	1420.86	1457.63	1374.12	83.51	1.7	267.58	0.312
4/2/07	1424.55	1456.38	1374.12	82.26	3.7	269.22	0.306
4/3/07	1437.77	1451.19	1374.12	77.07	13.2	281.19	0.274
4/4/07	1439.37	1449.37	1374.12	75.25	1.6	277.6	0.271
4/5/07	1443.76	1443.76	1374.12	69.64	4.4	280.17	0.249

Column	Formula
C	= MAX(B9:B36)
D	= MIN(B9:B36)
E	= C36-D36
F	= ABS(B36-B35)
G	= SUM(F9:F36)
H	= E36/G36

TABLE 16.8 Example of Calculating CI in Excel. The second, third and fourth columns are the S&P 500 high, low and closing prices respectively. Column E is the highest high of the last 28 days, Column F is the lowest low of the last 28 days, and Column G is the price percent change during the last 28 days. In column H is the percent daily price difference and in the last column is the CI.

A	B	C	D	E	F	G	H	I
Date	High	Low	Close	H H	L L	ROC	(HH-LL)/LL	CI
3/19/07	1403.2	1386.95	1402.06	1461.57	1363.98	−3.31	0.07	−46.23
3/20/07	1411.53	1400.7	1410.94	1461.57	1363.98	−2.58	0.07	−36.06
3/21/07	1437.77	1409.75	1435.04	1461.57	1363.98	−0.21	0.07	−2.94
3/22/07	1437.66	1429.88	1434.54	1461.57	1363.98	0.08	0.07	1.14
3/23/07	1438.89	1433.21	1436.11	1461.57	1363.98	−0.48	0.07	−6.68
3/26/07	1437.65	1423.28	1437.5	1461.57	1363.98	−1.22	0.07	−17.10
3/27/07	1437.49	1425.54	1428.61	1461.57	1363.98	−1.94	0.07	−27.06
3/28/07	1428.35	1414.07	1417.23	1461.57	1363.98	−2.63	0.07	−36.79
3/29/07	1426.24	1413.27	1422.53	1461.57	1363.98	−2.55	0.07	−35.57
3/30/07	1429.22	1408.9	1420.86	1461.57	1363.98	−2.52	0.07	−35.26
4/2/07	1425.49	1416.37	1424.55	1461.57	1363.98	−2.19	0.07	−30.55
4/3/07	1440.57	1424.27	1437.77	1456.95	1363.98	−0.92	0.07	−13.57
4/4/07	1440.16	1435.08	1439.37	1456.95	1363.98	−0.69	0.07	−10.12
4/5/07	1444.88	1436.67	1443.76	1449.25	1363.98	3.20	0.06	51.13

Column	Formula
E	= MAX(B22:B49)
F	= MIN(C22:C49)
G	= (D49-D22)/D22*100
H	= (E49-F49)/(F49+0.01)
I	= G49/H49

lower than the previous one. As a result the VHF was down on the actual breakout and the start of the trend! On the other hand the CI shot up from −13 to 51 during the next two days, confirming decisively the start of a possible trend.

■ Bibliography

Katsanos, Markos (2003). "Detecting Breakouts." *Technical Analysis of STOCKS & COMMODITIES*. Volume 21: April.

Katsanos, Markos (2004). "Volume Flow Performance." *Technical Analysis of STOCKS & COMMODITIES*. Volume 22: July.

Nison, Steve (1994). *Beyond Candlesticks: New Japanese Charting Techniques Revealed*. John Wiley & Sons Inc.

Ruggiero, Murray A. (1997). *Cybernetic Trading Strategies*. John Wiley & Sons Inc.

THE INTEGRATION OF TECHNICAL ANALYSIS

CHAPTER 17

Everything Is *Relative*; *Strength* Is Everything

Julius de Kempenaer

Taler Asset Management Ltd. & RRG Ltd.

From Paul Ciana, *New Frontiers in Technical Analysis* (Hoboken, New Jersey: Bloomberg Press, 2011), Chapter 2.

Learning Objective Statements

▪ Interpret Relative Rotation Graphs
▪ Explain how Relative Rotation Graphs are an example of a novel approach to visualizing relative strength

Everything is relative strength and relative strength is everything. What does this mean? Let's imagine we are listening to the beginning of a sales call:

JULIUS: Hi, George, how are you? It's Julius here. Have you got a few minutes to go over some technical ideas in European sectors?

GEORGE: Sorry mate, I'm focusing on technology stocks this week. I'm meet-ing with the technology analysts of some major investment banks as well as a few local companies who will all be bringing over their best technology companies in a road show. So I'll be really busy for the next few days. If you could quickly give me your top five picks in technology, that would be very helpful ...

This type of conversation was typical, and probably still is today, for a lot of sell-side analysts in the late 1990s and early 2000s. In an over-brokered market in which every portfolio manager and buy-side analyst receives hundreds of e-mails, reams of printed (research) reports, and dozens of phone calls every day, you need to offer something unique, something that adds value for them, and something they do not get anywhere else. You need to stand out from the crowd, one way or another. The bank where I was employed organized special training sessions to sharpen our "sales" skills. Let's say that some of these trainings were better than others, but one of the trainers had an appealing slogan: "You've got to make the facts sizzle." It could be the subject line of your e-mail that determines whether the recipient is going to open the mail at all, let alone read it. Or it could be your tone of voice when you leave a voicemail or the way that you communicate your message when you get to talk to a fund manager or an analyst in person.

In the early 2000s, I was working as a technical analyst on the trading floor of a midsized investment bank in Amsterdam. My primary job was being an analyst and producing technical reports for our institutional clients, and it involved a lot of client contact. I was confronted with the issues described above. Being the worst salesman in the business, I decided that my content should be the "sizzle" factor. The content I identified to be of most use to my clients was, and still is, Relative Strength Analysis. Over the years, the methods I've used to give my clients this information have evolved into some unique approaches, including the Relative Rotation Graph.

■ "This Time It's Different"

One of the cornerstones of technical analysis is that history repeats itself. We have seen that a lot of investors react to specific situations in a similar way. They display the same characteristics over and over again, even if there are generations between the occurrences of events. Recall these important events in financial history:

The Stock Market Crash of 1929
Black Monday, October 1987
The Russian Ruble Crisis of 1998
The Dot-com Bubble of 2000
The Credit Crunch of 2008

It is remarkable to see how similar the discussions and comments were in the wake of these previous shocks. Perhaps the most-heard comment was "This time it's different." Usually such a statement would be followed by a discussion or explanation as to why the current crisis or shock could not be compared to a previous one.

When such discussions develop, I usually bring up the following quote:

> Today's youth loves luxury. They are bad mannered, despise all authority, show no respect and talk when they should be working. The youngsters do not rise from their seats when elderly people enter, they go against their parents, chat in company, gobble down their food and tyrannize their teachers.

Then I ask: "Do you subscribe to the statement?" followed by "Do you think it applies today?" Most people will answer positively to both these questions. These same people will be surprised when they find out who I am quoting: the Greek philosopher Socrates, in 400 B.C.

FIGURE 17.1 1934 *Chicago Tribune* Cartoon: "Planned Economy or Planned Destruction?"

Source: www.chicagotribune.com/health/sns-pod-1934-cartoon-pic,0,7114709.photo.

The point is, most of the time things are *not* different. They may look a little different from the outside, but at the end of the day it is history repeating itself. Investors just do not believe it. The cartoon in Figure 17.1 is a perfect example. It comes from a 1934 edition of the *Chicago Tribune* and shows striking similarities with the 2008 "credit crunch" situation.

▪ What Is Comparative Relative Strength?

It did not take very long to figure out that institutional (equity) investors had different needs from private investors. Obviously, the size of their portfolios differs hugely, but also their investment goals or mandates are absolutely not comparable.

Private investors, 99% of the time, are looking for absolute return, whereas institutional investors, most of the time, are interested in relative returns.

A professional fund manager typically is given a benchmark for a portfolio and his or her job is to beat that benchmark. The portfolio manager who oversees the European equity portfolio within a large institution has only to beat the benchmark attached to that specific portfolio—for example, the Euro STOXX 50 index. In a very large institution, they may even have a separate portfolio manager for each sector. The allocation to European equities is not the manager's decision but instead comes from a chief investment officer or an investment committee.

No matter where you are in the professional decision pyramid, professional investing, like many other things in life, is all about making choices. A private investor has a choice as to whether to invest. For a professional investor who oversees a portfolio for a pension fund or an insurance company, for example, *not* investing is not a real choice.

A lot of academic work, started by Brinson, Hood, and Beebower in 1986, has shown that the majority of the variance in the return of a typical (pension fund) portfolio comes from asset allocation. It therefore makes sense to follow a top-down approach, which creates a decision pyramid or tree. This decision tree can be very simple or very complex.

Imagine a very simple asset allocation choice, as shown in Figure 17.2. The choice that the fund manager is facing is whether she should invest in bonds or equities, or perhaps more realistically, whether she should overweight bonds versus equities, or the other way around. In order to answer this question, technical analysts have a toolbox full of a wide variety of graphs and indicators. These range from very simple—for example, Figure 17.3 presents a plain-vanilla bar-chart of the S&P 500 index—to very complex—for example, Figure 17.4 shows the same S&P 500 index, but now with a number of technical indicators plotted below the price chart.

Using any type of chart or combination of graphs, any technician can come up with a more-or-less informed opinion on the equity market or the bond market. The problem is that these single security graphs will answer only the question of whether to invest in that specific security. Viewing the market in a broader context is more difficult. In the technician's toolbox there is only one technique that helps to make choices and to distinguish between two securities, and that is *relative strength* (RS). Relative strength, as used here, should not be confused with Wilder's Relative Strength Index (RSI), which is a single-security indicator. Relative strength is used

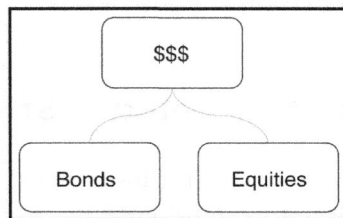

FIGURE 17.2 Simple Asset Allocation Choice.

FIGURE 17.3 Simple Bar Chart of S&P 500 Index.

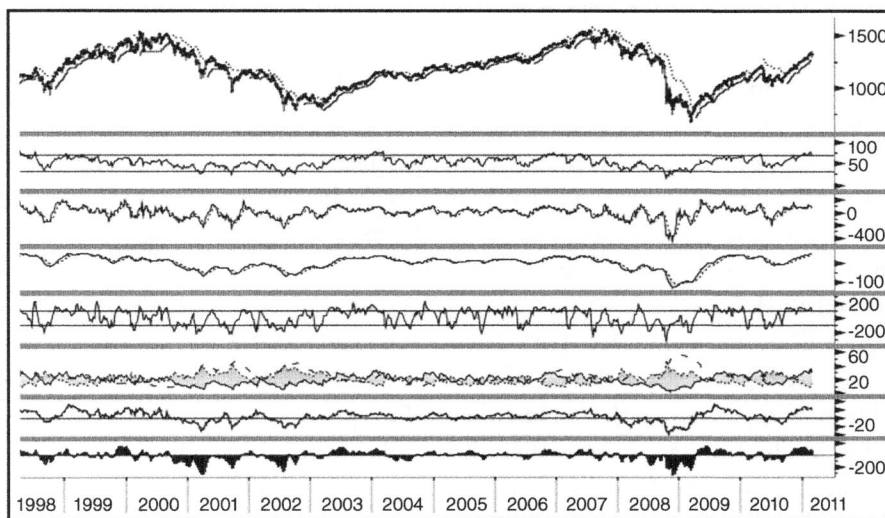

FIGURE 17.4 Complex Chart of S&P 500 Index with Indicators.

to measure the strength of two securities or indices against each other. It is therefore often referred to as *comparative* relative strength.

The standard relative strength line is simply defined as:

$$RS = Close\ security\ A / Close\ security\ B$$

The close can be the close of any timeframe from one-minute intraday series to monthly or even longer data series. Very often such an RS line is used to compare the performance of an individual stock against an index, for example, or two stocks

FIGURE 17.5 Euro STOXX 50 Index with RS Line against Bund Future.

against each other. When plotted in combination with a standard bar graph, the RS line appears as shown in Figure 17.5.

The interpretation of a RS line is very straightforward. If the RS line moves up, security A is outperforming security B, and obviously if the RS line is moving down, security B is outperforming security A.

All techniques, tools, and indicators as we know them in technical analysis are used to make only one decision: "Do I buy or sell this security?" The RS line is the only tool in the technician's toolbox that can be used to make wider choices. It helps to distinguish between two securities and to declare a preference, for example, "Do I buy security A or security B?"

Figure 17.5 shows the price (bar) chart of the Euro STOXX 50 index in the upper pane and the relative strength line of the Euro STOXX 50 index against the 10-year Bund future (the benchmark bond market in Europe) in the lower pane.

When we look at a number of these RS graphs, we can conclude that the RS line moves and behaves like the price chart of a single security. This means that an RS line can be analyzed as if it were a security in its own right. We can draw trend lines on them, use moving averages (MA), use indicators, and much more.

After a strong decline from mid-2007 into a low that was formed in the beginning of 2009, the RS line started to move up, breaking the falling trend lines and making higher highs and higher lows. That was enough to indicate that equities were outperforming bonds again, therefore suggesting a preference of equities over bonds in the asset allocation of a portfolio. The relative up-trend continued until the beginning of 2010, when the RS line failed to set a new higher high and then broke down through the rising trend line.

The RS line can be drawn on different periodicities ranging from daily to monthly, but also on intraday timeframes (5-minute periods, 10-minute periods, hourly periods, etc.). During my career as a sell-side analyst, I primarily used the weekly

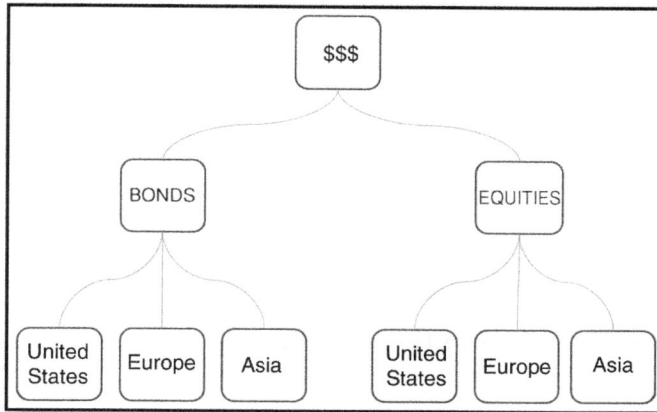

FIGURE 17.6   More Complex Asset Allocation Decision Tree.

timeframe in my reports. I found that it suited the longer time horizon of most institutions and showed less noise than a daily timeframe. Although I will usually use weekly graphs in the examples, please bear in mind that the method can be used on every other timeframe as well.

Using a relative strength chart like the one in Figure 17.5 will help the technical analyst to make an informed decision on the equity/bond choice.

If we then step down one level in the decision tree to where, for example, a choice has to be made on which region to invest in (e.g., United States, Europe, or Asia), our decision tree starts to look like the one in Figure 17.6.

The example with the United States, Europe, or Asia is still a universe that is limited in the number of elements. Only a small number of charts have to be studied to get guidance on the proper asset allocation or over-/under-weighting of the various regions.

The relationships that have to be analyzed and decided upon in the three regions can be found by using the matrix shown in Table 17.1.

The possible combinations that can be derived from the table are United States versus Europe, United States versus Asia, or Europe versus Asia. Obviously we do not have to look at United States versus United States, but we also may forget to look at Europe versus United States, as it is the reverse of United States versus Europe, which we already included in our list. Therefore, a 3 x 3 matrix presents three combinations for analysis.

The formula that can be applied to calculate the number of combinations to analyze is:

$$[(\text{Elements in the universe})^2 - \text{Elements in the universe}] : 2$$

TABLE 17.1   **Matrix of Relationships to Be Analyzed**

	United States	Europe	Asia
United States	✗	✓	✓
Europe		✗	✓
Asia			✗

In this case

$$(3^2 - 3) : 2 = 3$$

Another level down in the decision tree, we could find a sector decision for each region, for example. Assume that for the U.S. region, the sector universe consists of the 10 GICS level I economic sectors. This would give:

$$(10^2 - 10) : 2 = 45 \text{ charts to look at and 45 judgments to make.}$$

In Europe, where the Euro STOXX family of (sector) indices is often used, it comes down to:

$$(19^2 - 19) : 2 = 171 \text{ charts}$$

Imagine going into the selection of individual equities. The first thing to do to get on the radar screen of a portfolio manager is to offer them a piece of research that adds value to their process. As a technical analyst, I translated that into a monthly technical research report based on relative strength. In a very original mood, I dubbed it "The European Sector Report." That report formed the foundation for the relative rotation graphs that I will introduce later in this chapter.

In the early days I used a very straightforward relative strength approach. Figure 17.7 shows the weekly bar chart of the S&P 500 Financial sector (1998-2003) and the RS line of the Financials sector against the S&P 500 index. Overall, the rising RS line from 2000 to 2003 tells us that financial stocks were outperforming the broader S&P 500 index. Considering the movements in more detail, starting from the RS low in March 2000 through 2001, the line was rising, or the financials were outperforming the S&P 500. Toward the end of 2001, the RS line began

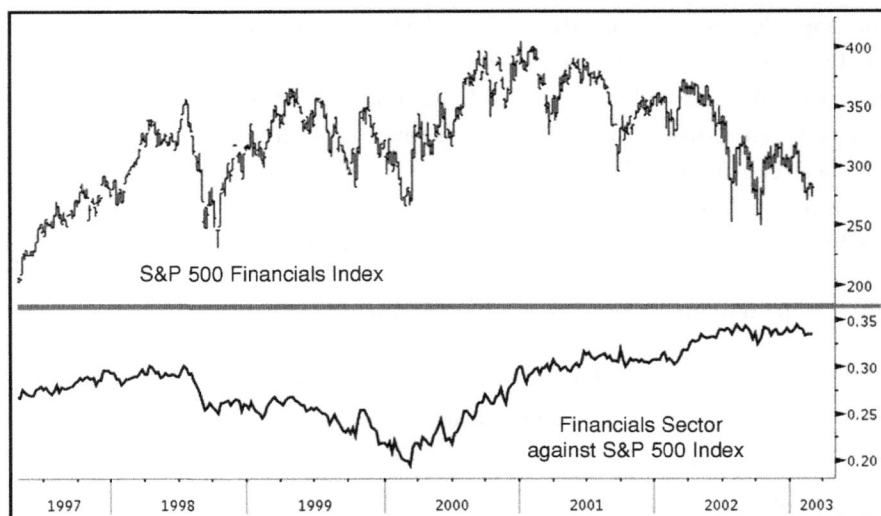

FIGURE 17.7 **S&P 500 Financials Index with RS Line against S&P 500 Index.**

moving sideways, or equally performing the S&P 500 index. During this time, the price of the financial index was making some lower highs and lower lows, but wasn't underperforming the benchmark. At the start of 2002 and into 2003, equal performance turned back into outperformance. The broader market was declining more than this sector. By 2003, the financials index was at the same value as at the start of 2000. During that same period, the S&P 500 index dropped from highs near 1500 to lows around 800-900. Investors holding financial stocks during that period didn't lose much at all, while those who owned the broader market lost upward of 40%.

Although the RS line itself is already very helpful, it is still a fairly volatile line. While it clearly shows relative trends, there is still a lot of noise present and gauging the direction of "trend" remains a subjective call. In order to overcome some of these issues, I reverted to the use of some "old friends" in technical analysis, namely moving averages. Just as we use moving averages on price charts and in many other indicators, we can use moving averages on RS graphs in order to determine trends.

Figure 17.8 shows the weekly bar chart of the S&P 500 Energy sector with the relative strength line against the S&P 500 index. Through the RS line I have drawn two moving averages, one with a look-back period of 10 weeks and one with a look-back period of 30 weeks.[1] The crossings of the two trigger a change in the trend of the RS line. When the 10-week moving average is above the 30-week moving average, we rate the RS line as being in an uptrend. When the 10-week moving average is below the 30-week moving average, we rate the RS line as being in a downtrend. This is the same application as applying moving averages to a price chart. The only difference to keep in mind is that we are now looking at relative movements. So when we have an RS line that is in an uptrend (10-week above 30-week), then we could still have

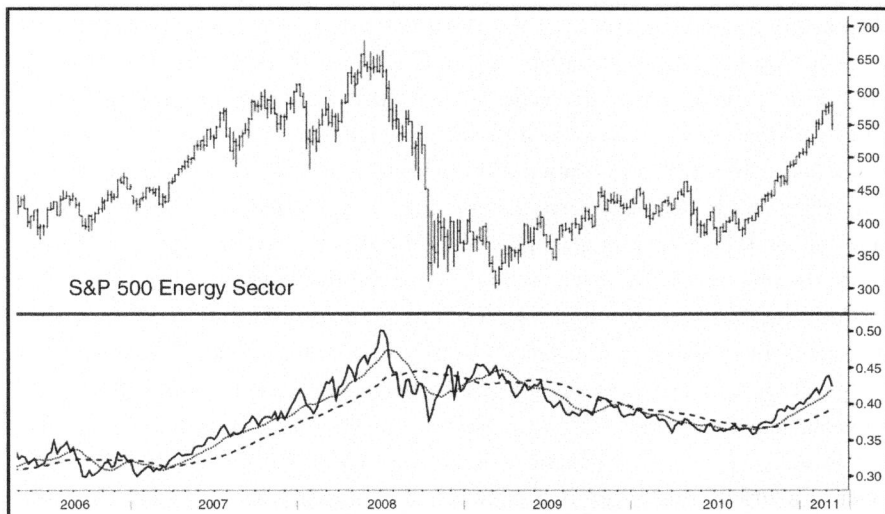

FIGURE 17.8   S&P Energy Index with RS Line against the S&P 500 Index.

[1] I have been using the combination of 10- and 30-week look-back periods since 1994. They continue to serve my purposes, but anyone can change these values according to their preferences.

a situation where the security we are looking at is dropping but the benchmark, for example, the S&P index, is dropping even faster. Although the result will be negative in absolute terms, the security is outperforming the benchmark, and that is exactly what professional money managers are looking for. Clearly the reverse is true as well: When the S&P index is rising, we are looking for sectors or stocks that are rising even faster.

Interpreting the trend of the RS line on the basis of the position of the moving averages takes a lot of the guesswork out of the analysis and makes it less subjective. However, the use of moving averages, by definition, introduces a lag. As a result, we can distinguish one more situation and that is when the 10-week moving average has crossed above the 30-week moving average, which signals an uptrend, but the raw RS line has already crossed back below both the 10- and the 30-week moving average. Such a situation will be seen as a warning signal that maybe something is cooking. So when the 10-week average is still above the 30-week average, but the raw RS line has dropped below both averages, the trend is rated neutral. The same goes for the reverse when the 10-week average is below the 30-week average (a downtrend), but the raw RS line has crossed above both of the moving averages.

This is better illustrated in Figure 17.9. This is the same view as shown in Figure 17.8, but zoomed in on the November 2007 to November 2008 period. Up until August 2008, the 10-week moving average is clearly above the 30-week moving average, indicating an uptrend, and thus an "outperformance" condition for the Energy sector. At the first dashed vertical line, the RS line drops below both moving averages, while the 10-week moving average is still above the 30-week moving average. This characterizes a "neutral" condition (something is cooking). A few weeks later in September, at the second dashed vertical line, the 10-week moving average crosses below the 30-week moving average, triggering an "underperformance" condition. Finally in November, at the third dashed vertical line, the RS line crosses above both moving averages, triggering another neutral condition.

For a long time this was the type of chart that I used in communications with institutional investors, and it served its purpose fairly well.

At the end of the 1990s, a number of these RS lines started to overshoot to the upside, creating huge differences between the moving averages and RS lines way above the 10- and 30-week moving averages. This created a situation where the raw RS line, and therefore the price of the security, could drop substantially before triggering a change in trend. Basically, they were giving away a lot of the gains that were run up during the rally.

In an attempt to speed up the signals from my RS graphs in combination with their moving averages, or at least to get an early warning signal, I started to experiment with overlaying some other indicators on the raw RS line. I ended up using the well-known moving average convergence/divergence (MACD) technique. This indicator looks at and draws the difference between two moving averages on a price chart (usually 12- and 26-periods, but they can be varied to suit the individual investor's needs), resulting in a line that oscillates around zero. If the MACD reads positive, it means that the shorter moving average lies above the longer moving average; that is, the market is moving up, and vice versa. The higher the reading of the MACD, the

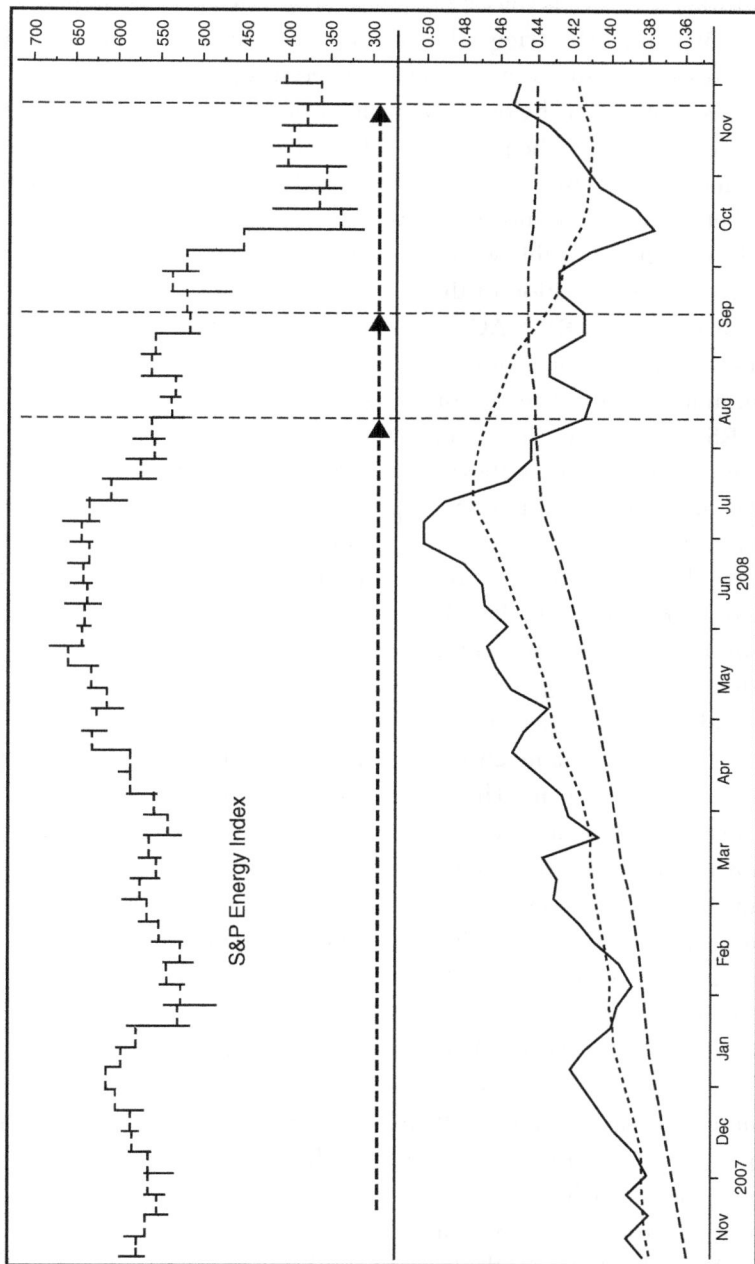

FIGURE 17.9 S&P Energy Index with RS Line against S&P 500 Index, Close-Up View.

EVERYTHING IS *RELATIVE*; *STRENGTH* IS EVERYTHING

bigger the difference between the two moving averages, hence the more price action in the opposite direction is needed to push the MACD line below (or above) the zero line. In order to detect the moment where the difference between the shorter and the longer moving averages is starting to decrease, a so-called trigger-line is drawn through the MACD line. This trigger-line is simply a 9-period moving average of the MACD line (this time frame can be varied). Therefore, in the default setting, the MACD line crosses above and below the zero line when the 12- and 26-period moving averages cross each other on the price chart. The crossings of the MACD-line and its own trigger-line are then used as an early warning indicator, alerting the trader that the distance between the two moving averages is shrinking.

With slight modification, this whole exercise can also be executed on a raw RS line. I usually use a combination of the 10- and 30-period moving averages on the raw RS line. If we draw a RS-MACD that looks at the difference between the 10- and 30-period moving averages of the raw RS line, we will get a line that oscillates around zero, indicating the strength of the *relative* trend. The higher (or lower) the value of the RS-MACD line, the stronger the trend of the underlying RS line. This RS-MACD line will then cross above and below the zero line, when the 10- and 30-period moving averages in the RS-graph cross each other. To get early warning signals and detect the point in time when the distance between the two moving averages starts to decrease, a trigger-line (9-period moving average of the RS-MACD line) is drawn. A crossing of the RS-MACD line below its trigger-line indicates that the relative uptrend is losing momentum and turning the other way. A crossing of the RS-MACD line above its trigger-line indicates that the relative downtrend is losing momentum and starting to turn around.

Figure 17.10 shows the same chart as in Figure 17.9, but now the RSMACD has been added in the bottom pane. The rally from early 2007 into mid-2008 is a good example of a very strong market that starts to turn. Due to the lag that's introduced by using moving averages, the 10- and 30-week averages on the RS line (middle pane in Figure 17.10) were very far apart. The RS-MACD catches the deterioration in a very early stage by setting a peak in mid-2008 (see label 1) and turning sharply down, giving an early warning signal that the relative outperformance of this sector might have come to an end. By the time the averages on the RS line are crossing each other (see label 2), the RS-MACD line crosses below zero.

This approach works well when only one item is analyzed against a benchmark at a time. The numerical values of the raw RS line cannot be used and have no real meaning. It is the slope of the line on the chart that gives the clues. The numerical readings of one security against a benchmark cannot be compared with the numerical readings of another security against the same benchmark. See the examples in the next two graphs. Figure 17.11 shows the RS line of the European utilities sector against the STOXX 600 index. This RS line is clearly trending down from high values near 1.70 to low values around 1.10. Figure 17.12 shows the RS line of the European Travel & Leisure sector against the STOXX 600 index. This RS line is clearly trending up but has much lower numerical values, from lows near 0.40 up to levels around 0.50.

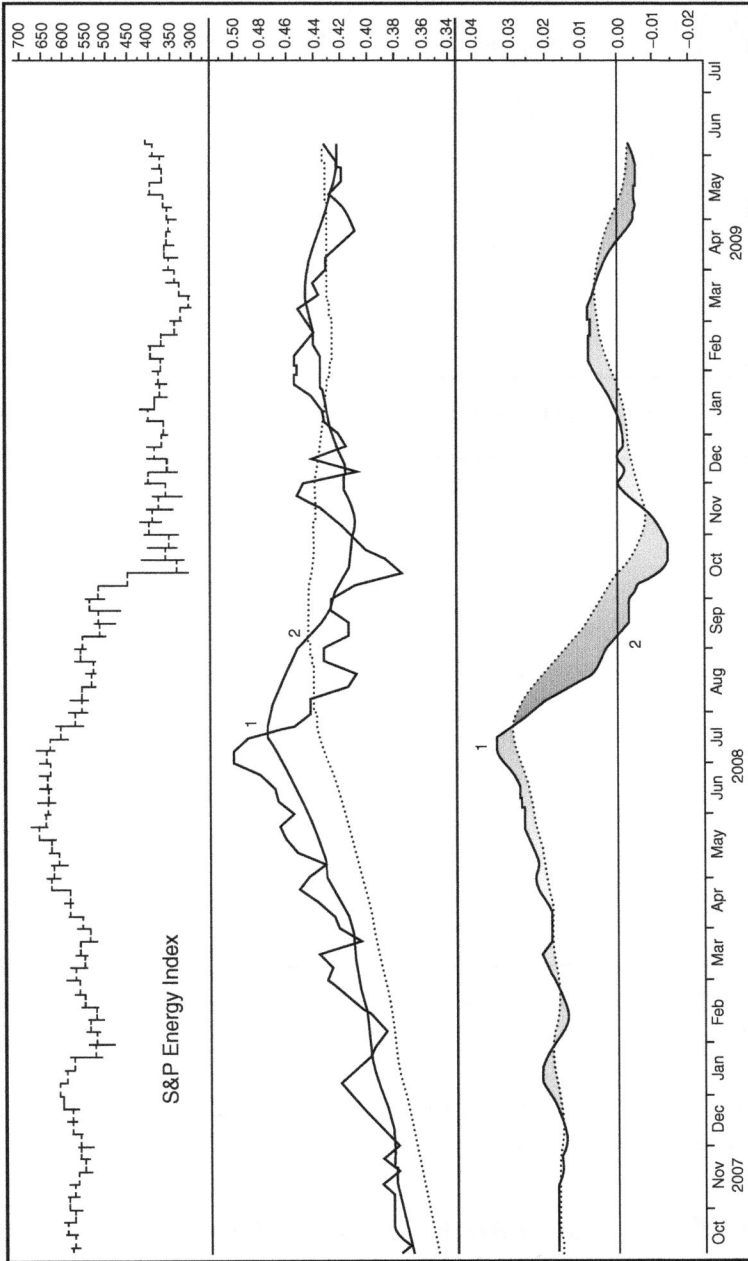

FIGURE 17.10 S&P Energy Index with RS Line and RS-MACD against S&P 500 Index.

EVERYTHING IS *RELATIVE*; *STRENGTH* IS EVERYTHING

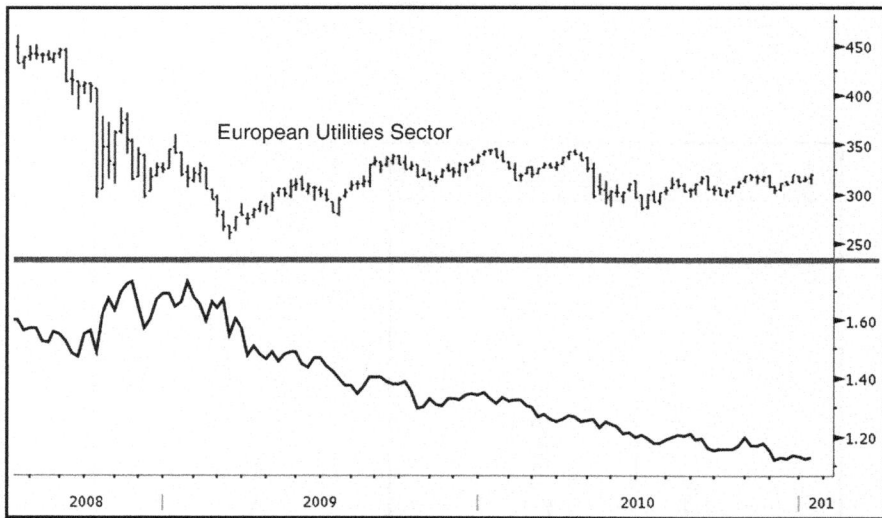

FIGURE 17.11 European Utilities Sector with RS Line against STOXX 600 Index.

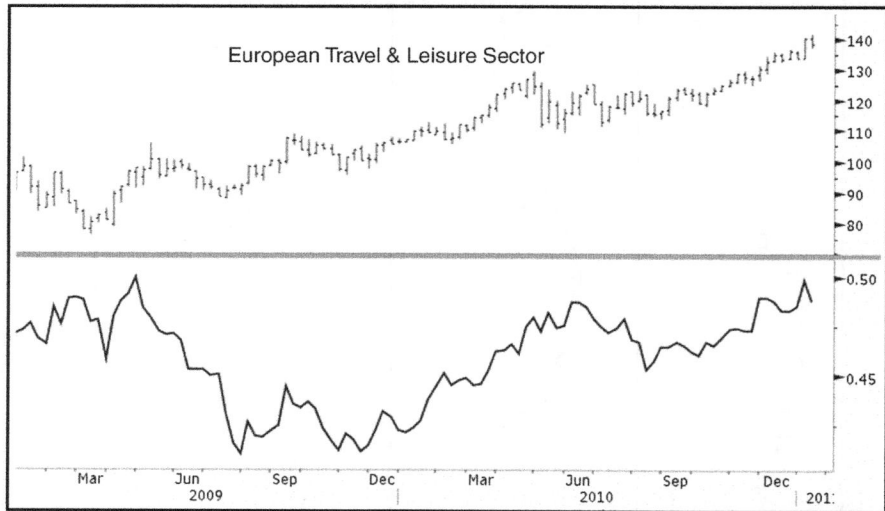

FIGURE 17.12 European Travel & Leisure Sector with RS Line against STOXX 600 Index.

Given this situation, the resulting values for the RS-MACD line and its trigger-line will therefore have no real meaning, either.

▪ The JdK RS-Ratio and JdK RS-Momentum

In order to be able to compare all elements in a universe and rank them based on their numerical readings—that is, high values are good and low values are bad—we need something else. What we are looking for is a uniform measure of relative strength that can be used across all the elements in a universe against the benchmark for that universe, but also to measure the relative strength of one element against another element. My search for such a measure resulted in the development of the (proprietary) JdK RS-Ratio.[2] This indicator measures the relative strength of all elements in a universe in such a way that the numerical results are all comparable. Not only are the values of the JdK RS-Ratio telling whether an element of the universe is doing better than the benchmark, they are also telling if an element is doing better or worse than another element.

The JdK RS-Ratio can therefore be used to rank a universe based on relative strength and answer the question, "What are the five best sectors, stocks, and so forth?" (see Table 17.2).

Table 17.2 shows an example of the STOXX universe ranked on the value of the JdK RS-Ratio indicator. The differences are clearly visible. There is only one problem with this table: it is a table—and technicians do not like tables. We like to see graphs! The snapshot of values that is printed in the table definitely gives valuable information regarding the current relative status of all elements in the universe. But how does that value compare to its own history? How did that element get to its JdK RS-Ratio value and the accompanying position in the table? In what direction is the JdK RS-Ratio value heading, up or down? To answer these questions, we need the graphical history of the JdK RS-Ratio. Figure 17.13 shows the JdK RS-Ratio line of the European Retail sector versus the STOXX index.

TABLE 17.2 European Sectors Ranked by JdK RS-Ratio Value	
Index Name	**JdK RS-Ratio**
STXE 600 Au&Pt € Pr	112.03
STXE 600 BsRs € Pr	107.95
STXE 600 Chem € Pr	105.62
STXE 600 Ig&S € Pr	104.00
STXE 600 FnSv € Pr	103.09
STXE 600 Cn&Mt € Pr	102.67
STXE 600 Tr&Ls € Pr	102.45
STXE 600 Oil&G € Pr	102.18
STXE 600 Pr&Ho € Pr	101.78
STXE 600 Tech € Pr	100.80
STXE 600 ReEs € Pr	100.05
STXE 600 Fd&Bv € Pr	100.02
STXE 600 Mda € Pr	99.40
STXE 600 Ins € Pr	98.14
STXE 600 Tel € Pr	98.13
STXE 600 HeCr € Pr	97.74
STXE 600 Rtl € Pr	97.51
STXE 600 Util € Pr	97.47
STXE 600 Bnk € Pr	92.66

[2] The JdK RS-Ratio indicator is available on the Bloomberg terminal.

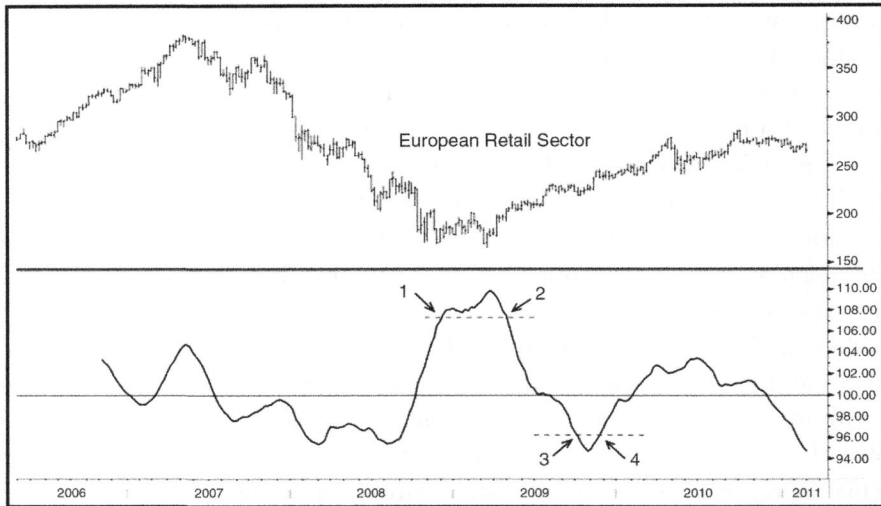

FIGURE 17.13 Europe Retail Sector with JdK RS-Ratio Line versus STOXX Index.

When we plot the JdK RS-Ratio below the price graph, it gives a pretty good indication of the relative strength of the security being analyzed against its benchmark. The visual inspection of that line is as straightforward as the interpretation of the raw relative strength line; a rising JdK RS-Ratio is good, that is, the stock is "outperforming," and a declining JdK RS-Ratio is bad, that is, the stock is "underperforming." Despite the fact that we can use the JdK RS-Ratio as a uniform measure of relative strength by interpreting high values as strong and low values as weak, and that we can plot the indicator on a regular price chart in order to get an indication of the relative position of that element, it's still not painting a complete picture of the market.

The problem that surfaces here is that one "high value" may not be the same as another "high value." This is better explained using Figure 17.13. Toward the end of 2008 (see label 1), the JdK RS-Ratio line is moving around 108, which is a relatively high value. A couple of months later, in April 2009 (see label 2), the JdK RS-Ratio line is again moving around 108, at the same relatively high value. But this time the line is clearly moving down as opposed to up, with acceleration on the first occasion. Obviously, the first situation is preferred over the second one.

A similar situation occurs at low(er) levels. In September 2009 (see label 3) the JdK RS-Ratio line is moving around 96, which is a relatively low level. In December (see label 4) the line is once again around 96, which is still a low level, but now the line has started to move up again and could be more interesting.

What we need here is an objective way to determine whether the JdK RS-Ratio line is moving up or down. In order to achieve this, we borrow the technique of using a trigger-line, as it is used in the construction of the MACD indicator. So a 9-period trigger-line (moving average) is drawn through the values of the JdK RS-Ratio line. When the JdK RS-Ratio line is above its trigger-line, the trend of the JdK RS-Ratio line is *up*. When the JdK RS-Ratio line is moving below its trigger-line, the trend is considered to be *down*. Such an example is shown in Figure 17.14.

FIGURE 17.14 Europe Retail Sector with JdK RS-Ratio Line versus STOXX Index and Trigger-Line.

The graph once again shows the European retail sector with the JdK RS-Ratio line, but now also the trigger-line has also been added. The use of this trigger-line helps to determine when the trend of the JdK RS-Ratio line has changed from up to down (see label 1) and the other way around from down to up (see label 2).

When the JdK RS-Ratio line is moving above the 100-level and crosses below its trigger-line, the momentum of the JdK RS-Ratio line starts to deteriorate and decline. This deterioration of momentum can be the prelude to the JdK RS-Ratio line eventually crossing below the 100-level. This is a definite signal that relative strength has turned negative.

Similarly, when the JdK RS-Ratio line is moving below the zero line and crosses above its trigger-line, that is the moment when the momentum of the JdK RS-Ratio line is starting to improve. If the improvement of this momentum continues, the JdK RS-Ratio line will eventually cross above the 100-line, signaling positive relative strength for the instrument at hand.

The graph in Figure 17.14 is an excellent example of the fact that a measure of relative strength can move up while prices are moving down, and can move down while prices are moving up. In the last quarter of 2008, when equity markets worldwide were going through serious declines, the JdK RS-Ratio line of the European retail sector started to move up, indicating an outperformance of this sector. At that time, the European retail sector index also fell in price, but far less than the broader benchmark against which its relative strength is measured. Similarly, when equity markets in general started to move up again in March 2009, the JdK RS-Ratio line crossed below its trigger-line, indicating a weakening of the positive relative strength, and finally the JdK RS-Ratio dropped below the 100-level, which definitely signals underperformance. All this happened while the index itself showed rising prices, but they did not rise rapidly enough. Other sectors were doing much better than retail during that period.

In fact what the trigger-line helps to measure is the momentum of the JdK RS-Ratio line. Once again, in order to be able to use a measure of momentum across a universe, it needs to be reworked into a uniform indicator: this became the JdK RS-Momentum indicator. This uniform measure of relative momentum can be used to further compare elements in a universe against a benchmark and against each other.

An example of the JdK RS-Ratio line and the JdK RS-Momentum line together in one graph is shown in Figure 17.15. This graph again shows the European retail sector, but this time in combination with the JdK RSRatio line (solid) and the JdK RS-Momentum line (dotted) plotted in one graph below the price chart. By plotting the two uniformed measures on one chart, the interaction between JdK RS-Ratio and -Momentum becomes clear. JdK RS-Ratio is considered to be the most important and most influential numerical measure. However, it is clear in the chart that JdK RS-Momentum is leading the JdK RS-Ratio and thus serves as an early warning signal. When JdK RS-Momentum drops below the 100-level, the JdK RS-Ratio has formed a peak and has started to move down. When JdK RS-Momentum crosses above the 100-level, the JdK RS-Ratio line has formed a low and has started to move up.

By using the indicators and the graphs described above you get a structured approach to analyzing the relative position (attractiveness) of the elements in a universe vis-á-vis a benchmark. This "universe" can be any group of securities or indices that are comparable. It can be a group of sector-indices against a broad index like the 10 S&P 500 economic sectors (GICS level I) against the S&P 500 index or the 19 STOXX sector indices against the STOXX 600 index. Or it can be all members (individual equities) of a sector index, for example, banks, against the appropriate sector index (the banking sector index, in this case).

Be careful when the universe contains, for example, both equity and interest-rate-related instruments. Make sure that all elements are on the same footing; usually the

FIGURE 17.15 European Retail Sector with JdK RS-Ratio and JdK RS-Momentum Lines versus STOXX Index.

best thing to do is to use fixed income (total return) indices in order to compare them against equities.

In my European Sector Report, I used the STOXX 600 universe and presented the charts of all 19 sector indices with their relative strength against the STOXX 600 index, with comments on their relative attractiveness and expectations or the relative trends going forward. In the comments I highlighted some interesting equities that were showing strong relative pictures against their sector index. In this way I wanted to present a top-down approach for fund managers. First I identified the sectors that were expected to outperform the general index, and then I selected individual equities that were expected to outperform their sector index. The selection of individual equities was also done on sectors that, as a whole, were showing a downtrend against the broader market. The rationale behind that is that a professional fund manager who oversees a portfolio of European stocks is very unlikely to have, for example, no banking stocks whatsoever in his portfolio. He may have an underweighting of banks against the weight of banking stocks in the broader benchmark, but will rarely have none. So there is still a need for some guidance toward which banking stocks to hold, even if the sector is underperforming.

After putting together the report on a monthly basis, which is fun, the hard work started: calling the fund managers and trying to get my message across and hopefully pick up some trades. This was desperately needed to finance the fun! This was the moment when the question posed at the beginning of the chapter used to pop up: "What are your five best picks?" Now I was able to answer that question and even back it up with some numbers!

This routine continued for a number of months with reasonable success, both in terms of results of the recommendations as well as sales success. At some stage I was given an intern on the desk, an econometrics student who was going to write his thesis on the use of technical analysis in investment analysis. Among other things, one of the studies he conducted was to evaluate the results of the recommendation that had been published in the European Sector Report for the four years it had been published at that time. The recommendations that were used in that report were "outperform," "underperform," and "neutral." After evaluating all the recommendations from the four years' worth of reports, he found that the recommendations produced a "significant outperformance compared to the benchmark." A good start, but not good enough as it covered only four years of monthly data, that is, 48 observations. As the data for the indices used in the report (STOXX family) went back to 1987 and the "rules" to get to the recommendations were fairly clear, the next study he did was to take the data set starting in 1987 and run the rules to get the recommendations and evaluate the hypothetical results again. Once again, the outcome of the test was that the results showed a significant outperformance compared to the benchmark. To me it was proof that the approach was valid and that we were actually adding value to the investment process for clients.

With that whole dataset and all the results (albeit, hypothetical results), some more tests were used to validate the approach. One of these tests was to look at all the recommendations (1987–2003 = 16 × 12 = 192 months × 18 sectors = 3,456) and see what the excess return compared to the benchmark was three months after the recommendation had been issued. The result of that test was that both the out-performance and the underperformance recommendations, on average, generated an excess return. But what was very interesting to see was that the average excess return of the underperform recommendations was significantly higher than the excess return of the outperform recommendations.

Now, this observation puts the question, "What are your five best picks?" in a whole different light. Basically, it is the wrong question. The right question to ask is "Which five stocks, sectors, and so forth, should I avoid?" As a matter of fact, the rationale behind this is probably very recognizable for many of us. If we look back at the end of a year, we will always recognize a number of positions about which we can say "If we had not had those . . ." If we are able to avoid the bleeders, the results (i.e., outperformance) will more or less follow automatically.

So we moved from raw relative strength to two measures of relative strength that make all elements in a universe comparable. On the one hand, there is the JdK RS-Ratio that measures the relative strength of the security against its benchmark, and on the other hand, there is the JdK RS-Momentum, which measures the direction and the rate of change of the RS-Ratio line. This basically tells us if relative strength is getting stronger or weaker and whether it is turning up or down. We also found that identifying the underperformers in a universe is more important than finding the outperformers. The only thing missing was a good way to get this information to clients in a simple and understandable way.

With this knowledge I changed the layout of the report somewhat to also include the underperformers in a universe both on a sector level as well as on individual equities. I kept the graph of the broad market index (STOXX 600) followed by graphs of each individual sector with a pane showing JdK RS-Ratio and JdK RS-Momentum of the sector against the broad market index. But instead of highlighting some interesting individual names in a written comment, I ranked the whole universe based on the JdK RS-Ratio and added a table for each sector showing the best (i.e., strongest) five stocks of that sector, but more importantly the table also showed the worst (i.e., weakest) five stocks of that sector in an attempt to (also) draw attention to the weaker sectors or stocks of a universe!

Once again, this proved to be an improvement of the format as it answered a lot of questions beforehand that clients were going to pose. The problem that persisted was that either the analyst who was going to give ideas to the portfolio manager, or the portfolio manager himself, still had to browse through all the individual elements of a universe to determine which sectors or stocks inside a sector were going to be good candidates to overweight or underweight. The desire to better visualize all these relationships and present them to clients in an easy-to-understand way was very much there, but the method for how to go about this was missing.

I experimented with many different chart formats and tables. With hindsight I can now say that most technicians are so accustomed to the classical way of charting prices, with time on the horizontal (x-) axis and prices and/or the values of indicators on the vertical (y-) axis, that it is difficult to alter that routine.

I must have had a very bright moment when pulling up a very basic x,y scatter plot and starting to fill it with the JdK RS-Ratio as the x-value and JdK RS-Momentum as the y-value. The first time I did this, I was working with the 19 STOXX sectors in the European universe. Filling the plot with the x,y values for these 19 sectors gave me a picture like the one in Figure 17.16, which became a very revealing picture.

But what are we looking at? The best way to describe this and build the picture is to start with a schematic overview of what is going on in the scatter diagram as shown in Figure 17.17.

On the horizontal axis the JdK RS-Ratio is plotted, while the JdK RS-Momentum values are plotted on the vertical axis. That is done for all elements in the universe. Both axes are crossing at the 100-level, which is the midpoint of the chart. As all elements are scaled against a benchmark, this benchmark becomes the anchor point of the chart at the 100,100 crossing. The interpretation for both measures is that values above 100 are good and values below 100 are bad. The higher the value, the stronger it is, and the lower the value, the weaker it is.

The top-right quadrant is where we will find the elements that have a strong relative strength, that is, high JdK RS-Ratio values, and where that relative strength is still rising further. So this is the area where you will find the elements that you want to be overweight or long in a portfolio. Before the JdK RS-Ratio values start to decline and eventually cross below the 100-level, first JdK RS-Momentum will start to level off and then begin to decline. When that happens the element drops into the bottom-right quadrant. These are the elements in which the relative strength is still positive—JdK RS-Ratio at levels above 100—but momentum is declining. If relative strength

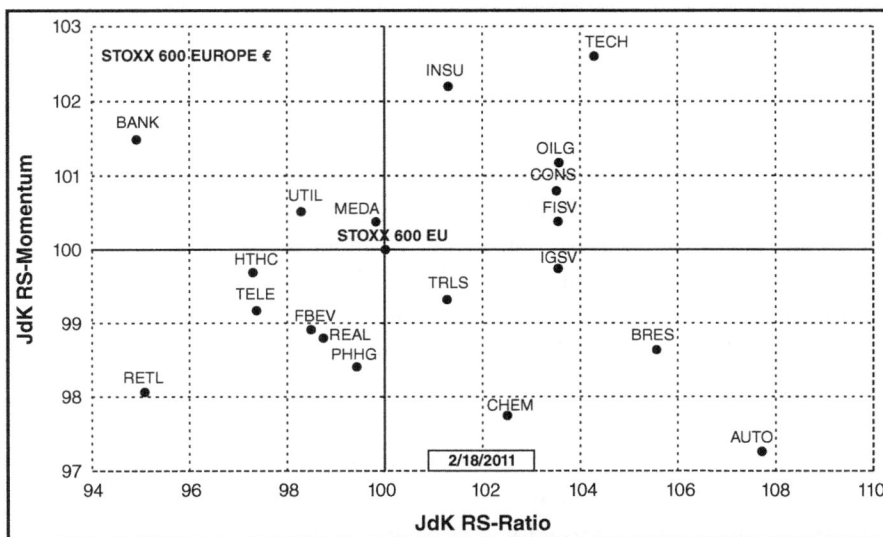

FIGURE 17.16   Scatter Plot with 19 STOXX Sectors.

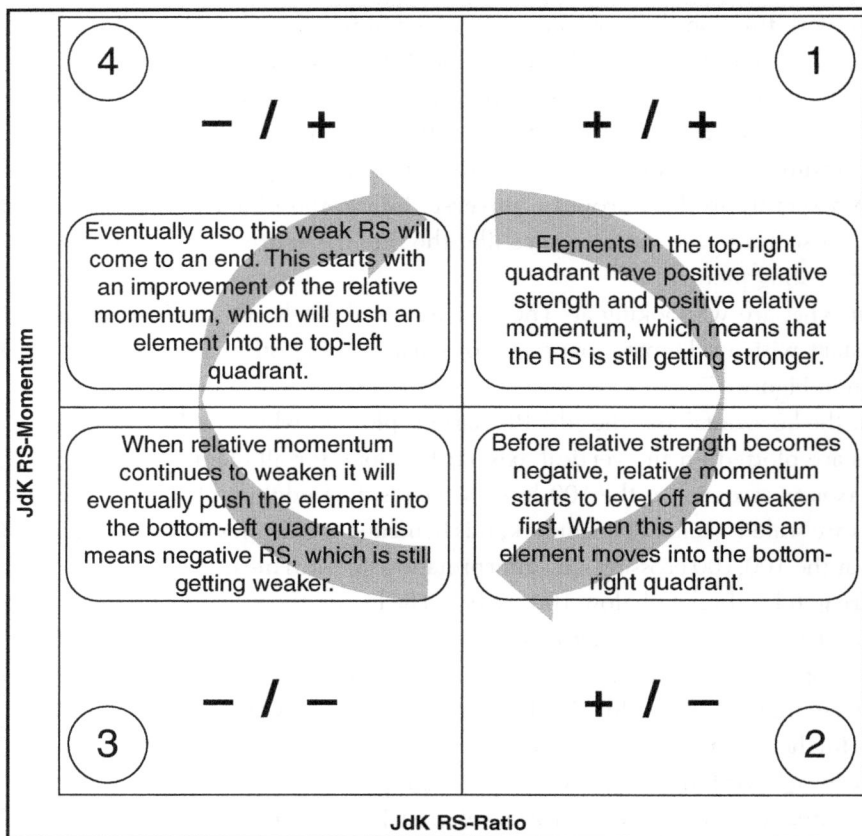

FIGURE 17.17 Schematic Overview of Rotation inside the Scatter Plot.

continues to weaken and momentum continues to accelerate on the downside, the element will eventually be pushed into the lower-left quadrant. These are the elements that are showing weak relative strength, that is, JdK RS-Ratio levels below 100 and the negative momentum continues to push them further down on the JdK RS-Ratio axis. These are the elements you want to be underweight or short in a portfolio.

Just as all good things come to an end, also all bad things will eventually come to an end. At some stage the acceleration of the downward JdK RS-Momentum will level off and turn back up again. This is the moment at which an element will be pushed from the lower-left quadrant into the top-left quadrant. At that stage the JdK RS-Ratio line is still in negative territory but moving up already. When that improvement continues the element will be pushed into the top-right quadrant again, and rotation has come full circle.

The first time I saw this rotation in action was what Germans would call an *Aha erlebnis* for me. Until then, I had often heard traders talking about sector-rotation but no one had ever been able to show me that sectors were actually rotating around a center/benchmark. With this tool I was now able to show people that markets actually do rotate, and that they do so in a clockwise fashion.

THE INTEGRATION OF TECHNICAL ANALYSIS

These pictures eventually became the Relative Rotation Graphs (RRGs) that I have been using in my research reports for institutional clients (available through our web sites) in various developing formats since 2005 and that have been available on the Bloomberg terminal since January 2011. So how are they going to help, and who are they going to help?

◼ Relative Rotation Graphs

The picture in Figure 17.16 shows only a snapshot of the last observations of all sectors, similar to the ranking on JdK RS-Ratio we saw in Table 17.2. In order to get a clearer picture and to put things into perspective, some historical data needs to be added to the graph. This is shown in Figure 17.18.

This picture shows the 10 economic sectors according to the Global Industry Classification System (GICS) level I of the S&P 500 universe. In this case, however, three weeks of history have been added to every sector, creating a "trail" that makes it possible to gauge the direction and the pace of the movement. Depending on the number of elements displayed in the scatter plot, trails can be longer or shorter. With a lot of elements displayed, long tails will make the graph look like spaghetti and make it more or less unreadable.

Try to find a balance between the number of elements and the length of the tails. If you want to study the rotation of individual elements over a longer time period, it's best to show just one or two elements with a long tail (see Figure 17.19). If you want

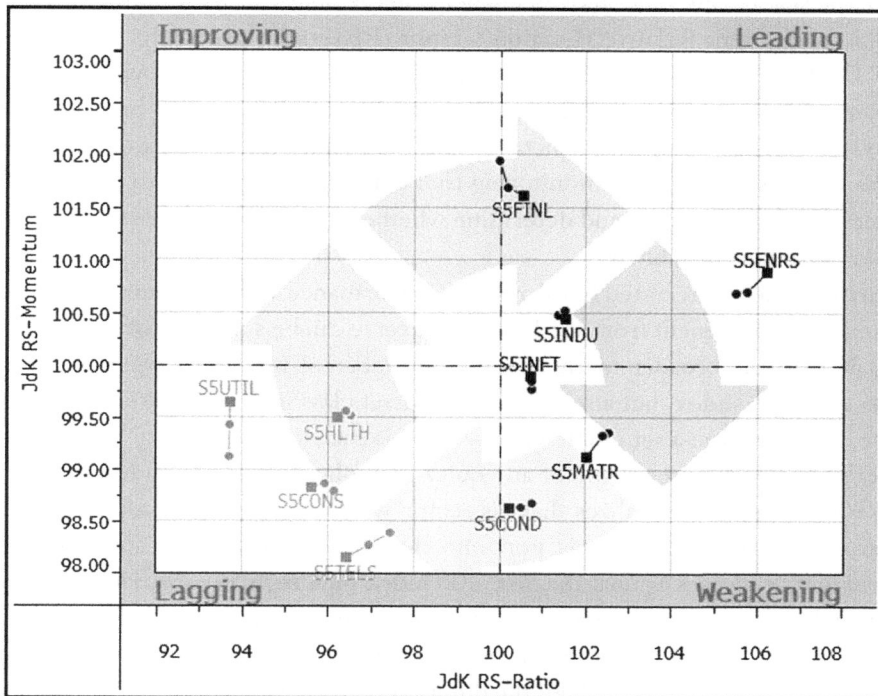

FIGURE 17.18   RRG of 10 Economic Sectors (GICS Level I) of S&P 500 Index.

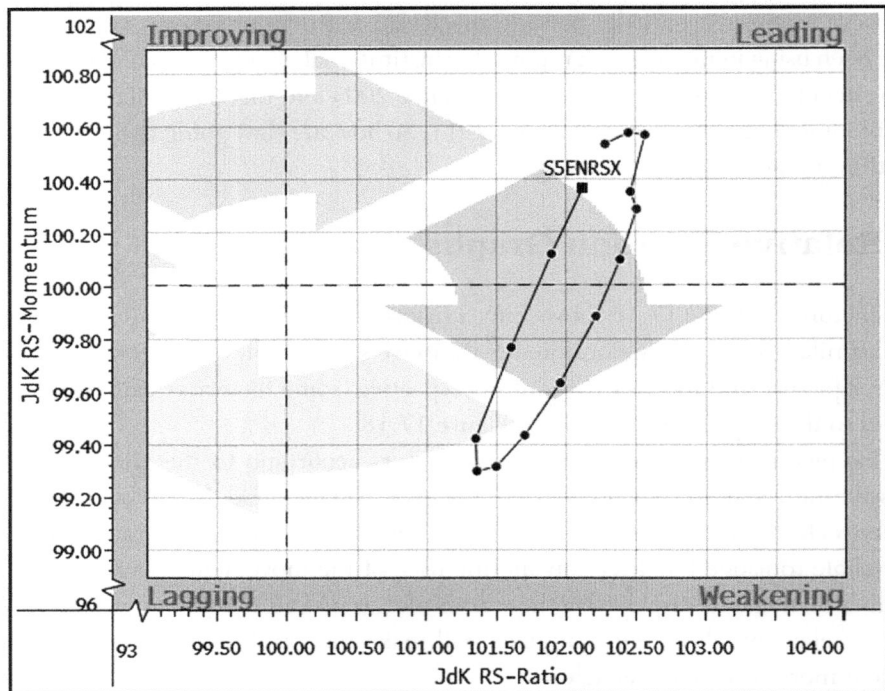

FIGURE 17.19 **RRG of S&P Energy Sector on a Daily Basis Showing Rotation in Positive Territory.**

to see the relative interaction of all elements in the universe, then show all elements with a shorter tail. Relative Rotation Graphs (RRGs) are primarily a visualization tool. The biggest advantage of this type of visualization is that it shows the user the relative positions of all elements in a universe, not only against a benchmark but also vis-á-vis each other in *one* picture—the *big* picture in *one* picture, so to speak. In this way RRGs serve as a monitoring tool that investors can use to monitor their universe or their portfolio and determine whether their holdings are still on track to outperform their benchmark.

Anyone who is interested in the relative performance and positioning of elements in a universe can benefit from the RRG. A universe can be a number of sector indices compared to the broader market index, a number of individual equities against a market (sector) index, but also a number of asset class indices (equities, bonds, real estate, etc.), or even a set of currencies vis-á-vis each other.

Let's start with an example of an equity portfolio manager who has to beat the S&P 500 index. As he realizes that his sector weightings will have a big impact on the overall performance of his portfolio, he checks the relative strength of the various sector indices against the S&P 500 index on a regular basis. He wants to be overweight in sectors with a strong relative strength and underweight in sectors with a weak relative strength vis-á-vis the broader market.

Instead of browsing through all the different sectors with a relative strength chart against the S&P 500, he could start with a look at a Relative Rotation Graph, similar

THE INTEGRATION OF TECHNICAL ANALYSIS

to the one shown in Figure 17.18, which shows the 10 economic sectors of the S&P 500 index against the S&P 500 index.

At one glance we can see that Energy is the leading sector and that Financials just entered the top-right quadrant and looks likely to continue higher on the JdK RS-Ratio scale. Overweight or long positions in these two sectors make sense. The Industrials sector is inside the top-right quadrant, but shows little momentum, and Information Technology is just inside the bottom-right quadrant, but also displays hardly any movement over the past three weeks. Sectors, or elements in a universe, that move very close to the benchmark are unlikely to generate a strong out- or underperformance as they move in line with the benchmark. In a large universe, and therefore a crowded Relative Rotation Graph, one can safely ignore the elements that are moving in a small circle around the benchmark. Concentrate on the elements that are moving on the outskirts of the diagram: this is where the real moves take place.

It is also quickly apparent that Materials and Consumer Discretionary are heading toward the bottom-left quadrant and very likely to arrive there soon. So these are sectors to keep an eye on, and if overweight or long positions still exist, it is time to start reducing them.

In negative territory, the bottom-left quadrant, we find Utilities, Health Care, Consumer Staples, and Telecom Services. The latter three are without doubt candidates for underweight or short positions.

Utilities need some extra examination as over the past three weeks relative momentum has been picking up rapidly. When this happens at low (or high) JdK RS-Ratio levels, it can happen that the pickup of relative momentum is a temporary thing and that a rotation takes place at levels < 100 (or > 100) on the JdK RS-Ratio scale, that is, without crossing to the right or the left of the diagram. This means that the security is still leading but it took some time to consolidate its prior outperformance. An example of such a rotation is seen in Figure 17.19.

The use of RRG as described above is a good way to monitor the current holdings in a portfolio and provides a quick visual check of whether the over- and under-weightings for specific sectors are still valid and justifiable.

RRG can also be used for pair-trade idea generation. The most obvious strategy is to be or to go long the sectors or elements that are crossing into or have just crossed into the top-right quadrant, and to be or to go short on the sectors or elements that are crossing or have just crossed into the bottom-left quadrant. These moves are considered to bear the least amount of risk, as the relative moves of the sectors at hand have already been confirmed. In the top-right quadrant are the sectors that are showing positive relative strength (high JdK RS-Ratio) with a positive relative momentum (high JdK RS-Momentum), indicating that relative strength is still getting stronger. The bottom-left quadrant are the sectors that are showing weak relative strength with relative momentum accelerating to the downside, indicating that relative strength is still getting weaker. An example of such a strategy is shown in Figure 17.20.

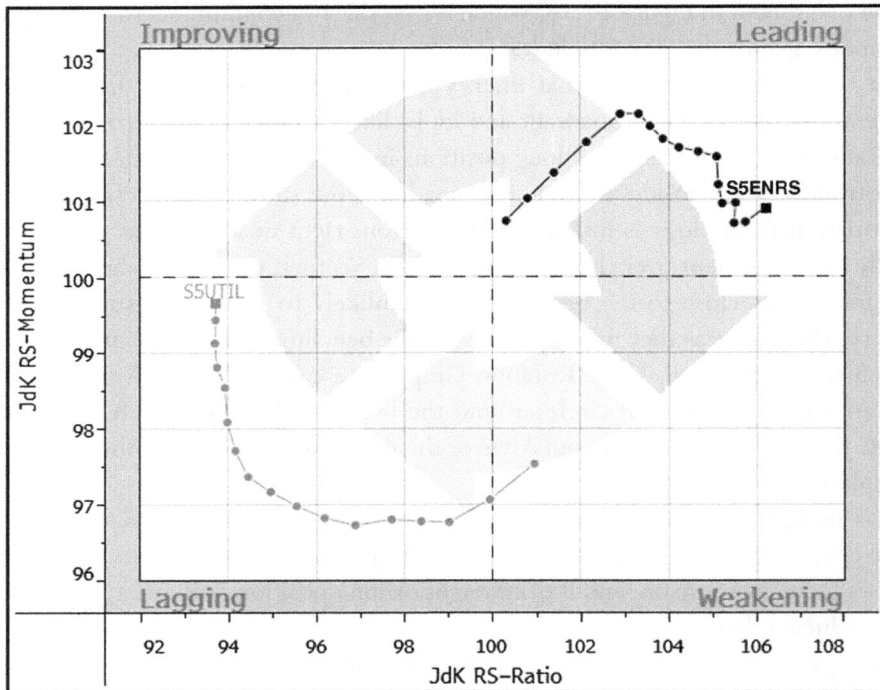

FIGURE 17.20 RRG of Energy and Utilities with a 17-Week Trail.

This RRG shows only two sectors of the S&P universe with a 17-week trail. At the beginning of the trail (the most recent point of the series is the bigger square marker with the label on top and therefore the beginning is the opposite end) the Energy sector (S5ENRS) had just entered the top-right quadrant and could be expected to show further outperformance versus the S&P 500 index. At the same time the Utilities sector was on the verge of crossing into the bottom-left quadrant and therefore very likely to show an underperformance versus the S&P500 going forward. The idea to be captured here is to overweight or go long the Energy sector and underweight or go short the Utilities sector. When looking at a RRG, conclusions like this are easily reached and do not require browsing through numerous charts. To get a better grasp of how the paths of these two trails translate back to a "normal" RS-line on a traditional chart, see Figure 17.21.

The top pane shows the weekly bar chart of the Energy sector, the middle pane shows the weekly bar chart of the Utilities sector, and the bottom pane is the RS line of Energy versus Utilities. The dashed vertical line shows the date mark of the beginning of the trail in the RRG in Figure 17.19.

At the beginning of the trail (11/5/2010) the Energy index traded at 465.12 and the Utilities at 162.54. At the end of the trail (2/25/11) Energy was at 577.37, a 24.1% gain, while Utilities were at 160.58, a 1.2% decline. This results in a 25.3% outperformance of Energy over Utilities in this period. As the trigger in this case was the entry of the top-right and the bottom-left quadrant this can be seen as a relatively "safe" strategy as the JdK RS-Ratio line at that time is confirmed above the 100-level.

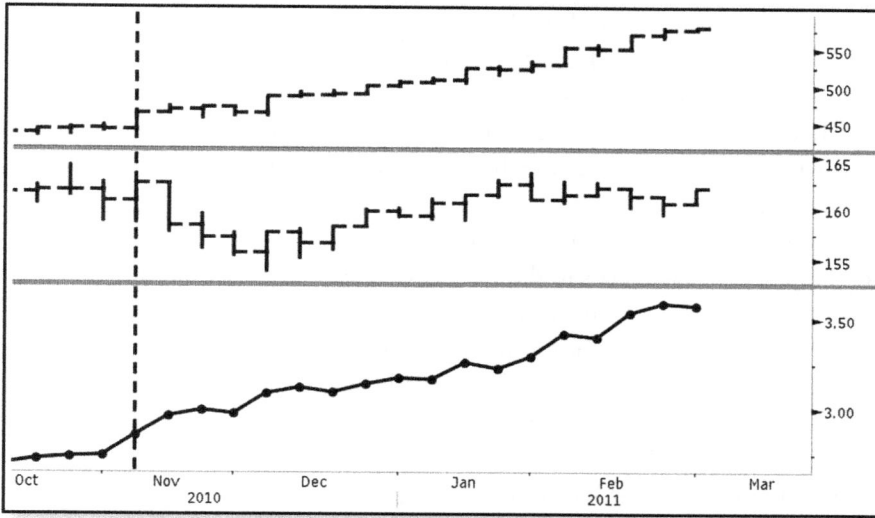

FIGURE 17.21 Bar Charts of Energy and Utilities with RS Line.

As the calculation of the JdK RS-Ratio line involves the use of moving averages, by definition some lag is introduced. This means that sectors have already gone through a decent move before entering into the top-right or the bottom-left quadrant. More adventurous or more aggressive investors could therefore also look for sectors in, or very close to, the top-left and bottom-right quadrants for trading opportunities, assuming that a rotation will continue in the expected direction. Such an example is shown in Figure 17.22.

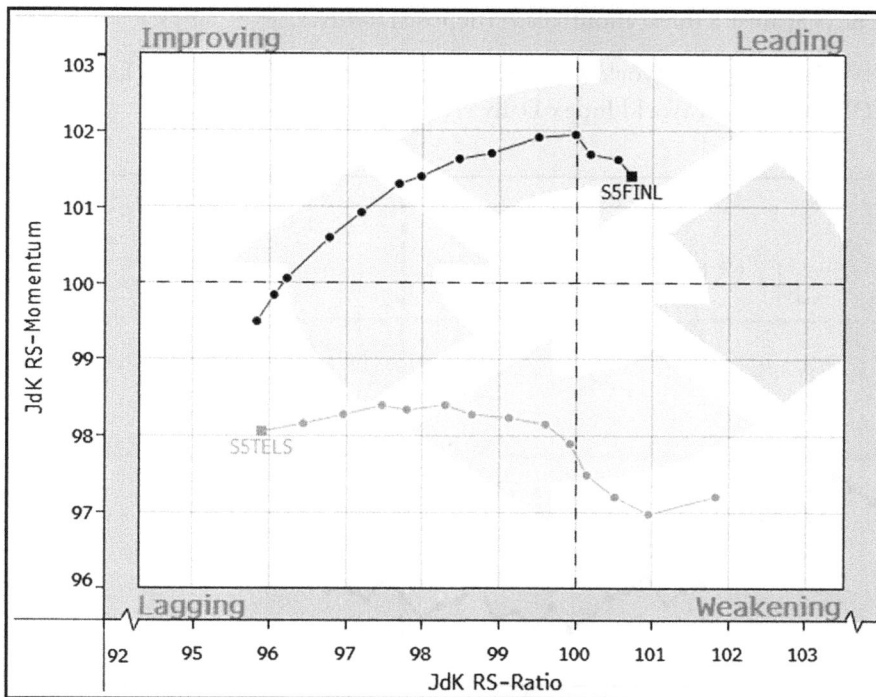

FIGURE 17.22 RRG of Financials and Telecom Services with a 14-Week Trail.

At the beginning of the trail the Financials sector is still in the bottom-left quadrant but heading toward, and nearly in, the top-left quadrant. The Telecom Services sector at the same time is well inside the bottom-right quadrant and heading for the bottom-left quadrant. Assuming a continuation of the rotation, investors or traders could start going long or overweight on Financials and short or underweight on Telecom Services.

In Figure 17.23 the 14-period trail is displayed in a regular chart containing the weekly bar chart of Financials in the top pane, Telecom Services in the middle pane, and the RS line of Financials to Telecoms in the bottom pane. The dashed vertical line marks the beginning of the trails in the RRG in Figure 17.22.

At the beginning of the trail (12/3/2010) Financials were trading at 203.97 and Telecom Services at 122.75. At the ends of the trail so far (2/25/2011), Financials were at 225.73 and Telecom Services at 124.84. This represents a gain of 10.3% for Financials and 1.7% for Telecom Services, that is, an outperformance of 8.6% at a point in time when Financials have just pushed into the top-right quadrant while Telecom Services are heading deeper into the bottom-left quadrant. The relative trend is therefore fully intact and may be expected to continue.

This type of analysis and idea generation using RRGs can be used in a lot of different markets, on a lot of different levels, and in all timeframes. Strategists and investment committees, for example, can use Relative Rotation Graphs to help determine dynamic asset allocations using a universe of indices representing various asset classes vis-á-vis some portfolio benchmark. Such an example is shown in Figure 17.24.

This RRG shows a number of asset class indices (all total return and all in local currency) against a three-month cash (deposit) index.

SBWGL: Citigroup World Government Bond Index all maturities Local
NDDLWI: MSCI World Index Daily Net TR Local

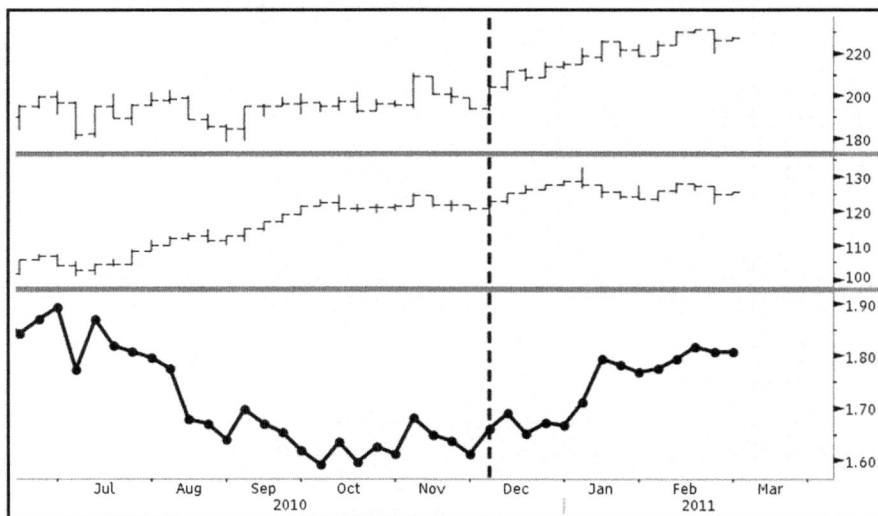

FIGURE 17.23   Bar Charts of Financials and Telecom Services with RS Line.

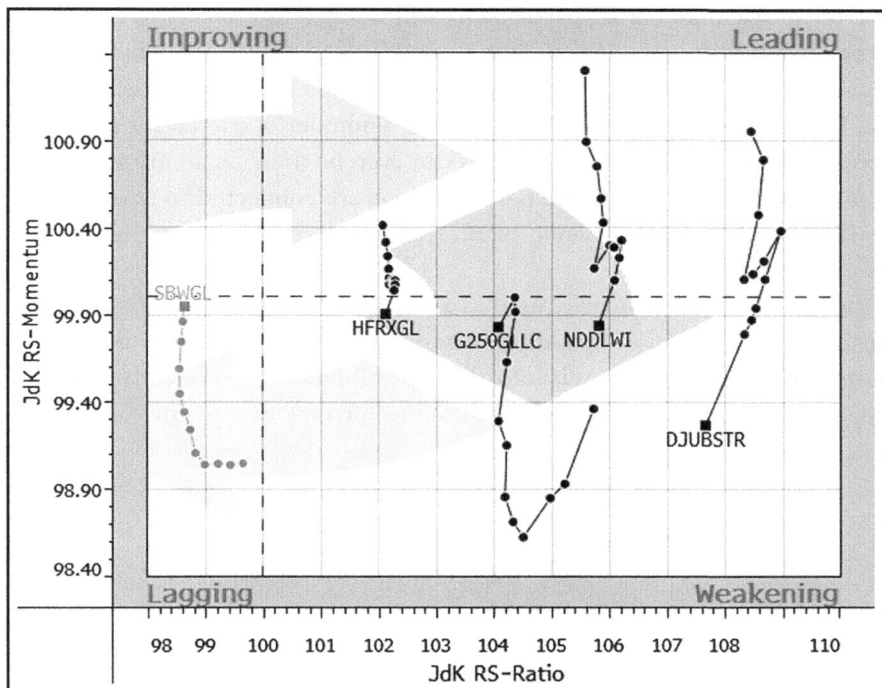

FIGURE 17.24 X RRG of Asset Classes against a Cash Index.

G250GLLC: GPR 250 Property Shares Index World Local
DJUBSTR: Dow Jones UBS Commodity TR
HFRXGL: HFRX Global Hedge Fund Index

The RRG shows that "risk assets" are still very strong, with high readings on the JdK RS-Ratio scale, but they are all losing relative momentum, with declining JdK RS-Momentum values, while bonds are picking up relative momentum. So far at this stage risk assets are still leading but as all are in the bottom-right quadrant, a close eye should be kept on any further deterioration that could warrant a shift of money out of risk assets into nonrisk assets (i.e., bonds and deposits). Of course, an RRG showing regional equity indices against the MSCI world equity index can then give clues as to which regions to prefer over others for the money that still remains invested in equity markets, assuming allocation to equities will not go down to zero. Another step down the decision tree can then be to draw an RRG of sector indices against the regional benchmark to determine which sectors to prefer, and so forth.

■ Conclusion

The application of Relative Strength analysis through the use of RRGs can aid investors at every level of the decision tree, from asset allocation to selection of individual equities. Usually the more active traders will use shorter timeframes, while longer-term-oriented market participants will want to use weekly or even monthly timeframes. Fixed-income investors can use RRGs to determine which type (government or corporate), region, or credit-level to pick, and at which part of the curve. Forex traders can use an RRG showing a number of currencies against a base currency to generate trade ideas. All this can even be done on an intraday basis, for example, hourly or in 10- minute periods. If you are connected to a real-time feed, this will generate a very dynamic picture, showing real-time rotation during the course of the trading day.

Although RRGs are primarily used as a visualization tool, that does not rule out using this method for more quantitative and rule-based approaches to markets. We are conducting further research into these possibilities and are actively designing trading strategies and tailor-made visualizations for various types of clients.

CHAPTER 18

Analyzing the Macro-Finance Environment

From Robert A. Weigand, *Applied Equity Analysis and Portfolio Management* (Hoboken, New Jersey: John Wiley & Sons, 2014), Chapter 2.

Learning Objective Statements

- Forecast possible progression of a business cycle model
- Explain the relationship between the business and financial cycles
- Identify leading, coincident and lagging indicators of economic activity

This chapter presents a system for analyzing the strength of U.S. economic activity, identifying the current stage of the business and financial cycle, and using the results of this analysis to identify stock sectors to over- and underweight in an actively managed portfolio. The learning objectives for this chapter are:

1. Explain the relation between the business and financial cycles.
2. Explain how the current stage of the financial cycle suggests which stock sectors are most likely to outperform or underperform the overall stock market over the coming year.
3. Explain what each of The Conference Board's leading, coincident and lagging indicators communicates about the strength and robustness of future, current, or past economic activity.
4. Analyze the signals conveyed by each Conference Board indicator and reduce these analyses to short written descriptions.
5. Synthesize these written descriptions into a Market Outlook Newsletter.
6. Recommend changes to a stock portfolio's active sector weights based on the analysis and conclusions contained in the Market Outlook Newsletter.

Economic Analysis: The First Step of a Top-Down Fundamental Process

This chapter guides you through the "top" part of the top-down analysis process. Before analyzing individual stocks, we will gauge the strength and resiliency of the U.S. economy to improve our investment decision-making process. For example, if our analysis indicates that economic growth is slowing or contracting, but equity values do not fully reflect the extent to which the slowing economy will impact corporate profits and cash flows, we might increase our portfolio cash position by selling off some of our weaker stocks (the ones we think are most vulnerable to a downturn). Or, if we're managing a fund with a mandate to be fully invested in equities at all times, we might practice *sector rotation* (explained in greater detail below), and take profits in some of our high-risk positions in more aggressive sectors. We can redeploy the proceeds from selling these securities into safer, low-beta stocks in defensive sectors such as consumer staples and utilities, or chase attractive dividend yields (during the 2008–2009 market downturn, for example, Bristol-Myers was yielding 5.5% and Verizon Communications' dividend yield reached 7.0%). The main point of this chapter is that having a good understanding of the relation between the macroeconomy and financial markets and the value of equities—what we'll call the macro-finance environment—can help you make better market timing and stock selection decisions.

Gauging the robustness of the U.S. economy is the first step in our process. The second step involves using the results of our macro analysis to identify the current stage of the U.S. *business cycle*—the alternating periods of expansion and contraction that occur in free-market economies. As shown in Figure 18.1, we will classify

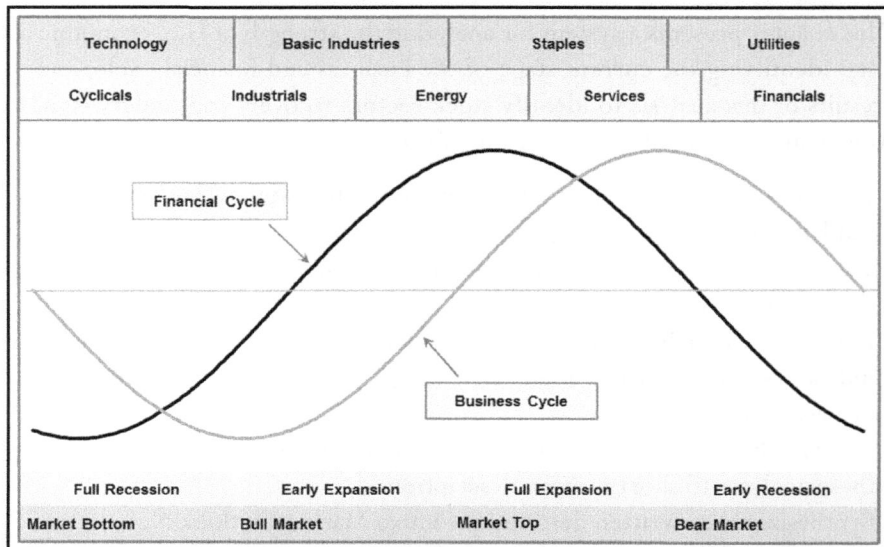

FIGURE 18.1 Stock Sectors and the Business and Financial Cycles.

the U.S. economy into one of four stages: (1) full recession, (2) early expansion, (3) full expansion, or (4) early recession.

Figure 18.1 depicts how the *financial cycle* leads the business cycle. Research shows that stocks tend to lead the economy by approximately six to nine months on average. For example, the stock market usually reaches a trough and begins rising while the U.S. economy is still in full recession mode and contracting. Similarly, stocks tend to top out and begin their next bear market decline while the economy is still in full expansion mode and growing.

Sector Rotation

Once we complete our analysis and are reasonably confident about the current stage of the business and financial cycle, the final step of the process involves mapping our location in the financial cycle to the suggested stock sectors shown in Figure 18.1. If our analysis shows that the market has bottomed and is due to begin rising in anticipation of an *economic expansion*, conventional wisdom suggests that it's best to lighten up on *defensive sectors* and put new money to work in aggressive or *cyclical sectors* (featuring stocks whose prices tend to rise and fall with economic conditions). Examples would include autos and other durable goods manufacturers and technology stocks, because businesses and consumers delay large-ticket purchases when the economy is weak, and then catch up on these purchases when economic conditions improve. If we think the economy is already expanding and the stock market is well into its bull market phase, however, increasing our allocations to industrial, basic material and energy stocks is recommended, because inflation runs hotter later in the business cycle, and rising commodity prices usually boost these companies' profits.

As we begin, a broad question to consider is, "What exactly is *the economy?*" More specifically, what free, publicly-available information could we research to depict economic activity from a variety of perspectives, and how would we analyze this information? This chapter provides you with tools that make it easy to research key economic indicators on your own and interpret them within a structured framework. Every individual indicator analyzed below is available for free from the Federal Reserve Economic Data (FRED) database at http://research .stlouisfed.org/fred2/. The first chapter spreadsheet (Ch02-Graphs) provides you with historical values of the indicators (through 2012), a template for graphing each indicator, and each indicator's FRED data code for accessing new values of each series. These data can be easily downloaded from FRED and pasted into the spreadsheet, so you can update your data and graphs over time and refresh your economic outlook.[1]

The chapter analysis system begins by first examining several big-picture economic indicators to obtain a broad overview of trends in national income, corporate profits, and job creation. Next, we will analyze 21 economic indicators compiled by The Conference Board, a private, nonprofit research organization based in the United States. Finally, I suggest several supplementary variables to complete our view of trends in economic activity. The Conference Board indicators are organized into three groups:

1. The 10 *leading indicators* are thought to change in advance of economic conditions. These are used for forecasting the *future* strength and direction of the business cycle.
2. The four *coincident indicators* are thought to change in sync with economic conditions. These are used for interpreting *current* economic strength or weakness.
3. The seven *lagging indicators* are thought to change after changes in economic conditions. These are used for corroborating that the economy has been expanding or contracting in accordance with our expectations and previous analyses we may have conducted.

The first chapter learning activity involves analyzing and interpreting the indicators, and writing short descriptions of each. Business writing guidelines for this activity are provided below, and sample solutions to several homework questions regarding each type of indicator are provided at the end of the chapter, so there are examples for you to follow to get a running start on this exercise.

As soon as you're comfortable analyzing and describing the behavior of the indicators, use the first chapter companion spreadsheet (Ch02-Graphs) to download and graph the most recent values of the indicators from the FRED database. The FRED data codes for each variable can be found on each variable's worksheet in the Ch02-Graphs spreadsheet. Follow the method described below and write three to five short sentences interpreting each indicator. This exercise teaches you to analyze each indicator in a consistent, systematic manner. Your written descriptions and the graphs created by the spreadsheet can be published as a Market Outlook Newsletter, which is the first major output this learning system coaches you to create.

Next, use the second chapter spreadsheet (Ch02-Scorecard) to fill out the economic scorecard template based on your written descriptions for each indicator. Reduce your written analyses to a −1, 0, +1 scale and rate each indicator as mainly negative for the economy and stocks (−1), neutral or not currently relevant (0), or mainly positive (+1). The spreadsheet will compile and graph the results of your rankings into a system for analyzing the strength of economic activity known as a *diffusion index*, which is just a technical term for the weighted average of all your −1, 0 and +1 variable rankings.

The Ch02-Scorecard spreadsheet computes two diffusion indexes. The first weights each indicator equally, and the second uses The Conference Board's weighting system, based on their proprietary statistical analysis of the relative importance of each indicator. Both diffusion indexes have a minimum possible value of −100%, which would represent negative signals from every indicator, and a maximum possible value of +100%, representing positive signals from every indicator. Figure 18.2 shows a sample scorecard for The Conference Board's 10 leading economic indicators and their recommended weightings for each indicator.

The first diffusion index (in the "Score" column) is calculated as a simple average of the rankings. Thus, with four scores of +1, five scores of zero, and one score

Leading Indicators	Score	Weight
Avg. Length Manufacturing Workweek	1	0.2781
ISM New Orders Index	0	0.1651
Consumer Sentiment	1	0.1551
Int. Rate Spread (10-yr minus Fed Funds)	0	0.1069
Manufacturers' New Orders-Consumers	0	0.0811
Leading Credit Index ™	1	0.0794
Stock Prices, S&P 500	1	0.0381
Manufacturers' New Orders-Capital Goods	0	0.0356
Avg. Weekly Initial Unemployment Claims	0	0.0334
Building Permits, New Private Housing	-1	0.0272
Leading Indicators Diffusion Index	**30%**	**52%**

FIGURE 18.2   Leading Indicators Sample Scorecard.

of −1, the equally weighted diffusion index equals +30%, which would indicate moderate acceleration of future economic activity relative to current economic conditions. The weighted diffusion index value of +52% is higher than the equally weighted diffusion index value because several of the more heavily weighted indicators (the manufacturing workweek and consumer sentiment) received scores of +1, but the only score of −1 was applied to the most lightly weighted indicator (building permits for new private housing units). Because the more heavily weighted components received positive scores, and the most lightly weighted component received the only negative score, the weighted diffusion index value is considerably higher than the equally weighted value. In this case, a score of +52% would indicate that future economic activity was expected to substantially accelerate relative to current economic conditions.

The scorecard spreadsheet also compiles your rankings of the lagging, coincident and leading indicators into a single graph that depicts an overview of your economic analysis, based on how you ranked each component of The Conference Board's three indexes. An example is shown as Figure 18.3.

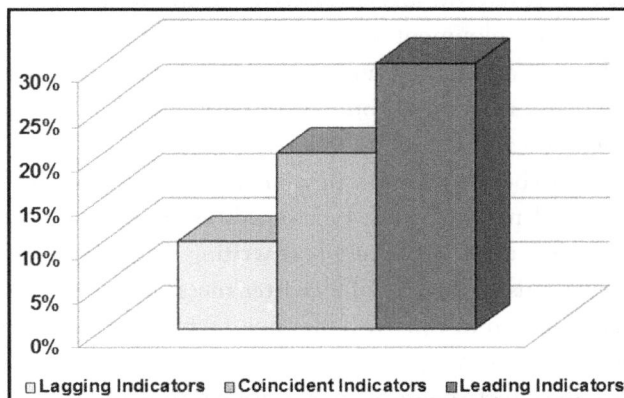

FIGURE 18.3   Example 1: Sample Rankings for the Lagging, Coincident, and Leading Indicators.

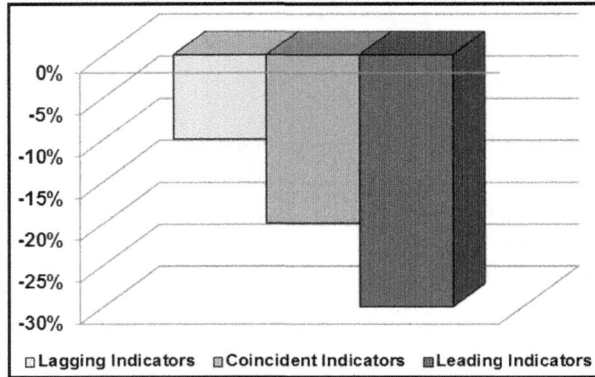

FIGURE 18.4 Example 2: Sample Rankings for the Lagging, Coincident, and Leading Indicators.

The graph progresses from lagging to coincident to leading indicators, so the perspective is (1) looking *back* at the recent behavior of the economy over the past six to nine months, (2) looking at the *current* state of the economy, and (3) looking *forward* to gauge the expected strength of the economy over the next six to nine months. Figure 18.3 depicts an economy that has been expanding slowly over the past six to nine months (indicated by the +10% ranking for the lagging indicators), is currently experiencing a further acceleration of business activity (+20% for the coincident indicators), and is forecasted to undergo additional positive acceleration in the next six to nine months (+30% for the leading indicators).

Next, let's consider Figure 18.4. If our rankings of the lagging, coincident, and leading indicators had instead resulted in diffusion index scores of −10%, −20%, and −30%, respectively, the graph would depict an economy that recently slowed, is currently slowing further, and is forecasted to undergo additional contraction before the slowdown cycle ends.

Writing Guidelines

Practicing concise, accurate business writing is an important part of all business students' professional development. Remember that you're only going to be able to capture your audience's attention span for a limited period. Your writing has to be concise, interesting and relevant if you expect busy end users to keep turning the pages of the reports you author.

It's important not to be too informal in your writing. Business professionals don't expect to see writing that contains the type of abbreviations you would use in a text message (as in "here's a tip 4 u"). One good writing discipline would be to try to confine your descriptions to the size of a Twitter message (140 characters). You can even take the writing down to concise bullet points, which would work great in this exercise. Remember to always get right to the point—make every word count. A great way to check the effectiveness of your writing is to read each sentence out loud and ask "So what?" after each statement you make. If the statement does not present relevant, compelling information, it needs to be rewritten or removed entirely.

Your goal should be to construct short, well-organized, readable paragraphs. Your paragraphs should be three to five sentences long (three is the minimum, five is the maximum). They should start with an introduction and finish with a sentence that begins: Conclusion. This concluding statement *tells the reader what to think about the metric*, based on the points you raise in the preceding sentences. Practicing telling the reader what to think is a particularly effective way to learn to write convincingly. Notice that a fine balance must be maintained: your writing should be persuasive and convicted, but your arguments should always be objectively plausible, and never purely partisan (economics and politics may often overlap, but they are two distinct disciplines—keep them separate!). When you learn how to support your conclusions in this manner, you will find that your business writing becomes more effective, because you'll be writing statements that are always accurate. Being fanatical over accuracy is important if your career path involves distinguishing yourself as an analyst.

At first, you may find it helpful to follow the rubric below for writing a five-sentence paragraph. Sentences (or bullet points) 1 through 5 should be written to communicate the following information:

1. As briefly as possible, describe what the indicator measures about past, current, or expected future economic activity (for each lagging, coincident, and leading indicator, respectively).
2. Interpret the behavior of the indicator during previous business cycles, noting if the indicator consistently lags, coincides, or leads economic activity as expected.
3. Direct the reader to either observe something interesting about the current behavior of the indicator, or to further consider how the variables presented should relate to each other (why the variables are, or aren't, behaving as expected).
4. Make a factual statement about the most important idea conveyed by the graph; be sure the implications for stocks and the economy are clear.
5. Conclusion: Tell the reader the most important thing to remember about the indicator. This is where you're telling the reader what to think, based on your objective interpretation of the data presented in sentences 1 through 4.

Data Considerations: Nominal and Real Time Series

Financial data are often reported in *nominal* terms, meaning that changes in any variables include the effects of inflation. Year-over-year earnings changes are usually reported in nominal terms, as are stock market returns (as in, "the market's up 5% year to date"). It's important to focus on real (inflation-adjusted) data when the long-term trend is of greater interest, however. This is the case when growth in gross domestic product (GDP) is reported, for example.

The ultimate achievement in investing is to outperform whatever market you're invested in *adjusted for inflation* (and risk, as we'll learn later), because that's the true measure of how wealth is changing in value over time. Many of the time series below are therefore interpreted net of inflation. Stripping away the effects of inflation allows us to observe and analyze the long-term trend in genuine economic growth and wealth creation.[2]

497

ANALYZING THE MACRO-FINANCE ENVIRONMENT

National Income, Corporate Profits, and Job Creation

We'll begin by taking a big-picture overview of economic activity by examining trends in national income, profits, and job creation. Figure 18.5 depicts the year-over-year growth rate in real gross domestic product (GDP), which is an estimate of the total output of goods and services produced in the United States. GDP includes consumer spending, private investment, net exports, and government spending. Note how GDP growth falls off sharply and often turns negative during recessions. In the 1980s to 1990s, growth in real GDP fluctuated around an average of 3.0%, but average growth has slowed slightly since the beginning of the 2000s. GDP growth has remained positive following the deep recession of 2008–2009, indicating a period of economic expansion.

Figure 18.6 depicts real disposable personal income and after-tax corporate profits. Increasing income and profits are signs of a healthy, growing economy. The graph

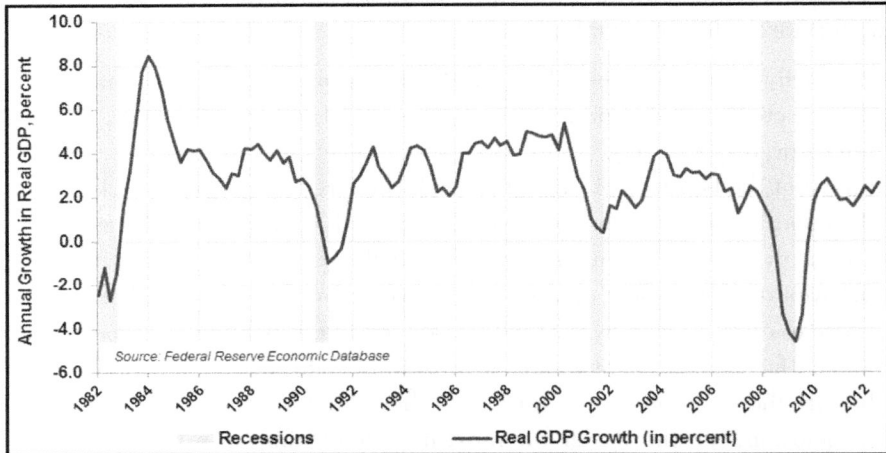

FIGURE 18.5   Annual Real GDP Growth.

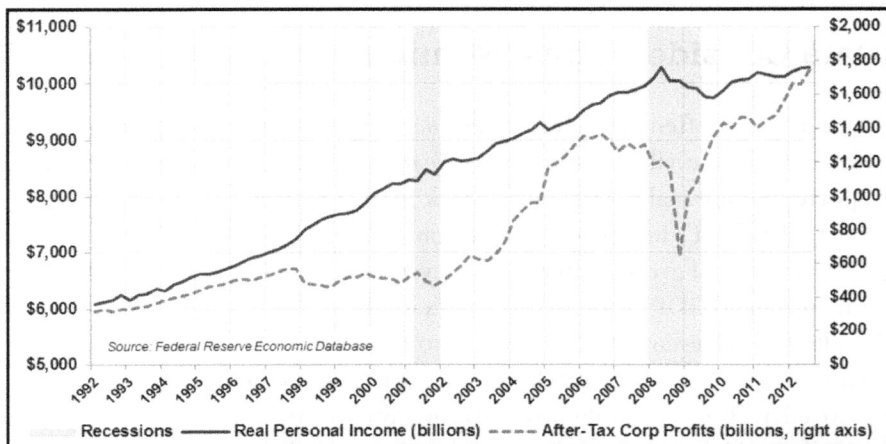

FIGURE 18.6   Real Disposable Income and After–Tax Corporate Profits.

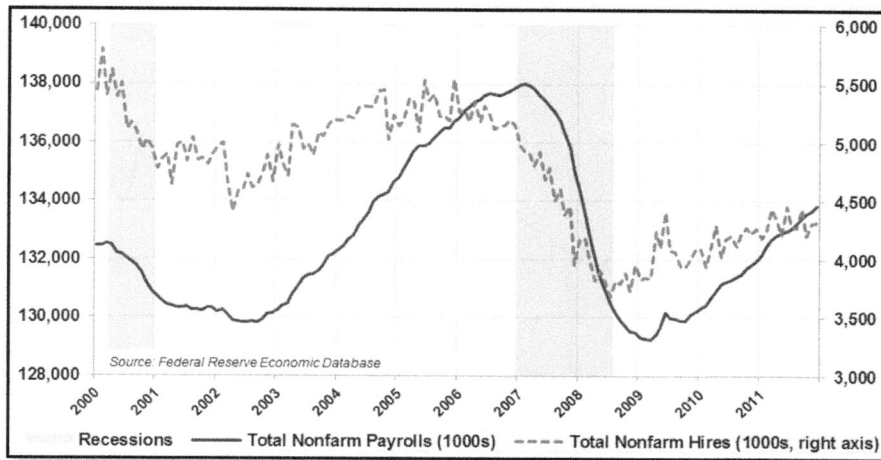

FIGURE 18.7   Total Nonfarm Payrolls and Total Nonfarm Hires.

shows that the 2008–2009 recession interrupted the positive trend in these variables, although both have subsequently resumed their upward trajectory. After-tax corporate profits have gone on to achieve record highs, while real personal income has shifted to more of a sideways trend since the end of the most recent recession.

We'll conclude our big-picture overview of the economy with a look at job creation. Figure 18.7 depicts total nonfarm payrolls and total nonfarm hires from 2000 to 2012. The 2008–2009 recession sharply reduced the total number of employed persons in the United States. Following the recession, job creation has rebounded, although the pace at which new workers are being hired remains sluggish. As of the end of 2012, there were approximately 4 million fewer employed persons in the United States than at the 2007 peak.

Our big-picture overview variables paint a mixed picture of the U.S. economy as of year-end 2012. Gross domestic product has grown steadily since 2009, although at a slower pace than in previous decades. After-tax corporate profits are at an all-time high, but real disposable personal income has grown more slowly than has been the case in previous economic expansions. Finally, job creation remains sluggish—the total number of employed persons is the same as in 2004, and the pace at which new workers are being hired is slower than any time during the 2000 recession. In the following section, we will examine each of The Conference Board's leading economic indicators.

■ Leading Economic Indicators

The Conference Board averages 10 indicators, 3 financial and 7 nonfinancial, into a forecasting tool known as the Leading Economic Index® (LEI). The LEI index is thought to change in advance of the general economy; thus, it is used to gauge whether the pace of future business activity is expected to accelerate, decelerate, or trend sideways. We are going to examine and interpret all 10 of the LEI components. The related learning activity for this section involves a business writing exercise to interpret the implications

FIGURE 18.8 The Conference Board's Leading Economic Index® (LEI) for the United States, 1982–2013.

of each indicator for the economy. Once you've practiced enough of the homework to be comfortable writing concise, accurate interpretations of the indicators, you should complete the learning activity by downloading the most recent values of each indicator from the FRED database, updating the Ch02-Graphs spreadsheet, and finish drafting your macro newsletter as you engage in the business writing exercise.

The LEI index is shown as Figure 18.8 (the 10 individual components of the LEI index were presented in Figure 18.2). Notice how the index reliably turns down before the start of recessions and begins increasing before the start of the next economic expansion.

LE-1. The Average Length of the Manufacturing Workweek (weight = 27.8%)

This indicator is depicted in Figure 18.9 along with the average length of the construction workweek. The manufacturing workweek is the most heavily weighted component of the leading indicators. The interpretation of this indicator is if U.S. manufacturers need employees to work longer hours, new manufacturing orders and overall economic activity are accelerating, and additional hiring may follow. Conversely, when the workweek trends downward, the implication is that new orders and overall economic activity are decelerating, and layoffs may also occur soon. A sideways trend implies stability in the sector and the overall economy. The average length of the construction workweek is also depicted in the graph. Although this is not an official component of the LEI, a similar interpretation applies to this indicator, and we get another closely related data point to further inform our analysis. In this case, both indicators are growing, suggesting strength in the manufacturing and construction sectors.

Notice that the LEI index only takes the length of the manufacturing workweek into account but ignores total employment in the sector. Figure 18.10 depicts two

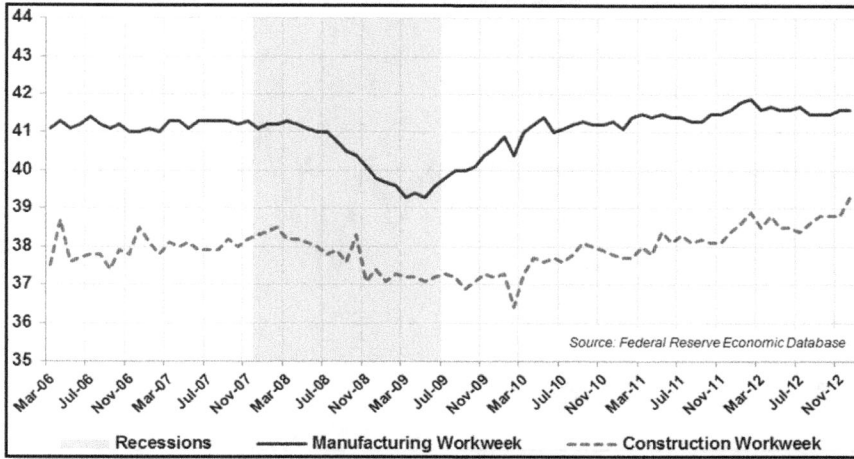

FIGURE 18.9 Average Length of the Manufacturing and Construction Workweeks.

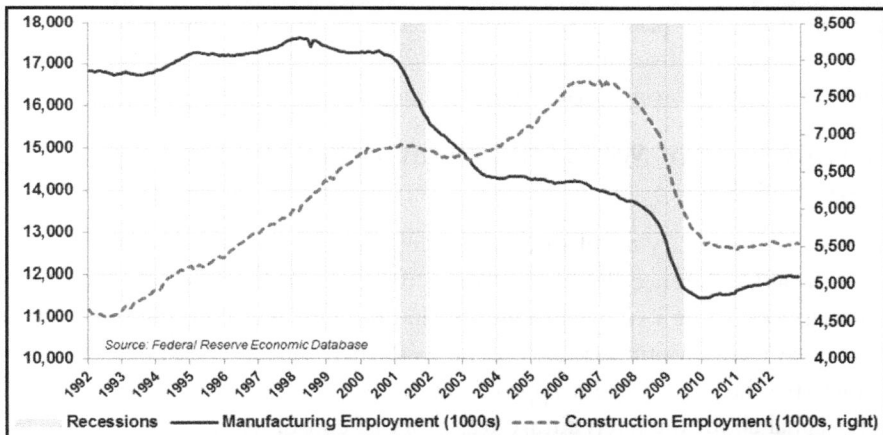

FIGURE 18.10 Total Manufacturing and Construction Employment in the United States.

additional, closely related variables: total manufacturing and construction employment in the United States. Due to outsourcing of manufacturing abroad and steady increases in manufacturing productivity, there are at least 5 million fewer workers employed in U.S. manufacturing since 2001, and 2.5 million fewer in construction since 2007. These findings temper our enthusiasm for the more positive signal conveyed by the manufacturing workweek indicator.

LE-2. Institute for Supply Management New Manufacturing Orders Index (weight = 16.5%)

The ISM New Orders Index indicates whether manufacturing orders are expanding or contracting. The index is constructed so that a value greater than 50 means new orders are increasing, while a number less than 50 indicates new orders are generally decreasing.

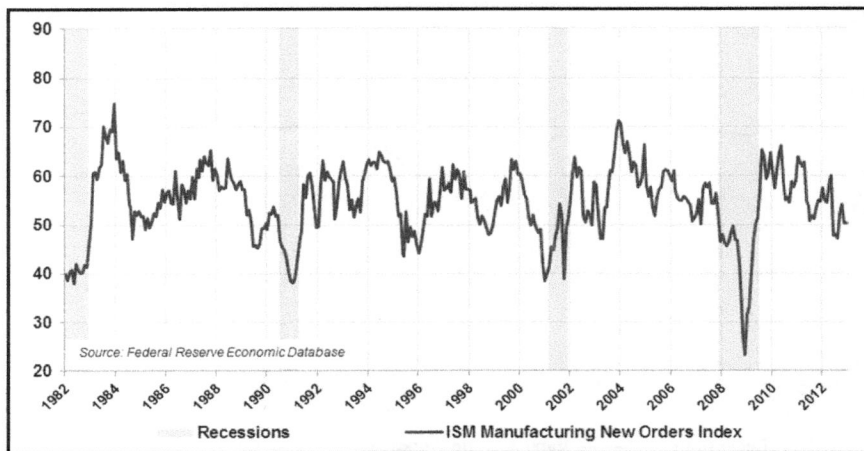

FIGURE 18.11   ISM New Manufacturing Orders Index.

Figure 18.11 shows the index since 1982. The index functions well as a leading indicator, reliably decreasing prior to the start of recessions and increasing before recessions end. After a strong positive surge following the 2008–2009 recession, the index has been trending downward, however, with several readings below the key level of 50.

LE-3. University of Michigan Consumer Sentiment Index (weight = 15.5%)

In this case it is necessary to substitute a publicly available consumer sentiment survey for the official Conference Board consumer confidence index, which is available only via subscription. There's common sense behind the idea that consumers spend more when they're feeling optimistic and spend less when they're pessimistic. Given that consumer spending accounts for approximately 70% of U.S. GDP, this indicator sends a strong signal about the likely future trajectory of consumer spending in the United States. Figure 18.12 depicts the University of Michigan Survey of Consumer Sentiment from 1982 to 2012.

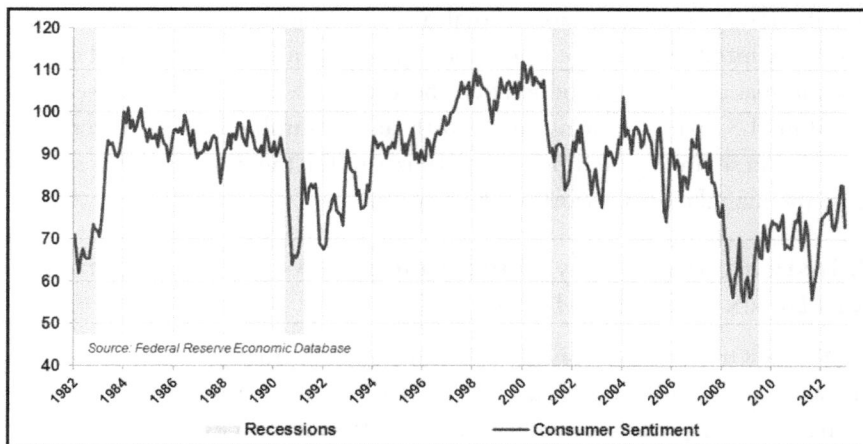

FIGURE 18.12   University of Michigan Consumer Sentiment Index.

While consumer sentiment has rebounded from the depths of the great recession, it still has a long way to climb before it registers the same sort of enthusiasm consumers felt during the 1980s, 1990s, and most of the 2000s. The overall trend following the 2008–2009 recession remains positive, however.

LE-4. Interest Rate Spread, 10-Year Treasury Yield Minus Fed Funds Rate (weight = 10.7%)

The "spread," or difference, between the yield (interest rate) on a 10-year Treasury note and the shorter-term Federal Funds rate is a proxy for one of the most popular business cycle forecasting indicators, the slope of the **Treasury yield curve**. The Treasury yield curve plots the interest rates on government securities at a range of maturities from 3 months to 30 years. First, we'll explore why the slope of the yield curve can be interpreted as an indicator of future economic activity, then we'll examine the current interest rate spread between the 10-year T-note yield and the Fed Funds rate.

The yield curve is influenced by two main factors. The first is Federal Reserve policy, which primarily impacts rates on the short end of the curve. The second is the preferences of borrowers and lenders (based on their expectations of future inflation and interest rates), which affect the intermediate- and long-term interest rates that comprise the middle and end sections of the curve. The easiest way to interpret the slope of the yield curve is to first picture what's known as the "expectations hypothesis of interest rates." This explanation of the forces that determine the shape of the yield curve says that investors believe that longer-term interest rates are the geometric (or compound) average of current and expected future short-term rates. As depicted in Equation 18.1, the yield on a 3-year T-note at time zero can be thought of as the average of the current 1-year rate of interest (now, at time zero) and the 1-year interest rates investors expect over the next two years (1 and 2 time periods in the future):

$$i_0^3 = \left[\left(1 + i_0^1\right)\left(1 + i_1^1\right)\left(1 + i_2^1\right) \right]^{\frac{1}{3}} - 1 \qquad (18.1)$$

$$\left(1 + i_0^3\right)^3 = \left(1 + i_0^1\right)\left(1 + i_1^1\right)\left(1 + i_2^1\right) \qquad (18.2)$$

This makes sense because an investor with a 3-year holding period has two basic ways to invest in bonds over this horizon:

1. Buy a 3-year bond and earn that yield for the next three years (depicted as the left-hand side of Equation 18.2), or
2. Buy a 1-year bond and hold it to maturity, then use the proceeds from that bond to buy another 1-year bond at the expected rate one year from now, and reinvest again at the 1-year rate expected two years from now (as shown on the right-hand side of Equation 18.2).

Further notice from Equation 18.2 that if investors believe that future rates will fall, the yield curve will flatten out, perhaps to the point that it eventually "inverts"

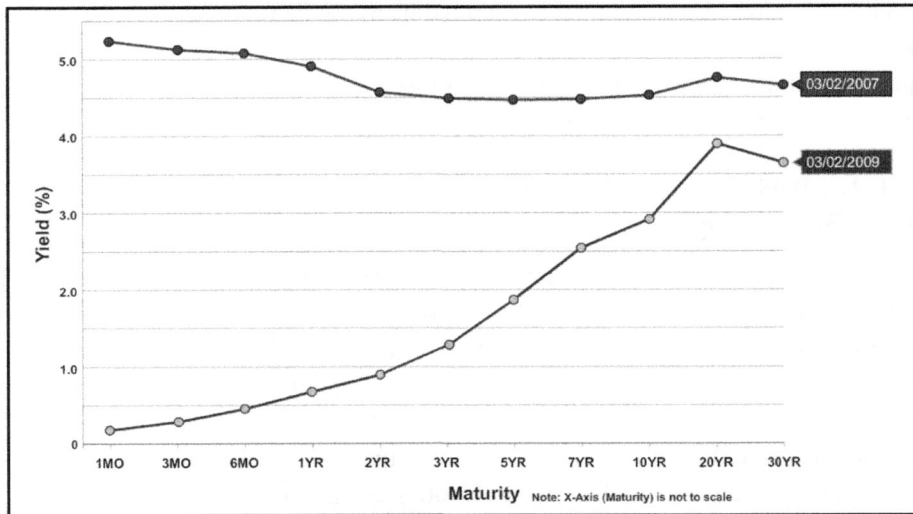

FIGURE 18.13 Examples of an Inverted and Upward-Sloping Treasury Yield Curve.
Source: treasury.gov.

(meaning that short rates are higher than long rates). This occurs because a decline in any of expected future 1-year interest rates on the right-hand side of Equations 18.1 and 18.2 will cause the long-term interest rate on the left-hand side to fall.

Figure 18.13 depicts two yield curves, the first from March 2007, immediately preceding the onset of the 2008–2009 recession, and the second from March 2009, the period in which the most recent economic expansion began (www.treasury .gov). The 2007 yield curve is inverted because short-term interest rates are higher than long-term rates. This inversion of the yield curve signals recession because bond traders reason that economic weakness will reduce the demand for borrowed funds, which would make future interest rates fall as investors desire less credit (interest rates are the price of credit). Traders therefore find it rational to buy long-term bonds now and lock in higher interest rates before they decline. This increased demand raises bond prices and reduces bond yields.

The yield curve regains its upward slope as traders look to the future and anticipate when the worst of the economic weakness will pass and the economy will begin expanding again. This can be seen in the March 2009 yield curve in Figure 2.13. The yield curve has an upward slope prior to and during economic expansions because investors expect future interest rates to rise as the demand for borrowed funds increases during expansionary periods. This increased demand for borrowed funds results in upward pressure on interest rates as lenders raise the price of credit. Traders therefore sell bonds because they know that the expected increase in interest rates will cause bond prices to fall. As traders sell, bond prices fall and rates rise in sync with investors' expectations.

Figure 18.14 depicts the official Conference Board indicator, the spread between the 10-year T-note yield and the Fed Funds rate. When the interest rate spread in the graph is increasing, the yield on the 10-year T-note is increasing faster than the Fed

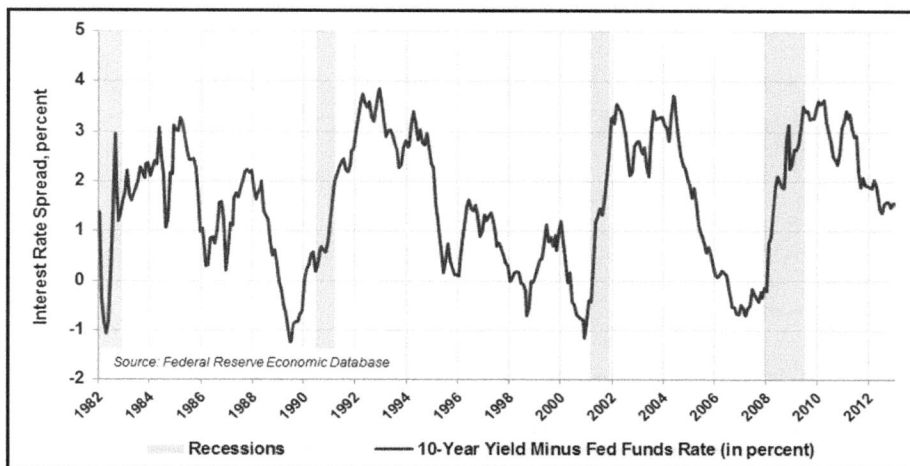

FIGURE 18.14   Interest Rate Spread: 10-Year T-Note Yield Minus Fed Funds Rate.

Funds rate, and when the interest rate spread is decreasing, the yield on the 10-year T-note is decreasing faster than the Fed Funds rate. When the yield spread falls below zero, the short-term Fed Funds rate is greater than the yield on the 10-year T-note. Figure 18.14 shows that full inversions of the yield curve such as this have reliably signaled the last four recessions.

Figure 18.14 also shows that the yield spread peaked at 3.5% in early 2010, after the official recession ended, but has fallen to only 1.5% in late 2012, indicating that the Treasury yield curve has been steadily flattening throughout the most recent economic expansion. Due to the Federal Reserve's efforts at pegging the Fed Funds rate as close to zero as possible, this means that the yield curve is not technically inverted, however, so the indicator is signaling only an economic slowdown rather than an outright recession.

LE-5. Manufacturers' New Orders for Consumer Goods and Materials (weight = 8.1%)

The rationale behind this indicator is straightforward: If consumers are willing to commit to larger-ticket purchases, known as durable goods (because the items last longer than one year), they are probably feeling more confident about future economic activity.

Figure 18.15 depicts manufacturers' new orders for durable goods from 1992 to 2012. Both the nominal and real (inflation-adjusted) series are displayed. It's easy to see how these large-ticket purchases fall sharply preceding recessions, particularly the 2008–2009 recession. The graph also shows that new orders for durable goods rebounded during the most recent economic expansion, which sends a positive signal regarding future economic activity. This trend reverses and declines for most of 2012, however, which bears close watching. The longer-term trend in real durable goods orders is more concerning, as the series peaks at lower highs in 2007 and 2011 before beginning its 2012 decline.

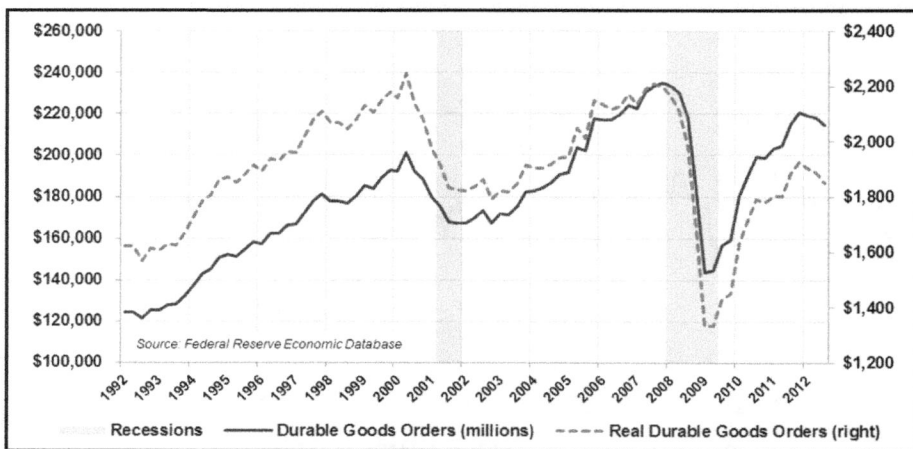

FIGURE 18.15 Nominal and Real Durable Goods Orders.

LE-6. Chicago Federal Reserve's National Credit Conditions Index (weight = 7.9%)

We are once again substituting a free publicly available indicator (the Chicago Federal Reserve Bank's National Credit Conditions Index) for The Conference Board's new Leading Credit Index™, which is available only via subscription. The Chicago Fed index is also a diffusion index, but instead of being anchored around a neutral value of 50, in this case the anchoring point is zero. A value below zero indicates "loose" financial conditions, meaning that as the index value declines, borrowing conditions are getting easier, and as the index climbs above zero, borrowing conditions are getting tighter.

Figure 18.16 depicts the Chicago Fed's Financial Conditions Index. This indicator climbs steeply during the mid-2000s and peaks during the onset of the 2008 financial crisis and recession. The index declines during recessions and continues falling early

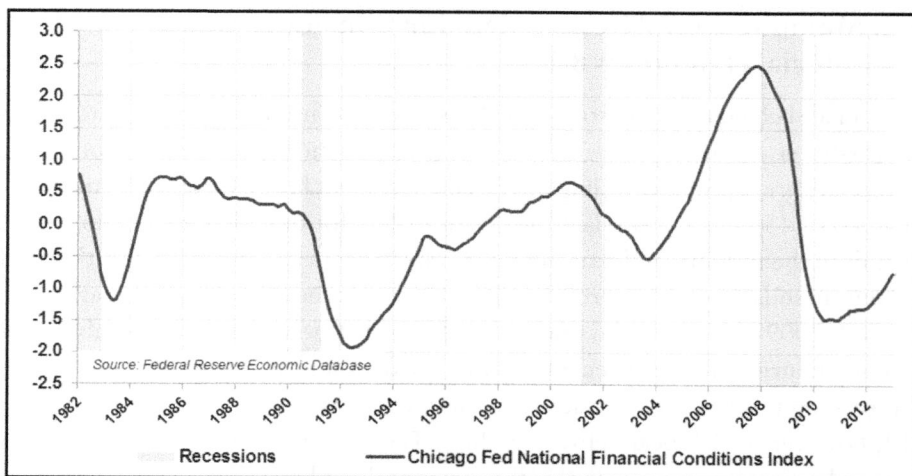

FIGURE 18.16 Chicago Fed National Financial Conditions Index.

in economic recoveries as the U.S. Federal Reserve keeps the Fed Funds rate low and engages in other activities that promote easy access to credit. The index begins rising after expansions gain traction and are more self-sustaining and the Federal Reserve reduces its efforts to stimulate borrowing. The current level of −0.7 indicates that borrowing conditions remain relatively easy in the United States, suggesting there are few factors impeding consumers' and businesses' access to credit. Conditions have tightened only slightly since the index reached its most recent trough in early 2010.

LE-7. Stock Prices, S&P 500 Index (weight = 3.8%)

It has long been thought that the stock market is a forward-looking "discounting" mechanism, where stock returns anticipate changes in economic conditions six to nine months ahead. As with many of the longer time series analyzed in this chapter, we will consider both nominal and real values of the S&P 500 index.

Figure 18.17 shows that the nominal S&P 500 declines in advance of the 1991 and 2001 recessions, but it continues falling well past the business cycle trough in 2001, and thus fails to predict the economic expansion. Stock values don't do a great job of anticipating the 2008–2009 recession, either, which seems to have taken investors by surprise, although stocks turn sharply upward in March 2009, several months before the end of the last recession. In terms of calling recent expansions and recessions, the stock market deserves only mixed reviews. The strong performance of stocks from 2009 to 2012 forecasts continued economic expansion.

Examining the real value of the index reveals additional interesting information. The U.S. stock market has been in what's known as a "secular" bear market (spanning multiple business cycles) for the past 12 years. The bull markets from 2003 to 2007 and 2009 to 2012 are what's known as "cyclical" bulls: run-ups associated with increases in business cycle activity. But the longer bear trend is what's known as a "secular" bear, one that spans several ups and downs of the business cycle.

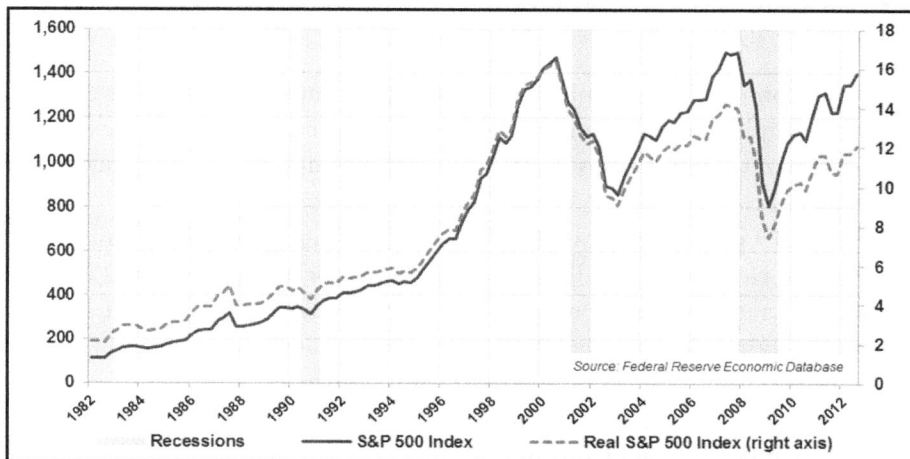

FIGURE 18.17 Nominal and Real S&P 500 Index.

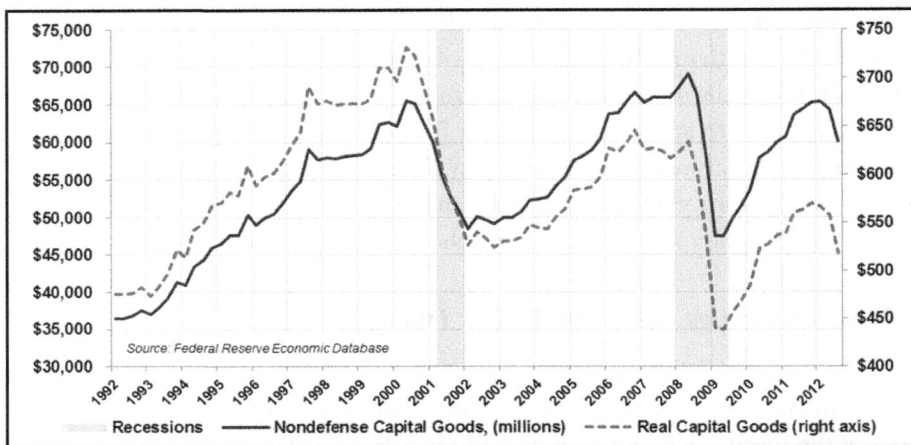

FIGURE 18.18 Nominal and Real Nondefense Capital Goods Orders (ex-aircraft).

LE-8. Manufacturers' New Orders, Nondefense Capital Goods (weight = 3.6%)

Capital goods are the long-lived assets in which businesses invest. Increased long-term investment by businesses signals optimism for the U.S. economy. Figure 18.18 depicts both the nominal and real time series of capital goods orders. Although nominal capital goods orders peak at a new high early in the 2008 recession, the real (inflation-adjusted) series falls short of its all-time record in 2000. The real capital goods series peaks at the end of 2011, although this peak was considerably lower than the level achieved in 2008. The series has contracted for most of 2012. U.S. businesses have not increased capital investment over the past 12 years. Real capital spending remains in a long-term decline (because business spending on capital goods has been increasing more slowly than the rate of inflation). The series behaves similarly to the nominal and real S&P 500 index.

LE-9. Average Weekly Claims for Unemployment Insurance (weight = 3.3%)

When the economy is weakening, business lay off more workers and initial filings for unemployment insurance increase. Conversely, economic expansions are characterized by increases in employment and decreases in unemployment insurance claims.

Figure 18.19 depicts the four-week moving average of initial unemployment claims. This series worked well as a leading indicator before the 1990 and 2001 recessions, increasing sharply many months before the official start of each economic contraction. Notice that initial unemployment claims do not decrease prior to the start of each economic expansion, however, but function more like coincident indicators as the economy transitions from contraction to expansion. Further notice that initial claims did not increase significantly in anticipation of the 2008–2009 recession.

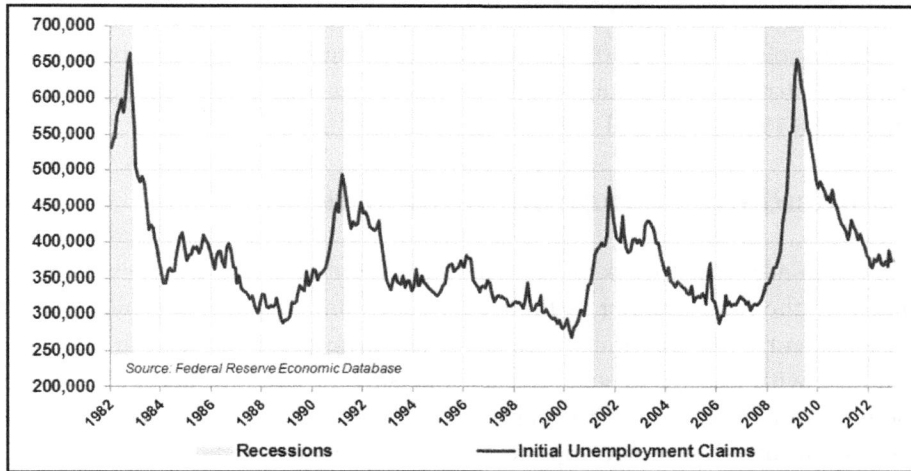

FIGURE 18.19 Average Weekly Claims for Unemployment Insurance.

Although the U.S. economy is currently several years into an expansionary mode, new initial unemployment claims remain close to the key level of 400,000, which is generally regarded as recessionary. The pace of layoffs remains elevated, considering the U.S. economy is supposed to be several years into an expansionary phase.

LE-10. Building Permits, New Private Housing Units (weight = 2.7%)

This indicator is thought to be predictive of future building activity. An increase in the number of permits for new private housing signals optimism on the part of homebuilders and prospective buyers. A decrease in the number of permits signals pessimism.

Figure 18.20 depicts new building permits since 1982. The series generally functions well as a leading indicator, with the exception of the 2001 recession, when

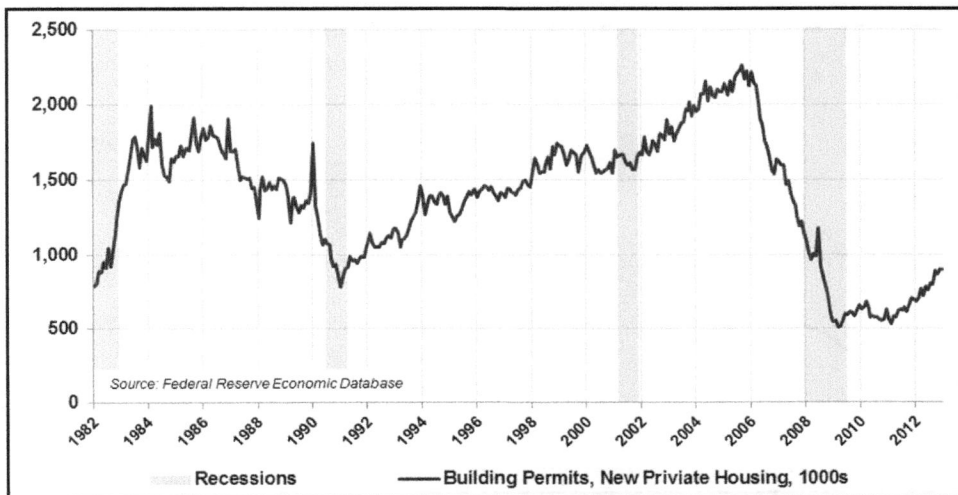

FIGURE 18.20 Building Permits for New Private Housing.

it failed to decline significantly. This indicator began plunging as early as 2006, finally reaching bottom in early 2009. Although new private housing permits have been rising since that time, the number of permits remains at lows associated with the depths of the 1981–1982 and 1991 recessions.

■ Coincident Economic Indicators

The Conference Board tracks four coincident indicators and averages them into an index in the same manner as the leading economic index. This index is called the Coincident Economic Index® (CEI). Changes in these variables are expected to coincide with changes in economic activity, so your diffusion index rankings for these indicators will be used to gauge the strength and resilience of current economic conditions. The four components of the coincident index and The Conference Board's recommended weights are shown in Figure 18.21.

It's interesting to note that the first two components of the CEI, manufacturing and trade sales and total nonfarm payrolls, make up 79% of The Conference Board's weighted index. This suggests that one can get a reasonably accurate indication of the strength of current economic conditions by merely consulting the trend in and current level of total sales and total employment.

Figure 18.22 depicts the Coincident Economic Index®. The index generally turns at the beginning of recessions and expansions, although it led slightly heading into

Coincident Indicators	Score	Weight
Manufacturing and Trade Sales		0.5318
Total Nonfarm Payrolls		0.2597
Personal Income Less Transfer Payments		0.1357
Industrial Production		0.0728

FIGURE 18.21   The Conference Board's Coincident Indicators.

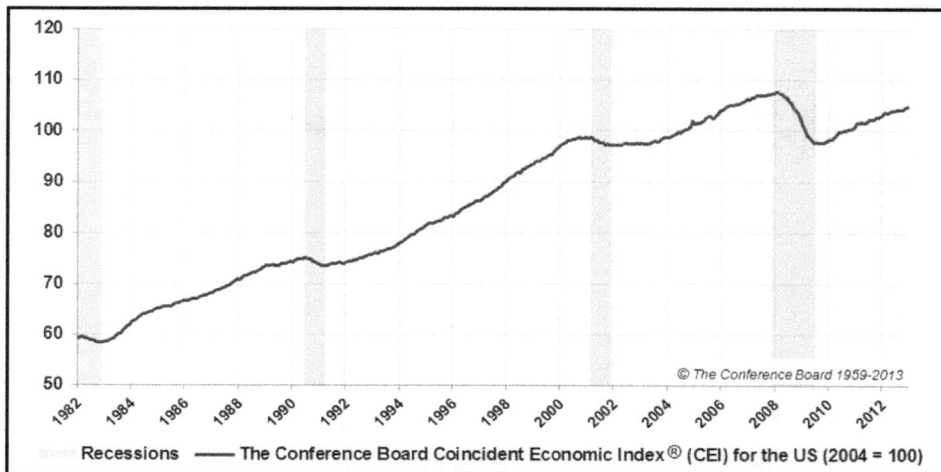

© The Conference Board 1959-2013

Recessions ——— The Conference Board Coincident Economic Index® (CEI) for the US (2004 = 100)

FIGURE 18.22   The Conference Board's Coincident Economic Index® for the United States, 1982–2013.

the 2001 recession. It has risen steadily since the end of the 2008–2009 recession, indicating that the United States remains in an economic expansion. Next, we'll consider each individual component of the CEI.

CO-1. Nominal and Real Total Retail Sales (weight = 53.2%)

Once again, we are using the closest match from the FRED database, substituting total retail sales including food services for The Conference Board's manufacturing and trade sales indicator. The total retail sales series has a straightforward interpretation: when total sales are rising, consumers and businesses feel more confident about current (and probably future) economic activity, and vice versa when sales are falling.

Figure 18.23 depicts the nominal and real total retail sales series. Notice how the upward trajectory of real retail sales changes to a sideways trend in anticipation of the 2001 and 2008–2009 recessions. Further notice the plunge in both series during the 2008–2009 recession and the slow, gradual recovery of this key indicator. Total real retail sales at the end of 2012 have finally regained their level from December 2007, which helps bring into perspective just how severe a setback the most recent recession dealt to the U.S. (and global) economy.

CO-2. Employees on Nonagricultural Payrolls (weight = 26.0%)

Total nonfarm payrolls measures the total number of people in the United States with a job, full- or part-time, temporary or permanent. This indicator is closely watched by investors. When employment is rising, it signals a bullish attitude on the part of both businesses and consumers, and vice versa when the economy is shedding jobs and layoffs are increasing. Nonfarm payrolls is depicted in Figure 18.24.

The series functions well as a coincident indicator, rising during economic expansions and falling during economic contractions. As has been the case with many of the indicators, the 2008–2009 recession resulted in a large reduction in the number of employed persons in the United States. The series has yet to regain its peak level, which occurred in early 2008.

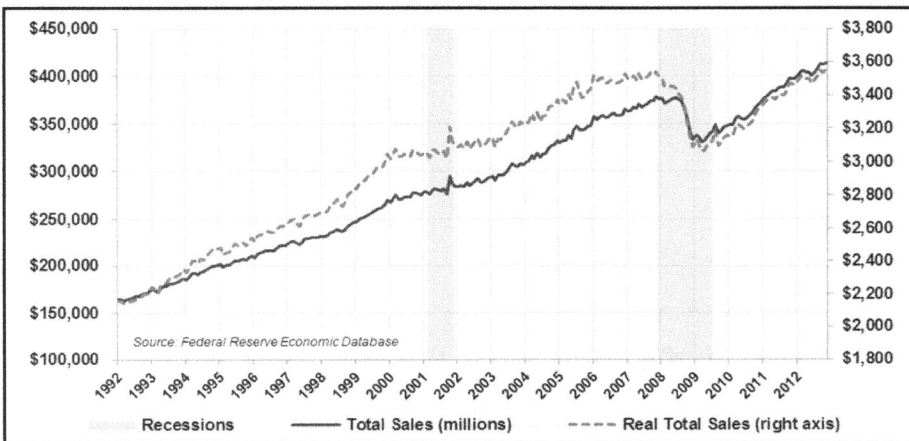

FIGURE 18.23 Nominal and Real Retail and Food Service Sales.

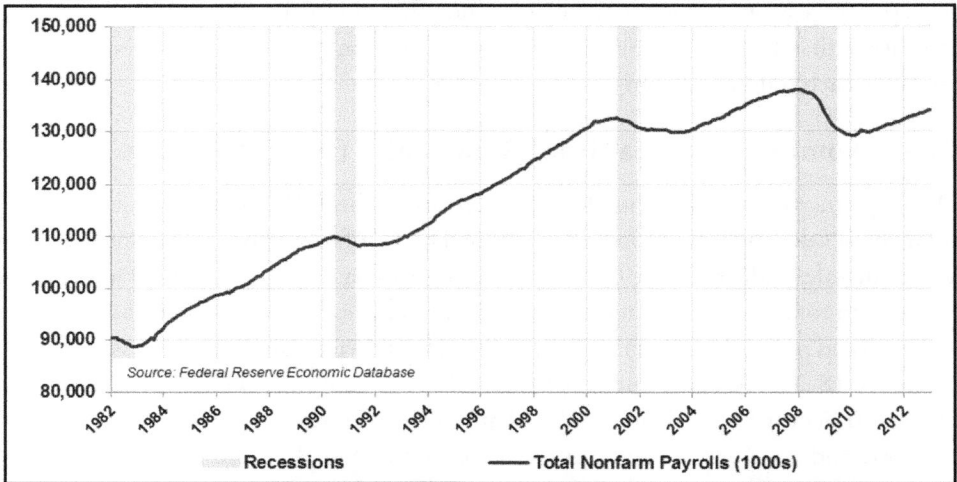

FIGURE 18.24   Total Nonfarm Payrolls.

CO-3. Personal Income Less Transfer Payments (weight = 13.6%)

With its consumer-driven economy, U.S. GDP grows by a greater amount when consumers spend freely. Personal income is the main source of consumer spending. Transfer payments are redistributions of tax revenue by the government, including Social Security, welfare, and business subsidies. Personal income less transfer payments measures the extent to which incomes in the United States are growing from market-based sources, excluding any government redistribution of income. The series is depicted in Figure 18.25.

The series worked well as a coincident indicator until the 2008–2009 recession, when it lagged changes in economic conditions by several months. Personal income less transfer payments has achieved new all-time highs every year since

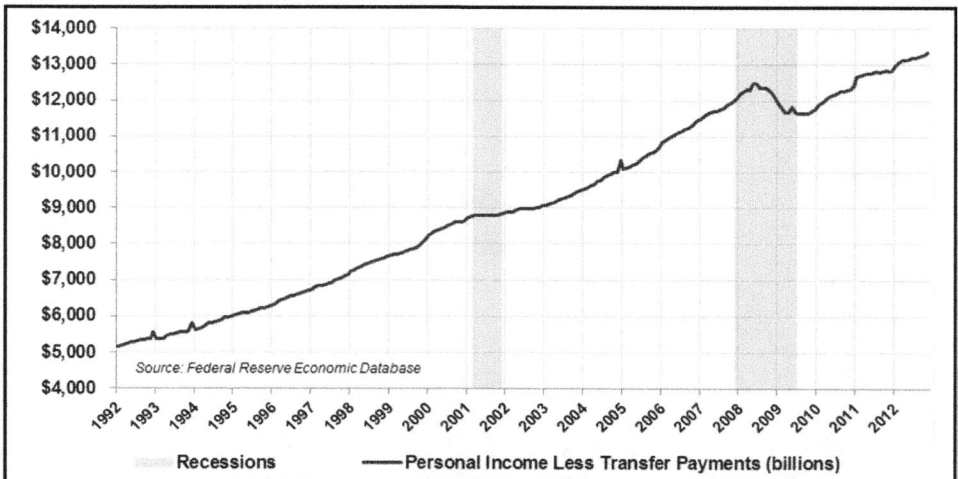

FIGURE 18.25   Personal Income Less Transfer Payments.

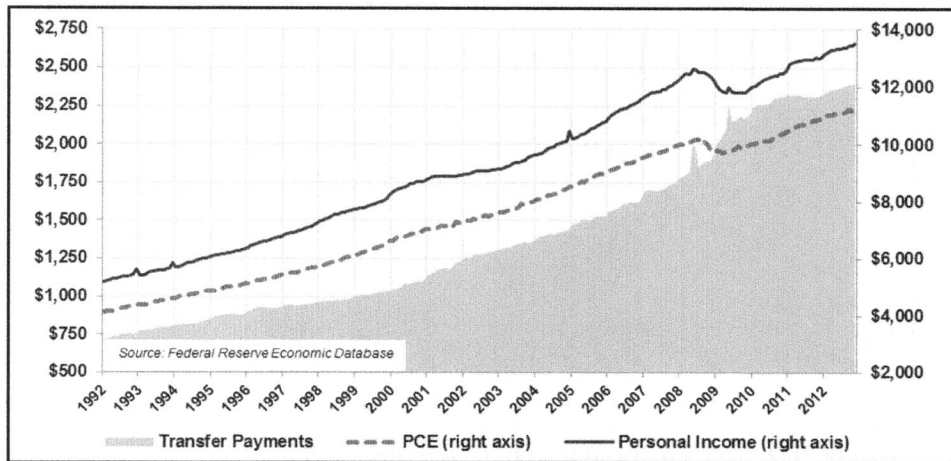

FIGURE 18.26 Transfer Payments, Personal Income, and Personal Consumption Expenditures.

the end of the last recession. Figure 18.26 takes a closer look at personal income, personal consumption expenditures (PCEs—the total amount of *spending* by consumers), and transfer payments. Notice how personal income and PCEs dip during the last recession, while transfer payments increase and grow along a higher trajectory until recently, as the U.S. federal government has finally slowed the rate at which it is redistributing income. The abrupt peaks in transfer payments associated with the federal government stimulus programs in May 2008 and May 2009 are easy to discern in the graph. The key question for the personal income less transfers indicator is how well consumer spending (PCE) will hold up if the federal government begins reducing transfer payments in the future, a move that is widely expected.

CO-4. Index of Industrial Production (weight = 7.3%)

The index of industrial production measures physical output at all stages of production in the manufacturing, mining, and gas and electric utility industries. Although the industrial sector represents only a fraction of the total U.S. economy, this index is thought to have a strong positive correlation with changes in total output. Both the nominal and real values of the index are depicted in Figure 18.27.

The nominal series works well as a coincident indicator, increasing and decreasing in sync with economic expansions and contractions, although it led the onset of the 2001 recession. Note that the inflation-adjusted industrial production index fails to increase during the 2002–2007 expansion, although it decreases sharply with the 2008–2009 recession, and rebounds weakly before resuming its sideways trend. This suggests that total industrial output in the United States has grown more slowly than the rate of inflation since the beginning of the twenty-first century.

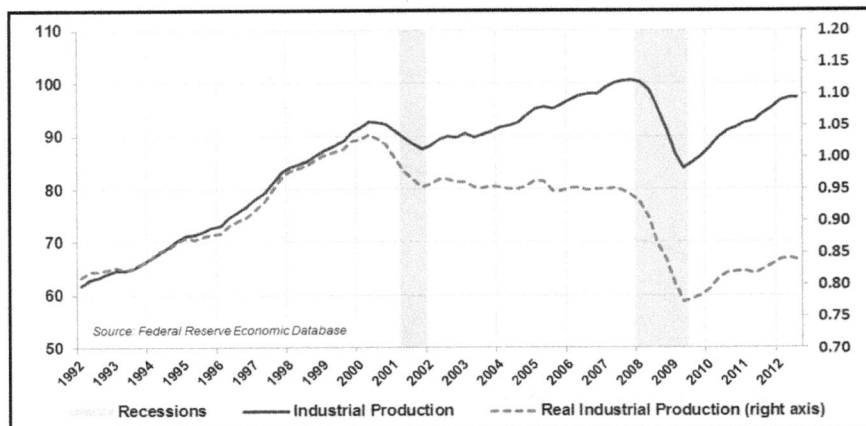

FIGURE 18.27 Nominal and Real Industrial Production.

Lagging Economic Indicators

The Conference Board tracks seven lagging indicators that are thought to change *after* changes in economic activity. These indicators are backward-looking, or corroborative, and are thus used to confirm the recent strength or weakness of economic activity. The Lagging Economic Index® (LAG) and the weights assigned to each indicator by The Conference Board are shown in Figure 18.28.

Figure 18.29 depicts the Lagging Economic Index®. The index generally reacts after the start of recessions and expansions, although it behaves more like a leading index heading into the 2001 recession. The index's steady upward trajectory since the end of the last recession confirms that the U.S. economy has been in an expansionary phase. Next, we'll review the seven components of the lagging index.

LA-1. Average Prime Rate (weight = 28.2%)

The average prime interest rate, depicted in Figure 18.30, is a benchmark interest rate used by lenders for setting the interest rates at which new loans are created. Highly creditworthy businesses and individuals might borrow at "prime minus 1," while less creditworthy borrowers might pay prime plus 1 to 2%, or more, depending on circumstances. The indicator trails the economy as banks adjust the price of credit. Once

Lagging Indicators	Score	Weight
Average Prime Rate		0.2815
Consumer Credit to Personal Income		0.2101
Consumer Price Index for Services		0.1955
Inventory to Sales, Manufacturing		0.1211
Commercial and Industrial Loans		0.0970
Unit Labor Cost, Manufacturing		0.0587
Average Duration of Unemployment		0.0361

FIGURE 18.28 The Conference Board's Lagging Indicators.

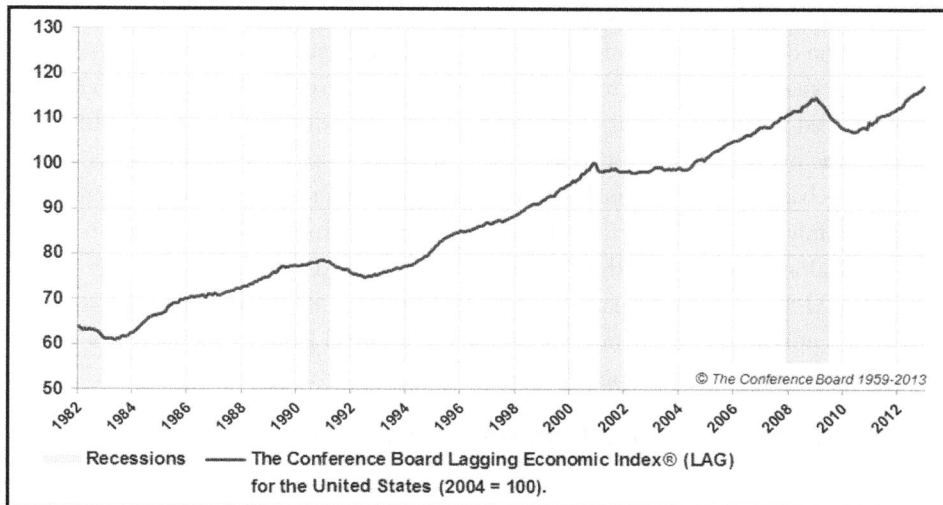

FIGURE 18.29 The Conference Board's Index of Lagging Economic Indicators.

the economy has been expanding for a while, and the demand for credit is growing, banks can mark up the price of credit and charge more. After the economy has slowed, and demand for credit weakens, banks need to put credit "on sale" to attract new borrowers, and interest rates fall. Total commercial and industrial loans are also depicted in the graph, because The Conference Board's Lagging Economic Index considers only the *level* of the interest rate; it does not consider whether total loans outstanding are expanding or contracting. Simply having low interest rates for a protracted period of time is not necessarily expansionary in and of itself—if new credit is not being created as a result of low rates, the economy has probably not been expanding robustly.

The first thing to notice in Figure 18.30 is that the bank prime rate has been in a secular downtrend for 30 years, declining with the general decrease in inflation and interest rates over the same period. Further notice that the prime rate acts more like a leading

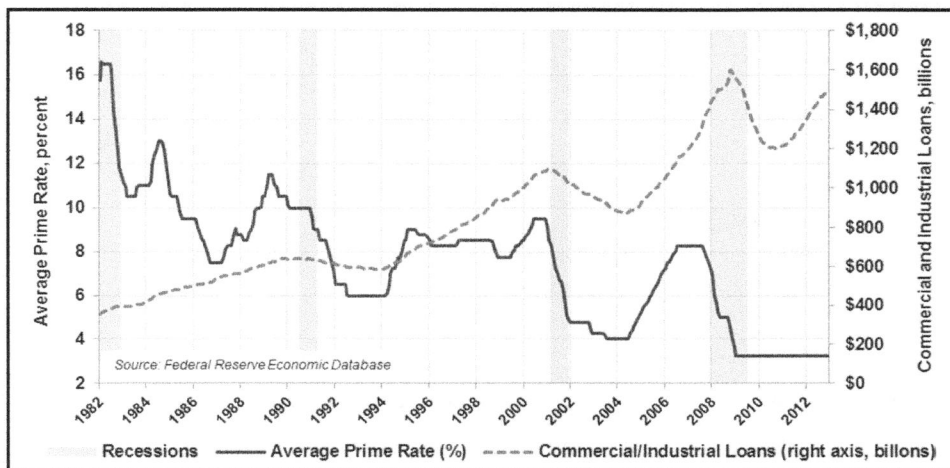

FIGURE 18.30 Average Prime Rate and Commercial and Industrial Loans.

indicator heading into recessions, as the U.S. Federal Reserve begins cutting interest rates in anticipation of future economic weakness. During the last three expansions, the prime rate functions as a lagging indicator, increasing well after the end of the previous recession. Due to the Fed's commitment to a zero interest rate policy (ZIRP) since the 2008–2009 recession, the prime rate has yet to increase. This suggests past and continued economic weakness, as banks have been unable to raise the price of credit. Low interest rates have almost certainly contributed to the rebound in commercial and industrial loans, however. Considered alone, the fact that the prime rate has not increased would fail to corroborate the current U.S. economic expansion. Considered along with the Fed's aggressive low interest rate policy and the strong rebound in commercial lending, the indicator's signal can be interpreted somewhat more positively.

LA-2. Ratio of Consumer Installment Credit/Personal Income (weight = 21.0%)

The ratio of consumer credit to personal income, depicted as Figure 18.31, behaves like a lagging indicator because consumers wait to increase borrowing for at least several months after a recession ends, when they can see tangible signs of economic recovery. Additionally, this ratio tends to reach a trough after personal income has risen for a year or longer, as consumers try to maintain a balance between their income and debt levels.

The ratio functions well as a lagging indicator around the 1981–1982 and 1991–1992 recessions, but the credit bubble that formed during the 2000s makes interpreting the current value of the series more challenging. Recall that personal income less transfer payments began a sharp decrease early in the 2008–2009 recession (Figure 18.25). As seen in Figure 18.31, consumers offset this loss of income during the latter part of the recession by increasing borrowing relative to income. Once the recovery begins, the ratio declines as incomes grow and consumers reduce debt. More recently, the series has resumed an upward trajectory, which suggests that personal income has grown to the point that consumers feel comfortable increasing their total borrowing once again.

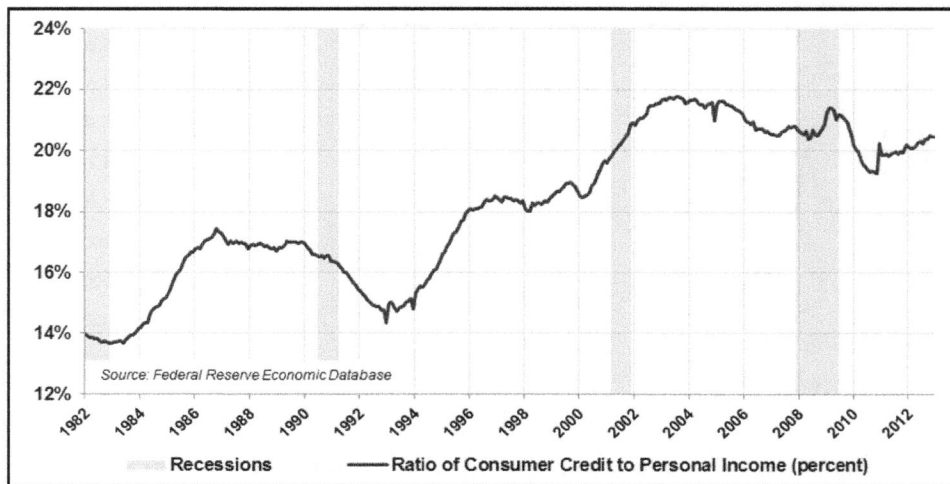

FIGURE 18.31 Ratio of Consumer Credit to Personal Income.

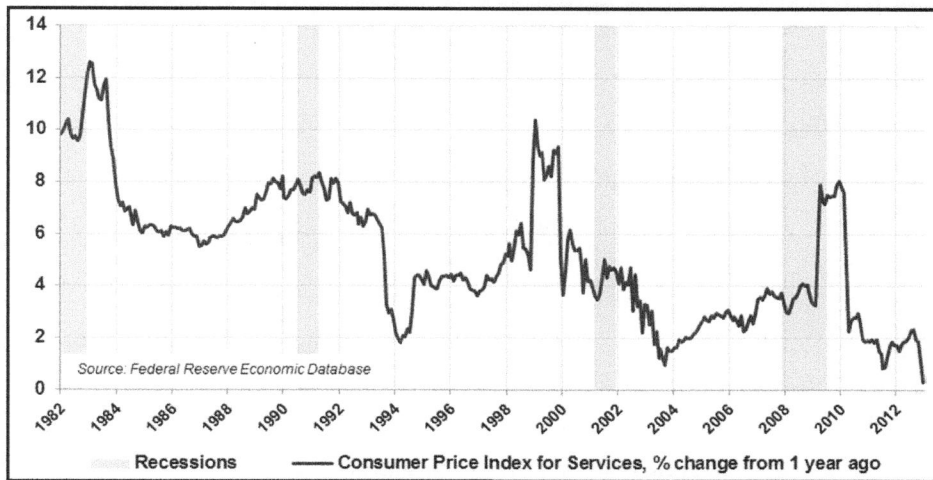

FIGURE 18.32   Consumer Price Index for Services.

LA-3. Consumer Price Index for Services (weight = 19.6%)

Service sector inflation, depicted as Figure 18.32, is expected to increase several months after the start of a recession, and decrease several months after the start of an expansion. This inflation measure displays a long-term decline, along with the general level of inflation and interest rates. The service sector CPI works well as a lagging indicator, and has decreased sharply during the most recent expansion, which corroborates that the U.S. economy has been in an expansionary phase.

LA-4. Inventory to Sales Ratio, Manufacturing and Trade (weight = 12.6%)

The ratio tends to peak in the middle of a recession, as businesses find it harder to sell existing inventory. The ratio declines during periods of economic expansion.

The secular downtrend in the inventory to sales ratio is evident in Figure 18.33, driven by continuous improvement in supply chain management and just-in-time inventory practices. The dramatic peak in the series midway through the previous recession is driven by the precipitous decline in retail sales (Figure 18.23). The ratio quickly snaps back to its pre-recessionary levels shortly after the end of the recession, which confirms that the U.S. economy remained in an economic expansion during 2012.

LA-5. Commercial and Industrial Loans (weight = 9.7%)

Total commercial and industrial loans are depicted in Figure 18.34, along with total consumer credit. Total business loans are expected to peak after an expansion (as declining profits increase the need for borrowed funds). Troughs usually occur a year or more after a recession ends. Both consumer and business credit continue expanding following their post-recessionary trough, which provides further confirmation that the U.S. economy has been in an expansionary phase.

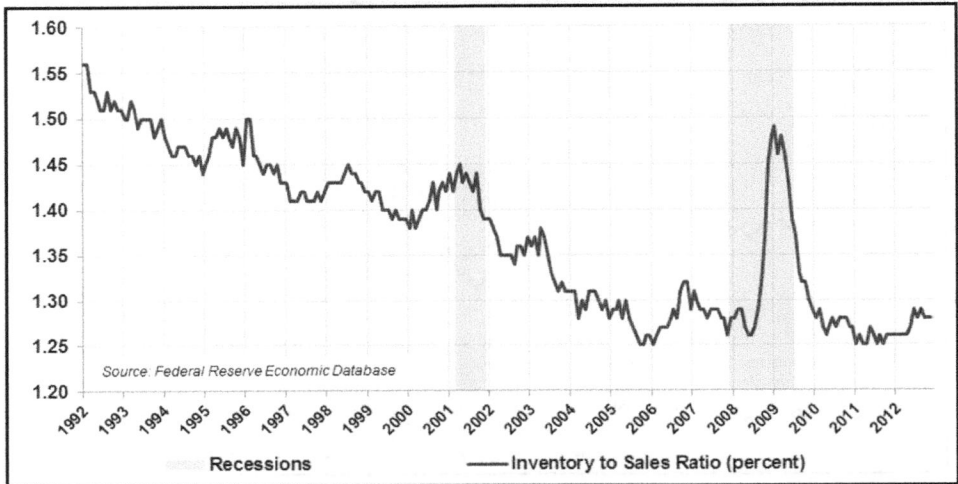

FIGURE 18.33   Inventory to Sales Ratio.

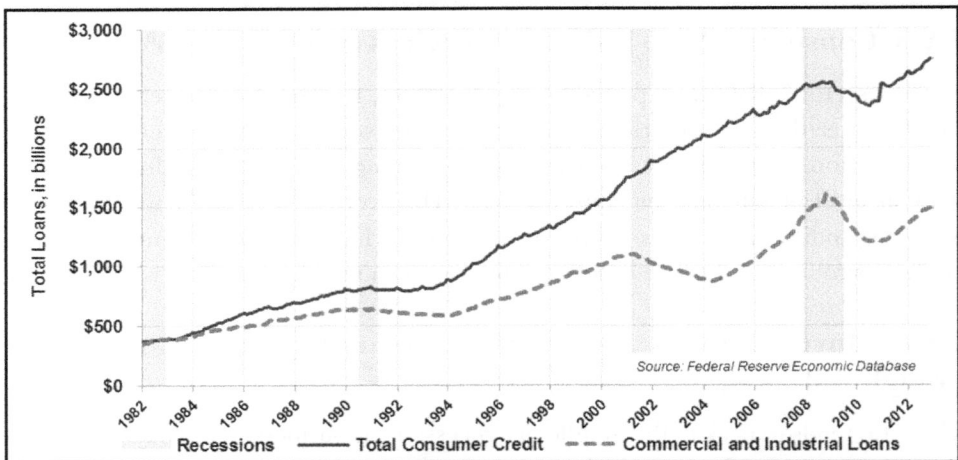

FIGURE 18.34   Total Consumer Credit and Commercial and Industrial Loans.

LA-6. Unit Labor Cost, Manufacturing (weight = 6.2%)

Unit labor costs are expected to peak midway through a recession, then decline or trend sideways until several months into the next economic expansion. Troughs are more difficult to identify and characterize. Nominal and real unit labor costs are depicted in Figure 18.35.

The long-term nominal and real series tell two different stories. The nominal series indicates that unit labor costs rose from 1992 to 2008, before leveling off in mid-2008. This would suggest U.S. businesses have had to accommodate and adapt to higher wage demands from workers. The real series is in a long-term downtrend, however, suggesting that these cost increases have been slower than the rate of inflation. The sideways trend in the nominal series since 2010 suggests an advantage for U.S. businesses, as this is the longest period in at least the past 20 years when unit labor costs have failed to increase significantly during a period of economic expansion.

THE INTEGRATION OF TECHNICAL ANALYSIS

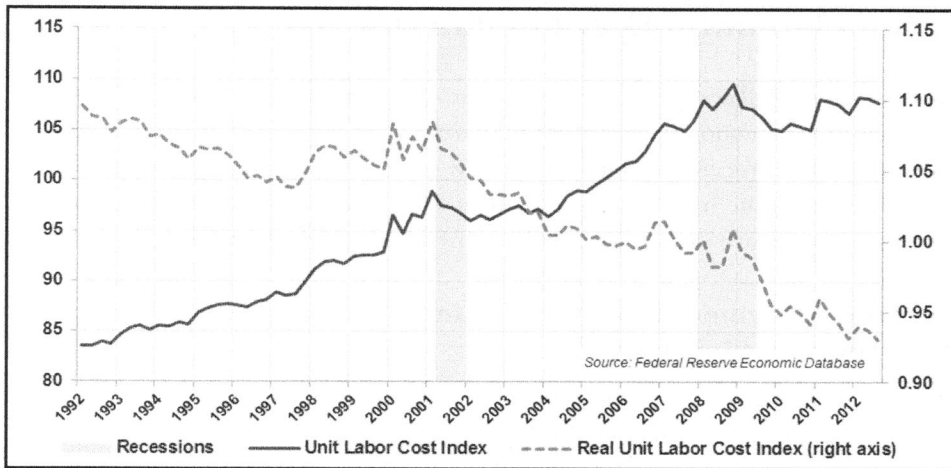

FIGURE 18.35 Nominal and Real Unit Labor Costs.

LA-7. Average Duration of Unemployment (weight = 3.7%)

Decreases in the average duration of unemployment tend to occur after an economic recovery gains traction and employers begin hiring in earnest. The series is graphed along with the labor force participation rate in Figure 18.36, which measures the percentage of the U.S. population that is working either full or part time or actively seeking work. (Note that FRED reports the median duration, rather than the mean.)

The length of time it takes laid off workers to find new employment remains elevated at a median duration of 18 weeks, which is significantly longer than its peak of 11 weeks following the 2001–2002 recession. Further note the decade-long downtrend in the U.S. labor force participation rate, which nosedives as unemployment duration skyrockets. The persistently high level of this indicator casts doubt on the robustness of the economic expansion that began in 2009.

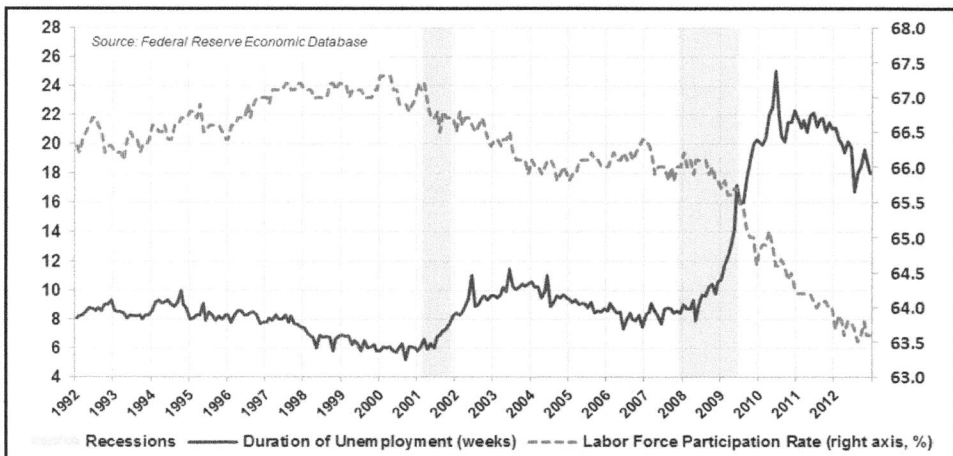

FIGURE 18.36 Duration of Unemployment and Labor Force Participation Rate.

■ Supplemental Economic Indicators

In this section we'll complete our view of the macro-finance environment by considering additional economic indicators that are widely discussed and have influenced investor attitudes recently. I'll interpret a few of my favorites. It's recommended that you customize your macro-finance analysis with some of your own supplemental indicators, which are easy to identify by browsing the FRED database.

S-1. Unemployment Rate and U6 Unemployment Plus Underemployment Rate

This indicator is displayed in Figure 18.37. The official unemployment rate doesn't count discouraged workers—unemployed individuals who have stopped looking for work altogether. Discouraged workers have become a much larger component of the United States' potential workforce since the end of the last recession. The U6 series is an "underemployment" rate, measuring the percentage of the population that is either unemployed, underemployed, or so discouraged that they have stopped looking for work altogether. The U.S. economy will find it difficult to sustain robust, rapid growth until more jobs are created.

S-2. Inflation

Figure 18.38 depicts the core consumer and producer price indexes, which measure inflation on the retail and wholesale levels, respectively. Core inflation measures exclude the effects of changing food and energy prices, which are excessively volatile and make the inflation series harder to interpret. Although inflation has declined for most of 2012, the core CPI remains above 4.0%, which is unacceptably high according to Federal Reserve standards. The Fed's loose monetary policy is expected to contribute further to rising inflation in coming years.

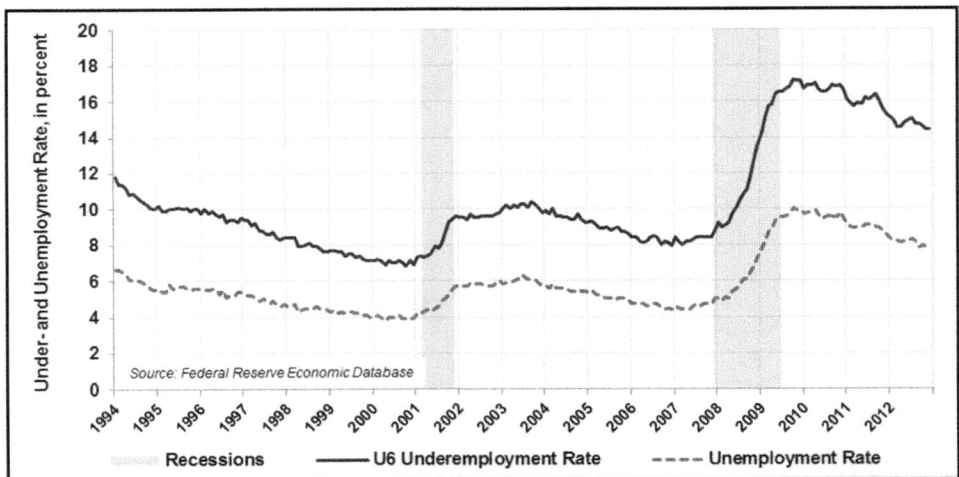

FIGURE 18.37 U6 Underemployment and Unemployment Rate.

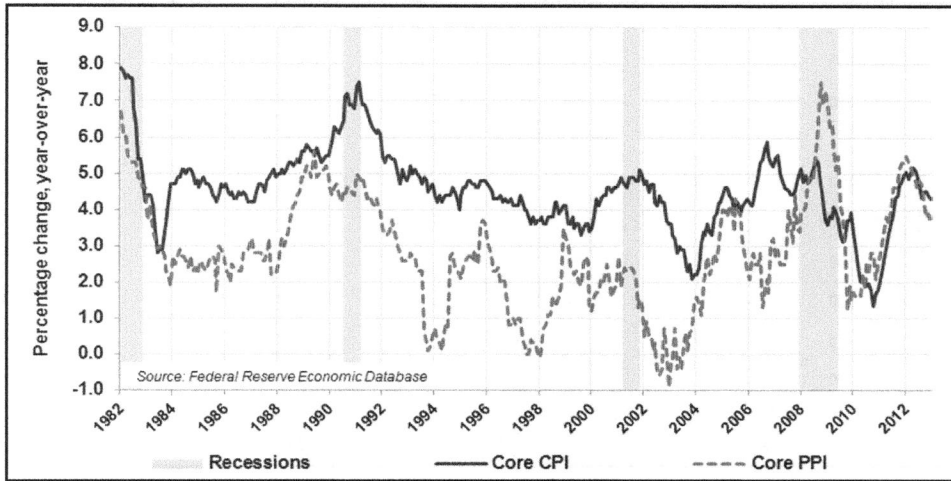

FIGURE 18.38 Consumer and Producer Price Indexes Ex-Food and Energy.

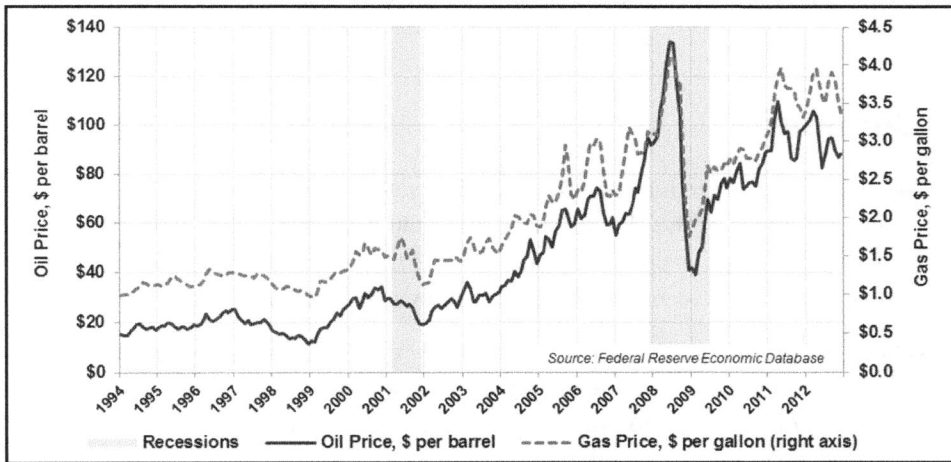

FIGURE 18.39 Gas and Oil Prices (West Texas Intermediate Crude).

S-3. Oil and Gas Prices

Rising energy prices act like a tax increase on businesses and consumers—there's less to spend on other things when more has to be spent on energy. Oil and gas prices are depicted in Figure 18.39.

S-4. Total U.S. Federal Debt and the U.S. Debt/GDP Ratio

For much of 2010–2012, the civilized world teetered on the edge over the *European* debt/banking crisis, while the United States—the world's alleged "safe haven"—faces its own severe debt problem.

Why does excessive debt matter? In their landmark study (which has recently faced substantial criticism), Rogoff and Reinhart (2009) show that nations' economies grow more slowly when their debt-to-GDP ratio exceeds 100%. Figure 18.40

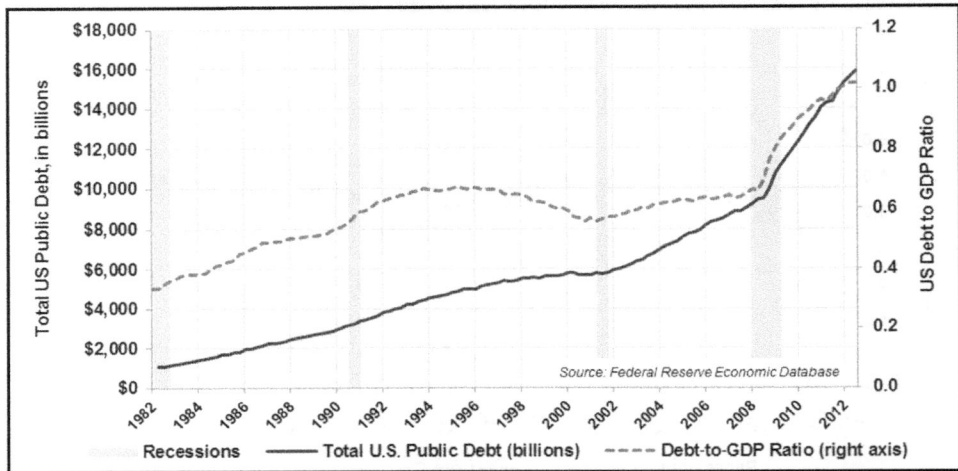

FIGURE 18.40 Total U.S. Public Debt and Debt-to-GDP Ratio.

shows that, as of early 2012, the United States surpassed the key 100% debt-to-GDP ratio.

Summary

- The business cycle tends to lead the financial cycle by six to nine months on average. Gauging the stage of the U.S. business cycle and mapping to the likely point in the financial cycle helps an analyst identify sectors to under- and overweight in pursuit of market-beating returns. This process is known as sector rotation.

- When analyzing long time series of economic data, it's important to consider the real (inflation-adjusted) values of the series, so that the genuine economic improvement or deterioration of the series can be easily identified.

- Economists often average the change in or ranking of economic time series into indicators known as diffusion indexes.

- Some of the most widely followed economic and business cycle indicators are grouped into leading, coincident and lagging diffusion indexes (that change before, in sync with, and after economic conditions) by The Conference Board.

- In addition to observing the trend in The Conference Board's indexes, examining the individual components of the indexes helps an analyst see more deeply into economic conditions and trends.

Questions

This chapter's learning activities require interpreting each individual component of The Conference Board's leading, coincident, and lagging indexes according to the business writing guidelines provided in the chapter. Next, these written descriptions

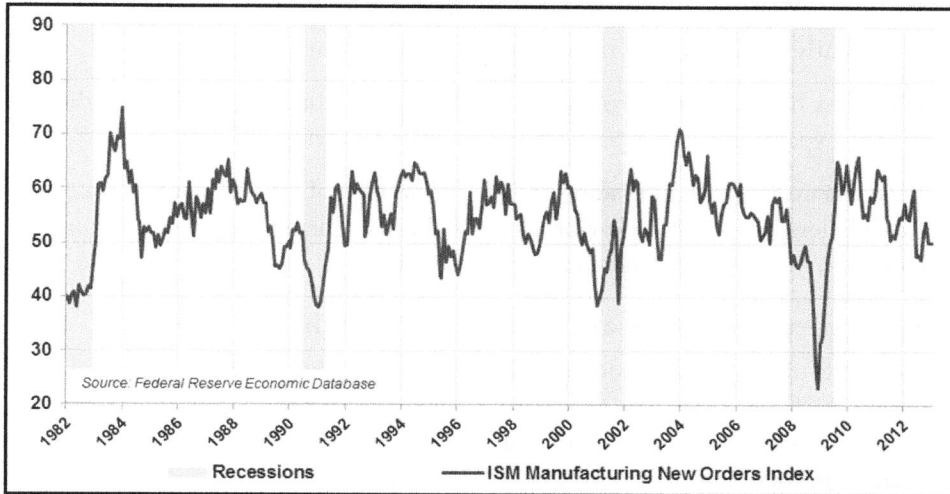

FIGURE 18.41   ISM New Manufacturing Orders Index.

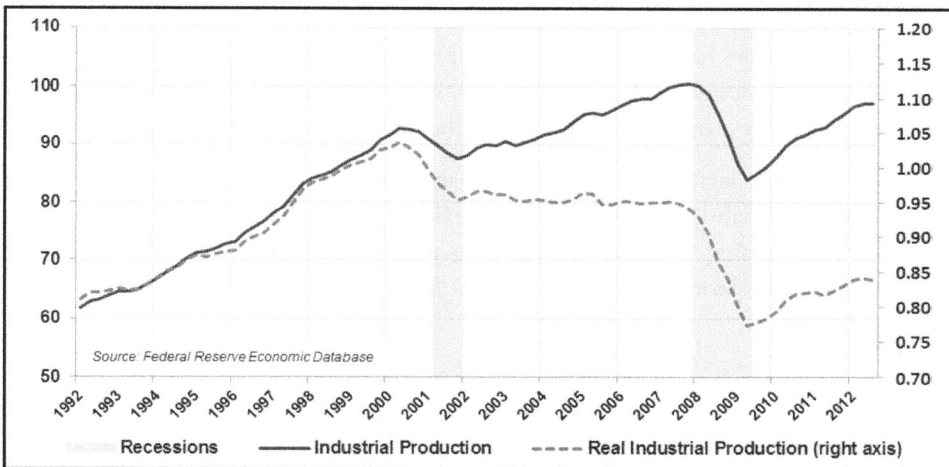

FIGURE 18.42   Nominal and Real Industrial Production.

should be synthesized into a −1, 0, or +1 ranking using the Ch02-Scorecard companion spreadsheet. Following are solved examples (see Figures 18.41 and 18.42), written in bullet-point format.

LE-2. Institute for Supply Management New Manufacturing Orders Index (Weight = 16.5%)

- The ISM New Orders Index is a leading indicator that measures the expansion (readings greater than 50) or contraction (readings less than 50) of new manufacturing orders.

- The index reliably increases and decreases before the start of recessions and expansions, although it also sends numerous false signals (every decline below the key level of 50 does not result in a recession).

- The index increased sharply beginning midway through the last recession, but has consistently trended lower throughout the most recent expansion.

- The index has fluctuated around the key level of 50 for much of 2012, indicating neither expansion nor contraction in new manufacturing orders.

- Note that every previous reading of 50 or below has not reliably signaled recession. Nonetheless, the weak behavior of the indicator during the current expansion merits no more than a *diffusion index score of zero*.

CO-4. Index of Industrial Production (Weight = 7.3%)

- The index of industrial production is a coincident indicator that measures physical output at all stages of production in the manufacturing, mining, and gas and electric utility industries. The index is thought to have a strong positive correlation with changes in total output.

- Both the nominal and real indexes work well as coincident indicators, although both series behaved more like leading indicators heading into the 2001 recession.

- The nominal series has trended sideways since 2000, and the inflation-adjusted industrial production index has trended lower, indicating that total industrial output in the United States has grown more slowly than the rate of inflation over the past 12 years.

- Although both series have been increasing since the end of the 2008–2009 recession, the inability of these series to exhibit any growth over the past 12 years sends a concerning signal regarding long-term economic growth in the United States. This indicator therefore merits a *diffusion index score of zero*.

Notes

1. FRED users can also create free accounts that allow you to save your favorite series into organized folders and create graphs of these series using FRED tools directly. There is also a spreadsheet add-in that allows you to download FRED data directly into Excel.
2. Whenever data in this chapter are reported in real terms, they are adjusted for inflation using the PCE (personal consumption expenditure) deflator. The major difference between the CPI (consumer price index) and PCE is that the CPI measures the change in the prices of a fixed basket of consumer goods, whereas the PCE deflator tracks the change in the prices of consumer goods taking into account how spending patterns have been changing over time.

References

The Conference Board. www.conference-board.org/data/bci/index.cfm?id=2160. Accessed January 28, 2013.

National Bureau of Economic Research. Dates of Business Cycle Expansions and Contractions. www.nber.org/cycles.html.

Reinhart, Carmen, and Kenneth Rogoff. 2009. *This Time Is Different; Eight Centuries of Financial Folly*. Princeton, NJ: Princeton University Press.

U.S. Treasury. www.treasury.gov/resource-center/data-chart-center/interest-rates/Pages/Historic-Yield-Data-Visualization.aspx.

CHAPTER 19

Portfolio Risk and Performance Attribution

From Robert A. Weigand, *Applied Equity Analysis and Portfolio Management* (Hoboken, New Jersey: John Wiley & Sons, 2014), Chapter 7.

Learning Objective Statements

- Explain the differences of various performance metrics and why one is more suitable than another for a given objective
- Interpret the Sharpe and Treynor ratios for individual stocks and portfolios
- Explain the characteristics of different alternative investment types and why a portfolio manager might consider using them

This chapter covers the calculation and interpretation of a variety of metrics for analyzing the risk of a stock portfolio and "performance attribution"—how to report returns and risk to illustrate how a portfolio's performance was achieved. We're going to take a pared-down, "what you need to know about risk" approach in this chapter. There are many outstanding sources that contain more comprehensive treatments of risk, ranging from entire books to textbooks that devote three to five chapters devoted to the topic. In an attempt to add some unique value, I am going to present more of a narrative-driven approach to the topic, starting from "square one" and building what I hope will be an easy-to-understand foundation for your deeper explorations of this topic as your careers progress.

The learning objectives for this chapter are:

1. Explain, interpret, and calculate basic statistics such as expected value, variance, standard deviation, covariance, and correlation.

2. Calculate and interpret the expected return and standard deviation of a stock portfolio and compare investment portfolios based on mean/variance efficiency.
3. Identify the subcomponents of portfolio volatility, interpret the type of risk each subcomponent represents, and explain why only one of the subcomponents is affected by diversification.
4. Identify and explain the two key drivers of beta.
5. Interpret the concept of beta in a linear regression context.
6. Explain why investing in stocks with solid fundamentals naturally leads to a low-beta portfolio.
7. Explain how a portfolio's active sector weights can cause it to under- or outperform its benchmark index.
8. Explain how comparing a fund's sector returns to the returns of the corresponding SPDR sector exchange-traded funds (ETFs) can illustrate how effective the fund's managers are as active investors.
9. Calculate and interpret the Sharpe and Treynor ratios for individual stocks and stock portfolios.
10. Explain how multifactor models represent an alternative approach to analyzing a portfolio's returns and exposure to risk.

■ Foundations: Risk and Expected Return

The sophisticated approaches to measuring and managing risk used by portfolio managers today did not exist prior to the 1960s. The key breakthrough was provided by Harry Markowitz (1952, 1959), who derived the formulas necessary for calculating the volatility and expected return of a diversified portfolio of assets. Markowitz's contributions to the finance literature were so profound that he was awarded the Nobel Prize in economics in 1990. Like all economic theoreticians, Markowitz's analysis employed several assumptions, the most important of which are:

■ Investors are generally risk-averse.
■ They base their portfolio decisions on risk and expected return only.
■ They measure risk as the variance (or standard deviation) of expected returns.

The third assumption allowed Markowitz to also develop the idea that an investment portfolio is mean-variance "efficient" if no other portfolio offers a higher expected return at a given level of risk, or lower risk for a given expected return. As we'll see below, creating portfolios that have higher mean-variance efficiency will depend upon certain statistical characteristics of the returns of the assets held in the portfolio. Armed with those perspectives, we're ready to begin our narrative.

Figure 19.1 displays the data we'll use for this chapter's extended example. I have calculated the annual returns for three stocks, Chevron (CVX), Yum! Brands (YUM), and Johnson & Johnson (JNJ), as well as the S&P 500 Index (^SPX). For this example, each year begins on the first trading day of May 2009, 2010, and so on, and ends on the last trading day of April of the year shown.[1]

Annual Returns (%)				
Year-End	CVX	YUM	JNJ	^SPX
30-Apr-10	22.81	33.01	22.70	39.34
29-Apr-11	36.92	29.27	2.18	15.13
30-Apr-12	-2.68	37.15	-1.05	2.59
30-Apr-13	14.41	-6.48	30.52	14.18

Datasource: S&P's Capital IQ

FIGURE 19.1 Annual Returns to CVX, YUM, JNJ, and the S&P 500.

Expected Value and Expected Returns

I can still recall, when I was first learning statistics, the terminology used to refer to the simple calculation of an arithmetic mean—adding up a sequence of numbers and dividing by the number of observations, depicted as Equation 19.1:

$$\bar{x} = \sum_{i=1}^{n} \frac{x_i}{n} \tag{19.1}$$

The professor kept referring to the mean as *expected value,* but he never explained this term—exactly what was "expected" was not immediately clear to me. It wasn't until later, when I was re-reading the textbook chapter as I studied for an exam, that the light bulb went off and my confusion was resolved. What the professor was saying is that the mean of a series represents the series' expected value in the same way that we use the historical average daily high temperature on a given date as a naïve forecast of the expected high temperature on that same date in subsequent years. If the average temperature on the 4th of July has been 90 degrees over the past 20 years, then, lacking a better forecast, it's reasonable to expect that the high temperature on the next 4th of July will be about the same. (Note how this simple method of forecasting is consistent with Keynes' observations as he describes the way people naïvely extrapolate the recent past into the future and assume these patterns will repeat.)

In addition to resolving my specific question, this realization had a larger benefit—it helped me see that statistics are numerical representations of concepts. As I practiced relating the concepts to what I was specifically being asked to calculate, metric by metric, my understanding and retention of the material increased significantly. This is the approach we'll take with all of the risk metrics covered in this chapter. We'll balance our emphasis on accurate calculations with an equal measure of interpretation, with the goal of making these metrics more meaningful to you.

Following from the above discussion, if we believe that the annual return histories of the four stocks depicted in Figure 19.1 represent an appropriate basis, we can calculate the arithmetic mean return for each stock and conceptualize these historical averages as each stock's forward-looking expected return for the next period.[2]

$$\overline{CVX} = \frac{22.81 + 36.92 - 2.68 + 14.41}{4} = 17.87 \tag{19.2}$$

$$\overline{YUM} = \frac{33.01 + 29.27 + 37.15 - 6.48}{4} = 23.24 \tag{19.3}$$

$$\overline{JNJ} = \frac{22.70 + 2.18 - 1.05 + 30.52}{4} = 13.59 \qquad (19.4)$$

YUM is our highest expected return stock at 23.24%, CVX's expected return is 17.87%, and JNJ's expected return equals 13.59%. In the next section we'll cover the basic terminology and calculations necessary for understanding how risk is conceptualized in finance.

Total Risk = Volatility = Standard Deviation of Returns

We'll begin our treatment of risk by reviewing some basic characteristics of the normal distribution, depicted in Figure 19.2. The normal distribution, sometimes called the *bell curve,* is symmetric around its central value, the arithmetic mean (as well as the median and mode, as these are all equal for normal distributions). The example depicts a special case known as the "unit" normal distribution, where the mean equals zero and the standard deviation equals 1.0—thus, the units of measure on the x-axis are expressed in terms of the distribution's standard deviation. Figure 19.2 depicts the idea that approximately 68% of a normal distribution's observations fall within +/− 1 standard deviation from the mean, about 95% fall within +/− 2 standard deviations, and about 99% fall within +/− 3 standard deviations.

Just as the mean of the distribution represents the concept of expected value, Figure 19.2 depicts the idea that the normal distribution's dispersion around the mean, or standard deviation, represents the concept of risk, or volatility, in finance. Distributions that are more dispersed around their mean have higher standard deviations, and distributions where the observations lie closer to their mean values have smaller standard deviations. Therefore, we can conceptualize standard deviation as a measure of risk because it describes how "far" outcomes are likely to be from a distribution's mean, or expected value. *As a time series' standard deviation increases, the probability—or risk—that successive observations will not equal expected value also increases.* Time series with

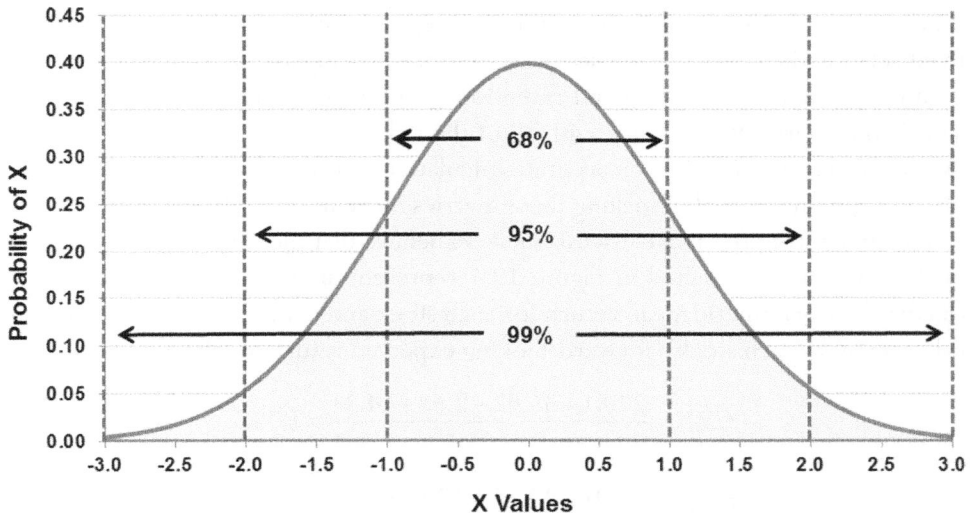

FIGURE 19.2 The Standard Normal Distribution.

higher standard deviations are therefore more risky (have higher volatility), and time series with lower standard deviations are less risky, or less volatile, because observations in the series have a higher probability of being close to the series' expected value.

The calculation of standard deviation will make it clear that this metric literally measures the average deviation from a series' mean, or expected value. Equation 19.5 depicts the formula for the variance of a time series, denoted by the lower case Greek letter σ ("sigma") squared. After calculating variance, we transform this metric into standard deviation by taking its square root (thus standard deviation is denoted by a lower case sigma without squaring).

$$\sigma_x^2 = \sum_{i=1}^{n} \frac{(x_i - \bar{x})^2}{n-1} \tag{19.5}$$

The variance formula tells us to take each observation (1 through n), subtract the arithmetic mean, and square that value. Next we add up the squared deviations from the mean, and divide them by $n - 1$, thus calculating the average squared deviation from expected value for the series.[3] After taking the square root, standard deviation therefore measures the average deviation from the series' expected value. The variance calculation for YUM is depicted in Equation 19.6, using the historical returns from Figure 19.1 and the arithmetic mean calculated in Equation 19.3.

$$\sigma_{YUM}^2 = \frac{(33.01 - 23.24)^2 + (29.27 - 23.24)^2 + (37.15 - 23.24)^2 + (-6.48 - 23.24)^2}{4 - 1}$$
$$= 402.81\% \tag{19.6}$$

Since we entered our inputs as percentage amounts (multiplying the decimal values by 100), the answer of 402.81 is also expressed as a percentage. And $\sqrt{402.81} = 20.07\%$, which in this case is YUM's standard deviation of annual returns. Figure 19.3 depicts the means, variances and standard deviations for the three stocks and S&P 500 market index that we'll be using throughout this chapter's extended example.

Note that there is a correspondence between the three stock's average returns and their standard deviation of returns. YUM has the highest expected return and standard deviation, CVX falls in the middle, and JNJ has the lowest expected return and standard deviation. This pattern conforms to a finance principle that asserts that assets' risk and expected returns should be positively related. In the next section, we'll further refine our understanding of volatility by considering the various factors that cause a stock's returns to be more or less volatile around their mean, or expected value.

	CVX	YUM	JNJ	^SPX
Mean	17.87	23.24	13.59	17.81
Variance	273.92	402.81	238.01	238.56
Std. Dev.	16.55	20.07	15.43	15.45

FIGURE 19.3 Summary Statistics: CVX, YUM, JNJ, and the S&P 500.

The Components of Volatility

In the previous section we defined a stock's total risk as its standard deviation of returns, also known as volatility. We next want to consider that volatility can have different drivers, meaning that various factors can cause a stock's price to change by larger or smaller amounts. Stocks' overall volatility depends on how sensitive stock prices are to these factors. We'll use a simple model that decomposes volatility into two drivers, the first pertaining to the macroeconomy, and the other pertaining to news that is specific to the company itself. This idea is depicted in Equation 19.7:

$$\text{Total risk} = \text{Market or Macroeconomic risk} + \text{Firm-specific risk} \qquad (19.7)$$

These volatility drivers go by several different names in finance. For example, the market or macroeconomic driver of volatility is also called "systematic" risk because macro factors affect the entire economic system, and thus all companies, to some degree. The firm-specific component of volatility is sometimes referred to as "unsystematic" risk, denoting that this type of news pertains to the company only. (These categories are somewhat oversimplified, of course, as company news can sometimes reflect larger macroeconomic realities, and there can also be additional types of risk, such as industry effects, but they nonetheless represent good starting points for understanding volatility.) Equation 19.7 can therefore be rewritten as shown in Equation 19.8:

$$\text{Total risk} = \text{Systematic risk} + \text{Unsystematic risk} \qquad (19.8)$$

As we are moving toward an understanding of how intelligent diversification makes an investment portfolio more "mean/variance efficient"—generating higher returns per unit of risk, or having lower volatility per unit of return—we'll next consider that these factors also go by names that reflect their respective contributions to portfolio volatility. As shown in Equation 19.9, the macroeconomic factors represent risk that cannot be reduced via diversification only—regardless of the number of securities in a portfolio, each stock will still be affected by the state of the macroeconomy. By default, this means that the firm-specific factors represent the type of risk that can be reduced by diversifying—the more stocks held in a portfolio, the less effect each stock's individual volatility has on the overall volatility of a portfolio.

$$\text{Total risk} = \text{Undiversifiable risk} + \text{Diversifiable risk} \qquad (19.9)$$

These definitions will carry us into the following section, where we will develop a deeper understanding of how to measure macroeconomic and firm-specific volatility effects in a portfolio. The key principle to remember from this section is that as more stocks are added to a portfolio, the risk of the portfolio declines due to the reduction in the firm-specific component of portfolio risk.

Statistical Representations of Macroeconomic and Firm-Specific Risk

Next, we'll develop statistical representations of the portfolio risk factors discussed in the previous section. As it turns out, we've already defined and calculated our first portfolio risk metric—an individual stock's standard deviation (or variance) of returns. Reexamining our calculation of YUM's variance of returns in Equation 19.6, we see that all of the inputs pertained specifically to YUM—the company's average and period-by-period returns, and the number of observations in the series (n). Standard deviation (or variance) of returns will therefore represent firm-specific risk in the portfolio risk calculations that follow.

Before we're ready to calculate portfolio volatility, however, we'll also need to develop metrics that measure the macroeconomic component of portfolio risk. Let's start by recalling that this risk factor is termed *systematic* because it affects all companies operating within an economic "system." We will therefore need a portfolio risk metric that reflects how companies' stock returns move together and co-respond to macroeconomic news. In this case, the metric we're looking for is called covariance. The formula for covariance is depicted in Equation 19.10:

$$\sigma_{xy} = \sum_{i=1}^{n} \frac{(x_i - \bar{x})(y_i - \bar{y})}{n-1} \qquad (19.10)$$

The easiest way to interpret what covariance measures is to compare the formula to the way variance is calculated. For convenience, I've rewritten the variance formula slightly differently, depicted as Equation 19.11:

$$\sigma_{x}^{2} = \sum_{i=1}^{n} \frac{(x_i - \bar{x})(x_i - \bar{x})}{n-1} \qquad (19.11)$$

The variance and covariance formulas are nearly identical, with one exception: when calculating covariance, instead of multiplying the first stock's deviation from its mean in each period by itself (squaring the quantity), we multiply it times the second stock's deviation from its mean. Therefore, if variance measures how one stock varies around its own mean, covariance measures how *two* stocks *co*-vary around their respective means.

Technically, covariance can range from negative infinity to positive infinity—there is no absolute limit on how low or high it can be. Covariance will take a positive value if the returns of two stocks tend to move together, or more precisely, if they tend to be above and below their means at the same time. Conversely, if the returns of two stocks tend to move oppositely, meaning that when one is above its mean the other tends to be below its mean (and vice versa), covariance will take a negative value. Looking at Equation 19.9, we can see why this is the case. If x is below (above) its mean when y is above (below) its mean, the numerator of covariance will equal the sum of primarily negative values, and covariance will be negative. However, if x and y are consistently above and below their means at the same time, the numerator of covariance will equal the sum of mainly positive values, and covariance will be positive.

Because covariance can take such a wide range of values, it can be difficult to interpret as a standalone metric. Fortunately, covariance is the key input to another statistic that is important in understanding how diversification reduces risk, and is also much easier to interpret: the correlation coefficient, depicted as Equation 19.12:

$$\rho_{xy} = \frac{\sigma_{xy}}{\sigma_x \sigma_y} \tag{19.12}$$

Equation 19.12 shows that the correlation coefficient equals the covariance between two series divided by the product of their standard deviations. By "scaling" covariance in this manner, we take this not particularly well-behaved statistic and force it to lie in a well-defined range. The lowest value the correlation coefficient can take is -1.0 (indicating perfect negative correlation), and the highest value is $+1.0$ (indicating perfect positive correlation). When the correlation coefficient is close to the midpoint of the range (zero), the interpretation is that the two series have no reliable statistical relation, either positive or negative. Therefore, whenever we talk about covariance or correlation, we're actually talking about the same statistical effect—the strength and direction of the relation between two series.

Next we're ready to demonstrate the calculation of covariance and correlation. We'll use Chevron and Johnson & Johnson's historical returns from Figure 19.1 and their mean returns, calculated in Equations 19.2 and 19.4 (equal to 17.87% and 13.59%, respectively). The calculation of the covariance between CVX and JNJ's returns is shown in Equation 19.13:

$$\sigma_{CVX,JNJ} = \frac{\begin{bmatrix} (22.81-17.87)(22.70-13.59)+(36.92-17.87)(2.18-13.59)+ \\ (-2.68-17.87)(-1.05-13.59)+(14.41-17.87)(30.52-13.59) \end{bmatrix}}{4-1}$$
$$= 23.26\% \tag{19.13}$$

The covariance between CVX and JNJ is extremely low (approximately one-tenth of the stocks' individual variances). Even before scaling this number to transform it into the correlation coefficient, we can infer that the annual returns of these two stocks were generally unrelated in a statistical sense from 2009 to 2013. Let's examine Equation 19.13 to understand why this is the case. Notice how in the first period the returns of both stocks are above their means, and how in the third period the returns of both stocks are below their means. Because their returns moved together in these periods, the first and third terms in the numerator of covariance are positive. In the second and fourth periods, however, their returns moved in opposite directions—when one was above its mean the other was below—thus, the second and fourth terms in the numerator of covariance are negative. Adding two positive values to two negative values results in a small numerator, and thus a low value for covariance.

Equation 19.14 depicts the calculation of the correlation coefficient between the returns of CVX and JNJ, which, as we expected, is low at 0.091. (Although the correlation coefficient is technically an index ranging from -1.0 to $+1.0$, it will sometimes be referred to as a percentage, which would be 0.091% in this case.)

$$\rho_{CVX,JN} = \frac{23.26}{16.55 \times 15.43} = 0.091 \qquad (19.14)$$

Now that we understand the calculation of covariance and correlation, and what these statistics measure about the strength and direction of the relation between two series, we are ready to move on and calculate portfolio volatility in the following section.

How Diversification Reduces Risk (and Why Only Firm-Specific Risk Is Reduced)

This section of the chapter covers several learning objectives. In addition to learning how to calculate portfolio volatility, you will want to pay close attention to differences in the calculations for a two- and three-stock portfolio. Observing how the variance and covariance terms proliferate as the number of stocks in a portfolio increases will be the key to understanding how diversification reduces risk, and why only the firm-specific risk component of portfolio volatility is reduced. We'll begin by considering the formula for the variance of a portfolio, depicted in Equation 19.15:

$$\sigma_p^2 = \sum_{i=1}^{n}\sum_{j=1}^{n} w_i w_j \sigma_{ij} \qquad (19.15)$$

If we were to put the formula into words, here's what it would say: "portfolio variance is a nonlinear weighted average of the covariances between each pair of securities in a portfolio." Despite its brevity, this formula can be difficult to figure out at first glance, so let's walk through it step by step. We can observe that covariance is the primary driver of portfolio variance, as σ_{ij} is the only purely statistical term in the formula. The "weights" for the weighted average are the w's, which will equal the percentage of the portfolio's total wealth invested in each security (with the weights always adding up to 1.0). The only other terms to account for are the two summation indexes (the capital sigma counters, ranging from i to n and j to n, where n is the number of securities in the portfolio). These indexes tell us that we have to sum the product of all the possible pairs of the stocks' weighted covariances. Whenever i and j are equal, notice that we'll be calculating the covariance of that stock's returns with its own returns (which is not as tricky as it first sounds). Take a moment and compare Equation 19.10 (covariance) with Equation 19.11 (variance). It should be clear that a stock's covariance with its own returns equals that stock's variance of returns (x with x equals variance, and x with y equals covariance). These will be the terms that represent the effect of each stock's individual variance of returns on overall portfolio volatility.

Next, we'll manipulate the portfolio variance formula to understand how it works. We'll start with a generic example using notation before plugging in the actual numerical inputs for our three stocks. Here's what to watch for in the following example: as the portfolio gets larger (n increases), the individual firm-specific variance terms will increase linearly (there will be n of them), but the covariance terms will increase exponentially (there will be $n^2 - n$ of them). As n gets larger, the covariance terms—which account for the macroeconomic factors that make stock returns move together to some degree—will increasingly dominate portfolio volatility. Once the portfolio contains 15 to 30 stocks, only the effect of the covariance terms matters (the exact n depends on the covariances and correlations between each pair of stocks in the portfolio—the lower the average correlation, the fewer securities necessary to achieve full diversification). At this point, the portfolio is fully diversified, meaning that virtually all the volatility stems from macro/covariance effects; these will dominate the firm-specific variance terms by sheer force of number. These points will be made clear by the following example, which will give you the chance to observe how the portfolio variance formula changes as we move from a portfolio of two assets to a portfolio of three assets. First, we'll expand Equation 19.15 for the case of a two-asset portfolio, depicted in Equation 19.16 (I'm going to switch the notation from x and y to stocks 1, 2, and 3 to make the counting easier).

$$\sigma_p^2 = w_1^2 \sigma_1^2 + w_2^2 \sigma_2^2 + 2 w_1 w_2 \sigma_{12} \tag{19.16}$$

The first two terms on the right-hand side of Equation 19.16 represent each stock's variance of returns multiplied by the square of the weight of each stock (w^2). The third term represents the covariance between each pair of stocks, weighted by the product of their portfolio weights. This last expression is multiplied by 2 because the i and j counters will pick up this combination twice (when $i = 1$ and $j = 2$, and when $i = 2$ and $j = 1$). Notice that there are n^2 terms (4 total), with n variance terms (2 total, one for each stock) and $n^2 - n$ covariance terms ($4 - 2 = 2$).

Next we'll expand Equation 19.15 for the case of a three-asset portfolio to illustrate how the weighted covariance terms eventually dominate the portfolio variance expression as n becomes large. This is shown as Equation 19.17:

$$\sigma_p^2 = w_1^2 \sigma_1^2 + w_2^2 \sigma_2^2 + w_3^2 \sigma_3^2 + 2 w_1 w_2 \sigma_{12} + 2 w_1 w_3 \sigma_{13} + 2 w_2 w_3 \sigma_{23} \tag{19.17}$$

The portfolio variance expression still has n^2 terms (9 total), with n weighted variance terms (3 total) and $n^2 - n$ weighted covariance terms (6 total). All we have to do is follow the pattern to understand how diversification reduces risk, and why only firm-specific risk is reduced. For a portfolio with 10 securities, there will be 100 total terms in the portfolio variance expression (n^2), but only 10 of these will be weighted variance terms (one for each stock's firm-specific risk). The remaining 90 terms will be weighted covariance terms, representing the macro forces that affect all companies. For a larger portfolio, say a mutual fund holding 50 stocks, there would be 2,500 terms in the portfolio variance expression, with only 50 weighted portfolio terms (n) and 2,450 weighted covariance terms ($n^2 - n$). This is why individual firm risk contributes little to the volatility of a well-diversified portfolio. As soon as the portfolio is reasonably large, the covariances between the assets—which represent macroeconomic risk effects in the portfolio—account for virtually all of the volatility.

Now that we understand the principles of how diversification works, in the following section we'll further extend our learning by creating a two- and three-asset portfolio using the historical annual returns for Chevron, Yum! Brands, and Johnson & Johnson.

Diversifying a Portfolio with CVX, YUM, and JNJ

In this section we will combine our stocks into a two- and three-asset portfolio and use Equations 19.16 and 19.17 to observe the effect on portfolio volatility. In addition to using the variances from Figure 19.3, we're also going to need each stock's covariance with all the other stocks, which I've calculated and depicted in Figure 19.4. Examining the table, we can corroborate a statement made above: a stock's covariance with its own returns equals its variance of returns. Notice how all the covariances on the diagonal (CVX with CVX, YUM with YUM, etc.) equal the variances reported in Figure 19.3.

To make it easy to interpret the results, I would also like you to examine the correlation coefficients between each pair of stock returns before we begin, depicted in Figure 19.5. Diversifying among these stocks is going to reduce a considerable amount of risk because their returns have unusually low correlations—some are even negative. The lower the correlations (and covariances), the greater the opportunity to reduce portfolio volatility.

Next, we'll calculate the variance and standard deviation of a portfolio consisting of 50% CVX and 50% YUM by plugging into Equation 19.16. The low correlation between the returns of these stocks (−0.02) indicates that there is a good opportunity to diversify away a substantial amount of volatility. The variance calculation for the 50/50 portfolio is shown as Equation 19.18:

$$\sigma_p^2 = \left(0.5^2 \times 273.92\right) + \left(0.5^2 \times 402.81\right) + \left(2 \times 0.5 \times 0.5 \times -6.64\right) = 165.86\% \quad (19.18)$$

	CVX	YUM	JNJ	^SPX
		Covariances		
CVX	273.92	-6.64	23.26	126.92
YUM	-6.64	402.81	-228.86	30.09
JNJ	23.26	-228.86	238.01	129.34
^SPX	126.92	30.09	129.34	238.56

FIGURE 19.4 Covariance Matrix: CVX, YUM, JNJ, and the S&P 500.

	CVX	YUM	JNJ	^SPX
		Correlations		
CVX	1.000	-0.020	0.091	0.496
YUM	-0.020	1.000	-0.739	0.097
JNJ	0.091	-0.739	1.000	0.543
^SPX	0.496	0.097	0.543	1.000

FIGURE 19.5 Correlation Matrix: CVX, YUM, JNJ, and the S&P 500.

The 50% CVX/50% YUM portfolio has a variance of 165.86%, and thus a standard deviation of 12.88%, as $\sqrt{165.86} = 12.88\%$. After calculating the expected return of the portfolio we can interpret its mean-variance efficiency and determine if diversifying between Chevron and Yum! Brands offers potential benefits for the average investor hypothesized by Markowitz (risk-averse, concerned only with expected returns and risk, and measures risk as the standard deviation of expected returns). The portfolio expected return calculation is not a nonlinear weighted average like portfolio variance, but just a simple linear weighted average of the expected returns of each security in the portfolio, as depicted in Equation 19.19. As was the case for portfolio variance, the weights are equal to the percentage of total portfolio wealth invested in each stock.

$$E(R_p) = \sum_{i=1}^{n} w_i E(R_i) \tag{19.19}$$

Plugging in the expected returns from Figure 19.3, the expected return of the 50/50 CVX/YUM portfolio equals 20.55%, as shown in Equation 19.20:

$$E(R_p) = (0.5 \times 17.87) + (0.5 \times 23.24) = 20.55\% \tag{19.20}$$

Figure 19.6 depicts the standard deviation (x-axis) and expected returns (y-axis) of CVX, YUM, the S&P 500 index, and the 50/50 portfolio.

If we consider CVX, YUM, and the 50/50 portfolio as three discrete investment choices for a typical Markowitz investor, one thing is immediately clear: no investor would want to hold CVX by itself, because the 50/50 portfolio dominates CVX in a mean-variance sense—it offers both a higher expected return and lower risk. Whether or not any Markowitz investors would want to hold YUM by itself it not as clear, however—there could be some investors whose individual risk tolerances make it worthwhile to pursue an extra 2.69% in expected return by exposing themselves to an extra 7.19% of standard deviation (although probably not too many).

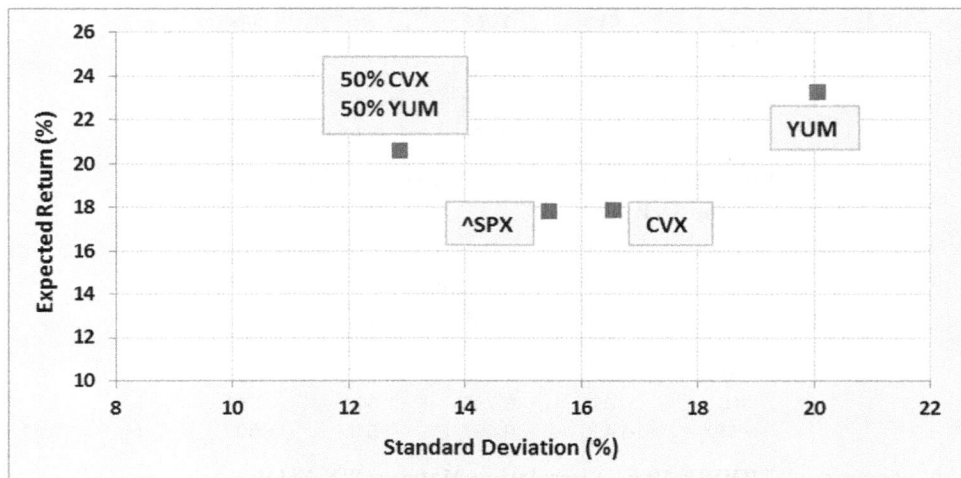

FIGURE 19.6 Expected Return and Standard Deviation of the 50/50 Portfolio.

We can also form a simple statistic that compares expected excess returns per unit of total risk for the three investment choices. The one we'll choose is called the "Sharpe ratio," named after William Sharpe (we'll consider his contributions to portfolio risk analysis further in the following section). The Sharpe ratio is calculated as an investment's excess investment return (above the prevailing risk-free rate) divided by its standard deviation of returns, as shown in Equation 19.21:

$$\text{Sharpe ratio} = \frac{\text{Expected return} - \text{Risk-free rate}}{\text{Standard deviation of returns}} \qquad (19.21)$$

The standard deviations, expected returns and Sharpe ratios for CVX, YUM, the S&P 500 index, and the 50/50 portfolio are shown in Figure 19.7 (we're using the yield on the 10-year Treasury Note as the risk-free rate, 2.02% as of May 23, 2013).

With a Sharpe ratio of 1.43, the 50/50 portfolio offers a substantially greater excess expected return per unit of risk than either CVX, YUM, or the S&P 500 index alone (which have Sharpe ratios of 0.95, 1.06, and 1.01, respectively). Because the portfolio is more efficient in a mean-variance sense, we can conclude that it will be preferred by most Markowitz-type investors.

Risk and Expected Return of a Three-Stock Portfolio

Next, we will extend our portfolio diversification example and introduce a third stock, JNJ. Figure 19.7 shows that JNJ has a low correlation with CVX (+0.09, similar to YUM's −0.02), and an extremely low correlation with YUM of −0.74. By adding a third stock to the portfolio before we're in the fully diversified range of 15 to 30 securities, we should expect to see further improvements in the mean-variance efficiency of the portfolio. Additionally, because we're adding a stock whose returns have such a low correlation with those of the other stocks, we can expect these benefits to be substantial.

Since YUM is our highest-expected-return stock, we'll leave its portfolio weight at 50%, and reallocate 20% of our position in CVX to JNJ, resulting in weights of 30% CVX, 50% YUM, and 20% JNJ. The expected return of the three-asset portfolio falls only slightly, from 20.55% to 19.70%, as shown in Equation 19.22:

$$E(R_p) = (0.3 \times 17.87) + (0.5 \times 23.24) + 0.2 \times 13.59) = 19.70\% \quad (19.22)$$

	Standard Deviation	Expected Return	Sharpe Ratio
CVX	16.55	17.87	0.95
YUM	20.07	23.24	1.05
^SPX	15.45	17.81	1.01
Portfolio	12.88	20.55	1.43

FIGURE 19.7 Sharpe Ratios: CVX, YUM, the S&P 500, and the 50/50 Portfolio.

Next we'll calculate the variance of the three-asset portfolio, depicted as Equation 19.23:

$$\sigma_p^2 = (0.3^2 \times 2.74) + (0.5^2 \times 4.03) + (0.2^2 \times 2.38) + (2 \times 0.3 \times 0.5 \times -0.07)$$
$$+ (2 \times 0.2 \times 0.5 \times -2.29) + (2 \times 0.3 \times 0.2 \times 0.23) = 0.899\% \qquad (19.23)$$

The portfolio's variance equals 0.899%, and the portfolio's standard deviation equals 9.48%, as $\sqrt{0.00899} = 0.0948$, or 9.48%. Now we're ready to compare the mean-variance efficiency of the three-asset portfolio to the three stocks individually and the 50/50 portfolio of CVX and YUM. First we'll take a graphical approach, depicted in Figure 19.8, which updates Figure 19.6 by adding the standard deviation and expected return of JNJ and the 30/50/20 portfolio of CVX, YUM and JNJ. Remember that each point on the graph represents an investment opportunity available to a Markowitz-type investor.

We can draw several conclusions from Figure 19.8. First, as was the case with CVX, no Markowitz investor would want to hold JNJ alone, as both portfolios offer higher expected returns and lower risk than either of these stocks. Second, the three-asset portfolio weighted 30/50/20 would represent a superior opportunity for most Markowitz investors vs. any of the other investment options. As shown in Figure 19.9, reallocating 20% of our CVX holdings to JNJ reduced the portfolio's expected return by only 0.86%, but the portfolio's standard deviation declines considerably, from 12.88% down to 9.48%. Strictly speaking, we cannot rule out that some risk-seeking investors might find it rational to expose themselves to an additional 3.40% of standard deviation to obtain an extra 0.86% of expected return (the 50/50 portfolio), or another 10.59% of standard deviation to obtain an additional 3.54% of expected return (YUM by itself). But it's safe to say that most Markowitz-type investors, who are averse to risk, would prefer the three-stock portfolio weighted 30/50/20, based on its Sharpe ratio of 1.85.

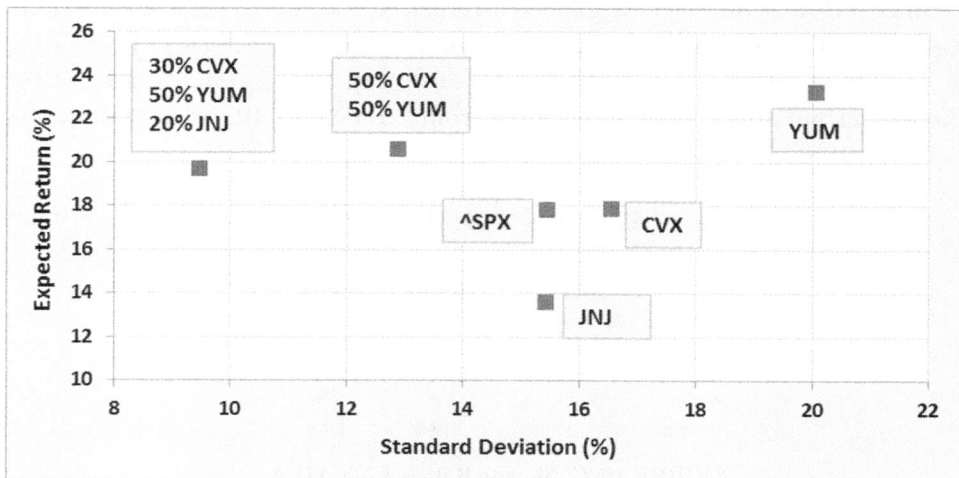

FIGURE 19.8 Expected Return and Standard Deviation of the 30/50/20 Portfolio.

	Standard Deviation	Expected Return	Sharpe Ratio
CVX	16.55	17.87	0.95
YUM	20.07	23.24	1.05
JNJ	15.43	13.59	0.74
^SPX	15.45	17.81	1.01
Portfolio 1	12.88	20.55	1.43
Portfolio 2	9.48	19.70	1.85

FIGURE 19.9   Sharpe Ratios: CVX, YUM, JNJ, the S&P 500, and the Two- and Three-Stock Portfolios.

That completes our coverage of how diversification reduces risk, and why only the firm-specific portion of risk is reduced. But this section leaves one significant question unanswered: Is it possible to fully understand the risk exposure of a large diversified portfolio without calculating (or having to think about) n^2 calculations? As we'll see in the next section, which introduces the concept of beta, the answer to that question is a resounding yes. The main points from this section are important to our understanding of risk nonetheless: the mechanics of covariance and correlation, and why portfolio risk management is more effective when we diversify among stocks with low correlations—the reason portfolio managers hold stocks from different sectors, a topic we'll cover later in this chapter.

Extending the Mean-Variance Framework: Beta

In the previous section we covered the nuts and bolts of how diversification works. We learned why the purely mechanical aspects of diversification only reduce a portfolio's firm-specific risk, leaving the portfolio's macroeconomic risk exposure unaffected. We also observed that when we diversified among stocks with low return correlations portfolio volatility could be further reduced because stocks with low return correlations tend to exhibit different responses to macroeconomic news. In this section we will further explore a portfolio's exposure to macroeconomic risk by introducing a new risk metric known as *beta*.

While the Markowitz framework is valuable for understanding how diversification works, and provides the most accurate calculations of portfolio volatility, there is something unsatisfying about the Markowitz depiction of portfolio risk. When managing even a modest-sized portfolio, the portfolio risk calculations can only be completed using Excel, or professional risk-management software. While this does not present a problem from a computational standpoint, it does mean that a portfolio manager has to sacrifice some intuition when thinking about the risk and expected return of the stocks in a portfolio—there are simply too many variables to hold in one mental snapshot.

Fortunately, our risk story does not end with Markowitz. A Stanford professor named William Sharpe (who shared the Nobel Prize with Markowitz in 1990) added further to our understanding of risk and expected returns with several contributions, most notably the capital asset pricing model (CAPM). We are going to focus on an important input to the CAPM, the index of stock and portfolio risk known as beta. We'll apply all the statistical foundations developed earlier in this chapter as we extend our understanding of portfolio risk management to include beta.

One More Assumption Leads Us to Beta

As we learned from studying Markowitz, economic and financial models employ assumptions, or simplifications, to obtain certain results. Transitioning from the Markowitz mean-variance framework to Sharpe's beta-based framework requires only one additional assumption, but it's a powerful one that will not only save us a lot of time and computing horsepower, but also allow us to obtain a more intuitive picture of a portfolio's risk exposure that would not be possible in the Markowitz framework.

Recall what happened as we transitioned from the volatility calculations for a two-asset portfolio to those for a three-asset portfolio (Equation 19.17): the most important driver of portfolio volatility, each stock's covariance with all the other stocks in the portfolio, proliferated rapidly and soon dominated the volatility calculations, even for modest-sized portfolio. Recall that every portfolio variance calculation has $n^2 - n$ of these cross-covariances, which means that fully understanding the volatility of even a 20-stock portfolio requires the calculation of 380 covariances.

So here's the additional assumption/simplification we need to employ: we're going to substitute "each stock's covariance with every other stock in the portfolio" ($n^2 - n$ calculations) with "each stock's covariance with an appropriate market index," such as the S&P 500 (n calculations). Can we do this without a huge loss of accuracy? Picture a reasonably diversified portfolio—let's say it has 20 stocks total. The average covariance of any one stock's returns with the other 19 will usually be extremely similar to that stock's covariance of returns with the overall stock market. This effect occurs because the remaining 19 stocks still represent a diversified portfolio, and their average returns will most likely be highly correlated with the returns of most market indexes (which are also diversified portfolios). That's the only simplification required to move from the mean-variance framework to beta.

Before moving on to a more technical understanding, let's review what we'll gain by measuring and managing portfolio risk using beta instead of Markowitz's mean-variance framework:

- Beta can be interpreted as an index that measures how much volatility a stock will contribute to a diversified portfolio. This will allow us to rank every stock's potential contribution to portfolio volatility using the same index scale.
- Similar to the way we scaled covariance and transformed it into the correlation coefficient to make it easier to interpret, beta is also a scaled version of covariance, and equally easy to interpret. The average beta of all stocks in the market will always equal 1.0, thus stocks with betas above 1.0 will be "high-beta," and stocks with betas below 1.0 will be "low-beta."

- A portfolio's average beta will be computed as a weighted average of each stock's individual beta. Instead of requiring n^2 calculations to fully understand portfolio risk (the Markowitz framework), we'll only need to calculate n betas—one for each stock. In terms of risk management, adding (deleting) a stock with a beta greater than the portfolio's weighted average beta will increase (decrease) portfolio volatility, and vice versa if we add or delete stocks with betas less than the portfolio's average beta. The portfolio's weighted average beta will be our measure of the portfolio's exposure to macroeconomic risk.

Estimating Beta

In this section we'll develop an understanding of how to estimate beta. We'll start by relating the calculation of beta to our discussion of covariance and correlation earlier in this chapter. Just as we scaled the covariance of two stocks' returns by the product of their standard deviations to create the correlation coefficient (which measured how their returns moved together, shown as Equation 19.12), we are now going to scale a stock's covariance of returns with the market by the variance of the market's returns to create a beta coefficient (shown in Equation 19.24):

$$\beta_x = \frac{\sigma_{x,m}}{\sigma_m^2} \qquad (19.24)$$

The covariance of a stock's returns with the market is the main driver of beta, just as the covariance of two stocks' returns was the main driver of the correlation coefficient. But Equation 19.24 represents more than plugging into a previous equation in an ad hoc manner—it derives from the statistical method known as linear regression. If we were to regress a stock's returns on those of a market index (depicted in Equation 19.25), the slope of the regression line—which is what beta measures in a statistical context—would be calculated as shown in Equation 19.24:

$$R_x = \alpha_x + \beta_x R_m + \varepsilon \qquad (19.25)$$

In Equation 19.25, R_x are the returns to an individual stock (x), usually termed the *dependent* variable. The individual stock returns are dependent because we're modeling these returns as a function of the returns to a stock market index, R_m, known as the *independent* variable. The regression line has an intercept, α (alpha), and a slope, β (beta). The variable ε (epsilon) represents a vector of residuals, or leftover terms, from the regression. The residuals are sometimes called the regression "errors" because the returns of stock x will not be perfectly correlated with the returns to the stock market index. The regression residuals are therefore considered errors because they represent the deviations from the relation between x and m predicted by the regression line.

More technically, the regression line is estimated as the line that most efficiently bisects an x-y scatterplot of the market and stock return data so that the sum of the squared deviations from the regression line is minimized. A scatterplot of Johnson & Johnson's monthly returns versus the S&P 500 and the resulting line of best fit from regressing JNJ's returns on those of the S&P 500 are shown as Figure 19.10 (based on 60 monthly observations from May 2008 to April 2013).

The slope of the regression line equals JNJ's beta—0.56 in this case. The regression intercept equals 0.283% per month, or 3.40% annually. We call this JNJ's *alpha,* or the annualized excess return over and above JNJ's fair expected return based on its volatility versus the market. Somewhat simplified, here's the intuition regarding JNJ's alpha: recall from Figure 19.5 that the S&P 500's average annual return over the prior period was 17.81% per year. JNJ is only expected to earn $0.56 \times 17.81 = 9.97\%$ per year because JNJ is only 56% as volatile as the market (beta = 0.56). JNJ's annual stock returns averaged 13.59% per year, however, so the annualized difference between $13.59\% - 9.97\% = 3.62\%$, which is roughly equal to JNJ's alpha of 3.40% estimated using linear regression. JNJ therefore earned more than its fair expected return based on its risk, with this outperformance being termed *positive alpha.*

Of course, when stocks earn less than their fair expected return, alpha can also be negative. Across the entire stock market for any given period, the sum of all the positive alpha must equal the sum of all the negative alpha, thus alpha is "zero sum," meaning that investors earn alpha from one another in the aggregate. Any investor's gains from generating positive alpha are equal to other investors' losses from their negative alphas. This is a statistical depiction of how competition among investors plays out in the stock market. Buy and hold investors earn the average market return, while active investors compete against each other to earn alpha, with their aggregate efforts totaling to zero—*before* fees. After accounting for the total cost of active investors' efforts to generate market-beating returns, their aggregate alpha is consistently negative.

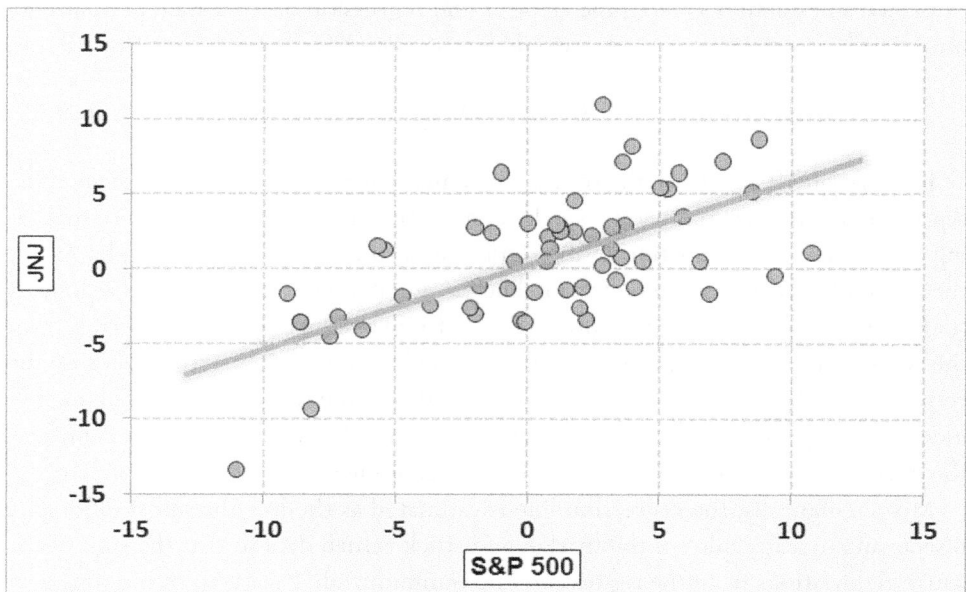

FIGURE 19.10   Scatterplot and Regression Line, JNJ versus the S&P 500.

The Drivers of Beta

In this section we will make a few substitutions into Equation 19.24 and rearrange our expression for beta to see more deeply into how this index of systematic risk works. Similar to the way we analyze various financial ratios, we're going to decompose beta into two key drivers: a stock's correlation with the market, and a stock's volatility relative to the market. We'll see that beta decreases with both of these factors, meaning that adding stocks that have either a lower correlation with the market (which makes the stock a better portfolio diversifier) or lower volatility versus the market (standard deviation of returns) will lead to a lower portfolio beta.

Previously, we saw that the correlation of a stock's returns with the market's returns equals their covariance scaled by the product of their standard deviations (Equation 19.12). In Equation 19.26 we rearrange that relation and derive an alternative expression for covariance, equal to the correlation coefficient times the product of the standard deviation of returns for the stock and the market index:

$$\rho_{x,m} = \frac{\sigma_{x,m}}{\sigma_x \sigma_m} \Rightarrow \sigma_{x,m} = \rho_{x,m} \sigma_x \sigma_m \tag{19.26}$$

Next, we will substitute this alternative expression for covariance into Equation 19.24, and then cancel out the extra σ_m terms in the numerator and denominator. This allows us to decompose beta into its two key drivers, a stock's correlation with the market and a stock's volatility relative to the market, as shown in Equation 19.27:

$$\beta_x = \frac{\rho_{x,m} \sigma_x \sigma_m}{\sigma_m^2} \Rightarrow \beta_x = \rho_{x,m} \times \frac{\sigma_x}{\sigma_m} \tag{19.27}$$

Equation 19.27 will help us better understand the factors that determine an individual stocks' beta. We'll use it to decompose the betas of the stocks in our portfolio to illustrate this point. We'll start with our lowest-beta stock, JNJ, which has a beta of 0.56, versus the S&P 500 (estimated via linear regression as shown in Equation 19.25, using 60 monthly returns from May 2008 to April 2013). The results are shown as Equation 19.28:

$$\beta_{JNJ} = \rho_{JNJ,\,SP500} \times \frac{\sigma_{JNJ}}{\sigma_{SP500}} = 0.679 \times \frac{4.490\%}{5.443\%} = 0.560 \tag{19.28}$$

Although JNJ's correlation with the market is moderately high at 0.679, JNJ has a low beta nonetheless, driven mainly by its low volatility versus the S&P 500 (few stocks have a lower standard deviation of returns than the market index). We repeat this decomposition in Equation 19.29, this time focusing on CVX's beta.

$$\beta_{CVX} = \rho_{CVX,\,SP500} \times \frac{\sigma_{CVX}}{\sigma_{SP500}} = 0.684 \times \frac{6.148\%}{5.443\%} = 0.773 \tag{19.29}$$

The two stocks' correlation coefficients with the market are virtually identical (0.679 vs. 0.684), but CVX's beta of 0.773 is substantially higher than JNJ's, driven by its higher standard deviation of returns. This makes sense, as CVX is in a more volatile industry (energy vs. health care), and their product offerings are less diversified than JNJ's (a diversified stream of revenues helps lower the volatility of a firm's earnings and free cash flows). Let's repeat the experiment with YUM (shown as Equation 19.30), which has the highest beta of the three stocks at 0.825.

$$\beta_{YUM} = \rho_{YUM, SP500} \times \frac{\sigma_{YUM}}{\sigma_{SP500}} = 0.665 \times \frac{6.752\%}{5.443\%} = 0.825 \qquad (19.30)$$

YUM actually has the lowest correlation of returns with the S&P 500, equal to 0.665. But YUM's beta is the highest of the three stocks due to its higher standard deviation of returns. McDonald's (MCD) modeled up well in its comparison with YUM, particularly in terms of per share intrinsic value. In addition to generating larger free cash flows, MCD's valuation received an additional boost from its lower cost of capital, due to its lower cost of equity (driven by its lower beta). Let's decompose MCD's beta of 0.389 into its two key drivers to understand why it's so much lower than YUM's (shown in Equation 19.31):

$$\beta_{MCD} = \rho_{MCD, SP500} \times \frac{\sigma_{MCD}}{\sigma_{SP500}} = 0.510 \times \frac{4.154\%}{5.443\%} = 0.389 \qquad (19.31)$$

To obtain a beta that low a stock has to have both drivers working for it, and MCD delivers. It has the lowest return correlation with the S&P 500 of all of our stocks (0.51), and the lowest standard deviation of returns (4.154%). Conversely, for most high-beta stocks, both the correlation and standard deviation of returns tend to be high. Equation 19.32 decomposes Caterpillar's (CAT) beta of 1.893 into its two key drivers.

$$\beta_{CAT} = \rho_{CAT, SP500} \times \frac{\sigma_{CAT}}{\sigma_{SP500}} = 0.820 \times \frac{12.562\%}{5.443\%} = 1.893 \qquad (19.32)$$

We see that CAT's returns not only have the highest correlation with the market of all the stocks we've examined (0.82) — this is what makes it a "cyclical" stock, one whose returns move in sync with the business cycle—it also has a much higher standard deviation of returns (12.562%).

Low Betas Derive from Solid Fundamentals Now that we've studied a variety of examples that explain how beta works, let's take a moment and reflect on the implications for portfolio risk management, as well as financial analysis and valuation. Because the main theme of this book revolves around fundamental analysis, a good question to consider is "What does beta tell us about a stocks' fundamentals?" In a paper I co-authored with Professor Ed Dyl of the University of Arizona in 1998, we found that companies initiating cash dividend payments not only had higher profits, but the betas of these stocks also declined around the time of the announcement. Our results suggested that companies begin paying dividends not only when the board of directors believes their earnings are permanently higher, but also when they believe that the volatility of their earnings is permanently lower, as both higher and less volatile (more predictable) earnings help the company sustain its commitment to paying dividends at a particular level.

For our purposes, the implication is that when you invest in stocks with tangible fundamentals that are defended by superior competitive positioning, the revenues, EBIT, NOPAT, earnings, free cash flows and dividends supporting their intrinsic value will also be less volatile. This is the essence of what it means to say that a low beta portfolio is "safer"—the prices of the stocks in the portfolio are less volatile because the fundamentals supporting their per-share intrinsic values are also less volatile. Stocks whose prices are better supported by fundamentals decline less during market downturns. This occurs because these stocks have superior fundamentals—not just higher than those of their competitors, but more stable as well.

These principles also extend to an entire portfolio. When a portfolio consists of the "best" stocks from each sector—where best means good growth opportunities, solid financial health, attractive intrinsic value, and superior competitive positioning—the portfolio has a better chance of outperforming its market index partly due to the stability of these stocks' returns. When a buy-and-hold portfolio suffers less severe drawdowns during corrections and bear markets, there are less losses to recoup, and the portfolio is back in profitable territory that much sooner. Portfolios comprised of stocks with superior fundamentals will therefore tend to be low-beta portfolios—at least over long horizons (we'll have more to say about this in the following section). The diligent fundamental process and the emphasis on competitive positioning not only help us earn higher returns, but they also help us create portfolios with lower volatility, which is another important component of success for the long-term investor who is focused on fundamentals.

■ Performance Attribution: Sector Weights, Dividend Yield, Beta, and Style

This section presents a variety of practical examples for reporting portfolio performance, including a portfolio's sector weightings, dividend yield and beta, and the portfolio's exposure to other macro- and style-based risk factors used in the practice of investment management.

We'll illustrate these examples by analyzing the performance of the Student Investment Fund (SIF) at my university. The students have managed the fund as a genuine buy-and-hold portfolio since its inception. Their goal is to trade and reinvest no more than 25 to 30% of the portfolio's net asset value per year, versus an average turnover rate of 100% for professionally managed mutual funds. The students target a low annual turnover rate to minimize transactions costs and cognitive errors. We structure our investment process so that the students have time to research all their buy and sell decisions thoroughly, which results in their having high conviction regarding the stocks in the portfolio. Figure 19.11 depicts the holdings of the SIF as of May 2013.

The SIF currently holds 22 stocks, with at least one stock from each sector. The weights of each stock in the portfolio vary considerably, based on students' conviction regarding the prospects for both the individual company and the company's sector.

Ticker	Company Name	Shares	Price	Position Size	Sector	Portfolio Weight
BMY	Bristol-Myers Squibb Company	183	$47.40	$8,686	Healthcare	7.5%
JNJ	Johnson & Johnson	96	$86.82	$8,376	Healthcare	7.3%
VZ	Verizon Communications Inc.	140	$51.39	$7,173	Telecommunication Services	6.2%
UTX	United Technologies Corp.	74	$95.04	$7,032	Industrials	6.1%
CVX	Chevron Corporation	54	$125.45	$6,743	Energy	5.9%
ACN	Accenture plc	80	$82.22	$6,578	Information Technology	5.7%
MCD	McDonald's Corp.	64	$100.29	$6,373	Consumer Discretionary	5.5%
PEP	Pepsico, Inc.	72	$82.58	$5,923	Consumer Staples	5.1%
EPB	El Paso Pipeline Partners, L.P.	135	$42.68	$5,762	Energy	5.0%
MDT	Medtronic, Inc.	111	$51.33	$5,704	Healthcare	5.0%
PG	Procter & Gamble Co.	69	$81.88	$5,626	Consumer Staples	4.9%
QCOM	QUALCOMM Incorporated	85	$64.26	$5,462	Information Technology	4.7%
BX	The Blackstone Group L.P.	228	$22.65	$5,165	Financials	4.5%
EMR	Emerson Electric Co.	90	$56.94	$5,125	Industrials	4.5%
DB:VOW	Volkswagen AG	30	$164.00	$5,000	Consumer Discretionary	4.3%
INTC	Intel Corporation	192	$23.92	$4,605	Information Technology	4.0%
DE	Deere & Company	50	$86.29	$4,273	Industrials	3.7%
MSFT	Microsoft Corporation	119	$34.27	$4,069	Information Technology	3.5%
EXC	Exelon Corporation	114	$34.65	$3,953	Utilities	3.4%
ABX	Barrick Gold Corporation	95	$19.69	$1,871	Materials	1.6%
MBT	Mobile Telesystems OJSC	68	$20.32	$1,382	Telecommunication Services	1.2%
FTR	Frontier Communications Corp	28	$4.40	$123	Telecommunication Services	0.1%
	Cash			$100		0.1%
	Total			$115,104		100.0%

FIGURE 19.11   Student Investment Fund Portfolio.

Our most heavily-weighted positions are in two health care stocks, Bristol-Myers and Johnson & Johnson. Although these stocks received a 5% allocation when we first purchased them for the fund, they have become overweighted relative to our other positions due to their superior long-term performance. The students have considered trimming these positions back to more modest portfolio weightings, but the stocks model up well each time they're reviewed and, most important, they continue outperforming, so the students decided to "let their winners run" in this case.

Sector Under- and Overweights

One way we analyze the fund's positioning is by our sector over- and underweights, a concept first introduced in Chapter 18. As students begin their review of the fund's holdings each year, they perform the macroeconomic analysis exercises from Chapter 18 to identify the current stage of the business and financial cycles. The students trim or sell positions in sectors thought to be poorly positioned, and add new positions in sectors thought to be more competitively positioned. Our sector weights relative to the S&P 500 are shown in Figure 19.12 (Standard & Poor's makes the current sector weights of the S&P 500 index available on their website: http://us.spindices.com/indices/equity/sp-500).

The SIF has overweights in three sectors: health care (Bristol-Myers, Johnson & Johnson, and Medtronic), telecom (mainly our position in Verizon) and industrials

Sector	Portfolio Weight	S&P 500 Weight	Over/Under Weight
Healthcare	19.8%	12.2%	7.6%
Telecommunication Services	7.5%	2.9%	4.6%
Industrials	14.3%	10.3%	4.0%
Utilities	3.4%	3.4%	0.0%
Information Technology	18.0%	18.3%	-0.3%
Energy	10.9%	11.2%	-0.3%
Consumer Staples	10.0%	10.6%	-0.6%
Consumer Discretionary	9.9%	11.7%	-1.8%
Materials	1.6%	3.6%	-2.0%
Financials	4.5%	15.8%	-11.3%
Total	100.0%	100.0%	0.0%

Datasource: Standard & Poor's

FIGURE 19.12   **Student Investment Fund Active Portfolio Weights.**

(United Technologies, Emerson, and Deere, the latter representing a position that was trimmed after a period of strong outperformance). Our biggest underweights are in materials stocks (the worst performing sector from late 2012 through mid-2013) and financials. The students decided to obtain minimal exposure to the financial sector via Blackstone, a publicly traded private-equity firm, and otherwise accept a large underweight in financials. Although financials have had strong recent performance, this sector has also been increasingly difficult to analyze since the U.S. Federal Reserve began implementing its bizarre policies during the global financial crisis in 2008. (In this case the students are following Peter Lynch's (1990) timeless advice to invest only in stocks they can genuinely understand.)

Returns by Sector

We also analyze the SIF returns by sector, shown in Figure 19.13. The goal of this exercise is to identify the sectors in which we earned higher returns (implying that

Sector	Sector Return	Weighted Sector Return	Portfolio Return	Weighted Port. Return	Higher/Lower Return
Financials	27.1%	1.2%	75.7%	3.4%	2.2%
Telecommunication Services	15.2%	1.1%	27.9%	2.1%	1.0%
Energy	15.4%	1.7%	21.2%	2.3%	0.6%
Information Technology	5.5%	1.0%	7.8%	1.4%	0.4%
Consumer Staples	21.7%	2.2%	25.5%	2.6%	0.4%
Healthcare	30.9%	6.1%	32.7%	6.5%	0.4%
Industrials	17.0%	2.4%	13.2%	1.9%	-0.5%
Utilities	9.0%	0.3%	-9.7%	-0.3%	-0.6%
Materials	9.9%	0.2%	-54.3%	-0.9%	-1.0%
Consumer Discretionary	23.8%	2.4%	12.0%	1.2%	-1.2%
Average	17.6%	18.6%	15.2%	20.1%	1.5%

Datasource: S&P's Capital IQ

FIGURE 19.13   **Student Investment Fund Returns by Sector.**

active management is paying off for us), as well as the sectors in which we earned lower returns (in which case we would have been better off investing passively and obtaining exposure to these sectors by buying the sector ETF).

Sector returns equal the 12-month trailing returns to the SPDR ETFs for each stock market sector (ETF ticker symbols are available at www.spdrs.com). The "Sector Return" column in Figure 19.13 shows the return to each sector ETF. These ETFs have low management fees, so their returns are good estimates of the passive returns we would have earned if we had simply bought the sector ETF instead of actively selecting individual stocks from each sector. The "Portfolio Return" column shows the average return to the stocks in our fund from each sector. The "Weighted Sector Return" and "Weighted Port. Return" columns weight the returns to both the sector ETFs and our stocks by multiplying them times the portfolio sector weights from Figure 19.12. The sum of the "Weighted Sector Return" column equals what our annual portfolio return would have been (18.6%) if we had bought each sector ETF and held them in proportion to our active portfolio weights. The sum of the "Weighted Port. Return" column equals our actual portfolio return (20.1%), which was 1.5% higher overall over the trailing 12 month period. The last column (higher/lower return) calculates the difference between the weighted portfolio return and weighted sector return. Positive values indicate that our active stock selections outperformed the sector average, while negative values indicate that our active stock selections underperformed the sector average.

Figure 19.13 shows that the SIF stocks outperformed the sector averages for financial, telecom, energy, information technology, consumer staples and health care stocks, and underperformed for industrials, utilities, materials and consumer discretionary stocks. The results of this exercise tells us that our fundamental stock-picking process is working for the first six sectors, but we have not been as skilled in picking stocks in the latter four sectors (there's always something to work on, of course). Notice that our overweights in health care and telecom paid off, as the returns to our stocks in these sectors exceed those of the sector ETFs. Our small overweight in industrials was not as profitable, as our stocks slightly trailed the sector ETF. Moreover, notice that we outperformed the weighted return to the financial sector ETF despite our large underweight. This occurred because our one financial stock, Blackstone, delivered an annual return of 75% over the trailing 12 months. Sector weightings and discriminating stock selection both contributed to the SIF's modest outperformance over the past year. The rest of this chapter will be devoted to better understanding what drove this outperformance, as well as identifying things we can do to further improve our performance in the future.

Dividend Yield by Sector

Because we (and most student investment funds) manage stocks for a not-for-profit entity (university endowments and foundations), dividends are a favored source of returns, as we pay no taxes on dividends and other distributions to shareholders. Figure 19.14 shows the dividend yield of the SIF by sector, organized in the same manner as Figure 19.13.

Sector	Sector Yield	Weighted Sector Yield	Portfolio Yield	Weighted Portfolio Yield	Higher/Lower Yield
Energy	1.47%	0.16%	4.43%	0.48%	0.32%
Healthcare	1.58%	0.31%	2.78%	0.55%	0.24%
Information Technology	1.39%	0.25%	2.54%	0.46%	0.21%
Financials	1.30%	0.06%	5.38%	0.24%	0.18%
Consumer Discretionary	1.18%	0.12%	2.69%	0.27%	0.15%
Telecommunication Services	2.87%	0.22%	4.33%	0.33%	0.11%
Industrials	1.83%	0.26%	2.46%	0.35%	0.09%
Consumer Staples	2.32%	0.23%	2.92%	0.29%	0.06%
Materials	1.84%	0.03%	4.04%	0.07%	0.04%
Utilities	3.78%	0.13%	3.91%	0.13%	0.00%
Average	1.96%	1.77%	3.55%	3.17%	1.40%

Datasource: S&P's Capital IQ

FIGURE 19.14 Student Investment Fund Dividend Yield by Sector.

The "Sector Yield" column shows the dividend yield for each SPDR sector ETF, and the "Weighted Sector Yield" column weights each yield by our portfolio sector weights from Figure 19.12. The sum of this column equals what our portfolio dividend yield would be (1.77%) if we held only sector ETFs in proportion to our active portfolio weights. The "Portfolio Yield" column shows the average yield of the stocks in our SIF by sector. Since dividends are a key part of our process, it's no surprise that our average sector yield is higher than the yield of most of the sector ETFs. The "Weighted Portfolio Yield" column weights each average yield according to our active sector weights. The sum of this column equals our actual portfolio dividend yield (3.17%). The "Higher/Lower Yield" column calculates the difference between our actual weighted sector yield and the weighted yield of the sector ETFs. The results show that our SIF is gaining additional weighted dividend yield from 9 out of the 10 sectors, for a total extra yield of 1.40%.

Recall that Figure 19.13 showed that the SIF outperformed an all-ETF strategy by 1.5% over the past 12 months. Our portfolio's higher dividend yield of 1.4% therefore accounts for most of our return outperformance. Prioritizing dividend yield in our stock selection process is therefore paying off, and thus a strategy that we will continue to follow.

Portfolio Alpha and Beta

Figure 19.15 shows the performance of the fund for the prior 60 months, beginning in May 2008. The previous points regarding the stability of a fundamentals-based portfolio are evident from the graph. As the market accumulated losses totaling almost −50% by March 2009, the SIF experienced a decline of only −32%. Over the entire five-year period shown, the SIF earned a total return of 16.2% while the S&P 500 index increased 16.6% (3.04% and 3.12% annualized, respectively). The students therefore matched their benchmark based on total returns over the five-year period.

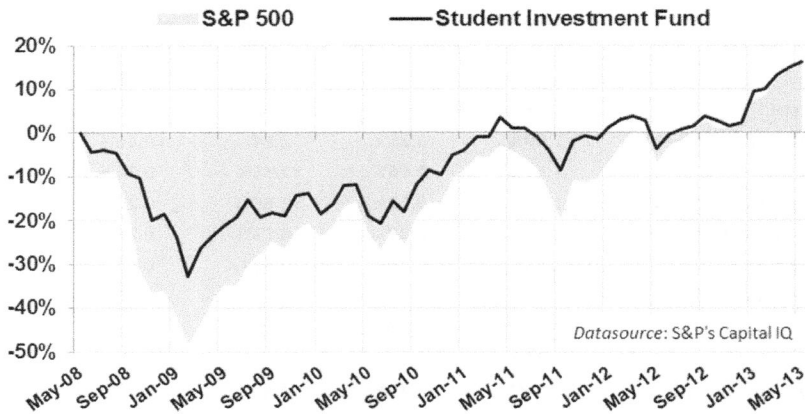

FIGURE 19.15 Student Investment Fund Returns versus the S&P 500, May 2008 through May 2013.

The performance of relative return investment vehicles must also be assessed based on risk, of course, so we'll use the single-index regression model first introduced as Equation 19.25 to estimate the alpha and beta of the SIF from May 2008 to May 2013. Because Sharpe's beta framework actually describes the relation between *excess* returns and systematic risk, we'll adjust our monthly portfolio and S&P 500 index returns by subtracting the 1-month yield on the 10-year T-note and run the regression using these excess returns. The regression model is depicted as Equation 19.33:

$$(R_{SIF} - RF) = \alpha_{SIF} + \beta_{SIF} (R_m - RF) + \varepsilon \qquad (19.33)$$

The regression fits the data well, resulting in an R-squared of 75.0%, which indicates that the excess returns of the S&P 500 explain 75% of the variation in the excess returns of the SIF. The regression intercept equals 0.11% — this is the portfolio's alpha, indicating a small average monthly outperformance (1.0011^{12} − 1 = 1.33% annualized). The regression beta coefficient equals 0.67, which indicates that the SIF earned these returns with only two-thirds of the volatility of the S&P 500. The SIF's low beta is earned mainly during the market's bear phase, when the fund's losses (−32%) are only about two-thirds of the market's losses (−50%). This is exactly the type of conservative, low-volatility performance we're targeting, as our only client is a university foundation. These results once again demonstrate that the stability of stocks with solid fundamentals also extends to entire stock portfolios.

The next interesting thing to observe is how a portfolio consisting of stocks with solid fundamentals and superior competitive positioning behaves during a bull market phase. The monthly returns to the SIF and S&P 500 from May 2012 to May 2013 are shown in Figure 19.16.

I reestimated the performance attribution regression shown in Equation 19.33 using monthly excess returns from this one-year period. The regression intercept (alpha) equals 1.0%, and the portfolio beta expands to 1.07 during what was

THE INTEGRATION OF TECHNICAL ANALYSIS

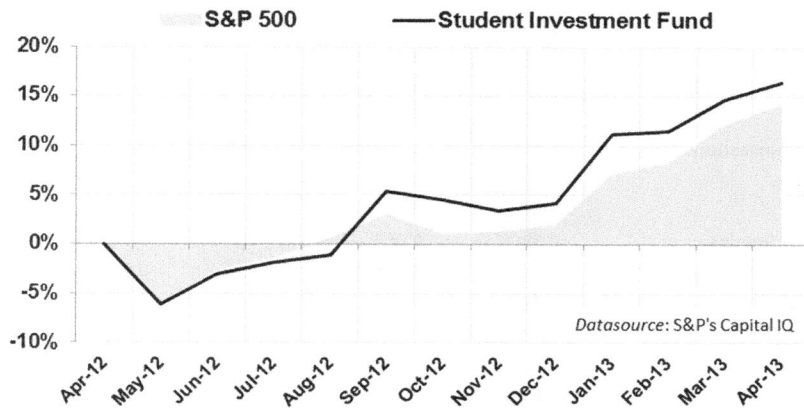

FIGURE 19.16 Student Investment Fund Returns versus the S&P 500, April 2012 through April 2013.

primarily a bull market phase. Once again, this is exactly the type of performance we want to engineer. The real art of fundamental analysis involves selecting stocks and combining them into portfolios that have lower betas during bear markets, but more exposure to macro/systematic risk during bull markets. Most important, we want this characteristic to be an organic part of the portfolio itself, not something that the manager tries to achieve by overtrading the portfolio. Focusing on making a small number of high-conviction portfolio adjustments each year leads to a lower error rate than can be achieved by portfolios with turnover rates of 100% or higher. When a team turns over the entire net asset value of a portfolio in just one year's time, we can infer that they never had high conviction in many of their stocks in the first place.

In this section we saw how a portfolio consisting of stocks with solid fundamentals will tend to lose less value during a bear market, but the superior competitive positioning of the companies in the portfolio results in their stock prices increasing proportionately with the overall stock market during bull market phases. This is what buy-and-hold fundamental investing is all about—constructing high-return, low-risk, low-turnover portfolios that allow an investor to go on vacation for a week without having to check their stock prices three times a day (a skill that's becoming increasingly rare, and thus all-the-more valuable, in our era of quantitative-driven investing).[4]

Sector Betas and the Treynor Ratio

We also analyze the portfolio's beta by sector, following the format introduced earlier in this chapter. The results are depicted in Figure 19.17. The "Sector Beta" column shows the beta of each SPDR sector ETF, and the "Weighted Sector Beta" column multiplies each beta by our active sector weights from Figure 19.12. The sum of this column equals what our portfolio beta would be (0.981) if we held only sector ETFs in proportion to our active sector weights. The "portfolio beta" column shows the average beta of the stocks we hold from each sector, and the "weighted portfolio beta"

Sector	Sector Beta	Weighted Sector Beta	Portfolio Beta	Weighted Portfolio Beta	Higher/Lower Beta
Consumer Discretionary	1.130	0.112	0.101	0.010	-0.102
Energy	1.065	0.116	0.527	0.057	-0.059
Telecommunication Services	1.361	0.103	0.616	0.046	-0.056
Healthcare	0.675	0.134	0.601	0.119	-0.015
Materials	1.303	0.021	0.603	0.010	-0.011
Consumer Staples	0.580	0.058	0.483	0.049	-0.010
Information Technology	0.977	0.176	0.965	0.174	-0.002
Industrials	1.249	0.178	1.249	0.178	0.000
Utilities	0.466	0.016	0.540	0.019	0.003
Financials	1.504	0.068	2.206	0.099	0.032
Average	1.031	0.981	0.789	0.761	-0.220

Datasource: S&P's Capital IQ

FIGURE 19.17 Student Investment Fund Beta by Sector.

column weights these average betas by our active sector weights. The sum of this column equals our actual weighted portfolio beta (0.761), which is slightly higher than the portfolio beta we obtained by regressing our portfolio returns on the returns of the S&P 500 index.[5] The "higher/lower beta" column calculates the difference between the weighted ETF betas and our weighted portfolio sector betas. The results show that our process identifies stocks with lower betas in most sectors. The sum of the "Higher/Lower Beta" column equals the difference between our actual portfolio beta and what our beta would be if we owned sector ETFs with the same portfolio weights. In this case, our fundamental process resulted in a portfolio beta that was 0.22 lower than an all-ETF portfolio.

Equation 19.34 depicts the Treynor ratio — similar to the Sharpe ratio (Equation 19.21), except it scales an asset's or portfolio's excess return by its beta rather than total volatility (Treynor, 1965). The Treynor ratio can be interpreted as the excess return an investor receives per unit of beta risk exposure. A larger ratio indicates a higher payoff for exposure to beta risk, and a smaller ratio indicates the payoff for exposure to market risk was lower (or negative if the portfolio underperforms the risk-free rate, which can occur during bear market years).

$$\text{Treynor ratio} = \frac{\text{Return} - \text{Risk-free rate}}{\text{Beta}} \quad (19.34)$$

Figure 19.18 depicts the Treynor ratios for each sector ETF and the SIF portfolio. Our fundamental process identified stocks with higher Treynor ratios in 7 out of 10 sectors. Overall our portfolio Treynor ratio was 0.41 higher. The SIF portfolio therefore has a risk/return trade-off that is 24% "better" than the risk/return profile of a similarly weighted all-ETF portfolio. We previously saw that the SIF modestly outperformed its benchmark in terms of returns over the past year. After adjusting the excess returns of the SIF and sector ETFs for beta risk using the Treynor ratio, we can conclude that the SIF portfolio delivered 2.07% of excess returns per unit of beta risk, while a similarly-weighted all-ETF portfolio would have delivered only 1.67% of excess returns at the same level of risk.

Sector	Weighted Sector Return	Sector Treynor Ratio	Weighted Port. Return	Portfolio Treynor Ratio	Higher/Lower Treynor Ratio
Consumer Discretionary	2.4%	0.19	1.2%	0.98	0.79
Telecommunication Services	1.1%	0.11	2.1%	0.42	0.31
Energy	1.7%	0.12	2.3%	0.36	0.24
Financials	1.2%	0.13	3.4%	0.33	0.20
Consumer Staples	2.2%	0.33	2.6%	0.48	0.15
Healthcare	6.1%	0.44	6.5%	0.51	0.07
Information Technology	1.0%	0.03	1.4%	0.06	0.02
Industrials	2.4%	0.12	1.9%	0.09	-0.04
Utilities	0.3%	0.15	-0.3%	-0.22	-0.36
Materials	0.2%	0.04	-0.9%	-0.94	-0.98
Average	18.6%	1.67	20.1%	2.07	0.41

Datasource: S&P's Capital IQ

FIGURE 19.18   Student Investment Fund Treynor Ratio by Sector.

▉ Multifactor Models

In the previous section we used a single-factor performance attribution model that compared the excess returns of a portfolio to the excess returns of an index benchmark. We measured excess returns as the intercept of the regression model (alpha) and risk as the slope of the line of best fit (beta). In this section we'll see how money managers incorporate more than one factor into similar types of models, known as multifactor models.

Multifactor Models Based on Macro Factors

Multifactor models take a variety of approaches in an attempt to understand the forces that determine a portfolio's returns. One approach, which follows from Ross's (1976) arbitrage pricing theory, models excess returns as a function of various macroeconomic factors. In the single-factor model we used previously, the returns to the stock market index were assumed to capture all of the relevant macro information in one signal. A portfolio manager would use a multifactor macro model when he believes that it's important to understand how the returns of a portfolio might respond to individual macro factors. Macro multifactor models are used more often in a quantitative portfolio management process.

In the previous section we attributed the performance of our portfolio to our sector over- and underweights vs. the S&P 500. In a macro multifactor model, a portfolio's performance can be attributed to the portfolio's exposure to certain macroeconomic risk factors. Equation 19.35 depicts one of the first multifactor models, introduced by Chen, Roll, and Ross (1986). We'll estimate this model by regressing the monthly excess returns to the SIF from 2008 to 2013 on the following factors (all of which are available for free download from the Federal Reserve Economic Database, or FRED2):

$R_m - RF$:   the monthly excess return to the S&P 500 index
ΔIP: the monthly percentage change in U.S. industrial production

Variable	Regression Coefficient	t-statistic
Intercept	-0.0282	-10.81
Mkt-RF	0.7587	15.24
Δ IP	-0.6704	-2.76
Δ CPI	0.3595	0.51
Δ Baa Yield-RF	0.1356	4.24
Δ 30-Yr Yield-RF	-0.0201	-4.73

FIGURE 19.19 Regression of Student Investment Fund Returns on Various Macro Factors.

ΔCPI: the monthly percentage change in the U.S. consumer price index

$\Delta Baa - RF$: the monthly percentage change in the bond credit spread (Baa yield − risk-free rate)

$\Delta 30yr - RF$: the monthly percentage change in the slope of the term structure of interest rates (30-year T-bond yield − risk-free rate).

$$(R_{SIF} - RF) = \alpha_{SIF} + \beta_1(R_m - RF) + \beta_2(\Delta IP) + \beta_3(\Delta CPI)$$
$$+ \beta_4(\Delta Baa - RF) + \beta_5(\Delta 30yr - RF) + \varepsilon \quad (19.35)$$

The results of the regression model are shown in Figure 19.19. Including the individual macro factors improved the model's explanatory power — the regression R-squared increased to 83%. Each factor's regression coefficient and t-statistic are shown in Figure 19.19. (As a general rule, t-statistics greater than 2.0 in absolute value indicate statistical significance, meaning that the variable has a genuine statistical relation with the dependent variable being modeled.) All the macro factors are significant except for the rate of change of the consumer price index.

The results displayed in Figure 19.19 are unsurprising. The SIF is a diversified large-capitalization portfolio focused mainly on U.S. stocks. We therefore expect the returns to our portfolio to have a significant relation with most U.S. macro factors. Additionally, because most of the factors in this model are statistically significant and the regression R-squared is higher than the single-index regression model, we can conclude that this model provides a better fit for the data. This means that the coefficient on the Mkt-RF factor of 0.76 is a better estimate of our portfolio market beta than the value of 0.67 obtained from the single-index regression model (Equation 19.33). Further notice that the portfolio beta estimate of 0.76 from the multifactor macro model is exactly equal to our weighted portfolio beta shown in Figure 19.17.

Multifactor Models Based on Style Factors

The style factor approach to multifactor modeling provides a better match for portfolios managed based on a fundamental vs. quantitative process. Fama and French

(1993) and Carhartt (1997) identified a variety of style characteristics that represent subcomponents of systematic risk viewed from a micro perspective. The model, shown as Equation 19.36, expresses the excess returns of a stock or a portfolio as a function of the following factors:

$R_m - RF$: the monthly excess return to the S&P 500 index

SMB: "small minus big," equal to the returns to a small-capitalization portfolio minus the returns to a large-capitalization portfolio

HML: "high minus low," equal to the returns to a portfolio of stocks with high book-to-market ratios minus the returns to a portfolio of stocks with low book-to-market ratios

MOM: momentum, equal to the returns to a portfolio of stocks with the best performance over the past year minus the returns to a portfolio of stocks with the worst performance

$$(R_{SIF} - RF) = \alpha_{SIF} + \beta_1(R_m - RF) + \beta_2(SMB) + \beta_3(HML) + \beta_4(MOM) + \varepsilon \quad (19.36)$$

The SMB factor captures the risk premium associated with the small firm effect, as the market is known to price small-capitalization stocks to have higher expected returns due to the additional risks associated with being a smaller company. The HML factor captures the risk premium associated with the value effect, as the market discounts the prices of stocks with questionable prospects to the point that their price-to-earnings (P/E), price-to-book (P/B), and other relative valuation ratios become extremely low. The MOM factor captures the risk premium associated with the price momentum effect, whereby stocks with positive (negative) price momentum have a tendency to earn additional positive (negative) future returns.

The results of fitting the multifactor style model to the returns of the SIF and three individual stocks are depicted in Figure 19.20. The regression coefficients are shown in bold, with the relevant t-statistics appearing beneath each coefficient. The SIF has significant exposure to the Mkt-RF factor, as was the case in all the models we've estimated. It is not surprising that the SIF's returns have no significant relation

Stock	Mkt-RF	SMB	HML	MOM	R-Squared
SIF	0.6945	-0.0924	0.0691	0.0845	73.9%
t-stat	10.97	-0.70	0.61	1.66	
CVX	1.0801	-0.7395	0.0216	0.3732	59.3%
t-stat	9.10	-2.97	0.10	3.92	
ARII	1.7135	1.9731	0.6453	0.3728	44.7%
t-stat	4.35	2.39	0.92	1.18	
AMZN	1.0099	0.6002	-1.7123	-0.2242	34.6%
t-stat	4.19	1.19	-3.99	-1.15	

FIGURE 19.20 Style Factor Regressions for the Student Investment Fund, CVX, ARII, and AMZN.

with the size, value or momentum factors, as our stock selection process did not emphasize any of these factors (evidenced by all the *t*-statistics having absolute values less than 2.0). Our preference for larger companies that are dominant in their industries is reflected in the negative (but statistically insignificant) coefficient on the SMB factor. The model fits the SIF returns well, resulting in an R-squared of 73.9%.

The model also fits Chevron's (CVX) returns well, reflected in the regression R-squared of 59.3%. The Mkt-RF factor is highly significant, as are the SMB and MOM factors. The negative coefficient on the SMB factor reflects CVX's status as a large-capitalization company, meaning that their returns respond oppositely to the common factors that drive small-cap returns. The significant positive coefficient on the MOM factor means that, to some degree, CVX's returns exhibited a tendency to move in trends, both positively and negatively. The next stock modeled is American Railcar Industries (ARII), which designs and manufactures tank railcars in North America. With a market capitalization of only $677 million, it is no surprise that ARII not only has significant exposure to the Mkt-RF factor, but the small-cap SMB factor as well. ARII's returns have no significant relation with the HML or MOM factors, however. The final stock modeled is Amazon (AMZN), which also has significant exposure to the Mkt-RF factor. Notice that AMZN has a significantly negative coefficient on the value (HML) factor, implying that AMZN's returns are negatively correlated with the forces that affect the returns of value stocks. With years of strong stock price performance despite an undefined P/E ratio (due to negative earnings), AMZN is clearly a growth stock, which accounts for its negative HML factor exposure.

Managing a Portfolio Using Multifactor Models

Multifactor models provide different frameworks for managing investment portfolios. Practitioners often refer to the various risk categories to which they seek or avoid exposure as *buckets,* which is a particularly descriptive term in this case. Our preferred method for portfolio management (heavily emphasized in this chapter) is the sector allocation approach. We could therefore think of the wealth invested in our portfolio as being allocated among 10 possible sector "buckets." Similarly, managers implementing a more quantitatively focused process think in terms of adding stocks with strong exposure to desirable macro factors, and trimming positions that provide exposure to less desirable macro factors. For example, Figure 19.19 showed that our SIF had a strong negative exposure to the slope of the term structure (the $\Delta\ 30yr{-}RF$ factor), caused by our underweight in financial stocks (banks are usually more profitable when the yield curve is steeply sloped). If we thought the yield curve was going to steepen, adding financial stocks to the portfolio—which would increase our exposure to the $\Delta\ 30yr{-}RF$ factor—would make sense. However, the SIF had no significant exposure to any of the style factors besides the basic Mkt-RF factor. If we thought the market was at a point where small-capitalization stocks were due to outperform, trimming some of our large-cap exposure and adding several well-positioned small-cap names would be the right move.

Summary

- Basic statistical metrics such as the arithmetic average, standard deviation, covariance, and correlation provide the foundations of professional stock and portfolio risk analysis.
- The best way to learn statistics—and risk analysis—is to understand each risk metric conceptually.
- In finance, total risk (or volatility) is conceptualized as the standard deviation of returns.
- Total risk is conceptualized as having two main drivers: market or macroeconomic risk, and firm-specific risk.
- Only firm-specific risk is reduced by the mechanics of diversification.
- When calculating portfolio volatility, each stock's individual variance of returns represents firm-specific risk effects, and each stock's covariance with all the other stocks in the portfolio represent macro risk effects.
- Mechanically, diversification reduces firm-specific risk because the covariance terms in the portfolio volatility calculation proliferate exponentially (there are $n^2 - n$ of them), but the individual firm variance terms only proliferate linearly (there are n of them). As a portfolio becomes larger, the covariance (macro) effects eventually dominate the portfolio volatility calculation.
- Diversifying among stocks with low return correlations improves a portfolios' mean-variance efficiency.
- Analyzing and managing a portfolio's risk using beta simplifies the calculations necessary to understand a portfolio's exposure to market risk (the risk that is unaffected by diversification only).
- Building a portfolio of stocks with solid fundamentals naturally leads to low-beta portfolios, as these companies' fundamentals provide support for their stock prices during bear markets.
- In addition to beta-risk exposure, a portfolio's performance can be attributed to its active sector weights and dividend yield.
- Multifactor models depict a portfolio's risk exposure to other types of factors, such as specific macroeconomic risks or investment style factors, including the small-firm, value, or price momentum effects.

Questions and Problems

1. What are the three most important assumptions underlying Markowitz's (1952, 1959) contributions to the theory of portfolio risk?
2. What does it mean to say that a stock portfolio is "mean-variance" efficient?
3. Explain how a stock's historical mean return is conceptualized as its "expected value" in portfolio risk analysis.
4. Explain how a stock's historical standard deviation of returns is conceptualized as a measure of the stock's "total risk."

5. What are the two main subcomponents of total risk (volatility)?

6. Why is market or macroeconomic risk sometimes called "undiversifiable" risk?

7. What are the three factors that affect the volatility of a diversified portfolio?

8. What statistic represents each stock's individual contribution to overall portfolio volatility?

9. What portfolio metric represents the portfolio's exposure to macroeconomic factors?

10. Why is covariance a difficult statistic to interpret?

11. Why is the correlation coefficient easier to interpret than covariance?

12. Provide a technical explanation of why portfolio risk gradually becomes all systematic (market) as the number of securities in the portfolio (n) gets large.

13. What does a stock's (or portfolio's) Sharpe ratio measure?

14. How are Sharpe ratios related to the idea of Markowitz mean-variance efficiency?

15. What are the two key drivers of beta?

16. How does a sound fundamental investment process help identify low-beta stocks?

17. In what sense is a portfolio of stocks with good fundamental characteristics "safer?"

18. Figure 19.21 shows the sector weights of a hypothetical portfolio versus the sector weights of the S&P 500 index. Comment on whether the portfolio appears to be defensively or offensively positioned based on the portfolio manager's sector over- and underweights.

19. Figure 19.22 shows the sector weights of a hypothetical portfolio vs. the sector weights of the S&P 500 index. Comment on whether the portfolio appears to be defensively or offensively positioned based on the portfolio manager's sector over- and underweights.

20. Use the annual returns of Deere, Intel, Pfizer, and the S&P 500 (Figure 19.23) to answer questions 20 (a) through (n).

    a. Calculate the arithmetic mean return for DE, INTC, PFE, and the S&P 500.

Sector	Portfolio Weight	S&P 500 Weight	Over/Under Weight
Consumer Staples	18.4%	10.6%	7.8%
Healthcare	18.8%	12.2%	6.6%
Utilities	7.2%	3.4%	3.8%
Telecommunication Services	4.8%	2.9%	1.9%
Consumer Discretionary	10.8%	11.7%	-0.9%
Materials	2.2%	3.6%	-1.4%
Energy	9.4%	11.2%	-1.8%
Industrials	7.8%	10.3%	-2.5%
Financials	9.5%	15.8%	-6.3%
Information Technology	11.1%	18.3%	-7.2%
Total	100.0%	100.0%	0.0%

FIGURE 19.21 Hypothetical Active Sector Weights.

THE INTEGRATION OF TECHNICAL ANALYSIS

| | Portfolio | S&P 500 | Over/Under |
Sector	Weight	Weight	Weight
Industrials	13.7%	10.3%	3.4%
Consumer Discretionary	14.3%	11.7%	2.6%
Energy	13.4%	11.2%	2.2%
Materials	5.2%	3.6%	1.6%
Information Technology	19.4%	18.3%	1.1%
Financials	16.0%	15.8%	0.2%
Telecommunication Services	2.2%	2.9%	-0.7%
Utilities	2.0%	3.4%	-1.4%
Healthcare	8.0%	12.2%	-4.2%
Consumer Staples	5.8%	10.6%	-4.8%
Total	100.0%	100.0%	0.0%

FIGURE 19.22 Hypothetical Active Sector Weights.

| | Annual Returns (%) | | | |
Year-End	DE	INTC	PFE	^SPX
30-Apr-10	34.44	36.12	0.30	19.51
29-Apr-11	47.48	4.77	37.20	21.56
30-Apr-12	-12.52	14.38	2.00	-2.56
30-Apr-13	16.08	-5.49	23.41	22.92

Datasource: S&P's Capital IQ

FIGURE 19.23 Annual Returns: DE, INTC, PFE, and the S&P 500.

b. Calculate the variance and standard deviation of returns for DE, INTC, PFE, and the S&P 500.

c. Calculate the covariance and correlation of returns between all the pairs of stock and stock index returns. Create one table displaying all the covariances and another displaying all the correlations.

d. Calculate the betas for Deere, Intel, and Pfizer.

e. Before performing any calculations, do you think that Deere and Intel would be good stocks to combine into a portfolio? (Explain.)

f. Calculate the expected return and variance of a portfolio comprised of 50% Deere and 50% Intel.

g. Would some investors find the 50/50 portfolio preferable to holding Deere, Intel, or an S&P 500 index exchange-traded fund (ETF) alone? Draw an XY scatterplot of the expected return (y-axis) and standard deviation (x-axis) of both stocks, the S&P 500 index and the 50/50 portfolio and explain your reasoning based on each investment's mean-variance efficiency.

h. Calculate the Sharpe ratios for Deere, Intel, the S&P 500, and the 50/50 portfolio and organize them into a table that displays the standard deviation, expected return, and Sharpe ratio of each investment option (use a risk-free rate of 2.16%). In terms of Sharpe ratios (mean-variance efficiency), which investment option is preferred? Explain your reasoning.

i. Before performing any calculations, do you think that Pfizer would be a good stock to combine into a portfolio with Deere and Intel? (Explain.)

j. Calculate the expected return and variance of a portfolio comprised of 35% Deere, 35% Intel, and 30% Pfizer.

k. Would some investors find the 35/35/30 portfolio preferable to holding Deere, Intel, Pfizer, or the S&P 500 index alone? Draw an XY scatterplot of the expected return (y-axis) and standard deviation (x-axis) of the three stocks, the S&P 500 index, and both portfolios and explain your reasoning.

l. Calculate the Sharpe ratios for Pfizer and the 35/35/30 portfolio. Organize the Sharpe ratios for all five investment options into a table that displays their standard deviation, expected return, and Sharpe ratios (use a risk-free rate of 2.16%). In terms of Sharpe ratios (mean-variance efficiency), which investment option is preferred? Explain your reasoning.

m. Calculate the weighted average beta of the 50/50 and 35/35/30 portfolios.

n. Calculate the Treynor ratios for Deere, Intel, Pfizer, the S&P 500 index, and the 50/50 and 35/35/30 portfolios. Organize the Treynor ratios for all five investment options into a table that displays their betas, expected return, and Treynor ratios (use a risk-free rate of 2.16%). In terms of Treynor ratios (excess returns per unit of beta risk), which investment option is preferred? Explain your reasoning. (Also provide a comment on interpreting INTC's Treynor ratio, based on INTC's negative beta.)

21. Use the annual returns of Coca-Cola, Heinz, Merck, and the S&P 500 (Figure 19.24) to answer questions 21 (a) through (m).

a. Calculate the arithmetic mean return for KO, HNZ, MRK, and the S&P 500.

b. Calculate the variance and standard deviation of returns for KO, HNZ, MRK, and the S&P 500.

c. Calculate the covariance and correlation of returns between all the pairs of stock and stock index returns. Create one table displaying all the covariances and another displaying all the correlations.

d. Calculate the betas for Coca-Cola, Heinz, and Merck.

e. Before performing any calculations, do you think that KO and HNZ would be good stocks to combine into a portfolio? (Explain.)

f. Calculate the expected return and variance of a portfolio comprised of 50% Coca-Cola and 50% Heinz.

g. Would some investors find the 50/50 portfolio preferable to holding KO, HNZ, or an S&P 500 index exchange-traded fund (ETF) alone? Draw an XY

Year-End	KO	HNZ	MRK	^SPX
28-May-10	5.20	22.08	25.21	19.51
31-May-11	28.83	22.91	8.73	21.56
31-May-12	11.74	-3.59	2.31	-2.56
31-May-13	6.88	36.17	23.24	22.92

Datasource: S&P's Capital IQ

FIGURE 19.24 Annual Returns: KO, HNZ, MRK, and the S&P 500.

scatterplot of the expected return (*y*-axis) and standard deviation (*x*-axis) of both stocks, the S&P 500 index and the 50/50 portfolio and explain your reasoning based on each investment's mean-variance efficiency.

h. Calculate the Sharpe ratios for KO, HNZ, the S&P 500, and the 50/50 portfolio and organize them into a table that displays the standard deviation, expected return, and Sharpe ratio of each investment option (use a risk-free rate of 2.16%). In terms of Sharpe ratios (mean-variance efficiency), which investment option is preferred? Explain your reasoning.

i. Before performing any calculations, do you think that Merck would be a good stock to combine into a portfolio with Coca-Cola and Heinz? (Explain.)

j. Calculate the expected return and variance of a portfolio comprised of 35% KO, 35% HNZ, and 30% MRK.

k. Would some investors find the 35/35/30 portfolio preferable to holding Coca-Cola, Heinz, Merck, or the S&P 500 index alone? Draw an XY scatterplot of the expected return (*y*-axis) and standard deviation (*x*-axis) of the three stocks, the S&P 500 index, and both portfolios and explain your reasoning.

l. Calculate the Sharpe ratios for Merck and the 35/35/30 portfolio. Organize the Sharpe ratios for all five investment options into a table that also displays their standard deviation, expected return, and Sharpe ratio (use a risk-free rate of 2.16%). In terms of Sharpe ratios (mean-variance efficiency), which investment option is preferred? Explain your reasoning.

m. Calculate the Treynor ratios for Coca-Cola, Heinz, Merck, the S&P 500 index, and the 50/50 and 35/35/30 portfolios. Organize the Treynor ratios for all five investment options into a table that displays their betas, expected return and Treynor ratios (use a risk-free rate of 2.16%). In terms of Treynor ratios (excess returns per unit of beta risk), which investment option is preferred? Explain your reasoning.

Answers to Selected Questions and Problems

1. Investors are generally risk-averse, they base their portfolio decisions on risk and expected return only, and they measure risk as the variance (or standard deviation) of expected returns.

3. The mean of a series represents the series' expected value in the same way that we use the historical average daily high temperature on a given date as a naïve forecast of the expected high temperature on that same date in subsequent years. If the average temperature on the 4th of July has been 90 degrees over the past 20 years, then, lacking a better forecast, it's reasonable to expect that the high temperature on the next 4th of July will be about the same. What are the two main subcomponents of total risk (volatility)?

5. Total Risk = Market or Macroeconomic Risk + Firm-Specific Risk, or
Total Risk = Systematic Risk + Unsystematic Risk, or
Total Risk = Undiversifiable Risk + Diversifiable Risk

7. The factors influencing portfolio volatility are (1) the total volatility of the component securities or assets, (2) the correlation (covariance) among the returns of these assets, and (3) the fraction of the total portfolio wealth invested in each asset.

9. Each stock's covariance of returns with every other stock in the portfolio.

11. By scaling two stocks' covariance of returns by the product of their standard deviations, covariance is transformed into the correlation coefficient, which lies in a strict range between -1.0 and $+1.0$.

13. The Sharpe ratio measures excess returns per unit of total risk.

15. The two key drivers of beta are a stock's return correlation with its relevant market index and a stock's volatility of returns relative to the market index's volatility of returns.

17. The prices of fundamentally sound stocks in the portfolio are less volatile because the fundamentals supporting their per share intrinsic values are also less volatile.

19. (See Figure 19.25.) This portfolio is positioned more offensively, with over-weights in classic high-beta, "risk-on" sectors such as industrials, consumer discretionary, energy, and materials stocks, and underweights in lower-beta defensive sectors such as utilities, health care, and consumer staples.

20. a.(See Figure 19.26.)

$$\overline{DE} = (34.4 + 47.5 - 12.5 + 16.1)/4 = 21.37\%$$
$$\overline{INTC} = (36.1 + 4.8 + 14.4 - 5.5)/4 = 12.45\%$$
$$\overline{PFE} = (0.3 + 37.2 + 2.0 + 23.4)/4 = 15.73\%$$
$$\overline{SP500} = (19.5 + 21.6 - 2.6 + 22.9)/4 = 15.36\%$$

b. $\sigma^2_{DE} = \dfrac{\begin{bmatrix}(34.44 - 21.37)^2 + (47.48 - 21.37)^2 + (-12.52 - 21.37)^2 \\ + (16.08 - 21.37)^2 \end{bmatrix}}{3} = 676.370$

Sector	Portfolio Weight	S&P 500 Weight	Over/Under Weight
Industrials	13.7%	10.3%	3.4%
Consumer Discretionary	14.3%	11.7%	2.6%
Energy	13.4%	11.2%	2.2%
Materials	5.2%	3.6%	1.6%
Information Technology	19.4%	18.3%	1.1%
Financials	16.0%	15.8%	0.2%
Telecommunication Services	2.2%	2.9%	-0.7%
Utilities	2.0%	3.4%	-1.4%
Healthcare	8.0%	12.2%	-4.2%
Consumer Staples	5.8%	10.6%	-4.8%
Total	100.0%	100.0%	0.0%

FIGURE 19.25 Hypothetical Active Sector Weights.

Annual Returns (%)				
Year-End	DE	INTC	PFE	^SPX
30-Apr-10	34.44	36.12	0.30	19.51
29-Apr-11	47.48	4.77	37.20	21.56
30-Apr-12	-12.52	14.38	2.00	-2.56
30-Apr-13	16.08	-5.49	23.41	22.92

Datasource: S&P's Capital IQ

FIGURE 19.26 Annual Returns: DE, INTC, PFE, and the S&P 500.

$$\sigma_{DE} = \sqrt{\sigma_{DE}^2} = \sqrt{676.370} = 26.01\%$$

$$\sigma_{INTC}^2 = \frac{\left[\begin{array}{c}(36.12+12.45)^2 + (4.77-12.45)^2 + (14.38-12.45)^2 \\ + (-5.49-12.45)^2\end{array}\right]}{3} = 315.007$$

$$\sigma_{INTC} = \sqrt{\sigma_{INTC}^2} = \sqrt{315.007} = 17.75\%$$

$$\sigma_{PFE}^2 = \frac{\left[\begin{array}{c}(0.30-15.73)^2 + (37.20-15.73)^2 + (2.00-15.73)^2 \\ + (23.41-15.73)^2\end{array}\right]}{3} = 315.487$$

$$\sigma_{PFE} = \sqrt{\sigma_{PFE}^2} = \sqrt{315.487} = 17.76\%$$

$$\sigma_{SP500}^2 = \frac{\left[\begin{array}{c}(19.51-15.36)^2 + (21.56-15.36)^2 + (-2.56-15.36)^2 \\ + (22.92-15.36)^2\end{array}\right]}{3} = 144.590$$

$$\sigma_{SP500} = \sqrt{\sigma_{SP500}^2} = \sqrt{144.590} = 12.02\%$$

c. Refer to the following calculations and Figures 19.27 and 19.28.

$$\sigma_{xy} = \frac{\sum_{i=1}^{n}(x_i - \bar{x})(y_i - \bar{y})}{n-1}$$

Covariances				
	DE	INTC	PFE	^SPX
DE	676.37	46.13	261.15	261.06
INTC	46.13	315.01	-231.47	-39.90
PFE	261.15	-231.47	315.49	124.33
^SPX	261.06	-39.90	124.33	144.59

FIGURE 19.27 Covariance Matrix: DE, INTC, PFE and the S&P 500.

Correlations				
	DE	**INTC**	**PFE**	**^SPX**
DE	1.000	0.100	0.565	0.835
INTC	0.100	1.000	-0.734	-0.187
PFE	0.565	-0.734	1.000	0.582
^SPX	0.835	-0.187	0.582	1.000

FIGURE 19.28   Correlation Matrix: DE, INTC, PFE and the S&P 500.

$$\sigma_{DE,INTC} = \frac{\begin{bmatrix}(34.44-21.37)(36.12-12.45)+(47.48-21.37)(4.77-12.45)+\\(-12.52-21.37)(14.38-12.45)+(16.08-21.37)(-5.49-12.45)\end{bmatrix}}{3}$$

$$= 46.13$$

$$\rho_{DE,INTC} = \frac{\sigma_{DE,INTC}}{\sigma_{DE}\sigma_{INTC}} = \frac{46.13}{(26.01)(17.75)} = +0.100$$

$$\sigma_{DE,PFE} = \frac{\begin{bmatrix}(34.44-21.37)(0.30-15.73)+(47.48-21.37)(37.20-15.73)+\\(-12.52-21.37)(2.00-15.73)+(16.08-21.37)(23.41-15.73)\end{bmatrix}}{3}$$

$$= 261.15$$

$$\rho_{DE,PFE} = \frac{\sigma_{DE,PFE}}{\sigma_{DE}\sigma_{PFE}} = \frac{261.15}{(26.01)(17.76)} = +0.565$$

$$\sigma_{DE,SP500} = \frac{\begin{bmatrix}(34.44-21.37)(19.51-15.36)+(47.48-21.37)(21.56-15.36)+\\(-12.52-21.37)(-2.56-15.36)+(16.08-21.37)(22.92-15.36)\end{bmatrix}}{3}$$

$$= 261.06$$

$$\rho_{DE,SP500} = \frac{\sigma_{DE,SP500}}{\sigma_{DE}\sigma_{SP500}} = \frac{261.06}{(26.01)(12.02)} = +0.835$$

$$\sigma_{INTC,PFE} = \frac{\begin{bmatrix}(36.12-12.45)(0.30-15.73)+(4.77-12.45)(37.20-15.73)+\\(14.38-12.45)(2.00-15.73)+(-5.49-12.45)(23.41-15.73)\end{bmatrix}}{3}$$

$$= -231.47$$

$$\rho_{INTC,PFE} = \frac{\sigma_{INTC,PFE}}{\sigma_{INTC}\sigma_{PFE}} = \frac{-231.47}{(17.75)(17.76)} = -0.734$$

$$\sigma_{INTC,SP500} = \frac{\begin{bmatrix}(36.12-12.45)(19.51-15.36)+(4.77-12.45)(21.56-15.36)+\\(14.38-12.45)(-2.56-15.36)+(-5.49-12.45)(22.92-15.36)\end{bmatrix}}{3}$$

$$= -39.90$$

$$\rho_{INTC,SP500} = \frac{\sigma_{INTC,SP500}}{\sigma_{INTC}\sigma_{SP500}} = \frac{-39.90}{(17.75)(12.02)} = -0.187$$

$$\sigma_{PFE,SP500} = \frac{\begin{bmatrix}(0.30-15.73)(19.51-15.36)+(37.20-15.73)(21.56-15.36)+\\(2.00-15.73)(-2.56-15.36)+(23.41-15.73)(22.92-15.36)\end{bmatrix}}{3}$$

$$= 124.33$$

$$\rho_{PFE,SP500} = \frac{\sigma_{PFE,SP500}}{\sigma_{PFE}\sigma_{SP500}} = \frac{124.33}{(17.76)(12.02)} = +0.582$$

d. $\beta_{DE} = \dfrac{\sigma_{DE,SP500}}{\sigma_{SP500}^2} = \dfrac{261.06}{144.59} = 1.81$, or

$$\beta_{DE} = \rho_{DE,SP500} \times \frac{\sigma_{DE}}{\sigma_{SP500}} = 0.835 \times \frac{26.01}{12.02} = 1.81$$

$$\beta_{INTC} = \frac{\sigma_{INTC,SP500}}{\sigma_{SP500}^2} = \frac{-39.90}{144.59} = -0.28, \text{ or}$$

$$\beta_{INTC} = \rho_{INTC,SP500} \times \frac{\sigma_{INTC}}{\sigma_{SP500}} = -0.187 \times \frac{17.75}{12.02} = -0.28$$

$$\beta_{PFE} = \frac{\sigma_{PFE,SP500}}{\sigma_{SP500}^2} = \frac{124.33}{144.59} = 0.86, \text{ or}$$

$$\beta_{PFE} = \rho_{PFE,SP500} \times \frac{\sigma_{PFE}}{\sigma_{SP500}} = 0.582 \times \frac{17.76}{12.02} = 0.86$$

e. The low positive correlation ($\rho = +0.100$) between the returns of Deere and Intel indicates the opportunity to diversify away a substantial amount of firm-specific volatility.

f. $E(r_p) = \sum_{i=1}^{n} w_i r_i = (0.5 \times 21.37) + (0.5 \times 12.45) = 16.91\%$

$$\sigma_p^2 = w_x^2 \sigma_x^2 + w_y^2 \sigma_y^2 + 2w_x w_y \sigma_{x,y}$$

$$\sigma_p^2 = (0.5)^2(676.37) + (0.5)^2(315.01) + 2(0.5)(0.5)(46.13) = 270.91$$

$$\sigma_p = \sqrt{\sigma_p^2} = \sqrt{270.91} = 16.46\%$$

g. (See Figure 19.29.)

For some investors the 50/50 Deere/Intel portfolio presents a risk/return trade-off that is preferable to holding Deere, Intel or the S&P 500 alone, but the portfolio only strictly dominates Intel on a mean-variance basis (because

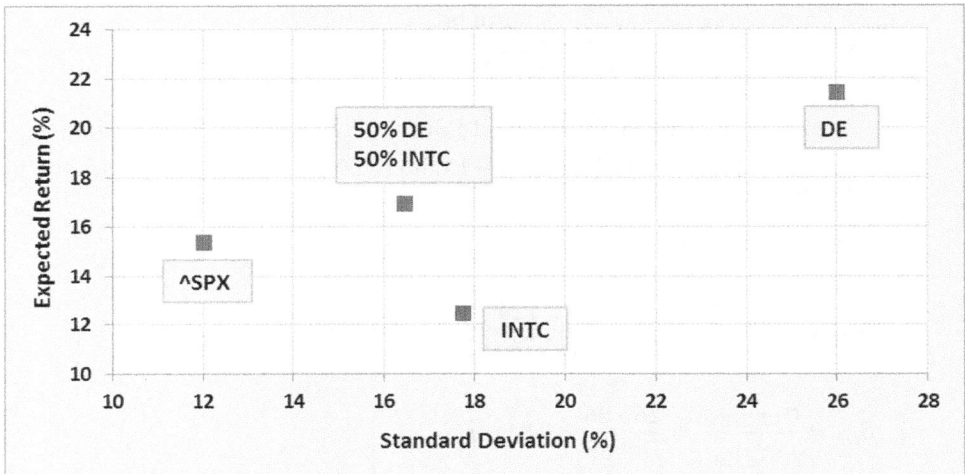

FIGURE 19.29 Expected Return and Standard Deviation, 50/50 Portfolio.

it has both a higher expected return and lower standard deviation). The expected return of the portfolio lies between that of Deere and Intel, while the standard deviation of the portfolio is lower than the standard deviation of either stock. There may be some risk-averse investors who prefer the trade-off offered by the S&P 500, however, and there may be some risk-seeking investors who prefer holding Deere alone.

h. (See Figure 19.30.)

$$\text{Sharpe ratio} = \frac{\text{Expected return} - \text{Risk-free rate}}{\text{Standard deviation of returns}}$$

$$\text{Sharpe ratio}_{DE} = \frac{21.37 - 2.16}{26.01} = 0.74$$

$$\text{Sharpe ratio}_{INTC} = \frac{12.45 - 2.16}{17.75} = 0.58$$

$$\text{Sharpe ratio}_{SP500} = \frac{15.36 - 2.16}{12.02} = 1.10$$

$$\text{Sharpe ratio}_{50/50} = \frac{16.91 - 2.16}{16.46} = 0.90$$

	Standard Deviation	Expected Return	Sharpe Ratio
DE	26.01	21.37	0.74
INTC	17.75	12.45	0.58
^SPX	12.02	15.36	1.10
Portfolio	16.46	16.91	0.90

FIGURE 19.30 Sharpe Ratios: DE, INTC, the S&P 500 and the 50/50 Portfolio.

The 50/50 portfolio has a higher Sharpe ratio (0.90) than either Deere or Intel alone, which means the 50/50 portfolio is expected to earn the highest excess return per unit of total risk, and is thus more mean-variance efficient than either DE or INTC alone. The S&P 500's Sharpe ratio is higher, however (1.10), so many investors would likely prefer an S&P 500 ETF to the portfolio.

i. The low negative correlation ($\rho = -0.734$) between the returns of Intel and Pfizer indicates the opportunity to diversify away a substantial amount of firm-specific volatility. Additionally, Pfizer has a moderate correlation with Deere (+0.565) and a low correlation with the S&P 500 (−0.187), and its expected return is over 3% higher than Intel's. Adding Pfizer to the portfolio in the right proportion should therefore boost the portfolio's Sharpe ratio further.

j. $E(r_p) = \sum_{i=1}^{n} w_i r_i = (0.35 \times 21.37) + (0.35 \times 12.45) + (0.30 \times 15.73) = 16.55\%$

$$\sigma_p^2 = w_x^2 \sigma_x^2 + w_y^2 \sigma_y^2 + w_z^2 \sigma_z^2 + 2w_x w_y \sigma_{x,y} + 2w_x w_z \sigma_{x,z} + 2w_y w_z \sigma_{y,z}$$

$$\sigma_p^2 = (0.35)^2 (676.37) + (0.35)^2 (315.01) + (0.30)^2 (315.49) + 2(0.35)(0.35)(46.13)$$
$$+ 2(0.35)(0.30)(261.15) + 2(0.35)(0.30)(-231.47) = 167.37$$

$$\sigma_p = \sqrt{\sigma_p^2} = \sqrt{167.37} = 12.94\%$$

k. (See Figure 19.31.)The mean-variance efficient options now become the S&P 500 index, the 35/35/30 portfolio, and, for a risk-seeking investor, Deere alone. These dominate the other investment choices. Most Markowitz investors would prefer either the S&P 500 index (lower risk) or the 35/35/30 portfolio (higher expected return).

l. Refer to the following calculations and Figure 19.32.

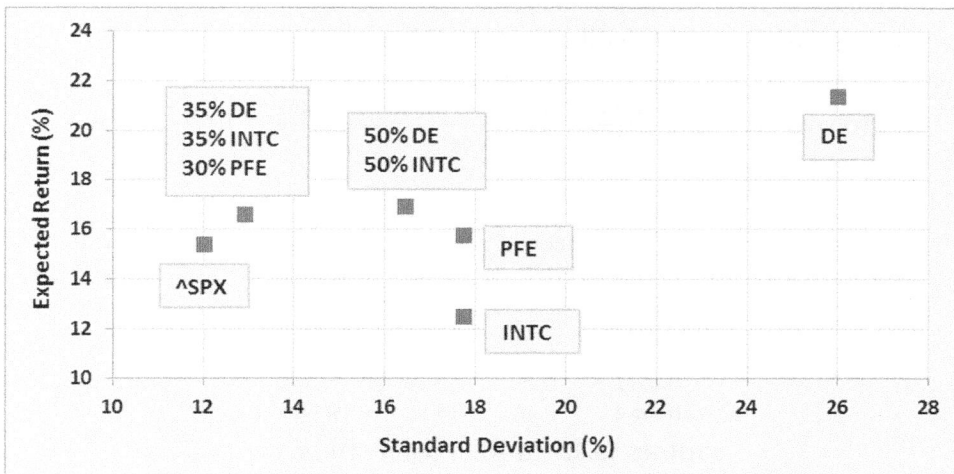

FIGURE 19.31 Expected Return and Standard Deviation, 35/35/30 Portfolio.

	Standard Deviation	Expected Return	Sharpe Ratio
DE	26.01	21.37	0.74
INTC	17.75	12.45	0.58
PFE	17.76	15.73	0.76
^SPX	12.02	15.36	1.10
Portfolio 1	16.46	16.91	0.90
Portfolio 2	12.94	16.55	1.11

FIGURE 19.32 Sharpe Ratios: DE, INTC, PFE, the S&P 500, and the 2- and 3-Stock Portfolios.

$$\text{Sharp ratio} = \frac{\text{Expected return} - \text{Risk-free rate}}{\text{Standard deviation of returns}}$$

$$\text{Sharp ratio}_{PFE} = \frac{15.36 - 2.16}{12.02} = 0.76$$

$$\text{Sharp ratio}_{35/35/30} = \frac{16.55 - 2.16}{12.94} = 1.11$$

The 35/35/30 portfolio has a slightly higher Sharpe ratio (1.11) than the S&P 50 index alone (1.10), which means it is expected to earn the highest excess return per unit of total risk, and is thus more mean-variance efficient than any of the other investment choices. Most Markowitz investors would prefer the portfolio or the S&P 500 index.

m. $$\beta_{50/50} = \sum_{i=1}^{n} w_i \beta_i = (0.50 \times 1.81) + (0.50 \times -0.28) = 0.76$$

$$\beta_{35/35/30} = \sum_{i=1}^{n} w_i \beta_i = (0.35 \times 1.81) + (0.35 \times -0.28) + (0.30 \times 0.86) = 0.79$$

n. Refer to the following calculations and Figure 19.33.

$$\text{Treynor ratio} = \frac{\text{Expected return} - \text{Risk-free rate}}{\text{Beta}}$$

	Beta	Expected Return	Treynor Ratio
DE	1.81	21.37	10.64
INTC	-0.28	12.45	N/A
PFE	0.86	15.73	15.78
^SPX	1.00	15.36	13.20
Portfolio 1	0.76	16.91	19.28
Portfolio 2	0.79	16.55	18.14

FIGURE 19.33 Treynor Ratios: DE, INTC, PFE, the S&P 500, and the Two- and Three-Stock Portfolios.

$$\text{Treynor ratio}_{DE} = \frac{21.37 - 2.16}{1.81} = 10.64$$

$$\text{Treynor ratio}_{INTC} = \frac{12.45 - 2.16}{-0.28} = -37.27$$

The Treynor ratio is not applicable when a stock has a negative beta.

$$\text{Treynor ratio}_{PFE} = \frac{15.73 - 2.16}{0.86} = 15.78$$

$$\text{Treynor ratio}_{SP500} = \frac{15.36 - 2.16}{1.00} = 13.20$$

$$\text{Treynor ratio}_{50/50} = \frac{16.91 - 2.16}{0.76} = 19.28$$

$$\text{Treynor ratio}_{35/35/30} = \frac{16.55 - 2.16}{0.79} = 18.14$$

Although adding PFE to the portfolio increased its mean-variance efficiency (Sharpe ratio), it decreased its Treynor ratio. This occurred because it diverted some of the portfolio weight away from a higher expected return stock (DE) and a lower beta stock (INTC). In terms of Treynor ratios, the 50/50 Deere/Intel portfolio offers greater excess expected returns per unit of beta risk, and is thus preferred to the 35/35/30 portfolio consisting of Deere, Intel and Pfizer.

▨ Notes

1. We will illustrate the statistical principles that follow using annual returns to keep the sample computations manageable. In the real world, we would perform these calculations using statistical software or Excel with more frequent data—usually at least five years of monthly returns—to improve the accuracy of the estimates. In most cases, using a long time series of monthly data for the chapter calculations would yield materially different results.

2. This depiction of a stock's historical average return as its expected value is only valid for the statistical calculations that follow. The capital asset pricing model is the theoretically correct method for estimating a stock's expected return, and the method we should use outside of any strictly statistical context.

3. Dividing by $n - 1$ instead of n corrects for a small statistical bias, but the calculation represents a type of average nonetheless.

4. Research supports the idea that fundamental techniques outperform quantitative techniques, including papers by Gregory-Allen, Shawky, and Stangl (2009) and Wermers, Yao, and Zhao (2010).

5. The betas reported in this table are obtained from S&P's Capital IQ—you will usually find small discrepancies between betas you estimate yourself versus betas obtained from professional data vendors.

References

Carhartt, M. 1997. "On Persistence in Mutual Fund Performance." *Journal of Finance* 52: 57–82.

Chen, N., R. Roll, and S. Ross. 1986. "Economic Forces and the Stock Market." *Journal of Business* 59: 383–404.

Dyl, E., and R. Weigand. 1998. "The Information Content of Dividend Initiations: Additional Evidence." *Financial Management* 27(3): 27–35.

Fama, E., and K. French. 1993. "Common Risk Factors in the Returns of Stocks and Bonds." *Journal of Financial Economics* 33: 3–56.

Gregory-Allen, R., H. Shawky, and J. Stangl. 2009. "Quantitative vs. Fundamental Analysis in Institutional Money Management: Where's the Beef?" *Journal of Investing,* Winter: 42–52.

Lynch, P., and J. Rothchild, J. 1990. *One Up on Wall Street: How to Use What You Already Know to Make Money in the Market*. New York: Penguin Books.

Markowitz, H. 1952. "Portfolio Selection." Journal of Finance 7, no. 1, 77–91.

Markowitz, H. 1959. *Portfolio Selection: Efficient Diversification of Investments*. Cowles Foundation Monograph # 16 (Wiley, New York).

Ross, S. 1976. "The Arbitrage Theory of Capital Asset Pricing." *Journal of Economic Theory* 13: 341–360.

Treynor, Jack. 1965. "How to Rate Management of Investment Funds." *Harvard Business Review* 43: 63–75.

Wermers, R., T. Yao, and J. Zhao. 2010. "The Investment Value of Mutual Fund Portfolio Disclosure." Working paper, University of Maryland.

THE INTEGRATION OF TECHNICAL ANALYSIS

CHAPTER 20

Statistical Analysis

From David Aronson, Evidence-Based Technical
Analysis (Hoboken, New Jersey: John Wiley &
Sons, 2006), Chapter 4.

Learning Objective Statements

- Differentiate between random and nonrandom trends in data from system performance
- Analyze fat-tailed distributions among returns data
- Explain how to measure probability of price change and returns over a given time frame
- Explain how to calculate relative frequency
- Derive a sampling distribution

Statistics is the science of data.[1] In the late nineteenth century, renowned British scientist and author H.G. Wells (1866–1946) said that an intelligent citizen in a twentieth-century free society would need to understand statistical methods. It can be said that an intelligent twenty-first-century practitioner or consumer of TA has the same need.

Statistical methods are not needed when a body of data conveys a message loudly and clearly. If all people drinking from a certain well die of cholera but all those drinking from a different well remain healthy, there is no uncertainty about which well is infected and no need for statistical analysis. However, when the implications of data are uncertain, statistical analysis is the best, perhaps the only, way to draw reasonable conclusions.

Identifying which TA methods have genuine predictive power is highly uncertain. Even the most potent rules display highly variable performance from one data set to the next. Therefore, statistical analysis is the only practical way to distinguish methods that are useful from those that are not.

Whether or not its practitioners acknowledge it, the essence of TA is statistical inference. It attempts to discover generalizations from historical data in the form of patterns, rules, and so forth and then extrapolate them to the future. Extrapolation is inherently uncertain. Uncertainty is uncomfortable.

The discomfort can be dealt with in two ways. One way is to pretend it does not exist. The other is the way of statistics, which meets uncertainty head on by acknowledging it, quantifying it, and then making the best decision possible in the face of it. Bertrand Russell, the renowned British mathematician and philosopher said, "Uncertainty, in the presence of vivid hopes and fears, is painful, but must be endured if we wish to live without the support of comforting fairy tales."[2]

Many people are distrustful or disdainful of statistical analysis and statisticians are often portrayed as nerdy number-crunching geeks divorced from reality. This shows up in jokes. We deride what we do not understand. There is the story about the six-foot-tall man who drowns in a pond with an average depth of only two feet. There's the tale about three statisticians who go duck hunting. They spot a bird flying overhead. The first shoots a foot too far to the left. The second shoots a foot too far to the right. The third jumps up and exclaims, "We got it!!" Even though the average error was zero, there was no duck for dinner.

Powerful tools can be put to bad purpose. Critics often charge that statistics are used to distort and deceive. Of course, similar ends can be achieved with words, although language is not held liable. A more rational stance is needed. Rather than viewing all claims based on statistics with suspicion or taking them all at face value, "a more mature response would be to learn enough about statistics to distinguish honest, useful conclusions from skullduggery or foolishness."[3] "He who accepts statistics indiscriminately will often be duped unnecessarily. But, he who distrusts statistics indiscriminately will often be ignorant unnecessarily. The middle ground we seek between blind distrust and blind gullibility is an open-minded skepticism. That takes an ability to interpret data skillfully."[4]

■ A Preview of Statistical Reasoning

Statistical reasoning is new terrain for many practitioners and consumers of TA. Trips to strange places are easier when you know what to expect.

It is wise to start with the assumption that all TA rules are without predictive power and that a profitable back test was due to luck. This assumption is called the null hypothesis. *Luck*, in this case, means a favorable but accidental correspondence between the rule's signals and subsequent market trends in the historical data sample in which the rule was tested. Although this hypothesis is a reasonable starting point, it is open to refutation with empirical evidence. In other words, if observations contradict predictions made by the null hypothesis, it is abandoned and the alternative hypothesis, that the rule has predictive power, would be adopted. In the context of rule testing, evidence that would refute the null hypothesis is a back-tested rate of return that is too high to be reasonably attributed to mere luck.

If a TA rule has no predictive power, its expected rate of return will be zero on de-trended[5] data. However, over any small sample of data, the profitability of a rule with no predictive power can deviate considerably from zero. These deviations are manifestations of chance—good or bad luck. This phenomenon can be seen in a coin-toss experiment. Over a small number of tosses, the proportion of heads can deviate considerably from 0.50, which is the expected proportion of heads in a very large number of tosses.

Generally, the chance deviations of a useless rule from a zero return are small. Sometimes, however, a useless rule will generate significant profits by sheer luck. These rare instances can fool us into believing a useless rule has predictive power.

The best protection against being fooled is to understand the degree to which profits can result from luck. This is best accomplished with a mathematical function that specifies the deviations from zero profits that can occur by chance. That is what statistics can do for us.

This function, called a probability density function, gives the probability of every possible positive or negative deviation from zero. In other words, it shows the degree to which chance can cause a useless rule to generate profits. Figure 20.1 shows a probability density function.[6] The fact that the density curve is centered at a value of zero reflects the null hypothesis assertion that the rule has an expected return of zero.

In Figure 20.2, the arrow indicates the positive rate of return earned by a rule when it was back tested. This raises the question: Is the observed rate of return sufficiently positive to warrant a rejection of the null hypothesis that the rule's true rate of return is zero? If the observed performance falls well within the range of the deviations that are probably attributable to chance, the evidence is considered to be insufficient to reject the null hypothesis. In such a case, the null hypothesis has withstood the empirical challenge of the back-test evidence, and a conservative interpretation of the evidence would suggest that the rule has no predictive power.

The strength of the back-test evidence is quantified by the fractional area[7] of the probability density function that lies at values equal to or greater than the rule's observed performance. This portion of the density function is depicted by the darkened area to the right of the vertical arrow in Figure 20.2. The size of this area can be interpreted as the probability that a rate of return this high or higher could have

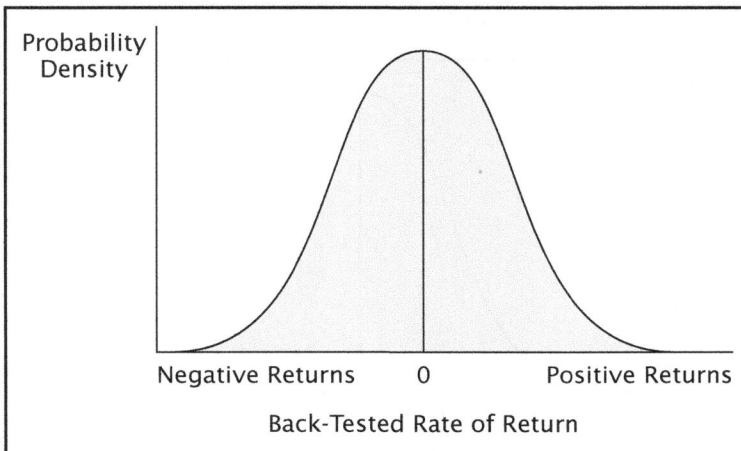

FIGURE 20.1 Probability Density of Chance Performance— Range of Possible Performance for a Useless TA Rule.

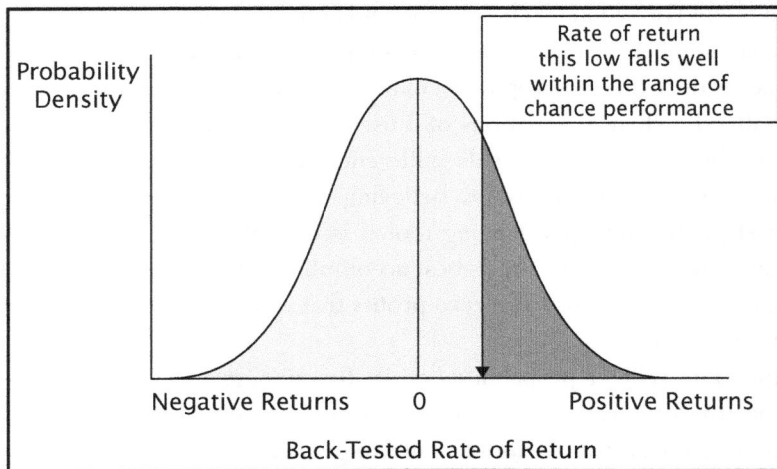

FIGURE 20.2 Probability of Chance Performance for a Useless Rule.

occurred by chance under the condition that the rule has no predictive power (expected return = 0, or the null hypothesis is true). When this area occupies a relatively large fraction of the density curve, it means that there is an equivalently large probability that the positive performance was due to chance. When this is the case, there is no justification for concluding that the null hypothesis is false. In other words, there is no justification for concluding that the rule does have predictive power.

However, if the observed performance is far above zero, the portion of the probability density function lying at even more extreme values is small. Performance this positive would be inconsistent with the assertion that the rule has no predictive power. In other words, the evidence would be sufficient to refute the null hypothesis. Another way to think of this is as follows: If the null hypothesis were true, a level of performance this positive would have a low probability of occurrence. This probability is quantified by the proportion of the density function that lies at values equal to or greater than the observed performance. This is illustrated in Figure 20.3. Note

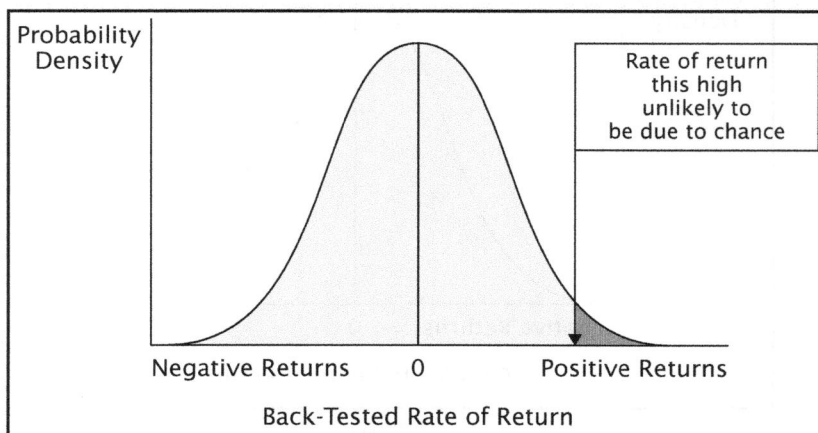

FIGURE 20.3 Probability of Chance Performance for a Good Rule.

that the observed performance lies in the extreme right tail of the density curve that would pertain if the rule were devoid of predictive power.

It is important to understand what this evidence does not tell us. It tells us nothing about the probability that either the null hypothesis or the alternative hypothesis is true. It only speaks to the probability that the evidence could have occurred under the assumption that the null hypothesis is, in fact, true. Thus, the probability speaks to the likelihood of the evidence, not the likelihood of the truth of the hypothesis. Observed evidence that would be highly improbable, under the condition that the null hypothesis is true, permits an inference that the null hypothesis is false.

Just because a creature has four legs, one cannot conclusively establish the truth of the hypothesis: *The creature is a dog*. Although evidence of four legs would be consistent with the hypothesis that the creature is a dog, it is not sufficient to prove, deductively, that the creature is a dog. Similarly, while the observation of positive performance would be consistent with the hypothesis that a rule has predictive power, it is not sufficient to prove that it does. An argument that attempts to prove the truth of a hypothesis with observed evidence that is consistent with the hypothesis commits the logical fallacy of affirming the consequent.

> *If the creature is a dog,* **then** *it has four legs.*
> *The creature has four legs.*
> Invalid Conclusion: *Therefore, the creature is a dog.*

> *If a rule has predictive power,* **then** *it will have a profitable back test.*
> *Back test was profitable.*
> Invalid Conclusion: *Therefore, rule has predictive power.*

However, the absence of four legs is sufficient to prove that the hypothesis, *the creature is a dog*, is false.[8] In other words, observed evidence can be used to conclusively prove that a hypothesis is false. Such an argument uses the valid deductive form, *denial of the consequent*. The general form of an argument, in which the consequent is denied, is as shown:

> *If P is true,* **then** Q *is true.*
> Q *is not true.*
> Valid Conclusion: *Therefore, P is not true (i.e., P is false).*

> *If the creature is a dog,* **then** *it has four legs.*
> *Creature does not have four legs.*
> Valid Conclusion: *Therefore, it is false that the creature is a dog.*

The argument just given uses the evidence, the absence of four legs, to conclusively falsify the notion that the creature is a dog. However, this level of certitude is not possible in matters of science and statistics. One can never conclusively falsify a hypothesis. Nevertheless, a similar logic can be used to show that certain evidence is highly unlikely if the hypothesis were true. In other words, the evidence gives us grounds to challenge the hypothesis. Thus, a highly profitable back test can be used to challenge the hypothesis that the rule has no predictive power (i.e., that it has an expected return of zero).

> **If** a rule's expected return is equal to zero or less, **then** a back test should generate profits that are reasonably close to zero.
>
> The back-tested performance was not reasonably close to zero; in fact, it was significantly above zero.
>
> Valid Conclusion: Therefore, the contention that the rule's expected return is equal to zero or less is likely to be false.

How unlikely or rare must the positive performance be to reject the notion that the rule is devoid of predictive power? There is no hard and fast rule. By convention most scientists would not be willing to reject a hypothesis so unless the observed performance has a 0.05 probability or less of occurrence under the assumption the null is true. This value is called the statistical significance of the observation.

The discussion so far pertains to the case where only one rule is back tested. In practice, however, TA rule research is typically not restricted to testing a single rule. Economical computing power, versatile back-testing software, and plentiful historical data make it easy, almost inviting, to test many rules with the aim of selecting the one with the best performance. This practice is known as data mining.

Although data mining is an effective research method, testing many rules increases the chance of a lucky performance. Therefore, the threshold of performance needed to reject the null hypothesis must be set higher, perhaps much higher. This higher threshold compensates for the greater likelihood of stumbling upon a useless rule that got lucky in a back test.

Figure 20.4 compares two probability density functions. The top one would be appropriate for evaluating the significance for a single rule back test. The lower density curve would be appropriate for evaluating the significance of the best-performing rule out of 1,000 back-tested rules. This density curve takes into account the increased likelihood of luck that results from data mining. Notice that if this best rule's observed performance were to be evaluated with the density curve appropriate for a single rule, it would appear significant because the performance is far out in the right tail of the distribution. However, when the best rule's performance is evaluated with the appropriate probability density function it does not appear statistically significant. That is to say, the rule's rather high performance would not warrant the conclusion that it has predictive power or an expected return that is greater than zero.

■ The Need for Rigorous Statistical Analysis

The tools and methods of a discipline limit what it can discover. Improvements in them pave the way to greater knowledge. Astronomy took a great leap forward with the invention of the telescope. Though crude by today's standards, the earliest instruments

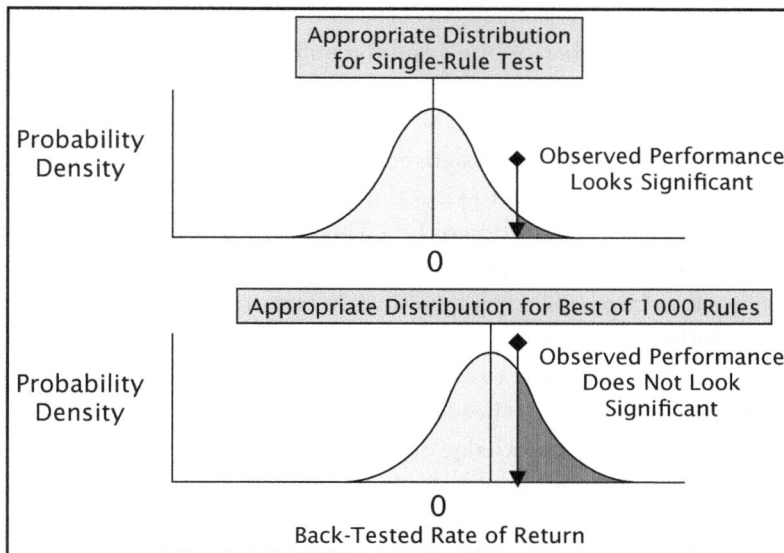

FIGURE 20.4 **Great Performance in a Single Rule Back Test Is Only Mediocre When 1,000 Rules Are Tested.**

had 10 times the resolving power of the unaided eye. Technical analysis has a similar opportunity, but it must replace informal data analysis with rigorous statistical methods.

Informal data analysis is simply not up to the task of extracting valid knowledge from financial markets. The data blossoms with illusory patterns whereas valid patterns are veiled by noise and complexity. Rigorous statistical analysis is far better suited to this difficult task.

Statistical analysis is a set of well-defined procedures for the collection, analysis, and interpretation of data. This chapter will introduce the way statistical tools and reasoning can be used to identify TA rules that work. This overview is necessarily condensed, and in many instances I have sacrificed mathematical rigor for the sake of clarity. However, these departures do not dilute the essential message: If TA is to deliver on its claims, it must be grounded in a scientific approach that uses formal statistical analysis.

■ An Example of Sampling and Statistical Inference

Statistical reasoning is abstract and often runs against the grain of common sense. This is good and bad. Logic that runs counter to informal inference is good because it can help us where ordinary thinking lets us down. However, this is exactly what makes it difficult to understand. So we should start with a concrete example.

The central concept of statistical inference is extrapolating from samples. A sample of observations is studied, a pattern is discerned, and this pattern is expected to hold for (extrapolated to) cases outside the observed sample. For example, a rule observed to be profitable in a sample of history is projected to be profitable in the future.

Let's begin to think about the concept in the context of a problem that has nothing to do with technical analysis. It comes from an excellent book: *Statistics, A New Approach* by Wallis and Roberts.[9] The problem concerns a box filled with a mixture of white and grey beads. The total number of beads and the numbers of grey and white beads are unknown. The task is to determine the fraction of beads that are grey in the entire box. For purposes of brevity, this value will be designated as *F-G* (fraction-grey in box).

To make this situation similar to statistical problems faced in the real world, there is a wrinkle. We are not allowed to view the entire contents of the box at one time, thus preventing a direct observation of F-G. This constraint makes the problem realistic because, in actual problems, observing all the items of interest, such as all beads in the box, is either impossible or impractical. In fact, it is this constraint that creates the need for statistical inference.

Although we are not allowed to examine the box's contents in its entirety, we are permitted to take samples of 20 beads at a time from the box and observe them. So our strategy for acquiring knowledge about F-G will be to observe the fraction of grey beads in a multitude of samples. In this example 50 samples will be taken. The lowercase f-g stands for the fraction of grey beads in a sample.

A sample is obtained as follows: The bottom of the box contains a sliding panel with 20 small depressions, sized so that a single bead is captured in each depression. The panel can be slid out of the box by pushing it with a similar panel that takes its place. This keeps the remaining beads from dropping out of the bottom. Consequently, each time the panel is removed, we obtain a sample of 20 beads and have the opportunity to observe the fraction grey (f-g) in that sample. This is illustrated in Figure 20.5.

After the fraction of grey beads (f-g) in a given sample has been determined, the sample beads are placed back into the box and it is given a thorough shaking before taking another sample of 20. This gives each bead an equal chance of winding up in the next sample of 20. In the parlance of statistics, we are making sure that each sample is random. The entire process of taking a sample, noting the value f-g, putting the sample back in the box, and shaking the box is repeated 50 times. At the end of the whole procedure we end up with 50 different values for f-g, one value for each sample examined.

By placing each sample back in the box before taking another sample, we are maintaining a stable concentration for the fraction of grey beads in the box. That is to say, the value for F-G is kept constant over the course of the 50 samplings. Problems

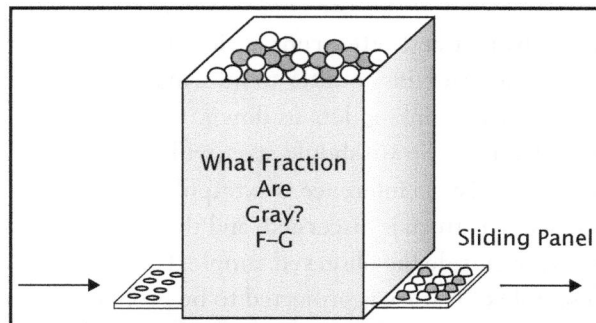

FIGURE 20.5 Determining f-g for Each Sample.

in which the statistical characteristics remain stable over time are said to be stationary. If the beads were not replaced after each sample the value F-G would change over the course of the 50 samplings, as groups of beads were permanently removed from the box. A problem in which the statistical characteristics change over time is said to be nonstationary. Financial markets may indeed be nonstationary, but for pedagogical purposes, the box-of-beads problem is designed to be stationary.

It is important to keep in mind the distinction between F-G and f-g. F-G refers to the fraction of grey beads in the entire box. In the language of statistics, all the observations in which we are interested are called a *population*. In this example, the term population refers to the color of all the beads in the box. The term *sample* refers to a subset of the population. Thus, F-G refers to the population while f-g refers to the sample. Our assigned task is to gain as much knowledge as possible about the value of F-G by observing the value f-g over 50 separate samples.

It is also important to keep clear the distinction between two numbers: the number of observations comprising a sample—in this case 20 beads—and the number of samples taken—in this case 50.

■ Probability Experiments and Random Variables

Probability is the mathematics of chance.[10] A *probability experiment* is an observation on or a manipulation of our environment that has an uncertain outcome.[11] This would include actions such as noting the precise time of arrival after a long trip, observing the number of inches of snow that falls in a storm or the face of a coin that appears after the tossing of a coin.

The quantity or quality observed in a probability experiment is called a *random variable* such as the face of a coin after a flip, the number of inches of snow that fell, or a value that summarizes a sample of observations (e.g., a sample average). This quantity or quality is said to be random because it is affected by chance. Whereas, an individual observation of a random variable is unpredictable, by definition, a large number of observations made on a random variable may have highly predictable features. For example, on a given coin toss, it is impossible to predict head or tails. However, given one thousand tosses, that the number of heads will lie within a specified range of 500 is highly predictable.

Depending on how it is defined, a random variable assumes at least two different values, though it can assume more—perhaps even an infinite number. The random variable in a coin toss, the face visible after the toss, can assume two possible values (heads or tails). The random variable, defined as the temperature at noon taken at the base of the Statue of Liberty, can assume a very large number of values, with the number limited only by the precision of the thermometer.

Sampling: The Most Important Probability Experiment

The most important probability experiment in statistical analysis is sampling. It involves the extraction of a subset of observations from a population. Here the random variable at issue is called a sample statistic. It is any computable characteristic of the sample. The value f-g is an example of a sample statistic.

Sampling can be done in a number of different ways, but it is crucial that the observations that are selected for the sample be chosen in a random manner and that they be selected independently of each other. This means that all observations that could possibly end up in the sample have an equal chance of doing so. Because no particular observation has a better chance of appearing in the sample than any other, the observations that wind up in the sample do so by chance. Samples must be constructed in this manner because the principles of probability, upon which statistical reasoning rests, assume that the observations that wind up in the sample got there randomly.

Consider the test of a new medicine on a sample of volunteers. The sample must be constructed so that anyone who might eventually take the medicine has an equal chance of being selected for the test group. If the subjects in the experiment are not selected this way, the results of the test will not lead to a sound conclusion. A medical experiment that selects test subjects who are expected to respond favorably to the medication will produce biased conclusions. In other words, the estimates of the medication's efficacy in the general population will be too optimistic.

Imagine taking a single bead at random from the box with your eyes closed and then observing its color. This is a sampling experiment with a sample size of one. The bead's color, grey or white, is the random variable. Now imagine randomly selecting 20 beads from the box. Here the sample size is 20 and the fraction grey in that sample (f-g) is a sample statistic that is also a random variable.

As discussed earlier, we will call this random variable f-g. It is a random variable because its value is affected by chance. It can assume 21 different values {0, 0.05, 0.10, 0.15, . . . , 1.0}. Now let's get back to the goal: increasing our knowledge about the value of F-G.

The Knowledge Gleaned from One Sample

Suppose the first sample contains 13 grey beads out of 20. The value of the sample statistic f-g is 0.65 (13/20). What does this tell us about F-G? With only this information, some might be tempted to conclude that we have solved the problem, and that 0.65 is the fraction grey for the entire box (i.e., F-G = 0.65). This view tacitly and naively assumes that a single sample can provide perfect knowledge. At the opposite extreme are those who just as wrongly conclude that the sample is too small to supply any information.

Both conclusions are wrong. First, there is no basis for thinking that we could acquire perfect knowledge from one sample. Though it is possible that a single sample of 20 beads might be a perfect replica of the entire contents of the box, it is not likely. For example, if the true value of F-G were 0.568, a 20-bead sample could never produce such a value. An f-g value of 0.55 (11 grey of 20) is as close as one could get. Ten grey beads in the sample would give an f-g of 0.50, 11 would give 0.55, and 12 would give 0.60.

Those who assert that nothing has been learned are also mistaken. On the basis of this sample alone, two possibilities can be eliminated. We can reject with absolute certainty that F-G = 1.0 (i.e., all beads grey) because there were 7 white beads in the sample. With equal certainty, we can reject the proposition that F-G is 0, because there were 13 grey beads in the sample.

However, more precise estimates of F-G on the basis of the single observed value of f-g are subject to uncertainty. Even if we were to take numerous samples and have numerous values of f-g, the value of F-G would remain uncertain. This is because a sample is, by definition, a partial representation of the full contents of the box. Only by observing every bead in the population could all uncertainty about F-G be eliminated. And this is prohibited.

However, with what has been learned from the single sample, some intelligent guesses can be made that go beyond the certain knowledge that F-G is neither 0 nor 1.0. For example, although a claim that F-G is as low as 0.10 cannot be conclusively ruled out; no one would take it seriously. The observed f-g value of 0.65 obtained from the first sample is too far above 0.10 for it to be a credible estimate of F-G. If F-G really were as low 0.10, the probability of getting a sample with an f-g of 0.65 would seem unlikely just based on common sense. We could apply the same kind of logic to dispense with a claim that F-G = 0.95. An f-g reading of 0.65 would seem too low if the entire box were composed of 95% grey beads. The bottom line: It is fair to say that a single sample does provide some knowledge about F-G.

What Can Be Learned from 50 Samples?

Greater knowledge about F-G can be obtained by analyzing more samples. Assume another 49 samples are taken and the value f-g for each sample is measured. The first thing we would notice is that f-g varies in an unpredictable fashion from sample to sample. This particular form of random behavior is one of the most important phenomena in all of statistics. It is called *sampling variability* or sampling variation.

Sampling variation is important because it is responsible for the uncertainty in statistical conclusions. Greater sampling variability translates to greater uncertainty. The greater the fluctuations in f-g from one sample to the next, the greater will be the uncertainty about the value of F-G.

Regrettably, this important phenomenon, sampling variability, is unfamiliar to many people who analyze data. This is understandable because real world problems do not offer the luxury of looking at more than one independent sample. The box-of-beads provides this opportunity.

As will be seen, by conducting 50 sampling experiments, the random variation in f-g becomes obvious. This is quite different from the situation faced by rule researchers. They typically have a single historical sample of the market, and if all that data is used to test a rule, only one observed value of the performance statistic is obtained. This provides no opportunity to see how the rule's performance would vary if it were tested in numerous independent samples. The bottom line is this: Sampling variation is an important fact that may not be obvious to data analysts unfamiliar with statistical analysis. This is a huge blind spot!

Sampling variation can be seen in a table of the 50 f-g values. See Table 20.1.

TABLE 20.1 **Fraction of Grey Beads in 50 Different Samples**

Sample	f-g	Sample Number	f-g	Sample	f-g
1	0.65	18	0.60	35	0.60
2	0.60	19	0.40	36	0.55
3	0.45	20	0.60	37	0.50
4	0.60	21	0.45	38	0.50
5	0.45	22	0.55	39	0.45
6	0.45	23	0.45	40	0.50
7	0.55	24	0.50	41	0.55
8	0.40	25	0.70	42	0.45
9	0.55	26	0.55	43	0.55
10	0.40	27	0.60	44	0.60
11	0.55	28	0.70	45	0.60
12	0.50	29	0.50	46	0.60
13	0.35	30	0.70	47	0.65
14	0.40	31	0.50	48	0.50
15	0.65	32	0.90	49	0.50
16	0.65	33	0.40	50	0.65
17	0.60	34	0.75		

Not surprisingly, the value of f-g, a random variable, fluctuates from sample to sample. This is an example of chance in operation. However, f-g's value is not entirely determined by chance. Its value is also strongly influenced by the value of F-G, the proportion of grey beads in the entire box.

Thus, it can be said that each observed value of f-g is the result of two influences; the underlying phenomenon, F-G, and randomness caused by sampling. F-G acts like a center of gravity, always keeping f-g within a certain range. In some samples, randomness nudged the value f-g above F-G. In other samples, randomness nudged f-g below F-G. From sample to sample the value of f-g oscillates randomly around this center of gravity. This is sampling variability.

Another important aspect of this situation is that the number of observations impacts our level of uncertainty about the value of F-G. The greater the number of observations comprising the sample, the more precisely the value f-g will reflect the value F-G. Suppose that, instead of taking a 20-bead sample, we took a 200-bead sample. The random variation in f-g around F-G would be smaller. In fact, it would be about one third of what it is for a 20-bead sample. This is a very important point: the larger the sample size, the smaller the impact of randomness. Two hundred beads dampen the ability of any single bead to push f-g away from F-G. In a one-bead sample, the single selected bead will produce an f-g of either 0 or 1.0. In a two-bead sample, f-g can be 0, 0.50 or 1.0. In a three-bead sample, f-g can be 0, 0.33, 0.66, or 1.0. Thus, the larger the sample size, the smaller will be the magnitude of random variation in f-g. Large samples give F-G, the truth that we wish to know, the ability to reveal itself. This is an effect of the *Law of Large Numbers*: Large samples reduce the role of chance. In other words, it can be stated that the larger the size of a sample, the more tightly the values of f-g will cluster about the value F-G. This is one of the most important principles in statistics.

We have learned an important concept of statistics that can be stated as follows: even though the value of F-G does not change over the course of the 50 sampling experiments, the value f-g can vary considerably from sample to sample. The phenomenon is called *sampling variability*. It is present whenever a random sample of observations is used to form a conclusion about a larger universe (i.e., population). Sampling variability is the source of the uncertainty that is addressed by statistical inference.[12]

Frequency Distribution of the Sample Statistic f-g

In the box-of-beads experiment, the random variable f-g can assume 21 possible values ranging from zero, when there are no grey beads in a sample, to 1.0, when the sample is composed entirely of grey beads. The 50 observed values of f-g are shown in Table 20.1. A casual examination shows that some values of f-g occurred with greater frequency than others. Values in the range of 0.40 to 0.65 occurred quite often, whereas values less than 0.40 and greater than 0.65 almost never occurred. In the 50 samples taken, f-g assumed the value 0.50 nine times, 0.55 eight times, and 0.60 ten times. Note that the value 0.65, which characterized the first sample, appeared only five times. Therefore, that value was not among the most common values, but it was not particularly unusual either.

A plot called a frequency distribution or frequency histogram communicates this information more forcefully than words or a table. It displays how frequently each of f-g's possible values occurred over the 50 sampling experiments. The term *distribution* is apt, because it depicts how a set of observations on a random variable are distributed or sprinkled across the variable's range of possible values.

Arrayed along the horizontal axis of the frequency distribution is a sequence of intervals, or bins, one for each possible value of f-g. The height of the vertical bar over each interval represents the number of times that a specific value of f-g occurred. Figure 20.6 shows the frequency distribution of the 50 f-g values.

The Equivalence of Frequency and Area

Frequency distributions depict an important relationship between the frequency of a particular value or set of values and the area covered by the bars representing that value or set of values. This concept can be understood if we first consider the entire distribution. In Figure 20.6, all the grey bars comprising the frequency distribution represent all 50 of the observed values of f-g. Thus, the area covered by all the vertical bars corresponds to 50 observations. You can verify this by summing the counts associated with all of the vertical bars. They will add up to 50.

The same principle applies to any fraction of the distribution's area. If you were to determine the fraction of the frequency distribution's total area covered by the area of a single bar, you would find that the bar's fractional area is equal to the fraction

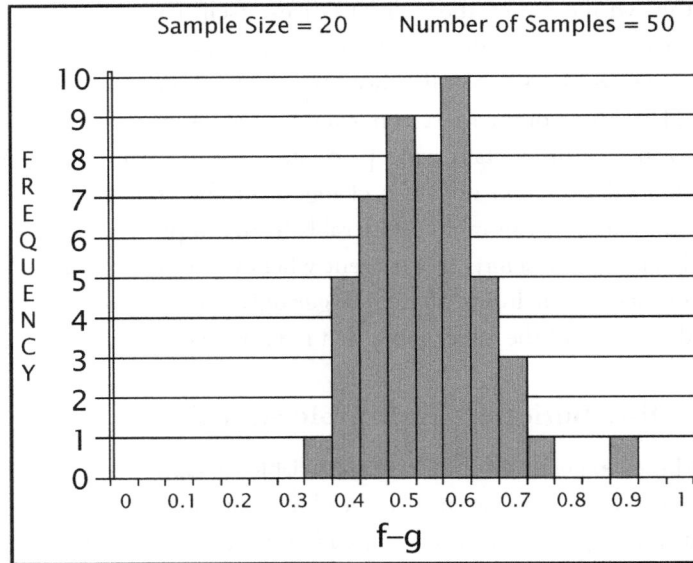

FIGURE 20.6   Frequency Distribution: (f-g).

of the total observations represented by that bar. For example, the vertical bar associated with the f-g value 0.60 shows a count (frequency) of 10. Thus, the bar represents 20% (10/50) of the observed values. If you were to then measure the area covered by this vertical bar, you would find that its area represents 0.20 of the total area covered by the entire distribution. This idea is illustrated in Figure 20.7.

Although this idea may seem obvious, even trivial, it is an essential aspect of statistical reasoning. Ultimately, we will use the fractional area of a distribution

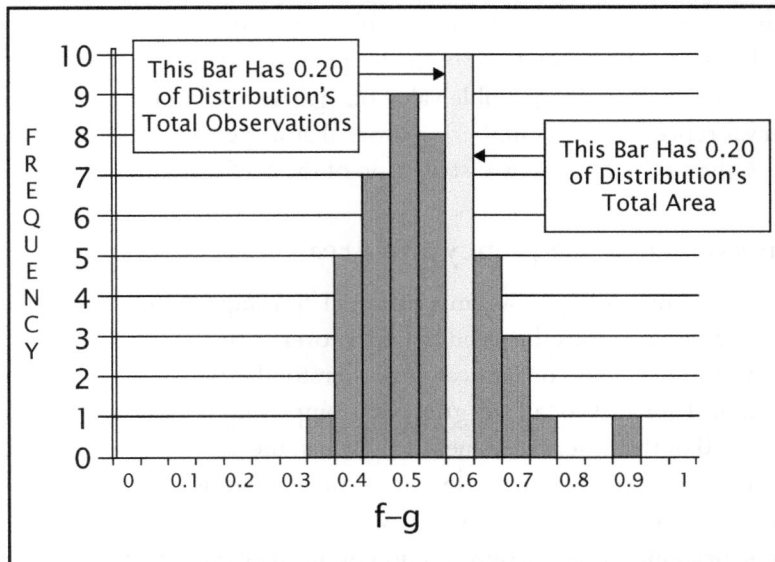

FIGURE 20.7   Proportion of Observations Equals Proportion of Distribution's Total Area.

to measure the probability that the back-test profits of a rule could have occurred by chance under the assumption that the rule has no predictive power. When that probability is small, we are led to the conclusion that the rule does have predictive power.

Relative Frequency Distribution of f-g

The relative frequency distribution is similar to the ordinary frequency distribution discussed earlier. The height of a bar in an ordinary frequency distribution represents an absolute number or count of the number of times a particular value of a random variable was observed to occur. In the relative frequency distribution, the height of a bar represents the number of observed occurrences relative to (divided by) the total number of observations comprising the distribution. For example, f-g assumed the value 0.60 on 10 out of 50 observations. Thus the value 0.60 had a relative frequency of 10/50 or 0.20. The distribution's bar for the value 0.60 would be drawn to a height of 0.20 along the vertical scale. This is illustrated in Figure 20.8.

The equivalence between frequency and area that applies to ordinary frequency distributions also applies to relative frequency distributions. The relative frequency of all bars is equal (adds up) to 1.0. This simply says that a random variable always (1.0 of the time) assumes a value somewhere in the range encompassed by all bars. If you were to add up the relative frequencies associated with all of the individual bars comprising the distribution, they would sum to 1.0 (100% of the observations). This has to be so because each bar represents the fraction of observations falling into that interval, and, by definition, all the bars together represent all (1.0) the observations.

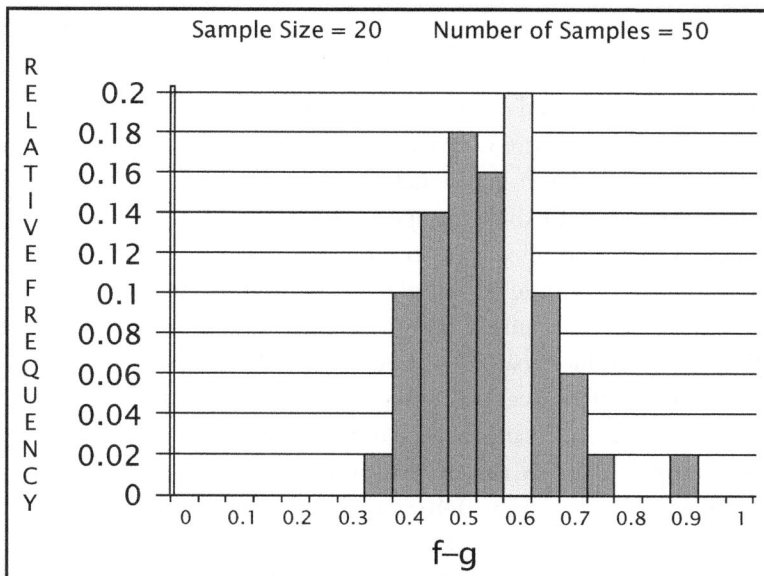

FIGURE 20.8 Relative Frequency Distribution: (F-G).

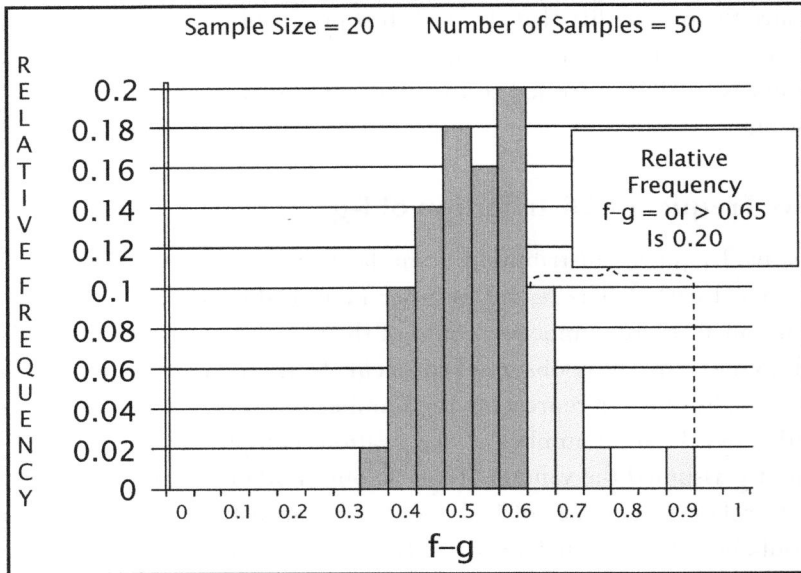

FIGURE 20.9 Relative Frequency Distribution: (F-G).

The relative frequency of any single bar or group of contiguous bars is equal to their proportion of the distribution's total area. Thus the relative frequency of an f-g value of 0.65 and larger is equal to $0.10 + 0.06 + 0.02 + 0.02 = 0.20$. This is equivalent to saying that the combined area of the contiguous bars associated with f-g values of 0.65 and larger is 20% of the distribution's total area. We will be making statements similar to this when testing claims about TA rules. Based on this, it can be said that the relative frequency of f-g values equal to or greater than 0.65 is 0.20. This is illustrated in Figure 20.9.

What Knowledge Has Been Gained about F-G from Sampling?

So far, sampling has increased our level of knowledge about F-G. In the first 20-bead sample, f-g had a value of 0.65. Based on this observation, two possibilities were conclusively ruled out: that F-G is equal to 0, and that F-G is equal to 1.0.

Not being content with these meager morsels of wisdom, another 49 samples were taken, and the value f-g was observed in each. These 50 values showed that f-g varies randomly from sample to sample. However, despite the unpredictability of any single f-g value, an organized pattern emerged from the randomness that was informative. The f-g values coalesced about a central value forming a well-organized hump. We suspect that this central tendency is related to the value F-G, yet F-G's precise value remains uncertain because of the random variation in f-g. However, in light of the hump's relatively narrow width, it seems reasonable to conjecture that F-G lies somewhere in the range 0.40 to 0.65.

Given that we started with no knowledge of F-G and given that we were precluded from examining the contents of the box in its entirety, a lot was learned from these 50 samples.

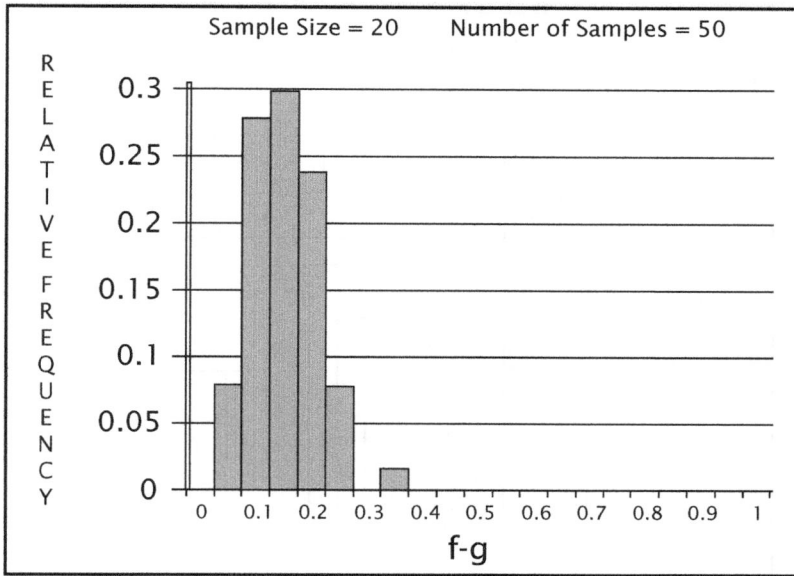

FIGURE 20.10 Relative Frequency Distribution Box 2: (f-g).

A Second Box of Beads

Now we will use sampling to learn the color proportions of a second box of beads. It too is a mixture of grey and white. The objective is the same—to learn the relative proportion of grey beads to the total number of beads in a second box. We call this quantity F-G 2.

As before, we are not allowed to examine the full contents of box 2, but we are permitted to take 50 samples, each composed of 20 beads. The value f-g 2, which refers to the proportion of grey beads in a sample from box 2, is measured in each sample. Again, note the distinction between the terms F-G 2 and f-g 2. F-G 2 refers to the proportion of grey beads in the entire box 2 whereas f-g 2 refers to the proportion of grey beads in an individual sample. F-G 2 is not observable while f-g 2 is.

Figure 20.10 is the relative frequency distribution for 50 values of f-g 2. There are several things to notice:

1. The general shape of the distribution for box 2 is similar to that of box 1, a hump clustering about a central value.
2. The central value of the distribution for box 2 is different than that of box 1. The distribution for box 1 was centered near a value of 0.55. The central value for box 2's distribution is near 0.15. This is clearly seen in Figure 20.11, which shows both distributions on the same horizontal scale. An arrow has been placed above each distribution at their approximate central values. Thus the arrows represent average values for f-g and f-g 2. From this we can conclude that box 1 has a higher concentration of grey beads than box 2.
3. Even though the samples from box 1 and box 2 were both affected by random variation, the degree of random variation differs. Box 2's results are less variable than those of box 1. This is evidenced by box 2's narrower clustering about its central

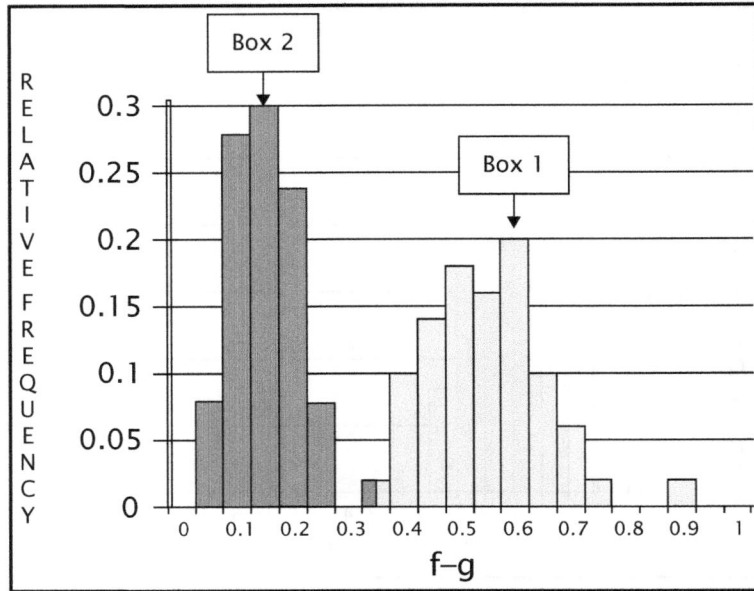

FIGURE 20.11 **Relative Frequency Distributions Compared.**

value. Given the lower degree of sampling variation in box 2, it would be fair to say that we know the value of F-G 2 with greater certainty than we know F-G.

What the Box Experiments Taught Us about Statistics

Yogi Berra, former manager of the New York Yankees, said you can observe a lot just by looking. If he were a statistician, he might have said that you can learn a lot just by sampling. Even though a sample is only a portion of a larger universe (population), it can teach us a lot about that population. However, there are limits to what a sample can tell us, limits imposed by randomness.

A fundamental task of statistics is to quantify the uncertainty due to sampling variability. This makes it possible to quantify the reliability of statements of knowledge based on samples. Without such quantification, such statements are of limited value. Statistics cannot eliminate uncertainty, but it can inform us about it, and in so doing, it tempers assessments of how much we know or how accurately we know it. Thus, statistical analysis is a powerful antidote to the tendency to be overconfident.

■ Statistical Theory

The box-of-beads experiments touched on many of the key ideas of statistical inference. We will now mix in some theory to extend those ideas to the evaluation of TA rules.

The Six Elements of a Statistical Inference Problem

Evaluating a claim that a TA rule has predictive power, that a new vaccine can prevent illness, or any other claim of knowledge are examples of a statistical inference problem.

Generally, such problems can be reduced to six key elements: (1) a population, (2) a sample consisting of a set of observations randomly selected from the population, (3) a population parameter, (4) a sample statistic, (5) an inference, and (6) a statement about the reliability of the inference. Each of these elements will be discussed as they relate to the box-of-beads experiments and then to the evaluation of TA rules.

The Population   A population consists of all possible observations of a random variable. It is a large—perhaps infinitely large—but a well-defined universe of observations. In the typical statistical inference problem, we want to learn some fact about the population, but it is either impractical or impossible to observe the population in its entirety. In the box-of-beads experiments, the population consisted of the set of beads filling a box. The color was the random variable. With respect to testing a TA rule, the population consists of all conceivable daily returns13 that would be earned by the rule's signal over the *immediate practical future*.

To what does the term *immediate practical future* refer? It would be unreasonable to assume that the dynamics of financial markets are stationary, and so it would be unreasonable to expect that the profitability of a rule will endure in perpetuity. For this reason, the population with respect to TA rules cannot refer to returns occurring over an infinite future.

A more reasonable notion is what I refer to as the *immediate practical future*. The immediate practical future refers to a finite future time period, over which it would be reasonable to expect a useful rule's profitability to persist, even though markets are non-stationary. Any endeavor to find predictive patterns must make some assumption about the continuity of predictive power. In other words, unless one is willing to assume some persistence in predictive power, all forms of TA are pointless. The assumption being made here is that a rule will continue to work long enough to compensate the researcher for the effort of discovering it. This is consistent with the position taken by Grossman and Stiglitz in "On the impossibility of informationally efficient markets."[14] It is also consistent with the idea that profitable rules signal opportunities to earn a risk premium.[15]

Therefore, the immediate practical future refers to all possible random realizations of market behavior over a finite future. It is as if there were an infinite number of parallel universes, where all universes are an exact duplicate except for the random component of the market's behavior. In each realization, or universe, the pattern that accounts for the rule's profitability is the same, but the random component of the market is different. This idea is illustrated in Figure 20.12.

The Sample   The sample is a subset of the population that is available for observation. In the box-of-beads case, we were able to observe 50 independent samples. In the case of a TA rule, we typically observe a single sample of the rule's performance by back testing it over a segment of market history. This sample is composed of a sequence of daily returns generated by the rule's signals. The sequence of returns is reduced to a single number, a sample performance statistic.

The Population Parameter   The population parameter is a fact or characteristic about the population that we would like to know. It is typically numerical, but it need not be.

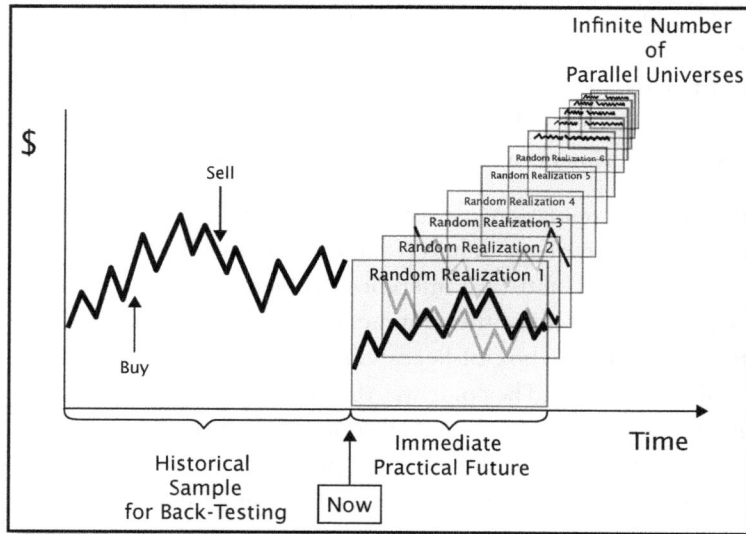

FIGURE 20.12 Different Realizations of Randomness in an Infinitude of Parallel Universes.

Unfortunately, the population parameter is unknown because the entire population cannot be observed. The essence of statistical inference is the attempt to increase our knowledge about a population parameter, despite the impossibility of observing the population in its entirety. In the box-of-beads case, the population parameter of interest was the fraction of grey beads in the box (i.e., F-G, and F-G 2). In the case of a TA rule, the population parameter is the rule's expected performance over the immediate practical future. Performance can be defined in many ways. Some common measures include average rate of return, Sharpe ratio, profit factor, and so forth. In this book, our measure of performance is the annualized average daily return on detrended market (zero-centered) data.

In many statistical problems, it is safe to assume the population parameter never changes (i.e., it is a constant). In the box-of-beads experiment, the proportion of grey beads remained constant. Statistical problems in which the population parameter remains fixed are said to be stationary.[16] Now imagine a wrinkle on that situation. Suppose, unbeknownst to the experimenter, an invisible demon secretly removes or adds grey beads between samplings. Now the population parameter, F-G, is unstable, or nonstationary.[17]

Earlier in this chapter, I said that it is best to start with an assumption that any rule we test has no predictive power. That is, we assume that it has an expected return equal to zero. Or, to put it in statistical terms, the population parameter is assumed equal to be zero.

The Sample Statistic A sample statistic is a measurable attribute of a sample.[18] Its value is known because it has been observed. In this book, the term *sample statistic* is restricted to numerical facts, for example a proportion, a percentage, a standard

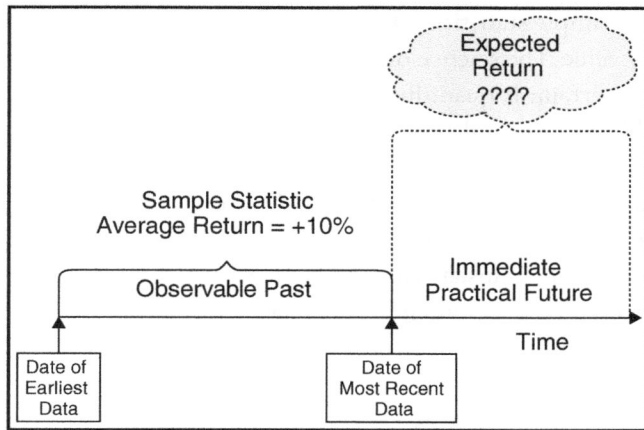

FIGURE 20.13 Is the Parameter's Value Greater than Zero?

deviation, an average rate of return, a trimmed average,[19] a Sharpe ratio, and so forth. In a statistical inference problem, the *sample statistic* typically refers to the same measurable attribute as the population parameter. In the case of the box-of-beads, the sample statistic, f-g, referred to the fraction of grey beads in an individual sample. The population parameter, F-G, referred to the fraction of grey beads in the whole box.

The bottom line is this: A sample statistic is important because it sheds light on the population parameter. Beyond this, it is a fact of no particular importance. Some market historians seem to be unmindful of this essential truth.

If a back test should result in a positive rate of return, it raises the following question: Is the positive performance a random deviation above zero due to sampling variability or is it attributable to the rule's predictive power (i.e., the rule has an expected return greater than zero)? Answering this question requires the tools of statistical inference. This is illustrated in Figure 20.13.

An Inference Statistical inference is the inductive leap from the observed value of a sample statistic, which is known with certainty but which is true only for a specific sample of data, to the value of a population parameter, which is uncertain but which is deemed to hold true for a wide, perhaps infinite, number of unobserved cases.

When a rule's positive past performance can reasonably be attributed to sampling variability, the reasonable inference is that its expected return over the immediate practical future is zero or less. However, if the positive performance is too high to be reasonably attributed to sampling variability (luck), the reasonable inference would be that the rule possesses genuine predictive power and has a positive expected return over the immediate practical future.

A Statement about the Reliability of the Inference Because a sample cannot represent the population perfectly, inferences based on a sample statistic are subject to uncertainty. In other words, it is possible that the inference is wrong. We have already seen how sample statistics vary randomly around the true value of the population parameter value. The science of statistics goes beyond simply admitting that its inferences are uncertain. It quantifies their reliability. This makes statistical conclusions considerably more useful than those reached by informal methods that do not provide such information.

The inference can be wrong in two ways. One error is concluding the rule has predictive power when it does not. This is a case of good luck shining on a worthless rule. This type of mistake translates into taking market risks that will not be compensated. The other error is concluding the rule has no predictive ability when it really does. This mistake results in missed trading opportunities.

Descriptive Statistics

The field of statistics subdivides into two main areas: descriptive and inferential. The most important for TA is statistical inference, which was discussed in the preceding sections. However, before making an inference, we must describe the sample data in a succinct and informative way. The tools of descriptive statistics serve this purpose.

The goal of descriptive statistics is data reduction, that is, reducing a large set of observed values to a smaller, more intelligible set of numbers and plots. Descriptive statistics tell the story of the forest rather than the individual trees. Three descriptive tools will be important for the work that lies ahead: (1) frequency distributions, (2) measures of central tendency, and (3) measures of variation.

Frequency Distributions

Frequency distributions have already been discussed in connection with the box-of-beads experiments. They were used to reduce a set of 50 observations on random variable f-g into an informative plot.

With only 50 observations, one might be able to form an overall impression of the data simply by looking at a table of numbers. Then again, if the number of observations were 500 or 5,000, a table would not be as informative as a frequency distribution.

Plotting a frequency distribution is usually the first step in analyzing a set of data. It provides a quick visual impression of two key features of a sample of observations: the central tendency (e.g., average value) and the degree of dispersion or variation about the central value. For example, Figure 20.11 showed that the two boxes of beads had different central values and different degrees of dispersion.

A visual impression of a sample is useful, but quantification improves matters. For our purposes, we will need to quantify two features of the frequency distribution: its central tendency and its variability or dispersion about its central tendency.

Statistics That Measure Central Tendency

There are many measures of central tendency. Three of the most common are the average, the median, and the mode. The average, also known as the arithmetic mean,

$$\boxed{\begin{array}{c} \text{Sample Mean for Variable } X \\[1em] \bar{X} = \dfrac{X_1 + X_2 + X_3 + \ldots X_n}{n} \\[2em] \bar{X} = \dfrac{\sum\limits_{i=1}^{n} X_i}{n} \\[1em] \textit{Where } x_i \textit{ is an individual observation on variable } X \end{array}}$$

FIGURE 20.14 Sample Mean for Variable X.

is used in many TA applications and is the summary statistic used in this book. It is the sum of the observed values divided by the number of observations.

It is important to distinguish the population mean from the sample mean. The sample mean is a statistic, a known quantity that is computed from observed values and varies randomly from one sample to the next. The population mean, in contrast, is unknown and does not vary in stationary problems. The formula for the mean of a sample is given in Figure 20.14 in two forms.

Statistical Measures of Variability (Dispersion)

Measures of variability describe the degree to which the observations in a sample are dispersed about their central tendency. In other words, measures of variability quantify the width of a frequency distribution.

Among the widely used measures of dispersion are the variance, the mean absolute deviation, and the standard deviation. They are important in the traditional approach to statistics (i.e., classical statistics). The standard deviation is the square root of the average squared deviation of each observation from the mean of the data. The formula for the standard deviation of a sample is shown in Figure 20.15.

An intuitive notion of dispersion is best conveyed with pictures. Figure 20.16 shows a number of idealized frequency distributions with differing degrees of variation and different central tendencies. They are idealized in the sense that the stair-step look that characterizes real frequency distributions has been smoothed away. The key point of Figure 20.16 is that central tendency and variation (dispersion) are independent characteristics of a frequency distribution. In row 1 of Figure 20.16, the four distributions have the same degree of variation but different central values. In row 2 the distributions have the same central value but different degrees of variation. In row 3 all distributions have different central values and different degrees of variation.

$$ s = \sqrt{\frac{\sum (X_i - \overline{X})^2}{n}} $$

Standard Deviation of a Sample of Observations

Where:

X_i Is an individual observation on variable X

$\overline{X}$ Is the sample mean on variable X

n Is number of observations in the sample

FIGURE 20.15   Standard Deviation of a Sample of Observations.

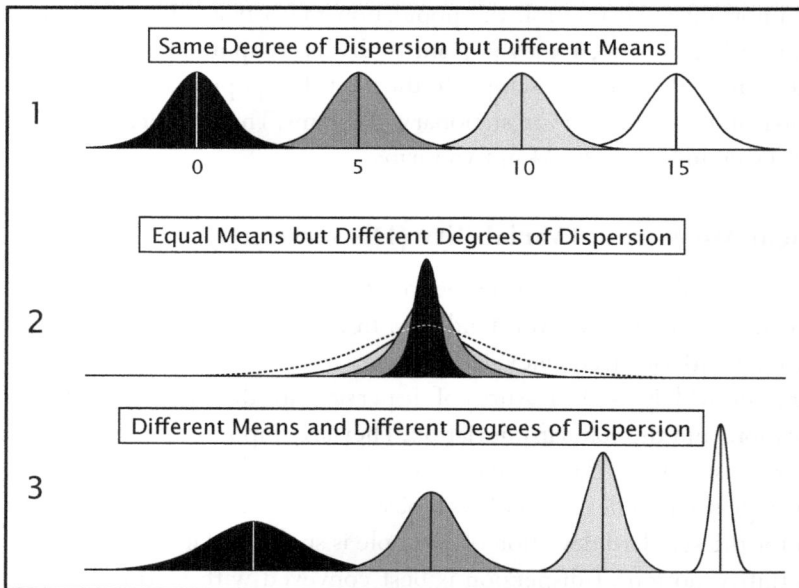

Same Degree of Dispersion but Different Means

Equal Means but Different Degrees of Dispersion

Different Means and Different Degrees of Dispersion

FIGURE 20.16   Central Tendency and Dispersion Are Distinct Attributes of a Distribution.

■ Probability

The notion of probability is important in statistics because it is used to quantify uncertainty. A conclusion reached via statistical inference is uncertain; that is, there is a chance of error. Thus, an inference about the value of a population parameter has some chance of being wrong. This chance is given in terms of a probability.

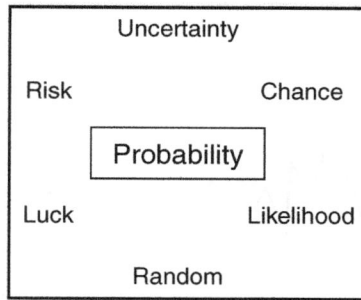

FIGURE 20.17 Common Notions of Probability.

We routinely use informal notions of probability to form expectations and make choices. Is the person I find so wonderful now, likely to remain so after marriage? What is the chance I will find gold if I dig in a certain spot? Is it probable I will feel fulfilled pursing a career in law? Should I buy that stock, and if I do, how much profit am I likely to make?

The informal usage of probability is connected to a cluster of interchangeable terms illustrated in Figure 20.17.

For our purposes, something more definitive is required. The definition of probability that makes the most sense for the work that lies ahead is based on the notion of relative frequency. The relative frequency of an event is the number of times the event actually occurred divided by the total number of opportunities on which the event could have occurred. Relative frequency is given as a fraction between 0 and 1. It could rain every day, but in the month of April the relative frequency of rain has actually been 0.366 (11 out of 30 days). If rain never occurred, then its relative frequency would be 0. If rain occurred every day, its relative frequency is 1.0. Thus, the relative frequency of an outcome is equal to:

$$\frac{\text{Number of occurrences of an event}}{\text{Number of possible opportunities for the event to occur}}$$

In the box-of-beads experiment the value of f-g was measured 50 times. This was the maximum number of opportunities for any specific f-g value to occur. In fact, the value f-g = 0.65 occurred on 5 out of 50. Therefore, it had a relative frequency of 5/50 or 0.10.

Probability is the relative frequency of an event over the long run—the very long run. That is to say, the probability of an event is its relative frequency of occurrence given an infinite number of opportunities for its occurrence. Probability is stated as a number that lies in the range of 0 to 1 inclusive. A probability value of 0 means the event never occurs, whereas a value of 1.0 means it always occurs.

Probability is a theoretical notion because it is never possible to observe an infinite number of anything. For practical purposes, however, when the number of observations becomes very large, relative frequency approaches theoretical probability.

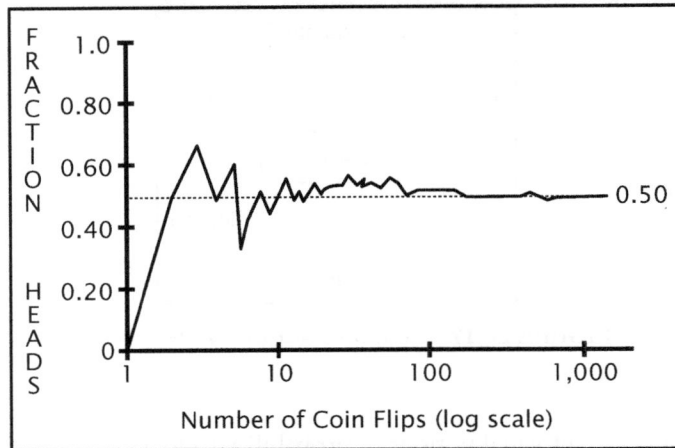

FIGURE 20.18   Law of Large Numbers.

The Law of Large Numbers

The tendency of relative frequencies to converge to theoretical probabilities, as the number of observations becomes large, is called the Law of Large Numbers.[20] The operation of the Law of Large Numbers can be illustrated with coin tossing. The possible outcomes (events) are heads or tails and the probability of heads is known to be 0.50. The Law tells us that the relative frequency of heads will *converge* to its theoretical value, 0.5, as the number of coin tosses becomes large. However, even for a large number of tosses, a departure from 0.50 can still occur, though the likely size of the departures decreases as the number of tosses increases. For small samples, however, The Law of Large Numbers warns us that the relative frequency of heads can differ substantially from 0.50. When the number of tosses is only three, a value of 1.0 can easily occur—three heads in three tosses.

Figure 20.18 shows the fraction of heads in a coin-toss experiment as the number of tosses grows from one to one thousand. When the number of tosses (observations) is less than 10, the fraction of heads experienced two large deviations from 0.50. At 3 tosses the fraction of heads reached 0.66 (2 out of 3). At 8, the fraction was 0.375 (3 out of 8). However, as the number of tosses increased the random variable, fraction heads, experienced progressively smaller deviations from the expected value of 0.50. This is exactly what the Law of Large Numbers predicts.

Now imagine a naive coin flipper. Upon observing five heads in five tosses, he loudly proclaims, "I've found the holy grail of coins. It always comes up heads." The Law of Large Numbers says that the poor fellow's optimism is unwarranted. This is also likely to be true for the TA researcher who finds a rule with five historical signals, all of which were correct. Optimism is most likely unwarranted. This rule was selected because it was the best performing rule out of a large universe of back-tested rules, that is to say, it was discovered by data mining, there would be even less reason to be optimistic about its future performance.

Theoretical versus Empirical Probability

There are two kinds of probabilities: theoretical and empirical. "Theoretical probabilities can be determined with a good degree of confidence purely on logical grounds. They are derived independent of prior experience, most often based on arguments of symmetry."[21] In other words, they can be deduced without any reference to the world of experience. The probability of a head in a coin toss is a theoretical probability. There is no need to toss it 10,000 times to predict that over the long run the probability of heads is 0.50. Simply the fact that the coin is fair, that it has two faces, and that it is unlikely to land on its edge is sufficient grounds for suspecting heads and tails are equally likely. The probabilities for being dealt a royal flush in poker, the occurrence of a six in a dice roll, and the chance of winning Lotto are also theoretical because each can be determined by a logical analysis of the situation.

Empirical probabilities are based on observed frequencies. Technical analysis is concerned with this type of probability. The chance of new snowfall on Mount Hood during the month of July or the likelihood of a rise in the stock market following a 2% drop in interest rates are examples of empirical probabilities. They can only be determined by observing numerous past instances of the specified conditions (Mount Hood in July), and determining the relative frequency of the event (new snow).

When determining empirical probabilities, it is vitally important that each instance be characterized by the same set of conditions. In TA this is a practical impossibility. Each past instance of a 2% drop in interest rates is similar with respect to that specific condition, but there are numerous other conditions that may not be the same. For example, the level of interest rates prior to the 2% drop may differ from observation to observation. In one instance, interest rates were at 5% prior to the drop whereas in another they were 10%. Of course, the level of interest rates could be added to the set of conditions that define each instance, but that has the downside of reducing the number of comparable instances. Moreover, there will always be other conditions that are not part of the specified condition set. The inability to control all potentially relevant variables is an unfortunate fact of life in nonexperimental/observational sciences. In contrast, the experimental scientist enjoys the supreme advantage of being able to hold constant all or nearly all relevant variables except the one being investigated. Imagine being able to do that in TA! I am told this is how it is in the afterlife.

▓ Probability Distributions of Random Variables

A probability distribution shows how often we can expect the different possible values of a random variable to occur (i.e., their relative frequencies). The probability distribution of a random variable is a relative frequency distribution built from an infinite number of observations.

The concept of a probability distribution can be understood by thinking of a sequence of relative frequency distributions, each built from increasing numbers of observations and progressively narrower bins or intervals. Gradually, the relative frequency distribution becomes a probability distribution. With increasing numbers of observations, more discrete intervals of decreasing width can be created.[22] As the number of observations approaches infinity, the number of intervals approaches infinity and their widths shrink to zero. Thus, the relative frequency distribution morphs into what is called a probability distribution, more technically referred to as a probability density function.[23]

Figures 20.19 though 20.23 show how a relative frequency distribution evolves into a probability density function as the number of intervals is increased and their interval widths are decreased. The height of each bar represents the relative frequency of events falling within the bar's interval. The figures presume that the random variable is a measure of price change.

This succession of diagrams shows that a probability density function is, in effect, a relative frequency distribution composed of an infinite number of observations whose intervals are infinitely narrow. Here is where things get a bit strange. If the intervals of a probability distribution have zero width, then there are zero observations per interval. This seems to make no sense! However, it is quite common for

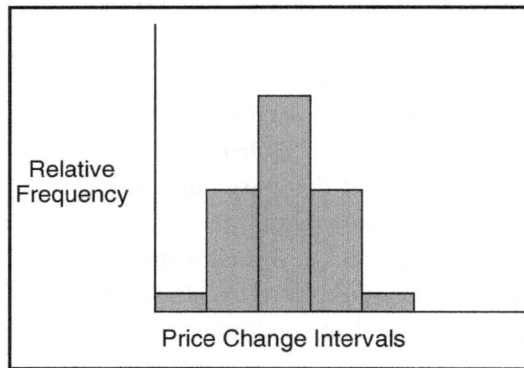

FIGURE 20.19 Relative Frequency Distribution Based on Five Intervals.

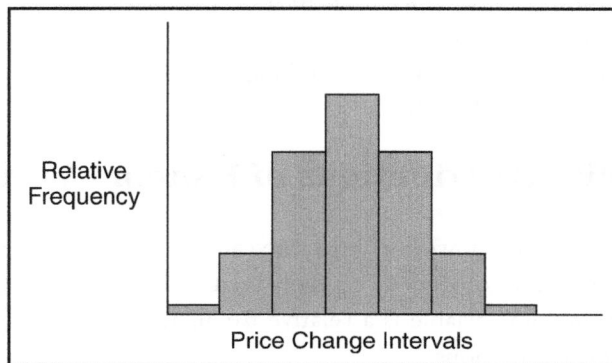

FIGURE 20.20 Relative Frequency Distribution Based on Seven Intervals.

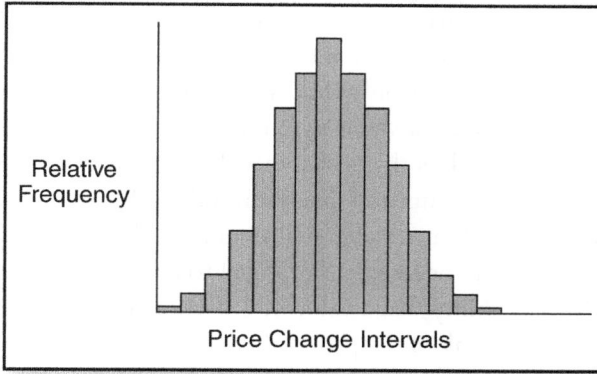

FIGURE 20.21 Relative Frequency Distribution Based on 15 Intervals.

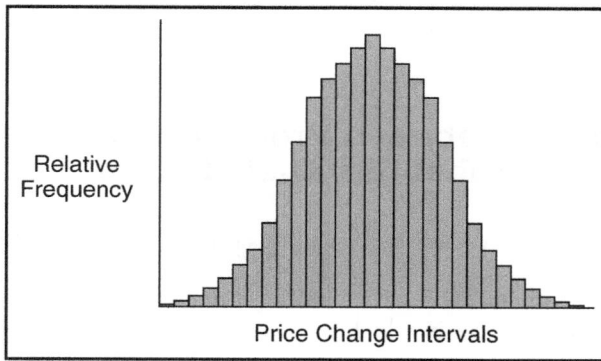

FIGURE 20.22 Relative Frequency Distribution Based on 29 Intervals.

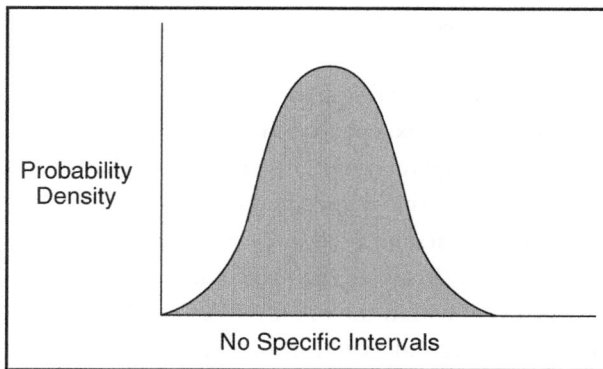

FIGURE 20.23 Probability Density Function.

mathematical concepts to be at odds with common sense. In geometry, a point has location but occupies no space (i.e., length, width, and breadth equal zero), a line has length but zero width, and so forth.

The fact that an interval has zero observations has a strange implication—the probability that any single value of a continuous random variable will ever occur is equal to zero. For this reason, it only makes sense to speak of the probability that a random variable will assume a value within a specified range of values. In other words, it makes sense to speak of the probability that a random variable will assume a value between specified minimum and maximum values. It also makes sense to speak of the probability that a random variable will assume a value that is equal to or greater than some specified value or less than or equal to a specified value. For example, we can speak of the probability that a value of 3.0 or greater will occur. However, it would make no sense to speak of the probability of a value of exactly 3.0.[24]

This somewhat counterintuitive idea fits nicely with rule testing. When testing the statistical significance of a rule's past rate of return, we will be concerned with the probability that a rate of return of 10% or higher could have occurred by chance under the condition that the rule has no predictive power. Probability density functions can provide such information.

Relationship Between Probability and Fractional Area of the Probability Distribution

Let's recap what has been established up to this point:

1. The probability of an event is its relative frequency of occurrence given an infinite number of instances in which the event could have occurred.
2. A probability density function is a relative frequency distribution built from an infinite number of observations and intervals of zero width.
3. The relative frequency of a random variable taking on a value within a given interval is equal to the fractional area of the frequency distribution sitting on top of that interval. See Figure 20.24.

We are now ready to take the final step in this sequence of thinking. It is analogous to point 3 in the preceding list, except that the term *relative frequency* distribution is replaced with *probability density function*. The probability that a continuous random variable will assume a value within a specified range is equal to the fraction of the probability density function encompassed by (sitting above) that range. This concept is illustrated in Figure 20.25. It shows the probability that X, a continuous random variable, will assume a value within the range A-B is equal to 0.70.

In many instances, the interval in question refers to the extreme or tail of the distribution. For example, Figure 20.26 shows the probability that random variable X will assume a value of B or greater. The probability is 0.15.

The probability distribution of a random variable is a very useful concept. Even though an individual future observation on random variable X is not predictable, a large number of observations form a highly predictable pattern. This pattern is the random variable's probability density function.

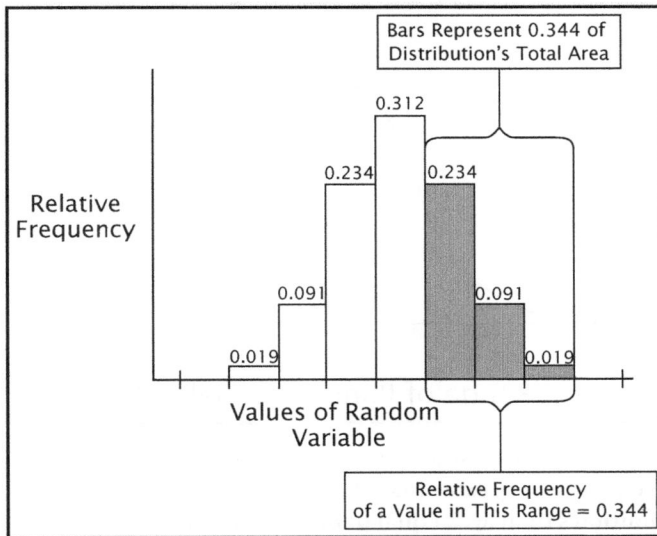

FIGURE 20.24 The Correspondence of Relative Frequency and Fractional Area of a Distribution.

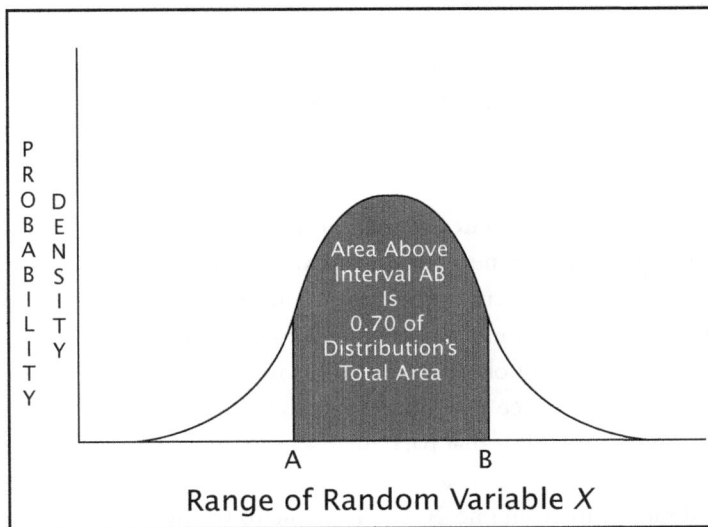

FIGURE 20.25 The probability random variable X will assume a value between A and B equals the fraction of the distribution's total area above the interval A,B.

Now, here is where these ideas start to come together for us. When a hypothesis is represented by the probability distribution of a random variable we will be able to use an observed value of the random variable to test the veracity of the hypothesis. This will enable us to conclude if a rule's back-tested profitability was due to luck or genuine predictive power.

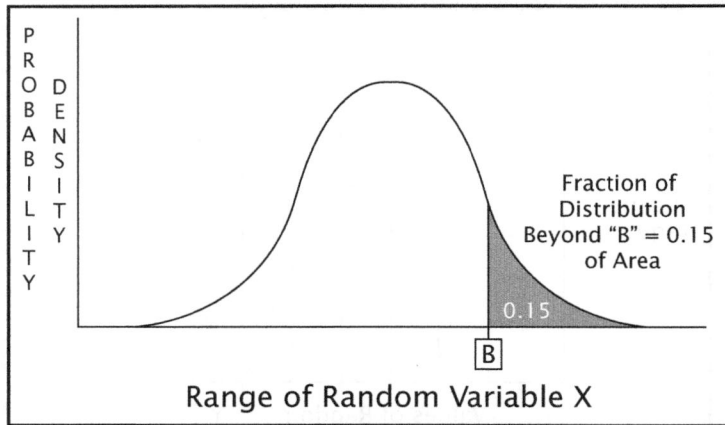

FIGURE 20.26 The probability random variable X will assume a value equal to or greater than B equals the fraction of the distribution's total area equal to or greater than B.

The probability distribution used for this purpose is a specific type. It is called a sampling distribution—perhaps the most important one in all of statistics and certainly the most important for TA analysts.

The Sampling Distribution: The Most Important Concept in Statistical Inference

To recap:

1. A random variable is the outcome of a probability experiment.
2. Taking a sample of a given number of observations from a population and computing the value of a statistic such as *the sample's* mean is a probability experiment.[25]
3. A sample statistic[26] is a random variable in the sense that it fluctuates unpredictably from one sample of observations to the next. The sample statistic fluctuates randomly because chance determines which specific observations wind up in a particular sample, and it is that particular set of observations that determines the value of the statistic for that sample. In the box-of-beads experiment, the value f-g varied randomly from one 20-bead sample to the next because the particular set of beads that wound up in a given sample was determined by chance.
4. A relative frequency distribution describes how often the possible values of a random variable occur over a very large number of observations.

We are now ready to meet the sampling distribution, the most important concept in statistical inference.

The Sampling Distribution Defined

The sampling distribution is the probability distribution of a random variable, and that random variable happens to be a sample statistic. In other words, the sampling distribution shows the various possible values the sample statistic can assume, and their associated probabilities.[27] For example, "the sampling distribution of the sample mean refers to the probability distribution of all possible means for all possible random samples of a given size from some population."[28] Here, the sample statistic is the mean.

The sample statistic in the box-of-beads experiments was f-g. Its random variation across 50 samples, each comprised of 20 beads, was shown by the relative frequency distribution in Figure 20.8. If, instead of 50 values we were to take all possible 20-bead samples—a very large number—this theoretical distribution would be f-g's sampling distribution.

In rule back testing, the sample statistic is a measure of performance observed in a back test. In this book that sample statistic will be the rule's average rate of return. A back test typically produces a single observed value for the performance statistic because we have a single sample of market history. Now imagine what it would be like if we were able to test a rule in an infinite number of independent samples of market history. This would provide an infinite number of values for the performance statistic. If this set of data were then converted into a relative frequency distribution, it would be the statistic's exact sampling distribution. This is obviously not possible because we do not have an infinite number of independent samples of historical data. However, statisticians have developed several methods to get something that approximates the exact sampling distribution closely enough to be useful, despite the fact that we have only one sample of historical data and one value of the sample statistic. Two of these methods will be discussed later in this chapter.

The Sampling Distribution Quantifies Uncertainty

The sampling distribution of a statistic is the foundation of statistical inference because it quantifies the uncertainty caused by the randomness of sampling (sampling variability).

As stated above, the sampling distribution displays the relative frequencies of a statistic if it were to be measured in an infinite number of random samples of the same size, drawn from the same parent population. The box-of-beads experiments showed that the value of a statistic, f-g fluctuated randomly from sample to sample. Figure 20.8 showed that these values tend to fall into a well-behaved pattern, not a random chaotic mess. The fact that the pattern of random variation is well behaved is what makes statistical inference possible.

It may seem ironic that a sample statistic would show such a regular pattern given that it is, in fact, a random variable. Thankfully for statisticians, it does. Figure 20.8 revealed a central value (i.e., the mean of the sampling distribution) of approximately 0.55. It also showed a well-defined pattern of dispersion about this central value. This pattern allowed us to conclude, with a fair degree of assurance, that the value of the population parameter F-G was contained within the range 0.40 to 0.65. It also allowed us to conclude, although with somewhat diminished confidence, that F-G was more accurately pinned in the range between 0.50 and 0.60. It was the degree of dispersion in f-g's sampling distribution that permitted these statements to be made about the value of the population parameter F-G.

The dispersion of the sampling distribution quantifies the uncertainty of our knowledge about the population parameter F-G. The distribution's central tendency conveys information about the most likely value of F-G, approximately 0.55. Knowing this is nice, but it is not enough. It is also important to know about the reliability of the value 0.55. In other words, how accurately does the sampling distribution's central tendency of 0.55 portray the true value of F-G?

The reliability (degree of certainty) is conveyed by the dispersion of the sampling distribution. The greater the distribution's dispersion around its central value, 0.55, the less certain we can be that 0.55 accurately informs us about the true value F-G, the proportion of grey beads in the entire box.

To illustrate this point consider the two following sampling distributions. Both have central values of 0.55 but their dispersions are quite different. The first shown in Figure 20.27 is a narrow dispersion thereby delivering a strong impression that F-G is in the vicinity of 0.55. The distribution in Figure 20.28 is wider thus conveying a less certain message about F-G value. It is saying that the true value F-G may be considerably different from the central value of the sampling distribution.

In summary, certainty is directly related to the dispersion of the sampling distribution. And the certainty of a conclusion about a population parameter depends upon the width of the statistic's sampling distribution—greater width means greater uncertainty.

Suppose it is hypothesized that a rule's expected return is equal to zero. Also suppose the rule's back-tested return turns out to be greater than zero. Is the positive return sufficient evidence to conclude that the hypothesized value of

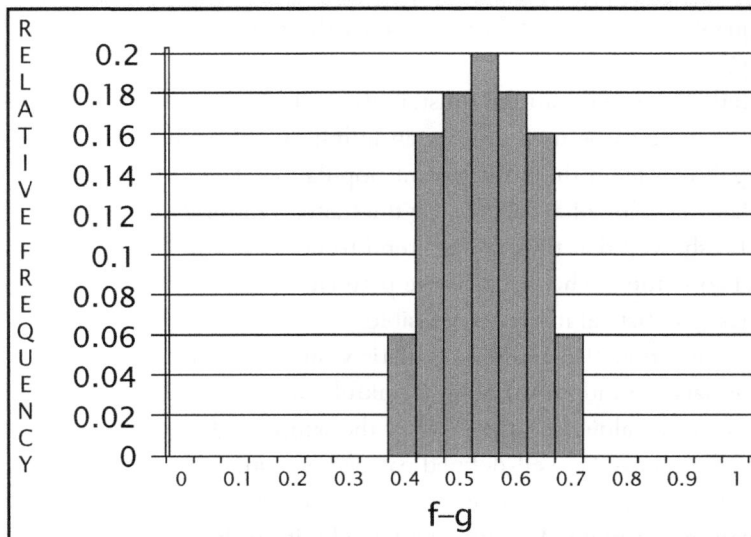

FIGURE 20.27 Relative Frequency Distribution: F-G. (Sample Size = 20, Number of Samples = 50).

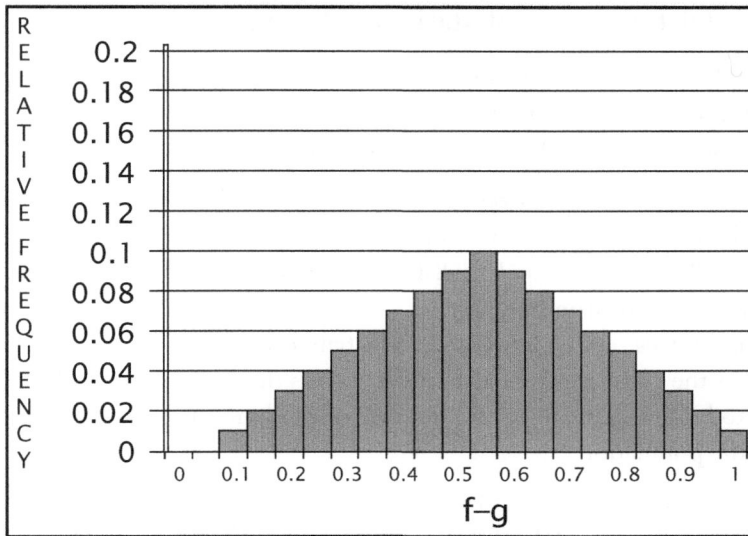

FIGURE 20.28 Relative Frequency Distribution: f-g. (Sample size = 20, Number of Samples = 50).

zero is false? The answer will depend on how far above zero the back-tested return is relative to the width of the sampling distribution. If the relative deviation is large the hypothesis can be rejected. The important point for now is that the width of the sampling distribution is critically important in answering this question.

Sampling Distribution of Trading Performance

A sampling distribution can be formed for any statistic: the average (mean), the median, the standard deviation, and many other statistics used in statistical inference.[29] Each has its own sampling distribution.

This discussion here is confined to the sampling distribution of the mean because the performance statistic used to evaluate TA rules in this book is a rule's mean rate of return. However, there are many other performance measures that might be used: the Sharpe ratio,[30] the profit factor,[31] the mean return divided by the Ulcer Index,[32] and so forth. It should be pointed out that the sampling distributions of these alternative performance statistics would be different from the sampling distribution of the mean.

It should also be pointed out that the methods used in this book to generate the sampling distribution of the mean may be of limited value in generating sampling distributions for performance statistics with elongated right tails. This can occur with performance statistics that involve ratios such as the Sharpe ratio, the mean-return-to-Ulcer-Index ratio, and the profit factor. However, this problem can be mitigated by taking the log of the ratio to shorten the right tail.

The Three Distributions of Statistical Inference

Statistical inference actually involves three different distributions, one of which is the sampling distribution. They are easy to confuse. This section is intended to clarify their differences. In the context of rule testing the three distributions are:

1. *Data distribution of the population*: an infinite sized distribution comprised of all possible daily rule returns, which we assume extends into the immediate practical future.
2. *Data distribution of the sample*: a distribution comprised of a finite number (N) of daily rule returns from the past.
3. *Sampling distribution*: an infinite-sized distribution of the sample statistic—in this case it is the rule's mean return. It represents the mean returns of the rule, if it were to be tested in an infinite number of random samples of size N extracted from the population.

There are two points to emphasize. First, the observations comprising the data distribution of the population and the data distribution of the sample (1 and 2 in the preceding list) are comprised of single-day rule returns. In contrast, the observations comprising the sampling distribution are sample statistics in which each observation represents the mean return of the rule computed over a sample of days. Second, both the population distribution and the sampling distribution are theoretical in the sense that they refer to an infinite number of possible observations. In contrast, the data distribution of the sample is composed of a finite number of observations from a historical back test.

The relationship between these three distributions can be visualized by imagining an experiment similar to the box-of-beads experiment. In this case, however, you are to imagine a population distribution of daily rule returns that is infinite in size. Imagine taking 50 independent samples from the population, where each sample is comprised of a substantial number of daily rule returns. Next, determine the mean return for each sample and then plot the sampling distribution of the 50 means. This is illustrated in Figure 20.29.[33]

The Real World: The Problem of One Sample

The preceding discussion was theoretical in the sense that we imagined what it would be like if we could observe 50 independent samples from a parent population. In most real-world statistical problems, there is only one sample of observations and thus one value for the sample mean. The problem is that with only one sample mean available we have no notion of the sample statistic's variability. The problem of one sample and one mean is illustrated in Figure 20.30.

Fortunately, we can learn a lot about a sample statistic's variability and its sampling distribution by looking at the single available sample. The discovery of how to do this, early in the twentieth century, is what made the field of statistical inference possible. In fact, statisticians have developed two distinct approaches for estimating the sampling distribution of a statistic from a single sample of observations: classical and computer intensive.

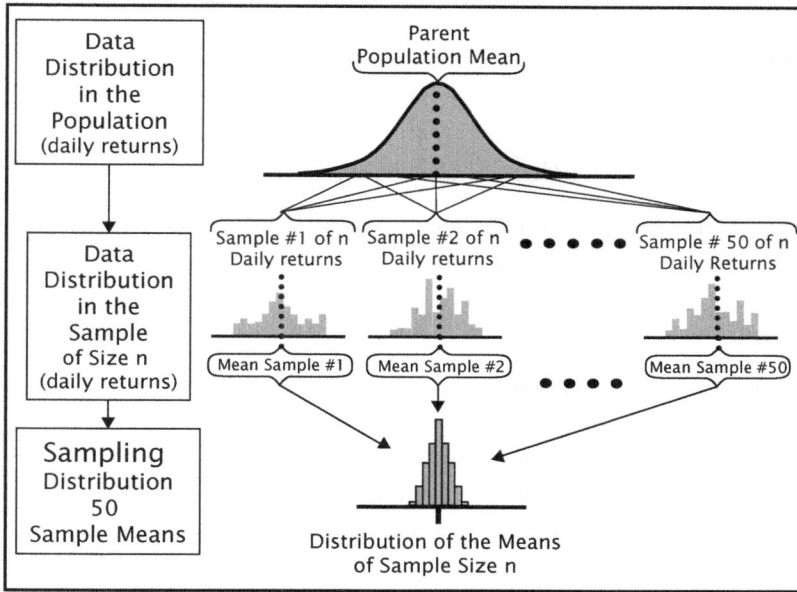

FIGURE 20.29 The Three Distributions of Statistical Inference.

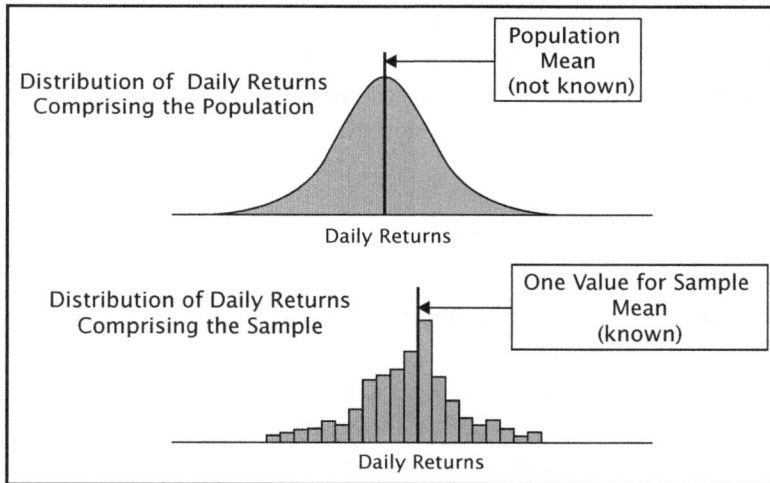

FIGURE 20.30 The Real World: One Sample and One Value of the Test Statistic.

Deriving the Sampling Distribution: The Classical Approach

This classical approach is the one most often taught in basic statistics courses. It is attributed to the two fathers of mathematical statistics, Sir Ronald Fisher (1890–1962) and Jerzy Neyman (1894–1981). It utilizes probability theory and integral calculus to derive the sampling distribution on the basis of a single observed sample. It provides estimates of the sampling distribution's dispersion, its mean, and its basic shape (normal). In other words, it provides everything needed to quantify the reliability of an inference based on a single sample of observations.

The Sampling Distribution of the Sample Mean

Every statistic has its own sampling distribution. This discussion will focus on the sampling distribution of the mean (average).

Classical statistical theory tells us several things about the sampling distribution of the mean.

1. The mean of a large sample is a good estimate of the mean of the population distribution from which the sample was obtained. The larger the sample, the more closely the sample mean conforms to the population mean.
2. The dispersion of the sampling distribution depends on the size of the sample. For a given population, the larger the sample, the narrower the sampling distribution.
3. The dispersion of the sampling distribution also depends on the amount of variation within the parent population data. The bigger the variation in the parent population, the wider the sampling distribution.
4. Under the conditions that apply to the evaluation of TA rules, the shape of the sampling distribution of the mean will tend towards the so-called normal or bell shape, with the conformity to the normal shape increasing as the sample size increases. Other sample statistics, such as ratios, can be profoundly nonnormal.

Each of these concepts is now explained.

The Mean of a Large Sample Is a Good Estimate of the Population Mean This is a manifestation of The Law of Large Numbers, which we met previously in the context of a coin-flipping experiment. To recap, The Law of Large Numbers tells us that the larger the number of observations comprising the sample, the more closely the sample mean will approximate the population mean. There are some qualifying conditions[34] attached to this promise, but they need not concern us here.

The graph of the coin-flipping experiment illustrated the action of the Law of Large Numbers (Figure 20.18). As the number of coin tosses increased, the proportion of heads gradually converged to its theoretically correct value of 0.50. In the early stages of the experiment, when the sample size was small, there were large departures from 0.50. These departures illustrate the large role that chance plays in small samples. In four tosses, though values of 0.75 or 0.25 are not the most probable, they are quite common. However, when the number of coin tosses reaches 60, the probability of 0.75 or 0.25 is less than 1 in 1,000. The important lesson: Increased sample size diminishes the role of chance.

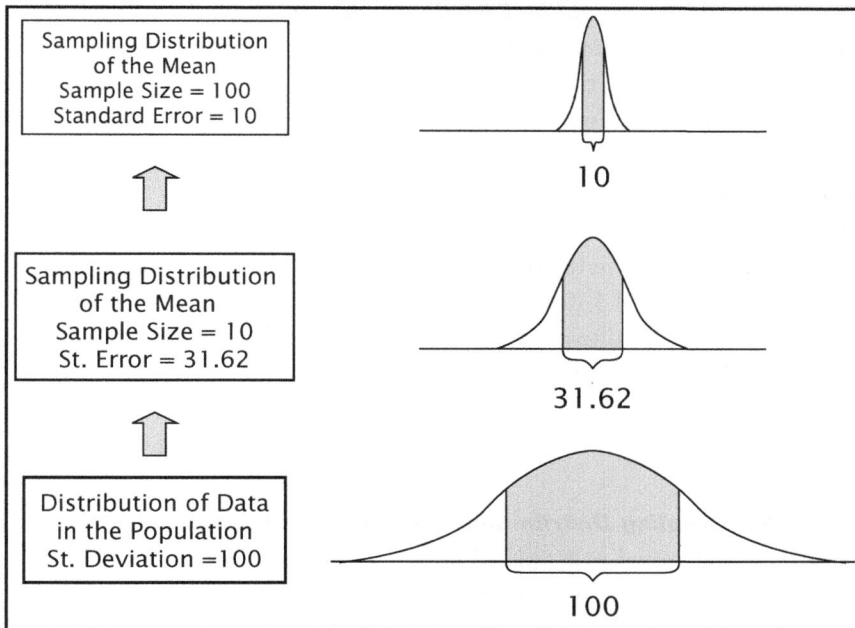

FIGURE 20.31 The Narrowing of the Sampling Distribution with Increased Sample Size.

The Dispersion of the Sampling Distribution Depends on the Size of the Sample: The Larger the Sample the Less the Dispersion Imagine a very large population of observations on some variable whose standard deviation is 100. Usually, we do not know the population standard deviation, but in this case we will assume that we do.

In Figure 20.31, I show the parent population distribution at the bottom. Above it are two sampling distributions for the variable's mean for sample sizes of 10 and 100. Notice that the width of the sampling distribution is cut by approximately one-third each time the sample size is increased by a factor of 10. One of the lessons from classical statistics is that the standard deviation of the sampling distribution of the mean is inversely proportional to the square root of the sample size.[35] Thus, if the sample size is increased by a factor of 10, the width of the sampling distribution is reduced a factor of 3.16, the square root of 10. The parent distribution can be thought of as a sampling distribution with a sample size of one (one mean—the population mean). The sampling distribution for a sample size of 100 is one-tenth the width of the parent population. The essential message is the larger the sample size, the less the uncertainty about the value of a sample statistic. Incidentally, the standard deviation of the sampling distribution of the mean is given a special name in statistics, the *standard error of the mean* (see later explanation).

With some qualifications,[36] the Law of Large Numbers tells us that the larger the sample size, the more accurate our knowledge of the population's average. With some caveats,[37] therefore, we would like to work with samples that are as large as possible so as to minimize the width of the sampling distribution as much as possible.

The Dispersion of the Sampling Distribution of the Mean Also Depends on the Amount of Variation within the Data Comprising the Parent Population There is another factor that impacts the width of the sampling distribution—the amount of variation within the parent population from which the sample was taken. The greater the variation within the population data, the greater will be the variation (dispersion) of the sampling distribution.

You can visualize this by thinking about a population that has no variation at all. For example, if all people in the population weighed 150 lbs, every sample is going to have an average weight of 150 lbs. Therefore, zero variation among the members of the population would lead to zero variation in the sample average, and consequently a sampling distribution that has no dispersion whatsoever. Conversely, if there is great variation among the individuals comprising the population, there is going to be greater variation in the sample averages, which translates to a fat sampling distribution.

Shape of the Sampling Distribution Tends Toward Normal The Central Limit Theorem, a foundational principle of classical statistics, states that as the size of a sample gets larger, the sampling distribution of the mean, with some qualifications,[38] converges toward a specific shape irrespective of the shape of the population distribution. In other words, no matter how weirdly shaped the distribution of the data in the parent population, the shape of the sampling distribution approaches a specific shape that statisticians refer to as the *normal distribution*, also known as the Gaussian distribution.

The *normal distribution* is the shape of the most common probability distribution. Often referred to as the bell curve because it has the silhouette of the Liberty Bell, the normal distribution characterizes continuous variables that describe many real-world phenomena.

There are a few points about the normal distribution that should be understood:

- It is completely described by its mean and its standard deviation. If these two facts are known, you know everything that there is to know about the distribution.

- About 68% of the observations lie within one standard deviation of the mean, and about 95% lie within two standard deviations of the mean.

- The tails of the distribution become quite thin beyond two standard deviations. Thus values beyond three standard deviations are rare and beyond four are extremely rare.

The normal distribution, which is illustrated in Figure 20.32, is so common that it has been called a fundamental feature of the natural world. Its shape is caused by the additive effects of many independent factors acting on the same situation. For example, systolic blood pressure is affected by genetic factors, diet, weight, lifestyle, aerobic conditioning, and a multitude of other factors. When they interact, the probability distribution of blood pressures in a large group of randomly selected people will have the bell-shaped distribution.

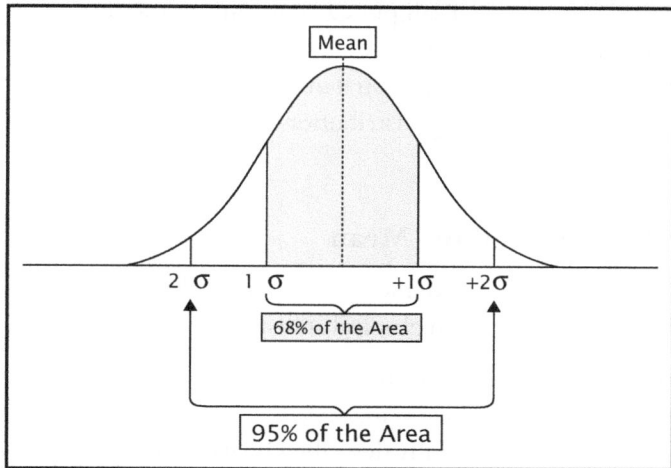

FIGURE 20.32   The Normal Distribution.

Figure 20.33[39] shows several very nonnormal population distributions along with the shape of the sampling distribution of the mean. Note how the sampling distribution converges to a normal shape as a sample size is increased irrespective of the shape of the distribution of the data in the parent population. There is nothing magical about the number 30. The rate at which the sampling distribution converges to a

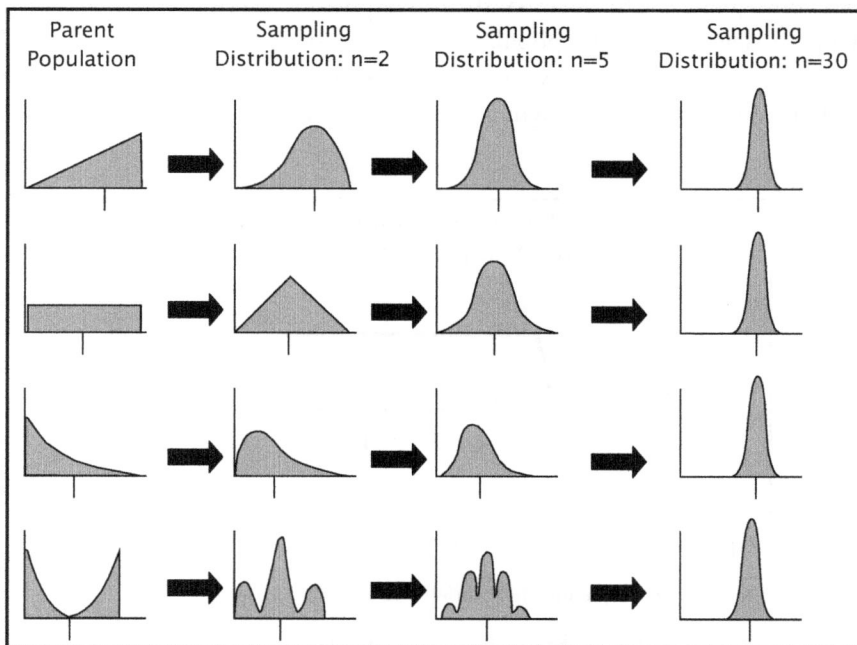

FIGURE 20.33   Given Sufficient Sample Size the Sampling Distribution of the Mean Approaches Normal Shape Irrespective of the Variable's Distributional Shape.

normal shape as a function of sample size depends on the shape of the parent distribution. Note that for three of the cases in the figure, a sample size of five produces a nearly normally shaped sampling distribution of the mean. However, for the bottom case in the figure, the sampling distribution of the mean does not become normal-like until a sample size of 30.

The Standard Error of the Mean

We are now in a position to take the final step toward defining the sampling distribution of the mean as it is done in classical statistics. So far, it has been established that:

1. The sampling distribution of the mean converges to the shape of a normal distribution as the sample size is increased.
2. A normal distribution is fully described by its mean and its standard deviation.
3. The standard deviation of the sampling distribution of the mean, also known as the standard error of the mean, is directly related to the standard deviation of the population from which the samples were taken.
4. The standard error of the mean is inversely related to the square root of the sample size.

The standard error of the mean is equal to the standard deviation of the population divided by the square root of the sample size. This is a true statement but not of practical use because the standard deviation of the population is not known. This is simply a consequence of the fact that the full population is not observable. However, the standard deviation of the population can be estimated from the sample. This estimate, which is designated by sigma-hat, is shown in equation in Figure 20.34. The little roof or hat over the sigma is statistical symbolism for a quantity that has

Estimate of Population Standard Deviation
Based on a Sample of Observations

$$\hat{\sigma} = \sqrt{\frac{\sum (x_i - \bar{x})^2}{n - 1}}$$

Where:

x_i Is an individual observation on variable X in the population

$\bar{X}$ Is the sample mean on variable X

n Is number of observations in the sample

FIGURE 20.34 Estimate of Population Standard Deviation Based on a Sample of Observations.

FIGURE 20.35 The Standard Error of the Mean.

been estimated. You will note that the divisor within the radical sign is $n - 1$, rather than n. This modification compensates for the fact that the sample standard deviation understates the standard deviation of the population.

This expression is used to estimate the standard deviation of the parent population, which is then used in the equation in Figure 20.35 to estimate the standard error of the mean.

With the standard error of the mean in hand, and the assumption that the sampling distribution is normal, it is now possible to form a good estimate of the sampling distribution of the mean. And recall all this was on the basis of a single sample.

There is one problem with the traditional approach. It assumes that the sampling distribution is normally shaped (bell curve). If this proves not to be so, the conclusions reached will be inaccurate. For this reason, I have chosen to use an alternative method for estimating the sampling distribution of the mean, based on computer simulation.

■ Notes

1. David S. Moore, *The Basic Practice of Statistics* (New York: W.H. Freeman, 1999).
2. B. Russell, *A History of Western Philosophy* (New York: Simon & Schuster, 1945).
3. R.P. Abelson, *Statistics as Principled Argument* (Mahwah, NJ: Lawrence Erlbaum, 1995).
4. A.W. Wallis and H.V. Roberts, *Statistics: A New Approach* (New York: The Free Press of Glencoe, 1956), 101–110.
5. The method for detrending or zero normalizing the market data series to which the rules are applied is discussed in Level I, Chapter 30.
6. Probability density is formally defined as the first derivative of the cumulative probability of a random variable. For the purposes of this discussion, it can be thought of as chance or probability that something will happen.
7. Fractional area refers to the proportion of the area of the density function lying to the right of the observed performance relative to the total area covered by the density function.
8. Instances of dogs missing limbs are excluded from this discussion for purposes of simplification.
9. Wallis and Roberts, *Statistics*, 101–110.
10. D.S. Moore, *The Basic Practice of Statistics* (New York: W.H. Freeman, 1999).
11. S. Kachigan, *Statistical Analysis* (New York: Radius Press, 1986), 77.
12. In this example, it is assumed that the underlying phenomenon is stationary; that is, it remains unchanged over time. Financial markets are most likely nonstationary systems. In general, statistical inference is not intended to cope with nonstationary phenomena. Nonstationary is a risk inherent when investing on the basis of any sort of rule, statistically derived or not.

13. Daily returns refers to returns earned by a rule on zero-centered or detrended market data as defined in Level I, Chapter 30.

14. S.J. Grossman and J.E. Stiglitz, "On the Impossibility of Informationally Efficient Markets," *American Economic Review* 70, no. 3 (1980), 393–408.

15. Level II, Chapter 19, Theories of Nonrandom Price Motion, discusses the possibility that TA rules may be profitable because they signal opportunities to earn risk premiums. Under this notion, TA rule profits are compensation to the technical trader for providing valuable services to other market participants, such as liquidity, information in the form of price discovery, or risk transference. Because these are ongoing needs, profits earned by rules that result from fulfilling said needs are likely to persist.

16. This definition of stationary is not strictly correct but close enough for purposes of this discussion.

17. N.N. Taleb, *Fooled by Randomness—The Hidden Role of Chance in the Markets and in Life* (New York: Texere, 2001), 97.

18. The rigorous definition of a statistic is a function of the cases in the sample that does not depend on any unknown parameter. Thus, if computing the statistic requires a piece of information that is unknown, then it is not a statistic.

19. The trimmed mean is computed after removing the largest 5% wins and losses. This can provide a more accurate estimate of the population mean by removing outliers that can skew results.

20. In fact, the Law of Large Numbers refers to the convergence between a sample average and a population average. However, a *relative frequency* is the same as an average if the occurrence of an event is given the value of 1 and the nonoccurrence a value of 0. Relative frequency refers to the proportion of event occurrences within an observed sample, whereas the theoretical idea of probability refers to the relative frequency of the event in the unlimited number of trials that constitutes the population of observations.

21. Kachigan, *Statistical Analysis,* 75.

22. The Law of Large Numbers requires that the number of observations in each interval be sufficiently large to reveal the true relative frequency of the values represented by that interval.

23. Probability density is the slope of the cumulative distribution function. For any point on the horizontal axis, the height of the probability density function at that point is the first derivative of the probability that an observation will be less than or equal to the point on the horizontal axis.

24. For example, the probability of obtaining the value 4.23 is zero. This is not so strange because a continuous random variable never assumes a value of exactly 4.23. The real value is either slightly higher or lower than 4.23, if it were given with additional accuracy (e.g., 4.229).

25. In fact each individual observation that winds up in the sample is a probability experiment.

26. A more technical definition of sample statistic: A function of one or more random variables that does not depend on any unknown parameters. This implies that a statistic is itself a random variable.

27. Kachigan, *Statistical Analysis,* 101.

28. R.S. Witte and J.S. Witte, *Statistics,* 7th ed. (New York: John Wiley & Sons, 2004), 230.

29. Other statistics include: Z, t, F-ratio, chi-square, and so forth. There are many.

30. The Sharpe ratio is defined as the annualized average return in excess of the risk-free rate (e.g., 90-day treasury bills) divided by the standard deviation of the returns stated on an annualized basis.

31. The profit factor is defined as a ratio of the sum of gains of profitable transactions to the sum of all losses on unprofitable transactions. The denominator is stated as an absolute value (no sign) so the value of the profit factor is always positive. A value of 1 would indicate the rule is break even. A superior way to calculate the profit factor to transform it to have a natural zero point is to take the log of the ratio.

32. The Ulcer Index is an alternative and possibly superior measure of risk that considers the magnitude of equity retracements, which are not directly considered by the Sharpe ratio. The standard deviation, the risk measure employed by the Sharpe ratio, does not take into account the sequence of winning and losing periods. For a definition of the Ulcer Index, see P.G. Martin and B.B. McCann, *The Investor's Guide to Fidelity Funds* (New York: John Wiley & Sons, 1989), 75–79. A similar concept, the return to retracement ratio, is described by J.D. Schwager, *Schwager on Futures—Technical Analysis* (New York: John Wiley & Sons, 1996).

33. This figure was inspired by a similar figure in Lawrence Lapin, *Statistics for Modern Business Decisions*, 2nd ed. (New York: Harcourt Brace Jovanovich, 1978), Figure 6-10, 186.

34. The qualifying condition for the mean of a sample to approach the mean of the parent population is that the mean in the parent population be finite.

35. This is true when the test statistic is the sample mean, but it is not true in general. A critical assumption is that the observations comprising the sample are independent. If the observations are serially correlated, as might be the case in a time series, the variance reduction is slower than the square root rule suggests.

36. The population has a finite mean and a finite standard deviation.

37. The general principle that bigger samples are better applies to stationary processes. In the context of financial market time series, which are most likely not stationary, old data may be irrelevant, or even misleading. For example, indicators based on short selling volume by NYSE specialists seem to have suffered a decline in predictive power. Larger samples may not be better.

38. The Central Limit Theorem applies to a sample for which observations are drawn from the same parent population, which are independent, and in which the mean and standard deviation of the parent population are finite.

39. This figure was inspired by a similar figure in Lawrence Lapin, *Statistics for Modern Business Decisions*, 2nd ed. (New York: Harcourt Brace Jovanovich, 1978), 216–217.

CHAPTER 21

Hypothesis Tests and Confidence Intervals

From David Aronson, *Evidence-Based Technical Analysis: Applying the Scientific Method and Statistical Inference to Trading Signals* (Hoboken, New Jersey: John Wiley & Sons, 2006), Chapter 5.

Learning Objective Statements

- Explain why the null hypothesis should be the target of any system developer's research
- Interpret data used for statistical inference

▨ Two Types of Statistical Inference

Statistical inference encompasses two procedures: hypothesis testing and parameter estimation. Both are concerned with the unknown value of a population parameter. A hypothesis test determines if a sample of data is consistent with or contradicts a hypothesis about the value of a population parameter, for example, the hypothesis that its value is less than or equal to zero. The other inference procedure, parameter estimation, uses the information in a sample to determine the approximate value of a population parameter.[1] Thus, a hypothesis test tells us if an effect is present or not, whereas an estimate tells us about the size of an effect.

In some ways both forms of inference are similar. Both attempt to draw a conclusion about an entire population based only on what has been observed in a sample drawn from the population. In going beyond what is known, both hypothesis testing and parameter estimation take the inductive leap from the certain value of a sample statistic to the uncertain value of a population parameter. As such, both are subject to error.

However, important differences distinguish parameter estimation from hypothesis testing. Their goals are different. The hypothesis test evaluates the veracity of a conjecture about a population parameter leading to an acceptance or rejection of that conjecture. In contrast, estimation is aimed at providing a plausible value or range of values for the population parameter. In this sense, estimation is a bolder endeavor and offers potentially more useful information. Rather than merely telling us whether we should accept or reject a specific claim such as a rule's average return is less than or equal to zero, estimation approximates the average return and provides a range of values within which the rule's true rate of return should lie at a specified level of probability. For example, it may tell us that the rule's estimated return is 10% and there is a 95% probability that it falls within the range of 5% to 15%. This statement contains two kinds of estimates; a *point estimate*, that the rule's return is 10%, and an *interval estimate*, that the return lies in the range 5% to 15%. The rule studies discussed in Part Two use estimation as an adjunct to the hypothesis tests.

■ Hypothesis Tests versus Informal Inference

If a rule has been profitable in a sample of historical data, this sample statistic is an indisputable fact. However, from this fact, what can be inferred about the rule's future performance? Is it likely to be profitable because it possesses genuine predictive power or are profits unlikely because its past profits were due to chance? The hypothesis test is a formal and rigorous inference procedure for deciding which of these alternatives is more likely to be correct, and so can help us decide if it would be rational to use the rule for actual trading in the future.

Confirmatory Evidence: It's Nice, It's Necessary, but It Ain't Sufficient

Informal inference is biased in favor of confirmatory evidence. That is to say, when we use common sense to test the validity of an idea, we tend to look for confirmatory evidence—facts consistent with the idea's truth. At the same time, we tend to ignore or give too little weight to contradictory evidence. Common sense tells us, and rightly so, that if the idea is true, instances where the idea worked (confirmatory evidence) should exist. However, informal inference makes the mistake of assuming that confirmatory evidence is sufficient to establish its truth. This is a logical error. Confirmatory evidence does not compel the conclusion that the idea is true. Because it is consistent with the idea's truth, it merely allows for the possibility that the idea is true.

The crucial distinction between necessary evidence and sufficient evidence can be illustrated with the following example. Suppose we wish to test the truth of the assertion: *The creature I observe is a dog.* We observe that the creature has four legs (the evidence). This evidence is consistent with (i.e., confirmatory of) the creature being a dog. In other words, if the creature is a dog, then it will necessarily have four legs. However, four legs are not *sufficient* evidence to establish that the creature is a dog. It may very well be another four-legged creature (cat, rhino, and so forth).

Popular articles on TA will often try to argue that a pattern has predictive power by presenting instances where the pattern made successful predictions. It is true that, if the pattern has predictive power, then there will be historical cases where the pattern gave successful predictions. However, such confirmatory evidence, while necessary, is not sufficient to logically establish that the pattern has predictive power. It is no more able to compel the conclusion that the pattern has predictive power than the presence of four legs is able to compel the conclusion that the creature is a dog.

To argue that confirmatory instances are sufficient commits the fallacy of affirming the consequent.

> *If p is true, then q is true.*
>
> *q is true.*
>
> Invalid Conclusion: *Therefore, p is true.*
>
> *If the pattern has predictive power, then past examples of success should exist.*
>
> *Past examples of success exist, and here they are.*
>
> *Therefore, the pattern has predictive power.*

A discussion in Level II shows that although confirmatory evidence is not sufficient to prove the truth of an assertion, contradictory evidence—evidence that is incompatible with an assertion's truth—is sufficient to establish that the assertion is false. The fact that a creature lacks four legs is sufficient to falsify the assertion that the creature is a dog. This is the valid form of argument called denial of the consequent.

> *If p is true, then q is true.*
>
> *q is not true.*
>
> *Therefore, p is not true (i.e., p is false).*
>
> *If the creature is a dog, then the creature has four legs.*
>
> *Creature does not have for legs.*
>
> *Therefore, creature is not a dog.*

The logical basis of the hypothesis test is falsification of the consequent. As such, it is a potent antidote to the confirmation bias of informal inference and an effective preventative of erroneous belief.

What Is a Statistical Hypothesis?

A statistical hypothesis is a conjecture about the value of a population parameter. Often this is a numerical characteristic, such as the average return of a rule. The population parameter's value is unknown because it is unobservable. For reasons previously discussed, it is assumed to have value equal to or less than zero.

What an observer does know is the value of a sample statistic for a sample that has been drawn from the population. Thus, the observer is faced with a question: Is the observed value of the sample statistic consistent with the hypothesized value of the population parameter? If the observed value is *close* to the hypothesized value, the reasonable inference would be that the hypothesis is correct. If, on the other hand, the value of the sample value is *far away* from the hypothesized value, the truth of the hypothesis is called into question.

Close and *far* are ambiguous terms. The hypothesis test quantifies these terms making it possible to a draw a conclusion about the veracity of the hypothesis. The test's conclusion is typically given as a number between 0 and 1.0. This number indicates the probability that the observed value of the sample statistic could have occurred by chance under the condition that (given that or assuming that) the hypothesized value is true. For example, suppose it is hypothesized that a rule's expected return is equal to zero, but the back test produced a return of +20%. The conclusion of the hypothesis test may say something like the following: *If the rule's expected rate of return were truly equal to zero, there is a 0.03 probability that the back-tested return could be equal to or greater than +20% due to chance.* Because there is only a 3% probability that a 20% return could have occurred by chance if the rule were truly devoid of predictive power, then we can be quite confident that the rule was not simply lucky in the back test.

Falsifying a Hypothesis with Improbable Evidence

A hypothesis test begins by assuming that the hypothesis being tested is true. Based on this assumption, predictions are deduced from the hypothesis about the likelihood of various new observations. In other words, if the hypothesis is true, then certain outcomes would be probable to occur whereas other outcomes would be improbable. Armed with this set of expectations an observer is in a position to compare the predictions with subsequent observations. If predictions and observations agree, there is no reason to question the hypothesis. However, if low probability outcomes are observed—outcomes that would be inconsistent with the truth of the hypothesis—the hypothesis is deemed falsified. Thus, it is the occurrence of unexpected evidence that is the basis for refuting a hypothesis. Though this line of reasoning is counterintuitive, it is logically correct (denial of the consequent) and extremely powerful. It is the logical basis of scientific discovery.

To give a concrete example, suppose I view myself as an excellent social tennis player. My *hypothesis* is *David Aronson is an excellent social tennis player.* I join a tennis club with members whose age and years of play are similar to mine. On the basis of my hypothesis, I confidently predict to other club members that I will win at least three-quarters of my games (predicted win rate = 0.75). This prediction is merely a deductive consequence of my hypothesis. I test the hypothesis by keeping track of my first 20 games. After 20 games I am shocked and disappointed. Not only have I not scored a single victory (observed win rate = 0), but most losses have been by wide margins. This outcome is clearly inconsistent with the prediction deduced from my hypothesis. Said differently, my hypothesis implied that this evidence had a very low probability of occurrence. Such surprising evidence forcefully calls for a revision (falsification) of my hypothesis. Unless I prefer feel-good delusions to observed evidence, it is time to abandon my delusions of tennis grandeur.[2]

In the preceding situation, the evidence was overwhelmingly clear. I lost every one of 20 games. However, what if the evidence had been ambiguous? Suppose I had won two-thirds of my games. An observed win rate of 0.66 is below the predicted win rate of 0.75 but not dramatically so. Was this merely a random negative deviation from the predicted win rate or was the deviation of sufficient magnitude to indicate the hypothesis about my tennis ability was faulty? This is where statistical analysis becomes necessary. It attempts to answer the question: Was the difference between the observed win rate (0.66) and the win rate predicted by my hypothesis (0.75) large enough to raise doubts about the veracity of the hypothesis? Or, alternatively: Was the difference between 0.66 and 0.75 merely random variation in that particular sample of tennis matches? The hypothesis test attempts to distinguish prediction errors that are small enough to be the result of random sampling from errors so large that they indicate a faulty hypothesis.

Dueling Hypotheses: The Null Hypothesis versus the Alternative Hypothesis

A hypothesis test relies on the method of indirect proof. That is, it establishes the truth of something by showing that something else is false. Therefore, to prove the hypothesis that we would like to demonstrate as correct, we show that an opposing hypothesis is incorrect. To establish that hypothesis A is true, we show that the opposing hypothesis *Not-A* is false.

A hypothesis test, therefore, involves two hypotheses. One is called the *null hypothesis* and the other the *alternative hypothesis*. The names are strange, but they are so well entrenched that they will be used here. The alternative hypothesis, the one the scientist would like to prove, asserts the discovery of important new knowledge. The opposing or null hypothesis simply asserts that nothing new has been discovered. For example, Jonas Salk, inventor of the polio vaccine, put forward the alternative hypothesis that his new vaccine would prevent polio more effectively than a placebo. The null hypothesis asserted that the Salk vaccine would not prevent polio more effectively than a placebo. For the TA rules tested in this book, the alternative hypothesis asserts the rule has an expected return greater than zero. The null hypothesis asserts that the rule does *not* have an expected return greater than zero.

For purposes of brevity, I will adopt the conventional notation: H_A for the alternative hypothesis, and H_0 for the null hypothesis. A way to remember this is the null hypothesis asserts that zero new knowledge has been discovered, thus the symbol H_0.

It is crucial to the logic of a hypothesis test that H_A and H_0 be defined as mutually exclusive and exhaustive propositions. What does this mean? Two propositions are said to be *exhaustive* if, when taken together, they cover all possibilities. H_A and H_0 cover all possibilities. Either the polio vaccine has a preventive effect or it does not. There is no other possibility. Either a TA rule generates returns greater than zero or it does not.

The two hypotheses must also be defined as mutually exclusive. Mutually exclusive propositions cannot both be true at the same time, so if H_0 is shown to be false, then H_A must be true and vice versa. By defining the hypotheses as exhaustive and mutually exclusive statements, if it can be shown that one hypothesis is false, then we are left with the inescapable conclusion that the other hypothesis must be true. Proving truth in this fashion is called the method of indirect proof. These concepts are illustrated in the Figure 21.1.

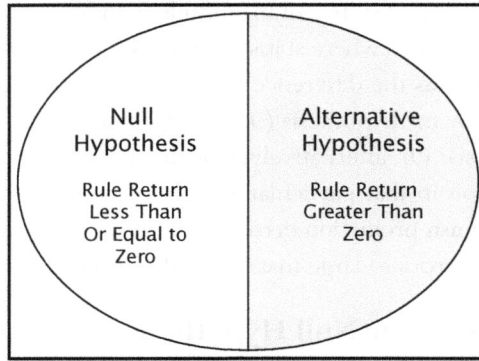

FIGURE 21.1 Mutually Exclusive and Exhaustive Hypotheses.

■ Rationale of the Hypothesis Test

Two aspects of the hypothesis test warrant explanation. First, why the test is focused on the null hypothesis. Second, why the null hypothesis is assumed to be true rather than the alternative hypothesis. This section explains the reasoning behind both aspects.

Why Is the Null Hypothesis the Target of the Test?

As discussed in Level II, evidence can be used to logically deduce that a hypothesis is false, but it cannot be used to deduce that it is true.[3] Therefore, hypothesis testing must be about trying to falsify something. The question is: Which of the hypotheses, H_0 or H_A, should be the target of this effort?

Of the two competing claims, H_0 presents a better target for falsification because it can be reduced to a single claim about the value of the parameter. This means that only one test must be performed. If that single value can be successfully challenged with evidence, H_0 will have been falsified. In contrast, the alternative hypothesis represents an infinite number of claims about the parameter's value. With no unique value to shoot at, an infinite number of tests would have to be performed to falsify the alternative hypothesis.

In fact, both H_0 and H_A represent an infinite number of claims about the rule's expected return, but H_0 can be reduced to a single claim. First, let's consider why H_A represents an infinite number of claims. In asserting that the rule's return is greater than zero, H_A effectively says that the rule's expected return, over the immediate practical future, might be any one of an infinite set of values greater than zero: +0.1%, or +2% or +6% or any other positive value. This is illustrated in Figure 21.2. Given that H_A makes an infinite number of claims, an infinite number of tests would have to be conducted to conclusively refute it. Clearly this is impractical.

H_0 also makes an infinite number of claims about the value of the population parameter. It asserts that the rule's average return is equal to zero or some value less than zero. However, only one of these claims really matters—that the rule's average return is equal to zero. The attempt to falsify a single claim is a practical

THE INTEGRATION OF TECHNICAL ANALYSIS

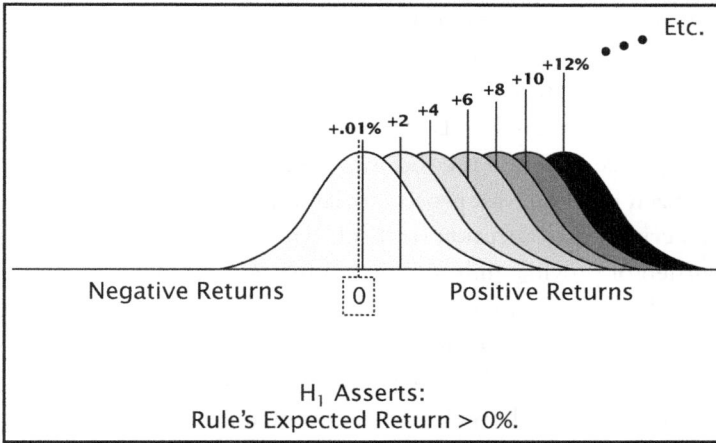

FIGURE 21.2 The Alternative Hypothesis Makes an Infinite Number of Claims about the Rule's Expected Rate of Return.

goal. If the most positive of these claims (return $= 0$) can be called into question by the rule's back-test profitability, then all lesser claims (e.g., the rule's return $= -1.3\%$) are contradicted but to an even greater degree. This is how H_0 reduces to the single claim that the rule's return is zero. This is illustrated in Figure 21.3.

Why Is the Null Hypothesis Assumed to Be True?

The hypothesis test assumes H_0 is true on two grounds: scientific skepticism and the principle of simplicity (parsimony).

Skepticism The assumption that H_0 is true is consistent with science's skeptical attitude toward all new claims of knowledge. As explained in Level II, this conservative

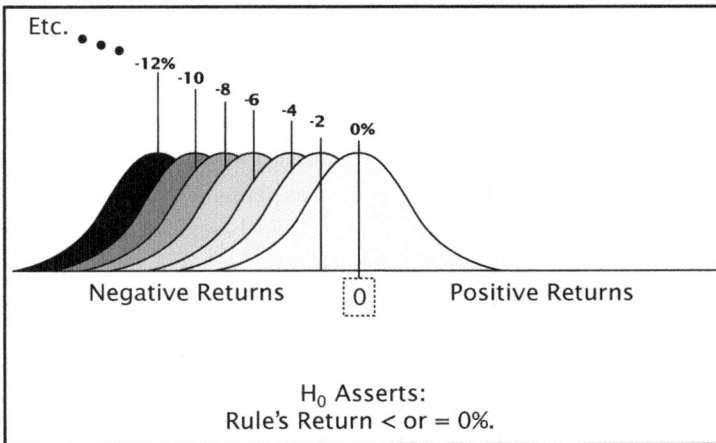

FIGURE 21.3 The Null Hypothesis Makes an Infinite Number of Claims about the Population Mean, but Only One Matters.

stance is justified because making claims is easy but making genuine discoveries is hard. The burden of proof should be on the claimant.

Science has a legitimate concern with protecting the storehouse of knowledge from contamination with falsehoods and weird beliefs. A useful analogy can be made to the criminal justice system. Free societies have a legitimate concern with protecting the lone citizen from the vast prosecutorial power of the state. For this reason the defendant in a criminal prosecution starts off with a presumption of innocence. This places the burden of proving guilt—falsifying the assumption of innocence—on the state, and it is indeed a substantial burden. To gain a conviction, the state must provide evidence of guilt beyond a reasonable doubt, a very high threshold. The initial assumption of innocence and the high threshold of proof can be seen as the legal system's way of preventing the jails and gallows from being contaminated with innocent citizens.

Following the scientific tradition, the hypothesis test places the burden of proof on those asserting new knowledge. In fact, whenever the back-tested performance of a rule is greater than zero, the sample evidence actually favors H_A—that the rule's expected return is greater than zero. However, the hypothesis test demands more than merely reasonable evidence. It demands compelling evidence before abandoning the assumed truth of H_0. Those asserting that a TA rule has predictive power (H_A) must meet a large burden of proof before they can reasonably expect their claim to be accepted by scientific practitioners of TA.

Simplicity   An additional reason to grant priority to H_0 is the principle of simplicity. This fundamental precept of science says that simpler theories are more likely to capture the true patterns of nature than more elaborate ones. This principle, known as *Occam's Razor*, says that if a phenomenon can be explained by more than one hypothesis, then the simplest hypothesis is more likely to be correct. H_0, which explains a rule's past success as luck, is simpler than H_A, which asserts that profits stem from a recurring market pattern with predictive power.

Simpler explanations (theories, rules, hypotheses, models, and so forth) are more likely to be correct because they are less likely to fit data by chance. The more complex an explanation—that is, the more numerous its assumptions, its conditions, and constraints—the more likely it is to fit a set of observations by chance. This is illustrated when fitting a mathematical function to a set of data. A function can be thought of as a mathematical hypothesis that explains a given set of observations. In Figure 21.4, two mathematical functions have been fitted to the same set of data. One function is linear. It is relatively simple in that it is defined by only two coefficients or degrees of freedom: its slope and where it cuts the vertical axis (*Y*-intercept). In other words, the line's fit to the data can be improved by manipulating only these two factors.

The other function is a complex polynomial with 10 coefficients. Each coefficient allows the curve to make an additional bend. With this degree of flexibility, the curve can weave and bend so that it touches every data point. In fact, when a function is fit to data using a method called least-squares regression, a perfect fit is guaranteed

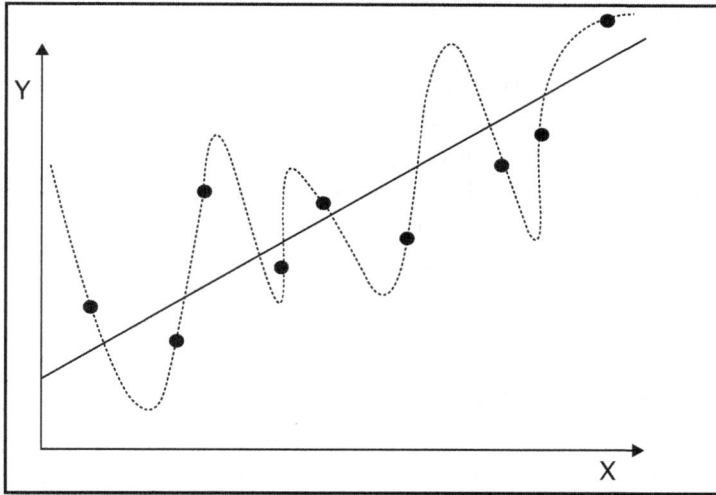

FIGURE 21.4 The Superiority of Simplicity—All Else Being Equal.

if the function is allowed to contain as many degrees of freedom (coefficients) as there are data points. Although the linear function does not manage to touch every observed point, it does describe the general tendency of the data; increasing values of X are associated with increasing values of Y. In other words, the simple function captures the essential feature of the data, making it more likely that it represents the real relationship between X and Y. In contrast, the complex function is most likely a detailed description of the data's random fluctuations in addition to the positive correlation between X and Y.

This is not to suggest that complex curves are never justified. If there is enough data and it was generated by a complex process, an elaborate model may very well be justified. However, all else being equal, the simpler explanation is more likely to be correct.

Strong and Weak Decisions

A hypothesis test leads to one of two decisions; reject H_0 or retain H_0. The decisions are qualitatively different: the first is a strong decision while the second is a weak one.[4] Rejection is a strong decision because it is compelled by improbable, informative evidence that forcefully contradicts H_0. In contrast, the decision to retain H_0 is a relatively weaker choice because the evidence is nothing more than consistent with what we had already expected and assumed to be so, that H_0 is true. In others words, the observed value of the test statistic is unsurprising and hence uninformative.

Had tests of Salk's polio vaccine shown that recipients of the real vaccine had the same risk of getting the disease as recipients of the placebo, H_0 would be left intact, and no one would have been surprised by the vaccine's failure. Nothing had worked up to that point, so it would have been just another frustrating day at the lab. Of course this is not what actually happened, and the course of medical history was changed. Salk's decision to reject H_0 was compelled by a rate of infection in the treated group that was surprisingly less than the placebo group.

It is in this way that a decision to reject H_0 is fundamentally a stronger decision than one to retain H_0. It is a decision forced by evidence that is strong enough to rebut an initial and entirely reasonable doubt that new knowledge has been discovered. In contrast, the decision to retain H_0 is due to an absence of compelling evidence. The absence of compelling evidence does not mean the null is necessarily true or even probably true.[5] It simply means that it could be true. Because science takes a conservative stance toward new knowledge, in the absence of compelling evidence, the more reasonable conclusion is that nothing new has been discovered.

■ Hypothesis Testing: The Mechanics

"Three ingredients are usually necessary for a hypothesis test: (1) a hypothesis, (2) a *test statistic*, and (3) some means of generating the probability distribution (sampling distribution) of the test statistic under the assumption that the hypothesis is true."[6] The term *test statistic* refers to the sample statistic that is being used to test a hypothesis. Thus, the terms are interchangeable.

To recap these items as they pertain to rule testing: (1) the hypothesis H_0 is that the rule has an expected return of zero or less, (2) the test statistic is the rule's mean return obtained by back testing it in a historical sample of data, and (3) the sampling distribution represents the random variation in the rule's mean return if it were to be tested in many independent samples. The sampling distribution is centered at a mean return of zero, reflecting the assumption asserted by H_0.

The sampling distribution can be derived in two ways: the analytical approach of classical statistics and via computer simulation. There are two computer-based approaches: Monte-Carlo permutation and the bootstrap. Both will be used in the case study presented in Part Two.

The Question: Is the Test Statistic Improbable?

The basic idea of a hypothesis test is simple: an outcome (observation) that would rarely happen under the condition that the hypothesis were true is good evidence that the hypothesis is not true."[7] If my hypothesis that *I am a good tennis player* were true, then it would be rare (improbable) for me to lose 20 games in a row. To my surprise and embarrassment I did lose 20 games in a row. That evidence implies my hypothesis is false.

Suppose a TA rule called MA50 is back tested. The MA50 rule is defined as follows: If S&P 500 close is greater than a 50-day moving average, hold a long position in the S&P 500, otherwise hold a short position. The alternative hypothesis (H_A) asserts that the rule has predictive power and is, therefore, expected to earn a rate of return greater than zero on detrended data.[8] Zero is the rate of return expected for a rule with no predictive power. The null hypothesis (H_0) asserts that the MA50's expected return is equal to zero or less. H_0's assertion is depicted in Figure 21.5. The horizontal axis represents expected return over the immediate practical future.

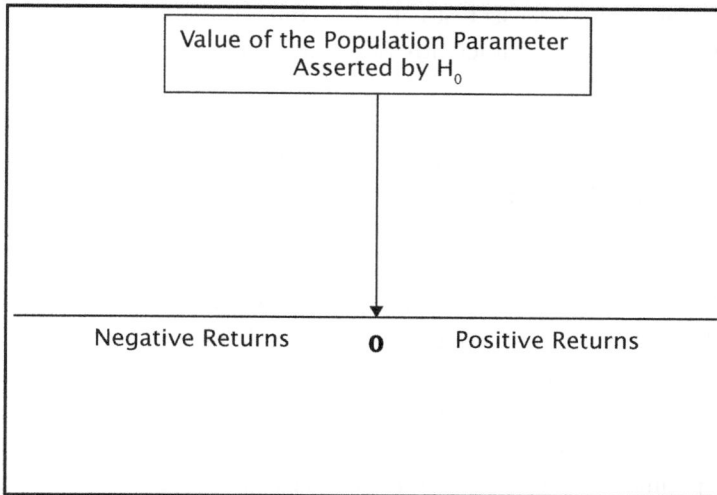

FIGURE 21.5 Value of Population Parameter Asserted by H_0.

MA50's mean return is obtained by back testing the rule in a sample of historical data. When this value is plotted on the same axis as the hypothesized value for population parameter, we get Figure 21.6.

Note that in Figure 21.6 there is a positive deviation between the value predicted by H_0 and the performance of the rule obtained in the back test. This raises the question: Is the positive deviation so surprising that H_0 should be rejected as an implausible hypothesis?

There are two possible explanations for the positive deviation. It could simply be due to sampling error—the rule got lucky in the particular sample of data used for back-testing—or, it could be because the hypothesized value of zero is wrong—the rule does have predictive power and its expected return is indeed greater than zero.

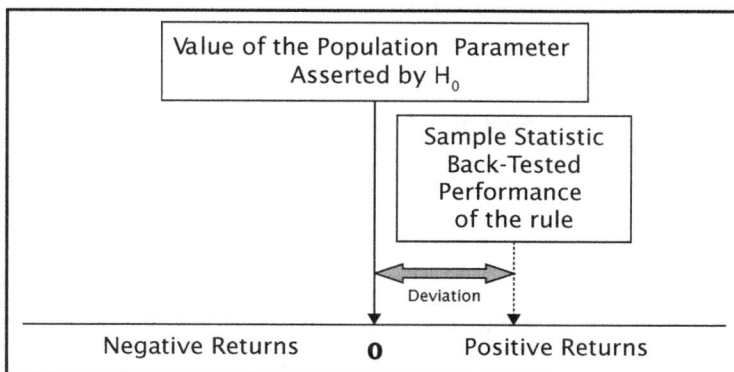

FIGURE 21.6 Hypothesized Value of Population Parameter Compared to Back-Tested Performance.

The objective of the hypothesis test is to determine if the evidence, specifically the size of positive deviation, is sufficiently rare, surprising, or improbable that it would warrant a rejection of H_0.

To assess the improbability of the evidence, the observed average return, in particular its deviation from the hypothesized value, is evaluated in light of the sampling distribution. Recall, the sampling gives the probability for various sized deviations between the observed value of the sample statistic and its expected value due to sampling error. If the observed value's deviation is greater than what could reasonably be attributed to sampling error, then H_0 is rejected and the alternative hypothesis, H_A, is adopted. In other words, we conclude that the rule has predictive power.

Figure 21.7 gives us an intuitive sense of the values of the sample statistic that could occur due to sampling variability. Note that the sampling distribution is positioned so that the most likely value of the return is zero. This merely reflects the value of the population parameter asserted by H_0. Also note that the observed (back tested) value of the rule's average return falls well within the range of random variation allowed by the sampling distribution. This is an unsurprising result. In other words, the deviation between the observed value of the test statistic and the hypothesized (predicted) value could easily be due to sampling error. Hence the evidence is not strong enough to warrant a rejection of H_0.

Figure 21.7 makes it clear that the width of the sampling distribution is critical in deciding if the deviation between the observed return and the hypothesized return is large enough to warrant a rejection of H_0. The width of a statistic's sampling distribution is determined by two factors: (1) the amount of variation within the parent population which gave rise to the sample, and (2) the number of observations comprising the sample. With respect to the first factor, the greater the variability of the data comprising the population, in this case daily rule returns, the larger the

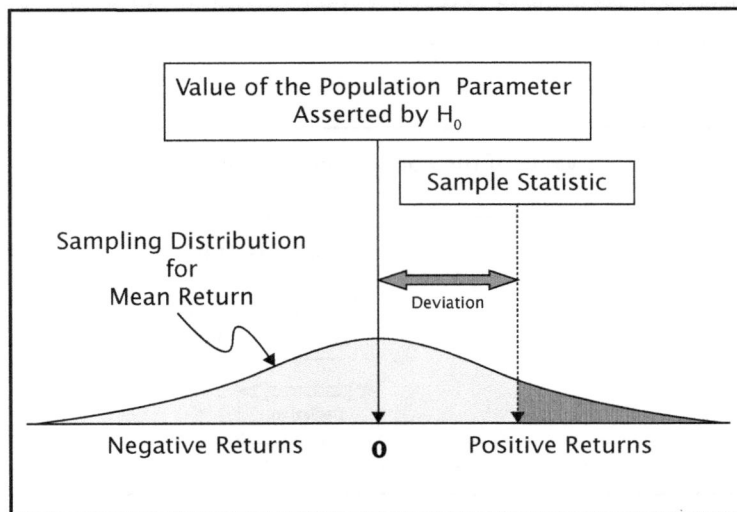

FIGURE 21.7 **Unsurprising Evidence Lies well within the Range of Sampling Variation; H_0 Not Rejected.**

width of the sampling distribution. With respect to the second factor, the larger the number of observations comprising the sample, the smaller the width of the sampling distribution.

In Figure 21.8 the sampling distribution is relatively narrow. The observed value of the sample statistic lies in the outer right tail of the sampling distribution. This would be considered an improbable or surprising observation and one that would be incompatible with the hypothesized value. Such evidence would warrant a rejection of H_0.

These diagrams convey an intuitive sense of how the size of the deviation between an observed value and a hypothesized value (the value predicted by the hypothesis) is used to falsify a hypothesis. To be rigorous, this intuition must be quantified. This is done by translating the observed value's deviation into a probability—specifically the probability of observing a deviation that large under the condition that the hypothesized value is true. A probability that is contingent on the existence of a specified condition, in this case that the hypothesized value is true, is called a *conditional probability*. Said differently, a conditional probability is a probability that is conditional upon some other fact being true.

In a hypothesis test, this conditional probability is given the special name *p-value*. Specifically, it is the probability that the observed value of the test statistic could have occurred conditioned upon (given that) the hypothesis being tested (H_0) is true. The smaller the p-value, the greater is our justification for calling into question the truth of H_0. If the p-value is less than a threshold, which must be defined before the test is carried out, H_0 is rejected and H_A accepted. The p-value can also be interpreted as the probability H_0 will be erroneously rejected when H_0 is in fact true. P-value also has a graphical interpretation. It is equal to the fraction of the sampling distribution's total area that lies at values equal to and greater than the observed value of the test statistic.

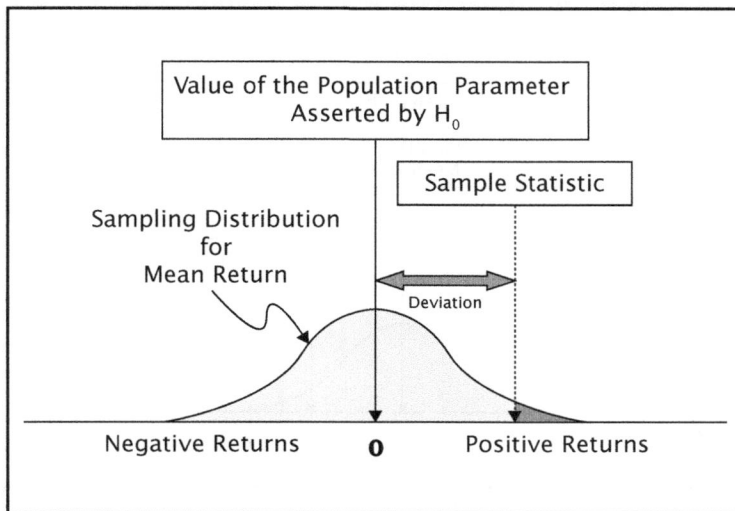

FIGURE 21.8 **Surprising (Improbable) Evidence at the Outer Edge of the Range of Sampling Variation; H_0 Rejected.**

Let's consider how all of this pertains to the test of a rule. For example, if a rule's return in a back test was +3.5%, we mark the value +3.5% on the horizontal axis upon which the sampling distribution sits. We then determine the fraction of the sampling distribution's area occupying values equal to or greater than +3.5%. Suppose that this area equals 0.10 of the sampling distribution's total area. The value 0.10 is the sample statistic's p-value. This fact is equivalent to saying that if the rule's true return were zero, there is a 0.10 probability that its return in a back test would attain a value as high as +3.5% or higher due to sampling variability (chance). This is illustrated in Figure 21.9.

p-value, Statistical Significance, and Rejecting the Null Hypothesis

A second name for the p-value of the test statistic is the *statistical significance of the test*. The smaller the p-value, the more statistically significant the test result. A *statistically significant* result is one for which the p-value is low enough to warrant a rejection of H_0.

The smaller the p-value of a test statistic, the more confident we can be that a rejection of the null hypothesis is a correct decision. The p-value can be looked upon as the degree to which the observed value of the test statistic conforms to the null hypothesis (H_0). Larger p-values mean greater conformity, and smaller values mean less conformity. This is simply another way of saying that the more surprising (improbable) an observation is in relation to a given view of the world (the hypothesis), the more likely it is that world view is false.

How small does the p-value need to be to justify a rejection of the H_0? This is problem specific and relates to the cost that would be incurred by an erroneous rejection. We will deal with the matter of errors and their costs in a moment. However, there are some standards that are commonly used. A p-value of 0.10 is often called possibly significant. A p-value of 0.05 or less is typically termed statistically

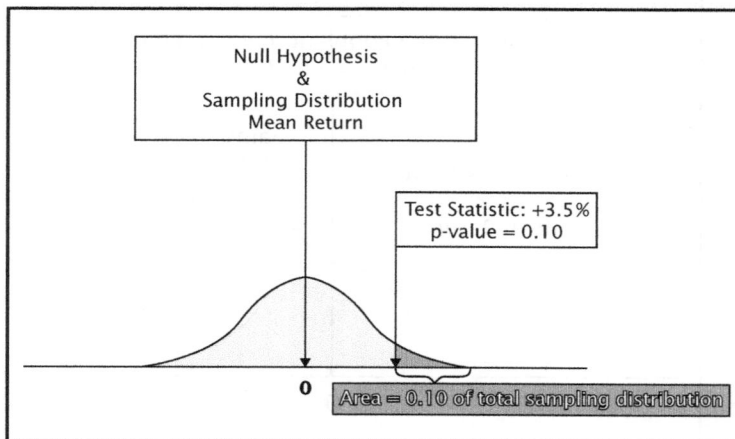

FIGURE 21.9 **P-Value: Fractional Area of Sampling Distribution Greater Than +3.5%, Conditional Probability of +3.5% or More Given That H_0 Is True.**

significant and is usually considered to be the largest p-value that would give a scientist license to reject H_0. When the p-value is 0.01 or less it is called called very significant and values of 0.001 or less are termed highly significant.

Test Conclusions and Errors

A hypothesis test leads to one of two possible conclusions: (1) reject H_0, or (2) accept H_0. What is actually true also has two possibilities: (1) H_0 is true, that is, the expected return of the rule is zero or less); or (2) H_0 is in fact false, that is, the rule's expected return is greater than zero because it possesses some degree of predictive power. Given that the test has two possible conclusions, and the truth has two possible states, there are four possible outcomes. They can be illustrated by a table with four cells shown in Figure 21.10.

The hypothesis test can err in two ways. A *type I error* is said to occur when a low p-value leads us to reject H_0, but in reality H_0 is true. This would be the case when a rule is truly devoid of predictive power, but by luck it generates a sufficiently profitable back test that its p-value is low enough to justify rejecting H_0. This is a case of the rule researcher being fooled by randomness. The second type of error, called a *type II error*, occurs when a high p-value leads us to retain H_0, when it is in fact false. In other words, the back test fooled us into concluding the rule has no predictive power, but it actually does and its expected return is greater than zero.

At the time the hypothesis test is conducted, only God knows for certain if an error has occurred and of which type. Mere mortals relying on statistical inference must accept the reality that the test's conclusion may be in error.

From the standpoint of an objective technician, the two types of errors have different consequences. A type I error, where H_0 is mistakenly rejected, leads to the use of a worthless rule. This exposes trading capital to risk without the prospect of compensation. A type II error causes a useful rule to be ignored, resulting in lost trading opportunities. Of the two kinds of error, type I is more serious. Lost trading

		Truth (The Reality Only Known to God)	
		H_0 True Rule Return $< = 0$	H_0 False Rule Return > 0
Test Result & Conclusion	High P-value H_0 Not Rejected	**Correct Decision** TA Rule Useless We Discard It	**Type II Error** TA Rule Good We Don't Use It Opportunity Loss
	Low P-value H_0 Rejected	**Type I Error** TA Rule Useless We Use it Earn Zero Return & Take Risk	**Correct Decision** TA Rule Good We Use Rule & Make Profits

FIGURE 21.10 Possible Outcomes of a Hypothesis Test.

capital is worse than lost opportunities. When capital is exhausted one is out of the game, whereas there will always be other trading opportunities.

The hypothesis test can also be right in two ways: a correct rejection of H_0, when the rule does have merit, and a correct acceptance of the H_0, when the TA rule is useless.

Computer-Intensive Methods for Generating the Sampling Distribution

As previously mentioned, hypothesis testing requires a method for estimating the shape of the sampling distribution of the test statistic. There are two ways to do this: the traditional approach of mathematical statistics, and the more recently developed computer-intensive randomization methods. This section discusses two computer-based methods: bootstrapping and the Monte Carlo permutation.

Both the traditional and computer-intensive approaches solve the problem of estimating the degree of random variation in a test statistic when there is only a single sample of data and, therefore, only a single value of the test statistic. As previously stated, a single value of a statistic cannot convey a sense of its variability.

Computer-intensive methods estimate the sampling distribution's shape by randomly resampling (reusing) the original sample of observation so as to produce new computer- generated samples. A test statistic is then computed for each resample. This procedure can be repeated as many times as desired, perhaps thousands of times, thus producing a large set of values for the sample statistic. The sampling distribution is developed from this large set of computer-generated values. It might seem strange that reusing the original sample of observations over and over again would allow one to approximate the variability of a sample statistic, yet it does! Not only does this work quite well in practice, the approach is grounded in sound mathematical theory.

The two computer-intensive methods, the bootstrap and Monte Carlo permutation, are similar in that they both rely on randomization. That is, they randomly resample the original sample. However, the two methods are different in several important respects. First, they test slightly different versions of H_0. Although, in both, H_0 asserts that the rule being tested has no predictive power, they do so in slightly different ways. The H_0 tested by the bootstrap asserts that the population distribution of rule returns has an expected value of zero or less. In contrast, the H_0 tested by the Monte Carlo permutation method asserts that the rule's output values ($+1$ and -1) are randomly paired[9] with future market price changes. In other words, it asserts that the rule's output is uninformative noise that could have just as easily been generated by a roulette wheel.

Because the bootstrap and the Monte Carlo methods test somewhat different versions of the null hypothesis, they require different data. The bootstrap utilizes a daily history of rule returns. The Monte Carlo uses a daily history of the rule's output values (i.e., a sequence of $+1$ and -1's) and a daily history of price changes for the market being traded.

The two methods also use different random sampling methods. The bootstrap uses a randomization method called resampling with replacement, whereas the Monte

Carlo randomly pairs rule output values with market returns without replacement. This distinction will be clarified in the description of each method's algorithm.

Because of these differences, the methods generate somewhat different sampling distributions. Therefore, it is possible that the conclusion to reject or not to reject H_0 may not always be the same. However, extensive simulations conducted by Dr. Timothy Masters, developer of the Monte Carlo permutation method, show that both methods generally do agree when they are applied to detrended market data. For this reason, the hypothesis tests conducted in this book use detrended market data for both the bootstrap and Monte Carlo methods.

The final distinction of the Monte Carlo permutation method is that it is in the public domain, whereas the bootstrap method that is suitable for rule testing is a patented product that is available only from its developer, Quantmetrics.[10]

The Bootstrap

The bootstrap method was first described by Efron[11] in 1979 and then refined in several later publications cited in Eric Noreen's *Computer Intensive Methods for Testing Hypotheses*.[12] The bootstrap derives a sampling distribution of the test statistic by resampling with replacement from an original sample.

The bootstrap is based on a truly amazing mathematical fact, the bootstrap theorem. A mathematical theorem deduces a previously unrecognized truth from the established theorems and foundational assumptions (axioms) of a mathematical system. Assuming that certain reasonable conditions are satisfied, the bootstrap theorem assures us that it will converge to a correct sampling distribution as the sample size goes to infinity. From a practical standpoint, this means that given a single sample of observations bootstrapping can produce the sampling distribution needed to test the significance of a TA rule.

In its basic form, the bootstrap is not suitable for evaluating the statistical significance of rules discovered by data mining. However, a modification invented and patented by Dr. Halbert White, professor of economics at the University of California, San Diego, extended the application of the bootstrap to rules discovered by data mining. This modification to the bootstrap, which is incorporated in software called "Forecaster's Reality Check," and can be used to evaluate the statistical significance of over 6,000 rules for trading the S&P 500.

Bootstrap Procedure: White's Reality Check The description that follows pertains to the use of bootstrapping in the context of testing the statistical significance test of a single TA rule. Thus, the following description does not address the issue of data mining. Figure 21.11 illustrates the bootstrap procedure. The double arrows between each resample and the original sample indicate that the sampling is being done with replacement (explained below).

There are several things worthy of note in Figure 21.11. First, the original sample, represented by the large oval, is comprised of the daily returns earned by the rule on detrended data. As discussed in Level I, the detrended market data has an average daily change of zero.

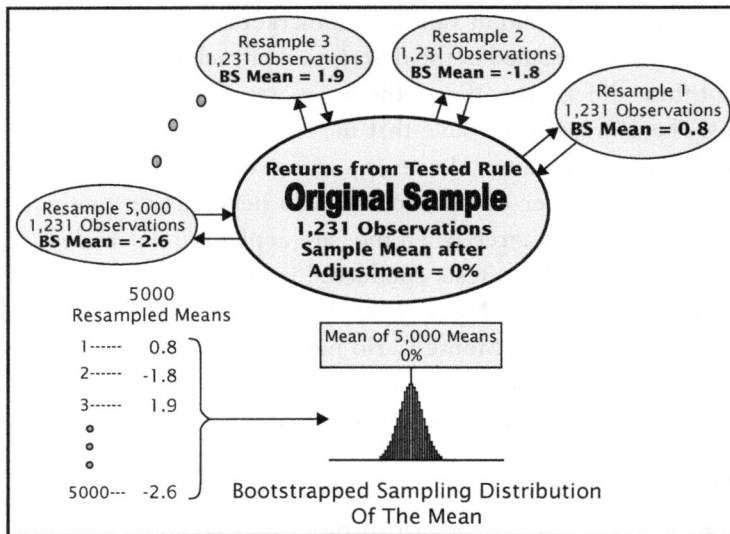

FIGURE 21.11 How Bootstrapping Produces the Sampling Distribution for the Sample Mean Return.

Second, before the resampling operation begins, the daily returns of the rule are adjusted by a procedure called zero-centering, not to be confused with the detrending. The zero-centering adjustment makes the mean daily return of the rule equal to zero. In other words, if the rule was able to earn a nonzero return on detrended data, its returns must be zero centered. This serves the purpose of bringing the daily returns into conformity with the H_0, which asserts that their average value is equal to zero. This step is accomplished by first computing the mean daily return of the rule and then subtracting that mean value from each daily rule return. Once the rule's daily returns have been zero centered in this fashion we are in a position to generate a sampling distribution that conforms to H_0's assumption.

Third, the number of daily observations comprising each resample must be exactly equal to the number of observations in the original sample. The bootstrap theorem only holds true if the number of observations in each resample is equal to the number of observations in the original sample. In the figure, the original sample is composed of 1,231 observations. Thus, each bootstrapped resample is also comprised of 1,231 observations.

Fourth, each resample is produced by sampling with replacement. This means that after a daily rule return has been selected at random from the original sample and its value has been noted, it is then replaced back into the original sample before another daily return is selected at random. This makes it possible for an individual daily return to be selected more than once or for it never to be selected at all for a given resample. It is this element of randomness that enables the bootstrap procedure to model the variability in the sample statistic.

Fifth, the diagram shows 5,000 resamples being taken. A mean is computed for each resample. These 5,000 means are used to construct the sampling distribution of the mean.

The sequence of steps involved in bootstrapping the sampling distribution of the mean is:

1. Calculate the mean daily return for the rule over the observations in the original sample (1,231 in Figure 21.11).
2. Zero centering: Subtract the mean daily return from each day's return in the original sample.
3. Place the zero-centered data in a bucket.
4. Select a daily return at random from the bucket and note its value.
5. Place that return back in the bucket, and then thoroughly stir the bucket (some statisticians prefer their samples shaken rather than stirred).
6. Perform steps 4 and 5 exactly N − 1 more times (e.g., 1,230) creating a total of N (1,231) randomly selected observations. This completes the first bootstrapped sample.
7. Compute the mean return for the N (1,231) observations in the first resample. This is one value of the bootstrapped mean.
8. Perform steps 6 through 9 a large number of times (5,000) yielding a large number of bootstrapped means.
9. Form the sampling distribution of the means.
10. Compare the observed mean return of the rule to the sampling distribution and determine the fraction of the 5,000 means comprising the sampling distribution that exceed the observed mean return of the rule to determine the p-value. See Figure 21.12.

Monte Carlo Permutation Method [MCP]

Monte Carlo simulation, invented by Stanislaw Ulam (1909–1984), is a general method for solving mathematical problems by random sampling. The Monte Carlo permutation method for rule testing was developed by Dr. Timothy Masters. He is the first to propose this approach as a way to produce the sampling distribution to test

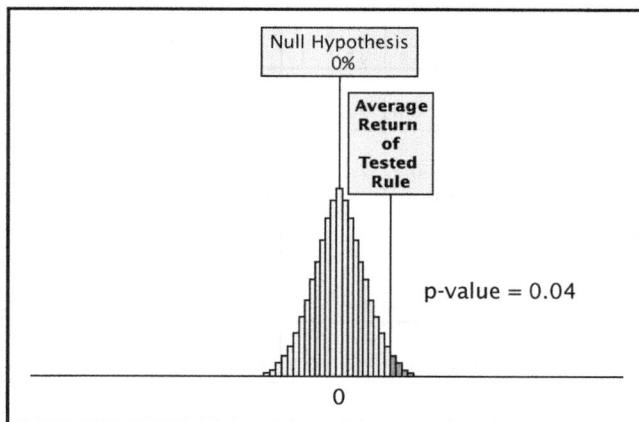

FIGURE 21.12 Comparing the Rule's Mean Return to the Bootstrapped Sampling Distribution of the Mean.

the statistical significance of a rule's back-tested performance. It is presented as an alternative to White's reality check.

Although the Monte Carlo method has been in existence for a long time, it had not been previously applied to rule testing. This was made possible by Dr. Masters' insight that the Monte Carlo method could generate the sampling distribution of a rule with no predictive power. This is accomplished by randomly pairing or permuting the detrended daily returns of the market (e.g., S&P 500) with the ordered[13] times series representing the sequence of daily rule output values. Recall that the H_0 tested by the Monte Carlo permutation method asserts that the returns of the rule being evaluated are a sample from a population of returns that were generated by a rule with no predictive power. The daily returns of such a rule can be simulated by randomly pairing the rule's output values (+1 and −1) with the market's price changes. The random pairing of the rule output values with market changes destroys any predictive power that the rule may have had. I refer to this random pairing as a *noise rule*.

The process of randomly pairing market-price changes with rule output values is illustrated in Figure 21.13. The daily time series of rule output values are simply those that were produced by the rule that is being evaluated in their original order. After the sequence of output values has been randomly paired with what is effectively a scrambled version of the market's history, the mean daily return of the noise rule can be computed. This value appears in the grey box at the end of each row. To produce the sampling distribution we need many such values.

To produce additional values of noise rule mean returns, the same time series of actual rule output values is paired with (permuted with) numerous scrambled (randomized) versions of market-price changes. The illustration shows only three Monte Carlo permutations but in practice it would be done a large number of times, perhaps 5,000. The 5,000 values for average return are then used to form

Time Series of Rule Output Values	+1	+1	+1	+1	-1	-1	-1	-1	-1	-1	
Randomized SP500 Return₁	-0.8	+0.3	-0.9	-2.6	+3.1	+1.7	-0.8	-2.6	+1.2	-0.4	Mean Return₁
Randomized Rule Return₁	-0.8	+0.3	-0.9	-2.6	- 3.1	-1.7	+0.8	+2.6	-1.2	+0.4	**-0.62**
Randomized SP500 Return₂	-0.4	+1.2	-2.6	-0.8	+1.7	+3.1	-2.6	-0.9	+0.3	-0.8	Mean Return₂
Randomized Rule Return₂	-0.4	+1.2	-2.6	-0.8	-1.7	- 3.1	+2.6	+0.9	-0.3	+0.8	**-0.34**
Randomized SP500 Return₃	-2.6	+1.7	-0.4	-0.9	-0.8	-0.8	+0.3	+1.2	-2.6	+3.1	Mean Return₃
Randomized Rule Return₃	-2.6	+1.7	-0.4	-0.9	+0.8	+0.8	-0.3	-1.2	+2.6	-3.1	**-0.26**

FIGURE 21.13 Monte Carlo Permutation Method.

the sampling distribution of the mean return earned by a noise rule—a rule with no predictive power.

Procedure   The sequence of steps to generate the sampling distribution by the Monte Carlo permutation method is as follows:

1. Obtain a sample of one-day market-price changes for the period of time over which the TA rule was tested, detrended as described in Level I.
2. Obtain the time series of daily rule output values over the back-test period. Assume for this illustration that there were 1,231 such values, one rule output value for each day on which the rule was tested.
3. Place the market's detrended one-day-forward price changes on a piece of paper. Place them in a bin and stir.
4. Randomly select a market-price change from the bin and pair it with the first (earliest) rule output value. Do not put the price change back in the bin. In other words this sampling is being done without replacement.
5. Repeat step 4 until all the returns in the bin have been paired with a rule output value. In this example there will be a total of 1,231 such pairings.
6. Compute the return for each of the 1,231 random pairings. This is done by multiplying the rule's output value ($+1$ for long, -1 for short) by the market's one-day-forward price change.
7. Compute the average return for the 1,231 returns obtained in step 6.
8. Repeat steps 4 through 7 a large number of times (e.g., 5,000).
9. Form the sampling distribution of the 5,000 values obtained in step 8.
10. Place the tested rule's rate of return on the sampling distribution and compute the p-value (the fraction of random rule returns equal to or greater than the tested rule's return).

Application of Computer Intensive Methods to Back-Test of a Single Rule

This section demonstrates the application of the two computer-intensive hypothesis testing methods to a single rule: 91 day channel breakout[14] using the Dow Jones Transportation Index (input series 4) as the rule's input series. This rule, which is designated as TT-4-91, and all others tested in Part Two of this book are described in detail in Level II. The main point for current purposes is to demonstrate the hypothesis test. The rule was used to generate long and short signals on the S&P 500 index from November 1980 through June 2005. Over this period of time, the rule earned an annualized return of 4.84% using detrended S&P 500 data to compute the rule's daily returns. The expected annual return of a rule with no predictive power is zero on detrended data.

Both the bootstrap and the Monte Carlo permutation methods were used to test the null hypothesis that the rule has no predictive power. The question is this: Is TT-4-91's $+4.84\%$ return sufficient to reject the null hypothesis?

Testing Rule Performance Using Bootstrap: White's Reality Check To generate the sampling distribution of the average return, the specific steps taken starting with the detrended S&P 500 data are:

1. Zero Centering the Daily Rule Returns: Because the rule generates a positive return (+4.84%) on the detrended market data, the average daily return of the rule (approximately 0.0192% per day) is subtracted from the return earned by the rule each day. This transformation creates a set of daily returns whose average value is zero, thereby making the data conform to H_0. Note— this is not to be confused with the detrending of the S&P 500 data.
2. Resampling the Daily Returns: The zero-centered daily returns as computed in the preceding step are sampled with replacement. This must be done exactly 6,800 times (the number of observations in the original sample) for the Bootstrap Theorem to hold true.
3. Compute the Mean Return: The mean daily return is computed for the 6,800 resampled returns. This is the first bootstrapped mean.
4. Repeat steps 2 and 3 5,000 times. This obtains 5,000 values for the resampled mean.
5. Create the bootstrapped distribution of resampled means.
6. Compare rule's +4.84% return to the sampling distribution to determine the fraction of the sampling distribution's area that lies at values equal to or greater than +4.84% per annum. This is done by counting the fraction of the 5,000 bootstrapped means that have values equal to or greater than this return.

Results: H_0 Rejected—Rule Possibly Has Predictive Power Figure 21.14 shows the bootstrapped sampling distribution with the actual performance of rule

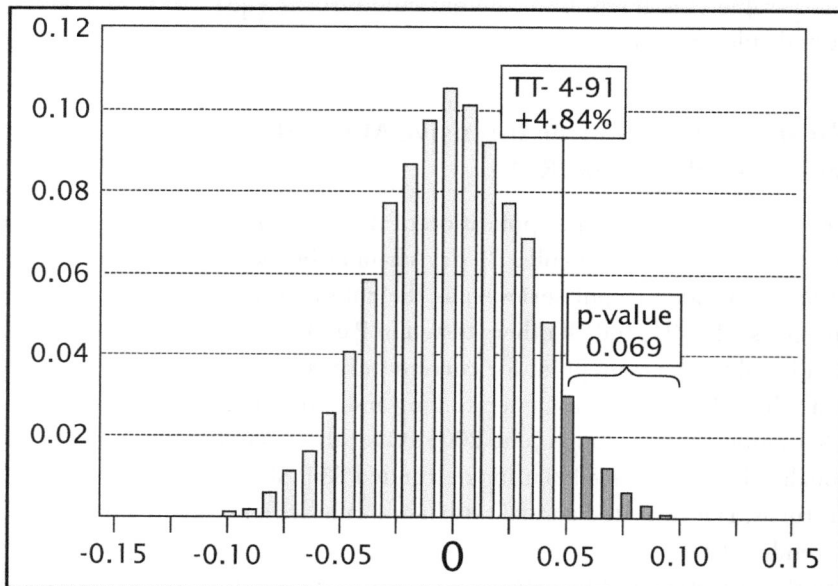

FIGURE 21.14 Bootstrapped Sampling Distribution for Rule TT-4-91 and Its p-Value.

THE INTEGRATION OF TECHNICAL ANALYSIS

TT-4-91 superimposed. The p-value of 0.0692 indicates that .069 of the 5,000 boot-strapped means were equal to or greater than +4.84%. This means that if the rule's expected return were truly equal to zero, about 7 times out of 100, the rule would earn a return of +4.84% or greater simply due to chance (sampling variability). Statisticians would regard such a result as possibly significant. The amount of search-ing that led to the discovery of the rule, specifically whether the rule was found amongst a large group of back-tested rules, can impact the p-value and the rule's significance. Consequently, the results quoted here assume that this was the only rule proposed for back testing.

Testing Rule Performance with Monte Carlo Permutation Method   The follow-ing steps describe the process of applying the Monte Carlo Permutation Method to a rule's back-tested performance:

1. The time series of daily rule output values is laid out in its proper sequence over the time period of the rule back test. As stated earlier there will be 6,800 of these daily +1 and −1 values.
2. Each of the 6,800 detrended one day forward price changes is inscribed on a ball. These 6,800 balls are placed in a bin.
3. The bin is shaken, and then, one at a time, the balls are drawn at random and paired with an individual rule output value. Thus, each of the rule's daily output values is matched with a single one day forward S&P 500 return. This is done without replacement until all balls have been paired with a rule output value. Because there are exactly 6,800 daily market returns and 6,800 rule output values, the bin will be empty when this step is complete.
4. Multiply each rule value (+1 or −1) by the associated S&P 500 return. This gives the return that would be earned by the noise rule over the next day. This step will produce 6,800 daily rule returns.
5. Average the 6,800 values obtained in step 4. This is the first Monte Carlo per-muted mean return for a noise rule.
6. Steps 3 through 5 must be repeated 5,000 times.
7. Produce the sampling distribution from the 5,000 Monte Carlo means.
8. Compare the return of the TT-4-91 rule with the sampling distribution and determine the fraction of Monte Carlo means that equal or exceed the return earned by the rule. This is the p-value.

Monte Carlo Results: Rule Possibly Has Predictive Power   Confirming the bootstrapped result, the Monte Carlo method gives a p-value that is almost identical.

▨ Estimation

Estimation is the other form of statistical inference. In contrast to hypothesis test-ing, which is oriented to the acceptance or rejection of a claim made about the value of a population parameter, estimation's purpose is to approximate the value of the population parameter. In our case, it will be used to estimate the expected return of a rule.

Point Estimates

There are two kinds of estimates: point and interval. A point estimate is a single value that approximates the population parameter, for example *the rule has an expected return of 10%*. An interval estimate is a range of values within which the population parameter lies with a given level of probability. The following statement would exemplify this: *The rule's expected return lies within the range 5% to 15% with a probability of 0.95*.

Actually, we already have been making point estimates, but they have not been described as such. Every time we compute a sample mean and use it to approximate the population mean, we are making a point estimate. This fact is easily overlooked. Some commonly used point estimators are: the mean, median, standard deviation, and the variance. The estimate is computed from a sample of observations taken from the population. In other words, a point estimate is a sample statistic. The formula to compute a sample mean is shown in Figure 21.15.

The use of means (averages) is so ubiquitous in TA that it is taken for granted, yet the sample mean turns out to be an elegant and powerful estimator. It provides a single value that is, in an important sense, the best (most informative) estimate of the population's mean. This is an important fact.

Just how informative the sample mean is becomes clear when we consider the criteria used to judge the quality of an estimator. Good estimators should be: *unbiased, consistent, efficient, and sufficient*. In terms of these four criteria, it can be shown that the sample mean is the best estimator of the population mean.[15]

An estimator is unbiased if its expected value is equal to the population value. Said differently, if an estimator is unbiased its deviations from the true population value have an average value of zero. The sample mean's deviations from the population

$$\overline{X} = \frac{X_1 + X_2 + X_3 + \ldots X_n}{n}$$

$$\overline{X} = \frac{\sum_{i=1}^{n} X_i}{n}$$

Where X_i is an individual observation on variable X

FIGURE 21.15 Sample Mean of Variable X.

mean are unbiased. This allows us to say that a rule's mean return in a historical sample is an unbiased estimate of its mean return in the immediate practical future.

Another criterion of a point estimator's goodness is its *consistency*. An estimator is said to be consistent if its value converges to the value of the population parameter as sample size is increased. The Law of Large Numbers tells us that this is so for the sample mean.

Estimators should also be *efficient*. This criterion relates to the width of its sampling distribution. As mentioned earlier, an estimator is a sample statistic, and thus has a sampling distribution. The most efficient estimator is the one that produces the narrowest sampling distribution. In other words, the most efficient estimator has the smallest standard error.[16] Both the sample mean and the sample median are unbiased and consistent estimators of the population mean for populations that are distributed symmetrically. However, the sample mean is more efficient than the sample median. For large samples, the standard error of the mean is about 80% smaller than the sample median's standard error.[17]

The final trait of a good point estimator is called its *sufficiency*. "An estimator is sufficient if it makes such use of all the available sample data that no other estimator would add any information about the parameter being estimated."[18] The sample mean is sufficient in this sense.

Interval Estimates—The Confidence Interval

More informative than the point estimate is the interval estimate, also known as a confidence interval. It is described in this section.

What Do Confidence Intervals Tell Us? A point estimate has limited value because it conveys no sense of the uncertainty in the estimate due to sampling error. The confidence interval solves this problem by combining the information of the point estimate with the information about the estimator's sampling distribution.

A confidence interval is a range of values that surround the point estimate. The interval is defined by upper and lower values called bounds. In addition, the interval is accompanied by a probability number that tells us how likely it is that the true value of the population parameter falls within the bounds of the confidence interval. By convention the probability is stated as a percentage rather than a fraction. Thus, a 90% confidence interval for the mean has a 0.90 probability of enclosing within its bounds the population's true mean value.

When thinking about what a confidence interval tells us, it is best to think of what would happen if one were to construct a large number of 90% confidence intervals, each based on an independent sample of data taken from the population. If this were to be done, about 90% of the intervals would actually encompass the value of the population's parameter. By extension, about 10% of the confidence intervals would fail to include the population parameter. This is illustrated in Figure 21.16 for 10 confidence intervals. Ten is a small number, which I used to keep the figure simple. The true, but unknown, population mean is indicated by the Greek letter μ (mu). The sample mean is identified by the dot within each confidence interval. Note that one of the confidence intervals fails to enclose the population mean.

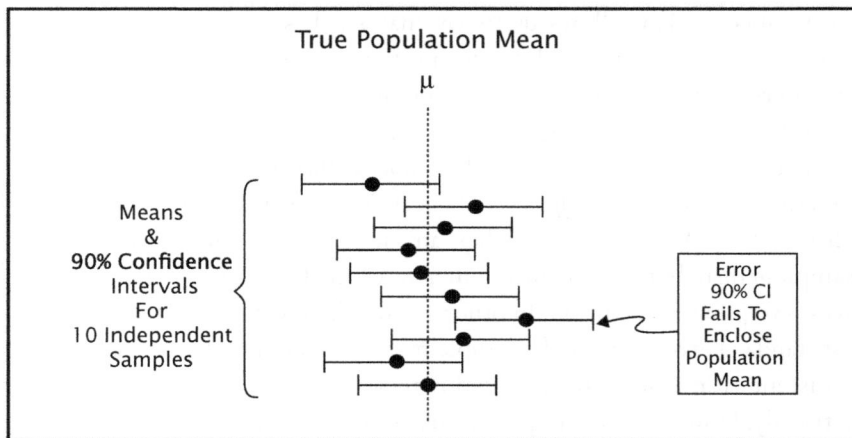

FIGURE 21.16   90% Confidence Intervals (.90 probability correct).

The researcher can choose whatever confidence level is desired. For example a 99% confidence level contains the true population mean with a probability of 0.99. Of course, there is a price to be paid for the higher level of confidence—the interval is wider. In other words, the price for higher confidence is reduced precision. Note in Figure 21.17, by increasing the confidence level to 99%, the error made by the 90% confidence interval in Figure 21.16 has been eliminated. The reduced error rate was accomplished by using a wider (less precise) confidence interval.

If a rule were to be back tested on one hundred independent samples of data and a 90% confidence interval were constructed about the mean return observed in each sample, approximately 90% of these confidence intervals would contain the rule's true or expected return in the population. Figure 21.18 shows a 90% confidence interval for a rule that earned a 7% return in a back test. We can be certain, with a probability of 0.90, that the rule has an expected return between 2% and 12%.

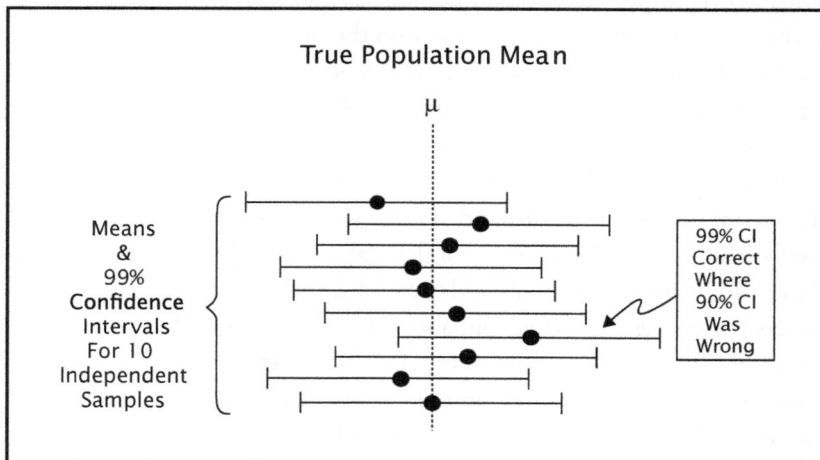

FIGURE 21.17   99% Confidence Intervals (.99 probability correct).

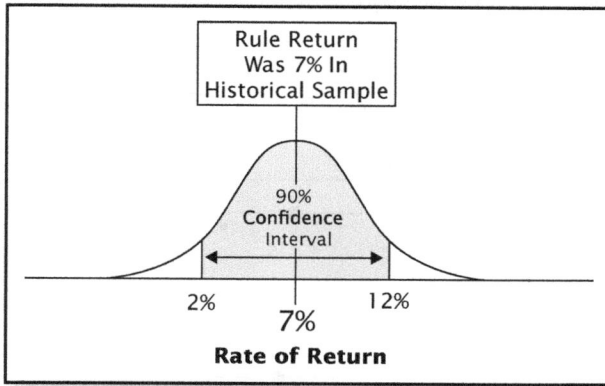

FIGURE 21.18 90% Confidence Interval for Rule Back Test.

The Confidence Interval and Its Connection to the Sampling Distribution

Confidence intervals are derived from the same sampling distribution that is used to compute the p-values for a hypothesis test. Given what we have already learned about sampling error (sampling variability), it can be said that the value of a sample mean is equal to the unknown value of the population mean, plus or minus its sampling error. This relationship is shown by the upper formula in Figure 21.19. By rearranging the terms of this formula we get the lower formula in Figure 21.19. It says that the value of the population mean is equal to the known value of the sample mean plus or minus sampling error.

The bottom formula tells us that, although we do not know the precise value of the population mean, we can take the value of the sample mean, which we do know, and the sampling distribution of the mean, which we also know, and obtain a range of values that contains the population mean with a specified level of probability. In operational terms, this tells us that if we were to repeat the following procedure

FIGURE 21.19 The Known Sample Mean Is the Unknown Population Mean with Error.

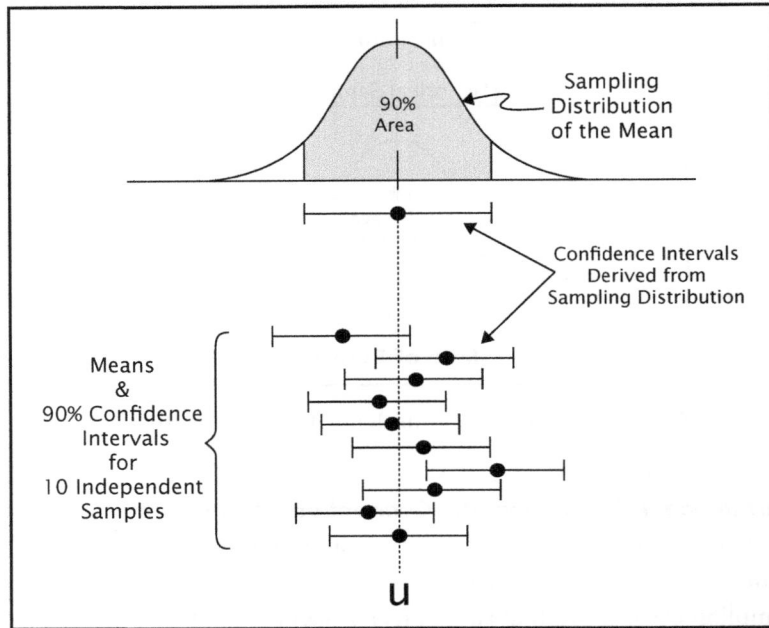

FIGURE 21.20 The Connection between the Confidence Interval and the Sampling Distribution.

1,000 times—*compute a sample mean and a 90% confidence interval*—the population mean would lie within approximately 900 of the 1,000 confidence intervals. This concept is illustrated when the procedure is repeated only 10 times in Figure 21.20. Note that one of the 10 confidence intervals fails to include the population mean. The point of this section is that the confidence interval's width is derived from the width of the sampling distribution.

As was said earlier, the confidence interval is based on the same sampling distribution that is used in the hypothesis test. However, in the case of the confidence interval, the sampling distribution is simply shifted from the position it occupies in a hypothesis test. In the hypothesis test, the sampling distribution is centered at the hypothesized value of the population mean, for example, zero. In the case of a confidence interval, the sampling distribution is centered over the sample mean, for example, 7%. This concept is illustrated in Figure 21.21.

Generating Confidence Intervals with the Bootstrap. Bootstrapping can be used to derive confidence intervals. The procedure is almost identical to the one used to generate the sampling distribution for a hypothesis test.

There are numerous methods for computing bootstrap confidence intervals. The one presented here, the *bootstrap percentile method*, is popular, easy to use, and generally gives good results. More sophisticated methods are beyond the scope of this text.

It should be pointed out that the Monte Carlo permutation method cannot be used to generate confidence intervals. This is because the method has nothing to do

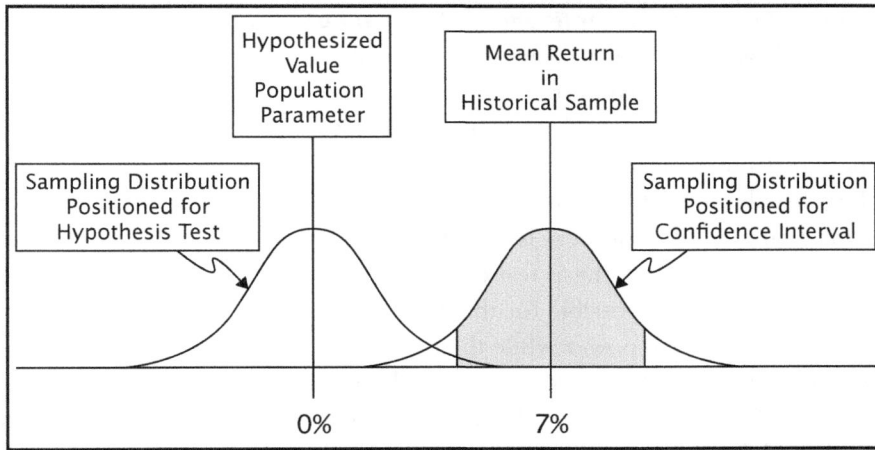

FIGURE 21.21 The Sampling Distribution Positioned for a Hypothesis Test and Positioned for a Confidence Interval.

with estimating the value of a population parameter or testing a claim made about its value. As previously mentioned, the Monte Carlo permutation method tests a claim about the information content of the rule's signals. Specifically, the H_0 asserted under the Monte Carlo permutation method is that the long and short positions dictated by the rule are devoid of useful information about future market changes. Because there is no reference to a population parameter (e.g., mean rule return) there is nothing to create a confidence interval for!

The bootstrap percentile procedure for constructing the confidence intervals works as follows: Suppose the rule's returns have been resampled 5,000 times and a mean is computed for each resample. This would result in 5,000 different values for the resampled mean return. We know that because of sampling variability, these means will differ. Next suppose that the set of 5,000 values is arranged in rank order from highest mean to lowest. Then, depending on the confidence interval desired, the highest x percent and lowest >x percent of values are removed from the ordered list, where

$$X = \frac{100 - \text{Confidence interval desired}}{2}$$

So if a 90% confidence interval is desired, one would remove the highest 5% and the lowest 5% of the values in the 5,000 resampled means. This would require removing the highest 250 and the 250 lowest values of the resampled mean. After these extreme values are removed, the highest remaining resampled mean would be the upper bound of the 90% confidence interval and the lowest remaining resampled mean is the lower bound. The 99% confidence interval would result by removing only the highest 25 (top .5%) and the lowest 25 (bottom .5%) from the set of 5,000 resampled means comprising the sampling distribution.

Some astute readers may have envisioned a problem. It is possible for a hypothesis test and a confidence interval to lead to different conclusions about a rule's expected return. This prospect stems from the fact that a hypothesis test focuses on the right tail of the sampling distribution whereas the confidence interval focuses on the left tail of the sampling distribution. This means it is possible for the lower bound of a 90% confidence interval to imply that there is a 5% probability that a rule's expected return is less than zero, while a hypothesis test conducted at the .05 significance level rejects H_0. In other words, it is possible for the confidence interval to tell us that the rule does not have predictive power while the hypothesis tells us that it does. In theory, the hypothesis test and the confidence interval should come to the same conclusion on this issue. That is to say, if the lower bound of a 90% confidence interval tells us that the rule's expected return is less than 0%, then a hypothesis test at the .05 significance level would presumably not reject the null hypothesis.

Conflicting conclusions can arise when the sampling distribution is not symmetrical (i.e., is skewed to the right or left). This is illustrated in Figure 21.22. The sampling distribution, which is clearly skewed to the left, is shown in two positions. In the lower portion of Figure 21.22, the sampling distribution is positioned as it would be for conducting a test of H_0. Because less than 5% of the sampling distribution's right tail lies above the mean return of the back-tested rule, the test indicates the rule is significant at the .05 level. In other words, H_0 can be rejected in favor of the alternative hypothesis, H_A, that claims the rule has an expected return that is greater than zero.

The upper portion of Figure 21.22 shows the sampling distribution as it would be positioned to construct a 90% confidence interval using the bootstrap percentile method. Note that the lower bound of the confidence interval is below a zero rate of return. This tells us there is greater than a .05 probability that the rule's true rate of return is less than zero. In other words, the 90% confidence interval leads to a

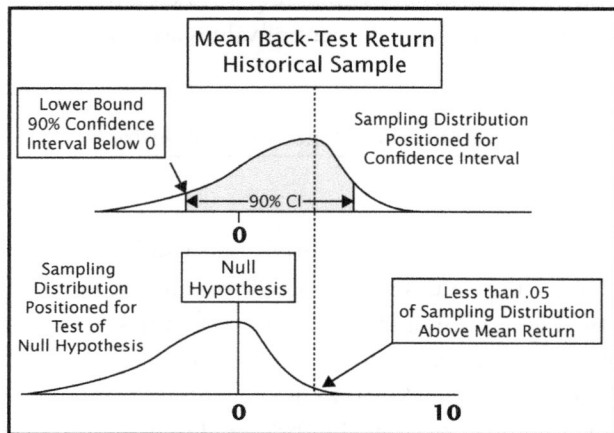

FIGURE 21.22 Potentially Conflicting Conclusions: Hypothesis Test versus Confidence Interval.

conclusion that is opposite to the conclusion of the hypothesis test. The figure shows that the ambiguity is due to the asymmetrical shape of the sampling distribution.

Fortunately this problem does not afflict the research conducted in this book, which uses the sample mean as a performance statistic. The all-important Central Limit Theorem assures us that the sampling distribution of the mean will not be seriously skewed (asymmetrical) as long as the sample size is large. To recap, the Central Limit Theorem tells us that, as sample size increases, the sampling distribution of the mean tends toward a symmetrical bell shape. Other performance statistics may not behave this way. In situations where the sampling distribution is not symmetrical, there are bootstrap techniques, which involve pivoting the sampling distribution to alleviate this problem. Unfortunately, these other methods can have problems of their own. In any case, this all makes the mean return an attractive performance statistic to use in rule testing.

Confidence Intervals for the TT-4-91 Rule   This section gives an example of the confidence interval for the rule TT-4-91. Figure 21.23 shows the 80% confidence interval superimposed on the bootstrapped sampling distribution positioned at the rule's observed back-tested return of +4.84%. The lower bound of the 80% confidence interval is +0.62%. The upper bound is +9.06%. This tells us that if rule TT-4-91 were to be back tested on 100 independent samples of data and an 80% confidence interval were to be placed around the mean return in each sample, in approximately 80 of the samples, the true expected return of the rule would be enclosed by the confidence interval.

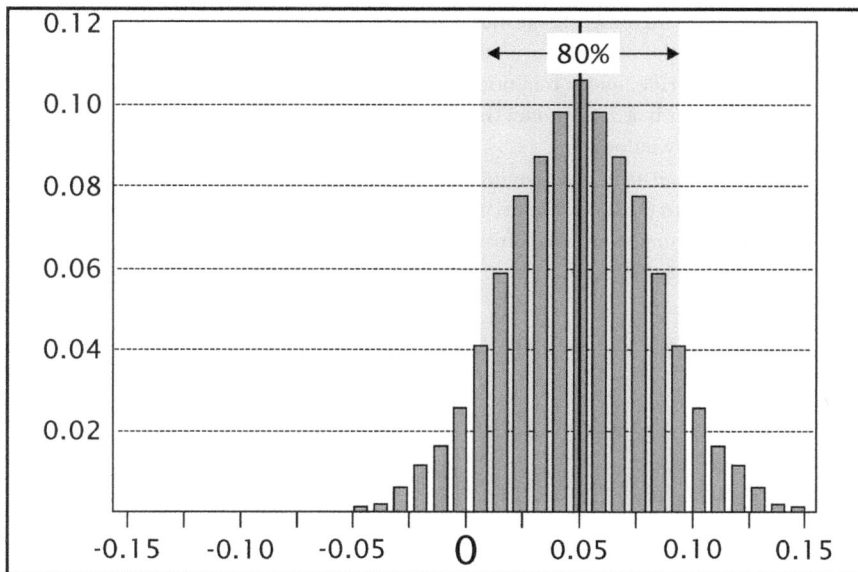

FIGURE 21.23   Sampling Distribution and 80% Confidence Interval for Rule TT-4-91.

■ Notes

1. J.E. Burt and G.M. Barber, *Elementary Statistics for Geographers*, 2nd ed. (New York: The Guilford Press, 1996), 5.

2. Because of the self-attribution bias, people can maintain a delusion by rationalizing a loss: headache, shoelaces were untied, argued with wife before game, the other player put an evil eye on me, and so on. Distasteful evidence can always be explained away if loose evidence standards are applied.

3. According to Popper and Hume, no amount of confirmatory evidence can provide certitude for a claim. However, evidence can be used to falsify a claim. For this reason, a science test claims by focusing on evidence that has the potential to show that the claim is false rather than on evidence that might confirm the claim.

4. R.S. Witte and J.S. Witte, *Statistics*, 7th ed. (Hoboken, NJ: John Wiley & Sons, 2004), 264.

5. Ibid.

6. Eric W. Noreen, *Computer Intensive Methods for Testing Hypotheses: An Introduction* (New York: John Wiley & Sons, 1989), 2.

7. David S. Moore, *The Basic Practice of Statistics*, 2nd ed. (New York: W. H. Freeman, 2000), 314.

8. Detrending transforms the market data such that it has a mean daily change of zero. This eliminates the distortion in a rules performance due to the conjoint effects of position bias and the market's trend during the back-test period.

9. Randomly paired means that the historical daily price changes of the market are scrambled, and then each is randomly paired with a rule output value (+1 or −1).

10. Quantmetrics, 2214 El Amigo Road, Del Mar, CA 92014.

11. B. Efron, "Bootstrap Methods: Another Look at the Jackknife," *Annals of Statistics* 7(1979), 1–26.

12. E.W. Noreen in *Computer Intensive Methods for Testing Hypotheses* cites the following references to bootstrapping: B. Efron and G. Gong, "A Leisurely Look at the Bootstrap, the Jacknife and Cross-Validation," *American Staistican* 37 (February 1984), 36–48; B. Efron, "Better Bootstrap Confidence Intervals," *LCS Technical Report No. 14*, Department of Statistics and Stanford Linear Accelerator; B. Efron and R. Tibshirani, "Bootstrap Methods for Standard Errors, Confidence Intervals, and Other Methods of Statistical Accuracy," *Statistical Science* 1 (1984), 54–77.

13. Here, *ordered* means the values occur in their proper temporal order.

14. A channel breakout rule, under traditional TA interpretation, registers a buy (sell) signal when the rule's input series is at a maximum (minimum) value for the current day and all prior days in the rule's look-back window.

15. L.J. Kazmier, *Statistical Analysis for Business and Economics* (New York: McGraw-Hill, 1978), 217.

16. *Standard error* refers to the standard deviation of sample means around the population mean when many independent samples are taken from the same population.

17. Kazmier, *Statistical Analysis*, 216.

18. Ibid.

CHAPTER 22

Causality and Statistics

From Edwin T. Burton and Sunit N. Shah,
Behavioral Finance (Hoboken, New Jersey:
John Wiley & Sons, 2013), Chapter 12.

Learning Objective Statement

- Explain why most people make the error of drawing conclusions from data and identify the kinds of errors they are likely to make

In each of our daily lives, we face a myriad of instances of using data from past observations to draw conclusions about particular hypotheses. From deciding what tie to wear for an interview, or how to approach a friend or colleague to ask a question, or even what to eat for breakfast in the morning, we are taking past data on similar events and trying to ascertain specific details about the given situation.

The process humans use to draw conclusions based on observable data has not evolved in a flawless way. We often overweight particular data points and underweight others in ways that can lead us to draw misinformed conclusions. Some of these mistakes can be rather innocuous, while others can lead to catastrophic outcomes.

In this chapter, we discuss some of the errors people commonly make when drawing conclusions from sets of information, as well as the potential consequences of some of these actions.

■ Representativeness

Representativeness reflects the tendency of most people to read too much into stereotypes. As an example, consider the following problem, taken from Kahneman:[1]

Tom W. is a graduate student at the main university of your state. Please rank the following disciplines in order of likelihood that Tom is now a student in each field:

- Business Administration

- Computer Science

---

[1] Daniel Kahneman, *Thinking, Fast and Slow* (New York: Farrar, Straus and Giroux, 2011), 146–154. Example reworded slightly here.

- Engineering

- Humanities and Education

- Law

- Medicine

- Library Science

- Physical and Life Science

- Social Science and Social Work

Most ranked the disciplines in size order of the fields, which is the correct method to rank them without any further information. Subjects were then given the following description and told it was created by a psychologist "on the basis of psychological tests of uncertain validity":[2]

> Tom W. is of high intelligence, although lacking in true creativity. He has a need for order and clarity, and for neat and tidy systems in which every detail finds its appropriate place. His writing is rather dull and mechanical, occasionally enlivened by somewhat corny puns and flashes of imagination of the sci-fi type. He has a strong drive for competence. He seems to have little feel and little sympathy for other people, and does not enjoy inter-acting with others. Self-centered, he nonetheless has a deep moral sense.

This description was designed specifically to conform to specific stereotypes of the departments listed above that tend to be smaller and not to correlate with the characteristics most ascribe to the departments listed above that tend to be larger. For example, one might think this description fits well with computer science but not as well with social science and social work.

The researchers found that individuals completely revamped their ordering of the various disciplines based solely on a simple description by a psychologist, even though they were warned that the description is of uncertain validity. Individuals adjusted their probability estimates far too much in the face of the additional, limited information. Most almost completely reversed their orderings, listing the smallest departments as the most likely, and the largest departments as the least likely.

Mathematically, the task at hand is to calculate the *conditional probability* that Tom W. is a member of each department and then rank those probabilities in order. One approach is to start with the first question's results, the unconditional probabilities that Tom W. is a member of each department, also known as the *base rates*, and then adjust those base rates based on the additional information they receive, namely Tom's personality profile.

However, most respondents adjust their estimates too far—in fact, the evidence shows they shift their estimates almost fully, as if the personality profile is the only information they have, eschewing any knowledge of department size completely.

---

[2] Kahneman, 147.

As an example, if the distribution of all graduate students in the university were as follows:

- Business Administration: 10%

- Computer Science: 5%

- Engineering: 10%

- Humanities and Education: 35%

- Law: 10%

- Medicine: 12%

- Library Science: 3%

- Physical and Life Science: 5%

- Social Science and Social Work: 10%

These probabilities then represent the base rates, or the probabilities that Tom W. is a member of each department unconditional on any information about his personality.

Once we receive his personality assessment, we have additional information we can use to approximate the likelihood Tom is in each department.[3] Let's say the proportion of all grad students in each department that fits this profile are as follows:

- Business Administration: 30%

- Computer Science: 70%

- Engineering: 45%

- Humanities and Education: 20%

- Law: 20%

- Medicine: 15%

- Library Science: 40%

- Physical and Life Science: 30%

- Social Science and Social Work: 5%

To calculate the probability Tom W. is in each department given his personality profile, we must utilize the *law of total probability*, which implies that:

$$P(A \mid B) = \frac{P(A \& B)}{P(B)} \tag{22.1}$$

---

[3] For the purposes of this example, consider the personality profile reliable.

for two events, A and B, where an event can be any occurrence, such as "it will rain tomorrow" or "the Redskins will win the Super Bowl." The vertical line means that that probability is calculated assuming everything to the right of the line is true. The intuition behind this equation is relatively straightforward—if one wants to know how likely it is to be above 80 degrees given that it is raining, he or she just needs to look at all the times in which it is raining at all and see what fraction of those times it is above 80 degrees in addition.

Here, the event A is that a specific grad student is in a particular department, and the event B is that a specific grad student has the listed personality profile. To calculate the proportion of all grad students that both have Tom's personality and are in a particular department, we simply multiply the unconditional probability of attendance in a department by the proportion of grad students in that department that have the given personality. For example, if 10% of grad students are in business administration, and 30% of those have the given personality, then 3% of all grad students are both in business administration and have the given personality. These percentages for each department are:

- Business Administration: 3%

- Computer Science: 3.5%

- Engineering: 4.5%

- Humanities and Education: 7%

- Law: 2%

- Medicine: 1.8%

- Library Science: 1.2%

- Physical and Life Science: 1.5%

- Social Science and Social Work: 0.5%

To calculate the percentage of grad students in all of these departments that fit Tom's personality profile, we can simply sum these numbers, which yields 25%. This is our $P(B)$ from the preceding equation. The last step, then, is to divide the above probabilities by 25%. Hence, the conditional probability that a grad student is in each department given he or she has Tom's personality profile is:

- Business Administration: 12%

- Computer Science: 14%

- Engineering: 18%

- Humanities and Education: 28%

- Law: 8%

- Medicine: 7.2%

- Library Science: 4.8%

- Physical and Life Science: 6%

- Social Science and Social Work: 2%

Compare these probabilities with the base rates given earlier. Those for departments that are heavily weighted with students like Tom increased noticeably, whereas departments with a dearth of Tom-like students generally had their probabilities decrease. However, the base rates still weigh heavy in the final outcome. For example, Tom is still twice as likely to come from "Humanities and Education" than from "Computer Science," even though students like Tom occur in the Computer Science department with 3.5 times the frequency they occur in Humanities.

Herein lies the mistake most individuals make. They overweight the effect of these kinds of stereotypes on the original base rates. Most in the survey ranked the departments very closely to the ordering that would exist if only considering the proportion of Tom-like students in each department, ignoring the size of the departments almost entirely.

Conjunction Fallacy

Following on the example from the previous section, assume one is given Tom W.'s personality profile, stated again here:

> Tom W. is of high intelligence, although lacking in true creativity. He has a need for order and clarity, and for neat and tidy systems in which every detail finds its appropriate place. His writing is rather dull and mechanical, occasionally enlivened by somewhat corny puns and flashes of imagination of the sci-fi type. He has a strong drive for competence. He seems to have little feel and little sympathy for other people, and does not enjoy interacting with others. Self-centered, he nonetheless has a deep moral sense.

And is asked to rank the following statements in order of likelihood:

- Tom W. is a computer technician.

- In the summers, Tom W. vacations in Maine.

- Tom W. enjoys watching baseball.

- Tom W. is an avid gardener.

- Sometimes Tom W. gets lost in his daydreams.

- About four times a year, Tom W. gets together with his extended family.

- Tom W. is an avid gardener and enjoys playing World of Warcraft.

This is very similar to an experiment run by Daniel Kahneman and Amos Tversky in the early 1980s.[4] The fourth and seventh statements are all the experimenters are interested in; the others serve only to make the similarity between these statements less obvious. It is impossible for the latter statement to be more likely than the former. The latter is a subset of the former, and hence any instance of the latter (that Tom W. is both an avid gardener and enjoys playing World of Warcraft) is also an instance of the former (that Tom W. is an avid gardener). However, most participants ranked the last statement as more likely than the fourth.

This persisted even when the subjects were asked to rank only the following statements:

- Tom W. is an avid gardener.

- Tom W. is an avid gardener and enjoys playing World of Warcraft.

What is going on here? From the description, individuals find it unlikely that Tom would be an avid gardener, so when they read the former statement, they simply think it is improbable. But when this statement is put in conjunction with a statement they think is likely, that Tom enjoys World of Warcraft, they ignore the conjunction and focus on the part of the sentence they think is likely, incorrectly rating this statement more likely than the former. Kahneman and Tversky termed this phenomenon *conjunction bias*.

This has important implications for financial markets. In the case of financial markets, imagine that a particular stock has exhibited a very high rate of return recently. From which of the following groups of stocks is that stock most likely a member?

- All common stocks.

- Technology stocks with very strong earnings.

If the conjunction bias were to come into play, we might find investors picking the latter group as more likely than the former, which includes it.

■ Reading into Randomness

Your friend decides to flip a coin ten times and track the results. If we call each landing of heads "H" and each landing of tails "T," which of the following results seems most likely to occur?

- HT HT HT HT HT

- HH HH HH HH HH

- TT TT TT TT TT

- HT TH HH HT HH

---

[4] Amos Tversky and Daniel Kahneman, "Extensional versus Intuitive Reasoning: The Conjunction Fallacy in Probability Judgment," *Psychological Review* 90 (1983): 293–315. Discussed extensively in Kahneman (2011), pp. 156–165.

The answer seems obvious to many—the first three results appear highly unlikely to happen, whereas the last seems more indicative of the random process. After all, the chances that 10 coin flips come out all heads, all tails, or alternates between heads and tails 5 times seems to be virtually zero, whereas a random pattern as in the last case could easily occur.

That logic is incorrect. There are 1,024 possible outcomes to this experiment, and each of them is equally likely, including all four of the outcomes listed above. Intuitively, however, the first three outcomes seem unlikely to be random, since they appear to follow a very clear pattern, whereas the fourth seems to follow no pattern at all and hence appears more random.

This reflects our nature as humans, attempting to find order in a sea of chaos. From an evolutionary standpoint, this outcome makes sense. Consider two gatherers from long ago that come across a dispersal of apple trees across a wide swath of land. One gatherer finds a pattern in the locations and uses that to predict where other apple trees might be, and the other does not. If there is a pattern to tree locations, the first is much more likely to find a source of food than the second, and if there is no pattern, the second garners no real benefit from having been right. Consequently, it was to our advantage as a species to err on the side of finding patterns in observable data and draw actionable conclusions from them, even when those patterns might not truly exist.

Those instincts can have disastrous consequences in finance. Many traders execute technical analysis trading strategies by looking for price trends, ceilings and areas of support, and so on. These traders make a living finding patterns in prices and acting on that information. But in this case, the trader that finds a pattern in a random assortment of data may pay a big price for his mistake.

This mistake can be very tempting to make. Returning to our coin flip example, if we assume every landing of heads is a $1 increase in a stock price, whereas every landing of tails is a $1 decrease in price, our four outcomes correspond to the following four graphs (Figure 22.1).

It is very tempting to say the first three are clearly a function of pattern and the fourth results from a random process, even though all four are equally likely outcomes of the same coin flip experiment.

Another even more costly potential example of reading patterns into randomness in the financial markets involves estimates of the money managers themselves. Many make the argument that some hedge funds must be capable of beating the market because of the track record of those funds over time. One will often hear sentiments such as "they have beaten their threshold return for 10 straight years—they clearly know how to invest money."

Burton Malkiel[5] makes the case that this seeming pattern does not necessarily reflect any innate ability of the fund itself. When considering the number of funds that have failed over the years, if each hedge fund's return for the year has a coin flip's chance of beating its threshold, the consequences of such a random process would look a lot like the "pattern" of returns history has witnessed. If 1,024 money

---

[5] Burton Malkiel, *A Random Walk Down Wall Street* (New York: W.W. Norton, 1973).

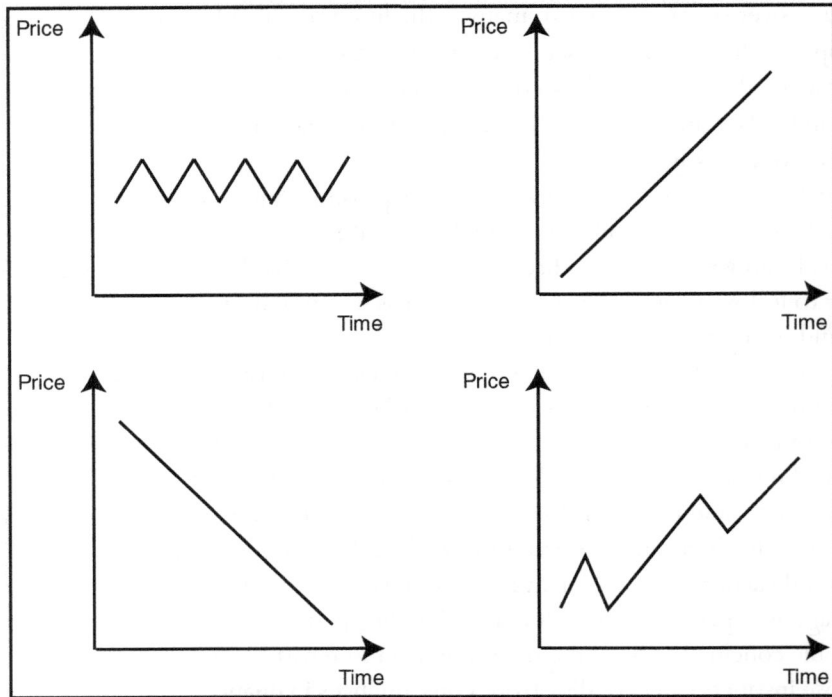

FIGURE 22.1

managers flip a coin 10 times in a row, one of them is likely to hit heads 10 straight times,[6] and that fund will be the one that survives and makes the news. When people see only that fund's returns, it is very difficult to get away from the thinking that that fund knew what they were doing, more so than every other.

■ Small Sample Bias

Imagine hearing the following statement: "A disproportionately large number of high-achieving high school senior classes belong to smaller schools." As you hear this statement, it might sound like it represents the result you would expect from smaller schools. Your mind likely floods with reasons why this makes sense—for example, smaller schools are probably able to give their students more attention, or many private schools are smaller than average and these schools probably also have more resources to dedicate to their students than other schools, or perhaps that schools for the gifted tend to be smaller in size and have students that are higher achieving going in.

Now imagine hearing this statement: "A disproportionately large number of low-achieving high school senior classes belong to smaller schools." Had you not heard the first statement, this statement likely would have made perfect sense upon hearing it, and your mind would likely fill with reasons why this is the expected result, such

---

[6]The probability that 10 fair coin flips will result in 10 heads in a row is 1 in 1,024.

as that smaller schools are more likely to belong to rural areas, where perhaps the quality of both the students and the pool of potential teachers are lower.

Of course, a below-average school size cannot explain students being both high-achieving and low-achieving. However, both statements are in fact true.[7] This might seem extraordinary, but it is a simple consequence of statistics.

To illustrate the cause, consider an experimenter flipping a coin four times. If one ran this experiment and reported a result of all heads, this result might be met with mild surprise, but it would not seem terribly unlikely. In fact, this has a 1 in 16, or approximately 6%, chance of occurring.

Now consider running the same experiment, but with 20 coin flips. A result of all heads would be met with a much larger element of surprise—in fact, one would probably doubt the results. Such an extreme result is significantly less likely with so many trials; the chance of all heads with 20 flips is about one in a million.

The natural intuition in these cases reflects a simple mathematical reality: extreme results are much less likely to occur as the sample size increases. If one thinks of each school as a number of draws from an urn with a large number of balls, some labeled "high-achieving," some "average," and some "low-achieving," the chance of getting a large majority of high-achieving draws is smaller when the overall number of draws increases. Conversely, the chance of getting a large majority of low-achieving draws is also smaller the larger the number of draws. This is because the probability of getting a large number of draws of any one given type goes down as the number of draws increases.

Returning to our example, it is not the size of the school that is causing or even correlated with factors that cause the students in those schools to be high or low achieving. It is simply the nature of having fewer students that makes the average achievement in these schools more variable—meaning smaller schools will have more extreme results for average achievement than larger schools will, in both directions. However, individuals tend to put more stock into the observations of a small sample of data than is warranted. Kahneman and Tversky dubbed this phenomenon the "law of small numbers."[8]

This statistical phenomenon has consequences for the scientists running experiments as well—consequences that the scientists often do not realize. One of the most important components of designing an experiment is determining how many data points to collect. The more data points collected, the lower the variance in the results and the more confidence the experimenter can have that the data acquired represents the population. But a larger data set also requires more time and resources to procure.

Consequently, before running an experiment, the scientist faces a trade-off between cost and improved accuracy of results and must determine the optimal data set size based on his or her estimation of the benefit of more data. Unfortunately, studies have shown that scientists are not very good at estimating the informational cost of having a small sample size. In a 1962 study,[9] Jacob Cohen showed that researchers

---

[7] Kahneman, 117.

[8] Amos Tverksy and Daniel Kahneman, "Belief in the Law of Small Numbers," *Psychological Bulletin* 76, no. 2 (1971): 105–110.

[9] Jacob Cohen, "The Statistical Power of Abnormal-Social Psychological Research: A Review," *Journal of Abnormal and Social Psychology* 65 (1962): 145–153.

CAUSALITY AND STATISTICS

commonly picked sample sizes so small that they undertook a 50% chance of having their true hypotheses appear false. Kahneman and Tversky found a similar result in an informal survey of their colleagues.[10]

These studies show that scientists routinely overestimate the conclusive power of small sample sizes. If professional researchers make such errors, surely laypeople make similar mistakes in everyday life. This result has consequences for financial markets as traders continuously are making decisions on trading strategies based on historical data. Consider a trader determining whether to execute a trading strategy of buying a particular stock after the company releases positive earnings announcements. Suppose that this company releases positive and negative announcements equally as often. The trader could very well think that 10 years of data is a substantial data set. Such a data set would provide only 20 positive earnings announcements[11] from which to derive an opinion. The trader would be putting too much stock into such a small data set. A similar problem might exist if the trader looks at the last 10 years of data to see which days of the week the market tends to move up or down, or the past 100 years of data to see which way months tend to trend.

▪ Probability Neglect

When most people are asked questions such as the following:[12]

- ▪ Do strokes kill more people each year than accidents?
- ▪ What causes more deaths—tornadoes or asthma?
- ▪ What is more likely—death by lightning or death by botulism?

they tend to overstate the probability of events for which they have a large bank of relevant memories or stories relative to the probability of other events. In this case, 80% of respondents mistakenly believed accidents kill more people than strokes, most thought tornadoes kill more people than asthma even though asthma is 20 times as deadly, and most thought death by lightning is less frequent than death by botulism, even though lightning kills 52 times as many people each year.

In these cases, it is clear that the level of media coverage of the various events is skewing the respondents' perceptions of each event's likelihood. News outlets are significantly more likely to report on the devastation of a tornado than on a local asthmatic episode, so respondents have a larger pool of memories regarding tornado-related deaths than they do deaths by asthma. Hence, the former seems more prevalent.

This manifests itself in a particular way when considering the probability of a specific event such as a potentially tragic one, a phenomenon that Cass Sunstein refers to as *probability neglect*.[13] If one is awaiting the arrival of a loved one's plane after

---

[10] Kahneman, 113.

[11] Earnings estimates are released four times a year.

[12] Kahneman, 138

[13] Kahneman, 144.

a long trip, and the plane is inexplicably an hour late, the individual's mind might flood with thoughts of horrible plane crashes from past news stories. This might quickly lead to the conclusion that something disastrous has happened. In the ratio representing the probability that a given plane crashes, the number of tragic plane crashes divided by total number of plane flights, one is considering the numerator when recalling past stories of such events while disregarding the denominator entirely, and hence exaggerating the probability that the event actually happened.

■ Conclusion

This chapter explored some of the psychological phenomena encountered when attempting to use an information set to draw statistical inferences or specific conclusions. The process humans use to evaluate conclusions based on observable data is often accurate but is far from perfect. Whether based on previously encountered stereotypes, or reading into patterns, or a misapplication of innate statistical methods, we often overweight certain data points and underweight others, and the mistaken conclusions that are reached can lead to unfortunate consequences. However, knowledge of these phenomena can help us to be cognizant of our own biases, allowing us to adjust or possibly even correct our natural inclinations toward such incorrect conclusions.

CHAPTER 23

Illusions

From Edwin T. Burton and Sunit N. Shah, *Behavioral Finance* (Hoboken, New Jersey: John Wiley & Sons, 2013), Chapter 13.

Learning Objective Statements

- Describe and identify the more common cognitive illusions that investors are prone to make

Our capacity to predict the likelihood of future events relies in part on our ability to draw inferences from past observations. Traditional economic theory assumes that individuals evaluate and learn from past occurrences in an objective fashion. Psychological studies, however, have shown that humans have persistent limitations in their ability to draw conclusions from historical data and hence often derive false conclusions from past experience.

Cognitive illusions, or biases, represent one subset of these limitations. A cognitive bias is a departure in inference or judgment from objective analysis that leads to a distortion in perception or understanding. From a set of observations on how one performs in a specific context, one may believe he or she is more capable at the given task than actually warranted. When comparing one's prediction to an actual outcome of events, one might tend to overstate the impact he or she had on the outcome. These illusions can have an acute impact on financial markets, as evaluations of investment possibilities and choices of professional managers can be affected significantly by them.

Illusion of Talent

One of the most successful franchises in video game history is Madden NFL, a series of football video games produced by EA Sports. Named after John Madden, a famous National Football League player, coach, and commentator, the label has sold more than 70 million copies across multiple gaming platforms since its inception in 1988. For about a decade, EA Sports decorated the Madden NFL game boxes primarily with a picture of John Madden on its cover. In 1999, the manufacturer shifted its strategy, instead picturing an athlete coming off a stellar year. Every year since, Madden NFL has had one or more popular players gracing the cover of its box.

Within a few years, the public began to notice that athletes who were on the Madden NFL cover suffered from a sharp drop in production the following year. Consistently, these cover athletes would underperform the expectations set by their recent production. In some cases, these athletes suffered injuries as well, causing them to miss playing time and stunt their production even further. Popular folklore recalls several examples of this phenomenon. In 2000, Eddie George of the Tennessee Titans graced the Madden cover. That year, the Titans lost in the playoffs, and his individual production dropped dramatically afterward; he would never have another season like that which earned him the cover.

In 2004, Ray Lewis of the Baltimore Ravens appeared on the cover. He subsequently broke his hand in the 15th week of the 17-week season and recorded no interceptions for the year. Shaun Alexander of the Seattle Seahawks was featured in 2006 as the league's reigning Most Valuable Player. The next season he sustained a foot injury that caused him to miss six games; his production would never return to the same level again.

Rather quickly, this trend gained widespread attention. Fans of the NFL began to fear their favorite players might grace the cover and suffer sharp drops in production or, even worse, become injured. When LaDainian Tomlinson considered appearing on the cover, his fans started the website SaveLTfromMadden.com in an attempt to dissuade him. [1]

Eventually, this trend gained a popular nickname: the Madden Curse. A similar phenomenon was observed for those who appeared on the cover of *Sports Illustrated,* dubbed the *Sports Illustrated* cover jinx.

The Madden Curse is an example of people providing too much attribution of a given observation to an individual's talent and not enough to luck. Each NFL player's output in each year is a function of two things: his skill and luck. A players' skill will not change much from year to year—a running back who has the speed and agility to gain a lot of rushing yards one year likely has the same skills the next. Luck behaves differently. Whether based on the output of his teammates, or themes in the offensive play calling, or how defenses play against him, many factors unrelated to the actual player will affect his performance the next year, and these can change significantly from year to year.

In a league as prominent as the NFL, the player who ends a given year with the most rushing yards is undoubtedly very talented. However, given the number of running backs in the league, it is unlikely he could have finished first without most of the items relating to luck falling his way as well. The next year, his talent will be unchanged, but to reach the same level of production, his luck would need to remain unchanged as well, which is very unlikely. Consequently, when one observes a production drop off after a stellar performance, it is more likely the first performance involved an element of luck that is not easily reproducible than it is that some outside force has cursed the athlete's performance the next year.

This is also an example of confirmation bias, the tendency for people to focus on evidence that confirms their beliefs rather than view the entire set of observations

THE INTEGRATION OF TECHNICAL ANALYSIS

---

[1] Tomlinson decided not to appear on the cover that year, reportedly due to contract disputes.

objectively. Those who believe in the Madden Curse or *Sports Illustrated* cover jinx ignore the fact that Larry Fitzgerald had a career year after his appearance on the cover and focus instead on the injury sustained by Troy Polamalu, with whom he shared the cover. They ignore the stellar year Drew Brees had the year after his appearance and focus instead on the fact that his team lost in the first round of the playoffs. They ignore the fact that Michael Jordan graced the cover of *Sports Illustrated* a record 49 times and never suffered any measurable disruption to his performance.

The illusion of talent is closely related to our tendency to see patterns in the outcomes of random processes. Human nature desires to see more order than may exist in chaotic processes, whether it is attempting to discern predictability in a set of random numbers or attempting to assign causation to a random trend of luck over time. Evidence that argues against these conclusions gets mentally discarded in favor of observations that jive with the desired results.

Kahneman[2] reports a similar finding with professional athletes in golf. Consider a golf tournament in which the average participant shot par in the first round. A golfer who shot six under par on that day is likely more talented than his average competitor, but it is also likely that he enjoyed above-average luck on that day. If asked to predict his score the next day, one would expect he would still have above-average talent, but there is no reason to expect he would have above-average luck again. Consequently, the best guess of his second-round score is slightly better than the average competitor, but not by as much as it was in the first round. The same logic would apply to golfers that had below-average scores the first day—they are likely less talented than their competitors, but also likely had below-average luck, so the best guesses of their second-round scores would be slightly worse than the mean but not by as much as on the first day.

That is exactly what one finds. Golf scores tend to regress to the mean as one moves from day one to day two. One might argue that this tendency arises for other reasons, such as overconfidence from having done well the first day or nerves from being atop the leader board. However, if one uses round two scores to try to predict the scores in round one, the same result appears: scores regress to the mean. Golfers with extreme outcomes on day 2 were likely impacted significantly by luck, and they tend to have had less luck on day 1.

Illusion of Skill

A closely related cognitive bias is the illusion of skill, or the tendency for people to think they have an ability to execute a particular task when the evidence shows they are no better at it than random chance. The classic example of this bias lies with the casual market trader who believes he can pick stocks that will beat the market. The universe of studies demonstrating that asset managers do not, on average, beat the market is voluminous. The most famous treatment of this subject comes from

---

[2] Daniel Kahneman, *Thinking, Fast and Slow* (New York: Farrar, Straus and Giroux, 2011), 177–178.

Burton Malkiel. In *A Random Walk Down Wall Street*,[3] Malkiel explores the world of money management and finds that managers are no more likely to beat market thresholds than one is to call the outcome of a coin flip correctly.

One of the most famous studies[4] on how amateur investors perform came from two University of California–Davis researchers, Brad Barber and Terrance Odean. With a data set of trades executed by over 60,000 households over a six-year period, Barber and Odean were able to analyze trading activity over a large cross-section of individuals. On average, each household turned over more than 75% of its portfolio annually. In total, their data set spanned over one million trades.

The study found clear evidence of overconfidence in one's ability to invest. One sells stocks when he or she expects the price to drop and buys when he or she expects appreciation. Hence, one measure of investor performance would be a comparison of how stocks that were sold did versus the stocks that were bought. On average, the stocks that individual traders sold outperformed those they bought by 3.2%.[5] Overall, households that traded the most frequently earned 11.4% annualized, versus 17.9% earned by the market over the same time span.[6]

Another measure of whether or not individuals have a skill in a given capacity is consistency of performance over time. Using the framework discussed earlier, if output is ability plus luck, output would be somewhat consistent if it is mainly a function of ability, whereas if it is rather sporadic over time, it is likely mainly luck. Kahneman[7] analyzed performance data on 25 wealth managers at a given firm over eight consecutive years. Ranking these managers each year, Kahneman calculated the correlation between the rankings in each year and every other year, yielding 28 pairwise comparisons overall. The average correlation across years was approximately zero; in other words, there was no performance persistence across time for these managers.

When he brought this to the firm's attention, his results were met with avoidance and self-delusion. The firm's managers yielded no reaction and continued along the same path of action as they had previously. The investment managers themselves reacted more strongly, though with only frustration and annoyance at the results. This is the nature of the illusion. Those who have dedicated themselves to a particular profession are loath to realize their success is a function of luck rather than their hard work and skill, which can be a dangerous mindset for market traders to have. It is much easier to conclude that the hours one has spent poring over company financials and analyst reports has yielded an expected return benefit than it is to decide the impact of one's investment decisions are still no less random than the roll of a die.

---

[3] Burton Malkiel, *A Random Walk Down Wall Street* (New York: W. W. Norton, 1973).

[4] Brad M. Barber and Terrance Odean, "Trading Is Hazardous to Your Wealth: The Common Stock Investment Performance of Individual Investors," *Journal of Finance* 55, no. 2 (2000): 773–806.

[5] Kahneman, 213.

[6] Barber and Odean, 774.

[7] Kahneman, 215–216.

■ Illusion of Superiority

The consequences of the last section are especially intriguing given the view of most traders on the market. Investment professionals tend to believe that most people cannot beat the market. But these same investment professions tend to believe that they are among the few who can. This is an example of the illusion of superiority, which can be summed up as follows: "the average person thinks he or she is above average."

People tend to associate positive attributes with themselves overwhelmingly more so than negative ones, and they rate themselves more favorably and less negatively than a hypothetical generalized individual such as "the average college student." This tendency is so pervasive that it even affects the process of memory. Positive personality information is recalled much more easily than negative personality information, which most find more difficult to process, and information regarding prior successes is more easily recalled than that relating to past failures.

These tendencies also affect perceptions. The aspects of oneself that he or she finds negative are judged to be both more common and less important than the aspects he or she finds positive. Similar findings exist for the tasks at which one is proficient versus tasks at which one has no actual skill. Individuals even create the illusion of improvement in areas that are thought to be important, even when no discernible improvement exists.[8]

Comparison with others' perceptions of a given individual confirm the tendency to overestimate one's abilities. A group of researchers[9] had individuals perform tasks involving group interaction while other individuals observed these interactions. The observers were then asked to rate the participants on a variety of metrics while the individuals rated themselves on the same metrics. Individuals consistently saw themselves more favorably than the observing group did.

This phenomenon has been broadly recognized in the academic literature and is discussed under a number of monikers, including the above average effect, the leniency effect, the primer inter pares effect, and the Lake Wobegon effect, named after the fictional town created by Garrison Keillor in which "all the women are strong, all the men are good looking, and all the children are above average." This tendency has broad implications for financial markets, where one wins simply by performing above average. If an asset manager can demonstrate above average results for years running, he or she would have little trouble raising a large pool of assets to manage. Conversely, if one believes he or she will perform above average consistently over time, he or she will unwarrantedly invest a sizeable amount of assets in their

---

[8] See Shelley E. Taylor, and Jonathan D. Brown, "Illusion and Well-Being: A Social Psychological Perspective on Mental Health," *Psychological Bulletin* 103, no. 2 (1988): 193–210; and C. Randall Colvin and Jack Block, "Overly Positive Self-Evaluations and Personality: Negative Implications for Mental Health," *Journal of Personality and Social Psychology* 68, no. 6 (1995): 1152–1162 for reviews on the literature on this topic.

[9] P. M. Lewinsohn, W. Mischel, W. Chaplin, and R. Barton, "Social Competence and Depression: The Role of Illusory Self-Perceptions," *Journal of Abnormal Psychology* 89 (1980): 203–212.

own abilities, likely with disastrous results. Based on the evidence reported by Burton Malkiel and others, many professional investment managers are likely suffering from this illusion.

■ Illusion of Validity

Kahneman[10] relays a tale from his days in the Israeli military in which he was tasked with identifying promising individuals for officer training from a pool of potential candidates. He and a colleague watched these candidates perform a task in which they were all stripped of symbols of rank and were asked to use a log to scale a six-foot-high wall without allowing the log to touch either the ground or the wall itself. If the log touched either item, the soldiers were to call it out and restart the exercise.

As the two evaluators watched these men interact, they saw a myriad of emotional cues to help ascertain how they reacted under pressure. Some men got angry when their ideas were challenged, some got increasingly frustrated as they grew physically tired, some decreased their own individual effort when their ideas were rejected by the group, some stepped up and took the reins to lead when the group was fatigued and frustrated. These observations gave Kahneman and his colleague a clear picture of what each soldier was like and his prospective chances of success in officer training. Whether a given candidate was rated very likely to succeed, very unlikely to succeed, or somewhere in between, the two observers were sure their conclusions were correct.

Several months later, the military gathered the data on how the candidates actually did in officer training and compared it to the evaluators' projections. They found that the projections were, at best, marginally predictive in separating good candidates from bad. In other words, the evaluations were barely more likely to be correct than a coin flip would have been. After the analysis was presented, the two evaluators went back to observe more candidates. Despite the clear evidence just presented to them, as each evaluated future candidates, they were again sure that their predictions would be right every time.

As Kahneman termed it, he and his colleague were suffering from the "illusion of validity." Individuals tend to believe the conclusions they draw from a brief set of observables are more likely to be valid than they actually are, and this tendency holds true even in the face of clear evidence to the contrary. This phenomenon closely resembles the representativeness heuristic. Each candidate has a base rate of success, representing the candidate's likelihood of success unconditional on any observation from the exercise. As the evaluators collected observations during the exercise, to the extent that these observations are predictive (which itself is debatable), they should adjust the base rates, but not by much. People tend to change the base rates by more than they should because they put too much faith in the power of their observations.

[10] Kahneman, 209–211.

This tendency is also closely related to the *illusion of control*. Individuals tend to believe they have more control over the outcome of random events than they actually have, even when the events are explicitly constructed as random. For example, people believe they have greater control over the outcome of a dice roll if they personally roll the dice rather than having someone else throw them. When anticipating a certain outcome occurring from a random process, if that outcome actually does occur, people tend to overestimate their contribution to its occurrence.[11]

Conversely, when individuals reflect on incorrect predictions they have made, they overestimate the effect of random chance on the outcome and underestimate their personal contribution to the error. Both situations reflect the human tendency to overestimate the validity of his or her predictions. Before they are judged by time or if they are judged correct, individuals tend to overestimate their contribution, whereas if they are instead judged incorrect, people create other reasons that caused them to be wrong to reconcile the outcome with their preconceived illusion of validity.

Experts in a specific content area are particularly likely to exhibit this behavior. Philip Tetlock, a psychologist then at University of California–Berkeley, interviewed over 200 people whose professions it was to identify and discuss trends. He asked each to predict the likelihood of specific events occurring in the future, totaling tens of thousands of predictions across individuals. Over time, he found that the experts were less accurate at predicting these events than random guesses would have been. When asked to reconcile the differences between their predictions and observation, experts were also the most likely to create excuses for their errors, such as they were right but had the timing wrong or had been wrong but for the right reasons.[12]

■ Conclusion

Cognitive illusions have a profound potential impact on financial markets. Substantial evidence already exists that traders—both casual and professional—suffer from the illusion of skill, predicting they are likely to pick stocks that beat the market even while thinking that most other people are not. Consequently, individuals overtrade their portfolios, thinking each trade will generate an above-market return. Instead, the stocks these individuals sell generally outperform the ones they buy in exchange.

A casual trader who recognizes this pattern and decides to invest with a professional manager may run into the same problem. Professional managers are certainly not immune to these tendencies. Compounding the issue, these illusions also make it difficult to pick a successful manager. Differentiating which managers are actually capable from those that have achieved good returns by random chance requires separating talent from luck, which is difficult for most to do. Humans tend to attribute too much of past performance to ability instead of random chance.

---

[11] Taylor and Brown, 196.
[12] Kahneman, 218–220.

Such inaccurate evaluation of past results has real economy effects. Resources may get allocated inefficiently as those with the most talent and most potential lose out to those who happened to strike the best luck in the past. Managers with stellar recent returns, which could just as easily have been caused by luck as by talent, may win out over those with good but more modest returns over a longer time period. The latter are less likely to have performed based on a string of good luck, but human tendencies may keep investors from evaluating performance records correctly, and inferior managers may end up with more assets under management.

A similar phenomenon can occur with stocks, as it did before the dot-com bubble. Technology stocks became the rage with investors because of their remarkable short-term returns. Older, more well-established stocks, or even indexes, which could not match the short-term track record of these new firms but had provided good returns over a longer time period tended to be neglected. Consequently, capital was over-allocated to these dot-com firms even though an objective look at their track records did not warrant such levels of investment.

CHAPTER 24

The Story Is the Thing (or the Allure of Growth)*

From James Montier, *Behavioural Investing: A Practitioner's Guide to Applying Behavioural Finance* (Hoboken, New Jersey: John Wiley & Sons, 2007), Chapter 15.

Learning Objective Statement

- Describe some common misconceptions investors make by looking for evidence of growth globally

> Shakespeare wrote "The play's the thing". For investors it appears that the story is the thing. In a rational world, we gather evidence, weight it and then decide. However, people rely on stories instead. We gather the evidence (in a biased fashion), construct a story to explain the evidence, and then match the story to a decision. This reliance on stories helps to drive investors into the growth trap.

- A former colleague of mine once wrote that 'stockbrokers exist to sell dreams'. I have long held that the corollary to this statement should be 'but they deliver nightmares'. Despite my scepticism, investors seem to love to listen to the siren songs of stockbrokers. Why?

- In a rational world, we would all go around gathering the evidence, and then evaluate it and weigh it before reaching our decision. However, real-world behaviour is a long way from the rational viewpoint. We collect evidence (usually in a biased fashion), then we construct a story to explain the evidence. This story (not the original evidence) is then used to reach a decision. Psychologists call this explanation-based decision-making.

---

*This article appeared in *Global Equity Strategy* on 18 November 2005. The material discussed was accurate at the time of publication.

- Experiments have shown that stories can have a massive impact upon decision-making. For instance, in a mock trial situation when the prosecution presented the evidence in a story order, but the defence presented evidence in witness order, 78% of jurors found the suspect guilty. However, when the formats were reversed only 31% of jurors found the suspect guilty!

- Other experiments have found that in simulation markets, participants trade on rumours (and lose money) but say that they don't believe the rumour and that it didn't impact their decision-making. The researchers found that to persuade participants to trade, the rumour merely needed to 'explain' current share price moves!

- New research shows that investors behave just like jurors. They map information into a story, and then use the story as a basis for making decisions. All too often investors are sucked into plausible sounding stories. For instance, the story that the internet would alter the way the world did business was probably true, but it doesn't necessarily translate into profits for investors.

- The current market obsession with China is another potential example of investors being sucked into a growth story. Those piling into commodities on the back of the fact that China is the largest consumer of just about everything are likely to end up ruing their decision.

- Indeed, trying to invest in the fastest growing emerging equity markets has been a very poor strategy in the past. Those economies with the highest GDP growth have delivered the lowest returns, while those economies with the lowest GDP growth have delivered the highest returns. Why? Because investors end up over-paying for the hope of growth. Beware the growth trap.

Way back in the dim and distant past, I studied English Literature (not that any of the literary genius I studied rubbed off on me!). However, one of the few things I remember from those long ago studies was a quote from Shakespeare that could be wheeled out whenever one was discussing his plays. In order to stress the importance of seeing a play in production rather than simply reading it, a quotation from Hamlet was most useful: "The play's the thing wherein I'll catch the conscience of the king."

With profound apologies to the bard, the investment equivalent would seem to be 'the story's the thing wherein I'll capture the conscience of the investor'. A former colleague of mine once wrote that 'stockbrokers exist to sell dreams', I have long held that the corollary to this statement should be 'but they deliver nightmares'. The only snag is that people love to listen to the siren songs of the stockbrokers. Why?

We appear to use stories to help us to reach decisions. In the 'rational' view of the world we observe the evidence, we then weigh the evidence, and finally we come to our decision. Of course, in the rational view we all collect the evidence in a well-behaved unbiased fashion. Readers will know that this isn't a good description of the way in which most evidence is gathered. Usually we are prone to only look for the information that happens to agree with us (confirmatory bias), etc.

However, the real world of behaviour is a long way from the rational viewpoint, and not just in the realm of information gathering. The second stage of the rational decision is weighing the evidence. However, as the diagram below shows, a more commonly encountered approach is to construct a narrative to explain the evidence that has been gathered (the story model of thinking).

The rational view

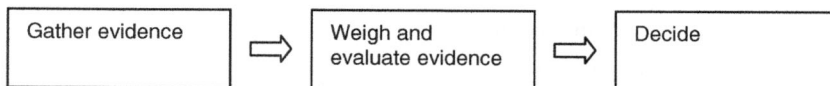

| Gather evidence | ⇨ | Weigh and evaluate evidence | ⇨ | Decide |

The story view

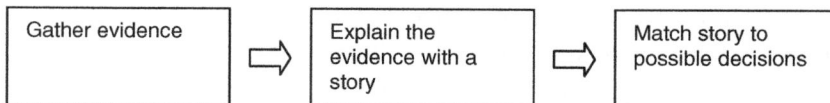

| Gather evidence | ⇨ | Explain the evidence with a story | ⇨ | Match story to possible decisions |

Hastie and Pennington (2000) are the leading advocates of the story view (also known as explanation-based decision-making).[1] The central hypothesis of the explanation-based view is that the decision maker constructs a summary story of the evidence and then uses this story, rather than the original raw evidence, to make their final decision.

Hastie and Pennington note

> This intermediate mental model of the decision facilitates evidence comprehension, directs inferencing, enables the decision maker to reach a decision, and determines the confidence assigned to the accuracy or expected success of the decision.

Much of the original work on the importance of stories has been investigated in the realm of jurors. However, the same mental processes are likely to be at work when it comes to investment decisions.

Consider Hastie and Pennington's description of the juror's decisions task:

> First, a massive 'database' of evidence is presented at trial, frequently comprising of several days of testimony, exhibits, and arguments. Second, the evidence comes in a scrambled sequence, usually many witnesses and exhibits convey pieces of the historical puzzle in a jumbled temporal sequence. Third, the evidence is piecemeal and gappy in its depiction of the historical events that are the focus of reconstruction: event descriptions are incomplete, usually some critical events were not observed by the available witnesses, and information about personal reactions and motivations is not presented . . . Finally, subparts of the evidence are interdependent in their probative implications for the verdict. The meaning of one statement cannot be assessed in isolation because it depends on the meanings of several other related statements.

---

[1] See Hastie and Pennington (2000) for an up to date summary of the field.

TABLE 24.1	Percentage of Jurors Returning a Guilty Verdict		
		Defence	
		Story order	Witness order
Prosecution	Story order	59%	78%
	Witness order	31%	63%

Source: Pennington and Hastie (1988).

In several empirical tests, Pennington and Hastie (1986, 1988) have investigated the decision-making process of jurors. They discovered that jurors who had reached different verdicts had constructed different stories with distinctly different configurations of events. Their study also revealed that people found it easier to construct a story when the evidence was ordered in a temporal and causal sequence that matched the original events.

Table 24.1 shows the results of a mock juror test in which participants were asked to listen to a 100-sentence summary of a trial, with 50 prosecution and 50 defence statements, and a judge's charge to choose between a first-degree murder verdict and a not guilty verdict. Exactly the same material was presented in each case, only the format of the statements was changed. Sometimes the information was presented in story order, and on other occasions it was presented in witness order.

The impact the format had was staggering. When the prosecution presented evidence in story order, and the defence used witness order, 78% of jurors returned a guilty verdict. Conversely, when the roles were reversed only 31% of jurors returned a guilty verdict!

Hastie *et al.* (1997) also investigated explanation-based decision-making in civil cases. They asked people to 'think aloud as you make your decisions about the verdict'. They noted that the first step was again the construction of a story to explain the evidence. This summary 'included the major events from evidence that the juror believed occurred, ordered in a temporal sequence. This narrative included causal linkages, many of them inferred, that serve as "glue" holding the story. . . together.'

If you are anything like me then the parallels between the juror and the investor are likely to leap out to you. Before giving you an example of one instance of explanation-based decisionmaking in real-world financial markets, I want to talk about two other studies.

The first is by DiFonzo and Bordia (1997). They tested the impact of rumours on financial markets. Having set up two experimental stock markets, they subjected one to news and the other to rumours. They found that when they introduced rumours, investors started to trade on them (but didn't make any money from them!). Participants claimed that the rumour sources weren't credible, and didn't impact upon their decision to trade. However, in a world in which actions speak louder than words, the participants were found to trade as if the rumours were news! In order to persuade participants to trade, the rumour merely needed to 'explain' current share price moves. This fits with the importance of the explanation-based view of the world.

TABLE 24.2	The Elements of the Story
Stage	**Type of information**
Context	Company's past success
Problem	Criticism or praise recently received
Reaction	Company's intention to work harder or continue as usual
Plan	Hiring or firing of employees
Outcome	Stated whether the new product was successful or not

Source: Mulligan and Hastie (2005).

The other study is a paper by Mulligan and Hastie (2005). They aim to test if 'qualitative information in the financial investment arena is mentally organized in a story structure, analogous to the stories jurors rely on to "find the facts"'.

Participants were given stories about firms working in the medical sector. Each story contained five elements (listed out in Table 24.2). The aim of the task was to pick investments over the next 2–5 years. After each line of text was revealed, participants were asked whether or not they would purchase the stock for a long time horizon, and how confident they were (on a scale of 1 to 5).

In one format the story was given in order, in the other the elements of the story were scrambled. Figure 24.1 shows the mean regression weights for each story component as a function of the presentation format. Note the spike upwards in the regression weight assigned to the outcome when the story is told in the correct order.

Mulligan and Hastie conclude

> Participants in the story order condition still relied primarily on the
> outcome piece when making decisions . . . Once a coherent mental representation of a story has been constructed, people do not break down
> the story into its component pieces and use them independently, even

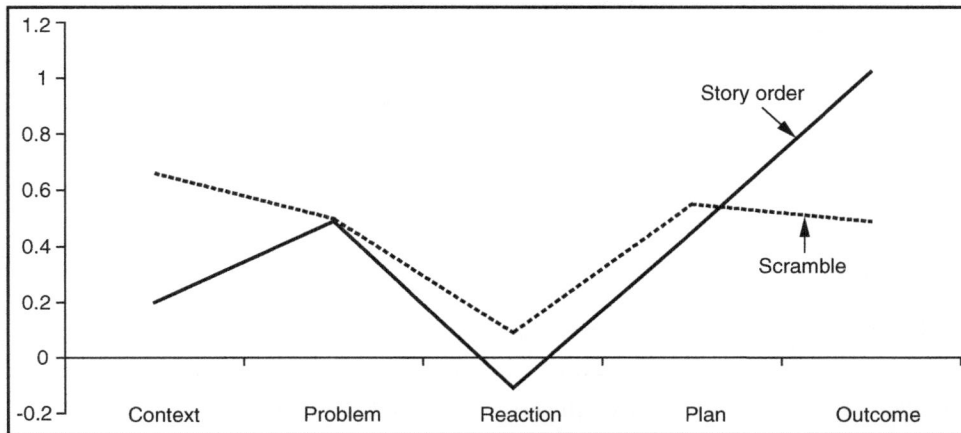

FIGURE 24.1 Mean Regression Weights for Each Story Component.

Source: Mulligan and Hastie (2005).

when it might be sensible, even rational, to do so . . . These order-of-information effects make sense in the context of an explanation-based theory of judgement, but they are patently irrational in the context of traditional theories of investment finance.

Just like jurors, investors seem to frame their worlds in terms of stories rather than facts. *It is exactly this trait that makes stories so dangerous.* All too often investors are sucked into plausible sounding stories. Indeed, underlying some of the most noted bubbles in history are kernels of truth. For instance, the story that the internet would alter the way the world did business is probably true, but it doesn't necessarily translate into profits for investors.

Indeed, we recently wrote on the dangers of growth investing based around the risks involved in listening to the stories at the stock level (see *Global Equity Strategy*, 16 March 2005). However, investors' love affair with China stands out as another great example of the seemingly insatiable thirst for growth.

Investors seem to be able to effortlessly trot out amazing facts and figures on Chinese demand for raw materials. One of my favourite examples is a well-known fund management house quoted in the FT as saying: "Chinese demand for commodities is revolutionizing global commodity markets. China has already overtaken the USA as the largest consumer of iron ore, steel and copper." The FT concludes, 'The China effect seems unstoppable'.[2] All of these may well be true, but does it make sense to base an investment decision on such stories?

Indeed, in the realm of emerging markets investors seem to be addicted to growth. Figures 24.2, 24.3 and 24.4 tell an interesting story. Figure 24.2 relates average GDP growth rates to average dollar stock returns. The relationship is the opposite of the one many investors believe exists. Those economies with the *lowest* growth

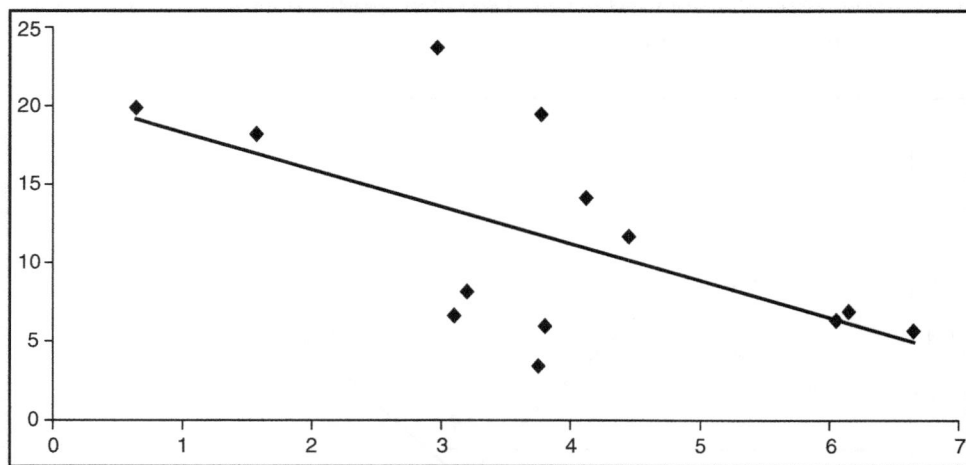

FIGURE 24.2 **Average GDP Growth versus Average Dollar Stock Returns (1988–2004).**

Source: MSCI, DrKW Macro research.

_____

[2] China effect convulses commodity markets, *Financial Times*, 15 November 2003.

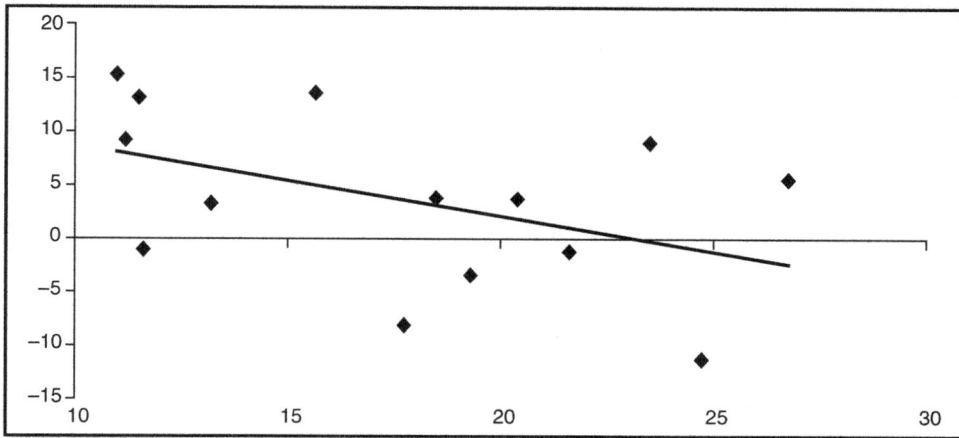

FIGURE 24.3   1995 PEs versus 10-Year Dollar Stock Market Returns.

Source: MSCI, DrKW Macro research.

rates seem to deliver the highest returns, while those with the highest growth rates deliver the lowest returns! Why? The most logical explanation is that investors end up overpaying for growth (much as they do at the stock level).

Figure 24.3 suggests that investors would be better off buying cheap emerging markets rather than being sucked into investing in fast-growing economies. The figure shows the relationship between PEs and subsequent returns over the next 10 years. The cheapest emerging markets have the highest returns, while the most expensive tend to have the lowest returns. This is the long-run counterpart of work we have previously done showing that cheap emerging markets outperform expensive ones [even in the relatively short term (see *Global Equity Strategy*, 12 January 2005, for details)].

Figure 24.4 is aimed at seeing if it is indeed fast growth that tempts investors to overpay. It shows the relationship between the GDP growth rates from 1990 to 1995

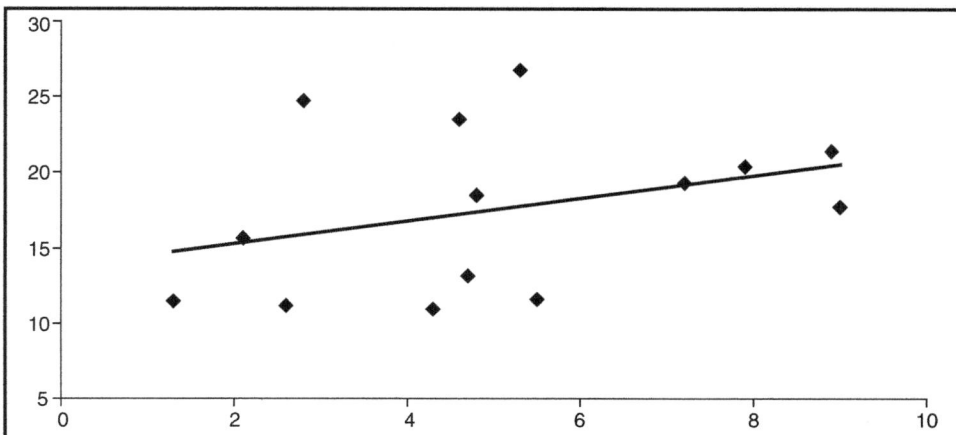

FIGURE 24.4   GDP Growth Rates 1990–1995 and 1995 PEs.

Source: MSCI, DrKW Macro research.

and the PEs at the end of 1995. While there is not a very strong relationship, there is nonetheless a relationship which suggests that investors do indeed end up paying too much for growth.

Investors enamoured with China, and its growth potential, would perhaps be well advised to study history and understand that growth is often not the panacea that it seems to be. Dependency upon stories for decision-making is one reason why investors keep stumbling into the growth trap year after year.

CHAPTER 25

Are Two Heads Better Than One?*

From James Montier, *Behavioural Investing: A Practitioner's Guide to Applying Behavioural Finance* (Hoboken, New Jersey: John Wiley & Sons, 2007), Chapter 17.

Learning Objective Statement

- Explain three possible means for reducing group biases

> Do you set your asset allocation by committee? Or perhaps sit on a stock selection team? If so, then read on. Psychologists have documented that group decisions are often among the worst decisions made. We explore why groups are prone to make mistakes, and offer some solutions for mitigating these errors.

- The eternal hope is that groups come together, exchange ideas, and reach sensible conclusions. The reality of group behaviour is frequently very different. Psychologists have documented that, on average, groups are more likely to amplify rather than alleviate decision-making biases.

- Groups tend to reduce the variance of opinions, and lead members to have more confidence in their decisions after group discussions (without improving accuracy). They also tend to be very bad at uncovering hidden information. Indeed, members of groups frequently enjoy enhanced competency and credibility in the eyes of their peers if they provide information that agrees with the group view!

- Groups also have a tendency to suffer cascades. Under cascades members abandon their individual information, choosing to agree with others because they think they know more.

---

*This article appeared in *Global Equity Strategy* on 18 November 2005. The material discussed was accurate at the time of publication.

- Groups are also at risk of suffering polarization and possibly groupthink. Polarization occurs when members of a group end up in a more extreme position in line with their original beliefs after discussion with the group. Groupthink is an extreme version of polarization leading to all sorts of problems.

- Beating the biases of group behaviour is every bit as difficult as overcoming individual biases. However, secret ballots may help to reduce social pressures to conform. The use of devil's advocates may help (but they must believe the case they are arguing, and run the risk of being ostracized). Having respect for the other group members can help, but we all know how difficult that can be!

Do you conduct your asset allocation via committee? Or perhaps you sit on a stock selection committee? If so perhaps you should read on. Psychologists have spent many years documenting the fact that group decisions are among the worst decisions ever made, effectively endorsing the view that committees are groups of people who keep minutes but waste hours! The key reason for this appears to be that when we come together as a group we not only have to deal with our own biases, but also with everyone else's biases.

The well-informed reader might point out that James Surowiecki (2004) has recently published a book entitled *The Wisdom of Crowds*.[1] The book purports to show that "the many are smarter than the few". The basic idea of the book is that groups outperform individuals in decision-making. Surely this is in direct contradiction of my opening paragraph?

However, Surowiecki is correct that groups outperform individuals, but only under a very strict set of circumstances. Psychologists have shown that statistical groups can outperform individuals and deliberative groups. A statistical group effectively involves asking a large number of people what they think the answer is and taking the mean. Such groups have a good track record when it comes to forecasting.

For instance, when judging the number of beans in a jar, the group average is almost always better than the vast majority of the individual members. In one such experiment, a group of 56 students was asked about a jar containing 850 beans; the group estimate was 871, a better guess than all but one of the students (see Surowiecki, 2004).

In another experiment, a group was asked to rank 10 piles of buckshot, which were only minimally different in size from each other. The group's guess was 94.5% accurate, far more so than that of almost all the group members (Bruce, 1935).

However, for a statistical group to be a useful device, three conditions must be met:

1. People must be unaffected by others' decisions (effectively their errors must be uncorrelated).
2. The probability of being correct must be independent of the probability of everyone else being correct.
3. The participants must be unaffected by their own vote possibly being decisive.

---

[1] A client and friend sent me a signed copy of this book. Thank you Rob.

If these conditions are broken the group's advantage is quickly lost. This is a particular cause for concern from a behavioural point of view. Critics of behavioural finance argue that if one person is overoptimistic and one is pessimistic, then their mistakes cancel out. One of the foundations of behavioural finance is that people, generally, err in a similar fashion. Hence, the mistakes they make are highly unlikely to be uncorrelated.

In addition, groups can be subject to anchors just like individuals (see *Global Equity Strategy*, 27 August). An anecdotal story may help to illustrate this point. Recently, my colleagues and I went to the Oval to watch England vs the West Indies. At about 5 pm, we decided to run a book on the total score for England's first innings. The run total was around 250 at that point. I went first and chose 350; the subsequent bets were surprisingly tightly clustered around the initial estimate. The group was at risk of anchoring. The eventual outturn was an England first innings of 470!

The other weak spot of statistical groups appears to be when the members have no idea of the answer to the question. For instance, Professor Sunstein (Sunstein, 2004) asked his fellow faculty the weight, in pounds, of the fuel cell that powers the space shuttle. The actual answer is 4 million pounds. The median response was 200,000; the mean was 55,790,555 (driven by a single outlier). Both answers are wildly inaccurate.

However, statistical groups are not a good description of the way in which the average asset allocation committee reaches decisions. Instead, the stereotypical asset allocation committee is formed of the regional heads of equity (i.e. Europe, USA, Japan and perhaps Global), the head of fixed income, the CIO, and an economist/strategist. This group then sits down and debates the issues before arriving at a conclusion. This is the prototypical set up for what psychologists call deliberative groups.

The eternal hope is that such groups will come together, exchange ideas, each bringing something different to the discussion. The aim is of course to uncover all the information the group has. If one member has an irrelevant anchor, then the hope is that the group will expose this anchor, hence beating the bias.

However, the reality of group behaviour is very different. As MacCoun (2002) notes, "Groups generally can be expected to amplify rather than correcting individual bias" (sic). For instance, psychologists have shown that, in general, deliberation tends to reduce variance. After talking together, the members of a group will tend to reach a consensus; hence the variance of views is diminished.

Additionally, group discussion tends to lead to group members having more confidence in their decisions after the group deliberations (Heath and Gonzalez, 1995). However, sadly, this increased confidence is not matched by increased accuracy. People simply become more sure about the views they hold rather than enjoying an improvement in performance.

This confidence seems to be driven by the simple repetition of the view. The more you hear a view, the more you tend to have confidence that the view is correct!

Sunstein (2004) — see also Stasson *et al.* (1988) and Sniezek and Henry (1989) — notes,

Groups have been found to amplify, rather than to attenuate, reliance on the representativeness heuristic; to reflect even larger framing effects; to show more confidence than individuals; . . . In addition, groups demonstrate essentially the same level of reliance on the availability heuristic.

Deliberative groups also show an alarming inability to uncover information that isn't common knowledge, and instead end up centred on the knowledge that is easily available to all the group members. Sunstein cites a wonderful example from Hightower and Sayeed (1995):

The purpose of the study was to see how groups might collaborate to make a personnel decision. Resumes for three candidates, applying for a marketing manager position, were placed before group members. The attributes of the candidates were rigged by the experimenters so that one applicant was clearly the best for the job described. Packets of information were given to subjects, each containing a subset of information from the resumes, so that each group member had only part of the relevant information. The groups consisted of three people, some operating face-to-face, some operating on-line. Almost none of the deliberating groups made what was conspicuously the right choice. The reason is simple: They failed to share information in a way that would permit the group to make that choice. Members tended to share positive information about the winning candidate and negative information about the losers. They suppressed negative information about the winner and positive information about the losers. Hence their statements served to 'reinforce the market toward group consensus rather than add complications and fuel debate'.

The general finding from a wide variety of such experiments is that unshared information is highly likely to be omitted from the discussion. Instead, members of the group will tend to concentrate on shared information leading to a hardening of view, creating an anchor for the subsequent discussions.

Why are groups so bad at uncovering unshared information? In part it is a function of the statistical fact that shared information is more likely to be discussed and repeated. Of course, this will tend to influence the individuals in the group, and hence influence the group's eventual outcome.

The other factor that helps to explain why groups are so bad at sharing information concerns social pressure. Those who perceive themselves to be of a relatively low status (admittedly not a major problem for many in our industry!) are particularly likely to refrain from sharing unique information (Wittenbaum and Park, 2001; Stasser and Titus, 2003). They are scared of looking stupid in front of their colleagues. The reputational risk is simply too high for low-status members to chance sharing information if it doesn't conform to the group.[2]

---

[2] We will explore a related issue on obedience to authority in a future weekly.

THE INTEGRATION OF TECHNICAL ANALYSIS

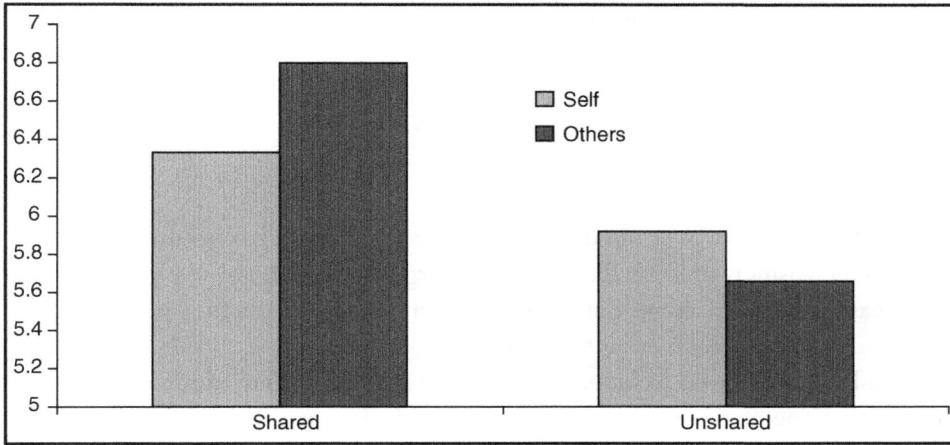

FIGURE 25.1 Communication Bias: Evaluation Ratings as a Function of the Type of Information.

Source: Wittenbaum *et al.* (1999).

Wittenbaum *et al.* (1999) have also shown that those who share information that confirms the group's views are seen as competent and more credible by their peers and by themselves! A situation Wittenbaum *et al.* call mutual enhancement.

Figure 25.1 shows the result of one of Wittenbaum *et al.*'s experiments. Once again information over candidates for a job was the topic. After hearing from the various members of the group, people were asked to rate the other members and themselves using a 0–9 scale (strongly disagree to strongly agree) on the following two questions (i) I feel competent at determining the better job candidate, (ii) the others are competent at determining the better job candidate.

Evidence of mutual enhancement would arise if participants evaluated themselves and the others more favourably when the information was common/shared by the group (i.e., they don't reveal unique information). And, when people relied on unique information, they rated themselves lower and the group would also rate them lower rather than on unique information. That was exactly what was uncovered.

The third major problem that groups encounter is the tendency to suffer cascades. We have previously discussed cascades in the context of markets in *Global Equity Strategy*, 13 January 2004 and 19 May 2004. However, cascades can also affect group decision processes.

A cascade is a situation whereby an individual's action is potentially independent of his private information, and totally dependent upon the observation of other's actions and/or words.

One of the key features of cascades is their tendency to exhibit idiosyncrasy. That is to say, the behaviour resulting from signals of just the first few individuals drastically affects the behaviour of numerous followers. Effectively, cascades are highly path dependent.

TABLE 25.1   **Cascade Creation: Actual Pot Used B**

Player	1	2	3	4	5	6
Private signal	a	a	b	b	b	b
Decision	A	A	A	A	A	A

Source: Anderson and Holt (2004).

Within the context of group discussions, once an opinion has been voiced then it becomes increasingly unlikely that others will argue against it. This is not only for the social reasons outlined above, but because they might assume that the person voicing the belief has more information than they do.

Cascades have proved to be easy to create in laboratory environments.[3] Players are told that one of two pots containing three balls is being used. One pot contains two red and one white ball (pot A), the other, two white and one red ball (pot B). Players are selected in a random order to announce which pot is being used after having received a private signal in the form of a draw from the pot.

The results from one of their experiments are shown in Table 25.1. The pot used was B. However, players 3 onwards decided that the other players knew more than they did and hence ignored their private signal, despite the fact that going with the private signal would be correct on two-thirds of occasions!

The fourth hurdle that deliberative groups must attempt to overcome is the risk of group polarization and possibly groupthink. Group polarization is the tendency for members of a group to end up in a more extreme position in line with their original beliefs after talking to one another. The increased confidence in view mentioned earlier begins to create feedback into the extremity of view, generally creating a loop of increased confidence in more and more extreme views.

Even more extreme than group polarization is groupthink. The term was coined by Irving Janis in 1972. In his original work Janis cited the Vietnam War and the Bay of Pigs invasion as prime examples of the groupthink mentality. However modern examples are all too prevalent. The recent Senate report on the intelligence gathering by the CIA over the war in Iraq explicitly accused the CIA of displaying many of the elements of groupthink.

Groupthink is often characterized by:

■ A tendency to examine too few alternatives

■ A lack of critical assessment of each other's ideas

■ A high degree of selectivity in information gathering

■ A lack of contingency plans

■ Rationalizing poor decisions

■ An illusion of invulnerability and shared morality by the group

---

[3] For a very up-to-date survey see Anderson and Holt (2004).

- Suppressing true feelings and beliefs

- Maintaining an illusion of unanimity

- Appointing mind guards (essentially information sentinels) to protect the group from negative information.

■ Beating the Biases

Can these various problems be overcome? As with all biases the solutions are never easy to implement. However, three possible routes to reducing group biases are given below:

Secret Ballots   The use of secret ballots obviously reduces the risk of group members coming under social pressure. So perhaps before the meeting starts members should write down their views and their preference for asset allocation, then count the votes, and debate the outcome if it is really necessary – bearing in mind the dangers inherent in this process.

Devil's Advocates   Appointing a devil's advocate[4] may help. However, all too often the person selected may not truly believe the role he is asked to play, and hence does not really try too hard to prevent the group reaching its consensus decision. Selecting prickly disagreeable individuals with a strong contrarian view and the ability and desire to argue on almost anything would be perfect. But such individuals are hard to find, and don't fit easily into most corporate cultures.

Respect for Other Group Members   The other factor that can help to reduce the dangers of group decisions is when the group members are acknowledged to be experts in their field, and hence disparate viewpoints are easier to deal with and unshared information may be easier to uncover. However, all too often people tend to believe that they know best on almost every subject and hence tend not to display respect for the views of others.

■ References

Anderson, L. and Holt, C. (2005) Information cascade experiments. In Plott, C. and Smith, V. (eds) *The Handbook of Experimental Economics Results, Vol 1*. Amsterdam: Elsevier Science.

Bruce, R.S. (1935) Group judgements in the field of lifted weights and visual discrimination, *Journal of Psychology*, 117, 1935–1936.

Global Equity Strategy (various issues).

Heath, F. and Gonzalez, R. (1995) Interaction with others increases decision confidence but not decision quality, *Organisation Behaviour and Human Decision Processes*, 61, 305–326.

---

[4]The term comes from the process of canonization. When the Pope considers conferring sainthood, a devil's advocate is appointed unofficially to argue against the decision.

Henry, R.A. (1989) Accuracy and confidence in group judgement, *Organisational Behaviour and Human Decision Processes*, 43, 1–55.

Hightower, R. and Sayeed, L. (1995) The impact of computer-mediated communication systems on biased group discussion, *Computers in Human Behaviour*, 11(1), 33–44.

MacCoun, R. (2002) Comparing micro and macro rationality. In Gowda, M.V.R. and Fox, J. (eds) *Judgements, Decisions and Public Policy*. Cambridge University Press: New York. (Also available from http://ist-socrates. berkeley.edu/~maccoun/index.html#B).

Stasser, G. and Titus, W. (2003) Hidden profiles: a brief history, *Psychological Inquiry*, 14, 304–313.

Stasson, M.F. and Ono, K. Zimmerman, S.K. and David, J.H. (1988) Group consensus processes to cognitive bias task, *Japanese Psychological Research*, 30, 68–77.

Sunstein, C.R. (2004) Group judgements: deliberation, statistical means and information markets. Chicago Law School working paper.

Surowiecki, J. (2004) The wisdom of crowds. Anchor.

Wittenbaum, G.M. and Park, E.S. (2001) The collective preference for shared information, *Current Directions in Psychological Science*, 10, 70–73.

Wittenbaum, G.M., Hubbell, A.P. and Zuckerman, C. (1999) Mutual enhancement: Toward an understanding of the collective preference for shared information, *Journal of Personality and Social Psychology*, 77, 967–978.

CHAPTER 26

The Anatomy of a Bubble*

From James Montier, *Behavioural Investing: A Practitioner's Guide to Applying Behavioural Finance* (Hoboken, New Jersey: John Wiley & Sons, 2007), Chapter 38.

Learning Objective Statement

■ Explain and recognize evidence for the five stages of a bubble

685

Despite the disparate nature of assets on which bubbles have formed, there is an uncanny similarity about the phases through which each moves. We identify five stages of bubbles. In 2002 the USA was only at the start of the fourth period and further downside was expected. Volumes may be a key indicator of the final stages.

■ Each bubble tends to move through five stages: displacement, credit creation, euphoria, financial distress and finally revulsion. Each stage is outlined inside. The experience of the US between 1991 and 2002 is mapped against our theoretical bubble pattern. During that period the US was at the early part of the financial distress stage.

■ The financial distress/critical stage is the point where a set of insiders decide to take their profits and cash out. Significant selling by insiders had been a hallmark of 2000/1. The fact that insiders were still selling four times the amount of stock they were buying should tell you something about how confident they were over the prospects for equity markets.

■ Financial distress refers to an awareness on the part of a considerable segment of the speculating community that a rush for liquidity may develop. Kindleberger

---

*This article appeared in *Global Equity Strategy* on 18 July 2002. The material discussed was accurate at the time of publication.

notes, "The specific signal that precipates the crisis may be . . . the revelation of a swindle." How prescient! We document how the USA compared with other past bubbles in this and other respects.

- We had yet to see capitulation or indeed revulsion. Trading volumes remained amazingly high. We took this as a sign that people had not yet fully adjusted to the post-bubble world. Valuations were far from supportive; if buyers of last resort emerged, we should have sold to them!

Despite the wide range of assets that have witnessed bouts of irrational exuberance (tulips, sugar, coins, bonds, cotton, wheat, land and, of course, equities to name but a few), bubbles seem to follow a similar pattern. As Marx noted, history repeats itself, first as tragedy, second as farce. This chapter attempts to outline the anatomy of an asset price bubble, and then assesses where we currently are along this path.

The model of bubbles that we wish to present is one promoted in Kindleberger's truly superb "Manias, panics and crashes". It is largely the result of work carried out by the economist Hyman Minsky. Hence we will refer to the framework as the Kindleberger/Minsky model. A diagrammatic outline of the bubble stages is presented below:

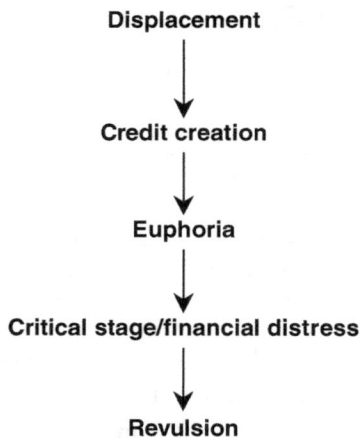

Displacement

$\downarrow$

Credit creation

$\downarrow$

Euphoria

$\downarrow$

Critical stage/financial distress

$\downarrow$

Revulsion

Displacement

Displacement is generally an exogenous shock that triggers the creation of profit opportunities in some sectors, while shutting down profit availability in other sectors. As long as the opportunities created are greater than those that get shut down, investment and production will pick up to exploit these new opportunities. Investment is likely to occur in both financial and physical assets. Essentially a boom is engendered.

In the most recent bubble in the US equity market, the exogenous shock was clearly the arrival of the internet. Here was something capable of revolutionizing the way in which so many of us conducted our businesses (and lives more generally).

▣ Credit Creation

The boom is then further exacerbated by monetary expansion and/or credit creation. Effectively the model holds money/credit as endogenous to the system, such that for any given banking system, monetary means of payment may be expanded not only within the existing system of banks, but also by the formation of new banks, the development of new credit instruments and the expansion of personal credit outside the banking system.

Sooner or later demand for the asset will outstrip supply, resulting in the perfectly natural response of price increases. These price increases give rise to yet more investment (both real and financial). A positive feedback loop ensues: new investment leads to increases in income which, in turn, stimulate further investment.

Monetary and credit creation in the US high-tech bubble were largely the result of overly accommodative monetary policy on the part of the Fed in 1998 (Figure 26.1). In response to the emerging market/LTCM crisis (and later Y2K), the Fed cut rates to protect the soundness of the financial system. However, we suspect (admittedly with the benefit of hindsight) that the Fed kept monetary policy too easy, resulting in a massive liquidity surge into financial assets.

This official monetary creation spurred on massive levels of private sector credit creation. Figure 26.2 shows the scale of margin buying as a percentage of household disposable income.

The prominent role that investment played in driving the US boom is immediately obvious from even a cursory glance at Figure 26.3, which shows that investment as a percentage of GDP soared from around 14% in the late 1980s to nearly 19% at the peak in 2000.

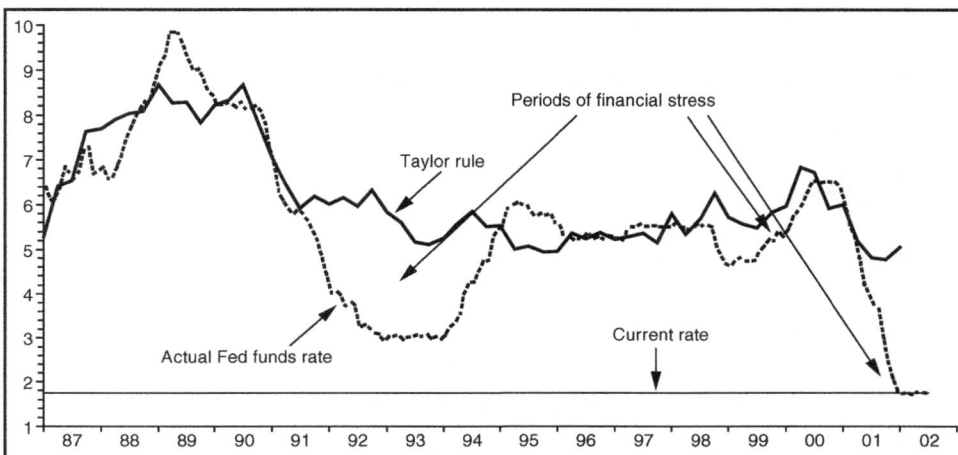

FIGURE 26.1   Fed Funds and the Taylor Rule (1987–2002).

Source: DrKW.

FIGURE 26.2 Buying on Margin – Margin Debt as Percentage of Personal Income (1980–2002).

Source: Thomson Financial Datastream.

FIGURE 26.3 Investment as a % of GDP (1980–2002).

Source: DrKW.

■ Euphoria

'Euphoria' is the term given when speculation for price increase is added to investment for production and sales. Effectively this is momentum trading or the "greater-fool-theory" of investment. Adam Smith referred to such developments as "overtrading". Kindleberger correctly notes that overtrading is a nebulous concept. However, he notes that overtrading may involve pure speculation, an overestimate of prospective returns or excessive gearing.

The US experience between 1991 and 2002 certainly fits all three of these elements. The massive popularity of such creations as aggressive growth funds testifies to the large purely speculative elements at work within the US equity market.

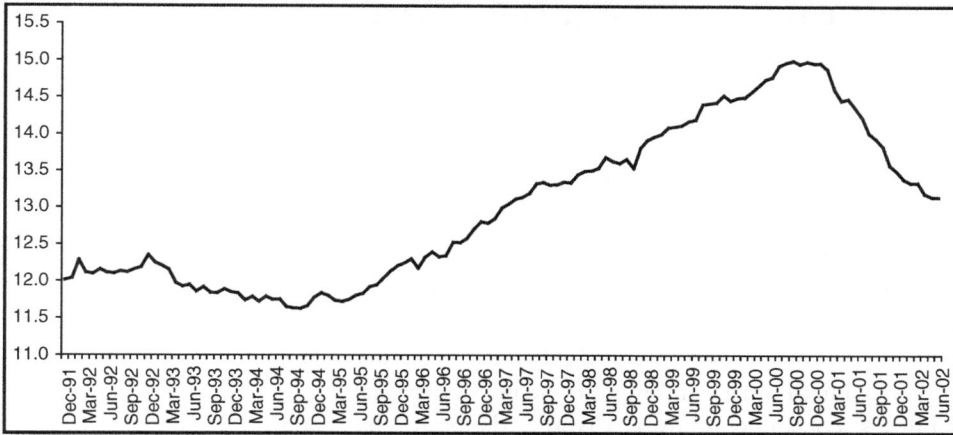

FIGURE 26.4 Bottom Up Consensus Expectations of Long-term Earnings Growth (%).

Source: DrKW.

Analysts clearly had excessive overestimates of the prospective returns at least in terms of the long-term earnings potential of US corporates (see Figure 26.4).

Given that analysts and corporates tend to work so closely, these estimates essentially receive sign off from the companies as well. As such, they reflect the ridiculous levels of overoptimism that infected corporate managers during the late 1990s.

Further reflections of overoptimism among corporate managers can be witnessed by the scale of recent goodwill write-downs. After all, a goodwill write-down is nothing more than an admission that a company overpaid for its acquisitions.

Overgearing is also a prominent feature of the recent US experience. Driven by a desire to meet or beat analysts' forecasts of ever-growing EPS (largely reflecting the dominance of option grants as a form of compensation), firms increased their gearing to truly awe-inspiring levels. Figure 26.5 shows the level of total liabilities to corporate GDP soaring in the late 1990s.

FIGURE 26.5 Liabilities to Corporate GDP.

Source: Thomson Financial Datastream.

▪ Critical Stage/Financial Distress

The fourth stage of the bubble process is labelled the critical stage or the financial distress stage. The critical stage is the point where a set of insiders decide to take their profits and cash out. Significant selling by insiders has been a hallmark of 2000/1 (Figure 26.6). The fact that, by 2002, insiders were still selling four times the amount of stock they were buying should tell you something about how confident they were over the prospect for equity appreciation over the following 12 months!

Financial distress usually follows straight on from the critical stage (indeed the two can be hard to separate, hence we have tacked them together). The term 'financial distress' is borrowed from the finance literature where it refers to a situation in which a firm must contemplate the possibility that it may not be able to meet its liabilities. For an economy as a whole, the equivalent condition is an awareness on the part of a considerable segment of the speculating community that a rush for liquidity (out of assets into cash) may develop.

As the distress persists, so the perception of crisis increases. Kindleberger notes, "The specific signal that precipates the crisis may be a failure of a bank, or a firm stretched too tight, the revelation of a swindle." His words, not mine, but oh so appropriate in the prevailing conditions.

The occurrence of swindling/fraud seems highly procyclical. Fraud follows Keynes's law that demand creates its own supply (rather than Say's law that supply creates it own demand). We will return to fraud and its role in bringing down bubbles later.

The USA was clearly in financial distress in both the finance and bubble interpretations of the word. Figure 26.7 shows Altman's Z-score for the S&P 500 (and the percentage of firms within the universe that are currently below the critical 1.8 level). It clearly shows the scale of financial distress that was being observed in the equity market.

The preference for liquidity is easily observable from the performance of the various asset classes shown in Figure 26.8. Government bonds outperformed corporate bonds which in turn outperformed equities.

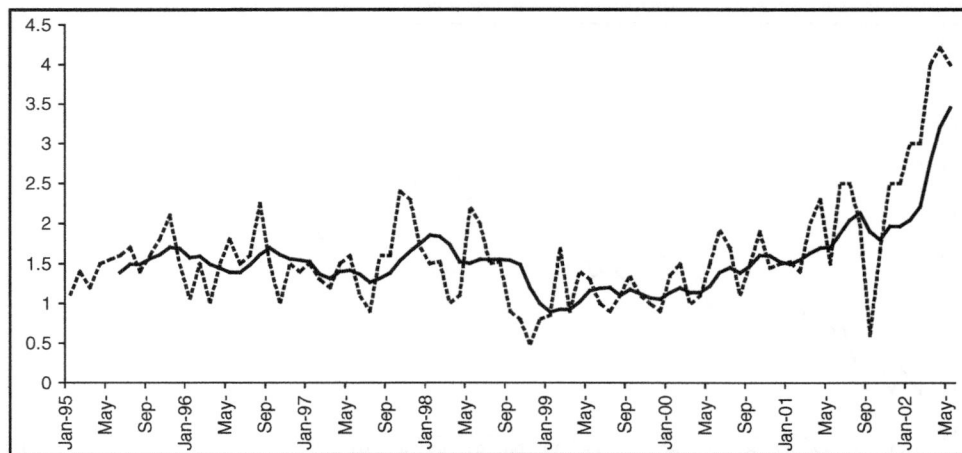

FIGURE 26.6 Insider Sales to Purchases Ratio (and 6mma).

Source: Thomson Financial Datastream.

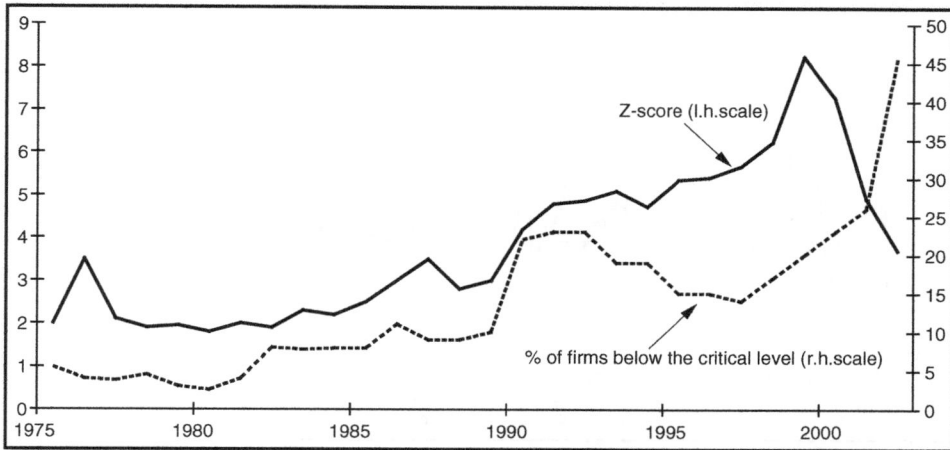

FIGURE 26.7 Altman's Z-score and the Percentage of Firms below the Critical Level.

Source: Thomson Financial Datastream.

FIGURE 26.8 Relative Performance: US Asset Classes.

Source: Thomson Financial Datastream.

The longer-term picture (Figure 26.9) shows the relative annual performance of equities vs bonds going back to 1926. It shows the scale of liquidity preference that had occurred. Bonds had delivered one of their best performances relative to equities since the 1930s!

An alternative perspective is given by Figure 26.10. This shows the peak to trough performance of the S&P 500. Surely no one can deny the severity of this bear market. No wonder people had a liquidity preference!

The role of swindles in bursting bubbles is intriguing. Later in this book we will illustrate just how prevalent swindles and wrong-doing have been at the peak of prolonged bull markets.

This is the stage the US post-bubble was going through. The wrong-doers were being exposed for all to see, and a strong liquidity preference existed.

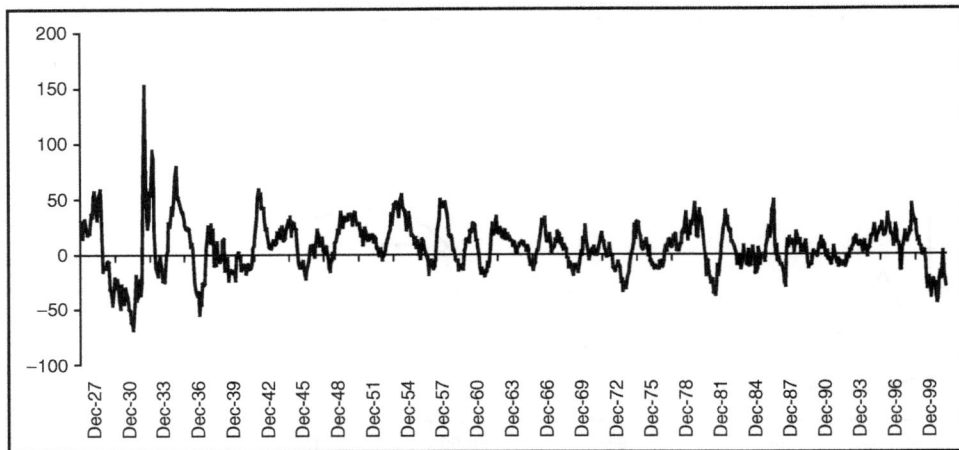

FIGURE 26.9 Long-term Relative Annual Performance: US Equities versus Bonds.

Source: Ibbotson, DRKW

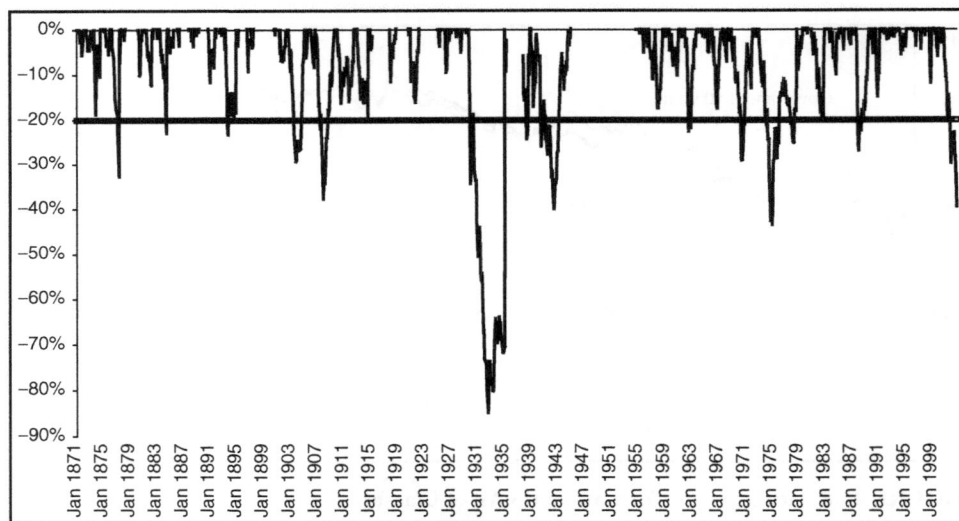

FIGURE 26.10 S&P 500 – Percent from Peak.

Source: DrKW.

■ Revulsion

Revulsion is the final stage of the bubble cycle. Revulsion refers to the fact that people are so badly scarred by the events in which they were embroiled that they can no longer bring themselves to participate in the market at all. It is clearly related to that most dreadful of current buzz words – capitulation. Capitulation is generally used to describe the point when the final bull admits defeat and throws in the towel. In the language of the Kindleberger/Minsky model, capitulation is described as degenerate panic. Revulsion is obviously not exactly the same thing, since it can (and frequently does) occur post-capitulation.

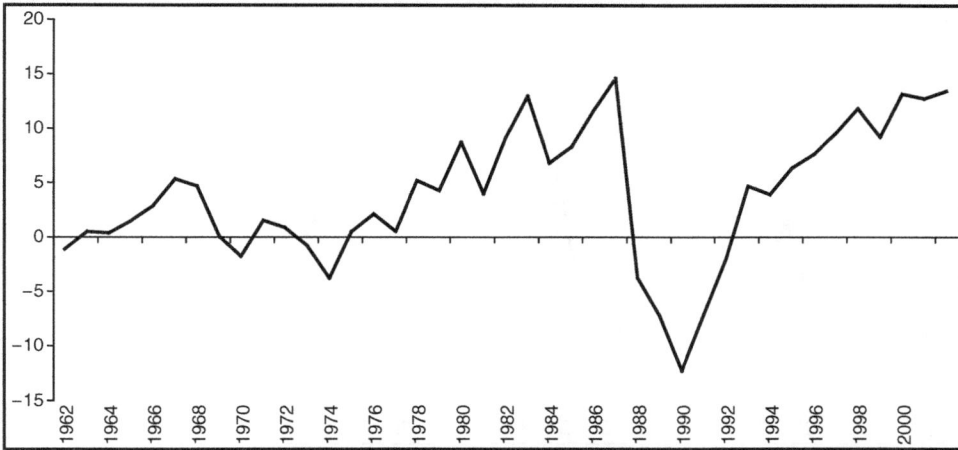

FIGURE 26.11 Detrended Turnover on the NYSE.

Source: DrKW.

In terms of the 2002 market we saw no signs of capitulation. Most strategists were still amazingly bullish. Perhaps more significantly volumes remained very high. We have written before on the use of volumes as a sentiment indicator (see *Global Strategy Weekly*, 29 November 2001). Figures 26.11 and 26.12 show some further evidence that capitulation remained some way off.

Figure 26.11 shows our measure of volumes. It is the detrended turnover on the NYSE (reported volume to average number of shares listed). Usually the end of bear markets is coincident with collapses in volume. No such sign emerged from Figure 26.12. Turnover remained massively high.

Figure 26.13 confirms this view of volumes, and shows volumes relative to market capitalization. Once again the extreme nature of optimism was plain for all to see. Volumes remained at amazingly high levels – comparable to the late 1920s!

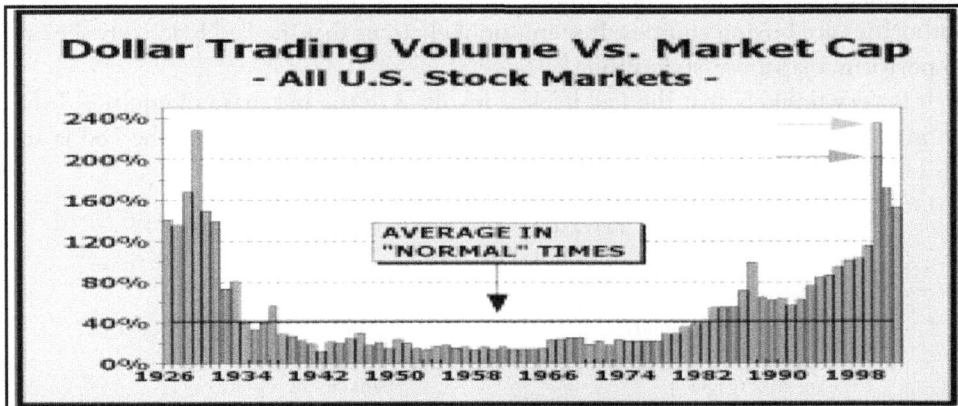

FIGURE 26.12 Dollar Trading Volume versus Market Cap.

Source: cross-currents.net.

FIGURE 26.13 Graham and Dodd PE – Based on 10-Year Moving Average of as Reported earnings.

Source: Shiller, DrKW.

The degenerate panic ends when one of three events occur:

- Prices fall so low that investors are tempted to move back in to the asset.
- Trade is cut off by setting limits on price declines.
- Lender of the last resort steps in.

So let's assume we get a degenerate panic. Which, if any, of these options will present itself as a potential escape route from the markets' declines? Well, equity prices have a considerable downside before we can start to claim valuation support. At the very least, 30% declines in prices are likely to be required before valuations look tempting to us.

The second route provides only temporary release from panic. A halt on trading may allow people to reassess, however, it may simply result in the market dropping in stages in the face of persistent panic.

The third route is perhaps the most appealing – a lender (or rather buyer) of the last resort emerges. This is a favourite of the current market rumours that the US authorities are buying equities. It seems unlikely to us that the Fed is actively seeking to perform a Japanese-style PKO.

It is very unlikely that the Fed itself is involved in the purchase of equities. It has no mandate to do so. Table 26.1 shows the private sector assets that the Fed is and isn't allowed to purchase.

TABLE 26.1	Private Sector Assets the Fed May, and May Not, Purchase	
No Express Authority		**May Purchase**
Corporate bonds		Gold
Commercial paper		Foreign exchange
Mortgages		Bankers' acceptances
Equity		Bills of exchange
Land		

Source: Clouse *et al.* (2000).

TABLE 26.2 Bubble Paths

	South Sea Bubble	First British Railway Boom	1920s US Equity Bubble	1960s Conglomerate Mergers Boom	1980s Japanese Land and Equity Bubble	1990s US Equity Bubble
Displacement	Profits from conversion of government debt, supposed monopoly on Spanish Americas	End of depression, new means of transport	Decade of fast growth, end of fears of WWI deflation, rapid expansion of mass production	Two decades of rising stock markets, the joys of growth investing	Financial liberalization. Monetary easing	Widespread acceptance of the internet, strong growth, and monetary easing
Smart money response	Insiders buy up debt in advance of the conversion scheme	Build a railroad	Expansion of supply of new shares, creation of new closed end funds	Emergence of professional conglomerates	Zaitech	Aggressive growth funds, stock options, start a dot.com
Sustaining the bubble	Development of coffee house network for speculation	?	Regional exchanges, growth of margin accounts and brokers loans	Stock swaps to create apparent earnings growth	Cross shareholdings, buybacks (tokkin funds), latent asset value, Q ratio, PKO in 1987 crash	Pro forma earnings, New valuation metrics, buybacks
Authoritive blessing	Government approval, royal involvement	Government approval for each railroad	Blessing from Coolidge, Hoover, Mellon and Irving Fisher	McGeorge Bundy	Nomura calls for 80,000 by 1995	Greenspan joins the New Era
Swindle/Fraud	Ponzi scheme	George Hudson paying dividends out of capital (Ponzi scheme)	Harold Russell Snyder, Samuel Insull buying binge and debt mountain	?	Recruit Cosmos, Bubble lady	Accounting fraud – Enron, WorldCom et al.
Political reaction	Ex post facto punishing of directors, restrictions on the use of corporate form	Reform of accounting standards, rules passed so that dividends must be paid out of earnings not capital	Glass-Steagall Act, creation of the SEC, holding company act	Reform of accounting practices, Williams Act	?	Sarbanes & Oxley Bills, voluntary option expensing as corporates seek moral high ground

Source: Shleifer, DrKW.

There is some room for discretion under the provision that if the Board of Governors found that there were "unusual and exigent circumstances" and at least five governors voted to authorize a broadish range of "notes, drafts and bills of exchange . . . indorsed or otherwise secured to the satisfaction of the Federal Reserve Bank". However, it is far from clear how broadly the Fed would interpret this ruling. In *extremis*, anything is possible.

Perhaps official inspired intervention *à la* Japan is more likely. Edward Chancellor in "Devil take the hindmost" points out that in 1987, "The day after the October crash, representatives of Japan's largest brokerages . . . were summoned to the Ministry of Finance. They were ordered to keep the Nikkei average above 21,000." Indeed similar intervention was attempted during the US crash of 1929, when bankers met at the offices of J.P. Morgan to supply funds and stabilize the market (their attempts failed dismally, by the way). In the context of the US this, of course, is idle speculation that can neither be proved nor disproved. Either way, our view is that should buyers of the last resort emerge, investors should be happy to sell to them!

Table 26.2 takes some of the major bubbles in history and maps them to the model we have outlined here. Our essential finding is that the Kindleberger/Minksy model fits the empirical evidence well.

CHAPTER 27

De-Bubbling: Alpha Generation*

From James Montier, *Behavioural Investing:
A Practitioner's Guide to Applying Behavioural
Finance* (Hoboken, New Jersey: John Wiley &
Sons, 2007), Chapter 57.

Learning Objective Statement

■ Identify and explain the three cross-section strategies that should benefit from a
  de-bubbling/deflationary period

> We map out our view of the de-bubbling process and tease out its implications for alpha
> generation. Old relationships between bonds and equities will be shown as illusory.
> Absolute returns are the way forward. Stock selection should focus on balance sheet
> strength, earnings quality, low capex and avoiding previous bubble winners.

■ Bursting bubbles pose a special danger to investors. Few will have ever experienced anything similar before. In order to understand survival strategies a reasonable knowledge of the causes and consequences of bubbles is required.

■ Bubbles contain the seeds of their own destruction. The excessive optimism and
  overconfidence that help to sustain bubbles form the Achilles' heel when it comes
  to bust time. Excessive expectations lead firms to gear up in order to overinvest.
  This can unleash a deflationary debt spiral during the bust.

■ The key lesson for asset allocators is that established relationships between bonds
  and equities break down. The illusory correlation of bull markets is exposed as the
  product of investors confusing real and nominal variables. Trading on the basis of
  old relationships is likely to be hazardous to your wealth.

■ Where possible, investors should focus on absolute returns via true equal long/
  short portfolios. Portfolios based around balance sheet strength, earnings quality,

---

*This article appeared in *Global Equity Strategy* on 6 November 2002. The material discussed was accurate at the time of publication.

and low capex stand out as obvious winners. Use this rally to position. Bubble winners do not usually lead us out of the bust, yet each of the major US rallies has been tech dominated. Until investors give up this hope, the bear market won't end.

Bursting bubbles pose special problems for investors. They alter the investment landscape massively. This note takes our previously proposed framework for analysing bubbles and busts and tries to draw out advice for both stock selection and asset allocation. In order to understand the optimal strategies in a post-bubble world, we need to understand bubbles in the first place. Let's start our journey in the laboratory.

■ Bubbles in the Laboratory

It strikes us as slightly evening up the scales, following Alan Greenspan's knighthood for services to bubble blowing, that Daniel Kahneman and Vernon Smith won the Nobel prize for economics. Kahneman helped to catalogue many of the psychological traits that underlie the bubble process, while Smith was the first economist to find a bubble in an experimental market.

Figure 27.1 shows the results from one of Smith's latest papers (see Caginalp *et al.*, 2000). The idea is simply to create a clean market in which a financial asset can be traded. The payoffs (dividends) on the asset are uncertain, but the distribution of the payoffs is known, and shown in Table 27.1.

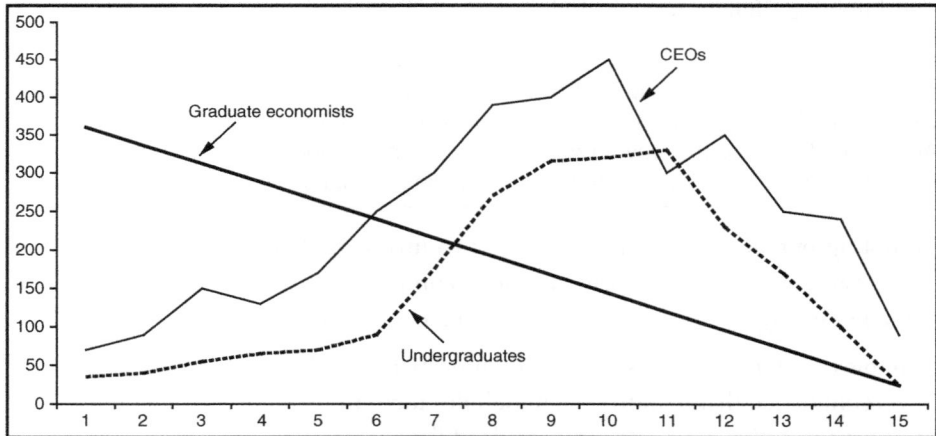

FIGURE 27.1   Bubbles in the Laboratory.

Source: Caginalp *et al.* (2000).

TABLE 27.1	Dividend Distribution
Probability	**Payoff**
0.25	0
0.25	8
0.25	28
0.25	60

Source: Caginalp *et al.* (2000).

We know that if investors followed the laws of classical finance then they would work out the expected value of the asset, which is 24. Since the experiment lasted for 15 periods, the price should have been 360, decreasing by 24 per period until the end of the game.

However, the results show the alarming ease with which bubbles can be created. When the game was played by graduate economists, the results were predictably dull. They managed to trade at the correct right price, although volumes were much higher than theory would have suggested.

Thankfully for the rest of us, the world isn't populated by graduate economists. When the game was played by undergraduates, a bubble was quickly created. The undergraduates started with a price that was just 10% of fundamental value, and at the height of the bubble, the disparity between price and value was a staggering 270%!

However, they weren't the worst players. When business executives were the traders, a truly awe-inspiring bubble was created. Price started off at 20% of fundamental value. At the peak of the bubble prices represented a breathtaking 570% of value! And remember this was in the simplest, cleanest possible market.

Experimentalists have uncovered many traits that make the creation of a bubble more likely. A bubble is more likely to be found when:

- The ratio of inexperienced to experienced traders is high.

- The uncertainty over fundamental value is greater.

- The lottery characteristics of the security are high (effectively a small chance of a big payoff increase the likelihood that people will overpay for an asset – growth stocks?).

- Buying on margin is possible.

- Short selling is difficult.

The last of these strikes us as particularly interesting given the recent debate over short selling in the UK. The experimental evidence shows that far from being an "evil", short selling helps to move the market towards efficiency.

Bubbles in the Field

However, enough of artificial bubbles; what of bubbles in the real world of financial markets (surely an oxymoron?) We have previously presented a framework for analysing bubbles (see *Global Equity Strategy*, 18 July, The anatomy of a bubble). In that note we explored bubbles in a very general way, drawing our examples from a wide range of historical events.

In this chapter, we will examine the US and Japanese bubbles in order to see what lessons we can derive from them. The framework we use to characterize the bubble process is drawn from the work of Irvine Fisher and Hyman Minsky, popularized by Charles Kindleberger in his *tour de force – Manias, Panics and Crashes*.

Fisher was among the leading economists in the USA at the time of the 1929 crash. Indeed, he is perhaps best remembered for his proclamation that stocks had reached a permanently high plateau in 1929! Steve Keen, in this entertaining book (Keen, 2001), notes that Fisher provided four key reasons why stock valuations were justified:

- Changed expectations of future earnings.

- The higher retained earnings of corporates (allowing for faster future growth).

- A change in risk premiums.

- Longer time horizons for investors.

It is a list that will seem uncannily familiar to modern-day investors. I can clearly recall having seen each of these arguments during the bubble (indeed I fear I even used one or two of them myself!).

However, Fisher's faith in the rationality of the market was cruelly stripped away by the crash of 1929. In the wake of such overwhelming evidence against his belief, Fisher turned his attentions to explaining how collapsing bubbles could cause deflation. He concluded that two factors stood out above all others in the creation of a depression: "over-indebtedness to start with and the deflation following soon after". As Keen notes, Fisher "has the dubious distinction of fathering both the conventional theory of finance – which, like his 1929 self, reassures finance markets that they are rational – and an unconventional theory that argues speculative bubbles can cause economic depressions".

Sadly, Fisher was largely ignored and treated as a leper, the economist's equivalent of a fallen angel. Thankfully, however, Minsky breathed new life into Fisher's work, and it is this work that provides us with a framework for analysing bubbles and their busts.

The Minsky/Kindleberger model can be simplified to five stages through which a bubble passes:

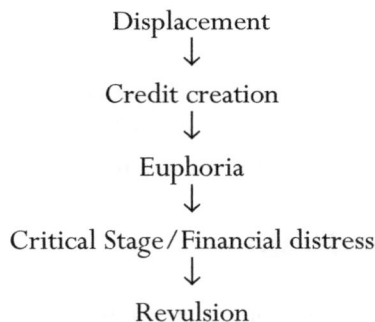

Displacement
↓
Credit creation
↓
Euphoria
↓
Critical Stage/Financial distress
↓
Revulsion

Let us examine each of these in turn.

■ Displacement: The Birth of a Boom

Displacement is generally an exogenous shock that triggers the creation of profit opportunities in some sectors, while closing down profit availability in other sectors. As long as the opportunities created are greater than those that get shut down, investment and production will pick up to exploit these new opportunities. Investment in both financial and physical assets is likely to occur. Effectively, we are witnessing the birth of a boom.

In Japan's case, massive liberalization of the financial system seems to have been the exogenous shock. In the USA, the widespread adoption of the internet was certainly a good candidate for a proximate displacement event.

■ Credit Creation: Nurturing the Boom

Just as fire can't grow without oxygen, so a boom needs liquidity to feed on. Minsky argued that monetary expansion and credit creation are largely endogenous to the system. Effectively, not only can money be created by the existing banking system, but also by the formation of new banks, the development of new credit instruments, and the expansion of personal credit outside the banking system.

Sooner or later demand for assets will outstrip supply, resulting in the perfectly natural response of price increases (*à la* Economics 101). These price increases give rise to yet more investment (both real and financial). A positive feedback loop ensues: new investment leads to an increase in income, which in turn stimulates yet further investment.

Figure 27.2 shows the role of monetary expansion in the creation of the Japanese bubble. It shows the McCallum rule for base money growth[1] against the actual rate of growth in base money. Even a cursory glance reveals the massive overcreation of liquidity during the mid and late 1980s.

Looking at the US experience shows that the bubble gained two liquidity injections. Figure 27.3 shows the Fed funds rate against a Taylor rule. It is certainly

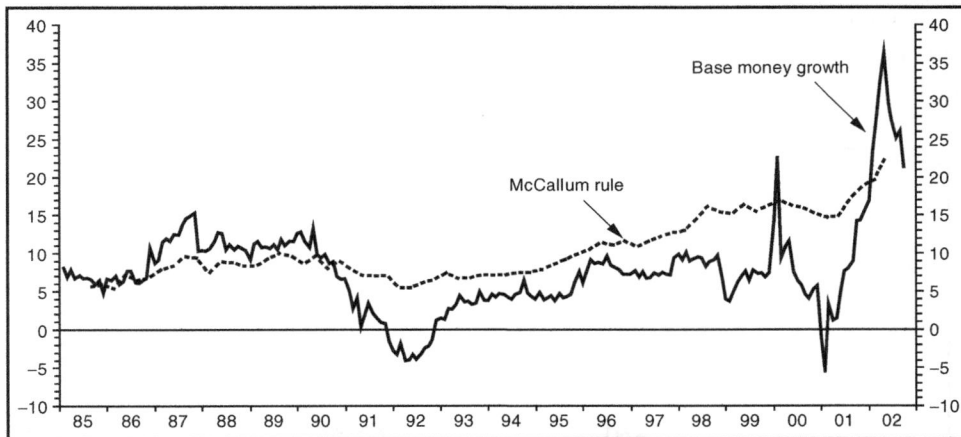

FIGURE 27.2 Base Money Growth in Japan and the McCallum Rule.

Source: Thomson Financial Datastream, DrKW.

---

[1] The McCallum rule relates growth rate of base money to the growth rate of nominal GDP adjusted for changes in technology (via the velocity of circulation). Technically: Change in base money growth = Potential nominal output growth rate − (4-year moving average in velocity of circulation) +0.5× Nominal output gap.

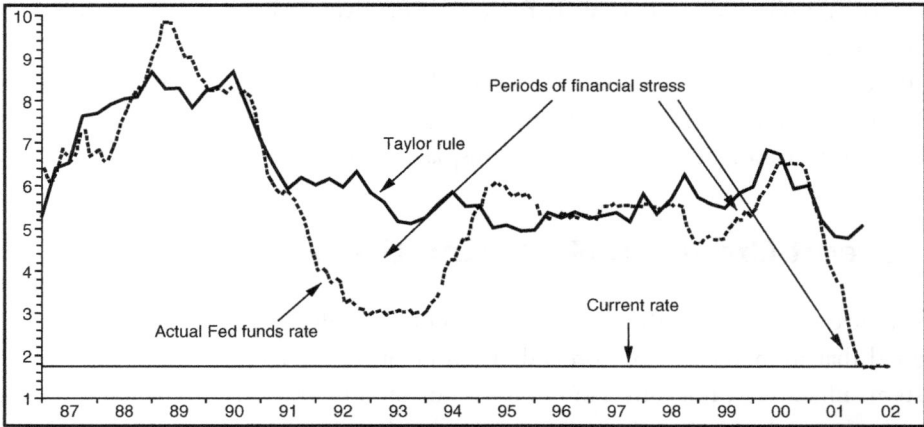

FIGURE 27.3 Fed Funds and the Taylor Rule.

Source: Thomson Financial Datastream.

possible to argue that in the wake of the S&L debacle in the early 1990s, the Fed kept interest rates too low for too long, and began to engender a boom. An additional flood of credit creation occurred in response to the emerging markets/LTCM crisis (and later Y2K). Of course, both of these are far easier to spot with the benefit of hindsight. At the time they may well have appeared totally rational, indeed even admirable responses by the central bank.

This official deluge of monetary creation spurred on massive levels of private sector credit creation (just as the model outlined). Figure 27.4 shows the scale of margin buying as a percentage of household disposable income.

Of course, this liquidity has to find a home. It usually ends up in a mixture of real and financial assets. The real proportion usually creates a massive investment boom – bubbles are rarely purely financial, but are all too often economic as well.

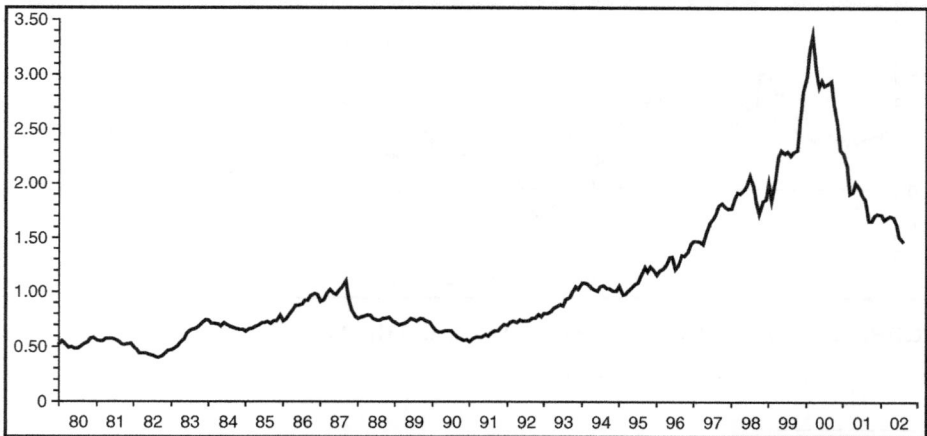

FIGURE 27.4 US Margin Buying (% of Disposable Income).

Source: Thomson Financial Datastream.

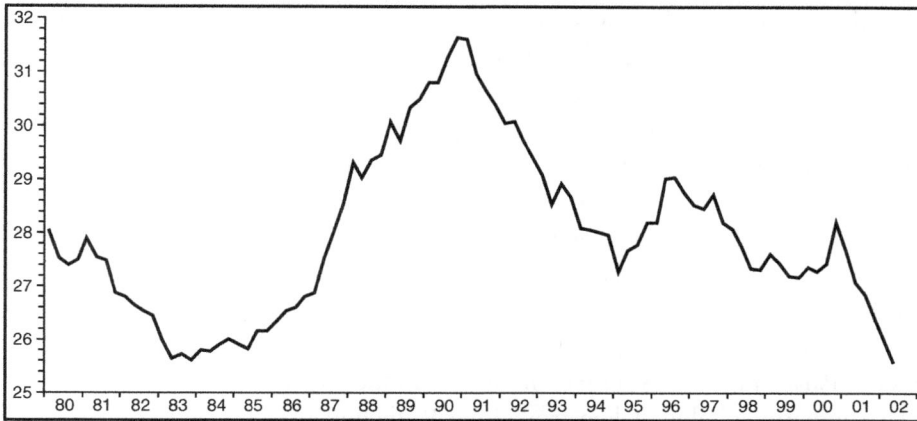

FIGURE 27.5 Japan: Investment to GDP Ratio.

Source: Thomson Financial Datastream.

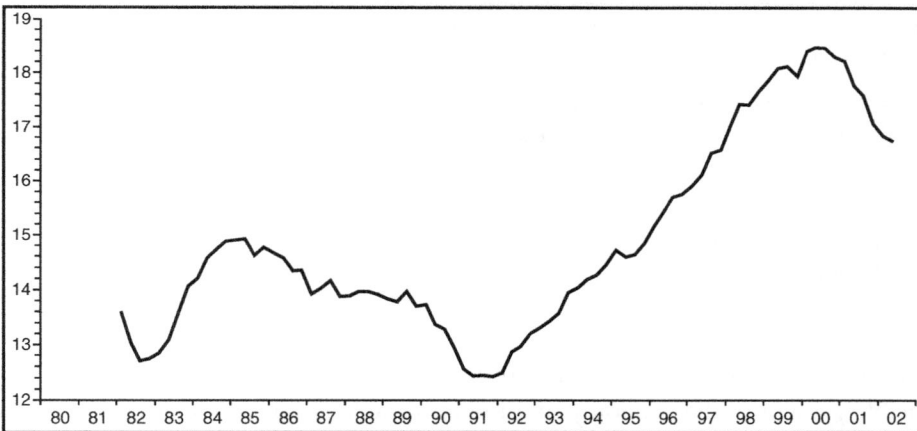

FIGURE 27.6 US Investment to GDP Ratio.

Source: Thomson Financial Datastream.

Figures 27.5 and 27.6 show the scale of the investment booms that were part of the bubbles in both Japan and the US. In Japan's case, investment as a percentage of GDP rose from 26% in the mid 1980s to a peak of just under 32% at the height of the bubble.

The US case shows investment rising from somewhere around 13/14% "normally" to a peak of nearly 19% at the zenith of the bubble.

▩ Euphoria

Everybody begins to buy into the "new era". During the Japanese bubble countless books were written on why Japanese management techniques were going to dominate the world, and why it would be a case of 'imitate or perish' for corporate managers around the rest of the world. Indeed, Peter Tasker, our consultant Japanese strategist, recalls that inside Japan there was much talk of Japan moving from being a production-driven economy to a new era of consumption-based economic development!

The other example of new era thinking is the creation of new valuation techniques in order to justify the soaring asset prices. In the USA, analysts moved up the income statement in order to justify stratospheric stock prices. When PEs based on net income were looking too stretched, analysts drifted up the statement reaching for price to sales. Then came along pro forma earnings – leaving out ad hoc elements of the income statement. Eventually, eyeballs, clicks and ARPU were all introduced!

In Japan, Tobin's Q was regularly wheeled out to justify stock prices, as were latent asset valuations techniques. Who can forget the time when the grounds of the Imperial Palace in Tokyo were worth more than the entire state of California.

The quotations below, taken from John Rothchild's book (1998), all show that previous bubbles in the USA have been accompanied by discussion over the arrival of a new age.

It seemed to be taken for granted in speculative circles that this is a market of "manifest destiny" and that destiny is to go continuously forward. (*New York Times*, September 1929)

At least two members of the Federal Reserve Board now are saying that prosperity can go on and on. (*US News & World Reports*, 15 November 1965)

Is the market crazy? Hardly. Underlying the equity boom is the emergence of a New Economy, built on the foundation of global markets and the Information Revolution. (*Business Week*, 30 December 1996)
   Source: Jim Stack

These developments spur a dangerous psychology into force. The seemingly invincible growth of the economy, and the inexorable rise in stock prices, leads to a marked increase in feelings of overoptimism and overconfidence. These traits are ever present, and largely a part of the human condition, but receive an extra boost during bubble periods.

Overoptimism and overconfidence are a potent combination. We have shown elsewhere (see Montier, 2002) that this combination leads people to overestimate their knowledge, understate the risks, and overestimate their ability to control the situation.

These traits lead to three developments in terms of the bubble framework. The greater fool theory kicks in. Investors begin to speculate for the sake of speculation. Indeed, one could see the rise in popularity of aggressive growth funds in the USA as a sign of such behaviour.

Because of the overconfidence and overoptimism, long-term growth expectations and long-term return expectations get ratcheted higher and higher. Unfortunately, investors and corporates believe these new expectations. Investors set themselves up to be disappointed. The corporate managers engage in excessive gearing. Because of their blind faith in the new era, firms take on debt in the belief that faster growth will generate the necessary payback with ease (see Figures 27.7 and 27.8).

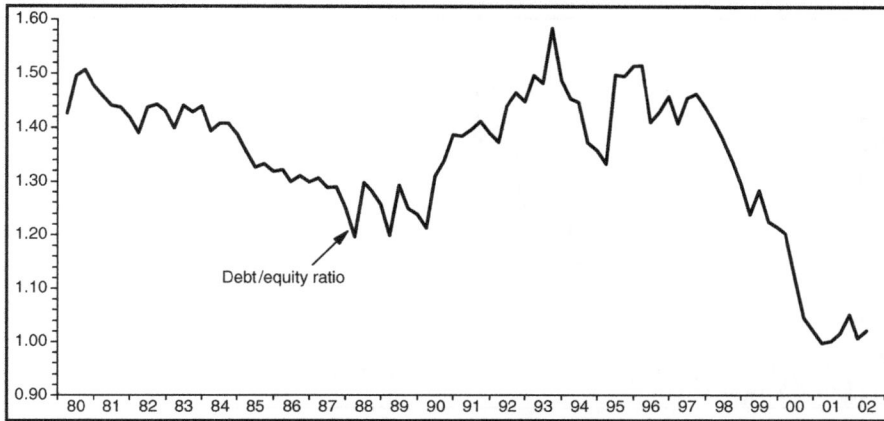

FIGURE 27.7 Debt/Equity Ratio of Corporate Japan.

Source: Thomson Financial Datastream.

FIGURE 27.8 US Corporate Debt to GDP Ratio.

Source: Thomson Financial Datastream.

■ Critical Stage/Financial Distress

Eventually the euphoria gives way to the critical stage. This is the point at which the insiders sell out. One good proxy for this is the number of firms conducting initial public offerings; after all this is a prime example of insiders selling out! Figures 27.9 and 27.10 suggest that tracking equity issuance can be a valuable tool in tracking bubble progress.

My favourite measure of insiders' behaviour during the previous US bubble is provided in a paper by Rau *et al.* (2001), who track the number of firms adding or deleting dot.com to or from their name (Figure 27.11).

Financial distress results when the over-leveraging of euphoria receives an economic reality check. It can be a cruel and painful experience for the overenthusiastic debt accumulators. In Figure 27.12 we show our work from 1975 to 2000 on one measure of balance sheet strain. We have used Altman's Z-score to track the

FIGURE 27.9   Number of IPOs per Month – Japan.

Source: Thomson Financial Datastream.

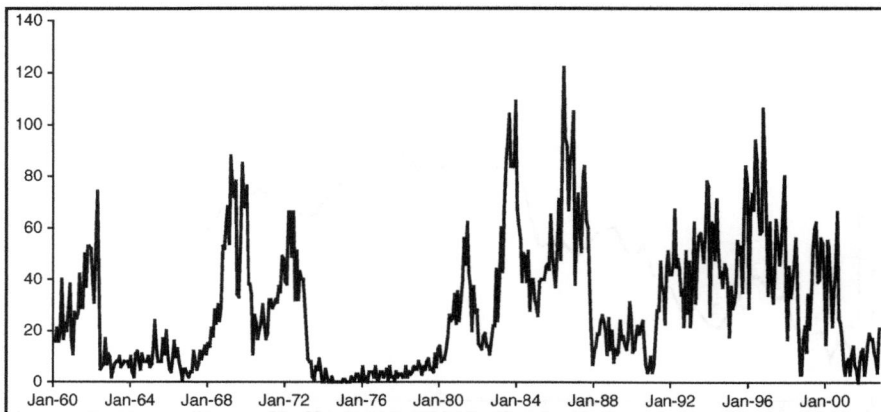

FIGURE 27.10   Number of IPOs per Month – US.

Source: Thomson Financial Datastream.

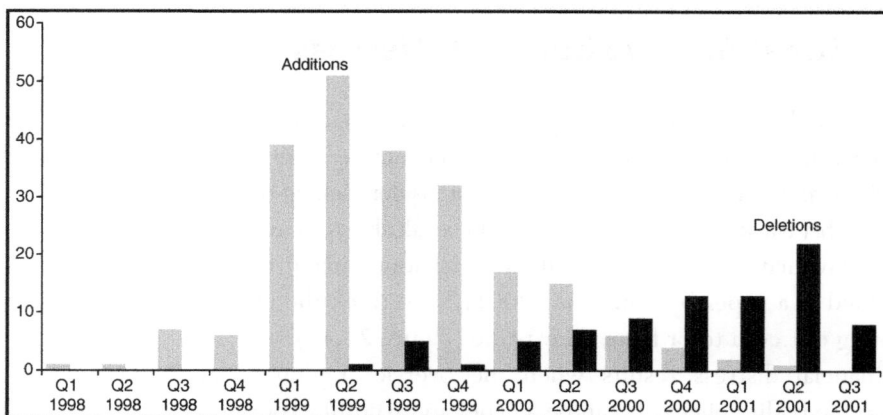

FIGURE 27.11   Number of Firms Changing Their Names to/from dot.com.

Source: Rau *et al.* (2001).

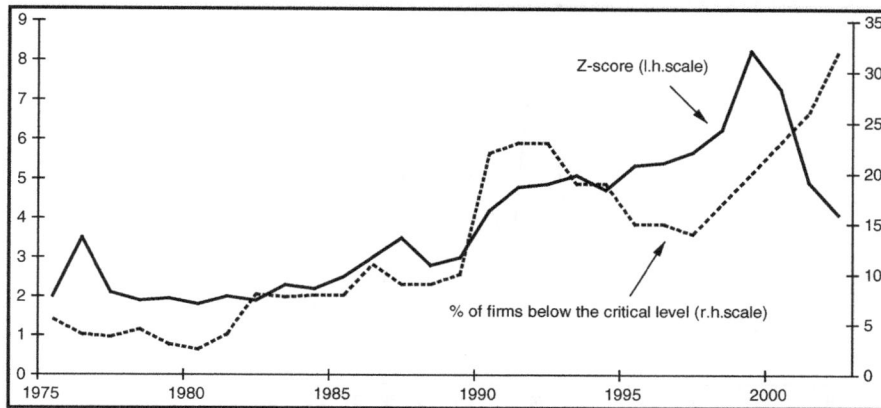

FIGURE 27.12 Z-score for the S&P 500 and Number of Firms in Distress.

Source: DrKW.

degree of financial distress in the USA. The chart shows not only the absolute level of Z for the S&P 500 (ex. financials) but also the percentage of firms that register a score below 1.8 (the critical level). This stands at a terrifying 33%!

It is this build-up in debt that poses the most critical danger in the bursting of the bubble. If deflation arrives while the overhang of debt is still massive, then a nightmare is created. Indeed, if inflation is low at the time the bubble bursts, that act alone can force the economy into deflation.

Cash flows will be inadequate to service the debt. Firms whose cash flows are exceeded by their interest payments will be forced to undertake extreme measures. They will be forced to attempt to create cash flows by capturing market share, effectively buying in volume. The most likely path to capturing market share is to lower prices – which of course only exacerbates the deflationary pressures.

The alternative route to raise cash flow is to seek to sell assets. Of course, if whole industries have created massive excess capacity, buyers of such assets will be few and far between. A fire sale results in a decline in asset prices as well. And any assets that are purchased are likely to be used to produce low-cost output, again undermining the already fragile pricing structure in the real economy, and in the markets.

The only other way out is to default and go bankrupt. Once again this results in asset fire sales, and more asset price depreciation. So all three paths to debt reduction are deflationary in the extreme.

Here we hit a fallacy of composition. In the immortal words of Inspector Clouseau "er, what?" A fallacy of composition is simply what may be true at the micro level does not hold at the macro level. For instance, every analyst thinks the firms he covers are capable of generating 15% long-term growth; however, we know that in aggregate this can't possibly be true. Hence, while it may be perfectly rational for each firm to pursue such cash flow generation policies, it can't possibly be true for the economy as a whole.

Of course, the saliency of this analysis depends entirely upon the starting level of inflation. In a portentous weekly, our colleague, Dylan Grice, noted that deflation is much closer than many currently believe (see *Global Economics for Investors*, 18

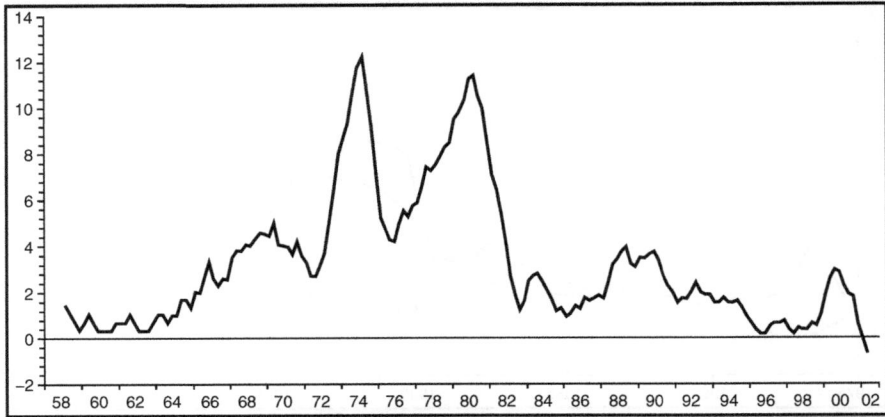

FIGURE 27.13   US Corporate Sector Deflator YoY Shows Deflation.

Source: Thomson Financial Datastream.

FIGURE 27.14   Core PPI Inflation in the US at Lowest Reading on Record.

Source: Thomson Financial Datastream.

October 2002). He estimates that some 50% of the US CPI components are already showing deflation (Figure 27.13) and the US corporate sector deflator is already in deflation, as is the core PPI measure (Figure 27.14).

Those arguing that the headline series remains well above deflation are running the risk of focusing too much upon the headline data. At our recent conference, Peter Tasker noted that the headline CPI (Figure 27.14) was one of the last measures to slip into deflation, by which time, it was too late for the BoJ (Figure 27.15) to do anything about it!

Keynes noted that deflation left firms with the unenviable situation of being long real assets and short nominal assets, exactly the wrong way round for a deflationary environment. The only way of closing this position is to shut down production. This is a hard reality for firms to face.

Figure 27.16 shows that it has taken almost a decade for Japan Inc. to realize that they need to shut down production and remove capacity (destroy the capital stock) in order to make any progress.

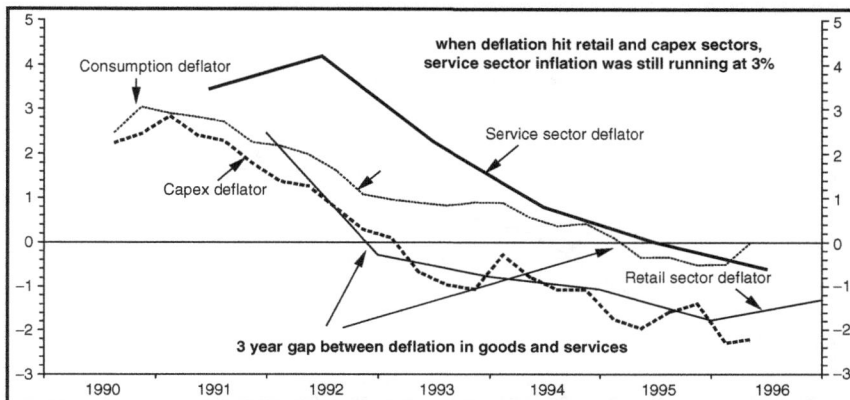

FIGURE 27.15 Japanese Service Sector Inflation Is the Last to Go Negative.

Source: Thomson Financial Datastream.

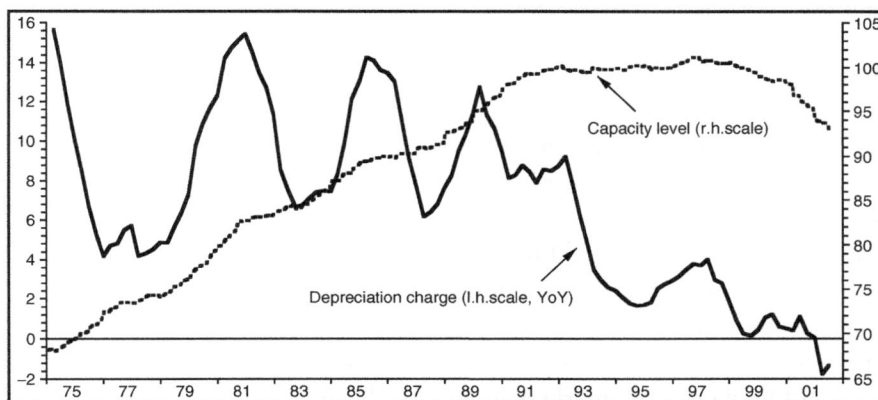

FIGURE 27.16 Japanese Capacity Level and Depreciation Charge (YoY).

Source: Thomson Financial Datastream.

The USA may just be learning a little quicker than Japan. As Dylan Grice noted (*Global Economics for Investors*, 1 November 2002) the USA has been reducing its capital stock (at least in the non-financial sector). However, it should be noted that the capacity reduction occurring in the early 1990s was much larger than reduction we have so far witnessed. Given the scale of the over-investment boom, a very large cut back in the capital stock would seem to be warranted (Figure 27.17).

Fraud also tends to emerge at this stage of the bubble process. Fraud follows Keynes's law that demand creates its own supply – that is to say, investors are so keen for growth that firms will deliberately seek to manufacture growth. In Japan, Recruit Cosmos was a scandal that embroiled several very high-profile Japanese ministers. My favourite tale is that of the bubble lady, a restaurant owner who managed with the help of a crooked bank manager to secure massive funds from one of Japan's leading banks. These funds were then invested on the basis of advice from a ceramic toad! The memories of recent US frauds are still fresh in investor's minds, from Enron to WorldCom and Tyco (and this time around a ceramic poodle umbrella stand!)

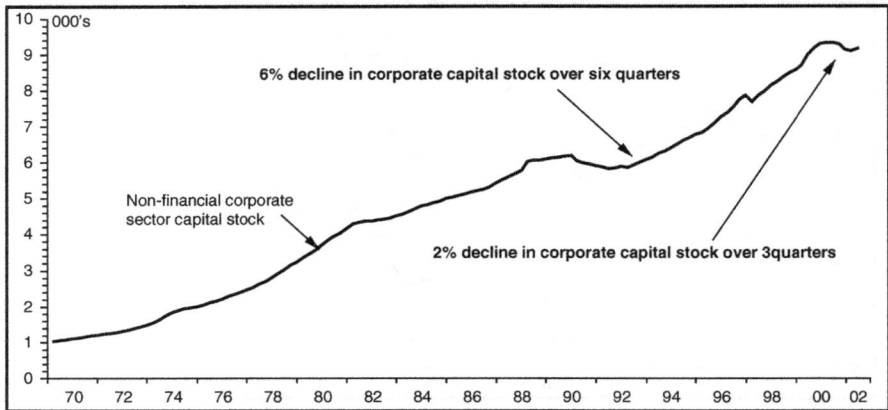

FIGURE 27.17 Flow of Funds Data Suggests Decline in Non-Financial Corporate Capital Stock.

Source: Thomson Financial Datastream.

Revulsion

The final stage of a bubble is revulsion. Investors are so scarred by the events in which they participated that they can no longer bring themselves to participate in the market at all.

Revulsion usually follows in the wake of a degenerate panic. However, this has been absent so far. Equity weightings remain extraordinarily high, both in terms of actual fund allocations and indeed in most strategists' recommendations.

It has become clear that institutional investors are all waiting for their fair value targets to be reached in order to buy stocks. However, as we noted in *Global Equity Strategy*, 18 October 2002, markets should be cheap rather than fair value. Clients know this too, so why are they opting to get back in at fair value?

Psychology and peer group benchmarking may help to explain this bizarre behaviour. There is a human tendency to feel the pain of regret at having made small errors, without putting those errors into any context. In common parlance, it is the same thing as kicking yourself for doing something foolish. If you wish to avoid the pain of regret, then you may act in ways that appear irrational unless the pain of regret is taken into account. Effectively, investors are more worried about the risk of missing the next move up, than about waiting for equities to become cheap.

Another group of investors have been arguing that bear markets only tend to last "X" number of months. However, that is like saying that simply because stocks have fallen a lot they must be cheap. It simply isn't true. There is no statute of limitations on bear market duration. As Tasker noted at the conference, in a world with deflation time is a killer rather than a healer!

Tasker also made an insightful observation that in the wake of previous bubbles it is not the stocks that led you into the bubble that will lead you out (Figure 27.18). For instance, the star performers in Japan post-bubble were the electricals and autos (Figure 27.19), however during the bubble these were laggards and considered to be an irrelevance to the changing economy.

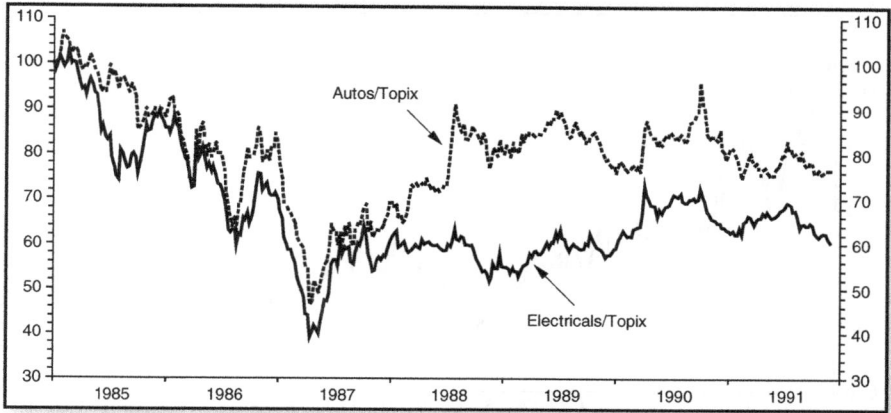

FIGURE 27.18 Laggards of the Bubble Years . . . .

Source: Thomson Financial Datastream.

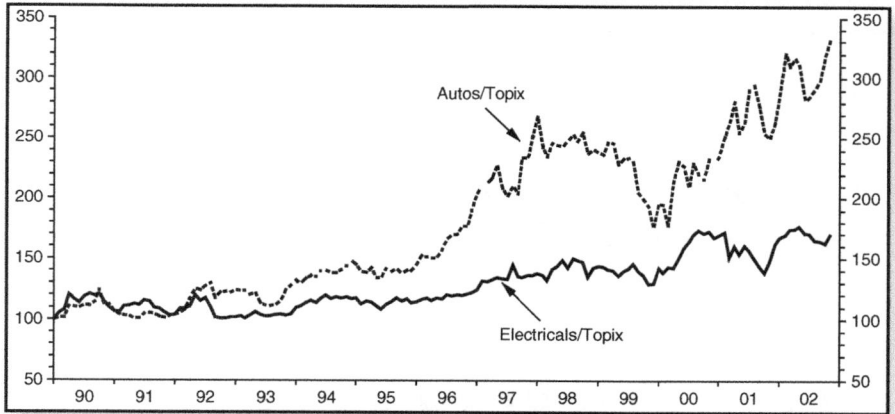

FIGURE 27.19 But Winners in the Post-Bubble Era.

Source: Thomson Financial Datastream.

This provides yet more evidence that the current rally in the USA is just another example of a bull snap in the overall bear market. Figure 27.20 shows the way in which technology has been leading each of the attempted rallies since the US bubble burst. The bear market won't end until investors finally give up hope on the tech stocks!

One of the hallmarks of the end of the bubble will be a collapse in volumes, a sign that investors have truly lost their faith in the equity culture. However, current volumes remain at massive levels. In order to track volumes we use a measure of turnover (reported volume relative to the average number of shares listed), then we detrend that series in order to remove the effect of an increasing habit of traders to trade with each other (Figure 27.21). Yet even after making this adjustment we find that volumes remain at record levels!

Let's assume that we eventually get to a degenerate panic. What will pull us out? We have recently explored two potential endgames that can be mapped out. Firstly,

FIGURE 27.20 Tech Driven Rallies Will Not End the Bear Market.

Source: Thomson Financial Datastream.

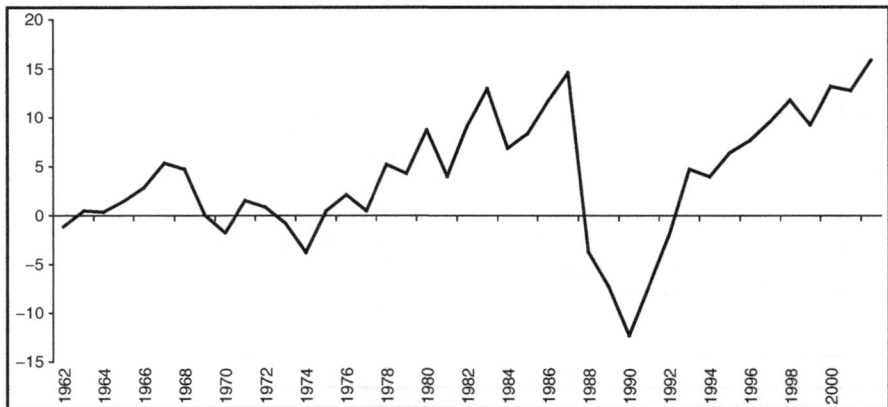

FIGURE 27.21 US Detrended Turnover Still at Manic Levels.

Source: NYSE, DrKW.

just as valuations get stretched beyond all reasonable levels in the bubble, so valuations should likewise fall to truly cheap levels during the burst.

We examined markets on both a top-down and bottom-up perspective in terms of valuation in our *Global Strategy Weekly*, 18 October 2002. The conclusion was that markets simply weren't cheap. Figure 27.22 shows our much loved Graham and Dodd PE (using a 10-year moving average of reported earnings) for the US market. It still stands at a lofty 25 times, against bear market bottoms of around 10 times.

The other mechanism was explored by Albert Edwards in *Global Strategy Weekly*, 1 November 2002, which was the path of unconventional policy response. Effectively a lender of the last resort steps in to provide a floor to the market. As Albert writes, "It may be a move to money targeting (base or broad). It may involve T-bond

FIGURE 27.22 US Graham and Dodd PE.

Source: DrKW.

purchases. It has to be something different and to be credible." However, before we see such a response "things will get much, much worse first".

◼ Applications

The above lays out the framework and provides some hints to the asset allocation and stock selection ideas that we will now seek to draw out more fully.

Asset Allocation

Japan offers asset allocators one simple lesson – forget everything you think you know about the nature of the relationship between bonds and equities. The arrival of deflation wreaks havoc upon prior relationships.

Too many investors have grown up only experiencing bull market conditions, and disinflationary bull market conditions at that. There is a lost generation of analysts because they spent so long preparing rather than analysing income statements, let alone balance sheets. Similarly, there is a lost generation of asset allocators who have only experienced bonds driving equities.

We have written many times before that this supposed relationship between bonds and equities is an illusory correlation. It results from equity investors trying to have their cake and eat it. Think of it this way, prices should be determined by discounted cash flow models. Such valuation models will have inflation factored into both their numerator and denominator; that is to say, cash flows projections will be in nominal terms, and the discount rate will be in nominal terms. Hence inflation should cancel out to leave the resulting value in "real terms".

However, investors have been willing to drop their discount rates as bond yields declined owing to low inflation. Of course, as inflation declines so should cash flow projections in nominal terms. But investors haven't done this, resulting in seriously overvalued equities, and an illusory correlation between nominal bonds and equities!

Figure 27.23 shows the relationship between bond and equity returns in Japan. We have overlaid inflation on the chart, and it is no coincidence that the correlation drops negative at the same time that deflation arrives on quite a permanent basis.

Of course, when the correlation between bonds and equities shifts so dramatically, it should be obvious that models based on positive correlations between bonds and equities will "break down". Figure 27.24 shows the Japanese bond equity earnings yield ratio. Unsurprisingly it breaks down when deflation arrives and the illusory correlation between bonds and equities is revealed for all to see.

Lest those of us who live in the Western world assume that the lessons from Japan are somehow irrelevant, take a look at the evidence presented below (Figure 27.25). In both Germany and the USA, the correlation between bond and equity returns is negative. Yet still bullish strategists insist on producing bond equity earnings yield

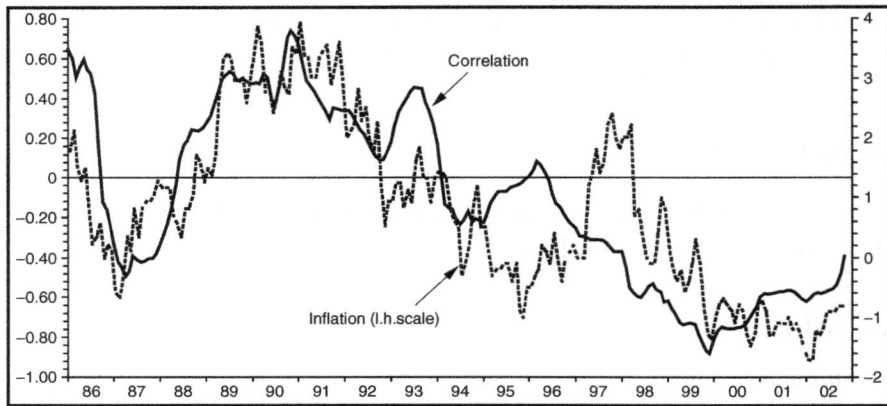

FIGURE 27.23 **Japanese Bond/Equity Return Correlation and Inflation.**

Source: Thomson Financial Datastream.

FIGURE 27.24 **Japanese BEER.**

Source: Thomson Financial Datastream.

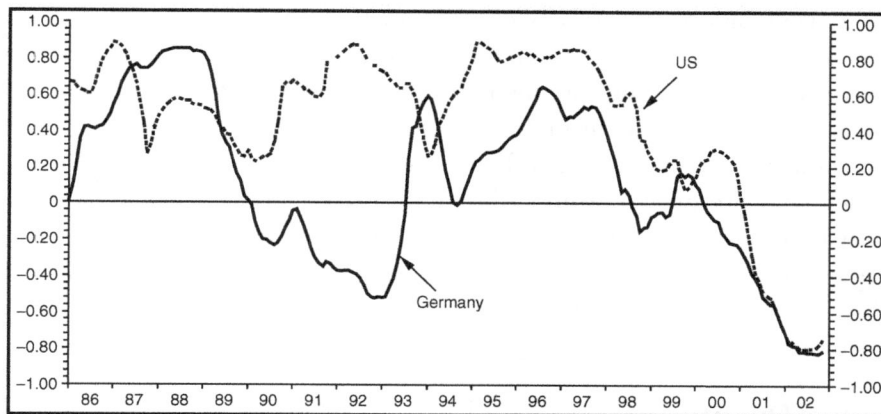

FIGURE 27.25 US and German Bond/Equity Return Correlations.

Source: Thomson Financial Datastream.

charts to illustrate that equities are cheap! Don't be fooled into relying on old valuation ranges. They simply aren't valid.

Alpha Generation

Unlike the long bull market, investors won't simply make money by being long equities. Effectively, investors will be forced to focus more and more on absolute returns rather than relative performance. This in turn should cause a shift from the time series to the cross-section of returns. Investors will need to exploit differences between firms more and more. The focus should be on true long/short portfolios. Too many of the so-called hedge funds set up over recent years are really nothing more than leveraged long funds. Active management should become more valuable, and index funds could find themselves out in the cold.

We can identify three such cross-section strategies that should be among the vanguard of those benefiting in a de-bubbling/deflationary period.

Balance Sheets

Given all we have said about the risks of firms taking on too much debt during the euphoria stage, it should come as little surprise that we feel that balance sheet strength should be a key component of any stock selection process in the post-bubble world.

As an example of the cross-section strategies mentioned earlier, Dichev (1998) shows that the lowest 10% of Z-scores underperform the market by 33% over 3 years. Investors only incorporate the information contained in a low Z-score slowly over time. Hence we see a pattern of prolonged adjustment. In terms of an equal long/short portfolio, Dichev shows that the annual average return to such a trade is around 7% p.a.

An alternative screen was created by Piotroski (2000). He set out to examine whether using a simple accounting screen could help with stock selection in a value universe. He found that a minority of value stocks created the long run outperformance of value stocks relative to growth stocks. In fact just 44% of the value universe created the entire value premium. He then asked if using historical accounting information could help find that minority. He found that it could indeed.

Piotroski then formed an equal long/short portfolio based around going long those with a score greater than 5 (the financially sound value stocks), and short those with a score of less than 5 (the financially vulnerable value stocks). Such a strategy yielded annual average returns of 9% p.a. for zero cost! Equally impressive, and highly relevant for absolute return funds, the trade only generated 2 years of negative returns between 1976 and 1996.

Earnings Quality

This should really be in the forefront of investors' minds at all times. However, the reality of overoptimism is that quality tends to take second place to quantity. However, with fraud rife once again, it would seem that a strategy designed to exploit high-quality earnings should merit investigation.

Of course, it is easy to talk of high-quality earnings but exactly how do we define such a concept? Well, one obvious way is to think about what earnings really represent. Earnings can be seen as the summation of two components, cash flows (about which we should care) and accruals (accountants' tricks).

It has long been known that accruals tend to be reversed, and that firms that use accruals tend to have high earnings at the time, naturally enough. However, they can't keep hiding the truth forever, and sooner or later the accruals are reversed to reveal a poor underlying earnings situation.

Table 27.2 shows the returns based on portfolios formed by the degree of accruals contained in the earnings numbers (and conversely, the same thing based on cash flows).

Houge and Loughran (2000) point out that this suggests a natural earnings quality trade. Investors should find firms with low earnings but a high cash flow percentage (or a low percentage of accruals) to those earnings. Conversely, firms with high earnings but low cash flows (or high accruals) should be shorted. They show that an equal long/short portfolio based on this generated returns of 16% p.a. (Table 27.3).

Capital Expenditure

The final alpha generation strategy that we wish to explore as relevant to a post-bubble world relates to the overinvestment hypothesis outlined above. Just as overinvestment is a major problem for the economy, so it can be for firms. We have witnessed countless examples of firms wasting shareholders' cash on massively expensive purchases of other firms, and a plethora of bizarre investment projects in general.

TABLE 27.2	Cash Flows vs Accruals – Raw Returns (% pa)		
Low accruals	18.4%	High accruals	10.2%
Low cash flows	10.4%	High cash flows	18.6%

Source: Houge and Loughran (2000).

THE INTEGRATION OF TECHNICAL ANALYSIS

TABLE 27.3	Earnings Quality Trade Construction	
	Low Earnings	**High Earnings**
Low cash flows	—	Earnings largely composed of accruals, implies poor earnings quality SELL
High cash flows	Earnings dominated by cash flows, implies high earnings quality BUY	—

Source: Houge and Loughran (2000).

Titman *et al.* (2001) show that firms that carry out high levels of cap ex relative to their sales (or total assets) underperform firms that resist the temptation to splurge on pointless expenditures. The variable they use is cap ex over sales in year 0 relative to the average of the same variable over the last 3 years. Although their results are remarkably robust to altering the definitions.

They find strong evidence that firms that carried out high levels of investment tend to underperform those that didn't. Being good academics they measure returns as the excess return after adjusting for style, size and momentum. Even then they show a 2% p.a. difference between the two groups. Now excess returns generally don't mean much to investors, but roughly speaking this is equivalent to an equal long/short portfolio generating 6–8% p.a. Again, in a world of low numbers, hardly a return to be sniffed at.

Long-Only Funds

While we believe that absolute returns are the way forward, we acknowledge that many clients are concerned largely with peer group relative performance, and many more are constrained to long-only positions. However, the same stock selection criteria can add value to such managers as well. Table 27.4 shows the annual percentage returns from the long-only side of the strategies outlined above, proving that the gains aren't all on the short side!

TABLE 27.4	Long Only Portfolio Returns	
Strategy	**Return**	**Market Return**
Z-scores	16%	14.4
Earnings quality	18%	15.4
Cap Ex	4%	16.2

Source: DrKW

Summary

This is an unusually long chapter by our standards; in general we prefer to follow Keynes's advice and "fling pamphlets to the wind". However, this is a complex topic, and a basic understanding of the causes of bubbles is necessary in order to understand the ways in which we can exploit the de-bubbling process.

The key points are:

- Starting from a point of low inflation, a bursting bubble can easily unleash debt deflation.

- Bear markets don't have time limits.

- Don't rely on the soundness of prior relationships.

- Deflation alters the investment landscape radically.

- Previous winners won't lead you out.

- Where possible concentrate on absolute returns.

- Balance sheets, earnings quality, and low cap ex are key stock selection criteria.

■ References

Caginalp, G., Porter, D. and Smith, V.L. (2000) Overreaction, momentum, liquidity and price bubbles in laboratory and field asset markets, *Journal of Psychology and Financial Markets*, 1(1), 24– 48.

Dichev, I.D. (1998) Is the risk of bankruptcy a systematic risk? *Journal of Finance*, 53(3), 1131–1147.

Global Equity Strategy (various issues).

Houge, T. and Loughran, T. (2000) Cash flow is king, *Journal of Psychology and Financial Markets*, 1(3&4), 161–175.

Keen, S. (2001) Debunking economics: The Naked Emperor of the Social Sciences. Zeb Books.

Montier, J. (2002) *Behavioural Finance: Insights in Irrational Minds and Markets*. John Wiley & Sons Ltd: Chichester.

Piotroski, J.D. (2000) Value Investing: The use of historical financial information to separate winners and losers, *Journal of Accounting Research*, 38, 1–14.

Rau, R., Patel, A., Osobov, I., Khorana, A. and Cooper, M. (2001) The game of the name: Value changes accompanying dot.com additions and deletions. Unpublished working paper.

Rothchild, J. (1998) *The Bear Book: Survive and Profit in Ferocious Markets*. John Wiley & Sons, Inc: Hoboken.

Titman, S., Wei, K.C.J. and Xie, F. (2004) Capital Investments and Stock Returns. *Journal of Financial and Quantitative Analysis*, 39, 677–700.

CHAPTER 28

The VIX as a Stock Market Indicator

From Russell Rhoads, *Trading VIX Derivatives: Trading and Hedging Strategies Using VIX Futures, Options, and Exchange Traded Notes* (Hoboken, New Jersey: John Wiley & Sons, 2007), Chapter 9.

Learning Objective Statements

- Contrast different measures of volatility
- Interpret changes in volatility as a signal useful for forecasting
- Explain how volatility can be an integral part of a market forecast

The high level of the VIX is often cited on the business networks when the overall stock market is under pressure. Usually the VIX level is cited and the term *fear and greed index* are associated with it. However, a good explanation of why the VIX tends to rise when the overall stock market is under pressure is not often shared. The implied volatility of option prices rises when there is more demand for than supply of option contracts. When the market comes under pressure, there is often a resulting increase in demand for option contracts. The relationship between increased demand for option contracts in times of panic will be discussed further. Then this concept will be taken another step, and how some traders apply the VIX as a technical indicator will be introduced.

Following the exploration of the relationship of the S&P 500 and VIX indexes, some other methods that have developed involving the VIX will be explored. Specifically, we will examine the VIX index alone, the VIX index combined with other volatility indexes, combining the VIX index with VIX futures trading, and an analysis of the VIX and gold prices. Finally, we'll discuss how to use the put-call ratio calculated through VIX option activity.

By no means should the sample strategies presented in this chapter be taken as absolute recommendations. They are simply basic examples of how powerful the VIX and VIX-related trading activity can be in analyzing market activity. The point behind this chapter is to demonstrate to traders who use technical or quantitative trading strategies that they may want to consider adding the VIX and other volatility-related securities to their technical toolbox.

■ The Inverse Relationship Between the Vix and the S&P 500

The inverse relationship between the stock market and the VIX requires a little explanation. This relationship is in place mainly due to the type of option trading that occurs in times of market weakness. When investors are most concerned regarding the direction of the S&P 500 index or overall market, they tend to seek out protection. One common strategy, to hedge in times of panic, is the purchase of S&P 500 index put options. In times of greater concern regarding the stock market, the purchase of put contracts may be more aggressive. This aggressive purchasing of S&P 500 index put options would result in a rise in implied volatility of S&P 500 index options. The VIX measures implied volatility of S&P 500 index options, so the VIX tends to rise when the overall stock market falls. In times of dramatic market weakness, the VIX will often rise at a magnitude that is greater than the drop in the market. For instance, Table 28.1 shows this relationship based on the 10 worst days for the S&P 500 since 1990.

The CBOE has applied the VIX calculation, which was developed in 2003, to existing data and has the index available from the beginning of 1990. Comparing that data to the daily performance of the S&P 500 index results in the data in Table 28.1. Note that on each of the 10 worst-performing days for the S&P 500 the VIX index was up more, on a percentage basis, than the market was down.

Also, comparing the size of a VIX move to the upside relative to the loss in the S&P 500 index over other periods yields interesting results. Table 28.2 shows the number of times the move to the upside in the VIX has been less than the loss in the S&P 500 index over a variety of days. Also included is the performance for the cutoff day in each

TABLE 28.1	Percent Change of the S&P 500 and VIX Index on the 10 Worst Days from 1/1/1990 to 10/31/2010	
	S&P 500 Index	**VIX Index**
10/15/2008	−9.03%	25.61%
12/1/2008	−8.93%	23.93%
9/29/2008	−8.81%	34.48%
10/9/2008	−7.62%	11.11%
10/27/1997	−6.87%	34.31%
8/31/1998	−6.80%	11.82%
11/20/2008	−6.71%	8.89%
11/19/2008	−6.12%	9.79%
10/22/2008	−6.10%	31.14%
4/14/2000	−5.83%	13.91%

	Day S&P 500	VIX Move Less	Percent VIX Move
Days	Performance	Than S&P 500	Less Than S&P 500
10	−5.83%	0	0.0%
25	−4.17%	1	4.0%
50	−3.23%	1	2.0%
100	−2.58%	6	6.0%
250	−1.82%	24	9.6%
500	−1.27%	41	8.2%
1000	−0.71%	132	13.2%

TABLE 28.2 Incidents of VIX Magnitude Being Lower Than S&P 500 Performance from 1/1/1990 to 10/31/2010

example. For instance, the first row, which shows what occurred over the 10 worst days for the S&P 500 index, shows that the S&P 500 index lost 5.83% on the 10th day.

On only one of the worst 50 performance days for the S&P 500 index was the VIX up less in magnitude than the S&P 500 was down. The 50th worst day was down over 3%. A 3% down move in the stock market is usually a newsworthy event for the day and one that will keep traders at their screens. The worst single day in this worst 50 of days was October 8, 2008, when the stock market lost over 5%, but the VIX was only up a little over 3%.

As the number of days increases, the magnitude of the drop of the S&P 500 index decreases. The result is smaller down days are included in the study, and the frequency of a VIX move to the upside being more than the loss for the S&P 500 index is lower. Note on the 500th day the market was down only 1.27% and on the 1,000th worst day the market loss less than 1% (down 0.71%). A loss of around 1% for the S&P 500 index is not exactly the kind of market activity that results in urgent buying of S&P 500 put options for protection. However, for the 500 worst days of performance, volatility actually increased more than the S&P 500 lost over 90% of the time. Even with the 1,000 worst days being measured, over 85% of the time volatility increases more than the market loses.

■ Vix Index as an Indicator

Before discussing the value of the VIX index as an indicator, look to a chart of the VIX versus the S&P 500 from 1990 to late 2010 in Figure 28.1.

On January 2, 1990, the VIX closed at 20.11. Almost 20 years later, the VIX closed at 21.20. The path the VIX took over that long period ranged from an intraday high of 89.53 to a low of 9.31. Over the same period the S&P 500 rose from 352.20 to 1,183.26. Although the VIX is basically flat and the S&P 500 has risen tremendously, the shorter-term inverse relationship between the S&P 500 and the VIX may be used to predict the future direction of stock prices.

For instance, consider using a 20-, 50-, and 200-day moving average for the S&P 500 as the only criteria to be long the index. As long as the S&P 500 closes above

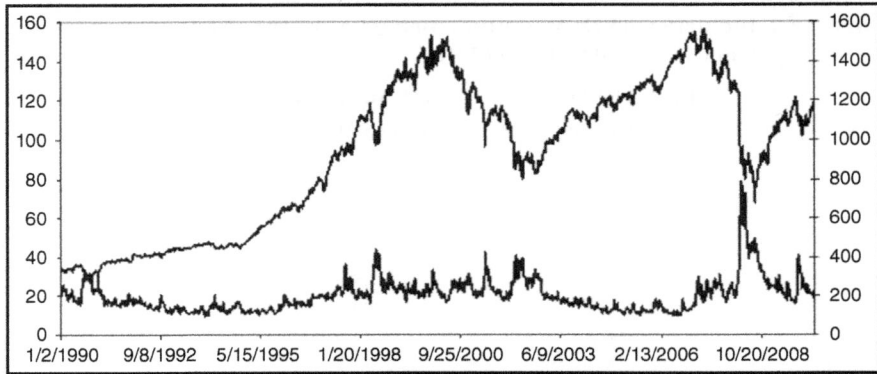

FIGURE 28.1 Weekly Chart of the VIX Index versus the S&P 500 Index, 1/1/1990 to 10/25/2010.

these moving averages, there is a long position in the index. When the closing price for the S&P 500 index is below the respective moving average, the system keeps investors on the sidelines and out of the market. For each of these moving averages, a profit would be made through being long the index. Now, if we add a filter that involves the VIX index, there is improvement for each of these moving average rules except for the 200-day moving average system. Table 28.3 shows the results from a simple S&P 500 index moving average and a system combining an S&P 500 moving average system and a VIX index moving average filter.

This test takes each of the moving averages from October 1990 to October 2010 and analyzes the performance of being long the S&P 500 as long as the index closes over the respective moving average. Then a VIX filter is added that involves only being long the S&P 500 in cases where the index is over the respective moving average and the VIX index close is below the same moving average.

The VIX as a filter improves using a 20-day moving average by about 45 S&P points and then it adds about 40 points of value when a 50-day moving average is applied. As the length of the moving average is increased, the effectiveness of using VIX decreases. The idea here is that VIX is much more of a short-term than a long-term market indicator. Spikes in volatility happen quickly, and then the market returns to normal over time. Therefore, as a long-term indicator, the VIX does not appear to be a useful supplement to an S&P 500 moving average system.

Also, it should be noted that buying and holding the S&P 500 index over the same period results in a gain of 880 points for the S&P 500. Admittedly, buy and hold would have

THE INTEGRATION OF TECHNICAL ANALYSIS

TABLE 28.3	S&P 500 Moving Averages Combined with VIX Indicator Results	
Moving Average	Stand-Alone S&P 500 Result	S&P 500 MA + VIX MA Result
20	95.65	140.22
50	331.83	370.66
200	847.73	626.10

TABLE 28.4	Results of Buying the S&P 500 after a 1% Drop Combined with a VIX-Related Filter	
	S&P Down 1%	w/VIX Up 3%
Points gained	921.48	1,060.48

outperformed any of these systematic trading approaches. The goal was to display that the VIX index is better over the short term as a market tool as opposed to the long term.

Some of the best buying opportunities for stocks over the decades has occurred when the market appears to be at its worst. Another way to think of this is the best time to buy may be when there is so much fear in the market that there is nothing but sellers in the market. In those times, the result is high implied volatility. Combining market weakness and VIX strength has an interesting outcome.

As a basic analysis of this, buying the S&P for a one-day hold when the market is down 1% was tested. Then doing so only when the VIX had a day where it was higher was added to the mix. The result of each approach appears in Table 28.4.

Buying the S&P 500 only when it is down 1% or more and holding until the next day's close yields a return of 921.48 S&P 500 points. There is an assumption that there are no transaction costs involved in this system and that a long position mirroring the S&P 500 index may be entered and exited with no slippage. This is a short-term strategy, so adding the VIX index into the mix actually improves the results a bit. To determine whether there is really fear in the marketplace, a filter of the VIX being up at least 3% on the same days was tested. This method takes into account only days on which the VIX moves in a larger magnitude than the S&P 500 index, indicating that fear in stocks combined with increased S&P 500 index option implied volatility based on aggressive option purchases. The result is an extra 120 S&P points over just buying daily weakness.

▪ Vix Futures as An Indicator

A more useful tool to use in market forecasting may be the VIX futures prices versus the VIX index. Also, the relationship between different VIX futures prices has shown promise as a market indicator. A VIX futures contract price is based on the market's outlook for volatility up to and on the expiration date of that contract. Stated another way, VIX futures anticipate the direction and level of the VIX index or the implied volatility of the overall market. With no financial relationship between the spot index and futures contract prices, the result is an indirect market prediction.

This indirect market outlook given by VIX futures works due to the inverse relationship between the S&P 500 and the VIX index. Since the VIX is expected to rally when the stock market moves lower and the VIX would be expected to trend lower during a market upturn, a prediction of where the VIX will be at a certain time in the future is also a bet on what will happen to the S&P 500 index.

If traders expect the S&P to rally, they should sell VIX futures. If they expect the S&P will sell off dramatically, they would take a long position in VIX futures.

When VIX futures prices are at a discount to the VIX index, this indicates VIX futures traders believe the S&P 500 index should trade higher and the VIX index should move lower. Conversely, when VIX futures contracts are at a dramatic premium to the VIX index, traders may be anticipating weakness from the overall stock market.

The front month future relative to the VIX index is usually the most active VIX future contract and also the best indicator of the market's expectation of volatility over a short period. This contract will settle in a special calculation of the VIX index, so as time approaches the future contract will trend closer to the value of the index. To eliminate this trend from analyzing the nearest expiring future contract, for testing purposes a new front month is designated the Friday before expiration.

For example, November 12, 2010, is the Friday before November VIX expiration. On this date, even though the November futures contract still has a few more days until expiration, the December 2010 contract becomes the front month for analysis purposes.

Any test or analysis using VIX futures contracts will originate only at the beginning of 2007. VIX futures trading has been taking place at the CBOE Futures Exchange since 2004, but the data starting in 2007 has more integrity than going back to the beginning of VIX futures trading. Also, there is a consistency of months available since 2007 that allows for comparisons between contracts. Comparing the worst days for the S&P 500 since the beginning of 2007 with the performance for the tradable front month VIX futures contract yields similar results to the comparison of the S&P 500 and VIX index. Table 28.5 shows this performance comparison.

In 9 out of the 10 worst days for the S&P 500 since 2007, the VIX future contract was up more in magnitude than the S&P 500 index lost. This could be considered more significant than comparing the S&P 500 performance to spot VIX index. The significance comes from the ability to actually trade the VIX future contract and benefit from this price move. The VIX future change is based on traders' anticipation of what may occur in the overall market. When traders buy VIX futures based on the market moving lower, they are anticipating that this trend may continue. Of interest

TABLE 28.5	The S&P 500 Index and VIX Front Month Futures Performance on the 10 Worst Days for the S&P 500 since 1/1/2007	
Date	S&P 500% Change	VIX Front Month% Change
10/15/2008	−9.03%	18.61%
12/1/2008	−8.93%	13.61%
9/29/2008	−8.81%	14.14%
10/9/2008	−7.62%	14.79%
11/20/2008	−6.71%	5.29%
11/19/2008	−6.12%	9.79%
10/22/2008	−6.10%	10.34%
10/7/2008	−5.74%	11.93%
1/20/2009	−5.28%	12.63%
11/5/2008	−5.27%	8.12%

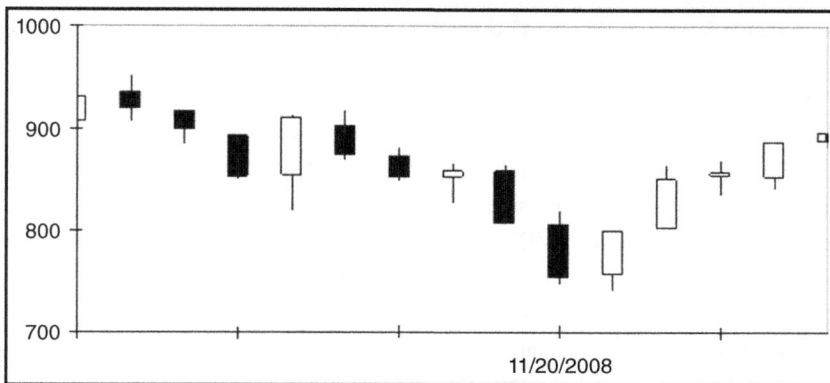

FIGURE 28.2   The S&P 500 Index, November 2008.

from this table is the day where the S&P 500 lost more on a percentage basis than the VIX future contract rose.

On November 20, 2008, the S&P 500 dropped from 806.58 to 752.44, a loss of 6.71%. The same day, the December 2008 VIX future contract gained 5.29%, rising from 62.90 to 66.23. Also, the spot VIX index was up from 74.26 to 80.86, a gain of 8.89%. Note that the index rose more than the S&P 500 lost, but the future contract did not follow suit. This disparity between the VIX futures, the VIX index, and the S&P 500 resulted in an interesting few days following November 20. This interesting response can be seen in Figure 28.2.

November 20 turned out to be a short-term bottom for the overall stock market. The S&P 500 index was up over 15% over the next four trading days following this divergence day, when the VIX futures market was not up as much as the S&P 500 was down. Table 28.6 is an overview of the number of times the S&P 500 was down more than the near-term VIX future contract was up on the day for a variety of lookback periods.

This table has pretty consistent results across the board as far as the VIX future contract being up more than the S&P is down about 10% of the time. This also translates into the VIX futures rising more than the S&P 500 lost around 90% of the time on bearish days. A bearish day in the stock market could easily be considered down more than 2.5% on the day, so using the 100 worst days is a fairly logical choice.

TABLE 28.6   Incidents of VIX Futures Magnitude Being Lower Than S&P 500 Performance from 1/1/2007 to 10/31/2010

Tests	Day S&P 500 Performance	VIX Future Move Less Than S&P 500	Percent VIX Move Less Than S&P 500
10	−5.27%	1	10%
25	−3.48%	2	8%
50	−3.23%	5	10%
100	−2.58%	13	13%

■ A Modified Vix Futures Contract

Using the VIX futures contract as an indicator does lead to issues related to time to expiration. As the VIX futures contract approaches expiration, the price gap between the future and the index continues to narrow. To adjust for this, a modified contract price based on the front two months has been created.

The method of developing a VIX reading based on futures to use for technical analysis follows. First, the next two expiration date settlement prices are determined. Then a weighted average of the two contracts is calculated. As time passes, the near-term contract is given less weighting and the longer-term contract is given more, based on their proportion of the combined time to expiration of both contracts.

The following steps would be taken to determine the weighted VIX futures calculation on August 18, 2010. First, the next two expirations would be determined, in this case September 2010 and October 2010. Next, the roll date for each contract is determined with September 23 days off and October 58 days. Finally, the prices of these two contracts will be needed.

Calculating A Modified VIX Futures Contract

Use the following key and steps to calculate a modified VIX futures contract.

Key

FMD Front month days to roll
BMD Back month days to roll
FMC Front month close price
BMC Back month close price

1. Determine total number of days (TD).
   $$TD = FMD + BMD$$
2. $((FMD/TD) \times FMC) + ((BMD/TD) \times BMC)$

As an example of determining the modified VIX futures contract, let's use the closing prices on August 18, 2010:

FMD = 23
BMD = 58
FMC = 29.00
BMC = 31.10

1. TD = 81
2. $(23/81) \times 29.00 + (58/81) \times 31.10 = 30.50$

By taking the two closing prices and weighting them in this manner, the outcome is a closing price of 30.50. This sort of smoothing of the data will allow a better comparison of the closing price of the VIX with the underlying index. As this sort of comparison eliminates the time factor, this calculation creates a better futures-based reading to use as an indicator.

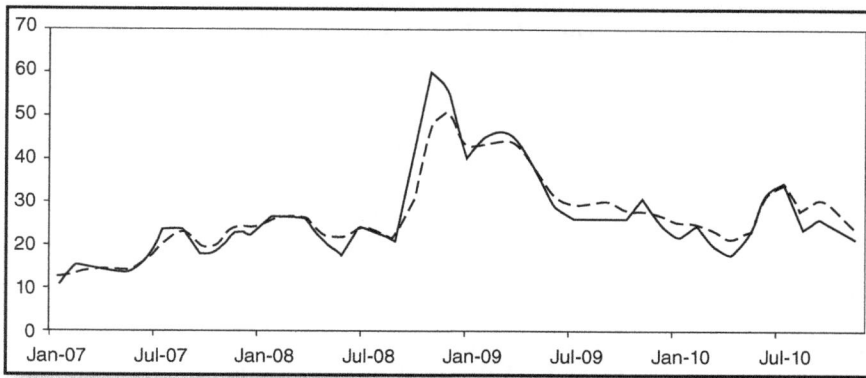

FIGURE 28.3 Monthly Modified VIX Future versus VIX Index, January 2007 to October 2010.

Figure 28.3 is a quick comparison of the spot VIX index and the VIX futures closing prices on a monthly basis from the beginning of 2007 to October 2010. Note that throughout the time period, the futures are at times at a premium or at a discount to the index, depending on the market's outlook for S&P 500 implied volatility.

The modified VIX futures contract is a useful method of smoothing VIX futures. When comparing the front month to the VIX index, the time to expiration may be a factor. Creating a modified contract analysis when comparing the future and index is more useful. The result is the comparison of futures trading versus the index—an easier process.

■ Combining Vix Futures and the Vix Index

Comparing the modified VIX future closing price to the index is a good indication of what the market place expects over the next few weeks regarding the direction of volatility. This comparison results in a prediction of where the S&P 500 is expected to go over the next few weeks. Table 28.7 shows the percentage of days that the VIX futures are at a premium to the index each year starting with 2007. This data was compiled before the end of 2010 so 2010 represents a partial year.

Note that in 2008 the S&P 500 index lost over 38% and the VIX futures closed at a discount much more frequently than in the other three years. The other years, with the futures at a premium more often than not, resulted in a positive year for the S&P

TABLE 28.7 Percent of Times the Closing VIX Futures Are at a Premium to the VIX Index

Year	Trading Days Futures above Index	Total Trading Days	% Trading Days above Index	S&P 500 Index Return
2007	177	251	70.5%	3.53%
2008	143	253	56.5%	−38.49%
2009	202	252	80.2%	23.45%
2010	180	209	86.1%	6.11%

TABLE 28.8 **S&P 500 Returns Using the VIX Future versus the VIX Index as a Signal**

Year	S&P 500 Performance	Long VIX Future Less Than VIX Index	VIX Future Less Than 95% VIX Index
2007	3.53%	14.79%	17.98%
2008	−38.49%	−11.47%	−6.51%
2009	23.45%	14.34%	9.69%
2010	6.11%	1.70%	2.73%
Average	−1.35%	4.84%	5.97%

500. However, using the futures relative to the index may be useful in gauging when it is time to buy in moments of panic.

Using the futures price relative to the index as an oversold or panic indicator would result in better performance relative to the S&P since 2007. Table 28.8 shows the performance of the S&P 500 index along with being only long the S&P 500 when the VIX future is at a discount to the VIX index. Also, the final column of this table shows applying a buffer of 5% to the VIX index versus the future contract.

Using the VIX futures relative to the index improves performance versus just holding the S&P 500 index. Although underperforming two years and outperforming in a couple of years, trading in this manner results in a return of about 5% per year.

The buffer of 5% also results in better results than just buying and holding for the S&P 500. Averaging the per-year returns results in an annual return of just about 6% per year. This 6% return beats the buy-and-hold strategy and is a slight improvement on the nonbuffered return.

■ Vix Index and Gold Price Indicator

A financially related instrument that has been historically associated with market fear is the price of gold. It is an asset that will appreciate in times of turbulence, just like volatility and the VIX. As gold and the VIX have similar reactions to crisis, it makes sense that using them together or related to each other may result in a useful market indicator.

To test the validity of using the price of gold and volatility, the GLD exchange-traded fund is used along with the spot VIX index to represent volatility. Pricing for the GLD goes back as far as late 2004, so testing runs from the beginning of 2005 through late 2010. Figure 28.4 is a price chart comparing the GLD and the VIX monthly closing prices from 2005 to late 2010.

The top line on this chart represents the monthly closing price of the GLD, with the lower line representing the VIX. It appears there are times when they track each other and times when there is some disparity in the direction of the two instruments. A specific time that stands out on this chart is late 2008. As there are times when there is a disconnection between gold and VIX prices, a ratio of the price of gold versus volatility was plotted.

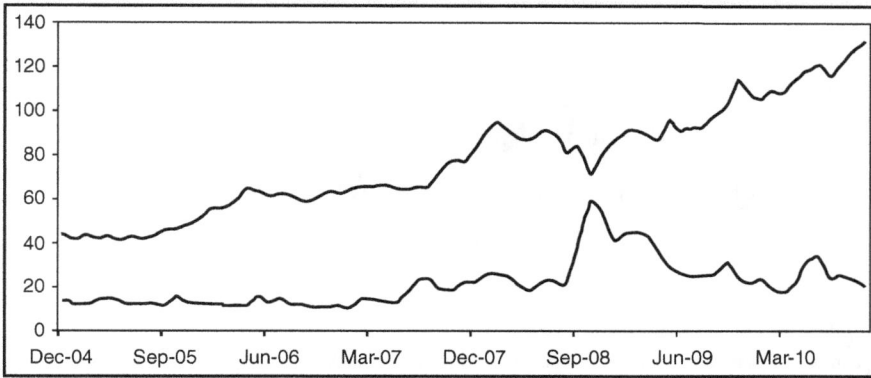

FIGURE 28.4 Monthly GLD versus VIX Index, January 2005 to October 2010.

FIGURE 28.5 Ratio of GLD ETF and VIX Index, January 2005 to October 2010.

Figure 28.5 shows the ratio of the GLD to the VIX over almost five years. Note that the range fluctuates from a low just below 1.00 to a high that breaches 7.00 a few times. There are times when the price of gold and the VIX index are in sync, but at other times they go in opposite directions.

Before exploring the benefit of this ratio as an indicator, Figure 28.6 shows this ratio compared to the S&P 500 index from January 2005 to October 2010. The lower

FIGURE 28.6 Ratio of GLD ETF to VIX Index versus S&P 500 Index, January 2005 to October 2010.

FIGURE 28.7 Ratio of GLD ETF to VIX Index January 2005 to October 2010 with Signal Levels Delineated.

line represents the GLD/VIX ratio, while the upper line shows the performance of the S&P 500 index over almost five years. Note there appears to be a closer correlation between this ratio and the S&P 500. Both tend to rise and fall in sync.

Applying this ratio as an indicator has some interesting results. This is a simple strategy, but it demonstrates the usefulness of comparing gold prices to implied volatility to create a market indicator. A buy signal on the S&P 500 index occurs when the GLD/VIX ratio crosses from under 2.75 to above 2.75. A sell signal occurs when the ratio crosses from a reading above 6.25 to below 6.25. The system enters on each of these signals and holds a position in the S&P 500 index for 15 days. Figure 28.7 shows the ratio with lines to indicate the buy and sell signal levels.

Note that when these levels are violated, often there is usually a pretty quick rebound of the ratio. However, a few instances of market turbulence have resulted in extreme readings that were maintained for days and even, in the case of 2008, for months. The tendency for this indicator to remain overbought or oversold at times led to developing a signal based on a return to the normal range of prices for the ratio. Table 28.9 is a summary of the results from taking the GLD/VIX ratio crossover as a signal to buy or sell the S&P 500 index.

TABLE 28.9 Summary of Ratio System Results

	Long System	Short System	Combined System
Total points	415.45	321.28	736.73
Maximum	75.14	81.25	81.25
Minimum	−28.36	−43.95	−43.95
Average	21.87	24.71	23.02
Signals	19	13	32
Winners	15	8	23
Percent win	78.95%	61.54%	71.88%

This system was tested from the beginning of 2005 to late 2010, covering 1,468 trading days. Only 32 signals were generated, so this is a case of very infrequent signals emanating from these rules. However, the results are fairly impressive for using this indicator as a stand-alone system.

Using this method of being long or short the market results in a total profit of 736 S&P 500 points, or 415 points from the long system and 321 from the short signals. Over the tested period, the S&P 500 index was down slightly, from 1,202 to 1,183 for a loss of 19 points, or basically flat. Even just using the long-only system would have added value.

On the long side, there were 19 signals with 15 of those trades resulting in a profit from holding the S&P 500 index over 15 trading days, or a win percentage of almost 79%. The short side had few signals and a slightly lower win rate. On the short side, there were 13 signals with 8 winners, for a winning percentage of just over 61%.

The average winners for both long and short came to about 20 S&P points, and the maximum loser for each was much lower than the points lost on the maximum losing trade. Again, this indicator has limited history, but it seems to have performed well signaling market reversals.

■ Vix Option Put-Call Ratio

Historically the most common use of option market data as some sort of market indicator has been the put-call ratio. This measure is a ratio of put volume to call volume, and the theory behind it is that an increase in put volume indicates an abundance of bearishness in the market. Too much bearishness in the market may be considered a contrarian indicator. This theory coincides with the thought behind some of the uses of the VIX index as an indicator. Basically, lower stock prices bring in put buying, this increase in put buying pushes implied volatility higher, and the result is a move higher in the VIX index.

There are flaws that go along with using option volume data as a predictive indicator for the overall market. A major one is the ability to create a bullish payout using all put options. In this case, put option volume would increase due to a bullish outlook. Selling call options to increase income in a portfolio due to the market or a stock appearing overbought to a trader is a situation where a neutral to slightly bearish outlook may prompt an increase in call volume. However, in general the put-call ratio has held up as a market indicator for some time.

The CBOE publishes a variety of put-call ratios going back as far back as 1995. Table 28.10 is a table of put-call ratios that are calculated by the CBOE along with their respective descriptions.

Due to the longevity of available and consistent data, the CBOE Equity Put-Call Ratio is the most commonly quoted version of a put-call ratio. Historical data going back to 1995 on some of these ratios are available for free from the CBOE at www.cboe.com/data/putcallratio.aspx.

TABLE 28.10	Put-Call Ratios Calculated and Published by the CBOE
Ratio	Description
Index put-call ratio	Ratio of all index option volume
Equity put-call ratio	Ratio of equity option volume
S&P 500 index put-call ratio	Ratio of S&P 500 index option volume
VIX put-call ratio	Ratio of VIX option volume
Total exchange put-call ratio	Ratio of all exchange option volume

Figure 28.8 is a typical put-call ratio chart depicting the ratio over a 10-month period in 2010. This chart is fairly normal, with the ratio oscillating around the 0.6 range. A reading of 0.6 would indicate that for every 10 call contracts traded there were 6 put contracts. Generally, call volume is higher than put volume. The exception to this occurs during periods of increased concern regarding the equity markets. When there is increased worry in the market regarding the direction of stocks, usually the result is higher than normal put volume relative to call volume.

A put-call ratio developed using option volume data from the VIX option marketplace is an interesting approach to this indicator. Activity in the VIX option market has increased tremendously over the past few years. A good portion of this trading is by institutions using VIX call options as a hedge against a bearish move in the equity market. The leverage provided by out of the money VIX call options can be tremendous in a bear market. Using VIX options as a portfolio hedge is discussed in the next chapter. Also, a study of the usefulness of out of the money VIX call options during the bear market of 2008 is discussed.

VIX call volume would be expected to increase when institutions are most concerned about bearishness in the equity market. Therefore, an indicator developed with VIX put and call volume would be viewed inversely to a traditional equity put-call ratio. That is, increased call volume would indicate market bearishness as

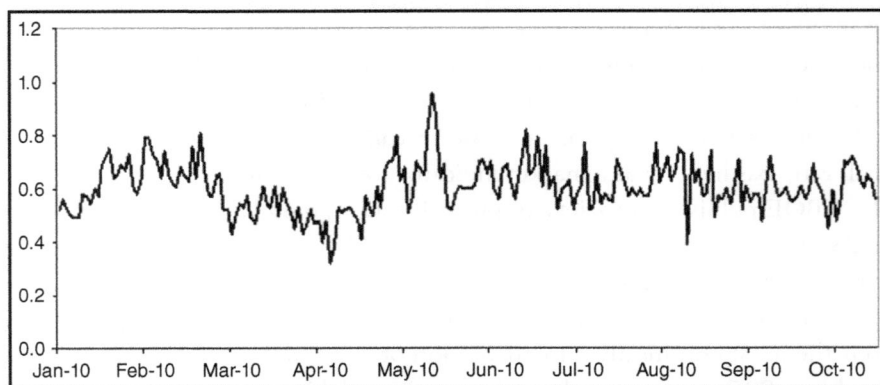

FIGURE 28.8 Chart of the CBOE Equity Put-Call Ratio.

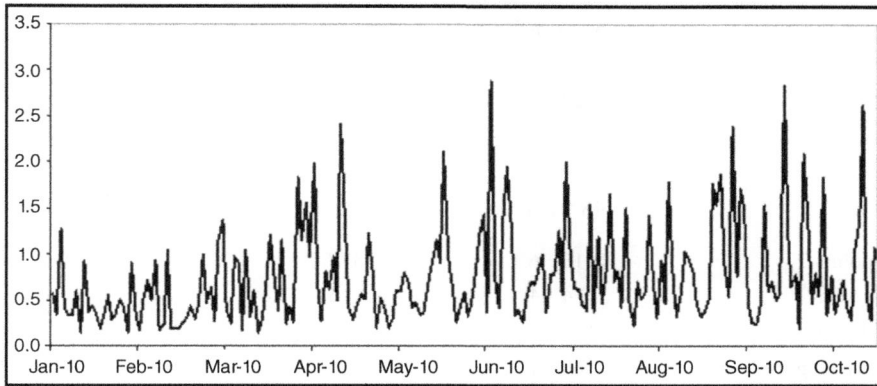

FIGURE 28.9 Chart of the VIX Index Put-Call Ratio.

opposed to an increase in equity put volume, which may be considered an indication of excessive bearishness.

Figure 28.9 is a chart of the VIX put-call ratio for January 2010 through October 2010. This is the same period covered by the previous chart of the equity put-call ratio. Note that there is a much wider range of readings for the VIX put-call ratio. Being based on a single product, especially one that experiences an abundance of very large institutional orders, results in this increase in the day-to-day volatility of this indicator. Specifically, the high for this ratio was 3.87 and the low was 0.02; a much wider range than was seen for the put-call ratio based on equity option volume. One interesting side note is that the average put-call ratio based on VIX option volume did result in 0.58, which is very close to the average for the equity option putcall ratio.

Another cause of some of the extreme moves in this specific put-call ratio results from low-volume days that can occur in the VIX option arena. Table 28.11 is a summary of VIX index option volume by year from 2007 to late 2010. Note the average volume has steadily increased and been pretty strong. However, there are days when the low end of the spectrum can skew these results. In order to adjust for this, when testing a trading system, a slight modification was applied to adjust for low-volume days.

The approach to using a VIX-related put-call ratio involves using the ratio to indicate that professionals anticipate bearishness in the marketplace. Increased VIX index call volume relative to VIX index put volume would be a sign that VIX option traders anticipate weakness in the overall stock market. With this specific use of VIX call

TABLE 28.11 Average Daily VIX Option Volume Statistics

	2007	2008	2009	2010
Maximum volume	361,120	426,661	717,330	605,235
Minimum volume	5,822	6,701	13,661	58,161
Average volume	104,668	102,560	132,732	240,237

Figure	Long Trades	Short Trades	Total Trades
Trades	229	100	329
Winners	112	59	171
Win %	48.91%	59.00%	51.98%
Total points	1015.96	377.47	1393.43
Average trade	4.44	3.77	4.24
Biggest winning trade	118.05	88.09	118.05
Biggest losing trade	−60.79	−56.92	−60.79

options in mind, the displayed system will take only a short position on the S&P 500 based on a signal from the VIX put-call ratio. A long version is included, but the short system seems to have more validity than the long version. The long S&P 500 system also screens out days with volume below 75,000 contracts on the day and takes a long position in the S&P 500 for three days if the VIX put-call ratio closes above 1.00 on a day. This rule was added to eliminate those days when low trading volume would result in a signal that may be less than valid based on the fundamental concept.

As with all systems shown in this chapter, the rules behind this test are simple. If the VIX put-call ratio is under .33, indicating three times as much VIX call volume as VIX put volume, then a short position is taken in the S&P 500. This position would be held for three days from close to close. Table 28.12 is a summary of applying this system to short and long S&P 500 positions.

Note there are many more signals using the short system based on excessive VIX call volume relative to the signals created by more put than call volume. Also the short signal is based on three times the amount of calls traded than the number of puts, while the long version takes a position on days when the put volume just exceeds call volume.

Combining these systems would result in a gain of almost 1,400 S&P 500 points over 46 months. This gain in the S&P 500 from January 2007 to October 2010 is a stark contrast to a basically flat performance from the S&P 500 index over the same period.

Some concerns regarding this method would include the significant losses incurred from the biggest losing trades for both the long and short systems as well as the relatively low winning percentage of around 50%. However, this is just a single indicator that may be improved on through adding other analysis or even just using judgment when initiating trades.

Each of the methods for using the VIX as an indicator shows promise. The ideas in this chapter are meant to provide a basis for further work on the VIX as an indicator. Again, these methods of using the VIX or VIX trading vehicles to predict the direction of the stock market should be used in conjunction with other analysis or indicators. For example, combining a moving average or other indicator specific to the S&P 500 index with a VIX-related indicator is more successful than using a VIX-related indicator alone to develop an opinion on the overall market.

CHAPTER 29

Hedging with VIX Derivatives

From Russell Rhoads, *Trading VIX Derivatives: Trading and Hedging Strategies Using VIX Futures, Options, and Exchange Traded Notes* (Hoboken, New Jersey: John Wiley & Sons, 2007), Chapter 10.

Learning Objective Statements

- Identify the subcomponents of portfolio volatility
- Explain how portfolio volatility may be affected by diversification

The VIX futures and index option markets have experienced tremendous volume growth over the past few years. This has come as a result of institutions accepting volatility as an asset class. Both of these instruments are used as hedges against a drop in stock prices. This use of VIX derivatives comes into play due to the inverse relationship between market implied volatility and the direction of stocks. The performance of these trading vehicles during the bear market of late 2008 and early 2009 solidified their place as a legitimate method of portfolio diversification and hedging.

Although volatility-related trading vehicles continue to be introduced, the two most commonly used hedging vehicles are VIX index options and futures. The main focus of this chapter is how VIX index options and futures are used to hedge equity portfolios. In addition, this chapter covers how these products can be used in place of S&P 500 index options. Also, there is a study of how a consistent mix of VIX futures and long stock would have performed over the past few years. The end of this chapter touches on an academic study that looks at the use of VIX options and futures during a period of market weakness.

Hedging with VIX Options

The first two tables in this chapter depict open interest for S&P 500 index options and VIX index options. The S&P 500 option open interest is heavily weighted toward at the money contracts, while the VIX index options have the greatest open interest at strikes that are out of the money.

TABLE 29.1	**Dec S&P 500 Index Put Option Open Interest, Late November 2010**

Strike	Open Interest
800	133,159
825	32,240
850	83,403
875	43,693
900	191,613
925	68,617
950	163,341
975	93,561
1,000	207,753
1,025	110,481
1,050	125,175
1,075	110,834
1,100	236,583
1,125	120,129
1,150	**202,102**
1,175	**129,873**
1,200	**203,041**
1,225	18,743
1,250	25,772
1,275	1,683
1,300	48,269

Table 29.1 shows the open interest of S&P 500 index put options expiring in December 2010. This open interest was compiled in late November 2010 with the S&P 500 index closing at 1,170.

Two of the four put options that have open interest in excess of 200,000 contracts have strike prices very close to where the S&P 500 index is currently quoted. Contracts that have a strike very close to the underlying security price are referred to as being at the money. Higher open interest around the at the money contracts is typical of most option series, whether index, equity, or exchange-traded fund. Stated another way, the closer the strike price to the price of an underlying, the higher the open interest would be expected to be. In addition, the at the money option contracts are usually the most actively traded along with having the highest open interest.

The three strikes that are closest to the S&P 500 index level of 1,170 are highlighted in this table. There are levels of high open interest at other lower strike prices. Quickly checking the previous nine months' price history of the S&P 500 index resulted in a low of just over 1,000 and a high of around 1,200. Using that range of trading, any strike between 1,000 and 1,200 would be considered at the money at some time over the life of these option contracts.

Table 29.2 shows the open interest of VIX index call options expiring in December 2010 using data from the same date in late November of that year. The closing price for the VIX index on this date was 20.63 and the corresponding December VIX future contract

TABLE 29.2 **Dec VIX Index Call Option Open Interest, Late November 2010**

Strike	Open Interest	Strike	Open Interest
10.00	9,986	32.50	65,002
15.00	889	35.00	56,102
16.00	3,346	37.50	95,454
17.00	700	40.00	119,706
18.00	14,431	42.50	29,516
19.00	2,260	45.00	54,966
20.00	24,959	47.50	4,054
21.00	**35,115**	50.00	28,452
22.50	**61,854**	55.00	37,997
24.00	**19,361**	60.00	15,486
25.00	64,395	65.00	6,729
26.00	26,390	70.00	2,695
27.50	102,904	75.00	2,222
29.00	19,915	80.00	813
30.00	122,175		

had a closing price of 20.75. With a quick review of the table, an interesting observation can be made regarding the call option strikes that have the highest open interest.

The December 2010 30 Call has the highest open interest, followed closely by the 40 Call and the 27.50 Call. In fact, using the assumption that the VIX Dec 21 Call is the at the money option, there are eight further out of the money option contracts that have higher contract open interest than the at the money contract. This case of the open interest being highest at out of the money call strike prices is common and unique to VIX options.

The highest level for the December 2010 VIX future contract was 34.10. Therefore all strikes above 35.00 were never at the money contracts. The December VIX 40 Call with an open interest of almost 120,000 contracts was almost 6 points out of the money with the VIX futures at their peak. Considering this contract in another light, the call was almost 15% out of the money at the peak of the underlying contract. When this table was created, the 40 Call was almost 100% out of the money.

The reason behind high open interest for VIX index option contracts that are 10 to 20 points out of the money emanates from how investors have started to use VIX options for hedging. Many institutions will buy out of the money VIX calls as a version of disaster insurance on the overall equity market. The expectation is that the VIX index and futures contracts will rally in a magnitude that is in excess of the movement to the downside that would occur in the S&P 500 index.

In times of market turbulence, the VIX index often rallies in a magnitude that is many times that of the drop of the S&P 500 index. An excellent example of this occurred during the market turbulence in 2008. Table 29.3 compares the performance of the VIX index and futures contracts to that of the S&P 500 index.

On November 20, 2008, the S&P 500 index closed at 752.44. This closing price represented a loss of about 40% from the closing price of 1,260.31 on

	8/1/2008	11/20/2008	Change	% Change
S&P 500	1261.31	752.44	−508.87	−40%
VIX Index	22.57	80.86	+58.29	+258%
VIX Future	21.44	76.81	+55.37	+258%

August 1, 2008. Over the same period, both the VIX index and front month VIX futures markets gained over 250%. The expectation that a large equity market drop would be accompanied by a much larger rally in the VIX is behind the increased institutional use of out of the money VIX call options. By purchasing these calls, institutions may obtain cheap protection against a dramatic loss in the equity market. Based on the magnitude of the drawdown in stock prices, buying VIX calls may end up being a more attractive method of hedging relative to buying S&P 500 index put options.

In 2009 a study by Edward Szado of the University of Massachusetts analyzed the financial market activity in the last four months of 2008. A variety of model portfolios were combined with different weightings attributed to VIX derivatives. One conclusion of this study was how the use of VIX call options in this manner can provide superior hedging results to traditional hedging strategies. The specifics of this study will be discussed later in this chapter.

A couple of unique difficulties arise regarding using out of the money VIX call options to hedge an equity portfolio. What strike to choose would be an initial consideration with how many to purchase being a secondary concern.

Any option purchase or hedging strategy should begin with a price opinion on the underlying security. In this case, although VIX call options are being considered for purchase, the purchase is based on concern regarding the direction of the level of the S&P 500 index. An arbitrary 2.5% down move in the S&P 500 index on a single day will be the definition of a bearish day. Between 2007 and 2010 there have been 50 days where the S&P 500 index dropped more than 2.5% on a single day. Taking the days that the S&P 500 has dropped by 2.5% or more, the average move higher for the VIX index has been around 15%. The front month future contract has averaged a 9% move higher based on a drop of 2.5% or more in the S&P 500 index. Looking at even more bearish days of down 5% does not change the outcome, as the VIX index rallies on average 17.5% and the VIX futures increase on average about 11%. Although the index may be a more dramatic number, the future price has more significance as the option contracts are priced off this contract.

As a hypothetical exercise, on Friday, December 18, 2010, the S&P 500 index closed at 1,244, the VIX index closed at 16.11, and the January VIX future contract closed at 20.20. If there is concern regarding a 2.5% to 5% drop on Monday of the following week, the S&P 500 index put options from Table 29.4 might be considered to hedge an equity portfolio.

To hedge a $500,000 S&P 500 index portfolio, approximately four at the money SPX 1,245 put contracts would be purchased. The number of option contracts is

TABLE 29.4	December 31, 2010, SPX Put Option Quotes	
Put Contract	Bid	Ask
SPX 1160	0.65	1.20
SPX 1165	0.75	1.30
SPX 1170	0.95	1.40
SPX 1175	1.00	1.50
SPX 1180	1.35	1.65
SPX 1185	1.40	1.85
SPX 1190	1.45	2.20
SPX 1195	1.65	2.50
SPX 1200	2.00	2.70
SPX 1205	2.35	3.30
SPX 1210	2.85	3.80
SPX 1215	3.50	4.50
SPX 1220	4.20	5.40
SPX 1225	5.30	6.40
SPX 1230	6.80	7.70
SPX 1235	7.90	9.50
SPX 1240	10.00	11.10
SPX 1245	11.80	13.50

determined by dividing the dollar amount of the portfolio by the current index level times 100. As an equation, it would look like this:

$$\$500,000/(\$100 \times 1,244) = 4.02(4 \text{ contracts})$$

The hedging transaction would be a cost of $5,400, determined by purchasing four contracts at 13.50 each ($1,350). This amount comes to approximately 1% of the value of the portfolio. However, if the plan is to hedge for only a day so the cost can be estimated through estimating the price, the contract may be sold the following day if the S&P 500 index closed unchanged. All else staying the same, the SPX 1,245 Put could be sold the following day at 11.25, resulting in a loss of $900 (13.50 − 11.25 × 4 × 100). This change in price is due to the width of the bid-ask spread along with the impact of the passage of one day of time value.

Table 29.5 applies the cost of hedging for a day to a variety of S&P 500 put options. These dollar amounts may be considered the per contract one-day cost of hedging a portfolio against a drop in the S&P 500, but again the protection gained varies by strike. Table 29.6 shows the results of a 2.5% drop and resulting gain or loss by applying the full $5,400 to a variety of put option contracts. The result is a great number of contracts at lower strike price. Even though more puts may be purchased at lower strike prices, there is not an improvement protection received based on this 2.5% estimated price move. The best protection actually comes from the 1,245 strike contract.

TABLE 29.5 Cost of Hedging Based on One-Day Hold

Put Contract	Cost	Bid Next Day	Cost	$ Cost
SPX 1160	1.20	0.45	−0.75	$300
SPX 1165	1.30	0.55	−0.75	$300
SPX 1170	1.40	0.60	−0.80	$320
SPX 1175	1.50	0.75	−0.75	$300
SPX 1180	1.65	0.85	−0.80	$320
SPX 1185	1.85	1.00	−0.85	$340
SPX 1190	2.20	1.20	−1.00	$300
SPX 1195	2.50	1.40	−1.10	$440
SPX 1200	2.70	1.60	−1.10	$440
SPX 1205	3.30	1.95	−1.35	$540
SPX 1210	3.80	2.40	−1.40	$560
SPX 1215	4.50	3.05	−1.45	$580
SPX 1220	5.40	3.80	−1.60	$640
SPX 1225	6.40	4.80	−1.60	$640
SPX 1230	7.70	6.10	−1.60	$640
SPX 1235	9.50	7.60	−1.90	$760
SPX 1240	11.10	9.40	−1.70	$680
SPX 1245	13.50	11.25	−2.25	$900

TABLE 29.6 Hedged S&P 500 Portfolio Performance with 2.5% Drop in S&P 500 Index

Put Contract	Cost	Bid	Profit	% Profit	Puts	$ Profit	S&P Portfolio Loss	Net Gain/ Loss	% Port Gain/ Loss
SPX 1160	1.20	3.20	2.00	167	12	2,400	−12,500	−10,100	−2.02
SPX 1165	1.30	3.70	2.40	185	12	2,880	−12,500	−9,620	−1.92
SPX 1170	1.40	4.40	3.00	214	12	3,600	−12,500	−8,900	−1.78
SPX 1175	1.50	4.85	3.35	223	12	4,020	−12,500	−8,480	−1.70
SPX 1180	1.65	5.90	4.25	258	11	4,675	−12,500	−7,825	−1.57
SPX 1185	1.85	6.40	4.55	246	10	4,550	−12,500	−7,950	−1.59
SPX 1190	2.20	7.00	4.80	218	9	4,320	−12,500	−8,180	−1.64
SPX 1195	2.50	7.90	5.40	216	8	4,320	−12,500	−8,180	−1.64
SPX 1200	2.70	9.25	6.55	243	8	5,240	−12,500	−7,260	−1.45
SPX 1205	3.30	10.60	7.30	221	6	4,380	−12,500	−8,120	−1.62
SPX 1210	3.80	12.40	8.60	226	6	5,160	−12,500	−7,340	−1.47
SPX 1215	4.50	14.50	10.00	222	6	6,000	−12,500	−6,500	−1.30
SPX 1220	5.40	16.80	11.40	211	5	5,700	−12,500	−6,800	−1.36
SPX 1225	6.40	19.70	13.30	208	5	6,650	−12,500	−5,850	−1.17
SPX 1230	7.70	23.00	15.30	199	5	7,650	−12,500	−4,850	−0.97
SPX 1235	9.50	26.00	16.50	174	5	8,250	−12,500	−4,250	−0.85
SPX 1240	11.10	29.95	18.85	170	4	7,540	−12,500	−4,960	−0.99
SPX 1245	13.50	36.00	22.50	167	4	9,000	−12,500	−3,500	−0.70

TABLE 29.7 Hedged S&P 500 Portfolio Performance with 5% Drop in S&P 500 Index

Put Contract	Cost	Bid	Profit	% Profit	Puts	$ Profit	S&P Portfolio Loss	Net Gain/ Loss	% Port
SPX 1160	1.20	9.70	8.50	708	12	10,200	−25,000	−14,800	−2.96
SPX 1165	1.30	11.05	9.75	750	12	11,700	−25,000	−13,300	−2.66
SPX 1170	1.40	12.80	11.40	814	12	13,680	−25,000	−11,320	−2.26
SPX 1175	1.50	14.10	12.60	840	12	15,120	−25,000	−9,880	−1.98
SPX 1180	1.65	16.45	14.80	897	11	16,280	−25,000	−8,720	−1.74
SPX 1185	1.85	18.00	16.15	873	10	16,150	−25,000	−8,850	−1.77
SPX 1190	2.20	19.85	17.65	802	9	15,885	−25,000	−9,115	−1.82
SPX 1195	2.50	22.25	19.75	790	8	15,800	−25,000	−9,200	−1.84
SPX 1200	2.70	25.15	22.45	831	8	17,960	−25,000	−7,040	−1.41
SPX 1205	3.30	28.20	24.90	755	6	14,940	−25,000	−10,060	−2.01
SPX 1210	3.80	31.70	27.90	734	6	16,740	−25,000	−8,260	−1.65
SPX 1215	4.50	35.50	31.00	689	6	18,600	−25,000	−6,400	−1.28
SPX 1220	5.40	39.50	34.10	631	5	17,050	−25,000	−7,950	−1.59
SPX 1225	6.40	43.85	37.45	585	5	18,725	−25,000	−6,275	−1.26
SPX 1230	7.70	48.45	40.75	529	5	20,375	−25,000	−4,625	−0.93
SPX 1235	9.50	53.50	44.00	463	5	22,000	−25,000	−3,000	−0.60
SPX 1240	11.10	57.75	46.65	420	4	18,660	−25,000	−6,340	−1.27
SPX 1245	13.50	62.70	49.20	364	4	19,680	−25,000	−5,320	−1.06

Table 29.7 shows the results of using the same number of option contracts, but looking at the portfolio results of a 5% drop in the stock market. With a more dramatic drop in the stock market, the 1,235 strike put is the best choice with the portfolio losing only 0.60% of value instead of losing 5% for the portfolio that was not hedged.

An alternative to hedging with S&P 500 put options would be to purchase January 2011 VIX calls. VIX call option choices appear in Table 29.8. For a quick comparison using the at the money VIX call options a couple of methods are

TABLE 29.8 January VIX Call Option Quotes

VIX Call	Bid	Ask
Jan 20.00	2.00	2.10
Jan 21.00	1.60	1.80
Jan 22.50	1.30	1.40
Jan 24.00	1.00	1.10
Jan 25.00	0.90	0.95
Jan 26.00	0.75	0.85
Jan 27.50	0.60	0.70
Jan 30.00	0.50	0.55
Jan 32.50	0.35	0.40
Jan 35.00	0.25	0.30

TABLE 29.9	Cost of Hedging with Various VIX Calls Based on One-Day Hold				
VIX Call	Ask	Next Day Bid	Cost	% Cost	Contracts
Jan 20.00	2.10	1.95	−0.15	−7	60
Jan 21.00	1.70	1.55	−0.15	−9	60
Jan 22.50	1.40	1.25	−0.15	−11	60
Jan 24.00	1.10	0.95	−0.15	−14	60
Jan 25.00	1.00	0.85	−0.15	−15	60
Jan 26.00	0.85	0.70	−0.15	−18	60
Jan 27.50	0.70	0.55	−0.15	−21	60
Jan 30.00	0.55	0.45	−0.10	−18	90
Jan 32.50	0.40	0.30	−0.10	−25	90
Jan 35.00	0.30	0.20	−0.10	−33	90

available for a direct comparison with the cost of hedging for a single day using at the money SPX put options. First, the one-day dollar amount of protection using the at the money 1,245 strike put contracts was estimated at $900. Using this as the one-day cost of hedging could result in determining how many VIX call options may be purchased in place of buying S&P 500 put contracts. A one-day passage of time would lower the bid price of the VIX Jan 20.00 Call to 1.95. Using $900 as the willing cost of the hedge along with an expected loss of 0.15 over the course of the passage of a day results in the formula:

$$\$900/(\$100 \times 0.15) = 60 \text{ contracts}$$

The result is if $900 is the cost of hedging, 60 of the VIX Jan 20.00 Call options could be purchased with the same expectation for a loss.

Depending on the contract and cost associated with the spread and the passage of a day, either 60 or 90 VIX Calls may be purchased as a hedge against a drop in the S&P 500. These potential weightings appear in Table 29.9.

The results for using a variety of long call positions appear in Table 29.10. The actual result is pretty similar protection that is offered by S&P 500 index option contracts. A portfolio loss of just over 1% is realized using the Jan 20.00 Calls for a single-day hold.

When traders or portfolio managers are concerned about potential portfolio losses, but not willing to pay the option premium for protection, there is a viable alternative. This alternative is known as a collar. A traditional collar consists of buying a put for protection and funding the cost of this protection by selling a call option. The result would be protection against a downside move, but it would sacrifice profits if there were a bullish move out of the underlying.

For example, 100 shares of XYZ stock are owned at 37.50. With concern regarding a bearish move out of XYZ in the next 30 days, purchasing a put option is considered. A 35 strike put is trading at 2.00, which may be considered a bit expensive by the trader. However, a 30-day 40 strike call is also trading at 2.00. To gain protection, a trader may sell the 40 strike call and purchase the 35 strike put for no cost. No cost

TABLE 29.10   Outcome of 10% Rise in VIX

VIX Call	Cost	Bid	Profit	% Profit	Calls	$ Profit	S&P Portfolio Loss	Net Gain/ Loss	% Port
Jan 20.00	2.10	3.25	1.15	55	60	6900	−12,500	−5,600	−1.12
Jan 21.00	1.70	2.65	0.95	56	60	5700	−12,500	−6,800	−1.36
Jan 22.50	1.40	2.15	0.75	54	60	4500	−12,500	−8,000	−1.60
Jan 24.00	1.10	1.70	0.60	55	60	3600	−12,500	−8,900	−1.78
Jan 25.00	1.00	1.52	0.52	52	60	3120	−12,500	−9,380	−1.88
Jan 26.00	0.85	1.28	0.43	51	60	2580	−12,500	−9,920	−1.98
Jan 27.50	0.70	1.05	0.35	50	60	2100	−12,500	−10,400	−2.08
Jan 30.00	0.55	0.85	0.30	55	90	2700	−12,500	−9,800	−1.96
Jan 32.50	0.40	0.60	0.20	50	90	1800	−12,500	−10,700	−2.14
Jan 35.00	0.30	0.40	0.10	33	90	900	−12,500	−11,600	−2.32

is the result of taking in 2.00 on the call and paying 2.00 for the put. For the next 30 days the trader now has protection below 35.00 for XYZ but also has sacrificed upside over 40.00 on XYZ.

Using VIX options as a collar would involve selling a put to fund a call. If the collar is initiated to protect against a downside move in the overall stock market, then the position should be set up to benefit from a rise in the VIX. The long call should increase in value, while the short put should lose value in a case of a rising VIX based on a drop in the market.

On November 9, 2010, the November VIX futures contract was trading at 18.90 and the spot VIX index was at 19.08. If there were concern over a drop in the S&P 500 over the next week and a feeling that the market would not rise dramatically over the same period, a collar may be considered using VIX options. Some of the November VIX option quotes appear in Table 29.11.

With the S&P 500 index at 1,213.40, a portfolio manager is concerned about a drop in the index over the next week. He checks the markets and sees an opportunity to place a favorable hedge using VIX options. A collar that would expire in seven days could be initiated by purchasing a November 20.00 Call at 0.60 and selling the November 19.00 Put for 0.85. The result is actually a credit of 0.25. As a bonus for this position, as the VIX index is currently trading at 19.08, if the VIX is unchanged

TABLE 29.11   VIX November Option Quotes, November 9, 2010

Call	Bid	Ask	Put	Bid	Ask
Nov 18.00	1.25	1.35	Nov 18.00	0.35	0.45
Nov 19.00	0.75	0.85	Nov 19.00	0.85	1.00
Nov 20.00	0.50	0.60	Nov 20.00	1.55	1.70
Nov 21.00	0.35	0.40	Nov 21.00	2.40	2.55
Nov 22.50	0.20	0.25	Nov 22.50	3.70	4.00

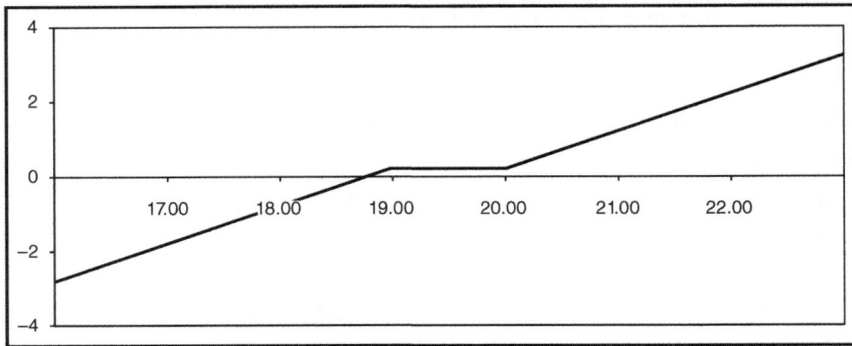

FIGURE 29.1 VIX Collar Payout at November Expiration

at expiration this trade would actually yield a small profit. In fact, at any price above 18.75 this collar there would be a profititable trade. This is shown in the payout diagram in Figure 29.1.

Remember, this position is initiated in conjunction with long exposure to the S&P 500. Below 18.75 on the VIX, there would be losses incurred for the option spread, but there should be S&P 500 gains associated with those losses.

November VIX expiration came in at 22.21, so the portfolio manager was correct in his short-term outlook for the overall market. The profit on this trade would be 2.46, or $246 per contract. At the same time, the S&P 500 came under pressure, dropping about 3% to 1,178.34.

The hedging decision would start with an outlook for the overall stock market. After establishing this outlook, the cost of VIX calls relative to S&P 500 index put options hedging would need to be analyzed. There may be times when VIX calls are a favorable method for hedging market exposure, especially in situations where a dramatic drop in the overall market is feared.

▣ Hedging with Vix Futures

VIX futures may also benefit from periods of equity market bearishness and a subsequent rally in volatility. However, a consistent hedging program with front month VIX futures contracts would be costly and the result would be a benefit in bearish market environments, underperformance in bullish markets, and an overall underperformance versus a pure long portfolio of stocks. This underperformance would be a result of how VIX futures contract prices gravitate to the index over time. Using the front two month VIX futures as opposed to just the front month contract will avoid this constant gravitation to the index by the front month.

Table 29.12 shows the return based on holding a portfolio that matches the performance of the S&P 500 index monthly from 2007 to 2010. This will be representative of a buy-and-hold portfolio. The next table shows the performance of a portfolio with weightings in the front two-month futures contracts.

TABLE 29.12	Monthly S&P 500 Index Returns			
	2007	2008	2009	2010
Jan	1.41%	−6.12%	−8.57%	−3.70%
Feb	−2.18%	−3.48%	−10.99%	2.85%
Mar	1.00%	−0.60%	8.54%	5.88%
Apr	4.33%	4.75%	9.39%	1.48%
May	3.25%	1.07%	5.31%	−8.20%
Jun	−1.78%	−8.60%	0.02%	−5.39%
Jul	−3.20%	−0.99%	7.41%	6.88%
Aug	1.29%	1.22%	3.36%	−4.74%
Sep	3.58%	−9.08%	3.57%	8.76%
Oct	1.48%	−16.94%	−1.98%	3.69%
Nov	−4.40%	−7.48%	5.74%	−0.23%
Dec	−0.86%	0.78%	1.78%	6.53%
Annual	**3.53%**	**−38.49%**	**23.45%**	**13.27%**

Table 29.13 is a return calculation based on holding a continuously rebalanced portfolio representing the next two expiring VIX futures contracts. This return is based on there being no rebalancing costs associated with this portfolio. To replicate this performance, trading would occur every day. Note the strong performance of this strategy in 2007 and 2008 and then the resulting dropoff over the latter two years.

Table 29.14 assumes a portfolio with 90% exposure to the S&P 500 combined with 10% exposure to the VIX futures portfolio. Note the outperformance in 2007 and 2008 with underperformance in 2009 and 2010. This relative performance can be attributed to an uptrend in volatility through 2007 and 2008 and basically a downtrending to flat volatility market in 2009 and 2010.

TABLE 29.13	Monthly VIX Futures Portfolio Returns			
	2007	2008	2009	2010
Jan	−5.73%	5.89%	0.51%	0.54%
Feb	10.89%	3.54%	2.70%	−9.42%
Mar	6.49%	−0.19%	0.21%	−10.34%
Apr	−4.45%	−16.55%	−16.19%	10.74%
May	2.24%	−3.42%	−15.53%	37.31%
Jun	14.81%	13.36%	−7.44%	9.59%
Jul	28.05%	−4.51%	0.58%	−18.40%
Aug	10.86%	−0.84%	4.78%	10.17%
Sep	−14.61%	27.25%	−9.74%	−10.29%
Oct	1.90%	63.87%	0.83%	−13.94%
Nov	21.81%	8.11%	−4.24%	6.05%
Dec	−1.40%	−16.64%	−5.69%	−22.50%
Annual	**85.20%**	**77.90%**	**−41.29%**	**−22.81%**

TABLE 29.14 Monthly 90% S&P 500 + 10% VIX Portfolio Performance

	2007	2008	2009	2010
Jan	0.69%	−4.92%	−7.66%	−3.27%
Feb	−0.88%	−2.77%	−9.62%	1.62%
Mar	1.55%	−0.56%	7.71%	4.26%
Apr	3.45%	2.62%	6.83%	2.40%
May	3.15%	0.62%	3.22%	−3.65%
Jun	−0.12%	−6.40%	−0.73%	−3.89%
Jul	−0.07%	−1.34%	6.73%	4.35%
Aug	2.24%	1.01%	3.50%	−3.25%
Sep	1.76%	−5.45%	2.24%	6.85%
Oct	1.52%	−8.86%	−1.70%	1.92%
Nov	−1.78%	−5.93%	4.74%	0.40%
Dec	−0.92%	−0.96%	1.03%	3.63%
Annual	**11.70%**	**−26.85%**	**16.98%**	**11.16%**

For a final and possibly better comparison, the next two tables display the result of investing $10,000 in either the balanced portfolio or purely in an S&P 500 index portfolio. Table 29.15 shows the result of $10,000 invested in the S&P 500 and compounded monthly.

Ten thousand dollars invested in the S&P 500 at the end of 2006 and held through the end of 2010 would result in a portfolio worth $8,867. This is based on the index return and not total returns that may be earned if dividends were also received.

The result from the combined portfolio with exposure to VIX has superior results to the S&P 500 portfolio. Table 29.16 shows the result of 90% of a portfolio invested in the S&P 500 and 10% of a portfolio with exposure to the balanced VIX future strategy.

TABLE 29.15 Performance of $10,000 Invested in the S&P 500 Index Compounded Monthly

	2007	2008	2009	2010
Jan	$10,141	$9,720	$5,823	$7,572
Feb	$9,919	$9,382	$5,183	$7,787
Mar	$10,018	$9,326	$5,626	$8,245
Apr	$10,452	$9,769	$6,154	$8,367
May	$10,792	$9,874	$6,481	$7,681
Jun	$10,600	$9,025	$6,482	$7,267
Jul	$10,261	$8,936	$6,962	$7,767
Aug	$10,393	$9,045	$7,196	$7,399
Sep	$10,765	$8,224	$7,453	$8,046
Oct	$10,924	$6,830	$7,306	$8,343
Nov	$10,443	$6,319	$7,725	$8,324
Dec	$10,353	$6,369	$7,862	$8,867

TABLE 29.16	Performance of $10,000 with 90% Exposure to the S&P 500 Index and 10% in VIX Futures Compounded Monthly			
	2007	2008	2009	2010
Jan	$10,069	$10,551	$7,285	$8,822
Feb	$9,981	$10,258	$6,584	$8,966
Mar	$10,135	$10,201	$7,091	$9,347
Apr	$10,485	$10,469	$7,576	$9,572
May	$10,816	$10,533	$7,820	$9,223
Jun	$10,802	$9,859	$7,764	$8,864
Jul	$10,794	$9,727	$8,286	$9,250
Aug	$11,037	$9,826	$8,576	$8,949
Sep	$11,231	$9,291	$8,768	$9,562
Oct	$11,402	$8,467	$8,619	$9,746
Nov	$11,199	$7,966	$9,028	$9,784
Dec	$11,096	$7,889	$9,121	$10,139

As of the end of 2010, regular exposure to VIX futures does result in superior performance to the buy-and-hold S&P 500 index portfolio. Ten thousand dollars in the balanced portfolio would have held up better than the S&P 500, and at the end of 2010 it would have been worth $10,139, for a result of just above breakeven.

As the VIX and VIX futures have gone through periods of high and low levels, an approach that dynamically hedges based on some sort of indicator or market analysis may result in stronger outperformance. This outperformance may be achieved through increasing and decreasing exposure to volatility based on some systematic approach.

University of Massachusetts Study

After the market turmoil of 2008, a study was conducted at the University of Massachusetts–Amherst, to determine the potential benefits of VIX futures and options as hedging vehicles. The study, "VIX Futures and Options—A Case Study of Portfolio Diversification During the 2008 Financial Crisis," appeared in the *Journal of Alternative Investments*. (The full report and a two-page summary are available for download from the CBOE at www.cboe.com/Institutional/reports.aspx.)

The key question was whether these two VIX-related derivatives would have served as useful diversification tools during the financial crisis of 2008. Specifically, returns based on performance of assets from August 1, 2008, to December 31, 2008, were studied. Several traditionally constructed portfolios were analyzed with a variety of VIX derivative weightings added to the portfolio. The types of portfolios studied were 100% longonly equity portfolio, mixed portfolio with 60 % stocks and 40% bonds, and fully diversified portfolio with multiple asset classes. VIX weightings that were added to these standard portfolios included a long 2.5%

VIX futures weighting, a 10% long VIX futures weighting, 1% long at the money VIX calls, 3% long at the money VIX calls, 1% long out of the money VIX calls, and 3% long out of the money VIX calls. Out of the money calls were strikes that were 25% higher than the VIX index.

One interesting outcome involved the returns for the fully diversified portfolio when weightings of out of the money VIX call options were included. From August 1, 2008, to December 31, 2008, the fully diversified model portfolio lost 19.68% in value. Contributing 1% out of the money VIX calls to the portfolio resulted in a portfolio return of 17.70%. A 3% weighting of out of the money VIX calls resulted in a portfolio return of 97.18%. These results show the dramatic benefits of the leverage gained from out of the money VIX calls. This leverage resulted from the dramatic magnitude of the inverse relationship between the VIX index and the S&P 500 combined with the normal leverage that comes with using out of the money options.

Two findings were determined by the study. First, in a period of dramatic market losses, such as this four-month period in 2008, all financial assets tend to lose value, so a portfolio that is considered diversified may not hold up as well as anticipated. The second finding involves the use of volatility as a diversification tool. The result is that during a period of a market downturn, VIX diversification results in protection. However, over the long term, exposure to the VIX for diversification purposes may result in underperformance.

The growth of VIX option and futures contracts can be directly attributed to the use of these instruments to hedge an equity portfolio. A consistent program of hedging an equity portfolio with VIX instruments can result in underperformance of a portfolio. However, there are often instances when using VIX options or futures to hedge an equity portfolio would result in cheaper protection that would result in strong performance in the case of a dramatic loss in the equity market.

CHAPTER 30

Introduction to Candlestick Charts

From Thomas N. Bulkowski, *Encyclopedia of Candlestick Charts* (Hoboken, New Jersey: John Wiley & Sons, 2008), Introduction.

Learning Objective Statements

- Identify and interpret candlestick patterns
- Validate a forecast with candlestick patterns

The candlestick trade I'm about to describe made me enough money to pay for three months of living expenses. That's not bad for an hour's work! In a moment, I'll outline the trading setup so you can tailor it to your liking.

On May 16, 2007, I went shopping for a stock to buy and found one in the diversified chemicals aisle of the market. What caught my eye first was a consolidation pattern called a descending triangle. Figure 30.1 shows the chart pattern in May. Descending triangles have a flat bottom and a downwardsloping top. They break out downward 64% of the time, but upward breakouts can post spectacular results. I was looking for an upward breakout.

The next pattern I noticed was the Big W. A tall left side (C to A) leads to a reversal pattern, such as the Eve & Eve double bottom AB. Eve bottoms are wide, rounded turns, unlikeAdam bottoms,which are narrow, often pointed—a single spike or two wide. Eve can have spikes like that shown at B, but the spikes are shorter and more numerous than what you see on Adam. The Eve & Eve double bottom is one of the more powerful and successful chart patterns. The theory behind a Big W is that the right side will mimic the left and price will climb after that.

The pattern that sealed the deal was the morning doji star candlestick. That candle pattern ended the day that price closed above the top of the descending triangle. My research said that the morning doji star is a highly reliable candle formation. Combined with additional analysis I did on the company, both fundamental and technical, the stock was a buy only if it gapped open higher. Why? Because the next day the company was holding a conference call before the market opened to discuss earnings. A higher open would mean the market liked its story.

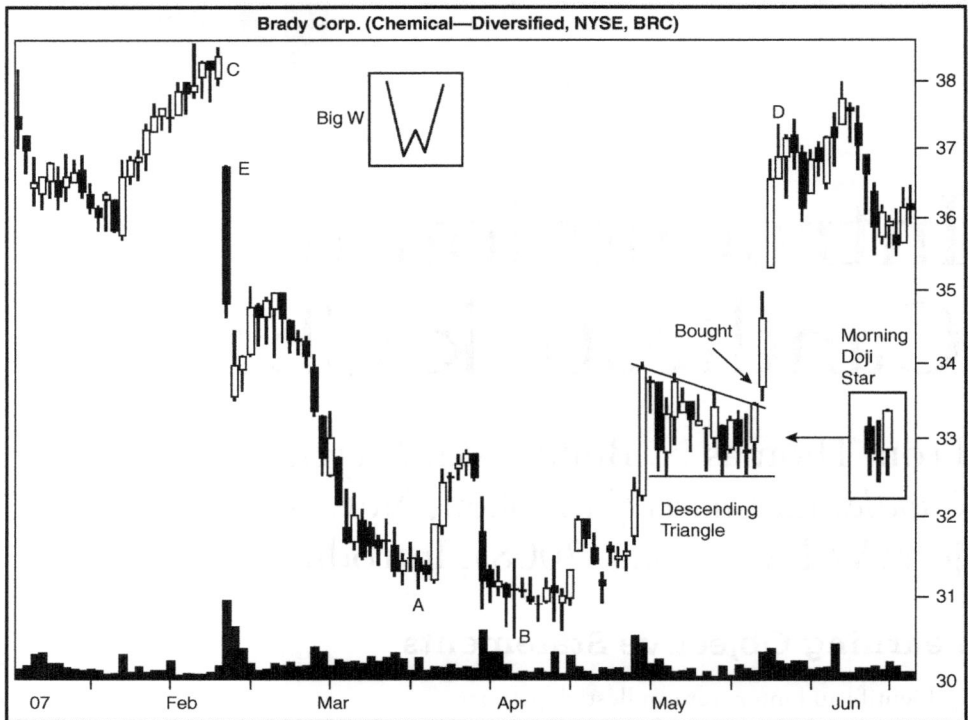

FIGURE 30.1 The Combination of a Descending Triangle, Big W, and Morning Doji Star Set Up a Profitable Trade.

The news reports the night before the meeting said that net profit was 53 cents versus 61 cents during the year-ago quarter even as revenue climbed by 30%. Just 1% of the revenue gain was from higher internal sales, though. Most was from acquisitions or currency translation. Analyst estimates ranged from $0.52 to $0.58, so earnings came in at the low end. All of this sounded bearish to me, but the technicals were shouting, "Buy!"

My candle research says that opening gap confirmation from a morning doji star results in the best performance. That means trading with the trend as soon as possible.

The next day, I watched the stock open and price took off. In the first minute, it shot from the prior close of 33.46 to 34. That left a tall white candle on the chart. Again, my research and knowledge of candles said that the body of a tall candle is often a support zone. So, I placed a buy order halfway down the body, at 33.78.

Sure enough, price turned down and nailed my buy order, filling most of it before moving up again. I had trouble fitting through the door because the smile on my face was so wide. Five minutes later, the remainder of the order filled.

By day's end, the stock had recovered and closed higher by 1.16. The next day a brokerage firm upgraded the stock and price moved higher still, this time up another 1.93. The following day price coasted upward 33 cents (D).

Exit time. Why? This is one of those situations where you get a feeling that it's time to leave, so I started my analysis. The height of the candle lines was diminishing, suggesting a trend change. The Commodity Channel Index (CCI, with default settings of 20 bars for the lookback and 5 for the DCCI line—dual CCI, a smoothing of the CCI), an indicator, was rounding over and looked as if the next day would produce a sell signal. In other words, upward price momentum was slowing. I didn't want to hang around and give back my profits.

The falling window from C to E I thought added to overhead resistance, but my research said that happens only 25% of the time. The candle pattern at D also resembled a shooting star, with a tall upper shadow and small body after an upward price trend. This one wasn't perfect, because the body was too tall in relation to the height of the upper shadow. If you have no idea what an upper shadow and a body are, don't worry about it. I'll explain them later.

The day after D, I vowed that if the stock opened lower, I would sell. I thought of selling it all at the open but the futures market suggested a higher open for equities, so I decided to wait and see.

Volume was thin in the stock but it opened lower, just as I expected. I timed the exit as best as I could and got out just before price plummeted. By the day's close, however, the stock had gained it all back and then some. The candle that printed on the chart was a hanging man. Despite their reputation as a reversal, they act as a continuation pattern 59% of the time. That suggested more upside. But it doesn't matter because I don't own the stock anymore.

If you want to replicate this trading setup, look for:

- *Good industry relative strength*. If the stocks in the industry are doing well, then the chances improve that this stock will do well, too.

- *Better than expected earnings*. Only price can tell you how much the market likes the results, so watch the stock after the announcement of earnings. If price gaps upward, buy immediately or wait for a retracement and then buy.

- *A reason to buy the stock from a technical or fundamental perspective*. Even if price does not explode higher at the open, it should do well in the coming weeks based on your analysis.

I used an upward breakout from a descending triangle with a morning doji star inside a Big W pattern. The combination worked well but will be almost impossible to duplicate.

What Are Candlesticks?

Let's talk about candlesticks, starting at the beginning so everyone comes up to speed at the same time. I'll be brief because most people know what candle charts are. Figure 30.2 shows two examples of candlesticks. The *line* (a single price bar) on the left is a white candle. This one shows the relative positions of the open, high, low, and close. Notice that the closing price is higher than the opening price. When that occurs, the body is white. On the right, the candle is black because price closed below the open. The upper shadow is hair growing from the top of the candle, and

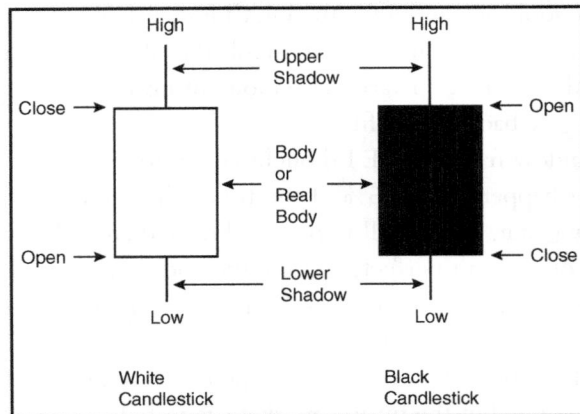

FIGURE 30.2 White and Black Candlestick Lines.

the lower shadow is a single leg dangling from the bottom of the candle. It may help to think of shadows as wicks.

Candles don't need either an upper or a lower shadow. They don't need a body, either (such as when the open and close are the same). The key concept to remember is that a black candle shows a close *below* the open and a white candle shows a close *above* the open. A black candle does not show price closing lower than the previous day, nor does a white candle show a higher close than the day before.

With this candle definition, you can have a stream of white candles in a declining price trend, and black candles forming a rising price trend. I've seen both situations, too.

That's all there is to candle configuration. Multiple candle lines along with variations in shadow and body length make up the many candle patterns.

■ The Data

I wrote a computer program to recognize all of the candlestick patterns in this book. With nearly five million candle lines to explore for *each* of over 100 candle patterns, doing it manually was not an option.

I created what I call the *standard database*, a collection of data that doesn't change in size. It contains the 500 stocks of the S&P 500 index for 10 years covering both bull and bear markets. From the standard database I derive the frequency rank and prorate the number of times a particular candlestick pattern is found to determine whether it appears more often in bull or bear markets.

If I find too few candles in the standard database, then I use up to three more databases, one containing archived stocks I no longer follow, one that is a five-year/500-stock database, and one that is the current database I use for trading. Together they comprise almost five million candle lines (price bars). I removed any duplicated candles between databases, and all four contain splitadjusted, clean data.

The Price Trend

Many candles have a defined price trend that leads to the start of the candle pattern. For example, a hanging man appears in an upward price trend, and a hammer appears in a downtrend.

How do you determine the trend? I use a 10-day exponential moving average as a starting point and season it with special rules to allow price trends of a day or two to override the result. The method is a bit complicated but it works well. It is, however, not perfect, but the large sample size I use helps compensate.

Candle Performance

How do you measure candle performance? Since candlestick patterns often lead to short-term moves, I used the closest minor high or low (swing high or swing low), depending on the breakout direction, to gauge performance. The straight-line move often isn't a long one, but it serves as a good proxy of what you can expect. The statistics in this book should be used to compare results from candle to candle, not as benchmarks of how well you will do trading candles.

Candles Post Breakout

How do you determine if a candle acts as a reversal or a continuation pattern? I tested three methods and checked the results visually using hundreds of candles. I chose the best method. Two were variations of an exponential moving average (the price trend) compared to the closing price over time. They were not as accurate or as simple as just looking for the breakout to determine reversal or continuation, success or failure.

An upward breakout occurs when price closes above the top (highest high) of the candle. A downward breakout occurs when price closes below the bottom (lowest low) of the candle. Marry the breakout direction with the price trend leading to the candle and you get either a reversal or a continuation of the prior trend. This is the same method I used with chart patterns. It's simple, it's repeatable, and it's a method everyone can agree with just by looking at the price trend surrounding a candle.

But there's a problem. Take a dragonfly doji as an example. The candle looks like the letter T with the close at the top of the candle. You would expect price to break out upward sooner than downward just because of where price closes in the candle.

First, the big surprise with such candlesticks is that price does not break out upward the next day. In one test I ran on 20,000 dragonfly doji patterns, it took an average of *four* days to break out upward in a bull market. Downward breakouts in a bear market took exactly the same time, four days, to make the journey. Yes, the position of the closing price *does* influence whether a candle acts as a reversal or a continuation, but not to the extent many believe.

Second, if a candle is supposed to act as a reversal, then price should reverse direction, regardless of where it closes in the candle. That's almost by definition. If you placed a stop-loss order a penny below a candle in a downtrend that failed to reverse, you'd be stopped out. So price should reverse quickly or it's useless as a reversal indicator.

To be fair, I'm not that stringent. I wait for price to close either above the top or below the bottom of the candle before I determine whether it's a reversal or a continuation. A hanging man, for example, takes an average of three days to prove it's a reversal.

Finally, I checked the statistical results, visually, with the candles themselves and found that the method agrees with how I would categorize each candlestick pattern. In other words, if the statistics said the candle acted as a reversal, then it did. If the stats said the candle acted as a continuation, then it did. I used my eyes and counted the results, then compared the results to the stats. Both agree.

Why am I making such a big deal about this? Because 31% of the candles in this book fail. That is, they don't work as advertised, and many work little better than random chance. There are exceptions, of course, and those are the candles you should rely on. That's why I wrote this book—to find those gems hidden on the floor of the exchange.

■ Results of Others

Other candlestick researchers may find different results than the ones presented here. Many factors can contribute to this, including pattern recognition methodology, data used for testing, time period studied, and rules for measuring performance.

I am reminded of the tests researchers do on drugs. Does aspirin reduce the occurrence of heart attacks? Out of 50 studies, for example, some will conclude that it does, some will say it doesn't, and some may decide that it works only for women. However, the preponderance of results one way or the other will tilt the scale to a conclusion. I offer the information in this book as just one more test to add to the pile. Your results may vary.

■ Don't Write This Book

I read a book that used nearly six pages to justify why writing an encyclopedia like this one is a bad idea. The primary argument was that candles don't work alone but in groups. That sounds wonderful, but my response is this: Imagine five blind men. You ask each blind man how to get to the nearest grocery store in a neighborhood that he's never visited. "I don't know," come the replies, one after another. Then you put the five men together in an empty room and—eureka!—do they magically discover how to get to the grocery store? I don't think so. If candles don't work alone, then it's unlikely they'll work together.

Now, imagine one of the men can see. The sighted man, working alone, looks out a window and sees the grocery store down the road. Put him together with the others and they can hatch a plan to get there. In other words, finding a candlestick that works alone might help the performance of other candlesticks, too. After all, many candles become part of other, more complicated, candle patterns.

Suppose that you start not with 5 men but with 103, the same number as candlestick patterns in this book. You don't know how many can see, but you assume there are some. So you test each one, and when you're done, you separate the blind folks from those who need reading glasses from those with perfect vision. Some might suffer from night blindness, so the quirks of each are important and you make note of them.

Wouldn't you like to avoid spending time learning about reversal candles that fail to reverse more often than not? Wouldn't you like to avoid candles that perform randomly or near randomly and concentrate on proven winners?

That's what this candlestick encyclopedia is all about. It's about finding the candles that can make you money whether you rely on them standing alone or in combinations with other candles. It's about making money. And if you choose not to buy this book and learn the secrets it reveals, that's okay. I'll be the one using a transporter to beam up a pound of $50 bills, and you'll be the one gripping an empty wallet or purse, wondering where your money went.

Knowledge is power. Knowledge is money.

CHAPTER 31

Findings

From Thomas N. Bulkowski, *Encyclopedia of Candlestick Charts* (Hoboken, New Jersey: John Wiley & Sons, 2008), Chapter 1.

Learning Objective Statement

- Point out one or more of the 18 findings in this chapter as supporting evidence for a forecast or other technical observation based on given chart data

A rguably, you are reading the most important chapter because it discusses the discoveries I made about candles while researching this book. You may already know some of them, but the others are new. I'll refer to many of them in later chapters.

▓ A Number of Candles Do Not Work as Expected

This is the big surprise for candle lovers. A candle that functions as a reversal of an upward trend should cause price to drop. Thus, a close above the top of the preceding candle would be a failure because price climbed instead of fell, whereas a close below the previous low would be a success. Similarly, a continuation candle should have price break out in the same direction as it entered. If price rose into the candle, for example, it should break out upward; a downward breakout would be a failure. How many of the 103 candles I looked at passed or failed according to this method?

Passed: 69%
Failed: 31%

If you listen closely, you may hear the half-glass-full people screaming. Yes, 69% of the candles worked, so let's discuss additional tests. If I say that a success rate of less than 60% is considered just random, then how many candles worked at least 60% of the time? There are 412 different combinations of 103 candles that acted as reversals or continuations in bull and bear markets. Of the 412, only 100 candles qualified, so the answer is 24%.

If I filter the group by using a frequency rank of 51 or better, then just 10% qualify. The 51 rank is about midway in the list of 103 candles. As a reference, the candle with rank 51 appeared 1,973 times out of 1,204,083 candle lines in 500 stocks over 10 years, including bull and bear markets. In other words, just 10% of candles work at least 60% of the time and occur frequently enough to be found.

If I raise the bar to a 66% success rate (meaning the candle should work as expected in two of three trades) and keep the frequency rank the same, then only 6% qualify. That means just 6% of the candles I consider to be investment grade.

Please remember that this applies only to stocks and not futures, exchange-traded funds, or other security types, so the results could change dramatically.

The following lists the investment grade candles:

Above the stomach
Belt hold, bearish and bullish
Deliberation
Doji star, bearish
Engulfing, bearish
Last engulfing bottom and top
Three outside up and down
Two black gapping candles
Rising and falling windows

These are the candle patterns in which price reverses or continues in the anticipated direction frequently, but it does not indicate how far price trends after that. For a more detailed description of performance over time, see Chapter 32, Statistics Summary.

■ An Unusually Tall Candle Often Has a Minor High or Minor Low Occurring within One Day of It

I looked at tens of thousands of candles to prove this, and the study details are on my web site, ThePatternSite.com.

Figure 31.1 shows examples of unusually tall candles highlighted by up arrows. A minor high or low occurs within a day of each of them (before or after) except for A and B. Out of 11 signals in this figure, the method got 9 of them right, a success rate of 82% (which is unusually good).

Follow these steps to use the results.

1. The tall candle must be above the highs of two and three days ago (for uptrends) or below the lows of two and three days ago (for downtrends).
2. Find the average high-low height of the prior 22 trading days (a calendar month), not including the current candle.
3. Multiply the average height by 146%. If the current candle height is above the result, then you have an unusually tall candle.

Expect a peak within a day from unusually tall candles 67% of the time during an uptrend and a valley within a day 72% of the time in a downtrend. Additional peaks

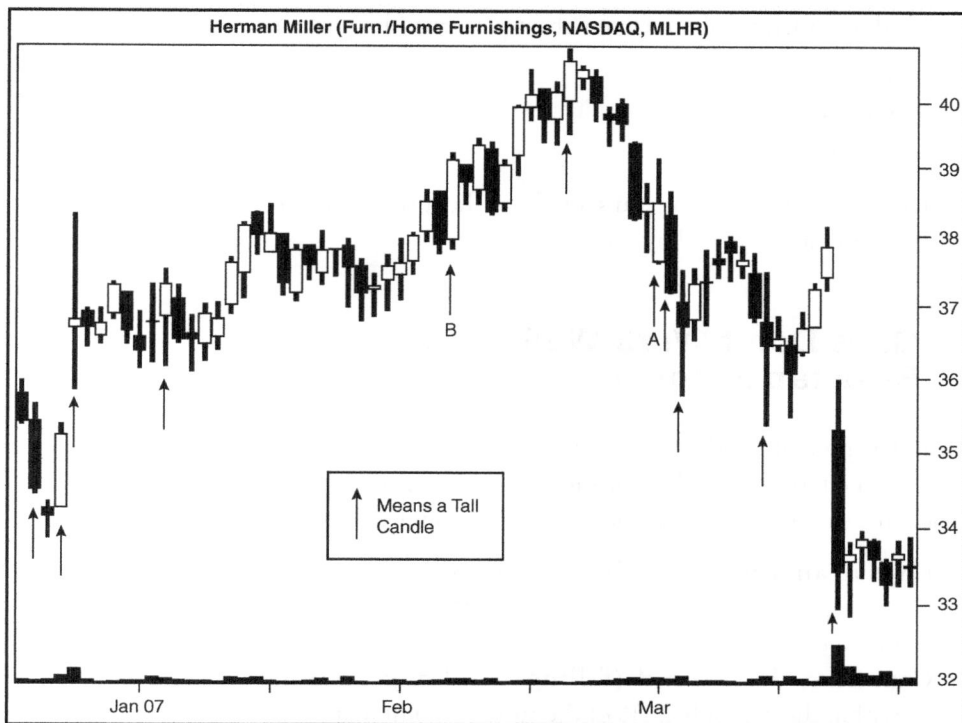

FIGURE 31.1 The Up Arrows Highlight Candles Taller Than Average. A Minor High or Minor Low Occurs within Plus or Minus One Day of Most of the Tall Candles.

or valleys can occur after that, so the minor high or low need not be wide or lasting. However, if you have a desire to buy a stock after a tall candle, consider waiting. The chances are that price will reverse and you should be able to buy at a better price.

■ The Best Performance Comes from Candles with Breakouts within a Third of the Yearly Low

This is true regardless of bull or bear markets, up or down breakouts. The percentages of chart patterns with breakouts within a third of the designated range that showed the best performance are:

Highest third: 5%
Middle third: 11%
Lowest third: 84%

I discovered another trend during chart pattern research that is similar. Here is where breakouts from the best-performing chart patterns with upward breakouts reside in the yearly price range:

Highest third: 27%
Middle third: 32%
Lowest third: 41%

For downward breakouts from chart patterns, the performance list is:

Highest third: 20%
Middle third: 25%
Lowest third: 55%

The results confirm that you should not short stocks making new highs but, rather, concentrate on those making new lows.

Gaps Don't Work Well as Support or Resistance Zones

Read Chapters 43 and 44 on windows (both rising and falling) if you don't believe me. I looked for minor highs or minor lows in a price gap and found that most often price just shoots through the gap without stopping. Here are the results:

Gaps in an uptrend (rising window): Price finds overhead resistance within the gap only 20% of the time in a bull market and 16% of the time in a bear market.

Gaps in a downtrend (falling window): Price finds underlying support within the gap only 25% of the time in a bull market and 33% of the time in a bear market.

Reversals Occur Most Often Near Price Extremes

I split the yearly price range into thirds and then mapped those patterns with reversals onto the yearly price range (based on the breakout price). I found that those within a third of the yearly high acted as reversals most often, followed closely by those within a third of the yearly low. Here are the results:

Highest third: 45%
Middle third: 12%
Lowest third: 43%

I would like to say that if you see a candle that usually acts as a reversal in the middle of the yearly price range you should ignore it—chances are price will not reverse, and if it does it probably won't be a lasting move. However, I'm not sure that's correct.

For continuations, here is where they appear most often, based on the location of the breakout price:

Highest third: 42%
Middle third: 10%
Lowest third: 48%

For reference, this is where all candle types (whether signaling a reversal, a continuation, or indecision) appear within the yearly price range. Some candles are neither a reversal nor a continuation, like a high wave, spinning top, or doji.

Highest third: 63%
Middle third: 9%
Lowest third: 28%

Opening Gap Confirmation Gives the Best Entry Signal

I tested three confirmation methods: closing price, candle color, and opening gap. Here is how often each confirmation method worked:

Closing price confirmation: 5%
Candle color confirmation: 13%
Opening gap confirmation: 82%

Candles with Breakouts below the 50-Day Moving Average Give the Best Performance

I tore apart my computer software at least three times checking to see if I had made a mistake on this one. I found that when the breakout from a candle is below the 50-trading-day moving average, performance is better than if the breakout is above the moving average. Here is how often each resulted in better performance:

Above the moving average: 14%
Below the moving average: 86%

Candles with Long Bodies Sometimes Show Support or Resistance

I looked at candle bodies (i.e., between the open and close, not the high-low price range) that were twice as tall as the one-month (22 trading days) average for the three years ending May 28, 2007, in 453 stocks. I found that minor highs or lows stop (i.e., show evidence of support or resistance) somewhere within the 41,301 tall candles 39% of the time. Candle color didn't show any performance difference (both show support or resistance 39% of the time).

Then I split the candle height into 10% divisions, did a frequency distribution of the results, and found that minor highs and minor lows stopped evenly across the candle. In other words, *the middle of a tall candle showed no greater likelihood of exhibiting support or resistance than anywhere else in a tall candle.*

A second study increased the candle height to four times the average and lengthened the time studied to 15 years. Few stocks actually covered the entire range. I found 25,285 tall candles that showed support or resistance 66% of the time. White candles showed support or resistance 65% of the time, and black candles showed support or resistance 67% of the time. The results were evenly distributed across the entire candle height, meaning the middle of the candle was *not* shown to have price stop there more often than any other part of the candle.

Let me also say that the taller a candle becomes, the higher the number of minor highs and lows that will appear within its body. That's why the hit rate increases from 39% to 66% for very tall candles. Imagine that a candle covers the entire price range, from yearly low to yearly high. It would include every minor low or high and consequently show a 100% success rate. Thus, I'm not sure that a tall candle is any more effective at showing support or resistance than any other candle.

Having said that, I have used tall candle support or resistance in my trading. For example, the trade I mentioned in the Introduction used a tall-bodied candle at the open. I cut the body price range in half and used it as a buy price. The stock dropped to the midpoint and most of the order filled before price climbed again.

As an example, look at Figure 31.2. I received a call from a broker when the Dow Jones Industrial Average plummeted 416 points in one session. I told him that on the way back up, the index would likely pause midway up the tall black candle. Point B shows the midpoint of body CD. Point A is where price paused. It's not exactly at the

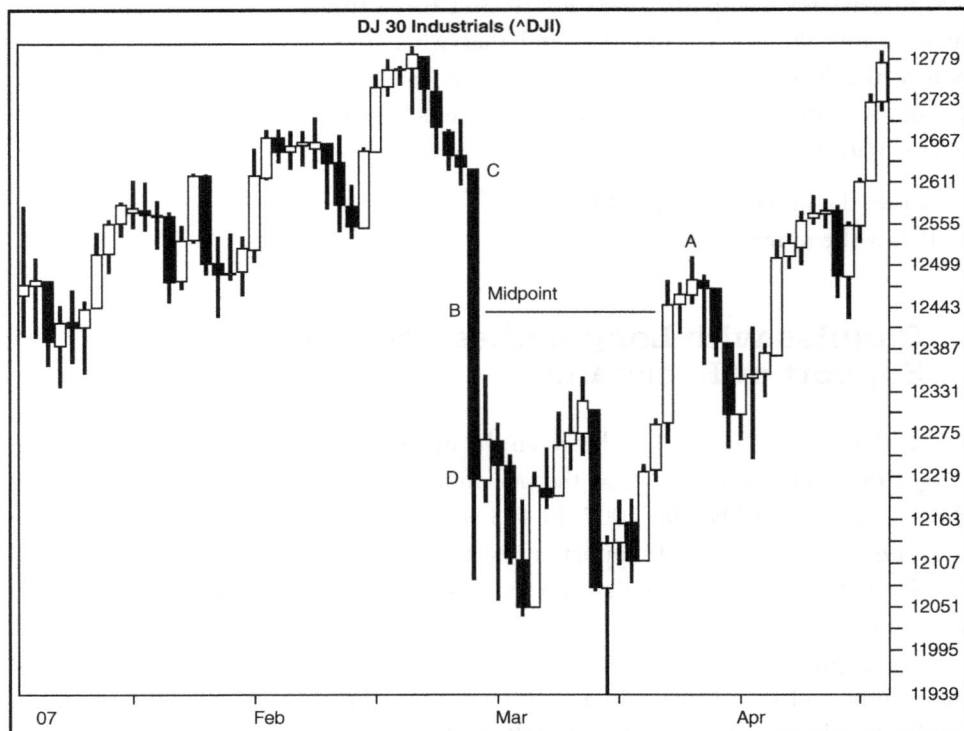

FIGURE 31.2   Price Finds Overhead Resistance Midway Up a Tall Black Candle.

midpoint, but it's close. Since I made that prediction, I've completed the analysis of tall candles, and it indicates that my prediction (of price stopping midway along the candle) was just a lucky guess.

Tall Candles Outperform Short Ones

This is the single best predictor of performance for both candles and chart patterns. It's worth the time to select candles taller than the median height. What is the median height? You'll have to refer to the individual chapter for the actual percentage because it varies slightly from candle to candle. I found it by taking the height of all of the candles of a particular type, dividing by the breakout price, and then finding the median. Candles with height/breakout price percentages greater than the median are tall candles. Here is how often tall or short candles performed better:

Tall: 96%
Short: 4%

Candles with Tall Shadows Get Better Performance

Candles with taller upper or lower shadows tend to perform better than do those with short shadows, regardless of the breakout direction or market condition (bull or bear). The following lists how often this worked:

Tall upper shadows: 87%
Short upper shadows: 13%
Tall lower shadows: 88%
Short lower shadows: 12%

Trade Bullish Candles in a Rising Primary Trend

If a reversal candle requires that the price trend leading to it is downward, then look for a downward retracement within an upward trend. Figure 31.3 shows an example of a morning doji star when the secondary trend is downward for a few days leading to the start of the candle formation. However, the underlying primary trend is upward.

After an upward breakout, the new trend joins the existing current and off it goes. You are much more likely to make a profit if the breakout joins the existing upward price trend than if the primary trend is downward and you expect a reversal to create a lasting trend change. That scenario *does* happen, but it's rare. This scenario is what I call the rise-retrace setup. Price retraces downward a portion of the prior up move before continuing the climb.

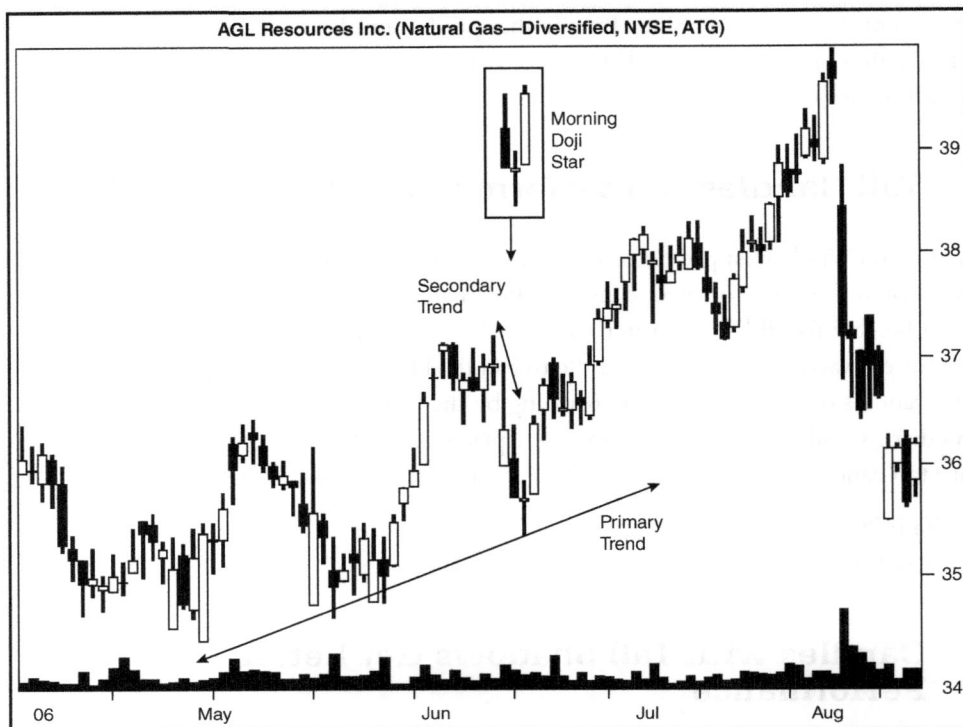

FIGURE 31.3 **A Morning Doji Star Appears in a Downward Price Trend (Secondary) When the Primary Trend Is Upward.**

If price closes below the lowest low in the candle pattern, then close out a long trade. That situation represents a downward breakout and price is apt to continue moving lower.

▪ Trade Bearish Candles in a Falling Primary Trend

This is the opposite situation of the prior tip. In this case, the best method to trade a bearish candle is when price is already tumbling. Price retraces a portion of the down move and then the bearish reversal candle appears. Once price breaks out downward, then it's off to the races.

What you don't want to do is depend on a bearish reversal candle in a primary uptrend to act as a trend reversal. It might, but the odds of a lasting decline are slim. Should price break out upward (i.e., it closes above the highest high in the preceding candle pattern), then close out your short position.

Avoid going long when the primary trend is downward. In that situation, you are trying to swim against the current; it's possible to do well, but it's unlikely. Upward breakouts tend to be short-lived in this scenario. If the primary trend is downward, then either remain in cash or go short. If you do find yourself in this situation, then exit a long trade if price closes below the lowest low in the preceding candle formation (a downward breakout).

THE INTEGRATION OF TECHNICAL ANALYSIS

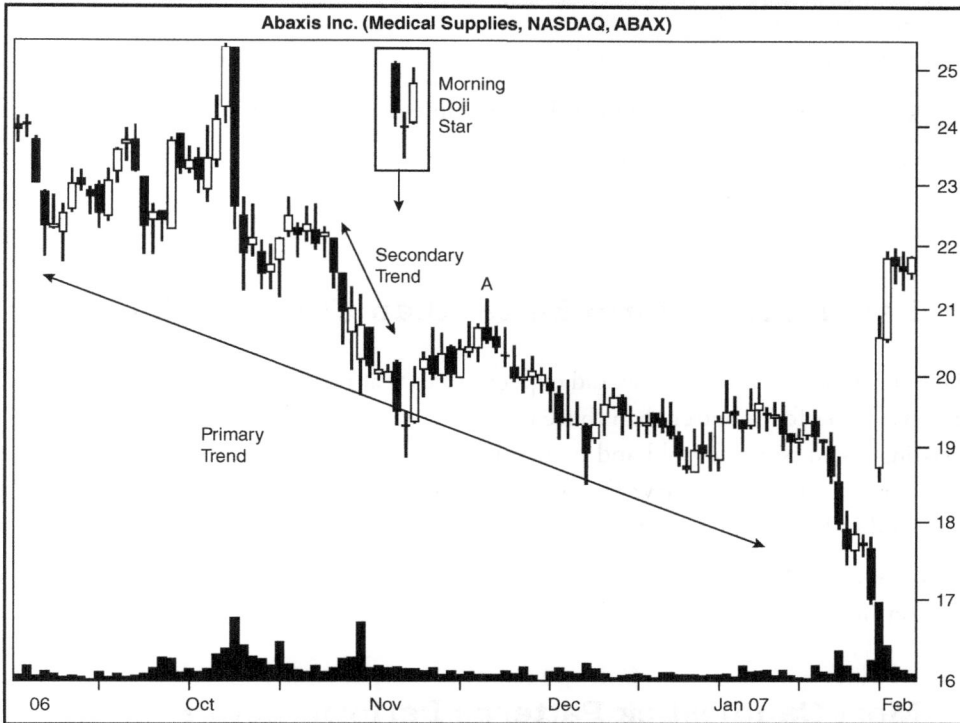

FIGURE 31.4 Both the Primary and Secondary Trends Are Downward, Leading to a Short Reversal.

Figure 31.4 shows this situation. Both the primary and secondary trends are downward when the morning doji star appears. Price reverses the trend but surfaces at A before being swept away by the downward-rushing current. If you traded this candle perfectly you would have made a dollar a share.

■ Candle Volume Is a Poor Predictor of Performance Except for Breakout Volume

I've never been a big fan of volume. I looked at volume four ways: the volume trend leading to the candle, the trend during the candle, the average during the candle, and breakout volume. I threw out the volume trend leading to the start of the candle because it didn't work well and made no sense anyway. What remained explores the relationship of volume inside the candle and during the breakout.

How often did candles perform better with a rising or falling volume trend?

Rising: 48%
Falling: 52%

How often did candles perform better if they had above- or below-average volume?

Above-average: 58%
Average or below-average: 42%

Howoften did heavy or light breakout volume lead to better performance?

Heavy breakout volume: 91%
Light breakout volume: 9%

■ Reversals Perform Better than Continuations

This is counterintuitive. You would expect prices that resume trending after a candle pattern to perform better than those candles that reverse the trend. But what if the existing trend is getting old and feeling tired, whereas a reversal is young, vibrant, and ready to start a new day? The following shows how often reversals or continuations led to better performance:

Reversals: 59%
Continuations: 41%

■ Most Candlestick Patterns Perform Better in a Bear Market, Regardless of the Breakout Direction

I can understand good performance of candles with downward breakouts in a bear market. They are going with the flow, riding a downward current in a falling market. But what about upward breakouts? Upward breakouts in a bear market often perform better than do those in a bull market! The only explanation I can think of is that the sample counts are fewer for bear markets (because of a shorter measurement period) and that has led to bogus results. That would make sense in a few isolated cases, but not all the time. Here is how often candles in different market conditions perform better:

Bear market: 96%
Bull market: 4%

■ Price Has to Have Something to Reverse

If the move leading to a candle is short, then don't expect a large move after the breakout. In other words, reversals work only if there is a trend to reverse. Price won't move far if it's mired in a congestion zone.

More Candles Appear within a Third of the Yearly High than Elsewhere in the Yearly Trading Range

You will find candles sprinkled throughout the yearly price range, but more will appear with breakouts within a third of the yearly high than in the other two thirds. Here is where the candle breakout resides in the yearly price range:

Highest third: 63%
Middle third: 9%
Lowest third: 28%

Where Price Closes in the Last Candle Line of the Pattern Helps Determine Performance

I split the candle line into thirds (except for candles like a gravestone doji where the close is expected to be pegged at one end) and looked at performance. Here is where the closing price resides for the best performance:

Highest third: 28%
Middle third: 32%
Lowest third: 40%

CHAPTER 32

Statistics Summary

From Thomas N. Bulkowski, *Encyclopedia of Candlestick Charts* (Hoboken, New Jersey: John Wiley & Sons, 2008), Chapter 2.

Learning Objective Statement

■ Identify the top three performing candle patterns (with more than 100 samples) in each of the categories listed in this chapter

The following pages show the top-performing candles. Candles with fewer than about 100 samples out of the 4.7 million studied mean you may never see them in the stock market. However, they may appear more often in other security types. Ties were not allowed. If a tie occurred, then I looked at the prior measurement period to break the tie. For example, both the bearish abandoned baby and downside Tasuki gap showed price climbing by 4.16% after 10 days in a bull market. To break the tie, I used the 5-day bull market/upward breakout measure (the abandoned baby won).

▨ Overall Rank

The following list shows candle patterns ranked by performance in bull and bear markets over one, three, five, and ten days after the candle ends. I summed the performance results (after multiplying downward breakout results by −1) and sorted them. The number after the candle is the performance sum.

The theory behind the list is that the best-performing candle patterns will post good numbers in bull and bear markets and over time.

1. Three-line strike, bearish: 67.38%
2. Three-line strike, bullish: 65.23%
3. Three black crows: 59.83%
4. Evening star: 55.85%
5. Upside Tasuki gap: 54.44%
6. Hammer, inverted: 51.73%
7. Matching low: 50.00%
8. Abandoned baby, bullish: 49.73%

9. Two black gapping candles: 49.64%
10. Breakaway, bearish: 49.24%
11. Morning star: 49.05%
12. Piercing: 48.37%
13. Stick sandwich: 48.20%
14. Thrusting: 48.10%
15. Meeting lines, bearish: 48.07%

The three-line strike patterns and the bearish breakaway had fewer than about 100 samples.

A falling window is a gap, and we are really measuring the price performance surrounding the gap, not the gap itself. If included in the list, a falling window would rank seventh, at 50.44%.

▪ Reversals: Bull Market

The top 15 best candles acting as reversals in bull markets are (based on how often price reverses, shown as a percentage):

1. Three stars in the South: 86%
2. Three-line strike, bearish: 84%
3. Three white soldiers: 82%
4. Identical three crows: 79%
5. Engulfing, bearish: 79%
6. Morning star: 78%
7. Three black crows: 78%
8. Morning doji star: 76%
9. Three outside up: 75%
10. Evening star: 72%
11. Belt hold, bullish: 71%
12. Evening doji star: 71%
13. Abandoned baby, bullish: 70%
14. Abandoned baby, bearish: 69%
15. Three outside down: 69%

The first two patterns had fewer than about 100 samples.

▪ Continuations: Bull Market

The top 15 best candles acting as continuations in bull markets are (based on how often price continues, shown as a percentage):

1. Mat hold: 78%
2. Deliberation: 77%
3. Concealing baby swallow: 75%

4. Rising three methods: 74%
5. Separating lines, bullish: 72%
6. Falling three methods: 71%
7. Doji star, bearish: 69%
8. Last engulfing top: 68%
9. Two black gapping candles: 68%
10. Side-by-side white lines, bullish: 66%
11. Hammer, inverted: 65%
12. Last engulfing bottom: 65%
13. Advance block: 64%
14. Doji star, bullish: 64%
15. Separating lines, bearish: 63%

The mat hold, concealing baby swallow, and rising and falling three methods patterns had fewer than about 100 samples.

I do not consider the rising and falling window patterns in the list because they are gaps, and the percentages associated with the candle patterns do not measure the gaps but, rather, the performance of the candle lines on either side of the gaps. If you include them in the list, the rising window would rank fourth, at 75%, and the falling window would rank 11th, at 67%.

■ Reversals: Bear Market

The top 15 best candles acting as reversals in bear markets are (based on how often price reverses, shown as a percentage):

1. Three stars in the South: 100%
2. Breakaway, bearish: 89%
3. Three white soldiers: 84%
4. Three-line strike, bullish: 83%
5. Engulfing, bearish: 82%
6. Three black crows: 79%
7. Three-line strike, bearish: 77%
8. Three outside up: 74%
9. Upside gap three methods: 72%
10. Identical three crows: 72%
11. Evening star: 72%
12. Breakaway, bullish: 71%
13. Morning doji star: 71%
14. Belt hold, bullish: 71%
15. Evening doji star: 71%

The three stars in the South, the breakaway (both bearish and bullish), and the three-line strike (both bullish and bearish) patterns had fewer than about 100 samples.

■ Continuations: Bear Market

The top 15 best candles acting as continuations in bear markets are (based on how often price continues, shown as a percentage):

1. Kicking, bearish: 80%
2. Rising three methods: 79%
3. Separating lines, bearish: 76%
4. Deliberation: 75%
5. 13 new price lines: 74%
6. Doji star, bullish: 70%
7. Two black gapping candles: 69%
8. Separating lines, bullish: 69%
9. Doji star, bearish: 67%
10. Last engulfing bottom: 67%
11. Hammer, inverted: 67%
12. Last engulfing top: 67%
13. Mat hold: 67%
14. Falling three methods: 67%
15. In neck: 65%

The bearish kicking, three methods (both rising and falling), 13 new price lines, and mat hold patterns had fewer than about 100 samples.

I do not consider the falling and rising window patterns in the list because they are gaps, and the percentages associated with the candle patterns do not measure the gaps but, rather, the performance of the candle lines on either side of the gaps. If you include them in the list, the falling window would rank sixth, at 73%, and the rising window would rank seventh, at 72%.

■ Performance after 10 Days: Bull Market/Up Breakouts

The top 15 candles sorted by average rise in a bull market 10 days after the candle ended are:

1. Doji star, collapsing: 7.32%
2. Three black crows: 6.95%
3. Breakaway, bearish: 6.66%
4. Concealing baby swallow: 5.92%
5. Identical three crows: 5.67%
6. Evening star: 5.37%
7. Long day, black: 5.11%
8. Doji star, bullish: 5.10%
9. Hammer, inverted: 5.03%
10. Separating lines, bearish: 4.93%
11. Upside gap three methods: 4.92%

12. Three outside down: 4.84%
13. Two black gapping candles: 4.83%
14. Evening doji star: 4.79%
15. Stick sandwich: 4.69%

The collapsing doji star, bearish breakaway, and concealing baby swallow patterns had fewer than about 100 samples.

A falling window is a gap, and we are really measuring the price performance surrounding the gap, not the gap itself. If included in the list, a falling window would rank fourth, at 5.93%.

▥ Performance after 10 Days: Bear Market/Up Breakouts

The top 15 candles sorted by average rise in a bear market 10 days after the candle ended are:

1. Three-line strike, bullish: 16.91%
2. Three black crows: 13.31%
3. Identical three crows: 10.03%
4. Evening star: 8.77%
5. Separating lines, bearish: 8.36%
6. On neck: 8.32%
7. Side-by-side white lines, bearish: 7.86%
8. Hammer, inverted: 7.74%
9. Three-line strike, bearish: 7.53%
10. Stick sandwich: 7.43%
11. Meeting lines, bearish: 7.16%
12. Matching low: 7.15%
13. Ladder bottom: 6.76%
14. Two black gapping candles: 6.45%
15. In neck: 6.34%

The bullish three-line strike had fewer than about 100 samples.

A falling window is a gap, and we are really measuring the price performance surrounding the gap, not the gap itself. If included in the list, a falling window would rank eighth, at 7.84%.

▥ Performance after 10 Days: Bull Market/Down Breakouts

The top 15 candles sorted by average decline in a bull market 10 days after the candle ended are:

1. Three-line strike, bearish: 8.81%
2. Mat hold: 7.21%
3. Concealing baby swallow: 7.10%

4. Three white soldiers: 6.41%
5. Abandoned baby, bullish: 6.04%
6. Deliberation: 5.24%
7. Rising three methods: 5.10%
8. Downside gap three methods: 4.97%
9. Breakaway, bearish: 4.71%
10. Three outside up: 4.50%
11. Morning star: 4.23%
12. Three-line strike, bullish: 4.23%
13. Doji star, bearish: 4.09%
14. Separating lines, bullish: 3.95%
15. Long day, white: 3.91%

The three-line strike (both bearish and bullish), mat hold, concealing baby swallow, and bearish breakaway had fewer than about 100 samples.

A rising window is a gap, and we are really measuring the price performance surrounding the gap, not the gap itself. If included in the list, a rising window would rank 11th, at 4.49%.

■ Performance after 10 Days: Bear Market/Down Breakouts

The top 15 candles sorted by average decline in a bear market 10 days after the candle ended are:

1. Abandoned baby, bullish: 10.31%
2. Upside Tasuki gap: 9.20%
3. Morning star: 8.53%
4. Separating lines, bullish: 8.05%
5. Three white soldiers: 7.66%
6. Three outside up: 7.14%
7. Ladder bottom: 7.07%
8. Three inside up: 7.00%
9. Mat hold: 6.89%
10. Three-line strike, bearish: 6.82%
11. Deliberation: 6.72%
12. Piercing: 6.57%
13. Engulfing, bullish: 6.31%
14. Morning doji star: 6.25%
15. Long day, white: 6.21%

The mat hold and bearish three-line strike patterns had fewer than about 100 samples.

A rising window is a gap, and we are really measuring the price performance surrounding the gap, not the gap itself. If included in the list, a rising window would rank fifth, at 7.74%.

CHAPTER 33

Above the Stomach

From Thomas N. Bulkowski, *Encyclopedia of Candlestick Charts* (Hoboken, New Jersey: John Wiley & Sons, 2008), Chapter 9.

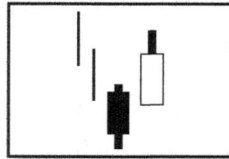

Learning Objective Statements

- Interpret potential price moves based on the patterns described in this chapter
- Calculate potential price targets
- Evaluate price levels for potential support or resistance
- Identify and interpret signals from various oscillators and technical studies

▦ Behavior and Rank

Theoretical: Bullish reversal.
Actual bull market: Bullish reversal 66% of the time (ranking 17).
Actual bear market: Bullish reversal 67% of the time (ranking 18).
Frequency: 32nd out of 103.
Overall performance over time: 31st out of 103.

It is refreshing to find a candle pattern that performs well and yet there are a gazillion of them in my database. The statistics are solid because of the high sample counts.

Above the stomach is a candle pattern that appears in a downtrend and begins with a black candle. The bears are enthusiastic until the next day when the bulls wrest control of the stock. Price opens above the middle of the black candle's body and closes above the middle, too. Not only are the bulls in control but they are not ceding any ground to the bears. Price climbs from there, but often the rise is brief, especially if the primary trend is downward.

As the rankings show, above the stomach is a refreshing change from other candle patterns that I have looked at. It works best as a bullish reversal in either bull or bear markets. For performance, it's in the lower reaches of the atmosphere, with an over-all rank of 31 out of 103, where 1 is best. That's quite good.

■ Identification Guidelines

When researching this candlestick pattern on the Internet, I found a one-sentence description and a thumbnail drawing at www.nisonmarketscan.com, but that was enough. Figure 33.1 shows an example. Price enters the stomach after a downtrend that begins at A, forming a black candle as the first line in the two-bar pattern. A white candle follows with price opening and closing above the middle of the black candle's body. Price breaks out upward in this example and rises to B, where it en-counters resistance at the price of A. Selling pressure pushes the stock down to C before bullish buying props it up again.

This rise-retrace pattern seems to be typical for the above the stomach pattern. However, the decline to C is usually not as severe as that shown here (meaning price often retraces only a fraction of the move up to B, not a full retracement as is shown here).

What should you look for when searching for an above-the-stomach? Table 33.1 lists the identification guidelines, all of which need little further explanation except for the last one. After a black candle appears on the first day of the

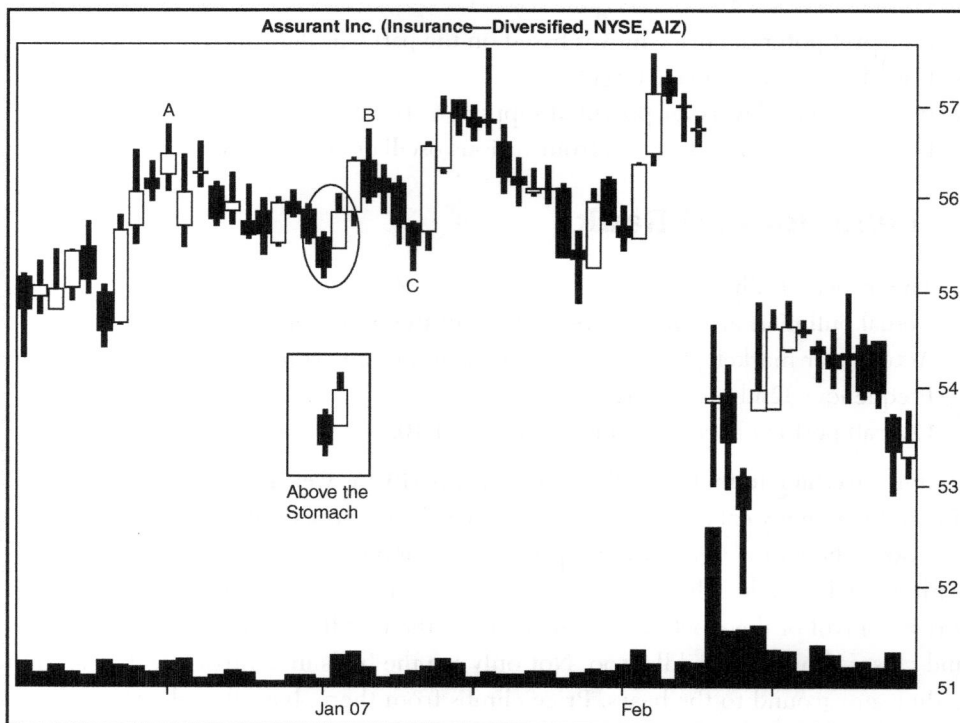

FIGURE 33.1 Price Rises after an Above-the-Stomach Candle Pattern, but Hits Overhead Resistance (A) at B and Drops to C.

TABLE 33.1	Identification Guidelines
Characteristic	**Discussion**
Number of candle lines	Two.
Price trend	Downward.
First day	Black candle.
Second day	White candle opening and closing at or above the midpoint of the prior black candle's body.

candlestick pattern, a white candle appears. Price in the white candle must open at or above the middle of the black candle's body and close at or above the middle as well.

■ Statistics

Table 33.2 shows general statistics.

Number found. I found 16,929 samples, so I did not need to resort to additional databases. That was enough to overload my spreadsheet. Most of the patterns came from a bull market.

Reversal or continuation performance. Since price trends downward into the pattern, an upward breakout is a reversal and a downward breakout is

TABLE 33.2	General Statistics			
Description	**Bull Market, Up Breakout**	**Bear Market, Up Breakout**	**Bull Market, Down Breakout**	**Bear Market, Down Breakout**
Number found	9,276	1,969	4,721	963
Reversal (R), continuation (C) performance	6.82% R	10.02% R	−5.17% C	−9.12% C
Standard & Poor's 500 change	1.39%	1.09%	−0.83%	−2.95%
Candle end to breakout (median, days)	3	3	5	5
Candle end to trend end (median, days)	7	8	7	8
Number of breakouts near the 12-month low (L), middle (M), or high (H)	L 2,183, M 2,481, H 3,734	L 734, M 642, H 562	L 1,550, M 1,381, H 1,305	L 473, M 327, H 149
Percentage move for each 12-month period	L 8.13%, M 6.41%, H 6.38%	L 13.90%, M 9.11%, H 7.25%	L −6.05%, M −4.82%, H −4.55%	L −9.67%, M −8.62%, H −8.64%
Candle end + 1 day	0.79%	1.35%	−1.14%	−1.78%
Candle end + 3 days	1.65%	2.78%	−2.36%	−3.91%
Candle end + 5 days	2.18%	3.68%	−2.95%	−4.95%
Candle end + 10 days	2.74%	3.50%	−3.05%	−4.86%
10-day performance rank	59	51	33	33

a continuation of the downtrend. The candle pattern performs better in a bear market, and upward breakouts do better than their corresponding downward breakout brothers (meaning that reversals perform better than continuations).

S&P performance. The candle pattern performs much better than the S&P 500 over the same periods.

Candle end to breakout. It takes between three and five days for price to break out, but the time is longer for downward breakouts. This makes sense because the close is usually nearer the candle's top than the bottom.

Candle end to trend end. It takes a median of seven or eight days to reach the trend end. Bear markets take a day longer than bull markets, perhaps because they travel farther and score better performance.

Yearly position, performance. Above-the-stomach candles appear most often near the yearly low, except for bull market/up breakouts, where a slight majority appear within a third of the yearly high. Performance is best when the breakout is near the yearly low in all categories.

Performance over time. Between 5 and 10 days, the performance suffers in a bear market (two columns), so this is not a robust performer. A well-performing candle would show higher performance numbers over time and in all categories.

The performance rank confirms the mid-list performance. Downward breakouts show better performance than upward ones when compared to other candle types.

Table 33.3 shows height statistics.

TABLE 33.3 **Height Statistics**

Description	Bull Market, Up Breakout	Bear Market, Up Breakout	Bull Market, Down Breakout	Bear Market, Down Breakout
Median candle height as a percentage of breakout price	3.82%	6.42%	3.69%	6.24%
Short candle, performance	5.41%	7.32%	−4.11%	−7.85%
Tall candle, performance	8.60%	12.87%	−6.65%	−10.63%
Percentage meeting price target (measure rule)	61%	57%	53%	55%
Median upper shadow as a percentage of breakout price	0.44%	0.90%	0.44%	0.92%
Short upper shadow, performance	6.27%	8.44%	−4.82%	−7.85%
Tall upper shadow, performance	7.26%	11.42%	−5.43%	−10.28%
Median lower shadow as a percentage of breakout price	0.58%	0.81%	0.63%	0.88%
Short lower shadow, performance	5.86%	8.53%	−4.42%	−8.75%
Tall lower shadow, performance	7.92%	11.62%	−6.10%	−9.54%

Candle height. Tall candles outperform. To determine whether the candle is short or tall, compute its height from highest high to lowest low price in the candle pattern and divide by the breakout price. If the result is higher than the median then you have a tall candle; otherwise it's short.

If Jake sees an above-the-stomach candle with a high of 18 and a low of 17, is the candle short or tall? The height is 18 − 17, or 1, so the measure would be 1/18, or 5.6% for an upward breakout. Assuming a bull market, the candle is tall.

Measure rule. Use the measure rule to help predict how far price will rise or fall. Compute the height of the candle and multiply it by the appropriate percentage shown in the table; then apply it to the breakout price.

Jake sees another above the stomach candle with the highest high at 75 and the lowest low at 71. What are the price targets? The height is 75 − 71, or 4. The upward target would be (for a bull market) 75 + (61% × 4), or 77.44. The downward target would be 71 − (53% × 4) or 68.88.

Shadows. The results in Table 33.3 pertain to the last candle line in the pattern. To determine whether the shadow is short or tall, compute the height of the shadow and divide by the breakout price. Compare the result to the median in the table. Tall shadows have a percentage higher than the median.

Candles with tall shadows perform better than those with shorter ones.

Table 33.4 shows volume statistics.

Candle volume trend. Excluding the tie in bear market/down breakouts, rising volume wins in two of three columns. Falling volume works slightly better in bull market/down breakouts.

Average candle volume. Candles with above-average volume perform well in all cases except bull market/down breakouts. Those do better if candle volume is light.

Breakout volume. In all categories heavy breakout-day volume suggests better performance postbreakout.

TABLE 33.4	Volume Statistics			
Description	Bull Market, Up Breakout	Bear Market, Up Breakout	Bull Market, Down Breakout	Bear Market, Down Breakout
Rising candle volume, performance	7.02%	10.22%	−5.13%	−9.13%
Falling candle volume, performance	6.57%	9.82%	−5.19%	−9.13%
Above-average candle volume, performance	6.97%	10.46%	−4.91%	−9.30%
Below-average candle volume, performance	6.65%	9.36%	−5.41%	−8.92%
Heavy breakout volume, performance	7.54%	11.18%	−5.18%	−10.09%
Light breakout volume, performance	6.07%	8.75%	−5.17%	−7.64%

▣ Trading Tactics

Like most bullish candles, this one does better as part of a downward retracement in an upward price trend. Be cautious about trading this one when the primary trend is downward. Price may make a lasting reversal, but the odds suggest otherwise.

Should price break out downward from this candle when the primary trend is also downward, then consider closing out any long positions and opening a short. Price is likely to continue moving lower.

In an upward trend with a downward breakout, trading is a tougher call. *Usually,* and I stress the word, price recovers in a few weeks after having dropped little, but the exception will burn you at the stake.

I split trading tactics into two basic studies, one concerning reversal rates and the other concerning performance. Of the two, reversal rates are more important, because it's better to trade in the direction of the trend and let price run as far as it can.

Table 33.5 gives tips to find the trend direction.

Confirmation reversal rates. If you want to detect a reversal, wait for price to close higher the next day. That works between 87% and 88% of the time.

Reversal, continuation rates. The breakout is upward from the stomach pattern most often.

Yearly range reversals. Reversals occur frequently within a third of the yearly high.

Table 33.6 shows performance indicators that can give hints as to how your stock will behave after the breakout from a candle pattern.

Confirmation, performance. Among the confirmation types, the opening gap method works best as a signal for reversal patterns. That means buying the stock if price gaps open higher the day after the candle pattern ends.

Moving average. Candles with breakouts below the 50-trading-day moving average do better than do those with breakouts above the average.

Closing position. Price closes all over the place in the last candle, so it's no help in predicting performance.

THE INTEGRATION OF TECHNICAL ANALYSIS

TABLE 33.5 Reversal Rates		
Description	Bull Market	Bear Market
Closing price confirmation reversal rate	88%	87%
Candle color confirmation reversal rate	85%	87%
Opening gap confirmation reversal rate	75%	74%
Reversal: trend down, breakout up	66%	67%
Continuation: trend down, breakout down	34%	33%
Percentage of reversals (R)/continuations (C) for each 12-month low (L), middle (M), or high (H)	L 58% R/42% C, M 64% R/36% C, H 74% R/26% C	L 61% R/39% C, M 66% R/34% C, H 79% R/21% C

| | TABLE 33.6 | Performance Indicators

Description	Bull Market, Up Breakout	Bear Market, Up Breakout	Bull Market, Down Breakout	Bear Market, Down Breakout
Closing price confirmation, performance	6.60%	9.63%	N/A	N/A
Candle color confirmation, performance	6.55%	9.41%	N/A	N/A
Opening gap confirmation, performance	7.44%	11.28%	N/A	N/A
Breakout above 50-day moving average, performance	6.34%	8.54%	−4.75%	−7.44%
Breakout below 50-day moving average, performance	7.49%	11.45%	−5.35%	−9.56%
Last candle: close in highest third, performance	6.96%	9.82%	−5.50%	−9.39%
Last candle: close in middle third, performance	6.88%	11.08%	−4.96%	−8.26%
Last candle: close in lowest third, performance	6.25%	8.33%	−4.97%	−10.28%

N/A means not applicable.

■ Sample Trade

Figure 33.2 shows a trade setup that intrigued Jake. Price moved in a straightline run from B to A. As expected, the stock then retraces a portion of that move. Most retraces reverse between 38% and 62% of the prior up move, and that's what happens here.

Sometimes Jake likes to place a buy order at the 62% retracement mark, and sometimes he'll wait to be sure price rebounds. If price closes below the 62% retracement level, then he is confident that price is heading lower. An upward turn doesn't happen all of the time, so it's a risky bet.

In this stock, he places a buy order at the 62% value, but price remains above it, so his buy order doesn't execute. He sees the above-the-stomach candle pattern and toys with trading the reversal.

He decides to evaluate the pattern first. Tall candles outperform, but is this a tall candle? The high is at 16.10 and the low at 33.25 for a height-to-breakout price of 2.85/16.10 or 7.9%. For a bull market with an upward breakout, that represents a tall candle. If price were to climb the average amount, it would move up 6.82% (from Table 33.2) above the candle high of 16.10, to 38.56. That's higher than the peak at A (37.84).

Looking at volume, the trend is rising, so that is good news. Candle volume is above average, so that also suggests good performance. Since the breakout has not occurred yet, Jake can't gauge breakout volume.

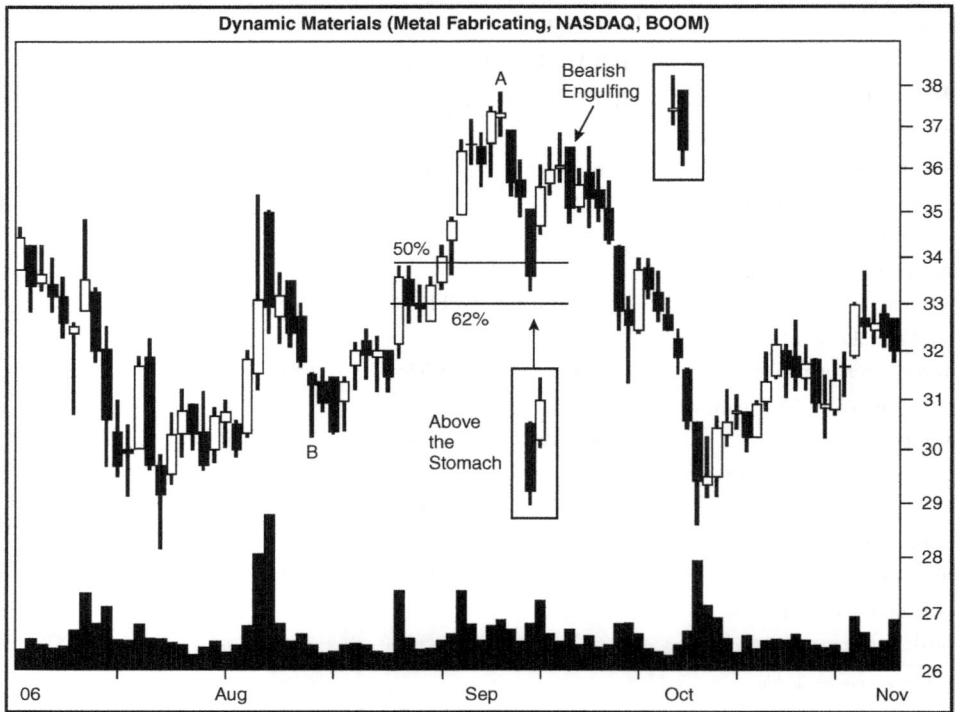

FIGURE 33.2 Price Retraces over 50% of the Move from B to A but Stays above Jake's Buy Order.

The best entry method is an opening gap (Table 33.6), so that's what he decides to use. The next day, price gaps open higher and he receives a fill 2 cents above that, or 35.67. He decides to play it conservatively and looks for a $2 gain per share, to 37.67, slightly below the high at A of 37.84. He places a sell order for that price because he knows trying to time the sale when it approaches an old high is difficult. It's best to have an order to sell already in place.

On the downside, he feels that if price drops below the stomach low, he'll sell. The low was at 33.25 so his stop is at 33.24, a penny below the low. That would represent a potential loss of 2.43 with a possible gain of 2. The win/loss ratio is below 1 when he wanted a minimum of 2 to 1.

He moves his stop closer, to 34.09, a penny below the last candle in the stomach. That means a potential giveback of 1.58 with a $2 gain. That still isn't great, but since he is already in the trade, it will have to do. Putting the stop closer he considers too risky.

The stock moves higher the next day, forming a high wave candle (a potential reversal since it appears at the top of an uptrend) followed by a bearish engulfing pattern. A bearish turn is all he needs to know. He cancels the sell order at 37.67 and sells at the open the next day, receiving a fill at 35.14, for a loss of 53 cents per share, not including commissions.

Looking over the trade, he realizes he made two mistakes. First, he decided to trade the above-the-stomach candle pattern instead of looking elsewhere for a more promising trade based on the 62% Fibonacci retracement (this stock didn't drop to 62%). And second, he evaluated the stop-loss location after he placed the trade. The good news is that he was able to exit sooner than he planned when the bearish engulfing candle appeared.

▪ For Best Performance

The following list offers tips and observations to help choose candles that perform well. Consult the associated table for more information.

- ▪ Use the identification guidelines to help select the pattern—Table 33.1.

- ▪ Candles within a third of the yearly low perform best—Table 33.2.

- ▪ Select tall candles—Table 33.3.

- ▪ Use the measure rule to predict a price target—Table 33.3.

- ▪ Candles with tall upper and lower shadows outperform—Table 33.3.

- ▪ Volume gives performance clues—Table 33.4.

- ▪ Trade this candle as part of a downward retracement in an uptrend—Trading Tactics discussion.

- ▪ The candle breaks out upward most often—Table 33.5.

- ▪ Patterns within a third of the yearly high tend to act as reversals most often—Table 33.5.

- ▪ Opening gap confirmation works best—Table 33.6.

- ▪ Breakouts below the 50-day moving average lead to the best performance—Table 33.6.

CHAPTER 34

Deliberation

From Thomas N. Bulkowski, *Encyclopedia of candlestick Charts* (Hoboken, New Jersey: John Wiley & Sons, 2008), Chapter 22.

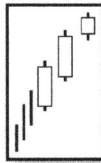

Learning Objective Statements

- Interpret potential price moves based on the patterns described in this chapter
- Calculate potential price targets
- Evaluate price levels for potential support or resistance
- Identify and interpret signals from various oscillators and technical studies

Behavior and Rank

Theoretical: Bearish reversal.

Actual bull market: Bullish continuation 77% of the time (ranking 2).

Actual bear market: Bullish continuation 75% of the time (ranking 4).

Frequency rank: 48th out of 103.

Overall performance over time: 93rd out of 103.

The first thing I thought was, "Deliberation! What a cool name but lousy performance." For a candle pattern that is supposed to act as a reversal, it doesn't. In fact, over 75% of the time price stages an upward breakout that continues the upward price trend. Upon closer inspection, I figured out why. In some cases, the pattern can be quite tall. To qualify as a reversal, price has to close below the candlestick's low. That can be difficult.

The reverse argument is that the candle is only three-days tall and a true price reversal should last longer than that. I agree, and that's why you see this pattern listed as a continuation. A visual check of the results confirms that this candle functions as a continuation pattern.

The deliberation candle pattern begins in an uptrend, so the bulls are in control. Their buying pressure pushes price up for two days, forming long white candles. On the third day, however, the bears counterattack. By day's end, the candle body is small even though it might support tall shadows. The small body emphasizes confusion and indecision over direction, a loss of bullish momentum when compared to the prior two days.

Nevertheless, I consider even a small white body to be bullish (but there is no rule that I could find to prevent the third day in the pattern from being black, which would be bearish, indeed). The day after the pattern ends is key. Since bullish momentum is slowing, judging by the shrinking body size, a black candle or other confirming pattern might put the bears in control to complete a reversal. Otherwise, expect price to continue trending up.

The numbers confirm the poor performance, with an overall rank of 93 out of 103, where 1 is best. Separating the overall rank into its component parts, we find that downward breakouts show very good performance but upward breakouts yank the rank back down. What appears to be happening is that price doesn't reverse immediately after an upward breakout, but sometimes does so within a week. That often means a small rise before price tumbles. As we will see in the statistics section, the performance over one, three, five, and ten days shows meager gains, as if the deliberation does not act as a reversal but perhaps warns of one coming.

■ Identification Guidelines

Figure 34.1 shows two examples of the deliberation candlestick pattern. Look closely at the deliberation in November. The breakout from this candle pattern is actually upward when price closes above the high in the three-day pattern. It acts as a continuation of the uptrend even though a trend reversal occurs two days later. This is an example of why the performance of the candle is so poor. Price climbs a small amount after the candle ends only to reverse in a few days.

The December deliberation shows price closing below the bottom of the candlestick, so the breakout is downward. Thus, the trend reverses after the candlestick.

Figure 34.2 shows another deliberation at D. If I were trading this candle, I would be concerned about overhead resistance set up by the trendline connecting peaks A, B, and C. With the appearance of the deliberation as price approaches the trendline, my bet would be on price reversing. Instead, price breaks out upward and moves closer to the trendline before reversing, but only for a few days. Price consolidates in a loose pattern and then resumes the uptrend, pushing through trendline resistance with a tall white candle.

Table 34.1 lists identification guidelines. Look for three white candles, each sporting a higher open and higher close. The first two candles should have tall bodies; the third candle line should be small and should open near where the prior candle closed. One source I checked indicated the third candle can be black or white, but other sources disagreed. I allow only white candles. Some sources require a gap above the prior day's close on the last day, but I do not.

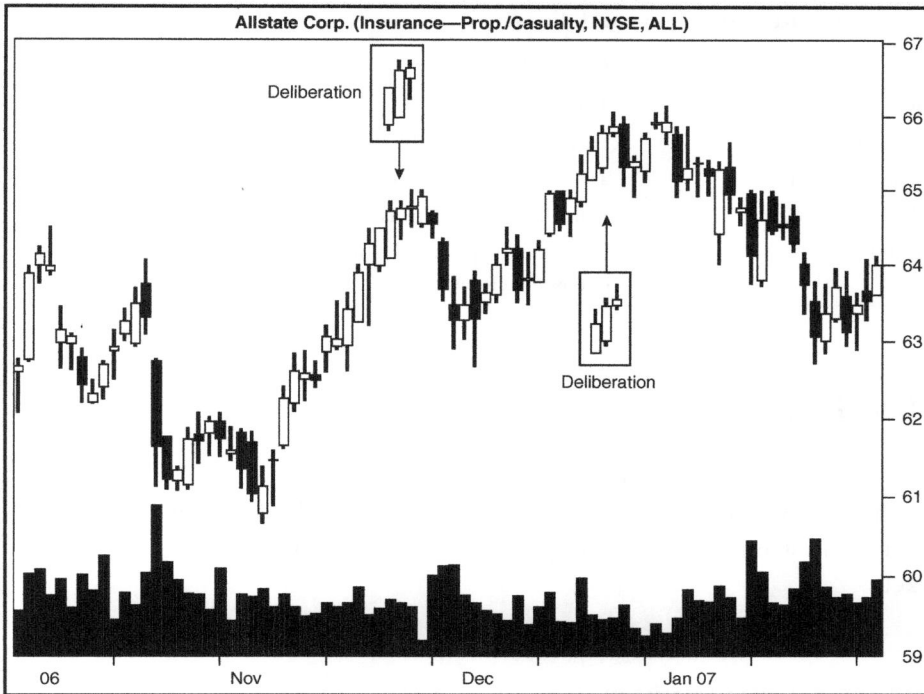

FIGURE 34.1 Two Examples of Deliberation; the First Is a Continuation of the Uptrend, and the Second Is a Reversal.

FIGURE 34.2 A Deliberation That Should Act as a Reversal but Doesn't.

TABLE 34.1　Identification Guidelines

Characteristic	Discussion
Number of candle lines	Three.
Price trend	Upward leading to the start of the candle pattern.
First and second days	Two long-bodied white candles.
Third day	A small body that opens near the second day's close.
Open and close	Each candle opens and closes higher than the previous ones' opens and closes.

■ Statistics

Table 34.2 shows general statistics.

Number found. I located 7,733 deliberations in the four databases I used. Prorating the standard database suggests deliberations appear most often in a bear market.

TABLE 34.2　General Statistics

Description	Bull Market, Up Breakout	Bear Market, Up Breakout	Bull Market, Down Breakout	Bear Market, Down Breakout
Number found	4,898	1,049	1,437	349
Reversal (R), continuation (C) performance	5.65% C	5.67% C	−5.16% R	−7.19% R
Standard & Poor's 500 change	1.12%	0.24%	−1.11%	−2.98%
Candle end to breakout (median, days)	4	4	9	8
Candle end to trend end (median, days)	7	7	11	11
Number of breakouts near the 12-month low (L), middle (M), or high (H)	L 402, M 901, H 3,098	L 139, M 348, H 555	L 212, M 322, H 755	L 84, M 105, H 159
Percentage move for each 12-month period	L 7.61%, M 5.58%, H 5.44%	L 8.46%, M 6.05%, H 4.93%	L −4.97%, M −5.24%, H −5.14%	L −6.71%, M −7.82%, H −7.05%
Candle end + 1 day	0.43%	0.23%	−1.43%	−1.69%
Candle end + 3 days	0.82%	0.53%	−3.24%	−4.06%
Candle end + 5 days	1.12%	0.92%	−4.24%	−5.56%
Candle end + 10 days	1.82%	1.29%	−5.24%	−6.72%
10-day performance rank	97	89	6	12

Reversal or continuation performance. Deliberations in a bear market performed better than did those in a bull market.

S&P performance. Candle performance beats the results from the S&P 500 over the same periods.

Candle end to breakout. Downward breakouts took much longer than did upward breakouts. Why? Because a downward breakout required a close below the candle's low price and that can be far from the current price. Upward breakouts need only close above the candle's high.

Candle end to trend end. It takes between 7 and 11 days to reach the trend end, longer for downward breakouts. Upward breakouts are moving in an existing uptrend, but downward breakouts have to start a new trend.

Yearly position, performance. The candle appears most often near the yearly high. Upward breakouts show the best performance within a third of the yearly low. That's typical for most candle types. Downward breakouts show the best performance comes from the middle of the yearly trading range, which is unusual.

Performance over time. The deliberation is a robust candlestick pattern, and by that I mean performance improves over time and in each category. What makes the rank so poor is that the gains over time (upward breakouts) are so meager. If they were 5% or 6%, then this candle would be near the top of the rankings, not the bottom at 93 (1 is best out of 103 candles).

Table 34.3 shows height statistics.

Candle height. Tall candles perform better than short ones. To determine whether the candle is short or tall, compute its height from highest high to lowest low

TABLE 34.3   Height Statistics

Description	Bull Market, Up Breakout	Bear Market, Up Breakout	Bull Market, Down Breakout	Bear Market, Down Breakout
Median candle height as a percentage of breakout price	6.03%	7.49%	6.50%	8.31%
Short candle, performance	4.46%	4.94%	−4.95%	−5.75%
Tall candle, performance	7.26%	6.52%	−5.45%	−9.26%
Percentage meeting price target (measure rule)	36%	29%	31%	32%
Median upper shadow as a percentage of breakout price	0.56%	0.76%	0.78%	0.91%
Short upper shadow, performance	4.80%	5.17%	−4.85%	−6.26%
Tall upper shadow, performance	6.64%	6.21%	−5.52%	−8.18%
Median lower shadow as a percentage of breakout price	0.60%	0.82%	0.55%	0.86%
Short lower shadow, performance	4.78%	5.01%	−4.99%	−6.14%
Tall lower shadow, performance	6.60%	6.30%	−5.33%	−8.56%

price in the candle pattern and divide by the breakout price. If the result is higher than the median, then you have a tall candle; otherwise it's short.

Suppose Jim sees a deliberation with a high of 93 and low of 87. Is the candle short or tall? The height is 93 − 87, or 6, so the measure would be 6/93, or 6.5%. Assuming a bull market with an upward breakout, the candle is tall.

Measure rule. Use the measure rule to help predict how far price will rise or fall. Compute the height of the candle pattern and multiply it by the appropriate percentage shown in the table; then apply it to the breakout price.

What are Jim's price targets for his candle? The upward target would be (6 × 36%) + 93, or 95.16, and the downward breakout would be 87 − (6 × 31%), or 85.14.

Shadows. The table's results pertain to the last candle line in the pattern. To determine whether the shadow is short or tall, compute the height of the shadow and divide by the breakout price. Compare the result to the median in the table. Tall shadows have a percentage higher than the median.

Candles with tall shadows perform better than do those with short ones.

Table 34.4 shows volume statistics.

Candle volume trend. The volume trend performance follows the breakout direction. Upward breakouts do better with a rising volume trend, and downward breakouts do better with a falling volume trend.

Average candle volume. Above-average volume works best for upward breakouts and below-average volume excels for downward breakouts.

Breakout volume. Deliberations showing heavy breakout volume perform best across all categories.

TABLE 34.4 Volume Statistics

Description	Bull Market, Up Breakout	Bear Market, Up Breakout	Bull Market, Down Breakout	Bear Market, Down Breakout
Rising candle volume, performance	5.77%	5.73%	−5.05%	−7.18%
Falling candle volume, performance	5.56%	5.61%	−5.27%	−7.21%
Above-average candle volume, performance	5.70%	5.69%	−4.53%	−6.49%
Below-average candle volume, performance	5.57%	5.64%	−6.13%	−8.27%
Heavy breakout volume, performance	6.09%	5.97%	−5.40%	−8.07%
Light breakout volume, performance	5.11%	5.30%	−4.86%	−6.05%

Trading Tactics

Figure 34.3 shows a deliberation that pulls back into the base of a descending triangle. If you want to trade a deliberation as a reversal, then look for them in a declining price trend. That means the primary trend (at least a month long, usually much longer) should be downward but the shorter trend (days or weeks) is upward leading to the candle pattern.

The chart shows an example. Price trends lower from the October high, breaks out downward from the triangle, and then moves lower. The deliberation appears as part of an upward retracement in a downward price trend.

Avoid trading deliberation candlesticks as reversals when the prevailing (longer-term) price trend is upward. Those tend to break out upward most often.

If a deliberation appears as part of a classic chart pattern, such as the right shoulder of a head-and-shoulders top or the second/third top of a double/triple top, then a reversal is more likely. If you can identify those situations properly, the deliberation works well as a reversal candlestick.

I split trading tactics into two basic studies, one concerning reversal rates and the other concerning performance. Of the two, reversal rates are more important, because it's better to trade in the direction of the trend and let price run as far as it can.

FIGURE 34.3 A Deliberation Appears as a Pullback to a Descending Triangle.

TABLE 34.5 **Reversal Rates**

Description	Bull Market	Bear Market
Closing price confirmation reversal rate	37%	38%
Candle color confirmation reversal rate	36%	38%
Opening gap confirmation reversal rate	28%	29%
Reversal rate: trend up, breakout down	23%	25%
Continuation rate: trend up, breakout up	77%	75%
Percentage of reversals (R)/continuations (C) for each 12-month low (L), middle (M), or high (H)	L 35% R/65% C, M 26% R/74% C, H 20% R/80% C	L 38% R/62% C, M 23% R/77% C, H 22% R/78% C

Table 34.5 gives tips to find the trend direction.

Confirmation reversal rates. To help predict a reversal, wait for price to close lower the day after the candle ends. Unfortunately, this works just over a third of the time.

Reversal, continuation rates. Most of the patterns acted as continuations of the uptrend due to the difficulty of closing below a tall three-candle pattern. Expect an upward breakout.

Yearly range reversals. Continuations occur most often when price is within a third of the yearly high.

Table 34.6 shows performance indicators that can give hints as to how your stock will behave after the breakout from this candle pattern.

TABLE 34.6 **Performance Indicators**

Description	Bull Market, Up Breakout	Bear Market, Up Breakout	Bull Market, Down Breakout	Bear Market, Down Breakout
Closing price confirmation, performance	N/A	N/A	−7.80%	−9.70%
Candle color confirmation, performance	N/A	N/A	−7.63%	−9.71%
Opening gap confirmation, performance	N/A	N/A	−7.51%	−9.11%
Breakout above 50-day moving average, performance	5.60%	5.51%	−4.73%	−7.18%
Breakout below 50-day moving average, performance	6.87%	7.87%	−6.26%	−7.21%
Last candle: close in highest third, performance	5.52%	5.67%	−4.75%	−6.93%
Last candle: close in middle third, performance	5.98%	5.54%	−5.37%	−7.15%
Last candle: close in lowest third, performance	5.08%	6.06%	−5.47%	−7.71%

N/A means not applicable.

Confirmation, performance. Usually the opening gap method works best, but not with deliberations. In a bull market, waiting for a lower close the next day to determine the trend direction works best. In a bear market, the next day's candle color (black) works better as a trading signal.

Moving average. Candles with breakouts below the 50-trading-day moving average result in performance better than those with breakouts above the moving average.

Closing position. Candles with a close in the last line of the candle pattern near its low tend to perform better than the other two areas. This is true in all cases except for bull market/up breakouts. Those do best when the close is in the middle of the candle line.

■ Sample Trade

Figure 34.4 shows an interesting situation that would have fooled me. Before I get to that, though, look at the March deliberation. Price trends up into the candle pattern, and at the end a black candle appears with a lower close. However, the next-day price breaks out upward, confirming the deliberation as a continuation pattern. Was that a clue to how the May deliberation would work?

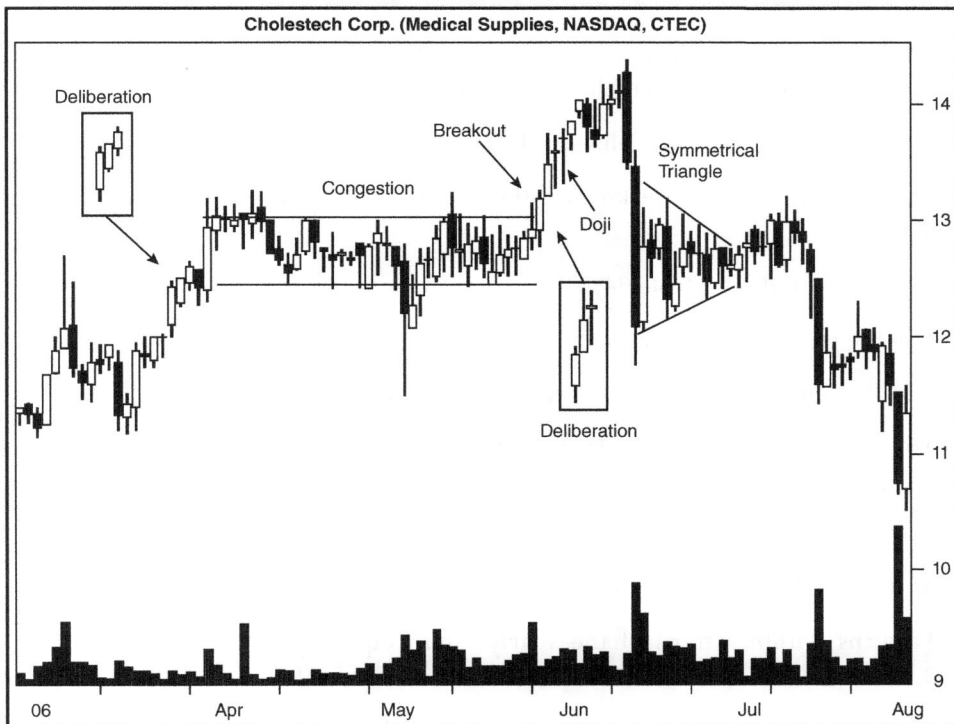

FIGURE 34.4 A Deliberation Appears at the Breakout from a Consolidation Region.

Avoid expecting a lasting reversal from a deliberation in a prolonged uptrend. This uptrend began in January 2006, well before the May deliberation appears. Although one could argue that the uptrend is getting tired (price moved horizontally for two months), I consider that a risky bet. The trend is up, so avoid going short.

A long congestion zone of price turnover churns the stock during April and May. Then price closes above the top of the congestion zone, staging an upward breakout. During the breakout process, a deliberation appears. If this were my trade, I would assume that the candle means price will fall back to the top of the congestion zone before continuing higher.

That's not what happens, though. After the deliberation completes, a doji forms, suggesting that the bulls and bears are undecided as to which way price should go. The next day, price closes above the top of the deliberation, confirming the pattern as a continuation. As the chart shows, the stock continues to rise for about two weeks before two huge black candles appear in a show of bearish power. The black candles are the final two lines of a three outside down candlestick pattern.

After that, a small symmetrical triangle takes shape with a breakout best described as horizontal. Price squeezes out the end of the funnel, wobbles up and down for two weeks or so, and then resumes dropping.

The moral of this example is to trade with the trend. The trend was upward, and the appearance of a deliberation candlestick didn't change that.

■ For Best Performance

The following list offers tips and observations to help choose candles that perform well. Consult the associated table for more information.

- Use the identification guidelines to help select the pattern—Table 34.1.

- Candles with upward breakouts within a third of the yearly low perform best—Table 34.2.

- Select tall candles—Table 34.3.

- Use the measure rule to predict a price target—Table 34.3.

- Candles with tall upper and lower shadows outperform—Table 34.3.

- Volume gives performance clues—Table 34.4.

- Trade deliberations as reversals only as part of an upward retracement in a primary downtrend—Trading Tactics discussion.

- The candle breaks out upward most often—Table 34.5.

- Patterns within a third of the yearly high frequently act as continuations—Table 34.5.

- Breakouts below the 50-day moving average lead to the best performance—Table 34.6.

CHAPTER 35

Doji Star, Bearish

From Thomas N. Bulkowski, *Encyclopedia of Candlestick Charts* (Hoboken, New Jersey: John Wiley & Sons, 2008), Chapter 30.

Learning Objective Statements

- Interpret potential price moves based on the patterns described in this chapter
- Calculate potential price targets
- Evaluate price levels for potential support or resistance
- Identify and interpret signals from various oscillators and technical studies

Behavior and Rank

Theoretical: Bearish reversal.
Actual bull market: Bullish continuation 69% of the time (ranking 8).
Actual bear market: Bullish continuation 67% of the time (ranking 11).
Frequency: 43rd out of 103.
Overall performance over time: 51st out of 103.

The bearish doji star reminds me of powering a bicycle uphill. My speed is higher at the bottom than when I crest the hill. With this candlestick pattern, price narrows from the first day to the second, showing a loss of momentum. This narrowing is a warning of a coming reversal—in theory.

In technical terms, the market trends upward, leading to a bullish white candle—a candle that closes well above the open, making it a tall, robust one. The next day, price gaps higher in a continuation of the bullish trend, but soon runs into selling pressure. Price trades in a narrow range all day as bulls and bears fight it out. When the battle is over, a doji prints on the chart.

Unfortunately, it rarely works that way. Most often, price just continues upward, closing above the candle high in a few days, never having reversed at all.

The 69% (bull market) and 67% (bear market) rates confirm the behavior not as a bearish reversal but as a bullish continuation pattern. Overall performance ranks 51 out of 103, with 1 being best, so this one is way down the list.

▪ Identification Guidelines

Figure 35.1 shows a good example of a doji star pattern and how it is supposed to work. After an uptrend, a doji follows a long white candle and then price drops. This doji star forms the head of a head-and-shoulders top. When price pierces the support line (neckline), price tumbles for several days before pulling back to the base of the head-and-shoulders formation and then resumes the slide.

Table 35.1 shows the identification guidelines for the doji star pattern. The characteristics are self-explanatory except for the following: The doji's body should remain above the close posted by the prior day. This forms a price gap between the bodies, even though the shadows may overlap. I do not allow ties between the price of the doji's body and that of the prior day's body.

In my tests, I began with a doji shadow height less than the average shadow height for each stock, but dismal were the number of doji star patterns qualifying (375). So

FIGURE 35.1 This Doji Star Forms the Head of a Head-and-Shoulders Top Chart Pattern.

TABLE 35.1	Identification Guidelines
Characteristic	**Discussion**
Number of candle lines	Two.
Price trend	Upward leading to the pattern.
First day	A long white candle.
Body gap	Price gaps higher, forming a body that is above the first day's body.
Second day	A doji. The open and close are at or near the same price.
Doji shadows	Avoid excessively long shadows on the doji. The sum of the doji shadows is less than the body height of the prior day.

I changed the algorithm to compare the total shadow height (sum of both upper and lower shadows) with the prior day's body height. If the combined shadow height was taller than the prior day's body, I excluded the candle. Simply put, when searching for a doji star, make sure the shadows on the doji look reasonable in length—not too long, whatever that may mean to you.

▓ Statistics

Table 35.2 shows general statistics.

TABLE 35.2	General Statistics			
Description	**Bull Market, Up Breakout**	**Bear Market, Up Breakout**	**Bull Market, Down Breakout**	**Bear Market, Down Breakout**
Number found	7,410	737	3,305	358
Reversal (R), continuation (C) performance	6.01% C	7.17% C	−5.59% R	−9.02% R
Standard & Poor's 500 change	1.05%	0.04%	−0.91%	−2.95%
Candle end to breakout (median, days)	3	3	6	5
Candle end to trend end (median, days)	6	7	10	10
Number of breakouts near the 12-month low (L), middle (M), or high (H)	L 888, M 1,499, H 4,106	L 145, M 213, H 373	L 607, M 759, H 1,543	L 97, M 111, H 145
Percentage move for each 12-month period	L 7.51%, M 5.68%, H 5.83%	L 10.46%, M 6.56%, H 6.05%	L −6.81%, M −5.29%, H −5.23%	L −11.01%, M −9.10%, H −8.32%
Candle end + 1 day	0.54%	0.69%	−1.35%	−1.95%
Candle end + 3 days	1.28%	1.52%	−2.86%	−3.99%
Candle end + 5 days	1.62%	1.94%	−3.65%	−4.92%
Candle end + 10 days	2.09%	2.50%	−4.09%	−5.77%
10-day performance rank	80	63	14	24

Number found. I found 11,810 doji stars on a cloudless night, separated into bull and bear markets, up and down breakouts. Most came from a bull market.

Reversal or continuation performance. Sorting performance by reversals and continuations, we see that the best performance comes from patterns in a bear market, regardless of the breakout direction (i.e., regardless of whether the doji acted as a reversal or continuation).

S&P performance. The doji candle performed better than the S&P 500 over the same period.

Candle end to breakout. Downward breakouts took two to three days longer to occur than upward breakouts. That is because price is closer to the top of the pattern than the bottom.

Candle end to trend end. The median time from candle end to trend end is 6 to 10 days. Downward breakouts take longer because price has to start a new trend whereas upward breakouts are closer to the end of an existing trend.

Yearly position, performance. The majority of bearish doji sars appeared within a third of the yearly high. However, the best performance came from those near the yearly low.

Performance over time. The bearish doji star is a robust pattern, meaning that performance improves over time and in each category. Unfortunately, the upward breakout percentage changes are too low to help the performance rank. Downward breakouts rank quite well.

Table 35.3 shows height statistics.

TABLE 35.3 Height Statistics

Description	Bull Market, Up Breakout	Bear Market, Up Breakout	Bull Market, Down Breakout	Bear Market, Down Breakout
Median candle height as a percentage of breakout price	4.21%	4.97%	4.42%	5.62%
Short candle, performance	4.82%	5.87%	−4.66%	−8.13%
Tall candle, performance	8.03%	9.05%	−7.08%	−10.33%
Percentage meeting price target (measure rule)	53%	55%	49%	54%
Median upper shadow as a percentage of breakout price	0.52%	0.61%	0.62%	0.81%
Short upper shadow, performance	5.21%	6.33%	−4.97%	−7.95%
Tall upper shadow, performance	6.89%	7.97%	−6.28%	−10.05%
Median lower shadow as a percentage of breakout price	0.64%	0.88%	0.65%	0.97%
Short lower shadow, performance	5.15%	6.46%	−4.91%	−7.62%
Tall lower shadow, performance	6.92%	7.99%	−6.27%	−10.67%

Candle height. Candles taller than the median outperform in all situations. To determine whether the candle is short or tall, compute its height from highest high to lowest low price in the candle pattern and divide by the breakout price. If the result is higher than the median, then you have a tall candle; otherwise it's short.

Doug has a bearish doji star with a high at 87 and a low at 85. Is the candle short or tall? The height is $87 - 85$, or 2, so the measure is 2/87, or 2.3%. In a bull market with an upward breakout the candle is short.

Measure rule. Use the measure rule to help predict how far price will rise or fall. Compute the height of the candle pattern and multiply it by the appropriate percentage shown in the table; then apply it to the breakout price.

What price targets does Doug's candle predict? The upward target is $87 + (2 \times 53\%)$, or 88.06, and the downward target is $85 - (2 \times 49\%)$, or 84.02.

Shadows. The table's results pertain to the last candle line in the pattern (the doji). To determine whether the shadow is short or tall, compute the height of the shadow and divide by the breakout price. Compare the result to the median in the table. Tall shadows have a percentage higher than the median.

Shadow performance. Candles with tall upper or lower shadows perform better than do those with short ones.

Table 35.4 shows volume statistics.

Candle volume trend. Candles with a falling volume trend perform better than do those with a rising trend in all categories.

Average candle volume. I compared the average candle volume for the two-day pattern with the one-month average and separated the performance results into above-average and below-average volume rows, which the table shows. Candles with below-average volume show better performance, with the exception of those in a bull market with an upward breakout. Those perform better if the candle pattern shows heavy volume.

Breakout volume. Candles with heavy breakout volume result in the best performance across the board.

TABLE 35.4	Volume Statistics			
Description	Bull Market, Up Breakout	Bear Market, Up Breakout	Bull Market, Down Breakout	Bear Market, Down Breakout
Rising candle volume, performance	5.76%	6.39%	−5.38%	−7.70%
Falling candle volume, performance	6.14%	7.69%	−5.71%	−9.82%
Above-average candle volume, performance	6.45%	6.89%	−5.54%	−8.60%
Below-average candle volume, performance	5.54%	7.49%	−5.65%	−9.57%
Heavy breakout volume, performance	6.78%	7.54%	−6.23%	−10.17%
Light breakout volume, performance	5.20%	6.78%	−5.07%	−7.77%

■ Trading Tactics

Figure 35.2 shows a reliable trading setup. In a downtrend that is usually at least a month long, a doji star sometimes appears just below a trendline like the one shown. Price bumps against overhead resistance, and usually within a week or so the decline resumes. The breakout may be upward, but it doesn't last long and the primary downtrend continues.

In cases where price pushes above the down-sloping trendline—that is, the upward breakout is a lasting one—it signals an extended advance, one worth hopping aboard.

I split trading tactics into two basic studies, one concerning reversal rates and the other concerning performance. Of the two, reversal rates are more important, because it's better to trade in the direction of the trend and let price run as far as it can.

Table 35.5 gives tips to find the trend direction.

Confirmation reversal rates. To help detect a reversal of the uptrend, wait for price to close lower after the bearish doji star. Unfortunately, that method works only randomly—50% in a bull market and 53% in a bear market.

Reversal, continuation rates. Over two-thirds of the time the bearish doji star acts as a continuation pattern, not a reversal. Expect an upward breakout.

Yearly range reversals. Continuation patterns populate the highest third of the yearly price range. Do not expect a reversal to occur.

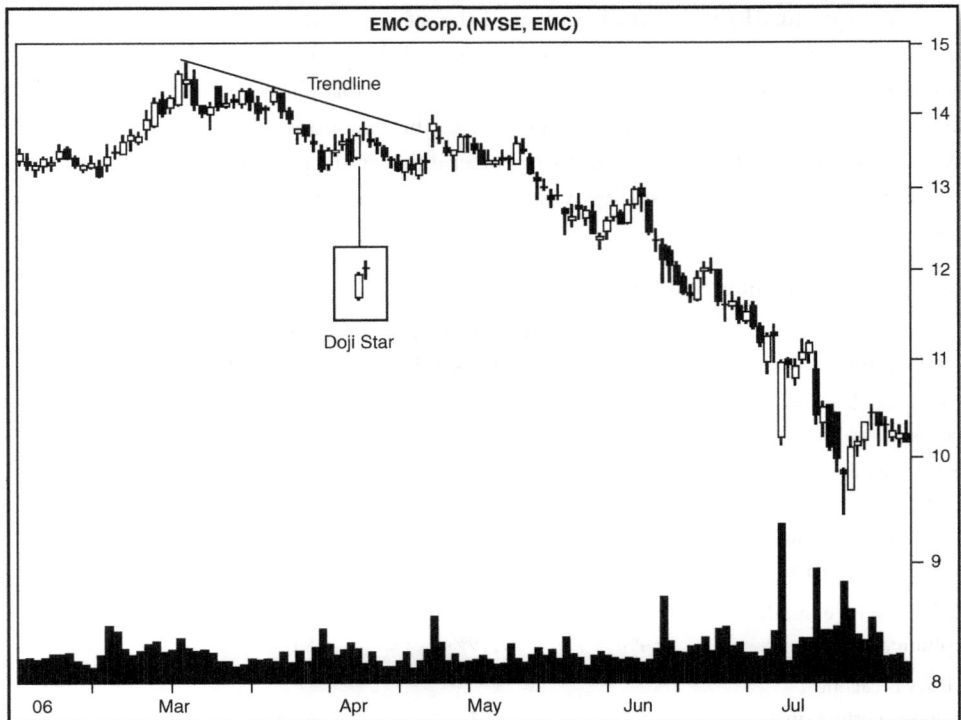

FIGURE 35.2   Resistance above This Doji Star, Coupled with a Downward Breakout, Suggests a Resumption of the Decline.

TABLE 35.5 Reversal Rates

Description	Bull Market	Bear Market
Closing price confirmation reversal rate	50%	53%
Candle color confirmation reversal rate	49%	50%
Opening gap confirmation reversal rate	39%	38%
Reversal rate: trend up, breakout down	31%	33%
Continuation rate: trend up, breakout up	69%	67%
Percentage of reversals (R)/ continuations (C) for each 12-month low (L), middle (M), or high (H)	L 41% R/59% C, M 34% R/66% C, H 27% R/73% C	L 40% R/60% C, M 34% R/66% C, H 28% R/72% C

TABLE 35.6 Performance Indicators

Description	Bull Market, Up Breakout	Bear Market, Up Breakout	Bull Market, Down Breakout	Bear Market, Down Breakout
Closing price confirmation, performance	N/A	N/A	−7.45%	−9.77%
Candle color confirmation, performance	N/A	N/A	−7.57%	−9.85%
Opening gap confirmation, performance	N/A	N/A	−7.46%	−10.73%
Breakout above 50-day moving average, performance	5.97%	6.85%	−5.19%	−8.29%
Breakout below 50-day moving average, performance	6.76%	9.67%	−6.42%	−10.58%
Last candle: close in highest third, performance	5.87%	7.56%	−5.69%	−8.15%
Last candle: close in middle third, performance	6.03%	6.56%	−5.56%	−10.15%
Last candle: close in lowest third, performance	6.21%	7.60%	−5.52%	−8.09%

N/A means not applicable.

Table 35.6 shows performance indicators that can give hints as to how your stock will behave after the breakout from this candle pattern.

Confirmation, performance. Since we are looking for reversals, only the downward breakout direction applies to all confirmation methods. If you wait for price to gap open lower the day after the doji star, the average decline to the trend low is 10.73%, the best of the bunch for a bear market. In a bull market, candle color works best as the confirmation method. That means trading only if a black candle appears the day after the doji star ends. Also notice that the numbers are close to each other, so it probably doesn't matter which method you use.

Moving average. Breakouts from bearish doji stars below the 50-day moving average lead to the best performance.

Closing position. Where price closes in the doji candle line (the last line in the candle) matters little for performance.

■ Sample Trade

Doug likes to search for support and resistance zones and then trade off those areas. For example, Figure 35.3 shows a trading setup that he finds appealing. A bearish doji star appears after a month's worth of price steadily climbing. (The move up the price mountain began in early May at a leisurely pace but quickened as June approached. Then the doji star appeared.)

The three peaks labeled A, B, and C are at nearly the same level, posing a barrier to any upward move—a ceiling, if you will, which Doug loves. He shorts the stock using the opening gap method on the day a hanging man appears.

How far will price fall? Use the measure rule for the doji star to get an idea. Subtract the candle low (the lower of the two price bars, 4.02) from the high (the higher of the

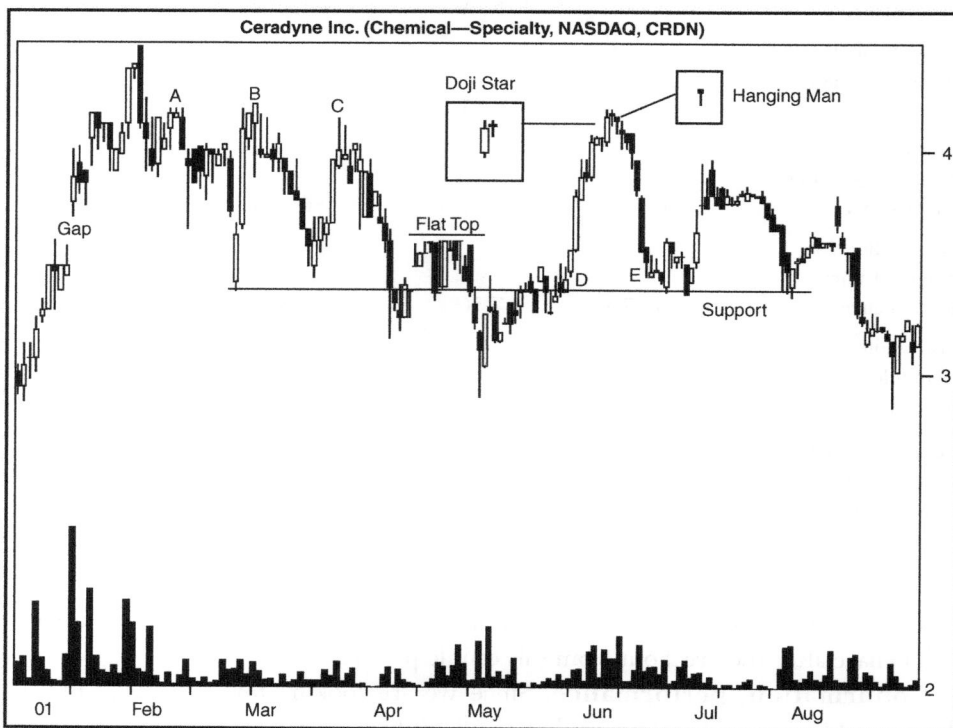

FIGURE 35.3 **This Doji Star Correctly Predicts a Reversal.**

two price bars, 4.22) for a height of 20 cents, and then subtract the height from the candle low. That gives a target of 3.82 (about 9% below the current close).

The measure rule works only 54% of the time (bear market/down breakout), so for a more likely target multiply the candle height by 54% and project the new height downward. That would give a closer target of 3.91.

Measure rules are fine, but I prefer to look for support zones. The flat top in April looks like a tasty landing zone. The flat top has a price of about 3.55, or 15% below the current close.

So what happens? As the chart shows, price can't pierce overhead resistance (peaks A, B, C), so it tumbles. Then price digs through the flat top as if it isn't there, finding support at a lower level. The decline mirrors the rise, making the path look like a bell-shaped curve (D to E). Such price mirrors happen from time to time and are worth factoring into your trading. Doug closes out his trade on the first tall white candle a few days after point E.

■ For Best Performance

The following list offers tips and observations to help choose candles that perform well. Consult the associated table for more information.

- Use the identification guidelines to help select the pattern—Table 35.1.

- Candles within a third of the yearly low perform best—Table 35.2.

- Select tall candles—Table 35.3.

- Use the measure rule to predict a price target—Table 35.3.

- Candles with tall upper or lower shadows outperform—Table 35.3.

- Volume gives performance clues—Table 35.4.

- Look for a bearish doji star to appear as an upward retracement in a downward price trend—Trading Tactics discussion.

- The candle breaks out upward most often—Table 35.5.

- Patterns within a third of the yearly high tend to act as continuations most often—Table 35.5.

- Breakouts below the 50-day moving average lead to the best performance—Table 35.6.

CHAPTER 36

Engulfing, Bearish

From Thomas N. Bulkowski, *Encyclopedia of Candlestick Charts* (Hoboken, New Jersey: John Wiley & Sons, 2008), Chapter 35.

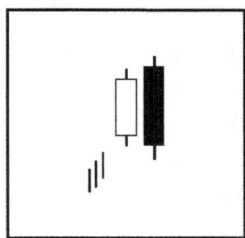

Learning Objective Statements

- Interpret potential price moves based on the patterns described in this chapter
- Calculate potential price targets
- Evaluate price levels for potential support or resistance
- Identify and interpret signals from various oscillators and technical studies

▓ Behavior and Rank

Theoretical: Bearish reversal.
Actual bull market: Bearish reversal 79% of the time (ranking 5).
Actual bear market: Bearish reversal 82% of the time (ranking 5).
Frequency: 11th out of 103.
Overall performance over time: 91st out of 103.

Bearish engulfing candlesticks are about as numerous as bees in a hive. I logged over 30,000 (candlesticks, not bees) in one database before I quit looking. What's more exciting, though, is that they work quite well as reversals, but that tells only part of the story. The rank of 5 as bearish reversals is very close to the best (1) out of 103 candlestick patterns. Unfortunately, although price may reverse it doesn't go far. Check out the overall performance ranking of 91. Ouch! Again, 1 is best out of 103. This candle pattern is like the time the fuel pump on my Chevette broke. As soon as I started an uphill climb, the car died. Don't depend on price after a reversal from this candle going anywhere, either.

Price trends upward leading to the first white candle in this pattern. With the bulls in control, a tall black candle appears that opens higher than the body of the first candle, indicating that the bulls still think they are masters of the domain. Then the bears come in and knock price down, with it closing below the body of the first day in a strong push of selling pressure. Price continues lower the vast majority of the time.

▣ Identification Guidelines

Figure 36.1 shows three examples of a bearish engulfing pattern. The first one in April appears after price trends up one day. This is a weak uptrend—more of a consolidation, really—so there's not much to reverse. Price breaks out downward nevertheless.

The middle bearish engulfing pattern is more successful. Price gaps lower and continues down for almost two weeks before finding solid ground upon which to stand.

The last engulfing pattern occurs near June. Price trends up leading to the candle pattern and continues moving up after the end, too. The shadows of the first candle are not engulfed and that's okay. It's an engulfed body that's important with this candle pattern.

Table 36.1 lists identification guidelines. This two-candle pattern begins with a white candle, followed by a black one. The black candle has a body that's taller than the white candle's body and it overlaps. That means the opening price of the black candle is equal to or above the prior close and the closing price of the black candle is

FIGURE 36.1 Three Bearish Engulfing Patterns, with Two Showing Reversals and One Not.

TABLE 36.1	Identification Guidelines
Characteristic	Discussion
Number of candle lines	Two.
Price trend	Upward leading to the start of the candle pattern.
First day	A white candle.
Second day	A black candle, the body of which overlaps the white candle's body.

equal to or below the prior open. Concerning the bodies, the two tops can be equal *or* the two bottoms can be equal, but not both. I don't make the rules; I just follow them.

■ Statistics

Table 36.2 shows general statistics.

Number found. I limited the number of candle patterns under study to 20,000 to keep things manageable. Most engulfing patterns came from a bull market.

Reversal or continuation performance. Candles with downward breakouts show the best performance. Those are also reversals.

S&P performance. Comparing the candle performance with the S&P 500, we see that the candle wallops the S&P's performance over the same period.

Candle end to breakout. It takes between two and four days for price to break out. Downward breakouts take about half the time to break out compared to upward ones. That's because price closes nearer the low than the high.

TABLE 36.2	General Statistics			
Description	Bull Market, Up Breakout	Bear Market, Up Breakout	Bull Market, Down Breakout	Bear Market, Down Breakout
Number found	3,059	933	11,745	4,263
Reversal (R), continuation (C) performance	2.79% C	3.67% C	−6.80% R	−11.26% R
Standard & Poor's 500 change	1.11%	0.38%	−1.06%	−2.69%
Candle end to breakout (median, days)	4	4	2	2
Candle end to trend end (median, days)	5	5	8	9
Number of breakouts near the 12-month low (L), middle (M), or high (H)	L 402, M 727, H 1,930	L 172, M 260, H 501	L 2,155, M 3,163, H 6,427	L 1,131, M 1,255, H 1,877
Percentage move for each 12-month period	L 3.73%, M 2.86%, H 2.63%	L 4.96%, M 3.44%, H 3.43%	L −7.39%, M −6.77%, H −6.68%	L −14.48%, M −10.70%, H −10.23%
Candle end + 1 day	1.27%	1.77%	−0.79%	−1.24%
Candle end + 3 days	2.01%	2.95%	−1.69%	−2.73%
Candle end + 5 days	1.36%	2.29%	−2.39%	−3.85%
Candle end + 10 days	−1.56%	−2.11%	−3.56%	−5.92%
10-day performance rank	103	100	25	21

Candle end to trend end. It takes between five and nine days for price to reach the trend end. Upward breakouts take less time to reach the trend end because the uptrend is already well along.

Yearly position, performance. Most of the bearish engulfing candles break out within a third of the yearly high. However, performance is best when the breakout is near the yearly low.

Performance over time. If you will recall, the reversal rate listed at the opening of this chapter was near the top of the list (5, where 1 is best). Looking at performance over time from the table tells you why the candle pattern ranks 91 out of 103. Performance does not climb over time and even goes negative when it should not. Downward breakouts do well but upward ones are pathetic. In fact, the bullmarket/ up breakout rank is the worst of any candle pattern.

Table 36.3 shows height statistics.

Candle height. Tall candles perform substantially better than short ones. To determine whether the candle is short or tall, compute its height from highest high to lowest low price in the candle pattern and divide by the breakout price. If the result is higher than the median, then you have a tall candle; otherwise it's short.

Rusty is considering shorting a stock that shows a bearish engulfing candle pattern with a high price of 37 and a low of 36. Is his candle tall? The height is 37 − 36, or 1, and the measure is 1/37, or 2.7%. That is above the median listed for bull market/ upward breakouts, so the candle is tall.

Measure rule. Use the measure rule to help predict how far price will rise or fall. Compute the height of the candle and multiply it by the appropriate percentage shown in the table; then apply it to the breakout price.

TABLE 36.3 Height Statistics

Description	Bull Market, Up Breakout	Bear Market, Up Breakout	Bull Market, Down Breakout	Bear Market, Down Breakout
Median candle height as a percentage of breakout price	2.62%	3.49%	3.07%	4.17%
Short candle, performance	2.19%	2.90%	−5.36%	−8.94%
Tall candle, performance	3.59%	4.55%	−8.73%	−13.95%
Percentage meeting price target (measure rule)	45%	41%	74%	76%
Median upper shadow as a percentage of breakout price	0.23%	0.27%	0.21%	0.30%
Short upper shadow, performance	2.57%	3.33%	−6.43%	−9.96%
Tall upper shadow, performance	3.02%	3.98%	−7.19%	−12.57%
Median lower shadow as a percentage of breakout price	0.45%	0.62%	0.37%	0.56%
Short lower shadow, performance	2.50%	3.22%	−6.21%	−10.72%
Tall lower shadow, performance	3.11%	4.13%	−7.47%	−11.84%

TABLE 36.4 Volume Statistics

Description	Bull Market, Up Breakout	Bear Market, Up Breakout	Bull Market, Down Breakout	Bear Market, Down Breakout
Rising candle volume, performance	2.80%	3.86%	−6.75%	−11.75%
Falling candle volume, performance	2.78%	3.51%	−6.86%	−10.80%
Above-average candle volume, performance	2.56%	3.61%	−6.81%	−11.24%
Below-average candle volume, performance	2.89%	3.69%	−6.80%	−11.28%
Heavy breakout volume, performance	3.06%	4.22%	−7.12%	−11.82%
Light breakout volume, performance	2.57%	3.24%	−6.55%	−10.83%

What are Rusty's price targets for his candle? The upward target becomes (1 × 45%) + 37, or 37.45, and the downward target would be 36 − (1 × 74%), or 35.26.

Shadows. The following results pertain to the last candle line in the pattern. To determine whether the shadow is short or tall, compute the height of the shadow and divide by the breakout price. Compare the result to the median in the table. Tall shadows have a percentage higher than the median. Candles with tall upper or lower shadows perform better than do those with short shadows.

Table 36.4 shows volume statistics.

Candle volume trend. A rising volume trend works better in all categories but one. Bull market/down breakouts work better with falling volume.

Average candle volume. Candles with below-average volume perform better than do those with above-average volume in all cases except bull market/down breakouts.

Breakout volume. Candles with heavy breakout volume perform best across the board.

▪ Trading Tactics

Figure 36.2 shows upward retracements in a downward price trend. Price peaks in May and then heads down in a stair-step decline. Along the way, three bearish engulfing patterns occur at the top of the upward retracements. They provide good trading signals to short the stock. Since the primary trend is downward, look for the brief upward retracements and take a position once price begins trending lower.

I split trading tactics into two basic studies, one concerning reversal rates and the other concerning performance. Of the two, reversal rates are more important, because it's better to trade in the direction of the trend and let price run as far as it can.

Table 36.5 gives tips to find the trend direction.

Confirmation reversal rates. To confirm that a reversal will occur, wait for price to close lower the day after the engulfing pattern ends. That method works 95% of the time.

Reversal, continuation rates. Looking at the breakout direction, the candle acts as a reversal more often. Expect a downward breakout.

FIGURE 36.2 Bearish Engulfing Patterns in a Downtrend Present Good Trading Opportunities.

Yearly range reversals. Most reversals occur within a third of the yearly low.

Table 36.6 shows performance indicators that can give hints as to how your stock will behave after the breakout from this candle pattern.

Confirmation, performance. Opening gap confirmation, where you short the stock if price gaps open lower, works best in both bull and bear markets.

Moving average. Candles with breakouts below the 50-trading-day moving average perform better than do those with breakouts above the moving average.

Closing position. Candles that close in the lowest third of the last candle line of the engulfing pattern perform better than do those that close elsewhere in the candle.

THE INTEGRATION OF TECHNICAL ANALYSIS

TABLE 36.5 Reversal Rates		
Description	Bull Market	Bear Market
Closing price confirmation reversal rate	95%	95%
Candle color confirmation reversal rate	92%	94%
Opening gap confirmation reversal rate	86%	87%
Reversal rate: trend up, breakout down	79%	82%
Continuation rate: trend up, breakout up	21%	18%
Percentage of reversals (R)/ continuations (C) for each 12-month low (L), middle (M), or high (H)	L 84% R/16% C, M 81% R/19% C, H 77% R/23% C	L 87% R/13% C, M 83% R/17% C, H 79% R/21% C

TABLE 36.6 **Performance Indicators**

Description	Bull Market, Up Breakout	Bear Market, Up Breakout	Bull Market, Down Breakout	Bear Market, Down Breakout
Closing price confirmation, performance	N/A	N/A	−6.09%	−10.29%
Candle color confirmation, performance	N/A	N/A	−6.06%	−10.59%
Opening gap confirmation, performance	N/A	N/A	−6.71%	−10.75%
Breakout above 50-day moving average, performance	2.69%	3.59%	−6.61%	−10.08%
Breakout below 50-day moving average, performance	3.36%	4.09%	−7.19%	−13.11%
Last candle: close in highest third, performance	2.50%	2.97%*	−6.08%	−10.24%
Last candle: close in middle third, performance	2.75%	3.64%	−6.45%	−9.41%
Last candle: close in lowest third, performance	2.81%	3.71%	−6.87%	−11.68%

N/A means not applicable.

*Fewer than 30 samples.

▪ Sample Trade

Rusty wants to trade the company shown in Figure 36.3. When the stock peaks at B and forms a bearish engulfing pattern, he gets excited. The peak is at the same height as point A, and that tells him overhead resistance will likely cause price to drop, but how far?

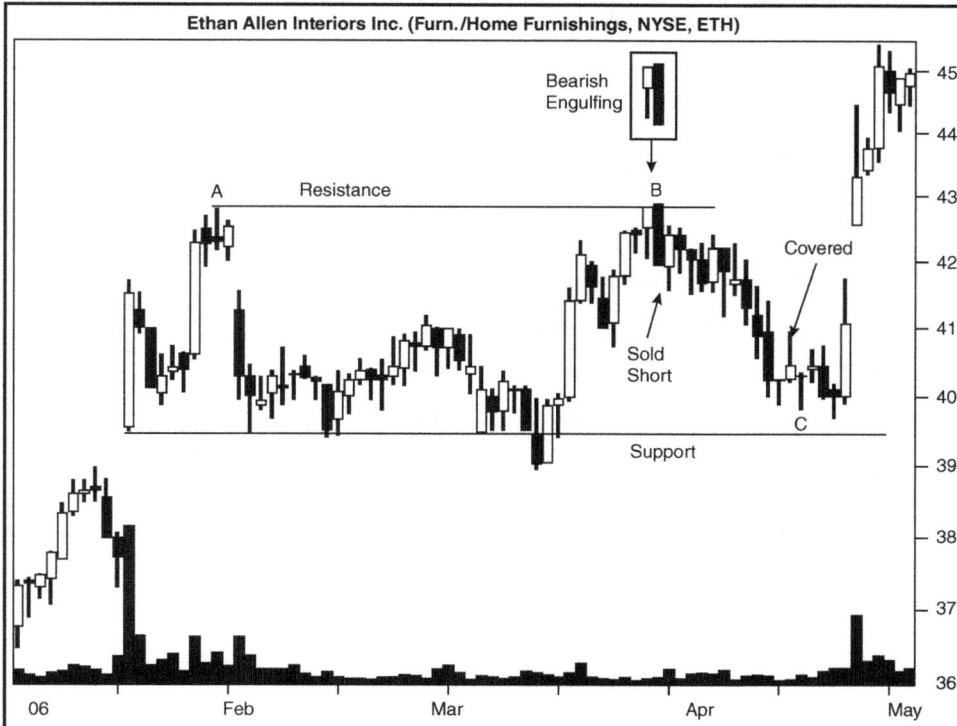

FIGURE 36.3 Price Hits Overhead Resistance and Forms a Bearish Engulfing Candle.

Below 40 is a horizontal support line. If all goes well, price will touch this line and then rebound. The price of the support line would be his target.

The next day, price gaps lower at the open and he sells short the stock (using opening gap confirmation). On that day, a white candle forms and it concerns him because the bulls are regaining control. Coupled with a long lower shadow, it confirms this bullish belief. Nevertheless, he decides to wait out the stock. For safety, he places a stop a penny above the high at B.

Price eases lower over time. When a gravestone doji appears at C, near underlying support, he believes the risk of a rise is much greater than the potential reward of an additional decline. The next day he closes out his short position for a near $2 profit per share.

"On a million shares, that's a nice chunk of change," he says. That's true, but it's too bad he didn't short a million shares.

▨ For Best Performance

The following list offers tips and observations to help choose candles that perform well. Consult the associated table for more information.

- ▪ Use the identification guidelines to help select the pattern—Table 36.1.

- ▪ Candles within a third of the yearly low perform best—Table 36.2.

- ▪ Select tall candles—Table 36.3.

- ▪ Use the measure rule to predict a price target—Table 36.3.

- ▪ Candles with tall upper or lower shadows outperform—Table 36.3.

- ▪ Volume gives performance clues—Table 36.4.

- ▪ Trade upward retracements in a downtrend—Trading Tactics discussion.

- ▪ The candle breaks out downward most often—Table 36.5.

- ▪ Patterns within a third of the yearly low tend to act as reversals most often—Table 36.5.

- ▪ Opening gap confirmation works best—Table 36.6.

- ▪ Breakouts below the 50-day moving average lead to the best performance—Table 36.6.

CHAPTER 37

Engulfing, Bullish

From Thomas N. Bulkowski, *Encyclopedia of candlestick Charts* (Hoboken, New Jersey: John Wiley & Sons, 2008), Chapter 36.

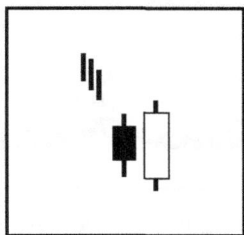

Learning Objective Statements

- Interpret potential price moves based on the patterns described in this chapter
- Calculate potential price targets
- Evaluate price levels for potential support or resistance
- Identify and interpret signals from various oscillators and technical studies

Behavior and Rank

Theoretical: Bullish reversal.

Actual bull market: Bullish reversal 63% of the time (ranking 22).

Actual bear market: Bullish reversal 62% of the time (ranking 25).

Frequency: 12th out of 103.

Overall performance over time: 84th out of 103.

The bullish engulfing pattern acts as a reversal almost two-thirds of the time (62% to 63%), but its performance suffers. It ranks 84 out of 103, where 1 is best. Downward breakouts show respectable performance, but upward breakouts yank the rank back like a bungee cord on the rebound. The candlestick appears most often at minor lows but less often at major turning points.

The psychology behind the pattern begins with a downward price trend leading to the engulfing pattern. The bears have control of the bank. A black candle prints

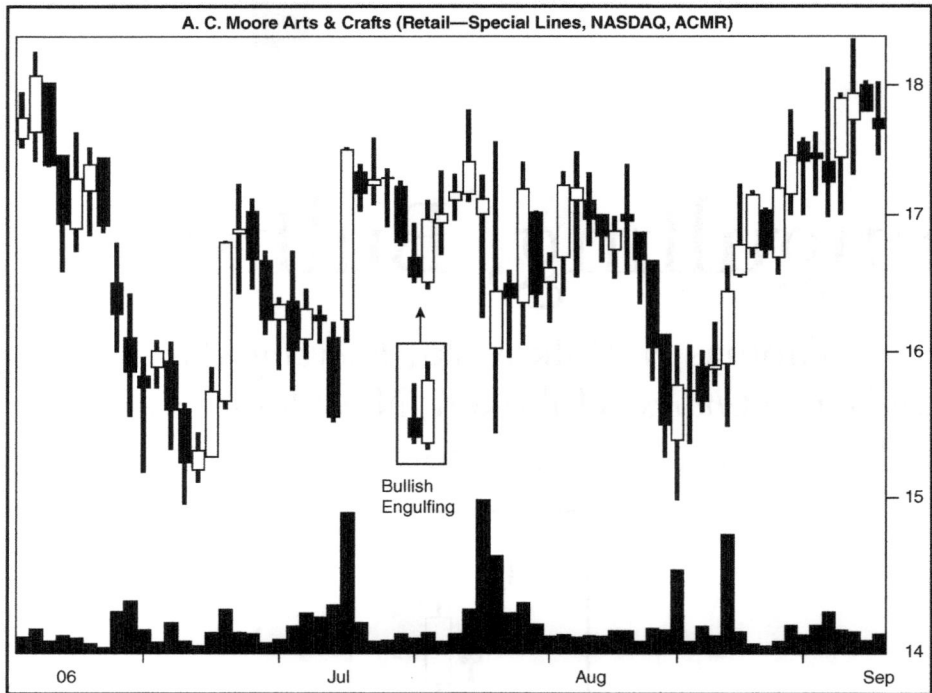

FIGURE 37.1 A Bullish Engulfing Pattern Occurs in a Downward Retracement of the Upward Trend.

on the chart as the opening move by the bears, but after price opens lower, the bulls storm the bank, taking over. Their buying demand pushes price up above the prior black body. At the close, the bulls still control the bank and price remains above the prior black body, completing the bullish engulfing candlestick.

■ Identification Guidelines

Figure 37.1 shows an example of where you will often see an engulfing pattern. Price moves up in a stair-step rise. At the bottom of the step, a bullish engulfing pattern sometimes appears. It's a signal for price to climb to the next step and that's what happens. Price moves higher, eventually closing above the top of the two-day candle pattern and staging an upward breakout. Table 37.1 lists what to look for when searching for bullish engulfing patterns.

TABLE 37.1 Identification Guidelines

Characteristic	Discussion
Number of candle lines	Two.
Price trend	Downward leading to the start of the candlestick pattern.
First day	A black candle.
Second day	A white candle opens below the prior body and closes above that body, too. Price need not engulf the shadows.

The candle pattern consists of two candle lines. The first line is black and the second white. The white candle engulfs or overlaps the black candle's body. That means the white candle opens at or below the black body and closes at or above the black body. The tops of the bodies or the bottoms of the bodies can share the same price, but not both. Ignore the shadows in this candle pattern.

■ Statistics

Table 37.2 shows general statistics.

Number found. I cut the sample size from a gazillion candle patterns to 20,000. Prorating the standard database reveals that the bullish engulfing pattern occurs more often in a bear market.

Reversal or continuation performance. The best-performing engulfing candles appear in a bear market. This isn't a fluke, because it occurs with many other candle types as well.

S&P performance. Comparing the candle breakout to the trend high or low with the performance of the S&P 500 over the same periods, we see that the engulfing candle does substantially better in all cases.

TABLE 37.2 General Statistics

Description	Bull Market, Up Breakout	Bear Market, Up Breakout	Bull Market, Down Breakout	Bear Market, Down Breakout
Number found	8,923	3,617	5,225	2,235
Reversal (R), continuation (C) performance	4.60% R	5.75% R	−5.91% C	−9.68% C
Standard & Poor's 500 change	1.32%	0.59%	−1.31%	−3.28%
Candle end to breakout (median, days)	2	2	4	4
Candle end to trend end (median, days)	6	6	8	8
Number of breakouts near the 12-month low (L), middle (M), or high (H)	L 2,130, M 2,589, H 4,204	L 1,083, M 1,161, H 1,373	L 1,696, M 1,680, H 1,849	L 896, M 718, H 621
Percentage move for each 12-month period	L 5.50%, M 4.63%, H 4.25%	L 7.56%, M 5.56%, H 4.84%	L −6.89%, M −5.84%, H −5.32%	L −12.12%, M −8.56%, H −8.31%
Candle end + 1 day	0.62%	0.95%	−1.34%	−1.88%
Candle end + 3 days	0.89%	1.22%	−2.69%	−4.11%
Candle end + 5 days	0.80%	0.92%	−3.32%	−5.02%
Candle end + 10 days	−0.05%	−1.18%	−3.77%	−6.31%
10-day performance rank	101	96	20	14

Candle end to breakout. It takes two to four days for price to break out. Upward breakouts take less time than downward ones because the close is nearer to the top of the candle.

Candle end to trend end. Upward breakouts take two days less time to reach the trend end than downward breakouts. Since the prevailing trend is downward, I find the result unusual. However, with price closing near the top of the second candle, a new uptrend would already be underway, so maybe that explains the shorter time.

Yearly position, performance. Most bullish engulfing candles appear within a third of the yearly high except for bearmarket/down breakouts. Those show more often near the yearly low. Candles within a third of the yearly low perform best.

Performance over time. First the good news. Performance after a downward breakout is exemplary. Performance increases over each measurement period, resulting in excellent performance rankings. The bad news is the bull market performance is dreadful. Price actually drops from days 5 to 10, so the performance rank suffers, too.

Table 37.3 shows height statistics.

Candle height. Tall patterns perform better than short ones. To determine whether the candle is short or tall, compute its height from highest high to lowest low price in the candle pattern and divide by the breakout price. If the result is higher than the median, then you have a tall candle; otherwise it's short.

John sees a bullish engulfing candle with a high of 77 and a low of 73. Is the candle short or tall? The height is 77 − 73, or 4, so the measure would be (assuming bull market/upward breakout) 4/77, or 5.2%. That is well above the median listed, so the candle is tall.

TABLE 37.3   Height Statistics

Description	Bull Market, Up Breakout	Bear Market, Up Breakout	Bull Market, Down Breakout	Bear Market, Down Breakout
Median candle height as a percentage of breakout price	3.17%	4.42%	3.06%	4.36%
Short candle, performance	3.83%	4.62%	−4.82%	−8.07%
Tall candle, performance	5.64%	7.08%	−7.35%	−11.71%
Percentage meeting price target (measure rule)	60%	54%	63%	67%
Median upper shadow as a percentage of breakout price	0.37%	0.49%	0.48%	0.67%
Short upper shadow, performance	4.32%	5.26%	−5.52%	−9.34%
Tall upper shadow, performance	4.92%	6.28%	−6.34%	−10.05%
Median lower shadow as a percentage of breakout price	0.24%	0.34%	0.24%	0.35%
Short lower shadow, performance	4.28%	5.23%	−5.51%	−9.23%
Tall lower shadow, performance	4.94%	6.28%	−6.33%	−10.16%

TABLE 37.4 Volume Statistics

Description	Bull Market, Up Breakout	Bear Market, Up Breakout	Bull Market, Down Breakout	Bear Market, Down Breakout
Rising candle volume, performance	4.61%	5.83%	−6.02%	−9.61%
Falling candle volume, performance	4.59%	5.64%	−5.78%	−9.76%
Above-average candle volume, performance	4.69%	6.07%	−5.95%	−10.06%
Below-average candle volume, performance	4.54%	5.53%	−5.89%	−9.43%
Heavy breakout volume, performance	4.90%	6.47%	−6.30%	−10.82%
Light breakout volume, performance	4.34%	5.20%	−5.53%	−8.45%

Measure rule. Use the measure rule to help predict how far price will rise or fall. Compute the height of the candle pattern and multiply it by the appropriate percentage shown in the table; then apply it to the breakout price.

What price targets can John expect? The upward target would be (4 × 60%) + 77, or 79.40, and the downward target would be 73 − (4 × 63%), or 70.48.

Shadows. The table's results pertain to the last candle line in the pattern. To determine whether the shadow is short or tall, compute the height of the shadow and divide by the breakout price. Compare the result to the median in the table. Tall shadows have a percentage higher than the median. Candles with tall upper or lower shadows perform better than do those with short shadows.

Table 37.4 shows volume statistics.

Candle volume trend. A rising volume trend within the candle leads to better performance in all categories except bear market/down breakout. Those show better postbreakout performance if volume trends lower within the candle pattern.

Average candle volume. Heavy (above-average) candle volume results in better postbreakout performance across the board. In many cases, however, the performances with above-average and below-average volume are close, so the results are not as startling as they may seem.

Breakout volume. Candles with heavy breakout volume perform better than do those with light volume.

■ Trading Tactics

Figure 37.2 shows a bullish engulfing candlestick that appears when price is trending downward. By this I mean the primary, longer-term trend, not the minor ripples that appear within the tide. It's rare that the engulfing pattern will act as a major turning point, so don't depend on it doing so.

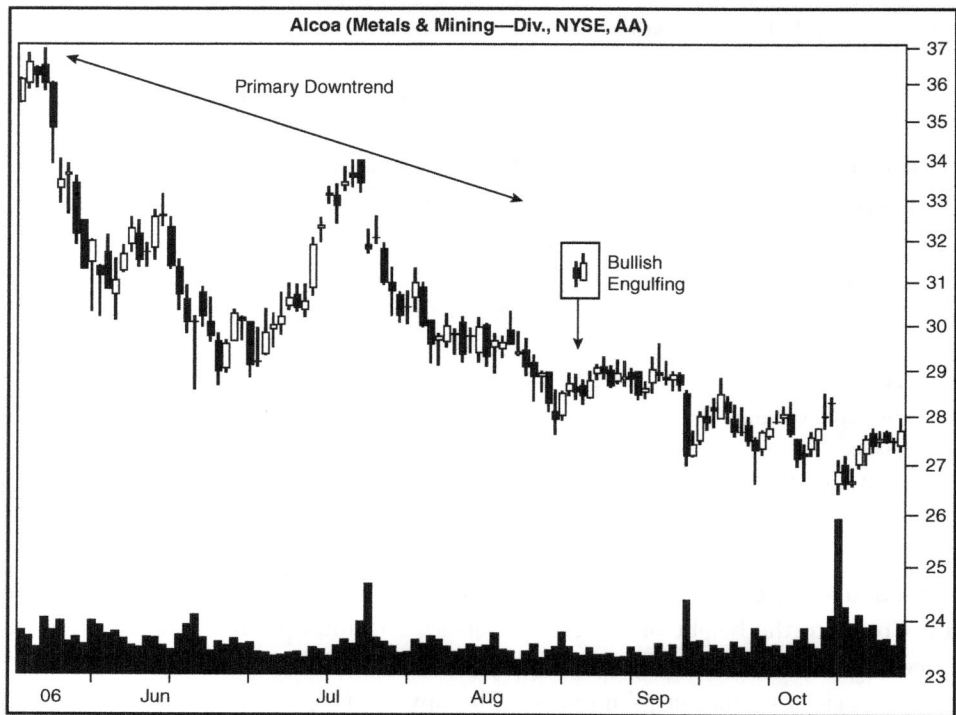

FIGURE 37.2 Avoid Trading a Bullish Engulfing Candle When the Primary Trend Is Down.

In this example, price moves higher, staging an upward breakout, but price resumes the downward trend soon after. Anyone taking a long position in this stock would lose money if they didn't sell quickly. Avoid going long when the primary price trend is downward.

I split trading tactics into two basic studies, one concerning reversal rates and the other concerning performance. Of the two, reversal rates are more important, because it's better to trade in the direction of the trend and let price run as far as it can.

Table 37.5 gives tips to find the trend direction.

TABLE 37.5 Reversal Rates

Description	Bull Market	Bear Market
Closing price confirmation reversal rate	89%	90%
Candle color confirmation reversal rate	86%	86%
Opening gap confirmation reversal rate	71%	70%
Reversal: trend down, breakout up	63%	62%
Continuation: trend down, breakout down	37%	38%
Percentage of reversals (R)/ continuations (C) for each 12-month low (L), middle (M), or high (H)	L 56% R/44% C, M 61% R/39% C, H 69% R/31% C	L 55% R/45% C, M 62% R/38% C, H 69% R/31% C

TABLE 37.6 Performance Indicators

Description	Bull Market, Up Breakout	Bear Market, Up Breakout	Bull Market, Down Breakout	Bear Market, Down Breakout
Closing price confirmation, performance	4.33%	5.52%	N/A	N/A
Candle color confirmation, performance	4.43%	5.63%	N/A	N/A
Opening gap confirmation, performance	5.67%	8.15%	N/A	N/A
Breakout above 50-day moving average, performance	4.35%	5.24%	−5.35%	−7.46%
Breakout below 50-day moving average, performance	4.91%	6.41%	−6.15%	−10.54%
Last candle: close in highest third, performance	4.67%	5.76%	−5.99%	−9.82%
Last candle: close in middle third, performance	4.30%	5.64%	−5.66%	−9.24%
Last candle: close in lowest third, performance	3.95%	6.44%	−5.58%	−9.20%

N/A means not applicable.

Confirmation reversal rates. To help detect a reversal of the downward price trend, wait for price to close higher the day after the engulfing candle ends. That is a reliable method, but it does not tell how long the new trend will last.

Reversal, continuation rates. Look for an upward breakout most often.

Yearly range reversals. Candles within a third of the yearly high tend to reverse more often than do those in the other ranges.

Table 37.6 shows performance indicators that can give hints as to how your stock will behave after the breakout from a candle pattern.

Confirmation, performance. Opening gap confirmation works better than the other methods. That means trading the day after the engulfing candle ends only if price gaps open higher.

Moving average. Candles with breakouts below the 50-trading-day moving average do better than do those with breakouts above the moving average.

Closing position. A close in the highest third of the last candle line in the pattern suggests better performance than a close elsewhere in the line except for bear market/up breakouts. Performance from those candles does best if the close is near the candle line's low.

▨ Sample Trade

Figure 37.3 shows a trade that John made. Price trends downward into A and then bounces up and returns to B. That's when a bullish engulfing candlestick appears. When price moves above the top of the engulfing pattern, John buys the stock, receiving a fill at 71.30.

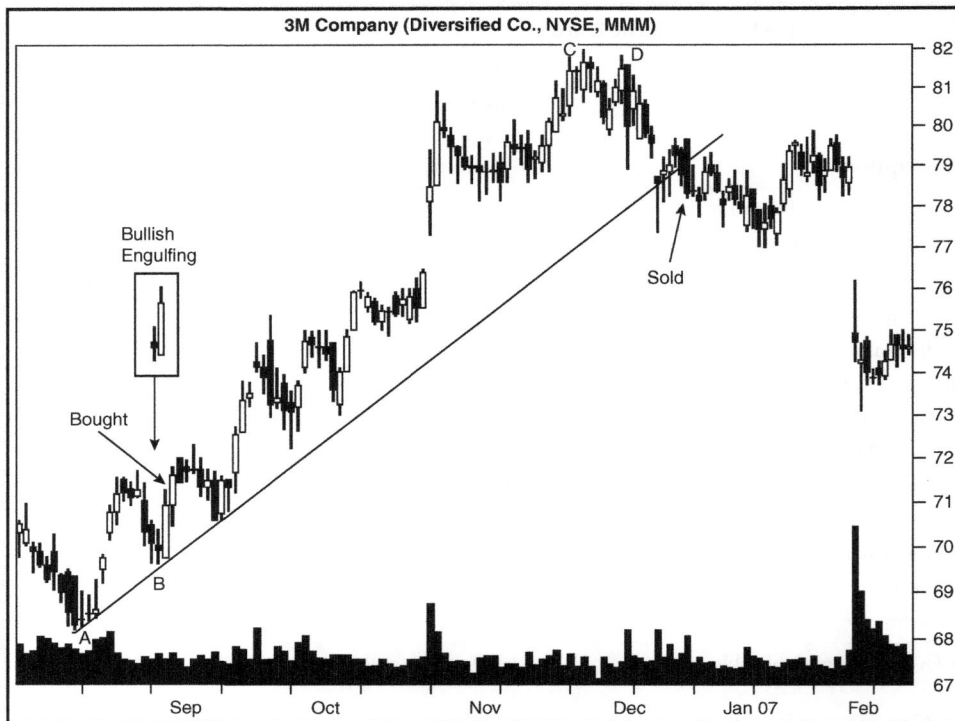

FIGURE 37.3 John Buys the Stock When the Primary Trend Is Up and Sells When Price Closes below the Trendline.

It's rare for price to trend upward in a straight-line run, so a return to a trendline connecting the lows of A and B is expected. That's what happens. John decides that if price closes below the trendline, he will get out. The sale will likely not be at the high, but at least he can keep most of his profit intact.

In subsequent months price moves up, loosely following the trendline upward. In mid-October price gaps higher, and John considers redrawing the trendline but decides against it. (That turns out to be a mistake, because a steeper trendline would have taken him out at a higher price.)

Price peaks to the right of C and then forms a lower high at D. A lower peak is a clue that the trend has changed from up to down. Why? "Because price attempted to make a new high and failed. The weakness suggests the bulls are tired," John says.

Price gaps downward in December but closes above the trendline. Four days later, price finally closes below the line. He sells the next day at the open and receives a fill of 78.31, making almost 10% on the trade.

■ For Best Performance

The following list offers tips and observations to help choose candles that perform well. Consult the associated table for more information.

- Use the identification guidelines to help select the pattern—Table 37.1.

- Candles within a third of the yearly low perform best—Table 37.2.

- Select tall candles—Table 37.3.

- Use the measure rule to predict a price target—Table 37.3.

- Candles with tall upper or lower shadows outperform—Table 37.3.

- Volume gives performance clues—Table 37.4.

- Avoid engulfing candles that appear in a downward primary trend—Trading Tactics discussion.

- The candle breaks out upward most often—Table 37.5.

- Patterns within a third of the yearly high tend to act as reversals most often—Table 37.5.

- Opening gap confirmation works best—Table 37.6.

- Breakouts below the 50-day moving average lead to the best performance—Table 37.6.

CHAPTER 38

Last Engulfing Bottom

From Thomas N. Bulkowski, *Encyclopedia of Candlestick Charts* (Hoboken, New Jersey: John Wiley & Sons, 2008), Chapter 54.

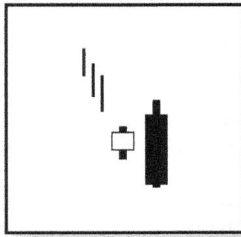

Learning Objective Statements

- Interpret potential price moves based on the patterns described in this chapter
- Calculate potential price targets
- Evaluate price levels for potential support or resistance
- Identify and interpret signals from various oscillators and technical studies

Behavior and Rank

Theoretical: Bullish reversal.
Actual bull market: Bearish continuation 65% of the time (ranking 14).
Actual bear market: Bearish continuation 67% of the time (ranking 12).
Frequency: 13th out of 103.
Overall performance over time: 48th out of 103.

The last engulfing bottom is yet another example of a dismal failure of a candle to act as a reversal. That's how it's supposed to behave, but my tests show that it acts as a continuation pattern 65% of the time (bull market) and 67% of the time (bear market). That's about two out of three. If you wait for an upward close the next day then you can reverse that. In that situation, price breaks out upward 61% of the time. As a continuation pattern, performance is middling, ranking 48 out of 103 candles, where 1 is best.

This candle pattern, which has a white candle followed by a black one, almost screams "bear!" The tall black candle engulfs the white one and somehow it's supposed to be bullish. Anytime I see a tall black candle it sends bearish shivers down my spine, like seeing a black funnel cloud heading for my house. That can't be good news, not for your house and not for the stock. Maybe this acts differently in securities other than stocks. We examine the behavior more closely in the Statistics section.

■ Identification Guidelines

Figure 38.1 shows a good example of a last engulfing bottom that's not a bottom. Price breaks out downward and then retraces a portion of the move from A before continuing lower. The retracement to B is typical for long downward moves, so don't think it's a delayed reaction to the engulfing pattern.

What do you look for when hunting last engulfing bottoms? Table 38.1 lists identification guidelines. The candle pattern uses two candle lines, the first is white and the second is black. The black candle engulfs the body of the white candle. That means the top of the black body is equal to or above the top of the white body and the black body bottom is equal to or below the bottom of the white body. Between the two candles, both the body tops and bottoms cannot be equal at the same time. The candle pair is similar to a bullish engulfing pattern except for color.

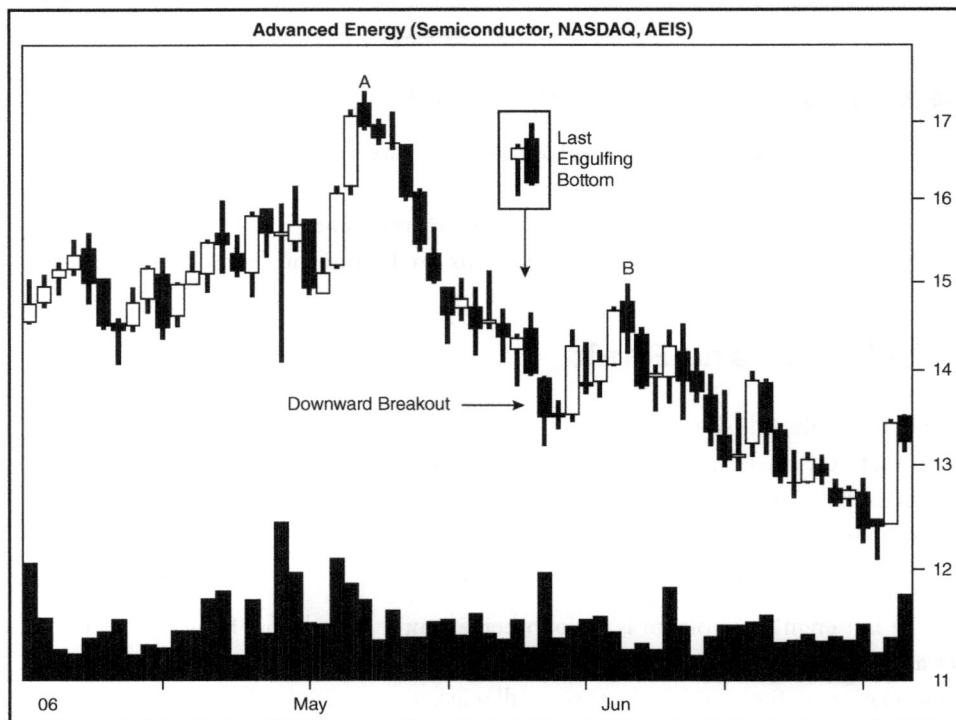

FIGURE 38.1   A Last Engulfing Pattern Acts as a Continuation Pattern When Price Breaks Out Downward.

TABLE 38.1 Identification Guidelines

Characteristic	Discussion
Number of candle lines	Two.
Price trend	Downward leading to the start of the candle pattern.
First day	A white candle.
Second day	A black candle opens above the prior body and closes below the prior body. Price need not engulf the shadows.

■ Statistics

Table 38.2 shows general statistics.

Number found. Prorating the standard database, the candle pattern appears most often in a bear market. However, I limited the selection to 20,000, which the table shows. Since the bull market was longer than the bear market, more appear there.

Reversal or continuation performance. The best performance comes from a bear market, regardless of the breakout direction.

S&P performance. Using the dates of the candle end to the trend end, I measured the performance of the S&P 500 and found that the candle beats the index by a wide margin.

TABLE 38.2 General Statistics

Description	Bull Market, Up Breakout	Bear Market, Up Breakout	Bull Market, Down Breakout	Bear Market, Down Breakout
Number found	5,183	1,723	9,559	3,535
Reversal (R), continuation (C) performance	6.63% R	8.12% R	−5.44% C	−10.20% C
Standard & Poor's 500 change	2.11%	1.09%	−0.82%	−2.53%
Candle end to breakout (median, days)	4	4	2	2
Candle end to trend end (median, days)	9	8	6	6
Number of breakouts near the 12-month low (L), middle (M), or high (H)	L 1,088, M 1,334, H 2,141	L 540, M 558, H 607	L 2,822, M 2,944, H 2,900	L 1,478, M 1,168, H 846
Percentage move for each 12-month period	L 7.68%, M 6.19%, H 6.34%	L 10.50%, M 7.83%, H 6.82%	L −6.00%, M −5.39%, H −5.12%	L −12.31%, M −9.24%, H −8.71%
Candle end + 1 day	1.46%	2.18%	−0.77%	−1.40%
Candle end + 3 days	2.96%	4.43%	−1.16%	−2.35%
Candle end + 5 days	3.58%	5.09%	−1.10%	−2.67%
Candle end + 10 days	3.99%	4.85%	−0.91%	−2.73%
10-day performance rank	31	31	98	74

Candle end to breakout. This describes the median time it takes price to close above or close below the candle pattern. Downward breakouts take half the time of upward ones because the close is near the pattern's low.

Candle end to trend end. How long can you expect price to trend? Again, downward breakouts take less time than do upward breakouts. The reason for this is probably because the downtrend is already underway, placing it closer to the trend end.

Yearly position, performance. Where a candle appears in the yearly price range sometimes affects performance. Upward breakouts appear within a third of the yearly high most often, but it's the yearly low where you'll find the best performance. In fact, the yearly low provides the best performance across the board.

Performance over time. Based on the performance rank, upward breakouts are where the money is to be made. The strength of this pattern softens between five and 10 days in the bear market/up breakout category and sooner (after three days) in the bull market/down breakout column. That weakness suggests this pattern is not a robust performer (or else it would be strong across all time periods and market conditions).

Table 38.3 shows height statistics.

Candle height. To determine whether the candle is short or tall, compute its height from highest high to lowest low price in the candle pattern and divide by the breakout price. If the result is higher than the median, then you have a tall candle; otherwise it's short.

For example, Aniston sees a last engulfing candle on her chart with a high price of 40 and a low of 39. Is the candle pattern short or tall? The height is 40 − 39, or 1, so the computation is 1/40, or 2.5%. Let's assume an upward breakout in a bull market, so the candle is short because the value is less than the median 2.93%.

TABLE 38.3 Height Statistics

Description	Bull Market, Up Breakout	Bear Market, Up Breakout	Bull Market, Down Breakout	Bear Market, Down Breakout
Median candle height as a percentage of breakout price	2.93%	4.25%	3.13%	4.53%
Short candle, performance	5.23%	6.16%	−4.47%	−8.23%
Tall candle, performance	8.44%	10.29%	−6.71%	−12.57%
Percentage meeting price target (measure rule)	70%	66%	61%	68%
Median upper shadow as a percentage of breakout price	0.26%	0.35%	0.24%	0.36%
Short upper shadow, performance	6.30%	7.67%	−5.22%	−9.29%
Tall upper shadow, performance	6.98%	8.58%	−5.67%	−11.10%
Median lower shadow as a percentage of breakout price	0.40%	0.62%	0.35%	0.52%
Short lower shadow, performance	5.89%	7.31%	−4.92%	−10.05%
Tall lower shadow, performance	7.48%	8.98%	−6.02%	−10.37%

TABLE 38.4   Volume Statistics

Description	Bull Market, Up Breakout	Bear Market, Up Breakout	Bull Market, Down Breakout	Bear Market, Down Breakout
Rising candle volume, performance	6.57%	7.67%	−5.41%	−10.28%
Falling candle volume, performance	6.70%	8.57%	−5.47%	−10.13%
Above-average candle volume, performance	6.67%	8.51%	−5.50%	−10.21%
Below-average candle volume, performance	6.62%	7.87%	−5.40%	−10.20%
Heavy breakout volume, performance	7.29%	8.68%	−5.76%	−11.22%
Light breakout volume, performance	6.01%	7.56%	−5.10%	−8.91%

Why is this important? Because candle height is one of the best predictors of post-breakout performance. Look at the performance results in the table and you'll see that tall candles beat the short ones in all columns.

Measure rule. Use the measure rule to help predict how far price will rise or fall. Compute the height of the candle pattern and multiply it by the appropriate percentage shown in the table; then apply it to the breakout price.

What are Aniston's price targets for her engulfing pattern, assuming a bull market? The height is 1, so the upward breakout target would be $(1 \times 70\%) + 40$, or 40.70 and the downward breakout target would be $39 - (1 \times 61\%)$, or 38.39.

Shadows. The shadows pertain to the last candle line in the pattern. To determine whether the shadow is short or tall, compute the height of the shadow and divide by the breakout price. Compare the result to the median in the table. Tall shadows have a percentage higher than the median. Tall upper and lower shadows perform better than their short counterparts.

Table 38.4 shows volume statistics.

Candle volume trend. A falling volume trend works best in all categories except for bear market/down breakouts. Those do better with a rising volume trend in the candle.

Average candle volume. Candles with above-average candle volume perform better after the breakout than do those with below-average volume.

Breakout volume. Heavy breakout volume suggests better performance across the board.

■ Trading Tactics

Trade a last engulfing bottom reversal only when the primary trend is upward. The short downward retracement in the uptrend provides a buying opportunity when price merges with the upward current already underway. Upward breakouts in a primary downtrend tend to be short-lived, so avoid that trading setup.

I split trading tactics into two basic studies, one concerning reversal rates and the other concerning performance. Of the two, reversal rates are more important, because it's better to trade in the direction of the trend and let price run as far as it can.

TABLE 38.5	Reversal Rates	
Description	Bull Market	Bear Market
Closing price confirmation reversal rate	61%	59%
Candle color confirmation reversal rate	59%	57%
Opening gap confirmation reversal rate	44%	42%
Reversal: trend down, breakout up	35%	33%
Continuation: trend down, breakout down	65%	67%
Percentage of reversals (R)/continuations (C) for each 12-month low (L), middle (M), or high (H)	L 28% R/72% C, M 31% R/69% C, H 42% R/58% C	L 27% R/73% C, M 32% R/68% C, H 42% R/58% C

Table 38.5 gives tips to find the trend direction.

Confirmation reversal rates. If you wait for an upward close the day after the candle pattern ends, price tends to continue moving higher 61% of the time in a bull market and 59% of the time in a bear market. That's the best of the bunch.

Reversal, continuation rates. Since the price trend is down, expect a downward breakout about 65% to 67% of the time.

Yearly range reversals. Patterns with breakouts in the two lowest thirds of the yearly price range act as continuations between 68% and 73% of the time. The highest third also favors continuation of the price trend, but the difference is not as startling.

Table 38.6 shows performance indicators that can give hints as to how your stock will behave after the breakout from a candle pattern.

Confirmation, performance. Candle theory says that when price closes higher after the black candle, it confirms the pattern as a reversal. That turns out to be true. If

TABLE 38.6	Performance Indicators			
Description	Bull Market, Up Breakout	Bear Market, Up Breakout	Bull Market, Down Breakout	Bear Market, Down Breakout
Closing price confirmation, performance	7.15%	10.62%	N/A	N/A
Candle color confirmation, performance	6.98%	10.31%	N/A	N/A
Opening gap confirmation, performance	7.16%	11.56%	N/A	N/A
Breakout above 50-day moving average, performance	6.41%	7.03%	−5.19%	−8.47%
Breakout below 50-day moving average, performance	6.79%	9.26%	−5.54%	−10.65%
Last candle: close in highest third, performance	6.38%	9.64%	−5.75%	−12.97%
Last candle: close in middle third, performance	6.67%	8.29%	−5.60%	−9.02%
Last candle: close in lowest third, performance	6.63%	8.03%	−5.41%	−10.37%

N/A means not applicable.

price closes higher the day after the candle ends, it breaks out upward 61% of the time. In other words, it acts as a reversal 61% of the time. That's quite a turnaround from being a continuation pattern 65% of the time when you don't wait for a higher close.

However, a higher closing price does not lead to the best performance. The opening gap method, where you wait for price to gap open higher, works better, especially in a bear market, as the numbers show.

Moving average. If the breakout price is below the 50-day moving average, post-breakout performance improves over those with breakouts above the moving average.

Closing position. A close within the highest third of the black candle suggests better performance in all categories except bull market/up breakouts. Those do better if price is in the middle third of the candle.

You may wonder how price can close in the top third of a black candle. The answer is the candle must have a long lower shadow. Few patterns qualify, so be skeptical and don't depend on this being accurate.

▥ Sample Trade

Figure 38.2 shows a trade Aniston made in the stock. Price trended lower during March, as the chart shows, and then found support. Price bobbled up and down,

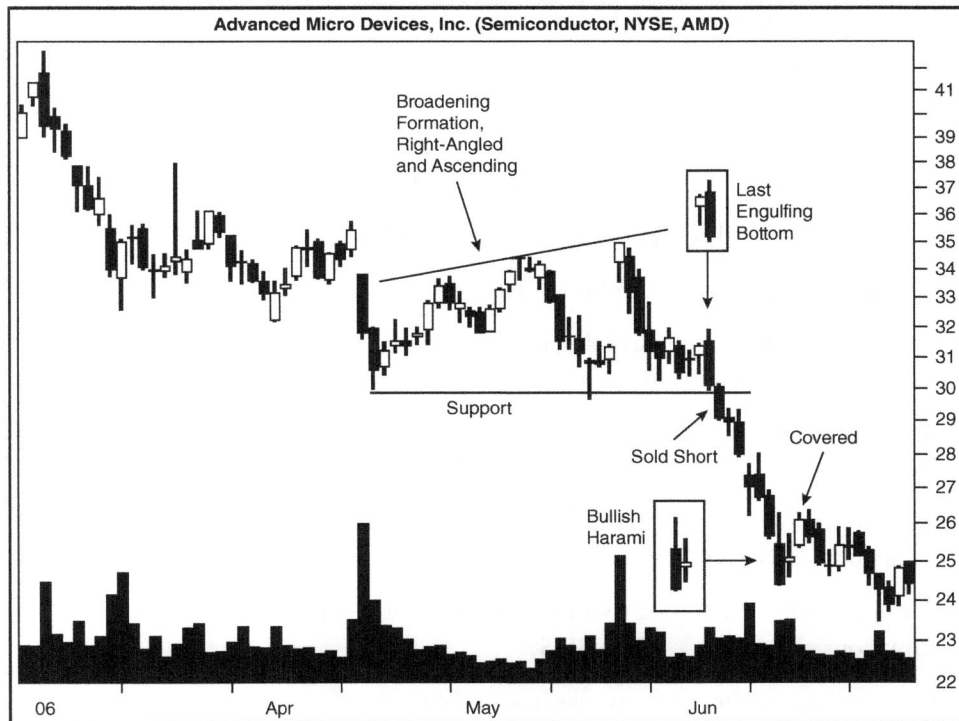

FIGURE 38.2   A Broadening Chart Pattern Appears with a Last Engulfing Bottom Pattern Pointing the Way Downward.

bottoming near the support line but forming higher peaks. Eventually, the pattern became a right-angled and ascending broadening chart pattern.

She followed price as it touched the support line and then formed a last engulfing bottom pattern. The breakout was in the middle third of the yearly price range, suggesting that the breakout would be downward (the last engulfing bottom would act as a continuation of the price trend). The candle was tall, as were both shadows, suggesting good postbreakout performance. The candle was comfortably below the 50-trading-day moving average, which was also good. Volume was rising in the candle (bad), but it was above average and breakout volume was also heavy (both suggest better performance). All of this pointed to, but did not guarantee, a profitable short trade.

She depended on opening gap confirmation the next day as the entry signal. When price gapped lower, she sold the stock short. Each day she got a quote and updated her charts. A spinning top and a series of black candles were all she saw until the bullish harami appeared—her signal to run for cover. When price gapped higher the next day, she covered her short and walked away with a profit in her purse and a smile on her face.

■ For Best Performance

The following list offers tips and observations to help choose candles that perform well. Consult the associated table for more information.

- ■ Use the identification guidelines to help select the pattern—Table 38.1.

- ■ Candles within a third of the yearly low perform best—Table 38.2.

- ■ Select tall candles—Table 38.3.

- ■ Use the measure rule to predict a price target—Table 38.3.

- ■ Candles with tall shadows outperform—Table 38.3.

- ■ Volume gives performance clues—Table 38.4.

- ■ Look to trade this candle in a downward retracement of an upward price trend—Trading Tactics discussion.

- ■ Wait for price to close higher a day after the candle ends to confirm a reversal—Table 38.5.

- ■ Use the trend leading to the start of the candle to help predict the likely breakout direction—Table 38.5.

- ■ Patterns within the lowest two-thirds of the yearly price range tend to act as continuations most often—Table 38.5.

- ■ Opening gap confirmation works best—Table 38.6.

- ■ Breakouts below the 50-day moving average lead to the best performance—Table 38.6.

CHAPTER 39

Last Engulfing Top

From Thomas N. Bulkowski, *Encyclopedia of Candlestick Charts* (Hoboken, New Jersey: John Wiley & Sons, 2008), Chapter 55.

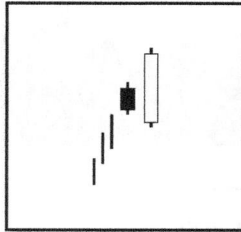

831

Learning Objective Statements

- Interpret potential price moves based on the patterns described in this chapter
- Calculate potential price targets
- Evaluate price levels for potential support or resistance
- Identify and interpret signals from various oscillators and technical studies

Behavior and Rank

Theoretical: Bearish reversal.
Actual bull market: Bullish continuation 68% of the time (ranking 9).
Actual bear market: Bullish continuation 67% of the time (ranking 14).
Frequency: 14th out of 103.
Overall performance over time: 79th out of 103.

The last engulfing top is supposed to act as a reversal candlestick, but my testing shows it acts as a continuation over two-thirds of the time. Even if you wait for a lower close, the reversal rate climbs to just 55%, which is a nickel above random. Do yourself a favor and trade this as a continuation pattern unless technical evidence says otherwise.

The last engulfing top is a continuation pattern that occurs frequently (rank of 14 out of 103 candles, where 1 is best) but performance suffers. It ranks 79. Based on the rank, you'll find the best performance after a downward breakout.

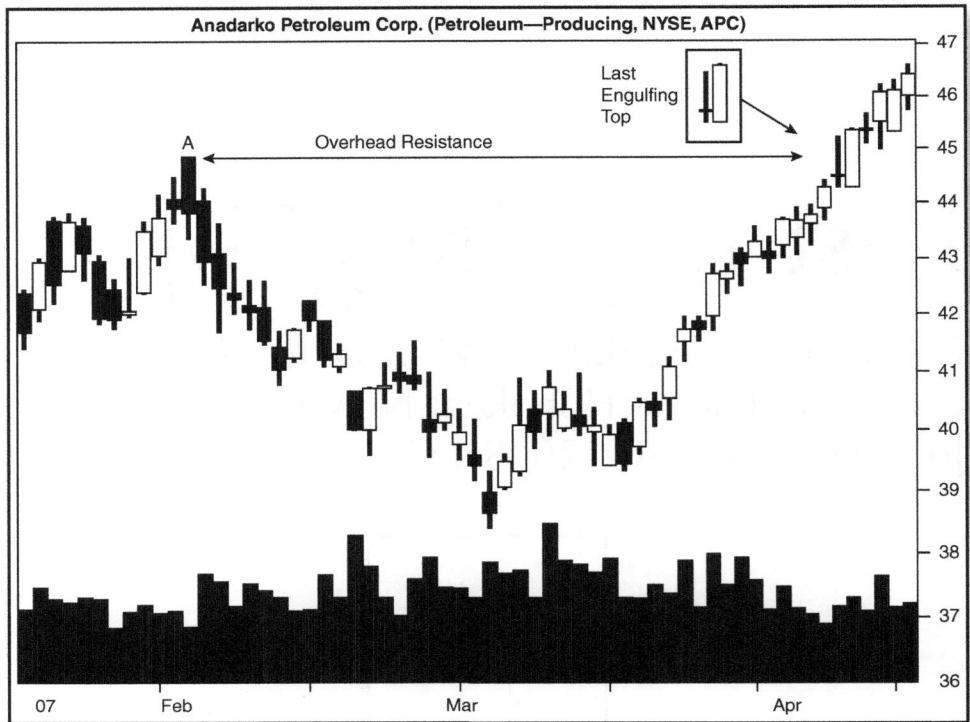

FIGURE 39.1 A Last Engulfing Top Suggests a Continuation of the Uptrend.

The psychology behind this pattern begins with a trend in which the bulls have pushed price upward. A black candle appears as a wake-up call to bulls who have grown fat and lazy from all of the money they've been gorging on. The next day sports a candle that wraps around the black body, engulfing it. It's a white candle and it says the bulls have gotten the message and are ready to tangle with the bears again. If price closes lower the next day, then the chances improve that price will reverse, but that's hardly a guarantee.

▪ Identification Guidelines

Figure 39.1 shows a last engulfing top that swallows the body of a doji. Many would expect price to reverse because of overhead resistance set up by the peak at A, but

TABLE 39.1 Identification Guidelines

Characteristic	Discussion
Number of candle lines	Two.
Price trend	Upward leading to the start of the candle pattern.
First day	A black candle.
Second day	A white candle, the body of which overlaps the prior black candle's body.

that's not what happens. Price continues rising, breaking out upward and tracking what is happening at the gas pump.

Table 39.1 lists identification guidelines. These are the same guidelines as those of a bearish engulfing pattern except for candle color. Look for a white candle to engulf the body of the prior black candle. That means the white body's top is at or above the black body's top and the white body's bottom is at or below the prior black body's bottom. Either the body tops or the body bottoms can be equal, but not both. Shadows are not important for candle recognition.

■ Statistics

Table 39.2 shows general statistics.

Number found. I prorated the results from my standard database (slightly different from the one used here) and found that the last engulfing top appears more often in a bear market. I limited the number of candles to 20,000 so my spreadsheet wouldn't cough up fur balls.

Reversal or continuation performance. The best performance comes from patterns in a bear market, regardless of the breakout direction.

S&P performance. Using the dates of the candle end to the trend end, I measured the performance of the S&P 500 and found that the candle outperforms the index.

TABLE 39.2	General Statistics			
Description	Bull Market, Up Breakout	Bear Market, Up Breakout	Bull Market, Down Breakout	Bear Market, Down Breakout
Number found	10,074	3,475	4,746	1,705
Reversal (R), continuation (C) performance	5.99% C	6.74% C	−5.45% R	−8.22% R
Standard & Poor's 500 change	1.37%	0.49%	−1.31%	−2.73%
Candle end to breakout (median, days)	2	3	4	4
Candle end to trend end (median, days)	7	6	8	9
Number of breakouts near the 12-month low (L), middle (M), or high (H)	L 1,113, M 2,018, H 5,250	L 668, M 1,015, H 1,737	L 687, M 1,104, H 2,319	L 377, M 553, H 740
Percentage move for each 12-month period	L 7.90%, M 5.85%, H 5.62%	L 10.03%, M 6.72%, H 5.82%	L −6.56%, M −5.68%, H −5.23%	L −10.42%, M −7.94%, H −7.53%
Candle end + 1 day	0.67%	0.96%	−1.28%	−1.71%
Candle end + 3 days	1.34%	1.41%	−2.52%	−3.47%
Candle end + 5 days	1.56%	1.58%	−2.92%	−4.08%
Candle end + 10 days	1.90%	1.45%	−2.79%	−4.42%
10-day performance rank	91	86	38	41

Candle end to breakout. It takes between a median of two and four days for price to break out. Since a white candle is the last line in the pattern, an upward breakout has less distance to travel so it takes less time than a downward breakout.

Candle end to trend end. Price trends for about a week before the trend stops. Downward breakouts take longer to reach the trend end than upward breakouts do.

Yearly position, performance. Most last engulfing tops appear within a third of the yearly high, but the best performers hide in the shallow end—within a third of the yearly low.

Performance over time. Compared to other candle results, these numbers are lousy. They also show that the candle pattern is a weak performer. For example, the middle two columns show weakness from 5 to 10 days. If this were a robust performer, the numbers would increase over time under all market conditions and breakout directions. The performance rank confirms that the pattern does better after a downward breakout.

Table 39.3 shows height statistics.

Candle height. Look for tall candles because they outperform. To determine whether the candle is short or tall, compute its height from highest high to lowest low price in the candle pattern and divide by the breakout price. If the result is higher than the median, then you have a tall candle; otherwise it's short.

Auntie Em sees a last engulfing top with a high price of 37 and a low of 36. Is the candle short or tall? The height is 37 − 36, or 1, so the result is 1/37, or 2.70%. In a bull market with an upward breakout, the candle is short.

Measure rule. Use the measure rule to help predict how far price will rise or fall. Compute the height of the candle pattern and multiply it by the appropriate percentage shown in the table; then apply it to the breakout price.

TABLE 39.3 Height Statistics				
Description	Bull Market, Up Breakout	Bear Market, Up Breakout	Bull Market, Down Breakout	Bear Market, Down Breakout
Median candle height as a percentage of breakout price	2.92%	3.92%	2.80%	3.90%
Short candle, performance	4.69%	5.49%	−4.42%	−7.31%
Tall candle, performance	7.66%	8.12%	−6.79%	−9.23%
Percentage meeting price target (measure rule)	67%	62%	65%	65%
Median upper shadow as a percentage of breakout price	0.32%	0.44%	0.40%	0.62%
Short upper shadow, performance	5.52%	5.95%	−5.13%	−7.74%
Tall upper shadow, performance	6.49%	7.59%	−5.79%	−8.72%
Median lower shadow as a percentage of breakout price	0.24%	0.32%	0.24%	0.34%
Short lower shadow, performance	5.55%	6.26%	−5.26%	−7.64%
Tall lower shadow, performance	6.44%	7.21%	−5.64%	−8.79%

TABLE 39.4 Volume Statistics

Description	Bull Market, Up Breakout	Bear Market, Up Breakout	Bull Market, Down Breakout	Bear Market, Down Breakout
Rising candle volume, performance	5.96%	6.85%	−5.53%	−8.41%
Falling candle volume, performance	6.03%	6.60%	−5.35%	−7.98%
Above-average candle volume, performance	6.12%	6.78%	−5.38%	−8.45%
Below-average candle volume, performance	5.92%	6.72%	−5.48%	−8.12%
Heavy breakout volume, performance	6.68%	7.60%	−5.77%	−8.88%
Light breakout volume, performance	5.33%	6.00%	−5.20%	−7.75%

Using Auntie Em's example, in a bull market the upward breakout target would be (1 × 67%) + 37, or 37.67, and the downward breakout target would be 36 − (1 × 65%), or 35.35.

Shadows. The results pertain to the last candle line in the pattern. To determine whether the shadow is short or tall, compute the height of the shadow and divide by the breakout price. Compare the result to the median in the table. Tall shadows have a percentage higher than the median. Candles with tall upper and lower shadows perform better than do their short counterparts.

Table 39.4 shows volume statistics.

Candle volume trend. A rising volume trend throughout the candle suggests better postbreakout performance in all cases except bull market/up breakouts. Those do better after falling volume.

Average candle volume. Heavy candle volume is better for performance except in a bull market with a downward breakout. That category does better with below-average volume.

Breakout volume. Heavy breakout volume suggests better performance across all categories.

■ Trading Tactics

If you see this candle form during a primary uptrend, it may signal a lasting reversal. However, more likely any turn down will be short-lived and the upward trend will resume. For a safer trade, look for an upward retracement in a downward price trend. When the candle breaks out downward it joins with the existing current and both sail off downstream.

I split trading tactics into two basic studies, one concerning reversal rates and the other concerning performance. Of the two, reversal rates are more important, because it's better to trade in the direction of the trend and let price run as far as it can.

Table 39.5 gives tips to find the trend direction.

Confirmation reversal rates. The last engulfing top acts as a continuation pattern 67.7% of the time. However, if you wait for a lower close the next day, price

TABLE 39.5 Reversal Rates

Description	Bull Market	Bear Market
Closing price confirmation reversal rate	55%	56%
Candle color confirmation reversal rate	52%	54%
Opening gap confirmation reversal rate	40%	41%
Reversal: trend down, breakout up	32%	33%
Continuation: trend down, breakout down	68%	67%
Percentage of reversals (R)/continuations (C) for each 12-month low (L), middle (M), or high (H)	L 38% R/62% C, M 35% R/65% C, H 31% R/69% C	L 36% R/64% C, M 35% R/65% C, H 30% R/70% C

breaks out downward 55% to 56% of the time. The other confirmation methods give less successful results.

Reversal, continuation rates. Since the price trend is up, expect an upward breakout between 67% and 68% of the time.

Yearly range reversals. Splitting the reversals and continuations into where they occur in the yearly price range, we find that they all behave similarly. Continuations rule regardless of where the candle appears. However, a continuation is most likely to occur within a third of the yearly high.

Table 39.6 shows performance indicators that can give hints as to how your stock will behave after the breakout from a candle pattern.

TABLE 39.6 Performance Indicators

Description	Bull Market, Up Breakout	Bear Market, Up Breakout	Bull Market, Down Breakout	Bear Market, Down Breakout
Closing price confirmation, performance	N/A	N/A	−6.73%	−9.11%
Candle color confirmation, performance	N/A	N/A	−6.66%	−8.93%
Opening gap confirmation, performance	N/A	N/A	−6.85%	−8.94%
Breakout above 50-day moving average, performance	5.85%	6.35%	−5.36%	−7.66%
Breakout below 50-day moving average, performance	6.95%	9.22%	−5.76%	−9.47%
Last candle: close in highest third, performance	6.01%	6.74%	−5.52%	−8.09%
Last candle: close in middle third, performance	5.93%	6.49%	−5.29%	−8.67%
Last candle: close in lowest third, performance	5.35%	9.04%	−4.40%	−7.30%

N/A means not applicable.

Confirmation, performance. In a bull market, the opening gap confirmation method leads to the best postbreakout performance. That's when you take a position if price gaps open lower the next day.

In a bear market, wait for a lower close the next day before shorting the stock.

Moving average. Last engulfing tops perform best if the breakout is below the 50-trading-day moving average.

Closing position. A close in the highest third of the last candle line of the engulfing top works best in all markets, regardless of the breakout direction except for bear market/up breakouts. Those do better when price closes near the low.

▦ Sample Trade

Auntie Em is shopping for stocks and sees a promising setup pictured in Figure 39.2. Price trends downward from the high at D to the low at A, bounces once like a stone skipping across water, and then bottoms at C. Price rises and forms another valley at B. The ABC formation is an ugly head-and-shoulders bottom chart pattern. By *ugly* I mean the two shoulders do not bottom near the same price.

FIGURE 39.2   A Last Engulfing Top Combined with a Head-and-Shoulders Bottom Suggests a Continued Rise.

A neckline drawn connecting the armpits of the pattern provides the traditional buy signal when price closes above it. That happens when price forms a last engulfing top. To Auntie Em, it's another signal that price will continue higher, so she buys the stock the next day.

Price rises in a series of white candles, and she believes it will reach the old high and stall. So she places a sell stop at the price of D, where the tallest body ends. In a few days, price reaches her stop and the stock sells for a tidy profit. She plans to use the money for Toto's vet bills.

■ For Best Performance

The following list offers tips and observations to help choose candles that perform well. Consult the associated table for more information.

- Use the identification guidelines to help select the pattern—Table 39.1.

- Candles within a third of the yearly low perform best—Table 39.2.

- Select tall candles—Table 39.3.

- Use the measure rule to predict a price target—Table 39.3.

- Candles with tall shadows outperform—Table 39.3.

- Volume gives performance clues—Table 39.4.

- Look for the candle in an upward retracement of a downward price trend—Trading Tactics discussion.

- Improve the reversal rate by waiting for a downward close a day after the candle formation ends—Table 39.5.

- The last engulfing top breaks out upward most often—Table 39.5.

- Opening gap confirmation works best in a bull market—Table 39.6.

- Breakouts below the 50-day moving average lead to the best performance—Table 39.6.

CHAPTER 40

Three Outside Down

From Thomas N. Bulkowski, *Encyclopedia of Candlestick Charts* (Hoboken, New Jersey: John Wiley & Sons, 2008), Chapter 89.

Learning Objective Statements

- Interpret potential price moves based on the patterns described in this chapter
- Calculate potential price targets
- Evaluate price levels for potential support or resistance
- Identify and interpret signals from various oscillators and technical studies

Behavior and Rank

Theoretical: Bearish reversal.
Actual bull market: Bearish reversal 69% of the time (ranking 15).
Actual bear market: Bearish reversal 70% of the time (ranking 16).
Frequency: 21st out of 103.
Overall performance over time: 39th out of 103.

The three outside down pattern was developed by Gregory Morris to confirm a bearish engulfing candle. An engulfing candle is a candle whose body covers the prior day's body. Morris requires the following candle to close lower to confirm the pattern.

The performance rank in a bull market is very good, 15, when 1 is best out of 103 candles. However, just because price reverses doesn't mean it moves far. That's where the overall rank of 39 comes into play. This is a gauge of how the pattern stacks up against other candle types, based on the percentage change over time in bull and bear markets, up and down breakouts. A rank of 39 is decent—not exceptional, mind you, but decent.

The psychology behind the pattern starts with an upward price trend. The bulls are in control, buying everything in sight, pushing price upward, and leaving a white candle on the chart. The next day, price opens higher but closes lower, disappointing the bulls. That's when the bears take over the party and tell everyone to go home. The next trading day confirms their authority when price closes lower.

■ Identification Guidelines

Figure 40.1 shows an example of the three outside down candle. Price trends upward for a few days leading to the start of the candle. When the pattern completes, price trends downward for about two weeks before recovering.

Table 40.1 lists identification guidelines. The three outside down candle is a bearish engulfing candle followed by a lower close. That means price forms a white candle on day one and a black candle the next day. The black candle has an open above the prior close and a close lower than the prior open. Thus, the black candle body is said to engulf the white one. The next day, price makes a lower close.

Ignore shadows in this candlestick pattern.

THE INTEGRATION OF TECHNICAL ANALYSIS

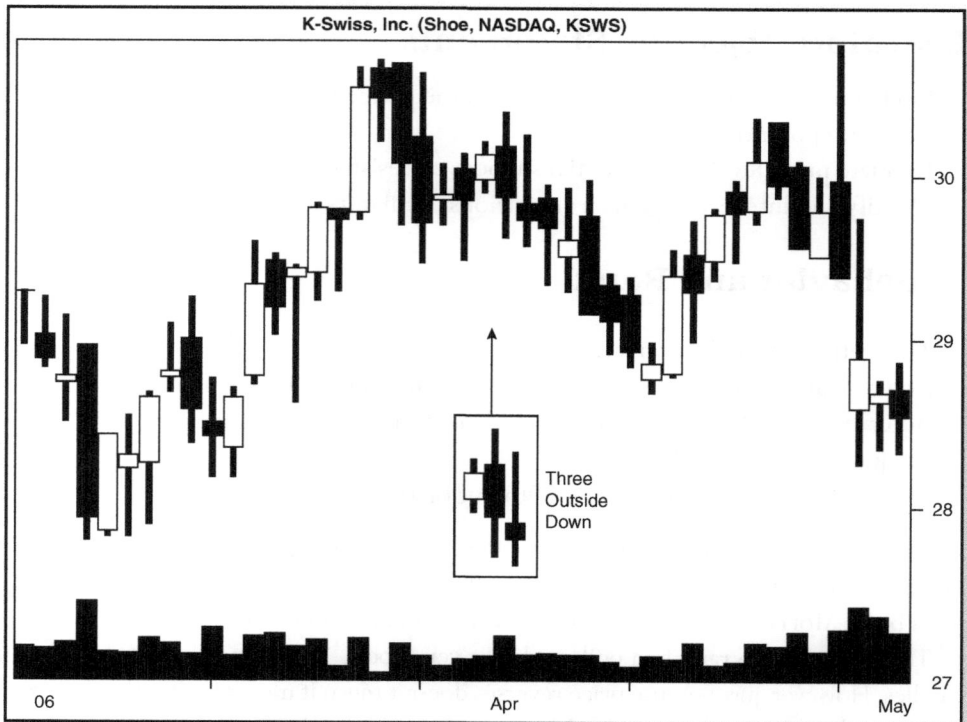

FIGURE 40.1 A Three Outside Down Candle Appears after a Slight Uptrend, and Price Reverses.

TABLE 40.1	Identification Guidelines
Characteristic	Discussion
Number of candle lines	Three.
Price trend	Upward leading to the start of the candle pattern.
First day	A white candle.
Second day	A black candle opens higher and closes lower than the prior candle's body, engulfing it.
Last day	A candle with a lower close.

■ Statistics

Table 40.2 shows general statistics.

Number found. This candle pattern is common. I found 17,569, with most of those coming from a bull market.

Reversal or continuation performance. Performance of the candle pattern in a bear market is better than that achieved in a bull market.

S&P performance. The candle does better than the S&P 500 index over the same time periods, regardless of market conditions and breakout directions.

Candle end to breakout. Downward breakouts take less time to occur than upward ones. This is because the closing price is nearer to the pattern's low.

Candle end to trend end. Downward breakouts also take less time to reach the trend end. This is a function of a downward trend already under way (two black

TABLE 40.2	General Statistics			
Description	Bull Market, Up Breakout	Bear Market, Up Breakout	Bull Market, Down Breakout	Bear Market, Down Breakout
Number found	4,069	1,332	9,059	3,109
Reversal (R), continuation (C) performance	6.26% C	6.83% C	−5.41% R	−9.38% R
Standard & Poor's 500 change	2.14%	1.26%	−0.77%	−2.21%
Candle end to breakout (median, days)	6	6	3	3
Candle end to trend end (median, days)	11	10	6	7
Number of breakouts near the 12-month low (L), middle (M), or high (H)	L 454, M 844, H 2,226	L 272, M 386, H 658	L 1,709, M 2,257, H 4,126	L 939, M 983, H 1,157
Percentage move for each 12-month period	L 7.87%, M 5.87%, H 6.14%	L 9.21%, M 7.28%, H 5.86%	L −5.96%, M −5.53%, H −5.22%	L −11.24%, M −9.32%, H −8.19%
Candle end + 1 day	1.47%	1.99%	−0.56%	−0.88%
Candle end + 3 days	3.11%	4.22%	−1.13%	−1.86%
Candle end + 5 days	3.94%	5.33%	−1.29%	−2.22%
Candle end + 10 days	4.84%	6.30%	−1.11%	−2.57%
10-day performance rank	13	18	92	76

candles suggests a declining price trend). Thus, a trend already under way is closer to the end than one just starting. An upward move would indeed start a new trend.

Yearly position, performance. Most three outside down patterns appear within a third of the yearly high, but performance is best when they appear within a third of the yearly low.

Performance over time. This candle pattern is not a strong performer. Weakness occurs during days 5 to 10 in bull market/down breakouts. A robust performer would show increasing numbers in all columns and over all time periods.

Based on a comparison with other candle types, this pattern excels during an upward breakout, meaning a continuation of the uptrend. Ranks of 13 and 18 are very good, whereas the 92 and 76 ranks for a downward breakout are very poor.

Table 40.3 shows height statistics.

Candle height. Tall candles perform better than short ones. To determine whether the candle is short or tall, compute its height from highest high to lowest low price in the candle pattern and divide by the breakout price. If the result is higher than the median, then you have a tall candle; otherwise it's short.

Cary sees a three outside down with a high of 53 and a low of 49. Is the candle short or tall? The height is 53 − 49, or 4. In a bull market with an upward breakout, the measure would be 4/53, or 7.5%. It's a tall candle.

Measure rule. Use the measure rule to help predict how far price will rise or fall. Compute the height of the candle pattern and multiply it by the appropriate percentage shown in the table; then apply it to the breakout price.

What are the price targets for Cary's candle? The upward target would be (4 × 55%) + 53, or 55.20, and the downward target would be 49 − (4 × 44%), or 47.24.

TABLE 40.3 Height Statistics

Description	Bull Market, Up Breakout	Bear Market, Up Breakout	Bull Market, Down Breakout	Bear Market, Down Breakout
Median candle height as a percentage of breakout price	4.08%	5.61%	4.59%	6.38%
Short candle, performance	4.89%	5.86%	−4.30%	−7.50%
Tall candle, performance	8.02%	7.85%	−6.86%	−11.49%
Percentage meeting price target (measure rule)	55%	48%	44%	47%
Median upper shadow as a percentage of breakout price	0.43%	0.50%	0.39%	0.56%
Short upper shadow, performance	5.50%	6.03%	−5.10%	−8.54%
Tall upper shadow, performance	7.06%	7.66%	−5.74%	−10.24%
Median lower shadow as a percentage of breakout price	0.53%	0.81%	0.46%	0.70%
Short lower shadow, performance	5.34%	6.46%	−4.86%	−8.90%
Tall lower shadow, performance	7.32%	7.20%	−6.04%	−9.88%

TABLE 40.4 **Volume Statistics**

Description	Bull Market, Up Breakout	Bear Market, Up Breakout	Bull Market, Down Breakout	Bear Market, Down Breakout
Rising candle volume, performance	5.89%	6.70%	−5.32%	−9.70%
Falling candle volume, performance	6.64%	6.96%	−5.51%	−9.02%
Above-average candle volume, performance	6.06%	6.32%	−5.38%	−9.15%
Below-average candle volume, performance	6.36%	7.09%	−5.43%	−9.53%
Heavy breakout volume, performance	6.82%	7.33%	−5.79%	−10.81%
Light breakout volume, performance	5.54%	6.26%	−5.06%	−7.98%

Shadows. The table's results pertain to the last candle line in the pattern. To determine whether the shadow is short or tall, compute the height of the shadow and divide by the breakout price. Compare the result to the median in the table. Tall shadows have a percentage higher than the median.

Tall upper or lower shadows result in better performance than short ones, in all cases.

Table 40.4 shows volume statistics.

Candle volume trend. A falling volume trend works best in all cases except for bear market/down breakouts. Those do better after rising candle volume.

Average candle volume. Below-average volume inside the candle pattern suggests better postbreakout performance.

Breakout volume. Candles with heavy breakout volume perform better than do those with light breakout volume.

■ Trading Tactics

The three outside down pattern works best when the primary price trend is downward and a short-term upward retracement occurs. When the three outside down candle occurs, price reverses the uptrend and is then free to resume the primary downtrend.

I split trading tactics into two basic studies, one concerning reversal rates and the other concerning performance. Of the two, reversal rates are more important, because it's better to trade in the direction of the trend and let price run as far as it can.

Table 40.5 gives tips to find the trend direction.

Confirmation reversal rates. Waiting for price to close lower the next day boosts the reversal rate to 90% or more.

Reversal, continuation rates. Most three outside down patterns break out downward.

Yearly range reversals. Most reversals appear within a third of the yearly low.

Table 40.6 shows performance indicators that can give hints as to how your stock will behave after the breakout from this candle pattern.

TABLE 40.5   Reversal Rates

Description	Bull Market	Bear Market
Closing price confirmation reversal rate	91%	90%
Candle color confirmation reversal rate	87%	88%
Opening gap confirmation reversal rate	78%	78%
Reversal: trend down, breakout up	69%	70%
Continuation: trend down, breakout down	31%	30%
Percentage of reversals (R)/continuations (C) for each 12-month low (L), middle (M), or high (H)	L 79% R/21% C, M 73% R/27% C, H 65% R/35% C	L 78% R/22% C, M 72% R/28% C, H 64% R/36% C

TABLE 40.6   Performance Indicators

Description	Bull Market, Up Breakout	Bear Market, Up Breakout	Bull Market, Down Breakout	Bear Market, Down Breakout
Closing price confirmation, performance	N/A	N/A	−5.40%	−9.38%
Candle color confirmation, performance	N/A	N/A	−5.70%	−9.57%
Opening gap confirmation, performance	N/A	N/A	−6.33%	−10.84%
Breakout above 50-day moving average, performance	6.23%	6.51%	−5.18%	−7.92%
Breakout below 50-day moving average, performance	6.34%	8.21%	−5.73%	−10.66%
Last candle: close in highest third, performance	5.73%	5.61%	−5.07%	−8.13%
Last candle: close in middle third, performance	6.68%	6.78%	−5.44%	−8.73%
Last candle: close in lowest third, performance	6.10%	7.13%	−5.43%	−9.82%

N/A means not applicable.

Confirmation, performance. Waiting for price to gap open lower the next day leads to better performance. Consider using that as the buy signal.

Moving average. Candles with breakouts below the 50-day moving average result in better postbreakout performance in all categories.

Closing position. In bull markets, a closing price in the middle of the last candle line leads to better performance. For bear markets, a close in the lowest third of the candle works best.

■ Sample Trade

Cary held the stock shown in Figure 40.2. Price gapped up to A on volume that dwarfed any other day on the chart. As is usual with such moves, price retraced a portion of the rise. In this case, the stock dropped to D before beginning another attempt at a new high.

At B, price tried to make a new high but failed. The failure was confirmed two days later when the three outside down pattern completed. Cary saw this failure and considered selling, but he wanted to be sure that price was headed lower. Often, it will drop some before resuming the uptrend. He didn't want to sell if price would continue higher, preferring to trade only if it changed trend from up to down for the long term.

He drew an up-sloping trendline along the valleys in October. When the stock dropped and closed below the line at C, it represented a tentative sell signal. A stronger signal occurred at E when price closed below the level of D, the valley between the two peaks A and B. That move confirmed the double top chart pattern, so he sold the stock.

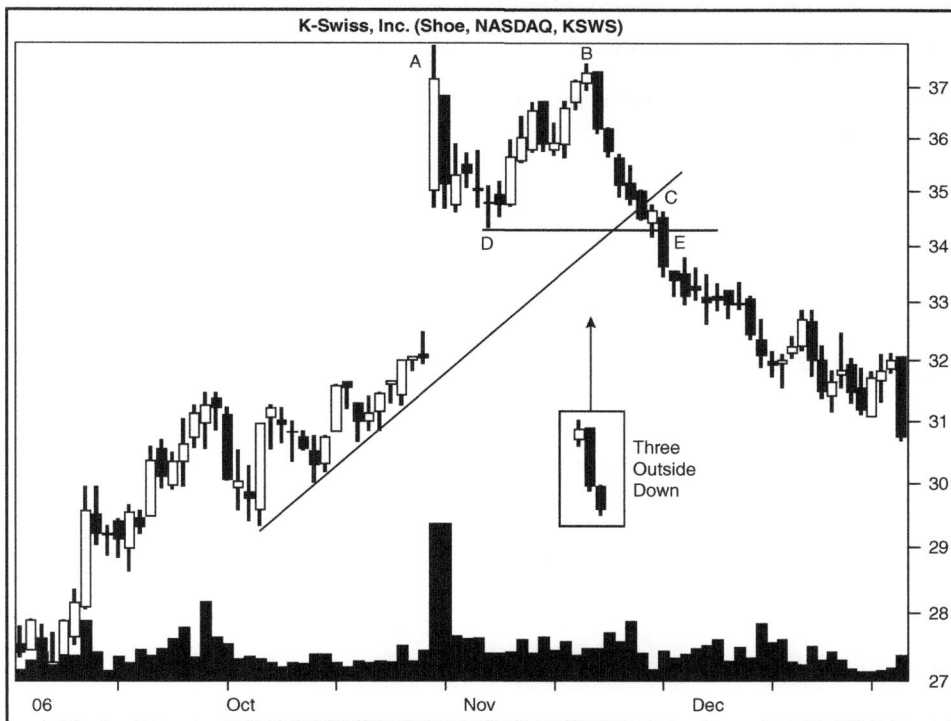

FIGURE 40.2 **A Three Outside Down Candle Hits Overhead Resistance and Price Reverses.**

■ For Best Performance

The following list offers tips and observations to help choose candles that perform well. Consult the associated table for more information.

- ■ Use the identification guidelines to help select the pattern—Table 40.1.
- ■ Candles within a third of the yearly low perform best—Table 40.2.
- ■ Select tall candles—Table 40.3.
- ■ Use the measure rule to predict a price target—Table 40.3.
- ■ Candles with tall upper and lower shadows outperform—Table 40.3.
- ■ Volume gives performance clues—Table 40.4.
- ■ Select three outside down candles in an upward retracement of the downward primary trend—Trading Tactics discussion.
- ■ Closing price confirmation boosts the reversal rate to 90%—Table 40.5.
- ■ Most three outside down candles break out downward—Table 40.5.
- ■ Opening gap confirmation works best—Table 40.6.
- ■ Breakouts below the 50-day moving average lead to the best performance—Table 40.6.

CHAPTER 41

Three Outside Up

From Thomas N. Bulkowski, *Encyclopedia of Candlestick Charts* (Hoboken, New Jersey: John Wiley & Sons, 2008), Chapter 90.

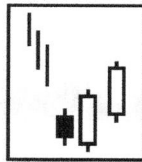

Learning Objective Statements

- Interpret potential price moves based on the patterns described in this chapter
- Calculate potential price targets
- Evaluate price levels for potential support or resistance
- Identify and interpret signals from various oscillators and technical studies

Behavior and Rank

Theoretical: Bullish reversal.
Actual bull market: Bullish reversal 75% of the time (ranking 9).
Actual bear market: Bullish reversal 74% of the time (ranking 8).
Frequency: 24th out of 103.
Overall performance over time: 34th out of 103.

Gregory Morris added a candle line to a bullish engulfing pattern and called it a three outside up candle. His intent was to change a yucky performing candle into one much better. The reversal rate of 75% in a bull market ranks 9 out of 103 candles, where 1 is best. It's a good score. With a high frequency, meaning the pattern appears often, the number should withstand rigorous testing. The overall performance is 34, and it's as good as it is because of the excellent performance of candles with downward breakouts, but is pulled down by the lousy performance of those with upward breakouts.

The psychology behind the pattern begins with a downward price trend and the bears in control. They dribble the ball and pass it often, but they can't score. Then the

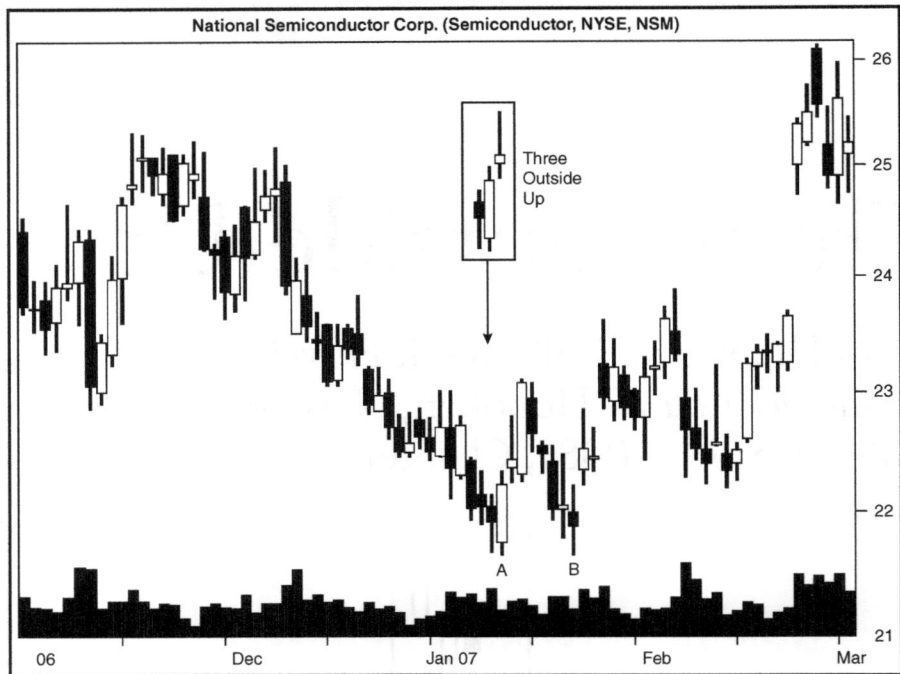

FIGURE 41.1 The First Bottom of a Double Bottom Chart Pattern Begins with the Three Outside Up Candle Pattern.

bulls grab the ball on the rebound: Price opens lower the next day but closes higher, high enough that the white body of the candle engulfs the prior black body. The bulls press their advantage, and the next day price posts a higher close. What happens in the game after that is anyone's guess, but price usually continues higher.

■ Identification Guidelines

Figure 41.1 shows an example of a three outside up candle pattern. Price trends downward from the high in November and stops at A. That candle line is in the middle of the three outside up candle formation. The white line at A engulfs the body of the prior candle, and the next candle, another white one, confirms the bullish engulfing pattern with a higher close.

Table 41.1 lists identification guidelines. Look for a bullish engulfing candle. That pattern begins with a black candle followed by a taller white candle. By *taller*, I mean

TABLE 41.1 Identification Guidelines

Characteristic	Discussion
Number of candle lines	Three.
Price trend	Downward leading to the start of the candle pattern.
First day	A black candle.
Second day	A white candle opens below the prior body and closes above the body, too. Price need not engulf the shadows.
Last day	A white candle in which price closes higher.

that price opens lower than the prior close and closes higher than the prior open, engulfing the body of the black candle. The next day closes higher, forming a white candle.

■ Statistics

Table 41.2 shows general statistics.

Number found. I found a bunch of these candles, so I limited selections to the first 20,000. Prorating the standard database means the candle appears most often in a bear market.

Reversal or continuation performance. Performance is best in a bear market, regardless of the breakout direction.

S&P performance. The candle beats the S&P 500 index in all columns.

Candle end to breakout. It takes price less time to break out upward than downward. This is due to the closing price ending near the candle's high. It doesn't take much for price to close above the top, thereby creating a breakout.

Candle end to trend end. Upward breakouts are closer to the trend end because price has been rising for a couple of days in the candle pattern. Downward breakouts would start a new trend, and that would take longer to reach the trend end than one midway along.

TABLE 41.2   General Statistics

Description	Bull Market, Up Breakout	Bear Market, Up Breakout	Bull Market, Down Breakout	Bear Market, Down Breakout
Number found	12,214	2,726	4,121	939
Reversal (R), continuation (C) performance	6.25% R	7.24% R	−5.51% C	−8.88% C
Standard & Poor's 500 change	1.39%	0.71%	−1.25%	−3.42%
Candle end to breakout (median, days)	3	3	7	6
Candle end to trend end (median, days)	7	7	10	10
Number of breakouts near the 12-month low (L), middle (M), or high (H)	L 2,116, M 2,791, H 5,273	L 754, M 810, H 1,128	L 1,110, M 1,157, H 1,221	L 338, M 313, H 276
Percentage move for each 12-month period	L 7.24%, M 5.79%, H 5.44%	L 9.39%, M 7.17%, H 6.11%	L −6.15%, M −5.65%, H −4.95%	L −10.67%, M −8.35%, H −7.53%
Candle end + 1 day	0.56%	0.51%	−1.36%	−2.04%
Candle end + 3 days	1.25%	1.30%	−2.96%	−4.54%
Candle end + 5 days	1.69%	1.71%	−3.84%	−5.92%
Candle end + 10 days	2.13%	1.68%	−4.50%	−7.14%
10-day performance rank	78	78	10	7

Yearly position, performance. Most three outside up candles appear within a third of the yearly high. The one exception is bear market/down breakouts, which appear most often near the yearly low. The yearly low is also where the candle performs best.

Performance over time. This candle pattern is not a top performer. In a bear market/up breakout scenario, performance weakens between 5 and 10 days. The upward breakout numbers must be considered poor because they are so low. Thus, if the breakout is upward, don't expect price to rise much.

Based on the performance of the candle against other candle types, downward breakouts show excellent ranks: 7 and 10. Upward breakouts are a pathetic lot.

Table 41.3 shows height statistics.

Candle height. Tall candles outperform. To determine whether the candle is short or tall, compute its height from highest high to lowest low price in the candle pattern and divide by the breakout price. If the result is higher than the median, then you have a tall candle; otherwise it's short.

If Robert sees a three outside up candle with a high of 56 and a low of 51, is the candle tall? The height is $56 - 51$, or 5, so the measure would be $5/56$, or 8.9% in a bull market with an upward breakout. The candle is tall.

Measure rule. Use the measure rule to help predict how far price will rise or fall. Compute the height of the candle pattern and multiply it by the appropriate percentage shown in the table; then apply it to the breakout price.

What are Robert's price targets for his candle? The upward target would be $(5 \times 47\%) + 56$, or 58.35, and the downward target would be $51 - (5 \times 44\%)$, or 48.80.

Shadows. The table's results pertain to the last candle line in the pattern. To determine whether the shadow is short or tall, compute the height of the shadow

TABLE 41.3 **Height Statistics**

Description	Bull Market, Up Breakout	Bear Market, Up Breakout	Bull Market, Down Breakout	Bear Market, Down Breakout
Median candle height as a percentage of breakout price	5.05%	6.56%	4.87%	6.58%
Short candle, performance	5.01%	5.70%	−4.57%	−7.30%
Tall candle, performance	7.99%	8.92%	−6.92%	−10.74%
Percentage meeting price target (measure rule)	47%	42%	44%	46%
Median upper shadow as a percentage of breakout price	0.45%	0.72%	0.57%	0.86%
Short upper shadow, performance	5.64%	6.08%	−5.08%	−7.95%
Tall upper shadow, performance	6.44%	8.45%	−5.98%	−9.93%
Median lower shadow as a percentage of breakout price	0.36%	0.53%	0.40%	0.61%
Short lower shadow, performance	5.69%	6.44%	−5.04%	−8.32%
Tall lower shadow, performance	6.84%	8.05%	−6.01%	−9.55%

TABLE 41.4   Volume Statistics

Description	Bull Market, Up Breakout	Bear Market, Up Breakout	Bull Market, Down Breakout	Bear Market, Down Breakout
Rising candle volume, performance	6.38%	7.14%	−5.55%	−8.61%
Falling candle volume, performance	6.07%	7.35%	−5.45%	−9.20%
Above-average candle volume, performance	6.34%	7.75%	−5.59%	−9.02%
Below-average candle volume, performance	6.17%	6.82%	−5.45%	−8.79%
Heavy breakout volume, performance	6.79%	7.70%	−6.05%	−9.78%
Light breakout volume, performance	5.68%	6.84%	−4.91%	−7.66%

and divide by the breakout price. Compare the result to the median in the table. Tall shadows have a percentage higher than the median.

Candles with tall upper or lower shadows perform better than candles with short shadows.

Table 41.4 shows volume statistics.

Candle volume trend. Rising candle volume in a bull market leads to better performance. In a bear market, falling volume leads to good performance.

Average candle volume. Candles with above-average volume perform better than do those with below-average volume.

Breakout volume. Look for candles with heavy breakout volume because they tend to do well.

▪ Trading Tactics

This pattern does well when the primary price trend is upward. Price retraces a portion of the up move until the three outside up candle appears, and then the downtrend ends with price climbing away. You will want to either avoid this candle pattern altogether in a primary downtrend or trade it cautiously. Even if it appears after a long downtrend, price might bounce around while trying to find a bottom.

I split trading tactics into two basic studies, one concerning reversal rates and the other concerning performance. Of the two, reversal rates are more important because it's better to trade in the direction of the trend and let price run as far as it can.

Table 41.5 gives tips to find the trend direction.

Confirmation reversal rates. If price closes higher after the three outside up, the chance is 93% that a reversal will occur (bull market). That's not saying much, though, because price is near the high of the pattern and all it has to do is close above the top to stage a reversal.

Reversal, continuation rates. Price breaks out upward most often.

Yearly range reversals. The highest third of the yearly price range shows the most reversals.

TABLE 41.5   Reversal Rates

Description	Bull Market	Bear Market
Closing price confirmation reversal rate	93%	91%
Candle color confirmation reversal rate	91%	44%
Opening gap confirmation reversal rate	81%	80%
Reversal: trend down, breakout up	75%	74%
Continuation: trend down, breakout down	25%	26%
Percentage of reversals (R)/continuations (C) for each 12-month low (L), middle (M), or high (H)	L 66% R/34% C, M 71% R/29% C, H 81% R/19% C	L 69% R/31% C, M 72% R/28% C, H 80% R/20% C

Table 41.6 shows performance indicators that can give hints as to how your stock will behave after the breakout from this candle pattern.

Confirmation, performance. Use the opening gap method as a trading signal. That means buy the stock if price gaps open higher a day after the candlestick ends.

Moving average. Candles with breakouts below the 50-day moving average tend to outperform.

Closing position. Patterns in a bull market with a close in the middle third of the intraday trading range (in the last candle line) tend to perform slightly better than the other two ranges. In a bear market, the lowest third works best.

TABLE 41.6   Performance Indicators

Description	Bull Market, Up Breakout	Bear Market, Up Breakout	Bull Market, Down Breakout	Bear Market, Down Breakout
Closing price confirmation, performance	5.80%	7.28%	N/A	N/A
Candle color confirmation, performance	5.44%	7.42%	N/A	N/A
Opening gap confirmation, performance	6.86%	9.09%	N/A	N/A
Breakout above 50-day moving average, performance	6.14%	6.67%	−4.89%	−6.78%
Breakout below 50-day moving average, performance	6.33%	8.28%	−5.77%	−9.69%
Last candle: close in highest third, performance	6.20%	7.08%	−5.38%	−8.28%
Last candle: close in middle third, performance	6.33%	7.35%	−5.87%	−8.91%
Last candle: close in lowest third, performance	6.32%	8.07%	−5.05%	−11.44%

N/A means not applicable.

Figure 41.2 shows a trade that Robert made. Price moved up in a smart advance from A to B and then retraced to C. The retracement ended at the 62% Fibonacci retracement level. That's when Robert became interested in the stock.

The small-bodied candle at C along with the prior few candles suggested indecision among traders about the stock. Since the candles were mostly black, the bias was downward. However, the 62% retracement level is often a strong support area, one that Robert has had success trading in the past.

He waited a day for price to signal a direction. That occurred with the white candle, which turned out to be part of a three outside up formation. The next day, he bought at the opening price, and the three outside up completed.

The stock cooperated by moving higher in a series of white candles, but then upward momentum slowed. Short candles with short shadows appeared as if the bulls and bears were waiting for the fundamentals to catch up.

Robert saw the bearish engulfing pattern appear, followed by a tweezers top. Because both candle patterns were bearish, he decided to sell the stock. He didn't want to ride price back down and risk giving away his profits in the process. The stock looked "tired," as he put it. He sold at the opening price after the tweezers top.

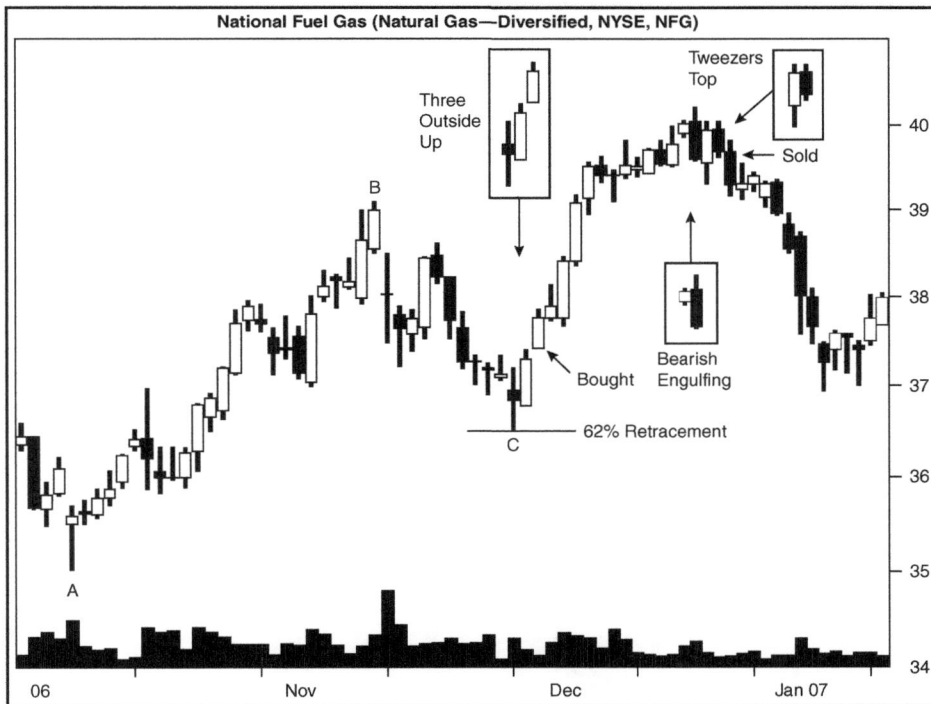

FIGURE 41.2 Price Finds Support at the 62% Retracement of the Prior Up Move, and Then a Three Outside Up Candle Pattern Forms.

■ For Best Performance

The following list offers tips and observations to help choose candles that perform well. Consult the associated table for more information.

■ Use the identification guidelines to help select the pattern—Table 41.1.

■ Candles within a third of the yearly low perform best—Table 41.2.

■ Select tall candles—Table 41.3.

■ Use the measure rule to predict a price target—Table 41.3.

■ Candles with tall upper and lower shadows outperform—Table 41.3.

■ Volume gives performance clues—Table 41.4.

■ Look for the pattern to appear as part of a downward retracement in an upward price trend—Trading Tactics discussion.

■ Price breaks out upward most often—Table 41.5.

■ Patterns within a third of the yearly high frequently act as reversals—Table 41.5.

■ Opening gap confirmation works best—Table 41.6.

■ Breakouts below the 50-day moving average lead to the best performance—Table 41.6.

CHAPTER 42

Two Black Gapping Candles

From Thomas N. Bulkowski, *Encyclopedia of Candlestick Charts* (Hoboken, New Jersey: John Wiley & Sons, 2008), Chapter 98.

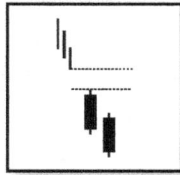

Learning Objective Statements

- Interpret potential price moves based on the patterns described in this chapter
- Calculate potential price targets
- Evaluate price levels for potential support or resistance
- Identify and interpret signals from various oscillators and technical studies

Behavior and Rank

Theoretical: Bearish continuation.
Actual bull market: Bearish continuation 68% of the time (ranking 10).
Actual bear market: Bearish continuation 69% of the time (ranking 9).
Frequency: 29th out of 103.
Overall performance over time: 10th out of 103.

Every time I see a continuation pattern, I wonder why anyone would hunt for one of those. The answer is clear: If I knew that price would continue trending downward tomorrow, then that's worth money.

A rank of 10 for the bull market continuation is close to the best, 1 out of 103 candles. The pattern occurs often (29 rank) and performance is stellar (10 rank) when compared to other candles. The performance over time suggests that upward breakouts

FIGURE 42.1 A Two Black Gapping Candles Pattern Sees Price Move Lower, Eventually.

are the direction in which to place your money. Of course, that would mean trading this candle pattern as a bullish reversal, not a bearish continuation pattern.

The psychology behind the two black gapping candles is a study in overhead resistance and downward momentum. In a falling price trend, the bears are strong enough to force price lower at the open the next day and keep the high price from closing the gap. That creates a falling window, or resistance against an up move. That day and the next, the bears continue forcing price lower, creating black candles. That completes the two black gapping candles pattern. What happens next is that price breaks out downward 68% of the time.

■ Identification Guidelines

Figure 42.1 shows an example of the two black gapping candles. Price gaps below candle A and then forms two black candles. After that, price recovers for a few days before the downtrend resumes. Even though a tall white candle closes higher than the prior candle after the candle pattern ends, the breakout is still downward because price first closed below the bottom of the entire pattern and not above the top.

Table 42.1 lists identification guidelines. I found only one source describing this candle, Nison's *Beyond Candlesticks* (John Wiley & Sons, 1994), and details were

TABLE 42.1 Identification Guidelines

Characteristic	Discussion
Number of candle lines	Two.
Price trend	Downward leading to the start of the candle pattern.
First day	Price gaps lower from the prior day and forms a black candle.
Second day	A lower high forms on the second black candle.

sketchy. Look for two black candles after price gaps lower. I require that the second candle have a lower high than the first one. That means price leaves the gap open. The black candles can be any size and the shadows any length, provided they are not tall enough to close the falling window (gap).

▪ Statistics

Table 42.2 shows general statistics.

Number found. Two black gapping candles happen a lot. I discovered 18,264 of them in two of the four databases I used, and if you prorate the standard database numbers, you'll find that they occur more often in a bear market.

Reversal or continuation performance. The candle pattern in a bear market performs better than it does in a bull market.

S&P performance. The S&P 500 index puts up good numbers, but the gapping candle puts up better ones.

Candle end to breakout. Downward moves take less time to break out than upward ones. This makes sense since the closing price is nearer the bottom of the candle than the top.

Candle end to trend end. Price takes less time to reach the trend end during downward breakouts than upward ones. That's because the downtrend is

TABLE 42.2	General Statistics			
Description	Bull Market, Up Breakout	Bear Market, Up Breakout	Bull Market, Down Breakout	Bear Market, Down Breakout
Number found	4,533	1,328	9,459	2,944
Reversal (R), continuation (C) performance	6.97% R	9.27% R	−6.09% C	−11.49% C
Standard & Poor's 500 change	2.28%	2.01%	−0.76%	−2.41%
Candle end to breakout (median, days)	5	5	3	3
Candle end to trend end (median, days)	11	11	6	6
Number of breakouts near the 12-month low (L), middle (M), or high (H)	L 1,010, M 1,265, H 1,905	L 468, M 468, H 377	L 3,076, M 3,046, H 2,571	L 1,495, M 944, H 452
Percentage move for each 12-month period	L 7.95%, M 6.61%, H 6.69%	L 11.73%, M 8.56%, H 7.75%	L −6.76%, M −6.03%, H −5.39%	L −13.08%, M −10.53%, H −9.22%
Candle end + 1 day	1.62%	2.58%	−0.79%	−1.09%
Candle end + 3 days	3.19%	5.34%	−1.43%	−2.61%
Candle end + 5 days	3.90%	6.85%	−1.67%	−2.54%
Candle end + 10 days	4.83%	6.45%	−1.64%	−3.11%
10-day performance rank	14	15	76	71

already well along the way to the end, whereas upward breakouts would start a new trend.

Yearly position, performance. Most candles appear within a third of the yearly low except in bull market/up breakouts. Those appear within a third of the yearly high most often. Performance is best when the candle is within a third of the yearly low.

Performance over time. Two black gapping candles are poor performers over time. I see weakness during days 5 to 10 in the middle two columns (bear market/up breakouts and bullmarket/down breakouts) and between days 3 and 5 in the last column (bear market/down breakouts).

When compared to other candle patterns, the performance is quite good after an upward breakout. That appears to be the direction to trade with this candle. Downward breakouts show that the percentage change over 10 days is unexciting, and that's why the ranks are so poor (76 and 71, where 1 is best out of 103 candles).

Table 42.3 shows height statistics.

Candle height. Tall candles outperform. To determine whether the candle is short or tall, compute its height from highest high to lowest low price in the candle pattern and divide by the breakout price. Do not include the gap in the computation. If the result is higher than the median, then you have a tall candle; otherwise it's short.

If Rusty sees two black gapping candles with a high of 87 and a low of 84, is the candle short or tall? The height is 87 − 84, or 3, so the measure in a bull market with a downward breakout would be 3/84, or 3.6%. That's a short candle.

Measure rule. Use the measure rule to help predict how far price will rise or fall. Compute the height of the candle pattern and multiply it by the appropriate percentage shown in the table; then apply it to the breakout price.

TABLE 42.3 Height Statistics

Description	Bull Market, Up Breakout	Bear Market, Up Breakout	Bull Market, Down Breakout	Bear Market, Down Breakout
Median candle height as a percentage of breakout price	4.16%	6.72%	4.57%	7.30%
Short candle, performance	5.73%	7.34%	−4.68%	−9.21%
Tall candle, performance	8.54%	11.27%	−7.76%	−14.06%
Percentage meeting price target (measure rule)	61%	55%	49%	53%
Median upper shadow as a percentage of breakout price	0.29%	0.44%	0.27%	0.52%
Short upper shadow, performance	6.50%	8.31%	−5.91%	−10.54%
Tall upper shadow, performance	7.37%	10.14%	−6.23%	−12.45%
Median lower shadow as a percentage of breakout price	0.62%	1.14%	0.49%	0.92%
Short lower shadow, performance	6.16%	7.97%	−5.30%	−11.35%
Tall lower shadow, performance	7.84%	10.55%	−6.86%	−11.64%

TABLE 42.4 Volume Statistics

Description	Bull Market, Up Breakout	Bear Market, Up Breakout	Bull Market, Down Breakout	Bear Market, Down Breakout
Rising candle volume, performance	7.47%	9.17%	−6.31%	−11.43%
Falling candle volume, performance	6.61%	9.35%	−5.94%	−11.54%
Above-average candle volume, performance	6.70%	9.22%	−5.95%	−11.48%
Below-average candle volume, performance	7.48%	9.35%	−6.36%	−11.53%
Heavy breakout volume, performance	7.38%	10.00%	−6.27%	−12.01%
Light breakout volume, performance	6.46%	8.43%	−5.81%	−10.52%

What are Rusty's price targets? The upward target would be (3 × 61%) + 87, or 88.83, and the downward target would be 84 − (3 × 49%), or 82.53.

Shadows. The table's results pertain to the last candle line in the pattern. To determine whether the shadow is short or tall, compute the height of the shadow and divide by the breakout price. Compare the result to the median in the table. Tall shadows have a percentage higher than the median.

Candles with tall upper or lower shadows perform better than do those with short shadows.

Table 42.4 shows volume statistics.

Candle volume trend. Patterns in a bull market perform better with rising candle volume, and those in a bear market do better after the candle shows falling volume.

Average candle volume. Candles with below-average volume tend to perform better than do those with above-average volume.

Breakout volume. Heavy breakout volume suggests better performance in all cases.

■ Trading Tactics

For downward breakouts, trade this candle when the primary price trend is also downward. That setup often leads to good moves. Avoid trading the pattern when the primary trend is upward and the gapping candlestick appears as a downward retracement.

I split trading tactics into two basic studies, one concerning reversal rates and the other concerning performance. Of the two, reversal rates are more important, because it's better to trade in the direction of the trend and let price run as far as it can.

Table 42.5 gives tips to find the trend direction.

Confirmation reversal rates. To help separate a potential reversal from a continuation pattern, wait for price to close higher the next day. If that happens, a reversal occurs 55% of the time in a bull market. Since random is 50%, waiting for a higher close is not much help.

Reversal, continuation rates. Price breaks out downward most often.

Yearly range reversals. Continuations occur frequently when price breaks out within a third of the yearly low.

Table 42.6 shows performance indicators that can give hints as to how your stock will behave after the breakout from this candle pattern.

Confirmation, performance. Use the opening gap confirmation method to trade this candle. That means waiting for price to gap open lower the next day before taking a position in the stock.

Moving average. Candles with breakouts below the 50-day moving average work better than do those with breakouts above the moving average.

Closing position. The best performance comes from candles when the closing price is within a third of the low, and it works in all cases except bull market/up

TABLE 42.5 Reversal Rates

Description	Bull Market	Bear Market
Closing price confirmation reversal rate	55%	52%
Candle color confirmation reversal rate	54%	51%
Opening gap confirmation reversal rate	41%	36%
Reversal: trend down, breakout up	32%	31%
Continuation: trend down, breakout down	68%	69%
Percentage of reversals (R)/continuations (C) for each 12-month low (L), middle (M), or high (H)	L 25% R/75% C, M 29% R/71% C, H 43% R/57% C	L 24% R/76% C, M 33% R/67% C, H 45% R/55% C

TABLE 42.6 Performance Indicators

Description	Bull Market, Up Breakout	Bear Market, Up Breakout	Bull Market, Down Breakout	Bear Market, Down Breakout
Closing price confirmation, performance	N/A	N/A	−5.95%	−10.89%
Candle color confirmation, performance	N/A	N/A	−6.31%	−11.44%
Opening gap confirmation, performance	N/A	N/A	−7.15%	−12.58%
Breakout above 50-day moving average, performance	6.84%	8.05%	−5.64%	−9.33%
Breakout below 50-day moving average, performance	7.04%	10.19%	−6.21%	−11.87%
Last candle: close in highest third, performance	6.85%	9.33%	−5.83%	−7.58%
Last candle: close in middle third, performance	7.34%	8.93%	−6.05%	−10.57%
Last candle: close in lowest third, performance	6.77%	9.50%	−6.12%	−12.27%

N/A means not applicable.

breakouts. Those do better when the close is in the middle of the candle. For this measure, use only the last candle line in the pattern and separate the line into thirds.

▦ Sample Trade

Figure 42.2 shows a trade that Rusty made. Price formed a double top created by the long peak at A and the sharper one at B. You could also call this a triple top, but Rusty didn't see it that way at first.

Along the bottom, he drew a neckline CD and extended it to E. A neckline is used most often for head-and-shoulders patterns, but in this case, it had absolutely no benefit over traditional methods. Go figure. The traditional method would be to sell once price closed below the lowest low in the double or triple top. Theoretically, the up-sloping neckline could get you out sooner, but the price difference between the two methods is negligible here.

Price formed two black gapping candles that ended at E. This told him that price was likely to continue lower, so the next day he sold his holdings in the stock at the open. As the chart shows, selling then was a timely move.

▦ For Best Performance

The following list offers tips and observations to help choose candles that perform well. Consult the associated table for more information.

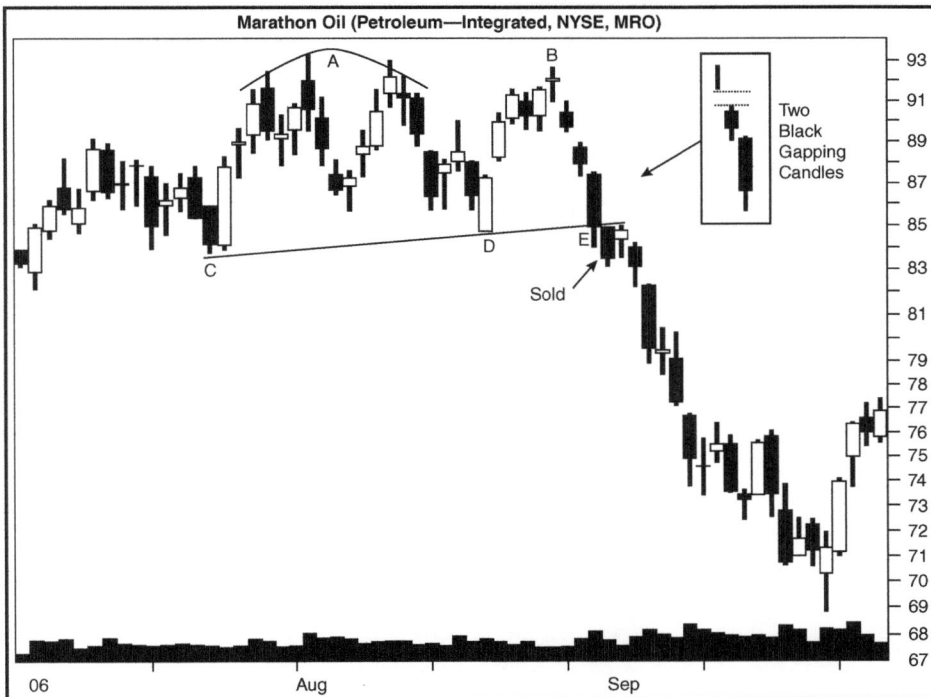

FIGURE 42.2 Two Black Gapping Candles Lead to a Timely Sale.

- Use the identification guidelines to help select the pattern—Table 42.1.

- Candles within a third of the yearly low perform best—Table 42.2.

- Select tall candles—Table 42.3.

- Use the measure rule to predict a price target—Table 42.3.

- Candles with tall upper or lower shadows outperform—Table 42.3.

- Volume gives performance clues—Table 42.4.

- Trade this candle pattern when the primary price trend is downward; avoid trading it in an uptrend—Trading Tactics discussion.

- The candle frequently breaks out downward—Table 42.5.

- Patterns within a third of the yearly low tend to act as continuations most often—Table 42.5.

- Opening gap confirmation works best—Table 42.6.

- Breakouts below the 50-day moving average lead to the best performance—Table 42.6.

CHAPTER 43

Window, Falling

From Thomas N. Bulkowski, *Encyclopedia of Candlestick Charts* (Hoboken, New Jersey: John Wiley & Sons, 2008), Chapter 104.

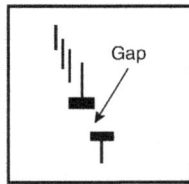

Learning Objective Statements

- Interpret potential price moves based on the patterns described in this chapter
- Calculate potential price targets
- Evaluate price levels for potential support or resistance
- Identify and interpret signals from various oscillators and technical studies

Behavior and Rank

Theoretical: Bearish continuation.
Actual bull market: Bearish continuation 67% of the time (ranking 11).
Actual bear market: Bearish continuation 73% of the time (ranking 6).
Frequency: 23rd out of 103.
Overall performance over time: 7th out of 103.

A falling window is a gap between two candles. How do you measure whether it acts as a reversal or continuation? You do that by including the two adjacent price bars. That's the approach I took.

As a continuation pattern, falling windows work well, ranking 11 in a bull market out of 103 candles, where 1 is best. Overall performance is also top-notch, ranking 7.

The psychology begins with the bears pushing price down. They do this with excessive selling pressure that overwhelms buying demand. At the open, this pressure is large enough that price gaps lower, leaving a falling window on the chart. Buying demand set up by hungry bulls is still no match for the selling pressure throughout the day. At day's end, if the bears have their way, the trading range of price throughout the day is not high enough to reach the prior day's low price. The falling window remains intact and appears as a space on the chart.

■ Identification Guidelines

Figure 43.1 shows an example of a falling window. Price at A forms a tall black candle. The next day, another black candle forms but this one (B) drops below the low of the prior candle, leaving a gap on the chart. In other words, the high at B is below the low at A.

Notice about a month later at D that price hesitates in its climb. About a quarter of the time the level of the falling window (the gap) offers resistance to future price movement. In this case, the stock pauses in its uphill run at D but is able to soldier on after a day's rest.

Another falling window occurs a month later at C. There price breaks away from congestion set up by short candles with long lower shadows in the week leading to the falling window. The long lower shadows are supposed to be a bullish omen, and price does make a strong advance but can't hold it. The candle above C sports a long upper shadow (bearish) and a small body with a small lower wick. It's a bearish sign, and price gaps lower the next day.

FIGURE 43.1   **A Falling Window Appears in a Declining Price Trend.**

TABLE 43.1 **Identification Guidelines**

Characteristic	Discussion
Number of candle lines	None.
Price trend	Downward leading to the start of the candle pattern.
Configuration	The high today is below the low of the prior day, leaving a gap on the chart.

Table 43.1 lists identification guidelines. A falling window refers to the gap left on the chart, so the pattern does not include any candle lines. What's important is that price gaps lower. That means today's high remains below the prior candle's low, leaving a gap on the chart.

■ Statistics

The statistics in the falling and rising windows chapters are different from others in this book due to the nature of the patterns. The most important questions that traders want answers to are: Does the gap act as a resistance zone? What happens to price over time? I answer those questions in the following paragraphs.

Table 43.2 shows general statistics for the falling window.

Number found. I looked at 13,997 candles from the standard database, and that was enough to get a good idea of how well falling windows acted as resistance zones.

Stopped in gap. This is the number of times a minor high appeared within the gap before price closed the gap. By *close the gap*, I mean price had to approach from below and *close* above the top of the gap before the end of data. This is also the same as how often a gap worked as a resistance zone to an upward price move.

I found all the minor highs from the day after the gap until price closed the gap (or end of data). Since this was a falling window, only minor highs mattered. I counted the number of times that the upper shadow of a candle stopped within the gap and the number of times price moved above the gap but didn't close it. In other words, the upper shadow of a candle was tall enough to span the gap but the candle closed

TABLE 43.2 **General Statistics**

Description	Bull Market	Bear Market
Number found	9,374	4,623
Stopped in gap	25%	33%
Average time to gap closed	55 days	86 days
Median time to gap closed	9 days	11 days
Number not closed	3%	2%
Average gap size	$0.30	$0.52
Median gap size	$0.12	$0.19

TABLE 43.3	Price Over Time Statistics	
Description	Bull Market	Bear Market
Gap+1	−1.9%	−3.3%
Gap+2	−1.8%	−3.3%
Gap+3	−1.7%	−3.5%
Gap+4	−1.6%	−3.5%
Gap+5	−1.5%	−3.3%
Gap+6	−1.5%	−3.1%
Gap+7	−1.3%	−3.5%
Gap+8	−1.3%	−3.3%
Gap+9	−1.2%	−3.1%
Gap+10	−1.2%	−3.4%

below the top of the gap. The day when it closed the gap, assuming it did before end of data, counted as the gap not showing overhead resistance.

In a bull market, 25% of the time the gap worked as overhead resistance to an upward price move.

Average/median time to gap closed. These are the average time and the median time it took for price to close above the top of the gap after approaching from below. The wide difference between the average and the median is due to several samples having large values, which tend to pull up the average but do not affect the median.

Number not closed. This is the percentage of gaps remaining open during the period of the study.

Average/median gap size. These measure from the top of the gap to the bottom of it. Again, the average is pulled up by large values.

Table 43.3 shows what happens to price over time after the gap ends. Gap+1 means the day after the gap completes; that is, if price gaps lower on Monday, then Gap+1 would be Tuesday. The table shows what happens to the closing price for two weeks after the gap.

To create the table, I found all gaps in stocks priced over $5 per share with an average daily volume over the prior 100 days of at least 250,000 shares. In other words, I wanted to eliminate thinly traded stocks. I found 12,706 samples that qualified.

In a bull market, price is 1.9% lower as measured from the high price the day the gap occurred (i.e., Monday's high price, continuing the analogy) to the following day's close (Tuesday's close). A day later, price has closed higher slightly, on average, to 1.8% below the gap. Two weeks later (Gap+10), price has narrowed the difference to 1.2% below the gap.

To be succinct, after a falling window, price in a bull market tends to rise during the next two weeks but not close the gap. In a bear market, price remains essentially constant.

CHAPTER 44

Window, Rising

From Thomas N. Bulkowski, *Encyclopedia of Candlestick Charts* (Hoboken, New Jersey: John Wiley & Sons, 2008), Chapter 105.

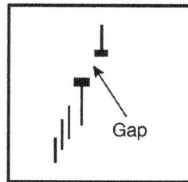

Learning Objective Statements

- Interpret potential price moves based on the patterns described in this chapter
- Calculate potential price targets
- Evaluate price levels for potential support or resistance
- Identify and interpret signals from various oscillators and technical studies

Behavior and Rank

Theoretical: Bullish continuation.
Actual bull market: Bullish continuation 75% of the time (ranking 4).
Actual bear market: Bullish continuation 72% of the time (ranking 7).
Frequency: 20th out of 103.
Overall performance over time: 42nd out of 103.

Now that I have completed researching rising and falling windows, I can see why stock traders don't put much emphasis on them. I certainly don't. A rising window will support price just 20% of the time in a bull market. That's once out of every five trades. Yuck. Maybe this works better in markets other than stocks.

The rank shows that a rising window acts as a bullish continuation 75% of the time, ranking 4, where 1 is best out of 103 candles. The overall performance is 42, a midlist rank.

The psychology begins with a rising price trend and bullish buying demand sending price higher. Before the open, the demand is so high that price gaps open and doesn't return to close the gap throughout the day. At day's end, price may have narrowed the gap but not closed it. What remains is a space on the chart, a rising window.

The theory behind a rising window is that it will act as a support zone. As we will see in the statistics section, that theory doesn't work well in the stock market on the daily scale.

■ Identification Guidelines

Figure 44.1 shows what a rising window looks like. This gap is an unusually tall one. Notice the tall white candle at B. Midway down the candle body is a support zone. I am more inclined to believe that a tall candle will support price midway down its body than I am that a rising window will support price. Just a few days ago, I placed an order to buy midway down a tall white candle. When price reached the midpoint, my order filled, and price climbed after that. It's a wonderful feeling when theory works in practice. Before I return to the rising window, research discussed in this book says that the mid-candle support or resistance area is a myth. Price is no more likely to find support or resistance there than anywhere else on a tall candle.

Table 44.1 lists identification guidelines. Rising windows appear in uptrends when price gaps higher. That means today's low price is above the prior high, leaving white space on the chart between the two price bars. A rising window is a gap and so it includes no candle lines.

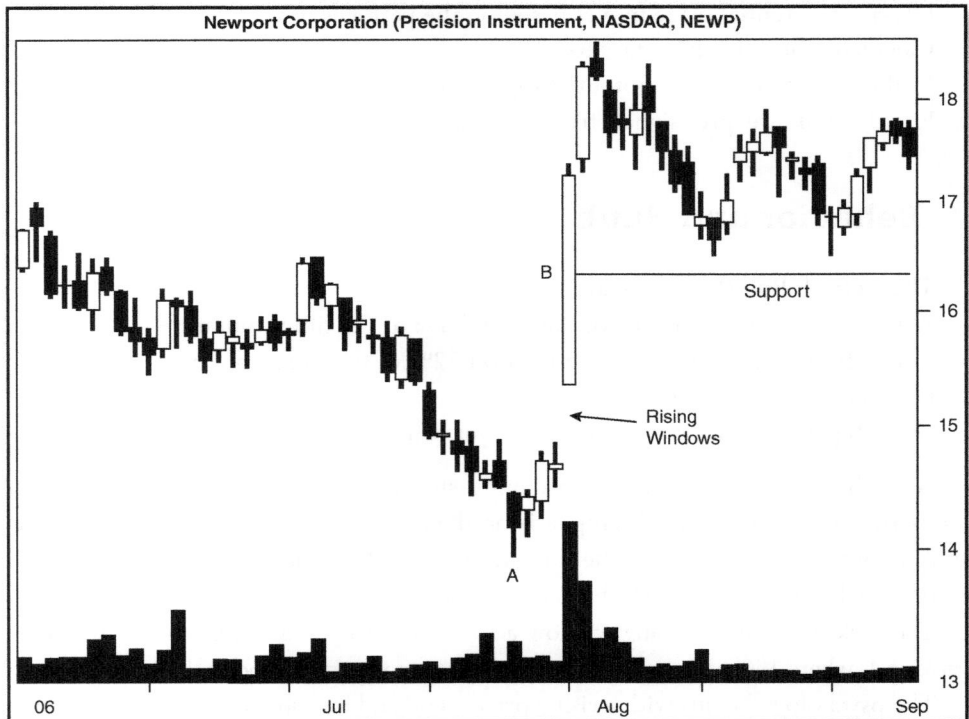

FIGURE 44.1 A Rising Window Appears Days after Price Changed Trend.

TABLE 44.1	Identification Guidelines
Characteristic	Discussion
Number of candle lines	None.
Price trend	Upward leading to the start of the candle pattern.
Configuration	The low today is above the high of the prior day, leaving a gap on the chart.

■ Statistics

The statistics in the falling and rising windows chapters are different from others in this book due to the nature of the patterns.

Table 44.2 shows general statistics for the rising window.

Number found. I found 18,229 rising windows in my standard database.

Stopped in gap. This tells how often price stopped within a gap. I used minor lows and compared the low price with the gap. If price entered the gap but didn't drop below the far side, then the gap acted as support (success). If the low price did drop below the far side, then that counted as a failure. The gap closed and the analysis ended when price closed below the high price the day before the gap.

I found that just 20% of the time price found support within the gap. The other 80% saw price continuing lower.

Average/median time to gap closed. The average and the median are two ways to look at the same data. The average can be swayed by several large values, as the results show. The median is just the midrange value in a sorted list of numbers. The median time to close the gap is 10 or 11 days. The average is much higher because some stocks had gaps that remained open for years.

Number not closed. This is the percentage of gaps that never closed by the end of data.

Average/median gap size. These show how tall the gap is using both the average and the median measures. I counted gaps as small as a penny in the analysis.

Table 44.3 shows what happens to price over time after the gap ends. Gap+1 means that if price gaps higher on Monday, then Gap+1 would be Tuesday. The table shows what happens to the closing price for two weeks after the gap as

TABLE 44.2	General Statistics	
Description	Bull Market	Bear Market
Number found	14,224	5,089
Stopped in gap	20%	16%c
Average time to gap closed	79 days	49 days
Median time to gap closed	11 days	10 days
Number not closed	9%	1%
Average gap size	$0.27	$0.33
Median gap size	$0.12	$0.15

TABLE 44.3	Price Over Time Statistics	
Description	Bull Market	Bear Market
Gap+1	1.8%	2.4%
Gap+2	1.9%	2.2%
Gap+3	2.0%	1.9%
Gap+4	2.1%	1.5%
Gap+5	2.0%	1.4%
Gap+6	2.1%	1.2%
Gap+7	2.1%	1.3%
Gap+8	2.1%	1.1%
Gap+9	2.2%	1.2%
Gap+10	2.2%	1.1%

measured from the top of the gap (i.e., Monday's low price, to continue the analogy).

To create the table, I found all gaps in stocks priced more than $5 per share with an average daily volume of at least 250,000 shares over the prior 100 days. In other words, I wanted to eliminate thinly traded stocks. I found 16,415 samples that qualified in the standard database.

Another research team found that upward gaps (rising windows) showed price trending lower over one day, two days, and a week later, but they did not separate bull and bear market data. I sorted the data by market condition and found that in a bull market, price coasted higher after the gap. In a bear market, the gap tended to narrow considerably (more than half) during the next two weeks.

CHAPTER 45

Dead-Cat Bounce

From Thomas N. Bulkowski, *Encyclopedia of Chart Patterns,* Second Edition (Hoboken, New Jersey: John Wiley & Sons, 2005), Chapter 54.

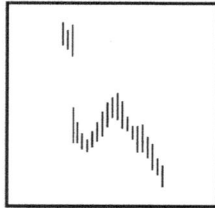

Learning Objective Statements

- Interpret potential price moves based on the patterns described in this chapter
- Calculate potential price targets
- Evaluate price levels for potential support or resistance
- Identify and interpret signals from various oscillators and technical studies

Results Snapshot

Event	An upward bounce and a declining price trend follow a dramatic decline.	
Reversal or continuation	Short-term bearish reversal	
	Bull Market	**Bear Market**
Performance rank	Not applicable	Not applicable
Event decline	31%	35%
Bounce	28%	35%
Postbounce decline	30%	40%
Surprising findings	About half the dead-cat bounce patterns with gaps close within 6 months. Over 75% decline below the event low after the bounce. In a bear market, a second large decline is likely within 6 months. Large bounces occur after large event losses but take longer to peak. Small bounces occur after small event losses but they peak quicker.	

If you trade stocks long enough, you will probably run across this puppy: the dead-cat bounce. (I could not resist the pun). It acts as a warning to exit the stock quickly after a dramatic decline.

The dead-cat bounce pattern (DCB) consists of three phases. First, the event sees prices decline over 30% in just a few sessions, the majority of the decline happening the first day. Second, prices bounce, recovering a portion of what they lost; and third, prices ease down, giving back all of their gains and more in the postbounce decline.

Surprising findings include the following. If price gaps down on the first day, how long does it take for prices to rise far enough to cover the gap, that is, to close the gap? About half the time, the gap closes within 6 months, leaving half of all patterns still lower than where they started. After prices bounce, they move lower and over 75% make a low below that posted during the event decline. In many stocks, one DCB follows another, especially in a bear market. The final surprise is that DCBs with large event losses tend to bounce higher but take longer to peak than events with small losses.

If a dead-cat bounce occurs in a stock you own, ride price upward in the bounce and then get out. Prices will likely move lower and another DCB may await 3 or 6 months down the line. Do not trade any bullish chart pattern less than 6 months after a stock shows a DCB.

Tour

The name "dead-cat bounce" comes from the behavior of a stock after an unexpected negative event. Figure 45.1 shows a typical example of a DCB. In late September, the smart money started selling their holdings, driving down the price and pushing up

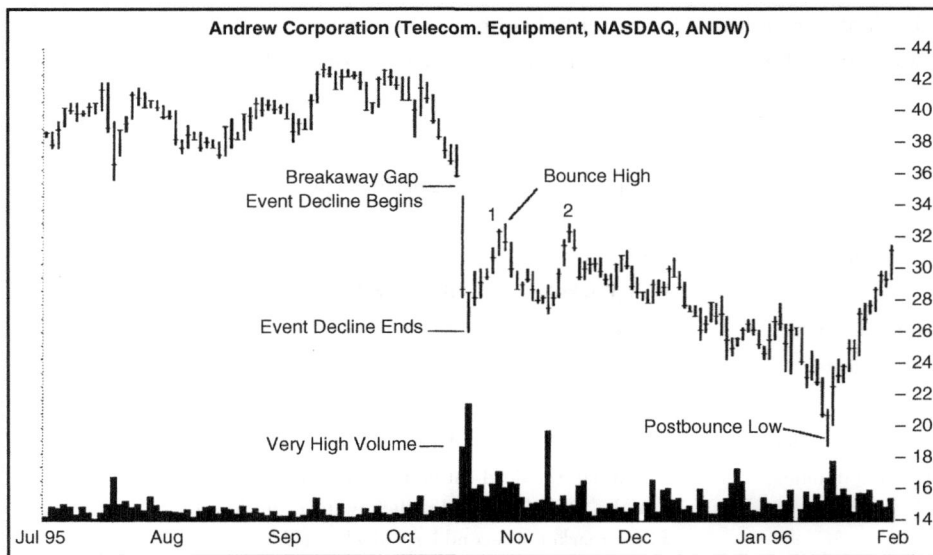

FIGURE 45.1   **A major brokerage firm lowered its rating on the stock, sending it tumbling 50% in about 3.5 months. The dead-cat bounce allowed astute investors to sell their holdings and minimize their losses before the decline resumed. The twin peaks in mid-October (1, 2) and early November are a double top signaling further declines.**

the volume trend. Prices declined from a high of 42.44 to 35.81 in just over a week. On October 9, a major brokerage house lowered its intermediate-term rating on the stock. Down it went. In 2 days the stock dropped over 30%.

For the next week and a half, the stock recovered somewhat, rising to 32.81 and enticing novice investors to buy the stock. The stock moved lower and then climbed again to form a double top. This rise was the end of the good news. From the second peak, it was all downhill until mid-January, when the stock bottomed. From the high before the event began to the ultimate low, the stock plunged 50%! Welcome to the dead-cat bounce.

■ Identification Guidelines

Are there characteristics common to the dead-cat bounce? Yes, and Table 45.1 lists them.

Price gap, plunge. Suppose a company announces a negative event, usually when the market is closed. The news surprises stockholders and they line up to sell. The overwhelming selling pressure forces the stock to gap lower on the open. For this study, I used a minimum event decline of 15% but most ranged from 25% to 45% and one was as high as 78%. Imagine waking up to find a $10,000 investment worth just $2,200. The plunge usually takes 1 or 2 days, but the downward trend before price begins to bounce can last longer, up to 8 days.

Bounce. Prices bounce up, recovering much of what they lost during the event decline. The recovery typically ranges between 15% and 35% and takes between 5 and 25 days to reach the top of the bounce.

Decline. After price peaks during the bounce, it drops, falling slowly, until reaching a trend low 15% to 45% below the bounce top. It makes this journey in 10 to 50 days, usually.

To put the numbers into perspective, consider Figure 45.2, a 47%, 1-day decline. The Food and Drug Administration's advisory panel rejected Cephalon's Myotrophin drug application. When the news hit the Street, the stock gapped down and traded at almost half its value. Volume was a massive 8.4 million shares, more than 15 times

TABLE 45.1 **Identification Characteristics**

Characteristic	Discussion
Price gap	The daily high is below the prior day's low, leaving a price gap (breakaway) on the chart.
Plunge	On the negative announcement, price gaps down and plunges, usually between 25% and 40% but can be as much as 70%.
Bounce	Prices recover between 15% and 35%. Do not be fooled; the decline is not over.
Decline	After the bounce finishes, another decline begins. This one is more sedate but prices typically decline another 15% to 30%.

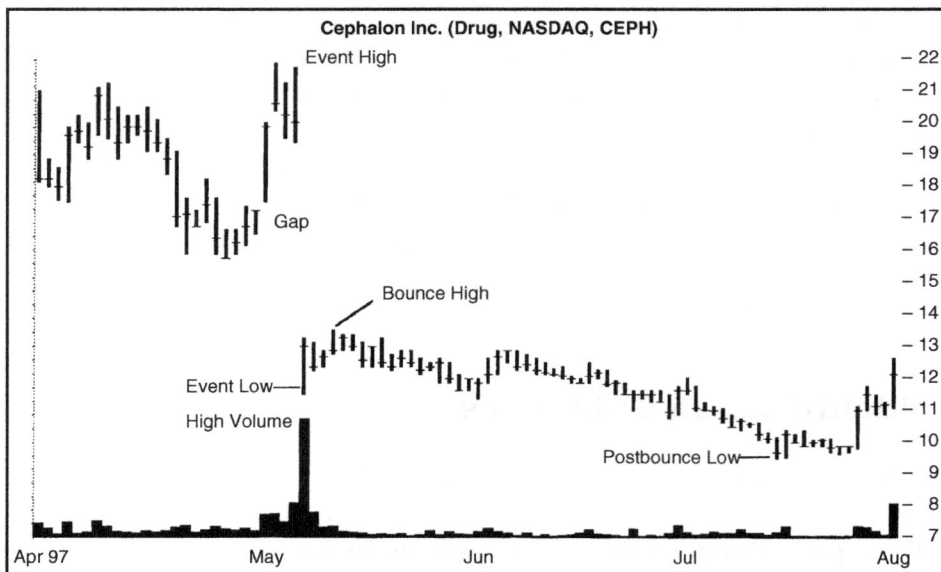

FIGURE 45.2 A negative announcement triggered the dead-cat bounce, which began when prices gapped down, bounced upward, and then trended lower.

normal. During the next 3 days, the stock recovered a portion of its decline by gaining $2 a share (low to high). Then the remainder of the decline set in. As if rubbing salt in the wound, the stock moved down again in an almost straight-line fashion. From the recovery high, the stock declined another 30%.

Figure 45.3 shows an even more alarming decline. Just 3 days before the massive decline, a brokerage firm reported that it believed the company would continue seeing strong sales and earnings trends. Perhaps this report boosted expectations, but when the company announced a quarterly loss—instead of the profit the Street was expecting—the stock dropped almost 43 points *in 1 day*. That is a decline of 62%.

The stock gapped downward, a characteristic that most DCBs share. A negative news announcement is so surprising that sell orders overwhelm buying demand. The stock opens at a much lower price. Volume shoots upward, typically several times the normal rate. Figure 45.3 shows that 49 million shares exchanged hands on the news, about 20 times normal.

Usually the 1-day decline establishes a new low and prices begin recovering almost immediately. Figure 45.3 shows that the stock made a new low the following day but then closed up a day later.

After a massive decline, the bounce phase begins. Most of the time, a stock will rise up and retrace some of its losses. However, the bounce phase for Oxford Health Plans was brief—only 1 day. In less than 2 months, the stock dropped by half.

What types of events cause these massive declines? Almost all the events are company specific: negative earnings surprises, bad same-store sales numbers, failed mergers, accounting sleight of hand, outright fraud—that sort of thing. Sometimes

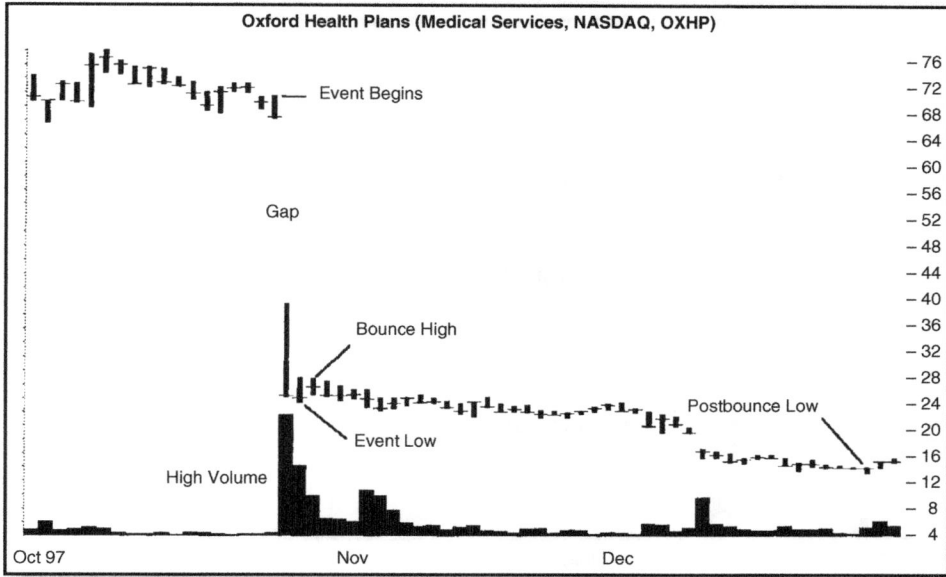

FIGURE 45.3 Negative news announcement triggered the massive 1-day decline, which saw prices drop by 43 points or over 60%, but the decline was not over as the stock fell an additional 43%.

the news affects more than one company. Figure 45.2 shows what happened to Cephalon, but Chiron stock was not immune. Chiron has a joint development and marketing agreement with Cephalon for the Myotrophin drug, so its stock also took a hit, but not nearly as large (less than 5%) as Cephalon.

Most of the time investors cannot predict the event. If you own the stock, you will lose your shirt. The question then becomes, how much of your remaining wardrobe do you want to lose? We see in the Trading Tactics section that it pays to sell quickly.

Focus on Failures

Not all massive declines end in a dead-cat bounce. Consider the event shown in Figure 45.4. On April 3, 1997, the company released earnings that fell short of expectations and announced that it terminated the merger with another company. Several brokerages downgraded the stock. Price tumbled 44%. Like all dead-cat bounces, the stock recovered. However, instead of bouncing up, then turning down and moving lower, this stock continued trending up. In less than 3 months, the stock recovered its entire loss.

Why did the stock fail to bounce and head lower? Events that take place just after the negative news announcement explain the stock's behavior. Several insiders bought the stock. Even the company got into the act and announced it was purchasing 10% of the stock. Together, the news sent the stock moving higher. Subsequent events kept the momentum building and the stock continued rising.

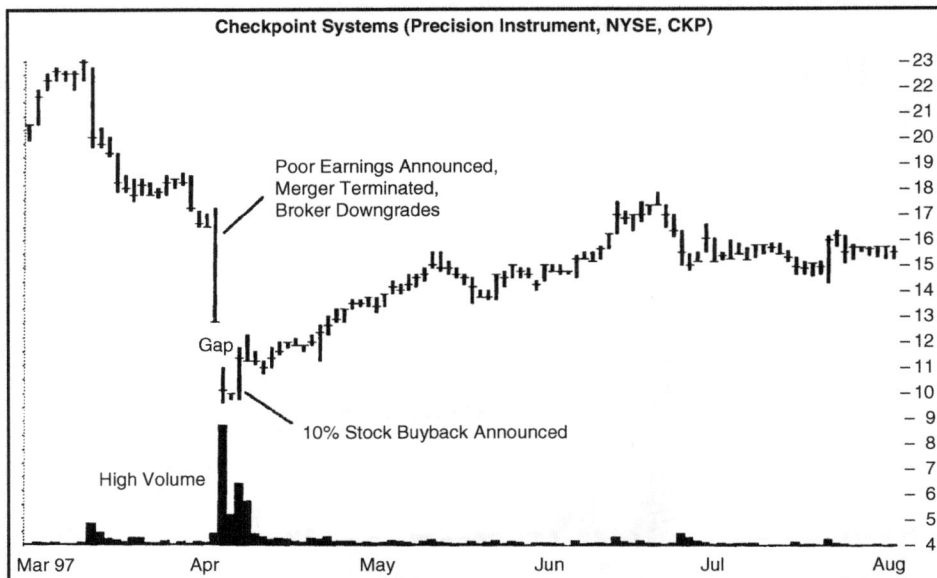

FIGURE 45.4 A Dead-Cat Bounce Formation Failure. After the decline, the stock moved higher and kept rising instead of moving back down.

■ Statistics

Table 45.2 shows general statistics for DCBs.

Number of formations. I used DCBs that I found when researching the first edition plus newer ones. I excluded those DCBs that showed event declines of less than 15%. I define the event decline as the move from the close the day before the event to the trend low, before the bounce begins. I used my database to match events to those large price moves; so if a stock dropped 20% but did not have an event associated with it, I ignored it. I found 676 DCBs from mid-1991 to mid-2004.

Reversal or continuation. Just 28 more DCBs acted as reversals of the price trend than continuations.

Yearly position. Using the closing price the day before the event as the reference in the yearly price range, we find that in a bull market DCBs appear most often in the middle of the range. In a bear market, they usually occur near the yearly low.

TABLE 45.2	General Statistics	
Description	Bull Market	Bear Market
Number of formations	454	222
Reversal (R), continuation (C)	237 R, 217 C	115 R, 107 C
Percentage occurring near the 12-month low (L), center (C), or high (H)[a]	L31%, C44%, H25%	L47%, C33%, H20%

[a] The reference used is the closing price the day before the event. The first edition of the *Encyclopedia* used the high price the day before the event, so results vary.

TABLE 45.3   Event Decline Statistics

Description	Bull Market	Bear Market
Number with event day gaps	337 or 74%	179 or 81%
Average gap size	$2.59	$4.06
Event decline (prior close to trend low)	31%	35%
Event duration (event day to trend low)	7 days	6 days
Number making a lower low the next day		
Event day + 1	207 or 46%	112 or 50%
Event day + 2	76 or 17%	61 or 27%
Event day + 3	39 or 9%	28 or 13%
Event day + 4	14 or 3%	12 or 5%

Table 45.3 shows event decline statistics.

Gaps. Between 74% and 81% of the dead-cat bounce patterns begin with a large price gap. This means the announcement came when the market was closed. When trading resumed, prices dropped significantly, far enough that subsequent intraday trading could not close the gap. By day's end, a gap averaging $2.59 in a bull market and over $4 in a bear market remained.

Event. The event decline, as measured from the close the day before the event to the trend low (before beginning a substantial rise to the bounce phase), averaged over 30%. The decline to the trend low took about a week, but that is an average pulled upward by several DCBs with long declines. If you use a frequency distribution, you find that about half the time, price makes a lower low the day after the event. Beyond that, fewer and fewer consecutive lower lows occur, as Table 45.3 shows.

What does this information mean? If you want to trade the bounce, place a buy order at the event day's low. The chances are about even that your order will fill and you can ride the bounce upward.

Table 45.4 shows the bounce statistics for DCBs.

Gaps closed. After the event occurs, prices bounce, but how high? In just under a quarter of the cases, prices bounce high enough to close the event day gap. That means prices rise at least to the low the day before the event.

In 3 months' time, over a third of the event day gaps were closed. In 6 months, over half were closed. Viewed another way, half a year after the massive event decline, prices had not fully recovered in almost half the stocks showing a DCB.

Bounce. The bounce height, as measured from the trend low after the event to the highest high in the bounce, averaged 28% in a bull market and 35% in a bear market. This finding surprises me. I would expect the bounce in a bull market to be higher than the one in a bear market, but Table 45.4 shows that such is not the case.

The time to complete the bounce was nearly the same for both market types: about 3 weeks. Notice that the rise in a bear market is higher and quicker than that in a bull market. Thus, if you want to trade the bounce, select DCBs in a bear market.

TABLE 45.4 Bounce Statistics

Description	Bull Market	Bear Market
Number of gaps closed during bounce (to bounce high)	74 or 22%	41 or 23%
Number of gaps closed in 3 months	127 or 38%	70 or 39%
Number of gaps closed in 6 months	195 or 58	96 or 54%
Average bounce height (event low to bounce high)	28%	35%
Bounce duration (event low to bounce high)	23 days	21 days
Median event loss	28.74%	33.32%
Large event loss, resulting bounce rise	35%	44%
Small event loss, resulting bounce rise	22%	29%
Large event loss, resulting bounce duration	25 days	25 days
Small event loss, resulting bounce duration	20 days	16 days

Event loss size. I compared the size of the event loss to the resulting bounce. Table 45.4 shows the median decline from the close the day before the event to the trend low before the bounce began. Losses higher than the median I call large events; losses smaller than the median are small events. Then I mapped the bounce height and duration and found that large event losses result in large bounces. Small event losses result in small bounces. For example, when the loss was large, prices bounced 35% in a bull market. Small event losses showed bounces averaging 22%.

The bounce duration contradicts what I found in the first edition of this book, but I use more samples here and do not rely on the interpretation of a scatter plot. I found that large event losses result in bounces that take longer to peak. For example, in a bull market, a large event loss takes an average of 25 days for price to peak in the bounce phase. Small event losses take 20 days to peak.

Table 45.5 shows the postbounce statistics. Postbounce is the decline measured from the highest high in the bounce to the postbounce low—the lowest low before the postbounce changes.

TABLE 45.5 Postbounce Statistics

Description	Bull Market	Bear Market
Postbounce decline (bounce high to postbounce low)	30%	40%
Postbounce duration (bounce high to postbounce low)	49 days	42 days
Event low to postbounce low	18%	27%
Number declining below event low	306 or 67%	167 or 75%
Decline from close day before event to postbounce low	38%	48%
Duration from day before event to postbounce low	79 days	69 days
Number with another 15% decline in 3 months	118 or 26%	105 or 47%
Number with another 15% decline in 6 months	174 or 38%	135 or 61%

Postbounce. Once prices peak in the bounce phase of a DCB, they decline 30% in a bull market and float like stones by plummeting 40% in a bear market. The time to make such a large drop is quicker in a bear market: 42 days versus 49 days in a bull market. If you want to short a stock after a DCB, try to time it so you open the short near the bounce peak and ride it down in a bear market.

Event low to postbounce low. This criterion measures the decline if you decided to ride out a DCB. The event low is the lowest low before price begins its rise to the bounce high. The postbounce low is the lowest low after the bounce. The difference between the event low and postbounce low is how bad things get after the large event decline. In a bull market, the additional decline measures 18% and in a bear market, it averages 27%. Over two-thirds of the stocks (67% to 75%) dropped below the event low.

What does all this information mean? Suppose someone catches the CFO with his hands in the cash register and the stock's price drops 40% in 2 days during a bear market. Should you ride the bounce upward and then get out, or just hold on? Answer: Ride it up and sell at the bounce high. Once the bounce completes, expect an additional decline of 27% for a combined loss of 67%.

Event start to postbounce low. The decline using the close the day before the event to the postbounce low measures 38% in a bull market and 48% in a bear market. This measure is the average decline suffered by investors holding onto the stock until they sell at the very bottom. It takes between 69 days and 79 days to inflict such pain.

Additional DCBs. I looked at the number of large declines (over 15%) in the days after a DCB. My contention is that a DCB follows a DCB because management cannot fix severe problems in just one quarter.

For DCBs for which data were available, 26% to 47% of the DCBs followed an existing DCB in 3 months, and 38% to 61% had another DCB within 6 months. Especially in a bear market, the numbers suggest that you make the best of a bad situation and get out of a long holding during the bounce phase. If you do not sell, you will suffer through the decline, and the chances of another DCB occurring are high.

Table 45.6 shows a frequency distribution of time for the three phases of a DCB, in calendar days, not trading days. What do the numbers tell us?

Event decline. Consider the event decline, the first block of numbers. This block shows how quickly price bottoms after a massive decline. For example, in a bear market 53% of the stocks with DCBs reach the trend low in 2 days or less. Since the columns are additive, 71% (53% + 8% + 10%) reach bottom in 6 days or less.

Bounce. The next block shows the time for prices to rise to the top of the bounce after reaching the event low. For example, in a bear market, 30% of the stocks showing a DCB take 5 days or less to reach the highest high before price begins another decline. In 10 days time, almost half—48% (30% + 18%)—will have reached the bounce high.

Postbounce. The last block shows how long it takes price to reach the postbounce low. For example, in a bear market, 19% take less than 10 days to reach the low. Within a month, 56% (19% + 20% + 17%) will have bottomed.

TABLE 45.6 Frequency Distribution of Time

Days:	2	4	6	8	10	12	14	16	18	>18
Event decline, bear market	53%	8%	10%	7%	4%	3%	3%	2%	1%	9%
Event decline, bull market	54%	6%	8%	8%	4%	3%	4%	2%	2%	11%

Days:	5	10	15	20	25	30	35	40	45	>45
Bounce rise, bear market	30%	18%	8%	10%	9%	5%	2%	3%	3%	11%
Bounce rise, bull market	26%	19%	12%	7%	7%	5%	4%	1%	4%	15%

Days:	10	20	30	40	50	60	70	80	90	>90
Postbounce decline, bear market	19%	20%	17%	6%	13%	5%	5%	4%	3%	9%
Postbounce decline, bull market	16%	20%	14%	11%	8%	5%	6%	4%	3%	15%

The table gives you some idea of how long it will take the average stock to navigate the three phases of a DCB: the event decline, the bounce phase, and the postbounce decline. Remember, though, that since we are dealing with probabilities here, anything can happen.

Table 45.7 is similar to Table 45.6 but concerns price.

Event decline. The first block of numbers shows the decline from the close the day before the event to the event low. For example, in a bear market 6% of the stocks with DCBs show declines of between 15% and 20%. Since the columns are additive,

TABLE 45.7 Frequency Distribution of Price

Percentage:	15	20	25	30	35	40	45	50	55	>55
Event decline, bear market	0%	6%	16%	17%	15%	11%	14%	6%	9%	6%
Event decline, bull market	0%	13%	19%	22%	15%	11%	8%	3%	6%	4%
Bounce rise, bear market	17%	11%	11%	9%	12%	8%	6%	2%	2%	22%
Bounce rise, bull market	23%	15%	10%	11%	7%	8%	6%	5%	3%	13%
Postbounce decline, bear market	5%	15%	10%	10%	9%	9%	11%	6%	7%	17%
Postbounce decline, bull market	16%	15%	15%	14%	9%	8%	7%	5%	4%	7%

39% (0% + 6% + 16% + 17%) have declines that range up to 30%. The table shows that most DCBs (73%) have declines that range from 25% to 45% (bear market) and 80% will decline between 20% and 40% in a bull market.

Bounce. The next block of numbers shows the height of the bounce as measured from the event low to the highest high in the bounce. In a bear market, for example, 17% of the stocks with DCBs have bounces that rise 15%. Most of the bounces (60% of them) will fall between 15% and 35%. In a bull market, most (59%) will bounce up to 30% higher.

Postbounce. The final block of numbers shows the depth of the postbounce decline as measured from the highest high in the bounce to the postbounce low. For example, in a bear market, 5% of the stocks showing DCBs will decline up to 15%. Another 15% will decline between 15% and 20%. Most of the stocks (64%) have postbounce declines that range from 20% to 45%. In a bull market, the decline is smaller, with most stocks (60%) declining between 15% and 30%.

Taken together, Tables 45.6 and 45.7 show how long and how far price will move during a dead-cat bounce. They can help you construct a trading plan to take advantage of a DCB.

■ Trading Tactics

Table 45.8 shows trading tactics for the dead-cat bounce event pattern, and Table 45.9 lists additional stocks with DCBs taken from my database on which you can hone your trading skills.

Sell long holdings. As bad as the event decline is, things will only get worse after prices finish bouncing higher. Table 45.5 shows that prices decline between 18% (bull market) and 27% (bear market) below the event low. Do you want to risk those additional losses?

Since you cannot avoid the event decline, ride it out, and wait for the bounce. Use Tables 45.6 and 45.7 to estimate how long and how far prices are likely to bounce. I have found that an up-sloping trend line drawn along the bottom of the minor lows as prices rise is effective in many cases. When price closes below the trend line, sell. You will not catch the bounce high and prices may resume rising without adding a postbounce decline, but selling is the best way to protect your wealth.

TABLE 45.8	Trading Tactics
Trading Tactic	**Explanation**
Sell long holdings	Wait for the bounce to peak and then sell.
Buy long	For swing traders, buy when price finishes the event decline. Sell when price peaks in the bounce phase. Never buy a stock showing a DCB just because it is cheap! It will be cheaper in the coming weeks.
Sell short	Short at the bounce high, ride prices lower, and cover when the trend changes.

If you happen to be short the stock and a DCB occurs, expect a bounce followed by an additional decline. Table 45.5 shows that between 67% (bull market) and 75% (bear market) of the stocks showing a DCB will drop below the event low. You may be looking at the exception, so if price rises to close the event gap (between 22% and 23% will, from Table 45.4), consider closing out your short position.

Whether price will decline again (after the bounce) largely depends on the actions the company takes. Are insiders buying the stock? Has the company announced a stock buyback? Is the problem company specific or is everyone in the industry getting beaten? If the industry is suffering, then look at other stocks in the industry. Are they showing signs of recovery? If so, then close out your short position. If the industry is suffering and the market is dropping, then consider riding out the bounce with the expectation that price will resume declining. Between a quarter (26%, bull market) and a half (47%, bear market) will have another DCB within 3 months. Usually, these are quarterly earnings–related events such as a weak retail environment (missed same-store sales, or missed earnings estimates). If the company cannot fix the problem in 3 months, then another DCB may follow.

Buy long. Trading the bounce is a risky maneuver and should be attempted only by seasoned swing traders. First, compute the event loss size from the closing price the day before the event to the event low. Is the decline large or small? Compare it to the median event loss shown in Table 45.4 for the associated bull or bear market. If you are trading a large event, expect a large bounce but one that takes longer than usual. If the event decline is small, expect a smaller but quicker bounce.

Look for DCBs in a historical price series and trade them on paper to sharpen your skills before committing real money. Table 45.9 lists stocks with DCBs on which you can practice. Print out the price chart and cover it with a sheet of paper. Slide the paper to the right, uncovering the event. When should you buy and when should you sell?

TABLE 45.9	Additional DCBs	
Company	**Symbol**	**Date**
Abbott Labs	ABT	6/11/2002
Abgenix	ABGX	8/19/2002
Administaff	ASF	5/1/2002, 8/1/2002
Advanced Micro Devices	AMD	1/14/1999, 7/6/2001, 4/18/2002, 10/3/2002, 1/17/2003
Airgas	ARG	4/27/1998, 4/28/2000
Any airline stock	ALK, CAL, DAL, FRNT, NWAC, LUV...	9/17/2001 (after 9-11 event)
Alkermes	ALKS	7/1/2002
Alpharma	ALO	7/30/2002, 8/15/2002, 9/9/2003
Amazon.com	AMZN	7/24/2001, 10/24/2001
American Power Conversion	APCC	7/31/2000

Buy when prices finish dropping during the event decline (as close to the event low as you can get). Price will bottom in 1 or 2 days (46% make a lower low the second day, as per Table 45.3). You can place a buy order at the low of the first day and then pray that the order is hit. The average rise will take 23 days (Table 45.4) in a bull market and 21 days in a bear market. Table 45.6 zooms in on the statistics to help you time your exit. The rise to the bounce high will be different from that shown in the tables, you can count on it. Be flexible and remember that the tables show what will *probably* happen, but it does not guarantee the results.

Use the same tips as discussed in "Sell long holdings" to exit the trade as close to the bounce high as possible.

Sell short. If you think you can make money shorting a stock, try practicing your technique on those listed in Table 45.9. Pull up the stocks shown in the figures accompanying this chapter and practice on those as well.

When prices stop climbing at the top of the bounce, consider shorting the stock. Use whatever method you normally use to spot the trend change. These methods may include indicators such as moving averages, stochastics, RSI, CCI, trend lines, chart patterns, support and resistance, and so on.

Count on the stock dropping to at least the event low (see Table 45.5). Not all stocks will do that, but that is the way to bet. If the drop to that price is not mouth-watering, then look elsewhere for a more promising trade unless you have a strong reason for believing the stock will tumble. It may not. Use stops to protect your position.

Check the fundamentals and understand why the stock took a tumble in the first place (the event decline). This knowledge will often give you a clue as to future DCBs. Many times, the problem cannot be fixed in the current quarter, so additional quarters may suffer as well.

■ Sample Trade

Consider Figure 45.5, a dead-cat bounce in Cerner Corporation. The stock dropped five points (25%) after the company said earnings would fall short of expectations and the outlook for the remainder of the year was grim. The stock closed higher on each of the next 4 days and then closed lower. Jill, after seeing the stock climb the hill, sold the stock short and received a fill at the closing price of 15. She then waited, watching the stock closely. It continued moving down—as predicted.

The earnings announcement forced the stock down another 20% in 2 days. Expecting another dead-cat bounce, Jill held onto her position. The stock rose in an uneven fashion over the next week or so, and then rounded over and headed lower.

She connected the tops from the preannouncement day onward in a down-sloping trend line. When price eventually closed above the trend line, she knew it was time to close out the position. The next day she bought the stock back and received a fill at 12, 0.25 below the daily close. She sat back and totaled up her profits and realized she made almost $3 a share, or about 20% in just 1 month.

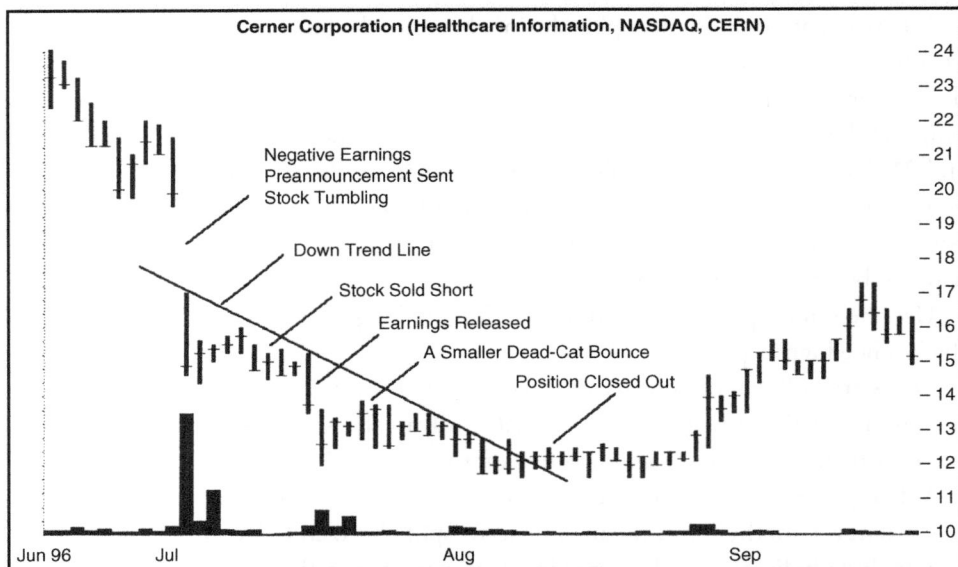

FIGURE 45.5 A Negative Earnings Announcement Triggers a Dead-Cat Bounce. As described in the sample trade, Jill sold the stock short just after the bounce high then covered when price closed above the trend line. The trade resulted in a 20% gain in 1 month.

As good as the trade was, had she waited until November to close out the position, she would have made an additional $1.50 a share (the stock reached a low of 10.50). However, between the time of covering the short and the ultimate low, the stock climbed back to 17.25. The moral is, you never go broke taking a profit.

■ For Best Performance

The following list includes tips and observations to help select DCBs that perform better after the breakout. Consult the associated table for more information.

■ Review the identification guidelines for correct selection—Table 45.1.

■ Nearly half the stocks make a lower low the day after the event—Table 45.3.

■ A quarter of the stocks with event day gaps close during the bounce—Table 45.4.

■ The larger the event day decline, the higher the bounce but the slower the rise—Table 45.4.

■ Prices decline faster and steeper in a bear market—Table 45.5.

■ Between 67% and 75% of stocks showing a DCB will drop below the event low after the bounce completes—Table 45.5.

■ Between 38% and 61% of the stocks exhibiting a DCB will suffer another 15% or larger decline in less than 6 months—Table 45.5.

CHAPTER 46

Dead-Cat Bounce, Inverted

From Thomas N. Bulkowski, *Encyclopedia of Chart Patterns,* Second Edition (Hoboken, New Jersey: John Wiley & Sons, 2005), Chapter 55.

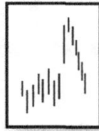

Learning Objective Statements

885

- Interpret potential price moves based on the patterns described in this chapter
- Calculate potential price targets
- Evaluate price levels for potential support or resistance
- Identify and interpret signals from various oscillators and technical studies

I call this event pattern an inverted dead-cat bounce, or iDCB, because of the way prices move after a surprisingly good event. I did not break out the statistics in the usual tables because I used a computer to find matches in the stocks I track. With more than 30,000 samples in some cases, reviewing them all would be too cumbersome. Thus, the format of this chapter differs from the others.

▓ Tour

What does an iDCB pattern look like? Figure 46.1 shows the first example, taken from a trade I made. The inverted dead-cat bounce pattern begins with a large, 1-day upward price move. In this example, the stock jumped 15% after the earnings announcement, gapping upward on high volume. The following day, it made a higher high, low, and close, but over the coming days, price dropped, returning to the launch point and then sinking moderately below it.

Here is my notebook entry for the trade: "2/6/04. I bought 400 shares, 300 filled at 30.30, 100 filled at 30.39. This is an earnings flag trade. I waited for a retrace before buying because of a weak general market. Price may retrace farther, but I expect a renewed climb. Downside is 50% retrace to 27.50–28. That is also the site of the

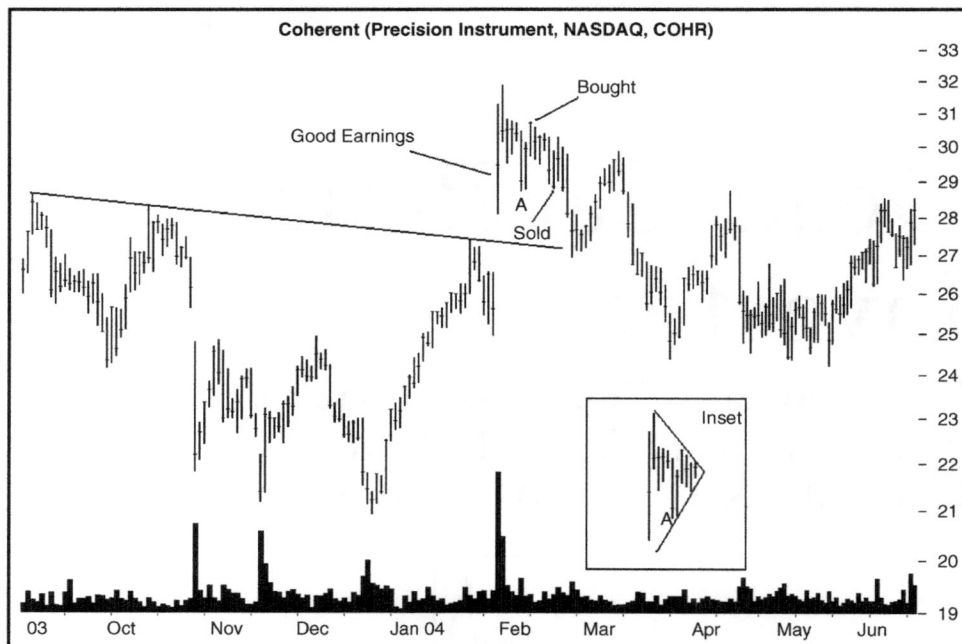

FIGURE 46.1 Good Earnings Propel the Stock Upward by 15%. Price Makes a Higher High the Next Day and Then Starts Declining.

THE INTEGRATION OF TECHNICAL ANALYSIS

August–November 2003 peaks. Expect a rise to 35. This could stall at 34 according to the point and figure chart. At 35, this goes up against a long-term down trend line from the March and July peaks in 2000. According to the 1-2-3 trend change rule, the stock is poised to move up. Price pierced the down trend line, retested the low, and is now breaking out to new highs."

Let me explain the entry. This was supposed to be an earnings flag trade, but as you can see, the flag was a failure because price dropped instead of moving to new highs. Had I studied the iDCB at the time, I would not have traded this one. Why? Large down moves often follow large up moves.

Since the odds of a successful trade improve with a rising stock, industry, and general market, I waited for the market to get on board. The S&P 500 index started moving up a few days before I bought. A retrace to the 27.50–28 area would find support from prior peaks but would also fill the gap. A gap usually supports the stock—as it did in late February—but price tunneled through in March.

The 35-price target comes from the earnings flag projection. From the low the day before the large up move, price bottomed at 25.24 and then peaked at 31.88 for a height of 6.64. From the flag low at point A, 28.75, the target would be 35.39. I played it conservative and rounded it down to 35.

A 50% retrace of the up move in the flagpole would put the stock at 28.56, just above the high end of the gap, and just below point A. I find that Fibonacci retracement numbers (such as 38%, 50%, and 62%) come in handy to help determine support and resistance zones. You can see that price approached the 50% retrace mark as it made a low at point A and then moved higher.

Sometimes I check the point and figure (PF) chart to help determine where support and resistance zones are. The PF chart shows overhead resistance at 34, and on the price chart, a solid block appears at that price in March and April of 2002 (not shown in Figure 46.1).

The 1-2-3 trend change rule is beyond the scope of this book (see *Trading Classic Chart Patterns,* Wiley, 2002, for an explanation), but it says price has changed trend from down to up when it breaks a down-sloping trend line, retests the low but fails, and rises above a prior minor high. Those three criteria were satisfied when price gapped above a down-sloping trend line connecting the September and October peaks, as shown.

Here is my notebook entry for the sale: "2/12/04. The Dow was up 123 points yesterday, but this stock hardly moved. Today, it has broken out downward from a pennant. Time to cut the loss. I'll sell at the market open tomorrow. This stock did not do as I expected, so it's time to sell. 2/13/04. The stock sold at 29.255."

Since my trading success depends on the market helping push prices upward, when the stock fails to participate in a market rally, that is often a red flag. Coupled with the breakout from the pennant (see inset in Figure 46.1), that signaled a sell. One key rule with trading chart or event patterns is that if price does not do as you expect, then close out your position. I did just that and cut my loss to about $450, or 3.8%. If I held on, I could have ridden it down to the May low for a 20% loss.

■ Statistics

For this pattern, instead of showing large tables of numbers, I show graphs. Let me issue this warning up front. The following graphs show averages of thousands of samples. Your trade will probably not act like the profile. Still, all of the graphs suggest selling on day 2, when price makes a higher high. Whether you buy back in later depends on the situation and price action. Use common sense and your trading experience to execute correctly.

The first graph, Figure 46.2, shows the price profile of between 29,600 and 37,100 event patterns in which the high, low, or closing price moved more than 5%. I used about 250 stocks to collect the data from as early as January 1988 to June 2004. Not all stocks had data covering that period.

The figure is a frequency distribution of the average price change over time. The vertical axis shows the average climb as measured from low to low, high to high, or close to close between the day before the large move (called the *reference day*) to succeeding days up to a month later. For example, on day 1, the intraday low and closing prices were 7.8% higher than the day before, and the intraday high was 7.9% higher. The following day, all three price components moved higher with the intraday high topping out at 8.7%, the low was 8.5% higher, and the close was 7.9% higher than the reference day's high, low, and close, respectively.

What does the chart mean? If you own stock and it jumps over 5%, Figure 46.2 shows the *average* price behavior for the next month. After the initial move, expect a higher high, higher low, and higher close the following day. That day is the time to sell. On average, price will drop in the coming sessions and will likely level out

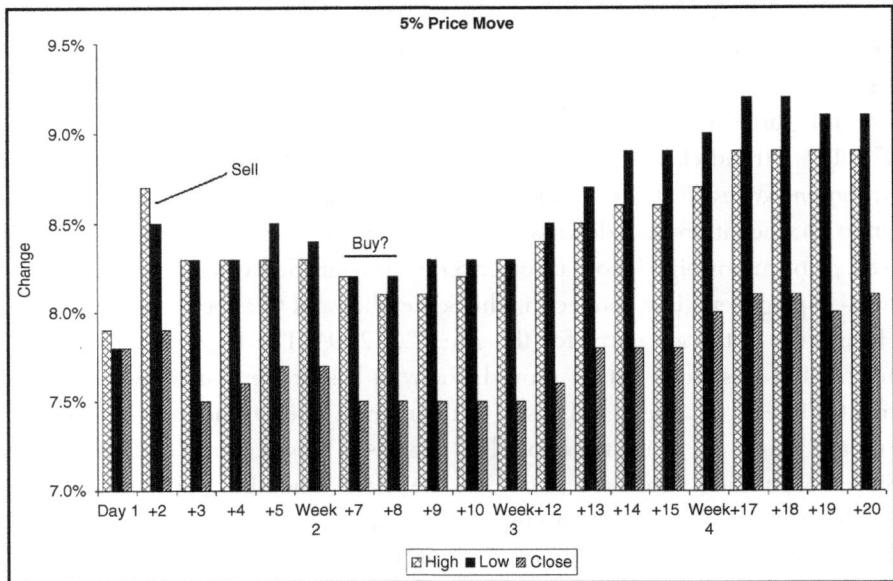

FIGURE 46.2 Price Climbs for 2 Days Then Drops and Levels Out before Beginning a Gentle Climb.

around the middle of week 2. That is when the intraday lows dip. Consider buying back in. Expect a shallow rise to begin in week 3 and continue upward into week 4.

Using the median instead of the average in the frequency distribution shows that the high price peaks on day 2 and then coasts downward until day 15, when it starts moving up. However, by the end of the month, the high price is still well below what it was on day 1. Another frequency distribution shows that 49% of iDCBs have a higher close on day 2. This percentage drops to 47% on day 3 but begins moving up on days 6 through 20. At month's end, 53% have higher highs.

In short, the data seem to indicate a sale on day 2 is the best course of action if you are a swing trader. For a position trader who holds a position for weeks, months, or even years, a 5% move may not warrant a sale. If price gives back all of its gains, they consider it no big deal. You may decide otherwise.

Figure 46.3 shows the price distribution for iDCBs in which price climbs at least 10%. I found between 9,300 and 11,500 samples qualifying in about 550 stocks from late 1987 to June 2004. Not all stocks covered the full range of data.

The profile is similar to that shown in Figure 46.2. Price climbs an average of 14.1% higher after the reference day and then makes a higher high (15.7% above the reference day) but closes at the same price. Day 2 is the day to sell as it shows the highest high for the coming month. Price does not climb back up to the average closing price until day 13, and by the end of the month, the close is below what it was at day 1 and 2. The intraday lows continue to rise, peaking near the middle of week 4. This finding suggests that once you sell, stay on the sidelines. With the intraday lows rising, the stock will only get more expensive.

The frequency distribution using the median high shows price peaking on day 2 and then dropping steadily until the end of the month. A third frequency distribution

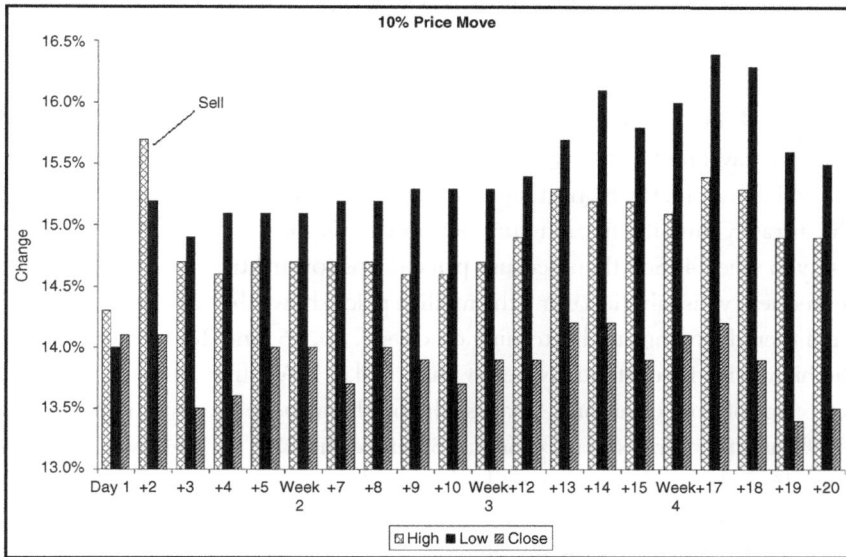

FIGURE 46.3 For Price Moves of 10%, the Best Time to Sell Is on the Second Day. That Day Represents the Highest Average High for the Next Month.

shows that 48% of the samples have higher highs on day 2. This percentage drops to 43% on days 4 and 5 then rises steadily until closing out the month at 50%, meaning that half the samples had intraday highs higher than day 1 and half were lower.

Figure 46.4 shows a more optimistic scenario. I used between 2,400 and 2,600 samples from 550 stocks covering January 1998 to June 2004. The difference in the

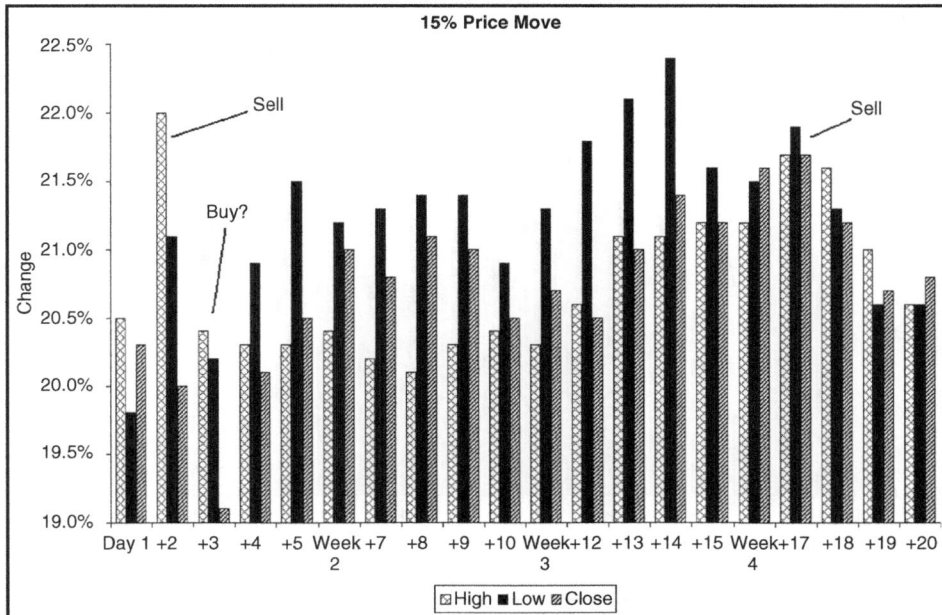

FIGURE 46.4 The Chart Shows Price Moves of at Least 15%. Sell the Second Day Near the High and Buy Back In during the Middle of Week 2. Ride Prices Higher into Week 4.

sample counts is a result of my collecting data individually in the three components: high, low, and close. Many times, the closing price has more samples moving higher than the other components.

The figure shows the average price change for minimum price moves of 15% above the reference day. The chart suggests selling on day 2 as close to the intraday high as you can get, which may be the highest high for the coming month. Buy back in the next day near the intraday low (if you can figure out how to do that) and then ride price upward until early in week 4. Sell then because price drops toward the end of the month.

The frequency distribution using the median price shows the intraday high peaking on day 1 and then dropping and bottoming on days 8, 10, 15, and 20. At month's end (day 20), the high price is substantially below that on day 1. Another frequency distribution shows a count of how often price makes a higher high above the high on day 1. It starts out at 46% and then drops to 40% on day 3 before climbing to 48% by month's end.

Figure 46.5 shows the price profile that used the fewest samples: between 1,000 and 1,300 covering 550 stocks from January 1988 to June 2004. Comparatively few stocks jumped at least 20% on any given day.

How do you use this information? On day 2, price reaches an average high 29% above the reference day's high, and then prices drop, closing lower at the end of day 3. If you can buy near the intraday low on day 3, consider doing so. Ride the stock up until early in week 2 (when intraday highs peak) or hold until the start of week 4 (high peaks again). Then sell. Price trends lower toward the end of the month.

Let me remind you that if you follow this advice, you might lose money. Selling on day 2 is a wise decision, but buying back in so soon may not be. The stock may

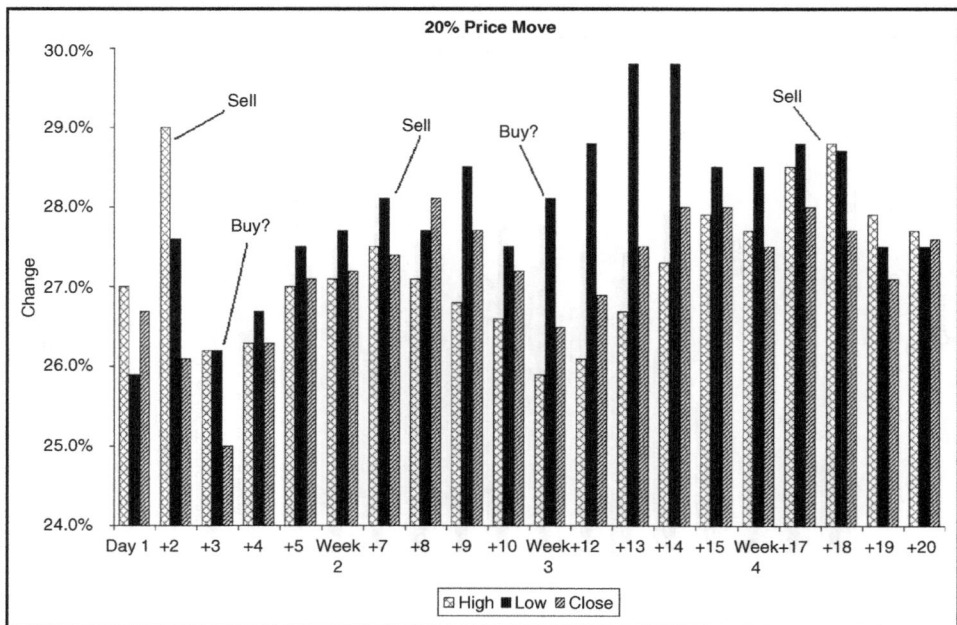

FIGURE 46.5 This Graph Shows Price Moves of at Least 20%. Sell on Day 2 and Buy Back in Near the Low on Day 3. Hold the Stock until the Middle of Week 4, and Then Sell.

continue to tumble. You may want to postpone buying until the start of week 3, or not at all.

A frequency distribution of intraday highs using the median instead of the average shows that price makes its highest high on day 1, drops until day 6, and then essentially moves horizontally until the end of the month. At month's end, the median high price is well below that posted on day 1. This behavior emphasizes the need to sell early.

A frequency distribution that counts the number of times price makes a new high above day 1 starts at 45% on day 2 and drops to its low, 37%, on days 3 and 4. Then it rises until finishing the month showing 47% with highs above day 1. The numbers suggest selling on the day that price makes a large move up and then looking elsewhere for another trade.

■ Trading Tactics

I bought 1,000 shares of Southwest Airlines for $15.81 a share. Less than 3 weeks later, on a Friday, the company announced that it reached a tentative accord with the flight attendants' union after 2 years of negotiations. The stock closed 8% higher on the news, at 17, giving me a profit of almost $1,200. Did I sell? No. I justified holding the stock because an 8% rise is nice, but still not enough when I am looking for 20% or 25%.

On the following Monday, the stock made a higher high but closed down 2% (16.64), as expected. It continued descending and eventually hit my stop at 15.41, cashing me out. I managed to change a potential $1,200 gain into a $430 loss. Oops. Now that I am a more active trader (to prevent such drawdowns), I know it is smart to take profit if price shoots up 5% or more.

Table 46.1 shows trading tactics for the inverted dead-cat bounce. I base the tactics on the graphs discussed in the Statistics section. Since the graphs represent

TABLE 46.1	Trading Tactics
Trading Tactic	Explanation
Measure the rise	Measure the close-to-close difference from the reference day to the next day (the day price zips 5% to 20% higher). Consult the appropriate graph in the Statistics section for the average price profile or use the following tips.
Close-to-close price rise 5%	Is a 5% move worth taking a profit on? Sell the day after the initial rise. Buy back in during week 2 for a rise that lasts through week 4.
10%	Sell the day after the initial rise. Do not buy back in, as price is likely to trend lower.
15%	Sell the day after the initial rise. For swing traders, consider the situation carefully before buying in near the low on day 3. Hold until early in week 4 when prices peak and then sell.
20%	Sell the day after the initial rise. For swing traders, consider buying back in near the low on days 3 or 11. Sell again early in week 2 or early in week 4. Prices trend down at the end of the month.

average price changes, your results will vary. Before trading, ask yourself if you should sell a holding to preserve profits. Remember, capital gains taxes may be important, and if the general market is trending upward, you may decide to hold on for the long term. However, if someone sells you a legal dollar bill for 80 cents, consider taking it. Twenty percent rises are rare in stocks, so sell because price will likely go down in the coming days. You can always buy back in once price bottoms.

Measure the rise. Say a stock you own jumps from a closing price of 10 to 12, for a 20% rise. Consult Figure 46.5 to see the average profile for price action over the coming month. Whether your situation will pan out like that shown in the figure is anyone's guess. Still, consider the profile as you make your trading plan.

Rises: 5% to 20%. All four profiles (Figures 46.2 through 46.5) suggest selling the day after a large rise. You may want to put a sell order at the intraday high price of the event day (day 1). For example, if price rises 10% and peaks at 20 but closes at 19, put a limit order to sell at 20 the next day and see if it hits. If price looks like it is peaking without reaching 20, change the limit order into a market order and get out. You may not reach the higher high on day 2, but you might be able to do better than the prior close. Remember, the frequency distribution says that fewer than half make a higher high the second day, so keep that in mind. If price looks like it has peaked on day 1, then sell. Do not wait for a higher high that may not happen on day 2.

Suppose you sell. What happens beyond that is usually stock, industry, and market related. If the stock market shoots up, chances are your stock will do well and post a higher high on day 2. Buy back in on weakness and watch the market, industry, and the stock closely. If price looks like it is peaking then sell. By *peaking*, I mean look for bearish chart patterns or indicators that show divergence (an indicator moves down forming lower lows, but the stock shows higher highs), failure swings (little M-shaped patterns at indicator extremes suggesting a short-term trend change), or overbought signals.

Let us take an example using the stock shown in Figure 46.6. First, measure the move. From a close on the reference day (the day "Bought" is pointing to in the figure), the stock closed at 14.70. The following day, it closed at 17.70, for a gain of 20%. Thus, Figure 46.5 shows the correct price profile. It says to sell on day 2 as close to the intraday high as possible, and that the high and low will be higher than the prior day, but the close is likely to be lower. That pattern means selling well before the market closes (at least an hour before because that is when the big boys start trading and activity picks up) to avoid the downward price trend leading to the close. In Figure 46.6, the stock did not make a higher high, but did make a higher low and close. Selling a day after the reference day turned out to be the best move, providing that your selling price was above the closing price (because the next day had a trading range above the prior day's close).

The profile says to buy if you can get in near the daily low on day 3 or 11. If you were successful buying at day 3 and sold early in week 2, you would have lost money as the stock trended down. If you bought on day 11 (see Figure 46.6) and sold early in week 4, that would have been a good call as price hit a minor high of 16.99 on May 18.

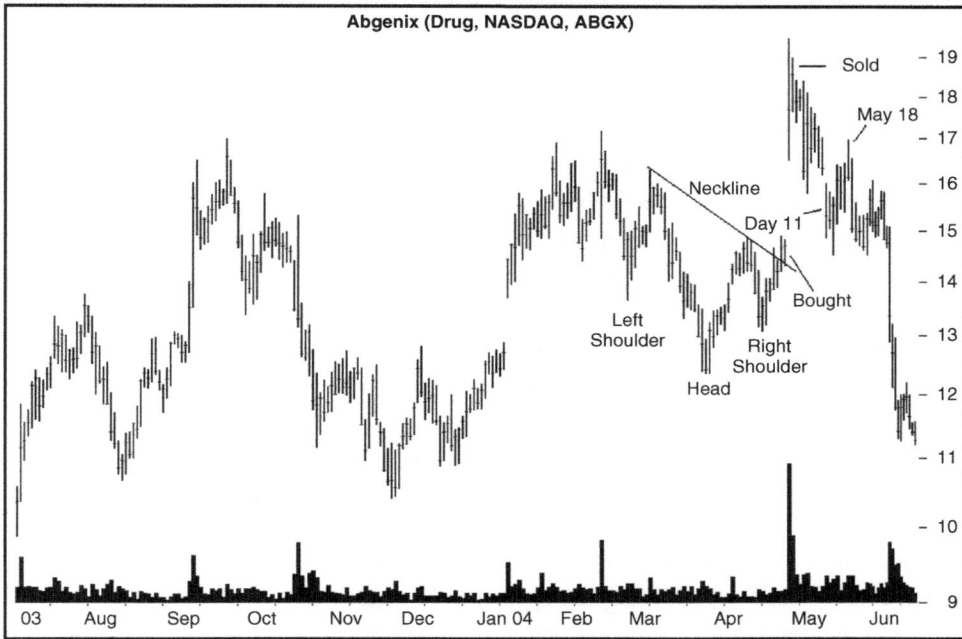

FIGURE 46.6 A Head-and-Shoulders Bottom Signaled a Buy. The Following Day, Price Shot Upward and the Next Day, the Stock Was Sold for a 25% Rise in 3 Days.

How did the profile do? The calls to sell on day 2 and early in week 4 were good calls as was the buy on day 11. The buy on day 3 was a losing trade, but not by much if you sold on May 18 (early in week 4).

This example should serve as a warning. Do not blindly follow investment advice. Do your own research. For example, how have other large up moves in your stock performed? Is the general market (use the S&P 500 index as a proxy) trending with you or against you? How are other stocks in the industry doing? If you are trading from the long side and other stocks in the industry and market are plunging, the chances of your trade performing as expected are diminished.

▇ Sample Trade

Figure 46.6 shows an actual trade I made in the stock. Here is my partial notebook entry for the buy: "4/23/04. I believe the stock will rise to 16–17, and, if lucky, push through to make new highs. Earnings are due a month from today, so that gives me room. Downside is 12.94, stop, for a loss of 12%. Shares: 600 filled at 14.668, 100 at 14.67, and 300 at 14.66. Buy reason: Head-and-shoulders bottom, upward breakout. Mood: buoyant but rushed. I wanted to get this in before the close and it may be a hip shot. I'm depending on the head-and-shoulders to perform. Future market direction (guess): Hard to tell. I expect the market to rise for a few days until tagging an earlier ascending triangle then declining, forming a large double top."

Here is the explanation of my notebook entry. I show the head-and-shoulders bottom in the figure. Price crossed the down-sloping neckline, signaling a buy. The head-and-shoulders pattern is not as pretty as one would hope, because the shoulders are not symmetrical about the head in either price or time.

I scored this pattern according to my book, *Trading Classic Chart Patterns*, as a +3, meaning that there was a good chance—but no guarantee—that price would climb to the target of 18.59. The measure rule for head-and-shoulders predicted a price rise to 17.51. Price met both predictions the day after I bought.

I expected the stock to reach the old high of 16–17 and stall there but eventually push through. If the trade went against me, then a stop at 12.94 (just below the round number 13) and below the right shoulder low of 13.08, would keep my loss to a rather large 12%.

I like to check when the next earnings announcement is due because I have learned not to trade within 3 weeks of the announcement (I just add 3 months onto the last announcement date or check a year earlier for a closer guess). Since the median hold time for my trading this year is 26 days (which is unusually short, but markets are volatile), following my typical hold time means I might sell just before the announcement. It also means that I might be buying as price declines into the earnings announcement. In many stocks, price will start dropping midway through the quarter—not always—but that is what I have noticed. Trading the stock a month before the earnings release I considered an acceptable risk.

I bought and the next day, the stock zoomed up 20%. I heard about it on the financial news that evening and took a closer look at the chart. I knew that a quick decline often follows a quick rise, so I decided to sell and protect my profit. Here is the notebook entry for the sale: "Date: 4/27/04. Shares: 1000, filled at 18.308. Sell reason: stock jumped three points yesterday on hype about cancer drugs. Mood: cautious. I expected the stock to give back almost all of its gains, but it was up this morning, coming down. A quick decline often follows a quick rise."

I sold well above the daily low but below the closing price. Still, I am happy with my 25% gain in three trading days. From that point, you can see what happened. In early June, the stock dropped 10% on good news about one of its cancer drugs in joint development with Amgen, putting the price well below the buy point.

I ended up having 3,611.79 reasons why I am glad I sold.

CHAPTER 47

Earnings Surprise, Bad

From Thomas N. Bulkowski, *Encyclopedia of Charts Patterns,* Second Edition (Hoboken, New Jersey: John Wiley & Sons, 2005), Chapter 56.

Learning Objective Statements

- Interpret potential price moves based on the patterns described in this chapter
- Calculate potential price targets
- Evaluate price levels for potential support or resistance
- Identify and interpret signals from various oscillators and technical studies in conjunction with the event-based patterns listed in these chapters

Results Snapshot
Downward Breakouts

Event	The company announces earnings and the stock price drops.	
Reversal or continuation	Short-term bearish continuation	
	Bull Market	**Bear Market**
Performance rank	3 out of 5	3 out of 4
Break-even failure rate	31%	26%
Average decline	13%	17%
Change after trend ends	51%	37%
Volume trend	Usually heavy on the announcement day	
Pullbacks	41%	45%
Percentage meeting price target	69%	68%
Surprising findings	Works best in a bear market and a downward price trend. Select patterns near the yearly low. A bad quarter usually follows a bad quarter. Pullbacks hurt performance. Tall patterns perform better than short ones.	
See also	Earnings Surprise, Good; Flag, Earnings	

No investor or trader likes surprises, so when a company announces earnings, what does the stock do? In a bear market, 61% of the 918 earnings announcements I looked at broke out *upward*! In a bull market, 43% of the 1,316 announcements I looked at broke out *downward*. The results surprised me, but market direction may have little to do with breakout direction.

In this chapter, I explore earnings announcements with downward breakouts only. I assumed that these were the bad earnings surprises. I also filtered the 2,234 announcements by those with intraday trading ranges that were wider than average.

The performance of what remained appears in the Results Snapshot. The event pattern usually acts as a short-term bearish continuation, not a reversal of the prevailing price trend. In many cases, the price trend leading to the pattern was down and so was the breakout. The break-even failure rate is high, 31% and 26%, for bull and bear markets, respectively. I consider anything above 20% to be unacceptable, so this event pattern is well out of the ballpark; trade it with care.

The decline is just a bit shy of other event patterns, averaging 13% and 17% for bull and bear markets. Once price reaches the ultimate low, it soars by 51% in a bull market and 37% in a bear market. If you can catch this turn, then you can make a lot of money.

On the announcement day, volume is heavy (above the monthly average). Pullbacks occur just over a third of the time (41% and 45% in bull and bear markets), which is somewhat less than the 50% return rate for other event patterns. Performance is also light with 69% and 68% of the stocks reaching their predicted price targets. Values above 80% I consider acceptable, but few patterns meet that benchmark.

Surprises are many but the notable ones are not really surprises at all. They confirm what many traders know. This pattern is bearish, so it works best in a bear market when the company's stock price is tumbling. The best performing patterns are those that appear within a third of the yearly low. Prices decline by 20%, on average. Finally, after examining over 2,000 patterns, I confirmed that a company having a bad quarter is likely to suffer in the next quarter as well.

▓ Tour

Figure 47.1 shows a typical example of a well-behaved stock after an earnings announcement. Many times, the announcement is not startlingly bad, so price does not gap downward or make a large move. Instead, price drifts lower without a rush, staging a downward breakout. That is what happened in this example. Price kept sliding until reaching the ultimate low. Price resumed its descent in late February, eventually reaching a new low of 15.31.

From the breakout price of 43.75 to the ultimate low of 27.25, the decline measured 38%. That figure is well above the usual 17% decline in a bear market.

▓ Identification Guidelines

Table 47.1 lists identification characteristics of the patterns resulting from bad earnings surprises.

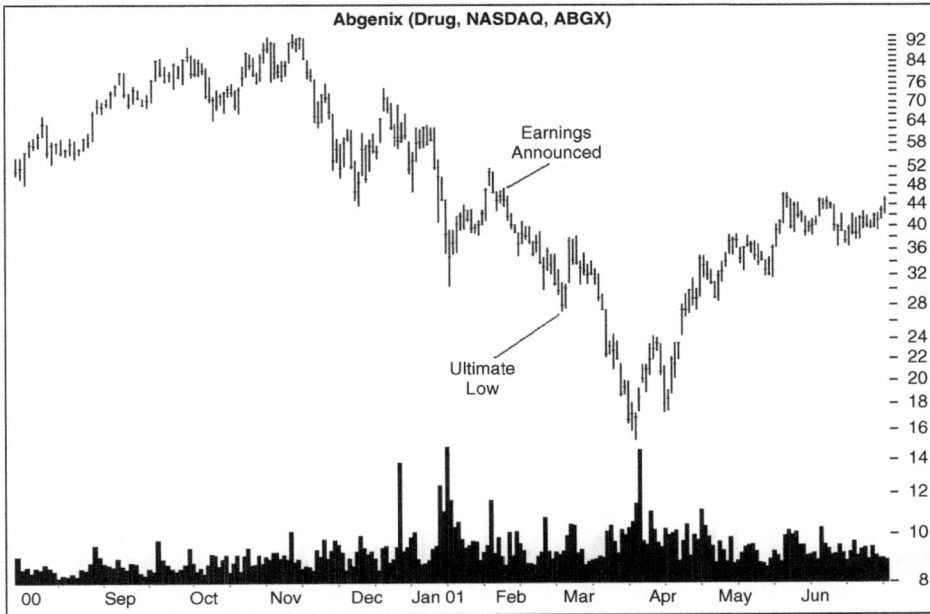

Abgenix (Drug, NASDAQ, ABGX)

Earnings
Announced

Ultimate
Low

FIGURE 47.1   Price Trends Down to This Earnings Announcement, Breaks Out Downward, and Then Continues Lower.

TABLE 47.1	**Identification Characteristics**
Characteristic	Discussion
Falling price trend	Look for the announcement to appear in a declining price trend, preferably in a bear market.
Earnings announced	The company announces earnings and the stock drops.
Breakout	Price must close below the intraday low posted on the announcement day.
Nearby support	Look for underlying support zones that might stop the decline.

Falling price trend. Performance improves when you trade with the trend. Since we are dealing with downward breakouts, look for a falling price trend leading to the earnings announcement.

Earnings announced. Wait for the earnings announcement. If a quarterly earnings announcement is less than 3 weeks away, defer the trade. Why? Because few things in life hurt more than losing money when your aim is to make money. If you were to trade the stock ahead of the breakout, the breakout could be in the adverse direction and you would lose money. Wait for the announcement and then wait longer for the breakout.

Breakout. A breakout occurs when price closes below the intraday low posted on the day of the announcement. Only then should you consider placing a trade. Wait for the downward breakout because a bad announcement could send the stock soaring. Why? Because the market was expecting worse results from the company.

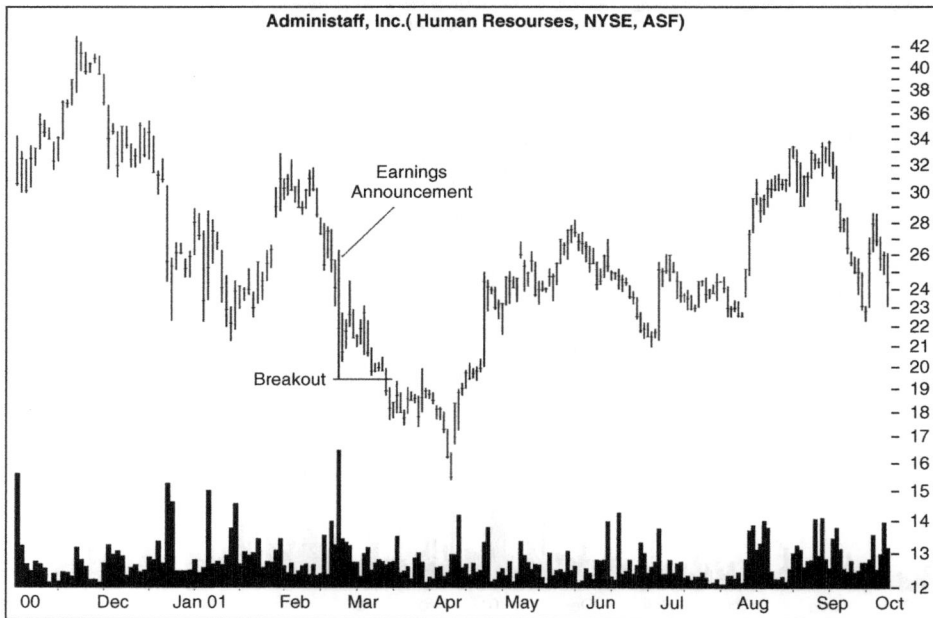

FIGURE 47.2 Price Has a Large Trading Range on the Earnings Announcement. Eventually, price closed below the intraday low, posting a breakout.

Nearby support. If you decide to short a stock after an earnings announcement, look for a support zone below where the stock is trading. This might be round number support or minor high/low support or any variety of other support mechanisms. If support is nearby, then look elsewhere for a more promising trade. It may be that the stock plummets through the support zone (and if support is less than 5% away, that will usually be the case), but why chance it?

Consider Figure 47.2 as an example. A falling price trend was in place before the earnings announcement, which suggested a continuation of the downward trend. On the day of the announcement, price moved in a large range, from 26.30 to 19.50, with a close at 21.90. After that, price rebounded somewhat and then curled down, eventually breaking out when it closed below the intraday low of 19.50. That was the safe time to short. Price moved horizontally for about a month before tumbling for 3 days and finding the ultimate low. The decline from the breakout to the low measured 21% in a bear market, slightly better than the average 17% decline.

■ Focus on Failures

With a break-even failure rate well above 20%, this pattern is not easy to trade profitably. One reason for the poor performance may be support below the pattern. Consider Figure 47.3. Price breaks out downward the day following the announcement. On that day, the trading range was wide and the close was near the daily low. This scenario suggested a lower low the next day, but the stock closed up sharply and then continued trending higher on following days.

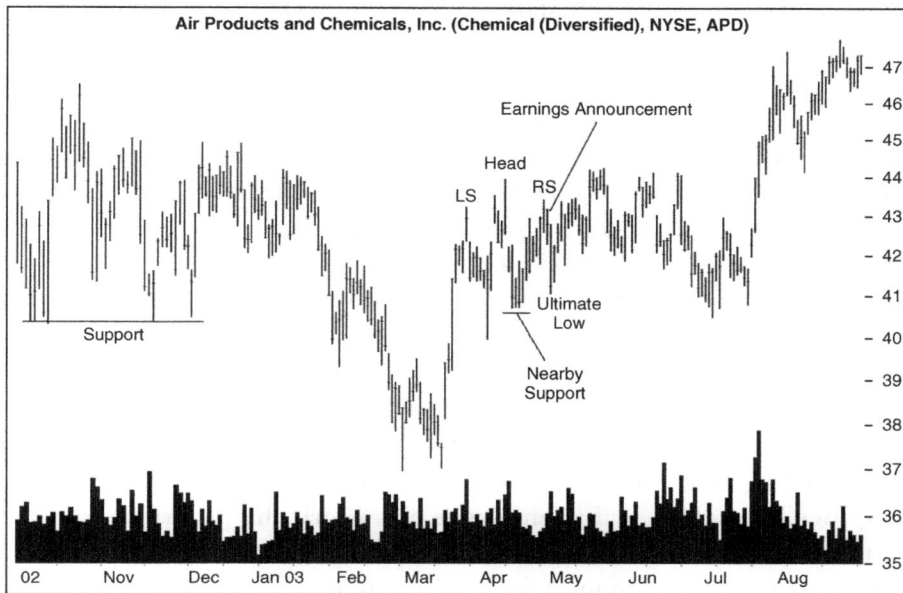

FIGURE 47.3 Price Broke Out Downward, Found Support, and Resumed Rising. Avoid taking a bearish position in a rising price trend.

The support zone in late 2002 stopped the decline in late January and April. Nearby support in early April suggested price might stop there, too.

Another clue to failure is a rising price trend. From the March low, price climbed quite rapidly for a week and then began rounding over. At the time of the earnings announcement, price looked like a spiky head-and-shoulders top (or a diamond), but the HST never confirmed. If you can, always trade with the prevailing price trend. Since the March price trend was up, skip this downward breakout.

▒ Statistics

Table 47.2 shows general statistics for this event pattern. I looked at just over 100 stocks beginning from early 1995 to mid 2003. Not all stocks had earnings

TABLE 47.2	General Statistics	
Description	Bull Market	Bear Market
Number of formations	450	276
Reversal (R) or continuation (C)	189 R, 261 C	111 R, 165 C
R/C performance	–12% R, –13% C	–16% R, –17% C
Average decline	13%	17%
Declines over 45%	13 or 3%	20 or 7%
Change after trend ends	51%	37%
Busted pattern performance	39%	25%
Standard & Poor's 500 change	–2%	–6%
Days to ultimate low	28	25

Note: Minus sign means decline.

announcements, and I used only those with downward breakouts with an *intraday trading range above the average range of the prior month*. These filters narrowed the 2,234 patterns to just 726. When the intraday trading range was twice or three times the average, the average decline improved (meaning prices declined farther) with lower failure rates. The wider the intraday trading range the better the performance.

Number of formations. The table shows that most of the earnings announcements with downward breakouts appeared in bull markets. This finding is not surprising as the bull market duration was substantially longer than the bear market.

Reversal or continuation. Most of the patterns acted as continuations of the prevailing price trend. Since the breakout is downward, select patterns in a downward price trend. They perform slightly better than reversals.

Average decline. The average decline matches the average posted by all event patterns as a group. With declines so meager, do you really want to trade this one? If the answer is yes, then find additional reasons to short the stock.

Declines over 45%. As if to emphasize how poorly this pattern performs, no more than 7% of the patterns I looked at dropped more than 45%. Yes, the 45% benchmark is a tough one to meet for bearish patterns, but the poor showing suggests you would do better looking for a different type of event pattern.

Change after trend ends. Once price reaches its ultimate low, it rebounds 51% in a bull market and 37% in a bear market. I like to see rebounds of 60% in a bull market, but for event patterns, a 51% rise is a good showing. If you can determine when the trend changes from down to up, buy the stock and ride the wave upward.

Busted pattern performance. If price drops less than 5% and then begins rebounding, consider buying the stock. In a bull market, the resulting rise averages 39% and in a bull market, it is 25%. Since the numbers are well below what is posted after the trend ends, there is reason for caution. The rise may not be as substantial as you hope. Use stops to protect your positions.

Standard & Poor's 500 change. In both bull and bear markets, the S&P 500 index dropped from the breakout to the ultimate low. That is good news if you believe a falling tide lowers all boats. The larger decline in a bear market that itself dropped 6% helped beat the 13% decline in a bull market (which dropped 2%).

Days to ultimate low. It took about a month for price to reach the ultimate low. Notice that the bear market decline is shorter than the bull market and yet the average decline is higher (17% versus 13%). Thus, the bear market decline must be steeper than the decline in a bull market.

Table 47.3 lists failure rates for the pattern. For bull markets, almost a third (31%) of the patterns fail to decline more than 5%. That is huge! Half turn around before declining 10%. Patterns in bear markets do better. A quarter (26%) drop less than 5%. Over half decline less than 15%.

As you can see in the table, the failure rates start out high and get worse, quickly. With half the patterns declining just 10% to 15%, does it make sense to trade this pattern?

Table 47.4 shows breakout- and postbreakout-related statistics for this event pattern.

TABLE 47.3 **Failure Rates**

Maximum Price Decline (%)	Bull Market	Bear Market
5 (breakeven)	138 or 31%	73 or 26%
10	230 or 51%	123 or 45%
15	302 or 67%	156 or 57%
20	347 or 77%	186 or 67%
25	377 or 84%	206 or 75%
30	406 or 90%	224 or 81%
35	420 or 93%	238 or 86%
50	442 or 98%	264 or 96%
75	450 or 100%	275 or 100%
Over 75	450 or 100%	276 or 100%

TABLE 47.4 **Breakout and Postbreakout Statistics**

Description	Bull Market	Bear Market
Formation end to breakout	4 days	5 days
Percentage of breakouts occurring near the 12-month low (L), center (C), or high (H)	L36%, C32%, H32%	L44%, C34%, H22%
Percentage decline for each 12-month lookback period	L14%, C11%, H13%	L20%, C16%, H14%
Pullbacks	41%	45%
Average time to pullback ends	11 days	11 days
Average decline for patterns with pullbacks	12%	15%
Average decline for patterns without pullbacks	14%	18%

Formation end to breakout. In both markets, price closed below the lowest low in the pattern within a week. That timing is about average for event patterns.

Yearly position. Where in the yearly price range does the breakout occur? Most often, the bad earnings surprise occurs near the yearly low. In bull markets, the range splits almost evenly. In bear markets, those stocks trading near the yearly high are the least likely to issue a bad earnings report. That makes sense. If investors sense trouble at the company, they punish the stock. Then, the company confirms what everyone knows: that they are having trouble.

Yearly position, performance. Where do the best performing patterns occur? Again, bull markets split evenly but the trend is clear. In both bull and bear markets, those earnings announcements with breakouts within a third of the yearly low perform best. Bull markets show average declines of 14%; bear markets do better with declines averaging 20%.

Pullbacks. A little less than half the time, the stock pulls back to the breakout price. This finding suggests that you not depend on a pullback to open a short position or add to an existing position. A pullback might not occur.

It took 11 days for price to return to the breakout price after a pullback, which is about average for all event pattern types. When a pullback occurs, it robs downward

TABLE 47.5	Frequency Distribution of Days to Ultimate Low										
Days:	7	14	21	28	35	42	49	56	63	70	>70
Bear market	48%	8%	8%	6%	7%	3%	2%	2%	4%	1%	11%
Bull market	47%	13%	7%	5%	4%	4%	4%	3%	1%	1%	11%

TABLE 47.6	Size and Volume Statistics	
Description	Bull Market	Bear Market
Tall pattern performance	–14%	–20%
Short pattern performance	–12%	–15%
Median height as a percentage of breakout price	5.01%	6.15%
Heavy announcement day volume, performance	–12%	–17%
Light announcement day volume, performance	–14%	–14%

Note: Minus sign means decline.

momentum and performance suffers. For example, when a pullback happens in a bull market, price drops an average of 12%; without a pullback, the drop measures 14%.

Table 47.5 shows a frequency distribution of the days to the ultimate low. For both markets, almost half (47% to 48%) of the patterns reached the ultimate low in less than a week. In a bull market, 67% (the sum of the 7, 14, and 21 day columns) reach the low in less than 3 weeks. This finding suggests that you should be ready to take profits quickly.

Notice the slight uptick in a bear market around the end of the month (7% reach the ultimate low then). I have seen this behavior in other patterns. A month after the event, slightly more stocks reach the ultimate low and start rebounding. When trading this pattern, be especially careful a month after the breakout.

Table 47.6 shows size and volume statistics.

Height. Do tall patterns perform better than short ones? Yes. The largest difference is in a bear market as price dropped 20% when the intraday trading range on the announcement day was wider than the median (as a percentage of the breakout price). In comparison, short patterns dropped just 15%.

For best performance, select patterns taller than the median. In fact, when the intraday trading range on the announcement day was 2 or 3 times that shown by the 1-month average, the pattern tended to outperform (an average of 16% decline in a bull market and 21% in a bear market). Select unusually tall patterns.

Announcement day volume. Conventional wisdom suggests that high volume pushes price farther. Table 47.6 does not show breakout volume, but announcement day volume. On announcement days when volume was above the 1-month average in a bear market, price dropped 17%. This finding compares to a drop of 14% when volume was below average. For bull markets, the results flipped. Event patterns with below average announcement day volume tended to do better.

Trading Tactics

Table 47.7 shows trading tactics should you decide to trade this pattern.

TABLE 47.7   Trading Tactics

Trading Tactic	Explanation
Sell signal	For intermediate- or long-term holders, do nothing, as the decline is likely to be small. For swing traders, consider selling immediately to minimize the loss. If price gaps down and the gap is small, price may retrace the next few days and cover the gap.
Sell short signal	In a bear market, wait for a close below the pattern's low and then short the stock. It may bottom in a week, so watch it closely. Use stops to protect your profits.
Measure rule	Used to predict a price target. On the announcement day, subtract the intraday low from the high, and subtract the difference from the intraday low. The result is the target price. Price hits the target 69% of the time in a bull market and 68% in a bear market.
Wait for confirmation	Traders can react to an announcement by pushing price in any direction. Thus, wait for the confirmation—a close below the intraday low before trading the event pattern.

Sell signal. If you own stock in a company and it issues an earnings report, what should you do? If the breakout is upward, then you are set. Sit tight and watch the stock rise. (Refer to Chapters 48 and 50.)

If the breakout is downward, then the decision becomes more difficult. In a bear market, consider selling because price may tumble 17%, on average. If the stock gaps down but the gap is small, it may close in a few days (an area gap). If the gap is wide, then you already have a loss or diminished profit. The stock may dead-cat bounce on you, so read Chapter 45. Wait for the bounce and then sell as price rounds over at the top just before a renewed decline.

Usually the decline from this pattern is not severe (see Table 47.3 to see how many patterns fail to drop far). If you can stomach the loss, then hang in there, especially if it is a bull market and price is trending upward. However, sometimes the pattern acts as a reversal of the uptrend. Sell immediately or wait for a correctly positioned stop loss to take you out of an existing position.

Remember, changes that affect earnings usually take longer than a quarter to fix, so if the company disappointed this quarter, there is a good chance it will do so again next quarter. I verified this prediction by looking at 1,963 earnings announcements. There were 866 *consecutive* earnings announcements with upward breakouts and 582 with downward breakouts (the pattern acted as a continuation of the price trend). In 515 additional cases, the breakout direction flipped from down to up or up to down from quarter to quarter (price reversals). Thus, 74% of the earnings announcements (866 + 582 out of 1,963) follow announcements having the same breakout direction. If one quarter is bad, there is a 74% probability that another bad quarter will follow.

Sell short signal. Performance from this pattern is poor, so I suggest you look for other event patterns to short. If you have a compelling situation, then review the "For Best Performance" section. The stock should be traded in a bear market and the price trend leading to the announcement should be downward. When price closes below the intraday low posted on the announcement day, then that is the sell short signal. Watch the stock closely as half the patterns bottom in the first week. Lower your stop as the stock declines. Keep an eye on the stock 4 to 5 weeks into the trade as price sometimes rebounds then.

Measure rule. How far will price drop? Pretend that a stock has an intraday high of 40 and a low of 38. The measure rule computes the pattern's height and then applies it to the breakout direction. In this example, the height is 2 (40 − 38) and the target price is 36 (38 − 2). Price reaches the target almost 70% of the time. This figure is below the 80% I like to see, so be conservative in your target estimate.

Wait for confirmation. Since the breakout direction is unknown until it happens, wait for price to close below the intraday low posted on the day of the announcement. When that happens, it confirms that you have a valid pattern and it signals a trade.

■ Sample Trade

How do you trade a bad earnings surprise? Look at Figure 47.4 for an example. In February, price tops out (point 1) after a sharp rise from the December low. Price moves horizontally for several months, forming a flat support zone (the confirmation line). As is often the case, price climbed to the level of the old high (point 2) and met resistance. The earnings announcement the day after the peak sent price skidding.

How low could we expect it to go? On the announcement day, the intraday high was 61.50; the low was 58.75. The measure rule predicted a decline to at least 55.94. Price reached the target just two days after the announcement.

If you shorted this stock, you could expect price to tumble to the confirmation line and stall there. Why? Because on four prior occasions, that is what happened

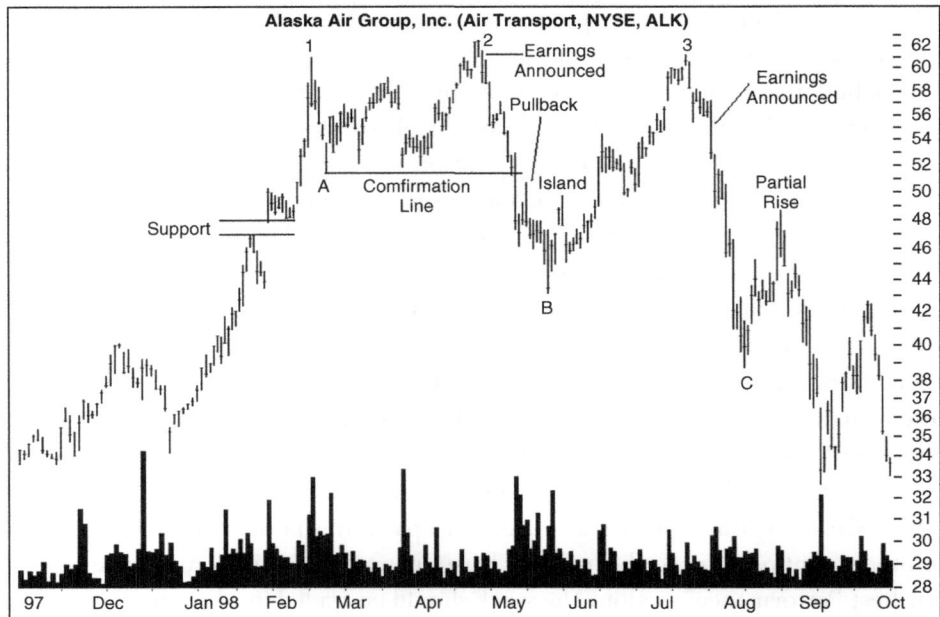

FIGURE 47.4 A Double Top Forms and Price Tumbles. A Second Downward Breakout from an Earnings Announcement Confirms That a Bad Quarter Follows a Bad Quarter.

(beginning in February and ending in March). If I saw price begin to rebound near that zone, I would cover my short.

Instead of stalling at the confirmation line, price confirmed the double top by closing below the line. The measure rule for the Adam & Eve double top suggested a decline to 40.38, which is the height of the double top subtracted from the price level of the confirmation line.

The mid-January price gap was another support zone. Since price plunged through the confirmation line, I would expect support at the January zone. For a week, that is what happened. Price returned to the confirmation line in a 1-day pullback and then struggled lower on declining volume.

When do you cover the short? I would be worried that price was climbing again after the small island on high volume in late May. The volume spike suggests renewed interest in the stock. I would have covered there.

As you can see, price fell short of the double top measure rule prediction (40.38) by dropping to a low of only 43.13. Notice the second earnings announcement (in July) that sent price lower. Remember that a bad quarter usually follows a bad quarter.

The three tops (1, 2, and 3) compose a triple top or a broadening formation, right-angled and descending (bottoms A, B, and C) with a partial rise in August, suggesting a downward breakout. A downward breakout is what happened in early September.

■ For Best Performance

The following list includes tips and observations to help you select better performing patterns. Consult the associated table for more information.

- Review the identification guidelines for correct selection—Table 47.1.

- Look for patterns in a downward price trend—Table 47.1.

- The pattern usually acts as a continuation of the prevailing price trend, so trade with the trend—Table 47.2.

- Trade this pattern only in a bear market for the largest average decline—Table 47.2.

- Failure rates start high and climb. For better performance, look for a wider intraday trading range (2 times or 3 times the range of the 1- month average) on the announcement day—Tables 47.3 and 47.6.

- Select patterns trading within a third of the yearly low—Table 47.4.

- Avoid pullbacks; look for underlying support that might cause a pullback—Table 47.4.

- Expect a quick but shallow decline. Almost half the patterns bottom in less than a week—Table 47.5.

- Select tall patterns—Table 47.6.

- The breakout direction will be the same from quarter to quarter 74% of the time. Thus, a bad quarter usually follows a bad quarter—Table 47.7.

CHAPTER 48

Earnings Surprise, Good

From Thomas N. Bulkowski, *Encyclopedia of Chart Patterns,* Second Edition (Hoboken, New Jersey: John Wiley & Sons, 2005), Chapter 57.

Learning Objective Statements

- Interpret potential price moves based on the patterns described in this chapter
- Calculate potential price targets
- Evaluate price levels for potential support or resistance
- Identify and interpret signals from various oscillators and technical studies in conjunction with the event-based patterns listed in these chapters

Results Snapshot

Upward Breakouts

Event	The company announces earnings and the stock price rises.	
Reversal or continuation	Short-term bullish continuation	
	Bull Market	**Bear Market**
Performance rank	5 out of 6	5 out of 5
Break-even failure rate	29%	28%
Average rise	24%	14%
Change after trend ends	−27%	−31%
Volume trend	Usually heavy on the announcement day	
Throwbacks	41%	44%
Percentage meeting price target	76%	74%
Surprising findings	Almost half the patterns fail to rise more than 10%. Patterns near the yearly low perform best. Throwbacks hurt performance. Tall patterns perform better than short ones.	
See also	Earnings Surprise, Bad; Flag, Earnings	

How many times have you heard a company announce good earnings and the stock drops? This pattern reflects the opposite of that situation. A company announces earnings that surprise the market. Traders like what they hear and buy the stock, pushing it higher. That is what a good earnings surprise (GES) is all about.

GES acts as a short-term bullish continuation. The failure rate is high, almost 30%, and I consider anything above 20% to be unacceptable. Most well-behaved chart patterns have single-digit break-even failure rates, but event patterns do much worse.

The average rise is in line with other event patterns. If you wait for price to reach the ultimate high and then short the stock, the average decline of 27% in a bull market and 31% in a bear market is mouthwatering. Unfortunately, you have to short at the exact peak and cover at the exact bottom, which is impossible to do consistently.

Of the surprising findings, there are many. Almost half of the GES patterns fail to rise more than 10%. That finding should serve as a wake-up call. You can improve your chance of success by selecting patterns with upward breakouts near the yearly low, avoiding patterns with nearby overhead resistance (to avoid a throwback), and selecting tall patterns. I explore these combinations later in the statistics section of this chapter.

■ Tour

What does a typical GES pattern look like? Figure 48.1 shows two examples. The July announcement occurred in a downward price trend. Even though the breakout was upward, the rise lasted a week before collapsing. Then price recovered and made

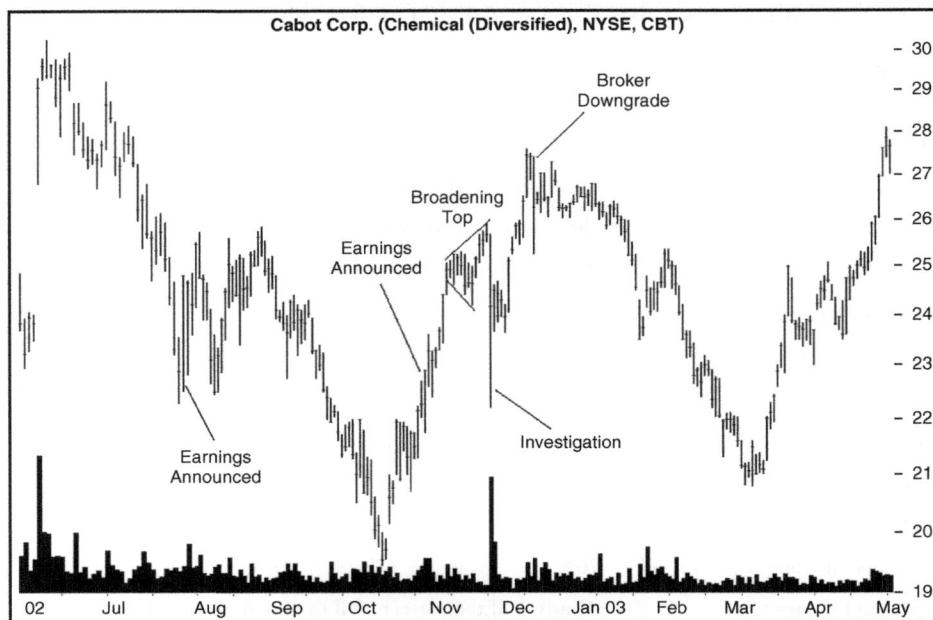

FIGURE 48.1 **The July Announcement Occurred in a Downward Price Trend. In October, the Announcement Sent Price Higher, but for Less Than 2 Months.**

a new minor high in August before resuming the downward trend. The lesson of this announcement is easy: Do not buy if price is trending down.

The stock performed better after the October announcement. Price climbed in a straight-line run until encountering overhead resistance and forming a broadening top. Then price tumbled in mid-November on news that U.S. and European regulators were reviewing documents as part of a joint investigation into possible price fixing in the carbon-black industry. After that, the stock recovered and made a new high. Then a broker downgraded the stock and that was enough to send price sliding.

■ Identification Guidelines

Table 48.1 lists identification guidelines for the GES pattern.

Rising price trend. With all chart and event patterns, you want to trade with the prevailing price trend. Since we are looking for an upward breakout (after all, this is a *good* earnings surprise, not a bad one), search for a rising price trend. That way you can ride the wave of a rising tide. It also helps to buy in a bull market.

Earnings announced. When the company announces earnings, price may move up sharply that day or the next if the announcement came after markets were closed (sometimes price gaps upward). You can find earnings announcements in the newspapers, on the Internet, or on financial television programs. Announcements usually occur quarterly, so add 3 months to the last release to estimate the date of the next release.

Large intraday range. To be included in the study, the announcement day's trading range needed to be larger than the 1-month average. The larger the day's price range, the better the performance (higher average rise with a lower failure rate), on average.

If price shoots upward on the announcement day and continues rising for several days, price will probably pause and form an earnings flag. (See Chapter 50 for tips on how to trade that pattern.) With the GES pattern, earnings are like hitting a single, not a home run. Price typically does not zip upward in a straight-line rise. Instead, the rise is more sedate.

Breakout. I only looked at upward breakouts. A breakout occurs when price closes above the intraday high posted on the announcement day.

TABLE 48.1 Identification Characteristics

Characteristic	Discussion
Rising price trend	Look for the announcement to appear in a rising price trend, preferably in a bull market.
Earnings announced	The company announces earnings. Price may have a wide trading range or, if the market is closed, price may gap upward the next trading day.
Large intraday range	Look for a large intraday price range on the announcement day, a range that is larger than the 1-month average.
Breakout	Upward breakouts only: Price must close above the intraday high posted on the announcement day.

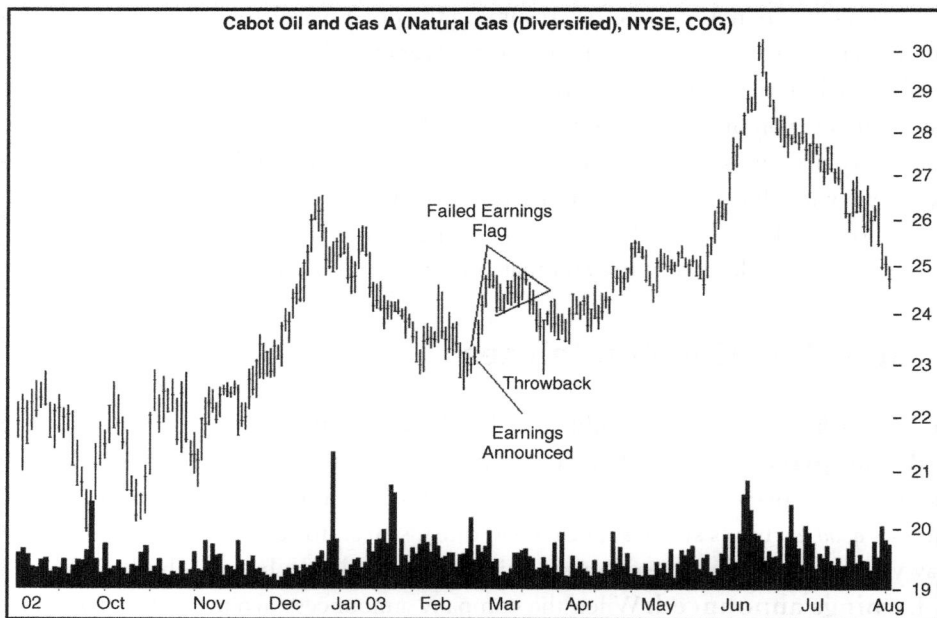

FIGURE 48.2 After a Short-Term Decline, the Earnings Announcement Acts as a Reversal, Sending Price Higher. A Throwback Drops the Stock to the Breakout Price before Recovering. This Is a Failed Earnings Flag Pattern because Price Breaks Out Downward from the Flag Portion of the Pattern.

Figure 48.2 shows an example of an earnings announcement acting as a reversal. After price declined for several months, the earnings announcement seemed to breathe life into the stock. Price jumped upward, but ran out of energy in a week. It then headed down and completed a throwback to the breakout price. Over the next several months, price climbed to just above 30, a rise of 30% from the breakout price.

This GES resembles an earnings flag pattern. Price makes a sharp, straight-line run and then pauses. Unfortunately, price breaks out downward from the pennant portion of the earnings flag, invalidating the pattern.

■ Focus on Failures

Pretend you own stock in CDI, pictured in Figure 48.3. It announces earnings in late April. Do you hold onto the stock, buy more, or sell? Answer: Sell. Why? Because price tumbles after the announcement—as shown in the figure— but what do you do if you cannot see the future?

A few technical clues give hints on how to trade this announcement. First, the earnings announcement did not send price moving much higher. It flatlined like somebody dying on the emergency room table. If earnings were truly better than expected, price would have moved up sharply.

Second, peak 1 is higher than peak 2, and peak 2 is above peak 3. Those three peaks represent a three falling peaks chart pattern—suggesting a bearish trend

FIGURE 48.3 Price Breaks Out Upward from this Earnings Announcement but Enters an Extended Decline. Why?

change. Peak 1 is also a bearish head-and-shoulders pattern. Paying attention to the surrounding price action would clue you in to the weakness of this situation.

Statistics

Table 48.2 shows general statistics for the GES pattern. I looked at just over 100 stocks with the earliest announcement occurring in January 1995. I used the identification guidelines listed in Table 48.1 to sift through the announcements. Table 48.2 shows only those patterns with upward breakouts and with an intraday trading range larger than the 1-month average.

TABLE 48.2	General Statistics	
Description	Bull Market	Bear Market
Number of formations	393	309
Reversal (R) or continuation (C)	152 R, 241 C	144 R, 165 C
R/C performance	24% R, 24% C	14% R, 13% C
Average rise	24%	14%
Rises over 45%	88 or 22%	25 or 8%
Change after trend ends	−27%	−31%
Busted pattern performance	−22%	−27%
Standard & Poor's 500 change	5%	1%
Days to ultimate high	69	40

Note: Minus sign means decline.

Number of formations. I uncovered roughly the same number of patterns in both markets, suggesting that more positive earnings surprises occur in a bear market (because the bear market was shorter). This suggestion may not be true because not all stocks contained quarterly earnings announcements (a limitation in the wimpy database I used), but it is a good guess. Consider that in a bear market, no one expects a good earnings report, so expectations are low. Thus, it is easier to surprise.

Reversal or continuation. The GES pattern acted as a continuation of the prevailing trend (57% of the time), not a reversal. Only in a bear market does a reversal outperform, and that is by one percentage point.

Average rise. The average rise is higher in a bull market than a bear market, as you would expect. It suggests you trade the GES pattern in a bull market.

Rises over 45%. Need I say that there are few rises over 45%? The bull market number, 22%, is almost triple the bear market tally, but still well below what other chart patterns do. On the other hand, for an event pattern, it holds up well when compared to other event patterns.

Change after trend ends. Once price reaches the ultimate high, it tumbles between 27% and 31%, depending on the market. If you can determine when the trend changes from up to down, then short the stock and ride it lower. Selling short is like rafting class 5 rapids: only the experienced should attempt it.

Busted pattern performance. If price rises less than 5% and then tumbles, the drop averages between 22% (bull market) and 27% (bear market) as measured from the highest high after the breakout to the ultimate low. If you were to trade busted patterns, your average return would be less because you should wait for price to breakout downward. If you do trade a busted pattern, do so in a bear market, preferably in a weak industry (other stocks are doing poorly).

Standard & Poor's 500 change. From the day of the breakout to the ultimate high, the S&P rose 5% in a bull market and 1% in a bear market. This finding compares to a price rise of 24% and 14% for the GES pattern over the same period.

Days to ultimate high. It took just over 1 month (bear market) to 2 months (bull market) to reach the ultimate high, on average, but a startling number top out in the first few weeks.

If you crunch the numbers, you will find that the slope of the rise in a bull market matches the rise in a bear market, which is unusual as bear markets typically rise faster.

Table 48.3 shows failure rates for the GES pattern in bull and bear markets. The break-even failure rate is too high, as I consider 20% the maximum acceptable. Twenty-nine percent of the patterns in a bull market and 28% of bear market patterns fail to rise just 5%. Almost half fail to rise 10%. Do not expect large gains from this pattern.

The numbers suggest that this pattern may be useful for swing traders, but others should avoid it. Why? Let me give you an example. If price rises by just 5% after a GES breakout in a bull market, it then tumbles at least 20% (by definition). Just to break even, 62% of the bull market patterns will fail to rise at least 20%. If you miss selling near the top, you could be taken to the cleaners.

TABLE 48.3 Failure Rates		
Maximum Price Rise (%)	Bull Market	Bear Market
5 (breakeven)	115 or 29%	86 or 28%
10	188 or 48%	147 or 48%
15	225 or 57%	201 or 65%
20	244 or 62%	227 or 73%
25	264 or 67%	249 or 81%
30	275 or 70%	267 or 86%
35	284 or 72%	276 or 89%
50	316 or 80%	290 or 94%
75	357 or 91%	303 or 98%
Over 75	393 or 100%	309 or 100%

Instead, use this pattern as just one tool of many in your trading toolbox. Think of it as confirming evidence of a bullish trade.

Table 48.4 shows breakout- and postbreakout-related statistics for this event pattern.

Formation end to breakout. For both bull and bear markets, it takes price 5 days to reach the breakout, on average. This movement may sound quick, but all price has to do is close above the intraday high posted on the announcement day.

Yearly position. Most GES patterns had breakouts within a third of the yearly high. Apparently, good news pushes the stock to new highs. Few surprisingly good earnings occur near the yearly low. Why? If traders drive by their favorite retailer and see a parking lot full of cars, they can expect good earnings. That anticipation pushes price higher. When the GES announcement comes, the stock is already out of the doghouse. Those GES patterns near the yearly low are true surprises, and the stock climbs. Want proof? Read on.

Yearly position, performance. Where in the yearly price range do the best performing GES patterns reside? For both bull and bear markets, the best performers have breakouts near the yearly low. In bull markets, price climbs 30%, and in bear

TABLE 48.4 Breakout and Postbreakout Statistics		
Description	Bull Market	Bear Market
Formation end to breakout	5 days	5 days
Percentage of breakouts occurring near the 12-month low (L), center (C), or high (H)	L26%, C32%, H41%	L30%, C33%, H36%
Percentage rise for each 12-month lookback period	L30%, C18%, H25%	L19%, C13%, H11%
Throwbacks	41%	44%
Average time to throwback ends	10 days	10 days
Average rise for patterns with throwbacks	21%	13%
Average rise for patterns without throwbacks	26%	14%

TABLE 48.5   Frequency Distribution of Days to Ultimate Low

Days:	7	14	21	28	35	42	49	56	63	70	>70
Bear market	41%	10%	9%	6%	6%	7%	2%	3%	1%	3%	13%
Bull market	41%	6%	6%	4%	3%	4%	4%	3%	2%	2%	25%

markets, it rises 19%, on average. Performance in this range is better than the other two-thirds of the yearly trading range.

Throwbacks. Throwbacks are comparatively rare, occurring between 41% and 44% of the time. When they do occur, it takes price 10 days to return to the breakout price.

When a throwback occurs, does performance suffer? Yes. In bull markets, price rises 21% when throwbacks occur, but 26% when they do not occur. The same trend happens in a bear market except that the performance difference is narrower.

Table 48.5 shows a frequency distribution of the days to the ultimate high. For example, 41% of the GES patterns in a bear market reached their high in less than a week. Just over half (51%, the sum of columns 7 and 14) summit in less than 2 weeks.

The table suggests that this pattern reaches the ultimate high quickly and the corresponding price rise is small. Notice that 7% top out after 42 days in a bear market. I have seen this slight blip a month after the breakout, so this one takes a bit longer to occur. Still, if you own a stock and it has been doing well, be aware of possible weakness in week 6. The stock may reach the ultimate high and then begin dropping.

Table 48.6 shows size and volume statistics.

Height. Do tall patterns perform better than short ones? Yes. In both markets, tall patterns do much better than short ones.

To use this feature, compute the GES pattern's height by subtracting the intraday low from the high posted on the announcement day. Divide the result by the breakout price (the intraday high). Then compare the result with the median in Table 48.6 for the appropriate market. If your value is above the median, then the pattern is tall, otherwise, it is short. For the best performance, select only tall patterns.

Announcement day volume. Does a GES pattern with above average volume perform better than do those with below average volume? Yes, but the differences are minimal. I compared volume on the announcement day with the 1-month average for the stock. Volume is the announcement day's volume, not the breakout day's volume.

TABLE 48.6   Size and Volume Statistics

Description	Bull Market	Bear Market
Tall pattern performance	27%	16%
Short pattern performance	21%	12%
Median height as a percentage of breakout price	4.57%	5.50%
Heavy announcement day volume, performance	24%	14%
Light announcement day volume, performance	22%	13%

◼ Trading Tactics

Table 48.7 shows trading tactics for the GES pattern. I do not recommend trading this pattern simply because a company announced good earnings. The performance is just not good enough to justify the risk of a trade. Look back at Table 48.3, the one showing failure rates. Almost half of all GES patterns rise 10% and then tumble by at least 20%. Those are not good odds.

Wait for announcement. Never try to guess the breakout direction and buy ahead of an earnings announcement. Before I trade, I always check when the next earnings announcement will be (typically, it is 3 months after the last one). If it is within 3 weeks, I will skip the trade because my holding time is usually longer than 3 weeks, and I do not want to hold it during the announcement. In the few times that I did, the earnings announcement may have been good, but the stock invariably tumbled. Why? Because traders were expecting better. The earnings missed the whisper number and prices dropped, sometimes dramatically.

Buy signal. If you have a compelling situation, buy when price closes above the announcement day's high. Only then is the pattern valid.

Trade with the trend. Only trade a GES pattern if price is moving up. Check the direction of the general market. If it is rising, then that will tend to support your stock as well. Look at other stocks in the same industry. Are they moving up (good)? Are they showing bearish patterns (bad)? Are the majority of them trending down even as the market is rising (bad)? Are they making new highs (good)?

Try filtering your selections using a moving average. Select only those in which the 50-day (or whatever period you are comfortable with) moving average is rising. Check other indicators for buy signals and weigh the evidence before taking a position.

Measure rule. Use the measure rule to predict a price target. For example, imagine that on the announcement day, the intraday high was 50 and the low was 48. The pattern's height is two (50 − 48). Add this difference to the intraday high (50) to get the target price of 52 (50 + 2). Price will meet or exceed the target between 74% (bear market) and 76% (bull market) of the time.

Limit order. Since event patterns are very short duration patterns, meaning that the rise associated from them lasts days to a few weeks, many swing traders will use

TABLE 48.7	Trading Tactics
Trading Tactic	**Explanation**
Wait for announcement	Never trade ahead of an earnings announcement.
Buy signal	Buy when price closes above the announcement day's high.
Trade with the trend	Buy if price is in an uptrend and other stocks in the industry are doing well.
Measure rule	Using prices from the announcement day, compute the difference between the intraday high and low. Add the difference to the intraday high to get the target price.
Limit order	For swing traders, put a limit order to sell at the target price. Price will hit it 75% of the time.

the measure rule to set a price target. They place a limit order to sell near the target price or just below overhead resistance. This method works about 75% of the time (see the Results Snapshot, "Percentage meeting price target").

■ Sample Trade

Figure 48.4 shows an example of how difficult it can be to make a profit trading the GES pattern. After price bottomed in November 2001, it started a long climb. In April, it formed a pennant leading to the earnings announcement. If price continued its normal pattern, we could expect price to fulfill the pennant measure rule and rise to about 56 (that is, a flagpole height of about 6, projected upward from the pennant low of 50). Call it 55 to be conservative.

The trading range on the announcement day was larger than the average over the prior month. That observation suggested a well-performing GES pattern. Volume on the announcement day was above the monthly average, too. Patterns with above average volume tend to outperform.

How high will price climb? On the announcement day, the intraday high was 50.90 and the low was 49.73, for a height of 1.17. Adding this difference to the intraday high gives a target of 52.07. A limit order set for 52 or just below the round number would work well. It took price 6 days to reach the target.

Despite good omens—a rising price trend, large announcement day trading range, and heavy volume—price moved up quickly and then tumbled. How would you have traded it?

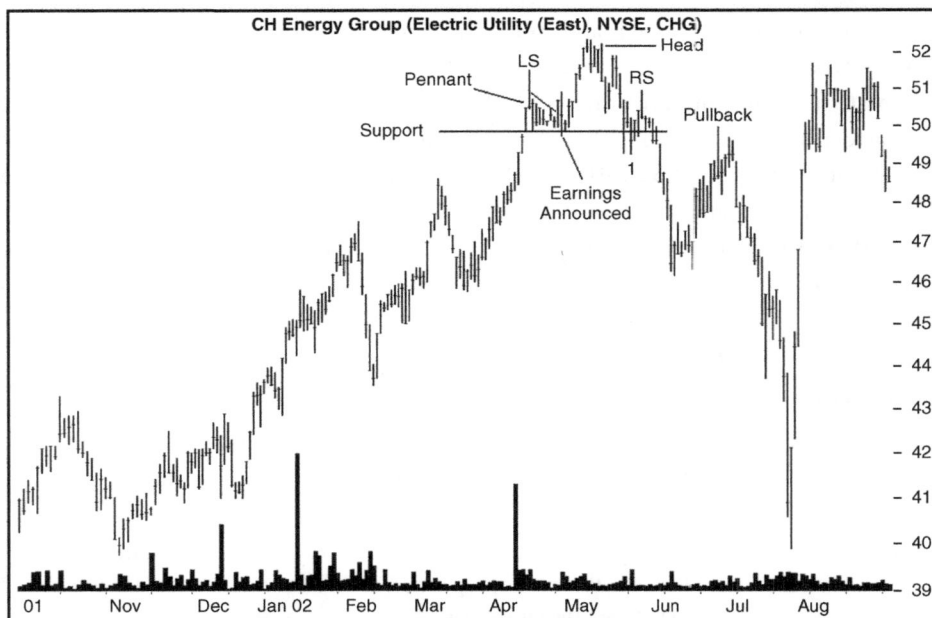

FIGURE 48.4 The Rise from an Earnings Announcement Is Often Brief, as This Figure Demonstrates.

If this were my trade, I would have placed a stop just below the support line. Even without a stop, a close below the support line was a sell signal, and you had a week to get out (starting at point 1). If you held on, the pullback gave you another opportunity to get out near breakeven, but it lasted only a day. If you missed selling, price dropped to the high 30s from about 50.

This behavior is typical of a good earnings announcement. Price breaks out upward, climbs (just 3% in this case), and then tumbles. Recall that Table 48.4 showed that those patterns in a bear market (as was this pattern) near the yearly high performed worst. I often trade event patterns in which the stock is making new highs (or nearing a new high). I much prefer them because price tends to keep moving up, especially if the general market is also doing well.

If a stock is making new lows (or anywhere except making a new high) and a GES pattern appears, I will not trade it. Chances are that price will throw back and continue down, resulting in a loss. Figure 48.4 shows a setup that I like to see, except that it occurs in a bear market. An upward breakout from a pennant with a long flagpole leading to it . . . what is not to like?

Once the unsymmetrical head-and-shoulders top appeared, that was another warning for traders to get out.

▓ For Best Performance

The following list includes tips and observations that may help you select GES patterns that outperform. Refer to the associated table for more information.

▪ Review the identifiction guidelines for correct selection—Table 48.1.

▪ Select patterns in a price uptrend, in a bull market, and with an upward breakout—Table 48.1.

▪ Pick GES patterns with a large intraday price range, larger than the 1-month average—Table 48.1.

▪ Trade with the trend since most GES patterns act as continuations of the prevailing trend—Table 48.2.

▪ Failure rates are high with this pattern, so be selective. Almost half fail to rise more than 10%—Table 48.3.

▪ Choose patterns near the yearly low but in a price uptrend—Table 48.4.

▪ Throwbacks hurt performance so avoid those patterns with nearby overhead resistance—Table 48.4.

▪ Half the patterns will top out in the first week or two—Table 48.5.

▪ Tall patterns perform better than short ones—Table 48.6.

▪ Select patterns with heavy announcement day volume—Table 48.6.

CHAPTER 49

FDA Drug Approvals

From Thomas N. Bulkowski, *Encyclopedia of Chart Patterns*, Second Edition (Hoboken, New Jersey: John Wiley & Sons, 2005), Chapter 58.

Learning Objective Statements

- Interpret potential price moves based on the patterns described in this chapter
- Calculate potential price targets
- Evaluate price levels for potential support or resistance
- Identify and interpret signals from various oscillators and technical studies in conjunction with the event-based patterns listed in these chapters

919

Results Snapshot

Upward Breakouts

Event	The FDA announces approval of a drug. The stock makes a large intraday price move with an upward breakout.
Reversal or continuation	Short-term bullish continuation
Performance rank	6 out of 6
Break-even failure rate	34%
Average rise	20%
Change after trend ends	−29%
Volume trend	Usually heavy on the announcement day
Throwbacks	61%
Percentage meeting price target	81%
Surprising findings	Reversals perform substantially better than continuations. Patterns with above average volume do better.

Downward Breakouts

Event	Same, but breakout is downward.
Reversal or continuation	Short-term bearish reversal
Performance rank	4 out of 5
Break-even failure rate	39%
Average decline	13%
Change after trend ends	52%
Volume trend	Same as for upward breakouts
Pullbacks	66%

Percentage meeting price target	78%
Surprising findings	Reversals perform substantially better than continuations.
	Patterns with above average volume do better.

Who would have thought that when the Food and Drug Administration (FDA) approves a new drug, the stock tumbles? If it does not tumble immediately, it soon will. I found that reaction when I searched for FDA drug approvals, and it surprised me. I expected to see an upward breakout followed by a flag or pennant pattern, and then a continuation of the climb. Instead, half the patterns had downward breakouts! If they broke out upward, 42% were trending downward within a week.

You might be thinking that this situation is a good example of the saying "Buy on the rumor; sell on the news." That is probably correct. Even after the drug approval comes, the company still has to get it into production and into the pharmacies. That process can take a long time and even longer for the drug profits to influence the bottom line.

The Results Snapshot shows the numbers for upward and downward breakouts, but there were not enough samples to split the results into bull and bear markets. The break-even failure rates for both breakout directions are well above the 20% maximum I consider acceptable. The average rise or decline, which represents a best-case scenario, is meager when you factor in commissions and trading costs, and that you will be late entering the trade and will not sell at the absolute peak or valley.

If you can determine when the trend changes (when price reaches the ultimate high or low), then sell short (upward breakouts) or buy long (downward breakouts) and profit from the move.

■ Tour

Figure 49.1 shows examples of what I found when I searched my database for instances of FDA drug approvals. This particular stock has the most drug approvals of any that I looked at. In July 1998, the first approval came and the stock price climbed. Then the stock dropped after another drug approval. The next three approvals show the stock *dropping* after the announcement. I thought that approvals were supposed to be good news for the company. . . .

Another surprise I found was the number of approvals each year. Some companies were busy getting new drugs approved and some were not. Let me tell you about the data. I used a popular Web site search engine and searched for the phrase "FDA drug approvals." The results took me to the FDA Web site where I found lists of approved drugs and devices, categorized by months. I copied that data and used my programming skills and brute force to extract the company name, application type, approval date, and drug name. I did not include the following: efficacy supplements, labeling revisions or supplements, nearly all medical or biological devices, or veterinarian approvals. I *did* use new drug applications and included tentative approvals.

Sound confusing? It gets worse. Imagine you are a drug company that has discovered a new aspirin. It comes in the form of a liquid that you inject. Later the researchers create formulations that come in the form of a solution (think eye

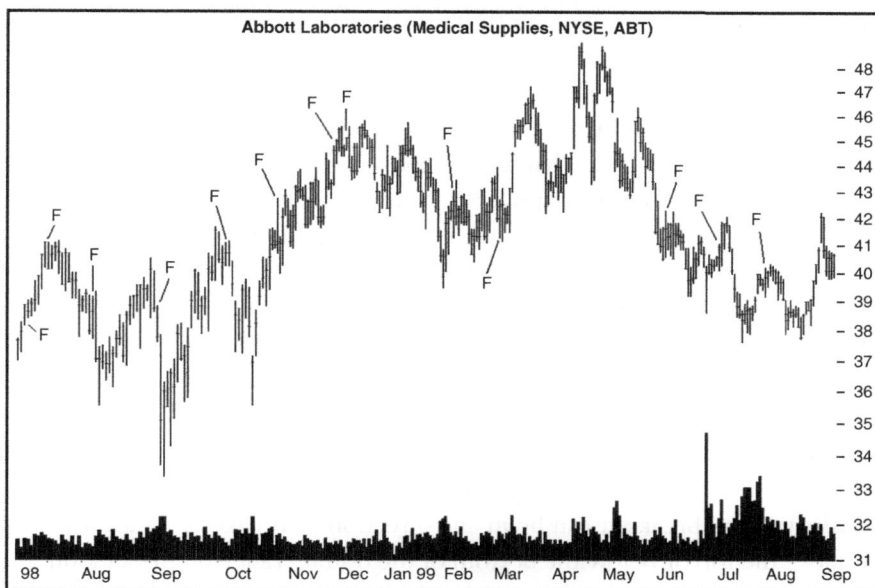

FIGURE 49.1 The F Symbols Mark Announcements of FDA Drug Approvals.

drops), gel, tablet, capsule, cream or ointment, and so forth, each having a variety of dosage levels. Those variations require FDA approval, and we have not even touched on over-the-counter and generics. Check out the FDA Web site and marvel at how inventive the companies can get with drug names.

■ Identification Guidelines

Table 49.1 shows identification guidelines for the patterns I selected.

TABLE 49.1 Identification Characteristics

Characteristic	Discussion
Announcement	News reports announce the approval of a drug by the FDA.
Large price move	The intraday price range on the announcement day or the next day must be wider than the 1-month average, or price must gap on the announcement day.
Breakout	The breakout can be in any direction, signaled by a close above the intraday high or below the intraday low posted on the announcement day.
Volume	Expect high volume on the announcement day.
J-Shaped Criteria	**Discussion**
Inverted J-shape	For upward breakouts, price trends up, then rounds over at the top, and finally tumbles, forming an inverted J shape.
Price rise	After the breakout, price rises from 3 to 6 weeks before cresting. Ignore patterns outside those limits unless the trade is compelling.
Trend-line pierce	Price usually moves upward following a trend. A line drawn along the bottom of the trend, when pierced, is the sell or sell short signal.

Announcement. I am not interested in trading a minor drug approval for a multibillion-dollar company. That type of random performance takes on the appearance of the chart shown in Figure 49.1. Rather, I scour the financial news for word of an FDA drug approval. Figure 49.2 shows an example of the pattern. It is not a terrific example, but it shows what to look for. On February 1, 2002, *The Wall Street Journal* reported that the FDA approved Neulasta, a longer-acting version of the company's Neupogen drug. That day, the stock gapped upward.

Large price move. I ran tests on the data and found that large price moves on the announcement day suggested larger profits ahead. Thus, I computed the average trading range of the stock over the month before the announcement and then compared it to the announcement day's range plus the next day. If either of those days were above the average, then I accepted the pattern. I included the next day in case the announcement did not make it during the normal trading day. In addition, I included days in which the price gapped, either up or down.

Breakout. The breakout can be in any direction. A breakout occurs when price closes above the top or below the bottom of the trading range on the announcement day. It might occur the next day or it may take 3 weeks, but it usually occurs quickly (4 days is the average for both up and down breakouts). In Figure 49.2, the breakout occurred the day after the announcement, when price gapped upward.

Volume. On the announcement day, expect volume to be above average. That reaction does not always happen, but when it does for upward breakouts, it usually suggests a larger move.

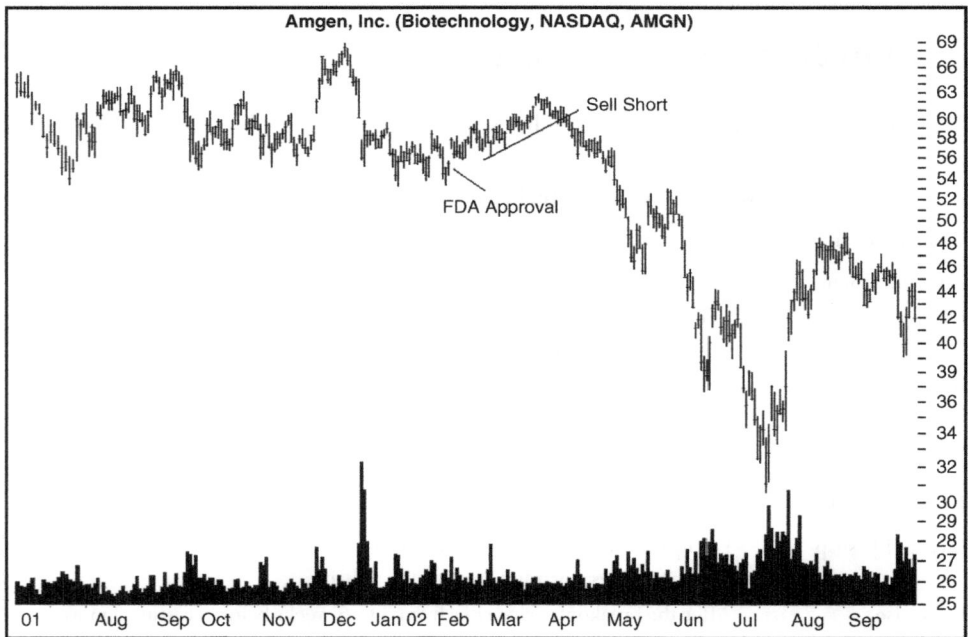

FIGURE 49.2 After the FDA Drug Approval, Price Gapped Up and then Topped Out about 6 Weeks Later. A Sell Short Signal Occurred When Price Closed below the Trend Line.

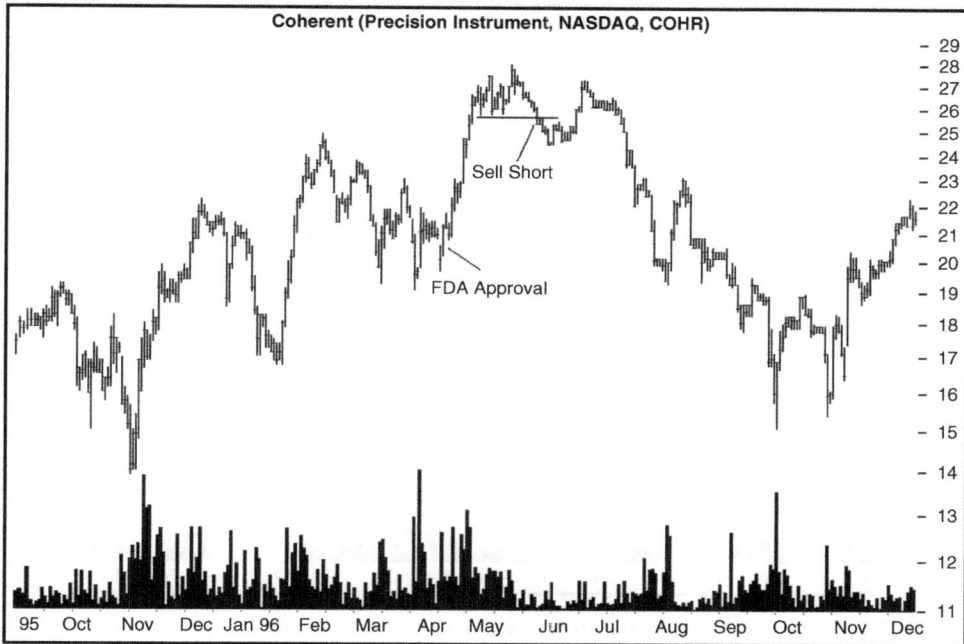

FIGURE 49.3 After the Company Received Approval of Its Laser, the Stock Climbed, Topped Out, and Then Tumbled.

Inverted J-shape criteria, price rise, and trend-line pierce. Here is a promising pattern to look for that is separate from the other identification guidelines. After an upward breakout, price climbs and then rounds over, forming an inverted J-shape that takes between 3 and 6 weeks to top out. The turn may not be graceful, but it often follows a trend line drawn along the low prices. Think of this behavior as a flag or pennant, perhaps one that slopes upward (a flag or pennant usually slopes opposite the prevailing price trend). A trend-line pierce is a signal to sell a long holding or short a new position. In Figure 49.2, price follows the trend line until piercing it, moving downward, in early April.

Figure 49.3 shows another example of the inverted J pattern. On April 10, 1996, a news report said that Coherent received FDA approval to market a laser that removed skin marks such as tattoos and birthmarks. The stock climbed, peaking in about 5 weeks before heading lower. A trend line drawn along the three minor lows in April–May set up a sell or sell short signal that occurred about 3 weeks later. The stock tumbled, but not before briefly climbing above the sell short price in mid-June. In September, the stock reached a low of about 15.

■ Focus on Failures

The major failure from this pattern comes from traders believing they can make money trading it. Consider Figure 49.4. The inverted J price pattern appears after news reports that the FDA approved a drug in July. Price reaches a minor high at point A before declining to D. With this decline, there is no trend-line break to signal

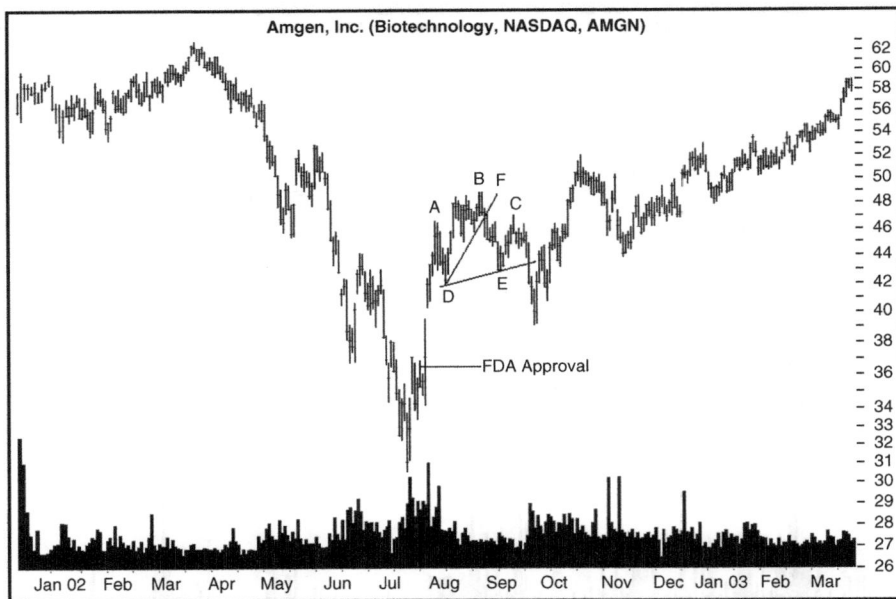

FIGURE 49.4 When Do You Short? A Head-and-Shoulders Pattern Appears as the Three Bumps, A, B, and C.

a short sale. The turn is quicker than the usual 3 to 6 week wait, suggesting that you postpone the trade.

Price then climbed from D to B. Now we can draw a trend line connecting the low at D to the low below B. The trend line, D–F, marks the sell short line. A close below this trend line is the signal. If you sold short at the close below the trend line and bought the stock back at the low—a perfect trade—you would have made just 16%. In the real world, no one trades perfectly, so your results after expenses would have been less. Would the trade have been worth the risk of a short?

A head-and-shoulders top appears as the pattern ABC. A close below the neckline, DE, is another sell signal. Even so, the stock does not decline much below the neckline before reversing.

When do you short? That is the major problem with the J-shaped chart pattern I have described. If you can correctly draw a trend line that price pierces, great! Otherwise, it becomes a guessing game. Imagine if Figure 49.4 shows price continuing the decline from point D. You would have kicked yourself for not shorting.

If you still think this pattern is tradable, cover Figure 49.1 with a sheet of paper. Slide the paper to the right and ask yourself if and when you would trade the associated drug approvals, (marked F) as they appear. How well did you do?

■ Statistics

The statistics shown in the following tables pertain to all FDA drug approvals that I looked at and that met the first set of identification guidelines, not those pertaining to the J-shaped pattern. (I did an informal study of the J-shaped pattern, and

TABLE 49.2 **General Statistics**

Description	Upward Breakout	Downward Breakout
Number of formations	95	96
Reversal (R) or continuation (C)	36 R, 59C	54 R, 42 C
R/C performance	24% R, 17% C	−15% R, −11% C
Average rise or decline	20%	−13%
Rises or declines over 45%	17 or 18%	2 or 2%
Change after trend ends	−29%	52%
Busted pattern performance	44%	−21%
Standard & Poor's 500 change	7%	−4%
Days to ultimate high or low	105	30

Note: Minus sign means decline.

the Trading Tactics section discusses those results.) The general statistics appear in Table 49.2.

Number of formations. The number of drug approvals split evenly between upward and downward breakouts but were not numerous enough to divide into bull and bear markets. For such a positive event as an FDA drug approval, it surprised me that price dropped half the time. I found 191 patterns in 31 unique stocks from 1995 to 2004 that met the identification guidelines.

Reversal or continuation. A slight majority of the patterns acted as continuations of the prevailing price trend, not reversals. This finding means that the approval did not change the direction of the trend. That result comes as a surprise as I would have expected an approval in a declining market to send a stock shooting upward. Even if it did not, I would expect price to be trending upward as the market anticipated an approval.

Reversals perform substantially better than do those acting as continuations. For example, in a bull market, price climbed 24% after a reversal but just 17% after a continuation.

Average rise or decline. For upward breakouts in all event patterns, price climbs an average of 24%; this pattern climbed just 20%. For downward breakouts, a good chart pattern will decline 18%, but this one drops just 13%. The performance of this pattern is disappointing.

Rises or declines over 45%. A good gauge of how well a pattern performs is the number of patterns that show postbreakout rises or declines over 45%. For upward breakouts, 18% of the patterns I looked at climbed more than 45%; only 2% made the cut in the downward direction. The poor showing for downward breakouts is typical as they never perform well in this test.

Change after trend ends. Once price reaches the ultimate high or low, it drops by 29% or rises by 52%, respectively. Thus, if you can determine when the trend changes, trade the stock, especially after a downward breakout. The 52% rise gives you plenty of time to verify that the trend has changed and to place a new trade. For the best results, check to be sure the general market and other stocks in the industry share the same trend as the stock you intend to trade.

Busted pattern performance. Patterns that drop by less than 5% turn around and soar an average of 44%. Those that break out upward and climb less than 5% drop by an average of 21%. Thus, if you see price reversing course after the breakout, wait for the new direction to be established, then take a position following the new trend.

Standard & Poor's 500 change. I like to think of the S&P index as the control group for how I collect statistics. As measured from the breakout day to the day of the ultimate high or low, the S&P 500 index climbed 7% for patterns with upward breakouts and dropped 4% for patterns with downward breakouts. Compare the results to the average rise or decline to see how much better the event pattern performed over the same period.

Days to ultimate high or low. It still surprises me that it takes over 3 months to climb an average of just 20%, but only a month to decline 13%. Thus, the declines are steeper than the rises, on average.

Table 49.3 shows the failure rate for this event pattern. Notice how many patterns fail to rise or decline more than 5%, the break-even failure rate. For example, 34% of the stocks having upward breakouts fail to rise more than 5%. Downward breakouts are even worse, with 39% failing to drop at least 5%. Well over half (59%) drop less than 10%.

This table serves as a warning to all those who think they can make money trading an FDA drug approval. They may make some bucks for a trade or two, but the long-term performance is apt to be dismal.

Table 49.4 shows breakout- and postbreakout-related statistics.

Formation end to breakout. This pattern takes 4 days to break out. It does not take long for price to close above the daily high or below the daily low to complete the breakout.

Yearly position. Where in the yearly price range do most breakouts occur? For both breakout directions, they occur most often within a third of the yearly high.

TABLE 49.3	Failure Rates	
Maximum Price Rise or Decline (%)	Upward Breakout	Downward Breakout
5 (breakeven)	32 or 34%	37 or 39%
10	46 or 48%	57 or 59%
15	59 or 62%	68 or 71%
20	67 or 71%	77 or 80%
25	71 or 75%	83 or 86%
30	74 or 78%	87 or 91%
35	76 or 80%	92 or 96%
50	80 or 84%	95 or 99%
75	87 or 92%	96 or 100%
Over 75	95 or 100%	96 or 100%

TABLE 49.4 **Breakout and Postbreakout Statistics**

Description	Upward Breakout	Downward Breakout
Formation end to breakout	4 days	4 days
Percentage of breakouts occurring near the 12-month low (L), center (C), or high (H)	L20%, C32%, H48%	L23%, C30%, H47%
Percentage rise or decline for each 12-month lookback period	L22%a, C14%, H23%	L11%a, C16%a, H12%
Throwbacks/pullbacks	61%	66%
Average time to throwback/pullback ends	8 days	11 days
Average rise/decline for patterns with a throwback/pullback	21%	−11%
Average rise/decline for patterns without a throwback/pullback	16%	−17%

Note: Minus sign means decline.

aFewer than 30 samples.

Yearly position, performance. Mapping performance over the yearly price range shows that FDA drug approval patterns with upward breakouts near the yearly high show gains of 23%. The middle of the yearly range does worst, showing gains of just 14%. For downward breakouts, the best performance comes from patterns that are in the middle of the yearly price range: They decline 16%.

Throwbacks and pullbacks. Throwbacks and pullbacks happen over 60% of the time. When they occur, it takes 8 to 11 days, on average, for price to return to the breakout price. That time frame is typical.

For many chart patterns, when a throwback or pullback occurs, performance suffers. You can see that with downward breakouts. When a pullback occurs, the resulting decline averages 11%. Without a pullback, the decline averages 17%. For upward breakouts, the results reverse: Those throwing back perform better.

Table 49.5 shows a frequency distribution of the time it takes to reach the ultimate high or low. The pattern either tops out (upward breakout at 42%) or reaches the ultimate low (55%) in the first week. A few lucky ones take over 70 days to reach the ultimate high or low.

Notice that 7% reach the ultimate high 56 days after the breakout. Thus, if you own a stock after an upward breakout, look for signs of it topping out 2 months after the breakout. Consider selling before price plummets (those 7% all dropped at least 20%, by definition of the ultimate high).

TABLE 49.5 **Frequency Distribution of Days to Ultimate High or Low**

Days:	7	14	21	28	35	42	49	56	63	70	>70
Upward breakout	42%	7%	3%	5%	2%	2%	1%	7%	1%	0%	28%
Downward breakout	55%	7%	6%	4%	1%	4%	2%	3%	0%	3%	14%

TABLE 49.6 **Size and Volume Statistics**

Description	Upward Breakout	Downward Breakout
Tall pattern performance	20%	−13%
Short pattern performance	18%	−13%
Median height as a percentage of breakout price	3.78%	3.26%
Heavy announcement day volume, performance	20%	−14%
Light announcement day volume, performance	19%	−11%

Note: Minus sign means decline.

Table 49.6 shows size and volume statistics, of which there are few.

Height. I computed the height of the 1-day pattern and divided the result by the breakout price. Then I sorted the results into short and tall categories and checked performance. For most chart and event patterns, tall ones outperform. For this pattern, upward breakouts do well, but downward breakouts show no performance difference. Remember, I only accepted those patterns that were taller than the 1-month average high–low price range (see Table 49.1, "Large price move").

Announcement day volume. I compared the announcement day volume with the 1-month average and then separated the patterns by those with above average volume and those with below average volume. Those with above average volume and upward breakouts climbed 20% above the breakout price. For those with low announcement day volume, price climbed 19%. For downward breakouts, the trend was the same but the results widened: declines of 14% versus 11%.

◼ Trading Tactics and Sample Trade

I do not recommend trading this pattern because the performance is so poor (low profit potential at high risk), and the low sample counts make some of the statistical results questionable. However, I do know one thing to be true: The wider the intraday trading range on the announcement (or the next day), the better the performance.

What does this finding mean? I measured the average trading range for the month leading to the pattern and compared it to the range on the announcement day. In mathematical terms, this is an average of the daily high–low differences of the prior month compared to the high–low range on the announcement day. If the announcement day high–low range (ADHLR) was larger than the average, the pattern tended to outperform. If the ADHLR was twice the average, the pattern did better still with a lower failure rate. When the ADHLR was 3 times the average, it did better still. Thus, look for a wide high–low price range on the day of the announcement for best performance.

As I mentioned in the Identification Guidelines section, one pattern shows promise. Here are a few statistics regarding an informal study of FDA drug approval patterns meeting the J-shaped identification guidelines.

I accepted patterns showing a price peak between 21 days and 48 days (3 to 6 weeks) after the breakout and then measured the decline from the closing price at the trend-line pierce to the ultimate low. The 20 patterns (in 15 stocks) I found

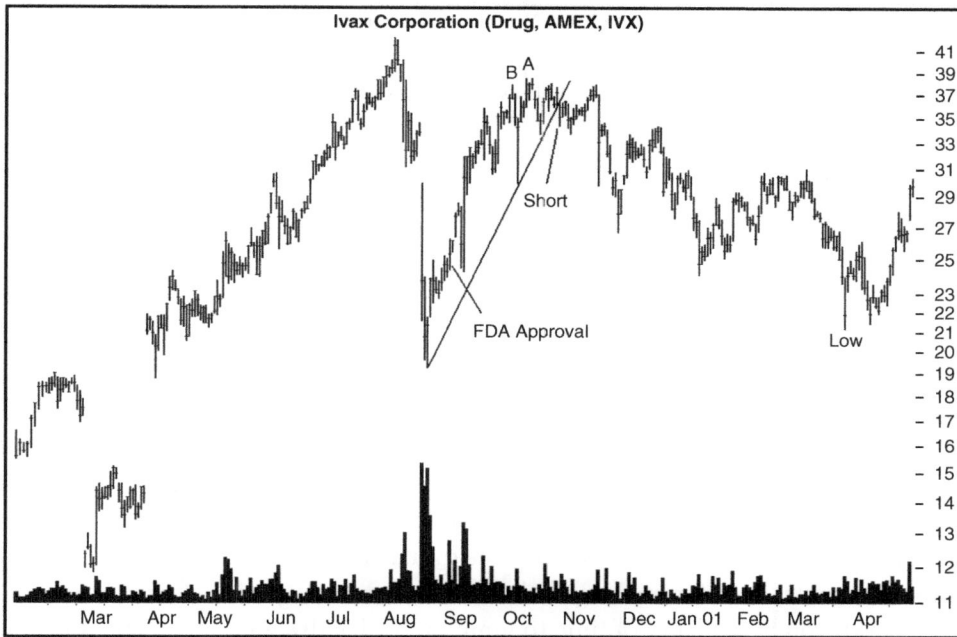

FIGURE 49.5 Look for the Peak to Round Over 4 to 6 Weeks after the Upward Breakout.

fitting the J-shaped criteria listed in Table 49.1 declined an average of 18%. That finding compares to a 13% decline for all FDA drug approvals with downward breakouts. The sample size is too small to consider statistically meaningful, but the results are promising.

Figure 49.5 shows one example of a pattern included in the J-shape study. Price climbed smartly after the FDA drug approval, but then topped out at point A, rounded over, and tumbled to the low at 21.19. Point A is 38 days after the approval. The short sale comes after price pierces the up-sloping trend line. The decline from the close the day following the trend-line pierce (35.20) to the ultimate low (21.19) measures 40%.

Look what would have happened if you used point B instead of point A as the peak. A steeper trend line meant you would short the day that price dropped to about 30 and then climbed to A. If you were an experienced trader, seeing prices climb above the high at B, you would have closed out your short position for a loss and then watched as price tumbled a week later.

I think you can make a less risky trade with other bearish formations without having to trade this pattern.

Table 49.7 shows statistics for trading FDA drug approvals once price reaches the ultimate high or low and then reverses.

Average decline or rise. If you wait for the ultimate high (upward breakouts) or ultimate low (downward breakouts), the table shows how well price performs from that point on. For upward breakouts, price drops by 29% after reaching the ultimate high. For downward breakouts, price rises an average of 51%.

TABLE 49.7	General Statistics for a New Trading Strategy	
Description	Upward Breakout Followed by a Decline	Downward Breakout Followed by a Rise
Average decline or rise	−29%	51%
Declines or rises over 45%	9 or 11%	49 or 55%
Days to ultimate low or high	86	220

Note: Minus sign means decline.

Declines or rises over 45%. I do not view the 11% of patterns declining more than 45% as exceptional, but the 55% climbing over 45% is huge.

Days to ultimate low or high. It takes almost 3 months to decline an average of 29% or 221 days to rise an average of 51%. Large moves take time.

What does all this information mean? If you can determine when a stock has topped or bottomed, *then* take a position and hold on. After an upward breakout from an FDA announcement, wait for price to start an extended decline. For downward breakouts, look for an extended rise. With an average rise of over 7 months (220 days), you have plenty of time to jump on the bandwagon. Of course, the key to this strategy is correctly calling the top or the bottom. How do you do that? Three answers: experience, luck, or both. You hate me now, right?

■ For Best Performance

The following list includes tips and observations to help you select patterns that outperform. Refer to the associated table for more information.

- Look for the inverted J-shaped pattern—Table 49.1.

- Select patterns that act as reversals of the prevailing trend—Table 49.2.

- Trade busted patterns—Table 49.2.

- Failure rates start high, so have a good reason for trading other than a drug approval—Table 49.3.

- For upward breakouts, avoid patterns in the middle of the yearly price range; for downward breakouts, those in the middle perform best—Table 49.4.

- Expect a throwback (good for performance) or pullback (bad)—Table 49.4.

- Between 42% and 55% of the patterns reach the ultimate high or low in the first week. Take profits quickly—Table 49.5.

- Trade patterns with above average volume on the announcement day—Table 49.6.

- Once price touches the ultimate high or low and then reverses, trade the stock—Table 49.7.

CHAPTER 50

Flag, Earnings

From Thomas N. Bulkowski, *Encyclopedia of Chart Patterns*, Second Edition (Hoboken, New Jersey: John Wiley & Sons, 2005), Chapter 59.

Learning Objective Statements

- Interpret potential price moves based on the patterns described in this chapter
- Calculate potential price targets
- Evaluate price levels for potential support or resistance
- Identify and interpret signals from various oscillators and technical studies in conjunction with the event-based patterns listed in these chapters

Results Snapshot

Upward Breakouts

Event	A company announces earnings and the stock breaks out upward. A flag, pennant, or other consolidation region forms near the top of a flagpole.	
Reversal or continuation	Short-term bullish continuation	
	Bull Market	**Bear Market**
Performance rank	**1 out of 6**	**1 out of 5**
Break-even failure rate	10%	16%
Average rise	34%	22%
Change after trend ends	−33%	−32%
Volume trend	Downward	Downward
Throwbacks	63%	58%
Percentage meeting price target	86%	84%

I discovered the earnings flag several years ago as I was wondering what happens after a good earnings announcement. I remember my eyes opening wide and my heart pounding, but I did not pursue the discovery until recently. I traded the pattern on several occasions without quite knowing how it behaved. This chapter puts my knowledge on paper and adds statistics to back it up. Now the pattern is one of my favorites because it is so easy to spot and often profitable.

The Results Snapshot lists the important details of the earnings flag, a pattern that sometimes occurs after a surprisingly good earnings announcement. With a comparatively low break-even failure rate in a bull market (10%) and decent average rise (34%), this pattern does well for both swing traders and position traders.

Surprises are the usual lot and I explain them in the Statistics section.

■ Tour

Figure 50.1 shows a good example of what I call an earnings flag. It appears when a company makes a good quarterly earnings announcement that surprises traders. Many times the announcement happens when the market is closed. *When* the announcement takes

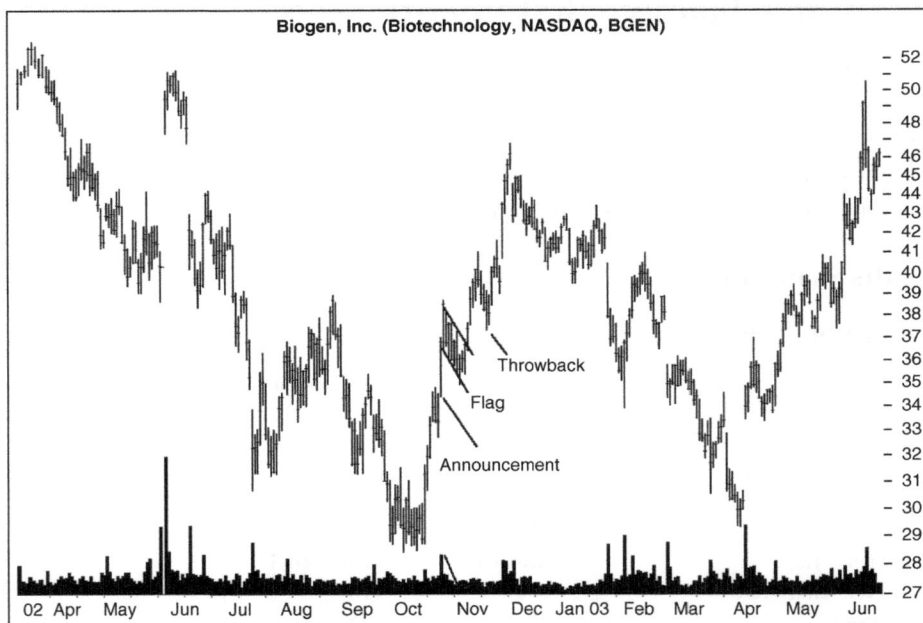

FIGURE 50.1 This Chart Shows a Good Example of the Earnings Flag Pattern. Price Zips Up on the Announcement Day, Pauses in the Flag Portion, and Then Resumes Rising. A Throwback Often Occurs. Volume in the Pattern Usually Trends Downward, Like That Shown.

place during the day is irrelevant unless you are a day trader or a nimble swing trader. I ignored the actual announcement and concentrated on how the market absorbed the news. I looked for a substantial up move within a day or two of the announcement.

In Figure 50.1 price started climbing about a week before the announcement, as if traders knew what was coming. On the day of the announcement, the stock zoomed up, made a higher high the next day, completing the flagpole. Price dropped into the characteristic flag pattern—usually a down-sloping rectangle (the rectangle can slope upward or horizontally). In my study of the pattern, I did not care what the flag looked like. It might resemble a pennant or just a bunch of squiggles.

After price pierced the flag trend line, staging a breakout, it moved up for another week and then threw back to near the breakout price before climbing to higher ground. This rise, pause, rise pattern is characteristic of the earnings flag.

Identification Guidelines

Table 50.1 lists identification guidelines for the earnings flag. Consider Figure 50.2 as I discuss the table.

Earnings announced. The earnings announcement is key to the pattern. If the newspapers proclaim that the earnings were better than the consensus estimate that is fine, but it does not mean anything to your wallet if price drops. And a drop happens regularly when good earnings are below the whisper number—the unofficial earnings estimate that traders use. Ignore any rumors or published facts and just watch what happens to the stock. If traders like what they hear from the company, they will buy. Increased buying demand will send the stock climbing, as it did beginning at point 1 in Figure 50.2.

TABLE 50.1 Identification Characteristics

Characteristic	Discussion
Earnings announced	An announcement of surprisingly good earnings sends the stock rocketing upward, usually on the same day as the announcement if the market is open. If too much time passes before the up move, say, more than 2 days, look elsewhere.
Flagpole	Price *usually* climbs in a near vertical run.
Flag	After leaving the flagpole, price trends downward, but not always. Price might meander upward or horizontally and it might not look like a rectangular flag at all. Expect any shape. The flag should look like a consolidation region separate from the vertical flagpole run.
Breakout	Price pierces the flag rectangle border, moving upward. If the flag portion has an irregular shape, use a close above the highest high.
Confirmation price	Confirmation is the price at which the earnings flag becomes a valid pattern. For testing, I used a *close* above the highest high in the formation as the confirmation price, but price piercing the upper flag boundary will get you in sooner.

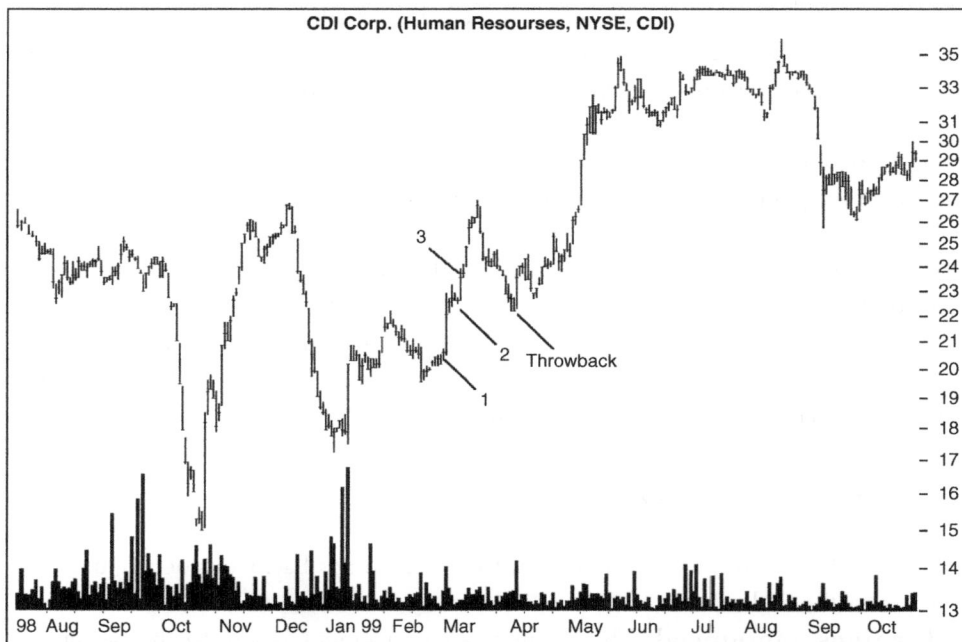

FIGURE 50.2 A Small Earnings Flag Reversal That Performs Well. Point 1 Shows the Earnings Announcement. Point 2 Is the Flag Consolidation Region. I Consider the Breakout to Be at Point 3—A Close above the Pattern High.

I like to see a straight-line advance for several days, but just 1 day is fine providing the rise is long enough. How long is "long enough?" Use your best judgment and consult the figures accompanying this chapter. Look for excitement reflected in the price. Beware price that gaps upward by small amounts. The gap often closes quickly (an area gap) and the move is not worth trading. The vast majority of earnings announcements do not affect the stock in a substantial way. With each stock having four earnings releases annually, you should be fussy and wait for the right opportunity before you invest.

Flagpole. As I mentioned, the best pattern is a straight-line run lasting several days (5 days is the median time to shimmy up the pole). That spurt forms the flagpole. The top of the pole is usually the highest high in the pattern. Whether the uphill run is nearly vertical or diagonal is not that important, just that the up move is significant. Again, use the figures in this chapter as guides.

Flag. The flag itself begins when price moves away from the flagpole (the horizontal cluster at point 2 in Figure 50.2). In this example, I would place a buy order once price closes above the flag, that is, at point 3; and in Figure 50.1, the order would go in the day after price pierces the upper flag trend line (the diagonal line on the top).

I call this pattern an earnings *flag* because most of the formations contain flags— rectangular-shaped boxes, usually sloping downward and hanging onto a flagpole. A pennant shape appears as the flag portion in Figure 50.3, for example. The *flag* portion in Figure 50.2 shows a random shape.

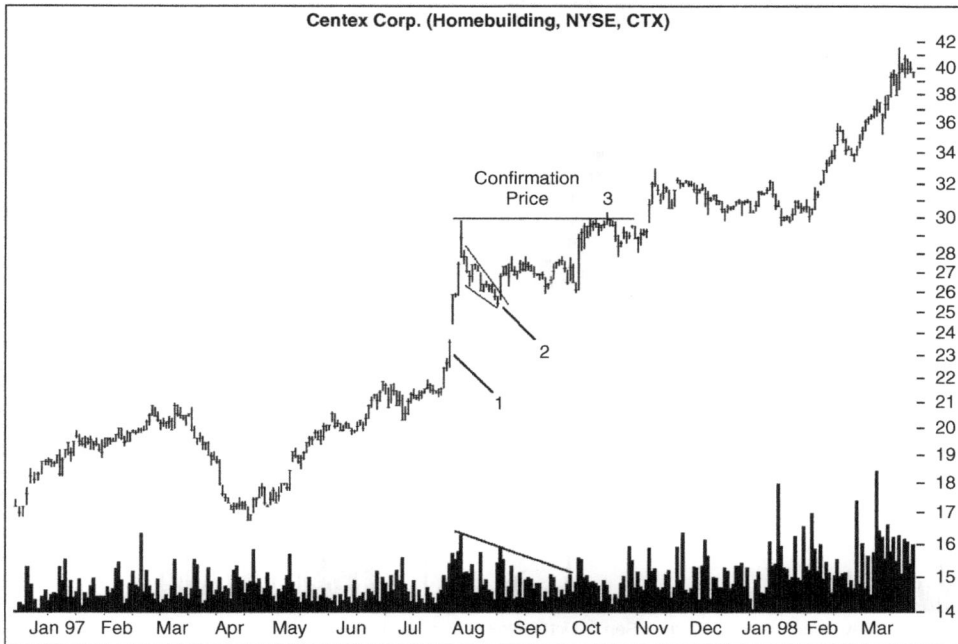

FIGURE 50.3 The Day after Point 2 Gives a Buy Signal. For the Statistics, I Waited for Price to Close above the Highest High in the Pattern before Buying. The Horizontal Line at Point 3 Shows the Breakout or Confirmation Price.

Breakout. A buy signal occurs when price closes above the formation high. That high is called the breakout price or confirmation price. You must wait for confirmation. In too many cases, price turns down and drops below the flag low, meaning a pattern failure and a loss if you own the stock. In some cases, like that shown in Figure 50.1, you can get a jump by buying when price pierces a trend line. That strategy is fine providing a trend line fits the shape of the flag portion.

Confirmation price. Look at Figure 50.3. For ease in gathering statistics, I used the highest high in the pattern as the confirmation price. When price closes above that price, then the pattern becomes a valid earnings flag. The figure shows the confirmation price as the horizontal line. However, if the flag slopes downward, as in this example and in Figure 50.1, consider buying near point 2, when price begins its uphill climb away from the flag. That timing gets you in earlier, saving you money and lowering your risk.

Always wait for confirmation, whether it is a close above the formation high or a piercing of the flag's trend line.

■ Focus on Failures

Figure 50.4 shows an example of a failure. I have highlighted the overhead resistance that appears like smog on the horizon. What I find important is the downward price trend leading to the pattern. Point 1 is the announcement and it happens after nearly 2 months of downward price movement. Avoid all flags that appear in a downtrend.

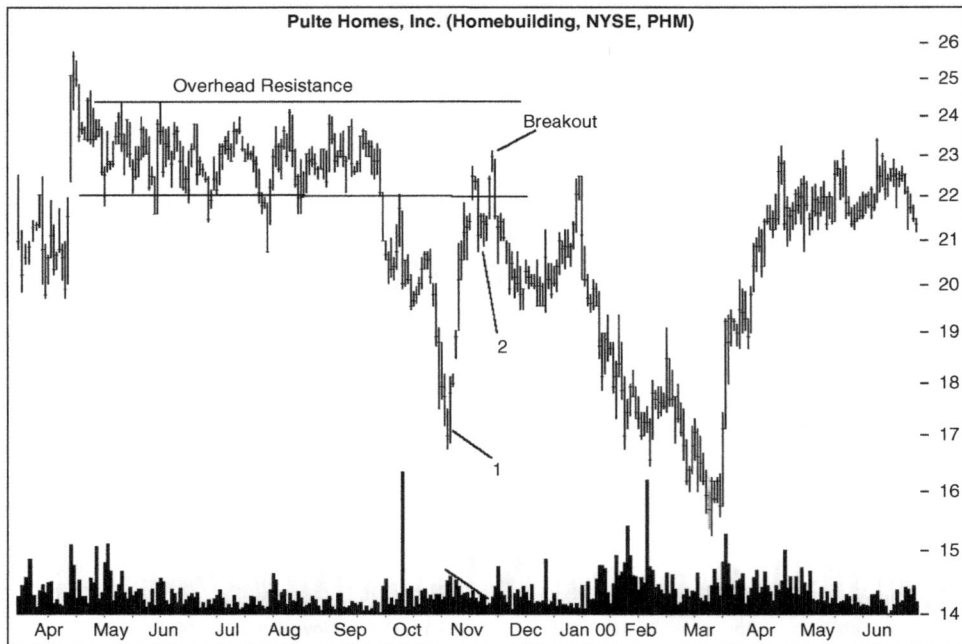

FIGURE 50.4 Overhead Resistance Stops This Earnings Flag (2) from Performing as Expected, but Another Clue Is to Avoid Selecting Earnings Flags in a Downward Price Trend. The Earnings Announcement Is at Point 1.

Why? The pattern *usually* acts as a continuation of the prevailing price trend, not as a reversal. If the price trend is down, the flag might send it up, but why chance it? Stick to flags in a rising price trend and that way your wallet can float on the rising tide.

Do not get excited about small gaps. I am talking about area gaps. When an earnings flag occurs, sometimes price gaps upward. Usually, in a few days, the up move collapses and closes the gap. This occurrence is not a problem if you wait for confirmation because the pattern never confirms. So, (1) beware earnings flags associated with area gaps and (2) wait for confirmation unless you enjoy losing money.

■ Statistics

I looked through my database of about 220 stocks from January 1995 to June 2004 to collect statistics about earnings flags. Due to database limitations, not all stocks had quarterly earnings releases. Still, I found 564 earnings flags, and Table 50.2 lists their general statistics.

Number of formations. I found 384 earnings flags in a bull market and 180 in a bear market. These numbers suggest that there are more earnings flags in a bear market than a bull market (because the bear market is shorter), but earnings at the start of the bull market period (1995) were scarce.

Reversal or continuation. Does the earnings flag act as a reversal or continuation of the prevailing price trend? Table 50.2 suggests that the pattern acts

TABLE 50.2 General Statistics

Description	Bull Market	Bear Market
Number of formations	384	180
Reversal (R) or continuation (C)	87 R, 297 C	48 R, 132 C
R/C performance	38% R, 33% C	22% R, 21% C
Average rise	34%	22%
Rises over 45%	111 or 29%	26 or 14%
Change after trend ends	−33%	−32%
Busted pattern performance	−30%	−28%[a]
Standard & Poor's 500 change	7%	1%
Days to ultimate high	114	80

Note: Minus sign means decline.

[a]Fewer than 30 samples.

as a continuation of the short-term trend 76% of the time. If the price trend was rising going into the earnings flag, chances are it will keep rising after the breakout; that is the way to trade it, anyway.

In a bull market, earnings flags that act as reversals perform substantially better than do those acting as continuations. In a bear market, the trend is the same but the results are narrower.

Average rise. The average rise in a bull market was 34%, but only 22% in a bear market. Both bull and bear market numbers are well above the 24% and 15% average rise for all event patterns, respectively.

Rises over 45%. Just over a quarter of the patterns (29%) in a bull market and 14% in a bear market rise more than 45%. Again, performance is quite good.

Change after trend ends. Once price reaches the ultimate high, it tumbles about 33%. Thus, if you can tell when the trend changes, you might consider shorting the stock. Use stops in case you guess wrong.

Busted pattern performance. Patterns that rise by less than 5% before plummeting drop an average of 28% to 30%. The drop measures from the highest high after the breakout to the lowest low—a perfect trade and one you are unlikely to make.

Standard & Poor's 500 change. Computing the change in the index from the date the earnings flag started to the ultimate high gives a 7% rise in a bull market and 1% gain in a bear market. This performance compares to a 34% and 22% average rise, respectively, for the earnings flag over the same period.

Days to ultimate high. If you trade this pattern perfectly, how long will it take to reach the point of maximum profit? Answer: in a bull market, 114 days, or about 4 months; in bear markets, just over 2 months (80 days). The rise in a bull market is slightly steeper than the rise in a bear market.

Table 50.3 shows a list of failure rates, beginning with the 5% or break-even failure rate. That is the rate I use to cover brokerage commissions, slippage, SEC fees,

TABLE 50.3	Failure Rates	
Maximum Price Rise (%)	Bull Market	Bear Market
5 (breakeven)	38 or 10%	28 or 16%
10	90 or 23%	56 or 31%
15	127 or 33%	86 or 48%
20	159 or 41%	107 or 59%
25	190 or 49%	121 or 67%
30	215 or 56%	134 or 74%
35	228 or 59%	141 or 78%
50	288 or 75%	157 or 87%
75	329 or 86%	169 or 94%
Over 75	384 or 100%	180 or 100%

and so forth. The table shows how often earnings flags fail to rise a given amount. For example, a third (33%) of the bull patterns and almost half of the bear patterns failed to rise more than 15% after the breakout.

What is alarming about the table, and seems to be the case for many chart and event patterns, is the rapid rise in failures for small changes in the maximum price rise. For example, the failure rate doubles from 5% to 10% and then leaps again. Since every trade is different, your results will vary. Play it safe and always use stops.

Suppose your trading costs amount to 5% and you want to make 10% on every trade. That totals 15%, but you know you will not win *every* trade. It has been your experience that you win every two out of three trades. Therefore, if you boost the profit margin to 20% (25% with expenses), that will compensate for the losers, leaving a 10% average profit on all three trades. How many flags will fail to deliver 25%? Answer: 49% in a bull market and 67% in a bear market. It sounds unlikely that you will reach your profit goals trading this event pattern.

Table 50.4 shows breakout- and postbreakout-related statistics.

Flagpole top to breakout. The flag portion of the formation averages just over 2 weeks long as measured from the day after the flagpole ends to the day of the breakout.

TABLE 50.4	Breakout and Postbreakout Statistics	
Description	Bull Market	Bear Market
Flagpole top to breakout	18 days	16 days
Percentage of breakouts occurring near the 12-month low (L), center (C), or high (H)	L14%, C27%, H59%	L17%, C32%, H50%
Percentage rise for each 12-month lookback period	L48%, C30%, H33%	L30%, C23%, H19%
Throwbacks	63%	58%
Average time to throwback ends	11 days	12 days
Average rise for patterns with throwbacks	30%	22%
Average rise for patterns without throwbacks	41%	22%

Yearly position. Using the highest high in the pattern (the breakout price) as the benchmark, where does the flag occur in the yearly price range? For both bull and bear markets, most of the patterns happen near the yearly high. This finding makes intuitive sense. If the stores are full of customers and the cash registers are ringing, investors like what they see and buy the stock. Buying demand pushes up the price, and then the company announces better than expected earnings, pushing the stock even higher.

Yearly position, performance. The best performance comes from patterns within a third of the yearly low. They had rises averaging 48% in a bull market and 30% in a bear market. Apparently, few expected earnings to surprise when the stock was so low.

Does that finding mean you should buy stocks with earnings flags near the yearly low? I checked the median percentage move and, sure enough, the lowest third showed the best performance, with a median rise of 36%. The middle range scored gains of 24% and the highest third had a median rise of 25%.

I will confess that I buy earnings flags if the stock is near the yearly high, never anywhere else, and always in a price uptrend. I have found that they work for me about two-thirds of the time. Since flags near the yearly low perform better, they are worth a closer look.

Throwbacks. Throwbacks occur between 58% and 63% of the time. If you miss trading a stock making an earnings flag, you may have another opportunity to invest if it throws back. Throwbacks also allow you to add to an existing position. It takes, on average, between 11 and 12 days for price to complete the throwback. In a bull market, a throwback hurts performance. Thus, look for overhead resistance before trading an earnings flag.

Table 50.5 shows a frequency distribution of the time it takes price to reach the ultimate high. Many earnings flags top out in the first week. At the other end of the scale, over a quarter of the patterns in a bear market take longer than 70 days to reach the ultimate high. In a bull market, nearly half (48%) take over 70 days to top out.

In a bear market, there is a slight tendency for flags to peak 35 days after the breakout. Thus, if other stocks in the same industry show weakness a month after the breakout or if the general market begins heading lower, raise your stop or be prepared to close out the trade.

Table 50.6 shows size statistics.

Height. With most chart patterns, tall ones perform better than short ones, and the earnings flag is no exception. Patterns taller than the median showed gains of 37% in bull markets and 24% in bear markets. Short patterns gained 31% and 20%, respectively. Thus, select patterns taller than the median for the best average performance.

TABLE 50.5	Frequency Distribution of Days to Ultimate High										
Days:	7	14	21	28	35	42	49	56	63	70	>70
Bear market	48%	8%	8%	6%	7%	3%	2%	2%	4%	1%	11%
Bull market	47%	13%	7%	5%	4%	4%	4%	3%	1%	1%	11%

TABLE 50.6	Size Statistics	
Description	Bull Market	Bear Market
Tall pattern performance	37%	24%
Short pattern performance	31%	20%
Median height as a percentage of breakout price	13.56%	14.67%
Narrow pattern performance	33%	26%
Wide pattern performance	35%	17%
Median length	14 days	12 days
Average formation length	15 days	14 days
Short and narrow performance	30%	25%
Short and wide performance	33%	14%
Tall and wide performance	36%	20%
Tall and narrow performance	39%	28%

TABLE 50.7	Volume Statistics	
Description	Bull Market	Bear Market
Rising volume trend performance	26%[a]	27%[a]
Falling volume trend performance	35%	21%
Heavy breakout volume performance	33%	20%
Light breakout volume performance	36%	24%

[a] Fewer than 30 samples.

Width. Do wide patterns perform better postbreakout than narrow ones? Yes and no. The median flag length was 14 days in a bull market and 12 days in a bear market, as measured from the announcement day to the breakout. In bull markets, wider flags performed better than narrow ones, 35% versus 33%; but in bear markets the results flipped, 26% versus 17%.

Average formation length. The average length from the start of the flagpole to the end of the flag was about 2 weeks.

Height and width combinations. The best performing combination of height and width goes to tall and narrow flags in both bull and bear markets. The worst combinations are short and narrow flags in a bull market and short and wide flags in a bear market.

Table 50.7 shows volume-related statistics.

Volume trend. The earnings flag shows a falling volume trend 93% of the time. I measured volume using linear regression from the announcement day to the day before the breakout. The performance results are not meaningful because of too few samples.

Breakout volume. In both markets, flags with light breakout volume tend to perform better after the breakout than do those with heavy breakout volume.

▥ Trading Tactics

Table 50.8 shows trading tactics for earnings flags.

Measure rule. The measure rule predicts how far price will rise, at a minimum. To use it, compute the formation height by subtracting the highest high in the pattern from the announcement day low. Add the difference to the lowest low in the flag portion of the pattern. The result is the predicted target price. Price reaches the target between 84% and 86% of the time.

For example, look at Figure 50.5. The formation high (point 2) is 21.19. The low price at the announcement day (point 1) is 17.25. Add the difference, 3.94, to the formation low in the flag (point 3) at 19.63 to get a target price of 23.57. Price met the target 4 days after the breakout.

Confirmation, buy signal. Price confirms the pattern when it breaks out above the highest high or pierces a trend line. Never buy before confirmation as price often moves lower without confirming the pattern.

There are two buy signals. Buy when price closes above the formation high. In Figure 50.5, the formation high is a close above point 2. The second buy signal is when price closes above a flag trend line. Figure 50.1 best describes the flag portion of the pattern. Two parallel down-sloping trend lines highlight the flag. When price pierces the upper trend line, buy. Sometimes though, the flag is irregular and does not lend itself to trend lines. Revert to the other buy signal—a close above the highest high in the pattern.

Sell signal. This is not an easy pattern to trade because price may rise quickly and then stage a massive decline. Be prepared to sell in the first week or so, before price throws back. If, after the throwback, price continues rising, then buy in again and ride the up wave.

Watch for throwback. A throwback occurs over half the time. Expect nearby overhead resistance to repel the upward price move and for price to throw back to the breakout price. Price may not make it all the way back down or it may throw back and continue lower. It is the latter situation you have to watch for. Few things hurt more than seeing a profitable trade turn into a loss. If you see price curling over

TABLE 50.8	Trading Tactics
Trading Tactic	**Explanation**
Measure rule	Used to predict a target price. Take the difference of the formation high from the announcement day low. Add this difference to the flag low (the lowest low to the right of the flagpole). The result is the target price. Price reaches the target 86% and 84% of the time in bull and bear markets, respectively.
Confirmation, buy signal	Buy when price closes above the formation high or pierces a flag trend line, but never before.
Sell signal	Price may top out in the first week. In bear markets, look for weakness a month into the trade.
Watch for throwback	A throwback occurs over half the time, so expect it. If it occurs and price begins rebounding, add to your position.

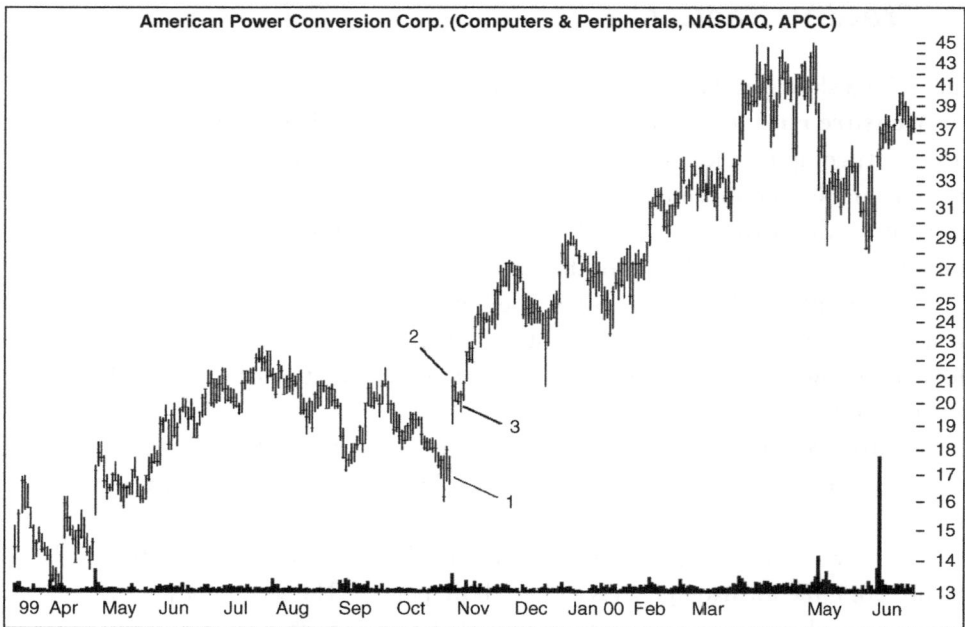

FIGURE 50.5 Prices Gapped Up after the Earnings Announcement. Apply the Measure Rule by Finding the Height (the highest high, Point 2, minus the lowest low on the announcement day, Point 1) Added to the Flag Low at Point 3. The Result Gives the Predicted Price Target.

within a week or so of the breakout, consider selling and capturing a profit. You can always buy again after price begins rebounding from the throwback.

■ Sample Trade

What is a real trade like? Figure 50.6 shows a trade I made in an earnings flag. Here is my notebook entry for the buy: "2/9/04. I bought 400 at market, filled at 31.75. This is an earnings flag trade. Upside is measured move up: $31.45 - 28.54 = 2.91$ measure. From 30.63, close at the low, the target is 33.54 or 33.50, rounded off. The recent diamond top should support this pattern. The measure rule worked for the October earnings surprise, and I expect this one will work as well. Competitor Michaels is doing well also. Downside is the most recent low, about 28 and change. That would give a 12% loss, a bit high. Tighten stop to closer to minor low when I get refreshed price data."

Stepping through the entry, I computed the target price using the measured move up method, which is also the earnings flag measure rule. Price reached the 33.50 target 3 days after I bought.

The October earnings flag begins at the base of the flagpole as shown on the figure. Price moves horizontally after the 1-day-wide pole then shoots up. A throwback gives back all of the profit and more in mid-November.

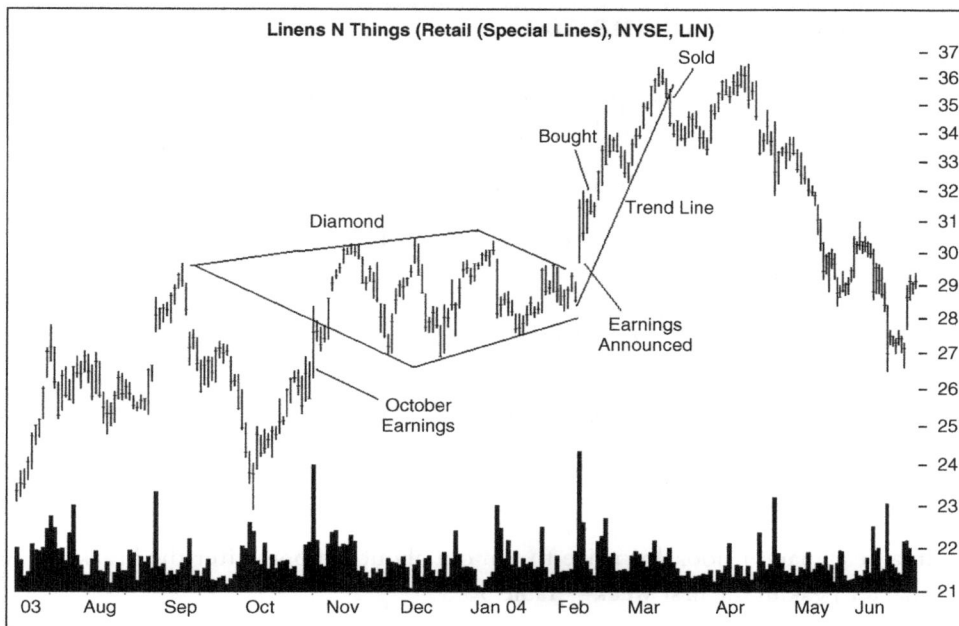

FIGURE 50.6 I Bought the Earnings Flag and Sold When the Technical Evidence Turned Negative.

The mention of Michaels Stores shows that I checked others in the industry, just to see how they were performing. I saw support, formed by the large diamond and horizontal price movement, centered near 28.

Here are additional notebook entries: "2/9/04 mental stop 28. 2/12/04 I placed a stop at 30.84, just below the minor low. 3/4/04 Stop raised to 32.13. 3/5/04 Stop raised to 33.23 after market close."

These entries show that I placed a stop and raised it as price climbed, beginning with the support zone at 28. When price broke out to a new high, I moved the stop up and placed it with my broker. The day before price peaked at a new yearly high, I raised the stop again to 32.13, just below a prior minor low, but too far away from the high of 36. The next day, I raised it again almost a buck.

Five days later, I sold the stock. Here is my entry: "3/10/04. I sold 400 at market because (1) CCI is diverging, (2) RSI is overbought a few days ago, (3) general market is down, (4) the stock is falling, and (5) the stock has pierced an up trend line. Stock filled at 35.20."

CCI is the commodity channel index and the indicator formed lower peaks even as price made higher highs. The relative strength index was in overbought territory but had moved into the neutral zone. The S&P 500 index started tumbling and that was like swimming against the current. The stock was also moving down and price had pierced the up-sloping trend line. Since everything looked bleak, I sold and made $1,350 on the trade.

You can see what happened to the stock. Price recovered to form a second high, an Eve & Eve double top, and then sank. Selling was the right move.

■ For Best Performance

The following list includes tips and observations to help select patterns that out-perform. Refer to the associated table for more information.

■ Select patterns that obey the identification guidelines—Table 50.1.

■ Earnings flags act as continuations of the upward price trend. Avoid flags in a bear market—Table 50.2.

■ Failure rates climb rapidly, so be prepared for a short trade. Take profits quickly—Table 50.3.

■ Buy earnings flags near the yearly low—Table 50.4.

■ In a bull market, earnings flags without throwbacks perform best, so avoid trading a stock with nearby overhead resistance—Table 50.4.

■ In a bear market, look for price to top out about a month after the breakout. A quarter peak in the first week—Table 50.5.

■ Select tall patterns—Table 50.6.

■ Flags both tall and narrow perform best—Table 50.6.

■ Select flags with light breakout volume—Table 50.7.

CHAPTER 51

Same-Store Sales, Bad

From Thomas N. Bulkowski, *Encyclopedia of Chart Patterns*, Second Edition (Hoboken, New Jersey: John Wiley & Sons, 2005), Chapter 60.

Learning Objective Statements

- Interpret potential price moves based on the patterns described in this chapter
- Calculate potential price targets
- Evaluate price levels for potential support or resistance
- Identify and interpret signals from various oscillators and technical studies in conjunction with the event-based patterns listed in these chapters

Results Snapshot

Downward Breakouts

Event	A retailer announces same-store sales numbers that the market interprets as bad, and the stock makes a large downward move that day or the next.	
Reversal or continuation	Short-term bearish continuation	
	Bull Market	**Bear Market**
Performance rank	**1 out of 5**	4 out of 4
Break-even failure rate	26%	27%
Average decline	12%	14%
Change after trend ends	54%	39%
Volume trend	Usually heavy on the announcement day	
Pullbacks	53%	60%
Percentage meeting price target	68%	69%
Surprising findings	Patterns in the middle of the yearly price range perform well. Pullbacks hurt performance. Tall patterns perform better than short ones.	
Synonyms	Comparable store sales, existing store sales	
See also	Same-Store Sales, Good	

John was excited. He called me and gushed over the phone that his favorite clothing retailer reported total sales up 30%. "Thirty percent! Can you believe that?" I popped his balloon when I asked about same-store sales. "Three percent," he said.

Same-store sales (3S) are sales from stores open longer than a year, sometimes two. For fast growing retailers, they are an important benchmark to gauge how well the chain is doing. If total sales grow by 25% each year but existing stores are suffering because the retailer is placing new stores just a mile away, then an investor might want to avoid the stock. Eventually, the chain will run out of places to build new stores . . . then what?

I looked at the retailing stocks I follow and searched for reports of same-store sales. I found hundreds of them, so I decided to limit the search to those with an above average trading range on the day of the announcement or the next day. After all, if a retailer announces bad 3S numbers and the stock goes nowhere, do investors care? The filtering improved results.

I used only downward breakouts so the pattern is bearish, and it usually occurs in a price downtrend. Thus, it is a continuation pattern of very short-term duration (about half reach the ultimate low in less than a week).

The break-even failure rate is over 25%, well above the normal single-digit values for well-behaved patterns (of all types), and it exceeds the 20% limit I consider acceptable. The average decline is meager, too (12% to 14%). After reaching the ultimate low, what happens to price? On average, it climbs 54% in bull markets and 39% in bear markets. Wow! This finding suggests a trading opportunity: Buy long after the stock bottoms. That sounds easy but is difficult to do. The Sample Trade in this chapter explores such a trade.

▓ Tour

What does the typical pattern look like? Figure 51.1 shows an example of a short sale opportunity we all would like to have. The stock was on a tear beginning in the summer of 1996 (not shown) and an almost straight-line run since October 1997. It made a broadening top pattern beginning in April, one I hesitate to show because of the amount of white space (it would look better if the mid-May peak touched the top trend line). Nothing is perfect in the chart pattern business, and it was not until prices peaked in June that the topping pattern appeared drawn properly. There were no hints of a coming decline.

Traders pulled the rug from under the home furnishings retailer when it reported same-store sales below expectations. The stock gapped down and then tried to close the gap, but failed. Price reached bottom in early September.

▓ Identification Guidelines

How do you identify a 3S pattern? By listening to the financial news. On a periodic basis, usually monthly but sometimes quarterly, many retailers disclose their sales numbers. Watch what happens next. If the stock makes a big up move, that is the kind of 3S

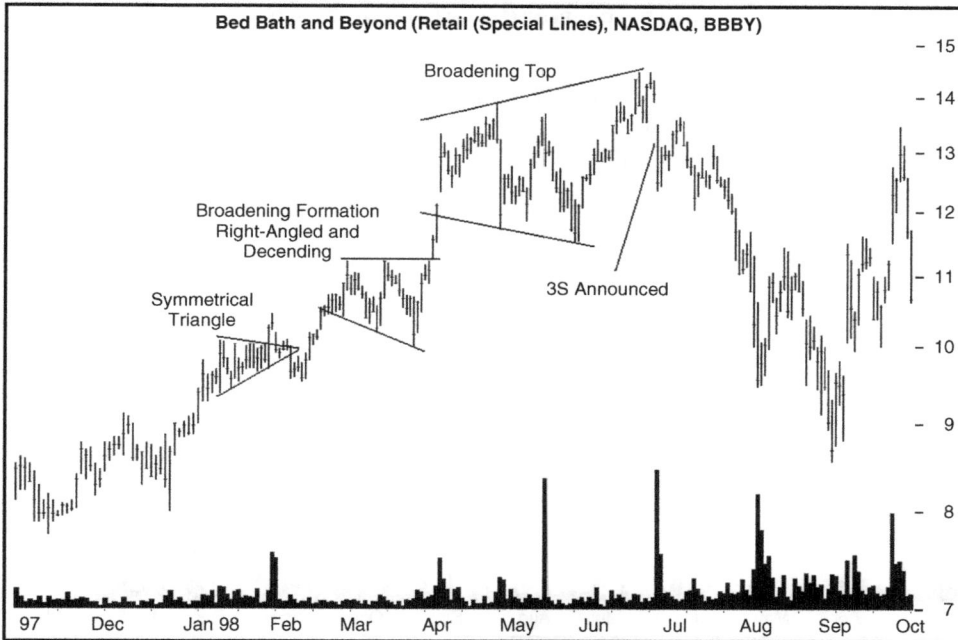

FIGURE 51.1 Price Declines When the Stock Reacts to the Bad Same-Store Sales Announcement.

pattern discussed in Chapter 52. If nothing exciting happens that day or the next, then the market is ignoring the result or is not excited enough to move the stock. However, if price drops, sometimes gapping down, or if it drops the next day (if the market was closed during the announcement), then that qualifies as a 3S pattern based on bad news.

Figure 51.2 shows another example of the 3S pattern. From the quarterly sales report in March 2000 (not shown), the retailer was doing well peddling camcorders, satellite systems, and televisions. The following quarter, ending in June, the company said sales of digital products were still strong, but why was the stock declining? Was this a case of the fundamentals chasing the technicals?

In September, the company reported that sales were sluggish but in line with consensus estimates. The stock gapped down 14% on the news but within about a week, it was trading at the same price, completing a pullback. Whew! A close call, some thought. Not if you owned the stock. Pullbacks and throwbacks are the last chance to get out of or into a trade, respectively. The figure shows what happened. From the close at 47.33 the day before the announcement, the stock dropped to 14, a decline of 70%. Notice the September support set up by the apex of the symmetrical triangle.

How do you identify a 3S pattern? Table 51.1 lists the characteristics I used.

Announcement. Many retailers announce their sales numbers either monthly or quarterly. I read about the numbers in the financial press or hear about it on the nightly television news broadcast. The Internet is also a good source for 3S news.

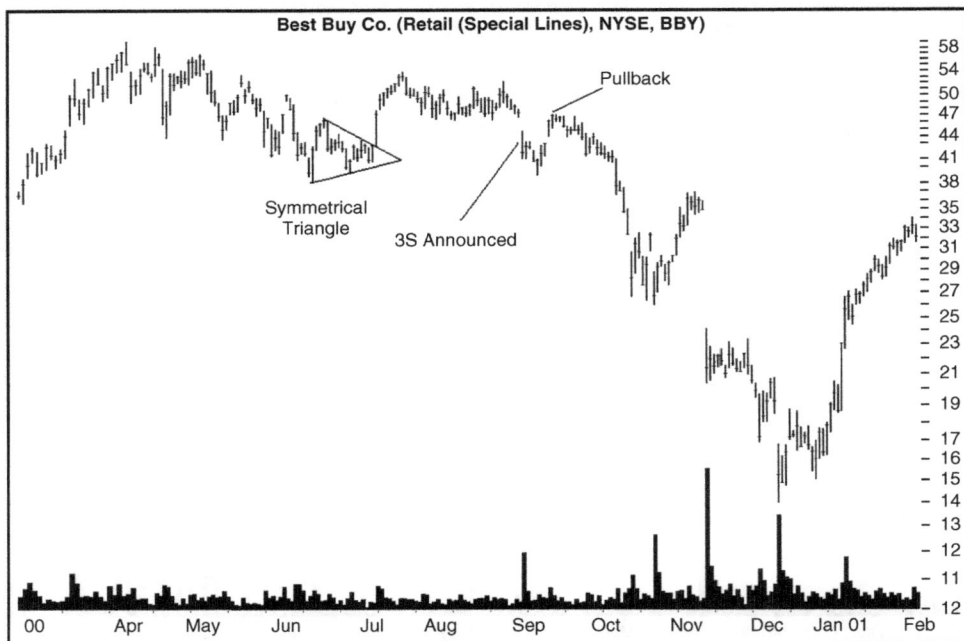

FIGURE 51.2 Price Completed a Pullback before Tumbling.

TABLE 51.1	Identification Characteristics
Characteristic	Discussion
Announcement	The company announces monthly or quarterly same-store sales numbers.
Large price decline	Price gaps downward or makes a large down move that day or the next. The daily trading range must be at least as large as the monthly average or it must gap lower.
Downward breakout	A breakout occurs when price closes below the intraday low posted on the day of the announcement.
Volume	Usually heavy.

Large price decline. The numbers may appear acceptable, but it is the perception of the market that is important. A same-store sales decline is never good, but if the market expected worse, look for the stock price to rise. However, if same-store sales were supposed to be 5% and they came in at 3%, that may well send the stock plunging. Expect the unexpected.

I computed the average trading range for the prior month and compared that to the range on the day of, or the day after, the announcement. If the intraday range was wider than the average, then I included the pattern in the study. I also included patterns that gapped downward on the announcement day, regardless of their intraday trading range.

For identification, look for a large price decline the day the announcement comes or the next day (in case of closed markets or if word is slow to disperse). Sometimes, a price gap occurs like that shown in Figures 51.1 and 51.2. I looked for gaps and large price moves but ignored everything else including decreasing same-store sales numbers. Gaps and large price moves mean a more promising (better performing) trade.

Downward breakout. What is a breakout? It is a close below the intraday low posted on the day of the announcement. Even if the stock gaps downward, I ignore it if the breakout was upward.

Volume. Expect heavy volume, volume that is above the average posted over the prior month.

▓ Focus on Failures

What can go wrong with the 3S pattern? Figure 51.3 shows the first example of a poor performer. At the time, the company was named Consolidated Stores and it reported same-store sales as those open for at least 2 years. In mid-July, the company said total sales for June were up a whopping 69%, but same-store sales were up just 3.4%. In the prior 8 weeks, sales were up 2.6% and year-to-date, up 3.9%.

What happened to the stock? It made a large down move that day and the next, pulled back to where it was trading before the announcement, and then formed an ascending scallop. Notice how price stops declining at the top of the March gap. Coincidence? Perhaps, but gaps set up support and resistance zones.

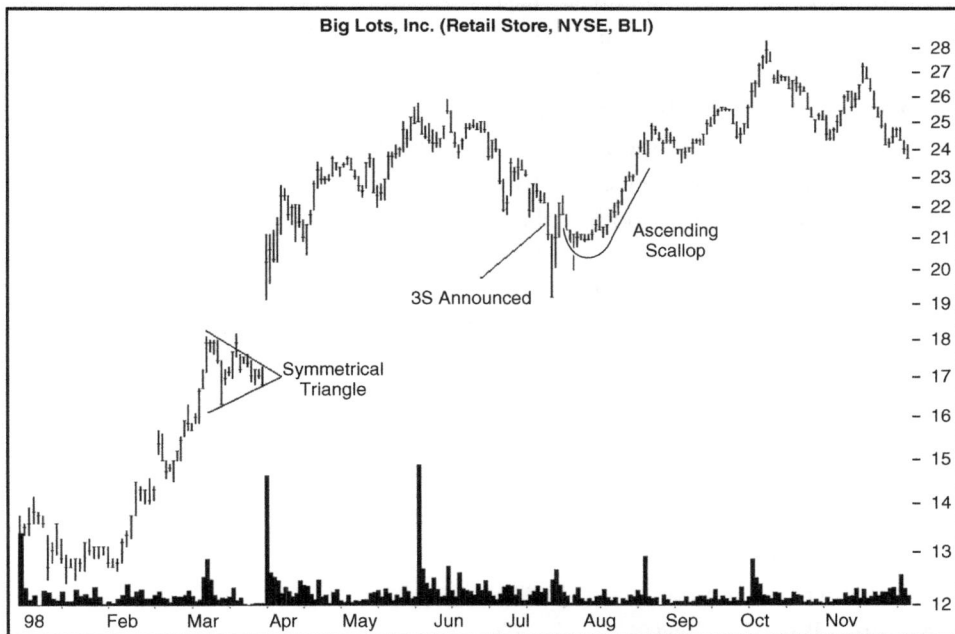

FIGURE 51.3   Price Dips on Release of Same-Store Sales. Price Quickly Recovers and Makes New Highs.

■ Statistics

Table 51.2 shows general statistics for the 3S pattern based on bad same-store sales.

Number of formations. I looked at all the retailers in my database of 500+ stocks and found only 28 with 3S patterns starting from early 1995. As you might guess, my data is limited and so are the samples. I found 258 valid patterns in bull markets, but just 78 in bear markets. Remember, these patterns all have intraday price ranges that are wider than the 1-month average. If I allowed all 3S patterns in, the performance would be worse, but I would have substantially more samples.

Reversal or continuation. Most of the 3S patterns I looked at acted as consolidations or continuations of the prevailing price trend. That finding means price dropped into the pattern and broke out downward. Reversals performed marginally better than continuations.

Average decline. The average decline, measured from the low price on the day of the announcement to the ultimate low, was 12% and 14% for bull and bear markets, respectively. If you used the closing price the day before the announcement to include any price gap that the announcement caused, the average decline measured a healthier 15% for bull markets and 17% for bear markets.

Declines over 45%. Just 1% of the 3S patterns declined more than 45%, so if you are expecting a large loss, you should look for another type of pattern to trade. In other words, consider taking profits quickly or there may be no profits to take.

Change after trend ends. Once price reaches the ultimate low, it soars 54% in a bull market and 39% in a bear market, on average. Thus, if you can tell when the trend ends—even if you are late—buy the stock. Use stops to protect your investment against adverse price moves.

Busted pattern performance. Busted patterns rise between 22% and 38%, depending on market conditions. Do not expect those types of gains in your trading as they are best-case values measured from the low after the breakout to the ultimate high. You probably will miss both of those turning points.

TABLE 51.2 General Statistics		
Description	Bull Market	Bear Market
Number of formations	258	78
Reversal (R) or continuation (C)	106 R, 152 C	36 R, 42 C
R/C performance	12% R, 11% C	16% R, 13% C
Average decline	12%	14%
Declines over 45%	3 or 1%	1 or 1%
Change after trend ends	54%	39%
Busted pattern performance	38%	22%
Standard & Poor's 500 change	−2%	−9%
Days to ultimate low	21	23

Note: Minus sign means decline.

TABLE 51.3	Failure Rates	
Maximum Price Decline (%)	Bull Market	Bear Market
5 (breakeven)	68 or 26%	21 or 27%
10	135 or 52%	34 or 43%
15	177 or 69%	44 or 56%
20	201 or 78%	57 or 73%
25	223 or 86%	63 or 81%
30	234 or 91%	69 or 88%
35	244 or 95%	74 or 95%
50	256 or 99%	78 or 100%
75	258 or 100%	78 or 100%
Over 75	258 or 100%	78 or 100%

Standard & Poor's 500 change. The S&P 500 index declined in both markets, by 2% in a bull market and 9% in a bear market over the same periods as the 3S patterns declined an average of 12% and 14%, respectively.

Days to ultimate low. How long does it take to reach the ultimate low? About 3 weeks. This information helps traders gauge the number of trades they can expect. A pattern that reaches the ultimate low in a week is valued more than one that takes a month (providing they decline the same amount).

Table 51.3 lists failure rates for this chapter's 3S pattern. In bull markets, the failure rate starts high, at 26%, and climbs rapidly. Half the patterns decline less than 10% after the breakout. Bear markets start out worse, with 27% failing to decline more than 5%. However, they perform better than patterns in a bull market because the failure rates are not as steep, but they are still much too high.

What do the numbers mean? Even though the announcement of poor same-store sales is a bummer, it appears that the impact is not as severe as one would expect. In other words, price does not decline far after the breakout. This finding suggests a quick trade. The failure rates also suggest trading the 3S patterns in a bear market as they have lower failure rates.

Table 51.4 shows breakout- and postbreakout-related statistics for this 3S pattern.

Formation end to breakout. It takes about 4 to 5 days before price closes below the intraday low posted on the announcement day. This finding is longer than I expected, so I checked the median time and found it to be 1 day in a bear market and 4 days in a bull market. Apparently, a few patterns pull the average upward.

Yearly position. Where in the yearly price range does the breakout from a 3S pattern appear most often? The answer depends on the market. In bull markets, the pattern appears near the yearly high and low most often, but in a bear market, patterns in the middle range appear more often.

Yearly position, performance. Mapping performance over the yearly price range, we find that the best performing 3S patterns have breakouts in the center third of the range.

TABLE 51.4	Breakout and Postbreakout Statistics	
Description	Bull Market	Bear Market
Formation end to breakout	5 days	4 days
Percentage of breakouts occurring near the 12-month low (L), center (C), or high (H)	L38%, C24%, H38%	L22%, C41%, H37%
Percentage decline for each 12-month lookback period	L12%, C14%, H10%	L13%^{a}, C16%, H12%^{a}
Pullbacks	53%	60%
Average time to pullback ends	11 days	11 days
Average decline for patterns with a pullback	10%	13%
Average decline for patterns without a pullback	13%	16%

^{a}Fewer than 30 samples.

One explanation for this finding is that companies with stocks making new highs are performing well. Then gray clouds gather and the stock begins easing down as if seeking shelter from the storm. Same-store sales come in below plan, and the stock tumbles in earnest. More 3S patterns occur, driving the stock into the middle range. As the stock nears the yearly low, things begin turning up and fewer 3S patterns appear. The stock recovers and starts the cycle again.

Pullbacks. How often does a pullback occur? Over half the time—53% and 60% for bull and bear markets, respectively. Thus, check for underlying support before you short a stock. A nearby support zone may cause a pullback. When a pullback occurs, it takes 11 days for price to return to the breakout price.

Pullbacks hurt performance. For example, patterns in a bull market showing a pullback decline 10%; those without a pullback decline 13%, on average.

I think of these results in terms of momentum. Price drops and downward momentum builds, but when a pullback occurs, the direction shifts upward, killing the downward momentum. When the pullback completes, the downward momentum resumes but with less enthusiasm. Thus, price tends not to decline as far after a pullback.

Table 51.5 shows a frequency distribution of the days to the ultimate low. Most of the bull market 3S patterns (50%) reach the low in less than a week. Price in over half (57%, the sum of the 7- and 14-day columns) of the bear market patterns trend upward within 2 weeks. Thus, expect your 3S pattern to bottom quickly. This finding suggests that the 3S pattern is most useful for swing traders.

Notice the bump in columns 42 and 49, bear market. It suggests price shows a tendency to rise 6 to 7 weeks after the breakout. Thus, be prepared to take profits then.

TABLE 51.5	Frequency Distribution of Days to Ultimate Low										
Days:	7	14	21	28	35	42	49	56	63	70	>70
Bear market	45%	12%	9%	1%	3%	9%	10%	0%	4%	0%	8%
Bull market	50%	12%	8%	6%	7%	2%	1%	2%	5%	1%	6%

TABLE 51.6	Size and Volume Statistics		
Description		Bull Market	Bear Market
Tall pattern performance		−14%	−15%
Short pattern performance		−10%	−14%
Median height as a percentage of breakout price		5.61%	5.32%
Heavy announcement day volume, performance		−12%	−15%
Light announcement day volume, performance		−12%	−12%[a]

Note: Minus sign means decline.

[a] Fewer than 30 samples.

Table 51.6 shows size and volume statistics for the 3S pattern.

Height. Tall patterns perform better than short ones. For example, in a bull market, short patterns dropped 10% but tall ones dropped 14%. I measured height by computing the pattern height on the announcement day (intraday low subtracted from the high) and divided the difference by the breakout price (which is the intraday low for this pattern). Then I sorted the results and chose the median as the divider between short and tall. Stick with trading tall patterns.

Announcement day volume. I compared the average volume for the month leading to the pattern with the volume on the day of the announcement. For those patterns with announcement day volume above the average, price declined 15% after the breakout in a bear market. Those patterns with below average volume suffered postbreakout declines averaging 12%. The results were unchanged for patterns in a bull market.

■ Trading Tactics

Table 51.7 shows trading tactics for the 3S pattern that forms in reaction to the announcement of bad same-store sales.

Measure rule. Use the measure rule to set a price target for the stock. Using announcement day prices, compute the pattern height by subtracting the intraday low from the high, and then subtract the difference from the intraday low. The result

TABLE 51.7	Identification Characteristics
Trading Tactic	Explanation
Measure rule	Used to predict a target price. Using the day of the announcement, compute the height by subtracting the intraday low from the intraday high. Subtract the difference from the intraday low for the target price. Price reaches the target 68% of the time.
Sell signal, sell short	Sell a long holding or sell short when price closes below the formation low, especially if the stock has been underperforming (prior 3S patterns, in a price downtrend).
Buy signal, cover the short	Buy once price bottoms and the stock begins recovering.

is the target price. Over two-thirds of the patterns decline to the target price or lower, but getting there may be bumpy. It may be that your pattern falls in the other 32%, so protect your wallet with stops.

For example, suppose a stock shows a 3S pattern with an intraday high of 10 and a low of 8. To what price may the stock decline after the downward breakout? Answer: 6. Find the pattern height (10 − 8 or $2). Subtract the difference (2) from the intraday low (8) to get the price target. If the result ever goes negative, then ignore it. Chances are your stock will not go bankrupt.

If the decline seems unusually large, check Table 51.3. In this example, the $2 decline represents a 25% drop from 8. What are the chances that the stock will fall that far? According to Table 51.3, 86% of the stocks in a bull market and 81% in a bear market have 3S patterns that *fail* to drop at least 25%. Thus, the table suggests the stock will *not* decline to 6.

Sell signal, sell short. If you own the stock, do nothing until the breakout. That is when price closes below the intraday low posted on the announcement day. If a breakout occurs, consider selling immediately. It may be that your stock decides to decline by 40%. Why chance it? Other 3S patterns may be coming in the following quarters, too. Weak same-store sales are like dogs digging through your trash. The day after you take the trash out, you find it strewn over your lawn. The dogs keep coming back. One 3S pattern often follows another.

Here is a caution for those who want to short a stock showing a 3S pattern: The pattern is not a good performer (high failure rate and low profit potential), so you should have solid reasons for shorting the stock. Just because the stock has a 3S pattern with a downward breakout is not enough. Is price falling? Is the announcement day volume high to propel price downward? Is the intraday trading range unusually large—well above the 1-month average? Is support nearby, suggesting a pullback? Check the fundamentals.

Buy signal, cover the short. If you can tell when the stock has bottomed, then buy. If you sold the stock short, cover your short or use protective stops to take you out when price reverses. For most 3S patterns, price will reach the ultimate low quickly, usually in a week or two (see Table 51.5).

■ Sample Trade

How do you profit from the information in this chapter? Consider Figure 51.4.

Sally is an experienced trader, but she is a shy, nonaggressive one. She will not short a stock because of the inherent risk involved. She saw the situation developing in Ross Stores and followed it closely, hoping she could profit from any trends.

In mid-October, a financial magazine reported that two insiders sold 70,000 shares in the company. For them, it was a good call as the stock tumbled. Earnings came out in mid-November and the market was not impressed: The stock continued down for a week and then recovered before sliding again in mid-December.

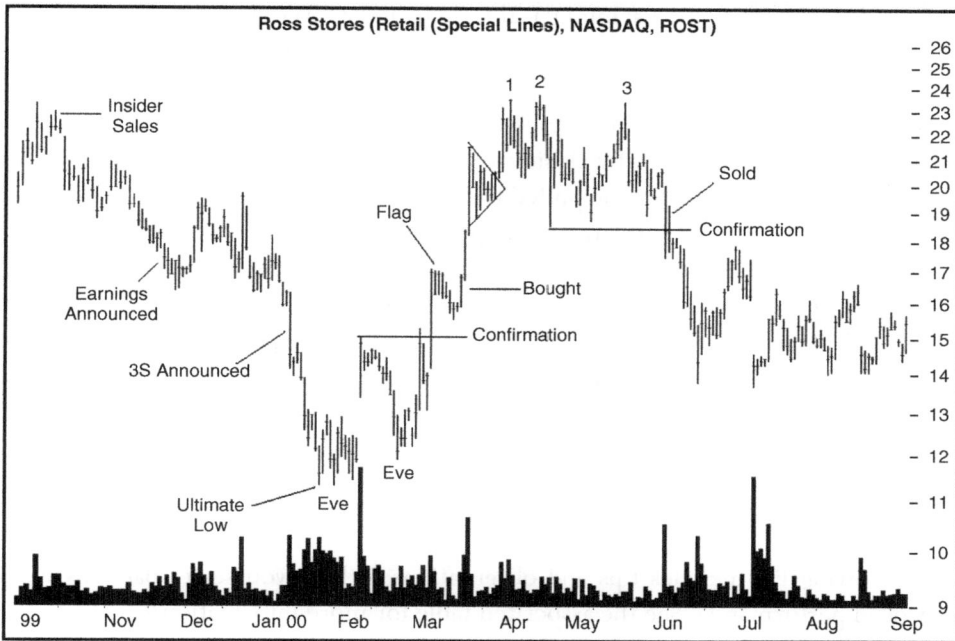

FIGURE 51.4 As Described in the Sample Trade, Sally Bought after the Eve & Eve Double Bottom Confirmed and Sold when the Triple Top Confirmed.

In early January, the newspaper said that same-store sales were flat. The stock tumbled almost 2 points on the news. It paused for 2 days and then closed lower on the third day, staging a downward breakout.

Eventually, the stock found footing in the new year at just above 11 (the ultimate low). Price consolidated at that level and then gapped upward on a good earnings forecast and a report that same-store sales were up 7% in January.

The rise was short-lived as price retraced almost all of its gain during the next 2 weeks. Price bottomed again, and it looked as if the stock was forming a double bottom. At that point, Sally started paying attention.

When price confirmed the double bottom by closing above the highest high between the two valleys, she got a quote on the stock and gasped. The stock was up several dollars over the prior day's close. She knows not to chase such quick moves, so she watched from the sidelines as the stock retraced its gains, forming a flag pattern.

Using the measure rule for flags, she computed the target price. From the start of the uptrend in February at 11.90 (the low of the second Eve bottom) to the flagpole top at 17.09, the pole height was 5.19. The bottom of the flag was at 15.53, giving a target price of 20.72, if everything worked as expected.

The day price climbed rapidly out of the flag, she caught the up move in midstream and bought, receiving a fill at 16.40. Since flags are half-staff patterns, she expected price to climb to the 20.72 target.

Just 2 days later, price hit the target when it reached a peak of 21.53. If she sold then, she would have made 31%. She did not sell. She hoped for better.

Price backpedaled into a symmetrical triangle in late March and then busted out upward. Was it time to sell now? Yes. Did she sell? No. Why not? When asked, she just shrugged her shoulders and then mumbled something about greed.

A wake-up call came when the stock triple topped (peaks 1, 2, and 3). When the pattern confirmed on June 1 by closing below the low posted in the triple top, she decided to sell. The next day she pulled the trigger and received a fill at 18.60. Her gain was 13%. If she sold at the triple top peak, she would have banked a tasty 45%.

Did she do anything wrong? She used two chart patterns as entry and exit signals. She bought in on the day of the flag's breakout and sold the day after the triple top confirmed, slightly above the confirmation price. In that respect, she did fine. However, if she placed an order to sell at the flag's target price, she would have more than doubled her profit. Greed, in this case, was her mistake.

■ For Best Performance

The following list includes tips and observations to help you select patterns with improved performance. See the associated table for more information.

- Use the identification guidelines to select a 3S pattern. Pay special attention to the large intraday trading range—above the 1-month average—Table 51.1.

- Reversals perform marginally better than continuations—Table 51.2.

- Do not expect a large decline (over 45%) from this pattern; just 1% decline that far—Table 51.2.

- Select patterns in a bear market for the lowest failure rates—Table 51.3.

- The best performing patterns occur in the middle of the yearly price range—Table 51.4.

- Pullbacks occur over half the time, and performance suffers when they do happen—Table 51.4.

- Price usually takes less than 2 weeks before bottoming. In a bear market, price may rise in weeks 6 and 7—Table 51.5.

- Select tall patterns—Table 51.6.

CHAPTER 52

Same-Store Sales, Good

From Thomas N. Bulkowski, *Encyclopedia of Chart Patterns,* Second Edition (Hoboken, New Jersey: John Wiley & Sons, 2005), Chapter 61.

Learning Objective Statements

- Interpret potential price moves based on the patterns described in this chapter
- Calculate potential price targets
- Evaluate price levels for potential support or resistance
- Identify and interpret signals from various oscillators and technical studies in conjunction with the event-based patterns listed in these chapters

Results Snapshot

Upward Breakouts

Event	A retailer announces surprisingly good same-store sales numbers and the stock moves up smartly that day or the next, but soon tumbles.	
Reversal or continuation	Short-term bullish continuation	
	Bull Market	**Bear Market**
Performance rank	4 out of 6	4 out of 5
Break-even failure rate	20%	27%
Average rise	23%	14%
Change after trend ends	−28%	−31%
Volume trend	Usually heavy on the announcement day	
Throwbacks	59%	70%
Percentage meeting price target	82%	72%
Surprising findings	Patterns near the yearly low perform better. Tall patterns perform better than short ones.	
Synonyms	Comparable store sales, existing store sales	
See also	Same-Store Sales, Bad	

If you follow the retailing industry, you know about same-store sales (3S) numbers. Some analysts call them comparable or existing store sales. They are sales from stores open longer than a year (but sometimes 2 years). The difference between 3S and regular sales is store openings. If a retailer opens new stores without closing old ones, expect sales volume to rise, perhaps substantially. Thus, year-to-year comparisons for fast growing retailers are difficult. Using 3S, the comparison is easier. If same-store sales rise by 8% this quarter compared to the same quarter last year, then that is better than if the retailer added 25% more outlets and *total* sales climbed by 8%. The sales climb might be due entirely to the new store sales volume even as existing stores suffered. Thus, same-store sales numbers are important to investors.

The Results Snapshot paints a picture of carnage. When a retailer announces monthly or quarterly 3S, the stock price can move up, down, or go nowhere. This chapter excludes the latter two possibilities. In fact, I only include above average price moves on the day of the announcement or the next day, or those with a discernible price gap on the announcement day. Thus, this chapter looks at *positive surprises*. The reason for using only positive surprises is to find tradable patterns. If a 3S day looks like any other day, do we care to trade the event?

Since I only included patterns with upward breakouts, the 3S pattern usually acts as a short-term continuation of the prevailing bullish price trend. The break-even failure rate is very high, at 20% in a bull market and a massive 27% in a bear market, with 20% being the threshold for awful. By comparison, well-behaved bullish chart patterns have break-even failure rates in the single digits. The average rise is a weak 23% and 14% in bull and bear markets, respectively, as measured from the breakout price.

Say you buy a stock showing a 3S pattern. What happens? Price rises, sure, but only for a few weeks. Half the patterns reach the ultimate high in 2 to 4 weeks. Then what happens? The drop is breathtaking—a 28% drop in a bull market and 31% in a bear market. Do you want to risk that size loss? If you are an experienced trader who loves risk, a 31% decline is mouthwatering. Short the stock and I explain what to look for later.

■ Tour

Figure 52.1 shows an example of a 3S pattern formed in response to better than expected same-store sales numbers. In early December, Circuit City reported November same-store sales were down 2% from the prior year and down 4% for the quarter. The stock gapped up on the news, suggesting that as bad as the numbers were, traders expected worse. Bad news was good news.

The day before the announcement, the stock closed at 18.69. It formed a shark-32 pattern, which looks like a midget symmetrical triangle, and then continued rising. Eventually, price topped out at 31.40, for a gain of 68%. If you exclude the gap and measure from the breakout price (the intraday high on the announcement day), then the rise is still a robust 45%.

That is how the 3S pattern *should* work.

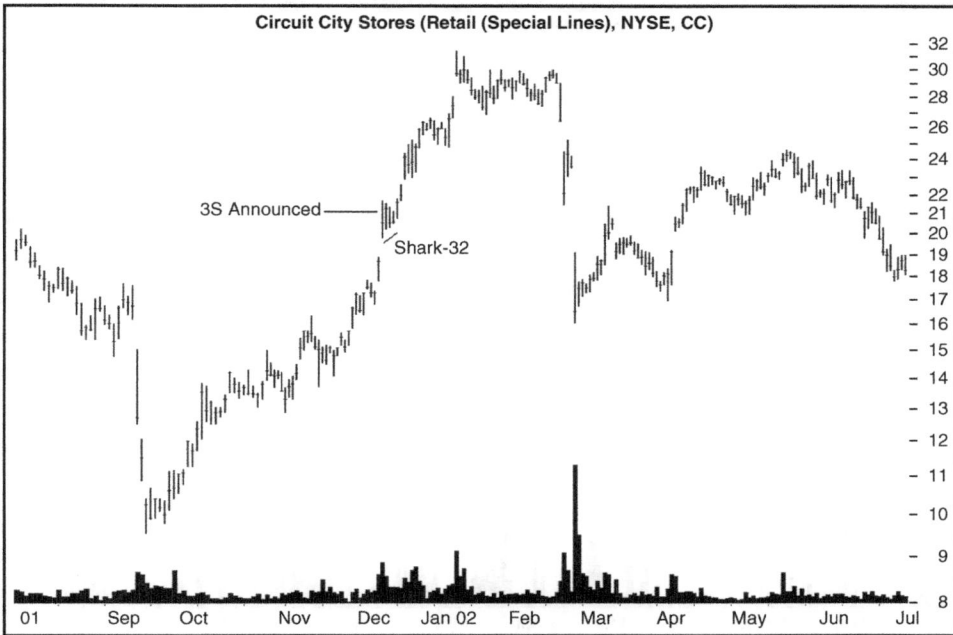

FIGURE 52.1   The Stock Gapped Up on News That Same-Store Sales for November Were Down 2%.

▓ Identification Guidelines

Identifying 3S patterns is simple; you just read the newspaper or listen to the financial news on television. On the day of the announcement, look for a large price swing (a wide trading range). Prices should move up, perhaps even gap upward. If they do not move much or if the trading range is unremarkable, then keep looking. Figure 52.2 shows three examples of good patterns.

In the first two cases, the daily low is near the prior day's high. In the August example, price gaps upward. We are looking for good news that surprises the market, boosting the price. How you choose to define a *large* move is up to you. I included days that gapped upward or had a large trading range that day or the following day. Why the next day? Because the markets may be closed during the announcement and any price move would occur the next day. If the stock did not react to the announcement, I ignored it. Table 52.1 lists what to look for.

Announcement. I learn of same-store sales announcements from the newspaper. Occasionally they appear on television, especially for the larger retailers. The Internet is also a source of 3S news.

Large price range. I grabbed all the 3S patterns I could find and then filtered them by comparing their intraday trading range (high minus the low) to the 1-month average. If the announcement day or the following day showed an above average trading range, or if prices gapped upward when trading began, then I accepted the pattern. Otherwise, I discarded it. After all, if the news is not a surprise to the market, ignore the announcement and keep looking for another 3S pattern.

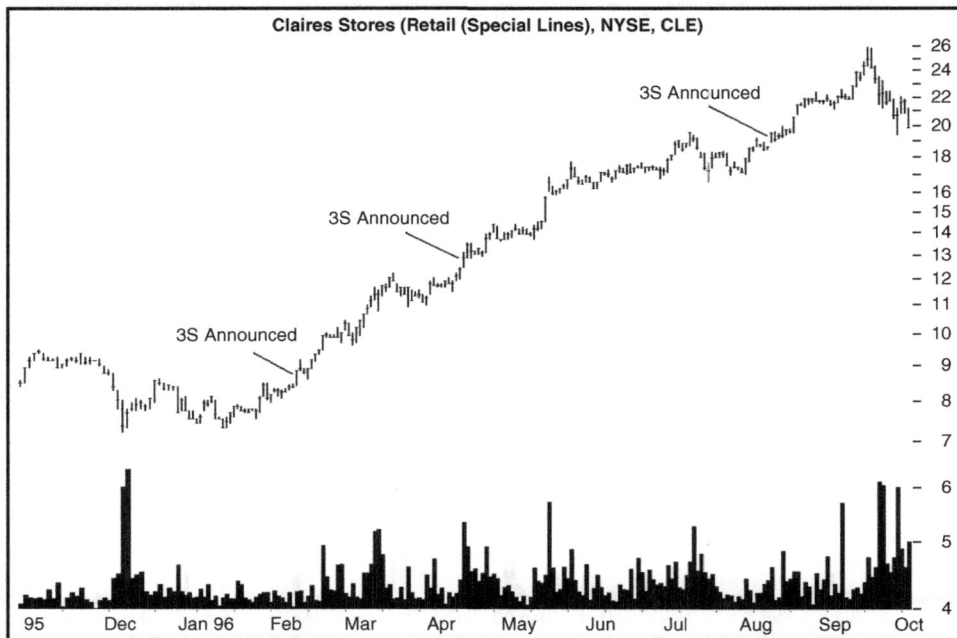

FIGURE 52.2 Price Moves Up or Gaps Up on Same-Store Sales News.

TABLE 52.1 Identification Characteristics

Characteristic	Discussion
Announcement	A retailer announces same-store sales.
Large price range	The intraday price range on the announcement day or the next day must be wider than the 1-month average, or price must gap upward when trading begins.
Upward breakout	In following days, price must close above the intraday high posted on the day of the announcement. Ignore downward breakouts.
Volume	Expect high volume on the announcement day.

If you filter the announcement day height as 2 or 3 times the 1-month average, performance improves (the rise to the ultimate high) and the failure rates decrease.

Upward breakout. I only looked at upward breakouts. I discuss downward breakouts in Chapter 51, "Same-Store Sales, Bad."

Volume. This is not a rule but a guideline: Volume is usually above average on the day of the sales announcement.

■ Focus on Failures

What can go wrong with the 3S pattern? In a moment, we look at the statistics, and they suggest that this is a risky pattern for traders. Why? Because price often returns to the breakout price and continues lower. Figure 52.3 shows an example.

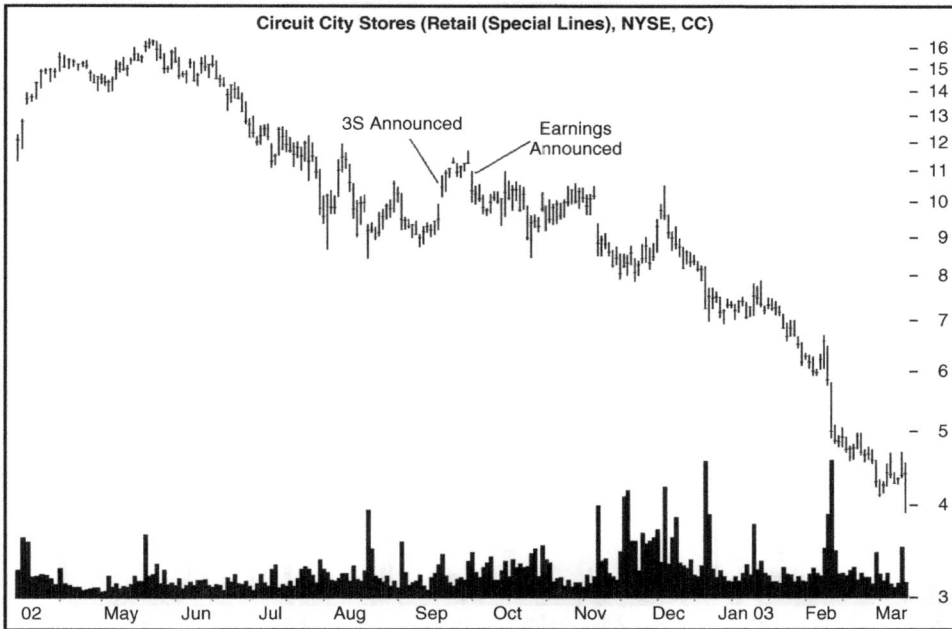

FIGURE 52.3 Price Trends Down Leading to the Pattern, Gaps Upward, Curls Over, and Drops.

Price was trending down leading to the pattern, so that trend is the first clue that you should trade this pattern with caution. If you obey the "trade with the trend" folklore, then you would short the stock after the announcement once a downturn becomes clear.

In early September, an announcement said that same-store sales were up 10% and earnings were in line with consensus estimates. Good news! Prices gapped upward. In following days, the upward momentum slowed. The saying "buy on the rumor, sell on the news" gripped traders, and price gapped down after the release of earnings.

Figure 52.4 shows another cautionary tale and a typical example of how the 3S pattern behaves: Price jumps up and peaks quickly, then tumbles. That happened in the March 3S pattern. Six insiders sold shares right at the March peak, and then the stock dropped to a low of 18.70 in April for a peak to trough decline of 24%, a large giveback if you owned the stock.

The June announcement of 12% same-store sales powered the stock up the price mountain. This time, nearly a dozen insiders dumped the stock. Another sales announcement occurred in July, and it was a surprise because price gapped upward. Price summits at 27.15 and then slips on the icy slope, starting an avalanche. Price snowballs downward until it rolls into base camp at 14 and change.

The point of these figures is a simple one. Pay attention. If price starts heading down, sell.

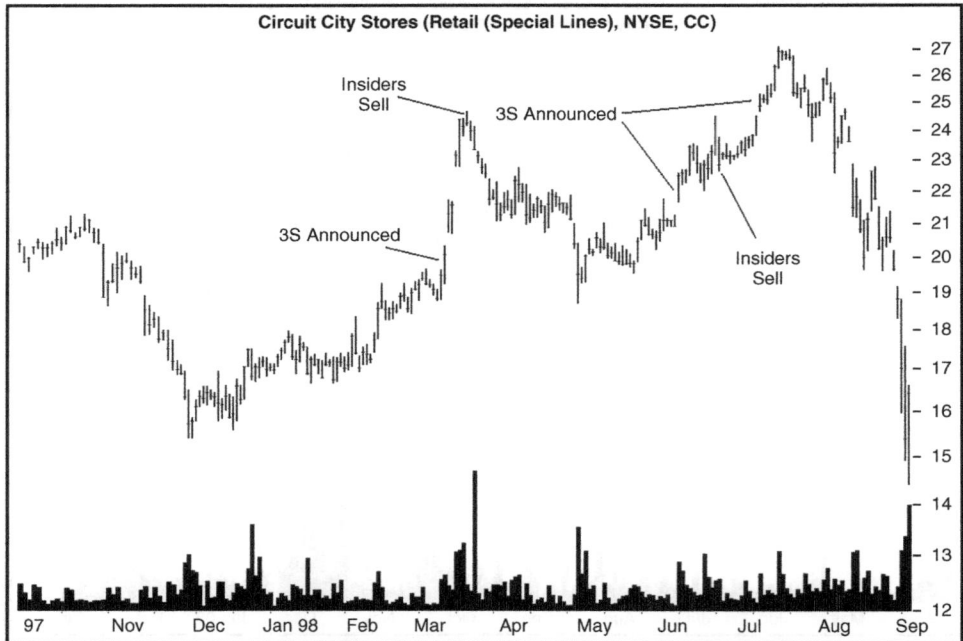

Circuit City Stores (Retail (Special Lines), NYSE, CC)

FIGURE 52.4 The 3S Pattern Shows a Tendency for a Quick Rise Followed by a Massive Decline within a Month.

Statistics

The following tables use data from over 500 stocks boiled down to just 29 retailers from early 1995 to late 2003. I tossed many of the patterns because they did not obey the identification guidelines shown in Table 52.1. Table 52.2 shows general performance statistics for the 3S patterns based on surprisingly good same-store sales.

Number of formations. I found enough patterns (354) to split them into bull and bear markets. Still, the 82 I found in bear markets is a bit slim, so remember that as we review the statistics.

TABLE 52.2 General Statistics

Description	Bull Market	Bear Market
Number of formations	272	82
Reversal (R) or continuation (C)	100 R, 172 C	28 R, 54 C
R/C performance	28% R, 20% C	14% R, 14% C
Average rise	23%	14%
Declines over 45%	59 or 22%	6 or 7%
Change after trend ends	−28%	−31%
Busted pattern performance	−20%	−27%
Standard & Poor's 500 change	7%	1%
Days to ultimate high	64	41

Note: Minus sign means decline.

Reversal or continuation. The vast majority of patterns acted as continuations of the prevailing price trend. That is, most had price rising into the pattern, and I only accepted those with upward breakouts. In a bull market, reversals vastly outperformed continuations, 28% to 20%.

Average rise. The average rise was an anemic 23% in bull markets and 14% in bear markets. Why the blood loss? Because I measured the rise from the formation high to the ultimate high. Thus, not included in the results were price gaps that sometimes occurred on the announcement day. Including the gaps, the rise measured 27% in a bull market and 18% in a bear market (from the prior close to the ultimate high). Those percentages are still below the average rise for all chart pattern types. Thus, no matter how long your ruler is, this pattern does not measure up.

Rises over 45%. In a bull market, 22% of the patterns rise more than 45%, but just 7% in a bear market rise over 45%. Both rates are small, suggesting that this pattern may lead you to poverty, not profit.

Change after trend ends. Once price reaches the ultimate high, it drops between 28% and 31%, on average. This finding shows how well you might do if you trade perfectly after a 3S pattern completes. Since this is a best-case scenario, your results will likely be lower.

Busted pattern performance. If prices rise less than 5% after the breakout, price then tumbles between 20% and 27%, depending on market conditions. Since busted patterns are easier to spot than trend changes, this characteristic shows how well you might do when shorting the pattern. Again, the results are best case, measured from the ultimate high after the breakout to the ultimate low. Your results will likely be less. I suggest you short after price closes below the low in the 3S pattern. That way you can be sure of a trend change, but use stops just in case.

Standard & Poor's 500 change. The S&P 500 index climbed an average of 7% and 1% in bull and bear markets, respectively, as measured from the 3S pattern's breakout date to the ultimate high date.

Days to ultimate high. How long did it take price to reach the ultimate high? About 2 months (64 days) in a bull market and about 6 weeks (41 days) in a bear market. In both markets, this is quick because the rise is so small. The numbers show that the slope of the rise in both markets is about the same.

Table 52.3 shows the failure rates for the 3S pattern. The results are about what I expect for an event pattern. The failure rate starts out high, with 20% failing to rise more than 5%, and that is in a bull market! That percentage nearly doubles to 38% of the patterns failing to reach a 10% rise. Half top out before rising more than 15%. Thus the data suggest that if you trade this pattern, you should be prepared to take profits quickly. Better yet, do not trade this pattern at all. An earnings flag is a more promising event pattern, for example.

The bear market results are even worse. Over a quarter (27%) of the patterns rise just 5% before dropping. Over half (54%) do not jump over a 10% hurdle. The results are clear: If you trade this pattern at all, stick to bull markets because they have lower failure rates.

TABLE 52.3 **Failure Rates**

Maximum Price Rise (%)	Bull Market	Bear Market
5 (breakeven)	54 or 20%	22 or 27%
10	104 or 38%	44 or 54%
15	135 or 50%	52 or 63%
20	160 or 59%	59 or 72%
25	175 or 64%	66 or 80%
30	189 or 69%	70 or 85%
35	197 or 72%	72 or 88%
50	221 or 81%	76 or 93%
75	245 or 90%	80 or 98%
Over 75	272 or 100%	82 or 100%

Table 52.4 shows breakout- and postbreakout-related statistics.

Formation end to breakout. The average time from the formation end (the day of the announcement) to the breakout was 4 days. This finding makes sense as a breakout occurs when price closes above the intraday high posted on the announcement day. Thus, it should not take long to stage a breakout.

Yearly position. I split the yearly price range into thirds and counted how often the 3S pattern occurred in each third. The winner for both bull and bear markets is the highest third as almost half the patterns showed breakouts within a third of the yearly high.

Yearly position, performance. Mapping the performance over the yearly price range shows that 3S patterns with breakouts within a third of the yearly low rise 33% in bull markets and 26% in bear markets, on average. Those figures handily beat the 16% and 10% rises for the highest thirds of the yearly price range.

Throwbacks. A throwback occurs between 59% and 70% of the time in bull and bear markets, respectively. Figure 52.5 shows an example of a throwback after the July announcement. When a throwback occurs, it takes about 10 or 11 days for price to return to the breakout price.

TABLE 52.4 **Breakout and Postbreakout Statistics**

Description	Bull Market	Bear Market
Formation end to breakout	4 days	4 days
Percentage of breakouts occurring near the 12-month low (L), center (C), or high (H)	L27%, C25%, H47%	L17%, C41%, H41%
Percentage rise for each 12-month lookback period	L33%, C28%, H16%	L26%[a], C16%, H10%
Throwbacks	59%	70%
Average time to throwback ends	10 days	11 days
Average rise for patterns with a throwback	19%	14%
Average rise for patterns without a throwback	29%	14%[a]

[a] Fewer than 30 samples.

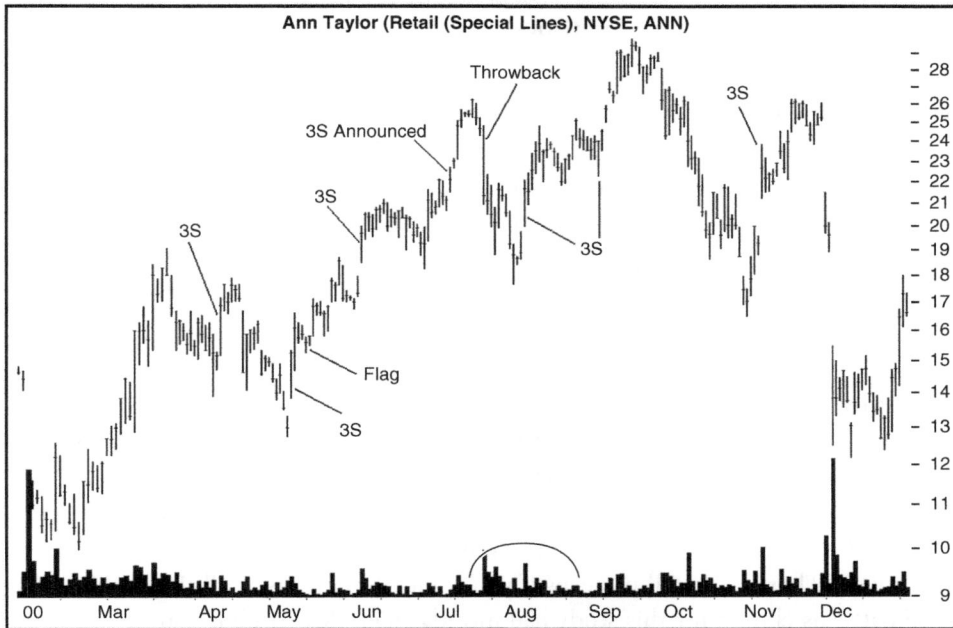

FIGURE 52.5 Price Rises for a Few Weeks and Then Tumbles, but Not Always.

Throwbacks hurt performance in a bull market. For example, those 3S patterns with a throwback showed rises averaging 19% in a bull market. Compared to an average rise of 29% for those patterns without a throwback, that is a huge difference. Thus, it pays to look for overhead resistance before placing a trade. That resistance level can repel price and cause a throwback.

Table 52.5 shows a frequency distribution of days to the ultimate high. I consider this table an important one because it gives you an insight into how long it will be before you may need to take profits. Since we are dealing with probabilities here, anything can happen, especially with low sample counts.

A substantial portion of the patterns reaches the ultimate high in the first week after a breakout (36% and 44% in bull and bear markets, respectively). In two weeks, 57% of the bear market patterns and 44% of the bull market ones have peaked.

Notice that 6% of the patterns top out 42 days after the breakout in a bear market. I have seen this behavior in other patterns. Thus, if you have a good trade going, watch for weakness about 6 weeks into the trade. It may be time to sell (bear market only).

TABLE 52.5 Frequency Distribution of Days to Ultimate High

Days:	7	14	21	28	35	42	49	56	63	70	>70
Bear market	44%	13%	7%	5%	2%	6%	1%	0%	2%	4%	15%
Bull market	36%	8%	4%	6%	6%	2%	3%	4%	1%	1%	29%

TABLE 52.6   Size and Volume Statistics

Description	Bull Market	Bear Market
Tall pattern performance	30%	18%
Short pattern performance	17%	11%
Median height as a percentage of breakout price	5.22%	5.68%
Heavy announcement day volume, performance	22%	14%
Light announcement day volume, performance	28%	13%[a]

[a] Fewer than 30 samples.

Table 52.6 shows size and volume statistics for this chapter's 3S pattern.

Height. I computed the height of the pattern by subtracting the intraday low from the high and dividing the result by the breakout price (which is the intraday high). Then I sorted the patterns into those shorter and taller than the median. Those 3S patterns taller than the median scored rises averaging 30% in a bull market and 18% in a bear market. Those below the median had rises averaging 17% and 11%, respectively. Thus, trade tall patterns if you trade 3S patterns at all. Remember that *all* 3S patterns chosen for this study had intraday high–low trading ranges above the 1-month average.

Announcement day volume. I compared the volume on the day of the same-store sales announcement with the average over the prior month. Those 3S patterns with above average volume in a bull market showed postbreakout gains averaging 22%. Those with below average volume showed gains averaging 28%. This finding is contrary to expectations, but sometimes patterns surprise me. The bear market trends show the expected results.

■ Trading Tactics

Table 52.7 shows trading tactics for the 3S pattern that forms in reaction to better-than-expected news of same-store sales.

TABLE 52.7 Trading Tactics	
Trading Tactic	**Explanation**
Measure rule	Used to predict a target price. Using the day of the announcement, compute the height by subtracting the daily low from the daily high. Add the result to the daily high for the target price. Price reaches the target 82% and 72% of the time in bull and bear markets, respectively.
Buy signal	Buy when price closes above the formation high and use a stoploss order to protect profits.
Sell signal	Expect to take profits in a week or two. Sell when price starts heading down.
Short the stock	After the upward breakout, price should reach the ultimate high quickly. Once they start heading back down, sell short. Watch for a throwback to stall price near support zones (including the announcement day gap). Protect your position with stops.

Measure rule. Consult Figure 52.5 to apply the measure rule. In the April announcement, price ranged from an intraday high of 17.17 to a low of 15.17, for a height of 2. Add the height to the high to get a target price of 19.17. In this example, price topped out 3 days later at a price of 17.92, well short of the target. However, in 82% of the bull market cases I looked at (and 72% in a bear market), price reached or exceeded the target before declining substantially (more than 20%).

Buy signal. The buy signal is a close above the intraday high posted on the announcement day. Since the 3S pattern consists of 1 day, it should not take long for price to wander off . . . typically 4 days (from Table 52.4). I do not recommend buying a stock just because it posted a good same-store sales number. Chances are the stock will tumble below the buy price in a few weeks.

Sell signal. When to sell is a difficult topic to cover in just a few paragraphs. Price should climb and then start rounding over in a week or two. When you sense the top has occurred and price is heading down, sell, or at least tighten up a stop. If price continues dropping, the stop will take you out. If you fail to sell, the decline after the ultimate high averages 28% in a bull market and 31% in a bear market, well above the 23% and 14% bull and bear rises posted by the 3S pattern. Thus, you give back all of your gains and more.

If you own the stock and the company announces good same-store sales, then watch the stock carefully. If it breaks out downward, consult Chapter 51 for more information. If it breaks out upward with gusto, watch for price to peak in a week or two and then start heading back down. If the stock peaks, the decline might be a massive one, so consider selling then. If you are in a raging bull market and you like the company, then hold the stock, especially if it is near the yearly low (the best performing 3S patterns start there). Eventually the stock is going to go down, just keep raising your stop until it takes you out.

Short the stock. Shorting a stock is a risky play as it depends on correctly predicting the top in a stock. If you suspect price has reached its high and is now heading down, consider selling short. Use a stop to protect yourself and have good reasons, based on both fundamental and technical analysis, before you place the trade. With this pattern, the top usually—but not always—comes quickly.

▥ Sample Trade

Look at Figure 52.5 for a sample trade. Ann Taylor announces same-store sales on a monthly basis. Thus, you have plenty of trading opportunities each year. The patterns marked on the chart are all valid 3S chart patterns. They have upward breakouts and they gap upward or show an above average trading range on the announcement day or the day after.

In the April announcement, price climbs and rounds over in a week and tumbles, ending well below the close the day before the announcement. That curling action is an example of a throwback. The May announcement shows an upward price gap, price rises for another day and then it retraces in a flag pattern. After the flag, price resumes its climb in a stair-step manner. The June 3S pattern is similar to April, only wider. Price rounds over and finds support at the announcement day gap. Most of the time (91%), price will stop before reaching the bottom of the gap.

The July pattern looks a lot like the April pattern, including the decline afterward. The August pattern behaves like the May pattern, with a rise-retrace climb. The September climb is a wider version of April, and so is the November pattern.

On this chart, we have five patterns that behave similarly (April, June, July, September, and November) with the other two showing extended rises. These patterns suggest that you avoid buying a stock expecting a long rise after a 3S pattern. A better plan is to actively trade the 3S pattern by buying quickly, riding it upward for a few days, and then selling. Alternatively, wait for price to top out and then short the stock.

Before you short a stock using the 3S pattern, use a sheet of paper to cover each figure in the chapter and slowly move it to the right. Decide where you would short a stock after the 3S pattern. Then move the sheet to the right and see where you would cover the short. How did you do?

Practice on stocks you follow to get comfortable with the idea. Hone your skills and test your trading technique on paper before trying it in the marketplace with real money. The 3S pattern is a risky way to short a stock, but it is easy to do. The tough part is making money doing it.

As I mentioned before, if you own the stock (a long holding) and it announces surprisingly good same-store sales, use a stop to protect yourself. Raise your stop until a declining price takes you out. All stocks tumble eventually, so a stop-loss order is a good way to lock in profits.

■ For Best Performance

The following list includes tips and observations to help you select patterns with improved performance. Refer to the associated table for more information on each tip.

- Use the identification guidelines to select a 3S pattern. Those with a wider daily trading range do better and show smaller failure rates—Table 52.1.

- Trade with the trend. Most patterns act as continuations of the upward price trend, but reversals outperform in a bull market—Table 52.2.

- Busted patterns may make shorting a 3S pattern easier—Table 52.2.

- Avoid this pattern in a bear market as 27% fail to rise more than 5% and 54% do not make a 10% rise—Table 52.3.

- Select 3S patterns that occur within a third of the yearly low—Table 52.4.

- Performance suffers after a throwback in a bull market, so check for overhead resistance before trading—Table 52.4.

- Be prepared to take profits quickly. Almost half (44%) of the bear market patterns reach the ultimate high in the first week—Table 52.5.

- Tall patterns perform better than short ones—Table 52.6.

CHAPTER 53

Stock Downgrades

From Thomas N. Bulkowski, *Encyclopedia of Chart Patterns*, Second Edition (Hoboken, New Jersey: John Wiley & Sons, 2005), Chapter 62.

Learning Objective Statements

- Interpret potential price moves based on the patterns described in this chapter
- Calculate potential price targets
- Evaluate price levels for potential support or resistance
- Identify and interpret signals from various oscillators and technical studies in conjunction with the event-based patterns listed in these chapters

Results Snapshot

Upward Breakouts

Event	A broker announces a downgrade and price rises for a week before tumbling.	
Reversal or continuation	Short-term bullish reversal	

	Bull Market	**Bear Market**
Performance rank	3 out of 6	3 out of 5
Break-even failure rate	25%	28%
Average rise	27%	14%
Change after trend ends	−30%	−34%
Volume trend	Usually heavy on the announcement day	
Throwbacks	49%	50%
Percentage meeting price target	71%	64%
Surprising findings	The best performers occur near the yearly low. When a throwback occurs, performance suffers. Tall patterns perform better than short ones.	

Downward Breakouts

Event	A broker announces a downgrade and price drops.	
Reversal or continuation	Short-term bearish continuation	

	Bull Market	**Bear Market**
Performance rank	2 out of 5	**1 out of 4**
Break-even failure rate	26%	17%

Average decline	14%	19%
Change after trend ends	50%	35%
Volume trend	Same as for upward breakouts	
Pullbacks	48%	45%
Percentage meeting price target	69%	72%
Surprising findings	The best performers occur near the yearly low. Pullbacks hurt performance. Tall patterns perform better than short ones.	

If you own a stock and a broker downgrades it, what happens? You get angry. But what happens to the stock price? In 39% of the cases I looked at, price climbs! However, the price usually did not climb for long and when it finally tumbled, it dropped at least 30%.

If you own a stock and a broker downgrades it, do you sell immediately or hold on and pray? On average, the stock price has already declined 71% and 67% of the way to the ultimate low in bull and bear markets, respectively. On a time basis, the results are similar, with 73% (bull market) and 71% (bear market) of the time gone before price bottoms. Chances are you would be selling near the bottom.

▨ Tour

Figure 53.1 shows a busy chart of announcements. A broker downgraded the stock in mid-March and what happened? Price *climbed* for 3 days and then moved horizontally. The downgrade was a good call, and it warned alert investors over a month before the stock started sliding. Less than 2 weeks later, another brokerage firm increased the price target for the stock (a bullish stance). Based on the resulting tumble, that increase was a bad call.

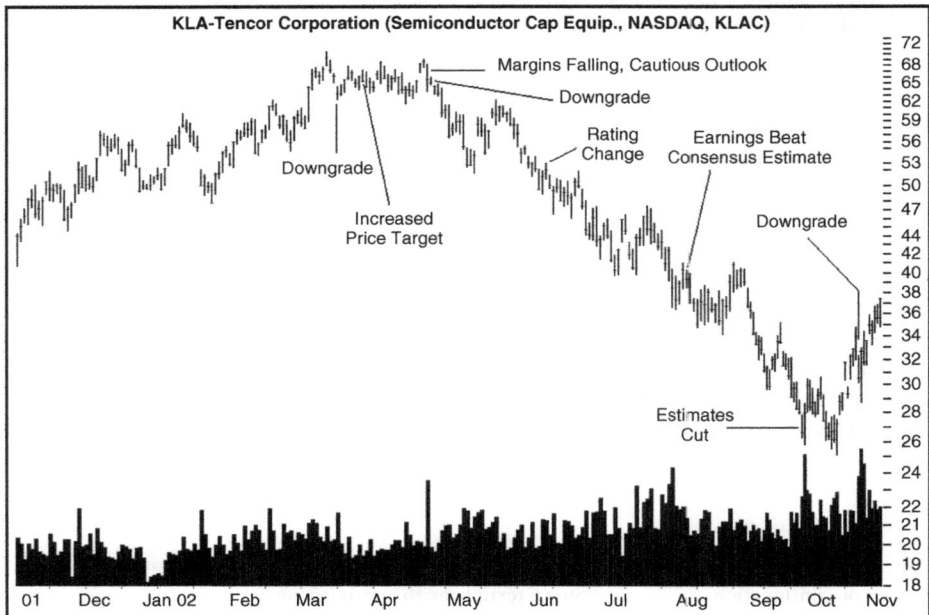

FIGURE 53.1 **The First Downgrade Occurred about a Month before Price Tumbled. The Last One Happened after the Stock Bottomed.**

Quarterly earnings arrived in mid-April, and even though the company reported better than expected earnings, a report warned of falling margins and a cautious outlook. A day later, another broker downgraded the stock. That combination of announcements sent the stock tumbling.

In early June, a broker changed its rating from "outperform" to "strong buy." That wording sounds like an upgrade, but what do I know? In my research, one firm changed its rating from "buy" to "add to," and left me scratching my head. In research for this chapter, I did not pay attention to the content of the downgrade, just that it happened.

Returning to Figure 53.1, earnings were better than expected but the company made negative comments. The stock continued down. In September, another brokerage firm cut estimates for the company just 2 weeks before the stock bottomed. Another broker downgraded the stock in October even as price was recovering.

■ Identification Guidelines

How do you identify a stock downgrade? You tune into the financial press. The important downgrades make the newspapers and the television news. Apparently, many are made during closed markets because price often gaps when the stock opens.

Figure 53.2 shows an example of the effects of a downgrade. Price gaps lower on the downgrade but moves higher and closes above the formation high, scoring an upward breakout. A few days later, price starts declining. From a closing price the day before the downgrade, 46.23, to a low of 29.31, the decline measured 37%. For the brokerage firm that made the call, it was a well-timed one.

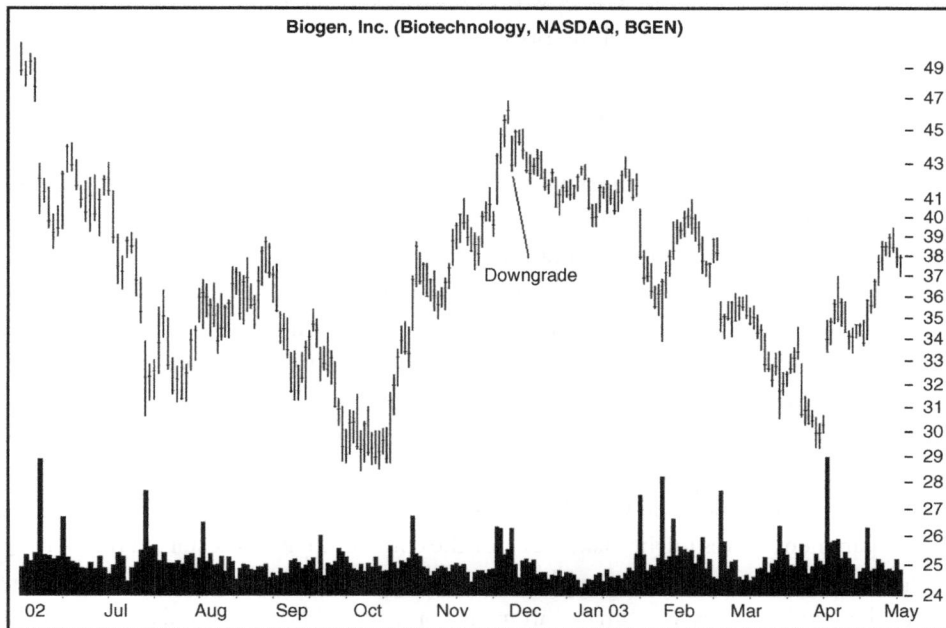

FIGURE 53.2 Price Gaps Downward, Breaks out Upward a Day Later, and Then Tumbles.

TABLE 53.1 Identification Characteristics

Characteristic	Discussion
Announcement	A broker downgrades the stock and the financial news reports it.
Large price range	Look for a large trading range on the announcement day, one that is above the monthly average.
Breakout	Usually downward.
Volume	Heavy on the announcement day.
Behavior	For upward breakouts, price rises, rounds over, and then declines. For downward breakouts, price drops but pulls back almost half the time.

Table 53.1 lists identification guidelines for patterns resulting from downgrades.

Announcement. In collecting statistics, I included only those downgrades that made the newspapers or television, not those posted on the Internet. Thus, the downgrades were from major brokerage firms on popular stocks.

Large price range. I tested the pattern and found that the wider the intraday trading range, the better the performance. I limited selection to patterns showing a trading range that was larger than the average over the prior month. If you use a high–low range that is 2 or 3 times the average, expect lower failure rates and higher average profit after the breakout.

Breakout. When the announcement occurs, anything can happen, but usually the breakout is downward.

Volume. When a major broker downgrades a stock, expect heavy volume during the current trading session, or the next one in case the stock is not trading.

Behavior. For downward breakouts, price drops but sometimes pulls back before resuming the decline. For upward breakouts, price rounds over and tumbles as fear overcomes greed and selling pressure overcomes buying demand.

■ Focus on Failures

I would like nothing more than to write, "sell all downgrades," but that is too simple. As I scan through hundreds of downgrades, I find a mixture of good timing with bad, downward breakouts with upward ones.

Figure 53.3 shows an example of bad timing. Investors started getting nervous in December after the announcement that same-store sales were up 4%. In early January, the stock gapped down on weak same-store sales. Two days later, the board authorized the buyback of additional shares, up to 90 million from 50 million. That helped boost the stock, but only for a time. When the company released earnings, they were worse than expected and two brokers downgraded the stock. Look how close to the bottom the February downgrade was. Wow! Just over a week later, a rumor circulated that May Department Stores might make a bid for the company. The stock started recovering.

Figure 53.4 shows another example of the downgrade confusion. In early December, two brokerage firms raised estimates after the company said strong holiday demand for computers would boost quarterly sales above forecast. A week later, a different firm

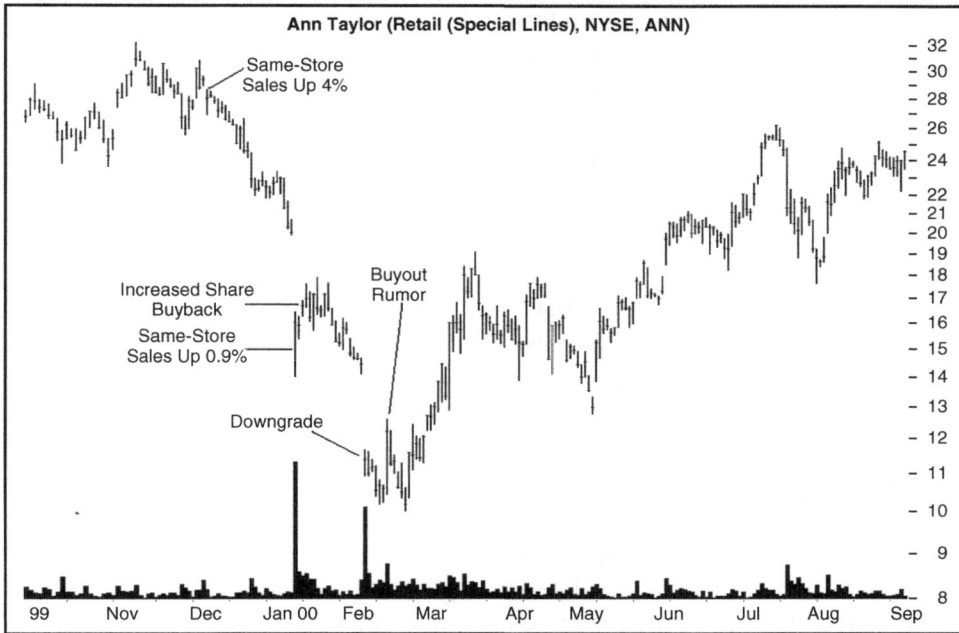

FIGURE 53.3 After the Downgrade, a Rumor Circulated That May Department Stores Might Buy the Company.

downgraded the stock. That was a good call, because the stock dropped . . . until another firm repeated a buy recommendation and made positive comments (early January). The price bubbled up. News of an earnings warning killed the rise (mid-January). That

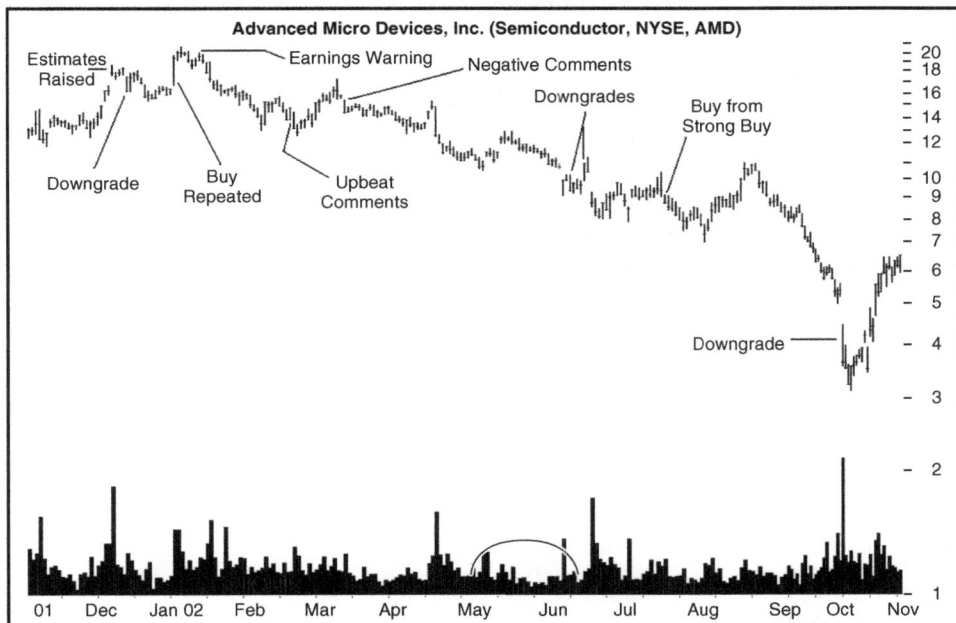

FIGURE 53.4 Some Brokers Were Praising the Stock, and Others Were Downgrading it. One Firm Downgraded the Stock 3 Days before the Bottom.

news did not stop a brokerage firm from issuing positive comments (mid-February). The stock closed near the daily high and then tumbled for two days before recovering. For a time, the upbeat comments seemed to hit the mark as price climbed. Then, the same firm made negative comments and cut earnings estimates (mid-March). The stock fell. Midway through the decline, two more brokers downgraded the stock in mid-June. A few days later, another firm downgraded the stock.

In mid-July, a broker downgraded the stock to "buy" from "strong buy." Had you taken that advice literally and bought the stock, you would have bought at about 9. The stock tumbled to 3.10 in less than 3 months.

News from the company was not good and the stock continued down. In October, the company warned of sharply lower sales. The next day, a brokerage firm downgraded the stock. That was just 3 days from the bottom. After that, the stock rebounded dramatically.

■ Statistics

Table 53.2 shows general statistics gathered in over 500 stocks from 1995 to mid-2004. Many of the stocks did not have downgrades as the companies were too small for analysts to follow, and if they did follow them, the downgrade did not make the news. Other companies were both popular and newsworthy.

Number of formations. I found more downgrades with downward breakouts, than those with upward breakouts in both bull and bear markets. This behavior is expected, but I also assumed that the number of upward breakouts would be fewer than the 39% I found.

Reversal or continuation. Upward breakouts were predominantly reversals that outperformed the continuations, and downward breakouts were continuations of the existing price trend, which performed better than reversals. For the best performance, buy after a downgrade in a bull market with an upward breakout or short in a bear market with a downward breakout.

TABLE 53.2	General Statistics			
Description	Bull Market, Up Breakout	Bear Market, Up Breakout	Bull Market, Down Breakout	Bear Market, Down Breakout
Number of formations	164	108	218	201
Reversal (R),	125 R,	92 R,	39 R,	30 R,
continuation (C)	39 C	16 C	179 C	171 C
R/C performance	27% R,	14% R,	–14% R,	–16% R,
	26% C	11% C	–14% C	–19% C
Average rise or decline	27%	14%	–14%	–19%
Rises or declines over 45%	47 or 29%	6 or 6%	11 or 5%	21 or 10%
Change after trend ends	–30%	–34%	50%	35%
Busted pattern performance	36%	21%	–21%	–34%
Standard & Poor's 500 change	7%	2%	–2%	–6%
Days to ultimate high or low	79	27	26	24

Note: Minus sign means decline.

Average rise or decline. When the breakout was upward, the stock gained between 14% and 27%, depending on the market direction. Downward breakouts showed postbreakout losses between 14% and 19%. The numbers suggest that, for the best performance, you trade with the trend: upward breakouts in a bull market and downward breakouts in a bear market.

Rises or declines over 45%. Do stocks really make large down moves? No. The best performance came from 29% of the downgrades with upward breakouts in a bull market. They climbed more than 45%. In second place were downward breakouts in a bear market: 10% declined more than 45%.

Change after trend ends. The post-ultimate high or low results are as expected. After peaking in an upward breakout, price tumbles at least 30%, on average. Downward breakouts, after bottoming, rise between 35% and 50%. Thus, if you can tell when the trend changes, you can make money. If you are wrong, of course, you may lose your shirt.

Busted pattern performance. In all cases, busted patterns perform better than the actual ones, but that may be because of the way I measured. I used the lowest low after a downward breakout to the highest high (or the reverse for upward breakouts).

For busted patterns, take a position once the breakout direction reverses and price closes above the highest high posted during the announcement for downward breakouts or below the lowest low for upward breakouts. Trading with the new direction will improve the risk profile.

Standard & Poor's 500 change. The S&P 500 index climbed after upward breakouts and dropped after downward breakouts. Notice the influence of the market on the average rise or decline, suggesting the importance of trading with the market trend.

Days to ultimate high or low. How long does it take price to reach the ultimate high or low? It took 24 days to tumble 19% (bear markets, down breakouts), but it took almost 3 times as long (79 days) to climb by 27% (bull markets, up breakouts). Thus, the decline in a bear market is steeper and shorter than is the rise in a bull market.

Table 53.3 shows the failure rates for the two breakout directions sorted by bull and bear markets. I consider 5% to be the break-even failure rate and the minimum

TABLE 53.3 **Failure Rates**

Maximum Price Rise or Decline (%)	Bull Market, Up Breakout	Bear Market, Up Breakout	Bull Market, Down Breakout	Bear Market, Down Breakout
5 (breakeven)	41 or 25%	30 or 28%	57 or 26%	34 or 17%
10	68 or 41%	55 or 51%	106 or 49%	68 or 34%
15	79 or 48%	68 or 63%	129 or 59%	92 or 46%
20	89 or 54%	75 or 69%	153 or 70%	117 or 58%
25	96 or 59%	82 or 76%	168 or 77%	133 or 66%
30	103 or 63%	90 or 83%	181 or 83%	149 or 74%
35	111 or 68%	99 or 92%	191 or 88%	159 or 79%
50	122 or 74%	102 or 94%	210 or 96%	186 or 93%
75	140 or 85%	108 or 100%	217 or 100%	200 or 100%
Over 75	164 or 100%	108 or 100%	218 or 100%	201 or 100%

amount that the stock must move to cover all trading costs. Your costs may be higher or lower than 5%.

The table may look intimidating but it is not. Take the first entry, bull market with an upward breakout. Twenty-five percent of the downgrades failed to rise more than 5% after the breakout. The next row down says that 41% failed to rise more than 10%. Downward breakouts read almost the same way. The first entry under bull markets with downward breakouts shows 26% of the patterns declined just 5% before hitting bottom.

As you scan down each column, you can see how the failure rates climb. More than half of all downgrades reach bottom or top out after moving less than 10% to 20%. Thus, if you expect a large move after a downgrade, you are probably wrong. It may happen, but that is not the way to bet if you trade this pattern often.

Table 53.4 shows breakout- and postbreakout-related statistics.

Formation end to breakout. How long does it take before price closes above the intraday high or low? Answer: between 4 and 6 days.

Yearly position. Where in the yearly price range do most breakouts occur? Splitting the yearly price range into thirds, we find that the majority occur within a third of the yearly low, regardless of the breakout direction and the market.

Think about the result for a moment. Most downgrades occur near the yearly low. That information is not very helpful if you own the stock because you have already suffered through most of the decline. In a perfect world, the downgrades should occur near the yearly high, not the low. Think of this another way: The downgrade may actually be a *buy* signal. However, I would not go that far because after the downgrade occurs, price makes new lows. Thus, wait for price to bottom, and then buy.

TABLE 53.4 **Breakout and Postbreakout Statistics**

Description	Bull Market, Up Breakout	Bear Market, Up Breakout	Bull Market, Down Breakout	Bear Market, Down Breakout
Formation end to breakout	6 days	6 days	5 days	4 days
Percentage of breakouts occurring near the 12-month low (L), center (C), or high (H)	L48%, C22%, H30%	L58%, C22%, H19%	L46%, C29%, H25%	L62%, C25%, H13%
Percentage rise/decline for each 12-month lookback period	L35%, C26%, H22%	L17%, C9%[a], H12%[a]	L20%, C13%, H9%	L21%, C18%, H14%[a]
Throwbacks/pullbacks	49%	50%	48%	45%
Average time to throwback/ pullback ends	11 days	10 days	10 days	10 days
Average rise/decline for patterns with throwback/pullback	27%	16%	−11%	−17%
Average rise/decline for patterns without throwback/pullback	27%	10%	−17%	−20%

Note: Minus sign means decline.
[a] Fewer than 30 samples.

Yearly position, performance. Mapping the performance into the yearly high–low range shows that the best performing downgrades occur within a third of the yearly low. The results obey the theory that you should short stocks making new lows, not those making new highs.

Throwbacks and pullbacks. About half of the stocks after a downgrade return to the breakout price within a month. However, their stay may be brief—in many cases only a day—before the move continues in the original breakout direction.

On average, it takes between 10 and 11 days for the stock to return to the breakout price. For downward breakouts, pullbacks hurt performance. For example, when a pullback occurs, price declines 11% in a bull market. Without a pullback, the decline averages 17%. Many other chart and event patterns show this same result for both bull and bear markets.

Table 53.5 shows a frequency distribution of the days to the ultimate high or low. Yawn, right? Nothing is more boring than staring at a table full of numbers. Would you like to know when to sell? The table will not tell you that, but it does hint that half the patterns reach their ultimate high or low in the first week or two. About two out of three will top or bottom in about three weeks. Bull markets with upward breakouts take longer to reach the ultimate high than the other combinations. This table reinforces the belief that you should be prepared to take profits quickly.

Table 53.6 shows size and volume statistics for patterns forming in reaction to stock downgrades.

Height. I found the median height for a given breakout direction as a percentage of the breakout price and then sorted the patterns into tall and short. Tall patterns performed substantially better than short ones in all combinations. For example, in a bear market with an upward breakout, short patterns had gains averaging 9%. Tall patterns scored rises averaging more than double—19%. This finding confirms one of my selection criteria: a large price range (taller than the 1-month average). Patterns 2 or 3 times the average height perform better still (higher profit) and have a lower failure rate.

Announcement day volume. I compared the announcement day volume with the average daily volume over the prior month and then looked at performance for above and below average volume announcements. In bear markets, patterns with above average volume performed better than those with below average volume. In

TABLE 53.5	Frequency Distribution of Days to Ultimate High or Low									
Days:	7	14	21	28	35	42	49	56	63	70	>70
Bear market, up breakout	52%	10%	10%	3%	5%	1%	3%	2%	2%	2%	11%
Bull market, up breakout	37%	7%	5%	3%	4%	3%	1%	2%	1%	2%	34%
Bear market, down breakout	45%	10%	9%	8%	5%	4%	3%	3%	2%	2%	7%
Bull market, down breakout	41%	9%	15%	6%	6%	3%	3%	3%	2%	1%	11%

TABLE 53.6 Size and Volume Statistics

Description	Bull Market, Up Breakout	Bear Market, Up Breakout	Bull Market, Down Breakout	Bear Market, Down Breakout
Tall pattern performance	32%	19%	−20%	−22%
Short pattern performance	23%	9%	−10%	−17%
Median height as a percentage of breakout price	5.76%	6.42%	6.52%	6.94%
Heavy announcement day volume, performance	25%	14%	−14%	−19%
Light announcement day volume, performance	38%[a]	8%[a]	−16%[a]	−15%[a]

Note: Minus sign means decline.
[a] Fewer than 30 samples.

bull markets, those with below average volume performed better. Since most downgrades occurred on heavy volume, the sample size is small and likely to change results.

Trading Tactics

Table 53.7 shows trading tactics for upward and downward breakouts.

Measure rule. Use the measure rule to predict the target price. First, find the height on the downgrade day by subtracting the intraday low from the high. For upward break-

TABLE 53.7 Trading Tactics

Trading Tactic	Explanation
Measure rule	Used to predict a target price. Using the day of the downgrade, compute the height by subtracting the intraday low from the intraday high. For upward breakouts, add the result to the daily high; for downward breakouts subtract it from the daily low. The result is the target price. This method works between 64% and 71% of the time.
Buy signal	None. Do not buy after a broker downgrades the stock. Most likely, price is going to drop.
Sell signal—down breakouts	For downward breakouts, sell a long holding immediately or sell after price turns down after a pullback.
Sell signal—up breakouts	Price peaks in 1 to 3 weeks after the downgrade, so consider selling as price rounds over after an upward breakout.
Short the stock—down breakouts	Selling short is risky and downgrades are not reliable short candidates. Too often, price drops for a week or two and then recovers. If you still want to short, sell immediately and use stops to limit losses. The best performance comes from downgrades within a third of the yearly low, so check for that.
Short the stock—up breakouts	If the breakout is upward, watch the stock as it climbs. It may top out quickly. When it starts heading down, short it. Use stops to protect your wallet (or purse). See Sample Trade—Upward Breakout—for an example.

outs, add the result to the intraday high; for downward breakouts, subtract it from the intraday low. The result is the target price, the minimum expected price move. The Result Snapshot ("Percentage meeting price target") shows how often this method works.

Buy signal. Do not buy a stock after a broker downgrade unless you have a compelling reason to do so. In many cases, the downgrade may be near a trend change (from down to up), meaning that the downgrade often comes near the yearly low, just as price is about to recover. Wait for it to bottom and then buy cautiously as more downside may become apparent.

Sell signal—down breakouts. If you own the stock, sell immediately, or pray for a pullback and sell then. If you decide to hold onto the stock, remember the statistics. The average decline is between 14% and 19%. Do you really want to hold onto a stock worth a buck today when it will be worth 81 cents in a few weeks?

If you own a stock and a downgrade comes, why are you still holding it? Chances are it has declined far from the peak price. What are you waiting for?

Sell signal—up breakouts. Some downgrades result in an upward breakout. See Sample Trade—Upward Breakout for an example of what this pattern looks like and how to trade it.

Short the stock—down breakouts. You are probably considering shorting *after* the downgrade and *after* any downward gap. Thus, a good portion of the decline may be behind you already. In many cases I have looked at, the downgrade comes just before the stock turns bullish. That is bad news if you hold a short position. Use stops to protect your position.

Short the stock—up breakouts. The sample trade for an upward breakout gives a good example of how to trade a downgrade when the breakout is upward. What you want to do is watch from shore as price rises, then jump in and take to the waves when price starts tumbling. Timing is everything, and getting in at the right time is perhaps the hardest timing to achieve.

■ Sample Trade—Downward Breakout

Don had a winning strategy of buying stocks low and selling them high. His win-loss ratio was strong. Not every trade was profitable, but he narrowed his losses and tried to let his profits run. He did everything right until he became bored with making money. Trading was no longer exciting, as if the bear market of the last 3 years took the fun out of it. He decided to try a new technique (see Figure 53.5).

Don kept his eye on Amgen and watched it rise from the July 2002 low near 30 (not shown). "Drug stocks are volatile, and volatility spells a profit opportunity." To prove his point, he sold the stock short 2 days after a broker downgrade and after news of another patent-infringement suit pushed the stock down. He received a fill at 44.55 and rubbed his hands with excitement as it closed lower.

The next few days did not worry him as prices climbed. He expected them to recover back to the gap top (when the stock was downgraded) and then start heading down. As recently as September, news reports said Wyeth would sell its 7.7% stake

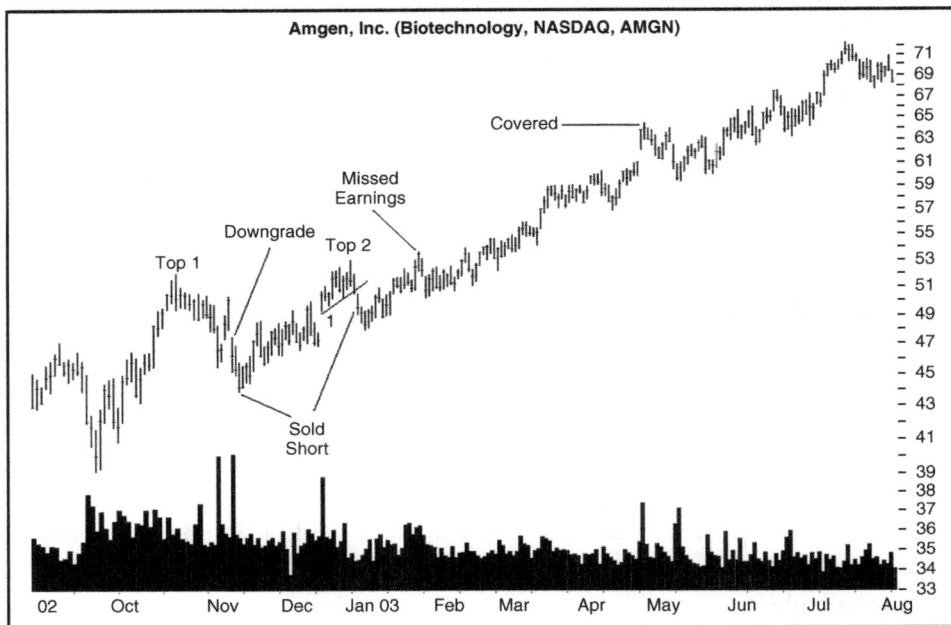

Amgen, Inc. (Biotechnology, NASDAQ, AMGN)

Covered

Missed
Earnings

Downgrade   Top 2

Top 1

1

Sold
Short

02   Oct   Nov   Dec   Jan 03   Feb   Mar   Apr   May   Jun   Jul   Aug

FIGURE 53.5   As Described in Sample Trade—Downward Breakout, Don Shorted the Stock and Then Sold Again When It Looked Like a Double Top.

in the company in chunks. Dumping nearly a 100 million shares over the coming year would help keep a lid on the price rise. Moreover, insiders were selling, too, as recently as July and August (not shown).

He was confident of his position even as shares approached the price level of top 1. At point 1 on the figure, four insiders sold their holdings. When the people running the company do not like the stock that is never a good sign . . . except when you have bet the stock would fall. Meanwhile, the news from the company was good. As a present, the FDA approved a manufacturing plant in Rhode Island 2 days before Christmas.

Price pushed higher, rounded over, and started down, forming top 2. The day after Christmas, a judge dismissed the company's lawsuit about Medicare reimbursement for one of its drugs. The stock dropped on the news. With the bad news fresh in his mind and seeing a budding double top chart pattern (tops 1 and 2), he shorted the stock again when price pierced the short trend line. The order filled at 49.76.

The decline lasted just two more days before price started up again. Over the coming month, he fumed about his losing position. Then the company reported that sales climbed 57% and net nearly tripled. But the results missed the consensus estimate. The stock declined for 2 days then rebounded.

Over the next few months, insiders continued to sell their shares and yet the price kept climbing. In late April, he finally threw in the towel and covered his short position after the company made a good earnings report and lifted forecasts. He received a fill at 64. On the first short, he lost 44% and the second trade lost 29%.

"I think I've had enough excitement." He is back to his old style of trading and is making money again.

■ Sample Trade—Upward Breakout

Figure 53.6 shows a sample trade based on an upward breakout in response to a downgrade. After reaching a peak, the stock tumbled when a broker cut earnings estimates in mid-August. The next day, another broker downgraded the stock and it gapped lower. This plunge put the stock below the up-sloping May trend line. Since a trend line is a known resistance line and so is the gap, there was a good chance that price would not recover to the old high soon. That, of course, is easy to say in hindsight.

Confusing news came from brokerage firms. Some were downgrading the stock even as the company announced better-than-expected earnings. Others made positive comments, then changed their minds and downgraded the stock after it peaked. The day after the gap, another brokerage firm made positive comments and set a new price target. That news helped push the price up. The stock pulled back to the diagonal May trend line but could not jump over the gap before declining.

Any time after point A was the time to short the stock. A pullback often precedes a decline, and that is the way to trade this chart. If you draw a trend line connecting the lows, you could short the stock once it closed below that trend line (the short diagonal trend line starting in August, as shown).

How far would price decline? I would expect a pause at the bottom of the late May to July horizontal consolidation (at about 20), for a meager 10% decline. If price bored through that level, then the next support zone was the two valleys in April and May at around 17, for a 23% decline (the horizontal support line).

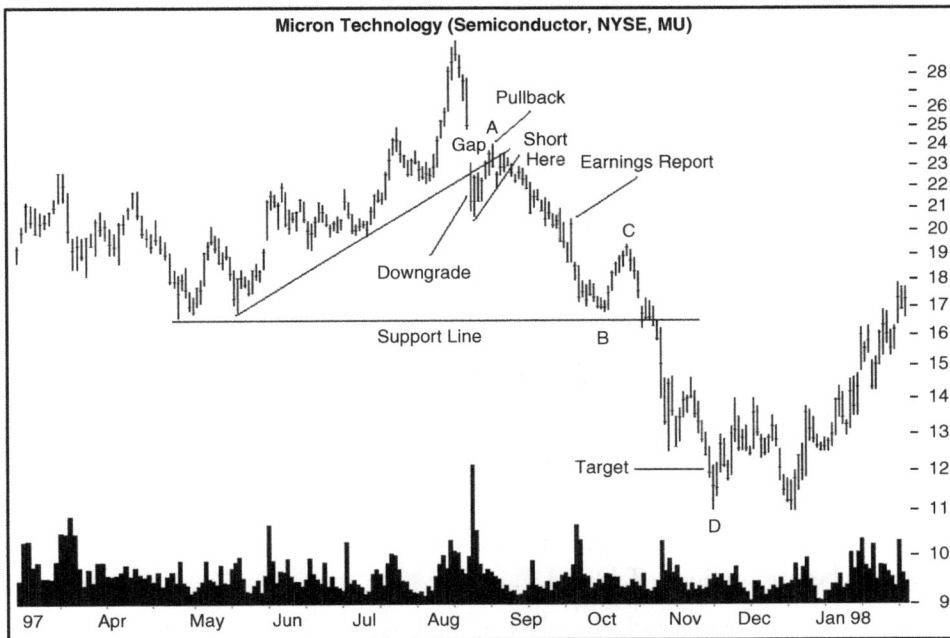

FIGURE 53.6 These Situations, When Traded by an Expert, Can Lead to Handsome Profits.

As you can see, price drilled through the first support zone at 20. The company released earnings and they were well below what was expected, but the stock soared that day. The next day, several large brokerage firms stampeded for the door in their hurry to cut estimates. The stock gave back all it gained from the prior day, and more.

Price did find support at the next zone, as shown (point B). Price climbed to C, the level of the prior support/resistance zone at 20, and then dropped.

The ABCD pattern is a measured move down formation. The move from C to D should mirror the decline from A to B. Thus, if you do the math, it gives a target as shown, just above point D. The stock declined to the target and dropped to D before double bottoming (point D and the December low).

To exit the trade, you can get out as the target neared. Waiting for price to actually meet the target is not wise because it often falls short. In this case, everything worked out.

Shorting a stock is not for the novice. It entails unlimited risk, as Don discovered in the first sample trade. However, if you discover a downgrade with an upward breakout that rounds over, keep this chapter in mind. Do your homework on the fundamentals and make sure you have valid technical and fundaments reasons for shorting a stock. Use proper money management techniques to limit losses if you decide to trade it.

■ For Best Performance

The following list includes tips and observations that may help you select patterns to improve your trading performance. Refer to the associated table for more information.

■ Use the identification guidelines to select a tradable pattern—Table 53.1.

■ Select downgrades that have a wide intraday trading range, 2 or 3 times the monthly average—Table 53.1.

■ Sell short a downward breakout in a bear market, not in a bull market—Table 53.2.

■ If a busted pattern appears, trade it, because price moving less than 5% in the breakout direction before reversing suggests that the new trend may be a strong one—Table 53.2.

■ Select patterns with downward breakouts in a bear market. They have the lowest failure rates for moves up to 20%—Table 53.3.

■ The best performance comes from downgrades near the yearly low. Stocks making new lows tend to continue making new lows—Table 53.4.

■ When a pullback occurs, performance suffers. Look for nearby underlying support before trading—Table 53.4.

■ Half the downgrades reach the ultimate high or low in a week or two. Almost two-thirds reverse in less than 3 weeks—Table 53.5.

■ Tall patterns perform better than short ones—Table 53.6.

CHAPTER 54

Stock Upgrades

From Thomas N. Bulkowski, *Encyclopedia of Chart Patterns*, Second Edition (Hoboken, New Jersey: John Wiley & Sons, 2005), Chapter 63.

Learning Objective Statements

- Interpret potential price moves based on the patterns described in this chapter
- Calculate potential price targets
- Evaluate price levels for potential support or resistance
- Identify and interpret signals from various oscillators and technical studies in conjunction with the event-based patterns listed in these chapters

983

Results Snapshot

Upward Breakouts

Event	A broker upgrades the stock and price breaks out upward.	
Reversal or continuation	Short-term bullish continuation	
	Bull Market	**Bear Market**
Performance rank	2 out of 6	2 out of 5
Break-even failure rate	18%	21%
Average rise	24%	16%
Change after trend ends	−30%	−32%
Volume trend	Heavy on the announcement day	
Throwbacks	63%	59%
Percentage meeting price target	81%	77%
Surprising findings	Continuations perform better than reversals. Tall patterns perform better than short ones. Price drops by at least 20% within 2 weeks in nearly half the patterns.	

Downward Breakouts

Event	Same, but breakout is downward.	
Reversal or continuation	Short-term bearish continuation	
	Bull Market	**Bear Market**
Performance rank	5 out of 5	2 out of 4
Break-even failure rate	38%	23%
Average decline	12%	18%

Change after trend ends	44%	35%
Volume trend	Same as for upward breakouts	
Pullbacks	37%	17%
Percentage meeting price target	67%	77%
Surprising findings	Tall patterns perform better than short ones. The stock *drops* after the upgrade 35% of the time. Half surge upward within a week.	

What happens to price after a broker upgrades a stock? Stock upgrades should be good for the stock and good for the owners of the stock. Right? Well, not always.

The Results Snapshot begins to tell the story. After the upgrade, anything can happen. For example, suppose you own a stock in XYZ Company and a broker upgrades the stock. You hear about the announcement on the television or read about it in the newspaper the next day. Which way will price move? About two out of three times (65%), the stock will move higher, as expected, and break out upward, climbing an average of 24% in a bull market. Then price tumbles 30%, giving back its gains and more.

If the stock has a downward breakout, expect price to continue moving down an average of 12% in a bull market before the decline stops. Then price climbs by 44%. Both breakout directions spell a trading opportunity, but not in the direction you expect. More about the new trading patterns later.

Surprising findings include the usual culprits and new ones as well. A large number (35%) of stocks have downward breakouts after an upgrade. If the breakout is downward, over half begin a sustained rise (over 20%) within a week. For upward breakouts, the reverse is true: Nearly half decline substantially (over 20%) within 2 weeks. I discuss these surprises later in the chapter.

■ Tour

Figure 54.1 shows what I expected to see after a brokerage firm upgraded Dell. On the day of the announcement, price closed at the daily high. On succeeding days, prices climbed even higher and then took a rest for a week or so before resuming their climb. This stair-step pattern continued until October, when price reached the ultimate high. The breakout price was 3.75, and price completed its climb at 12.98, for a gain of 246%.

That is how I *thought* the pattern would work and in a few cases, it did. The figure shows the best performing stock in the database for this pattern. Most of the time, though, you will be disappointed. A stock upgrade is often a premature sell signal. In the majority of the patterns I looked at, prices either dropped immediately or declined within 3 weeks. Thus, if a brokerage firm upgrades a stock you own, be ready to sell. It is not an automatic sell as it might turn out like Figure 54.1. If the stock drops after the upgrade, wait for a buying opportunity.

■ Identification Guidelines

Figure 54.2 shows a typical example of a pattern I discovered when researching what happens after a stock upgrade. Most of the time, the stock climbs after the announcement.

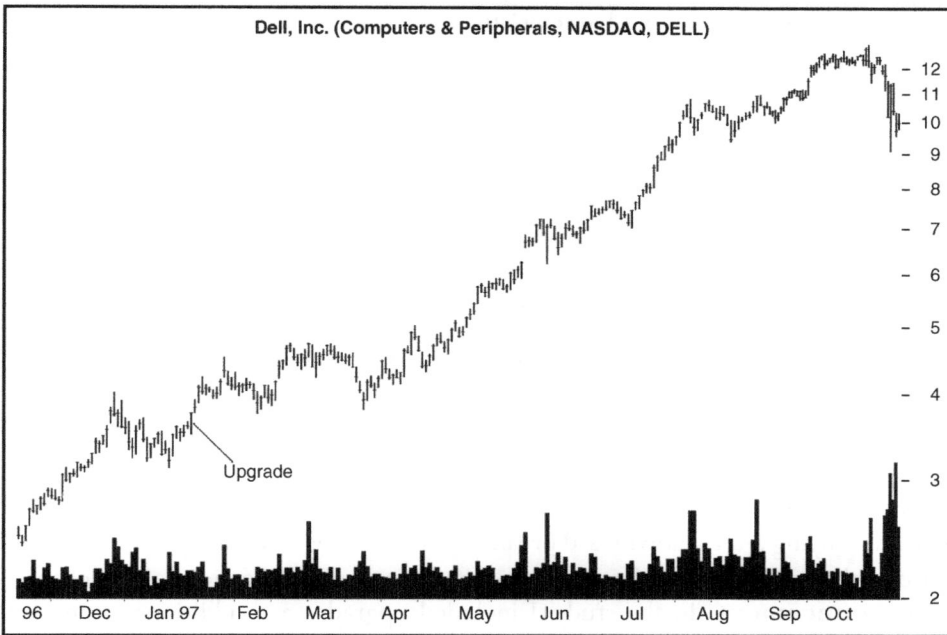

FIGURE 54.1 This Chart Shows How Price Should React after an Upgrade.

Thus, the breakout is upward, signaled when price closes above the daily high posted on the day of the upgrade. Price continues climbing, usually in a stair-step pattern.

In this figure, prices climbed just 11%. Then the world ended and prices tumbled, plunging through the trend line drawn along the minor lows (a sell signal). The decline measured 43% to the May low.

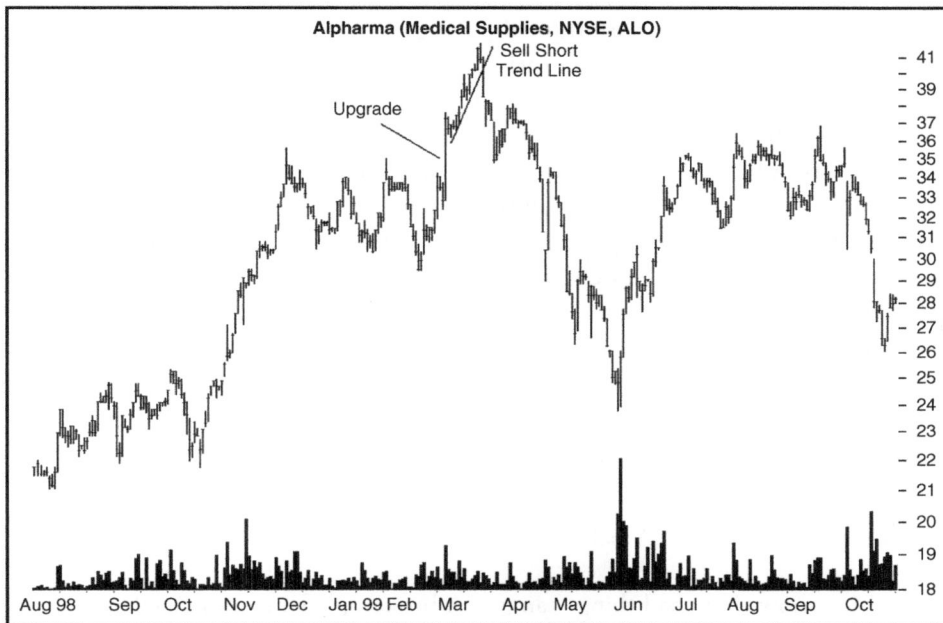

FIGURE 54.2 Prices Climb but Soon Tumble. Here, the Decline Measures 43%.

TABLE 54.1	Identification Characteristics
Characteristic	Discussion
Announcement	A brokerage firm announces an upgrade to the stock's rating or is adding the stock to its recommended list, priority list, or focus list.
Large price range	On the announcement day, look for an intraday high–low range that is above the 1-month average.
Breakout	Occurs when price closes above the intraday high or below the intraday low posted on the announcement day.
Price decline	For downward breakouts, look for a decline that stops in less than 2 weeks and then begins to recover.
Price rise	For upward breakouts, prices rise usually from 1 to 3 weeks before cresting and then tumbling.
Volume	Expect heavy volume on the announcement day.

Table 54.1 shows the identification characteristics for upgrades using two new patterns: buying after a downward breakout and shorting after an upward breakout. I discuss the patterns in the Trading Tactics and Sample Trade sections of this chapter.

Announcement. In the study, I included upgrades and additions to any list, such as a recommended list, priority list, or focus list. I ignored reiterated ratings or upgrades in the debt rating of the company. I also ignored the type of rating upgrade (buy, sell, hold, add, and so on). I included upgrades that were significant enough that either they made the financial press (newspapers) or I heard of them on television. I did not search the Internet for upgrades in the stocks I follow nor did I visit the company or brokerage firm's Web site.

Large price range. I included only those upgrades in which price showed an above average trading range on the day of the announcement or the following day (in case markets were closed), or if price gapped upward or downward. I used the average trading range over the prior 30 days as the benchmark. Performance improves in both breakout directions and markets, and failure rates improve, too, with a larger intraday trading range (like 2 or 3 times the average range).

Breakout. A breakout occurs when price *closes* above the intraday high posted on the announcement day or below the intraday low.

Price decline. Look for prices to bottom within a week or so (about half do). After reaching bottom, prices climb substantially. The pattern should look like the upgrade in Figure 54.5.

Price rise. For upward breakouts, prices climb, and the downward turn takes longer, with about half posting substantial declines within 3 weeks. The pattern should look like Figure 54.2.

Volume. Volume is unusually heavy on the day the stock is upgraded.

Focus on Failures

Figure 54.3 shows how bad things can get. A brokerage firm announced an upgrade to the stock just 6 days after it posted a new high. Then the stock tumbled from a

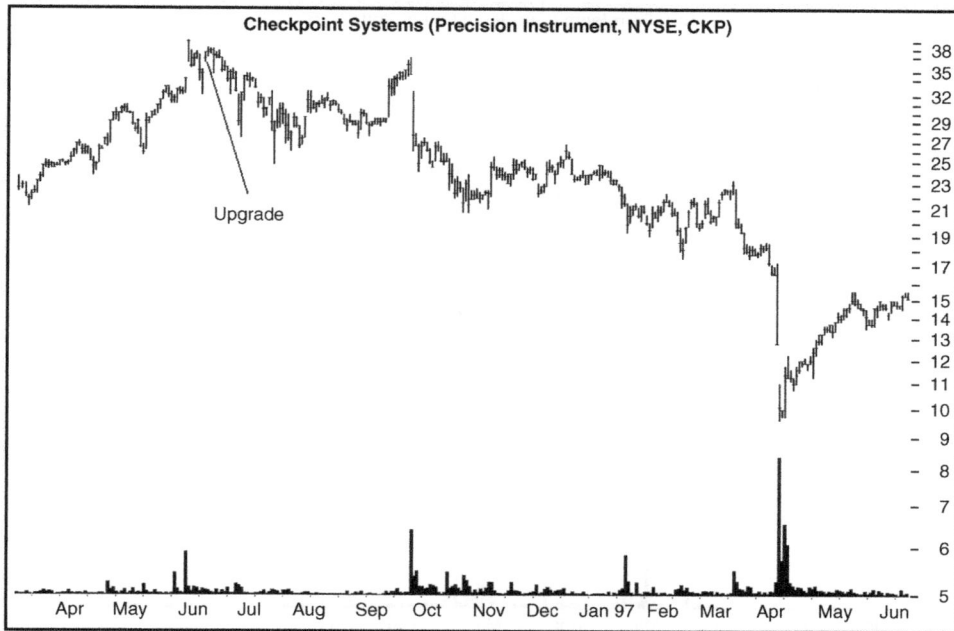

FIGURE 54.3 A Week after Reaching a High of 39, a Broker Upgraded the Stock. Prices Begin a Long Slide That Ends at a Low of 9.62.

high of 39 at the peak to a low of 9.62 almost a year later. If the intent of the upgrade was for performance over the coming year, you can see how awful the upgrade was. This is not an isolated incident, as the figures in this chapter attest.

Let me hasten to add that I am not picking on brokerage firms, analysts, or the brokers themselves. The research from this chapter shows that the market's reaction to a broker's optimistic upgrade is not what many expect. It may be a case of Wall Street saying, "buy on the rumor, and sell on the news." In some cases, the upgrade is prescient as prices climb. However, in too many examples, the climb is brief and prices tumble.

Figure 54.4 is another example of bad timing. The stock started down in April as if the investment community knew the refinery industry was having trouble. Then the company announced quarterly results and the loss was larger than expected. Multiple brokers downgraded the stock. The stock tumbled on very high volume and proceeded to dead-cat bounce. Amidst the rubble, a lone broker, one of the largest in the United States, upgraded the stock. The stock climbed on the news but soon rolled over and tumbled . . . dramatically, reaching a low of 1.24, a decline of 87% from the high on the day of the upgrade. Wow!

Earlier in the year, in January, another broker added the stock to its recommended list from an even higher price, 14.05. The stock peaked at 15.29 and then dropped to 11.60 when another broker reduced financial projections for the industry. If you sold the stock then, it would have meant a 17% loss. Large, sure, but nothing like holding it to the October low (a 91% loss).

If an upgrade means optimism about the prospects of a company and its stock, then anything except an upward price climb means a failure.

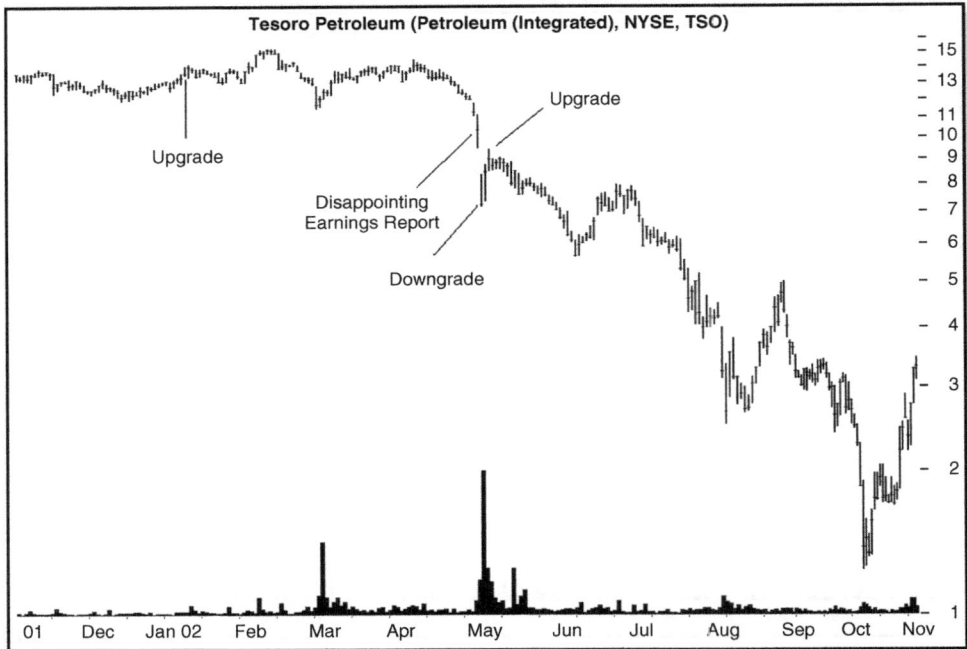

FIGURE 54.4 **The Stock Dropped from a High of 9.43 to a Low of 1.24.**

▦ Statistics

Table 54.2 shows general statistics for traders' reactions to stock upgrades.

Number of formations. I found 698 upgrades in about 500 stocks from early 1995 to mid-2004 that passed the identification guidelines listed in Table 54.1. Many of the stocks did not have any upgrade information. Active stocks, like Intel, had many

TABLE 54.2 **General Statistics**

Description	Bull Market, Up Breakout	Bear Market, Up Breakout	Bull Market, Down Breakout	Bear Market, Down Breakout
Number of formations	325	129	174	70
Reversal (R), continuation (C)	42 R, 283 C	34 R, 95 C	129 R, 45 C	43 R, 27 C
R/C performance	16% R, 25% C	14% R, 16% C	−12% R, −13% C	−19% R, −16% C
Average rise or decline	24%	16%	−12%	−18%
Rises or declines over 45%	63 or 19%	16 or 12%	6 or 3%	4 or 6%
Change after trend ends	−30%	−32%	44%	35%
Busted pattern performance	38%	16%	−22%	−30%
Standard & Poor's 500 change	5%	1%	−2%	−6%
Days to ultimate high or low	61	43	25	25

Note: Minus sign means decline.

upgrades (a dozen for the company). The statistics are not a definitive study of stock upgrades, but they capture several brokerage recommendations on popular stocks.

Reversal or continuation. Most stock upgrades occurred as prices climbed (an uptrend), resulting in an upward breakout. Thus, they acted as continuations of the current trend, not as reversals. In all but one case, the best performance came from stocks that acted as continuations. The exception was from downward breakouts in a bear market. Under those conditions, reversals performed better than continuations.

Average rise or decline. The average rise in a bull market, 24%, was superior to the other combinations of market type and breakout direction. For downward breakouts, the best performance came when the breakout direction agreed with the market trend. Thus, for best results, trade this pattern in the direction of the prevailing market trend (upward breakout in a bull market or downward breakout in a bear market).

Rises or declines over 45%. This measure of how well a formation performs shows that for upward breakouts, 19% climbed more than 45%. For downward breakouts, just 6% made the cut. Notice the performance difference between bull and bear markets for the same breakout direction. Again, trade with the trend.

Change after trend ends. Once price reaches its ultimate high or low, it reverses and makes a dramatic move. Thus, if you can call the turn accurately, you can make a lot of money. Unfortunately, the performance after a downward breakout is not like the 60% posted by some chart patterns. Even the downward move after an upward breakout seems less than robust.

Busted pattern performance. The virtue of a busted pattern is its easy identification. For safety, take a position in the stock once price confirms a breakout in the new direction.

Standard & Poor's 500 change. The index did not make dramatic moves during this pattern (from the announcement day to the ultimate high or low). However, the theory "a rising tide lifts all boats" is intact as the average rise or decline mirrored the rise or fall in the index.

Days to ultimate high or low. How long does it take to reach the ultimate high or low? On average, 2 months or less for upward breakouts and about a month otherwise. The comparatively short time to the ultimate high or low is probably a reflection of the meager gains or losses posted by the pattern. If you compare the days to the ultimate high or low with the average rise or decline, you will find that bear market drops are steeper than are the rises in bull markets. This finding suggests you should monitor any trade in a bear market closely.

Table 54.3 shows the failure rates for upward and downward breakouts. Notice how the values start in double digits and get worse, quickly. These results suggest that you should avoid trading the pattern unless you are selective. Bull markets with upward breakouts and bear markets with downward breakouts perform best. That makes sense as it is trading with the trend. The countertrend trades suffer higher failure rates.

Let me give you some examples to make the table clear. Over a third of the upgrades (37%) in a bull market fail to rise at least 10% after the breakout. Almost half top out with gains of less than 15%. The worst performer is in a bull market with a

TABLE 54.3 Failure Rates

Maximum Price Rise or Decline (%)	Bull Market, Up Breakout	Bear Market, Up Breakout	Bull Market, Down Breakout	Bear Market, Down Breakout
5 (breakeven)	57 or 18%	27 or 21%	66 or 38%	16 or 23%
10	120 or 37%	60 or 47%	104 or 60%	27 or 39%
15	157 or 48%	73 or 57%	123 or 71%	34 or 49%
20	182 or 56%	86 or 67%	140 or 80%	41 or 59%
25	197 or 61%	94 or 73%	149 or 86%	51 or 73%
30	216 or 66%	102 or 79%	155 or 89%	55 or 79%
35	233 or 72%	108 or 84%	162 or 93%	60 or 86%
50	266 or 82%	120 or 93%	169 or 97%	66 or 94%
75	293 or 90%	126 or 98%	174 or 100%	70 or 100%
Over 75	325 or 100%	129 or 100%	174 or 100%	70 or 100%

downward breakout. A full 71% fail to drop at least 15%. Do not trade an upgrade with a downward breakout in a bull market.

Table 54.4 shows breakout- and postbreakout-related statistics.

Formation end to breakout. Since the upgrade occurs in a single day, it should not take long for price to close above the daily high or below the daily low, but it took longer than the 2 to 3 days I expected. The average ranges between 3 and 5 days.

Yearly position. I looked at the breakout price and placed it within the yearly high–low price range. For most markets and breakout directions, the breakout occurred within a third of the yearly high, as if brokers were playing the momentum

TABLE 54.4 Breakout and Postbreakout Statistics

Description	Bull Market, Up Breakout	Bear Market, Up Breakout	Bull Market, Down Breakout	Bear Market, Down Breakout
Formation end to breakout	4 days	3 days	5 days	5 days
Percentage of breakouts occurring near the 12-month low (L), center (C), or high (H)	L18%, C28%, H54%	L27%, C33%, H40%	L24%, C31%, H45%	L38%, C33%, H29%
Percentage rise/decline for each 12-month lookback period	L21%, C23%, H25%	L20%, C15%, H14%	L16%, C12%, H10%	L21%[a], C16%[a], H17%[a]
Throwbacks/pullbacks	63%	59%	37%	50%
Average time to throwback/ pullback ends	10 days	10 days	11 days	10 days
Average rise/decline for patterns with throwback/pullback	24%	15%	−11%	−17%
Average rise/decline for patterns without throwback/pullback	23%	16%	−13%	−19%

Note: Minus sign means decline.

[a] Fewer than 30 samples.

card and hoping for a continued uptrend. The one out of synch is upgrades in bear markets with downward breakouts. They broke out most often near the yearly low.

What does this information mean? Frequently, brokers upgrade the stock near the yearly high, just before the stock tumbles!

Yearly position, performance. Where in the yearly price range do breakouts occur that show the best performance? Most often, upgrades near the yearly low perform best in three out of the four combinations. The exception is in a bull market with an upward breakout. Those do well near the yearly high.

Throwbacks and pullbacks. Throwbacks and pullbacks occur about half the time, with downward breakouts in a bull market showing the lowest pullback rate: 37%. The average time to return to the breakout price is 10 or 11 days.

Most of the time, a throwback or pullback hurts performance, but the performance differences are minor. The one exception is for upward breakouts in a bull market. Those perform marginally better after a throwback.

Table 54.5 is an exciting table. Let me tell you why. By definition, the ultimate high comes once price reaches a high and then declines by at least 20%. In a similar manner, the ultimate low is a low point before price climbs by at least 20%. The behavior we are seeing with this pattern is that prices climb a bit after an upward breakout and then drop dramatically. With a downward breakout, prices drop a bit then climb dramatically. Thus, you should short upward breakouts and buy downward ones; just do not enter the trade immediately after the breakout. More about trading tactics later in the chapter.

The table shows how quickly prices reach the floor or ceiling. For downward breakouts in a bull market, 53% reach the ultimate low in a week and then climb by at least 20%. Bear markets with downward breakouts are similar, with 50% hitting bottom in the first week. In another week, 66% bottom out (50% + 16%). Only bull markets with up breakouts take their time reaching the ultimate high. Over a third (35%) top out in the first week. A quarter of the patterns (29%) do not reach the high in less than 2 months (over 70 days).

Table 54.6 shows size and volume statistics.

TABLE 54.5 **Frequency Distribution of Days to Ultimate High or Low**

Days:	7	14	21	28	35	42	49	56	63	70	>70
Bear market, up breakout	43%	10%	12%	2%	3%	5%	3%	1%	2%	2%	18%
Bull market, up breakout	35%	9%	8%	4%	4%	3%	2%	1%	3%	2%	29%
Bear market, down breakout	50%	16%	3%	4%	1%	1%	7%	0%	1%	1%	14%
Bull market, down breakout	53%	7%	9%	3%	6%	3%	4%	1%	1%	1%	10%

TABLE 54.6   Size and Volume Statistics

Description	Bull Market, Up Breakout	Bear Market, Up Breakout	Bull Market, Down Breakout	Bear Market, Down Breakout
Tall pattern performance	29%	22%	−15%	−22%
Short pattern performance	20%	11%	−11%	−14%
Median height as a percentage of breakout price	5.61%	6.10%	5.32%	5.25%
Heavy announcement day volume, performance	23%	16%	−12%	−18%
Light announcement day volume, performance	30%[a]	11%[a]	−12%[a]	−13%[a]

Note: Minus sign means decline.
[a] Fewer than 30 samples.

Height. Tall patterns perform substantially better than short ones. Upward breakouts in bear markets, for example, do twice as well as short patterns—with rises of 22% versus 11%, respectively.

To use this finding, compute the formation height by subtracting the intraday low from the high using prices from the day of the stock upgrade. Divide the result by the breakout price, which for upward breakouts is the intraday high; for downward breakouts, use the intraday low. Compare the result by the median listed in the table to determine whether your pattern is short or tall. For best average results, select tall patterns and ignore short ones.

Announcement day volume. I compared the announcement day volume with the average of the prior month and then mapped performance according to whether the announcement day volume was above or below average. Announcements accompanying high volume performed better than did those with low volume, except bull markets with upward breakouts. They climbed 30% on light announcement day volume and 23% when volume was above average. In all cases, the sample size was small, so the results may change.

◼ Trading Tactics

Table 54.7 lists a brief explanation of trading tactics. I do not discuss them individually as they are self-explanatory. In addition, the following sample trades use most of them.

◼ Sample Trade—Downward Breakout

Figure 54.5 illustrates a sample trade when a stock breaks out downward after an upgrade. In mid-February, the stock received an upgrade from a broker and it gapped higher. The next day, prices dropped, closing below the low of the prior day and signaling a downward breakout.

TABLE 54.7 Trading Tactics

Trading Tactic	Explanation
Measure rule	Used to predict a target price. Using the day of the upgrade, compute the height by subtracting the intraday low from the intraday high. For upward breakouts, add the result to the intraday high; for downward breakouts subtract it from the intraday low. The result is the target price. Price meets the target between 67% and 81% of the time (see Results Snapshot, "Percentage meeting price target").
Buy signal	After a downward breakout, prices drop and then start recovering. Buy when you are sure prices are rising. Use stops in case you are wrong and to lock in profits.
Sell signal	After an upward breakout, prices rise, curl over, and then head down. Sell short near the peak and use stops to protect your gains.
If you own the stock	If you own the stock, watch the breakout direction. If it breaks out downward, sell immediately or buy more after the stock bottoms. If the breakout is upward, hold onto your stock until it peaks and then consider selling.
Wait for confirmation	Wait for price to close above the daily high or below the daily low before trading.

Bill's hobby is trading stocks when it is too inclement to play golf, and he is an experienced trader. He liked Big Lots and watched the stock for months. When a broker announced the upgrade in February, that boosted his confidence in the stock.

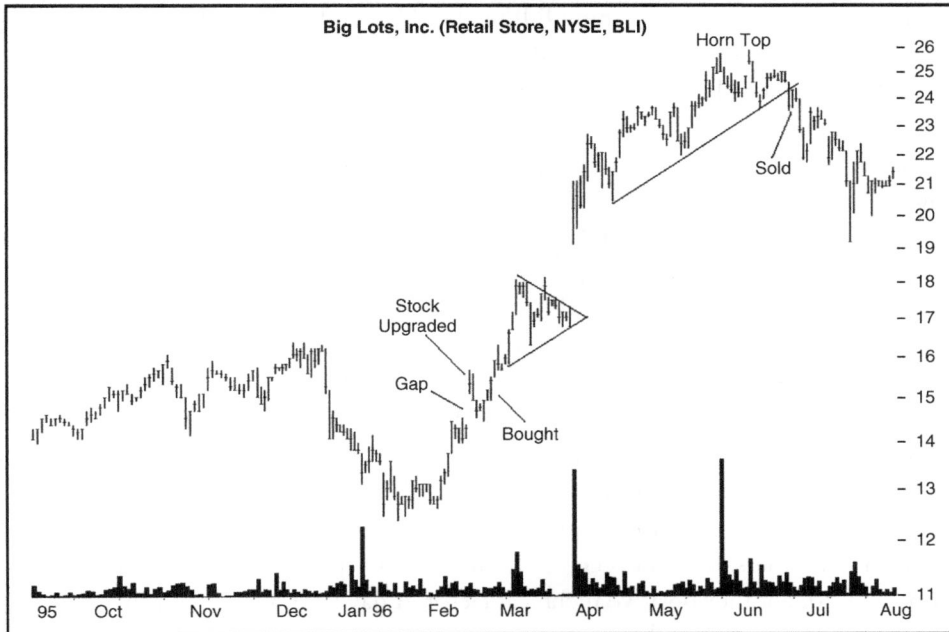

FIGURE 54.5 As Described in the Sample Trade—Downward Breakout, When Prices Stopped Dropping after the Upgrade, Bill Bought the Stock and Sold it When it Pierced the Trend Line.

Since the breakout was downward, he held off buying, suspecting that the gap would support the stock. He was right as prices paused there. However, he knew that sometimes they continued down, so he waited to place his buy order.

He applied the measure rule to the upgrade. On that day, the stock reached an intraday high of 15.68 and a low of 15.12, giving a height of 56 cents. Since the breakout was downward, he subtracted the height from the intraday low (15.12 − 0.56), giving the target price of 14.56. The stock reached that price 2 days after the upgrade. When prices started climbing again, he bought and received a fill at 15.20.

Over the coming days, prices climbed until moving sideways in the March symmetrical triangle. When it prematurely broke out upward in early March, it was still too soon to recognize the triangle as a pattern (not enough trend-line touches).

On March 26, the market reacted favorably to news that the company was buying Kay-Bee Toys. The stock gapped up and at least one broker upgraded the stock.

The stock continued climbing. In May–June, on the weekly scale, a horn top appeared, suggesting a trend reversal. That worried Bill. He drew a trend line along the minor lows, and the day after price closed below the trend line, he sold and received a fill at 24. He made 58% on the trade and spent the money on a set of shiny new golf clubs.

■ Sample Trade—Upward Breakout

Figure 54.6 shows an earlier trade Bill made, this one from the short side. In mid-March, a broker raised his rating on the stock and it gapped upward. It took another 3 days before price closed above the high on the day of the upgrade. The stock rose, following an up trend line drawn along the price bottoms.

For kicks, Bill pulled out a ruler, held it up to the monitor, and measured the height of the day when the upgrade occurred. It measured three-eighths of an inch. He slid the ruler to the right and saw that prices met the measure rule 6 days after the upgrade (a day before prices peaked).

When prices gapped through the trend line on news that same-store sales declined, Bill considered shorting the stock. He does not like shorting stocks, but the fundamentals seemed to be on his side. Still, he worried about the support level at 21 to 22 and expected prices to stall there. He did not short the stock.

Two days later, prices pierced the lower boundary of the support zone. Still he waited. Another week saw prices dip below the zone, then pull back into the zone, and then begin heading down again. Resumption of the decline was another short sell signal.

He shorted the stock and received a fill at 19.90, just below the round number support at 20, another positive technical factor. A day later, the stock gapped down, then bounced up, rounded over, and gapped down again in early May. There, the stock made a one-day reversal with a long tail and a closing price near the daily high. That pattern worried him as it suggested a short-term trend reversal.

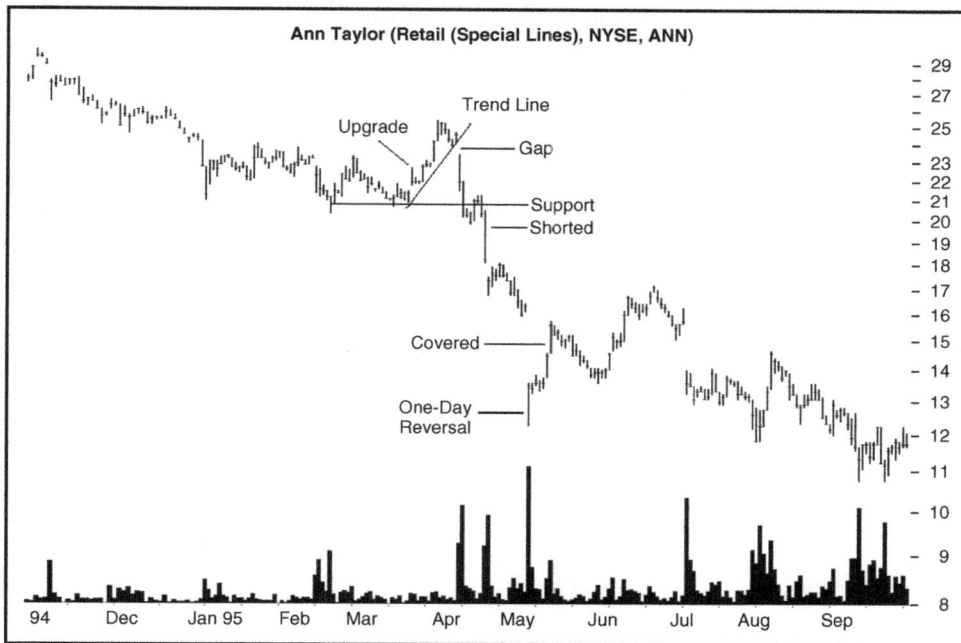

FIGURE 54.6 As Described in Sample Trade—Upward Breakout, Bill Shorted the Stock after It Pierced a Support Zone and Then Panicked on the Sharp Move Up in May.

When prices jumped upward, he put in an order to close out his position and covered his short at 15, for a 25% gain in about 3 weeks.

Prices declined after that, eventually reaching a low of just over 6 in January 1996. If he had held onto his position, he could have made a lot more money. Did the missed profit opportunity bother him? No, because short positions worry him, and worry interferes with his golf game.

■ For Best Performance

The following list includes tips and observations to improve your trading performance. Consult the associated table for more information.

■ Performance improves with wider intraday price range—Table 54.1.

■ Buy or hold in a bull market during an upgrade with an upward breakout. The average rise measures 24%, well above the other combinations—Table 54.2.

■ Select patterns that continue the rising price trend (continuations) by breaking out upward—Table 54.2.

■ The lowest failure rates associate with upgrades in a bull market and an upward breakout—Table 54.3.

■ In bull markets, upward breakouts near the yearly high perform best—Table 54.4.

- Downward breakouts near the yearly low perform best—Table 54.4.

- Pullbacks hurt performance—Table 54.4.

- Half the upgrades with downward breakouts reach the ultimate low in the first week. Most upward breakouts peak in less than 3 weeks—Table 54.5.

- High volume in upgrades usually improves postbreakout performance—Table 54.6.

- Select tall patterns—Table 54.6.

CHAPTER 55

Statistics Summary

From Thomas N. Bulkowski, *Encyclopedia of Chart Patterns,* Second Edition (Hoboken, New Jersey: John Wiley & Sons, 2005), "Statistics Summary" Appendix.

Learning Objective Statements

- Interpret potential price moves based on the patterns described in this chapter
- Calculate potential price targets
- Evaluate price levels for potential support or resistance
- Identify and interpret signals from various oscillators and technical studies in conjunction with the event-based patterns listed in these chapters

This summary is an alphabetical list, sorted by market direction, showing performance statistics for the chart and event patterns covered in this book. The patterns are also ranked and sorted by market direction.

In the following tables, a minus sign means a decline and N/A means not applicable. Where rank is listed, it is the sum of the columns to the left of it, sorted and then renumbered. Ties share the same value with no breaks in the numbering.

Chart Patterns: Bull Markets

Formation	Average Rise or Decline (%)	Break-even Failure Rate (%)	Change After Trend Ends (%)	Throwback or Pullback Occurrence (%)
Broadening Bottoms, down breakout	−15	16	52	42
Broadening Bottoms, up breakout	27	10	−34	41
Broadening Formations, Right-Angled and Ascending, down breakout	−15	20	53	65
Broadening Formations, Right-Angled and Ascending, up breakout	29	11	−31	47

Continued

Formation	Average Rise or Decline (%)	Break-even Failure Rate (%)	Change After Trend Ends (%)	Throwback or Pullback Occurrence (%)
Broadening Formations, Right-Angled and Descending, down breakout	−15	14	55	51
Broadening Formations, Right-Angled and Descending, up breakout	28	19	−26	52
Broadening Tops, down breakout	−15	18	53	48
Broadening Tops, up breakout	29	15	−33	54
Broadening Wedges, Ascending, down breakout	−17	11	49	57
Broadening Wedges, Ascending, up breakout	38	2	−31	50
Broadening Wedges, Descending, down breakout	−20	9	47	53
Broadening Wedges, Descending, up breakout	33	6	−33	53
Bump-and-Run Reversal Bottoms, up breakout	38	2	−29	59
Bump-and-Run Reversal Tops, down breakout	−19	5	53	62
Cup with Handle, up breakout	34	5	−30	58
Cup with Handle, Inverted, down breakout	−16	11	56	54
Diamond Bottoms, down breakout	−21	10	59	71
Diamond Bottoms, up breakout	36	4	−33	53
Diamond Tops, down breakout	−21	6	47	57
Diamond Tops, up breakout	27	10	−29	59
Double Bottoms, Adam & Adam, up breakout	35	5	−33	64
Double Bottoms, Adam & Eve, up breakout	37	5	−33	59
Double Bottoms, Eve & Adam, up breakout	35	4	−31	57
Double Bottoms, Eve & Eve, up breakout	40	4	−31	55
Double Tops, Adam & Adam, down breakout	−19	8	54	61
Double Tops, Adam & Eve, down breakout	−18	14	50	59
Double Tops, Eve & Adam, down breakout	−15	13	54	64
Double Tops, Eve & Eve, down breakout	−18	11	63	59
Flags, down breakout	−16[a]	2	41	46

Formation	Average Rise or Decline (%)	Break-even Failure Rate (%)	Change After Trend Ends (%)	Throwback or Pullback Occurrence (%)
Flags, up breakout	23[a]	4	−22	43
Flags, High and Tight, up breakout	69	0	−36	54
Gaps	N/A	N/A	N/A	N/A
Head-and-Shoulders Bottoms, up breakout	38	3	−31	45
Head-and-Shoulders Bottoms, Complex, up breakout	39	4	−29	63
Head-and-Shoulders Tops, down breakout	−22	4	51	50
Head-and-Shoulders Tops, Complex, down breakout	−23	4	48	67
Horn Bottoms, up breakout	35	9	−32	29
Horn Tops, down breakout	−21	7	51	33
Island Reversals, down breakout	−17	17	45	65
Island Reversals, up breakout	23	18	−28	70
Islands, Long, down breakout	−22	5	46	54
Islands, Long, up breakout	31	11	−35	67
Measured Move Down	N/A	N/A	46	N/A
Measured Move up	N/A	N/A	−26	N/A
Pennants, down breakout	−19[a]	4	40	31
Pennants, up breakout	25[a]	2	−25	47
Pipe Bottoms, up breakout	45	5	−33	44
Pipe Tops, down breakout	−20	11	56	41
Rectangles Bottoms, down breakout	−14	16	62	69
Rectangles Bottoms, up breakout	46	10	−28	53
Rectangles Tops, down breakout	−17	11	57	58
Rectangles Tops, up breakout	39	9	−30	64
Rounding Bottoms, up breakout	43	5	−31	40
Rounding Tops, down breakout	−19	12	57	48
Rounding Tops, up breakout	37	9	−31	53
Scallops, Ascending, down breakout	−14	27	54	56
Scallops, Ascending, up breakout	31	10	−32	58

Continued

	Chart Patterns: Bull Markets (*Continued*)			
Formation	Average Rise or Decline (%)	Break-even Failure Rate (%)	Change After Trend Ends (%)	Throwback or Pullback Occurrence (%)
Scallops, Ascending and Inverted, up breakout	43	4	−32	61
Scallops, Descending, down breakout	−17	15	51	55
Scallops, Descending, up breakout	22	22	−32	62
Scallops, Inverted and Descending, down breakout	−18	10	55	58
Three Falling Peaks, down breakout	−17	12	56	59
Three Rising Valleys, up breakout	41	5	−33	60
Triangles, Ascending, down breakout	−19	11	52	49
Triangles, Ascending, up breakout	35	13	−29	57
Triangles, Descending, down breakout	−16	16	60	54
Triangles, Descending, up breakout	47	7	−30	37
Triangles, Symmetrical, down breakout	−17	13	50	59
Triangles, Symmetrical, up breakout	31	9	−31	37
Triple Bottoms, up breakout	37	4	−33	64
Triple Tops, down breakout	−19	10	53	61
Wedges, Falling, down breakout	−15	15	51	69
Wedges, Falling, up breakout	32	11	−28	56
Wedges, Rising, down breakout	−14	24	53	63
Wedges, Rising, up breakout	28	8	−30	73

[a]Flags and pennants measure performance to the trend high or low, not the ultimate high or low.

Event Patterns: Bull Markets

Formation	Average Rise or Decline (%)	Break-even Failure Rate (%)	Change After Trend Ends (%)	Throwback or Pullback Occurrence (%)
Dead-Cat Bounce	N/A	N/A	N/A	N/A
Dead-Cat Bounce, Inverted	N/A	N/A	N/A	N/A
Earnings Surprise, Bad, down breakout	−13	31	51	41
Earnings Surprise, Good, up breakout	24	29	−27	41
FDA Drug Approvals, down breakout	−13	39	52	66
FDA Drug Approvals, up breakout	20	34	−29	61
Flag, Earnings, up breakout	34	10	−33	63
Same-Store Sales, Bad, down breakout	−12	26	54	53
Same-Store Sales, Good, up breakout	23	20	−28	59
Stock Downgrades, down breakout	−14	26	50	48
Stock Downgrades, up breakout	27	25	−30	49
Stock Upgrades, down breakout	−12	38	44	37
Stock Upgrades, up breakout	24	18	−30	63

Rank: Bull Market Chart Patterns

Formation	Average Rise or Decline Rank	+	Break-even Failure Rate Rank	+	Change After Trend Ends Rank	=	Overall Rank
Head-and-Shoulders Tops, down breakout	2		2		11		1
Diamond Bottoms, down breakout	3		8		4		1
Measured Move Down	N/A		N/A		16		—
Double Tops, Eve & Eve, down breakout	6		9		1		2
Head-and-Shoulders Tops, Complex, down breakout	1		2		14		3

Continued

Formation	Average Rise or Decline Rank	+	Break-even Failure Rate Rank	+	Change After Trend Ends Rank	=	Overall Rank
Bump-and-Run Reversal Tops, down breakout	5		3		9		3
Horn Tops, down breakout	3		5		11		4
Double Tops, Adam & Adam, down breakout	5		6		8		4
Pipe Tops, down breakout	4		9		6		4
Rounding Tops, down breakout	5		10		5		5
Islands, Long, down breakout	2		3		16		6
Scallops, Inverted and Descending, down breakout	6		8		7		6
Rectangles Tops, down breakout	7		9		5		6
Diamond Tops, down breakout	3		4		15		7
Triple Tops, down breakout	5		8		9		7
Cup with Handle, Inverted, down breakout	8		9		6		8
Three Falling Peaks, down breakout	7		10		6		8
Triangles, Ascending, down breakout	5		9		10		9
Triangles, Descending, down breakout	8		14		3		10
Pennants, down breakout	N/A		2		19		—
Broadening Wedges, Descending, down breakout	4		7		15		11
Flags, down breakout	N/A		1		18		—
Rectangles Bottoms, down breakout	10		15		2		12
Double Tops, Eve & Adam, down breakout	9		11		8		13
Broadening Formations, Right-Angled and Descending, down breakout	9		12		7		13
Broadening Wedges, Ascending, down breakout	7		9		13		14
Triangles, Symmetrical, down breakout	7		11		12		15
Double Tops, Adam & Eve, down breakout	6		12		12		15

Formation	Average Rise or Decline Rank	+	Break-even Failure Rate Rank	+	Change After Trend Ends Rank	=	Overall Rank
Scallops, Descending, down breakout	7		13		11		16
Wedges, Falling, down breakout	9		13		11		17
Broadening Bottoms, down breakout	9		14		10		17
Broadening Tops, down breakout	9		16		9		18
Broadening Formations, Right-Angled and Ascending, down breakout	9		17		9		19
Wedges, Rising, down breakout	10		18		9		20
Scallops, Ascending, down breakout	10		19		8		20
Island Reversals, down breakout	7		15		17		21
Gaps	N/A		N/A		N/A		—
Flags, High and Tight, up breakout	1		1		1		1
Measured Move Up	N/A		N/A		10		—
Pipe Bottom, up breakout	4		5		4		2
Scallops, Ascending and Inverted, up breakout	5		4		5		3
Three Rising Valleys, up breakout	6		5		4		4
Rounding Bottoms, up breakout	5		5		6		5
Triangles, Descending, up breakout	2		7		7		5
Broadening Wedges, Ascending, up breakout	9		2		6		6
Double Bottoms, Eve & Eve, up breakout	7		4		6		6
Triple Bottoms, up breakout	10		4		4		7
Head-and-Shoulders Bottoms, up breakout	9		3		6		7
Diamond Bottoms, up breakout	11		4		4		8
Double Bottoms, Adam & Eve, up breakout	10		5		4		8
Bump-and-Run Reversal Bottoms, up breakout	9		2		8		8

Continued

Formation	Average Rise or Decline Rank	+	Break-even Failure Rate Rank	+	Change After Trend Ends Rank	=	Overall Rank
Head-and-Shoulders Bottoms, Complex, up breakout	8		4		8		9
Double Bottoms, Adam & Adam, up breakout	12		5		4		10
Double Bottoms, Eve & Adam, up breakout	12		4		6		11
Rectangles Bottoms, up breakout	3		10		9		11
Broadening Wedges, Descending, up breakout	14		6		4		12
Rectangles Tops, up breakout	8		9		7		12
Rounding Tops, up breakout	10		9		6		13
Cup with Handle, up breakout	13		5		7		13
Horn Bottoms, up breakout	12		9		5		14
Islands, Long, up breakout	16		11		2		15
Scallops, Ascending, up breakout	16		10		5		16
Triangles, Symmetrical, up breakout	16		9		6		16
Broadening Bottoms, up breakout	19		10		3		17
Triangles, Ascending, up breakout	12		12		8		17
Wedges, Rising, up breakout	18		8		7		18
Pennants, up breakout	N/A		2		11		—
Broadening Tops, up breakout	17		13		4		19
Broadening Formations, Right-Angled and Ascending, up breakout	17		11		6		19
Wedges, Falling, up breakout	15		11		9		20
Diamond Tops, up breakout	19		10		8		21
Flags, up breakout	N/A		4		12		—
Scallops, Descending, up breakout	21		16		5		22
Broadening Formations, Right-Angled and Descending, up breakout	18		15		10		23
Island Reversals, up breakout	20		14		9		23

Rank: Bull Market Event Patterns

Formation	Average Rise or Decline Rank	+	Break-even Failure Rate Rank	+	Change After Trend Ends Rank	=	Overall Rank
Dead-Cat Bounce	N/A		N/A		N/A		—
Dead-Cat Bounce, Inverted	N/A		N/A		N/A		—
Same-Store Sales, Bad, down breakout	3		1		1		1
Stock Downgrades, down breakout	1		1		4		2
Earnings Surprise, Bad, down breakout	2		2		3		3
FDA Drug Approvals, down breakout	2		4		2		4
Stock Upgrade, down breakout	3		3		5		5
Flag, Earnings, up breakout	1		1		1		1
Stock Upgrades, up breakout	3		2		2		2
Stock Downgrades, up breakout	2		4		2		3
Same-Store Sales, Good, up breakout	4		3		4		4
Earnings Surprise, Good, up breakout	3		5		5		5
FDA Drug Approvals, up breakout	5		6		3		6

Chart Patterns: Bear Markets

Formation	Average Rise or Decline (%)	Break-even Failure Rate (%)	Change After Trend Ends (%)	Throwback or Pullback Occurrence (%)
Broadening Bottoms, down breakout	−18	9	46	56
Broadening Bottoms, up breakout	21	9	−35	44
Broadening Formations, Right-Angled and Ascending, down breakout	−22	8	47	52
Broadening Formations, Right-Angled and Ascending, up breakout	15	11	−38	43

Continued

	Chart Patterns: Bear Markets (*Continued*)			
Formation	Average Rise or Decline (%)	Break-even Failure Rate (%)	Change After Trend Ends (%)	Throwback or Pullback Occurrence (%)
Broadening Formations, Right-Angled and Descending, down breakout	−23	4	55	57
Broadening Formations, Right-Angled and Descending, up breakout	23	6	−35	50
Broadening Tops, down breakout	−20	3	49	62
Broadening Tops, up breakout	24	11	−33	53
Broadening Wedges, Ascending, down breakout	−21	14	37	52
Broadening Wedges, Ascending, up breakout	18	0	−30	70
Broadening Wedges, Descending, down breakout	−25	2	49	66
Broadening Wedges, Descending, up breakout	24	11	−32	61
Bump-and-Run Reversal Bottoms, up breakout	31	1	−34	73
Bump-and-Run Reversal Tops, down breakout	−27	1	48	65
Cup with Handle, up breakout	23	7	−34	42
Cup with Handle, Inverted, down breakout	−26	2	54	48
Diamond Bottoms, down breakout	−44[a]	0	48	40
Diamond Bottoms, up breakout	36	3	−36	60
Diamond Tops, down breakout	−24	4	47	57
Diamond Tops, up breakout	33	0	−34	54
Double Bottoms, Adam & Adam, up breakout	24	7	−32	61
Double Bottoms, Adam & Eve, up breakout	33	4	−35	54
Double Bottoms, Eve & Adam, up breakout	23	8	−36	56
Double Bottoms, Eve & Eve, up breakout	24	7	−34	46
Double Tops, Adam & Adam, down breakout	−19	11	47	48
Double Tops, Adam & Eve, down breakout	−22	7	43	58

Formation	Average Rise or Decline (%)	Break-even Failure Rate (%)	Change After Trend Ends (%)	Throwback or Pullback Occurrence (%)
Double Tops, Eve & Adam, down breakout	−24	5	51	54
Double Tops, Eve & Eve, down breakout	−25	2	45	51
Flags, down breakout	−25[b]	0	40	44
Flags, up breakout	17[b]	3	−25	53
Flags, High and Tight, up breakout	42	0	−35	65
Gaps	N/A	N/A	N/A	N/A
Head-and-Shoulders Bottoms, up breakout	30	4	−33	51
Head-and-Shoulders Bottoms, Complex, up breakout	31	3	−33	66
Head-and-Shoulders Tops, down breakout	−29	1	45	64
Head-and-Shoulders Tops, Complex, down breakout	−27	1	42	60
Horn Bottoms, up breakout	27	7	−37	58
Horn Tops, down breakout	−22	2	47	44
Island Reversals, down breakout	−23	5	46	59
Island Reversals, up breakout	21	10	−37	75
Islands, Long, down breakout	−26	2	48	54
Islands, Long, up breakout	25	4	−37	74
Measured Move Down	N/A	N/A	49	N/A
Measured Move up	N/A	N/A	−27	N/A
Pennants, down breakout	−25[b]	0	50	54
Pennants, up breakout	21[b]	2	−24	54
Pipe Bottoms, up breakout	32	4	−36	52
Pipe Tops, down breakout	−27	2	50	37
Rectangles Bottoms, down breakout	−25	4	48	53
Rectangles Bottoms, up breakout	24	11	−35	60
Rectangles Tops, down breakout	−21	9	45	65
Rectangles Tops, up breakout	20	16	−33	71
Rounding Bottoms, up breakout	31	5	−33	43
Rounding Tops, down breakout	−23	9	53	57

1007

STATISTICS SUMMARY

Continued

Formation	Average Rise or Decline (%)	Break-even Failure Rate (%)	Change After Trend Ends (%)	Throwback or Pullback Occurrence (%)
Rounding Tops, up breakout	19	16	−35	52
Scallops, Ascending, down breakout	−19	14	46	57
Scallops, Ascending, up breakout	19	16	−34	42
Scallops, Ascending and Inverted, up breakout	26	7	−33	65
Scallops, Descending, down breakout	−23	8	51	52
Scallops, Descending, up breakout	20	20	−36	58
Scallops, Inverted and Descending, down breakout	−23	5	55	50
Three Falling Peaks, down breakout	−24	4	52	62
Three Rising Valleys, up breakout	22	9	−33	65
Triangles, Ascending, down breakout	−24	3	47	45
Triangles, Ascending, up breakout	30	12	−32	54
Triangles, Descending, down breakout	−25	11	50	59
Triangles, Descending, up breakout	27	9	−34	52
Triangles, Symmetrical, down breakout	−19	9	45	62
Triangles, Symmetrical, up breakout	26	7	−33	55
Triple Bottoms, up breakout	23	8	−36	61
Triple Tops, down breakout	−24	5	46	64
Wedges, Falling, down breakout	−24	6	52	72
Wedges, Falling, up breakout	26	11	−33	61
Wedges, Rising, down breakout	−20	15	36	63
Wedges, Rising, up breakout	17	14	−35	66

[a]This decline is so large because only 20 samples are used.
[b]Flags and pennants measure performance to the trend high or low, not the ultimate high or low.

Event Patterns: Bear Markets				
Formation	Average Rise or Decline (%)	Break-even Failure Rate (%)	Change After Trend Ends (%)	Throwback or Pullback Occurrence (%)
Dead-Cat Bounce	N/A	N/A	N/A	N/A
Dead-Cat Bounce, Inverted	N/A	N/A	N/A	N/A
Earnings Surprise, Bad, down breakout	−17	26	37	45
Earnings Surprise, Good, up breakout	14	28	−31	44
FDA Drug Approvals, down breakout	N/A	N/A	N/A	N/A
FDA Drug Approvals, up breakout	N/A	N/A	N/A	N/A
Flag, Earnings, up breakout	22	16	32	58
Same-Store Sales, Bad, down breakout	−14	27	39	60
Same-Store Sales, Good, up breakout	14	27	−31	70
Stock Downgrades, down breakout	−19	17	35	45
Stock Downgrades, up breakout	14	28	−34	50
Stock Upgrades, down breakout	−18	23	35	17
Stock Upgrades, up breakout	16	21	−32	59

Rank: Bear Market Chart Patterns				
Formation	Average Rise or Decline Rank +	Break-even Failure Rate Rank +	Change After Trend Ends Rank =	Overall Rank
Measured Move Down	N/A	N/A	7	—
Cup with Handle, Inverted, down breakout	4	3	2	1
Diamond Bottoms, down breakout	1[a]	1	8	2[a]
Pennants, down breakout	N/A	1	6	—
Pipe Tops, down breakout	3	3	6	3
Bump-and-Run Reversal Tops, down breakout	3	2	8	4

Continued

Formation	Average Rise or Decline Rank	+	Break-even Failure Rate Rank	+	Change After Trend Ends Rank	=	Overall Rank
Broadening Formations, Right-Angled and Descending, down breakout	7		5		1		4
Scallops, Inverted and Descending, down breakout	7		6		1		5
Head-and-Shoulders Tops, down breakout	2		2		11		6
Islands, Long, down breakout	4		3		8		6
Broadening Wedges, Descending, down breakout	5		3		7		6
Three Falling Peaks, down breakout	6		5		4		6
Double Tops, Eve & Adam, down breakout	6		6		5		7
Wedges, Falling, down breakout	6		7		4		7
Head-and-Shoulders Tops, Complex, down breakout	3		2		13		8
Rectangles Bottoms, down breakout	5		5		8		8
Double Tops, Eve & Eve, down breakout	5		3		11		9
Triangles, Ascending, down breakout	6		4		9		9
Flags, down breakout	N/A		1		14		—
Horn Tops, down breakout	8		3		9		10
Diamond Tops, down breakout	6		5		9		10
Rounding Tops, down breakout	7		10		3		10
Broadening Tops, down breakout	10		4		7		11
Scallops, Descending, down breakout	7		9		5		11
Triple Tops, down breakout	6		6		10		12
Triangles, Descending, down breakout	5		11		6		12
Island Reversals, down breakout	7		6		10		13
Broadening Formations, Right-Angled and Ascending, down breakout	8		9		9		14

Formation	Average Rise or Decline Rank	+	Break-even Failure Rate Rank	+	Change After Trend Ends Rank	=	Overall Rank
Double Tops, Adam & Eve, down breakout	8		8		12		15
Rectangles Tops, down breakout	9		10		11		16
Double Tops, Adam & Adam, down breakout	11		11		9		17
Triangles, Symmetrical, down breakout	11		10		11		18
Broadening Bottoms, down breakout	12		10		10		18
Scallops, Ascending, down breakout	11		12		10		19
Broadening Wedges, Ascending, down breakout	9		12		15		20
Wedges, Rising, down breakout	10		13		16		21
Flags, High and Tight, up breakout	1		1		4		1
Diamond Bottoms, up breakout	2		4		3		2
Diamond Tops, up breakout	3		1		5		2
Measured Move Up	N/A		N/A		9		—
Pipe Bottom, up breakout	4		5		3		3
Double Bottoms, Adam & Eve, up breakout	3		5		4		3
Bump-and-Run Reversal Bottoms, up breakout	5		2		5		3
Head-and-Shoulders Bottoms, Complex, up breakout	5		4		6		4
Islands, Long, up breakout	9		5		2		5
Horn Bottoms, up breakout	7		8		2		6
Head-and-Shoulders Bottoms, up breakout	6		5		6		6
Rounding Bottoms, up breakout	5		6		6		6
Broadening Formations, Right-Angled and Descending, up breakout	11		7		4		7
Triangles, Descending, up breakout	7		10		5		7

Continued

Formation	Average Rise or Decline Rank	+	Break-even Failure Rate Rank	+	Change After Trend Ends Rank	=	Overall Rank
Scallops, Ascending and Inverted, up breakout	8		8		6		7
Triangles, Symmetrical, up breakout	8		8		6		7
Double Bottoms, Eve & Adam, up breakout	11		9		3		8
Triple Bottoms, up breakout	11		9		3		8
Double Bottoms, Eve & Eve, up breakout	10		8		5		8
Cup with Handle, up breakout	11		8		5		9
Double Bottoms, Adam & Adam, up breakout	10		8		7		10
Broadening Wedges, Ascending, up breakout	16		1		8		10
Island Reversals, up breakout	13		11		2		11
Rectangles Bottoms, up breakout	10		12		4		11
Wedges, Falling, up breakout	8		12		6		11
Triangles, Ascending, up breakout	6		13		7		11
Broadening Bottoms, up breakout	13		10		4		12
Pennants, up breakout	N/A		3		11		—
Three Rising Valleys, up breakout	12		10		6		13
Broadening Tops, up breakout	10		12		6		13
Broadening Wedges, Descending, up breakout	10		12		7		14
Broadening Formations, Right-Angled and Ascending, up breakout	18		12		1		15
Flags, up breakout	N/A		4		10		—
Scallops, Descending, up breakout	14		17		3		16
Rounding Tops, up breakout	15		15		4		16
Wedges, Rising, up breakout	17		14		4		17
Scallops, Ascending, up breakout	15		16		5		18
Rectangles Tops, up breakout	14		16		6		19
Gaps	N/A		N/A		N/A		—

*a*This rank is high because only 20 samples are used.

Formation	Average Rise or Decline Rank	+	Break-even Failure Rate Rank	+	Change After Trend Ends Rank	=	Overall Rank
Stock Downgrades, down breakout	1		1		3		1
Stock Upgrades, down breakout	2		2		3		2
Earnings Surprise, Bad, down breakout	3		3		2		3
Same-Store Sales, Bad, down breakout	4		4		1		4
FDA Drug Approvals, down breakout	N/A		N/A		N/A		—
Flag, Earnings, up breakout	1		1		2		1
Stock Upgrades, up breakout	2		2		2		2
Stock Downgrades, up breakout	3		4		1		3
Same-Store Sales, Good, up breakout	3		3		3		4
Earnings Surprise, Good, up breakout	3		4		3		5
Dead-Cat Bounce	N/A		N/A		N/A		—
Dead-Cat Bounce, Inverted	N/A		N/A		N/A		—
FDA Drug Approvals, up breakout	N/A		N/A		N/A		—

CHAPTER 56

Fact, Fiction, and Momentum Investing

From Clifford S. Asness, Andrea Frazzini, Ronen Israel, and Tobias J. Moskowitz, *Journal of Portfolio Management*, Fall 2014 (New York: *Institutional Investor Journals*).

Learning Objective Statement

- Explain valid reasons for establishing strategies based on momentum investing styles and momentum-based price patterns

It's been over 20 years since the academic discovery of momentum investing (Jegadeesh and Titman (1993), Asness (1994)), yet much confusion and debate remains regarding its efficacy and its use as a practical investment tool. In some cases "confusion and debate" is us attempting to be polite, as it is near impossible for informed practitioners and academics to still believe some of the myths uttered about momentum — but that impossibility is often belied by real world statements. In this article, we aim to clear up much of the confusion by documenting what we know about momentum and disproving many of the often-repeated myths. We highlight ten myths about momentum and refute them, using results from widely circulated academic papers and analysis from the simplest and best publicly available data.

[1] Clifford S. Asness, Andrea Frazzini, and Ronen Israel: AQR Capital Management, 2 Greenwich Plaza, Greenwich, CT, 06830. Tobias J. Moskowitz: University of Chicago Booth School of Business and NBER. We thank Antti Ilmanen, Sarah Jiang, John Liew, Scott Richardson, Laura Serban, and Daniel Villalon for useful comments and suggestions.

Momentum is the phenomenon that securities that have performed well relative to peers (winners) on average continue to outperform, and securities that have performed relatively poorly (losers) tend to continue to underperform.[2]

The existence of momentum is a well-established empirical fact. The return premium is evident in 212 years (yes, this is not a typo, *two hundred and twelve years* of data from 1801 to 2012) of U.S. equity data,[3] dating back to the Victorian age in U.K. equity data,[4] in over 20 years of out-of-sample evidence from its original discovery, in 40 other countries, and in more than a dozen other asset classes.[5] Some of this evidence predates academic research in financial economics, suggesting that the momentum premium has been a part of markets since their very existence, well before researchers studied them as a science.

However, as momentum strategies have grown in popularity, so have myths around them. Some of the most common myths are that momentum is too "small and sporadic" a factor, works mostly on the short-side, works well only among small stocks, and doesn't survive trading costs. Furthermore, some argue that momentum is best used as a "screen", not as a regular factor in an investment process. Others will go so far as to say that momentum investing is like a game of "hot potato", implying that it isn't a serious investment strategy, with no theory or reasonable explanation to back it up.

Frankly, we're a little irked (if that was not clear) by those who should know better but continue to repeat these myths, stretching the limits of credulity. In this essay we address and refute these myths using academic papers (that have been widely circulated throughout the academic and practitioner communities, have been presented and debated at top-level academic seminars and conferences, and have been published in peer-reviewed journals) and the simplest data taken from Kenneth French's publicly available website, a standard dataset used by both academics and practitioners. Anyone repeating these myths, in any dimension, after reading this piece is simply ignoring the facts.

Please note, of course, that we make no claim that momentum works all the time. In fact, of late (this year and the last few years), momentum as a strategy has had a

---

[2] The term "relative" is important. Momentum is sometimes confused with trend following — though related, these are not the same. The process behind momentum is to rank securities relative to their peers; in contrast, trend following typically focuses on absolute price changes. Unlike trends, which increase exposure during upswings and decrease exposure during downswings, momentum takes no explicit view on the market trend, but simply ranks securities relative to each other over the same time period (though in doing so some implicit, net directional market view may exist). Momentum's "winners" and "losers" are defined no matter how the market overall is doing. For example, during 2008 a winner would have only been down a few percent relative to other stocks that on average were down more than 30%. During market upswings, losers would similarly be defined as stocks that were only up a few percentage points.

[3] See Geczy and Samonov (2013) for evidence of momentum in U.S. stocks from 1801 to 2012 in what the authors call, with some justifiable pride, "the world's longest backtest".

[4] See Chabot, Ghysels, and Jagannathan (2009).

[5] See Asness, Moskowitz and Pedersen (2013).

more difficult time. Still, the fact is momentum is a risky variable factor (as they all are) with an impressive long-term average return that survives all the attacks (myths) hurled against it. In this essay, we defend momentum, including its use stand-alone (especially as a substitute for growth investing) and in combination with value, from these persistent attacks. We feel this, both myth busting and focusing on the long term, is especially important given momentum's recent performance, which only wrongly reinforces the resilience of its attackers. At the same time, our goal is not to denigrate other factors, most specifically value, although we occasionally note the irony that many of the myths we dispel come from value investors attempting to discredit momentum, even though several of these myths actually apply better to value investing itself! However, as we'll show in this essay, value and momentum work better when used as complements, and it is the combination of the two we stress and most strongly recommend. We are fans of both momentum and value but bigger fans of their combination (and not fans of myths at all).

Now, on to the myth busting.

■ Myth #1: Momentum Returns Are Too "Small and Sporadic"

While we have already cited some evidence in the introduction, given this precisely worded myth has been used in print, a further exploration of this most basic issue has to be myth #1. We start with gross of costs, long-short portfolios to establish base-line results. In later sections we debunk the myths surrounding shorting, transactions costs, and the general implementability of momentum for traditional long-only investors.

Momentum's presence and robustness are remarkably stable (and by this we don't mean that it doesn't have long stretches of poor performance, as does any factor, or short stretches of extreme performance; we mean the overall evidence across very long periods of time and in many places). Again, it is present in U.S. stocks over very long time periods and, following its academic "discovery" in the early 1990s, has been shown to be robust out-of-sample (an important exercise we will repeat here), in the individual stocks of other countries, for stock markets, and for completely different asset classes, such as bond markets, currencies, commodities, and others. It has become one of the preeminent empirical regularities studied by academics and practitioners. To see why, we will provide evidence that anyone can replicate. Most of the analysis is based on factors from Professor Kenneth French's website and focuses on momentum within U.S. stocks. Some definitions are needed, and we follow Professor French here:

- **RMRF** represents the equity market risk premium, or aggregate equity return minus the risk free rate. It is the return from simply being long equities at market capitalization weights and, unlike the other factors, is not a "spread" return between one set of stocks and another but between all stocks and cash;

- **SMB**, or "small minus big", represents a portfolio that is long small stocks and short big stocks to capture the "size" effect;

- **HML,** or "high minus low", represents a portfolio that is long high book-to-price stocks and short low book-to-price stocks representing "value" investing;

- **UMD,** or "up minus down", represents a portfolio that is long stocks that have high relative past one-year returns and short stocks that have low relative past one-year returns[6] to capture "momentum."[7]

For all factors, Kenneth French's data library provides returns of the long and short sides separately, for both large and small capitalization securities separately, all of which we use in this essay. Most of our analysis focuses on UMD and its components. A link to Kenneth French's data library can be found here if you want to use the data, update the series, or check the analysis yourself:

http://mba.tuck.dartmouth.edu/pages/faculty/ken.french/data_library.html

Table 56.1 reports the annualized mean spread returns and Sharpe ratios for each of the different portfolios described above over three different periods: 1) the longest period for which Kenneth French provides data on all factors (starting in January 1927 and running to the end of 2013), 2) beginning in July 1963, the start date of Fama and French's seminal papers (1992, 1993) on the 3-factor model and running to the end of 2013, and 3) the out-of-sample period since the original momentum papers (Jegadeesh and Titman (1993) and Asness (1994)), beginning January 1991 and running to the end

TABLE 56.1

Sample	Returns				Sharpe Ratios			
	RMRF	SMB	HML	UMD	RMRF	SMB	HML	UMD
1927–2013	7.7%	2.9%	4.7%	8.3%	0.41	0.26	0.39	0.50
1963–2013	6.0%	3.1%	4.5%	8.4%	0.39	0.29	0.45	0.57
1991–2013	8.2%	3.3%	3.6%	6.3%	0.54	0.29	0.32	0.36

---

[6] Specifically, this is defined as the past 12-month return, skipping the most recent month's return (to avoid microstructure and liquidity biases), as defined by Asness (1994) and now generally used as the standard definition of momentum.

[7] SMB and HML are formed by first splitting the universe of stocks into two size categories (S and B) using NYSE market cap medians and then splitting stocks into three groups based on book-to-market equity [highest 30% (H), middle 40% (M), and lowest 30% (L), using NYSE breakpoints]. The intersection of stocks across the six categories are value-weighed and used to form the portfolios SH (small, high BE/ME), SM (small, middle BE/ME), SL (small, low BE/ME), BH (big, high BE/ME), BM (big, middle BE/ME), and BL (big, low BE/ME), where SMB is the average of the three small stock portfolios (1/3SH+1/3SM+1/3SL) minus the average of the three big stock portfolios (1/3BH+1/3BM+1/3BL) and HML is the average of the two high book-to-market portfolios (1/2SH+1/2BH) minus the average of the two low book-to-market portfolios (1/2SL+1/2BL). UMD is constructed similarly to HML, in which two size groups and three momentum groups [highest 30% (U), middle 40% (M), lowest 30% (D)] are used to form six portfolios and UMD is the average of the small and big winners minus the average of the small and big losers.

of 2013.[8] Gross returns and Sharpe ratios for momentum (a.k.a., UMD) are large and, in fact, larger than both value and size. This is true over the full-sample period of 87-plus years of data, from 1963 onwards and in the out-of-sample period.

Critics of momentum who complain it is "volatile" may be pointing to some of the evidence implied in Table 56.1. Momentum's advantage over the other factors is somewhat smaller in Sharpe ratio terms than in raw spread returns. But, even considering its higher volatility, momentum still comes out on top! Stepping back and explaining a bit more, and focusing on the full period from 1927–2013, this means the spread of small stocks over large stocks averaged 2.9% a year, the spread of cheap stocks over expensive stocks averaged 4.7% a year, and the spread of recent winners over recent losers averaged 8.3% a year, all calculated using analogous methods (and these correspond to Sharpe ratios of 0.26, 0.39, and 0.50, respectively). This ordering, by return or Sharpe ratio, is the same over the much shorter out-of-sample period, too.

As for the word "sporadic" included in myth #1, it is not clear if this needs any more coverage as we have included Sharpe ratios above (which are adjusted, of course, for volatility, an imperfect yet very useful measure of "sporadicness").[9] But for those who like a more common-sense method of judging whether something is sporadic, we also present in Table 56.2 the percentage of times each strategy generates positive returns (i.e., the longs beat the shorts, so for value this is how often the cheap stocks beat the expensive stocks, for momentum it's how often winners beat losers, etc.) We focus on one- and five-year horizons, though results are not very sensitive to this choice.

At 1-year rolling horizons, UMD is the most consistent over the longest period. At 5-year horizons (any longer gets a bit silly for an out-of-sample period of 23 years), UMD is edged by HML, perhaps (statistics on this are not dispositive) because value has more negative long-term autocorrelation than does momentum, or perhaps, as discussed in Asness and Frazzini (2013), because this version of HML is really a portfolio of mostly value with a little oddly constructed momentum thrown in.[10]

TABLE 56.2

Sample	% Positive, 1-Year Rolling Returns				% Positive, 5-Year Rolling Returns			
	RMRF	SMB	HML	UMD	RMRF	SMB	HML	UMD
1927–2013	71%	58%	63%	81%	82%	65%	89%	88%
1963–2013	72%	61%	64%	80%	77%	65%	87%	89%
1991–2013	78%	62%	61%	76%	73%	75%	74%	71%

[8] Another of the never-ending attempts to knock down momentum is a vague comparison to some other effects that did not hold up out-of-sample (e.g., http://www.dimensional.com/famafrench/questions-answers/qa-can-investors-profit-from-momentum.aspx). While examining out-of-sample results is always crucial, comments like this give us even more motivation to see if the analogy is valid.

[9] If that's not a word, it should be.

[10] See Asness and Frazzini (2013) for the argument that value, HML, as defined by Fama and French was logical for its time, before momentum had been studied, but accidentally mixes about 80% a pure value strategy and about 20% a very odd (accidentally and thus poorly constructed) momentum strategy. Asness and Frazzini (2013) find that a small, logical change in how value is defined produces what they call "pure value". This definition of value is positive 81% of the 5-year periods, below momentum's consistency.

TABLE 56.3

	RMRF	SMB	HML	UMD	60/40 HML/UMD
Sharpe Ratios	0.41	0.26	0.39	0.50	0.80
% positive, 1-year rolling returns	71%	58%	63%	81%	81%
% positive, 5-year rolling returns	82%	65%	89%	88%	92%

But we don't recommend one versus the other—we recommend using both value and momentum together; and neither, in any reasonable form, are what any knowledgeable analyst, economist, money manager, or academic should call "sporadic".

Finally, while not the direct point of this section, we elaborate a bit more on the statement above, recommending using value and momentum together. Below, in Table 56.3, are the statistics for a portfolio that combines HML and UMD, with 60% of the weight on HML and 40% of the weight on UMD.[11] We believe the 60/40 HML/UMD column speaks for itself.

Critics and myth makers would do well to remember that, even if a factor were sporadic, it's not the "sporadicness" of one factor that matters, but that of the portfolio. This is portfolio theory 101. Viewing momentum alone, the myth is wrong. Viewing momentum as part of a portfolio, the myth is very, very wrong.

Of course, again, the debate can still rage on about how much of the above (for each factor, not just momentum) can be captured by long-only investors,[12] after trading costs and, for some investors, taxes, and even how much history will repeat going forward in a possibly changing world. But, starting with the basic spreads between winners and losers, as do most other authors on this topic, it's undeniable that far from being "small", momentum returns are large, large after basic risk-adjustment (Sharpe ratio), and larger than other major factors, even those occasionally being promoted by the exact same crowd calling momentum "small and sporadic". If the myth-sayers think momentum is small and sporadic, then size, value, and even the equity premium must appear tiny and positively flighty to them.

So, to sum up, who you calling small and sporadic?

---

[11] We chose the 60/40 weights deliberately in an attempt to build a balanced portfolio of the two. Part of the reason for choosing 60/40 and not 50/50, another possible balanced allocation, is found in Asness and Frazzini (2013) who show that the classic HML is best thought of as an approximately 80/20 combination of value and momentum. Thus, a 60/40 combination of these factors is actually closer to a real 50/50 combination of pure value and momentum. Results are not sensitive to this choice; we're just being picky!

[12] The above are, again, long-short factors, which absolutely do indeed count as some trade this way directly. In fact, they were one of the original methodologies used by Fama and French (1993) to explore the value effect. But not all investors are able or willing to go long and short so we consider their situation as well.

Myth #2: Momentum Cannot be Captured by Long-Only Investors as "Momentum Can Only be Exploited on the Short Side"

In other words, the UMD factor is long winners and short losers, and those repeating this myth are asserting that most or all of the returns we show above for UMD come from being short the losers. This is patently and clearly false, which somehow does not stop it from being among the most-repeated momentum myths.

First, even if it were true (it's not), for a long-only investor, being underweight a security relative to the market is economically similar to being short the security (albeit with the constraint that your largest underweight can only be as large as a stock's weight in the benchmark or market). So, asking how much of a factor return comes from the long and short side is already only partially relevant. But, admittedly, if all of the returns came from the short-side, it would certainly weaken the factor's utility for long-only investors, as this constraint on the size you can underweight a stock could, depending on goals, bind quite often.

However, this is not the case, and disproving myth #2 is easy. Simply take Kenneth French's momentum factor, UMD, and look at the market-adjusted returns (alphas) of the up ("U") and down ("D") portfolios separately (market-adjusted returns are the intercept of a regression of returns in excess of the risk free rate on market returns in excess of the risk free rate).[13] Remember, Kenneth French's UMD portfolio is just a long (winners) portfolio plus a short (losers) portfolio, and now we're just going to examine these two sides separately (so if the short portfolio goes down, it records as a positive number here, as that is its contribution to UMD).

As the left panel of Table 56.4 indicates, there is little difference between the long and short sides of momentum. Historically, almost half of the UMD premium came from "up". For instance, over the full period, the short side contributed 5.1% to UMD (remember, that means the short portfolio fell 5.1% more than its market beta would imply it should and because it's held short, −5.1% becomes a +5.1% contribution) and the long side contributed 5.5%, which sum to the 10.6% of UMD itself. The long side is every bit as profitable as the short side! Furthermore, the table shows that whether you look at U vs. D over the whole sample period or over subsample periods (including the out-of-sample period), you cannot find any reliable evidence that the short side is more important than the long side—in fact, it's evenly split between them. If you do not like regressions and prefer to simply look at average returns versus the market (abstracting from the difference in market beta of the long and short portfolios), the right panel of Table 56.4 also indicates that, if anything, on average, the long side of UMD has contributed to most of its returns, the opposite of what critics often assert.

---

[13] For this exercise, it is important to look at market-adjusted returns since we know that the market returns are generally positive and a stand-alone short momentum portfolio (losers) has a different market beta than a stand-alone long momentum portfolio (winners), which will average higher betas. Though, for completeness we also show the results without market-adjustment and they hold up as well (in fact too well as the lack of proper risk adjustment favors the long side!)

TABLE 56.4

Sample	UMD Market-Adjusted Returns				UMD Returns Minus Market			
	Short Side	Long Side	UMD	% Long	Short Side	Long Side	UMD	% Long
1927–2013	71%	58%	63%	81%	82%	65%	89%	88%
1963–2013	72%	61%	64%	80%	77%	65%	87%	89%
1991–2013	78%	62%	61%	76%	73%	75%	74%	71%

We only present the data for momentum within U.S. stocks here. More formally, and with a plethora of tests and specifications, Israel and Moskowitz (2013a) show that the long and short side of momentum are equally profitable using 86 years of U.S. data as well as 40 years of international equity data, and another 40 years of data from five other asset classes outside of equities. Everywhere they looked and in every way, they could not find any evidence that the short side profits were systematically larger or more important than the long side. In other words, long-only momentum is quite profitable, equally so with the short side of momentum.

If you don't like what Israel and Moskowitz (2013a) do in their paper (or don't have time to read it), you can download Kenneth French's data and try it yourself as we have done. You will find what we find: momentum does not work better, or only, on the short-side.

■ Myth #3: Momentum Is Much Stronger among Small Cap Stocks Than Large Caps

Like the other myths, this is often claimed even more histrionically as "momentum only exists among small caps." And, like the other myths, it is false. But what it lacks in truth it makes up for with the amusing quality of being backwards, at least when uttered (as is often the case) by fans of value investing—this myth happens to be true if you replace the word "momentum" with "value" (yes, we still love value, despite its weakness among large caps).

For the most detailed study to date on this topic, see Israel and Moskowitz (2013a). In their paper, they find little to no evidence that momentum is related to size; it is almost equally as strong among large caps as it is among small caps. However, in an interesting twist, they find that though the value premium is strong among small caps, it's virtually non-existent among large caps. While we ourselves are big proponents of value investing (we just believe the ubiquitous data that it is better alongside momentum!), to argue that momentum is all about small stocks is completely inconsistent with the facts, and far more of an argument to lay at the feet of pure value investing. To promote this myth about momentum while simultaneously advocating value investing is bordering on absurd.

Returning to Kenneth French's data and carrying out some simple tests, Table 56.5 looks at "UMD Small", which goes long winners and short losers only among small stocks, "UMD Big", which does the same only among large caps, and repeats the

TABLE 56.5

Sample	Momentum			Value		
	UMD Small	UMD Big	UMD	HML Small	HML Big	HML
1927–2013	9.8%	6.8%	8.3%	5.9%	3.5%	4.7%
1963–2013	11.3%	5.5%	8.4%	6.4%	2.6%	4.5%
1991–2013	8.1%	4.5%	6.3%	6.5%	0.7%	3.6%

results for regular UMD, which is done over all stocks (see footnote 7 for exact specification). It also does the analogous exercise for HML. The table shows that momentum returns among big cap stocks are large and only slightly smaller in magnitude than returns among small cap stocks (most factor averages get larger among small stocks, either because risk premia are greater, inefficiencies are greater, or just because volatility is greater). Value returns are also smaller among large cap than small cap (comparing the HML Big column to the HML Small column).

Over the entire sample period, the return to value within small cap stocks is 5.9% per annum and within large it's 3.5% per annum (and, as it turns out, not statistically different from zero once you adjust for market beta). The return for momentum within small is 9.8% per annum, and within large it's 6.8% per annum (both highly statistically significant, even after adjusting for beta). Momentum is again better in both categories, with a smaller percentage drop-off in large versus small caps than for value.

Taking this a bit further reveals a dirty little secret of value investing. It turns out that value investing, as measured by HML, which is gross of everything and implemented long-short (the test usually most biased to find strong results), is highly sensitive to the fact that Fama and French chose to split the weight in HML half to large and half to small (try building that portfolio in real life by shorting expensive tiny stocks!). HML constructed among only large capitalization stocks is, dependent on the time horizon, quite a dodgy proposition (for instance if HML was done just among large cap stocks in the original Fama and French (1993) paper over the time frame used at that point in history, they would not have found a very strong value effect at all). Even over what we call the full out-of-sample period, 1991–2013, HML among only big stocks is a paltry 0.06 Sharpe ratio versus 0.51 within small stocks. In contrast, UMD over this period among large stocks is a 0.24 Sharpe versus 0.45 in small stocks (yes, not as big in large caps, but much closer for momentum than for value). Momentum, unlike value, is far more robust among large versus small stocks (and again makes others getting this backwards really odd—people who live in houses made of cheap stocks shouldn't …).

Putting it starkly: in-sample, out-of-sample, calculated in Greenwich Connecticut, Chicago, Boston, Palo Alto, Santa Monica, Austin, or in the library with a candlestick, wherever or however you want to look, along any dimension, those who make the claim that momentum fails for large caps, while being supporters of value investing, are not simply mistaken, they have it backwards.

You might wonder how myths #2 and #3 originated. Well, two papers in particular helped contribute to these myths, with one of the papers co-authored by an author of this article. In Hong, Lim, and Stein (2000) and Grinblatt and Moskowitz (2004), the authors show, using a more limited sample period predominantly from the 1980s and 1990s, that momentum is stronger among small stocks and on the short side (though to be clear, neither article ever claimed momentum was non-existent among large caps or on the long side; somehow the original evidence became twisted into something more extreme). We also showed above that, over an overlapping period from 1991–2013, momentum worked better in small than large caps (0.45 vs. 0.24 Sharpe ratios, respectively), but it held up in large caps, and fared far better than value did. It turns out even this difference, which is still a victory for momentum, is anomalously weak. These results have proven not to be robust out-of-sample by Israel and Moskowitz (2013a). As we've shown, over the much longer out-of-sample period from 1927 to 2013, and Israel and Moskowitz (2013a) have shown in international markets and other asset classes, the returns to momentum are really no stronger on the short side and are not related to size. So, if one of the authors of the original papers claiming these facts can admit that they do not hold up out of sample, certainly those without their names on these papers should accept the facts.

This sample-specific effect of size on momentum also explains other results in the literature that claim the same facts. For example, Fama and French (2012) look at momentum internationally and conclude that it is stronger among small cap stocks (again their evidence does show a healthy momentum premium among large caps, just not as strong as among small caps). However, their sample period is from 1989 to 2011, which is essentially the same period over which these other short-period papers, and our out-of-sample test, find a stronger small-cap momentum effect in the U.S. Over the longer sample period, there is little statistical evidence that momentum is much stronger among small cap stocks. And, most importantly, over no reasonable length sample period is there any evidence that momentum actually fails among large cap stocks.

Finally, these two myths—that momentum is dominated by the short side and mostly among small caps—are often voiced together, the motivation (we think) being to convey that it will be practically difficult and costly to implement. First, even if this were true, a long-only investor would still benefit from underweighting small cap losers as mentioned above. Second, and far more important, it isn't true or even close to true. This leads us to the next myth.

■ Myth #4: Momentum Does Not Survive, or Is Seriously Limited by, Trading Costs

Momentum is a higher turnover strategy than some other strategies (e.g., value) and hence the question arises as to whether the premium for momentum covers trading costs (a reasonable question for any strategy). Plus, if you believed in the myths that momentum was dominated by shorting small stocks, then trading costs might seem to be an even larger potential impediment. However, just like these previous myths, the statement that momentum does not survive trading costs is false.

While much of our other myth-dispelling can be done with Kenneth French's data, disproving this particular myth requires real world, net-of-costs data. To the best of our knowledge, the most comprehensive work to date that analyzes real-world trading costs of factors is Frazzini, Israel, and Moskowitz (2013), "FIM", which uses trades from a large institutional investor (AQR Capital) over a long period of time. Using a unique dataset containing more than a trillion dollars of live trades from 1998 to 2013 across 19 developed equity markets, the authors estimate what real-world trading costs are for momentum, value, and size-based strategies. Their conclusion is that per dollar trading costs for momentum are quite low, and thus, despite the higher turnover, momentum easily survives transactions costs.

Unlike testing real-world strategies as in FIM, most academic studies examine portfolios that do not consider transactions costs in their design and do not allow for tradeoffs that could lead to a reduction in trading costs. They simply rebalance as automatons, ignoring costs. Trading patiently (by breaking orders up into small sizes and setting limit order prices that provide, not demand, liquidity) and allowing some tracking error to a theoretical style portfolio can significantly reduce trading costs without changing the nature of the strategy. FIM show that allowing both innovations can result in trading cost estimates (and break-even fund sizes) that are significantly smaller (larger) relative to naïve implementations.

Where did this myth come from? Several academic papers (e.g., Korajczyk and Sadka (2004) and Lesmond, Schill, and Zhou (2003)) using trading cost estimates from daily or intradaily data found much larger effects from transactions costs on the viability of momentum strategies. However, two key differences can explain the different results. First, the studies that find much larger trading costs do so because they estimate costs for the average investor using aggregated daily or transaction-level data for all trades in the market, which turn out to be about ten times larger than the costs of a large institutional manager, which are the costs FIM implicitly measure. Second, as discussed above, these other studies examine portfolios that do not consider transactions costs in their design, which can significantly reduce turnover and therefore trading costs further. Both factors result in trading cost estimates (and break-even fund sizes) that are an order of magnitude smaller (larger) than previous studies suggest.

History provides an analogous myth. Decades ago when the first academic studies on the size premium came out, many declared "you can't trade it; the trading costs would wipe out any return premium." These statements were made without realistic trading costs data and without allowing for cost minimization through real-world, practical implementation. Similar to FIM, a paper by Keim (1999) that used real-world transactions costs from a large institutional investor—Dimensional Fund Advisors (DFA)—showed that these previous studies were flawed and had grossly overestimated transactions costs. A firm like DFA would never face the same costs as the average investor and is far smarter than to trade blindly to a set of dynamically changing strategy weights when even small modifications can greatly reduce costs. As the industry has proven for decades after these papers, small cap portfolios can indeed be traded in an efficient manner that does not wipe out their returns. Since the premium for momentum is much higher than it is for size, and the costs to trading momentum are slightly lower than those for size (momentum is higher turnover but small caps are more expensive to trade than other stocks), you don't have to do much math to realize that momentum can easily survive trading costs.

■ Myth #5: Momentum Does Not Work for a Taxable Investor

This myth is related to momentum's higher turnover relative to other strategies (e.g., value), so at face value it may seem reasonable. However, high turnover does not necessarily equal high taxes.

Papers by Israel and Moskowitz (2013b), Bergstresser and Pontiff (2013), and Sialm and Zhang (2013) show that momentum, despite having five to six times the annual turnover as value, actually has a similar tax burden as value. At first blush this seems counterintuitive, until you realize the following two facts. First, momentum actually has turnover that is biased to be tax advantageous—it tends to hold on to winners and sell losers—thus avoiding realizing short-term capital gains in favor of long-term capital gains and realizing short-term capital losses. From a tax perspective this is efficient and effectively lowers the tax burden of momentum strategies. Second, value strategies, despite their low turnover, have very high dividend income exposure, which is (in most tax regimes in history) tax inefficient. Momentum, on the other hand, more often than not has low dividend exposure. On net, this makes value and momentum roughly equally tax efficient. Since the premium for momentum is quite a bit higher than for value, yet they face similar tax rates, the after-tax returns to momentum are also higher than for value.

One more twist is worth mentioning. The analysis above didn't consider any "smart" trading, but just implicitly implemented the strategies from Kenneth French's data. Israel and Moskowitz (2013b) also look into tax-optimized versions of these strategies by designing portfolios that attempt to minimize taxes while not incurring meaningful style drift. The authors find that tax optimization is much easier to achieve through capital gains than through dividend income, which makes intuitive sense. Pushing the realization of gains from short-term to long-term status (which may often require only delaying a trade by a month) has a very small effect on the portfolio, but a large tax effect given the difference in tax rates between short- and long-term capital gains. There is a similar trade-off between short- and long-term loss realizations. But the only way to reduce dividend income is to not hold dividend paying stocks, which has a much more significant impact on a value portfolio and induces substantial style drift. Hence, tax optimization considerably improves the tax efficiency of a momentum strategy, whose tax burden comes mostly from capital gains, while it has a more limited effect on a value strategy, whose tax burden is driven primarily by dividend exposure.

The bottom line is that momentum survives taxes and has a tax burden roughly equal to or smaller than lower-turnover strategies such as value, especially if run optimally. Even for a taxable investor, momentum offers a healthy after-tax return premium and larger than what is provided by other strategies.

■ Myth #6: Momentum Is Best Used with Screens Rather than as a Direct Factor

A stronger form of this myth, and wording that has been used publicly, states "momentum is not useful as a factor in portfolio construction". Yet, those who say this, including those who demean momentum as a "hot potato", often leave the door open to use momentum in some other, ancillary way, typically as a "screen".

While a little confusing, we presume the position summed up as "momentum screens, yes; direct factor, no" means you wouldn't want to treat momentum like value (i.e., use both value and momentum to come up with a method of evaluating companies on both measures). But under this particular myth it still makes sense to use momentum as a "screen" where, after deciding, based on value, what to buy or sell, momentum is allowed some influence over the implementation of this rebalance. This seems like an attempt to incorporate momentum, as anyone looking at the literature and wealth of evidence (or the results above) should want to do, but not quite being willing to admit that it's a "real factor".

It is, in our opinion, an attempt to have your cake but denounce it too![14]

What's strange about using momentum as a screen but not a "real factor" is that it still requires a belief in momentum, albeit perhaps a milder one than ours. In other words, despite not giving it due credit, perhaps for fear it detracts from the value story or perhaps detracts from an efficient-markets-only point of view (we are believers that both risk-based efficient market and behavioral reasons likely contribute to the success of all of these factors), advocates of the "screen approach" want to find a way to use a little bit of it because of the strong evidence in its favor. The problem is (as the saying goes) "you can't be a little bit pregnant". Either you believe in momentum and acknowledge the data, or you don't.

Now, there is one possible way to save the "screen" story, and indeed claim to be just partially with child. In some sense the fable we are about to tell unifies a bunch of the myths we discuss under one untrue umbrella. The notion of using momentum as just a screen is consistent with some of the other myths we previously dispensed with: that momentum is mostly driven by the short side, works only among small cap stocks, and doesn't survive trading costs. If all three of these hold, using momentum only as a trading screen becomes more valid (how valid would depend on how strong these effects were). For example, imagine a long only investor who believed in momentum but thought (wrongly) that it worked only to underweight securities

---

[14] We leave it to the reader as to why one would denounce a cake.

(i.e., the short side), believed (wrongly) that it only worked in very small cap stocks, and believed (wrongly) that it would be too costly to implement alone. That investor might still look to avoid, or screen out, very small cap stocks that had poor momentum from his purchase list, as not buying something is free (i.e., no transactions costs) and he still believes momentum has efficacy for shorting small stocks (the signal momentum is giving here). Using the momentum factor in a long-only context at low weight would also achieve a similar outcome as a screen, namely not owning these stocks, but also have more influence on what is purchased (not simply what is not purchased), so it's possible, though still far from a certainty, that if all of these things were meaningfully true a screen could be preferred.

But, alas, the myth-makers are batting 200 points below the Mendoza line across each of these three assertions (that's 0.000 for you non-baseball fans).[15] Since momentum is very strong, is just as strong on the long side as the short side, works equally well among large cap as it does among small cap stocks, and is certainly profitable after trading costs, using momentum as a screen will be significantly suboptimal versus using momentum as a factor (there is no more reason to use a "screen" for momentum than for value; actually, there's even less given value's weakness among large cap stocks). Frazzini, Israel, Moskowitz, and Novy-Marx (2013) explore this issue empirically and show that a factor-based approach for momentum is superior to a screen-based approach.

■ Myth #7: One Should Be Particularly Worried about Momentum's Returns Disappearing

First, we find it odd that this is often said about momentum by supporters of other factors that also face this concern, as this concern can—and should—exist for any factor. We remember 1999-2000, when investors were abandoning value investing, many with the belief that it would never work again because "the world had changed". Every investor worries that the future may not reflect the past and that return expectations may be too optimistic. When others get this admittedly valid question about the future returns of their favorite factor, again, for instance, the value factor, I'm sure they roll their eyes and think "here we go again." That they'd turn around and unabashedly ask it only of momentum is odd to say the least, especially given the strength and stability of momentum's historical record. No other factor, save perhaps the market itself (and that is far from clear), has nearly as long a track record (remember, there is evidence of momentum for the past 212 years), as much out-of-sample evidence (including across time, geography and even security type), or as strong and reliable a return premium as momentum (see Table 56.1).

---

[15] Hitting below the Mendoza line has often been used in baseball to define incompetent hitting and is the threshold often used to claim that a player does not belong in major league baseball, regardless of his defensive prowess. It is named after Mario Mendoza, a good defensive shortstop who actually hit 0.215 in his career.

Our guesses as to why people ask this question more frequently about momentum are that 1) momentum is a newer factor in terms of academic attention than size or value and 2) behavioral explanations for its origin have been pushed more prominently (though not exclusively). The first reason does not make much sense once you've seen the data, since no other factor has as much evidence behind it. The second rationale is more plausible, yet it still requires a leap of faith in that it presumes that behavioral phenomena are somehow less likely to persist than risk-based ones and that other factors are 100% risk versus behavioral based (we know few of even the most ardent believers in the risk story who thought, when NASDAQ hit 5000 in the year 2000, that there was no behavioral component at all to the destruction being suffered by value).

The idea is that if something is driven by investor behavior, then arbitrage forces may eventually eliminate it. This is, of course, possible, but it is far from certain, and a risk-based factor can also disappear if tastes for risk change or the price of risk changes (even supporters of a pure risk-based story readily admit that the price of risk can and does change substantially through time).

Moreover, since the average investor has to, by definition, own the market, not everyone can be tilted toward the same risk factors. That is, for every value investor, there has to be a growth investor. If money managers continue to push value on everyone, then prices for value stocks will have to rise and will eventually eliminate the value premium.[16] So, yes, any factor can fail to produce returns in the future, but that possibility of failure exists for behavioral factors and risk-based factors. And, remember, the jury is still out on whether momentum is a behavioral or risk-based factor (we have not given up hope on improving upon the risk-based explanations). Perhaps the most important point is that both theories—behavioral and risk-based—provide good reasons for why the premium should persist (more on this in myth #10). Considering the overwhelming long-term evidence for *both* value and momentum investing, the onus is on anyone claiming future risk premia or behavior will change to these factors' detriment. This challenge has not been met, not close.

Having said that, we are of course interested in trying to answer whether momentum's returns are likely to disappear. Israel and Moskowitz (2013a) take up this issue by looking at a host of out-of-sample periods for momentum (after the original momentum studies were published) to see if there was any degradation in its returns. They did not find any evidence of degradation. They also looked at whether momentum's returns decreased with declines in trading costs (a proxy for the cost of arbitrageurs) and the growth in hedge fund and active mutual fund assets (a proxy for arbitrage activity). Again, the answer was "no" on both counts.

---

[16] Obviously, even in this scenario, there are still limits, as it requires investors remaining patiently invested in these strategies. We are not predicting this will happen, as we are actually actively betting it doesn't occur, but simply raising the analogous possibility here.

So, there is no evidence that momentum has weakened since it has become well known and once many institutional investors embraced it and trading costs declined. This doesn't mean momentum could never disappear, but at least in the more than 20 years since its original discovery, we've seen nothing to indicate that it is being arbitraged away. Israel and Moskowitz (2013a) also looked at value and size under the same light and found that these factors, especially size, had not fared as well as momentum out-of-sample (though, at the risk of repetition that annoys the reader, we mention again that we remain fans of *combining* value with momentum).

But let's forget all that and leave caution to the wind. What if the expected return on momentum were truly zero? Suppose, despite all of the evidence to the contrary and our strong belief it's positive, momentum had a *zero* expected return going forward. Would it still be a valuable investment tool? The answer is clearly, though perhaps surprisingly, yes. The reason is because of momentum's tremendous diversification benefits when combined with value.[17]

Again, we use Kenneth French's data to run simple optimizations where we maximize the Sharpe ratio of a portfolio combining the market (RMRF), size (SMB), value (HML), and momentum (UMD). Figure 56.1 shows the optimal weight of momentum as a function of momentum returns, while holding the expected returns of the other factors and the correlations between factors at their long-term averages (1927–2013). Using the average momentum premium observed in the full sample, this simple optimization would place about 38% of a portfolio in UMD, which is not surprising given the evidence discussed above (this is the rightmost of the two vertical dashed lines). Moreover, Figure 56.1 shows that even in the extreme case where we assume a *zero* return for momentum, the optimal portfolio still places a significant positive weight on momentum. The diversification benefits are so great that even a zero expected return would be valuable to your portfolio! The logic is simple. Since value is a good strategy and momentum is -0.4 correlated with it, one should expect momentum to lose money based only on that information. Yet, the fact that it does not lose but in this assumed case breaks even makes it a valuable hedge.

Put simply, even if the expected return on momentum were to disappear to zero, the benefits of diversification would still push you to want a significant weight on momentum in your portfolio (though admittedly the above is a theoretical exercise maximizing Sharpe ratio on gross of costs, long-short portfolios). While we believe

---

[17] The correlation between UMD and HML in Kenneth French's data is -0.4 over the full sample period (1927–2013). We have used the definition of HML as per Kenneth French's data for objectivity and to make it easy for the reader to replicate the results, but we note that using the definition of value in Asness and Frazzini (2013) dramatically increases the magnitude of this negative correlation (to -0.7) and the power of combining value and momentum. Following their methodology, the results of this section would be far stronger.

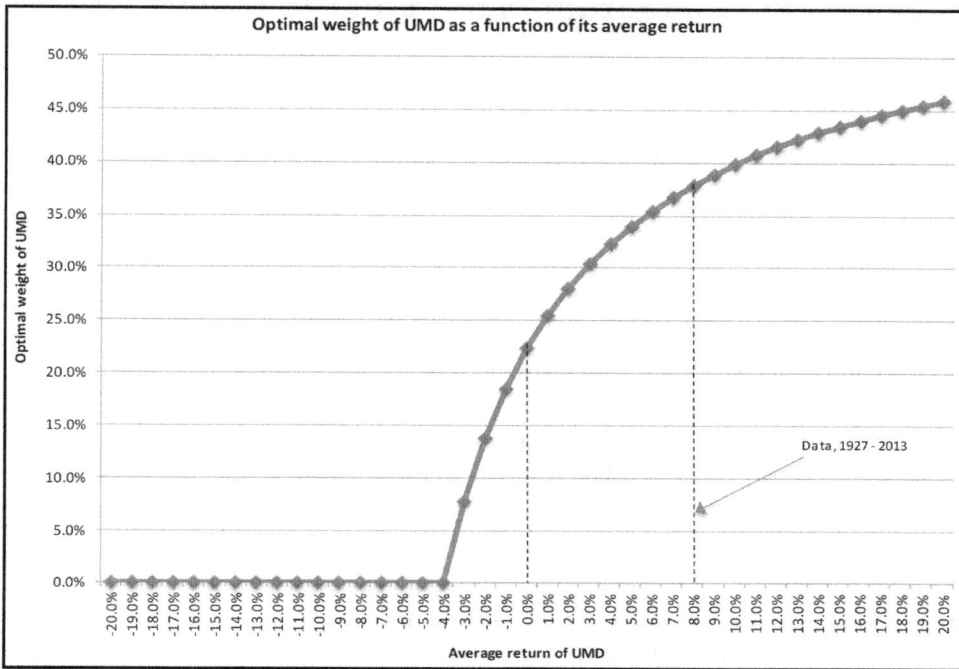

FIGURE 56.1

in momentum as a stand-alone factor, we've always advocated combining it into a broader portfolio, particularly with value.[18],[19] And, of course, we emphatically believe the going-forward expected premium is positive, not zero.

---

[18] By the way, we fully recognize and acknowledge that the past ten years have not been great for momentum, with the 10-year return for UMD falling in the 7th percentile of rolling 10-year returns (going back to 1927). At the same time the past ten years have not been great for value, either, with the 10-year return for HML falling in the 5th percentile of rolling 10-year returns. That, of course, makes the prior 10-year return of the 60/40 combination of the two low (2nd percentile), but still positive (12%). You know a strategy has a pretty great history when the 2nd percentile return is still positive. As Figure 56.1 indicates, even with the lower than normal returns for UMD over the prior 10-year period, the optimal weight on momentum would still be high (that is, if you knew the returns on UMD would be as low as in the past 10 years the ex-post highest Sharpe ratio portfolio still wants a lot of it as it hedges value so well). Also, if investors are basing their concerns about momentum's returns disappearing on the prior 10 years, despite the longer term evidence, it would seem odd that they wouldn't similarly be concerned about value's returns. For both value and momentum we, obviously, think the longer term evidence is most convincing.

[19] Asness (2012) shows a very similar thing in Japan. Momentum for choosing stocks within Japan is one of the few places we've seen a zero historical momentum premium (albeit over the much shorter international versus USA sample). Asness shows, among other arguments including the significant chance this was a random occurrence, that even with this result, a Sharpe ratio optimizing investor with perfect knowledge of this zero premium future would *still* put substantial weight on momentum for very similar diversification/hedging reasons to those discussed here in the hypothetical.

■ Myth #8: Momentum Is too Volatile to Rely On

Yep, they say it this way, too. Since this might just be the "sporadic" myth again, and since volatility is fully accounted for in momentum's reported Sharpe ratios (that's what a Sharpe ratio does!), we'll interpret this often-repeated myth as a different sort of attack, which it probably is as it's sometimes separately included by the same people at the same time attacking momentum. To the extent we are wrong and the myth-makers were just being repetitive, please consider this extra credit. But we think when people say something like this they don't mean regular old volatility but the admitted empirical tendency for momentum to suffer some very bad short-term periods, in particular for a few months in 2009.

As with any factor, momentum does not make money all the time and occasionally suffers large losses, and historically this has been somewhat worse for stand-alone momentum than the other factors discussed here. Spring 2009 was one of these times. But, while more extreme, this isn't unlike other factors. Every factor has its dark times. Witness value investing in the late 1990s (back then we vigorously defended value from its ubiquitous critics). Unfortunately, since this particular momentum episode was recent, it has prompted some of momentum's critics to overemphasize it. We think this is a gross overreaction and mischaracterization of the facts. Recall that momentum has a much higher Sharpe ratio than the size or value strategy, despite including this episode (again to emphasize, all of the numbers we have looked at above include the dark periods observed in the history for all of these factors, including the recent one for momentum). So, on a risk-return basis, momentum still comes out on top. If momentum had a superior return but a vastly inferior, and even unacceptable, Sharpe ratio due to very high volatility, then it might have made sense to criticize it this way, but that's just not close to true. In fact it's why we use Sharpe ratios!

Some critics of momentum use 2009 as a glaring example to imply that you don't want to invest in something that can ever have a really bad period. One prominent value manager, and prominent momentum myth spreader, says specifically, with no further explanation, as if none is necessary, "Momentum is also quite variable; in 2009, it was sharply negative for US stocks." That is a fairly amazing thing for a student of these factors to say. No doubt 2009 was a terrible year to be a momentum investor, particularly if momentum was all you did, however, so was 1999 for a value investor, and so was 2008 for passive equity investors. And, for those interested, 1932 was also very ugly for momentum, and 1930 ugly for value, and in each case the other came through and the 60/40 value/momentum portfolio results were reasonably calm (have we mentioned that we like value and momentum together, not as competitors?) We highlight this not to spend time analyzing Great Depression-era long-short returns but to highlight the silliness of pointing to specific-period results for attractive but risky factors one is supposed to invest in for the long-term and as part of a diversified portfolio. Of course, any decent researcher knows far better than to point to one bad period for a factor with long-term success (success that, again, *includes* that bad period) and impugn it while letting other factors have a free pass regarding events in their own histories.[20]

Nevertheless, the fact that momentum can be volatile and experience large left tails, admittedly stand-alone larger left tails than some other factors, shouldn't be ignored and deserves study. Daniel and Moskowitz (2013) look specifically at momentum crashes to try to understand these rare but turbulent times. They find that these crashes typically occur after a long bear market (say, over the last two years) followed by an abrupt market upswing. This almost perfectly characterizes the spring of 2009 and also the other most extreme momentum crash in late summer of 1932. The authors dig into what happens to momentum at these times and find that conditional market exposure is the culprit. That is, by buying winners and selling losers, a momentum strategy following a bear market will be long low beta stocks and short high beta stocks. Then, when the market suddenly upswings, being short high beta stocks will be a bad strategy. In fact, Daniel and Moskowitz (2013) show that all of the crashes to momentum are driven by being short the losers; the winners actually fare well. So, ironically given our discussion in myth #2, this is one circumstance where shorting losers distinguishes itself—it fully explains the crash episodes of momentum. Since these episodes are driven by market exposure, the authors further devise a way to hedge much of this risk and significantly reduce the crashes. Whether one uses this hedging strategy or not, it is important to note that these two crashes (the worst ones) for momentum come during very sharp market *upswings*, periods during which the portfolios of most investors are doing well otherwise, thus making the losses potentially more tolerable. Indeed, surprising to many is that momentum's long-term (1927–2013) average beta to the long-only stock market (RMRF in Kenneth French's data) is non-trivially negative, presumably influenced by these periods, and value's slightly positive, favoring momentum in a multi-factor portfolio including the all-important market factor over this longest test period.

But, there's an even simpler and equally effective way to mitigate these crashes, as we mention repeatedly: combining momentum with value. This combination has effectively eliminated these crashes in our long-term sample evidence—and not just those for momentum but also the crashes that can occur for value investing. In other words, the diversification benefits of combining momentum with value don't just

---

[20] By the way, for those students of the esoteric history of quant investing, in the period immediately before 2009 some quants (not the myth makers we discuss in this piece but quantitative investors who had embraced both value and momentum) made the decision to overweight momentum versus value and other factors as before the painful 2009 episode the long- and in particular the short-term track record for momentum versus value was even stronger (this overweight was a misguided, in our opinion, attempt to use the "momentum of momentum" to time itself as momentum was stronger than value in the 2007–2008 financial crisis). We get plenty wrong, none of which we will volunteer here, but as in early 2000, when many argued for abandoning value and we yelled no, we also argued against this soon-to-be-disastrous overweight of momentum immediately prior to 2009. We are cheerleaders for giving momentum a balanced, significant weight in a process, not for trying to overweight it at "the right time."

appear during normal times, but also during these extreme times, which makes their combination even more valuable. For example, Asness and Frazzini (2013) show that the combination of value and momentum did not suffer as badly in 2009. Going the other way, in 1999 momentum helped ameliorate value's pain. Both factors have worked well over the long-term, but neither has a Sharpe ratio of 10, meaning that both will have hard times occasionally, but when combined together they will have fewer hard times.

Using Kenneth French's data, we can show similarly that these very poor episodes for momentum and value are ameliorated.[21] The diversification benefits between momentum and value are evident, even during these extreme times. For example, the worst drawdown over the full sample is −43% for value, −77% for momentum[22], but only −30% for a 60/40 combination of value and momentum.

Pointing at one very bad period for momentum that doesn't substantially change the long-term results (and was quite survivable especially if one also included a meaningful value tilt, as we advocate), and then saying "see, look, it can be really rough sometimes, you'd better avoid it" is just not an intellectually defensible argument. There is a saying at the University of Chicago, "the plural of 'anecdote' is not 'data'". Neither 2009 for momentum nor 1999 for value are indicative of the overall health and strength of these strategies. Plus, again, their combination greatly mitigates these worst times.

▪ Myth #9: Different Measures of Momentum Can Give Different Results over a Given Period

OK, this isn't a myth, it's actually true, but it's tritely obvious and yet still often hurled as a critique of momentum so we've chosen to include it. The myth, more properly stated, would say "different measures of momentum give different results over a given time period and that's a terrible thing." But that just sounds too silly so people don't quite get that explicit (myth tellers often prefer their statements to be less obviously humorous). Yet, the statement is meant to imply that since different measures of momentum can give different results over a given period, momentum is not a stable process and possibly data mined. This is just false.

The notion that different measures can give different results is true with *any* strategy, as there are often several valid ways of measuring the same phenomenon. For instance, value measures usually contain some form of fundamental value to market value such as earnings-to-price, cash-flow-to-price, or book-to-market value. And, guess what,

---

[21] Using value as defined by Asness and Frazzini (2013), which we do not do here as we stick with the normal formulation, this amelioration is dramatically more pronounced. Constructing value properly, and focusing on the returns of value and momentum together, something we always encourage as they form a system, shows 2009 to be only a modest event to the properly defined combination.

[22] This is a bigger drop than for value but not by as much as it appears as, again, momentum's natural volatility is higher and value, as defined on Kenneth French's website, contains about 20% momentum as we have discussed, which acts as a hedge.

although all are effective over the long-term they give different results over any given period! In fact, Frazzini, Israel, Moskowitz, and Novy-Marx (2013) show that combining multiple measures of value, instead of relying on just one, can lead to stronger results for the factor.

As with value, momentum can be measured in various ways. The idea is to capture relative past performance. Often Occam's razor applies: the simplest measure is the best. For momentum, the past 12-month return, skipping the most recent month's return (to avoid microstructure and liquidity biases), is the most frequently used measure and has been since Asness (1994). Many other measures have been proposed, such as various return horizons ranging from 3–12 months,[23] consistency of the past returns,[24] or measures of "fundamental" momentum related to earnings announcement returns or analysts revisions.[25] While each of these other measures may add some incremental performance, the overall momentum effect over the long term is very similar across measures as shown in Chan, Jegadeesh, and Lakonishok (1996).

To guard against data mining, choosing the simplest measure or taking an average of all reasonable measures tends to yield better portfolios, as shown by Frazzini, Israel, Moskowitz, and Novy-Marx (2013). As a case in point that has oddly been used to impugn momentum's stability, Novy-Marx (2012) argues that momentum in U.S. equities is better measured by past returns from 7–12 months ago and that using the most recent six months of returns is not valuable. However, Goyal and Wahal (2012) replicate Novy-Marx's results in 36 international equity markets and find that in 35 out of 36 countries (the only exception being the U.S.), his result does not hold up and the past 12-month return is a superior measure of momentum, with the most recent 6 months of returns contributing equally to performance as the more distant 6 months of returns. Both ways work but simplest is best.

The fact that different measures of momentum yield substantially similar results should rationally be taken as a sign of robustness, not as a critique.

▪ Myth #10: There Is No Theory Behind Momentum

One of the myths often said about momentum is that "it has no theory" as those, for instance, who dismiss it as a "hot potato" strategy imply. This is false. Like other robust return premia, such as size and value, there is much debate regarding the explanation behind momentum, and again, like size and value, none of the models are so compelling that a consensus exists on their explanation. Still, there are several reasonable theories.

---

[23] Jegadeesh and Titman (1993).

[24] Grinblatt and Moskowitz (2004).

[25] Chan, Jegadeesh, and Lakonishok (1996).

Most theories fall into one of two categories: risk-based and behavioral. While the jury is still out on which of these explanations better fit the data, the same can also be said for the size and value premia.

The behavioral models typically explain momentum as either an underreaction or delayed overreaction phenomenon (it is of course possible that both occur, making it harder to empirically sort things out). In the case of underreaction, the idea is that information travels slowly into prices for a variety of reasons (e.g., investors being too conservative, being inattentive, facing liquidity issues, or displaying the disposition effect—the tendency to sell winners too quickly and hold onto losers too long). In the case of overreaction, investors may chase returns, providing a feedback mechanism that drives prices even higher.[26]

The other possibility is that the momentum premium is compensation for risk. One set of models argues that economic risks that affect firm investment and growth rates can impact the long-term cash flows and dividends of the firm that generate momentum patterns. The idea is that high-momentum stocks face greater cash flow risk because of their growth prospects or face greater discount rate risk because of their investment opportunities, causing them to face a higher cost of capital.[27] In addition, others argue that the presence of a correlation structure across markets and asset classes of momentum strategies is indicative of a shared economic risk.[28]

While academics debate whether risk or behavioral explanations matter more, for the practical investor the distinction is far less relevant. Why? Because both the risk and non-risk based explanations provide an economic reason for the premium to exist and, importantly, persist. From a risk-based perspective, as long as risks and tastes for risks don't change, the premium will remain stable and long-lived. Likewise, under the behavioral explanations, as long as the biases, behaviors, and limits to arbitrage remain stable, the premium will as well. The evidence from over 200 years of data, in dozens of financial markets, and in many different asset classes, suggests that these phenomena are not short-lived.

And remember, some of momentum's biggest myth spreaders still want to use it in some capacity (as a "screen" or in an "ancillary" way). While we've already discussed this in depth, it's important to again note this means they believe in momentum. Earlier we said "you can't be a little pregnant" so one wonders, since these folks are clearly expecting, was the father behavioral or risk-based?

Despite all this, there are still some that say *"the momentum premium is not large enough to trade profitably, because if it was it would be an example of market mispricing."* This statement seems to be based mostly on religion rather than fact. The idea is that if the momentum premium is really as large and robust as we show it to be, then it must be

---

[26] Some behavioral models that deliver momentum: DeLong, Shleifer, Summers, and Waldmann (1990), Daniel, Hirshleifer, and Subrahmanyam (1998), Barberis, Shleifer, and Vishny (1998), Hong and Stein (1999), Shefrin and Statman (1985), Grinblatt and Han (2005), and Frazzini (2006).

[27] Some risk-based models that deliver momentum: Berk, Green, and Naik (1999), Johnson (2002), Sagi and Seasholes (2007), and Zhang (2004).

[28] Asness, Moskowitz, and Pedersen (2013).

due to a market inefficiency and therefore (and here's where the religion comes in) it can't be real, as markets are obviously perfectly efficient. This thinking implies that if markets are efficient, then the data on momentum must be wrong. While we believe risk-based efficient market explanations play an important part in all of these factors' returns, we also believe there is a role in each, perhaps at different degrees, for behavioral explanations. Some believe it's all one or the other.[29] But, even if you believe that, the statement "what you're saying can't possibly be true despite the overwhelming evidence or my one-sided view of the world would be wrong" is not an argument but a tacit admission of defeat!

There are two alarming things with this myth. First, the data are undeniable, and (as history has shown repeatedly) rejecting data on the basis of theory can be dangerous (cf. Christopher Columbus 1492, Galileo Galilei 1615, and Salem Massachusetts 1692). Second, the statement denies any possible efficient markets stories for momentum, which, as discussed above, do indeed exist (and is ironic coming from the efficient-markets-only crowd).

Most importantly, while we can debate forever how efficient or inefficient markets are (indeed, the Nobel Prize committee this year couldn't decide and split the prize between the two camps), none of this debate should diminish momentum as a valuable investment tool. The point is not to confuse the theoretical debate (which is ongoing, not just for momentum, but for other premia, like value, as well) with the empirical consensus on the efficacy of momentum. We discovered the world wasn't flat before we understood and agreed why.

◼ Conclusion

Now that you've seen the evidence and know where to find it, those repeating the myths above regarding momentum should have a harder time maintaining credibility. They never had the facts on their side, but, while the myths have been around piecemeal, no one ever assembled a detailed refutation before nor tied some of the myths together (e.g., you need to believe myths about momentum's lack of small cap efficacy, short versus long side efficacy, and transactions costs, to believe the myth about screens). There has now been so much work done addressing and testing these myths that repeating them means ignoring the data. Given that most of these myths can be shattered by a quick visit to Kenneth French's website (like the infomercial says, "don't just take our word for it"), they should stop being repeated by those who want to be considered informed consumers of the research.

---

[29] Ironically the myth-spreading supporters of value come from both ends of the spectrum, some who believe value is purely a risk-based efficient markets effect, and some who believe value is instead only the product of "noise" in prices coming from inefficient markets (and rather oddly that they are the only ones to ever have advanced that possibility). Perhaps believing in extreme explanations is correlated with myth-making?

If one wants to challenge the evidence that is fine, too. For instance, doing your own research and/or building your own database to attempt to establish even the slightest truth behind these myths, and explaining why you find a different result than those found to date, or picking apart the above referenced papers to come up with a story for why you don't believe them, is fine. Momentum, or any empirical regularity, should, of course, not be immune from criticism. Quite the opposite. But, eventually you must confront the data. Barring new data or a new convincing interpretation, you don't get to repeat specific falsehoods, pretending that there isn't an abundance of research and evidence refuting your statements. If someone discovers something challenging or enlightening versus what we have shown, we welcome it and wish to understand more. On the other hand, if someone creates new false myths to replace the old, we stand ready! At the very least, we hope that our thorough refutation finally puts a stop to momentum critics repeating these same old myths.

■ References

Asness, C. S. (1994). "Variables that explain stock returns." Ph.D. Dissertation, University of Chicago.

Asness, C. S. (1997). "The Interaction of Value and Momentum Strategies." *Financial Analysts Journal.*

Asness, C. S. (2012). "Momentum in Japan." *Financial Analysts Journal.*

Asness, C. and A. Frazzini (2013). "The Devil in HML's Details." *Journal of Portfolio Management* 39(4), 49–68.

Asness, C., A. Ilmanen, R. Israel and T. Moskowitz (2013). "Investing with Style." *Journal of Investment Management*, forthcoming.

Asness, C., T. Moskowitz, and L. Pedersen (2013). "Value and Momentum Everywhere." *Journal of Finance* 68(3), 929–985.

Barberis, N., A. Shleifer, and R. Vishny (1998). "A Model of Investor Sentiment." *Journal of Financial Economics* 49, 307–334.

Bergstresser, D. and J. Pontiff (2013). "Investment Taxation and Portfolio Performance." *Journal of Public Economics* 97, 245–257.

Berk, J., R. Green, and V. Naik (1999). "Optimal Investment, Growth Options, and Security Returns." *Journal of Finance* 54, 1553–1607.

Booth, D. (2013). "The Evolution of Dimensional." Equius Partners, Inc. Asset Class Newsletter.

Carhart, M. (1997). "On Persistence in Mutual Fund Performance." *Journal of Finance* 53.

Chabot, B., E. Ghysels and R. Jagannathan (2009). "Price Momentum in Stocks: Insights from Victorian Age Data." National Bureau of Economic Research Working Papers 14500.

Chan, L., N. Jegadeesh, and J. Lakonishok (1997). "Momentum strategies." *Journal of Finance* 51, 1681–1713.

Daniel, K., D. Hirshleifer, and A. Subrahmanyam (1998). "A Theory of Overconfidence, Self-Attribution, and Security Market Under- and Over-Reactions." *Journal of Finance* 53, 1839–1885.

Daniel, K. and T. Moskowitz (2013). "Momentum Crashes." Working paper, University of Chicago.

DeLong, J.B., A. Shleifer, L. H. Summers, and R. J. Waldmann (1990). "Positive Feedback Investment Strategies and Destabilizing Rational Speculation." *Journal of Finance*, 45(2), 379–395.

Fama, E.F., and K.R. French (1992). "The cross-section of expected stock returns." *Journal of Finance* 47, 427–465.

Fama, E.F. and K.R. French (1993). "Common Risk Factors in the Returns on Stocks and Bonds." *Journal of Financial Economics* 33, 3–56.

Fama, E.F. and K.R. French (2008). "Dissecting Anomalies." *Journal of Finance* 63.

Fama, E.F. and K.R. French (2012). "Size, Value, and Momentum in International Stock Returns." *Journal of Financial Economics* 105, 457–472.

Frazzini, A. (2006). "The Disposition Effect and Underreaction to News." *Journal of Finance*, 61.

Frazzini, A., R. Israel, and T.J. Moskowitz (2013). "Trading Costs of Asset Pricing Anomalies." Working paper, University of Chicago.

Frazzini, A., R. Israel, T.J. Moskowitz and R. Novy-Marx (2013). "A New Core Equity Paradigm." Whitepaper, AQR Capital Management.

Geczy, C. and M. Samonov (2013). "212 Years of Price Momentum (The World's Longest Backtest: 1801–2012)." Working paper, University of Pennsylvania - The Wharton School.

Goyal, A. and S. Wahal (2013). "Is Momentum an Echo?" *Journal of Financial and Quantitative Analysis*, forthcoming.

Grinblatt, M. and B. Han (2005). "Prospect Theory, Mental Accounting, and Momentum." *Journal of Financial Economics*.

Grinblatt, M. and T.J. Moskowitz (2004). "Predicting Stock Price Movements from Past Returns: The Role of Consistency and Tax-Loss Selling." *Journal of Financial Economics*, 71, 541–579.

Hong, H., T. Lim, and J. Stein (2000). "Bad News Travels Slowly: Size, Analyst Coverage, and the Profitability of Momentum Strategies." *Journal of Finance*, 55, 265–295.

Hong, H. and J. Stein (1999). "A Unified Theory of Underreaction, Momentum Trading and Overreaction in Asset Markets." *Journal of Finance*, LIV, no. 6.

Huij, H., S. Lansdorp, D. Blitz, and P. Stein (2014). "Factor Investing: Long-Only versus Long-Short." Working paper, Erasmus School of Economics.

Israel, R. and T. Moskowitz (2012). "How Tax Efficient Are Equity Styles?" Working paper, University of Chicago Booth School of Business.

Israel, R. and T. Moskowitz (2013). "The Role of Shorting, Firm Size, and Time on Market Anomalies." *Journal of Financial Economics* 108(2), 275–301.

Jegadeesh, N. and S. Titman (1993). "Returns to Buying Winners and Selling Losers: Implications for Stock Market Efficiency." *Journal of Finance*, 48, 65–91.

Johnson, Timothy (2002). "Rational Momentum Effects." *Journal of Finance* 57, 585 – 608.

Kahneman, D. and A. Tversky (1979). "Prospect Theory: An Analysis of Decision Under Risk." Econometrica 47.

Keim, D.B. (1999), "An analysis of mutual fund design: the case of investing in small-cap stocks," *Journal of Financial Economics*, 51, 173–194.

Korajczyk, Robert A., and Ronnie Sadka (2004), "Are Momentum Profits Robust to Trading Costs?" *Journal of Finance*, 59, 1039–1082.

Larson, R. (2013). "Hot Potato: Momentum as an Investment Strategy." Research Affiliates Fundamentals Newsletter.

Lesmond, David A., Michael J. Schill, and Chunsheng Zhou (2003), "The Illusory Nature of momentum profits." *Journal of Financial Economics*, 71, 349–380.

Merton, Robert C. (1987). "A Simple Model of Capital Market Equilibrium with Incomplete Information." *Journal of Finance* 42, 483–510.

Novy-Marx, Robert (2012). "Is Momentum Really Momentum?" *Journal of Financial Economics*, 103(3), 429–453.

Pastor, L. and R. F. Stambaugh (2003). "Liquidity Risk and Expect Stock Returns." *Journal of Political Economy*, 111.

Sagi, J. and M.S. Seasholes (2007). "Firm-Specific Attributes and the Cross-Section of Momentum." *Journal of Financial Economics* 84, 389–434.

Shefrin, H. and M. Statman (1985). "The Disposition to Sell Winners Too Early and Ride Losers Too Long: Theory and Evidence." *Journal of Finance* 40, 777–791.

Sialm, C. and H. Zhang (2013). "Tax-Efficient Asset Management: Evidence from Equity Mutual Funds." Working paper, University of Texas at Austin.

Zhang, H. (2004). "Dynamic Beta, Time-Varying Risk Premium, and Momentum." Yale ICF Working Paper No. 04–26.

CHAPTER 57

Conclusions*

From Richard J. Bauer Jr. and Julie R. Dahlquist,
Technical Market Indicators: Analysis & Performance
(Hoboken, New Jersey: John Wiley & Sons,
1999), Chapter 10.

Learning Objective Statements

- Explain why each of the observations listed in this chapter are applicable as general guidelines of validity to most systems of trading or investment that are based on technical analysis
- Validate a trading system by comparing it to the observations stated in this chapter

W e have made many general summarizing comments at various points in the book. In this chapter, we bring them all together. What follows is a list of twelve major conclusions from our tests. Before you launch into technically based trading, we think that each point needs to be fully understood. Technical analysis can quickly become a sinkhole of time and money. We hope these points will save you many hours and many dollars. Each point will be briefly explained. For a complete understanding of each point, refer back to the relevant section of the book.

▥ Major Conclusions

1. If you trade strictly following the signals from technical indicators, you will, on average, do worse than a buy-and-hold strategy.

This is a sweeping conclusion, based on average results. What we are saying here is that if you were to just randomly pick one of the sixty indicators, randomly pick a stock, and begin trading, then you will probably not fare as well as you would have with a buy-and-hold strategy. You might get lucky and beat a buy-and-hold strategy. You might even have a string of successful results, just as a few people do from Las Vegas

---

* Editor's Note: This chapter was written at the conclusion of a study of more than 60 technical indicators. The references to the results of the study apply to those indicators only; however, the principles captured in this chapter can be generally applied to insights available from the majority of technical indicators.

slot machines. But, on average, you are likely to be disappointed. If you keep playing a random picking game long enough, you will probably lose. The odds for the technical analysis slot machine are against you. Conclusion 2, next, partially explains what is causing the underperformance relative to a buy-and-hold strategy. Before you write off technical analysis as a complete waste of time, however, see Conclusion 4.

2. Technical indicators are, on average, conservative; they signal a high proportion of cash positions.

This is, perhaps, a surprising conclusion. Many people view technical analysis as fairly risky. However, most indicators seem to provide definite buy or sell signals only when reasonably restrictive criteria are met. They are not just saying buy or sell in a willy-nilly manner. Therefore, they are actually somewhat cautious. Imagine that Joe is a technical analyst who strictly follows the Bollinger Band Crossover indicator in making his buy and sell recommendations. When Joe says buy or sell, he is probably worth listening to. However, much of the time he throws up his hands and says, "I don't know what to do here; maybe you should just park your money in cash until the situation gets a little clearer." Joe's behavior is basically what is going on with most of the technical indicators. There are many "I don't know" messages.

You might ask: "What's the harm?" The problem is that, on average, stock prices rise. The long-run historical performance of stocks is quite good. There is an opportunity cost to sitting on the sidelines, staying in cash. The opportunity cost is the forgone return. Because the forgone return is generally positive, holding cash too frequently hurts overall performance. The balance between positive and negative returns is somewhat delicate. For the stocks we examined and the time period we examined, the optimal percentage of long positions was 45.6 percent. This, coupled with the fact that the magnitude of positive returns is greater than the magnitude of negative returns, means that it is beneficial, on average, to be long. The opportunity cost of a cash position is significant.

3. Technical indicators generally outperform a buy-and-hold strategy for stocks that are declining in price, and they underperform stocks that are rising in price.

Part of the explanation here goes back to Conclusion 2. If the strategy you are using tends to leave you invested in cash much of the time, then you will miss many good days in rising markets and avoid many bad days in falling markets. Thus, you will underperform a buy-and-hold strategy in rising markets and outperform it during falling markets. This is, in fact, what we observed. It could also be true that technical indicators inherently have this tendency, even above and beyond what happens from the tendency toward cash positions. Our results point in this direction, but we would need to do more analysis before we could feel comfortable making a definite assertion in this regard. Our advice here is mainly to be somewhat cautious about good results you might be getting in falling markets.

4. The trading signals from technical indicators do, on average, contain information that may be of value in trading.

The easiest way to understand this conclusion is to go back to the buy-and-hold strategy and its underlying philosophy. Buy-and-hold is a simple no-brainer approach;

you just buy the stock and continue holding the stock throughout your investment horizon. This approach will give you a certain average daily return, which for our sample of stocks and time period was 0.055 percent per day. The buy-and-hold strategy treats all days as equal, essentially settling for the average return over time. There will be some good days and some bad days, but they will all average out to a decent return; that's the philosophy.

If you use technical indicators, then you are assuming that you can differentiate between good and bad days. If the indicator says to go long, then you expect to receive an above-average return for that day; you expect something better than the average daily return you would get from the buy-and-hold return. At least, that's what you expect on average. You know that some days might have a return lower than 0.055 percent and some days will have a return higher than 0.055 percent, but you expect the overall average return on days that are marked with long signals to be higher than 0.055 percent. Our results show that this appears to be a reasonable expectation, at least using certain indicators.

Many of the technical indicators do seem to be providing useful information concerning days to go long. Fifty of the sixty indicators had an average daily long return above the 0.055 percent buy-and-hold average return. Twelve had averages above 0.070 percent, which is more than one-fourth, or 25 percent, greater than the buy-and-hold average.

The results concerning short signals were not as strong, but the short signals still contain value. Ideally, if a technical indicator signals to go short, you would want the stock price to be going down, resulting in a negative return. If you have shorted the stock, then this negative change in price leads to positive returns on your short position. However, the average short signal return is lower than the average buy-and-hold return for more than half of the sixty indicators. Therefore, the short signals do contain information. Essentially, they are saying: "It looks like a worse-than-average day ahead." They seem to be pointing toward days when the average return is likely to be below the buy-and-hold return; you will likely earn less than 0.055 percent on days when a short signal has occurred.

We have qualified our remarks with phrases like "seem to be." The reason is that we tested a certain sample of stocks over a certain time period. Results for other stocks might point to a different conclusion. Results in other time periods might point toward other conclusions. Future results for our sample of stocks may be different. There is always some uncertainty with these types of investigations. However, our sample was quite broad and did cover a reasonably extensive period of time. The signals from the technical indicators do, in general, seem to contain valuable information.

5. Trading only long positions or only short positions with technical indicators generally will not beat a buy-and-hold strategy; you must be willing to utilize both long and short signals.

As discussed above, following only the long signals or only the short signals leaves you doing nothing a high proportion of the time. The returns on days when long signals have occurred are generally above average. The problem is that those signals don't occur frequently enough. If you are not long and not short, then you must be in a cash position. The opportunity cost of cash, the forgone return, is high when the return for an average day is 0.055 percent.

Therefore, something more is required, other than just acting on either the long signals or the short signals. The problem is: What is the *something more*? As we have explained above, the short signals do contain information, but the information is not as good as one would like. Because the average return on days when short signals occur is positive, the issue is not simply a matter of going short on those days and long on the days when long signals occur.

To beat a buy-and-hold strategy, you will have to somehow use the information from the short signals. This is not easy to do without creating other problems. Conclusions 6 and 12 have more thoughts along these lines.

6. Portfolio management is an important issue in technically based trading systems.

Portfolio management has many different aspects. There are many different things to consider in the construction and implementation of a trading system. However, we will focus on one specific portfolio management issue.

Earlier, we talked about how the low frequency of long and short signals creates problems. To see the problems, let's look first at a situation that would be easy to manage. Assume that you only want to trade long signals with one indicator, you are going to trade just five different stocks, and you are starting with $10,000. For Monday, your indicator signals a long position only for stock A. You invest all your money in stock A. For Tuesday, you receive a long signal only for stock B, so you close out your position in A and move your money into stock B. For Wednesday, you receive a long signal only for stock C. You repeat the earlier actions, moving your money out of B into C. For Thursday you receive a long signal only for stock D, and you follow the actions along the same lines as before. For Friday, the same thing occurs with stock E. If this pattern occurred repeatedly, week after week, and you were getting good average returns from your long positions, then life would be relatively simple. The problem that we have discussed concerning the low frequency of long signals would be solved, owing to the distribution of the signals. You would be getting one signal per day, so you could have a long position 100 percent of the days. But you would be invested in different stocks on different days.

The situation we just described is quite unrealistic. There are numerous possible complications. For example, what if, on Tuesday, you had received long signals for stocks A and B? Would you sell some of stock A and split your money between A and B, or just ignore the signal about B and continue with all of your money in A? Or, what if long signals always occurred on Monday for all five stocks and there were no long signals during the rest of the week? You would still have the problem that on 80 percent of the days you would be uninvested, holding your money in cash. These examples show that the distribution of the long signals, day by day, for the stocks that you are considering will be quite important.

Deciding how you will manage a portfolio of stocks when faced with a variety of long and/or short signal patterns is what we are referring to here as a portfolio management issue. There are many different ways you could decide to approach this issue, and your approach will have a major bearing on your overall results. We have not tested various methods of handling this problem. Our purpose here is just to alert you to an important issue that should be considered.

7. Results vary widely from stock to stock.

The performance of different indicators varies considerably from stock to stock. Just because an indicator has good average results over the entire sample does not mean that it will have that same performance for each stock. One indicator may work extremely well for one stock and somewhat poorly for another stock. Averaging across the two stocks, we might say the performance is moderately good.

It would be nice to be able to predict the performance of a particular indicator for a particular stock. We have no guidance to offer about that. Our primary results deal with *average* performance.

8. For a single stock, results can vary significantly from one time period to the next.

9. Transactions costs, slippage, and interest need to be considered.

Our results represent somewhat of a best-case scenario because we have totally ignored transactions costs. Our results do not give technical indicators a rave review, but rather a more modest positive review, and this is disturbing for those wanting to implement technically based trading systems. We are looking at daily long/short signals, so it might seem that transactions costs would be extremely high as a result of a lot of switching in and out of positions. However, the technical indicators generally give signals in streaks. For example, consider a twenty-day trading period. If an indicator gives ten long signals over this period, it is more likely to come in the form of seven days long, ten days in cash, followed by three days long, and not long/cash/long/cash/long/cash, and so on. The signals tend to come in runs or streaks, so the transactions costs issue is not the major concern that it potentially could be.

Slippage refers to the ability to transact at the prices we were using. This too is a definite problem. If, on average, you were only able to buy at higher prices than we used and sell at lower prices, the results would be much worse. Omni-Trader and some other technical analysis software packages allow the user to explicitly factor in a user-defined level of slippage when performing historical backtesting.

We have ignored the possibility of earning interest in the cash positions. This extra return would improve the performance of all of the indicators we tested. However, even in quarters with money market rates of 12 percent annually, this would only raise the overall return by about $1\frac{1}{2}$ percent (assuming 3 percent quarterly and a 50 percent cash position). This is still not enough extra return to outperform a buy-and-hold strategy in most cases.

The bottom line here is that transactions costs and slippage will probably dampen our results. This is clearly worrisome to those wanting to implement technically based systems.

10. Combining indicators may result in better signals, but they will be less frequent.

You may have heard the free lunch theorem: There is no free lunch. Two indicators may be better than one, but the extra reliability comes with a price: frequency. As you try to combine indicators in an effort to get a more reliable signal, you will sacrifice frequency. The combined signal may be great when it comes, but what do you do while you wait for it to arrive? If you are parked in a cash position while you wait, you are forgoing opportunities. Because the average daily return for stocks is a decent positive return, cash positions carry an opportunity cost. The high frequency of cash positions when using indicator combinations creates a major drag on overall return.

11. Changing the interpretation of signals may be useful in some cases.

Assume that Joe gives you investment advice on a regular basis. You notice that nine times out of ten he is dead wrong. When he says to buy, it would have been better to sell, and vice versa. Is Joe's investment advice valuable? Yes. Just do the opposite of what Joe says to do. As long as Joe gives consistently bad advice, then you should pay attention to his recommendations. We can carry this same idea over to our interpretation of signals from indicators.

Some of the indicators in our results actually had returns, on days of short signals, that were higher than the average buy-and-hold return. One way to use these signals would be to consider the short signals to actually be long signals.

Based on our results, the short signals generally should be viewed more as a yellow caution flag than a red flag saying "Stop." If you are going to go short, then you want the price change in the stock to be negative, not positive. Our results showed that the price changes, or returns, on days when short signals occurred were generally positive. However, the returns were lower than average on those days. Thus, the short signals may need to be interpreted as days of gentle warning.

The indicators give one of three signals: long, cash, or short. When you combine two indicators, there are nine possible outcomes: short/short, short/cash, short/long, cash/short, cash/cash, cash/long, long/short, long/cash, and long/long. If, in studying the returns for each of these nine possibilities, you saw that only the cash/cash combination had returns that were, on average, negative, then you might want to use a cash/cash combination signal to mean "Go short" and interpret the other eight combinations as "Go long."

12. Leveraged positions may be necessary to exploit certain opportunities.

What do we mean by a leveraged position? We mean a position that involves using borrowed funds, such as buying stocks on margin. Let's assume that you have $10,000 to invest. Let's also assume that you have found an indicator that gives good long signals. The returns on days of long signals from this indicator average 0.130 percent, which is more than twice that of the average buy-and-hold return of 0.055 percent. The problem is that these signals occur only 50 percent of the time. To keep things simple, assume that you can borrow at no cost. So, every time you go long, you invest your $10,000 and another $10,000 that you have borrowed. Because you are doubling the amount invested, this will compensate for the fact that these signals occur only 50 percent of the time. You would be using leverage to capitalize on the long signals from your indicator.

One way to leverage an investment is through buying on margin. Another possibility is using options. Options contracts have inherent leverage. So, if the stock you are following has options traded on it, you might be able to implement an options-based strategy that would allow you to capitalize on indicators that give good, but infrequent, signals.

The basic idea here definitely has merit, but we want to issue three caveats.

1. Make sure that you thoroughly understand any leveraged strategy that you try to employ. Many people lose money in options because they simply do not understand the characteristics of what they have bought.

2. Based on our results, fairly high levels of leverage might be necessary. For example, the Directional Movement Crossover (DMI-C) indicator had an average long signal return of 0.100 percent, which is not quite twice that of the buy-and-hold average return of 0.055 percent. But this signal occurs only 22.3 percent of the time. Therefore, you would need to employ significant leverage, more than just doubling up your capital, to compensate for the low frequency of signals. The higher the leverage, the higher the risk.

3. As a former colleague once said, repeated games of Russian roulette have a certain, not an uncertain, outcome. Leverage magnifies outcomes. If you are highly leveraged during a severe market downturn such as the crash of October 1987, then you may lose all of your capital. Borrower, beware!